1987

1987

The Nonprofit Sector

THE NONPROFIT SECTOR

A Research Handbook

EDITED BY WALTER W. POWELL

YALE UNIVERSITY PRESS
New Haven and London

Designed by Susan P. Fillion
and set in Optima display and Times Roman text type.
Typeset by Keystone Typesetting Company, Orwigsburg, Pa.
Printed in the United States of America by Murray Printing Co.,
Westford, Mass.

Library of Congress Cataloging-in-Publication Data

The Nonprofit sector.
    Includes index.
    1. Corporations, Nonprofit—Management.
2. Corporations, Nonprofit.   3. Charitable uses,
trusts and foundations.   I. Powell, Walter W.
HD62.6.N67 1987   338.7′4   86–15984
ISBN 0–300–03702–3

The paper in this book meets the guidelines for permanence and
durability of the Committee on Production Guidelines for Book
Longevity of the Council on Library Resources.

10   9   8   7   6   5   4   3   2   1

Contents

Tables

Figures

Preface

This handbook is a collective effort to produce a state-of-the-art review and assessment of scholarly research on the nonprofit sector. Over the past ten years or so, public attention to and scholarly analysis of the voluntary sector have increased substantially. The range of services and activities provided, in part or exclusively, by nonprofit organizations has expanded, and public awareness of the importance of nonprofits appears to have grown commensurately. Some of the stimulus for scholarly inquiry on the voluntary sector was generated by the Commission on Private Philanthropy and Public Needs (referred to as the Filer Commission, after its chairman, John Filer). These research papers provided scholars and policymakers with a baseline knowledge, circa the mid-1970s, of the scope and operations of the nonprofit sector. More recently, scholars have been attracted to the study of nonprofits because of a growing recognition of their many unique organizational attributes. Moreover, these features—often analytically fascinating in their own right—cast in sharp relief the different roles played by government and the private sector. This body of research has now grown to the point that a stocktaking seems in order; thus the decision to produce this handbook was made.

The majority of the contributors to this volume have been associated with the Program on Non-Profit Organizations, an interdisciplinary research program based at the Institution for Social and Policy Studies at Yale University. It is under the program's auspices that the handbook appears, and it is the program's support of scholarly debate and inquiry that has made the volume possible. The program began in 1976 with the goals of studying the role, character, organization, and impact of the voluntary sector in the United States and abroad and of building a substantial body of information, analysis, and theory relating to nonprofit organizations. It has engaged approximately 150 scholars, at Yale and many other institutions, as participants in this research agenda. They come from a wide spectrum of academic disciplines—all the social

sciences, history, law, and medicine—and their efforts have produced numerous working papers, journal articles, chapters, and books. This healthy output, however, is not readily accessible: there is no single compendium that summarizes the research of program-affiliated scholars, as well as the work of many others, not affiliated with the program, who have been studying the voluntary sector.

The purpose of this handbook, then, is to build a solid foundation under the burgeoning field of multidisciplinary scholarship on the nonprofit sector. We have attempted to meet this goal in a volume that we hope will be widely used by scholars who teach and conduct research on nonprofit organizations and by practitioners who work in or advise nonprofits. The authors have prepared chapters that speak both to scholars in their own disciplines and to others who may be unfamiliar with the author's disciplinary language and assumptions. This is by no means an easy task for an academic, but many of the contributors have succeeded admirably.

The authors present a thorough and realistic appraisal of current knowledge in their respective fields; moreover, they provide integrative frameworks that will help readers interpret previous research on the subject. They have emphasized issues of importance and persistence so that these chapters will remain salient for many years. But we also want the essays to provoke debate and stimulate new lines of research; in doing so they will, in a sense, hasten their own obsolescence. Our aims are to pinpoint those issues and problems of the nonprofit sector that require more research and theory development and to highlight the unresolved challenges that face nonprofit managers and their staffs and thus demand the attention of policymakers.

The handbook is organized into six parts and twenty-four chapters. Part I of the volume offers an overview of the nonprofit sector. Peter Hall maps the changing terrain of the sector, providing a backdrop that allows us to see how the environment of the nonprofit sector has evolved over the past two hundred years. Henry Hansmann and James Douglas introduce us to the two disciplines—economics and political science—that have contributed the most to our theoretical understanding of the reasons for the existence of the nonprofit sector. Gabriel Rudney presents a much-needed empirical survey of the size and scope of the nonprofit sector. The second section of the volume deals with the relationship of the voluntary sector to government and private enterprise. John Simon gives us a comprehensive analysis of the theory and practice of federal and state tax treatment of nonprofits. Lester Salamon draws our attention to the fact that many government-funded services are actually delivered by nonprofit organizations. Turning from the role of the state to that of the private sector, Richard Steinberg shows us the various ways in which nonprofits differ from private firms as well as the ways in which they resemble and compete with them.

The third part of the volume focuses on crucial organizational and management issues. Melissa Middleton looks at the governance role played by nonprofit boards of directors. Rosabeth Kanter and David Summers tackle the thorny question of effectiveness: what standards of success or failure are available to an organization to which the more conventional standards of market and ballot do not apply? Dennis Young addresses the role of leadership and the unique problems and opportunities for entrepreneurial management that are afforded by nonprofit organizations. Rebecca Freidkin and I examine the literature on organizational change and discern some of the critical factors that have been responsible for changes in the missions and goals of nonprofit organizations.

The functions of the nonprofit sector are many and varied. The chapters constituting part IV by no means exhaust the range of activities and services that are undertaken or offered by nonprofits. Rather, we have chosen to focus on what we regard as the core functions—that is, the activities in which nonprofits play either a preponderant or a particularly vital role (and, secondarily, on which sufficient research has been carried out to justify a review). One of the most helpful features of these chapters is their comparative institutional focus. Paul DiMaggio looks at both popular and high culture and accounts for the differential presence of nonprofit and for-profit organizations in these areas. Theodore Marmor, Mark Schlesinger, and Richard Smithey discuss the contribution of nonprofits to health care and contrast this effort with that of public and for-profit health care providers. Daniel Levy compares public and private educational institutions in the United States and abroad with specific attention to their differences in focus and scope. Ralph Kramer gives us a thorough assessment of the role played by nonprofits in delivering personal social services. Carl Milofsky examines the key features of community-based nonprofits. Craig Jenkins addresses the role of nonprofit social movements in the political process and suggests under what circumstances nonprofits play a vital advocacy role.

The fifth part of the handbook deals with the fundamental issue of financing. Here we are concerned with basic questions about the nature and scope of charity and patronage.

Christopher Jencks does a marvelous job of pulling together various data sources in order to ascertain who gives what to the nonprofit sector. His focus is on individual contributions of money; more research on the donation of time and services is sorely needed. Michael Useem looks at the role played by private corporations in supporting the voluntary sector, a role that is growing rapidly in importance as government contributions to nonprofits have either remained stable or declined. Paul Ylvisaker addresses the substantial power and influence that foundations have over other nonprofit organizations. Useem and Ylvisaker discern important patterns in corporate and foundation giving. In both cases, a small number of organizations dominates grant giving. The authors suggest ways in which the pluralism of the voluntary sector may be harmed by this dominance as well as ways in which this degree of influence affords special opportunities. In response to increased competition for, and decreased availability of, sources of financial support, many nonprofits have turned their efforts to generating their own income. These attempts at producing earned income have met with mixed success: some fail and thereby weaken the organization's financial base, whereas others bring in healthy revenues but harm the organization's reputation and even threaten its tax-exempt status. Ed Skloot examines a number of cases of nonprofit entrepreneurship. He analyzes the ingredients that are necessary for success and illustrates the potential obstacles that cause many ventures to fail.

The last part of the handbook represents a foray into the important question of the role played by the nonprofit sector in other industrialized nations and in developing countries. The United States can be distinguished from all other societies (save, perhaps, for Israel) by the size of the work load it assigns to its voluntary nonprofit sector. Yet we do not understand why the United States is exceptional in this regard, nor have we devoted sufficient attention to studying the scope and dimensions of the nonprofit sector abroad. Estelle James, who knows a good deal more about these issues than anyone else, provides us with several answers to the question of the comparative vitality of the nonprofit sector. For example, she finds that the roles played by organized religion and cultural heterogeneity are critical in explaining the presence of the nonprofit sector. In the following chapter, we move from global comparisons to a specific region. Helmut Anheier, supplementing the literature with his field research, gives us insights into the operations of indigenous voluntary associations in West Africa. The final chapter, by Avner Ben-Ner, deals with producer cooperatives, that is, worker-owned firms, which exist in varying numbers in many capitalist societies. There are, to be sure, many variants on this type of organizational form (for example, worker-owned service firms like taxicab companies; consumer cooperatives; and mutual benefit life insurance and savings and loan associations). These different types of organizational arrangements point to the need for more comparative research—particularly cross-national, but also across sectors and across different forms of organization. The chapters in part VI provide an important foothold on this territory. We hope others will join us in enhancing our knowledge and understanding of these key topics.

Producing this handbook entailed a great deal of work—and not just on the part of the authors, the advisory editors, or myself. Several people whose names do not appear on the title page or the table of contents played a major role in this large project. It was a task that at times seemed overwhelming. But the advice and helpful blue pencil of our editor, Gladys Topkis, was a steadying source of support. Luisa Dato did a marvelous job in helping to manage the project—keeping track of authors and their chapters, staying in touch with the contributors, and urging them to the swift completion of their work. Cecile Watters copyedited the entire manuscript—an unenviable task she performed with both skill and speed. Finally, we are indebted to the Lilly Endowment, Inc., whose generous grant supported the production of this volume.

Walter W. Powell

New Haven, Connecticut
May 1986

AN OVERVIEW OF THE NONPROFIT SECTOR

1

A Historical Overview of the Private Nonprofit Sector

PETER DOBKIN HALL

Historians have tended to ignore the nonprofit sector. The existing scholarship examines only particular fields (education, health care, social welfare, the professions, philanthropy), the development of specific institutions, and the lives of individuals prominent in nonprofit areas. But little of the literature deals meaningfully with nonprofit institutions as a distinctive sector of activity. Thus I will draw on this research, fragmentary as it is, to delineate a historical model of the origins and development of the nonprofit sector in the United States and its relation to the for-profit and public sectors.

I define a nonprofit organization as a body of individuals who associate for any of three purposes: (1) to perform public tasks that have been delegated to them by the state; (2) to perform public tasks for which there is a demand that neither the state nor for-profit organizations are willing to fulfill; or (3) to influence the direction of policy in the state, the for-profit sector, or other nonprofit organizations.

Nonprofit organizations exist under a particular combination of ideological, political, social, and economic conditions that are, in turn, the products of a unique set of historical experiences. Ideologically, the nonprofit organization and its supporters see the will of the state as the collective will of the individuals who compose it. Politically, this view that sovereignty resides in the people is expressed institutionally in such legislative forms as grants of incorporation, tax exemptions, and tax regulations providing incentives to individuals to make donations to nonprofit organizations; it is expressed through such juridical devices as the creation of equity jurisdiction, which facilitates private collective action by permitting the allocation and administration of property

This research has been supported by grants from the Exxon Education Foundation, the Teagle Foundation, the American Council of Learned Societies, and the Program on Non-Profit Organizations, Institution for Social and Policy Studies, Yale University.

for future purposes. These ideological and political conditions can exist only in a social context in which individuals are socialized to responsible autonomy and the modes of authority are geared to compliance rather than coercion. Paralleling all three sets of conditions is an economic system in which individuals' financial resources and productive energies are subject to their discretionary disposal. The nonprofit sector is, then, a distinctive product of democracy and capitalism.

With the exception of England, on whose legal precedents and institutional experience Americans have drawn extensively in creating their own institutions, no other nation has depended so heavily as has the United States on private nonprofit organizations for performing so many public activities. Compelling testimony to this fact is that, as developing nations in this century have looked to developed countries for institutional models, their embryonic nonprofit sectors have been based on American rather than British examples.

THE PRIVATE NONPROFIT SECTOR IN THE UNITED STATES, 1780–1844

Although the laws of corporations and of charitable trusts had undergone extensive development in England before the end of the eighteenth century, they had little impact on the colonies. Because of their subsidiary status to the British crown, colonial legislatures lacked the power to create corporations (although they sometimes did). Because of the primitiveness of legal conditions and the absence of a legal profession before the mid-eighteenth century, equity, the jurisdiction under which trusts are enforceable, was either ill understood or, more often, entirely lacking. Many colonies, particularly those in New England, expressed a pronounced hostility to private corporations and to equity, which they associated with the corruptions of the Stuart monarchy and the Church of England. As a result, few corporations existed in the colonies before 1780. And their status was not firmly established as for-profit or nonprofit, private or public.

The situation of Harvard College, the oldest corporation in the colonies, illustrates well the ambiguous status of all colonial corporations. Although possessing a charter and thus technically private, it was governed by boards composed of ministers of the state-established church and state officials sitting in ex-officio capacities. Although it possessed an endowment made largely of donations and bequests from private individuals, much of its funding came from periodic public appropriations. Moreover, it was regarded as a public institution. Early business corporations such as the Massachusetts Bank (1783) were similarly ambiguous in their status: their capital often consisted of combinations of public and private subscriptions; public representatives often sat on their boards; the state reserved a right to interfere with or abrogate their charters at will; extensive justifications of their public utility were usually necessary to persuade legislatures to grant their charters.

It was only, then, in the late eighteenth century, when political and economic independence and cultural nationalism impelled major changes in institutional life, that lawyers and legislators began—in a fashion dictated largely by local and regional concerns—to draw on the English legal and organizational precedents of the previous two centuries.'

The five decades following the Revolution determined how Americans would deliver educational and charitable services. The Revolution itself left moot fundamental questions affecting the private exercise of public power. In New England, the Revolution did not immediately alter traditional conceptions of social and economic organization (Buel 1969). Nor did the displacement of the Tory elements of the elite alter the conviction held by the privileged and apparently assented to by the less so that the wealthy, learned, and respectable were those to whom public responsibilities of every sort were best entrusted. There was a movement for the establishment of both what we would call private for-profit corporations, beginning with the Massachusetts Bank in 1783 and continuing into the 1790s with the creation of bridge, turnpike, and canal companies, and a host of nonprofit corporations such as medical societies (Hartz 1948; Handlin & Handlin 1969; Hall 1973, 1982b). Although these grants of incorporation were clearly delegations of power from the state to groups of individuals for the performance of public tasks, and although profits might accrue to some of those who provided the capital, they were not conceived of as private corporations in the modern sense (Davis 1917; Dodd 1960; Kutler 1971). Their charters were not perpetual, and as their language makes clear, the corporations were created to serve public purposes. Most important, legislatures made the grants selectively to groups of individuals who, as long as pre-Revolutionary conceptions of social authority remained intact, were viewed more as public stewards than as private profiteers.

Although Massachusetts, like many other former colo-

nies, wrote a new state constitution in 1780, the property qualifications it specified both for voting and officeholding were eloquent testimony to the successful grafting of the Puritan conception of social corporatism onto a new commercial mentality. The Revolution passed without a rejection of the English laws governing the establishment of charities. Although Massachusetts courts did not possess equity powers (which posed a potential obstacle for the creation and administration of charitable and testamentary trusts), this defect was remedied by the legislature in 1819. In Connecticut, the pre-Revolutionary social order and ideology remained similarly unshaken by the war, though it differed from Massachusetts. It retained its colonial charter and the legislative acts that had proceeded from it (Purcell 1918), and the status of charities remained unchanged. As in Massachusetts, the post-Revolutionary wave of corporation building was entrusted to the elite. Favored by ideology, legislation, juridical framework, and commercial resources, the New England states led the new nation in incorporations of both for-profit and nonprofit enterprises, with 60 percent of incorporations as against 20 percent for the more populous and wealthy mid-Atlantic states (New York, New Jersey, Pennsylvania, and Delaware) and 20 percent for the relatively undeveloped states of the South and West (Davis 1917, 2:28).

Outside New England, institutional life was profoundly changed by the Revolution. The end of royal government and the establishment of state constitutions created the political and legal conditions favorable to extensive corporate activity. But religious and political heterogeneity placed almost insurmountable obstacles in the way of for-profit and nonprofit incorporations. In Pennsylvania and New York, efforts to obtain corporate charters became entangled not only in jealousies among Anglicans, Quakers, Dutch Reformed, and Presbyterians but also in conflicting interests between commercial and agrarian sectors. Thus, as of 1800, the middle states had granted only sixty-seven charters (to New England's two hundred), only two more than the economically backward and war-ravaged South. New York, moreover, had repealed the Elizabethan Statute of Charitable Uses and had, by the establishment of the University of the State of New York (the Regents), placed the government of private charitable and educational organizations within a political structure of accountability (Whitehead 1973). This hostility to private eleemosynary corporations was elaborated during the next three decades, as the state legislature passed laws that not only restricted the ability of testators to make bequests to endowed institutions but also required the institutions to hold the size of their endowments within limits specified by their charters. By 1830, New York surpassed both Boston and Philadelphia in population and wealth. But its philanthropic resources were scattered among a host of competing institutions, none of them the equal of Harvard, the Boston Atheneum, Massachusetts General Hospital, or the Pennsylvania Hospital. Not until the 1890s, after a major set of legal reforms, would New York City's charitable and cultural organizations match its commercial eminence (Ames 1913, 286ff.; Scott 1951, 251ff.).

The situation of nonprofit organizations in Pennsylvania between 1780 and 1830 was complex and ambiguous. On the one hand, as early as 1776, the new state government had encouraged the incorporation of charities and protected the rights of unincorporated ones—actions that were reaffirmed in 1790 when the state revised its constitution (Wyllie 1959, 205–06; Miller 1961, 15–17). On the other hand, it deprived its courts of the equity powers necessary for the enforcement of charitable and testamentary trusts—vital elements in the creation of institutional endowments (Hitchler & Liverant 1933, 156ff.). Individuals were free to create such trusts—and many did—but the lack of institutional mechanisms for their enforcement posed problems. As a Masachusetts court had noted in 1804 (fifteen years before the legislature granted it equity jurisdiction) in a case in which a trustee refused to pay an annuity to a widow upon her remarriage even though the annuity had not been subject to such a condition, "If this conveyance was in *trust*, this court could not have compelled the execution of it; and until the legislature shall think it proper to give us further powers, we can do nothing on subjects of that nature (1 *Massachusetts Reports* 204 [1804]). This ambiguous juridical situation hardly encouraged the growth of charitable endowments!

Finally, Pennsylvania's diverse ethnic and religious makeup mirrored New York's in many respects. And although the state did not go so far as to establish a governmental oversight body comparable to the Regents, intense political and economic competition among Episcopalians, Presbyterians, Quakers, and Lutherans, between English-speaking and German-speaking groups, and between Jeffersonians and Federalists led to a scattering of philanthropic resources. Pennsylvania had many colleges by 1830, but none remotely comparable to Harvard or Yale. Only in the field of medicine, in which the Pennsylvania Hospital, along with newer institutions like the Jefferson Medical College, received broad charitable support, were the state's early nonprofits of major national significance.

The South, however, was the fountainhead of anticorporate legal doctrines (Hirchler 1939, 109–16; Miller 1961, 6–8). Thomas Jefferson was hostile to corporations of any kind, regarding them as unwarranted grants of public privilege and property to private persons. Having repealed the Statute of Charitable Uses in 1792, the Virginia legislature in 1801 seized all the properties owned by the recently disestablished Episcopal church, turning them over to county overseers of the poor for management (permitting them, however, to be applied to the uses designated by their donors). By 1806, the legislature had enacted a statute that provided that all property given for charitable purposes was to be turned over to the management of county overseers of the poor. Individuals were free to make charitable gifts and bequests and were assured by the statute that they would be used as directed, but their management by political bodies could hardly have been reassuring to the potentially benevolent. Between 1790 and 1830, the Old Dominion paralleled New York's hostility to private eleemosynary corporations, refusing to charter new organizations and restricting the ability of individuals to provide them with property by gift and bequest.

The divergent attitudes of the states on the status of corporations and charitable trusts were necessarily reflected at the federal level (Zollman 1924). Although there were no federal statutes dealing with charities and corporations during the early national period, by 1819 a number of crucial cases were pending before the Supreme Court. The case of *Dartmouth College* v. *Woodward* involved the right of the state of New Hampshire to alter the charter of a private corporation against the will of its trustees. In this decision Chief Justice Marshall defined corporate charters as contracts and barred unwarranted government interference in their performance. Daniel Webster's argument in favor of the college emphasized not only the importance of protecting private corporations from government interference but also the nature of the bond between donors and the corporation:

> The case before the court is not of ordinary importance, nor of every-day occurrence. It affects not this college only, but every college, and all literary institutions of the country. They have flourished, hitherto, and have become in a high degree respectable and useful to the community. They have all a common principle of existence—the inviolability of their charters. It will be dangerous, a most dangerous experiment, to hold these institutions subject to the rise and fall of popular parties, and the fluctuations of political opinions. If the franchise may be at any time taken away, or impaired, the property may also be taken away, or its use perverted. Benefactors will have no certainty of effecting the object of their bounty; and learned men will be deterred from devoting themselves to the service of such institutions, from the precarious title of their officers. Colleges and halls will be deserted by better spirits, and become a theater for the contention of politics. Party and faction will be cherished in places consecrated to piety and learning. The consequences are neither remote nor possible only. They are certain and immediate. (4 Wheat. 518 [1819])

Nevertheless, federal doctrines on private charity remained confused. Although the Supreme Court had supported the corporate side of the argument for private charitable corporations in the *Dartmouth College* case, its decision in *The Philadelphia Baptist Association* v. *Hart's Executors* undermined the rights of private donors (4 Wheat. 1 [1819]). In 1795, Silas Hart, a citizen of Virginia, bequeathed a small sum of money to the Philadelphia Baptist Association, to be used to educate young men for the ministry. His executors refused to surrender the bequest to the Baptists, arguing that, because the association was not incorporated at the time of Hart's death, it could not hold charitable property under Virginia law. Moreover, Hart's executors argued that the membership of the organization was too poorly defined to constitute a legal beneficiary. While such a bequest might be legal under English law, Virginia's repeal of the Statute of Charitable Uses rendered it void in that state. Chief Justice Marshall sustained the defendants.

Although the *Hart* decision did not affect the activities of states like Massachusetts and Connecticut where incorporated charitable organizations were well established in fact and in law, it created serious problems in New York and Pennsylvania where the status of these institutions had not yet been clarified. Not until 1844, when the Supreme Court ruled on the *Girard Will* case, were private nonprofit corporations placed on a firm legal footing under federal law (Wyllie 1959, 219–20). This case involved the will of Stephen Girard, an enormously wealthy merchant who, on his death, left $7 million for the establishment of a college for orphans in Philadelphia. Although the case raised many important issues, the central one was the status of charitable bequests in places where the Statute of Charitable Uses had been repealed, as it was in Pennsylvania. By 1844, the quality of American legal scholarship had improved, and the attorneys for the Girard estate were able to demonstrate that the Elizabethan statute had, in fact, merely been the codification of a long series of other statutes and that, therefore, charitable trusts still stood on a firm foundation regardless of the legal status of the Statute of Charitable Uses (43 *U.S.* 127 [1844]). Thus, after 1844, private charitable corporations were securely established under federal law, although this did not affect the actions of states like Virginia and New York, which continued to limit their activities.

THE NONPROFIT SECTOR AND THE TRANSFORMATION OF AMERICAN CULTURE, 1780–1860

The evolution of American law in the first half-century of the Republic was merely symptomatic of a more profound transformation of society, economics, politics, and ideology. This transformation began in New England as an effort to deal with a tension among Puritan ideology, institutions, and resources. It ultimately affected the entire country, as New Englanders migrated to other regions, carrying with them a distinctive set of social ideas, economic practices, and institutional forms (Johnson 1978, 20, 139; Ryan 1982, 18–59, 105–44; Hall 1982b, 151–77).

Puritanism was more than a body of religious beliefs; it was also a social ideology. As developed by New Englanders, it drew largely but selectively on the colonists' medieval heritage, especially from the traditions of manorial communalism, and from their readings of the Old Testament. The central institution of New England life was the household, in which all were required to live, submitting themselves to the authority of its head, the father. Under this system of "family government," formal institutions of political and social life were barely necessary. Fathers were the agents of social control in the communities, each taking responsibility for those under his care. And, as Peter Laslett (1965; 1–21) has noted, domestic organization in this tradi-

tional society was economic organization, for the majority of the population engaged in subsistence agriculture, each household providing basic necessities for its members (also see Morgan 1944, 133–60; Greven 1969, 72–99). Neither the state nor the church had any real independence in this system. The church was a gathering of believing heads of families with a minister who served at their pleasure. The state, as manifested in the government of the towns, was a gathering of the landowning heads of families of good character.

This system was maintained and perpetuated by the collective control of land resources (Greven 1969, 41–71). When a town was settled, a portion of the land granted its proprietors by the colony was immediately distributed, but the bulk was held in reserve for distribution to future generations. By the third and fourth generations of settlement—that is, by the last decades of the seventeenth century in New England's older communities—these land reserves were exhausted. Although still deeply committed to their Puritan beliefs, fathers had to encourage vocational and geographical mobility for their sons (Farber 1973; Hall 1982a). But buying land, whether in their own towns or in others, cost money. Apprenticeships in the trades and professions were also costly commitments. Sustaining the Puritan polity pushed New Englanders from subsistence agriculture toward market production.

Although it began in the older communities, the crisis of land and resources became pervasive by the mid-eighteenth century, affecting not only farmers but all occupations. Overwhelmed by applicants for apprenticeships and swelled by their own trainees and recent immigrants from Europe, the crafts became extremely competitive. Even the professions were affected: as pulpits became increasingly difficult to find, many who had been trained as clergymen took up medicine and law, transforming them from marginal occupations into learned vocations.

The crisis in the occupational structure, evident by the early decades of the eighteenth century, had a pronounced impact on the whole structure of society, especially on the mechanisms of authority. As it became increasingly difficult to reward the young materially for their obedience and the lower orders for their deference, it became less possible to sustain the authority of church, state, and parents. Further, as sons were forced by circumstances to seek new vocations in new places, modes of social control began to shift from an externalized shame orientation, suitable to the patriarchal and communitarian context, toward an internalized guilt orientation, more adaptive to situations requiring autonomy (Vine 1976). Finally, as market production externalized economic activity, it became increasingly difficult for households to sustain their role in the delivery of social services—educating the young, disciplining the deviant, and caring for the sick, the poor, and the disabled.

After the Revolution differences of outlook and interest among the major social, economic, and sectional groups in the new nation began to emerge. Traditionalists favored older social forms based on the patriarchal family, the established church, and communal deference to the wealthy, learned, and respectable. But the social crisis had also created a coalition of diverse interests that stood outside the established order for reasons ranging from religious dissent through economic rivalry. Initially, the traditionalists—or Federalists, as they came to be known—favored strong government and advocated the delegation of state power to groups of respectable individuals for public purposes. By the 1790s these purposes included eleemosynary ones such as the establishment of schools, colleges, and hospitals as well as such commercial enterprises as banks, bridges, canals, and turnpikes. The dissenters, who came to be known as the Democratic Republicans, favored minimal government and looked to individuals and unincorporated voluntary associations to perform the basic tasks of production and social palliation.

In the election of 1800, the dissenters, led by Thomas Jefferson, captured the federal government. And as their successes eroded traditional patterns of political deference and extended the franchise and the right to hold office to the lower orders, they became the majority party, even in New England. Their triumph brought about a major shift of attitudes about corporations. The forces of wealth, learning, and respectability, having lost control of the state, began to recognize that private action was the only way they could hope to regain their influence. The majority party, with its large constituency of ambitious artisans and small entrepreneurs, favored corporations for economic purposes, though opposing the special privileges—monopolies and tax exemptions—with which the early corporations had been favored. They remained, however, steadfastly hostile to private nonprofit corporations. Though they might disagree on the most appropriate uses for corporations, both Federalists and Democrats by the second decade of the nineteenth century were moving toward a view that differentiated private and public action—a view articulated in its clearest form in the *Dartmouth College* case in 1819.

Two groups were especially aggressive and effective in their use of corporations for both for-profit and nonprofit purposes. Both were elements of the Federalist "standing order" which had been displaced by the rise of political and economic democracy after 1800. The first consisted of members of the Congregational and Presbyterian churches of the Northeast, which had been disestablished by the rise of an organized political opposition. The churchmen, supported by the Federalist merchants, professionals, and magistrates, created an evangelical counteroffensive (Foster 1960). Its purpose was to ensure that American democracy, both in older areas of settlement and on the frontier, would be tempered by the restraining influence of religion and education.

The machinery of the evangelical counteroffensive was a complex of interrelated voluntary and nonprofit organizations. At its base were the churches and, in close association with them, a set of nondenominational organizations—temperance, Bible, and tract societies; a nationally linked network of lyceums (which presented public lectures and organized debates on current events); teachers' institutes; and private academies—all of them reaching out to the public for supporters. The young people who were drawn into these organizations gained opportunities, particularly educational ones, that were lacking in society at large (Allmendinger 1975). The evangelicals also formed societies that underwrote college educations for pious young men (Allmendinger 1971; Potts 1971) and created missionary societies, which found pulpits for young clerics and established evangelical outposts in American communities (Scott 1978; Mattingly 1975). Tied to them were a host of secular pursuits closely tied to evangelical purposes—teaching positions in the public and private schools, editorships of temperance, religious, and antislavery newspapers, and lyceum lectureships (Horlick 1975). Even for those who became lawyers, businessmen, or farmers after college, there were advantages to be gained from evangelical connections: they enhanced the availability of credit and opened up avenues of political influence. These laymen tended to assume positions of economic, political, and cultural leadership wherever they settled (Tocqueville 1945, 1:304).

By the 1850s, the evangelicals had created not only a personal and organizational network that embraced the nation but also a "culture of organization," a subgroup of individuals oriented to for-profit and nonprofit corporate activity. Although they were a political minority, their influence in their communities was astonishing. Even in western and southern states where the law remained hostile to private eleemosynary corporations, they often managed to insulate publicly funded cultural and welfare institutions from political control through the institution of relatively autonomous boards of trustees. Wherever an orphanage, a library, a college, a hospital, an academy, or a professional society operated, it was almost invariably the work of a migrant New Englander with evangelical connections (Hall 1982b). Much the same could be said about banks, telegraphs, and the major incorporated for-profit enterprises of the mid-nineteenth century.

Paralleling the evangelical counteroffensive was a movement among the Federalist merchants of Boston, who, in addition to being politically displaced by the rise of the Jeffersonians, also faced economic challenges (Hall 1973, 50–104; Story 1980, 160–82). The traditional familial basis of business enterprise had proved extremely adaptive to colonial commercial conditions, but it handicapped those who sought to take advantage of the seemingly boundless opportunities offered by independent nationhood.

The conditions of post-Revolutionary commerce were dramatically different from those of the colonial period. Freed from the strictures of British mercantilist trade regulations, which had limited the growth of manufacturing and restricted American activities in world markets, entrepreneurs nevertheless found themselves unable to take advantage of the new conditions. Their capital, encumbered with familial and social obligations, was insufficient to engage in ventures like trade with India and China. Required now were joint ventures among unrelated families and the mobilization of idle capital in the population as a whole. Such ventures, whether in trade or in newer corporate activities like banking, required operatives selected for competence rather than kinship. Finally, because the post-Revolutionary Boston mercantile community was remarkably heterogeneous, its leaders having come from Massachusetts's smaller towns and cities, there was a particular need for mechanisms to take the place of kinship in fostering reliability and trust.

The mercantile response was coherent and thorough. To disengage capital from earlier obligations, the merchants encouraged vocational diversity among their sons. Pushing them into the professions was not a repudiation of traditional patriarchalism, however, for this generation of fathers ensured their sons' success (and retained some control over them) by creating corporate organizations: medical societies and schools, hospitals, and infirmaries for the doctors; corporate directorships and testamentary and institutional trusteeships for the lawyers.

This strategy affected not only their own families and the institutions they funded but also society itself. By disengaging capital, the family freed it for investment in expanding markets. Institutional endowments were important as mechanisms for pooling capital and for controlling the economy, as well as facilitating the expansion of mercantile influence into noneconomic realms. These institutions, then, socialized the merchants' sons and also served as vehicles for the recruitment of talented outsiders.

The years between 1820 and 1860 have often been called the Age of the Common Man—a period in which artisans and farmers discovered their political and economic strength and overturned an older, more patrician order. Although this characterization is not inaccurate, it masks a less visible but no less important pattern of institutional growth that grew from the ruins of the Federalist-Congregational polity. Tocqueville noted the importance of associations for Americans of the antebellum period. But he did not note—as he surely would have had he visited America twenty years later—that some associations, particularly those of Federalist-Congregational ancestry, were more important than others. Even workingmens' societies of the 1820s and 1830s, though seeming to partake of the spirit of an upsurgent democracy, were often dominated by members of the old elite, for whom they served as mechanisms for the political education of the masses.

If the evangelicals had created a nonprofit machinery that provided a foundation for the economic success of their adherents, the Bostonians had, by 1850, created a for-profit machinery in which nonprofit organizations played crucial roles as recruiters and socializers of personnel and as sources of capital. Although the nonprofit organizations yielded particular benefits for their creators, they were no less effective in providing important services for the public. Both merchants and evangelicals were active organizers and supporters of schools, colleges, hospitals, medical societies, orphanages, asylums, and other charitable enterprises that offered essential services few governments or private groups would undertake. The willingness of the benevolently wealthy and the evangelicals to assume these responsibilities

both lent credibility to their claims for political leadership—which were based on a rhetoric of public stewardship—and legitimated their accumulation of wealth—which, as their charitable actions showed, they held as stewards (Griffin 1960). In the tumult of antebellum democracy and capitalism, which shattered traditional forms of authority, these two groups were distinctive in their willingness to devote their wealth to public purposes and to do so through private nonprofit corporations.

The Civil War made good the groups' claims against those of the more doctrinaire democrats. The art of administration had stagnated under Andrew Jackson and his successors (White 1954, 550–51). Even the army had been deprived of its most talented officers by Jacksonian hostility to professional elites. The early phases of the war effort drew on Jacksonian administrative practices, such as they were. The results were disastrous, as the Union armies were routed on every front. It was only when Lincoln, who had been profoundly influenced by Federalist-evangelical organizational activities as a young man, turned to those with significant experience in the private sectors that it became possible to transform the jerry-built prewar government into an effective and reasonably efficient administrative apparatus.

Although the significance of the New England-based culture of organization was first identified by George Frederickson (1965) in his study of the U.S. Sanitary Commission, the private organization responsible for providing medical care to the Union army, it now seems apparent that the military and financial dimensions of the war effort also drew extensively on it. College-educated New Englanders and individuals influenced by evangelical institutions were disproportionately represented in the officer corps and key civilian positions. The evangelical enterprises provided the bureaucratic organizational models for the mobilization and produced both the levels of expertise and the personality types necessary for effective administration. The Union's victory was seen by its organizers and significant elements of the public as a legitimation of the claims of the organized private sector. By 1865, American culture had been transformed. The Jacksonian persuasion, with its prejudices against private power and the institutions and elites associated with it, was on the defensive in the face of a triumphant political nationality. But the national consolidation of economic and cultural energies still lay in the future.

THE NONPROFIT SECTOR AND THE SEARCH FOR ORDER, 1865–1920

The outcome of the Civil War made it possible for the advocates of private power to argue that the redemption of the Union was more than just a triumph of virtue. It was also a vindication of the private institutions whose strength was a product of their simultaneous commitment to reason, virtue, and science (Higginson 1866, iii–vi; Eliot 1874, 371–72). The notion of stewardship, of private responsibility for the public good, which had originated in religion, had been transformed by events and by new views of the place of man in nature into a scientific justification of the role of elites in America and their relation to the masses. This redefinition pointed to vast new responsibilities for private-sector institutions. For this reason elite educational reformers like Charles W. Eliot stressed the importance of the sciences at Harvard and the need to integrate them into the undergraduate curriculum.

If ideology and politics suggested new tasks for the private sector, the coalescence of the two strands of private institution building—the national evangelical network and the urban-intensive Boston institutional hierarchy—provided the means for undertaking these tasks. From 1865 on, the advocates of private power concentrated their energies in two areas: building private business corporations capable of operating on a national scale and transforming nonprofit institutions, especially colleges, into organizations that would facilitate that end. The two efforts were related. To establish and operate large-scale business organizations required new kinds of trained manpower and new technologies, as well as the ability to gather and interpret social and economic information (Lubove 1965; Haskell 1977). These were needs that colleges could best supply (Eliot 1869b), but they required the support of private wealth to expand facilities, to recruit students nationally and faculty internationally, to create new curricula, and to develop new fields for teaching and research. University administrators and progressive-minded business people sought one another out, with dramatically successful results: gifts and bequests to Harvard between 1866 and 1890 amounted to $5.9 million, compared to $1.6 million for the years 1841–65; gifts and bequests at Yale for the same period amounted to $5.3 million, compared to $1.0 million for the previous quarter century (Sears 1922, 23–24). Businessmen became so involved with the affairs of the major universities—all of them private—that it was hardly an exaggeration to claim, as Thorstein Veblen did, "men of affairs have taken over direction of the pursuit of knowledge" (1918, 57). University training became increasingly essential for the pursuit of careers in the larger business corporations. And businessmen were active in the founding of professional organizations like the American Social Science Association, the American Statistical Association, and the American Economic Association, which brought together nonprofit and for-profit institution builders in contexts of mutual concern (Buck 1965, 24–25, 82–88; Haskell 1977, 181ff.).

As important and powerful as the relationship between big business and the larger organizations of the nonprofit sector may have been in the years between 1865 and 1900, it was neither dominant nor unchallenged. Within the private sector, the power of business was resisted by antimodernists and avatars of "genteel culture" (Hawkins 1972, 216; Lears 1981). By the 1880s, groups of urban workers, intellectuals, farmers, and small businessmen in the South and West began organizing a coherent political opposition. Focusing first on national fiscal policy including hostility to big business and its cultural components, it became widespread.

The use of private nonprofit organizations grew enor-

mously during these years (Bremner 1956, 1960, 1980). Big business and private wealth underwrote the growth of universities, libraries, hospitals, professional organizations, and private clubs. But labor unions, mutual benefit societies, fraternal organizations, volunteer fire companies, building and loan associations, and even cooperatively owned nonprofit businesses came into their own during this period as institutional vehicles for the interests of the middle and lower classes. With the rise of urban poverty and growing awareness of it among the middle and upper classes, charitable organizations of every sort were established, ranging from traditional funds for the relief of the sick, poor, and disabled to new forms of nonprofit activity like the settlement house (Bremner 1956; Davis 1967; Huggins 1971; McCarthy 1982). With the rise of the "social gospel," churches, which until the 1860s dealt primarily with spiritual matters, became active in charitable affairs and in social, economic, and political reform efforts (Cross 1967; Smith-Rosenberg 1971). And a host of organizations—temperance societies, civil service reform associations, civic federations, and the like—became actively involved in the political process.

No less important than the nonprofit organizations directed to the reform of society was the rise of new kinds of cultural organizations whose primary constituencies were the well-to-do. The establishment and professionalization of museums and symphony orchestras (as well as the growth of the academic specialties that legitimated their activities) played a major role in recasting the nature of urban culture, transforming the market for artistic products, and reshaping the styles of the nation's upper classes (Fox 1963; Harris 1966; Horowitz 1976; DiMaggio 1981). By the 1880s, charitable activity itself became subject to the trend toward rationalization that was affecting business, as reformers attempted to make benevolence more effective through the creation of "united charities" organizations, which combined the resources of smaller enterprises, and state charity commissions, which oversaw the administration of public and private charitable activities.

As the public became more aware of violence, poverty, and disorder in the 1870s, it tended to indict foreigners and radical demagogues as sources of discontent (Hay 1877; Aldrich 1880). But between the great railroad strike of 1877 and the Haymarket bombing of 1886, public perception shifted to seeing disorder as a problem in social and economic organization. One of the first and most widely read products of this change was Henry George's *Progress and Poverty* (1879). In his introduction, George reviewed the optimistic expectations of most nineteenth-century Americans, who found them to be illusory in the new industrial age: the vast increases in production and wealth brought about by industrialization had neither abolished poverty nor made men more equal.

George was not alone in his condemnation of industrialism. Mark Twain's *Connecticut Yankee in King Arthur's Court* (1889) was a black comedy portraying industry as no more than a method for enlarging on the destructive capacity of the human race. Edward Bellamy's *Looking Backward*

(1886), while anticipating an evolutionary solution to the problems of inequality, similarly condemned the contemporary industrial order. As social and economic turbulence increased in the last quarter of the century, so too did criticism of business, the wealthy, and the institutions they supported.

But although they were perceived by many as enemies of social and economic justice, big business and its allies in the professions and the universities *were* concerned about poverty, corruption, and disorder. Very few businessmen were hard-line social Darwinists or reactionary advocates of laissez-faire (Kirkland 1956; Wiebe 1962; Heald 1970). Many were acutely uncomfortable with the growing contradictions between Christian social ethics and social reality and between democratic convictions about equality of condition and their extraordinary ability to concentrate private power in their own hands. Ironically, the severest critics of business, George and Bellamy, had their greatest following among the business and professional classes (Aaron 1951; Bowman 1958; Mann 1954; Sproat 1968). Upper-class churches, led by the Episcopalians, were the vanguard of socially concerned Christianity (Cross 1967). And businessmen themselves, most notably Andrew Carnegie, wrote influential analyses of the problems of industrial disorder (Carnegie 1886a, 1886b, 1889; Kirkland 1956).

By the turn of the century, a paradigm for the resolution of these problems began to be articulated, laying the foundation for what would become the dominant political consensus for the next eighty years. First, as Henry Adams would note in his *Education,* it had become clear by the mid-1890s that "a capitalistic system had been adopted, and if it were to be run at all, it must be run by capital and by capitalistic methods" (1918: 344). Large bureaucratically organized institutions were believed by many to be the most efficient mechanisms for achieving the social, economic, and political goals of reform. And if Americans wished to remain true to their democratic and Christian traditions—to "fulfill the Promise of American Life," as George Croly would put it in 1909—they would have to accept large organizations with their bureaucratic hierarchies, specialization of activity, and inherent inequality of condition. But if accepting inequality of condition were to be made consonant with democratic beliefs, it would have to be replaced by the creation of a rhetoric and a set of institutions that would dramatically equalize (or appear to equalize) opportunity and an ethos of service that would invest social, economic, and political hierarchies at all levels with a sense of common purpose. The new order, in other words, would take the form of a moral equivalent of war in which individuals attained their positions according to ability and talent and in which differentials of position and power, as well as a high degree of specialization, became recognized as essential to the pursuit of collective goals.

THE PRIVATE-SECTOR ALTERNATIVE, 1900–1935

Alternatives to capitalism and its legal basis, the private ownership of property, had been topics of discussion and experiment in some circles in America as early as the 1830s. But as long as socialism remained philosophical and utopian, it was not perceived as a threat to the established order. In the 1870s, however, the anticapitalist radicalisms began to be viewed in a new light, as events like the Paris Commune of 1871 and the emergence of radical organizations among farmers and urban industrial workers—capped by the great railroad strike and riots of 1877—propelled them to the forefront of public attention. Many of the more emotional journalists and politicians viewed radicalism as a moral issue. Some advocated the violent suppression of union activity, restriction of immigration (because immigrants were believed to be the vectors of socialism and anarchism), prohibition (because saloons were the centers of immigrant political activity), and restriction of the franchise. But those Americans with large business interests knew that social and political turbulence was a manifestation of fundamental problems in political, economic, and social institutions— problems that mere repression would not solve (Carnegie 1886a, 1886b; Croly 1919; Perry 1921, 329). These business leaders were also aware that leading European nations, particularly England and Germany, were responding through state action to popular demands for social and economic justice.

America's business leaders were averse to governmental solutions to social and economic problems, not so much from self-interest (neither German nor British industry suffered much from the implementation of the early social programs) as from the basic premises and historical experiences that had shaped American political culture. There was no precedent for large-scale federal action in peacetime, and even the effort to establish central control over the Federal armies during the Civil War had been fiercely resisted (Upton 1907; Ambrose 1962, 1964). Americans had rejected Whig programs of large-scale government scientific activity in the 1820s, and even conservatives had opposed efforts to establish a national university in the 1880s. Although the federal government had played an important role in the building of a transcontinental railroad and telegraph, it had done so only indirectly, through providing incentives and subsidies.

Philosophical opposition to big government dated from colonial times, was restated during the Revolution and in the drafting of the Constitution, and was reinforced by the pervasive, albeit vernacular, influence of social Darwinism. Most influential Americans saw progress as an open-ended phenomenon and feared that interference in "natural" social processes was both dangerous and, in terms of its effects on individuals, morally pernicious. Some Darwinists carried this viewpoint to extremes of laissez-faire brutalism; most, however, although disapproving of government action, viewed private-sector effects on social and economic activity as acceptable. Like the capitalist marketplace, private institutions of charity and culture were voluntary, in terms of both benefactors and beneficiaries. Their survival, like that of business corporations, was determined by how efficiently they were run, not by legislative edict. And their effect, like that of markets, was on the character of individuals who, in being better enabled to compete in the struggle for existence, would move the race forward.

Even if influential Americans in the last third of the nineteenth century had been able to overcome their philosophical objections to government activism, the disreputable, corrupt, and uncontrollable nature of American politics during that period would have discouraged them from increasing the powers of government over private action. Thus, it was incumbent upon the leaders of American business, culture, and charity to work toward a private-sector alternative to socialism.

It is in this light that the paradoxes of Progressivism, which emerged as an organized political force in the 1890s, appear less self-contradictory. Revisionist historians of the 1950s and 1960s made much of the Progressives' curious ability to combine antibusiness rhetoric (trust busting) with close ties to big business and remarkable inaction against business combinations like American Bell Telephone and U.S. Steel, which violated the spirit if not the letter of the Sherman and Clayton antitrust acts (Kolko 1963). Others, most notably Richard Hofstadter (1955), criticized Progressives' use of a democratic rhetoric that masked the movement's elite leadership and unrealistic and unduly moralistic concerns (1955). But, as the more recent work of Robert Wiebe (1967), Burton Bledstein (1976), and others has suggested, Progressivism was far more than a factional movement within the Republican party. It was a pervasive movement for cultural reform, and its roots, as Bledstein has shown, lay deep in the nineteenth-century history of private-sector institutions. The Progressive organizational style, with its emphasis on educated expertise and bureaucratic organization, affected both major political parties and, indeed, all realms of activity, from social work and government to business. But the common thread running through them all (leaving aside certain western Progressives, whose outlook owed much to populism and who came from states with poorly developed private cultural and charitable enterprises) was the recognition that social justice should come through the actions of the private sector assisted, but not directed by, government.

There was considerable disagreement among Progressives over the role of government. Some, especially literary intellectuals influenced by Marx, saw the movement as a form of evolutionary socialism. Others, including the more conservative business and professional reformers, emphasized the importance of efficiency in the private sector. World War I crystallized these viewpoints. To the Left, the war revealed the oppressive power of the capitalist state. To the Right, the war mobilization, which was an experiment in public-private partnership, both exposed the limitations of government bureaucratic centralization and underlined the value of planning and cooperation in the private sector (Galambos 1966; Cuff 1973). As the more radical elements in the movement spun off into bohemianism and third-party politics after the Armistice, the business Progressives were left free to develop a private-sector alternative to socialism.

This alternative grew out of two major sources, both

within the business community. The first involved the ideas about philanthropy articulated by industrialists like Andrew Carnegie. In his 1889 essay, "The Gospel of Wealth," Carnegie suggested that philanthropy, rather than being palliative, should orient itself to the prevention of social problems. By the turn of the century, Carnegie, John D. Rockefeller, and others began parceling out their fortunes to a new kind of philanthropic instrument: the charitable foundation. The foundation differed from previous eleemosynary vehicles in three major ways. First, its purpose was open-ended: rather than being devoted to some particular aim like better education or health care, the foundation included within its purposes any and all of the charitable uses covered by the Statute of Charitable Uses. Second, it performed its charitable purpose by giving money rather than by operating institutions. Third, although the process of money giving was to be entrusted to a board of self-perpetuating trustees, the identification of worthy aims was to be performed by a staff of expert individuals.

Although Carnegie can be credited with articulating the positive rationale for foundations and for large-scale philanthropy by the new industrial elite, his own charitable ventures moved only gradually toward the foundation form. The Carnegie Hero Fund Commission, established in 1901, had the conventional object of rewarding individuals who had demonstrated conspicuous courage in assisting others. But the three other foundations he created—the Foundation for the Advancement of Teaching (1905), the Endowment for International Peace (1910), and the Carnegie Corporation of New York (1911)—were progressively more open-ended in intention and in the discretion granted trustees.

The Rockefeller philanthropies followed a similar path from relatively conventional and clearly specified objects (such as his gifts to the University of Chicago in the 1890s) toward increasingly open-ended and flexible entities. In 1903, John D. Rockefeller endowed the Rockefeller Institute for Medical Research in New York, the first of a series of medical philanthropies. In the same year, he took a major step toward flexibility with the establishment of the General Education Board (Fosdick 1962). Originally modeled on the Peabody and Slater funds and serving similar purposes, the board by 1905 had acquired an expanded endowment of $10 million and the mission of improving higher education on a national basis. But the jewel in the crown of Rockefeller's benevolence was the foundation bearing his name, a fund of $100 million whose purpose was to be "the betterment of mankind." The Rockefellers had hoped to obtain a federal charter for the foundation, but encountered concerted congressional opposition (Collier & Horowitz 1976). After a series of acrimonious and highly publicized hearings, they abandoned the effort and in 1913 obtained a charter of incorporation from the New York State legislature.

Rockefeller, Carnegie, and their contemporaries proceeded cautiously in moving toward the foundation form. By the 1880s, the evolution of legal doctrine permitted great latitude to the founders of charitable trusts, exempting them from many of the constraints affecting private trusts. Rulings of the Supreme Judicial Court of Massachusetts had stated that a trust could be considered valid even if no particular object of charity was specified by the donor (*Schouler, Petitioner*, 134 *Massachusetts Reports* 426 [1883]; *Minot* v. *Baker*, 147 *Massachusetts Reports* 348 [1888]). A similar vagueness of intent was permitted with regard to the appointment and succession of trustees. Two of the earliest foundations, the Peabody Fund (1869) and the John F. Slater Fund (1882), although devoted to the education of southern Negroes, embodied many of the features of open-endedness and trustee discretion that would later characterize modern foundations.

The first genuinely open-ended foundation was established not by industrial giants like Carnegie or Rockefeller but by an enormously wealthy and charitably inclined widow, Margaret Olivia Slocum Sage (Mrs. Russell Sage). A champion of women's rights and a patron of conservation and medical research, Mrs. Sage, like Carnegie, was concerned about the problem of indiscriminate giving. Seeking advice about the ultimate disposition of her estate, she turned to her lawyer, Robert De Forest. A Wall Street lawyer and a director of many corporations, De Forest was also an experienced philanthropist: he had served as president of New York's Charity Organization Society since 1888, had chaired the New York State Tenement House Commission, was appointed New York City's first tenement house commissioner in 1902, and was elected president of the National Conference of Charities and Corrections in 1903 (Marquis 1925, 931; Smith, forthcoming).

By the time Mrs. Sage consulted him, De Forest's ideas about the need for fundamental changes in the nature of philanthropy were already well formed. As he wrote in the 1906 *Annual Report of the New York City Charitable Organization Society*, "the result to the community in eliminating and diminishing some of the more important causes of pauperism is of infinitely greater value than could have been brought about by the same amount of effort and the same amount of money expended for the relief of individual suffering" (De Forest 1906). He was prepared to sell Mrs. Sage on the idea of a philanthropic trust "elastic in form and method to work in different ways at different times" for "the permanent improvement of social conditions." The foundation was chartered by the New York State legislature in April 1907.

The Sage Foundation was unusual for its open-endedness and for its explicit public policy orientation. It intended to fund worthy objects and also to formulate and facilitate the reform of social, economic, and political life. These lofty ends were to be achieved by promoting surveys of social conditions, making their findings available to influential citizens, and mobilizing public opinion to bring about change. This relationship of academic experts, influential private groups, and government would become the paradigm for the public policy process that would be fostered by Herbert Hoover and other champions of the private-sector alternative.

It was precisely this relationship between industrial wealth and public policy that underlay the 1910–13 controversy over the chartering of the Rockefeller Foundation (*Rockefeller Foundation* 1913) and the 1915–16 hearings of the Senate Commission on Industrial Relations (*Industrial . . . 1916*). In a general sense, the fears of those who opposed the foundations were not ungrounded. The foundations, through their ability to channel huge amounts of money toward charitable objects at will, might become major instruments through which "the interests" could influence public policy. But the fierce controversy over their existence served to make philanthropists extraordinarily cautious. A few foundations, such as Russell Sage, the Brookings Institution (1916), and the Twentieth Century Fund (1919), addressed themselves fairly directly to public policy matters, but most acted with greater circumspection, either by funding relatively noncontroversial activities such as health care and education or by indirectly influencing public policy through grants to intermediary organizations like the Social Science Research Council, the American Council of Learned Societies, and the National Bureau of Economic Research. Foundation grants to these organizations and to the universities had a profound impact on the ordering of research priorities of universities and the growth of new disciplines, particularly the social sciences (Arnove 1982; Karl & Katz 1982; Stanfield 1985).

Philanthropy of the foundation type represented only one aspect of big business's recognition of its unique responsibilities. No less important—and, indeed, closely related— was the program of "welfare capitalism" that emerged in the 1880s. Commentators like Stuart Brandes (1970) have traced the origins of welfare capitalism to the mill villages of the early industrial age. But, although some of the welfare capitalist efforts did involve the construction of company towns, this model of employer-employee relations was a nostalgic attempt to reconstitute an idealized but vanished social context (Dalzell 1975). The main thrust of welfare capitalism in its motives and methods was more sophisticated than the crude paternalism indicted by Brandes. In fact, welfare capitalism appears to have stemmed from the same concerns with equity, efficiency, and expertise that gave rise to the general-purpose foundations.

The key issue for welfare capitalism was not whether charity had a seat on the board of directors but the extent to which firms could, by operating efficiently, also function more equitably. This approach involved not only improvements in technology and organization of production (particularly the introduction of statistical techniques that would permit quantitative assessments of efficiency and productivity) but also investments in human capital that would lead the worker to identify more closely with the firm and would, through improving his skills, make him more productive. Strictly speaking, this was not philanthropy, for it was not disinterested. At the same time, the impact of welfare capitalism on the work force and on the communities affected by it—as well as the motives underlying it, which saw doing well and doing good as inextricably linked—make it necessary to consider it as part of any overall assessment of philanthropy.

As Brandes's study suggests, welfare capitalism was not a clearly defined body of thought and practice. It was an uncoordinated set of managerial experiments that stemmed from a set of common concerns, but that varied enormously across the range of corporations and regions. Sometimes it involved direct corporate subsidies of nonprofit organizations, as, for example, with the massive support by the railroad industry of the Young Men's Christian Association. Between 1882 and 1911, the railroads contributed over a million dollars for the construction of 113 YMCA buildings and the underwriting of their operating expenses (Andrews 1952, 25). Other companies contributed to the creation of parks and playgrounds, schools, and libraries. But welfare capitalist programs most commonly were implemented either within particular firms or in the communities in which they operated. For this reason, they were not without their shortcomings. In some of its manifestations, welfare capitalism contained an intrinsic element of paternalism as in such places as George Pullman's model community outside of Chicago, where the company exercised extraordinary social and political control over its workers and facilities were more costly than they needed to be (Buder 1967; Brandes 1976). And, as the massacre of Carnegie's own workers at Homestead, Pennsylvania, in 1892 suggested, the freedom of the workers depended strongly on the forbearance of their employers. Nevertheless, welfare capitalism embraced a wide variety of possibilities, ranging from the exploitative company towns of the textile and mining regions through more open-ended provisions of health care and insurance, education, pensions, and profit-sharing plans for workers to subsidization of social and cultural services for the communities in which they lived.

Welfare capitalism, especially as articulated by Carnegie in his 1886 and 1887 articles on labor relations, focused less on the company-town concept than on the relationship between corporation and community. Carnegie's establishment of public libraries and donations for church organs pointed in this direction, but the major developers of this variant of corporate philanthropy were the entrepreneurs who operated in diversified economic contexts, many of them in smaller towns. This movement had several sources. One, which developed in the troubled period between 1873 and 1896, was the board of trade movement, the association of established businesses in a given location for the purpose of encouraging economic growth—not only through promotional activities, but also through programs of tax abatements, low-interest bank loans, and low-cost real estate (Hall & Hall 1982). Often these efforts derived from the recognition that the attractiveness of a community for plant location depended on noneconomic factors, such as the purity of the water supply, the quality of public education, the accessibility of recreational facilities, and the character of social amenities, from housing to class relations. Given the

calculable economic advantages to be gained from social investment, the business communities of many towns moved toward patterns of cooperation among business, government, and nonprofit institutions. By the 1890s, these efforts gave rise to the civic federation movement, which sought to reconcile the diverse concerns of different interests within American communities. One of the movement's major proponents was Marcus Alonzo Hanna, a powerful national figure in the Republican party and a major iron and coal operator (Croly 1919).

The boards of trade and civic federations, both dependent on business for their primary support, gave rise to the establishment of community foundations, a rationalization and centralization of the charitable resources of communities. The earliest of these was established in Cleveland: in 1900, the Committee on Benevolent Associations of the Cleveland Chamber of Commerce began to specify a list of agencies permitted to solicit funds within the city; in 1913, after some years of study, the chamber organized the Federation of Charities and Philanthropy, later incorporated as the Cleveland Foundation (Seely et al. 1957, 18–19). The early community foundations were not, as most are now, primarily trustees of endowments. They solicited and directed the distribution of charitable funds on a current basis, in the manner of the modern United Way. Thus, they provided a model for the Red Cross and War Chest campaigns of World War I, which were institutionalized during the 1920s in the form of Community Chest organizations.

By the end of the war, the basic elements were in place for the attempt to create a private-sector alternative to socialism. And the success of the Bolshevists in Russia, the almost successful socialist revolutions in Germany and Hungary, and a wave of radical-led strikes in the United States in 1919 made the creation of such an alternative an urgent task. The central figure in the effort was Herbert Hoover, a millionaire mining engineer turned public servant, who, as administrator of European food relief during and after the war, had seen the horrors of social upheaval firsthand.

Hoover's 1922 book, *American Individualism,* set forth his model for a "New Era." The professionalization of management with its connotations of trained expertise and public service led, in Hoover's view, to new kinds of institutional relationships. The most important of these were cooperative in nature. For Hoover, the rise of cooperative organizations had specific implications for the future of American politics and society. Rather than implying a move in the direction of socialism, it promised a private-sector alternative to socialism that would embody the efficiencies of centralized planning without stifling individual initiative. This model of an "associative state" is summarized by Ellis Hawley:

> The key to this achievement [the accommodation of individualism to industrial organization] lay in the development and proper use of cooperative institutions, particularly trade associations, professional societies,

and similar organizations among farmers and laborers. These, Hoover and other associationists believed, would form a type of private government, one that would meet the need for national reform, greater stability, and steady expansion, yet avoid the evils long associated with "capital consolidations," politicized cartels, and government bureaucracies. Unlike the earlier trusts, these newer institutions would preserve and work through individual units, committing them voluntarily to service, efficiency, and ethical behavior and developing for them a new and enlightened leadership capable of seeing the larger picture. And unlike government bureaus, they would be flexible, responsive, and productive, built on service and efficiency rather than coercion and politics, and staffed by men of expertise and vision, not by self-serving politicians or petty drudges. (1977, 132)

Hoover's ideas were widely shared in the business community. An examination of the twenty-fifth reunion class books of the major universities between 1890 and 1915 reveals a striking number of graduates who not only became progressive businessmen but were also broadly involved in progressive organizational activities on national and local levels. Typical of these was Walter S. Gifford who, upon graduating from Harvard in 1905, went to work at Western Electric in Chicago (Harvard College 1930, 238–40). While there, he lived at Hull House. His work and his social interests were not casually related, however, for his field of expertise at Western Electric was statistics, a specialty that had deep roots in and remained closely connected to the enterprise of social reform. His outstanding work brought him to the attention of AT&T's management. After moving to its New York headquarters, he organized the company's statistical department. He spent the war in Washington, serving as head of the Council of National Defense. By 1925 he had become president of AT&T, which he transformed into a model of welfare capitalist enterprise. The basis for reordering the corporation was financial: in order to enlarge its responsibilities to its workers and to the communities it served, production costs had to be lowered and the volume of business increased. Analyzing AT&T's business, Gifford realized that more profits could be made by tapping the mass consumer market than by devoting primary attention to commercial users (Gifford 1928, 97–106). Accordingly, he targeted domestic telephones as the company's primary market. An important part of his campaign to sell the telephone to a mass consumer market was the reshaping of AT&T's corporate image from that of a mere private company to that of a private company in the public service (Danielian 1939, 291–325). Also significant was his emphasis on improving communications technology to lower operating costs. For this, Gifford established the Bell Labs, which were active not only in lowering the costs of telephones but also in developing related communications technologies that, would prove enormously valuable to the company (Gifford 1928, 78–80). Finally, Gifford was attentive to the needs of his work force.

Realizing that employee loyalty was valuable and that employees were also consumers, AT&T under Gifford's leadership steadily increased wages and salaries through the 1920s and introduced a full range of benefits. Gifford was active in the associational network of nonprofit organizations, serving on the boards of the Rockefeller Foundation and the National Research Fund and acting as an adviser to the National Bureau of Economic Research.

Associational and welfare capitalist activity was not restricted to large quasi monopolies like AT&T and General Electric, nor was it limited to intrafirm strategies. For many, the community itself was the primary arena of action. This was especially true for communities with diversified economies. In Allentown, Pennsylvania, for example, industrialist Harry Clay Trexler fostered cooperative entrepreneurship and charitable activity on all levels within the community (Hall 1981; Hall & Hall 1982, 97–133). Like Gifford's innovations at AT&T and Gerard Swope's at General Electric, the work of Trexler and his associates was based not solely on humanitarian impulses but on quantitative reasoning, too. The Allentown business progressives actively subsidized surveys of the town's physical and social problems, which in turn became the bases for the policies they pursued (Bossard 1918; Holben 1923). When Trexler died in 1933, he left his $50 million estate to the community as a charitable trust, which, through the investment of its endowment, continued to encourage economic cooperation among the city's businesses and, through its grants program, subsidized the city's rich associational life.

Hoover's vision of the central role of the private sectors in shaping the nation's future appears to have been widely accepted in the business and professional communities. This acceptance was reflected in the emergence of a coordinated network of private organizations that included progressively managed corporations, corporate and independent foundations, policy institutes, private universities, and intermediary bodies, including trade associations and scholarly bodies like the National Bureau of Economic Research, the American Council of Learned Societies, and the Social Science Research Council. among the more important efforts of these linked organizations were the National Research Fund, which involved a $10 million commitment from major corporations to underwrite basic scientific research in the universities, and the President's Research Committee on Social Trends, which was a comprehensive attempt, using scholarly teamwork, accurately to assess the present and future direction of American life in the twentieth century. Though a federally sponsored effort, the committee's work was funded by the Rockefeller Foundation and staffed by the Social Science Research Council.

The real measure of the ubiquity of Hoover's ideas, however, was the extent to which they formed the basis for the first phase of the New Deal. The centerpiece of Roosevelt's first-term program was the National Recovery Administration (NRA), essentially a formalization of the private-sector alternative Hoover had been building during the 1920s. Designed to revive industrial and business activity and to reduce unemployment, the NRA was based on the principle of industrial self-regulation operating under government supervision through a system of fair competition codes. Based on earlier fair trade codes, these collective security arrangements were designed to prevent wage and price cutting, which in turn would enable corporations to maintain employment levels and benefits packages and support nonprofit welfare agencies. Although Hoover himself denounced the NRA, it was in fact a direct offshoot of his ideas and the programs he had fostered during the 1920s; it also owed much to the ideas of his colleagues in the business world. The Swope plan of 1931, for example, embodied many of its essentials and constituted the intellectual and institutional bridge between the private-sector emphasis of the New Era and the more statist tendencies of the New Deal (Loth 1958, 201–15). In many respects the NRA was little more than a formalization of the private-sector alternative through which the private for-profit sector and the nonprofits that depended on it would be guaranteed stability, thus generating employment and delivering social services that had been provided under welfare capitalist programs. The private sector could also continue its philanthropic activities in society at large.

THE PRIVATE NONPROFIT SECTOR IN THE WELFARE STATE, 1935–1980

After some fifty years, a bewildering variety of nonprofit organizations existed. Although they were broadly supported by Americans from all walks of life, their major support came increasingly from the business community. Wealth derived from business was passed by its owners either directly to nonprofit organizations or indirectly to foundations that in turn devoted it to charitable ends. But the role of small givers nevertheless remained important. In the 1920s organized fund-raising efforts had aimed particularly at mobilizing the resources of the middle classes, and the Community Chests, the YMCA, and the universities all professionalized their revenue-generating operations (Cutlip 1965). Finally, the corporations themselves grew in significance as charitable actors with the rise of professional management and the broad acceptance of welfare capitalist doctrines. Collective security arrangements fostered by the trade associations and later incorporated into the NRA codes permitted firms to devote significant portions of their income to social investment.

Although government figures on charitable giving are generally reliable after 1917 when the charitable deduction for individuals was incorporated into the tax code, it was only after 1936 when firms were allowed the same privilege that exact figures became available on the level of corporate contributions. Nevertheless, what evidence exists suggests their importance. Between 1920 and 1929, for example, thirty-five thousand corporations gave over $300 million to Community Chests in 129 American cities (Williams & Croxton 1930, 93). During the same period, corporate contributions to YMCA/YWCA, hospital, and other welfare service building funds in 37 cities amounted to $6.5 million. The proportion of corporate contributions to the totals raised in these fund drives ranged from 0 to 47 percent, with the average nearly 20 percent (Williams & Croxton 1930, 221–22). Contributions to Harvard from corporations and their officers during 1924–25 alone totaled almost 35 percent of annual capital and current giving (Harvard University 1925, 119–55). Thus, even though there was no tax incentive for charitable giving by corporations and in fact it was illegal in many states, the practice continued on a surprisingly large scale and was beginning to be professionalized, with the establishment of the Altman Foundation in 1913.

Nevertheless, even with the NRA in operation, the resources of the private sector were inadequate to the massive challenges of the Great Depression. The economic crisis of the thirties was national and international in scope, and most foundations and private social welfare agencies operated at the local level. In the end, their dependence on business proved to be a handicap rather than an advantage, for the business of the corporations first of all was to make money. When they were pressed, welfare and benefits programs were often the first areas attacked by cost cutters. Some firms, notably AT&T, acted quickly both to curtail benefits programs and to lay off workers (Danielian 1939, 200–42). Others, like General Electric and Bethlehem and U.S. Steel, struggled to maintain their commitments to their employees (Loth 1958, 216–40; Brody 1980, 66–78). But ultimately, as Bethlehem Steel's Charles Schwab admitted, "None of us can escape the inexorable law of the balance sheet." In any event, because welfare capitalism was based on voluntary compliance, it was effective only in the most centralized industries, such as steel, communications, and electrical equipment manufacturing. Many industrial sectors were relatively unaffected by trade associations. And many workers labored in small enterprises that stood entirely outside the associationist system. In some cases, this made little difference. In Allentown, Pennsylvania, for example, cooperative relationships among businesses and among the for-profit, nonprofit, and public sectors worked so well that the impact of unemployment and deflation were minimized (Fricke 1974). In fact, more plants were in operation in the city by 1939 than in 1929. Overall, however, the private-sector alternative did not withstand the depression.

The death blow to this alternative was the 1935 Supreme Court decision in *Schecter* v. *The United States* (295 U.S. 495; 55 S. Ct. 837; 79 L. Ed. 1570 [1935]). This case did not address itself directly to the trade associations and other collective security arrangements that had made welfare capitalism possible. Rather, it was concerned with Congress's ability to delegate legislative power to the executive branch, the power on which the government had based the writing and enforcement of the NRA codes. Without federal authority, the codes were meaningless. When the NRA went, so did the private-sector alternative, for even massive increases in individual giving could not compensate for the loss of business support.

Deprived of a consolidated private sector on which it could depend for the delivery of basic social and cultural services, the federal government had no choice but to turn to direct action. From the standpoint of Franklin Roosevelt's electoral constituency, which was in effect the populist alliance of southern and western farmers and urban workers who had always opposed big business, the turn away from the private sector and toward federal action was politically advantageous. It enabled Roosevelt to cast off his ties to the business community and commit his administration to a rhetoric and a set of policies that had profound public appeal. They yielded immediate political benefits, even if they did not succeed in bringing about recovery. But their long-term consequences, in terms of the inherent dangers of big government and of their impact on the nonprofit sector and the business community as a charitable support constituency, would not become evident for many years.

Roosevelt did not entirely rule out a charitable role for big business. His 1936 tax act for the first time permitted corporations to deduct charitable contributions from their federal income taxes. (He first opposed the deduction, but finally accepted it after intensive lobbying by the Community Chest [Heald 1970, 148–73].) And as their tax burden increased, both corporations and individuals in upper-income brackets turned to large-scale giving to reduce their obligation.

A difficult problem in the history of the private nonprofit sector is that of assessing the impact of Roosevelt's post-1935 redistributional ("soak the rich") policies. Their impact on individual givers as a group was minimal: between 1922 and 1938, the percentage of total gross income contributed to charity never exceeded 2 percent except in 1932 (Jones 1940, 10). Only the very richest, those earning $300,000 or more, increased their level of giving substantially after 1935 (Jones 1940, 8–10). Because the government did not gather statistics about business giving before 1936, we can only speculate about the impact of the corporate charitable deduction. Emerson Andrew's figures on the corporate share of contributions to Community Chests between 1920 and 1951 show surprisingly little change until World War II, when a combination of patriotism and high excess-profits taxes undoubtedly encouraged firms to give more than they had in the past (Andrews 1952, 158). The level of corporation giving in support of research in the natural sciences actually fell after 1936, in spite of its deductibility between 1930 and 1935, industry contributed between 60 and 75 percent of all funds devoted to scientific research; by 1940, contributions had dropped to less than 20 percent (Andrews 1952, 209). The response to tax incentives appears to have been pronounced only as it affected foundations, whose rate of formation increased dramatically. Where 239 foundations had been established before 1929, 294 were set up between 1930 and 1939 (Foundation Center 1970, 29).

These figures suggest that, except with regard to foundations, the coercive character of Roosevelt's tax legislation may actually have had a negative impact on charitable contributions in that it altered the rationale for giving. Whereas individuals and firms formerly had given because they believed in a cause or an institution, now their motive was the negative one of tax avoidance. Moreover, as Roosevelt's

rhetoric and policies became more stridently opposed to business and private wealth, corporate activities became subject to critical scrutiny by congressional committees, regulatory agencies, labor unions, and profit-starved stockholders. This discouraged managers—even the most idealistic—from straying far from the conventional kinds of charitable activities. In an atmosphere of distrust, corporate social and cultural investment, involving active efforts by companies to affect the environments in which they operated, became a relatively bland and unimaginative corporate philanthropy. One measure of the demotion of corporation giving to a subsidiary role is the fact that, although allowed by tax regulations to deduct up to 5 percent of pretax income for charitable gifts, business giving during the period 1936–80 never exceeded 2 percent (Harris & Klepper 1977).

It is interesting to speculate on what giving patterns would have been without a public policy emphasis on tax coercion. Unfortunately, virtually all the scholarship on the nonprofit sector has emphasized the negative aspects. Thus, F. Emerson Andrews wrote in 1967 that

> the extraordinary variations [in corporate foundation formation] are clearly related to corporate tax chronology. Excess profits tax, when combined with normal tax increases, began to rise sharply from 1940, reaching very high levels by 1945 [172 corporate foundations were formed between 1942 and 1945; only 36 had been formed in all previous years], at the close of which excess profits taxes were rescinded. They were again put into effect during the Korean crisis, from 1 July 1950 through 1953, at the close of which the combined tax rate for affected corporations was 82 per cent. More than 42 per cent of these foundations were established during those four years. (29)

Although these increases can be accounted for solely in terms of tax chronology, there were other powerful forces influencing corporate givers after 1940 and particularly between 1947 and 1955. One was the growing conviction in the business community that the growth of federal power could be checked only by a concerted effort to marshal the financial and cultural resources of the private sector. The Arthur Page Papers, which contain correspondence between Page, the leading figure in American corporate public relations during the years 1930–55, and a host of major foundation and corporation executives, reflect this concern. The first efforts to coordinate and consolidate business support for higher education (movements in which Page played a leading role) occurred during this period (Curti 1965a, 238–58). And the major challenge to the legal restrictions on corporation giving was mounted by a group of which Page was a part, its language reflecting their concerns. As the chief justice of the Supreme Court of New Jersey noted in his endorsement of a broader mandate for business philanthropy:

> I am strongly persuaded by the evidence that the only hope for the survival of the privately supported American college and university lies in the willingness of cor-

porate wealth to furnish in moderation some support to institutions which are so essential to public welfare. . . . I cannot conceive of any greater benefit to corporations in this country than to build and continue to build, respect for and adherence to a system of free enterprise and democratic government, the serious impairment of either of which may well spell the destruction of all corporate enterprise. (*A. P. Smith Manufacturing Company* v. *Barlow et al.,* 13 N.J. Sup. Ct. 147 [1954)])

The effort to counter the socialist tendencies that men like Page and his associates saw in the growth of federal power after 1936 was ultimately limited, however. These men had constituted the first generation of progressive business managers—the avatars of the private-sector alternative. By the late 1940s and early 1950s, they were dying or passing the reins of power to younger men. Their successors were men for whom (if Hays and Abernathy are to be believed) management was more a matter of technique than of vision, and they were more than willing to accommodate themselves to the welfare state (1980). As Allen Matusow characterized them, these corporate liberals ''were not reactionary champions of laissez-faire, as myth would have it, but sophisticated managers seeking to secure their hegemony with governmental assistance'' (1984, 32). Their attitudes about corporation giving mirrored their managerial outlook. Just as the new managerial approach emphasized short-term over long-term returns on investment, tax avoidance, and public relations, the dispensing of corporate charity as an executive prerequisite became the dominant characteristic of corporation giving (White & Bartolomeo 1982).

If they did not affect giving levels as dramatically as they might have, the policies of the emerging welfare state nevertheless had a pronounced impact on the nonprofit sector. Higher tax rates during World War II and the Korean War, the liberalization of legal doctrines on corporate giving, the refinement of conceptions of corporate social responsibility, and generational factors interacted to increase the wealth and influence of the nonprofit sector. The generational factor appears to have been especially important in swelling the assets of foundations and, in turn, accounts for their growing share of the total assets of the nonprofit sector. In 1929 foundations' assets represented only 10.7 percent of the assets of nonprofits (the total includes private religious, educational, health-care, and other charitable organizations), their share had increased by 1949 to 11.3 percent and by 1973, to 21.7 percent (Wood, Struthers & Co. 1932, 6; Andrews 1950, 70; Copeland 1977, 144).

The dramatic growth of the assets and number of foundations after 1940 (5,400 were formed between 1940 and 1959, compared to 591 before 1940) appears to have stemmed from four major sources. First, the war and postwar years internationalized America's outlook, bringing into sharp focus the confrontation between the capitalist democracies and totalitarianism. If the war had cast America in the role of ''arsenal of democracy,'' the emerging postwar situation suggested that the coming decades would be the ''American century.'' This redefinition of the scope of national responsibilities led to a systematic reexamination of American institutions and values and to a reconstruction of a positive rationale for private giving. (It was during this period, for example, that the American studies movement began. An important component of the effort was the examination of fundamental institutions of education and philanthropy under the leadership of scholars like Merle Curti and Bernard Bailyn. The role of foundation funding in this enterprise is covered in detail in the Arthur W. Page Papers, Wisconsin State Historical Society, Madison.) Second, the prosperity of the war and postwar years brought with it enormous increases in individual and corporate income, which, coupled with high tax rates, stimulated charitable giving. Third, increases in the federal inheritance tax after 1936 created a major tax-avoidance incentive for the wealthy, among whom were many of the founders of the great industrial fortunes of the twentieth century—Ford, Sloan, Lilly, Kettering, Pew, and others. Fourth, wealthy families were quick to recognize the utility of the foundation as a device for maintaining dynastic control over firms. Through their positions on the boards of family foundations they could maintain control over family corporations, draw substantial salaries, and extend their political and cultural influence (Marcus, 1983). Some of these post-1935 family foundations, notably the enormous Ford Foundation (1936) and the substantial Lilly Endowment (1937), performed a genuine public service, but many were little more than tax dodges. This would eventually lead to serious problems for the foundation world as a whole.

Overall, the growth of the welfare state after 1936 appears to have stimulated rather than discouraged the growth of the private nonprofit sector, but the direction of its growth changed markedly. Before the second New Deal, its major thrust was in the direction of a comprehensive associational system of private for-profit and nonprofit sectors working with encouragement from government to deliver basic social, cultural, and welfare services. After World War II, when the assets and numbers of nonprofit organizations began to increase dramatically, the thrust veered in the direction of a public-private partnership, with the private sector assisting the government in the delivery of basic services.

A major factor in this directional shift, aside from the changing of the guard in the ranks of business management, apparently was the experience of World War II. Although alienated by the Roosevelt administration's domestic policies in the late 1930s, important elements of big business shared with the president an understanding of the extent to which America's interests were threatened by the rise of fascism and, more distantly, by the power of the Soviet Union. Nonprofit lobbying and public information organizations like the Foreign Policy Association, the Council on Foreign Relations, and the Committee to Defend America by Aiding the Allies, as well as the foundations themselves, played a key role in preparing the public to accept the inevitability of America's involvement in the world conflict (Chadwin 1965). And as the nation began to prepare for war,

Roosevelt shifted his rhetorical gears and welcomed major business figures (Dulles, Forrestal, Stimson, and others) back into his administration. As in World War I, individuals from the private corporations, the foundations, and the universities proved to be essential in organizing the war effort and planning the postwar world order.

But unlike World War I, from which the leaders of the private sectors emerged disenchanted with big government, World War II encouraged closer ties between the two. Although some wariness remained, especially among older business progressives, the prospect of the United States becoming the dominant world power appears to have sustained the public-private partnership in the postwar era. Surely a major factor in this reconciliation was the parallel growth of foreign policy activism in government and the internationalist orientation of business. Another factor was the influence of Keynesian economic thought, which led both business and government leaders to recognize their common interest in economic stability. In addition, the Pax America, which necessitated big government, transformed government itself into the nation's largest single consumer of goods and services, a situation with considerable appeal to managers concerned with stability and reliable short-term returns on investment. Finally, the commitment of government as the primary actor in the fulfillment of basic social, cultural, and welfare needs altered conceptions of corporate responsibility and freed their funds for more clearly economic purposes.

The ensuing redefinition of the place of the private nonprofit sector in a world of big government was incremental rather than concerted, arising on the one hand from expansion of government activity in areas previously dominated by the private sector and on the other from an explicit reexamination by the private sector of its future role in American life. The expansion of government was comprehensive. With the creation of the National Security Council and the Council of Economic Advisors in 1948, the government assumed a central role in national economic, social, and political stabilization, a planning function performed earlier by a coalition of private groups. Government's assumption of this role became increasingly acceptable, even to the business community, as it became clear that America's struggle with the Soviet Union would involve a long-term commitment requiring a high degree of national unity and as Dwight D. Eisenhower's probusiness administration allayed fears about Washington's leftward drift. Another factor making an enhanced federal role acceptable was its inclusive character. Policy formation increasingly involved private-sector organizations (universities, foundations, policy institutes, and such quasi trade associations as the Business Advisory Council), and larger numbers of business managers and academicians put in stints of public service, coming to constitute over time an informal policy establishment (Burch 1981, 69–167).

Accompanying this accommodation of the public and private sectors was the emergence of the federal government as a major supporter of the private sector. In the early 1940s, when the war effort magnified the need for basic and applied research, government became the largest single contributor to the incomes of private universities, a role made permanent during the postwar effort to defend the peace. The National Science Foundation, established in 1950, and subsequently the National Institutes of Health made grants on a very large scale to private hospitals and universities. The passage of the GI bill in 1944, its renewal in 1952, and the National Defense Education Act in 1958 siphoned massive indirect subsidies into the private nonprofit sector. Finally, the Hospital Construction Act of 1945 and the postwar growth of private nonprofit health insurance plans transformed the federal government into a major actor in the health care field, though in this case it was still acting largely through organizations in the private sector (Fox 1985). In the 1960s, when international rivalries in arms and space exploration intensified and the War on Poverty got underway, federal funding of and influence over the private nonprofit sector become even more pronounced.

Between the 1960s and the election of Ronald Reagan, students of the nonprofit sector tended to view the growth of government power as an encroachment on areas of activity that had traditionally been private. Only recently—with Salamon and Abramson's 1982 analysis of the impact of cutbacks in federal social expenditure—has it become clear that the enormous growth of the private nonprofit sector after 1940 was in large part funded by government, which depended on private-sector organizations to implement its policies. The interdependence involved more than the government's use of the nonprofits to deliver social services. One of the ironies of the growth of the machinery of government in the postwar decades was its surprising failure to develop its own capacity for policy formulation and analysis. Instead it became increasingly dependent for implementation ideas on universities, foundations, and policy research institutes. And these institutional relationships were paralleled by the career patterns of policymakers, who tended to move back and forth between government, the universities, the foundations, the research institutes, and the corporations. We are only beginning to grasp the extent and implications of this institutional hybridization (DiMaggio & Powell, 1983). It is clear, however, that the relatively simple tripartite view of intersectoral relations relevant to the years before 1940 is not an adequate basis for understanding the development of organizations in our own time.

THE ASSAULT ON THE PRIVATE NONPROFIT SECTOR, 1940–1980

The growing importance of the private nonprofit sector after 1940 was not viewed positively by all Americans. Rumblings of discontent could be heard even in the late 1930s. The Temporary National Economic Committee investigations of corporate and private wealth, although sharply questioning the humanitarian intentions of the welfare capitalists, were curiously silent about the power of foundations and charitable trusts. Individuals in the foundations world, however, worried about their vulnerability to legislative attack.

In 1938, Frederick W. Keppel, president of the Carnegie Corporation, wrote:

> It would carry the writer too far afield to reenter the discussions as to the proportion of American Foundations which make no public record of their activities whatsoever—thereby failing to recognize their responsibility to the public as organizations enjoying exemption from taxation, a privilege shared with religious, educational, and charitable institutions. The instances in which it seems impossible to obtain pertinent information is disquietingly large. The question is not whether the funds of these silent trusts are put to useful purposes—indeed, some of the so-called family foundations are to the writer's knowledge making their grants with intelligence and discretion—it is rather whether public confidence in the foundation as a social instrument, a confidence which is in no small degree based upon the policy of complete publicity adopted by the better known foundations, may not be endangered. (Coon 1939, 334–35).

The real danger, as it turned out, would come from the Right, particularly from the realignment of political loyalties as the nation moved toward involvement in World War II. As early as 1940, many isolationists had already identified what they saw as an internationalist conspiracy to draw America into the war, and they were quick to question the role of foundations and a variety of nonprofit interest groups in advocating American intervention. These charges, however, did not find legislative expression until 1944 when, in the context of a Senate debate over tax legislation, John A. Danahar of Connecticut proposed an amendment to restrict the amount of losses from secondary businesses that could be allowed as deductions (Becker 1964, 241–48). On the face of it, the amendment was aimed at wealthy individuals who used expensive money-losing businesses to avoid taxation. But as the debate proceeded, it became clear that it was aimed at the activities of Marshall Field III, one of the nation's richest and most politically liberal businessmen and philanthropists. On the eve of the war Field had recognized the problems that isolationist control of the press (by men like Hearst and Robert McCormick) posed for internationalists trying to prepare the nation for the inevitability of war. To combat the isolationists, he established two newspapers, *PM* in New York and the *Sun-Times* in Chicago. Although both newspapers consistently lost money, they were widely read and effectively promoted internationalism.

But as the war drew to a close, the isolationist coalition, a curious alliance of Irish-Americans and other Americans with populist roots, began to sharpen their knives. The former group, mostly Democrats, had never forgiven Roosevelt for coming to the aid of the British. The latter, mostly Republicans, had never forgiven the internationalists for depriving their candidate, Robert Taft, of the party's presidential nomination in 1940 and 1944. Rather than attacking the charitable deduction, which would have aroused opposition from a wide range of charitable organizations, they

pursued the more politically viable strategy of favoring the Danahar amendment with its veiled attack on liberals like Field. (It should be noted, however, that there was a close historical association between the kind of populist sentiment that favored "soaking the rich" and isolationism.) The proposal was ultimately defeated, not because Field's friends rallied to his cause, but because the amendment would have had an especially severe impact on livestock breeders.

The start of the cold war, the breakup of wartime domestic and international political alliances, and the deaths of the nation's leading internationalists, Franklin Roosevelt and Wendell Willkie, opened the door to an assault, cloaked in anticommunist rhetoric, against liberal internationalism. The antisubversive movement, which included the investigations of the House Committee on Un-American Activities and the Senate Internal Security Subcommittee under Sen. Joseph McCarthy, was directed in large part against private universities and foundations, viewed by the radical Right as centers of subversion. Their animus in fact represented a revival of the old populist hostility against the private sector, reinforced by earlier factional struggles within the Republican party over its commitment to internationalism (Hofstadter 1955; Rogin 1969). It was no coincidence that the primary target of the antisubversives was Alger Hiss, president of the Carnegie Endowment for International Peace, who personified the liberal internationalist policy elite. In 1952, the Select (Cox) Committee of the House of Representatives launched an attack on the foundations that made explicit the charges that had been merely implicit since the Hiss case. The Cox Committee carried on an extremely thorough investigation of foundations, requiring the larger ones to answer an exhaustive questionnaire. The committee's real purposes were made clear in its final report, which is concluded with this question: "Have foundations supported or assisted persons, organizations, and projects which, if not subversive in the extreme sense of the word, tend to weaken or discredit the capitalistic system as it exists in the United States and to favor Marxist socialism?" (*Hearings . . . [Cox] Committee . . .* 1953, 9).

Shortly after the Cox Committee disbanded, one of its members, Rep. B. Carroll Reece, who felt that the inquiry had not had enough time to complete its work, received funding for an additional investigation. The hearings of the Special Committee to Investigate Tax Exempt Foundations were premised on a single issue: "that great change has occurred in America in the direction of socialism and collectivism . . . [and that] these changes were aided . . . through a 'diabolical conspiracy' of foundations and certain educational and research organizations" (Andrews 1968, 3). Coming as they did during the censure proceedings against Senator McCarthy, the findings of the committee had little credibility. The establishment stood firm, and not until the early 1960s would the enemies of the private nonprofit sector succeed in subjecting it to government regulation and public scrutiny.

As foundations and other nonprofit organizations became an increasingly important part of the American polity through the 1950s, resentment grew, especially among old populists like Rep. Wright Patman of Texas and other southerners and westerners. Their resentment was unquestionably reinforced by the role of certain foundations in underwriting political action, particularly in the area of civil rights. In May 1961, Patman began a sustained attack on private foundations, questioning their power and influence, their failure to provide adequate financial reports, the impact of their tax-free status on the nation's tax base, their role in perpetuating dynastic wealth and corporate control, and a host of other issues (Andrews 1968). Patman used the same sensationalistic technique as the red-baiters and was notably careless with the facts, but much of what he said was true. Foundations *did* hold enormous assets, they *were* frequently employed as devices to ensure control of corporations and to maintain the power and influence of particular families, and, most important, they *were* neither carefully scrutinized by the IRS nor, because they were not required to render annual reports, subject to public oversight. Patman's investigations, the findings of which were widely publicized in Ferdinand Lundberg's 1968 best-seller, *The Rich and the Super Rich,* culminated in the 1969 Tax Reform Act, which placed the foundations under strict federal oversight, setting standards for public reporting, the kinds of assets they could hold, and the proportion of annual grants to income. Almost two decades after the passage of the act, the nonprofits world still remains divided on the wisdom of foundation regulation. Although most concede the need for elimination of obvious abuses, those who see foundations as an important counterforce to government power have decried the act's chilling effect on social activism and advocacy activities by foundations.

Vengeful populists and advocates of self-policing were not the only threats to the autonomy of the nonprofits in the 1960s. Perhaps the most significant attack on the sector arose from the impact of federal aid on private institutions, especially universities and health-care facilities. In line with the decisions of the Warren Court, the federal government began attaching affirmative-action guidelines to its aid. Private institutions, having become extraordinarily dependent on federal funds in the postwar years, were in no position to refuse the government's demands. A number of issues were at stake in this struggle. One involved the maintenance of hallowed traditions of gender exclusivity and religious and racial quotas in the older private universities. Although they had much to gain by accepting federal guidelines, they justifiably feared the impact of coeducation and other changes on their financial base among older and wealthier alumni. A second issue involved the radicalization of faculty and students as a result of the civil rights movement and the Vietnam War. By the late 1960s, the various constituencies of the private universities tended to favor the antiwar and civil rights struggles. Because of this, the prowar elements who remained dominant in government threatened to punish the universities by attaching further conditions to federal aid and otherwise interfering with university operations. In 1967, for example, the Selective Service System adopted the policy of declaring students with low grade point averages eligible for the draft, a move that prompted the adoption of nonletter grading systems by many universities. The government's punitive actions became even more threatening when leading business conservatives William E. Simon and David Packard suggested that it was inappropriate for business to support universities whose faculties and students advocated position inimical to private enterprise and government policies.

Under these conditions, the federal aid that had been so crucial to the growth and modernization of the private universities and had served as a major factor in their maintaining their competitive position relative to the enormous expansion of the public sector in higher education began to look like a Trojan horse. To many the nonprofit independent sector appeared to be in grave danger, and by 1973, serious enquiries into its future were underway. The most notable of them, the Commission on Private Philanthropy and Public Needs (the Filer Commission), was privately sponsored but strongly encouraged by major political figures, including Democrat Wilbur Mills, chairman of the House Ways and Means Committee, and Treasury Department officials George P. Shultz and William E. Simon (Commission . . . 1977).

The result of the Filer Commission's work was published by the Department of the Treasury in seven weighty volumes in 1977. This comprehensive multidisciplinary survey of the nonprofit sector described and analyzed the continuing importance of nonprofit organizations as employers, as sources of essential health, educational, welfare, and cultural services, and as forces in political life. It also considered the regulatory and tax issues affecting the well-being of the sector. But while highlighting the sector's importance, it also revealed how little was really known about it—a fact that would become evident with the election of Ronald Reagan in 1980. The Filer Commission's work had posited a degree of sectoral autonomy that proved unfounded. And as the new administration began to cut federal social spending and shift the federal social role toward localities and the private nonprofit sector, the need became acute for knowledge not only about the nonprofits as an independent sector but also about the patterns of interdependence between public and private institutions and how fundamental social responsibilities were to be allocated between the two.

The new administration attempted to address these issues by forming a Task Force on Private Initiatives under the chairmanship of industrialist William Verity. Although this approach was originally predicated on the expectation that business, the nonprofits, and other voluntary groups could compensate for the losses that social, cultural, and welfare services would suffer from federal cutbacks, disagreement among members of the task force combined with the unwillingness of many corporations to commit themselves to giving at even the 2 percent level (much less the 10 percent permitted under the new administration's tax legislation) quickly transformed a search for policy alternatives to an exercise in public relations. The most serious blow to the effort came from policy analysts like Lester Salamon and

Alan Abramson of the Urban Institute who in 1982 demonstrated the interdependence of the public and private sectors for the delivery of basic services— meaning that private groups could not compensate for federal cutbacks, for they themselves had become largely dependent on public money. The two men further cited historic trends in giving and the then-depressed economy as other negative factors.

Since 1982, neither the Reagan administration nor the defenders of the private nonprofit sector have managed to develop a coherent policy on the independent sector. The administration has put forth sets of contradictory proposals—on the one hand pursuing its efforts to pare federal social and cultural expenditure while rhetorically supporting private voluntarism, and on the other favoring tax reform plans that would eliminate or reduce the giving incentives contained in the charitable deduction. Similar contradictions were evident in its education policy, which appeared to favor private institutions through proposals for the establishment of tuition tax credits, but then advocated cuts both in direct aid to higher education and in student loan programs, making attendance at private universities possible only for the very wealthy.

The combination of federal cutbacks in a time of recession and threats to the charitable deduction and to the financial base of universities did have the effect of drawing the diverse organizations of the nonprofit sector into a common defense of their privileged position under the tax code and other federal programs. The Foundation Center, although continuing its work as a generator and coordinator of information on the nonprofit sector, also became an active representative of the legislative interests of foundations. (One measure of this shift in purpose was its move from New York to Washington.) New organizations were formed to articulate and publicize the goals of the nonprofit sector, most notably Independent Sector, whose research and publication programs have helped push the frontiers of knowledge about the sector well beyond those established by the Filer Commission.

But even those favoring the nonprofit sector have not spoken with one voice on all issues. Although there has been virtual unanimity among the institutions of the nonprofit sector on the importance of the charitable deduction, some economists have questioned its efficiency as an incentive, especially with regard to small donors. Other more conservative economists, most notably Milton Friedman, have questioned the diversion of capital, particularly corporate resources, for philanthropic purposes, believing that firms serve society best by engaging as efficiently as possible in the task of making products and profits (MacAvoy & Millstein 1982). Still others, like the revisionist historians led by David Rothman, have challenged the concept of benevolence itself, arguing that ''a claim once considered to be of the most benevolent sort, the claim to be acting benevolently, had now become—to understate the point—suspect: if the last refuge of the scoundrel was once patriotism, it now appeared to be the activity of 'doing good' for others, acting in the best interests of someone else.'' (Rothman et al. 1978).

As the debate over the most effective way of serving public needs has proceeded, differences have also emerged among the institutions themselves in the nonprofit sector. In particular, there have been disagreements over the professionalization of nonprofit staffs, the application of affirmative-action guidelines, and the concept of public accountability. The Council on Foundations, led by James Joseph, has tended to favor not only affirmative action within the foundation world but also a giving agenda more responsive to public needs. Although this has been acceptable to many foundations, others, led by the conservative Institute for Educational Affairs (1983), have resisted the effort to lead foundations into following what it views as a liberal policy agenda.

The lack of unanimity, disheartening to some, is seen as an exciting intellectual challenge by others. The debate has generated important questions about the future of the nonprofit sector in the United States and, as we have come to recognize the centrality of independent institutions in American life, about the future of America itself. Although these questions are far from resolution, the first step toward resolving them is to accept the fact that the sector's problems and prospects are entwined with the broadest questions of political, economic, and social organization. And they rest, as Robert Payton, president of the Exxon Educational Foundation, has pointed out, on our fundamental values and the quality of our moral imagination (1984).

REFERENCES

BOOKS AND ARTICLES

Aaron, Daniel. 1951. *Men of Good Hope: A Story of American Progressives*. New York: Oxford University Press.

Adams, Henry. 1918. *The Education of Henry Adams*. Boston: Massachusetts Historical Society.

Aldrich, Thomas Bailey. 1880. *The Stillwater Tragedy*. Boston: Houghton, Mifflin.

Allmendinger, David F. 1971. "The Strangeness of the American Education Society." *History of Education Quarterly* 11:3–22.

———. 1975. *Paupers and Scholars: The Transformation of Student Life in Nineteenth Century New England*. New York: St. Martins Press.

Ambrose, Stephen E. 1962. *Halleck: Lincoln's Chief of Staff*. Baton Rouge: Louisiana State University Press.

———. 1964. *Upton and the Army*. Baton Rouge: Louisiana State University Press.

Ames, James Barr. 1913. *Essays in Legal History*. Cambridge, Mass.: Harvard University Press.

Andrews, F. Emerson. 1946. *American Foundations for Social Welfare*. New York: Russell Sage Foundation.

———. 1950. *Philanthropic Giving*. New York: Russell Sage Foundation.

———. 1952. *Corporation Giving*. New York: Russell Sage Foundation.

———. 1967. Introduction to *The Foundation Directory*, edited by Marianna Lewis, 7–51. New York: Foundation Center.

———. 1968. *Patman and the Foundations*. Occasional Papers, no. 3. New York: Foundation Center.

Arnove, Robert F. 1982. *Philanthropy and Cultural Pluralism*. Bloomington: Indiana University Press.

Bailyn, Bernard. 1955. *The New England Merchants of the Seventeenth Century*. Cambridge, Mass.: Harvard University Press.

———. 1960. *Education in the Forming of American Society*. Chapel Hill: University of North Carolina Press.

Baltzell, E. Digby. 1979. *Puritan Boston and Quaker Philadelphia: Two Protestant Ethics and the Spirit of Authority and Leadership*. New York: Free Press.

Becker, Stephen. 1964. *Marshall Field III: A Biography*. New York: Simon & Schuster.

Bellamy, Edward. 1886. *Looking Backward, 2000–1887*. Boston: Ticknor & Co.

Bledstein, Burton J. 1976. *The Culture of Professionalism: The Middle Class and the Development of Higher Education in America*. New York: W. W. Norton & Co.

Blumberg, Philip I. 1970. "Corporate Social Responsibility and the Social Crisis." *Boston University Law Review* 50, no. 2:157–210.

Bossard, James H. 1918. *The Churches of Allentown—A Study in Statistics*. Allentown, Pa.: Privately printed.

Bowman, Sylvia E. 1958. *The Year 2000: A Critical Biography of Edward Bellamy*. New York: Bookman Associates.

Brandes, Stewart. 1976. *American Welfare Capitalism*. Chicago: University of Chicago Press.

Bremner, Robert M. 1956. *From the Depths: The Discovery of Poverty in the United States*. New York: New York University Press.

———. 1960. *American Philanthropy*. Chicago: University of Chicago Press.

———. 1980. *The Public Good: Philanthropy and Welfare in the Civil War Era*. New York: Alfred A. Knopf.

Brewster, Kingman. 1981. *The Voluntary Society*. Tanner Lectures on Human Values delivered at Clare Hall, Cambridge University, October 29 and 30, 1981.

Brody, David. 1980. "The Rise and Decline of American Welfare Capitalism." In *Workers in Industrial America*, edited by David Brody, 48–81. New York: Oxford University Press.

Buck, Paul, ed. 1965. *The Social Sciences at Harvard*. Cambridge, Mass.: Harvard University Press.

Buder, Stanley. 1967. *Pullman: An Experiment in Industrial Order and Community Planning, 1880–1930*. New York: Oxford University Press.

Buel, Richard. 1969. *Securing the Revolution: Ideology and Politics in America, 1789–1815*. Ithaca, N.Y.: Cornell University Press.

Burch, Philip. 1981. *Elites in American Society*. New York: Holmes & Meier Publishers.

Carnegie, Andrew. 1886a. "An Employer's View of the Labor Question." *Forum* 1:114–25.

———. 1886b. "Results of the Labor Struggle." *Forum* 1:538–51.

———. 1889. "The Gospel of Wealth." *North American Review* 148:653–64 and 149:682–98.

Carosso, Vincent P. 1970. *Investment Banking in America: A History*. Cambridge, Mass.: Harvard University Press.

Chadwin, Mark L. 1965. *The Warhawks: American Interventionists before Pearl Harbor*. New York: W. W. Norton & Co.

Chandler, Alfred D. 1977. *The Visible Hand: The Managerial Revolution in American Business*. Cambridge, Mass.: Harvard University Press.

Collier, Peter, and Horowitz, David. 1976. *The Rockefellers: An American Dynasty*. New York: New American Library.

Commission on Private Philanthropy and Public Needs. 1977. *Research Papers*. Washington, D.C.: Department of the Treasury.

Coon, Horace. 1939. *Money to Burn: What the Great American Foundations Do with Their Money*. London, New York, and Toronto: Longmans, Green.

Copeland, John. 1977. "Financial Data from Form 990 Returns for Exempt Charitable, Religious, and Educational Organizations and Private Foundations." In Commission on Private Philanthropy and Public Needs, *Research Papers,* 143–55. Washington, D.C.: Department of the Treasury.

Corner, George W. 1964. *A History of the Rockefeller Institute, 1901–1953: Origins and Growth.* New York: Rockefeller Institute Press.

Croly, Herbert. 1909. *The Promise of American Life.* New York: Macmillan Co.

———. 1919. *Marcus Alonzo Hanna: His Life and Work.* New York: Macmillan Co.

Cross, Robert D., ed. 1967. *The Church and the City.* Indianapolis: Bobbs-Merrill.

Croxton, Frederick E., and Williams, Pierce. 1930. *Corporation Contributions to Organized Community Services.* New York: National Bureau of Economic Research.

Cuff, Robert D. 1973. *The War Industries Board: Business Government Relations during World War I.* Baltimore: Johns Hopkins University Press.

Curti, Merle, and Nash, Roderick. 1965a. *Philanthropy and the Shaping of American Higher Education.* New Brunswick, N.J.: Rutgers University Press.

———. 1965b. *American Philanthropy Abroad.* New Brunswick, N.J.: Rutgers University Press.

Cutlip, Scott M. 1965. *Fund Raising in the United States: Its Role in America's Philanthropy.* New Brunswick, N.J.: Rutgers University Press.

Dalzell, Robert F., Jr. 1975. "The Rise of the Waltham Lowell System and Some Thoughts on the Political Economy of Modernization in Ante-Bellum Massachusetts." *Perspectives in American History* 9:229–68.

Danielian, N. R. 1939. *A.T.&T.: The Story of Industrial Conquest.* New York: Vanguard Press.

Davis, Allen F. 1967. *Spearheads for Reform: The Social Settlements and the Progressive Movement, 1890–1914.* New York: Oxford University Press.

Davis, Joseph S. 1917. *Essays in the Earlier History of American Corporations.* 2 vols. Cambridge, Mass.: Harvard University Press.

Davis, Lance E., and Kevles, Daniel J. 1974. "The National Research Fund: A Case Study in the Industrial Support of Academic Science." *Minerva* 12:206–20.

De Forest, Robert. 1906. *Annual Report of the New York City Charitable Organization Society.* New York: Charitable Organization Society.

DiMaggio, Paul J. 1981. "Cultural Entrepreneurship in Nineteenth Century Boston: The Creation of an Organizational Base for High Culture in Early America." *Media, Culture, and Society* 4:33–50.

DiMaggio, Paul J., and Powell, Walter W. 1983. "The Iron Cage Revisited: Conformity and Diversity in Organization Fields." Yale University, Program on Nonprofit Organizations Working Paper no. 52.

Dodd, Edwin M. 1960. *American Business Corporations until 1860 with Special Reference to Massachusetts.* Cambridge, Mass.: Harvard Univesity Press.

Eliot, Charles W. 1869a. "The New Education." *Atlantic Monthly* 23:203–20, 358–67.

———. 1869b (1898). "Inaugural Address as President of Harvard University." In *Educational Reform: Essays and Addresses,* 1–38. New York: Macmillan Co.

———. 1874. "Views Respecting the Present Exemption from Taxation of Property Used for Religious, Educational, and Charitable Purposes." In *Annual Report of the President and Treasurer of Harvard University,* 369–94. Cambridge, Mass.: Harvard University Press.

Eliot, Samuel Atkins. 1845. "Public and Private Charities in Boston." *North American Review* 61:135–59.

———. 1848. *A Sketch of the History of Harvard College and Its Present State.* Boston: Ticknor & Fields.

———. 1860. "Charities of Boston." *North American Review* 91:154–61.

Farber, Bernard. 1973. *Guardians of Virtue: Salem Families in 1800.* New York: St. Martin's Press.

Fosdick, Raymond B. 1952. *The Story of the Rockefeller Foundation.* New York: Harper & Row.

———. 1962. *Adventure in Giving: The Story of the General Education Board.* New York: Harper & Row.

Foster, Charles I. 1960. *An Errand of Mercy: The Evangelical United Front, 1790–1837.* Chapel Hill: University of North Carolina Press.

Foster, Margery S. 1962. *"Out of Smalle Beginnings": An Economic History of Harvard College in the Puritan Period. 1636–1712.* Cambridge, Mass.: Harvard University Press.

Foundation Center. 1970. *Foundations and the Tax Reform Act of 1969.* New York: Foundation Center.

Fox, Daniel M. 1963. *Engines of Culture: Philanthropy and Art Museums.* Madison: State Historical Society of Wisconsin.

———. 1985. "Organizing Health Policy in the United States." Paper presented at the Davis Center Colloquium on Charity and Welfare, Princeton University, March 16.

Frederickson, George M. 1965. *The Inner Civil War: Northern Intellectuals and the Crisis of the Union.* New York: Harper & Row.

Fricke, Ernest V. 1974. "The Impact of the Depression on Allentown, Pennsylvania, 1929–1940." Ph.D. diss., New York University.

Galambos, Louis. 1966. *Competition and Cooperation: The Emergence of a National Trade Association.* Baltimore: Johns Hopkins University Press.

———. 1970 (1977). "The Emerging Organizational Synthesis in Modern American History." In *Men and Organizations: The American Economy in the Twentieth Century,* edited by Edwin J. Perkins, 3–15. New York: G. P. Putnam's Sons.

———. 1983. "Technology, Political Economy, and Professionalization: Central Themes of the Organizational Synthesis." *Business History Review* 57:471–93.

George, Henry. 1879 (1940). *Progress and Poverty.* New York: Henry George School of Social Science.

Gifford, Walter S. 1928–49. *Addresses, Papers, and Interviews.* New York: American Telephone & Telegraph Co.

Greven, Philip J., Jr. 1969. *Four Generations: Population, Family and Land in Colonial Andover, Massachusetts.* Ithaca, N.Y.: Cornell University Press.

Griffin, Clifford S. 1960. *Their Brothers' Keepers: Moral Stewardship in the United States, 1800–1865.* New Brunswick, N.J.: Rutgers University Press.

Hall, Peter Dobkin. 1973. "Family Structure and Class Consolidation among the Boston Brahmins." Ph.D. diss., SUNY-Stony Brook.

———. 1975. "The Model of Boston Charity: A Theory of

Charitable Benevolence and Class Development." *Science and Society* 38, no. 4:464–77.

———. 1981. "The Community Foundation and The Foundations of Community: The H. C. Trexler Estate of Allentown, Pennsylvania." Yale University, Program on Non-Profit Organizations Working Paper no. 34.

———. 1982a. "Philanthropy as Investment." *History of Education Quarterly* 22: 2: 185–191.

———. 1982b. *The Organization of American Culture, 1700–1900: Institutions, Elites, and the Origins of American Nationality.* New York: New York University Press.

Hall, Peter Dobkin, and Hall, Karyl Lee Kibler. 1982. *The Lehigh Valley—An Illustrated History.* Woodland Hills, Calif.: Windsor Publications.

Handlin, Oscar, and Handlin, Mary F. 1969. *Commonwealth: A Study of the Role of Government in the American Economy, 1774–1861.* Cambridge, Mass.: Harvard University Press.

Harris, James F., and Klepper, Anne. 1977. "Corporate Public Service Activities." In Commission on Public Needs and Private Philanthropy, *Research Papers,* 1174–88. Washington, D.C.: Department of the Treasury.

Harris, Neil. 1966. *The Artist in American Society: The Formative Years, 1790–1860.* New York: G. Braziller.

Harris, Seymour. 1970. *The Economics of Harvard.* New York: McGraw-Hill.

Harriss, C. Lowell. 1975. "Corporate Giving: Rationale, Issues, and Opportunities." In Commission on Private Philanthropy and Public Needs, *Research Papers,* 1789–1822. Washington, D.C.: Department of the Treasury.

Hartz, Louis. 1948. *Economic Policy and Democratic Thought in Pennsylvania, 1776–1860.* Cambridge, Mass.: Harvard University Press.

Harvard College. Class of 1903. 1928. *Sixth Report.* Cambridge, Mass.: Harvard University Press.

———. Class of 1905. 1930. *Sixth Report.* Cambridge, Mass.: Harvard University Press.

Harvard University. 1925. *Report of the President and Treasurer.* Cambridge: Printed for the university.

Haskell, Thomas. 1977. *The Emergence of Professional Social Science: The American Social Science Association and the Nineteenth Century Crisis of Authority.* Urbana: University of Illinois Press.

Hawkins, Hugh. 1972. *Between Harvard and America: The Educational Leadership of Charles W. Eliot.* New York: Oxford University Press.

Hawley, Ellis W., ed. 1974. *Herbert Hoover as Secretary of Commerce: Studies in New Era Thought and Practice.* Iowa City: University of Iowa Press.

Hawley, Ellis W. 1977. "Herbert Hoover, the Commerce Secretariat, and the Vision of an 'Associative State.'" In *Men and Organizations: The American Economy in the Twentieth Century,* edited by Edwin J. Perkins, 131–48. New York: G. P. Putnam's Sons.

Hay, John. 1877 (1900). *The Breadwinners: A Social Study.* New York: Harper & Brothers.

Hays, Robert H., and Abernathy, William J. 1980. "Managing Our Way to Economic Decline." *Harvard Business Review* 58, no. 4:67–77.

Heald, Morrill. 1970. *The Social Responsibilities of Business: Company and Community, 1900–1960.* Cleveland: The Press of Case Western Reserve University.

Higginson, Thomas W., ed. 1866. *Harvard Memorial Biographies.* Cambridge, Mass.: Sever & Francis.

Hirchler, Edward S. 1939. "A Survey of Charitable Trusts in Virginia." *Virginia Law Review* 25:109–16.

Hitchler, W. H., and Liverant, S. R. 1933. "A History of Equity in Pennsylvania." *Dickinson Law Review* 32:156ff.

Hofstadter, Richard. 1955. *The Age of Reform.* New York: Alfred A. Knopf.

Holben, Ralph P. 1923. *Poverty with Relation to Education.* Philadelphia: N.p.

Hoover, Herbert Clark. 1922. *American Individualism.* Garden City, N.Y.: Doubleday, Doran & Co.

Horlick, Allen S. 1975. *Country Boys and Merchant Princes: The Social Control of Young Men in New York.* Lewisburg, Pa.: Bucknell University Press.

Horowitz, Helen Lefkowitz. 1976. *Culture and the City: Cultural Philanthropy in Chicago, 1880–1917.* Chicago: University of Chicago Press.

Howard, Charles M. 1937. "Charitable Trusts in Maryland." *Maryland Law Review* 1:105–27.

Huggins, Nathan I. 1971. *Protestants against Poverty: Boston's Charities, 1870–1900.* Westport, Conn.: Greenwood Press.

Institute for Educational Affairs. 1982. *The Future of Private Philanthropy.* Foundation Officers Forum Occasional Paper 5. New York: Institute for Educational Affairs.

———. 1983. *Independent Philanthropy.* New York: Institute for Educational Affairs.

Johnson, Paul E. 1978. *Shopkeeper's Millennium: Society and Revivals in Rochester, New York, 1815–1837.* New York: Hill & Wang.

Jones, John Price. 1940. *The Yearbook of Philanthropy 1940, Presenting Information and Statistics Covering American Philanthropy since the Year 1920.* New York: Inter-River Press.

Karl, Barry D. 1982. "Corporate Philanthropy: Historical Background." In *Corporate Philanthropy,* edited by Mary E. Cadette, 132–35. Washington, D.C.: Council on Foundations.

Karl, Barry D., and Katz, Stanley N. 1982. "The American Private Philanthropic Foundation and the Public Sphere, 1890–1930." *Minerva* 19:236–70.

King, Wilford I. 1928. *Trends in Philanthropy: A Study of a Typical American City.* New York: National Bureau of Economic Research.

Kirkland, Edward Chase. 1956. *Dream and Thought in the Business Community, 1860–1900.* Ithaca, N.Y.: Cornell University Press.

Kolko, Gabriel. 1963. *The Triumph of Conservatism: A Reinterpretation of Progressivism, 1900–1916.* Chicago: Quadrangle Books.

———. 1967. "Brahmins and Businessmen." In *The Critical Spirit: Essays in Honor of Herbert Marcuse.* Boston: Beacon Press.

Kutler, Stanley I. 1971. *Privilege and Creative Destruction:*

The Charles River Bridge Case. Philadelphia: J. B. Lippencott.

Laslett, Peter, 1965. *The World We Have Lost: England Before the Industrial Age.* New York: Charles Scribner's Sons.

Lears, T. J. Jackson. 1981. *No Place of Grace: Antimodernism and the Transformation of American Culture, 1880–1920.* New York: Pantheon Books.

Lindemann, Eduard C. 1936. *Wealth and Culture: A Study of One Hundred Foundations and Community Trusts and Their Operations during the Decade 1921–1930.* New York: Harcourt, Brace & Co.

Loth, David. 1958. *Swope of G.E.* New York: Simon & Schuster.

Lubove, Ray. 1965. *The Professional Altruist: The Emergence of Social Work as a Career, 1880–1930.* Cambridge, Mass.: Harvard University Press.

MacAvoy, Paul W., and Millstein, Ira M. 1982. "Corporate Philanthropy vs. Corporate Purpose." In *Corporate Philanthropy,* edited by Alice Muckler. Washington, D.C.: Council on Foundations.

McCarthy, Kathleen D. 1982. *Noblesse Oblige: Charity and Cultural Philanthropy in Chicago, 1849–1929.* Chicago: University of Chicago Press.

Mann, Arthur. 1954. *Yankee Reformers in the Urban Age: Social Reform in Boston, 1880–1900.* Cambridge, Mass.: Harvard University Press.

Marcus, George. 1982. "Law in the Development of Dynastic Families among American Business Elites: The Domestication of Family Capital." *Law and Society Review* 14:4.

———. 1983. "The Fiduciary Role in American Family Dynasties and Their Institutional Legacy." In *Elites: Ethnographic Issues,* edited by George Marcus, 221–56. Albuquerque: University of New Mexico Press.

Marquis, Albert N. 1925. *Who's Who in America.* Chicago: A. A. Marquis & Co.

Mattingly, Paul H. 1975. *The Classless Profession: American Schoolmen in the Nineteenth Century.* New York: New York University Press.

Matusow, Allen J. 1984. *The Unraveling of America: A History of American Liberalism in the 1960s.* New York: Harper & Row.

Miller, Howard S. 1961. *The Legal Foundations of American Philanthropy, 1776–1844.* Madison: Historical Society of Wisconsin.

Morgan, Edmund S. 1944. *The Puritan Family: Religion and Domestic Relations in Seventeenth Century New England.* Boston: Boston Public Library.

Morison, Samuel Eliot. 1936. *Three Centuries of Harvard.* Cambridge, Mass.: Harvard University Press.

Morison, Samuel Eliot, ed. 1936. *The Development of Harvard University.* Cambridge, Mass.: Harvard University Press.

Noble, David F. 1977. *America by Design: Science, Technology, and the Rise of Corporate Capitalism.* New York: Oxford University Press.

Page, Arthur W. 1941. *The Bell Telephone System.* New York: Harper & Brothers.

Payton, Robert L. 1984. *Major Challenges to Philanthropy.* Washington, D.C.: Independent Sector.

Perry, Bliss. 1921. *The Life and Letters of Henry Lee Higginson.* Boston: Atlantic Monthly Press.

Potts, David. 1971. "American Colleges in the Nineteenth Century: From Localism to Denominationalism." *History of Education Quarterly* 10:72–86.

Purcell, Richard J. 1918. *Connecticut in Transition, 1775–1918.* New Haven: Yale University Press.

Research Committee on Recent Social Trends, Inc. 1933. *Recent Social Trends in the United States.* New York: McGraw-Hill Book Co.

Rogin, Michael Paul. 1969. *The Intellectuals and McCarthy: The Radical Specter.* Cambridge: MIT Press.

Rothman, David J. 1971. *Discovery of the Asylum: Social Order and Disorder in the New Republic.* Boston: Little, Brown & Co.

Rothman, David J.; Gaylin, Willard; Glasser, Ira; and Marcus, Steven. 1978. *Doing Good: The Limits of Benevolence.* New York: Pantheon Books.

Rudick, Harry J. 1952. "Legal Aspects of Corporation Giving." In *The Manual of Corporation Giving,* edited by Beardsley Ruml, 35–78. New York: National Planning Association.

Ryan, Mary P. 1982. *The Cradle of the Middle Class: The Family in Oneida County, New York, 1790–1865.* New York: Cambridge University Press.

Salamon, Lester M., and Abramson, Alan J. 1982. *The Federal Budget and the Non-Profit Sector.* Washington, D.C.: Urban Institute Press.

Scott, Austin W. 1967. *The Law of Trusts.* Boston: Little, Brown & Co.

———. 1951. "Charitable Trusts in New York." *New York University Law Review* 26: 152–75.

Scott, Donald M. 1978. *From Office to Profession: The New England Ministry, 1750–1850.* Philadelphia: University of Pennsylvania Press.

Sears, Jesse B. 1922. *Philanthropy in the History of American Higher Education.* Washington, D.C.: Bureau of Education, Department of the Interior.

Seeley, John R., et al. 1957. *Community Chest: A Case Study in Philanthropy.* Toronto: University of Toronto Press.

Smith, Hayden W. 1983. *A Profile of Corporate Contributions.* New York: Council for Financial Aid to Education.

———. 1984. "Corporate Contributions Research since the Filer Commission." New York: Council for Financial Aid to Education.

Smith, James. Forthcoming. *A Commonwealth of Experts: Public Policy Research Institutes in the United States.* New York: Twentieth Century Fund.

Smith-Rosenberg, Carol. 1971. *Religion and the Rise of the American City: The New York City Mission Movement, 1812–1870.* Ithaca: Cornell University Press.

Sproat, John G. 1968. *"The Best Men": Liberal Reformers in the Gilded Age.* New York: Oxford University Press.

Stanfield, John. 1985. *Philanthropy and Jim Crow in American Social Science.* Westport, Conn.: Greenwood Press.

Story, Ronald. 1980. *The Forging of an Aristocracy: Harvard and Boston's Upper Class, 1800–1870.* Middletown, Conn.: Wesleyan University Press.

Tocqueville, Alexis. 1945. *Democracy in America*. 2 vols. New York: Alfred A. Knopf.

Twain, Mark. 1889 (1971). *A Connecticut Yankee in King Arthur's Court*. New York: Penguin Books.

Upton, Emory. 1907. *The Military Policy of the United States*. Washington, D.C.: U.S. Government Printing Office.

Vasquez, Thomas. 1975. "Corporation Giving Measures." In Commission on Private Philanthropy and Public Needs, *Research Papers*, 1839–52. Washington, D.C.: Department of the Treasury.

Veblen, Thorstein. 1918. *The Higher Learning in America*. New York: B. W. Huebsch.

Vine, Phyllis. 1976. "Preparation for Republicanism: Honor and Shame in the Eighteenth Century College." Paper presented at the Annual Meeting of the Organization of American Historians, New York City, April.

Warner, Sam Bass. 1968. *The Private City: Philadelphia*. Philadelphia: University of Pennsylvania Press.

Weaver, Warren. 1967. *U.S. Philanthropic Foundations: Their History, Structure, Management, and Record*. Washington, D.C.: America Academy of Arts and Sciences.

White, Gerald T. 1955. *The Massachusetts Hospital Life Insurance Company*. Cambridge, Mass.: Harvard University Press.

White, Arthur, and Bartolomeo, John. 1982. *Corporate Giving: The Views of Chief Executive Officers of Major American Corporations*. Washington, D.C.: Council on Foundations.

White, Leonard D. 1954. *The Jacksonians: A Study in Administrative History*. New York: Macmillan Co.

Whitehead, John S. 1973. *The Separation of College and State: Columbia, Dartmouth, Harvard, and Yale, 1776–1876*. New Haven: Yale University Press.

Wiebe, Robert. 1967. *The Search for Order*. New York: Hill & Wang.

Williams, Pierce, and Croxton, Frederick E. 1930. *Corporate Contributions to Organized Community Welfare Services*. New York: National Bureau of Economic Research.

Wood, Struthers & Co. 1932. *The Trusteeship of Charitable Endowments*. New York: Macmillan Co.

Wyllie, Irvin G. 1959. "The Search for an American Law of Charity." *Mississippi Valley Historical Review* 46, no. 2:203–21.

Zollmann, Carl. 1924. *American Law of Charities*. Milwaukee: N.p.

CASES AND STATUTES

A. P. Smith Manufacturing Company v. *Barlow*. 13 N.J. Sup. Ct. 147 (1954).

Dartmouth College v. *Woodward*. 4 Wheat. 518 (1819).

Minot v. *Baker*. 147 Mass. Rep. 348 (1888).

Philadelphia Baptist Association v. *Hart's Executors*. 4 Wheat. 1 (1819)

Prescott v. *Tarbell*. 1 Mass. Rep. 204 (1804).

Schecter v. *The United States*. 295 U.S. 495, 55 S. Ct. 837, 79 L. ed. 1570 (1935).

Schouler, Petitioner. 134 Mass Rep. 426 (1883).

Statute of Charitable Uses. 43 Elizabeth, c. 4 (1601).

Tilden v. *Green*. 130 N.Y. 29, 28 N.E. 880 (1891).

Vidal v. *Girard's Executors*. 2 How. 27, 11 L. ed. 205 (1844).

GOVERNMENT DOCUMENTS

Final Report of the Select Committee to Investigate Foundations and Other Organizations. 1953. 82d Cong., 2d sess., H. Rep. 2514. Washington, D.C.: U.S. Government Printing Office.

Hearings before the Select (Cox) Committee to Investigate Tax-Exempt Foundations. 1953. U.S. House, 82d Cong., 2d sess. Washington, D.C.: U.S. Government Printing Office.

Hearings before the Special (Reece) Committee to Investigate Tax-Exempt Foundations and Comparable Organizations. 1954. U.S. House, 83rd Cong., 2d sess. Washington, D.C.: U.S. Government Printing Office.

Incorporation of the Rockefeller Foundation. 1910. U.S. Senate, 61st Cong., 2d sess. Rep. 405. Washington, D.C.: U.S. Government Printing Office.

Industrial Relations: Final Report and Testimony Submitted to Congress by the Commission on Industrial Relations. 1916. 64th Cong., 1st sess. S. Doc. 154. Washington, D.C.: U.S. Government Printing Office.

Report of the Special Committee to Investigate Tax-Exempt Foundations and Comparable Organizations. 1954. 83rd Cong. 2d sess. H. Rep. 2681. Washington, D.C.: U.S. Government Printing Office.

Tax-Exempt Foundations and Charitable Trusts: Their Impact on Our Economy. 1962–68. Chairman's Report to the Select Committee on Small Business. House. 87th Cong. Washington, D.C.: U.S. Government Printing Office.

The Rockefeller Foundation. 1913. U.S. Senate, 62d Cong., 3d sess. Washington, D.C.: U.S. Government Printing Office.

2

Economic Theories of Nonprofit Organization

HENRY HANSMANN

Serious work on the economics of the nonprofit sector began only in the early 1970s. This timing probably reflects, in part, the recent growth in the size and scope of the nonprofit sector. Until the 1950s, the sector was largely composed of traditional charities that received a substantial portion of their income from philanthropic contributions. Consequently, economic theorizing about the nonprofit sector, to the extent that it was undertaken at all, focused primarily on philanthropic behavior (for example, Dickinson 1962).

By the late 1960s, however, the character of the nonprofit sector had begun to change noticeably, its structure and performance assuming obvious importance for public policy. This change was most conspicuous in health care, particularly in the hospital industry. The implementation of Medicare and Medicaid in 1965 completed a process of evolution through which nonprofit hospitals were freed from dependence on charitable contributions and came to be potentially profitable institutions deriving virtually all their revenue from patient billings. Large publicly held business corporations owning chains of for-profit hospitals emerged for the first time. Simultaneously, hospital cost inflation appeared as a serious policy problem. The hospital industry in general, and the role and behavior of nonprofit hospitals in particular, thus became the subject of serious economic inquiry. It is not surprising, then, that the first efforts to develop economic models of nonprofit institutions focused almost exclusively on hospitals (for example, Newhouse 1970; Feldstein 1971; Lee 1971; Pauly & Redisch 1973).

Change was conspicuous in other parts of the nonprofit sector as well, however. Higher education, for example, underwent enormous expansion in the 1950s and 1960s and then fell into serious financial difficulty in the early 1970s. The live performing arts exhibited the paradox of constant fiscal crisis in the midst of rapid growth.[1] The day-care and nursing home industries, which had scarcely existed before World War II, became enormous. These industries—and many others like them—were all characterized by a mix of nonprofit, for-profit, and governmental firms, thus raising questions as to the relative functions and behavior of these three types of organization. Moreover, because all these industries received large and growing public subsidies, an understanding of their underlying economics was of obvious relevance for purposes of policy. The resulting prominence of such industries has led, over the past fifteen years, to the development of a substantial body of work concerning the economics of the nonprofit sector in general.

The economic theories of nonprofit organization appearing in the literature can conveniently, if somewhat artificially, be divided into two types: theories of the *role* of nonprofit institutions and theories of their *behavior*. Theories of the first type address such questions as these: Why do nonprofit organizations exist in our economy? What economic functions do they perform? Why, in particular, are nonprofit firms to be found in some industries and not in others? Why, among those industries in which nonprofit firms are found, does their market share—vis-à-vis both for-profit firms and governmental firms—vary so radically from one industry to another?

Theories of the second type address such questions as these: What objectives are pursued by nonprofit organiza-

A number of individuals provided helpful comments on an earlier draft, including Avner Ben-Ner, Eugene Fama, Estelle James, Michael Jensen, Richard Nelson, Susan Rose-Ackerman, John G. Simon, Richard Steinberg, Burton Weisbrod, and Dennis Young; I am grateful to them all. If the work of these or other authors is nevertheless mis- or underrepresented here, the responsibility is mine. I am also grateful to Walter Powell for his thoughtful editing.

1. The fiscal problems of the performing arts were documented by Baumol and Bowen (1965, 1966) in work that helped bring particular attention to the economics of that industry.

tions? What are the motivations of managers and entrepreneurs in the nonprofit sector? How do nonprofit organizations differ in these respects from for-profit and governmental organizations? How does the productive efficiency of nonprofit organizations differ from that of for-profit and governmental organizations? In what ways are such differences attributable to the special characteristics of the nonprofit form?

Ultimately, of course, questions of role and questions of behavior cannot be separated. To understand why it is that nonprofit firms arise in one industry and not in another, one must understand something about the firms' characteristic behavior. Nevertheless, economic theories of nonprofit institutions have tended to focus primarily on only one or the other of these two broad areas of concern, and thus the division will be employed here as a means of organizing the literature.

In this survey I shall focus primarily on firms organized as "true" nonprofits—that is, firms that are formally organized as either nonprofit corporations or charitable trusts. These organizations are all characterized by the fact that they are subject, by the laws of the state in which they were formed, to a constraint—which I shall call the "nondistribution constraint"—that prohibits the distribution of residual earnings to individuals who exercise control over the firm, such as officers, directors, or members (Hansmann 1980, 1981d). Note that nonprofits are *not* prohibited from earning profits; rather, they must simply devote any surplus to financing future services or distribute it to noncontrolling persons. Theories of the nonprofit firm are, then, essentially theories of the way in which the presence of a nondistribution constraint affects a firm's role or behavior. I shall not deal here, except for purposes of comparison, with cooperatives (producer or consumer), which are discussed in chapter 24, or with mutual companies, such as mutual insurance companies or banks; such organizations are empowered to distribute net earnings to their members and thus are not formally subject to a nondistribution constraint. Also, except for purposes of comparison, I shall not discuss public enterprise, but shall rather confine myself to private nonprofits.

TYPES OF NONPROFIT ORGANIZATIONS

The organizations that populate the nonprofit sector are structurally rather diverse. For ease of reference, I shall adopt here a classification scheme offered elsewhere (Hansmann 1980) under which firms are distinguished according to (1) their source of income and (2) the way in which they are controlled.

Nonprofits that receive a substantial portion of their income in the form of donations will be referred to here as "donative" nonprofits; firms whose income derives primarily or exclusively from sales of goods or services will be called "commercial" nonprofits. The Red Cross is an example of the former; most nonprofit hospitals and nursing homes today would be in the latter category. The term *patrons* will be used to denote those individuals who are the ultimate

TABLE 2.1   A FOUR-WAY CATEGORIZATION OF NONPROFIT FIRMS

	Mutual	Entrepreneurial
Donative	Common Cause National Audubon Society Political Clubs	CARE March of Dimes Art Museums
Commercial	American Automobile Association Consumers Union[a] Country clubs	National Geographic Society[b] Educational Testing Service Hospitals Nursing homes

Source: Adapted from Hausmann 1980.
a. Publisher of *Consumer Reports*
b. Publisher of *National Geographic*

source of the organization's income. Thus, in a donative nonprofit the patrons are the donors, whereas in a commercial nonprofit they are the firm's customers. In the case of nonprofits that have both donors and customers, the term comprises both.

Firms in which ultimate control (the power to elect the board of directors) is in the hands of the organization's patrons will be referred to as "mutual" nonprofits. Other nonprofits—including, in particular, those in which the board of directors is self-perpetuating—will be called "entrepreneurial" nonprofits.

The intersections of these two two-way classifications yield four types of nonprofits: donative mutual, donative entrepreneurial, commercial mutual, and commercial entrepreneurial. Table 2.1 gives some examples of each type.

The boundaries between the four categories are, of course, blurred. Many private universities, for example, depend heavily on both tuition and donations for their income and thus are to some extent both donative and commercial. Also, university boards of trustees commonly comprise some individuals who are elected by the alumni (who are past customers and present donors) and some who are self-perpetuating, with the result that the universities cannot be categorized as clearly mutual or clearly entrepreneurial. The four categories are, then, simply polar or ideal types, offered for the sake of clarifying discussion.

THE ROLE OF NONPROFIT ORGANIZATIONS

Several theories have been advanced to date to explain the economic role of nonprofit organizations. These theories are sometimes competing and sometimes complementary.

The Public Goods Theory

The first general economic theory of the role of nonprofit enterprise was offered by Weisbrod (1974, 1977), who suggested that nonprofits serve as private producers of public goods (in economists' sense of that term).[2] Governmental entities, Weisbrod argued, will tend to provide public goods only at the level that satisfies the median voter; consequently, there will be some residual unsatisfied demand for public goods among those individuals whose taste for such goods is greater than the median.[3] Nonprofit organizations arise to meet this residual demand by providing public goods in amounts supplemental to those provided by government.[4]

Weisbrod's theory captures an important phenomenon. Many nonprofit firms provide services that have the character of public goods, at least for a limited segment of the public. This is conspicuously true, for example, of those donative nonprofits (such as the American Heart Association, the National Cancer Society, and the March of Dimes) that collect private donations to finance medical research. As originally presented, however, the public goods theory left two questions open. First, the services provided by many nonprofits do not seem to be public goods but rather appear to be private ones. This is true especially of commercial nonprofits, whose share of the nonprofit sector has increased impressively in recent years. For example, the appendectomy performed in a nonprofit hospital, the child care provided by a nonprofit day-care center, the education provided by a nonprofit preparatory school, the nursing care provided by a nonprofit nursing home, and the entertainment provided by a nonprofit symphony orchestra are all difficult to characterize as public goods in the usual sense. Second, Weisbrod's theory stops short of explaining why nonprofit, rather than for-profit, firms arise to fill an unsatisfied demand for public goods. What is it about nonprofit firms that permits them to

serve as private suppliers of public goods when proprietary firms cannot or will not?

The Contract Failure Theory

The elements of a somewhat different theory of the role of nonprofits were set forth in an essay on day care by Nelson and Krashinsky (1973; Nelson 1977), who noted that the quality of service offered by a day-care center can be difficult for a parent to judge. Consequently, they suggested, parents might wish to patronize a service provider in which they can place more trust than they can in a proprietary firm, which they might reasonably fear could take advantage of them by providing services of inferior quality. The strong presence of nonprofit firms in the day-care industry, they argued, could perhaps be explained as a response to this demand. Similar notions had been hinted at in an earlier essay on health care by Arrow (1963), who suggested in passing that hospitals may be nonprofit in part as a response to the asymmetry in information between patients and providers of health care.

The theme advanced by Nelson and Krashinsky was fleshed out and generalized in an article by Hansmann (1980), where it is argued that nonprofits of all types typically arise in situations in which, owing either to the circumstances under which a service is purchased or consumed or to the nature of the service itself, consumers feel unable to evaluate accurately the quantity or quality of the service a firm produces for them. In such circumstances, a for-profit firm has both the incentive and the opportunity to take advantage of customers by providing less service to them than was promised and paid for. A nonprofit firm, in contrast, offers consumers the advantage that, owing to the nondistribution constraint, those who control the organization are constrained in their ability to benefit personally from providing low-quality services and thus have less incentive to take advantage of their customers than do the managers of a for-profit firm.[5] Nonprofits arise (or, rather, have a comparative survival advantage over for-profit firms) where the value of such protection outweighs the inefficiencies that evidently accompany the nonprofit form, such as limited access to capital and poor incentives for cost minimization (see below). Because this theory suggests, in essence, that nonprofits arise where ordinary contractual mechanisms do not provide consumers with adequate means to police producers,

---

2. A public good, in the economists' sense, is a good that has two special attributes: first, it costs no more to provide the good to many persons than it does to provide it to one, because one person's enjoyment of the good does not interfere with the ability of others to enjoy it at the same time; second, once the good has been provided to one person there is no easy way to prevent others from consuming it as well. Air pollution control, defense against nuclear attack, and radio broadcasts are common examples of public goods.

3. Logrolling and other devices, of course, often lead to establishment of government programs that cater to supramedian demands. Consequently, the median voter model should probably not be taken too literally here. Nevertheless, extremely intense or idiosyncratic demands for public goods are unlikely to be fully satisfied by governmental programs.

4. Weisbrod's theory has recently been illustrated and refined, with an emphasis on welfare considerations, in a formal model developed by Weiss (1986). In that model, Weiss demonstrates that, while a Pareto superior allocation of resources might well result when high demanders of a public good supplement public production with privately financed production, this is not a necessary result; it is possible that, even where there is cooperation between the public and private providers of the public good, the welfare of the high demanders will be lower when they can undertake supplemental private production than when they cannot. The reason for this result is that the low demanders, foreseeing the incentive for the high demanders to supplement public production with their own private production, might vote to support a substantially lower level of public production than they would otherwise and free ride on the private production, which will, as a consequence, be larger (and costlier to the high demanders) than it would be otherwise.

5. The emphasis in the text here is on the role of the nondistribution constraint as a direct bar to opportunistic conduct on the part of a nonprofit's managers. The nondistribution constraint might also, however, serve the same function through indirect means by screening for managers who place an unusually low value on pecuniary compensation and an unusually high value on having the organization they run produce large quantities of services or services that are of especially high quality. A simple model along these lines is offered by Hansmann (1980, Appendix). Data that lend some support to such a theory are presented, in the context of public interest law firms, by Weisbrod (1983). Young (1983; this volume, chap. 10) discusses screening for entrepreneurs at length, exploring a rich set of personal characteristics for which nonprofit firms might serve as a screen.

it has been termed the "contract failure" theory of the role of nonprofits (Hansmann 1980).

Donative Nonprofits

Although the contract failure theory has its roots in the work of authors (Arrow 1963; Nelson & Krashinsky 1973) who are primarily concerned with the role of commercial nonprofits, its most obvious application is in fact to donative nonprofits (Hansmann 1980; Thompson 1980; Fama & Jensen 1983a).[6] A donor is, in an important sense, a purchaser of services, differing from the customers of commercial nonprofits (and of for-profit firms) only in that the services he or she is purchasing are either (1) delivery of goods to a third party (as in the case of charities for the relief of the poor or distressed) or (2) collective consumption goods produced in such aggregate magnitude that the increment purchased by a single individual cannot be easily discerned. In either case, the purchaser is in a poor position to determine whether the seller has actually performed the services promised; hence the purchaser has an incentive to patronize a nonprofit firm.

For example, individuals commonly contribute to CARE in order to provide food to malnourished individuals overseas. A for-profit firm could conceivably offer a similar arrangement, promising to provide a specified quantity of food to such people in return for a contribution of a given amount. The difficulty is that the purchaser (donor), who has no contact with the intended beneficiaries, has little or no ability to determine whether the firm performs the service at all, much less whether the firm performs it well. In such circumstances, a proprietary firm might well succumb to the temptation to provide less or worse service than was promised.

The situation is similar with public goods. If an individual contributes to, say, a listener-sponsored radio station, then, unlike the situation with CARE, she is at least among the recipients of the service and can tell whether it is being rendered adequately. What she cannot tell is whether her contribution of fifty dollars in fact purchased a marginal increment of corresponding value in the quantity or quality of service provided by the station or simply went into somebody's pocket. A for-profit firm that operated such a radio station would have an incentive to solicit payments far in excess of the amounts necessary to provide their programming. In situations such as these, the nonprofit organizational form, owing to the nondistribution constraint, offers the individual some additional assurance that her payment is in fact being used to provide the services she wishes to purchase.[7]

As this example suggests, the contract failure theory is complementary to the public goods theory described above. Indeed, the public goods theory can be seen as a special case of the contract failure theory. For the reasons described by Weisbrod, there may be residual demand for public goods—such as noncommercial broadcasting—that is unsatisfied by government. Yet even if individuals are prepared to overcome their incentive to free ride and will donate toward financing of a public good, they will have an incentive to contribute to a nonprofit rather than a for-profit firm because of the monitoring problems just described.

We have been proceeding here on the implicit assumption that the donors to the nonprofit firm will be private persons. In many cases, however, the government is an important donor, and in some cases it is the only donor. Sometimes government donations are direct, as in the case of grants made by the National Endowment for the Arts to nonprofit performing arts companies or (now discontinued) Hill-Burton Act capital grants to nonprofit hospitals. In other instances, government donations are indirect, as in the case of tax exemption or reduced postal rates for nonprofits. Regardless of the way in which such donations are made, however, the government is often subject to the same problems of contract failure that face a private donor: it cannot easily determine directly whether its donation is being devoted in its entirety to the purposes for which it was made. Consequently, the government, like a private donor, has an incentive to confine its subsidies to nonprofit rather than for-profit firms, and it commonly does so. And this, in turn, creates further demand for the services of nonprofit firms.

Commercial Nonprofits

The contract failure theory can also help explain the role of commercial nonprofits. The types of services that commercial nonprofits commonly provide—such as day care, nursing care, and education—are often complex and difficult for the purchaser to evaluate. Further, the actual purchaser of the service is often not the individual to whom the service is directly rendered and thus is at a disadvantage in judging the quality of performance: parents buy day care for their children, and relatives or the state buy nursing care for the elderly. Finally, the services provided by commercial nonprofits are commonly provided on a continuing long-term basis, and the costs to the recipient of switching from one firm to another are often considerable. Consequently, purchasers are to some extent locked in to a particular firm once they have begun patronizing it, and thus the firm, if unconstrained, is in a position to behave opportunistically.[8] For all

6. Fama and Jensen (1983a, 342) seek to distinguish their briefly sketched theory of donative nonprofits from that offered by Hansmann (1980). The difference, however, is difficult to discern.

7. The same arguments presumably apply to situations in which individuals donate their own labor or other goods or services in kind. If a volunteer were to donate his services to a for-profit hospital, for example, he might find it difficult to determine whether the result was in fact an equivalent increase in the services rendered by the hospital without a corresponding increase in price or whether, alternatively, the owners

used him as a replacement for labor they would otherwise have paid for and thus simply increased their own profits. Consequently, individuals generally volunteer their services only to nonprofit organizations.

8. Ellman (1982) offers useful terminology for making distinctions between different forms of contract failure. On the one hand, there are problems of "quality monitoring," which involve situations in which the consumer can determine whether performance took place but has

these reasons, patrons might have an incentive to patronize a firm subject to a nondistribution constraint as additional protection against exploitation.[9]

Where commercial nonprofits are concerned, contract failure is presumably a less serious problem than with donative nonprofits. Consequently, it is not surprising that commercial nonprofits nearly always share their market with for-profit firms providing similar services. For example, roughly 20 percent of all private hospitals, 60 percent of all private day-care centers, and 80 percent of all private nursing homes are for-profit enterprises (Hansmann 1985a). If the contract failure theory explains the presence of commercial nonprofits in these industries, then the presence of both types of firms may reflect some division of the market: patrons who are reasonably confident of their ability to police the quality of the services they receive patronize the for-profit firms, whereas those who are less confident in this respect patronize the nonprofit firms, perhaps paying a premium for the service on account of the productive inefficiencies associated with the nonprofit form.

Although this theory is plausible as applied to most types of commercial nonprofits, it does not, interestingly, seem particularly persuasive when applied to hospitals, which constitute (in terms of GNP) the largest class of nonprofit institutions. There are two reasons for this. First, the hospital itself does not provide the patient care services that are the most sensitive and difficult to evaluate—namely, the services of the attending physicians. Rather, the physicians are usually independent contractors who deal separately with the patient. The hospital itself is largely confined to providing relatively simple services such as room and board, nursing care, and medicines. Second, the patient herself does not order the hospital services she receives; rather, they are ordered and monitored for her by a skilled and knowledgeable purchasing agent, namely, her physician. Consequently, it is not at all obvious that the nondistribution constraint offers the hospital patient any special protection that she would clearly be lacking without it.

Why, then, are hospitals nonprofit? It may be that, if we allow for a little historical lag, the contract failure theory in fact explains it. Until the end of the nineteenth century, hospitals were almost exclusively donative institutions serving the poor; the prosperous were treated in doctors' offices or in their own homes. The nonprofit form was therefore

efficient for the reasons of contract failure discussed above with respect to donative institutions in general. Then, however, a revolution in medical technology turned hospitals into places where people of all classes went for treatment of serious illness. Subsequently, the development of public hospitals took from the nonprofit hospitals much of the burden of caring for the poor. Finally, the spread of private, and more recently public, health insurance made it possible for the great majority of patients to pay their hospital bills without the aid of charity. The result is that today—which is to say, since the appearance of Medicare and Medicaid in 1965—most nonprofit hospitals have become more or less pure commercial nonprofits, receiving no appreciable portion of their income through donations and providing little or no charity care. The continuing predominance of nonprofit firms may simply be the consequence of institutional lag and of the various subsidies and exemptions that continue to be available to nonprofit but not to for-profit hospitals (Hansmann 1980, 866–68; Clark 1980). Indeed, since the late 1960s there has been substantial entry of large for-profit firms into the industry.

Contract Failure as an Agency Problem

In essence, the contract failure theory views the nonprofit firm as a response to agency problems. In situations like those just described, the purchaser (donor) is in the role of a principal who cannot easily monitor the performance of the agent (here, the firm) that has contracted to provide services to her. Consequently, there is a strong incentive to embed the relationship in a contractual framework, or "governance structure" (Williamson 1979), that mitigates the incentives of the agent to act contrary to the interests of the principal. The nonprofit corporate form, with its nondistribution constraint, serves this purpose.

It is worth noting, in this respect, that the relationship between the donors to a donative nonprofit firm and the managers of such a firm is analogous to the already much analyzed agency relationship between the shareholders in a publicly held business corporation and the managers of the corporation (see, for example, Jensen & Meckling 1976; Fama & Jensen 1983a, 1983b). The purchaser of a share of newly issued stock in a widely held business corporation, like a donor to CARE, is in no position to see for himself how the management is using the corporation's funds in general, much less what use is being made of his own marginal contribution to the corporation's assets. The shareholder is simply turning over funds to the corporation's management to be combined with other such funds and used however management chooses, subject only to the general constraints that (1) management will seek to obtain a reasonable rate of return for the shareholders on their contributed funds, and (2) management will take for itself no more than reasonable compensation for services rendered. These two constraints are precisely parallel to those that bind the management of a nonprofit firm, differing only in that, in the case of the nonprofit enterprise, the first constraint is replaced by one

---

difficulty judging the quality of the goods or services delivered. On the other hand, there are problems of "marginal impact monitoring," which involve situations in which the consumer can judge the quality of services performed by the firm but has difficulty determining whether the quantity or quality of services produced is higher than it would have been if he had not contributed. Commercial nonprofits presumably arise primarily in situations in which quality monitoring is a problem. Listener-supported broadcasting, in turn, presents a clear problem of marginal impact monitoring, and charities like CARE seem to involve both quality monitoring and marginal impact monitoring problems.

9. See Williamson (1979) for analysis of other contractual and organizational devices for mitigating opportunistic behavior in long-term complex transactions.

calling for management to devote the corporation's funds to the purposes specified in its charter. As in the case of the nonprofit firm, these two constraints are imposed upon the management of a business corporation by the terms of the corporation's charter and the legal framework in which that charter is embedded. Moreover, it is the second of these two constraints, which is effectively a nondistribution constraint, that has the more bite of the two; the very forgiving "business judgment rule" that the law applies to the decisions of corporate management makes the first constraint a largely nominal obligation.

In short, in the business corporation as in the nonprofit corporation, the only real contractual check on the behavior of the corporation's management is embodied in the nondistribution constraint imposed on management by the corporation's charter. The difference between the two types of corporations lies primarily in the class of individuals in whose favor the nondistribution constraint runs: the patrons (customers) or the investors of equity capital.

There are, to be sure, some important differences in the way the obligations of management are enforced in these two types of firms. The patrons of a nonprofit firm lack the mechanism of the derivative suit to enforce the nondistribution constraint against management. Rather, in most states only the state attorney general and/or the tax authorities have the right to bring suit in case of managerial malfeasance. Further, only in the case of mutual nonprofits do the patrons have any voting rights. And finally, patrons in both commercial and mutual nonprofits lack the advantage of a market for corporate control[10] as a means of sanctioning management.

Easley and O'Hara (1983) have sought to capture the contract failure theory in a formal model, treating it as a principal/agent problem. In this model the manager of the firm (the agent) has sole knowledge of the firm's level of output, the firm's cost function, and the extent to which the manager's own effort exceeds some minimal observable level; a customer of the firm (the principal) knows none of these things but can only verify that the manager has expended the minimal level of effort. The authors interpret a for-profit firm as one that contracts with the customer only in terms of price and output, the firm (or rather its manager/owner) promising to produce a given level of output in return for a given price. In this model, such a for-profit firm will produce no output (since the customer cannot observe it); rather, the manager will simply pocket the whole purchase price, expending no effort and using none of the purchase price to cover other costs of production.

A nonprofit firm, in turn, is interpreted as a contract that specifies (1) the amount of compensation to be received by the manager, (2) that the remainder of the purchase price is to be devoted to other costs of production, and (3) that the manager is to expend at least the minimal observable level of effort—all of which features of the contract are assumed to be verifiable by the customer. Easley and O'Hara show that this contract will result in a positive level of output in those cases in which the manager's minimal observable effort level (together with the other inputs acquired by the firm with that part of the purchase price that does not go to the manager as compensation) is sufficient to produce such a positive level of output. Thus, in this model, the nonprofit firm performs more efficiently than the for-profit firm, since the nonprofit produces a positive level of output in at least some cases, whereas the for-profit firm always produces zero output.

What is most interesting about this result is the nature of the assumptions necessary to establish it. In order for the nonprofit form to perform more efficiently than the for-profit form when output is unobservable, it is not sufficient simply to put a verifiable cap on the manager's compensation; the manager's level of effort and her use of the remainder of the purchase price must also be observable. In short, in this model the nonprofit firm involves policing inputs rather than outputs. If inputs were also completely unobservable, the nonprofit form would do no better than the for-profit form; both would always produce zero output.

This model probably captures the essential features of reality. In effect, the nonprofit corporate form is a device whereby the state (via the tax and corporation law authorities), on behalf of the customer, undertakes a certain minimal level of policing of inputs and of managerial compensation.

Note that an entrepreneur (or manager, in the model) will presumably submit herself and her firm willingly to such policing when she realizes that otherwise she will receive no patronage at all (and when the return permitted her by the nonprofit form is greater than her opportunity cost). It is in this sense that the nonprofit form is essentially a contract voluntarily entered into between a firm (more accurately, those in control of the firm) and its customers.

Empirical Tests

Weisbrod and Schlesinger (1986) have undertaken empirical work to test the contract failure theory as applied to commercial nonprofits, using data on Wisconsin nursing homes. These authors used consumer complaints to regulatory authorities as a proxy for quality of service. They found that nonprofit nursing homes are the subject of significantly fewer complaints than their proprietary counterparts, and they interpret this result as tentative support for the conclusion that nonprofit homes are less likely than proprietary homes to exploit the information asymmetry that exists between the homes and their consumers. These results must, however, be

10. The "market for corporate control" refers to the process whereby one business corporation can acquire effective control of another (the target corporation) by purchasing a majority of the target's stock, generally through a tender offer to the target's shareholders. Where the target corporation has been managed inefficiently in the past, such an acquisition opens the way for the acquiring corporation to replace the old management of the target with new, more effective managers, thus raising the value of the target's stock and producing a profit for the acquiring corporation. The mere threat of such a takeover, it has been suggested, may be an important incentive for the management of business corporations to perform with reasonable efficiency (Manne 1965).

interpreted with caution, since consumer complaints are a very indirect measure of quality of service, and the authors' regressions do not control for price or cost of service.[11]

Indeed, it is not obvious that the contract failure theory implies that, in equilibrium, nonprofit firms will exhibit a higher quality/price ratio than their for-profit competitors. If, as suggested above, patrons sort themselves among the two types of firms according to their ability to police the quality of service they receive, one would in fact expect to find, ceteris paribus, a lower quality/price ratio in nonprofit firms (since patrons of nonprofits are paying a premium for the added protection they receive). Yet such an effect may be obscured in empirical data by the fact that nonprofit firms, but not for-profit firms, have the benefit of tax exemption and other explicit and implicit subsidies, and these will tend to create an offsetting reduction in the cost of service.

In any event, the contract failure theory is a theory of consumer expectations, not of actual performance. Individuals who are uncertain of their ability to monitor quality might patronize nonprofit firms in preference to for-profit firms in the belief that the nonprofits are most trustworthy, yet be mistaken in that belief. An incongruity between performance and consumer expectations that persisted over the long run would, however, require some explaining.

Some efforts have been made to test the contract failure theory as applied to commercial nonprofits by determining, through surveys, whether patrons in fact believe that commercial nonprofits are more to be trusted than their for-profit competitors. The results are thin and ambiguous, though arguably somewhat supportive of the contract failure theory (Newton 1980; Permut 1981; Hansmann 1981a).

Subsidy Theories

In most industries in which they are common, nonprofit firms benefit from a variety of explicit and implicit subsidies, including exemption from federal, state, and local taxes, special postal rates, financing via tax-exempt bonds, and favorable treatment under the unemployment tax system. It is often suggested that such subsidies are in large part responsible for the proliferation of nonprofit firms (for example, Fama & Jensen, 1983a, 344), particularly in those industries in which nonprofits compete with for-profit firms.

Given the structure and administration of these subsidies, however, there is reason to doubt that they have had much effect in determining the industries in which nonprofits have and have not developed. In general, the scope of the subsidies seems to have adjusted over the years to include the new industries into which nonprofits have proliferated, rather than vice versa (Hansmann 1980). On the other hand, it seems reasonable to expect that the presence of these subsidies has had an impact on the overall extent of nonprofit development in those industries in which such firms appear.

11. The regressions do, however, control for the certification level of the home—that is, whether the home has been certified as a "skilled," "intermediate," or "personal and residential" care facility.

An empirical study using cross-sectional (state-by-state) data on four industries in which nonprofit firms and for-profit firms compete—hospitals, nursing homes, private primary and secondary education, and postsecondary vocational education—in fact provides tentative evidence that the availability of state property, sales, and income tax exemptions has a significant effect in enhancing the market share of nonprofit firms vis-à-vis their proprietary competitors (Hansmann 1985a).

The Consumer Control Theory

There are some types of nonprofits—in particular, some types of mutual nonprofits—that do not seem to have arisen in response to contract failure.

For example, it appears that exclusive social clubs, such as country clubs, constitute a distinct exception to the contract failure theory (Hansmann 1980, 1986). In such organizations, the patrons seem as capable of judging the quality of services as they would at, say, a resort hotel. The nonprofit form is evidently adopted here simply as a means of establishing patron control over the enterprise. Such control serves the purpose of preventing monopolistic exploitation of the patrons by the owners of the firm. The source of such monopoly power in social clubs is the personal characteristics of the members of the club. A substantial part of the appeal of belonging to an exclusive club lies in the opportunity to associate with the other members, who presumably have qualities or connections that make them unusually attractive companions. Consequently, if such a club were for-profit, its owner would have an incentive to charge a membership fee high enough not just to cover costs but also to capture some portion of the value to each member of associating with the other members. That is, so long as individuals who would make equally desirable clubmates were insufficiently numerous to populate a number of competing clubs, the owner of a proprietary club could charge a monopoly price to each member for the privilege of associating with the other members. Thus the members as a group have an incentive to exercise control over the club themselves to avoid such exploitation. Exclusive social clubs, under this view, therefore play an economic role that has more in common with that of consumer cooperatives—which, as discussed below, typically seem to be formed to cope with problems of simple monopoly—than with that of other types of nonprofits.

Ben-Ner (1986) takes a broader view of the role of patron control, arguing that *most* nonprofit organizations are formed primarily in order to provide consumers with direct control over the firm from which they purchase goods or services. He points, in particular, to three possible circumstances in which consumers might desire to have direct control over a firm rather than simply exercise control via the market. The first is contract failure (asymmetric information about quantity or quality of output), although Ben-Ner focuses on consumer control as a means of eliminating the information asymmetry rather than on the nondistribution constraint as a means of curtailing incentives for the firm to exploit that asymmetry. The second circumstance is that in which the firm is a monopolist and, although product quality is easily observable, there is a broad range of potential quality levels for the product, only one of which can be chosen. The problem here is that market signals alone may lead the firm to choose a quality level that appeals to marginal rather than average consumer evaluations of quality; direct consumer control could mitigate this problem. The third circumstance is that in which the firm produces price-excludable collective consumption goods. In such a case, consumer control might lead to a superior form of price discrimination, and thus higher aggregate welfare, than would control by profit-seeking investors.

Ben-Ner gives few examples of industries in which these factors constitute important sources of the demand for nonprofit, as opposed to for-profit, enterprise. Moreover, the few examples he does offer—such as the performing arts—may be better explained by other theories (see Hansmann 1981b). Consequently, although the factors examined by Ben-Ner may possibly play an important role in some industries, it is not obvious that they have broad application.

In developing his theories, Ben-Ner does not distinguish between nonprofit organizations and consumer cooperatives, but rather suggests that his theory explains the appearance of both types of firms. As the following section suggests, however, these two organizational forms generally seem to occupy distinct economic niches, and thus we need a theory of role that distinguishes between them.

Nonprofits versus Other Forms of Limited-Profit Enterprise

Nonprofits are not the only common form of profit-constrained enterprise. Privately owned public utilities typically operate under a form of price regulation designed to permit them no more than a competitive return on invested capital. Limited dividend companies, which are restricted by contract or statute to a stated maximum rate of cash return on equity, are common in the construction and operation of publicly subsidized housing. Producer and consumer cooperatives are constrained by the cooperative corporation statutes to pay a return on capital shares that does not exceed a specified percentage rate. And finally, cost-plus contracts, which provide for no more (and no less) than a stated rate of return to the seller, are common in situations such as defense procurement.

One might be tempted to suppose that all such forms of limited-profit enterprise, being so similar in form, must play similiar economic roles. In fact, this is not the case. To be sure, limited-dividend companies do seem to occupy a role similar to that of donative nonprofits: in particular, they seem to be used by the government as a means of ensuring that public subsidies are passed through to housing consumers rather than accruing entirely to developers. Regulated utilities, however, are a response to the potential for pricing abuses that accompany natural monopoly, a role that nonprofits seem rarely to play. (Indeed, the industries in which

nonprofits are commonly found are almost all characterized by a substantial number of competing suppliers.) Consumer cooperatives also generally seem to represent a response to monopoly. Like public utilities, and in contrast to nonprofits, they usually sell only simple standardized goods and hence do not typically seem to arise as a response to contract failure (Hansmann 1980; Heflebower 1980). There are exceptions, however. For example, mutual life insurance companies—which are formally structured as consumer cooperatives—originally arose in large part as a response to contract failure in the insurance market (Hansmann 1985b).

Cost-plus contracts, in turn, commonly serve as a device for shifting risk to the purchaser when *both* parties face ex ante cost uncertainty. Easley and O'Hara (1984) argue that a particular form of cost-plus contract—the cost-plus-variable-fee contract—may arise not exclusively as a risk-sharing device but also or instead as a response to situations of information asymmetry in which producers know more about cost of performance than consumers do. They are careful to distinguish this situation, however, from the type of information asymmetry concerning quality of performance that seems to give rise to nonprofits.

Nonprofit versus Governmental Enterprise

As the preceding discussion suggests, most work on the role of nonprofit enterprise has focused on the choice of the nonprofit versus the for-profit form of organization. In particular, this has been true of the work that has sought to explain the development of nonprofits as a response to contract failure, subsidies, or a need for consumer control to counter monopoly power. Relatively little work has been done to date comparing and contrasting the role of nonprofit and governmental enterprise. This is unfortunate because nonprofit firms typically operate in industries in which the organization of firms as governmental entities is a serious alternative. In fact, in the United States, governmental firms have a significant share of the market in many industries in which nonprofits are common, including hospital care, nursing care, primary and secondary education, and postsecondary and vocational education. Moreover, many of the activities that in this country are performed in substantial part by nonprofits are performed in most other developed countries almost exclusively by governmental firms; health care, higher education, and the performing arts are conspicuous examples.

An important explanation for this gap in existing theory undoubtedly lies in the fact that contemporary economic theory offers a much more coherent view of the role of for-profit enterprise than it does of the role of governmental enterprise, and thus the proprietary form of organization offers a much firmer basis for comparison than does governmental organization. Nevertheless, there has been some useful work illuminating various aspects of the relationship of nonprofit and governmental enterprise.

To begin with, Weisbrod's work on the public goods theory (1974, 1977), discussed above, suggests that nonprofits tend to serve a gap-filling role vis-à-vis governmental enterprise, meeting some of the supramedian or idiosyncratic demand for public goods that is left unmet by government provision. This theory leads to the prediction that the market share of nonprofit versus governmental firms will be larger in those jurisdictions in which demand is unusually heterogeneous. Lee and Weisbrod (1977) have sought to test this implication with respect to hospitals using cross-sectional (state-by-state) U.S. data. In particular, they regressed nonprofit hospitals as a fraction of total nonprofit and governmental hospitals against various proxies for heterogeneity of demand, including variance within the population in age, education, income, and religion. The results are mixed, but arguably mildly supportive of the theory. James, whose work is discussed in chapter 22, has also tried to test this implication of the public goods theory by exploring the relative shares of nonprofit and governmental provision of services in several foreign countries and seeking to correlate these relative shares with the apparent heterogeneity of the populations involved. She too finds some support for the theory.

Further considerations bearing on the choice of nonprofit versus governmental organization are offered by Nelson and Krashinsky (1973) and by Hansmann (1980). For example, governmental firms have the advantage, through use of the taxing power, of more reliable access to capital and to operating revenues (especially in the case of public goods). Also, governmental organizations are usually linked by an organizational chain of command to the central executive of the government in order to provide the government with the requisite degree of information and control. This chain of command can serve as an additional mechanism for ensuring accountability in situations of contract failure. On the other hand, it also imposes a degree of bureaucratization that can make governmental organizations more costly and less flexible than their nonprofit counterparts. The private nonprofit form of organization has the corresponding advantage that it permits the development of a number of independent firms and thus promises greater competition and responsiveness to market forces. Moreover, a nonprofit firm can be more easily tailored to serve a narrow patronage, since it need not respond to the interests of the public at large. These and other factors that might affect the relative market shares of governmental and nonprofit organizations are explored in a cross-national context by James in chapter 22.

Further questions involve the relationship between governmental action and donative nonprofits. Governmental policy can affect the amount and direction of activity undertaken by donative nonprofits in various ways. Much attention has been given in recent years to exploring, both theoretically and empirically, the extent to which the charitable deduction incorporated in the personal income tax serves to encourage larger donations and the way in which these increased donations are distributed across different types of charities (Feldstein 1975; Clotfelter & Salamon 1982; Jencks, this volume, chap. 18). Less well explored, but of equal interest, are the ways in which direct government grants to nonprofits, or governmental provision of services in competition with those

provided by nonprofits, may affect, positively or negatively, the amount or types of activity undertaken by nonprofits. Similarly, it is of interest to inquiry why it is that governments in some cases provide services directly and in other cases provide the same or similar services by means of grants to private nonprofit organizations (see Rose-Ackerman 1981; James, this volume, chap. 22).

The Role of Donative Financing

Another set of interesting questions concerns the role of donative financing. The contract failure theory provides a potential explanation for the fact that donatively financed organizations are almost universally organized as nonprofits: by definition, donations involve payments that, though usually intended to be used for specific purposes, are not made with the expectation that they will be used simply to finance private goods for the donor. Consequently, the donor is very likely to experience difficulty in overseeing the use made of his donation and feel the need for the kind of protection afforded by the nonprofit form. In itself, however, the contract failure theory does not explain why it is that some services are donatively financed and others are not. To be sure, some services—such as redistribution to the poor or the provision of public goods—must by their very nature be donatively financed if they are to be provided privately at all. But in the case of some services that are commonly provided by donative nonprofits, it is not obvious that either redistribution to the poor or the production of public goods is involved. In such cases, closer consideration sometimes suggests that donative financing has arisen as a means of coping with special types of market imperfections that are peculiar to particular industries.

Price Discrimination

It is interesting to inquire, for example, why donative financing plays such a large role in the high-culture live performing arts. The services provided by such organizations, after all, are seldom rendered to the poor and are not easily characterized as public goods whose benefits spill over to individuals who do not pay the price of admission.

One likely explanation is that donative financing in the performing arts serves as a form of voluntary price discrimination, the need for which is dictated by the unusual cost and demand structure in that industry (Hansmann 1981b). In the high-culture live performing arts, fixed costs (primarily those of preparing a show prior to the first performance, including the cost of rehearsals, costumes, and stage sets) are a large proportion of the total costs of a production; once a production has been staged, the marginal cost of adding another performance to the run or of admitting another person to the audience for a performance that has not sold out is relatively small. This is, of course, in part a reflection of the fact that the potential audience for the high-culture performing arts is limited, even in the largest cities. It appears that, as a consequence, for many productions there is no single ticket price that can cover total costs. If costs are to be met, some form of price discrimination must be employed so that high demanders pay more than low demanders for a given performance. Transferability of tickets, however, puts limits on the amount of price discrimination that can be accomplished through ticket pricing. Yet *voluntary* price discrimination has proven possible here: ticket purchasers with unusually high demand for performing arts productions can simply be asked to contribute some portion of the consumer surplus they would otherwise enjoy at the nominal ticket price—and, interestingly, a large proportion is in fact willing to do so.

The audiences for the popular performing arts such as movies and Broadway theater—in contrast to those for opera, symphonic music, and ballet—are large enough so that fixed costs can be spread widely, and thus fixed costs are low relative to marginal costs. Consequently, price discrimination is unnecessary for the viability of such productions, and they are usually produced by for-profit firms.

Although the performing arts seem to offer the best illustration of voluntary price discrimination, this may also be part of the function played by donative financing in other parts of the nonprofit sector, such as museums (which also experience fixed costs that are high relative to marginal costs), higher education, and health care.

Implicit Loans

The substantial role of donative financing in private education raises similar questions. In part it may serve to finance public goods or the provision of education to the poor. These explanations do not seem compelling, however, in the case of private primary or secondary schools or in the case of four-year private colleges, many of which emphasize teaching rather than research and have (at least until recently) served almost exclusively the relatively well-to-do. Further, such explanations do not entirely square with the fact that donations come largely from alumni of these colleges.

An alternative explanation, more consistent with such phenomena, is that donative financing in higher education serves at least in part as a system of voluntary repayments under an implicit loan system that has arisen to compensate for the absence of adequate loan markets for acquisition of human capital (Hansmann 1980). Many individuals for whom the present value of the long-run returns from higher education exceed the cost of that education are unable to finance it out of their own or their family's existing assets. If these individuals could take out a long-term loan against their future earnings, then this would be a worthwhile strategy for financing their education. Yet, since an individual cannot pledge human capital as security for such a loan (owing to laws against peonage, among other things), lenders will offer an inadequate supply of such loans. Private nonprofit schools provide a crude substitute for such loans. They supply education to many students at rates below cost, in return for an implicit commitment on the part of the students that they will

"repay" the school through donations during the course of their lives after graduation.

Option Demand

Weisbrod (1964; Weisbrod & Lee 1977) has argued that donations to nonprofits may in part reflect what he calls "option demand." In particular, he suggests, this may help explain why hospitals are organized as donative nonprofits. "An individual's uncertainty with respect to demand for hospital services that may become critical to life means that he will be willing to pay a sum to secure the physical availability of those facilities in the future. An option demand may be said to exist for stand-by capacity, which is capacity in excess of the expected level of utilization" (Weisbrod & Lee 1977, 94). Of course, the mere fact that future demand is unpredictable need not in itself lead to market failure. Simply because one's own future demand, or even the entire market's future demand, for personal computers, four-bedroom apartments, or penicillin is uncertain does not mean that for-profit producers will supply them at an inefficient level. Some reason must be given to explain why for-profit firms, in the face of uncertain demand, will provide an inefficiently low level of capacity. One such reason has recently been offered by Holtmann (1983), though Holtmann makes no reference to Weisbrod's earlier option demand theory.

Holtmann develops a model in which demand is stochastic and in which a producing firm must choose its price and its maximum capacity level (which will subsequently represent a fixed cost for the firm) before the level of demand is revealed. The socially efficient behavior for the firm is to select a capacity level for which marginal expected (social) benefits equal marginal expected costs, and then set price equal to marginal cost. Such a policy will, however, produce negative returns for the firm regardless of the level of demand that subsequently materializes, and hence it will not be chosen by a for-profit firm. Without developing the point formally, Holtmann suggests that a donatively financed nonprofit firm will choose a lower price and larger capacity level than will a for-profit firm, and hence will come closer to the social optimum. Hence, Holtmann intimates, donative nonprofit firms might arise to meet the ex ante demand for capacity that for-profit firms will leave unsatisfied.

Other Motivations for Donating

There are, to be sure, many other reasons for donating besides those surveyed here. For example, donations to performing arts organizations may often be a form of conspicuous consumption (a type of signaling). Donations to one's alma mater may in part be inspired by a desire to maintain its institutional prominence in order to ensure that one's own degree will retain its status or quality. And donations to performing arts organizations, local hospitals, and one's alma mater may in part be, in effect, dues for membership in a club—the club of active supporters of the institution involved—which may be valuable for companionship or contacts. I have focused here on voluntary price discrimination, implicit loans, and option demand—in addition to the familiar functions of redistribution and financing public goods—simply because these are functions served by donations that (1) are frequently overlooked, (2) come to light most clearly when nonprofits are examined with an economist's special facility for appreciating the functions and limits of markets, and (3) have been explicitly developed in the existing economics literature.

Why Not Free Ride?

We would also like to understand why, and under what conditions, individuals make contributions rather than succumb to the temptation to act as free riders in situations such as those just discussed. The contract failure theory, after all, suggests only why it is that, *given* that an individual wishes to make a donation, he is likely to direct that donation to a nonprofit rather than a for-profit firm; it does not explain why individuals are willing to make donations in the first place. Yet the question is obviously an important one: Americans *do* donate a substantial portion of their income to nonprofit organizations; moreover, they commonly make such donations in response to impersonal (for example, through-the-mail) appeals. At present, most of the wisdom we have on this subject focuses on aggregate phenomena and especially on the responsiveness of donations to changes in income and in price—in particular, tax incentives. (The available data and theories are surveyed in chapter 18.)

Demand-Side versus Supply-Side Theories

The various theories of the role of nonprofit enterprise that have been surveyed here are all essentially demand-side theories. That is, they present reasons consumers might choose to patronize nonprofit firms in preference to for-profit firms in particular industries. To date, much less systematic work has been done on developing supply-side theories that help explain why there is a supply of nonprofit firms in particular industries, and whether the current distribution of nonprofit firms across industries can be explained at least in part on the basis of differing conditions of supply. This is not to say, however, that there has been no work at all in this area; chapter 22, for example, offers some important observations on supply. Moreover, the behavioral theories discussed below also offer some insight into these issues.

THE BEHAVIOR OF NONPROFIT ORGANIZATIONS

The theories of the role of nonprofit organizations just surveyed are all based on the assumption that nonprofit firms are—or at least appear to their patrons to be—bound by a nondistribution constraint. This constraint, however, is consistent with a variety of forms of behavior on the part of nonprofit firms. Therefore, commitment to one of these theories of the role of nonprofit organizations does not necessarily

involve commitment to a particular theory of the behavior of nonprofit firms, and vice versa. Moreover, many of the early efforts to model the behavior of nonprofit firms—especially hospitals—were developed without concern for the reasons such firms developed and survived. Consequently, the behavioral models of nonprofit organizations developed to date have been to some degree disconnected from models of the role of such firms.

Optimizing Models

Following the neoclassical tradition, most models of the behavior of nonprofit firms have been optimizing models, typically focusing on firms in a particular industry. Hospitals have been the most common subject.

Choosing the maximand has been a problem in these models. In contrast to the case of the for-profit firm, there is obviously no reason to believe a priori that profit maximization is a reasonable goal to impute to the nonprofit firm. Most commonly, nonprofit firms have instead been assumed to maximize the quality and/or quantity of the service they produce. The first of these goals might seem reasonable for a nonprofit firm run by professionals who derive strong satisfaction from doing craftsmanlike work, independent of the needs or desires of their clientele. Quantity maximization, in turn, might be imputed to managers who are empire builders or who are altruists of a type that seeks to serve as broad a segment of the public as possible. Models of nonprofit firms that pursue one or both of these goals have been developed by Newhouse (1970) and Feldstein (1971) for hospitals, James and Neuberger (1981) for universities, James (1983) for nonprofits in general, and Hansmann (1981b) for performing arts organizations. Lee (1971), in contrast, presents a model of a hospital that maximizes (or, more accurately, satisfices) not output but rather its use of certain inputs.

Models of nonprofits that seek to maximize their budgets have also been common. Presumably budget maximization might be chosen as a goal because it enhances the apparent importance of (or justifies a higher salary for) the firm's managers or, alternatively, because it provides the preferred trade-off between quality and quantity maximization. Examples of budget-maximizing models have been offered by Tullock (1966), who considers a purely donative nonprofit, and Niskanen (1971, chap. 9), who considers a purely commercial nonprofit. Hansmann's previously mentioned paper on the performing arts (1981b) also models the behavior of a (partly donative and partly commercial) nonprofit budget maximizer.

Each of these optimizing models is employed by its author to some degree to explore the welfare implications of the type of behavior the model postulates. For example, Newhouse (1970) emphasizes that the quality/quantity-maximizing firm in his model will usually exhibit productive inefficiency when contrasted with the performance of a for-profit firm operating in an environment free of market failure. Hansmann's performing arts model assumes that the firm is operating under conditions of contract failure and that it must adhere to the nondistribution constraint; the model then explores the socially optimal objective function for the firm, *given* this constraint. It turns out that quantity, quality, or budget maximizing may or may not constitute efficient behavior for the firm, depending on the structure of consumers' preferences and the way in which donations respond to firm behavior. In Tullock's model (1966), the budget-maximizing donative nonprofit overspends considerably (from a social welfare point of view) on promotion: at the margin, it spends more than a dollar in promotional expenses in order to solicit an additional dollar in donations.

Pauly and Redisch (1973) offer a model of a hospital that is operated to maximize the financial returns to its affiliated doctors. This is not the same thing as profit maximization for the firm. Rather, since doctors do not receive payment directly from the hospital but instead bill patients separately, this theory implies that hospitals will bill patients only enough to cover costs and will procure inputs that enhance the physicians' productivity. Pauly and Redisch then develop an explicit model of the hospital as a Ward-Domar-type producer cooperative (with the physicians as the worker/owners) and thus predict for a hospital the same behavior that characterizes other models of this type—behavior that involves considerable inefficiency in the short run in the form of perverse supply response. Since the work behavior and compensation of hospital-based physicians do not follow the simple fixed-effort and equal-sharing rules assumed in this class of producer cooperative models, it is not clear that in fact we should expect perverse supply response to be an empirically important phenomenon in hospitals. Nevertheless, the general view of hospitals as serving indirectly the financial interests of doctors may capture an important aspect of reality.

Productive Inefficiency

Optimizing models of the types just surveyed implicitly assume that the firms involved minimize costs. Another line of behavioral theory has argued that, whatever objectives nonprofits may pursue with respect to quantity or quality of output, they are inherently subject to productive inefficiency (that is, failure to minimize costs) owing to the absence of ownership claims to residual earnings (Alchian & Demsetz 1972; Hansmann 1980). This argument is clearest when applied to entrepreneurial nonprofits, which constitute the great majority of financially significant nonprofits. Those who control such organizations—whether the managers or the board of directors who appoint the managers—are unable, by virtue of the nondistribution constraint, to appropriate for themselves the net earnings obtained by reducing costs, and thus they have little pecuniary incentive to operate the organization in a manner that minimizes costs.[12] Of

course, it could be that the managers of some nonprofits derive substantial utility from having the firm produce large amounts of output and thus have a desire to minimize costs that is independent of the income they derive from the firm. And there is reason to believe that nonprofit organizations tend to attract more managers of this type than do for-profit firms (see Young 1983 and chapter 10 in this volume). Nevertheless, nonprofit managers in general might be expected to indulge themselves in various perquisites of office—including some forms of nonpecuniary income as well as a more relaxed attitude toward their duties—to a greater extent than do their counterparts in for-profit firms. Clarkson (1972) presents empirical results comparing the behavior of nonprofit and for-profit hospitals that provide some support for this view.

It is almost certainly true that nonprofit firms are productively inefficient in the sense that, in the absence of subsidies or a substantial degree of market failure of some type (such as contract failure) in the product market, they will generally produce any given good or service at higher cost than would a for-profit firm. If it were otherwise, we would expect to find nonprofit firms operating successfully in a much broader range of industries than is actually the case. As emphasized in the preceding discussion of the role of nonprofits, nonprofit firms seem to have survivorship properties that are superior to for-profit firms only where particular forms of market failure give them an efficiency advantage sufficient to compensate for their failure to minimize costs. Thus, in general we do not find nonprofit firms producing, wholesaling, or retailing standard industrial goods or agricultural commodities (such as machine screws or cucumbers) for which contract failure is not a significant problem.

Supply Response

Empirical work (Steinwald & Neuhauser 1970; Hansmann 1985a) indicates strongly that nonprofit firms tend to respond much more slowly to increases in demand than do their for-profit counterparts. For example, in those industries populated by both nonprofit and for-profit firms, such as nursing care, hospital care, and primary and secondary education, the ratio of nonprofit to for-profit firms is much lower in markets in which demand has been expanding rapidly than it is in markets in which demand has remained stable or declined.

One likely explanation for this phenomenon is that, in comparison to for-profit firms, nonprofit firms are constrained in their access to capital. Unlike for-profit firms, nonprofit firms cannot raise capital by issuing equity shares; rather, they must rely on debt, donations, and retained earnings for this purpose—sources that, even in combination, offer a less responsive supply of capital than does the equity market.

---

12. In mutual nonprofits, ultimate control is by definition in the hands of the patrons of the organization, and the patrons have an incentive to have the organization minimize costs. If the organization has many patrons, however, transaction costs and free-rider problems

may prevent the patrons from exercising effective authority over the firm's management, thus leading to poor incentives for cost minimization in these firms as well.

An alternative explanation for nonprofits' relatively poor supply response points to problems of entrepreneurship. Owing to the nondistribution constraint, nonprofit entrepreneurs are unable to capture the full return that can be gained by establishing a new firm or expanding an old one in the face of increased demand. Consequently, their incentive to undertake such entry or expansion is limited relative to that of entrepreneurs in the for-profit sector.

At present we cannot say to what extent each, or either, of these explanations accounts for the relatively poor supply response exhibited by nonprofits. There is empirical evidence that nonprofit firms are sometimes capital constrained (Ginsburg 1970), but we do not know precisely how this translates into supply response. And entrepreneurship in the nonprofit sector presents an even more elusive problem. Young (whose work is surveyed in chapter 10) has undertaken case studies of nonprofit entrepreneurship that indicate, as one might expect, a substantial range of motivation and behavior. He describes a set of personality types into which nonprofit entrepreneurs can be divided and suggests that certain of these personality types are selected for disproportionately by particular types of nonprofit firms. Not surprisingly, some of these personality types are inconsistent with a strong emphasis on expansion of services.

James in chapter 22 notes that, particularly in countries other than the United States, both the entrepreneurial initiative and the necessary capital for founding a nonprofit institution, such as a school, are commonly supplied by an existing organization that is already well established and well financed—such as a major religious sect. This observation underlines the importance of both factors, though it does not clearly indicate which is generally the more important bottleneck.

Income-Generating Behavior

To the extent that a nonprofit seeks to provide a service of a quantity or quality that cannot be supported by market demand, some form of subsidy must be found. One source of such a subsidy, evidently commonly used by nonprofits, is cross subsidization: one service is produced and sold by the nonprofit at a profit, which is then used to finance provision of another service that is more highly valued by the firm. The net returns earned on the subsidy-generating service may result from the fact that the nonprofit firm has some degree of market power in providing that service or from the fact that the nonprofit firm has lower costs than its competitors owing to tax exemption or some other form of governmental favor. James (1981, 1983) illustrates this form of behavior with a simple model of a multiproduct nonprofit firm that places different degrees of (either positive or negative) utility on the quantities of the various products it sells, and then determines price and output for the full set of products in a fashion that maximizes utility to the firm while meeting a breakeven constraint. Harris (1979) presents a model of a nonprofit hospital illustrating how cross subsidization can be employed to compensate for distortions and inequities in health insur-

ance coverage and offers empirical results suggesting that to some extent hospitals behave consistently with this model.

Another way to raise funds to pay for services whose production provides positive utility to the firm is to solicit donations. To be sure, as suggested earlier, we can view donations simply as a price that is paid by persons who wish to finance provision of services for third parties. In this sense, then, donations are not a subsidy, and efforts to increase donations are simply efforts to market the firm's goods—that is, a form of advertising. Nevertheless, donation-seeking behavior presents some interesting questions, especially from a welfare standpoint. In particular—depending on one's assumptions about donor information and behavior—nonprofits may have an incentive to expend inefficiently large amounts of funds on solicitation, as Tullock (1966) suggests. Since theoretical and empirical work on donation-seeking behavior is surveyed in chapter 7, however, the issue will not be addressed further here.

Patron Control

The discussion so far has proceeded largely as if all nonprofits were entrepreneurial nonprofits whose management is constrained in its behavior only by market forces and the nondistribution constraint. However, many nonprofits (namely, those we have called mutual nonprofits) are ultimately controlled, at least formally, by their patrons. Thus, it remains to ask whether, and how, patrons influence the behavior of mutual nonprofits through the exercise of their voting power—that is, through voice rather than exit, to use Hirschman's now familiar terminology (1970).

The only general theoretical treatment of this subject is offered by Ben-Ner (1986; this volume, chap. 24), who sees patron control as the principal raison d'être for nonprofit firms and thus devotes considerable attention to the possible behavior of customer-controlled firms. He focuses in particular on coalition formation among customer-members, arguing that high-demand customers can frequently be expected to dominate the firm and to set price and output parameters that maximize their own welfare while exploiting other customers to the extent permitted by competition.

A more narrowly focused treatment is offered in Hansmann (1986) of social clubs, colleges, hospital medical staffs, and other membership organizations in which the personal characteristics of one's fellow patrons (or employees) are an important factor in the utility derived from membership. A simple model is presented to illustrate the way in which member control interacts with competition to determine the size, fees, and membership characteristics of individual clubs. In that model, each individual is assumed to be characterized by a unidimensional variable denoting "status." Individuals join clubs in order to associate with other individuals, and the value of a given club's membership as companions is given by their average status: the higher the better. Assuming limited economies of scale (in terms of membership size) in the operation of clubs, and assuming that a given club must charge all its members the same fee, free formation of clubs in this model results in roughly the pattern we see in reality: that is, a system of member-controlled clubs that are usually smaller than the size that minimizes average cost per member, and that are exclusive and stratified in the sense that the highest-status individuals will be in a single club of their own, the next highest will constitute the membership of a second club, and so on.

CONCLUSION: SOME POLICY APPLICATIONS

The theories concerning the role and behavior of nonprofit firms discussed above are of interest simply as a matter of positive social science. They are also of interest, however, from a policy perspective. Indeed, the most pressing current problems of policy concerning the nonprofit sector cannot be resolved intelligently without adopting one or another point of view concerning the role and behavior of nonprofit firms. This is not the place to consider policy problems in detail. But for purposes of illustration and as a means of providing some perspective on the theories that have been surveyed here, we shall look briefly at some examples.

As suggested earlier, the most dramatic development in the nonprofit sector in recent decades has been the rapid growth of commercial nonprofits. The appearance of large numbers of such firms, which derive their revenues largely from fees for service and commonly exist in competition with for-profit firms providing similar services, has brought with it some of the most difficult problems of policy that currently involve the nonprofit sector.

Tax Exemption

One important set of issues, for example, concerns tax exemption. At present, most nonprofit firms are exempt from taxation (including sales, property, and corporate income taxation) at the federal, state, and local levels. These exemptions were relatively unproblematic when they were first established many decades ago: most nonprofits were simple donative charities that provided either public goods or aid to the poor, thus offering a substantial rationale for public subsidy. In any event, the potential tax liability of the organizations involved was often quite small. Yet the scope of these exemptions has been extended to keep pace with the expansion of the nonprofit sector, so that today large numbers of commercial nonprofits are also exempt. And it is not obvious that the arguments for exempting traditional charities carry over to commercial nonprofits such as nursing homes or health maintenance organizations.

It is difficult to rationalize tax exemption for commercial nonprofits on the simple ground that the basic service they provide—nursing care for the elderly, day care, hospital care, or whatever—is for some reason worthy of subsidy in general, since that argument would seem to call for exempting not only the nonprofit firms in the industry but the for-profit firms as well. Of course, the exemption might be confined to nonprofit firms even under this rationale on the

theory that the nondistribution constraint ensures that the subsidy will actually be passed through to consumers (see the general discussion of government ''donations'' above). But, in industries like those in question, in which firms simply sell goods or services directly to consumers, it would seem that competition among competing firms would go far toward ensuring the same result for for-profit firms. Consequently, the exemption seems more easily justifiable if it can be established that nonprofit firms in the relevant industries offer a type of service that is different from that offered by their for-profit competitors and that would be undersupplied without subsidy.

A possible argument along these lines is that nonprofit firms provide services that have more of the character of public goods than do the services provided by for-profit firms in the same industry. Yet, as we have observed in discussing the public goods theory of nonprofits above, it is not at all obvious that this is the case for commercial nonprofits in most industries. An alternative possibility is that commercial nonprofits are in fact a response to contract failure and that they offer a higher degree of fiduciary responsibility toward their customers than do their for-profit competitors—a quality that is of special service to that subset of customers who do not trust their own ability to look out for their interests in the market. Yet even acceptance of the contract failure theory as applied to commercial nonprofits does not necessarily resolve the question of exemption. For we must ask why it is that customers who want the special protection of the nonprofit form cannot be left to seek it out and pay for it on their own. Do such customers constitute a class that is specially deserving of a subsidy? Or is it the case that such customers will myopically undervalue the special protection afforded by nonprofit firms and thus need a subsidy to encourage them to patronize such firms? Or is the subsidy provided by the exemption best justified as a way of compensating for problems of supply response among nonprofit firms that would otherwise develop too slowly to meet demand? (Note that the latter justification is persuasive only if the problem of supply response is primarily the result of lack of capital rather than lack of entrepreneurship.)

The object here is not to offer a resolution of these issues.[13] Rather, it is simply to emphasize that, if one is to take a thoughtful position on whether to continue or revoke the exemption for commercial nonprofits in any given industry, one must necessarily think carefully about the role and behavior of the firms involved.

Outlawing For-Profit Firms

In recent years considerable attention has been devoted to abuses in the nursing home industry involving shoddy patient care and shady finances. These exposés have brought proposals from several prominent quarters for public policies designed to eliminate for-profit nursing homes (for example,

13. For further theoretical and empirical discussion, see Hansmann (1981c, 1985a).

by denying them licenses) on the theory that for-profit homes are the source of most of the abuses and that the industry would perform better if it were composed only of nonprofit firms (Etzioni 1976; New York Temporary State Commission . . . 1975). Indeed, such proposals have not been confined to the nursing home industry; public measures disadvantaging or outlawing for-profit as opposed to nonprofit firms have been enacted or proposed at various times as well for aspects of medical practice, legal practice, and higher education.[14]

To accept such proposals, it seems, one must accept strongly the contract failure theory of the role of nonprofits. Indeed, one must presumably believe not just that existing nonprofit nursing homes serve a fiduciary role toward their customers but that even those customers who currently patronize proprietary nursing homes need the protection of the nondistribution constraint and were misguided in choosing a for-profit rather than a nonprofit provider.

Further, to accept such proposals one must also believe that outlawing proprietary homes will not have a significant

14. For a more thorough discussion of such policies see Hansmann (1981d, 548–53) and Young (1983, 141–44).

effect on the character of nonprofit homes—for example, by forcing profit-motivated entrepreneurs to utilize the nonprofit form, thus creating a group of nominally nonprofit firms that actively seek to evade the nondistribution constraint.

And finally, before implementing such a proposal, one must consider the problem of supply response. If one goes no further than simply outlawing for-profit homes, then there will presumably be a long period of excess demand for the services of the remaining nonprofit firms. Thus, many of the elderly may simply go from having poor service to having no service. If capital constraints are the chief cause of poor supply response among nonprofits, this problem might be remedied by governmental provision of loan or grant capital to nonprofit firms. If, on the other hand, the supply response problem has its roots in the lack of incentives for nonprofit entrepreneurship, then capital subsidies in themselves might be unavailing, and the problem, if remediable at all, must be dealt with through more complex policies.

Thus here, as with tax exemption, intelligent policy must necessarily be based on a sophisticated understanding of the role and behavior of nonprofit firms. Recent work on the economics of nonprofit organizations holds the promise, at last, of yielding such an understanding.

REFERENCES

Alchian, Armen, and Harold Demsetz. 1972. "Production, Information Costs, and Economic Organization." *American Economic Review* 62:777–95.

Arrow, Kenneth. 1963. "Uncertainty and the Welfare Economics of Medical Care." *American Economic Review* 53:941–73.

Baumol, William, and William Bowen. 1965. "On the Performing Arts: The Anatomy of Their Economic Problems." *American Economic Review Papers and Proceedings* 55:495–502.

———. 1966. *Performing Arts—The Economic Dilemma.* Cambridge, Mass.: MIT Press.

Ben-Ner, Avner. 1986. "Non-Profit Organizations: Why Do They Exist in Market Economies?" In *The Economics of Nonprofit Institutions: Studies in Structure and Policy,* ed. Susan Rose-Ackerman. Oxford: Oxford University Press.

Clark, Robert. 1980. "Does the Nonprofit Form Fit the Hospital Industry?" *Harvard Law Review* 93:1416–89.

Clarkson, Kenneth. 1972. "Some Implications of Property Rights in Hospital Management." *Journal of Law and Economics* 15:363–84.

Clotfelter, Charles, and Lester Salamon. 1982. "The Impact of the 1981 Tax Act on Individual Charitable Giving." *National Tax Journal* 35:171–87.

Dickinson, Frank. 1962. *Philanthropy and Public Policy.* New York: National Bureau of Economic Research.

Easley, David, and Maureen O'Hara. 1983. "The Economic Role of the Nonprofit Firm." *Bell Journal of Economics* 14:531–38.

———. 1984. "An Information-Based Theory of the Firm." Unpublished manuscript; Cornell University Department of Economics.

Ellman, Ira. 1982. "Another Theory of Nonprofit Corporations." *Michigan Law Review* 80:999–1050.

Etzioni, Amitai. 1976. "Profit in Not-for-Profit Institutions." *Philanthropy Monthly* 9:22–34.

Fama, Eugene, and Michael Jensen. 1983a. "Agency Problems and Residual Claims." *Journal of Law and Economics* 26:327–50.

———. 1983b. "Separation of Ownership and Control." *Journal of Law and Economics* 26:301–26.

Feldstein, Martin. 1971. "Hospital Price Inflation: A Study of Nonprofit Price Dynamics." *American Economic Review* 61:853–72.

———. 1975. "The Income Tax and Charitable Contributions." *National Tax Journal* 28:81–97, 209–28.

Ginsburg, Paul. 1970. *Capital in Non-Profit Hospitals.* Ph.D. diss., Harvard University.

Hansmann, Henry. 1980. ''The Role of Nonprofit Enterprise.'' *Yale Law Journal* 89:835–901.

———. 1981a. ''Consumer Perception of Nonprofit Enterprise: Reply.'' *Yale Law Journal* 90:1633–38.

———. 1981b. ''Nonprofit Enterprise in the Performing Arts.'' *Bell Journal of Economics* 12:341–61.

———. 1981c. ''The Rationale for Exempting Nonprofit Organizations from Corporate Income Taxation.'' *Yale Law Journal* 91:54–100.

———. 1981d. ''Reforming Nonprofit Corporation Law.'' *University of Pennsylvania Law Review* 129:497–623.

———. 1985a. ''The Effect of Tax Exemption and Other Factors on Competition between Nonprofit and For-Profit Enterprise.'' Yale University, Program on Non-Profit Organizations Working Paper no. 65.

———. 1985b. ''The Organization of Insurance Companies: Mutual versus Stock.'' *Journal of Law, Economics, and Organization* 1:125–53.

———. 1986. ''Status Organizations.'' *Journal of Law, Economics, and Organization* 2:119–30.

Harris, Jeffrey. 1979. ''Pricing Rules for Hospitals.'' *Bell Journal of Economics* 10:224–43.

Heflebower, Richard. 1980. *Cooperatives and Mutuals in the Market System.* Madison: University of Wisconsin Press.

Hirschman, Albert. 1970. *Exit, Voice and Loyalty.* Cambridge, Mass.: Harvard University Press.

Holtmann, A. G. 1983. ''A Theory of Non-Profit Firms.'' *Economica* 50:439–49.

James, Estelle. 1983. ''How Nonprofits Grow: A Model.'' *Journal of Policy Analysis and Management* 2:350–65.

James, Estelle, and Egon Neuberger. 1981. ''The University Department as a Non-Profit Labor Cooperative.'' *Public Choice* 36:585–612.

Jensen, Michael, and William Meckling. 1976. ''Theory of the Firm: Managerial Behavior, Agency Costs and Ownership Structure.'' *Journal of Financial Economics* 3:305–60.

Lee, A. James, and Burton Weisbrod. 1977. ''Collective Goods and the Voluntary Sector: The Case of the Hospital Industry.'' In Burton Weisbrod, *The Voluntary Nonprofit Sector.* Lexington, Mass.: Lexington Books.

Lee, M. L. 1971. ''A Conspicuous Production Theory of Hospital Behavior.'' *Southern Economic Journal* 38:48–59.

Manne, Henry. 1965. ''Mergers and the Market for Corporate Control.'' *Journal of Political Economy* 73:110–20.

Nelson, Richard. 1977. *The Moon and the Ghetto: An Essay on Public Policy Analysis.* New York: W. W. Norton & Co.

Nelson, Richard, and Michael Krashinsky. 1973. ''Two Major Issues of Public Policy: Public Policy and Organization of Supply.'' In *Public Subsidy for Day Care of Young Children,* edited by Richard Nelson and Dennis Young. Lexington, Mass.: D. C. Heath & Co.

Newhouse, Joseph. 1970. ''Toward a Theory of Non-Profit Institutions: An Economic Model of a Hospital.'' *American Economic Review* 60:64–74.

Newton, Jamie. 1980. ''Child Care Decision-Making Survey—Preliminary Report.'' Unpublished manuscript; Yale University, Program on Non-Profit Organizations.

New York Temporary State Commission on Living Costs and the Economy. 1975. *Report on Nursing Homes and Health-Related Facilities in New York State.* N.p.

Niskanen, William. 1971. *Bureaucracy and Representative Government.* Chicago: Aldine Publishing Co.

Pauly, Mark P., and Michael R. Redisch. 1973. ''The Not-for-Profit Hospital as a Physicians' Cooperative.'' *American Economic Review* 63:87–99.

Permut, Steven. 1981. ''Consumer Perceptions of Nonprofit Enterprise: A Comment on Hansmann.'' *Yale Law Journal* 90:1623–32.

Rose-Ackerman, Susan. 1981. ''Do Government Grants to Charity Reduce Private Donations?'' In *Nonprofit Firms in a Three-Sector Economy,* edited by Michelle White. Washington, D.C.: Urban Institute.

Steinwald, Bruce, and Duncan Neuhauser. 1970. ''The Role of the Proprietary Hospital.'' *Law and Contemporary Problems* 35:817–38.

Thompson, Earl. 1980. ''Charity and Nonprofit Organizations.'' In *The Economics of Nonproprietary Organizations,* edited by Kenneth Clarkson and Donald Martin. Greenwich, Conn.: JAI Press.

Tullock, Gordon. 1966. ''Information without Profit.'' In *Papers on Non-Market Decision Making,* edited by Gordon Tullock. Charlottesville: Thomas Jefferson Center for Political Economy, University of Virginia.

Weisbrod, Burton. 1964. ''Collective-Consumption Services of Individual-Consumption Goods.'' *Quarterly Journal of Economics* 78:471–77.

———. 1974. ''Toward a Theory of the Voluntary Non-Profit Sector in a Three-Sector Economy.'' In *Altruism, Morality, and Economic Theory,* edited by Edmund S. Phelps. New York: Russell Sage.

———. 1977. *The Voluntary Nonprofit Sector.* Lexington, Mass.: D. C. Heath & Co.

———. 1983. ''Nonprofit and Proprietary Sector Behavior: Wage Differentials among Lawyers.'' *Journal of Labor Economics* 1:246–63.

Weisbrod, Burton, and A. James Lee. 1977. ''Collective Goods and the Voluntary Sector: The Case of the Hospital Industry.'' In Burton Weisbrod, *The Voluntary Nonprofit Sector.* Lexington, Mass.: Lexington Books.

Weisbrod, Burton, and Mark Schlesinger. 1986. ''Ownership Form and Behavior in Regulated Markets with Asymmetric Information.'' In *The Economics of Nonprofit Institutions: Studies in Structure and Policy,* ed. Susan Rose-Ackerman. Oxford: Oxford University Press.

Weiss, Jeffrey. 1986. ''Donations: Can They Reduce a Donor's Welfare?'' In *The Economics of Nonprofit Institutions: Studies in Structure and Policy,* ed. Susan Rose-Ackerman. Oxford: Oxford University Press.

Williamson, Oliver. 1979. ''Transaction-Cost Economics: The Governance of Contractual Relations.'' *Journal of Law and Economics* 22:233–61.

Young, Dennis. 1983. *If Not for Profit, for What?* Lexington, Mass.: D. C. Heath & Co.

3

Political Theories of Nonprofit Organization

JAMES DOUGLAS

The fields of activity we most readily associate with nonprofit organizations include health care, education, religion, the arts, and a vast array of social welfare services. In medieval times, these activities would have come primarily within the jurisdiction of the church rather than the state. After the Reformation, they were brought within the purview of civil as distinct from canon law. In 1601, the English Parliament enacted the Statute of Charitable Uses (43 Eliz. I c4), which has been described as "the starting point of the modern law of charities" and remains to this day one of the bases for the definition of charity in both English and American law.[1]

Thus history accounts for the fact that a charitable nonprofit sector exists independent of the government. It does not explain, however, why some fields of activity remain in this sector, whereas others either have been taken over by government (like the maintenance of bridges,[2] for example, or the care of prisoners) or are normally carried out by for-profit business enterprises. Institutions, like other organisms, are subject to the laws of natural selection. What we need to identify are the characteristics of the "environmental niche" in which nonprofits thrive.

Private nonprofits are subject to competition for survival from three other forms of social organizations—the family, commercial for-profit enterprises, and government-run services. Competition from any family unit beyond the nuclear has been weakened by deep-seated social and economic trends for at least a century. However, a recent study of

voluntary organizations (Wolfenden Committee 1978) sees as a strength of the nonprofit sector its ability to work easily with and supplement the resources of family and informal networks of friends and neighbors. The committee saw this capability of voluntary organizations to be greater than that of either of its important contemporary competitors—commercial for-profit enterprises and government-run services and agencies.

Economists have developed a considerable body of theory, reviewed in chapter 2, that enables us to identify the conditions most appropriate to for-profit enterprises—their environmental niche. The environmental niche for government services remains ill defined. We need something that will serve the same function in political theory that market failure and its related concepts serve in economic theory.

The task of devising a political analogue to market failure bristles with difficulties. At a fundamental level economists have a common criterion or measuring rod—that of "utility"—for judging the desirability of a form of organization. They can say that market failure occurs when pursuit by individuals of their own utility is calculated not to result in maximum utility for society. But there is no similar single measure that can be applied to political institutions. We can say that a government agency should promote both welfare and efficiency—two criteria subsumed in the economic concept of utility. But they cannot be the only criteria. Government action must also be based on publicly defensible criteria of justice, and it must in some measure respond to the values and choices of the majority of citizens, although not in a way that infringes on the rights of minorities. This age-old problem of reconciling the will of the majority with the rights of minorities is only one of the cases of contradictory criteria encountered when one tries to define a good polity. The economic good, for all its ultimately unquantifiable aspects, remains a much tidier concept than the political good.

At a less fundamental level, economists have acquired a

I am grateful to Paul DiMaggio, Woody Powell, and John Simon for their helpful comments.

1. Today we tend to distinguish such private nonprofit organizations as churches, private universities, and schools from charitable institutions. Yet they all come within the legal definition of a charity.

2. The care of bridges was a common charitable purpose of monastic foundations. The term *pontiff* originally derived from a builder of bridges.

mass of empirical data against which they can test their theories, and these theories in turn have stimulated more empirical studies. In examining the boundary between the state and the autonomous nonprofit sector, however, we have no comparable wealth of empirical data upon which to draw. In this chapter I shall suggest some normative hypotheses in the hope that this will stimulate others to test them empirically.

Yet another difficulty is presented by the very term *nonprofit organization*. We use the legal form of incorporation as a basis of classification because it is convenient. Yet, as many contributors to this volume point out, the term includes a wide variety of organizations, and the legal form of incorporation may tell us little about their nature. It is not difficult to think of borderline cases in which there appears to be no clear-cut distinction between a for-profit enterprise and a nonprofit organization. In the case of children's day-care centers or old people's nursing homes, for example, the form of incorporation often seems to be, particularly in small ones, no more than a matter of convenience to the founders. In health care delivery, it is not uncommon to find organizations switching from one form to the other. The distinguishing line between a private nonprofit organization and a government agency may also be a fine one. As Salamon notes in chapter 6, some nonprofit organizations are financed entirely by public funds and may even have been set up by public officials. In such cases the decision makers in the allegedly private organization will be somewhat less accountable through political channels than if it had been established overtly as a government agency, although this is very much a matter of degree. (Incidentally, the same problem of borderline cases exists regarding the boundary between the public and the commercial sectors in such cases as nationalized industries and public utility companies.)

In this chapter, I shall confine my attention to private nonprofit organizations carrying out a public function. This, broadly speaking, is the legal definition of a public charity. The question I will discuss is why, given the extensive range of services provided by the public (or government) sector, we need to supplement them by private endeavors that are not accountable through the same political channels.

The most obvious distinctive characteristic of a state service is that it can invoke the coercive power of law. The state can invoke this coercive power to commandeer goods—for example, through compulsory purchase and laws of eminent domain. It can invoke this power to commandeer services—as in the case of compulsory military service. But, nowadays, this power is most frequently used to commandeer money through compulsory taxation. Organizations in the private sector have no such power to commandeer the resources they need. They must either exchange something they own (or to which they have some form of title) for something they need or rely on tapping some vein of generosity. Exchange of the specific kind usually referred to as a quid pro quo transaction is, of course, the basic mechanism used in the marketplaces of the commercial sector. Both the quid and the quo must be identifiable, and it must be possible

to transfer some form of exclusive title to them. Failing these two characteristics, market transactions simply cannot take place. The power of the state and access to the power of coercion are, of course, also necessary to market transactions. A market economy could not exist without the power of the state and the legal framework it provides in a variety of forms, not least the law of contract.

Exchange also plays a part in the transactions of the voluntary nonprofit sector. Indeed if we use the term *exchange* in a sufficiently broad sense, it can be made to cover even the most altruistic of voluntary endeavors. The problem arises when benefits from a transaction cannot be confined to those who have contributed to the exchange and there is nothing to stop noncontributors from taking a free ride on the backs of the contributors.

THE FREE-RIDER PROBLEM

Even when those who contribute to a voluntary enterprise—whether labor, goods, or money—receive in return no exclusive benefit for themselves, we have to assume that they derive some satisfaction from their contribution; they're getting something in return whether it is a psychic reward or a share in a collective good. But because that benefit is not exclusive, the link between their contribution and the benefit it helped create is weak.

To take a typical example of a public good, all citizens in a given state benefit from national defense. This is a benefit that cannot be made exclusive: if you are being protected from invasion by a foreign power, then I too am being protected from the same danger. This is not to say that all citizens place the same value on national defense, only that it is a value that cannot be assessed by market forces. The relative value to be placed on, and hence resources to be devoted to, national defense can be only politically determined. In the limiting case, some citizens may even *not* wish to be defended from foreign invasion. Conceivably, for example, some black South Africans might prefer to be invaded by a black neighbor than to remain under Afrikaner rule. Yet they are protected from foreign invasion whether they like it or not. Assuming, however, that I do wish to be protected from foreign invasion, I would be tempted, if the cost of national defense were left to voluntary contribution, to let others bear the cost and simply take a free ride. The same analysis will apply to any form of public or collective good. As a citizen of the United Kingdom, I may want to live in a society that provides free health care to those in need. (Note that this is not the same as saying that I want to be able to get free health care.) But the costs of maintaining the National Health Service are vast and my contribution to those costs is not going to make much difference one way or the other, so why should I bother to add my petty contribution?

The traditional model of public finance has tended to view the state as an agency for maximizing public welfare or collective utility. There are problems with this view. Most people think this is what the state *should* do, but would most think that this describes accurately what the balance of public revenue and expenditure *actually* seeks to achieve? More significant, the very concept of public welfare or collective utility offers major difficulties, including the problems of aggregating utilities demonstrated in Arrow's famous ''impossibility theorem'' (1963). Brennan and Buchanan (1980) have proposed an alternative model in which the state is seen as a revenue-maximizing Leviathan, which has very different implications. Neither model is wholly satisfactory and the state probably works in both these ways at different times. A combination of public provision and voluntary provision for public purposes makes it possible to accommodate the views and preferences of a greater range of the community than could public provision alone.

Only the state, by using the coercive power of law, can avoid free riders, and thus hopes it will achieve a distribution of resources that more closely approximates the collective interests of the community. What the free-rider argument suggests, then, is that the distribution of resources that most closely approximates what the community really wants—the Pareto optimum—will not be reached so long as individuals can avoid contributing to the cost of a collective good and still benefit from it. The possibilities both of taking a free ride oneself and of others taking a free ride will deter individuals from contributing voluntarily to the cost of a collective good. To return to the case of the National Health Service, it is manifestly more rational for me to pay my contribution to its cost if I know that all others are contributing their share than if I have no way of knowing how many others are going to skip their contributions and take a free ride.[3] Considerations of both equity and efficiency will thus tend to shift services from the voluntary to the state sector as the demand for the service becomes more widespread.

Olson (1971) develops an argument along these lines for determining when a service can be left to voluntary provision. The scale or size of the unit wanting the collective benefit is central to his argument. Relatively small groups can form viable organizations for providing collective goods because the individual members will be aware that their failure to contribute their share of the cost will have a significant effect on the provision of the collective good they all want. The link between their contribution and the benefit is close and apparent. On the other hand, a large group will have much more difficulty establishing such an organization because each member is likely to feel his contribution will make little difference and will thus be more tempted to take a free ride. Such large groups, Olson argues, are unlikely to succeed without some form of compulsion or some selective benefit for their members.

Olson is concerned primarily with self-seeking motives for collective action, but the same logic may apply to more altruistic motives. A self-seeking motive might be some privilege or benefit for members of a professional body, in

which case the collective good is the privilege achieved by the members' collective action. However, the collective good might reflect some social value the members have in common. For example, imagine a group of relatively wealthy citizens who believe that better housing should be provided for the poor. In this case, the good they collectively want is an altruistic one, but Olson's logic will still apply. If the group is small and knows that its views are not widely shared, it may set up a voluntary organization to provide housing for the poor—realizing that this is the only way the good it wants can be attained. Many such organizations were in fact set up toward the end of the nineteenth century and in the early years of this century. David Owen (1964) gives many examples of early philanthropic housing projects and shows how they ultimately led to the development of public housing policies. On the other hand, if many people share this view (or the group believes they do), they will seek to invoke the coercive power of the state and press for public housing subsidized from taxation. Although compulsion is most often achieved by invoking the power of the state, Olson recognizes that occasionally private organizations can achieve a form of compulsion. For example, trade unions may be able to make membership virtually compulsory by closed-shop agreements that restrict employment to union members. Similarly, private cartels and monopolies may have similar power, though it may be short-lived.

In a pluralist democracy both government and voluntary organizations provide public goods. Some authorities have even argued that the work of voluntary organizations can be viewed as a private analogue to the making and implementation of public policy (Mavity & Ylvisaker 1977). Frequently voluntary and state services run side by side. Voluntary philanthropic housing associations, for example, operate parallel to public housing policies, and in education, all the pluralist democracies contain both public and private schools.[4] Voluntary hospitals and welfare services also coexist with a wide variety of public government-run schemes. The relationship of private philanthropic activities to the state and the services it provides varies from country to country, but the freedom to form voluntary organizations to serve a public purpose is characteristic of all democracies.

Dahl (1982) presents a balanced picture of the merits of pluralist democracies in which more or less autonomous voluntary organizations play a part in the provision of public goods and in the development of public policy. First, and more important, the organizations present a mechanism through which conflicts of values, interests, and views can, if not be resolved, be at least accommodated. ''In practice if not in propaganda, each [organization] accepts the existence of the others and even concedes, if sometimes grudgingly, their legitimacy as spokesmen for the interests of their followers. Thereafter none seeks seriously to destroy the oth-

---

3. Note that in this formulation I implicitly assume both that there is a general desire for a national health service and that the tax system is ''fair.'' Both these assumptions will vary from country to country and from one period to another.

4. I use the term *public school* in the American sense of schools maintained by the public authorities and financed from public funds. Private schools are also found outside the pluralist democracies (see Levy 1982).

ers'' (p. 42). As I argue later in this chapter, interest groups do not always facilitate mutual accommodation among conflicting interests and may, when too narrowly based, even impede the process. Dahl argues that because each group prevents the others from making changes that might seriously damage its perceived interests, the system exerts a stabilizing and conservative influence. ''As a consequence, structural reforms that would significantly and rapidly redistribute control,'' he says, ''status, income, wealth and other resources are impossible to achieve—unless ironically, they are made at the expense of the unorganized. In this way, a powerful social force that in authoritarian countries carries with it the unmistakable odor of revolution can in democratic countries strongly reinforce the status quo'' (p. 43).

There are basic differences between the characteristics of a voluntary service and those of a public service. As I have indicated above, the principal advantage enjoyed by public services run by government agencies and financed by compulsory taxation is that the scale of the service and the resources devoted to it are not limited by the free-rider problem. There are limits, however, to the use of public services run by government agencies.

THE CATEGORICAL CONSTRAINT

As soon as we invoke the coercive power of law, ordinary principles of democratic freedom and justice require restraints that are not applicable to a purely voluntary service. If we ask ourselves why such and such a voluntary service should not be made statutory and financed through compulsory taxation, several normative constraints will occur to us immediately. One of these might be expressed as follows: ''This service reflects the views of a relatively small proportion of the population. Most people do not consider it either necessary or desirable.'' In these circumstances it would be manifestly impossible for democratic governments to establish such a service, and it would be arguable whether the state was justified in compelling those who disagreed with the program to pay for it through compulsory taxation. In fact these constraints of political feasibility and political justice are not entirely clear-cut. Is the state entitled to compel those who disapprove of abortion to pay for it by compulsory taxation? What about those who disapprove of various kinds of defense expenditures—MX missiles or CIA activities in Latin America? Nor can we resolve the issue simply by saying that in such cases the minority must bow to the wishes of the majority.

Constraints that must exist when a service is provided by the state will not exist when a service is provided by voluntary action. The question of political feasibility does not arise. In the private sector those who want to provide the service are free to do so. Only if the service is seen as actually harmful will the law be invoked to prevent it. Similarly, the question of the justice of the imposition of the cost does not arise so long as the service is provided voluntarily. There are clearly many services of the need for which a large propor-

tion of the population is unconvinced and yet are not seen as positively harmful. This is an area that voluntary organizations are free to explore.

Similarly, if we look at the service from the point of view of the benefits it provides, a democratic state is more constrained to ensure that benefits are distributed fairly and equitably than is a voluntary organization. The democratic state has to treat all its citizens equally, which is what we mean by equality before the law. Voluntary organizations are not similarly constrained. Like the owner of the vineyard in the parable, they can argue that they are free to do what they will with their own: they may not have enough resources to serve all those in need of the service they offer but they can serve at least some of them, an argument not available to the state. Furthermore, the state's distribution of benefits must not only be equitable; it must be *seen* to be equitable. One of the things we mean by political accountability is that state officials can be made to justify why they provide a benefit to one citizen and deny it to another. State action has to fit a pattern of rules. Voluntary action can be more spontaneous and even, if need be, aleatory. Spontaneity, in turn, can release that style of human warmth and loving care that a generalized pattern of defensible rules tends to crush. At its best, voluntary action can be based on true charity; ultimately state action has to be based on justice.

Soon after the great expansion of state welfare services that took place in Britain after World War II, a committee under the chairmanship of Lord Nathan was appointed to look into the law relating to charities. Reviewing the historical record and the impact of voluntary organizations on the development of state services, the Nathan Committee (1952) concluded, ''Historically, state action is voluntary action crystallized and made universal.'' The constraints on the use of government agencies implicit in this universalizing process are, I believe, the nearest we can get to the constraints on the use of market mechanisms implicit in the market failure concepts of welfare economics. Because universality seems to me a more important characteristic than formality—law has to be a categorical imperative—I call these the categorical constraints.

DIVERSITY

We can divide the categorical constraints into several subclassifications. Although a wide diversity of views and social values will exist in a state of any size, the law of that state can adopt only one at a time, although that one may reflect compromise between differing views. The private sector may comprise both prolife groups opposed to abortion and prochoice groups favoring it, but the state must ultimately choose. Similarly, it cannot simultaneously oppose the teaching of religion in its schools and encourage it. Within any given jurisdiction, contradictory policies on the same subject must be avoided. This presents no problem when the policy adopted reflects virtually unanimous views, but far more often, this aspect of the categorical constraint prevents the policy and law of the state from reflecting the full diversity of views and values it is the objective of pluralist democracy both to tolerate and to respect.[5]

The classic pluralist argument is that a voluntary nonprofit sector permits a greater diversity of social provisions than the state itself can achieve. Using Ylvisaker's interesting suggestion that we can regard the voluntary sector as a private version of government (Mavity & Ylvisaker 1977), we can say that the voluntary sector enables us to achieve a sort of diversity that would require the impossible combination of a secular, Catholic, Protestant, Jewish, Moslem, rightist, leftist, and centrist government operating simultaneously in the same jurisdiction!

This pluralist argument for diversity, which I have developed more fully elsewhere (Douglas 1983), is probably the most important from the point of view of political theory, for it addresses the central paradox of democracy—that the people are sovereign but many: there is not one will of the people but several, sometimes contradictory wills.

It is probably for this reason that a healthy voluntary sector is characteristic of a democracy. We lack comprehensive systematic comparative data, but anecdotal evidence (such as the suppression of free trade unions in Communist-bloc countries) suggests that autonomous voluntary organizations are among the first casualties of a totalitarian regime whether of the Right or of the Left. At the same time, such comparative data as we do possess suggest that there are limits to the extent to which a voluntary sector can heal the breaches caused by a seriously fractionalized society. Sri Lanka is one such society and, moreover, one in which the minority, the Tamils, are, on average, wealthier than the majority. Yet James's careful analysis of the nonprofit sector in Sri Lanka (1980) does not suggest that voluntary organizations have succeeded in greatly reducing ethnic tension. The same is true of Northern Ireland, where voluntary organizations have been unable to bridge the gulf between the two communities.[6] On the other hand, where tensions are less severe and less violent, a voluntary sector seems to provide the desired diversity. James's comparison of Sweden, a relatively homogeneous society, and Holland, a relatively heterogeneous one, supports the hypothesis that cultural heterogeneity is positively associated with provision of services through nonprofit organizations (1982).

Denominational education provides another illustration of the diversity argument. Only in the last hundred years or so has education become sufficiently widely recognized as a universal right for the state to provide education as a service financed by compulsory taxation. Earlier, education was a function of the voluntary sector.[7] Yet today some form of education, at least at the secondary level, is provided as a free service in all advanced industrial countries.

Denominational education, however, is not normally provided entirely at the taxpayer's expense. Because the separation of church and state is enshrined in the First Amendment of its Constitution, the United States excludes public funding of denominational education altogether. And such countries as France and Britain subsidize denominational education to a lesser extent than nondenominational public education, which tends to be justified on some such grounds as the saving of what would otherwise have to be spent on public education. The argument is presumably that it would be unfair to expect taxpayers to pay for a form of religious education in which they did not believe. So denominational education is provided on a voluntary basis. It is financed in part by students' fees but also by contributions from people who are not necessarily parents of the students. Such contributors presumably see a social value in denominational education over and above the direct benefit to the students themselves. But this is not a social value they share with the generality of their fellow citizens. In effect they are taxing themselves to provide what they consider to be a social service.

The distinctive factor is that the social value the contributors place on the service is not shared by all. In a state in which all citizens were of the same denomination and placed the same value on denominational education, a state service financed from taxation would presumably be the solution adopted. The same argument can, of course, be applied to other minority values in education and to other services. Even if some people support denominational education for nondenominational reasons—for example, that it provides a more disciplined or academic education than do the public schools—nothing in the diversity argument precludes diversification on more than one dimension.

In a much debated report, Coleman, Hoffer, and Kilgore (1982) provided evidence that private schools, and Catholic schools in particular, produced what they call ''better cognitive outcomes'' than do public schools. It would be reasonable to suppose that this would lead people to support such schools, and, indeed, the argument is often met in conversation. On the other hand, they also found that denominational schools led to more segregation not only on expected religious lines but also on social, income, and ethnic lines. Here we can see the way a voluntary sector permits the expression of differing social values. Although segregation has a pejorative connotation, it is not inconceivable that some people should put a positive social value on allowing children to be educated among their coreligionists, and although it is more difficult to imagine people putting a positive social value on social and ethnic segregation, it is likely that different elements in a diverse population will reach different

5. The abortion issue shows that even the private sector cannot always permit reflection of the full diversity of values, especially when both factions wish to engage the coercive power of the state. The prolife groups want to engage the coercive power to forbid abortion, and the prochoice groups want to engage the coercive power by compelling those who consider abortion to be murder to pay for it through taxation.

6. See, for example, Padraig O'Malley (1983) on the history of the Peace People.

7. In some late-developing nations, the order was reversed with state-run education coming first (Levy 1982).

value judgments regarding the trade-off between divisiveness and academic attainment.

In the case of denominational education, the relationship between voluntary provision and minority social values is clear-cut. In other areas the relationship may be more complex and subtle. In the case of research and higher education, distrust of too great a governmental influence is partly an attempt to achieve a greater diversity of approaches under a mixed regime of partly voluntary, partly statutory provision than in an entirely state-run system.

Sometimes the diversity of social values will be related to the scale of provision. The principle of some degree of social welfare provision is clearly widely accepted, but equally clearly there are great differences among different groups of the population regarding the scale of provision that should be made from taxation. Weisbrod (1975) has provided an elegant model showing how voluntary nonprofit provision enables those who believe in a greater degree of social provision to supplement the level the politicians believe their constituents will accept. In practice it is, of course, very difficult to judge the precise point at which taxpayers balance the trade-off between level of taxation and level of social provision, and it is by no means clear that politicians actually attempt any such assessment. However, Weisbrod's basic point that voluntary organizations permit those who want to do more than they are legally compelled to do remains valid. The diversity argument applies just as much to those who want to provide more of a public good as it does to those who want to provide different kinds of public goods.

EXPERIMENTATION

Closely allied to the diversity argument is the greater facility for experimentation possessed by the voluntary nonprofit sector. Before a democratic government can embark on any course of action, the case for it must be accepted by a relatively large section of the population. It is, of course, not literally true that the government—or the peoples' representatives whose role it is to check the government—has to be satisfied that the action is desired by more than half the population.[8] Governments cannot, as scientists would, readily say, "This is a reasonable hypothesis. It is not proven, but let us see what happens when we act in such and such a way." Governments, perhaps more by convention than by strict democratic theory, have to adopt the convinced approach of acting on certainties rather than the tentative approach of the experimentalist acting on the basis of trial and error. If the approach has already been tried by a voluntary body and proved viable, government can then follow using the experience and evidence gained by the voluntary organization. Voluntary bodies not infrequently adopt a course of

action precisely in order to make a case for subsequent government action on the same lines. One well-known example is the "green revolution" pioneered by the Rockefeller Foundation, subsequently supported by other private foundations, and now primarily financed by governmental and intergovernmental agencies. It is extremely unlikely that governments would have embarked on this trail if it had not been blazed by the Rockefeller Foundation.

Even if a government has been persuaded to adopt an experimental policy, the requirement of equal treatment will present special problems. Let us take a hypothetical example, again from the field of education.[9] A public education authority wants to find out the most cost-effective student-teacher ratio. The obvious way to do this would be to set up classes with different ratios—ten students per teacher, twenty, perhaps a hundred—and measure performance against cost in each case. It is not difficult to imagine the political reaction to this strategy! The parents of the children in the larger classes would rightly feel aggrieved that their children were being discriminated against as compared to the children in the smaller classes and soon would mount a campaign to stop the experiment. The experiment would probably not be much easier to adopt in any single private school, but it could be carried out through a number of private schools—schools with larger classes compensating by lower fees. This hypothetical example may have sacrificed realism for arithmetic simplicity, but readers will be able to imagine more complex variables than the student-teacher ratio where a diversity of experience would be valuable and yet resisted on grounds of equity.

Experimentation involves not only trying things that have not been proven; it involves also abandoning experiments when the results show them to be unjustified. Here again government is at a disadvantage as against both the for-profit sector and the private nonprofit sector. Precisely because governments cannot easily admit to an experimental approach, it is more difficult for a government, which has invested political capital as well as taxpayers' money, to recognize that an experiment is no longer worth pursuing. The checkered history of sunset legislation is testimony to the difficulty governments experience in abandoning a project once it has been embarked upon.

The voluntary sector has fulfilled the role of experimenter and initiator with distinction in the past. Almost without exception every major social service was originally undertaken by the voluntary sector.[10] But does the sector still fulfill

8. Or even necessarily that those in favor outnumber those opposed. The cases where they do not—for example, the abolition of capital punishment in the majority of civilized democracies—present some special problems for democratic theory.

9. I am indebted to Martin Landau for this hypothetical example.

10. Many schools, universities, and hospitals were established in medieval times (see Jordan 1959). It is a moot semantic point whether these should be classed as voluntary organizations. But certainly by the beginning of the seventeenth century, they had come under the rubric of charity. The eighteenth century saw a great proliferation of humanitarian charities, and the nineteenth century saw the establishment of many organizations both to combat poverty and to systematize and coordinate charitable endeavors. In the same century we find movements to spread

this role? Again we lack empirical data. After consulting the annual reports of the large foundations and the major charities, we could compile lists of the projects and programs of which they are most proud. Will they prove to be as significant as the philanthropies of a Carnegie, say, or the Rockefellers or George Peabody or Dorothea Dix? We may be too close in time to recognize the true significance of the current work of the philanthropic sector; nevertheless it often seems to lack the pioneering and innovative character of earlier endeavors. One obstacle I see today to the experiment-initiating role is the power of fashion and the tendency among established organizations toward conformity. In one decade the fight against poverty in the Third World is adopted by a wide range of voluntary organizations. In the next decade all eyes are turned on the urban problems of the industrial countries. While, on the one hand, governments have accepted a greatly expanded role in social services, on the other, the voluntary organizations themselves seem to have become more sensitive to public opinion than they were in, say, the nineteenth century, and so they solicit more public support. Thus the roles of government and the voluntary sector have become more difficult to distinguish. Yet this may be no more than an impression derived from the media's presentation of the sector's activities. We need much firmer empirical evidence before we can determine how the sector is fulfilling its initiating and experimental role in social policy.

In one way the voluntary sector still seems to cater to the diversity of values in a complex society: the sector as a whole covers a wide spectrum of political and religious values. Politically we find voluntary organizations from the far Right to the far Left with almost every shade of opinion represented. Similarly most Christian denominations have their own relatively strong voluntary organizations, as does a wide variety of Jewish organizations. In most Western democracies, Christian and Jewish organizations are usually well supported and often politically influential. Finally the agnostic and atheistic varieties of humanism are also well represented in the voluntary sector. What is not clear is whether political and religious values are represented by these organizations proportionate to their incidence in society.

Is it true, for example, that the political Right is better represented in the voluntary sector than the Left because it has easier access to money? An experiment to support or disprove this contention would be hard to design because "Left" and "Right" are not easily measured political characteristics. Abandoning the crude Left-Right spectrum, Arnove edited a collection of essays (1980) that develops the

more subtle argument that one section of the voluntary sector, the big foundations, have tended to support a sophisticated conservatism (with a small c). These foundations were established and endowed by successful men operating in a competitive economy, and they have continued to be controlled for the most part by those whom the status quo has served well. Not surprisingly, therefore, they have tended to support changes, both in the United States and internationally, that make the status quo more acceptable and efficient rather than altering it radically.

Fisher's chapter in Arnove's book is a carefully documented and detailed case study of the development and influence of the Rockefeller Foundations' policies regarding the social sciences in England during the interwar years. Fisher found that the Rockefeller administrators, although committed to capitalist democracy, recognized that there was something fundamentally wrong about the levels of poverty and unemployment of the time. To them, these were unmistakable signs that the system was maladjusted, and they believed that a more complete knowledge of the working of the economic system would supply a basis for planning a more effective economic organization. They used their funds to stimulate the development of remedial social and economic sciences. Fisher, working in the files and archives of the Rockefeller Foundations, examined the thinking that went into the development of these policies more closely than did scholars who were confined to published sources and interviews. His case study revealed attitudes that were probably representative of those of the big foundations at the time: mainstream thinking, moderate progressiveness, an emphasis on research, and faith in the ameliorative potential of improved knowledge. These attitudes still compose an important strand in the thinking of big foundations. Nielsen's classic history of the big foundations (1972) leaves the reader with a similar impression.

This is not to say that there are no foundations with more radical commitments either of the Left or of the Right, nor are foundations the largest part of the voluntary sector (religion accounts for by far the largest slice). But even within this relatively small and well-documented part, the precise political balance is difficult to establish. Balance, however, is not necessarily a desirable objective in the voluntary sector: enabling the unpopular, the eccentric, and the heterodox to survive and lend their vitality to mass society is not the least of its functions.

BUREAUCRATIZATION

The diversity argument emphasizes the extent to which a service is made universal when it is transferred to the government sector, thus inevitably sacrificing some diversity. But the categorical constraint also springs from the way a service is formalized when transferred to the public sector; it becomes accountable to the public or the public's representatives. It must treat equals equally and it must show that it is doing so. These needs—to ensure equality of treatment

---

education and improve housing for the laboring classes. In contrast, the state was not greatly involved in providing any of these traditionally philanthropic services until toward the end of the century (see Owen 1964; Bremner 1975). Thus, if we take education, health, housing, and welfare as the main contemporary social services of the state, their origins in all cases lie in the voluntary sector (see Nathan Committee 1952).

throughout a jurisdiction and to be able to defend its actions politically—together, generate the morass typical of bureaucratic red tape. The irony is that those who complain most about red tape are often those who are most vociferous in their demands for public accountability. What exactly constitutes bureaucratic red tape, as is the case with many such disparaging phrases, is rarely defined. Kaufman (1977) shows that the term has been used to indicate almost everything from a generalized dislike of any form of regulation to specific cases of maladministration. I use the term here to indicate the rigidly rule-bound requirements and restraints that administrators are almost forced to impose, since they may be called upon to defend their actions publicly in any specific case.

Voluntary organizations themselves are of course not totally free of bureaucratic constraints; there is always someone—be it trustees or contributors—to whom their executives are accountable. But they are usually freer than government agencies, partly because the scale of operations typically is smaller and partly because those to whom they are accountable are less numerous so that conditions of trust are more easily established. But, above all, those who contribute voluntarily to an enterprise have a safeguard that those who are compelled to contribute do not possess. The former can stop contributing; the latter cannot. Following Hirschman's terminology, we can call the safeguard enjoyed by the former "exit" and conclude that the latter must be compensated for its absence by stronger institutions of "voice" (1970).

The voluntary sector achieves diversity through the very diversity of its institutions, but it may also achieve a measure of freedom from bureaucratic red tape even within its constituent institutions. The private institution may be as zealous as any public agency in treating its clients equally, but because it is less politically accountable than the public agency, it needs to devote a smaller proportion of its resources to justifying (and producing evidence to justify) its actions if challenged.

Let us say, for example, that a denominational school is as committed as a public-sector school to providing the most promising students with an education their parents can afford (or whatever may be the rule by which its mission is defined). But the public school will have to do this in a way it can defend publicly and politically. Thus it is likely to develop fairly rigid rules—such as specified qualifications, income limits for the parents, and so on. It will also have to keep elaborate records and adopt elaborate procedures to ensure that the rules are in fact applied. The private school, on the other hand, because it is not legally and politically bound to its rules in the same way, can be more flexible. It can rely on more subjective criteria and trust more in the judgments of its officials.

In the matter of costs, the more elaborate administration of the public-sector institution inevitably is more expensive. But an economic price is paid, too, for the diversity achieved by fulfilling functions through voluntary endeavors. There is the cost of carrying free riders and the cost of fund-raising activities designed to reduce their numbers. On the other hand, the voluntary sector's relative freedom from accountability results in a savings and enables a greater proportion of available resources to be devoted to the institution's primary mission. There is clearly a trade-off here that will vary from case to case. An empirical study would be useful to ascertain whether voluntary organization in any given field actually leads to a more economical service.

The relative freedom of the private voluntary sector from bureaucratic constraints is so well established that governments frequently use the device of subsidizing existing voluntary bodies (or establishing new ones) to carry out functions somewhat protected from the usual requirements of political accountability. Kramer and Terrell (1984) conducted an extensive survey of the use of voluntary bodies by government agencies in the San Francisco Bay area. A significant proportion of the social services in the area are provided by private organizations under contract to government agencies. From their survey emerged a clear picture of the perceived advantages and disadvantages of services paid out of taxation and provided by voluntary organizations.

The advantages most often mentioned by government officials were greater flexibility—a program could be initiated (or terminated) more easily when the government agency did not itself have to engage staff—and a saving in costs—volunteers could be used and staffs given lower salaries and fewer fringe benefits. The claimed advantage in cost, however, was not universally accepted. Kramer and Terrell, in effect, returned a verdict of "not proven" because of the difficulties of comparing costs in the public and private sectors. Advantages less frequently mentioned were perhaps more interesting. The private agencies were seen as having greater competence in certain specialized areas—for example, providing day and residential care for adults, dealing with violence in the family, running suicide prevention centers, and maintaining sheltered workshops. It was also easier to use private agencies for controversial programs like family planning services. Voluntary bodies could make contact more easily with certain classes of clients, such as ethnic and cultural minorities and drug and child abusers, where a social stigma is attached to receiving services from government agencies.

The major disadvantage seen by public officials in using private agencies was the difficulty of achieving the degree of accountability required. Kramer and Terrell said, "Almost every public program manager involved in contracting noted the presence of accountability problems" (p. 23). Perhaps not surprisingly, given the difference in the administrative conventions of the public and private sectors, government managers also complained of inadequate management in the private agencies, poor personnel practices, weak budgeting (*virement*, anathema in public-sector budgeting, is almost meaningless in the private sector), and inadequate record keeping. They also complained of political pressures and attempts to avoid complying with contractual requirements. The general impression left by Kramer and Terrell fits our model of a trade-off between accountability in the public sector and flexibility and diversity in the private sector.

THREE CLASSES OF NONPROFIT ORGANIZATIONS

The nonprofit organization set up to provide a public benefit from private funds is the most interesting from a theoretical point of view. This form of nonprofit organization is, in a real sense, an alternative to government, permitting a greater diversity of social provision than the state itself can achieve. Thus it constitutes a distinctive element in the Western liberal democratic tradition. It is not the only or even the most common form of nonprofit organization, however. We can identify at least two others: the mutual benefit organization—which is established to provide collective benefits more or less exclusively for its members—and the pressure group, or political action organization—which aims not to provide benefits itself but to persuade government to do so.

Of these three classes, only the first is technically a charity "within the spirit and intendment" of the Elizabethan statute. Obviously, a mutual benefit association in which all the benefits are captured by the members and contributors themselves has no claim to special legal or tax privileges. It no more serves a public purpose than does a for-profit organization. Similarly, although the reasons for this are less obvious, organizations set up primarily to achieve a political objective are not regarded as charitable, at least in the Anglo-American common-law tradition.[11]

The distinctions among these three classes of nonprofit organizations are somewhat artificial and arbitrary. Actual organizations often straddle the classes to a greater or lesser extent. Mutual benefit organizations whose benefits seem at first sight exclusive to their members, such as motoring or golf clubs, may on closer examination be shown to provide forms of benefit to those who are not members. Motoring clubs usually seek to represent the interests of all motorists whether members or not, and golf clubs frequently have a beneficial effect on the value of properties in their vicinity. Similarly, the distinction between a charity and a political action organization may be difficult to discern. Charities frequently feel that their commitment to their clients requires them not only to provide the specific benefits for which they were founded but also to defend the interests of their clients in terms of public policy. For example, a charity established to provide financial assistance to impoverished senior citizens will find it a natural and almost inevitable extension of its role to lobby on questions of their social security.

The problem created by this blurring of categories is one with which lawyers have had to wrestle and have resolved in different ways in different countries. The resolution is rarely very satisfactory. Organizations that common sense suggests should be seen as charitable (such as Gingerbread, and English mutual benefit organization for single-parent families) are sometimes excluded by the legal definition. Conversely the legal definition occasionally includes organizations that do not seem particularly charitable. Charities seeking to remain within the legal definition frequently complain that their activities are unduly restricted.

Mutual Benefit Organizations

Mutual benefit organizations range from elitist social clubs to trade unions. In many ways these are closer to the for-profit sector than to the philanthropic. There is frequently very little altruism about the motivation of their members. They differ from the typical commercial for-profit enterprise in providing goods or services for their members collectively rather than on a quid pro quo transaction basis, which usually is why the nonprofit form is adopted.

Trade unions, for example, negotiate collectively for their members. As wages and working conditions are usually determined for a whole class of working people, they cannot charge clients individually for their services in the same way as, say, a lawyer or a doctor might do. Although they often represent individual members as a lawyer might do, their central activity cannot be organized on a commercial quid pro quo basis, and this determines the form of organization adopted.

Sporting and social clubs, another common form of mutual benefit organizations, typically provide premises and facilities for which theoretically members could be charged individually each time they were used. This, however, would be an expensive way of organizing things. It is cheaper and more satisfactory to make facilities available to the members collectively in return for membership fees—an example of the way the economic case for a nonprofit organization can be made in terms of "transaction costs." The concept of transaction cost was developed by Williamson (1979) originally to elucidate the economic reasons for-profit firms adopt different commercial strategies in such matters as deciding whether to subcontract or manufacture their own components, whether to maintain their own retailing organization or sell on the open market to retailers, and so on. The key element in the concept involves shifting attention from the subject of the transaction to the transaction itself. Each form of transaction has advantages and disadvantages that can be treated as the costs and benefits of that form. Although originally developed in the context of the organization of for-profit firms, the concept is readily applicable to the distinctions among for-profit, nonprofit, and government forms of organization.[12]

In the case of social clubs, the cost of organizing things on a quid pro quo basis (the cost of this form of transaction) is higher than the cost of organizing them on a collective basis, and the higher transaction cost is not compensated by any significant advantages. This does not wholly explain why the nonprofit form is adopted, however. A for-profit enterprise could as easily as a nonprofit enterprise allow access to its facilities on the basis of an annual subscription. This is what

---

11. Civil-law countries, such as France and Germany, approach the problem of charities from a different standpoint. They have no analogous law of charities, but the end result is similar (see Pomey 1980).

12. The application of transaction cost analysis (and other techniques drawn from the economics of organization) to political institutions is reviewed by Moe (1984).

proprietary clubs in fact do, and the provision of services on the basis of an annual subscription is a common device in the for-profit sector. Thus, we need a further explanation for the adoption of the nonprofit form. I suspect that in this case the explanation lies in the greater control the nonprofit form gives to the customers/members. It compensates for the weakening influence of "exit" when goods are provided collectively by a strengthening of "voice."

Political Nonprofit Organizations

The class of nonprofit organizations that have public policy objectives is crucially important to the workings of democratic government. Political parties are themselves members of this class, but, even apart from them, it is almost impossible to imagine the workings of a modern democratic system without a whole constellation of lobbies, interest groups, and the like to articulate the range of interests and values that must be reconciled by the political system (see chapter 17 for a discussion of policy advocacy organization). Because the literature devoted to political parties, pressure groups, and other political nonprofits is so extensive, it is not feasible to summarize it here.[13] Nonetheless, a few points are worth making because they bear on fairly general characteristics of the nonprofit sector.

Although a wide spectrum of interests is represented by pressure groups and lobbies, it is generally recognized that all interests do not get equally represented. For example, producers find it easier to organize than consumers do, and a wealthy industry can deploy more resources in creating a pressure group to lobby on its behalf than a poor section of the community can. Here political norms of equity come into conflict with the spontaneity and randomness—the general untidiness—of the nonprofit sector.

It should be noted that these characteristics of the nonprofit sector are not mere accidental by-products to be corrected by systematic legislation ensuring equal representation of varying interests. Any attempt by the state to tidy up the nonprofit sector would necessarily interfere with freedom of association and thus would undermine an essential source of vitality for the sector. For example, the voluntary principle leads to duplication when two or more voluntary organizations embark on the same mission. Yet to rationalize the situation by allowing only one to exist would forfeit the opportunity for competition between them. More serious, there is a seeming irrationality in encouraging the formation of two voluntary organizations with mutually incompatible goals (for example, pro- and antiabortion groups), but to suppress one or both would be gravely to restrict democratic freedom. Either we must follow Rousseau in his condemna-

tion of partial societies and allow nothing between the state and the individual or we must accept that the nonprofit sector will reflect some of the differences in power that exist within our society.

In a recent development of his argument regarding the logic of collective action, Olson (1982) does make a case against those partial societies which he calls "distributional coalitions." His argument is that these coalitions (which include trade unions, cartels, pressure groups, business lobbies, and the like) place a value on benefits to their own members many times greater than any cost of those benefits to the community as a whole. Thus, in pursuing the particular good of their members, such bodies act to depress the general good of the wider society. A similar argument was developed by Thurow in *The Zero-Sum Society* (1980).

In general, the institutions of the political nonprofit sector facilitate the nonviolent resolution of conflicts within society. They form part of the system by which conflicting interests are represented, expressed, and reconciled. This reconciliation is normally achieved by a process of bargaining, in which negotiators represent a sufficiently wide range of interests to be able to concede in one direction in return for concessions in another. In negotiations between management and labor, for example, concessions on hours or wages might be traded against concessions on staffing. The existence of representative voluntary organizations greatly helps this process. Management and labor negotiations would be virtually impossible without voluntary organizations in any large industry with hundreds of firms employing tens of thousands of employees. Similarly, a point of view widely scattered throughout the population can be made effective only after it has been gathered together by a voluntary organization, which represents that point of view in the legislative process and frequently confronts representatives of other points of view. The environmental lobbies are examples of this process.

Voluntary organizations, however, may sometimes impede rather than help the process of reaching societal decisions—for example, when voluntary pressure groups represent too narrow a range of interests. The tendency in recent years to develop single-issue groups rather than the older pattern of class-interest groups has accentuated this danger. A group representing, say, farmers will accommodate a wide range of interests and enter easily into a bargaining mode that sacrifices an interest here for a concession there. It is difficult to see how any basis for agreement could be reached between, say, a group that believes all nuclear power stations are anathema and one that believes nuclear power is the safest, most economical, and most socially desirable way of generating electricity. The difference lies in the specificity with which the issue is defined. If it is defined in terms of overall use of energy (coal, oil, natural gas), then there may be scope for bargaining, but if it is defined in here-and-now terms (whether a particular power station shall be run on nuclear energy), then deadlock is nearly inevitable. Similarly, in the agricultural case, an issue defined in terms of

13. Some references with which to start may be useful. Most contain bibliographies or suggestions for further reading. On political parties: Sorauf (1984), Keefe (1980), and Crotty (1980). On pressure groups and other political action organizations: Berry (1984) and two classics, Truman (1971) and Schattschneider (1975).

forms of agricultural protection will be easier to resolve than one defined in terms of, say, a specific provision of the European Common Agricultural Policy.

Moreover, when beliefs are held so intensely that compromise is impossible, the process of making societal decisions may break down. How can agreement be reached between a group that believes that any form of abortion under any circumstances is murder and a group that sees abortion as the inalienable right of women? Instead of facilitating compromise and negotiation between different elements of society, pressure groups like these may serve to accentuate differences, as they not only reflect the view of their constituent members but reinforce them. The process of organizing a group, bringing it together, holding meetings, and the like tends both to reinforce the members' views and to develop an adversary relation with groups representing different interests. Moreover, as Michels (1966) long ago recognized (in relation to political parties), the officials of such a group acquire a vested interest in its survival. They are not necessarily eager to recognize that their activities have resolved the problems that led to the establishment of the group or that a satisfactory modus vivendi has been established with their erstwhile adversaries.

Although I have written of three distinct sectors—government, business, and voluntary—and of different classes of nonprofits within the last sector, these are artificial and academic distinctions imposed on what is, in reality, the seamless web of the institutional fabric of society. The study of two of these sectors—business and government—developed into the disciplines of economics and political science. The third sector has tended to be neglected by the social sciences. Yet it touches on both of the others and is not only interesting in itself but a good vantage point from which to study the other two. Increasing concern with the third sector, which the issuing of this volume demonstrates, follows logically from the academic trend to return to the older conception of a political economy, in which economy and polity are seen as all of a piece. It is also appropriate that we should explore more fully the strengths and weaknesses of the third sector at a time when the public is becoming increasingly disillusioned with both government and business.

REFERENCES

Archer, M., ed. 1982. *The Sociology of Educational Expansion.* Beverly Hills, Calif.: Sage Publications.

Arnove, Robert, ed. 1980. *Philanthropy and Cultural Imperialism.* Boston: G. K. Hall.

Arrow, Kenneth. 1963. *Social Choice and Individual Values.* New Haven: Yale University Press.

Berry, Jeffrey M. 1984. *The Interest Group Society.* Boston: Little, Brown.

Brennan, G., and Buchanan, J. M. 1980. *The Power to Tax.* New York: Cambridge University Press.

Bremner, Robert H. 1975. "Private Philanthropy and Public Needs: Historical Perspective." In *Research Papers,* sponsored by the Commission on Private Philanthropy and Public Needs. Washington, D.C.: Department of the Treasury.

Coleman, James; Hoffer, Thomas; and Kilgore, Sally. 1982. *High School Achievement.* New York: Basic Books.

Crotty, William, 1984. *American Parties in Decline.* 2d ed. Boston: Little, Brown.

Dahl, Robert A. 1982. *Dilemmas of Pluralist Democracy.* New Haven: Yale University Press.

Douglas, James. 1983. *Why Charity?* Beverly Hills, Calif.: Sage Publications.

Fisher, Donald. 1980. "American Philanthropy and the Social Services." In *Philanthropy and Cultural Imperialism,* edited by Arnove, 1980.

Hirschman, Albert. 1970. *Exit, Voice and Loyalty.* Cambridge, Mass.: Harvard University Press.

James, Estelle. 1980. "The Non-Profit Sector in International Perspective: The Case of Sri Lanka." Yale University, Program on Non-Profit Organizations Working Paper no. 28.

———. 1982. "The Private Provision of Public Services: A Comparison of Sweden and Holland." Yale University, Program on Non-Profit Organizations Working Paper no. 60.

Jordan, W. K. 1959. *Philanthropy in England, 1480–1660.* London: Allen & Unwin.

Kaufman, Herbert. 1977. *Red Tape.* Washington, D.C.: Brookings Institution.

Keefe, William. 1980. *Parties, Politics and Public Policy in America.* 3d ed. New York: Holt, Rinehart & Winston.

Kramer, Ralph, and Terrell, Paul. 1984. *Social Service Contracting in the Bay Area.* Berkeley, Calif.: Institute of Governmental Studies.

Levy, Dan. 1982. "The Rise of Private Universities in Latin America and the United States." In *The Sociology of Educational Expansion,* edited by Archer, 1982, 93–132.

Mavity, Jane H., and Ylvisaker, Paul N. 1975. "Private Philanthropy and Public Affairs." In *Research Papers,* sponsored by the Commission on Private Philanthropy and Public Needs, vol. 2, pt. 1, 795–836. Washington, D.C.: Department of the Treasury.

Michels, Robert. 1966. *Political Parties*. New York: Free Press.

Moe, Terry M. 1984. "The New Economics of Organization." *American Journal of Political Science* 28, no. 4: 739–77.

Nathan Committee. 1952. *Report of the Committee on Law and Practice Relating to Charitable Trusts*. (Cmd. 8710). London: HMSO.

Nielsen, Waldemar. 1972. *The Big Foundations*. New York: Basic Books.

Olson, Mancur. 1971. *The Logic of Collective Action*. Cambridge, Mass.: Harvard University Press.

———. 1982. *The Rise and Decline of Nations*. New Haven: Yale University Press.

O'Malley, Padraig. 1983. *The Uncivil Wars*. Boston: Houghton Mifflin.

Owen, David. 1964. *English Philanthropy, 1660–1960*. Cambridge, Mass.: Harvard University Press.

Picarda, Hubert. 1977. *The Law and Practice Relating to Charities*. London: Butterworths.

Pomey, Michel. 1980. *Traité des foundations d'utilité publique*. Paris: Presses Universitaires de France.

Schattschneider, Elmer E. 1975. *The Semi-Sovereign People*. New York: Holt, Rinehart & Winston.

Sorauf, Frank. 1984. *Party Politics in America*. 5th ed. Boston: Little, Brown.

Thurow, Lester C. 1980. *The Zero-Sum Society*. New York: Basic Books.

Truman, David. 1971. *The Governmental Process*. New York: Alfred A. Knopf.

Weisbrod, Burton. 1975. "Towards a Theory of the Non-Profit Sector." In *Altruism, Morality and Economic Theory*, edited by Edmund S. Phelps. New York: Russell Sage Foundation.

Williamson, Oliver. 1979. "Transaction-Cost Economies: The Governance of Contractual Relations." *Journal of Law and Economics* 22:233–61.

Wolfenden Committee. 1978. *Report of the Future of Voluntary Organizations*. London: Croom Helm.

4

The Scope and Dimensions of Nonprofit Activity

GABRIEL RUDNEY

L
ike for-profit and public organizations, philanthropic organizations render services that satisfy individual and societal needs. Because of a lack of quantitative information about the nonprofit sector, however, public recognition of the significance of nonprofit activity has been limited largely to its social and ethical values. In order to extend our understanding of the nonprofit sector, I present in this chapter compilations of recent economic measures of the scope and dimensions of philanthropic activity. In addition, comparisons with data for the public and for-profit sectors will illustrate the relative importance of nonprofit organizations in the U.S. economy. Comparative data are necessary to inform public policy debates, such as those over the choice of government, private, or combined government-private initiatives for providing public services; the appropriateness of tax incentives to support and expand philanthropic activity; and the fairness of competition among for-profit and nonprofit organizations in specific areas.

Most of this chapter is concerned only with the philanthropic sector—privately controlled, tax-exempt organizations to which donor contributions are tax deductible. This classification includes religious, educational, health, scientific, cultural, and social service organizations, which constitute the large majority of nonprofit organizations. For example, philanthropic organizations account for 93 percent of all nonprofit employment, 91 percent of all nonprofit expenditures, and 94 percent of all nonprofit production (Rudney 1981; Rudney & Weitzman 1983). Data for philanthropic organizations are actually estimates based on several federal government sources (see Rudney & Weitzman 1983 for a complete discussion of methodology and data sources). In some cases, data sources do not permit analysis of the

I am grateful to Rebecca Friedkin, Woody Powell, and Paul DiMaggio for their helpful editorial comments.

philanthropic sector alone. Therefore, some figures are given for the more inclusive nonprofit sector, which embraces, in addition to philanthropic organizations, private nonprofit commercial enterprises and membership groups (social clubs, fraternal organizations, labor unions, chambers of commerce, trade associations, and business leagues) that are organized largely to confer mutual benefits on their members. These organizations are tax-exempt under federal law, but donations to them are not deductible.

THE NONPROFIT SECTOR AND THE SERVICE ECONOMY

Since World War II the United States has undergone a transition from a goods-producing economy to a service-producing economy. In fact, the United States was the first industrial nation to attain the stage of economic development in which a majority of the labor force produced services instead of goods (Fuchs 1968). The nonprofit sector has expanded rapidly during this transition and, although still small, continues to grow. In 1982, the nonprofit share of the service-producing economy in terms of employment was 14 percent. The position of the nonprofit sector in the economy in this respect is well demonstrated in table 4.1.

The importance of nonprofit organizations, and philanthropic ones in particular, is readily apparent when we consider the nature of their work. Philanthropic activity is concentrated in four areas: health care, education, social services, and religion (by legal definition, all religious organizations are nonprofit). Nonprofit organizations constitute the vast majority of private educational and social services. And, although for-profit organizations account for an increasing proportion of health care services (see chapter 13), the majority of private health care resources are nonprofit. The health care field is the single largest employer of nonprofit labor.

Changes in the labor force over time are good indicators

TABLE 4.1   EMPLOYMENT BY ECONOMIC SECTOR, 1972 AND 1982

	1972		1982			Share of Net Job Creation 1972–82 (%)
Sector	Number (000)	Percent of Total	Number (000)	Percent of Total	% Increase 1972–82	
Private for-profit	55,374	75	66,761	75	21	72
Goods-producing	23,668	32	23,907	27	1	2
Service-producing	31,707	43	42,854	48	35	70
Private nonprofit	4,966	7	7,032	8	42	13
Philanthropic	4,576	6	6,523	7	43	12
Other nonprofit	390	1	509	1	31	1
Government	13,333	18	15,803	18	19	16
Federal	2,684	4	2,739	3	2	*
State	2,859	4	3,632	4	27	5
Local	7,790	11	9,432	11	21	10
Total	73,674	100%	89,596	100%	22	15,922

Source: Rudney and Weitzman 1983.
Note: Includes full- and part-time employment.
*Less than .5%.

of the path of economic development. The rapid increase of the service economy is also well documented in table 4.1. The private-service sectors, both for-profit and nonprofit, experienced the fastest rates of employment growth between 1972 and 1982, and they were the only sectors to increase their relative shares of the labor force during that period. In contrast, the for-profit goods-producing sector experienced virtually no employment growth, and its share of the labor force incurred a considerable loss—from 32 percent to 27 percent. Increases in employment growth in local and state governments during this period were 21 percent and 27 percent, respectively, comparable with employment growth in the economy as a whole. Federal government employment remained almost constant, increasing by only 2 percent over ten years, and its relative share of the labor force declined slightly.

Over four-fifths of all new jobs were created in the service sectors, where nonprofit organizations are prominent. Although the nonprofit sector employed only 8 percent of the total labor force in 1982, it accounted for 13 percent of all jobs created between 1972 and 1982. The for-profit-service sector increased employment at a slightly slower pace, but because of its larger size, it contributed the greatest number of new jobs to the economy during the same period. Seventy percent of net job creation was in the for-profit-service sector, although it accounted for only 48 percent of all employment in 1982.

Changes in the relative contributions to gross national product (GNP) also reflects the rise of the service economy and the growth of the nonprofit sector (see table 4.2). Although the nonprofit sector accounted for only 3.2 percent of the 1975 GNP, that share was more than 50 percent greater than in 1960. The government sector also increased its relative contribution to GNP, while the for-profit sector lost ground. (Note that because these data do not separate the goods-producing and service-producing sectors of the for-

profit economy, the relative decline of the goods-producing sector is somewhat masked.)

Although the nonprofit sector is the smallest of the three economic sectors, its size is nonetheless impressive. In 1980, the entire nonprofit sector in the United States purchased goods and services amounting to $142.2 billion (Rudney 1981). Philanthropic organizations accounted for $129.2 billion of these expenditures, a sum exceeding the total budget of any nation in the world except the United States, France, West Germany, the United Kingdom, Japan, and probably China and the Soviet Union. Gross expenditures, however, overstate the production of any economic sector since they include costs of goods and services purchased from other organizations. The contribution to GNP is the value added by a sector through the employment of labor and the use of capital resources. In 1980, philanthropic organizations purchased $42.6 billion worth of goods and services produced by others (Rudney 1981). Thus, the value added to its output

TABLE 4.2   DISTRIBUTION OF GROSS NATIONAL PRODUCT ORIGINATING IN FOR-PROFIT, NONPROFIT, AND GOVERNMENT SECTORS, 1960 AND 1975

	Amount ($ in billion)		Percentage Distribution	
Sector	1960	1975	1960	1975
For-profit	$409.4	$1,166.8	86.4%	81.6%
Nonprofit	10.0	45.4	2.1	3.2
Government	53.5	202.9	11.3	14.2
Total	$473.7	$1,430.6	100.0%	100.0%

Source: Ruggles and Ruggles 1980.
Note: Market transactions only. Because of conceptual differences, these data differ from the Department of Commerce's National Account data, but the variation does not significantly alter the general trends.

by the philanthropic sector amounted to $86.6 billion, or 67 percent of the sector's gross expenditures.

The remainder of this chapter will examine the nature of philanthropic and nonprofit production. A detailed discussion of the two components of value added, labor and capital, is followed by a look at the revenues and subsidies of nonprofits and the consumption of nonprofit services.

PHILANTHROPIC EMPLOYMENT

Philanthropic organizations are service organizations and tend to be labor-intensive. The cost of labor is by far the major expense, representing 58 percent of the cost of production and 87 percent of value added by the philanthropic sector in 1980 (Rudney 1981). For this reason, a careful examination of the employment patterns of philanthropic organizations will provide a good understanding of the shape of the nonprofit sector. This section presents two kinds of data about the philanthropic labor force. First, an account of the magnitude of philanthropic employment and its distribution across occupation categories and subsectors provides a descriptive overview of the philanthropic labor force. Second, a further perspective on the sector's employment profile is provided by comparing employment growth rates for important areas of the philanthropic sector.

In 1982 philanthropic organizations employed over 6.5 million people, including part-time workers. This labor force constituted 73 percent of all private employment in those subsectors (for example, hospitals or individual and family social services) in which such organizations operate (Rudney & Weitzman 1983).

Most philanthropic employees fall in one of two major occupational categories. In 1980, almost 40 percent of the philanthropic labor force comprised professionals, and about 36 percent, service workers. Philanthropic organizations employ a disproportionately large share of these workers. In 1980, philanthropic organizations employed only 5.7 percent of the total labor force but 14.1 percent of all professionals and technical workers and 15.3 percent of all service workers (Rudney 1981).

Although nonprofit organizations provide a wide range of services, they are most heavily concentrated in four areas. Table 4.3 shows the distribution of paid philanthropic employment by subsector for 1972 and 1982. Considering first the distribution of employment in 1982, we see that health care organizations (primarily hospitals) account for almost 50 percent of all philanthropic employment. Education and research organizations (primarily colleges and universities) employ the second largest proportion of philanthropic labor, almost 20 percent. Social service organizations and religious

TABLE 4.3 DISTRIBUTION OF PHILANTHROPIC EMPLOYMENT, 1972 AND 1982

Subsectors	Total Full- and Part-time Philanthropic Employment (000)		% of Philanthropic Total		% Change 1972–82
	1972	1982	1972	1982	
Health services	1,931.4	3,052.3	42.2	46.8	58
Nursing and personal care	141.9	255.5	3.1	3.9	80
Hospitals	1,703.8	2,593.2	37.2	39.8	52
Other health services	85.7	203.6	1.9	3.1	138
Education and research	966.7	1,202.5	21.1	18.4	24
Elementary and secondary education	235.2	322.1	5.1	4.9	37
Colleges and universities	637.2	752.6	13.9	11.5	18
Libraries and information centers	14.6	12.4	.3	.2	−15
Correspondence and vocational schools	11.5	13.0	.3	.2	13
Other educational, scientific, and research organizations	68.2	102.4	1.5	1.6	50
Social services	454.6	959.2	9.9	14.7	111
Individual and family services	71.7	220.7	1.6	3.4	208
Job training and related services	84.0	183.0	1.8	2.8	118
Child day-care services	82.6	163.2	1.8	2.5	98
Residential care	84.1	181.6	1.8	2.8	116
Other social services	132.1	210.7	2.9	3.2	60
Membership organizations	1,146.8	1,198.7	25.1	18.4	5
Civic, social, and fraternal	278.3	301.6	6.1	4.6	8
Religious	868.5	897.1	19.0	13.8	3
Culture, entertainment, recreation	51.3	79.7	1.9	1.2	55
Performing arts (theater, orchestra, etc.)	23.5	32.4	.5	.5	38
Radio and television broadcasting	6.6	11.6	.1	.2	76
Visual arts (museums, botanical and zoological gardens)	21.2	35.7	.5	.5	68
Legal services	12.4	12.4	.3	.2	0
Educational, religious, charitable trusts	13.1	18.3	.3	.3	40
Total philanthropic employment	4,576.3	6,523.1	100.0	100.0	43

Source: Rudney and Weitzman 1983.

organizations are the other major philanthropic employers, each accounting for almost 15 percent of the sector's work force.

Turning to employment growth, we see further evidence of the sector's strength. Employment increased by 43 percent between 1972 and 1982, adding more than 1.9 million jobs to the sector. As table 4.3 illustrates, however, there was considerable variation in the rate of increase across subsectors, ranging from a loss of jobs in libraries and information centers to more than a tripling of the number of jobs in individual and family services. In general, health care and social service organizations increased their relative shares of the philanthropic labor force, while educational and religious organizations lost ground. The social services enjoyed the largest increase in employment, more than doubling the absolute size of their labor force and increasing by half their share of the philanthropic total. Significant increases occurred among all components of the social services: individual family services, job training and related services, child day-care services, residential care, and other areas. This increase occurred primarily between 1972 and 1980, however. Between 1980 and 1982 employment growth slowed considerably, accounting for only 5 percent of all social service jobs created during the decade.

An aging population, increased availability of private health insurance, and increased government financial support for Medicaid and Medicare programs contributed sub-

stantially to increased demand for hospital services, the largest subset of the health care field. Health care employment increased by 58 percent, compared to an overall average for the philanthropic sector of 43 percent. Thus, health services increased its already large share of the philanthropic labor force.

The problems of colleges and universities over the last decade are reflected in the employment patterns for the educational field. Employment increased at a far slower rate than in the philanthropic sector as a whole, resulting in a decrease in education's share of philanthropic labor from 21 percent to 18 percent.

Religious organizations fared even more poorly than colleges and universities, increasing their labor force by only 3 percent over the course of the decade. Religious organizations accounted for 19 percent of philanthropic employment in 1972, but for less than 14 percent in 1982.

The distribution of labor within the philanthropic sector is only one indicator of the relative importance of various subsectors. Also important is a comparison with for-profit employment in the same areas. As table 4.4 shows, philanthropic organizations are vital to the service economy. They tend to dominate the subsectors in which they operate, accounting for the majority of private employment. (Note that these figures do not include public-sector employment, which in some cases is considerable.) For example, 69 percent of the private employment in health services is in philan-

TABLE 4.4 PHILANTHROPIC EMPLOYMENT AS PERCENTAGE OF ALL PRIVATE EMPLOYMENT, 1982

Subsectors	Total Private Full- and Part-time Employment (000)	Share in Philanthropic Sector (%)
Health services	4,411.8	69
Nursing and personal care	1,064.4	24
Hospitals	3,013.9	86
Other health services	333.5	61
Education and research	1,274.9	94
Elementary and secondary education	322.1	100
Colleges and universities	752.6	100
Libraries and information centers	12.4	100
Correspondence and vocational schools	50.7	26
Other educational, scientific, and research organizations	137.1	75
Social services	1,166.6	82
Individual and family services	230.4	96
Job training and related services	191.4	96
Child day-care services	289.0	56
Residential care	237.1	77
Other social services	218.7	96
Membership organizations	1,198.7	100
Civic, social, and fraternal	301.6	100
Religious	897.1	100
Culture, entertainment, recreation	338.1	24
Performing arts (theater, orchestra, etc.)	86.0	38
Radio and television broadcasting	216.4	5
Visual arts (museums, botanical and zoological gardens)	35.7	100
Legal services	565.4	2
Educational, religious, charitable trusts	18.3	100
Total of subsectors	8,973.8	73
All service-producing sectors	49,886.0	13

Source: Rudney and Weitzman 1983.

thropic organizations, primarily hospitals. Nursing homes and other personal care organizations, on the other hand, are predominantly for-profit employers.

Nonprofit organizations are even more crucial in the education and research subsector, accounting for an estimated 100 percent of all nonpublic employment in elementary and secondary schools, colleges and universities, and libraries and information centers. For-profit employers, however, are dominant in correspondence and vocational schools and employ one-quarter of the private labor force in scientific and research organizations and other educational organizations.

Nonprofit organizations are also predominant, numerically, in the social services, accounting for 82 percent of all private employment. In fact, for-profit organizations account for a significant amount of employment in only two areas: residential care (23 percent of private employment) and child day care (44 percent of private employment).

In contrast, for-profit organizations are the major private employers in the areas of culture, entertainment, and recreation, accounting for 76 percent of all private employment. Philanthropic organizations account for only 5 percent of radio and television employment and 26 percent of employment in the performing arts, but 100 percent of private employment in the smaller field of the visual arts (including museums, botanical gardens, and zoological gardens).

PHILANTHROPIC PAYROLL

The philanthropic sector's payroll for 1982 was $81.7 billion, representing 5.4 percent of the total U.S. payroll for that year. Employees of philanthropic organizations earn substantially less, on average, than those employed by private for-profit industries and governments. In 1982 the average wage in the philanthropic sector was $12,525, just three-quarters of the average wage for all employees, $16,797, and half the average federal government wage of $25,046 (Rudney & Weitzman 1983).

Payroll costs vary, of course, by subsector. The subsectors are affected by different demands, and their abilities to respond to these demands vary. The wage bill they must finance depends on the skills needed to supply services, the degree of staff professionalization, the balance of full-time and part-time labor and the relative strength of unions and management in wage bargaining. The total wage bill and average wage for various philanthropic subsectors in 1972 and 1982 are given in table 4.5. Not surprisingly, the 1982 average wage was highest in the most professionalized subsectors, legal and health services ($16,129 and $15,038 per year, respectively). Employees in social service and membership organizations earned the lowest average wages ($8,340 and $9,010, respectively).

TABLE 4.5   EARNINGS IN THE PHILANTHROPIC SECTOR, 1972 AND 1982

Subsectors	Wages and Salaries (in billions)		Average Earnings	
	1972	1982	1972	1982
Health services	$10.7	$45.9	$5,540	$15,038
Nursing and personal care	.6	2.3	4,228	9,002
Hospitals	9.4	39.8	5,517	15,348
Other health services	.7	3.8	8,168	18,664
Education and research	7.1	15.5	7,345	12,890
Elementary and secondary education	1.0	3.2	4,252	9,935
Colleges and universities	5.3	10.3	8,318	13,686
Libraries and information centers	.1	.1	6,849	8,065
Correspondence and vocational schools	.1	.2	8,696	15,385
Other educational, scientific, and research organizations	.6	1.7	8,798	16,602
Social services	2.1	8.0	4,619	8,340
Individual and family services	.4	2.1	5,579	9,515
Job training and related services	.3	1.0	3,571	5,464
Child day-care services	.3	1.2	3,632	7,353
Residential care	.4	1.7	4,756	9,361
Other social services	.7	2.1	5,299	9,967
Membership organizations	4.9	10.8	4,273	9,010
Civic, social, and fraternal	1.0	2.1	3,593	6,963
Religious	3.9	8.7	4,491	9,698
Culture, entertainment, recreation	.3	1.1	5,848	13,802
Performing arts (theater, orchestra, etc.)	.1	.5	4,255	15,432
Radio and television broadcasting	.1	.2	7,576	17,241
Visual arts (museums, botanical and zoological gardens)	.1	.4	4,717	11,204
Legal services	.1	.2	8,065	16,129
Educational, religious, charitable trusts	.1	.2	7,634	10,929
Total philanthropic earnings	$25.3	$81.7	$5,528	$12,525

Source: Rudney and Weitzman 1983.

Between 1972 and 1982 the philanthropic payroll more than tripled, from an estimated $25.3 billion to $81.7 billion. Most of this increase can be attributed to sharp rises in average salary, which in turn reflect both changes in hours worked and earnings per hour. Although the philanthropic labor force increased by almost 50 percent during the decade, the average wage more than doubled. But the rate of salary increase was comparable to the rate of inflation for the period, resulting in no real increase in workers' earning power. Philanthropic wages did increase, relative to those of all non-farm workers. In 1972 the philanthropic wage averaged 67.9 percent of the average wage for all non-farm workers. That proportion had increased to 74.6 percent by 1982. Average wages increased most for hospital employees, almost tripling over the decade. College and university employees experienced a substantially slower increase in their wages, only 64 percent, over the decade.

VOLUNTEER LABOR FORCE

Volunteer labor is a major resource for nonprofit organizations and is unique to the nonprofit sector. In 1980, about 80 million people donated time and effort to nonprofit organizations, compared to 6.7 million paid employees, a ratio of almost twelve unpaid volunteers for every paid employee in the sector (Weitzman 1983). There is some overlap between volunteers and employees, since employees of nonprofits often donate spare time to other nonprofits, and businesses sometimes donate their employees' services during work hours. The volunteer contribution to nonprofit activity is substantial, however, and is increasing. Since 1964, the number of volunteer hours donated to nonprofit organizations has increased almost threefold (Weitzman 1983).

In spite of the large number of volunteers, their total labor time is less than that of the paid nonprofit labor force. In 1980, the average volunteer donated just over 100 hours of time during the year, for a total of approximately 8.4 billion hours. Based on a work year of 1,700 hours, this volunteer labor is equivalent to approximately 4.9 million full-time employees. Based on an hourly wage rate of $7.45, volunteer labor was worth approximately $62.6 billion to the nonprofit sector in 1980.

Volunteer labor is a form of donation-in-kind, and economists more often than accountants include the value of such labor on the revenue side of the nonprofit income-and-expense statement. In economic terms, it is equally logical to include the value of volunteer labor as a labor cost on the expenditure side of the same statement. If the two are included in the statement, they would, of course, counteract each other, but the income-and-expense statement would more accurately represent the amount of labor input (paid and volunteer) needed to produce nonprofit services and the contribution of donated labor to the financing of that input. In 1980, the estimated $62.6 billion of volunteer labor would increase the estimated nonprofit revenues of $142 billion (Rudney 1981) by almost half and would nearly double the $70 billion labor bill (Rudney & Weitzman 1983).

INDIRECT LABOR REQUIREMENTS

In addition to direct labor requirements (paid and unpaid) nonprofit activity also has indirect labor requirements. These arise because of the sector's need for goods and services produced by others who in turn must employ labor. These secondary economic consequences of nonprofit activity make an important contribution to the U.S. economy.

In 1980, the nonprofit sector purchased $50.2 billion worth of goods and services from firms in predominantly for-profit industries. The employment that these purchases indirectly generated is estimated to be 1.5 million people (Rudney 1981), compared to 6.7 million paid employees in the nonprofit sector. Indirect employment generated by the nonprofit sector has tripled since 1960, compared to a doubling of direct employment. This disparity reflects, in part, the reaping by nonprofits of the economic benefits from increasing specialization by others—for example, their use of external specialized laboratories and contract maintenance services.

NONPROFIT CAPITAL RESOURCES

In addition to human resources, nonprofit organizations need capital resources—facilities, residences, equipment, and so on—in order to produce goods and services. We now turn to a description of the capital resources employed by the nonprofit sector.

Capital Stock and Financial Investments

The nonprofit sector's capital stock is composed of the physical assets employed in providing services. The capital stock together with financial assets represent the sector's accumulated investments. This discussion begins with a description of the nonprofit sector's capital stock and financial investments, followed by comparisons with the for-profit sector and finally comparisons among nonprofit subsectors.

Ruggles and Ruggles (1980) estimated that at the end of 1975 the nonprofit sector's capital stock was valued at $154 billion, net current value (that is, reflecting both appreciation and depreciation over time) (see table 4.6). These physical assets, primarily nonresidential structures, represented over three-quarters of the sector's total assets of over $201 billion. Because relatively little investment is financed by borrowing, 83 percent of asset holdings were free and clear of debt at the end of 1975. Thus, the sector's net worth totaled $168 billion. Net worth represents acquisition value, or original cost, corrected for appreciation and depreciation.

The following analysis considers only reproducible physical assets, that is, plant, equipment, and other physical assets but not land. (Land could have been included if considered reproducible.) The net current value, at year end 1975, of reproducible assets was $126 billion. This represents original costs of $94 billion, plus appreciation of $102 billion, minus depreciation of $70 billion (Ruggles & Ruggles 1980). Since the reproducible assets are mainly real estate, the experience

TABLE 4.6 ASSETS AND LIABILITIES OF NONPROFIT SECTOR, 1975 (NET CURRENT VALUE, IN BILLIONS OF DOLLARS)

Total assets	$201.8
Physical assets	154.0
Residential structures	11.4
Nonresidential structures	110.2
Equipment	4.8
Land	27.6
Financial assets	47.8
Cash	0.3
Government bonds	2.8
Mortgages	1.4
Corporate bonds	11.9
Corporate stock	31.4
Total liabilities	33.8
Mortgage debt	24.8
Other debt	9.0
Net worth (assets minus liabilities)	$168.0

Source: Ruggles and Ruggles 1980, Table 2.25.

has been that such assets appreciate more than they depreciate.

Capital stock over time becomes used up or obsolete. Moreover, largely because of inflation, the costs of replacement increase over time. The cost of replacing capital stock includes original cost and appreciation in value over time. Thus, in 1975, the nonprofit sector's capital stock had a replacement value of $196 billion, or more than double its original cost.

Some comparisons with the for-profit sector are instructive. Between 1960 and 1975 the historical cost of reproducible assets in the nonprofit sector tripled, increasing at an annual rate of 13.4 percent. This rate of growth was slightly higher than the average annual rate of increase of 12.2 percent for the for-profit sector (see table 4.7). It is important

TABLE 4.7 GROWTH IN HISTORICAL COST OF PHYSICAL ASSETS, NONPROFIT AND FOR-PROFIT SECTORS, 1960 AND 1975

	1960	1975	Average Annual
	($ in billions)		% Increase
Nonprofit Organizations			
Reproducible assets	$31.3	$94.0	13.4%
Residential structures	3.9	7.7	6.5
Nonresidential structures	25.1	79.5	14.4
Equipment	2.3	6.8	13.0
Land	11.0	27.6	10.1
Total Physical Assets	$46.3	$121.6	12.5%
For-Profit Organizations			
Reproducible assets	$669.8	$1,976.8	12.2%
Residential structures	87.5	214.4	9.7
Nonresidential structures	208.7	577.2	11.8
Equipment	267.4	756.9	12.2
Inventories	136.2	428.3	14.3
Land	175.0	759.9	11.8
Total Physical Assets	$974.8	$2,736.7	12.0%

Source: Ruggles and Ruggles 1980.

to note that the rate of capital growth is not always indicative of economic progress. There may be very little capital growth, and yet new technologically advanced capital may replace old capital. The improvement in the quality of capital may increase productivity even if the stock of capital does not increase.

The physical assets of the nonprofit sector are primarily in nonresidential structures, whereas those of the for-profit sector are more evenly divided among plant, equipment, and land (see table 4.7). This pattern is also suggested by the different depreciation rates for the two sectors. By the end of 1975, $70 billion, or 36 percent of the replacement value, of nonprofits' plant and equipment had been depreciated. In contrast, 50 percent of reproducible assets in the for-profit sector had been depreciated (Ruggles & Ruggles 1980). The greater percentage of depreciation for for-profits reflects both the greater reliance on equipment, which has a shorter life than buildings, and the methods of depreciation used by for-profit organizations among which the choice is usually influenced by tax consequences.

The relationships among debt, assets, and production, for nonprofit and corporate enterprises, are given in table 4.8. The nonprofit sector is characterized by a lower ratio of debt to reproducible assets (27 percent) than that of the for-profit sector (62 percent). Several factors explain this difference. Nonprofits have less access to credit when acquiring buildings, equipment, or working capital. Often nonprofit capital and current operating needs are financed by gifts. In contrast, debt financing in the for-profit sector is substantially encouraged by the federal tax code.

The ratio of a sector's contribution to GNP to its reproducible assets (see table 4.8) is a measure of the sector's productivity per dollar of capital. According to this measure, the corporate sector is almost twice as productive as the nonprofit sector (with a ratio of .66, compared to .36). Unfortunately, this measure is not strictly comparable for the two sectors because the costs of nonprofit production do not include taxes paid and return on investment, both of which are included in the costs of corporate production.

An examination of the asset holdings of organizations in the two largest philanthropic sectors, education and health (see table 4.9), reveals an almost inverse pattern of asset

TABLE 4.8 RELATIONSHIPS AMONG ASSETS, DEBT, AND PRODUCTION IN NONPROFIT AND CORPORATE SECTORS, 1975

	Nonprofit	Corporate
	($ in billions)	
Total reproducible assets (net current value)	$126.4	$1,336.0
Debt (fixed claim liabilities)	$33.8	$822.7
GNP originating in sector (market transactions only)	$45.4	$875.4
Debt/Assets	.27	.62
GNP/Assets	.36	.66

Source: Ruggles and Ruggles 1980.

TABLE 4.9 DISTRIBUTION OF ASSETS BY ORGANIZATION SIZE, HEALTH AND EDUCATIONAL PHILANTHROPIC ORGANIZATIONS, 1975

	Total Assets	Physical Assets	Financial Assets
Health Organizations			
Organizations with assets of under $50 million	71.8%	80.2%	57.8%
Organizations with assets of $50 million or more	28.2	19.8	42.2
Total	100.0%	100.0%	100.0%
Educational Organizations			
Organizations with assets of under $50 million	30.4%	47.1%	23.0%
Organizations with assets of $50 million or more	69.6	52.9	77.0
Total	100.0%	100.0%	100.0%

Source: Rudney 1981.

distribution. Both sectors require considerable physical plant and equipment. The education sector relies heavily on investment income for operations and has 69 percent of its holdings in financial assets. In contrast, only 37 percent of the health sector's assets are financial. Distribution of assets among organizations within each of these sectors also varies. The largest institutions (those with holdings of $50 million or more) account for less than 1 percent of the organizations in each subsector. Large educational institutions, however, hold 70 percent of all educational assets and over three-quarters of financial assets. In contrast, although the largest health institutions account for a disproportionately large share of the subsector's assets, especially financial assets, the degree of concentration is far less than in education. Indeed, smaller organizations hold 72 percent of the health sector's total assets.

Use of Physical Capital

Capital stock is the value of physical capital as of a given moment in time, usually the end of an accounting period. The use of physical capital represents the costs of depreciation, maintenance and repair incurred over time, usually during the organization's accounting period.

The continuing cost of maintaining land, buildings, and equipment is the third and smallest component of the cost of providing nonprofit services (the other two being labor and purchases from other organizations). In 1980, the total cost to nonprofits of using and maintaining owned capital was $9 billion.

The $9 billion was partly real and partly implicit costs. Real outlays were made for maintenance and repair. Depreciation is an implicit outlay, which should be includable in nonprofit expenditures. Often depreciation is not reflected in nonprofit financial reports. Economists also may be inclined to include the $9 billion in nonprofit revenues, viewing the amount as implicit rents that could be earned if the same capital were leased rather than used for the organiza-

tions' own purposes. Even though the inclusions of $9 billion on both sides of an accounting statement cancel each other, the total revenues and expenditures more correctly reflect this important economic activity.

PHILANTHROPIC REVENUES

Philanthropic organizations are unique in that the prices for services (hospital charges, tuition, admission fees, and so on) are not intended to cover the costs of producing these services. Philanthropic production is only partially financed by sales of services; the remainder is covered by various subsidies.

Philanthropic Sales

In 1980, philanthropic receipts totaled $61.5 billion for sales of services to businesses, households, and government (see table 4.10). Households are the major consumers of philanthropic services, accounting for just over half of all sales, with governments accounting for another 43 percent.

Subsidies

In 1980, sales of services recovered only 48 cents of every dollar spent on production. The shortfall of 52 cents was financed by various subsidies. Because all philanthropic organizations depend on these subsidies, both the individual who consumes a nonprofit service free of charge (for example, a person who receives medical care at a clinic for indigents) and one who actually pays a charge (such as a museum admission fee) for a nonprofit service normally receive a subsidy.

The process of subsidization can be viewed as one in which the donors or grantors ''purchase'' nonprofit goods or services that are consumed by others. Donations may be cash, property (tangible or intangible), or the time and effort of volunteer labor for current or future use. Donations to university or hospital endowments, capital gifts for future construction, and premiums on nonprofit old-age, health,

TABLE 4.10 SOURCES OF REVENUE FOR PHILANTHROPIC ORGANIZATIONS, 1980

Source of Revenue	$ in Billions	% of Total
Sales of services	$61.5	48
To businesses	3.7	3
To households	31.5	24
To governments	26.3	20
Subsidies	$67.7	52
Private donations	44.3	34
Government grants	7.6	6
Investment income	6.7	5
Rental value of buildings owned and used	9.1	7
Total Revenues (gross product)	$129.2	100

Source: Rudney 1981.

life, casualty, fire, and accident insurance are examples of current purchases or donations intended for future use.

Donations from individuals and businesses are the most important direct subsidy, providing 34 cents of every dollar of production costs, or two-thirds of the necessary subsidy. The ratio of individual contributions to operating expenses, however, has been decreasing. Although philanthropic operating expenditures per capita increased by almost 70 percent (from $200 to $338) between 1960 and 1980, contributions per capita increased by only 11 percent (from $103 to $114) during that period (Hodgkinson & Weitzman 1984).

The remaining 18 cents of direct subsidy is provided by three other sources in roughly equivalent proportions. Earnings on accumulated savings, or endowments, account for 5 cents of every dollar, government grants for 6 cents, and implicit income from owned property (equivalent rental costs) for 7 cents.

The extent of direct government support of philanthropic organizations is perhaps better understood if we exclude religious organizations, which are atypical. In 1980, approximately $22.2 billion, or half of all private donations, went to religious organizations, which receive the overwhelming majority of their support from private donors (Rudney 1981). In contrast, governments account for over one-third of the direct support of nonreligious organizations (see table 4.11), compared to only 26 percent of the support of all philanthropic organizations including religion (cf. table 4.10). As chapter 6 indicates, increased federal support has been responsible for much of the recent growth of the nonprofit sector. Moreover, government spending also affects the amount of private donations to nonprofits (see chapter 7).

The government subsidy of philanthropic activity is actually underestimated in the above calculations, which exclude various indirect subsidies, such as lower-than-market interest rates on government loans, government guarantees of private loans to nonprofits, preferential postal service rates, and tax concessions.[1] The largest of these is the tax deduction of $44.3 billion for private donations and the resulting loss of tax revenues. In 1980, this revenue loss amounted to $8.7 billion, $1.1 billion more than the total amount of government grants to philanthropic organizations. Important indirect tax subsidies include those portions of investment earnings and property values that are tax-exempt. Taking these indirect subsidies into account would increase government's

1. On the debate regarding classification of charitable deductions as an indirect subsidy, see S. Surrey, ''Federal Income Tax Reform,'' *Harvard Law Review*, 84, no. 352 (1970), and B. Bittker, ''Accounting for Federal Tax Subsidies in the National Budget,'' *National Tax Journal*, 22, no. 244 (1969).

TABLE 4.11   SOURCES OF SUPPORT FOR NONRELIGIOUS PHILANTHROPICS, 1980

Source of Support	$ in Billions	% of Total
Private	$64.0	65
Donations	22.1	22
Sales to households	31.5	32
Sales to businesses	3.7	4
Investment income	6.7	7
Government	$33.9	35
Sales to government	26.3	27
Government grants	7.6	8
Total Support	$97.9	100

Source: Rudney, 1981.

Note: The relatively small component of rental value of owned property is excluded because of the difficulty of dividing it into religious and nonreligious components.

relative share of philanthropic subsidy and decrease the private sector's share.

The philanthropic sector also benefits from indirect *private* subsidies, such as bank, corporate, and foundation loans at below-market interest rates. These implicit subsidies reduce operating costs and increase revenues for philanthropic organizations.

CONCLUSION

This chapter presented a quantitative overview of the nonprofit sector. Measures were provided of nonprofit production of services, labor and capital requirements and their costs, and the means of financing production costs. The estimates require continuing improvement and expansion but are highly dependent on the availability of basic source data at government agencies. A serious constraint in government that inhibits data collection is that nonprofit organizations as productive enterprises go unrecognized in the official U.S. National Accounts. The National Accounts are intended to provide a realistic economic model of the economy. Yet nonprofits are included as consumers, like households, of the nation's output and not as contributors to the nation's output. The unrealistic treatment tends to constrain data collection on nonprofit organizations by government agencies. Fortunately a movement led by Richard and Nancy Ruggles seeks to restructure the National Accounts and more realistically represent productive enterprise, including nonprofit organizations. Although the restructuring of the National Accounts in the near future is not anticipated, public discussion of nonprofit organizations as productive enterprises will no doubt lead to more and better development of data sources on nonprofits.

REFERENCES

Fuchs, Victor. 1968. *The Service Economy*. New York: Columbia University Press.

Hodgkinson, Virginia, and Murray Weitzman. 1984. *Dimensions of the Independent Sector*. Washington, D.C.: Independent Sector.

Rudney, Gabriel. 1981. ''A Quantitative Profile of the Nonprofit Sector.'' Yale University, Program on Non-Profit Organizations Working Paper no. 40.

Rudney, Gabriel, and Murray Weitzman. 1983. ''Significance of Employment and Earnings in the Philanthropic Sector, 1972–1982.'' Yale University, Program on Non-Profit Organizations Working Paper no. 77.

Ruggles, Richard, and Nancy D. Ruggles. 1980. ''Integrated Economic Accounts for the United States, 1947–1978.'' Yale University, Institution for Social and Policy Studies Working Paper no. 841.

Weitzman, Murray. 1983. *Measuring the Number of Hours Spent and Dollar Value of Volunteer Activity of Americans*. Washington, D.C.: Independent Sector Working Papers.

II

THE NONPROFIT SECTOR, THE STATE, AND PRIVATE ENTERPRISE

5

The Tax Treatment of Nonprofit Organizations: A Review of Federal and State Policies

JOHN G. SIMON

n the long history of charity and nonprofit institutions, there may never have been an epoch free of controversy over taxation, but the past forty post–World War II years have witnessed an unremitting state of siege. Since the days of the pharaohs and continuing through the church-state conflicts of the Middle Ages, there have been occasional perturbations over the granting—and termination—of tax relief for churches (Genesis 47:26; Adler 1922; Larson & Lowell 1969). Skirmishes of the past, however, were no more than isolated forerunners of the strife—over the taxation of both religious and secular nonprofits—that has prevailed in contemporary America. Since 1945, concern with federal, state, and local tax treatment of nonprofit institutions has produced at least eight congressional investigations and hearings, half a dozen major federal statutes (taking up some five hundred pages in the Internal Revenue Code and Regulations), and a succession of state and local wars over real property tax exemption. Indeed, this chapter has been written in the midst of yet another storm generated by Treasury tax-reform proposals, which, even as softened by President Reagan and the House of Representatives, would significantly reduce the tax incentives for charitable

giving.[1] With nonprofits receiving $50 billion in federally deductible contributions, generating roughly $110 billion in fee, sale, and investment revenue exempt from federal income tax, and holding an estimated $300 billion in real estate exempt from state and local property taxes,[2] it is little wonder that hard-pressed nonprofit institutions and deficit-ridden governments find themselves recurrently at war.

There are those who yearn, in different ways and for different reasons, for the status quo ante tax. Thus, many nonprofit managers would prefer a life uncomplicated by tax rules; champions of altruism would rather see charitable behavior flowering without tax inducement; and some tax

I am grateful to Boris I. Bittker, Paul J. DiMaggio, Henry Hansmann, Michael Krashinsky, and Walter W. Powell for detailed and thoughtful criticism of a draft of this chapter, and to the dozens of colleagues and students at the Yale Program on Non-Profit Organizations and the Yale Law School with whom, over the years, I have explored the issues covered in this chapter. I also express appreciation to the Rockefeller Foundation for the opportunity to work on this project during a period of resident study at the foundation's Bellagio Conference and Research Center.

1. These proposed changes are described in n5, and in the text.

2. These are the author's rough estimates for 1985. The revenue estimate is based on the conservatively low 1980 figure of $76 billion for charitable organizations (see text under "Support Function in Practice"), increased by 30 percent to account for inflation and by another 10 percent to include noncharitable nonprofits; the 10 percent figure is derived from chapter 4 in this volume. The revenue figure is not the same as a taxable income figure (see text below), but it is used here because revenue data are often used in the debates over tax exemption. The deductible contribution figure is based on a 1982 estimate derived from Clotfelter (1985, 6) and U.S. Internal Revenue Service (1982), increased to take account of inflation and the estimated amount of nonitemizers' contributions not deductible in 1982 but deductible in 1985. The real estate figure is derived from chapter 4 in this volume (based on Ruggles & Ruggles 1980) and increased for inflation, resulting in a figure of roughly $300 billion for the entire nonprofit sector, including organizations whose property is not tax-exempt. I have estimated that the amount of real estate held by such organizations is so small in comparison to the property held by exempt organizations, that the $300 billion figure can be used for the exempt group as well as the slightly larger nonprofit universe.

scholars and reformers would like to rededicate the tax system to revenue production, freed from the ancillary baggage of charitable ''subsidy.'' In a society suffused with taxes and reliant on them as engines of social and economic policy, however, the union of charity and taxes is in reality indissoluble—and controversy therefore inevitable. Charity seems destined to be enmeshed in tax policy debate not only because so is everything in our society but also because, over the years, we have come to entrust to the tax system a central role in the nourishment and regulation of the nonprofit sector.

Thus, at the federal and state levels, we use the taxing laws for these purposes:

1. To encourage through relief from tax—what some call subsidy (to be discussed below)—the continuation and expansion of the nonprofit sector. We may call this the *support* function.

2. To bring about through application of certain exemption criteria a degree of equalization or redistribution of resources and opportunities, or at least a discouragement of unacceptable forms of discrimination. We may call this the *equity* function.

3. To regulate through tax mechanisms the fiduciary behavior of nonprofit managers. We may call this the *police* function.

4. To regulate through tax mechanisms the capacity to which nonprofit organizations can operate in the business and public sectors by competing with, controlling, or influencing the behavior of commercial or governmental entities. We may call this the *border patrol* function.

Each of these functions is a major focus of tax policy debate (with the most elaborate controversy surrounding the first), and each, in turn, will be analyzed in this chapter, along with a summary of the research—both empirical and theoretical—that has been done, or needs to be done, under each heading. To carry out this analysis, however, we need to disaggregate the nonprofit sector; its subspecies (some of them legal artifacts) are subject to very disparate treatment under the tax laws and require separate scrutiny. Indeed, the manner in which the tax laws have carved up the sector is itself an important object of policy controversy that deserves to be dealt with under each of the four headings.

We start, therefore, with a taxonomy of these subspecies and the way they are treated under the federal tax system. It will serve as a rudimentary review of the federal tax treatment of the nonprofit sector. The federal taxonomy will then be used as the framework for a tabular outline of the way in which state laws categorize and treat the nonprofit sector and of the federal nontax consequences that are influenced by the tax system rules. After that, we will plunge into the policy analysis.

AN OUTLINE OF THE TAX TREATMENT OF THE NONPROFIT SECTOR

A Federal Tax Taxonomy

The nonprofit sector is subject to special treatment under federal individual and corporate income taxes, estate and gift

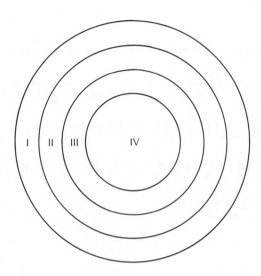

FIGURE 5.1 A SCHEMATIC SKETCH OF NONPROFIT TAX CATEGORIES

taxes, and certain excise taxes. There are, in fact, four separate treatments, one for each of four principal categories into which the federal tax laws divide the nonprofit sector. In figure 5.1 each category is represented by a ring embracing a set of organizations that are subject to a substantially similar tax regime, distinct from the regimes applicable to the adjoining rings. The rings are so arranged that together they make up a group of concentric circles, which, as one moves outward from Ring IV, contain increasingly larger portions of the nonprofit world.

Thus, the full circle, encompassing Rings I through IV, includes all entities that are exempt from federal income tax (the tax otherwise imposed on corporations, unincorporated associations, or trusts) under the principal exemption statute, §501 of the Internal Revenue Code. Almost all these groups share the condition of being organized on a not-for-profit basis, which means not that the entity is forbidden to generate a profit but that any such profits may not be distributed to owners or other private persons;[3] Hansmann (1980) refers to this rule as the ''nondistribution constraint.'' This constraint is imposed on these institutions by the legal instrument under which they are organized under state law—the ''charter'' or ''articles'' in the case of a nonprofit corporation or an unincorporated association, or the ''deed of trust'' or other trust instrument in the case of a charitable trust (Fremont-Smith 1965). (Which of these legal forms of organization a nonprofit group adopts is almost wholly irrelevant for determining that group's federal tax treatment.)

3. Membership corporations that finance farm crop operations and are exempt under §501(c)(16) are permitted to issue capital stock and distribute dividends to participating members, subject to certain constraints.

The Charitable-Noncharitable Distinction

There is a basic distinction between Ring I and the Rings II–IV circle, however. Groups in Rings II–IV are not only nonprofit but also what are loosely referred to by tax lawyers as the "charitables"—organizations described in §501(c)(3) of the code as serving "religious, charitable, scientific, testing for public safety, literary or educational purposes." The shorthand "charitable" is used for these Rings II–IV groups, even though it is only one of several adjectives used in §501(c)(3), because "charitable" is the residual category used to classify these groups when they do not fit under any of the other adjectives and also because the Supreme Court has held that all §501(c)(3) groups must conform to common-law charitable criteria.

In Ring I are the *non*charitable nonprofits that are listed throughout the succeeding subsections of the exemption statute, in §§501(c)(4)–(21); here we have social clubs, veterans' organizations, labor unions, burial societies, chambers of commerce, marketing cooperatives, and other associations that may roughly be described as carrying forward the private interests of the members but subject to the nondistribution constraint. Bittker and Rahdert (1976) describe these as "mutual benefit" organizations, as distinct from the §501(c)(3) charitable groups, which they characterize as "public service" organizations. Weisbrod (1980) distinguishes the Ring I from the Rings II–IV groups (to use our labels) on the basis of the greater tendency of the latter groups to provide "collective goods," often referred to as "public goods"—benefits that are not captured only by the persons or institutions generating the benefits. The tax system criteria for §501(c)(3)—Rings II–IV—treatment will be further described later in this chapter. Apart from criteria, what are the *results* of landing in the Rings II–IV circle—within the charitable §501(c)(3) set? Several consequences will be described below, but the most celebrated one is that contributions of cash or property (but not services) to these charitable groups are deductible by individuals and corporations for income tax purposes (under §170 of the code) and also deductible for estate and gift tax purposes (under §§2055, 2522). Gifts to Ring I organizations are not deductible, except for veterans' groups, nonprofit cemetery companies, and fraternal beneficiary organizations that use the gift for charitable purposes. (Further details of the deductibility distinctions are set forth in table 5.1.)

Distinctions within the Charitable World

Starting in 1954, and more ambitiously in 1969, Congress made distinctions—created a class system, some would say (Bittker 1973)—*within* the §501(c)(3) charitable world, which is why it is shown as a three-ring circle (II–IV) in our diagram. The charity world was first divided into two parts: the "private foundations" (Rings III and IV) and the groups that were *not* "private foundations" (Ring II). The private foundations were defined as constituting all groups that flunked certain tests set up by §509 of the code. To pass these tests, a group must be a school, a church, a hospital (or hospital-related research entity), or a group that meets one of

several alternative (and fairly complicated) definitions of a "publicly supported" organization. Organizations meeting these tests (and certain variations upon them)[4] are, in the language of the tax bar, "public charities" (not to be confused with the broader set of §501(c)(3) charities), and they escape private foundation classification, with all the disabilities that attach to that status. This subdivision was meant to separate grant-making organizations (embracing the Ford Foundation and lesser dispensers) from the operating charities. It was in the former camp that more fiscal abuses were thought to lie, more political activism, more "unaccountable" wealth, more of all kinds of other problems, and, in any event, it was thought that dollars given to grant-making foundations entered the stream of active charitable use more slowly than gifts to operating nonprofits (a proposition discussed below).

Distinctions within the Foundation Category

In the midst of the 1969 congressional deliberations, however, it was discovered that the private foundation category, as pending legislation defined it, included all kinds of non-grant-making bodies that did not happen to be schools, churches, hospitals, or publicly supported. Many research institutions, social action groups, museums, and other nonprofits would fall afoul of the private foundation strictures. Congress could have moved them into public charity (Ring II) status, but, instead, it subdivided the foundation world (the Rings III–IV circle) into the "operating foundations"—Ring III—and the "nonoperating foundations" (the grant-making ones)—Ring IV. Probably the most important legal feature of the operating foundation is that it spends 85 percent of its income on the active conduct of its charitable program (as compared to grant making). Operating foundations receive more favorable treatment in several respects than do their nonoperating counterparts, as we shall see when we summarize the ring-to-ring progression in terms of tax benefit and regulatory burden.

This somewhat amoebic subdivision repeated itself in August 1984. For the purpose of giving certain operating foundations the benefit of public charity treatment in two respects (cited below), Congress carved out a subset of the Ring III world and called it the "exempt operating foundation"—an operating foundation that (1) had that status at the start of 1983 or, if not, had a past history of being publicly supported, and (2) had a board that was "broadly representative of the general public" and was not donor controlled—no officers and not more than a quarter of the board were persons

---

4. One variant that permits a donor to retain some of the features of a private foundation but at the same time to operate free of private foundation rules is the supporting organization—one that is operated in close conjunction with, and is intended to benefit, one or more public charities (§509(a)(3)). (This section contains the following classic example of code-speak: "For the purposes of this subsection, an organization described in paragraph (2) shall be deemed to include an organization described in section 501(c)(4), (5), or (6) which would be described in paragraph (2) if it were an organization described in section 501(c)(3).")

TABLE 5.1   AERIAL VIEW OF FEDERAL TAX TREATMENT OF NONPROFITS

Glossary: Ring I: groups covered by §§501(c)(4)–(23)—noncharitable nonprofits. *Rings II–IV:* all §501(c)(3) groups—the charitable nonprofits. *Ring II:* the subset of §501(c)(3) groups covered by §509—groups exempted from private foundation status, known as public charities. *Rings III–IV:* the subset of §501(c)(3) groups *not* covered by §509—the private foundations. *Ring III:* private operating foundations. *Ring IV:* private nonoperating foundations.

A.   Numbers (all estimated)

	Ring I	Ring II	Ring III	Ring IV
Number of units filing returns plus churches[a]	477,000 ('84)	690,000 ('84)	2126 ('83)	23,600 ('83)
Assets	N.A.	$480B ('82)	$7B ('83)	$64.5B ('81)
Revenue	$10B ('84)	$196B ('82)	N.A.	$6B ('81)
Expenditures	N.A.	$194B ('84)	$457M ('83)	$5B ('83)
Employees	.5M ('82)	6.5M ('82)	N.A.	7,000 ('85)
Value of volunteer labor	$8B ('85)	$52B ('80)	N.A.	N.A.

Sources: American Association of Fund-Raising Counsel, 1985; Foundation Center, 1985; Hodgkinson and Weitzman (1984, and the 1986 2d edition); chapter 4 and chapter 20 in this volume; author's extrapolations from the foregoing.
N.A.: Not available; M: Millions; B: Billions.

B.   Exemption and Eligibility for Deductible Gifts and Foundation Grants

	Ring I	Ring II	Ring III	Ring IV
Exempt from corporate (and trust) income tax?	Yes	Yes	Yes	Yes
		Exception for I–IV: tax on unrelated business income		
			Exception for III, IV: excise taxes, see below	
Individuals' gifts to the organization deductible for income tax purposes?	No (except for veterans' organizations, cemetery associations, and some fraternal organizations)	Yes (up to 50% AGI)	Yes (up to 50% AGI)	Yes (up to 30% AGI) (Property gifts limited to 20% AGI and not always deductible at full value)
		(II–III: limit of 30% AGI for property gifts)		
Corporations' gifts to the organization deductible for income tax purposes?	No (except for veterans' organizations, cemetery associations, and some fraternal organizations)	Yes (up to 10% taxable income)	Yes (up to 10% taxable income)	Yes (up to 10% taxable income)
Bequests to the organization deductible for estate and gift tax purposes?	No	Yes (no limit)	Yes (no limit)	Yes (no limit)
Eligible for foundation grants?	No (unless special controls to assure exempt use)	Yes	Yes (but expenditure responsibility on grantor to police grantee use of funds)	Yes (but expenditure responsibility on grantor; see also pass-through rules under payout requirement)

AGI: Adjusted gross income

C.   Regulation (general)

	Ring I	Ring II	Ring III	Ring IV
Degree of regulation of fiduciary conduct and exempt behavior	Light; mainly limited to checks on personal gain	Substantial: mainly under "operated exclusively for charitable purposes" clause	III–IV: Intense. Rules on self-dealing, §4941; payout, §4942; corporate control, §4943; speculative investing, §4944; miscellaneous, §4945[b]	
Required reporting and level of audit	Form 990: rare audit	Form 990; more audit than for Ring I	Form 990–PF; very detailed and heavy level of audit (paid for by §4940 audit fee tax)	
Liability for excise taxes in support of regulatory system	None	Imposed only for exceeding lobbying limits (see Part D)	III–IV: 2% audit fee[c] and penalty taxes on foundations and managers for violating above rules	

TABLE 5.1 *(Continued)*

D. Regulation of Certain "Political" Activities

	Ring I	Ring II	Ring III	Ring IV
Electoral campaigning	OK for most organizations	Banned	Banned	Banned
Nonpartisan voter registration	OK	OK	III–IV: OK if carried out on 5-state, multidonor basis	
Legislative lobbying	OK	OK if (a) "insubstantial" or (b) within percentage spending limits[d]	Banned except to defend legal status, for "nonpartisan analysis study and research," and in response to legislative request	
Monitoring executive branch activity	OK	OK	OK	OK
Public interest litigation	OK	II–IV: OK but subject to IRS rules to prevent abuses, limit fees		
Publishing "political" material not violative of above prohibitions	OK	II–IV: OK but if organization is classed "educational," presentation must be "full and fair" (this rule held unconstitutional by a federal court)[e]		

E. Eligibility under Other Federal Tax Provisions

	Ring I	Ring II	Ring III	Ring IV
Ability to offer employees annuities with tax benefits similar to those under a qualified pension plan?	No	Yes	Yes	Yes
Exemption under Federal Unemployment Tax Act?	No	Yes	Yes	Yes
Tax-exempt bonds issued by state or local government for support of the organization subject to volume limitations?	Yes	No	No	No
Exemption from federal gambling tax?	No	Yes	Yes	Yes

a. Ring I and II figures are misleadingly low because they are based on the number of units in the IRS Exempt Organizations Master File, which does not include (a) branches of national Ring I or II organizations filing on a consolidated basis, (b) Ring II organizations excused from filing because their annual revenues are below certain floors established by the Treasury (currently $25,000), and (c) churches. An estimate of the number of churches has been added to Ring II; no estimate was possible with respect to the other two categories.

b. The payout rule does not apply to Ring III foundations (although they are required to make annual direct (essentially nongrant) expenditures in an amount close to the payout required of Ring IV organizations). One of the miscellaneous rules ("expenditure responsibility") does not apply to the new "exempt operating foundation" subspecies referred to in the text.

c. The audit fee is not imposed on "exempt operating foundations."

d. To come within these percentage limits, an election must be filed. Churches are not permitted to file such an election.

e. See footnote 50, this chapter.

related to major donors. Because of the limited (though not trivial) legal consequences of exempt operating foundation status, we have not created a separate ring (perhaps Ring II.5) for this subsubspecies.

Other Nonprofit Species

The reader may wonder where among these rings certain nonprofits reside. Take community foundations, for example. These grant-making pools of many endowed funds dedicated to local or statewide purposes and administered by a broadly representative distribution committee (for philanthropic decisions) and by trustee banks (for investment decisions) qualify, for the most part, as public charities (Ring II) because of the multiplicity of their funders. They are not to be confused with community chests (typically part of the United Way system), another form of Ring II organization that solicits mainly nonendowment contributions from the public

TABLE 5.2   AERIAL VIEW OF STATE TAX TREATMENT AND FEDERAL NONTAX TREATMENT OF NONPROFITS

	Ring I	Ring II	Ring III	Ring IV
A. State Tax Issues				
Exemption from real property tax?	No (except cemeteries and often veterans', fraternal, labor, agricultural groups)	Yes (but some exceptions)	Yes	Usually
Exempt from corporate income tax?	Yes	Yes	Yes	Yes
Eligible for income tax-deductible gifts?	No	Often (sometimes "tracks" federal rules)	Often	Often
B. Federal Nontax Issues				
Eligible for nonprofit postal rates?	Mostly no	Yes	Yes	Yes
Exempt from involuntary bankruptcy proceedings?	No	Yes	Yes	Yes
Exempt from antitrust laws and F.T.C. Act?	No	For most purposes, no		
Exempt from securities regulation laws?	No	For some puposes, yes		
Exempt from buyer liability under Robinson-Patman Act?	No	Yes	Yes	Yes

Sources: Federal statutes; Lashbrooke 1985; Hansmann 1980.

and channels them largely to member agency public charities. Corporate foundations are treated like any other grant-making Ring IV foundation, except that their resources come from a corporate donor (which often provides trustees and staff to the foundation from among company personnel). Lying outside these rings are still other nonprofits. Political parties are treated by a separate part of the code that both exempts part of their income and taxes part of it (for example, investment income). The funds that finance pension plans are covered by yet other code sections that exempt their investment income if they meet various qualifying criteria. Although some cooperatives are found within Ring I, consumer and farmer cooperatives are covered by special sections that, directly or indirectly, permit cooperative income to go untaxed.

Consequences of the Categories

What consequences attach to landing in one or another of the four rings? Table 5.1 answers this question in summary fashion, compressing in an inevitably oversimplified chart a complex regulatory scheme. After providing a few items of quantitative information about the organizations, the table provides highlights of federal tax treatment of nonprofits—and thereby displays certain overall legislative patterns. With respect to the *degree of regulation*, the reader will notice that here, as in Dante's circles of hell, the situation worsens (from the perspective of the nonprofit organization) as we move from outer to inner circles: the scope of the regulation, the strictness of standards, the strength of sanctions, and the obligations of disclosure all increase. When we look at the *degree of tax benefit*, however, the progression across the rings is rather different. We travel from the least-favored-nation status of Ring I to the most-favored position

of Ring II and then part (but not all) of the way back down the benefit scale as we cross Rings III and IV. Combining these patterns, we see that, as we go from mutual benefit groups (Ring I) to the public interest organizations (Rings II–IV), Congress increases the level of benefit and, in rough exchange, imposes a higher behavioral standard. However, *within* the public interest or §501(c)(3) realm (the Rings II–IV circle), the benefit-regulation trade-off ends, resulting in decreasing benefits *and* increasing regulation as we move from the most- to the least-favored charitable classes—from the public charities of Ring II to the grant-making foundations of Ring IV. (This pattern, however, does not apply to section E of the table, which refers to some miscellaneous tax provisions not involving tax exemption or deductibility.)

Table 5.1, it should be noted, represents the legal situation as of early 1986. Tax-reform legislation passed by the House of Representatives in late 1985—and awaiting an uncertain fate in the Senate—would affect a few of the provisions summarized in this table,[5] but not its overall configuration.

5. The House bill would affect various provisions summarized under part B of table 5.1: as noted in the text, the bill would end tax exemption for some of the organizations referred to in part B of table 5.1 that are nonprofit commercial-type insurance companies; the bill would limit the deductibility of gifts of appreciated property because of the alternative minimum tax provisions referred to in the text; and the bill would require any tax-exempt organization owning more than 5 percent of the shares of a corporation to pay an unrelated business income tax on the 10 percent of the dividends received from the corporation that was deducted by the corporation under the provisions of the bill. In addition, the House bill would reduce the ability of charitable organizations to offer tax-sheltered annuities to their employees and would impose a ceiling on the volume of tax-exempt bond financing that could be used to assist such organizations; these are issues listed in part E of table 5.1. As this chapter was being sent to press, the Senate Finance Committee had tentatively decided to oppose some of the House strictures but no bill had been reported out of committee.

State Tax and Federal Nontax Taxonomies

As a sequel to the federal tax chart, we look at a similar picture of the *state* tax consequences and the federal *nontax* consequences that flow from an organization's placement in one of the four rings (table 5.2). The state tax picture is necessarily vague and sketchy, for it seeks to summarize briefly the varying tax treatments of fifty states (some of which give local option to municipalities), treatments that usually employ definitions of nonprofit species that do not neatly fit within the federal tax categories (see Lashbrooke 1985).

This brief *tour d'horizon* has touched glancingly upon some aspects of the four main functions—support, equity, police, and border patrol—served by the tax treatment of the nonprofit sector. Thus, we have observed the greater degree of *support* provided to Rings II–IV organizations compared to Ring I groups; the less-favored treatment of private foundations (Rings III and IV), partly reflecting *equity* concerns provoked by the wealth associated with foundations; the fiduciary regulation to which the tax laws subject all nonprofits in varying degrees—a *police* function; and the limits on political activity imposed with differential intensity on Rings II–IV groups as an aspect of *border patrol*. We now turn to a closer look at these four functions, examining the policy controversies relating to each of them under federal and (less intensively) state tax law, as well as the research that informs, or might yet inform, these issues.

THE SUPPORT FUNCTION OF NONPROFIT TAX LAW

The assistance provided by the federal tax system is widely perceived as an important part of the explanation for America's robust nonprofit sector. Even though Schuster (1985) has noted that Western European tax systems provide more support to nonprofit arts organizations than is usually recognized, his study demonstrates (pp. 5–6) that the deductibility features of American tax law are more favorable to charitable organizations than any Western European tax regime. What is the rationale for this tax largesse and what arguments surround it? What are the consequences of this support? What can research tell us about these matters?

The Support Function in Theory: Search for a Rationale

Is Support the Rationale for Exemption and Deductibility?

Controversy greets us at the very mention of a support function. Some tax scholars, while acknowledging that tax exemption and deductibility nourish nonprofit organizations, deny that support is the point of these provisions. Instead, it is contended that an accurate and internally consistent definition of taxable income for federal purposes, or of taxable property for state purposes, explains exemption and deduct-

ibility and that a support or subsidy rationale is neither needed nor accurate. In other words, if an item of revenue or property is not a proper part of the tax base in the first place, then the nontaxable treatment of that item should not be characterized or explained as support for the nonprofit sector.

The Tax-Base-Defining Rationales. First, we consider rationales for the *exemption from federal income tax*. Bittker and Rahdert (1976) argue that, for charitable nonprofits (Rings II–IV), this exemption arises from (1) the fact that the income tax focuses on business and other activities pursued for personal gain—an underlying objective that does not apply to charitable entities, and (2) the fact that we cannot calculate the tax that would be imposed on these organizations. With respect to the latter point, the tax system does not tell us which expenditures made by charities are offsets to gross income, and we therefore cannot calculate taxable income. Moreover, our ignorance of the tax posture of the ultimate charitable beneficiaries makes it impossible to calculate the tax rate that ought to be imposed on the charitable entity that is supposed to be the surrogate for these beneficiaries.

For what we have called the Ring I groups (the mutual benefit entities), Bittker and Rahdert explain the exemption not as a subsidy but as a recognition of the fact that some activities "consist simply in the members' doing together what they could do separately without income tax consequences" (p. 358); on the other hand, they contend, revenue from investments or sales to nonmembers should not be entitled to exemption at all.

With respect to all Rings I–IV groups, exemption from corporate income tax can be understood in another way: Goode (1951, 40) states that one possible rationale for the corporate income tax is that it reduces inequalities of wealth and income among individuals resulting from stock-ownership and dividends; Goode points out that the corporate tax supplements the individual income tax by "reduc[ing] the amount of capital gains on stock which are traceable to retained profits, and in view of the preferential taxation of capital gains this narrows an important loophole in the individual income tax" (p. 205). The corporate income tax, however, has no inequality-reducing or loophole-narrowing function to perform with respect to a *nonprofit* corporation's taxable shareholders, for, by definition, the nonprofit has no such shareholders. This rationale, like those mentioned earlier, is in the tax-base-defining category; it has no "subsidy" elements.

Second, turning to the *deductibility under the federal income tax* of charitable contributions to Rings II–IV organizations, Andrews (1972) and Bittker (1972) have started with the venerable Haig-Simons definition of taxable income as the sum of a taxpayer's (1) consumption and (2) wealth accumulation (increase in net worth) during a given tax-reckoning period (Simons 1938). An item of revenue received by the taxpayer and then given away to charity during the same period does not increase the taxpayer's net worth. Moreover, it is argued that this pair of transactions does not constitute consumption, which, for income tax purposes, "may well be thought to encompass only the private consumption of divisible goods and services whose consumption by one household precludes their direct enjoyment by others"—private goods and services, in economics terminology (Andrews 1972); by contrast, charitable contributions buy only *public* goods and services. The charitable deduction simply gives effect (somewhat indirectly) to this proposition that income, when properly defined, does not include receipts thereafter contributed to charity (see also McNulty 1984). It should be noted that this rationale for deductibility does not necessarily justify a deduction for the full market value of appreciated property gifts; thus, Andrews (1972) suggests that, even under his theory, the gain portion of such property should not escape capital gains tax by reason of being given to charity.

Third, although Bittker and Andrews have not advanced an analogue to the income-defining rationale that would explain the *estate tax charitable deduction*, I have briefly explored such an estate-defining theory (Simon 1978, 22–23):

> Just as income is based on consumption and accumulation and the [income-defining] rationale asserts that this consumption is the private consumption of non-"public" . . . goods and services, we can perhaps say that the definition of personal wealth for estate tax purposes should refer to those assets available for the private accumulation or consumption of non-"public" . . . goods and services. A testamentary charitable contribution reduces the amount of assets available for such private consumption and accumulation; hence, under this analysis, it is logical to exclude these contributions from the definition of wealth for purposes of the estate tax.

Fourth, turning to the *state property tax exemption* of charitable organizations, Heller has provided what might be called a "property tax-base-defining" explanation for nontaxation (Yale University Program . . . 1982). Searching for theories that may be used to construct or define the property tax base, that is, "the general regime that defines which forms of . . . wealth are property to be taxed," he comes up with five alternative rationales: the property tax as an indirect charge for benefits, the property tax as a complement to the federal income tax, the property tax as land use regulator, the property tax as a wealth tax, and the "customary" definition of the property tax. Heller looks at each of these rationales to determine whether any of them necessarily suggests the inclusion of nonprofit organizations in the property tax base. His answer is that none of them does, and that therefore the exemption of charities can be explained on a tax-base-defining rather than a support or subsidy basis. (Tax-base rationales are discussed further in Swords 1981, 200–26.)

Implications of These Rationales. All four of these accounts point toward a rejection of the customary assumption that federal or state tax exemption or deductibility for the nonprofit sector represents an act of subvention, a bestowal

of largesse.[6] The implications of rejecting this assumption are profound. Quantitative limitations on exemption or deductibility become very difficult to justify: how and why do we limit a taxpayer's charitable deductions to 50 percent of adjusted gross income for an individual or 10 percent of net income for a corporation, and how and why do we impose a 2 percent tax on a foundation's investment income,[7] or how can we contemplate a ceiling on the estate tax charitable deduction (see Bittker 1976), if the amounts involved should not be included in the income or estate tax base to begin with?[8] And how and why does a state grant property tax exemption to some charities and not to others (Swords 1981), if their property is excluded from the tax base from the start?

Moreover, acceptance of an income, estate, or property tax-base-defining rationale avoids the adverse pressure on tax exemption or deductibility that arises out of "tax expenditure" accounting for these tax provisions—accounting that yields the estimate, for example, that in fiscal 1984 the federal government "spent" $9.2 billion in forgone tax revenues resulting from charitable deductions. Such tax expenditure calculations buttressed the Treasury Department's explanation of its 1984 recommendations for a floor on charitable deductions equal to 2 percent of adjusted gross income (U.S. Treasury Department 1984). In addition, a rejection of subsidy labels also makes it more difficult to challenge, under the First Amendment's Establishment Clause, the current tax treatment of churches (Joblove 1980); if this treatment does not represent subsidy, how can it represent constitutionally impermissible support of religion?

As a final set of consequences of accepting the tax-base-defining approach, instead of a support or subsidy approach, consider the impact on the equity, police, and border patrol functions of nonprofit tax policy. If exemption and deductibility do not represent a subsidy, the protests against *inequitable* subsidy (tilted in various ways more toward the rich than the poor) lose much of their force. Similarly, it is much more difficult to justify the federal government policing role discussed below—regulating the fiduciary conduct of nonprofit managers through the tax system—if the policing is not tied to what can be called a federal subsidy. Finally, the justification for border patrol restrictions under the tax code—fenc-

6. For example, this assumption was made without discussion in two *New York Times* opinion pieces one week apart. An op-ed article by Amitai Etzioni on March 4, 1985, argued that charities deserve "government support" but that this support should be provided "outright" rather than "indirectly, via the tax code." And an editorial on March 11, 1985, referred to charitable deductions as a "government subsidy."

7. §4940, I.R.C. This excise tax, originally set at 4 percent under the Tax Reform Act of 1969, was justified by the tax-writing committees of Congress principally as a fee to compensate the government for the special auditing expenses said to be associated with foundations. Nevertheless, it has been characterized as an incursion on the principle of tax exemption for charities (Bittker & Rahdert 1976).

8. Michael Krashinsky, in a memo to me, has pointed out that a limit on deductibility may not be inconsistent with the tax-base-defining rationale; the limit may only be a way of cutting down on some forms of abuse that are correlated with donations beyond certain percentages of incomes or estates.

ing nonprofits out of adjoining sectors—recedes if these constraints cannot be considered to be a condition of subsidy. A subsidy rationale, for example, undergirded a 1983 U.S. Supreme Court decision upholding one important aspect of border patrol: lobbying restrictions. These rules were attacked as an unconstitutional discrimination between charities, subject to lobbying restrictions, and veterans' organizations, *not* subject to lobbying restrictions, even though both types of organization enjoy the right to receive deductible contributions.[9] The Court stated, without explanation, that "tax exemptions and tax deductibility are a form of subsidy that is administered through the tax system," having "much the same effect as" or being "similar to cash grants," and, indeed, constituting an expenditure of "public moneys."[10] Having assumed the existence of a subsidy, the Court went on to hold that it is "not irrational for Congress to decide that, even though it will not subsidize substantial lobbying by charities generally, it will subsidize lobbying by veterans' organizations."[11] If tax exemption and deductibility were not regarded as subsidies, the Court could not have reasoned as it did, and the case might have had a different outcome.

The Limited Popularity of the Tax-Base-Defining Approach. The Supreme Court's subsidy assumptions are not idiosyncratic. Despite (or perhaps in part because of) the dramatic consequences that would flow from acceptance of the tax-base-defining rationales for tax exemption and deductibility, they have not been widely embraced (see, for example, Surrey 1973). Part of the explanation may lie in their novelty. To be sure, Harvard president Charles William Eliot attacked the idea of exemption as subsidy a century ago (Commission . . . 1975, 107), and one of the arguments for the charitable deduction when it entered the present tax law in 1917 resembled the not-part-of-consumption theory mentioned above (Commission . . . 1975, 106). But very little of the literature advancing a no-subsidy rationale appeared before 1972, and some of it came even later.

In addition, some aspects of this rationale appear to be inconsistent with long-standing tax doctrines or provisions. Thus, the income-defining and estate-defining theories of deductibility "bump into a countervailing theme in tax law: the ability to control the disposition of assets has often seemed to be a touchstone of taxability. . . . When one makes a gift to charity, this very act controls the disposition of assets—a fact that may therefore seem inconsistent with the notion that these same gifts reduce the . . . taxpayer's income or estate" (Simon 1978, 23). Similarly, the concept that federal income tax and state property tax exemption is tax-base-defining rather than subsidy depends in part on viewing "charitable organizations as conduit-type entities, a perspective which requires us to look at the beneficiaries of the nonprofit organizations—and their ability to pay" (Yale

University Program . . . 1982, 6). Standard tax doctrine, however, resists the conduit characterization of a corporation or trust (Bittker 1981, chaps. 81, 90). Congress has explicitly departed from standard doctrine to provide for conduit treatment of certain Ring I organizations—social clubs, homeowners' associations, and mutual savings banks (Hopkins 1983, 4, 16)—as well as for-profit corporation-partnership hybrids (so-called subchapter S corporations, §§1361–79, I.R.C.), but it is not clear that it meant to relax the no-conduit doctrine in the case of charitable corporations and trusts.

Some tax code provisions on charity, too, are awkward for those advancing a tax-base-defining rationale. The percentage limitations on individual and corporate deductibility and the excise tax on foundation investment income, already mentioned as difficult to justify under a tax-base-defining rationale, are themselves suggestive that the Congress did not have such a rationale in mind.[12] It may also be argued that the no-consumption theme—crucial to the Andrews-Bittker income-defining rationale for deductibility—is undermined by the fact that no deduction is allowed for gifts to *individuals,* as compared to organizations, outside of the family or household; it is hard to see why a gift to a stranger, poor or rich, is consumption, whereas the gift to a charity is not.[13] However, administrative reasons that are consistent with the no-consumption theory—rather than doctrinal muddiness—may explain the rule that only organizations are eligible; it is a way of making it "practical to establish and audit the amount of redistribution from donors to recipients" (Andrews 1972, 351).

A further source of rebuttal to the tax-base-defining rationales lies in the history, ancient and recent, of tax policy for nonprofits. Early exemption of churches from royal or feudal taxes was based on the need to promote God's works, and the legislative history of the American tax code is punctuated with support explanations.

True, there are several historical supports for a tax-base-defining theory. An early reason advanced in favor of deductibility, as already noted, had an income-defining ring to it. Moreover, one basis for exemption of church property was that "it ceased to be under human control when it was devoted to God" (Belknap 1977, 2027, quoting Stimpson)—the property was no longer part of any human tax base. Added support for the tax-base-defining approach comes from a statutory antecedent to the modern income tax, the Civil War income tax statute, which specified the organizations subject to taxation without including charitable entities, thus implying that the income of charities was not thought to be part of the tax base at all. Rusk (1961, 10–11) suggests that "exemption" language was included in the later (1894) general income tax "just to be sure," and that therefore "the notion of exemption is something of an accident of legislative drafting convenience." And the draftsman of the 1913 Revenue Act "argued in Congress against an explicit expansion of its exemption clauses to embrace 'be-

9. *Regan* v. *Taxation Without Representation of Washington,* 461 U.S. 540 (1983). With respect to the differential treatment, see part B of table 5.1.

10. 461 U.S. at 544–5.

11. Ibid., at 550.

12. But see Krashinsky's rebuttal, *n* 8.

13. I am indebted to Paul DiMaggio for this point about strangers.

nevolent' and 'scientific' organizations, on the ground that the statutory reference to 'net income' automatically excluded all non-profit organizations'' (Bittker & Rahdert 1976, 303).

Most of the argumentation in favor of the tax exemption and deductibility, however, has sounded other themes—of public benefit or reduction of government burdens. The burdens point is said to explain state property tax exemptions enacted in the nineteenth century (Adler 1922). And public benefit was the argument made in 1917 by Senator Hollis, one of the authors of the charitable deduction provision: that the imposition of heavy World War I taxes would hurt charitable institutions by tempting ''wealthy men . . . to economize. . . . They will say, 'Charity begins at home' '' (Commission . . . 1975, 106).

Adverting to these problems with the tax-base-defining rationales does not mean that they should be rejected. There are rebutting arguments that can be offered, such as the point that it is an odd subsidy to charity whose size is adventitiously determined by reference to a variable—the tax rate schedule—that is not fixed with charitable subsidy in mind.[14] Some day the tax-base-defining rationales, and the counterarguments, will receive the full-fledged analysis they deserve as an important part of the nonprofit tax policy research agenda. At this time, I can do no more than sketch the broad outlines and implications of this important set of explanations for exemption and deductibility, and some of the difficulties—and then proceed, as now, to consider the rationales that accept the premise of support or subsidy.

Support or Subsidy-Based Rationales

Even after tax-base rationales have been put aside, the search for a straightforward justification of tax exemption and deductibility for nonprofits, on the ground that they serve important values and need support, does not turn out to be trouble-free. The quest bumps into several issues raised by those who have studied some of its dimensions.

Why a Subsidy for Nonprofits? The issue of support through tax exemption and deductibility is prefaced with the question: why a government subsidy at all? And this question comes in two parts: Why a subsidy for this particular social function (for example, health or education)? And why a subsidy to *nonprofits* carrying out this social function? The first question has a fairly familiar answer: where the production of certain goods or services yields external benefits to the larger society, and where normal market operations result in a less than socially optimum supply of that good or service, public subsidy is in order.[15] But, turning to the second question, we have to ask why direct government provision, or a subsidy to for-profit providers, would not be a satisfac-

tory way of subsidizing production, without relying on nonprofit organizations.

Direct government provision is, of course, the way we obtain armies and most of our police, roads, and sewers. For goods and services like culture, health, welfare, education, and protection of civil rights and the environment, however, nongovernmental provision is often assumed to be preferable, for any one of a number of reasons:[16]

- Because only a part of the polity wants the good or service, despite its public or collective goods character—a circumstance especially likely to obtain in relatively heterogeneous societies like ours (Weisbrod 1977, and see chapter 22 in this volume).

- Because, even if the good or service is widely demanded, its provision by the government may be constitutionally prohibited (notably in the case of religion under the First Amendment) or inherently impractical (as in the case of monitoring, evaluation and criticism of government activities).

- Because, even if the good or service is in fact forthcoming, the *manner* in which it is provided will be constrained if the government itself offers it, as a result of majoritarian and egalitarian norms that bind the government and may be inconsistent with the values of innovation, quality, and freedom of inquiry in educational, cultural, and scientific affairs (see chapter 3 in this volume, where this is called the categorical constraint).

- Because government provision may be less efficient than nonprofit provision (in terms of cost per unit of production) as a result of the ability of the nonprofit to impose user fees where the government would find it hard to do so, or the nonprofit's ability to attract volunteer labor to the enterprise (see chapter 22 in this volume).

- Because use of nonprofits offers the possibility of decentralization of decision-making authority, thus serving the values of heterodoxy and participation.

These arguments against government provision are not universally accepted. They provoke protest, for example, that is based on a preference for majoritarian governance at all levels and in all contexts,[17] or based on fear of factionalism resulting from atomized decision making,[18] or based on

14. I am indebted to Michael Krashinsky for this observation.
15. These are typically circumstances in which the good or service is, in whole or in part, what economists call a ''public good'' or ''collective good'' (referred to above), the benefits of which cannot be captured by any one user to the exclusion of others.

16. Here and in other places in this chapter I recite arguments for or against various policies, arguments that may sound either normative (what makes good policy sense?) or positive (what explains policy decisions?). For the most part, I mean to set forth positive arguments, even though the considerations that lead policymakers to behave the way they do are often normative in nature.
17. This preference is reflected in the opposition to the practice of municipal (governmental) hospitals contracting with voluntary (private nonprofit) hospitals for the delivery of medical services and in a June 30, 1978, *New York Times* article headlined ''Private Charity Going Out of Style in West Europe's Welfare States.''
18. Although a supporter of the nonprofit sector, Lyman (1981) has discussed the possibility that its vaunted pluralism can lead to factional-

equity concerns about the power held by the more affluent participants in the nonprofit sector (to be discussed below). It is beyond the scope of this essay to resolve these dilemmas; I seek only a plausible, not a dispositive, explanation for the subsidization of nonprofit institutions, and the concerns about government "monopoly" clearly contribute to such an explanation.

Reluctance to rely exclusively on government providers, however, does not necessarily point us in the direction of nonprofits. Why not subsidize *for-profit* enterprises to carry out these functions? (See chapter 2 in this volume.) Subsidizing proprietary organizations is, after all, a familiar American activity, which nourished many of our infant industries and continues apace, as any opponent of oil-drilling expense deductions or the Lockheed or Chrysler "bailouts" will readily recount. The contract failure theory (Hansmann 1980; Nelson & Krashinsky 1973) suggests one problem with using for-profits: difficulties in obtaining or evaluating information may make it difficult for donors or consumers to police their contracts or the use of their gifts. This contract failure steers donors and consumers toward nonprofits whose managers are prevented by law from retaining profits and who thus have less incentive to engage in exploitive behavior. (For comments on contract failure, see Krashinsky [1984] and Ellman [1982].) An important research task, as contract failure's principal exponent readily agrees (Hansmann 1980), is to test empirically the trusting behavior, on the part of donors and consumers, that the theory hypothesizes,[19] and also to test the notion that nonprofit managers are *in fact* worthy of this trust (see Clark's critique [1980] of this notion).

If contract failure passes its empirical tests, that may qualify the theory as an explanation for the existence of nonprofit organizations but not necessarily as a justification for *preferential subsidy* for these organizations. Hansmann has doubts on that score (chapter 2), but James (chapter 22) argues that one element of contract failure theory—the difficulty of monitoring for-profit performance—helps justify choosing nonprofits rather than for-profits as the objects of any subsidizing that is to take place (apparently including tax subsidy). James states that government, viewed as "one large donor with the power to set certain basic contractual terms," finds it easier to monitor nonprofits than for-profits (and may also regard nonprofits as politically safer objects of subsidization).

Even as applied to nongovernmental donors and consumers, the contract failure theory helps build the case for subsidization of nonprofits, by suggesting their comparative advantage in the production of certain goods and service. An

alternative economic justification for subsidy is given by Krashinsky (1984), who suggests that "transactions costs" restrict the government in the direct provision of services. Other, noneconomic claims on behalf of nonprofit organizations, as compared to for-profits, point in the same direction: that the associational and participatory aspects of nonprofits contribute to the building of community life (Milofsky 1979); that the rendering of service to others meets important socioemotional needs, including the perception of self-worth; that the nonprofit setting is hospitable to "professional ideology and practice" and fosters professional self-regulation (Majone 1980); that, from the perspective of moral philosophy, there is intrinsic merit in voluntary associational activity for public purposes (Gamwell 1984); and an efficiency claim, involving the ability of nonprofits to deploy voluntary labor (see chapter 22 in this volume).[20] Without rehearsing or analyzing the counterarguments to these claims, I simply note that in many situations there are plausible grounds for relying on nonprofits rather than for-profits— and therefore for directing subsidies to nonprofits rather than to for-profits where some sort of subsidization is desirable.

An alternative rationale for subsidizing nonprofit organizations instead of for-profit organizations—one not based on the comparative advantage of nonprofits—has to do with the capital formation needs of both types of organizations. Hansmann (1981b) notes that the legal prohibition on the distribution of earnings by nonprofits effectively precludes them from issuing equity stock as a way of acquiring capital, and he suggests that in a very crude way the exemption of nonprofits from corporate income tax makes up for this disadvantage by permitting nonprofits to expand with untaxed retained earnings.

If a Subsidy for Nonprofits, Why Through the Tax System? We have, then, several alternate rationales for subsidizing nonprofit organizations, but, for the most part, they are not specifically tied to tax exemption or deductibility. In the search for a support or subsidy rationale for these tax provisions, we encounter, at this point, the contention that, granting the wisdom of subsidization, doing it through the tax system is a mistake (Surrey 1973). Tax subsidies, it is contended, are cumbersome (because it is difficult to pinpoint preferred objects of governmental aid through tax allowance systems), inefficient (because the government may lose more in revenue than is realized in subsidy dollars), inequitable (because of the allocational power they give to higher-income taxpayers), and immovable (because it is harder to amend tax laws than to delete subsidies from appropriations bills).

Postponing the equity point to the next section, we note

---

ism precluding effective pursuit of common goals; he quotes John Gardner on the danger of letting the *pluribus* crowd out the *unum* in "E pluribus unum."

19. Early efforts to test the theory empirically have been made by Permut (1981) and by James Newton, whose work in progress examines consumer choice between nonprofits and for-profits in the child-care area.

20. The theories mentioned here and in the nonprofit-government comparison do not exhaust the list of possible explanations of the origins and scope of America's third sector: for example, theories grounded in religion (Payton 1984), business history (chapter 1 in this volume), "national character" (DiMaggio 1983), or state expansion (DiMaggio 1983). In the text I have referred only to theories that explain the frequent *preference* for nonprofit as compared to government or business entities.

that, whatever the strength of these laments for tax subsidy in general, there is reason to regard them as less accurate or less serious when directed to subsidies for charity. Thus, with respect to efficiency, although early research indicated that, in aggregate effect, the charitable deduction cost the federal treasury more than the charities gained, subsequent studies by Feldstein and others (all of them summarized in Clotfelter 1985, 56–63) have been widely accepted as demonstrating that the opposite is true—a point to be returned to in our discussion of incentive measures. The defenders of the present system can accept the cumbersomeness point as a strength rather than a weakness, on the ground that the special genius of subsidy via the tax system—instead of governmental pinpointing of subsidy targets—is that it permits decentralized decision making through individual taxpayer choice. (See Hochman and Rodgers 1977, 2–3.) This "calculated anarchy of dispersed initiative, individuality and variety" (Brewster 1965) is consistent with the pluralism the nonprofit sector is valued for promoting.[21] As to the immovability point, its accuracy is in question: perhaps sacred-cow direct appropriations become just as politically imbedded as do tax law provisions, especially in an era of constant tax reform. Moreover, immovability can be defended as a way of buffering the process of individual, idiosyncratic charitable allocations, by subsidizing all of it despite shifts in legislative passions or prejudices.

Assuming that an alternative to direct appropriations is sought for subsidizing of nonprofits, the tax system is not the only option. In a dramatic challenge to the present arrangements, for example, Brannon and Strnad (1977) propose that we consider scrapping, in large part, the subsidization of contributors through tax allowances in favor of a client payment subsidy approach: the government gives vouchers, scholarships, and other forms of subsidies to consumers of the goods and services furnished by nonprofit organizations. This strategy is advanced as a way not only to avoid the equity problems associated with tax deductions but also to moderate various evils flowing from the tax system's subsidization of contributors rather than clients: the programmatic control that large contributors are said to have on some donees (particularly universities); the bizarre allocations that one finds, for example, in the health research field as a result of the mass marketing of some disease charities; and the gross escalation of art prices as a result of excessive tax valuations.

A rich array of empirical, analytical, and normative issues is raised by the Brannon and Strnad proposal (as the authors acknowledge). By way of brief example: What impact would the client payment subsidy system have on the behavior of nonprofit health, education, and welfare organizations now

required more than before to market their services to consumers? Would the process of fixing the level of client payments, subject to budget constraints, require the government to make allocational choices, among nonprofit industries and among types of organizations within those industries, that are distinguishable from the choices that have to be made in a direct appropriation system? And who are the clients to receive subsidies in a field like health research? Not the sick people themselves, Brannon and Strnad say, but perhaps disease organizations selected by "a vote of certified M.D.s" (p. 2378). Issues such as these deserve but have not yet received close study.

If Subsidy through the Tax System, Is the Present Method Appropriate? If one resolves these issues in favor of tax assistance as a way of subsidizing nonprofits, the question remains: is the *present* tax system the best approach? Most of the argument under this heading focuses on income and estate tax deductibility. Apart from its efficiency aspects, already discussed, the deduction has been attacked on distributional grounds. These criticisms, and proposals that the deduction be replaced by a tax credit, matching grant, or other allowance not tied to a donor's tax bracket, will be summarized in the equity discussion below.

The debate over the charitable deduction involves not only distributive consequences but also the rationale for selecting this particular form of tax assistance. We have already discussed nonsubsidy rationales; there are also a variety of subsidy theories to choose from. Bittker (1972) considers, as one of several ways of looking at the charitable deduction, that it may function as an award to the donor for a deed highly prized by the society. McConnell (1976) views the deduction as an "alternative tax" (not to be confused with the "alternative minimum tax" imposed under the present code): in effect, both the tax that is collected and the tax that is forgiven as a result of the charitable deduction represent taxes paid, but the latter component is one that the taxpayer is permitted to direct to a chosen public interest activity, in place of activities selected by the central government.

These deductibility theories point to additional research needs. In the absence of sufficient data and analysis relating to these and other issues, this chapter cannot complete the search for an overall rationale for tax exemption and deductibility. Some rationale questions remain, however, directed not to nonprofit tax treatment as a whole but to the differential *coverage* of that treatment—differential as to subject matter and as to type of nonprofit instrumentality.

If the Present Method Is Appropriate, Are Its Distinctions Defensible? As to subject matter, and returning to the four rings of table 5.1, what explains the extra subsidy (if subsidy is what it is) that flows to Rings II–IV, as compared to Ring I? Possible explanatory distinctions have been mentioned: public service versus mutual benefit; public or collective goods versus private goods. How well do the facts fit these distinctions? Weisbrod (1980) has constructed an empirical test for the collective-private goods distinction, based on the ratio between gift support (suggesting collective) and

---

21. The property tax exemption, James and Rose-Ackerman have in effect argued (1985, 92–93), presents a special case of cumbersomeness. They say that a general real property tax exemption may be too broad a subsidy mechanism if the social objective is to subsidize the costs of a particular geographical location that itself confers public benefits. "This . . . is an argument for subsidizing land rent, not for a general tax exemption that includes real property."

other revenues (suggesting private). One cannot be confident, however, that contributions support is a reliable proxy for public goods provision. Parental contributions to a private school may be a more or less explicitly constructed tuition substitute (Stewart 1973), and alumni contributions may be a form of deferred repayment of prior benefits received (Hansmann 1980). Contributions to the performing arts institutions can be looked upon as a way of charging higher prices to richer patrons without dislocating the explicit price schedule (Hansmann 1981a).

The past twenty-five years have seen a fairly steady expansion in the nonprofit activities regarded as on the public interest or public goods side of the Ring I versus Rings II–IV boundary. Congress has moved some organizations over the line—Olympic support organizations, societies for prevention of cruelty to animals—by including them in §501(c)(3). A 1960 Treasury regulation placed organizations that combat discrimination and "community deterioration" in the charmed circle (Reg. §§1.501(c)(3)–1(d)(2)). And a series of individual Treasury rulings and court decisions has given the same treatment to a variety of organizations that might earlier have had some sort of Ring I status, including voter education and registration projects (in a private letter ruling issued in 1961), organizations investing in private businesses located in poor communities (Rev. Rul. 74–587, 1974–2 Cum. Bull. 162), and health maintenance organizations organized on a membership basis (Hopkins 1983, 94).[22] For reasons that may or may not have much to do with public interest or public goods theory and that have not been closely examined, Congress has picked some organizations lying within Ring I and, without moving them out of the ring, has declared them eligible to receive deductible contributions: veterans' organizations, fraternal lodges insofar as they carry on charitable activities, and nonprofit cemetery companies (§§170(c)(3),(4),(5), I.R.C.).

Despite apparent departures, one can detect a fairly consistent adherence to principle in the federal tax system's assignment of organizations to what we have called Rings I and II–IV. It is much harder to discern the logic of the criteria for exemption from state property tax laws. As I suggested when introducing table 5.2, the states vary widely in their use of descriptive adjectives. Even within given states the theory behind the distinctions is not always evident; scholars, for example, have been puzzled at the New York courts' restrictive interpretation of "education" for property tax exemption purposes (Swords 1981, 168–74). A comprehensive examination of the state criteria, and the sense that can be made of them, remains to be done.

Some uncharted territory—regarding the criteria for exemption and deductibility—remains in the federal field as well. For example, what are the implications of the public

interest or public goods rationales—or of the tax-base-defining rationale—for the tax treatment of the following?

1. Groups whose purposes are predominately thought to be antisocial but that have explicit public interest goals. The Ku Klux Klan and the Communist party are frequently cited but little studied illustrations.[23] The charitable trust law doctrine that charities may not pursue purposes that violate "public policy"—a doctrine invoked by the Supreme Court to deny 501(c)(3) status to a racially discriminatory university (*Bob Jones University* v. *United States*, 461 U.S. 574 [1983])—can be invoked to deny exemption in these cases, but the possible impact of this doctrine on the heterodoxy of the nonprofit sector has caused some concern (Simon, Powers, & Gunnemann 1972, 152–53, and see below).

2. Organizations whose goals are regarded as hopelessly unrealistic or scientifically impossible, or whose programs do not seem destined to succeed. In the mid-1970s the IRS denied exempt status to two environmental litigation groups on the ground, among others, that it was "not clear that the overall effect of the litigation will be beneficial to the area," and the IRS questioned a third applicant: "Are the consequences of your legal activity clearly predictable and obviously beneficial to the community affected?" (Sowles 1980). How would the IRS (or the courts) handle an exemption application from the Flat Earth Society or from a group dedicated to building a perpetual motion machine or communicating with the dead?

Without pausing to explore further the implications of various exemption and deductibility rationales for *subject matter* coverage, we turn to a second coverage issue—that of *types of organization* and, specifically, the question of the distinction among Rings II (public charities), III (operating foundations), and IV (nonoperating foundations). To some extent, the special restrictions on the foundation categories are informed by overall exemption rationales, of either the tax-base-defining or the support-subsidy variety. Thus, language found in the legislative history of the 1969 Tax Reform Act—or the earlier legislation of 1950, 1954 and 1964 that created a precedent for treating nonfoundation charities more favorably than foundations—refers to the greater degree of fiscal abuse thought to inhabit the foundation world (Bittker 1973), or to the greater degree of power or influence over governmental and business institutions (Simon 1978), or to the foundations as repositories of private, "nonaccountable," and usually donor-controlled wealth (Karl & Katz 1981; Simon 1969). Each of these grievances (to be discussed below) contributed to the climate that led to "third-class charity" treatment for foundations, although, as Bittker (1973) makes clear, none of these charges received adequate empirical and analytical study. With varying degrees of difficulty, one can connect these grievances either to a tax-base-defining rationale (for example, because self-serving

22. As a result of giving §501(c)(3) status to groups that also fall in the Ring I social welfare category [§501(c)(4)], the coverage of these sections is quite similar except for the lobbying restrictions imposed on the latter category (Hopkins 1983, 274–75).

23. Exemption was denied to "Communist-controlled organizations" by the Internal Security Act of 1950 (64 Stat. 997; 50 U.S.C. 790(b)); see Hopkins (1983, 355).

fiscal benefits add up to "consumption" and therefore point toward taxability) or to a public interest or public goods subsidy rationale (for example, because fiscal self-dealing negates a public benefit).

There were other objections to foundations that more directly invoked a subsidy rationale: quantitative and qualitative complaints about the role of the foundation in creating public goods and services. On the *quantitative* front, it was contended that a dollar given to a foundation produced a direct charitable benefit that was too little and too late compared to a dollar given to a Ring II entity.

"Too little": the yield from foundation endowments, or the payout of those yields, was said to be inferior. Even for years before the 1969 Tax Reform Act (which forced a minimum level of annual payout [§4942, I.R.C.]), the available data did not support this complaint (Simon 1969). A major study of foundation fiscal practices being conducted (as of early 1986) by the Council on Foundations should throw new light on the "too little" story.

"Too late": it was assumed that gifts to foundations become part of endowment,[24] emerging only slowly as income grants to public charities, whereas a gift to a public charity is deployed at once for operational use. In economic terms, to be sure, there is no difference between X dollars given to public charities now and X dollars given to a foundation to be paid out to those charities over time. But from the perspective of hard-pressed human service or cultural institutions confronting an ocean of demand, current cash flow is critical and may not be obtainable in the face of borrowing constraints. Some gifts to conduit-type foundations, however, *are* paid out currently. Moreover, even direct gifts to public charities are not always disbursed currently; they may be locked up as part of the endowment funds of the college, church, hospital, or other recipient because of donor instruction or institutional policy. This is particularly true for large-scale gifts (often of appreciated property) made by the wealthiest donors—the very kinds of gifts that are likely to flow to foundations if not given to public charities. In short, public charities may accumulate their funds, and foundations may disburse at once, contrary to the "too late" assumptions. These and other aspects of the "too late" problem could use more empirical scrutiny.

Legislative objections to the foundations' production of public goods and services were not only quantitative but *qualitative*. Some critics objected to what they perceived as an eastern establishment bias, others to a radical hue, still others to "esoteric" grants (that is how the late Rep. Wright Patman, a leading critic, characterized some of his favorite targets, such as Bollingen Foundation support for study of Bosnian tombstones).[25] A more general qualitative concern

24. With very few exceptions, foundations do not receive their funds as true legal endowments—that is, funds burdened by a restriction on expenditure of capital—but many foundations (and most big ones) treat their funds that way.

25. Bittker (1973, 158–59) points out that similar criticism of "esoteric" tombstone research could have been directed at public charities, such as universities, churches, art galleries, historical societies, and the D.A.R.

seemed to involve "a judgment that publicly supported charities satisfy more pressing social needs than private charities, or that public support constitutes an informal referendum conferring an endorsement on public charities that private charities have not elicited" (Bittker 1973, 143). From a variety of perspectives, therefore, the "value added" by foundations was reckoned to be insufficient to justify "first-class" tax treatment. Other foundation appraisers have struck a more favorable trial balance (chapter 20 in this volume). The task of attempting a systematic analysis of the value-added question is another (and exceedingly difficult) task on the nonprofit research agenda.

As of mid-1984, despite the absence of thoroughgoing research on either the quantitative or the qualitative aspects of foundation performance, there was some evidence that congressional concern on these points had receded. In the Tax Reform Act of 1984, Congress deleted or moderated four provisions enacted in 1969 or earlier that disfavored private nonoperating (Ring IV) foundations:

1. The percentage of adjusted gross income that an individual can deduct for contributions to these foundations (in the form of cash) was increased from 20 percent to 30 percent, as compared to 50 percent for cash gifts to public charities (§170(b)(1)(B)(i)).

2. Individuals giving to these foundations in excess of percentage limitations were given the right, previously denied, to carry over the excess into five succeeding years (§§170(b)(1)(B), (D)(ii)).

3. The excise tax on foundation investment income was reduced from 2 percent to 1 percent for foundations making distributions that exceeded the legally required payout figure by an amount equal to the 1 percent tax reduction (§4940(e)).

4. Perhaps most important, Congress partially repealed the 1969 rule sharply distinguishing between foundations and public charities with respect to gifts of appreciated property; under that rule a taxpayer could deduct the full market value when giving to a public charity but could deduct only 60 percent of the appreciation when giving to a nonoperating foundation unless the foundation quickly "passed through" the gift to public charities. The 1984 legislation treats the foundation as favorably as the public charity when the gift to the foundation consists of publicly traded stock not representing a major interest in the company (§170(e)(5)).

The original (pre-1984) enactment of these four provisions—as compared to the *regulatory* legislation controlling various aspects of foundation behavior (self-dealing, and so on)—was less likely to have been motivated by particular "abuse" concerns and more likely to have been informed by general doubts about the quantitative and qualitative performance of foundations. What is notable about the 1984 modification of these provisions, therefore, is that it appears to reflect a judgment that the support-subsidy rationales undergirding exemption and deductibility for charities in general, whatever these rationales may be, also justify, in almost equal measure, exemption and deductibility for the Ring IV foundations. True, these foundations were still subject to regulatory measures significantly more stringent than those imposed on public (Ring II) charities, but the 1984 narrowing of the gap with respect to the nonregulatory restrictions could be considered to have moved foundations at least from third-class to second-class status.

The Support Function in Practice: Effects of Tax Relief

We turn from a look at the rationales for tax exemption and deductibility to an examination of impact: what support for the nonprofit sector do these federal and state tax blessings in fact provide? We start with the impact of present law and then briefly consider change proposals.

Consequences of Present Law

Superficially, it would appear that the impact of federal or state tax *exemption* is more readily discernible than the impact of income or estate tax *deductibility,* for the latter requires a difficult estimate of incentive effects. It turns out, however, that exemption-effect calculations are not straightforward either—which probably accounts for the paucity of estimates on this impact question.

Exemption under Federal Income Tax. If we try to calculate the effect of exemption of nonprofits under the federal income tax, we can obtain detailed revenue figures from each organization filing an information return (Forms 990 or 990–PF), and aggregate estimates have been made from this and other data that seek to take account of organizations not required to file—churches and public charities with less than $25,000 in revenues. One study estimates 1980 revenues for charitable organizations (Rings II–IV) at $129 billion (chapter 4 in this volume). In order to get closer to a taxable income figure, we subtract philanthropic contributions (but not government grants, which more nearly represent payment for services), and the result is $76 billion. But how much of this nondonative revenue represents taxable income? As already mentioned, Bittker and Rahdert (1976) have written about the difficulties in determining what parts of a nonprofit's expenditures should offset revenue to produce taxable income. Moreover, even if we had clearer guidance about how to prepare a putative tax bill, the aggregate expenditure information we have is not satisfactory, for it has been put together from a set of sources different from those that generate revenue numbers (chapter 4 in this volume).

The resulting difficulties are demonstrated by examining the Hodgkinson and Weitzman (1984, 36) data on "total use of resources" for what are, roughly speaking, our Rings II–IV groups in 1980. The known expenditures uncovered by the authors amount to $137.5 billion, which is $22.4 billion less than revenue estimated from other sources at $159.9 billion (somewhat higher than the Rudney estimate in chapter 4). If the $22.4 billion were surplus, that might be taxable income (if we knew how to define it); if we then applied conventional corporate tax rates and made certain assumptions about the corporate tax brackets into which the non-

profits fall,[26] we might end up with a forgiven-tax figure of about $10 billion for 1980. But Hodgkinson and Weitzman have not been able to characterize the $22.4 billion figure as surplus. (As surplus, it would represent a return on "sales" of about 15 percent.) Instead, this figure is "a residual account" which "includes funds for which there is no information about their designated use, and errors of estimation"; it is, in short, a balancing entry.

Although we are bereft of usable data, it seems fair to offer this generalization about the impact of income tax exemption: if we make what strikes me as the reasonable assumptions that (1) in the absence of exemption, a nonprofit would be allowed an offset for its program and administrative expenditures (as its cost of doing business), and (2) after deducting these expenditures, most nonprofits would show very little surplus or profit, then it follows that the amount of forgiven tax—and therefore the amount of this type of support provided to nonprofits—is quite minimal.[27]

Exemption from State Property Tax. The minimal-support generalization is probably not applicable to the state property tax exemption. Although, as we have noted, the theory of property taxation might exclude nonprofit holdings from the base even in the absence of an exemption, that does not mean that state and local governments would act upon that theory and fail to tax a nonprofit deprived of exemption. Accordingly, the property tax exemption offers a great deal more than "quite minimal" support to those nonprofits that own real estate and are eligible for the exemption. To put numbers on this statement, however, is another matter. Although Rudney in chapter 4 of this volume provides estimates of the total assets held by charitable organizations, it is not broken down by type of asset; nor does the IRS publish such information (Hodgkinson & Weitzman 1984, 40). Local governments have offered estimates of the value of tax-exempt property, and some aggregate figures have been set forth on the basis of such estimates (Balk 1971), but the local figures often fail to distinguish between property owned by nonprofits, on the one hand, and property owned by governmental bodies or other exempt holders, on the other hand. (This is not true, however, for Swords [1981] on New York State.) Moreover, all estimates of the value of exempt property are subject to serious cavils: such property is not subject to regular appraisal; it is more difficult to appraise because it so rarely resembles conventional commercial or residential property. The foregoing factors make it easy for governmental officials to indulge an understandable tendency to make the losses to the state or local treasury look as large as possible.

Federal Income and Estate Tax Deductibility. When we go from exemption to federal income and estate tax deductibility, we encounter a different challenge. Here, the amount of deductions is calculated by the IRS with reasonable

26. An average rate of 40 percent has been rather arbitrarily assumed. Note, however, the doubt expressed by Bittker and Rahdert (1976) about reliance on corporate tax rates for making this calculation.

27. Hansmann in chapter 2 in this volume offers a substantially less modest estimate of the amount of profit earned by certain categories of nonprofits.

accuracy, and fairly solid estimates can be derived therefrom of the taxes saved by contributors. For example, in 1983 the deductions amounted to approximately $36 billion (American Association . . . 1985), resulting in an estimated tax-saving of $10 billion for fiscal 1983. How much of this $10 billion represented nonprofit-sector support that is attributable to tax deductibility, however, depends on how much the taxpayers contributed to charity in relation to what they would have given in the absence of deductibility. The "price elasticity of giving" enables us to determine this amount; it tells us how much increased giving is induced by a given reduction in the "price" of the gift (through tax savings resulting from deductions). Feldstein's research for the Filer Commission (Commission . . . 1975, 129) presented widely accepted evidence of price elasticities between −1.15 and −1.29, meaning that each dollar of tax saved by taxpayers results in $1.15 to $1.29 in increased giving. Jencks (chapter 18 in this volume) reports that several studies, using different approaches, agree on elasticities between −1.0 and −1.5, or "on the order of −1.25." Multiplying this figure by the $10 billion in tax savings for fiscal 1983 (and lumping corporate donors with individuals for want of disaggregated data), one may surmise that charitable organizations received roughly $12.5 billion in support attributable to income tax deductibility in fiscal 1983, at a cost to the Treasury of approximately $10 billion.

Information on the support provided by the *estate* tax deduction (or its efficiency) is more difficult to find. We do not have data on how much of the $4.5 billion in bequests received by charities in 1983 had been deducted for federal estate tax purposes, but it is a plausible surmise that most of these bequest dollars came from taxable estates in which a deduction had been taken. Speculating that roughly $4 billion in deductions were involved and that the average marginal estate tax bracket was 50 percent, and splitting the difference between the estate tax price elasticity estimates of Feldstein (1977) and Boskin (1977)—both of which were greater than one—we come up with a rough guess that in 1983 charities received slightly more than $2 billion in support attributable to estate tax deductibility. Again, the elasticities also tell us that this support is efficient in terms of revenue losses.

Consequences of Proposed Changes

From time to time, state and local government officials talk about eliminating the charitable property tax deduction, and occasionally a state (such as New York in 1971) cuts back on the scope of the exemption, permitting localities to place groups back on the tax rolls (Swords 1981). And although there has been no similar talk about ending the federal income tax exemption for charities, inroads were made in this exemption when taxes were imposed on unrelated business income, on foundation investment income, and on political organization income (Bittker & Rahdert 1976). Moreover, Hansmann (1985, 12) contends that the 1984 Treasury proposals to repeal the exemption for nonprofit insurance com-

panies, coupled with the proposed repeal of some other exemptions (interest on municipal bonds that benefit tax-exempt institutions and credit unions), represent a "serious sign of trouble for the corporate tax exemption for non-profits." The tax reform bill passed by the House of Representatives in December 1985 followed up on the Treasury's insurance proposal: it would repeal tax-exempt status for nonprofit organizations "providing commercial-type insurance," including Blue Cross and Blue Shield (with some exceptions) and TIAA-CREF, the major provider of teacher pensions.[28] Should this provision become law or a broader repeal of federal income tax or state property tax exemptions be enacted, our earlier discussion of support levels points to methods—and difficulties—of calculating the consequences for nonprofits and suggests that repeal of property tax exemption may be more injurious than repeal of income tax exemption.

In recent years, however, most of the movement for change in tax support for the nonprofit sector has focused on deductibility under the federal income tax and (to a lesser extent) the estate tax. The major estate tax proposal came in the mid-1970s: to limit the charitable deduction to 50 percent of the gross estate (criticized in Bittker 1976). On the basis of 1969 data, Boskin estimated that this change would cause testators to cut out half of the 1969 level of testamentary charitable giving ($338 million—about a tenth of the 1983 level), with only a $43 million revenue gain (Commission . . . 1975, 151).

The traffic in proposals concerning the income tax deduction has been prolific, some of it aimed at increasing support for charities, and some intended to achieve various tax reform objectives that are probably inconsistent with increased charitable support.

Federal Tax Proposals to Induce Higher Giving. Increased support proposals in recent years have included these measures, listed here with no attempt to quantify the consequences:

- Providing a 200 percent or 150 percent deduction, respectively, for low- and middle-income givers, recommended by the Filer Commission in 1975 (Commission . . . 1975, 141–42).

- Substitution of a flat tax *credit* for the present deduction (for example, a credit against tax of 30 percent or 50 percent of each contributed dollar), or an optional credit to be used in place of the deduction (Commission . . . 1975, 127–33). While sometimes advocated as a way of overcoming the regressive tilt of the deduction, a credit at these levels would also have the effect of increasing total giving. The commission, however, did not endorse a credit as a substitute for the deduction because of its

28. §1012 of the House bill, adding §501(m) of the code. The Ways and Means Committee report states that this insurance activity is "so inherently commercial that tax-exempt status is inappropriate" and that it unfairly competes with commercial companies (House Report 99–426, 664).

allocational effect: under a 30 percent credit, giving to religion would increase, but giving to education and to hospitals—"among the financially hardest pressed of nonprofit organizations"—would drop substantially.

- Permitting corporations to take a 10 percent tax credit on top of charitable deductions (Commission . . . 1975, 155).

- Permitting artists who contribute their own creations to a museum to deduct at market value, as compared to the present-law deduction limited to the cost of materials (170(e), 1221(3)). This change would obviously increase the flow of art works to museums (see Frankel 1979), but no dollar estimates are available. The change might also result in additional valuation problems, as artists sought generous deductions for works that had never been the subject of a bargained-for valuation.[29]

- Easing restrictions on giving to foundations beyond the liberalizations enacted in 1984 (referred to above). New steps would permit donors to Ring IV organizations to deduct as high a percentage of adjusted gross income as donors to Rings II and III organizations, repeal the excise tax on foundation investment income, and eliminate some or all of the several regulatory restrictions imposed on Rings III–IV but not Ring II organizations.[30]

Federal Tax Proposals with Negative Effects on Giving. Several other recent or pending proposals, although not aimed at altering the level of giving to charities, could be expected to have a negative effect. The proposals listed below were part of various "flat," "fair," and/or "simplified" tax proposals that were being debated in 1984 and 1985, some of which were adopted by the House of Representatives in December 1985. They are briefly summarized here because they typify initiatives that can be expected to arise in the modern tax reform era and that, if enacted, would affect support levels for the nonprofit sector.

1. Tax reform proposals submitted by President Reagan in May 1985:

- Reduction of marginal tax rates, with the top rate declining from 50 percent to 38 percent (in the December 1985 House bill). Because a rate reduction increases the "price" of giving, this change by itself (and even giving effect to the increased after-tax income made available) is reckoned to have more of an impact on annual giving than any other changes listed below.

- Elimination of the deduction for state and local taxes. This change would make it unrewarding for many taxpayers to itemize their deductions—it is estimated that the nonitemizing percentage of taxpayers would rise from 62 percent to 75 percent—thus reducing the numbers of persons with a tax factor in their giving decisions. A decline in itemizers would not, however, have an effect on charitable giving if *non*itemizers were permitted to deduct their gifts—the subject of the next item.

- Repeal of the legislation that, by the year of full phase-in, 1986, would have allowed *non*itemizing taxpayers to claim charitable deductions on an equal footing with itemizers.

2. Tax reform proposals made by the Treasury in November 1984 not included in the above list:

- Denying donors the ability to deduct the market value of appreciated property gifts and permitting them to deduct only the original cost adjusted for inflation. This change was estimated to result in a significant decline in giving to higher education and arts institutions, the principal recipients of appreciated property gifts.

- If the foregoing provision was *not* enacted, requiring—as a substitute measure—that the amount of appreciation deducted by a property donor be designated a "tax preference item," thus subjecting it to a possible 20 to 25 percent "alternative minimum tax," with the impact falling mainly on educational and cultural institutions. The House of Representatives passed a modified version of this proposal in December 1985 as part of the tax reform bill.

- Imposing a floor of 2 percent of adjusted gross income, below which an individual taxpayer could not deduct contributions.[31]

Economists who studied the 1984–85 proposals have agreed on the general (downward) direction of the giving changes that would result and on their nontrivial dimensions (Clotfelter 1985; Lindsey 1985; Rudney & Auten 1985), but they have disagreed about magnitudes.[32] These discrepancies derived in part from the fact that even the most sophisticated econometric work has difficulty accounting for new contexts. For example, will price elasticity estimates based on 1981 or an earlier period apply to the philanthropic environment of the late 1980s? Will cross-sectional data comparing itemizers with nonitemizers at a single point in time

---

29. In 1984 Congress required the Treasury to issue new appraisal and substantiation rules to cope with art valuation problems (Public Law 98–369, §155(a)(1)–(6)).

30. The impact of existing law on giving to foundations is being considered as part of a study of the trends in the birth, growth, and death of foundations, and of the determinants of these trends, launched in 1983 by the Yale Program on Non-Profit Organizations and the Council on Foundations, scheduled for completion in 1986.

31. The one Treasury recommendation in the charitable field that cuts in the other direction is a recommendation that the 50 percent ceiling on the amount of adjusted gross income that can be given to charity be eliminated. This change was estimated, however, to induce only modest increases in charitable giving.

32. These studies were discussed at a February 1985 Brookings Institution conference. A comparison of the three studies appears in Zimmerman (1985).

predict what happens, over time, if and when nonitemizers lose their ability to take charitable deductions?

What reduces confidence in econometric predictions as one moves from context to context is that the elasticities and other statistical formulations are not informed by a body of behavioral learning on the dynamics of charitable giving. Although psychologists, social psychologists, and sociologists have developed a considerable body of research on individual helping behavior and altruism (reviewed in Gonzalez & Tetlock 1980), no comparable corpus addresses the determinants of money or labor contributions to nonprofit organizations. Survey research has been undertaken that asks respondents to explain their donative patterns (see Jencks, chapter 18 in this volume, and a forthcoming study by White [1986]), but neither the academy nor the fund-raising profession and industry has mounted a full-fledged effort to develop testable hypotheses regarding the factors shaping donative behavior and to test these theories empirically with simulated or naturally occurring data. Scholars and fund-raisers alike speculate about such (often overlapping) factors as identification with others, guilt, redistributional passion, religious belief and/or obedience, social or business pressures, self-esteem, feelings of indebtedness, quest for power over others, and desire to obtain pecuniary or educational advantage for family members—as well as less individually oriented behavioral explanations that invoke cultural norms or social mechanisms such as "network matching" (Boorman & Levitt 1981).[33] The mix of possible motives and influences is staggering, and some academically trained observers wonder if the subject is, in fact, researchable. Yet it seems odd that an industry that currently "sells" $75 billion of charitable wares per annum to individual and institutional donors, and hopes to do a great deal better, should go about its work using such a slender knowledge base. No other industry of remotely comparable size and complexity conducts its business relying on such a high ratio of art to science.

Until the nature of philanthropic giving is studied with more energy, system, and imagination, econometric predictions will have to be received with caution, and, indeed, the more general question of the efficiency of the support function of nonprofit tax policy will remain in at least partial darkness.

THE EQUITY FUNCTION OF NONPROFIT TAX LAW

Service to a wide spectrum of the public—including its least advantaged members—is a venerable and transcendent theme in the history of charity. It has roots in ancient Egypt (Gladstone 1982), in the Old and New Testaments (Isaiah 61:1; Luke 4:17), and in the 1601 English statute that still

dominates Anglo-American charity law (Statute of Charitable Uses, 43 Eliz. I ch. 4 [1601]; Gladstone 1982, 56–57). It has long been urged that the tax treatment of nonprofits reinforce this notion of "equity" (as the word is often used in this context), or at least not undermine it. These equity claims, however, sometimes seem to contravene other values that charity seeks to serve—such as the encouragement, in the name of pluralism, of new cultural traditions and the preservation of old ones—interests that do not have high priority for many disadvantaged citizens.

The tax policy questions that flow from these and other value clashes involving equity fall into four broad categories, of which the first most directly poses the historic equity issue and the other three are corollary.

1. How much should nonprofit tax policy insist on service to the poor, or, more generally, how much must it incorporate a redistributional ethic? (Redistribution, of course, need not benefit only the poor; it takes place, as Bittker has pointed out, when a middle-class art lover visits the Getty Museum.)

2. How much private benefit may the donor derive from his or her gift? This question relates to the first because a high degree of gain to an affluent donor may dilute any redistributional thrust of the gift.

3. How much allocative power should donors be permitted to wield? Here, the allocative capacity per se is the subject of equity concern, apart from the redistributional impact of the gift itself (question 1), and apart from any other aspects of private benefit (question 2).

4. To what extent is discrimination or preference based on the race, gender, religion, or ethnicity of the beneficiaries acceptable? This question may but need not overlap with the redistributional issue under question 1.

This discussion focuses on aspects of each topic that have received research attention.

The Redistributional Issue

Those who seek an explicit link between the legal criteria for tax-blessed charitable activity and assistance to the poor will only occasionally be able to find it. Even assuming that redistribution is a sine qua non of the tax law, the ways of effecting it in an economy as complicated as ours cannot be spelled out with sufficient precision to become a legal standard. Indeed, it is at least difficult and perhaps impossible to determine the redistributional impact of many or most forms of charitable endeavor. The one author who has tried, in a prefatory manner, to trace the degree to which charity results in a downward shift of income and wealth, concluded that "the redistributional effects of philanthropy are incalculable in the most literal sense of the word" (Schenkkan 1974, 50).[34] Moreover, the methods employed by both governments and nonprofit institutions to address poverty have

---

33. Some of these factors, along with class, ethnic, and other background variables, are discussed in chapter 18 of this volume. A comprehensive endeavor to speculate on many of these factors, against a background of philosophical and religious thought, appears in Payton (1984).

34. Schenkkan's essay sets forth an outline for further research on this subject that merits follow-up by scholars interested in the subject of distributive justice or philanthropy, or both.

necessarily become more sophisticated and indirect as the social order becomes more complex and also as charitable agencies, over the centuries, have moved away from alms-giving remedies.[35]

In any event, it is not at all clear that legislative bodies, federal or state, American or British, have adopted the assumption of the previous paragraph: that redistribution is a sine qua non of charitable exemption and deductibility. The British Parliament continued the charitable exemption when the income tax was reintroduced in 1842 with no effort to exclude "schools for the sons of gentlemen," and these schools had recently been determined to be charitable for nontax purposes (Gladstone 1982, 58). Congress has never imposed redistributional requirements. State court decisions during the period 1927–62 in Connecticut, Ohio, and Pennsylvania, interpreting the word *charitable* in property tax exemption statutes, declared the American counterparts to "schools for the sons of gentlemen" to be ineligible for property tax exemption because of failure to make an effort, within reasonable financial limits, to include less advantaged students. In Connecticut, however, the legislature amended the exemption statute to restore tax-free status for such schools (Stewart 1973). And in other jurisdictions the word *educational* in an exemption law has not been held to require such redistributional efforts.

In the face of societal complexity and legislative ambiguity, plus uncertainty about the basic rationale for exemption and deductibility, it is little wonder that taxing authorities and courts have not consistently required that claimants of charitable tax status demonstrate service to the poor (Swain 1984; Persons et al. 1977). Educational institutions need not meet such a test under federal law or under many state property tax laws. Treasury regulations once required that hospitals offer free or reduced-cost services, within the limits of financial feasibility, in order to enjoy §501(c)(3) status, but the IRS relaxed this rule in 1969 to require only that, if there is an emergency room, it must be open to all and that patients having third-party financing must not be turned away from the rest of the hospital. (The 1969 change was struck down by a federal district court but upheld by a federal court of appeals, with the Supreme Court then dismissing the case on procedural grounds [Hopkins 1983, 81–82].)

On the other hand, the IRS has required that consumer credit counseling agencies exclusively serve low-income persons if they wish §501(c)(3) status (Hopkins 1983, 82)—a ruling akin to the IRS position on other service agencies that resemble for-profit firms. The IRS appears willing to treat these agencies as charitable only if they distinguish themselves from their commercial counterparts by providing below-cost services (Persons et al. 1977). Somewhere in be-

tween is the position taken by the IRS on nursing homes: if they provide housing and health services tailored to the needs of the aged, they meet exemption standards by providing services "at the lowest feasible cost" and by not discharging residents who, after being admitted, thereafter "become unable to pay their regular charges" (Hopkins 1983, 93).

Returning to the less regulated end of the spectrum, cultural institutions (so long as they aim to make artistic works widely available) qualify for §501(c)(3) status without redistributive objection from the IRS. Even though the Tax Court has recited the fact that nonprofit theater groups have "the desire to keep ticket prices at a level which is affordable to most of the community,"[36] the IRS has made no significant effort to ensure that either prices or programs of cultural organizations are designed to attract low-income audiences; nor has an attempt been made to raise this issue in legislative, judicial, or academic forums considering federal tax issues. One sometimes reads in the press, as an argument against state property tax exemption for museums or concert halls in elegant locations, the assertion that they are not accessible to low-income members of the community, but I am not aware of any denials of exemption on such redistributional grounds.

Should such a denial be attempted at a federal or state level, addressed to cultural or educational exemptions, it would surely be met with the objection that modern-day charity, and modern-day charitable tax law, serve other important values (some mentioned at the start of this section). In weighing this objection, one would be cast back to basics: to the search for a rationale for exemption or deductibility, or indeed to even more fundamental issues relating to the primacy of redistributional norms in American law.

The Retained Private Benefit Issue

Although the tax case law, rulings, and literature on the redistributional question are fairly thin—in some contexts it is not even discussed—the issue of private benefit retained by the donor has been more fully ventilated. As a result, something approaching a "bright-line standard" has been developed. On the one hand, the receipt of cash or other directly realizable material benefits—or benefits not readily realizable but nevertheless contractually assured—will disqualify or limit a donor's deduction and can cause a denial or revocation of the recipient organization's exemption.[37] Thus, deductions for theater benefits must be reduced by the market value of the tickets received; gifts for environmental projects that enhance the value of the donor's land are nondeductible; an alumni fund-raising program that promised a

---

35. The trend in Great Britain from the seventeenth to the twentieth century is chronicled by Owen (1964); see also chapter 1 in this volume. In the twelfth century, Maimonides anticipated this movement by listing, at the highest level of charitable purity, not alms but loans or gifts that would assist "a poor Jew to put himself on his feet" (Marcus 1938, 364–65).

36. *Plumstead Theatre Society, Inc.* v. *Commissioner*, 74 T.C. 1324 (1980), aff'd 675 F.2d 244 (9th Cir. 1982).

37. A challenge to the deduction is usually based on the notion that, in whole or part, no true contribution was made; an attack on the exemption is based on the notion that the organization is not "organized and operated exclusively for . . . charitable . . . purposes" or that "net earnings" have "inure[d] to the benefit" of the donor (§501(c)(3)). The exemption rules are treated in Treusch and Sugarman (1983) and Hopkins (1983).

priority claim on the best football seats (but no tickets) led to nondeductibility (with the contractual nature of the arrangement playing a major part); and Congress has worked out an elaborate set of rules to preclude donors from retaining economic benefit, at the expense of charity, as a result of making "split interest" gifts—where, for example, the donor retains a life interest or a remainder interest in the donated property (Kurz & Robinson 1977).[38]

On the other hand, private benefits that are not directly realizable in material terms (or contractually assured) do not count. Deductions are not lost because the donor enjoys memorialization on the front of a building or at a testimonial dinner, enhanced college admission opportunities for the donor's child or business relationships for the donor, hopes for salvation or at least the expectation of perpetual prayers, the shared benefits that come with public goods like parks or cleaner air, or the general expectation that somewhere, somehow, the giver will benefit. ("Cast thy bread upon the waters: for thou shalt find it after many days" [Ecclesiastes 11:1; see Ross 1968].) Nor does the fact that the donor's motives were other than selfless defeat the deduction; neither charitable trust law (Bogert & Bogert 1973, 202) nor charitable tax law (Hopkins 1983) requires subjective altruism, despite the teaching of St. Paul: "And though I bestow all my goods to feed the poor . . . and have not charity, it profiteth me nothing" (1 Corinthians 13:3).

Ignoring motive may be a necessity for the tax system; the search for purity of charitable intention would be an unmanageable task, even ignoring the complications caused by psychoanalytic theory. But the *benefit* rules we have canvassed, even though fairly well set forth in the law and literature, have been subjected to demanding scrutiny by very few writers. One of these (Jones 1985) believes that private benefit to the donor is not the issue; the only pertinent question is whether the *charity* gets a "net benefit" commensurate with the donor's tax deduction. This formulation will be resisted by those who are particularly concerned with redistribution and who see it undermined if the donor comes out ahead, even where the charity does not come out behind. It will also be resisted by those who subscribe to the income-defining rationale for deductibility; the retained donor benefit will seem to represent a form of consumption under the Haig-Simons approach.

The Allocative Power Issue

Under this heading we consider not the way in which material benefits are distributed or the way they are captured by the donor but the fact that the income and estate tax deductibility "permits wealthy citizens to outweigh less-wealthy persons in controlling the disposition of taxable income and wealth and, as a corollary, . . . makes it easier for wealthy citizens

to use taxable income or wealth to influence the behavior of others" (Simon 1978, 56). The apparent power imbalance results from the proposition, noted earlier, that, under the present deduction system, the price of giving is lower for an affluent, high-bracket taxpayer than for a poorer one, and that the "after-tax cost of exercising power in the charitable world is cheaper for the rich than the poor" (p. 24).[39] The late Stanley Surrey (1973, 229–30) attacked this process as one that subsidizes the wealthy in a "bizarre upside-down fashion" (see also McDaniel 1977; Good & Wildavsky 1977).

One answer to this challenge lies in the income- and estate-defining rationales. As noted earlier, if they are accepted, the notion of a subsidy drops out and, with it, the claim that the deduction subsidizes the rich. Even apart from the subsidy issue, these theories provide a possible rebuttal to the notion that the deduction reduces the "after-tax cost . . . for the rich": if the donated funds are viewed as never part of the contributor's income subject to taxation, then the after-tax cost is the same for rich and poor. In an earlier essay, however, I suggested that this is an "excessively strenuous application" of these tax-base-defining rationales (Simon 1978, 24n42).

Putting aside alternative rationales for deductibility, a dramatic version of the power allocation phenomenon arises in the foundation context: the foundation mechanism enables a wealthy person to make deductible gifts of assets over which the donor and donor's family can maintain long-term dynastic control involving both managerial and dispositive powers. Congressional critics (Select Committee . . . 1962), the U.S. Treasury Department (1965), and scholarly writers (Stone 1977) have all assaulted the donor control phenomenon, although from differing perspectives. This phenomenon may have contributed to "third-class" treatment for foundations in 1969, and in the 1984 Tax Reform Act, Congress singled out non-donor-controlled entities for exemption from two of the restrictions normally imposed on operating (Ring III) foundations (§§4940(d), 4945(d)(4); see table 5.1).

Is dynastic control of foundations significantly different in kind from the more general allocative power that accrues to a wealthy donor as a result of tax deductibility? I have argued that it is not—that "mainly a balance of convenience distinguishes the power of foundation donors from the power of non-foundation donors" (Simon 1978, 18). "In various ways it is simply easier, through the foundation, to achieve personal or dynastic managerial or dispositive power" (p. 17).

My essay then analyzes the more general allocative power phenomenon, asking whether it violates (1) norms of progressive income and estate taxation or (2) principles of equity and fairness against which all legislation should be judged. Under the first heading, the study examines legislative, judi-

---

38. Retained benefit of this kind would also undermine the case for deductibility under the income- or estate-defining rationales discussed earlier, for such retention can be viewed as personal consumption that is unacceptable under these rationales.

39. The study suggests that, even if the deduction system were replaced by a credit arrangement (discussed above), the allocative power issue would remain, although in muted form.

cial, and scholarly materials to determine whether "the lev-
eling of dynastic power . . . is a significant goal of tax
progressivity," and reaches a negative conclusion (p. 55).
Under the second heading, the study acknowledges the non-
egalitarian tilt of the deduction system but notes that our
society has accepted other forms of class-biased legislation
that seem to meet four criteria set forth in the essay. The first
of these criteria is advancing an "important affirmative social purpose . . . that benefits the classes of persons who are
the 'victims' of the inequality"; the deduction system is
thought to meet this test by encouraging large-scale single-
source gifts—the kind of philanthropy that appears to promote "individuality and variety" within the nonprofit sector
and "the diffusion of power within the larger society" (pp.
62–75). In a subsequent essay, Strnad (1986) lends support
to the benefit-the-victims argument; his economic model of
subsidy structures leads him to conclude that "the deduction's higher subsidy for high-income individuals may be just
a way of insuring economic efficiency and an allocative
mechanism that accords with the preferences of *all* voters
including lower-income and middle-income people who are
not the apparent beneficiaries of the deduction." Strnad thus
takes issue with Hochman and Rodgers (1977), who believe
that a flat-rate tax credit will come closer than a deduction to
achieving such an evenhanded outcome.[40]

The other criteria my essay advances relate to the gravity
and reversibility of the inequality[41] and to the availability of
more egalitarian alternative routes to the same social purpose. Applying the four criteria to the deduction system, the
study concludes that it "comes out with passing grades. It
seems to present a plausible case for survival in a democratic
order" (pp. 84–85).

This analysis of the allocative power problem teems with
theoretical propositions and empirical assumptions that require testing and challenge. Unfortunately, there has been no
in-depth debate that would call forth such scrutiny.[42]

---

40. Zimmerman (1985, 28) suggests that a credit would mitigate the
tendency of the tax subsidy system (in its deduction mode) to favor gifts
to cultural and higher education institutions that are not "generally
targeted on the poor," as compared to religious organizations where
"much of the charitable work . . . is devoted to the poor." But Andrews
(1972, 354) argues that "the net effect of substituting a credit for a
deduction would be to tax some contributors on their contributions while
subsidizing others."

41. The reversibility criterion raises the question of ease of repeal of
an inegalitarian measure. The charitable deduction confers what its
critics deem disproportionate allocational power on a small fraction of
the population (those in higher brackets) and is, therefore, readily
reversible by a disapproving majority. In fact, however, the public
overwhelmingly favors it (Simon 1978, 84), although, of course, that
may be a function of not understanding how it works. This phenomenon
is dealt with in detail by Strnad (1986).

42. Michael Fitts, however, has been preparing a rebuttal of one
important part of my essay, which will be published by the Yale Program
on Non-Profit Organizations. Among other things, Fitts questions the
assumption that encouraging large-scale giving by high-income donors
necessarily results in the large-scale *gifts* on which my analysis places a
high value.

The Discrimination or Preference Issue

The general debate that has been missing in the allocative
power field has been flowering in the discrimination-prefer-
ence area, triggered by the controversy over the tax status of
"segregation academies" in the South (including IRS denial
of tax-exempt status and congressional response thereto
[Schwarz & Hutton 1984]) and by the prolonged *Bob Jones
University* litigation (ending with a Supreme Court denial of
exempt status on grounds of racial discrimination [*Bob Jones
University* v. *United States*, 461 U.S. 574 (1983)]).

Some of the debate about tax exemption and deductibility
for racially discriminatory groups involves the constitutional
question whether the acts of an entity enjoying §501(c)(3)
status constitute "state action," thus invoking the constraints imposed by the Equal Protection and Due Process
Clauses of the Constitution and the implementing provisions
of the 1866 Civil Rights Acts. A panel of the federal Court of
Appeals so held in the context of a private foundation accused of employment discrimination; a tie vote of the full
court defeated an effort to obtain reconsideration by that
court (*Jackson* v. *Statler Foundation*, 496 F.2d 623 [2d Cir.
1974]). And a federal district court held that the exemption of
investment income earned by a fraternal organization (Ring I
on our chart) was a sufficient government benefit to bring the
state action doctrine into play and bar racial discrimination
(*McGlotten* v. *Connally*, 338 F.Supp. 448 [D.D.C. 1972]).
Yet the latter decision has been criticized for the way it has
gone about "constitutionalizing" the tax code (Bittker &
Kaufman 1972), and the former decision has been condemned for blurring the time-honored distinction between
public and private institutions and threatening the autonomy
of private nonprofit groups (Judge Henry Friendly's dissent,
496 F.2d at 636). Fears and objections of this kind dissuaded
the nonprofit organizations filing briefs in the *Bob Jones* case
from seeking a constitutional decision from the Supreme
Court.

In point of fact, the IRS attack on the tax status of discriminating organizations and the Supreme Court's treatment of
Bob Jones University have employed a *non*constitutional
approach based on §501(c)(3), which, the Supreme Court
held, incorporates the common law of charity.[43] That law in
turn can be said to deny charitable status to racially discriminatory groups on two similar-sounding but significantly different grounds: (1) the doctrine that a charitable gift or trust
fails if its terms violate some public policy embodied in the
criminal law or otherwise clearly enunciated as a legal norm,
and (2) the concept that a charitable body must serve some
public purpose and confer a public benefit. The IRS had relied
on the first of these approaches in denying exempt status to
discriminatory schools (Rev. Rul. 71–447, 1971–2 C.B.
230), and a federal three-judge court came out the same way

---

43. Although the Court did not use a constitutional avenue to its
outcome, it had to consider—and rejected—a constitutional challenge
by Bob Jones University, which claimed that denial of tax exemption
infringed its free exercise of religion.

on the same ground.[44] The Supreme Court's decision in *Bob Jones,* however, seemed to rely on *both* of these approaches, despite the concern of commentators that the second approach opened the door to IRS determinations that unorthodox or unpopular groups do not advance the public purpose and therefore should not enjoy §501(c)(3) treatment (K. Simon 1981; Galston 1981). The first approach, requiring a finding that the challenged activity directly violates some clearly enunciated legal norm, appears to be more narrowly constructed and thus less open to official manipulation. Yet there is a degree of danger in any resort to public policy or public interest criteria for tax exemption, as Justice Powell observed in his *Bob Jones* concurring opinion (103 S.Ct. at 2038–9; see also Simon et al. 1972, 152–53). It is conceivable, if not likely, that these standards could be used to deny tax deductibility to groups favoring homosexual rights or *opposing* (through lawful means) black or women's rights, with grave consequences for the pluralism the nonprofit sector is widely valued for nurturing.

These possible outcroppings—and the resistance to them—are one aspect of the unfinished business of the *Bob Jones* case. Another has to do with the treatment of gender discrimination or preferential arrangements that favor minority or disadvantaged groups—the subject of a great deal of landmark litigation outside the tax field (for example, *Regents* v. *Bakke,* 438 U.S. 265 [1978]) but largely unplowed soil in the tax area. Schwarz and Hutton (1984, 657–58) mention some of the pending issues:

> Will a school practicing gender discrimination qualify as "charitable"? What about a church that discriminates on the basis of race or an orthodox Jewish school with no minority enrollment? Does a charitable trust that grants scholarships only to Caucasians violate the public policy standard of *Bob Jones?* What about a foundation that makes scholarship awards only to students of minority races?

The authors report that early returns suggest that the IRS is not opposed to §501(c)(3) status for either the Caucasian-only or the minority-only funds (p. 658). The questions the authors pose, however, will continue to be troublesome for the IRS, the courts, and tax policy scholars.[45]

THE POLICE FUNCTION OF NONPROFIT TAX LAW

The police function involves the federal tax system in an extensive program of regulating the fiduciary behavior of nonprofit trustees, managers, and donors. As we contemplate this central fact, the obvious first question is: why is this function within the jurisdiction of the tax system? Upon a slightly closer look, we ask a second question: why are the foundations (Rings III and IV) regulated so much more rigorously than the public charities (Ring II) or the noncharitable nonprofits (Ring I)?

The Jurisdictional Puzzle

What sharpens the first, jurisdictional question is the contrast with the support and equity functions. These are strongly linked to the definition of charitable activity—and therefore to definitional questions that must be taken into account in granting or denying exempt status—whereas the police function is less closely connected to these questions. To be sure, it can be contended that fiduciary regulation is essential to ensure that a group is "organized and operated exclusively for . . . charitable purposes." Yet Hooper (1985) suggests that this is true only with respect to one of the two main branches of fiduciary duty: the duty of loyalty (to the ultimate charitable beneficiaries and the commands of the charitable charter). With respect to the other fiduciary branch, the duty of care, a fiduciary's negligent and wasteful administration impairs a nonprofit's ability to perform but does not affect its charitable purpose and character[46]—presumably the central concerns of the exemption and deductibility statutes.

Moreover, if one takes into account the availability of alternative regulatory mechanisms (that is, other than the tax system's police function) for handling fiduciary enforcement, questions arise about whether either the duty of loyalty or the duty of care needs IRS policing. Both of these duties are the historic concern of the state courts, successors to the English chancellors in equity who regulated the fiduciary conduct of private trustees; these courts and the state attorneys general, who are the moving parties in fiduciary enforcement, have jurisdiction over nonprofits chartered or operating in their territories. The customary response to the suggestion that the tax system yield fiduciary jurisdiction to the states is that many of the state attorneys general are understaffed, inexperienced, or uninterested, or (along with some judges) in thrall to local nonprofit barons. In rebuttal, it has been suggested that some of the states are well equipped to carry out the enforcement function, that there are ways of assisting the other states to improve, and that perhaps "a decent regard for the desirable features of federalism" should encourage exploration of these possibilities (Simon 1965, 70).[47]

---

44. *Green* v. *Connally,* 330 F.Supp. 1150 (D.D.C. 1971), *aff'd mem. sub. nom. Coit* v. *Green,* 404 U.S. 997 (1971).

45. The ability of courts to deal with these matters at all will depend in part on the ability of contesting parties to obtain standing to be heard in court. The Supreme Court held in 1984 that persons cannot complain about IRS policies unless they can show direct personal injury traceable to those policies (*Allen* v. *Wright,* 104 S.Ct. 3315 [1984]).

46. Paul DiMaggio points out that gross mismanagement could result in such a shortfall in service, or force such a dramatic shift to fee-paying clientele, as to alter the character and defeat the purpose of the nonprofit organization.

47. Some observers have suggested a solution involving neither the IRS nor the states: assigning supervisory responsibility to a special (non-IRS) unit within the Treasury Department or creating a new, specialized federal agency for charitable supervision somewhat on the British model (see Ginsburg et al. 1977; Carson & Hodson, 1973). These proposals and arguments raise both theoretical issues (as to the allocation of regulatory functions within our federal structure) and empirical questions (as to the relative efficacy and capacity of IRS and other federal and state agencies) that await further exploration.

It must be said, however, that there is little movement in the mid-1980s for altering the present IRS-based policing system. Indeed, the foundation legislation of 1969 represented a move toward even greater reliance on the IRS, as the following discussion makes clear.

Policing the Foundations

Although there is no specific code of fiduciary behavior that informs tax policing of Ring I or Ring II organizations—the general "organized and operated exclusively for . . . charitable purposes" language is the global legislation on which IRS and courts rely—the *foundations* operate under a much more detailed set of legislative rules. These rules, referred to in table 5.1, are the following:

1. The "self-dealing" rules (§4941) impose outright prohibitions on certain kinds of transactions between a foundation and its fiduciaries or donors, whether or not the transactions are unfair to the foundation—as compared to the standards applicable to public charities, where the test is fairness: would the transaction have resulted from arms-length bargaining between strangers?

2. The "pay-out" rule (§4942), which requires annual distributions equalling 5 percent of investment assets, can affect fiduciary behavior by inducing foundation managers to make investment assets more productive of current income in order to reach the required distribution level without a forced sale of foundation assets. Public charities operate under no comparable strictures, although an excessively stingy pay-out policy might lead to attack under the "operated exclusively" clause.

3. The "jeopardizing investment" rule (§4944) directly regulates the investment practices of foundation managers. Even though the Treasury regulations call for a "whole portfolio" approach rather than scrutiny of each individual investment (Reg. §53.4944–1(a)(2)), the constraints on speculation or nondiversification are considerably greater than those applying to public charities under the "operated exclusively" clause (Bittker 1973).

4. The "excess business holding" rule (§4943), which effectively precludes foundation or joint foundation-donor control of a business corporation and which will be discussed further below, represents another form of fiduciary regulation not imposed on public charities. Some, but not all, of the objections to foundation-donor corporate control were framed in terms of breach of fiduciary duty.

The 1969 act policed other foundation practices not related to fiduciary duty. Two such provisions regulate a foundation's granting of travel-study funds to individuals and require a foundation to exercise "expenditure responsibility" over its grants to nonpublic charities (§§4945(d)(3),(4)(B)).

Not only does the 1969 law impose a more detailed and stringent set of substantive rules on foundations than on public charities; it sets up a more assiduous sanctioning system. Public charities accused of fiduciary misconduct risk loss of exemption. Although draconian, this result does not derive from a deliberate congressional sanctioning decision but is the natural consequence of an IRS determination that the organization no longer meets the §501(c)(3) test of "operated exclusively for . . . charitable purposes." Moreover, such an "all or nothing sanction" leads to "breakdown of enforcement" (New York State Bar . . . 1965, 713), for the IRS hesitates to request such an outcome, and the courts even more rarely decree it. By contrast, when enacting the 1969 law for foundations, Congress created a special set of sanctions: penalty taxes imposed on both the foundations and the managers or donors involved in the transaction—a set of sanctions that, with a single exception unrelated to the police function, is not imposed on public charities. Ironically, at the same time as it created these penalty taxes, Congress paid at least formal respect to the role of the states. The 1969 act required that the charter (or other controlling instrument) of every foundation be amended to include all the policing restrictions imposed by Congress through the tax system, thus giving state attorneys general and courts an extra enforcement tool: the capacity to complain of a violation of the foundation's own charter. But this bow to the states was accompanied by the imposition, for the first time, of a direct federal penalty unrelated to the tax exemption or deductibility status of the foundation.

Accordingly, the jurisdictional questions that arise generally in connection with the police function take on special force in the foundation area; here, Congress went beyond imposing conditions on exemption (as in the case of the public charities) and created a special regulatory tax. Constitutionally, the taxing power is virtually unchallengeable, but as a matter of legislative appropriateness, eyebrows may well be raised about the use of the taxing power to regulate conduct traditionally consigned to state control and with no conventional federal interest present (such as protection of interstate commerce or enforcement of federal constitutional rights). This subject has received surprisingly scant treatment from the research community.[48] The substantive question—the justification for the foundation policing rules themselves—has received somewhat greater attention; the rules have been defended in U.S. Treasury Department (1965, 1969) and congressional reports (for example, Senate Report no. 91–552) and questioned by some scholars (Bittker 1973). Once again, however, full theoretical and empirical examination remains to be performed.

THE BORDER PATROL FUNCTION OF NONPROFIT TAX LAW

In its efforts to keep nonprofit organizations from wandering off their reservation into the territory of government and

---

48. I have raised questions about the use of federal power in this area (1965). Specifically on the issue of federal excise taxes, Loeser (1986) is examining the use of this taxing power in the special context of the lobbying restrictions applicable to public charities. And see Troyer (1973) on the constitutionality of excise taxes imposed on foundations that engage in lobbying.

business, the tax system reaches far and wide. Here we sketch the scope of this border patrol function, outline the arguments surrounding it, and briefly discuss the research, past and potential, that bears on these arguments.

The Government Border

The Restraints

The federal tax code limits the channels through which non-profits can participate in public affairs activities, here defined as "those activities which seek to study, criticize, inform people about, and modify the actions of the executive, legislative, and judicial branches of government at all levels" (Simon 1973, 61). The prohibitions bind some groups more than others. Although Ring I organizations are minimally restricted (see table 5.1), public charities (Ring II) operate under these constraints:

- They are totally prohibited from engaging in electoral politics (§501(c)(3)), although educational programs may indirectly assist a candidate's cause.

- They are prevented from engaging in legislative activity beyond an "insubstantial" degree, unless they elect to come under an optional rule imposing certain percentage ceilings on direct lobbying and lower ceilings on grassroots legislative action (§4911).[49] These limitations do give way to fairly substantial exceptions; for example, legislative activity does not include disseminating the results of "nonpartisan analysis, study or research" or providing testimony in response to a written request from a legislative committee. Where these exceptions do not apply, the lobbying charity must either (1) navigate within the vague "insubstantiality" rule in order to retain exemption (a restraint, as noted above, upheld by the Supreme Court as a valid condition on a federal "subsidy") or (2), if the charity elects the percentage option, face special penalty taxes if the ceiling is breached.

- They are subject to special rules regulating the financing and control of public interest litigation (Hopkins 1983, 109–11).

Some public charities seek to gain their public affairs ends through public education rather than through direct participation in the governmental arena. These groups may have to meet a rule recently proposed by the IRS making §501(c)(3) status depend on the degree to which the educational program relies on unsupported views, factually distorted presentations, and emotionally based inflammatory statements (Schwarz & Hutton 1984).[50]

If the nonprofit organization is a foundation (Rings III or IV) rather than a public charity, the foregoing restrictions are augmented by the following:

- An absolute prohibition on lobbying, that is, without the ability either to rely on an "insubstantiality" defense or to elect a percentage ceiling option, although most of the exceptions to the public charity lobbying rules apply to foundations as well, and a foundation is not chargeable with lobbying by public charities using the foundation's grant if it was not earmarked for lobbying (§4945(d)(1), Reg. §53.4945–2(a)(5)).

- A rigorous restriction on conduct or support of voter registration activities, including a requirement that the voter program be conducted on a multistate, multifunder basis (§4945(d)(2)).

Moreover, these foundation rules are backed up by the penalty tax sanctions described in the police function discussion above, and by a regular foundation audit program under which the agents appear to devote special effort to the search for evidence of possible violations of the lobbying restrictions.[51]

Looking at both the public charity and the foundation rules, it appears that the only variety of public affairs activity that is unrestricted for all nonprofits is the monitoring of the policies and performance of government agencies (Fleming 1972; Douglas & Wildavsky 1978). This activity, too, would have been barred to foundations under a tentative proposal by the House Committee on Ways and Means (1969, 4) that foundations be precluded from "any activities intended . . . to influence the decision of any government body." The proposal was soon dropped by the committee, although, in a nontax setting, a rule very much like the Ways and Means proposal was temporarily adopted by the Office of Management and Budget in 1981 as a criterion for federal grant and contract eligibility for nonprofit and for-profit entities.

Explaining the Restraints

What explains this network of tax law restraints? Postponing a discussion of the general theory of border patrol, let us briefly review the specific arguments that are made in behalf of fencing charities out of the public affairs arena—arguments categorized as follows in my essay on foundations in public affairs (1973):

- *Definitional* arguments, based largely on assumptions about the etymological and historical meaning of *charity,* or on the administrative difficulty of determining when political activity is charitable.

- *Effectiveness* arguments, contending that charitable involvement in public affairs controversy is either unneces-

---

49. The right to elect these percentage limitations is denied to church groups—at their own request. This somewhat surprising scenario is discussed by Alexander (1978).

50. An earlier IRS test, requiring the educational organization to present a "full and fair exposition of the pertinent facts," was held to be unconstitutionally vague (*Big Mama Rag, Inc.* v. *United States,* 631 F.2d 1030 [D.C. Cir. 1980]).

51. This statement is based on the author's own experience and conversations with foundation executives.

sary in terms of social need or dangerously divisive and polarizing.

- *Normative* arguments, contending that public affairs activity offends against "(1) a concept of fair play as between users of pre-tax and after-tax dollars (the 'unfair competition argument') and (2) a concept that it is undemocratic for 'nonaccountable' institutions to use 'public' funds to affect the outcome of governmental decisions (the 'shadow government argument')" (Simon 1973, 73).

- A *prudential* argument, suggesting that, at least as a matter of self-regulation, charities eschew public affairs activity because "politicization" of charity might provoke political reprisal and loss of legally favored status.

Full discussion of these arguments requires consideration of history, social science, and tax theory materials that cannot be addressed in this space. It is also true that

> the answer to all the arguments considered under both the "normative" and "effectiveness" headings is, to some degree, empirical. For example, . . . the answer to the "unfair competition" argument admits the possibility of litigation between an exempt organization and a nonexempt individual, but suggests that such a clash is in fact highly unlikely; and the answer to the "shadow government" objection concedes that a foundation might be able to swamp the decision-making processes in a small polity—but contends that this is a fairly remote possibility. (Simon 1973, 91)

In the absence of adequate data on these points, I resolved the public affairs controversy *against* government restrictions by relying on a threshold "presumption in favor of full participation, by all individuals and groups in society, in all of the processes by which our public policies are formulated" (p. 64). But although presumptions are a legitimate aid to near-term resolution of difficult policy matters, they do not obviate the need for research. In this field, a full and difficult agenda waits to be tackled.

The Business Border

Turning from the nonprofit-government border to the nonprofit-business border, we find that the federal tax law has erected two forms of fences that restrict (1) *commercial activity* by nonprofit entities and (2) *business ownership* by foundations.

Restraints on Commercial Activity

The commercial activity issue has come increasingly to the fore in the 1980s as voluntary organizations of all kinds have scrambled to cope with the combined impact of government reductions in the rate of social service and cultural spending (thus thrusting greater burdens on the nonprofits), government reductions in the rate of grant and contract support for the nonprofits themselves, and charitable giving levels that have not increased fast enough to make up the gap (Urban Institute 1983). The nonprofits' course, predictably enough, has been a rush toward earned income—increased reliance on fees for services, entry into new or expanded forms of commercial operations (whether or not related to the nonprofit's charter purposes), and acquisition of revenue-producing assets distinct from traditional passive investment holdings (Crimmins & Keil 1983; chapter 21 in this volume). The approach was foreshadowed in a *New Yorker* cartoon (December 15, 1976) depicting Santa Claus saying to his elves: "I've been thinking. This year, instead of *giving* everything away, why don't we charge a little something?" Some of the more colorful recent examples of "charging a little something" include the operation of a blackjack casino by North Dakota social service agencies and the acquisition of a Nevada brothel by the Moapa tribe of the Paiute Indians (*New York Times*, November 4, 1984, 31).

Earned income activities have been largely responsible, according to Salamon (see chapter 6 in this volume), for the fact that many nonprofits have weathered the recent fiscal climate better than might have been expected. But these activities have also generated fresh interest in tax law border patrol along the charity-commerce front. For one thing, there have been demands for strengthening of the principal border patrol instrument: the tax on unrelated business income of nonprofit organizations (§§511 ff.). This tax, originally enacted by Congress in 1950 in the wake of New York University's indirect acquisition of a macaroni company, is imposed on a "trade or business" that is "regularly carried on" by a nonprofit and not "substantially related" to the nonprofit's exempt purposes. The legislative history of the tax reflects a congressional desire to avoid "unfair competition" between taxable and nontaxable businesses, although alternative explanations of the tax, not based on competitive considerations, have been developed (Schwarz & Hutton 1984, 680).

As the traffic in nonprofit commerce has grown, the IRS has undertaken new and more controversial enforcement measures relating to the tax on unrelated business income, which have led to litigation over group insurance programs, advertising, sales of mailing lists, and many other income-generating activities (Schwarz & Hutton 1984, 681–92). Moreover, small business groups, including a branch of the U.S. Small Business Administration (1984), have sought to cut back on the large number of exceptions Congress has grafted on to the tax over the years (for example, an exception for nonprofits doing basic scientific research, an exception for work performed by volunteers)—and, indeed, to tax even the "related" business income of nonprofit organizations. Earlier efforts to expand the coverage of the tax resulted in a repeal of the special exemption for church groups (it probably would have been declared unconstitutional in any event [Joblove 1984]) and in a shrinkage of the exception for rental income (§514). The more recent efforts to strengthen the tax, however, have not yet achieved success, partly because of the fiscal woes recited by the charitable groups in opposing tougher rules—and partly, perhaps, because the theoretical and empirical justification for the unrelated business income tax is itself controversial.[52]

The theoretical controversy turns on alternative hypotheses about the impact of tax exemption on competitive fairness. There appears to be general agreement that property tax exemption assists a nonprofit in a contest with taxable competitors. With respect to the federal income tax, however, opinion is divided. The assumption underlying passage of the 1950 legislation appears to have been that exemption permitted charities to undercut the prices of their taxable competitors and also allowed expansion with "free" capital—in the form of nontaxed retained earnings—not available to nonexempt rivals. Some economists rebut the first of these propositions on the ground that income taxes are not a "factor of production" that enters into price setting. Similarly, Bittker and Rahdert (1976, 319) have questioned "why the price level that had maximized both the pretax and after-tax profits of the enterprise before [acquisition by a tax-exempt organization] would not continue to maximize its profits thereafter." Hansmann (1981b, 28) contends, however, that the "free" capital proposition makes sense if it is interpreted to mean that "exemption from income taxation does permit nonprofit firms to grow faster than they could if they were taxed, and it does give them an incentive to grow, and ultimately perhaps to take markets away from for-profit firms, in a broader range of conditions than would be the case without exemption."

Another perspective comes from Rose-Ackerman (1982), who argues that the relevant unfairness issue raised by exemption does not involve competition between firms in the same industry but competition between firms in industries with "tax-favored firms" and firms in those industries without "tax-favored firms." The latter problem, she contends, arises when nonprofits turn from "unrelated" (and therefore taxable) commercial activities to "related" commercial activities in industries whose firms had not previously faced competition from nonprofit, "tax-favored" enterprises.

To those who see the nonprofit firm as enjoying competitive tax advantages, the National Assembly has recently responded, on behalf of its nonprofit agency members, that small businesses enjoy a congeries of tax advantages of their own, buttressed with Small Business Administration preferences, that at least offset any benefits that accrue to the nonprofits (Wellford & Gallagher 1985).

Empirical work has not kept pace with the theoretical debate. Hansmann (1982) examined the impact of a variety of state taxes on the relative prevalence of nonprofit and for-profit firms in various jurisdictions, finding, inter alia, that state income taxes made a difference—thus suggesting that federal income tax exemption may give a competitive advantage to nonprofit competitors. Yet we lack field investiga-

tions that examine concrete competitive arenas—and the behavior of nonprofit and for-profit firms within them—in a way that would cast light on the various theories mentioned above (see Bittker & Rahdert 1976, 320–21). It does not appear, for example, that there have been detailed case studies of specific settings in which competitive unfairness has been alleged—for example, the research, travel, and stationery industries discussed by Spiro (1979) and the other industries listed by Pires (1985)—in order to examine what tax or nontax factors have played an influential role. Such evidence could help congressional committees weigh the claims made in the course of the current debate over the tax on unrelated business income. This evidence could also throw light on another tax fairness issue not usually mentioned in the literature: the question of whether the ability of a §501(c)(3) organization to receive deductible contributions and foundation grants provides it with a financing capacity that has competitive consequences distinct from the impact of tax exemption.

Controversies over *state* tax exemption for charities also raise the specter of competitive advantage from time to time. Complaints about nonprofits enjoying commercial income while occupying tax-exempt real estate include claims of a competitive foul. And such claims sometimes trigger action by state or local tax officials to revoke property tax exemptions of groups engaging in commercial activity.[53] Even though, as noted, there is more agreement about the effects of property tax exemption than about the effects of income tax exemption, the issue of competitive unfairness resulting from property tax relief has undergone a degree of theoretical and empirical scrutiny even less searching than similar issues arising under federal taxation.

Unfair competition is not the only rationale for patrol, via the tax system, of the charity-commerce border. Other concerns may provoke requests that the border be tightened: a desire to minimize revenue loss through exemption; a fear that if the world of charity, through a process of isomorphism (DiMaggio & Powell 1982), comes to look too much like the world of business, public support for the nonprofit sector—in terms of funds, volunteering, or legislative support—will weaken; the prospect of charitable goals and values being abandoned in the rush for revenue; and, more generally, the possible erosion of a sectoral division of labor in the society—to be returned to below. To each of these worries there is a possible answer, in addition to the more general response that the tax system should not be used to vindicate non-tax-related anxieties; these rebuttals, however, cannot be developed here.

Another border patrol issue involves commercial ventures between nonprofit and for-profit entities to enable both par-

---

52. Similar controversy regarding unfair competition issues is encountered in discussions of the possibility that "too much" commercial activity will not only trigger the tax on unrelated business income but result in a total revocation of the organization's exemption. The revocation question has been examined in great detail by Gallagher (1984).

53. The operation of fitness centers by nonprofit organizations, such as YMCAs, has prompted some of these tax-exemption controversies. Complaints by for-profit racquet clubs are reported to have led to revocation proceedings against the YMCA in Multanomak County (Portland), Oregon, which resulted in a county assessor's decision that all YMCA property should be restored to the tax rolls and taxes assessed for past years as well (*Wall Street Journal*, March 31, 1986, 2d sec., p. 1).

ties to benefit from income tax business deductions and credits captured by the for-profit. One such mechanism is the limited partnership, which the nonprofit organization forms and joins as a general partner in order to attract for-profit investors into, for example, a housing or theatrical venture; the investors can shelter their personal taxable income with partnership write-offs, and their capital is thereby attracted to the charitable enterprise. A second mechanism is the sale and lease-back: here, property owned by a nonprofit—property that could give rise to depreciation allowances, investment tax credits, and other write-offs in the hands of a taxable (for-profit) owner—is sold to such an entity, which leases it back to the nonprofit under terms that allow the two parties to share in the tax savings enjoyed by the taxable owner. The IRS has attacked some of the partnership arrangements on the ground that the nonprofit general partner, in order to honor its fiduciary duty to the other partners, may have to sacrifice the interests of charity, thereby violating the "operated exclusively for . . . charitable purposes" clause (Philanthropy Monthly 1984).[54] And both of these mechanisms have been restricted in recent tax legislation limiting depreciation allowances and the investment tax credit in these settings (§168(j)). Scholarly critiques have challenged these legislative and administrative border patrol measures (Schill 1984; Pang 1985), but here, as in the competitive unfairness case, empirical investigation—scrutinizing, for example, the factual basis for the IRS fiduciary concerns—has not been forthcoming.

Restraints on Business Ownership

The nonprofit-business border patrol measures mentioned so far—taxing unrelated business income and restricting joint ventures—apply to all nonprofits (Rings I through IV). However, here as elsewhere in nonprofit law, foundations are subject to an extra degree of constraint not imposed on the other nonprofits. Organizations in Rings I and II can hold corporate control stock, that is, a sufficient number of shares to give the nonprofit, alone or in conjunction with the donor of the stock, working control of the company. Foundations are effectively barred from these investments. The "excess business holdings" provision of the 1969 Tax Reform Act (§4943), crudely summarized (it may well be the most complicated section in the entire code), requires foundations to divest themselves of business interests that, combined with interests held by donors and other related persons, amount to more than 20 percent of the voting power of a company. Foundations possessing such excess business holdings as of May 1969 were given long periods of time (ten to thirty-five years, depending on control percentages) to achieve divestiture, but after May 1969 foundations were not permitted to acquire such holdings by purchase, and if they received them by gift or bequest, they were required to dispose of them in five years.

At lengthy hearings held before a House subcommittee in 1983 (Subcommittee on Oversight 1983), foundations expressed their concerns about the impact of these provisions, and the Treasury pointed to the evils §4943 was supposed to correct. The outcome, a year later, was a rather modest hardship relief provision for foundations subject to the five-year divestiture schedule (§4943(c)(7)). Perhaps the reason for the somewhat inconclusive outcome was the fact that so little data were available—in 1983 or when the original law was passed in 1969—to throw light on the claims and counterclaims about §4943.

Thus, the Senate Finance Committee report on the 1969 Tax Reform Act (Committee on Finance 1969) set forth three concerns about foundation participation in corporate control:

> [1]Those who wish to use a foundation's stockholdings to retain business control in some cases are relatively unconcerned about producing income to be used by the foundation for charitable purposes. . . . [2] Even when the foundation attains a degree of independence from its major donor, there is a temptation for the foundation's managers to divert their interest to the maintenance and improvement of the business and away from their charitable duties. . . . [3] Where the charitable purposes predominate, the business may be run in a way which unfairly competes with other businesses. (pp. 449–50; numbers added)[55]

Only in support of the first claim (low productivity) was any aggregate data submitted by the Treasury in 1969—information rebutted by my calculations (Simon 1965; revised data appear in Troyer 1966, 987–88)—and no subsequent effort was made to update this information. No evidence at all was offered in support of the second claim (diversion) (see Bittker 1973, 151–52). And only a single illustration was offered, in a U.S. Treasury Department report (1965), in support of the third claim (unfair competition).

On the other hand, there was a comparable absence of solid empirical grounding for the concerns, expressed in 1969 and 1983, about the negative impact of the excess business holdings rule. These asserted fears fell into the following categories, which I outlined in a statement for the 1983 House hearings (Subcommittee on Oversight 1983, 1626–47):

1. The provision may force stock divestiture at fire-sale prices, thus causing unintended windfalls for buyers or diverting investment resources from urgent capital needs.

2. The provision may cause sales of corporate control stock to chains or conglomerates, thus reducing the diversity of corporate ownership, frustrating the congressional policy

---

54. The Treasury does approve these arrangements where the partnership instrument permits the charity to act solely in the service of its exempt purposes (Schwarz & Hutton 1984, 693).

55. Another possible complaint about foundation corporate control—that it can facilitate dynastic control of business corporations, free of the impact of the estate tax—was not advanced by the House committee. It is discussed in Simon (1965, 1978). This is not an aspect of the corporate control problem that is amenable to empirical evaluation; the issues are largely normative.

that favors continuity of family businesses, or withdrawing jobs from local communities.

3. The provision may discourage the flow of funds into the foundation field, thus restricting the foundation birthrate (with adverse consequences for the strength and diversity of foundation funding) or reducing total resources going to the nonprofit sector at a time of need.

4. The provision limits the allocational freedom of persons whose wealth is tied up in an ongoing business, as compared to those with more liquid forms of property.

Although the fourth point is not susceptible to empirical proof, the others are, but they have been the object of very little investigation. A few foundations have testified about the difficulty of getting a fair price for their excess business holdings or about the scarcity of nonchain buyers, but the general situation does not appear to have been surveyed.[56]

A Larger View of Border Patrol

Analyzing the tax law's efforts to police both the nonprofit-government and the nonprofit-business borders reveals a slim body of theoretical work and an even thinner empirical base. Many of the research questions that deserve scholarly attention have been specified in these pages, with at least the implicit suggestion that this agenda be taken seriously. Candor, however, compels the speculation that border patrol may be one of those areas observed by Lindblom and Cohen (1979) where beliefs are too strongly held to be modified by research findings. It may seem farfetched to assume that Congress, or the American people, care very deeply about what we have called border patrol; it sounds like a fairly recondite topic to engage strong passions.

Power and *order*, however, are themes that generate heat, and both are implicated in the border patrol function. The notion of relatively nonaccountable groups wielding power over the country's governmental and business institutions may explain some of the tax measures we have canvassed. This surmise may be especially plausible when explaining the extraordinary rigor of border patrol constraints imposed on foundations, for, as noted earlier, they are the least "accountable" inhabitants of the nonprofit world (Simon 1978, 9). "Ironically, however, it is quite possible that 'foundation power' is less, rather than more, impressive outside the nonprofit bailiwick than it is within that sector," because of various political and legal control mechanisms that make it difficult for foundations—and for that matter other nonprofits—to wield power in the marketplace or polity (Simon 1978, 9–10).

An even broader ground for border patrol measures lies in the concept of order in institutional arrangements. That no-

tion probably buttresses our adherence to the concept of separation of powers (executive, legislative, judicial), our efforts to keep federal-state jurisdictional lines straight, and our fascination with organization charts. The nonprofit entities that stray from their territory are thus guilty of disorderly conduct, of minding someone else's business. This speculation may not survive sustained scrutiny. But if it does, then another irony presents itself: that in our quest for order via border patrol, we may have ignored another fundamental American credo—that of checks and balances. Although nonprofits may not be able to exert conclusive power over other institutions, they can at least question and challenge and suggest alternate approaches. Here, perhaps, we find the quintessential contribution that our third sector makes to the health of the social order. Do border patrol tax measures limit that check-and-balance role? In the scholarly tradition, we leave this section with that question.

CONCLUSION

The place that the tax system—particularly the federal tax system—occupies in the nonprofit sector has become ever more central in recent decades; the support and regulatory functions covered above have become an increasingly important factor shaping the behavior of America's third sector. To some extent, taxation's presence was bound to grow, given the historically indissoluble relationship between taxes and charity noted at the start of this chapter and given also the ineluctable tendency of governmental support to beget governmental regulation.

What is striking, however, is the degree to which the tax system's forays into the nonprofit realm have been unaccompanied by a coherent theory of intervention or by empirical support for intervention. Thus, as we have noted, the support function itself—when viewed as a system to induce giving—is not based on any well-developed motivational theory of giving or a comprehensive body of evidence on the subject. The equity function is not grounded on an adequate rationale for or against a redistributional role for charity, or any empirical data about its redistributional impact. The justification for part of the police function of the tax system is hard to discern, as are both the theoretical and the empirical underpinnings for much of the border patrol function.

So far, the consequences of this somewhat carefree growth in tax jurisdiction do not appear to have been baleful. True, there has been some impact on the overall configuration of the nonprofit sector. Thus, the foundation regulations, restricting corporate control and other behavior, may well have slowed the birthrate within the foundation field and therefore limited the diversity of the nonprofit sector's ecology. Despite the breadth and depth of the tax system's shadow, however, it has not yet appeared to affect the autonomy and health of the vast majority of nonprofit organizations. In part that happy result flows from the rather remarkable self-denying ordinance under which Congress and the IRS have lived: refusing, for the most part, to seek program-

---

56. The third point listed above—involving the flow of funds to foundations and the birthrate consequences—is the subject of a joint study being conducted by the Yale Program on Non-Profit Organizations and the Council on Foundations, referred to in *n*30.

matic control, that is, declining to intervene into the substantive decisions of nonprofit institutions and their donors. But further proliferation of tax regulation could have consequences for the program decisions—and therefore the independence—of the independent sector.

This may, therefore, be the moment for a moratorium on further tax regulation of the nonprofit sector—a time to catch our collective breaths, a time to think through and test the justification for where we are and where, in the years to come, we seem to be heading.

REFERENCES

Adler, Phillip. 1922. Historical origin of tax exemption of charitable institutions. In *Tax Exemption on Real Estate—An Increasing Menace, Part I*. Westchester County, N.Y.: Chamber of Commerce. (Quoted in Belknap, cited below.)

Alexander, James. 1978. The Tax Reform Act of 1976: Does it stand the constitutional challenge? Paper prepared for Yale Law School seminar, New Haven, Conn.

American Association of Fund-Raising Counsel. 1985. *Giving USA—Annual Report 1985*. New York: American Association of Fund-Raising Counsel.

Andrews, William D. 1972. Personal deductions in an ideal income tax. *Harvard Law Review* 86, no. 2 (December):309–85.

Balk, Alfred. 1971. *The Free List*. New York: Russell Sage Foundation.

Belknap, Chauncey. 1977. The federal income tax treatment of charitable organizations: Its origins and underlying policy. In Commission on Private Philanthropy and Public Needs, *Research Papers*. Vol. 4, 2025–43. Washington, D.C.: Treasury Department.

Bittker, Boris I. 1972. Charitable contributions: Tax deductions or matching grants? *Tax Law Review* 28, no. 1 (Fall):37–63.

———. 1973. Should foundations be third-class charities? In Fritz F. Heimann, ed., *The Future of Foundations*, 132–62. Englewood Cliffs, N.J.: Prentice-Hall.

———. 1976. Charitable bequests and the federal estate tax: Proposed restrictions in deductibility. *Record of the Bar Association of the City of New York* 31, no. 3 (March):159–78.

———. 1981. *Federal Taxation of Income, Estates and Gifts*. Boston: Warren, Gorham & Lamont.

Bittker, Boris I., and Kenneth M. Kaufman. 1972. Taxes and civil rights: "Constitutionalizing" the Internal Revenue Code. *Yale Law Journal* 82, no. 1 (November):51–87.

Bittker, Boris I., and George K. Rahdert. 1976. The exemption of nonprofit organizations from federal income taxation. *Yale Law Journal* 85, no. 3 (January):299–358.

Bogert, George G., and George T. Bogert. 1973. *Handbook of the Law of Trusts*. 5th ed. St. Paul, Minn.: West Publishing Co., sec. 364.

Boorman, Scott A., and Paul R. Levitt. 1981. Network match-

ing: Nonprofit structure and public policy. Yale University, Program on Non-Profit Organizations Working Paper no. 61, chap. 1.

Boskin, Michael. 1977. Estate taxation and charitable bequests. In Commission on Private Philanthropy and Public Needs, *Research Papers*. Vol. 3. Washington, D.C.: Treasury Department.

Brannon, Gerald, and James F. Strnad II. 1977. Alternative approaches to encouraging philanthropic activities. In Commission on Private Philanthropy and Public Needs, *Research Papers*. Vol. 4, 2361–88. Washington, D.C.: Treasury Department.

Brewster, Kingman. 1965. Address to Yale Alumni Fund dinner. *Yale Alumni Magazine* 28 (February):10–11.

Carson, John J., and Henry V. Hodson, eds. 1973. *Philanthropy in the '70's: An Anglo-American Discussion*. New York: Council on Foundations.

Clark, Robert C. 1980. Does the nonprofit form fit the hospital industry? *Harvard Law Review* 93, no. 7 (May):1416–89.

Clotfelter, Charles. 1985. *Federal Tax Policy and Charitable Giving*. Chicago: University of Chicago Press.

Commission on Private Philanthropy and Public Needs. 1975. *Giving in America*. Washington, D.C.: Commission on Private Philanthropy and Public Needs.

Committee on Finance, U.S. Senate. 1969. *Senate Report no. 91–552*.

Committee on Ways and Means, U.S. House. 1969. Press release, May 27.

Crimmins, James C., and Mary Keil. 1983. *Enterprise in the Nonprofit Sector*. Washington, D.C.: Partners for Livable Places; New York: Rockefeller Brothers Fund.

DiMaggio, Paul. 1983. Non-economic theories of the nonprofit sector. In Independent Sector, *Working Papers for Spring Research Forum: Since the Filer Commission*. Washington, D.C.: Independent Sector.

DiMaggio, Paul, and Walter W. Powell. 1982. The iron cage revisited: Conformity and diversity in organizational fields. Yale University, Program on Non-Profit Organizations Working Paper no. 52.

Douglas, James, and Aaron Wildavsky. 1978. The dilemma of

the knowledgeable foundation in the era of big government. In *1976–77 Report, Russell Sage Foundation*. New York: Russell Sage Foundation.

Ellman, Ira M. 1982. Another theory of nonprofit corporations. *Michigan Law Review* 80, no. 5 (April):999–1050.

Feldstein, Martin. 1977. Charitable bequests, estate taxation, and intergenerational wealth transfers. In Commission on Private Philanthropy and Public Needs, *Research Papers*. Vol. 3, 1485–1500. Washington, D.C.: Treasury Department.

Fleming, Harold C. 1972. Riding hard on government programs. *Foundation News* (May/June):5–7.

Foundation Center. 1985. *The Foundation Directory*. 10th ed. New York: Foundation Center.

Frankel, Morgan. 1979. Tax treatment of artists' charitable contributions. *Yale Law Journal* 89, no. 1 (November):144–67.

Fremont-Smith, Marion R. 1965. *Foundations and Government*. New York: Russell Sage Foundation.

Gallagher, Edward. 1984. Limits on the commercial involvement of nonprofit organizations. Paper prepared for Yale Law School seminar.

Galston, Miriam. 1981. Public policy constraints on charitable organizations. Paper prepared for Yale Law School seminar.

Gamwell, Franklin I. 1984. *Beyond Preference: Liberal Theories of Independent Associations*. Chicago: University of Chicago Press.

Ginsburg, David, Lee R. Marks, and Ronald P. Wertheim. 1977. Federal oversight of private philanthropy. In Commission on Private Philanthropy and Public Needs, *Research Papers*. Vol. 5, 2575–2696. Washington, D.C.: Treasury Department.

Gladstone, Francis. 1982. *Charity, Law, and Social Justice*. London: Bedford Square Press.

Gonzalez, A. Miren, and Philip Tetlock. 1980. A literature review of altruism and helping behavior. Yale University, Program on Non-Profit Organizations Working Paper no. 16.

Good, David A., and Aaron Wildavsky. 1977. A tax by any other name: The donor-directed automatic percentage contribution bonus. In Commission on Private Philanthropy and Public Needs, *Research Papers*. Vol. 4, 2389–2416. Washington, D.C.: Treasury Department.

Goode, Richard. 1951. *The Corporation Income Tax*. New York: John Wiley & Sons.

Hansmann, Henry. 1980. The role of nonprofit enterprise. *Yale Law Journal* 89, no. 5 (April):835–901.

———. 1981a. Nonprofit enterprise in the performing arts. *Bell Journal of Economics* 12, no 2:341–61.

———. 1981b. The rationale for exempting nonprofit organizations from corporate income taxation. Yale University, Program on Non-Profit Organizations Working Paper no. 23.

———. 1982. The effect of tax exemption and other factors on competition between nonprofit and for-profit enterprise. Yale University, Program on Non-Profit Organizations Working Paper no. 65.

———. 1985. The future of corporate income tax exemption for nonprofit organizations. Unpublished manuscript.

Hochman, Harold, and James Rodgers. 1977. The optimal tax treatment of charitable contributions. *National Tax Journal* 30 (March):1–19.

Hodgkinson, Virginia A., and Murray S. Weitzman. 1984. *Dimensions of the Independent Sector: A Statistical Profile*. Washington, D.C.: Independent Sector.

Hooper, Sharon. 1985. Systems of fiduciary enforcement. Paper prepared for Yale Law School seminar.

Hopkins, Bruce R. 1983. *The Law of Tax-Exempt Organizations*. 4th ed. New York: John Wiley & Sons.

James, Estelle, and Susan Rose-Ackerman. 1985. The nonprofit enterprise in market economies. Yale University, Program on Non-Profit Organizations Working Paper no. 95.

Joblove, Leonard. 1980. Special treatment of churches under the Internal Revenue Code. Yale University, Program on Non-Profit Organizations Working Paper no. 21.

Jones, Andrew. 1985. The private benefit problem and the net benefit solution. Paper prepared for Yale Law School seminar.

Karl, Barry B., and Stanley N. Katz. 1981. The American private philanthropic foundation and the public sphere, 1890–1930. *Minerva* 19, no. 2 (Summer):236–70.

Krashinsky, Michael. 1984. Transactions costs and a theory of the nonprofit organization. Yale University Program on Non-Profit Organizations Working Paper no. 84.

Kurz, Theodore, and Barbara Paul Robinson. 1977. Explanation and analysis of split-interest gifts to charity. In Commission on Private Philanthropy and Public Needs, *Research Papers*. Vol. 4, 2221–48. Washington, D.C.: Treasury Department.

Larson, Martin A., and C. Stanley Lowell. 1969. *Praise the Lord for Tax Exemption*. Washington, D.C.: Robert B. Luce.

Lashbrooke, E. C., Jr. 1985. *Tax Exempt Organizations*. Westport, Conn.: Quorum Books.

Lindblom, Charles E., and David K. Cohen. 1979. *Usable Knowledge: Social Science and Social Problem Solving*. New Haven: Yale University Press.

Lindsey, Lawrence B. 1985. The effect of the Treasury proposal on charitable giving. Paper prepared for Harvard University.

Loeser, Doron I. 1986. The constitutionality of the tax on lobbying by private foundations after *Regan* v. *Taxation with Representation of Washington*. Paper prepared for Yale Law School seminar.

Lyman, Richard. 1981. *What Kind of Society Shall We Have?* Washington, D.C.: Independent Sector.

Majone, Giandomenico. 1980. Professionalism and nonprofit organizations. Yale University, Program on Non-Profit Organizations Working Paper no. 24.

Marcus, Jacob R. 1938. *The Jew in the Medieval World*. Cincinnati, Ohio: Sinai Press.

McConnell, Ann. 1976. Justifying the charitable deduction. Paper prepared for Yale Law School seminar.

McDaniel, Paul. 1977. Study of federal matching grants for charitable contributions. In Commission on Private Philanthropy and Public Needs, *Research Papers*. Vol. 4, 2417–2534. Washington, D.C.: Treasury Department.

McNulty, John K. 1984. Public policy and private charity: A tax policy perspective. *Virginia Tax Review* 3, no. 2 (Winter):229–53.

Milofsky, Carl. 1979. Not-for-profit organizations and community: A review of the sociological literature. Yale University, Program on Non-Profit Organizations Working Paper no. 6.

Nelson, Richard R., and Michael Krashinsky. 1973. Two major issues of public policy: Public subsidy and organization of supply. In Richard R. Nelson and Dennis Young, eds., *Public Policy for Day Care of Young Children*. Lexington, Mass.: D. C. Heath.

New York State Bar Association Section on Taxation, Special Committee on Exempt Organizations. 1965. Comment on Treasury Foundation Report. In *Additional Written Statements . . . on Treasury Department Report on Private Foundations*. Committee Print, Committee on Ways and Means, U.S. House, 710–35.

Owen, David. 1964. *English Philanthropy, 1660–1960*. Cambridge, Mass.: Harvard University Press.

Pang, Presley W. 1985. Restricting tax benefits for property leased to nonprofit entities. Paper prepared for Yale Law School seminar.

Payton, Robert L. 1984. *Major Challenges to Philanthropy*. Washington, D.C.: Independent Sector.

Permut, Stephen. 1981. Consumer perceptions of nonprofit enterprise: A comment on Hansmann. *Yale Law Journal* 90, no. 7 (June):1623–32.

Persons, John P., John J. Osborn, and Charles F. Feldman. 1977. Criteria for exemption under Section 501(c)(3). In Commission on Private Philanthropy and Public Needs, *Research Papers*. Vol. 4, 1909–2025. Washington, D.C.: Treasury Department.

Philanthropy Monthly. 1984. The charity as the general partner in a limited partnership: A discussion at the Association of the Bar of the City of New York. *Philanthropy Monthly* 17, no. 5 (May):24–38.

Pires, Sheila. 1985. *Competition between the Nonprofit and For-Profit Sectors*. Washington, D.C.: National Assembly.

Rose-Ackerman, Susan. 1982. Unfair competition and corporate income taxation. *Stanford Law Review* 34, no. 5 (May):1017–39.

Ross, Aileen. 1968. Philanthropy. In *International Encyclopedia of the Social Sciences*. Vol. 12, 73–80. New York: Macmillan Co. and Free Press.

Rudney, Gabriel, and Gerald Auten. 1985. Charitable deductions and tax reform: New evidence on giving behavior. In *1984 Proceedings of the National Tax Association–Tax Institute of America*, 73–81. Washington, D.C.: National Tax Association.

Ruggles, Richard, and Nancy Ruggles. 1980. Integrated economic accounts for the United States, 1947–1978. Yale University, Institution for Social and Policy Studies Working Paper no. 841.

Rusk, Dean. 1961. *The Role of the Foundation in American Life*. Claremont, Calif.: Claremont University College.

Schenkkan, Dirk. 1974. Philanthropy and the distribution of wealth—a preliminary foray. Paper prepared for Yale Law School seminar.

Schill, Michael H. 1984. The participation of charities in limited partnerships. *Yale Law Journal* 96, no. 7 (June):1355–74.

Schuster, J. Mark Davidson. 1985. Tax incentives as arts policy in Western Europe. Yale University, Program on Non-Profit Organizations Working Paper no. 90.

Schwarz, Stephen, and William T. Hutton. 1984. Recent developments in tax-exempt organizations. *University of San Francisco Law Review* 18, no. 4 (Summer):649–94.

Select Committee on Small Business, U.S. House of Representatives. 1962. *Tax-Exempt Foundations and Charitable Trusts: Their Impact on Our Economy, Chairman's Report*. Committee Print, Select Committee on Small Business.

Simon, John G. 1965. The Patman report and the Treasury proposals. In New York University, *Proceedings of the Seventh Biennial Conference on Charitable Foundations*. Albany, N.Y.: Matthew Bender.

———. 1969. Statement on H.R. 13270, submitted to Senate Committee on Finance, 1969. In Foundation Center, *The Foundations and the Tax Bill*, 190–98. New York: Foundation Center.

———. 1973. Foundations and controversy: An affirmative view. In Fritz F. Heimann, ed., *The Future of Foundations*, 58–100. Englewood Cliffs, N.J.: Prentice-Hall.

———. 1978. Charity and dynasty under the federal tax system. *Probate Lawyer* 5 (Summer).

Simon, John G., Charles W. Powers, and John P. Gunnemann. 1972. *The Ethical Investor*. New Haven: Yale University Press.

Simon, Karla W. 1981. The tax-exempt status of racially discriminatory religious schools. *Tax Law Review* 36, no. 4 (Summer):477–516.

Simons, Henry C. 1938. *Personal Income Taxation*. Chicago: University of Chicago Press.

Sowles, Marcia K. 1980. The charitable status of public interest litigation groups: The mixed reaction of IRS and the need for a comprehensive theory. Paper prepared for Yale Law School seminar.

Spiro, Thomas. 1979. ''Unfair competition'' between taxable and tax-exempt organizations. Paper prepared for Yale Law School seminar.

Stewart, Joseph R. 1973. Federal tax benefits for elite private schools. Paper prepared for Yale Law School seminar.

Stone, Lawrence. 1977. The charitable foundation: Its governance. In Commission on Private Philanthropy and Public Needs, *Research Papers*. Vol. 3. Washington, D.C.: Treasury Department.

Strnad, Jeff. 1986. The charitable contribution deduction: A politico-economic analysis. In Susan Rose-Ackerman, ed., *The Economics of Nonprofit Institutions: Studies in Structure and Policy*. New York: Oxford University Press.

Subcommittee on Oversight, Committee on Ways and Means, U.S. House. 1983. *Hearings on Tax Rules Governing Private Foundations, June 27–28*. Washington, D.C.: U.S. Government Printing Office.

Surrey, Stanley S. 1973. *Pathways to Tax Reform*. Cambridge, Mass.: Harvard University Press.

Swain, John. 1984. Searching for a redistributional requirement for 501(c)(3) organizations. Paper prepared for Yale Law School seminar.

Swords, Peter. 1981. *Charitable Real Property Tax Exemptions in New York State—Menace or Measure of Social Progress?* New York: Association of the Bar of the City of New York.

Treusch, Paul E., and Norman A. Sugarman. 1983. *Tax-Exempt Charitable Organizations.* 2d ed. Philadelphia: American Bar Association–American Law Institute.

Troyer, Thomas A. 1966. The Treasury Department report on private foundations: A response to some critics. *UCLA Law Review* 13, no. 4 (May):965–95.

———. 1973. Charities, law-making, and the Constitution: The validity of the restrictions on influencing legislation. In *NYU Institute on Federal Taxation* 31:1415–69. New York: Matthew Bender.

Troyer, Thomas A., and Robert A. Boisture. 1983. Charities and the fiscal crisis: Creative approaches to income production. In New York University, *Thirteenth Conference on Charitable Organizations,* 4-1–4-31. New York: Matthew Bender.

U.S. Internal Revenue Service. 1982. *Statistics of Income, Individual Income Tax Returns, 1982.* Washington, D.C.: U.S. Government Printing Office.

U.S. Small Business Administration, Office of Advocacy. 1984. *Unfair Competition by Nonprofit Organizations with Small Business: An Issue for the 1980s.* 3d ed. Washington, D.C.: U.S. Small Business Administration.

U.S. Treasury Department. 1965. *Report on Private Foundations.* Committee Print, Senate Committee on Finance.

———. 1969. *Tax Reform Proposals.* Committee Print, Committee on Ways and Means.

———. 1984. *Tax Reform for Fairness, Simplicity, and Economic Growth: The Treasury Department Report to the President.* Washington, D.C.: Department of the Treasury.

Urban Institute. 1983. Serving community needs: The nonprofit sector in an era of governmental retrenchment. Nonprofit Sector Project Progress Report no. 3, September.

Weisbrod, Burton A. 1977. Toward a theory of the voluntary nonprofit sector in a three-sector economy. In Burton A. Weisbrod, ed., *The Voluntary Nonprofit Sector: An Economic Analysis.* Lexington, Mass.: Lexington Books.

———. 1980. Private goods, collective goods: The role of the nonprofit sector. In Kenneth W. Clarkson and Donald L. Martin, eds., *The Economics of Nonproprietary Organizations,* Suppl. 1, 139–69. Greenwich, Conn.: JAI Press.

Wellford, Harrison, and Janne G. Gallagher. 1985. *The Myth of Unfair Competition by Nonprofit Organizations—A Review of Government Assistance to Small Business.* Washington, D.C.: National Assembly and Family Service America.

White, Arthur H. 1986. *The Charitable Behavior of Americans.* Washington, D.C.: Independent Sector.

Yale University Program on Non-Profit Organizations. 1982. Parsing property tax policy. *Research Reports,* no. 2 (Fall):5–7.

Zimmerman, Dennis. 1985. 1985 tax reform options and charitable contributions. *Philanthropy Monthly* 18, no. 5 (May):23–31.

6

Partners in Public Service:
The Scope and Theory of
Government-Nonprofit Relations

LESTER M. SALAMON

When contributions are hard to get, when fairs and balls no longer net large sums, when endowments are slow to come, the managers of private charities frequently turn to the public authorities and ask them for a contribution from the public revenues. On the other hand, when local or State legislatures see the annual appropriations bills increasing too rapidly, and when they see existing public institutions made political spoils, and the administration wasteful and inefficient, they are apt to think of giving a subsidy to some private institution instead of providing for more public buildings and more public officials. (Warner 1894)

In recent years, government has emerged in the United States as . . . *the* major philanthropist in a number of the principal traditional areas of philanthropy. The nonprofit sector has become an increasingly mixed realm, part private, part public, in much the same sense that the profit-making sector has—and not unlike the nonprofit sector itself once was. (Commission on Private Philanthropy and Public Needs 1975)

When Alexander Fleisher pointed out in 1914 that no problem of social policy is "more harassing, more complex and perennial than that of determining the proper relation of the state to privately managed charities within its border" (p. 110), he was calling attention to a point that current observers of American society have tended to ignore: that the "welfare state" has taken a peculiar form in the American context, a form that involves

I am indebted to the Local Associates of the Urban Institute Nonprofit Sector Project, as well as to my colleagues on the national staff of this project—especially James C. Musselwhite, Jr., Alan Abramson, Michael Gutowski, and Carol De Vita—for their help in compiling and analyzing much of the data reported here. I am grateful to Woody Powell and John Simon for their editorial advice.

not simply the expansion of the state but also an extensive pattern of government reliance on private nonprofit groups to carry out public purposes. In fact, in a number of fields, government has turned more of the responsibility for delivering publicly financed services over to nonprofit organizations than it has retained for itself. In the process, government has become the single most important source of income for most types of nonprofit agencies, outdistancing private charity by roughly two to one. What Fleisher termed "the sore thumb of public administrative policy" has thus become the core of the nation's human service delivery system and the financial mainstay of the nation's private nonprofit sector.

Despite its importance, however, this pervasive partnership between government and the voluntary sector has attracted surprisingly little attention. Even the most basic statistical data on the scope of government support to the voluntary sector have long been unavailable, and more systematic assessments of the value and impact of the relationship have been virtually nonexistent.

This chapter argues that this inattention to the relationship between government and the nonprofit sector is the product not simply of an absence of research but more fundamentally of a weakness of theory. Both the theory of the welfare state and the theory of the voluntary sector have been deficient—the former because of its failure to differentiate between government's role as a provider of funds and its role as a deliverer of services, and the latter because of its tendency to explain the existence of the voluntary sector in terms of failures of government and the market, and thus to make involvement by these other sectors in the world of nonprofits appear suspect at best. To understand the relationship between government and the nonprofit sector, it is therefore necessary not only to add to our storehouse of facts but also to reshape the conceptual lenses through which we view both the American welfare state and the nonprofit sector.

Such an exercise is especially important at the present time, moreover, because of recent government policy changes that are supposed to expand the role of nonprofit organizations by reducing government activity in their fields. Because of their failure to take account of the scope of government-nonprofit interaction, however, these changes have instead posed a serious threat to the viability of the nonprofit sector (Salamon & Abramson 1982, 1985; Salamon 1984a, 1984b). Under these circumstances, it becomes all the more important to clarify how government and the nonprofit sector interact and how prevailing theories must be altered to come to terms with this interaction.

To contribute to this clarification, the following discussion (1) examines the dimensions of the support government provides to nonprofit institutions and documents the role government plays in nonprofit finances; (2) identifies the shortcomings in existing theories that help explain the widespread neglect of the interaction between the two sectors and suggests the need for a reorientation of both the theory of the welfare state and the theory of the voluntary sector in order to come to terms with it; and (3) assesses the way this partnership has actually operated in practice and the impact it has had on nonprofits and government.

Throughout this discussion, I will be using the terms *nonprofit, voluntary,* and *charitable* interchangeably to refer to a broad spectrum of institutions that are exempt from federal taxation, eligible to receive tax-exempt gifts, engaged in direct service activities aimed at benefiting persons beyond the organization's own members, and formally controlled by a private—normally unpaid—board of directors. This definition includes hospitals, universities, museums, arts groups, foster-care providers, health clinics, youth training centers, private nursing homes, advocacy groups, neighborhood revitalization organizations, and many more. It does *not* include three other groups of tax-exempt organizations: (1) those whose principal function is the granting of funds as opposed to the provision of services (for example, founda-

tions); (2) those primarily devoted to religious worship; or (3) those providing services primarily devoted to the organization's own members rather than to a broader public (such as trade associations, fraternities, sororities, labor unions). The terms *nonprofit* and *voluntary* are used interchangeably to depict this set of organizations even though many of the organizations covered earn income and much of the work they carry out is conducted by paid professionals.

GOVERNMENT SUPPORT OF NONPROFITS: THE SCOPE

According to conventional wisdom, government support of the voluntary sector is a relatively recent development in this country, and one that runs counter to the historic independence of the voluntary sector. In point of fact, however, government support of voluntary organizations has roots deep in American history. Well before the American Revolution, for example, colonial governments had established a tradition of assistance to private educational institutions, and this tradition persisted into the nineteenth century. In colonial Massachusetts, for example, the commonwealth government not only enacted a special tax for support of Harvard College but also paid part of the salary of the president until 1781 and elected the college's Board of Overseers until after the Civil War. The state of Connecticut had an equally intimate relationship with Yale, and the state's governor, lieutenant governor, and six state senators sat on the Yale Corporation from the founding of the school until the late 1800s. The prevailing sentiment was that education served a public purpose and therefore deserved public support regardless of whether it was provided in publicly or privately run institutions (see Whitehead 1973, 3–16).

A similar pattern was also evident in the hospital field. A survey of seventeen major private hospitals in 1889, for example, revealed that 12 to 13 percent of their income came from government (Stevens 1982). A special 1904 Census Bureau survey of benevolent institutions estimated the government share of private hospital income at closer to 8 percent nationwide, but reported that it exceeded 20 percent in a number of states (Stevens 1982). So widespread was the appropriation of public funds for the support of private voluntary hospitals, in fact, that an American Hospital Association report referred to it in 1909 as "the distinctively American practice" (Stevens 1982; Rosner 1980).

If government support was important to the early history of private, nonprofit hospitals and education institutions, however, it was even more important to the early history of private social service agencies. Hospitals and higher education institutions, after all, had access to fees and charges. Agencies providing care for the poor usually did not. As the social problems that accompanied urbanization and industrialization increased in the latter nineteenth century, therefore, governments were increasingly called on to respond. But in a substantial number of cases, public officials turned to private nonprofit agencies for help. In New York City, for example, the amount the city paid to private benevolent institutions for the care of prisoners and paupers grew even faster than total city expenditures for these purposes—from under $10,000 in 1850 to over $3 million in 1898, from 2 percent of total city expenditures on the poor to 57 percent (Fetter 1901–02, 376). Similarly, in the District of Columbia, about half of the public funds allocated for aid to the poor went to private charities as of 1892. What is more, private charitable institutions absorbed two-thirds of the funds the District granted between 1880 and 1892 for construction of charitable facilities (Warner 1894, 337). In other words, the Congress, which set the District budget, was willing not only to compensate private charities for services they were providing to the District poor but also to finance construction of the facilities these organizations needed.

Nor were these isolated instances. To the contrary, a 1901 survey of government subsidization of private charities found that "except possibly two territories and four western states, there is probably not a state in the union where some aid [to private charities] is not given either by the state or by counties and cities" (Fetter 1901–02, 360). In many places, moreover, this public support was extensive enough to replace private charity as the principal source of income for nonprofit organizations. A study of two hundred private organizations for orphan children and the friendless in New York State in the late 1880s showed, for example, that twice as much of their support came from the taxpayers as from legacies, donations, and private contributions. Similarly, private benevolence accounted for only 15 percent of the income of private charities in the District of Columbia as of 1899 (Warner 1894, 337; Fetter 1901–02, 376). In short, there is nothing novel about extensive interaction between government and the voluntary sector in this country. No wonder one close student could conclude that "collaboration, not separation or antagonism, between government and the Third Sector . . . has been the predominant characteristic" throughout most of our history (Nielsen 1980, 47).

Although government support of the voluntary sector has deep historical roots in this country, however, this support has grown considerably in scope and depth over the past thirty years. Unfortunately, the generation of data needed to chart this growth has not kept pace. Although the Office of Management and Budget prepares a yearly "special analysis" of federal support to state and local governments, for example, no governmentwide overview of federal support to nonprofit institutions is available. We know that nonprofit organizations are eligible participants in 564 out of the 988 separate federal programs listed in the *Catalogue of Federal Domestic Assistance,* but few of these programs maintain data systems that make it possible to identify the scale of program resources flowing to nonprofit institutions. Similarly, few state or local governments collect data on this facet of program operations. As a consequence, to examine government support to the voluntary sector it is necessary to stitch together data from a variety of disparate sources.

One of the more recent efforts to do this was the research conducted for the Commission on Private Philanthropy and Public Needs (the Filer Commission) by Rudney in the early 1970s. Rudney (1975) estimated that government support to private tax-exempt organizations totaled $23.2 billion in 1974. By comparison, these same organizations received an estimated $13.6 billion in private philanthropic support that same year. In other words, by Rudney's reckoning, private nonprofit organizations (exclusive of churches, which are not eligible for government support) received a larger share of their income from government as of 1974 than they did from all sources of private giving combined—corporate, foundation, and individual.

More recent research, including in particular a major project I directed at The Urban Institute,[1] has made it possible to bring the current status of government support to the nonprofit sector into clearer focus. In particular, on the basis of this work it is possible to identify five major characteristics of the existing pattern of government support to the nonprofit sector. Let us look at each of these characteristics in turn.

The Extent

The first notable dimension of government support to the voluntary sector is its considerable extent. According to our estimates, federal support to the nonprofit sector alone amounted to $40.4 billion in 1980, which represented about 36 percent of total federal spending in these fields (Salamon & Abramson 1982, 37–42). State and local government own-source revenues would likely add another $8 billion to $10 billion to this total. By comparison, private contributions to these same kinds of organizations in 1980 totaled approximately $25.5 billion (American Association . . . 1981), or about 40 percent less than the federal contribution and about 50 percent less than the overall government contribution. These findings confirm the central conclusion of the Filer Commission that government is a more important source of revenue to nonprofit service providers (exclusive of churches) than all private giving combined.

As can be seen in table 6.1, the extent of reliance on nonprofit organizations to deliver federally funded services varies widely among service fields. In the fields of research, arts and humanities, social services, and health, close to half or more of all federal funding goes to support services provided by nonprofit organizations. In the fields of community development, higher education, and foreign aid, in contrast, the nonprofit share of total federal spending is less than 25 percent.

1. This work has taken three principal forms: first, the development of national estimates of the share of federal spending flowing to nonprofits under each of the federal programs in which nonprofits are eligible recipients; second, the assembly of detailed data on the extent of spending by all levels of government—federal, state, and local—in fields where nonprofits are active and on the portion of this spending flowing to nonprofits in sixteen representative field sites; and third, a survey of over 3,400 nonprofit service organizations in the same sixteen sites. The field sites used for the latter two forms of work included one large, one medium-sized, and one small metropolitan area plus one rural county in each of the four major Census Bureau regions (Northeast, Midwest, West, and South).

TABLE 6.1 ESTIMATED FEDERAL SUPPORT OF NONPROFIT ORGANIZATIONS, FY 1980 ($ BILLIONS)

Field	Federal Spending	Federal Support to Nonprofits	
		Amount	As Percentage of Total Federal Spending
Research	$4.7	$2.5	54%
Social services	7.7	4.0[a]	52
Arts, humanities	0.6	0.3	50
Health	53.0	24.8	47
Employment and training	10.3	3.3	32
Elementary/secondary education	7.0	0.2	2
Higher education	10.3	2.6	25
Community development	11.5	1.8	16
Foreign aid	6.9	0.8	11
Total	$111.6	$40.4	36%

Source: Data on federal spending from U.S. Office of Management and Budget, *Budget of the United States Government for Fiscal Year 1982* (Washington, D.C.: U.S. Government Printing Office, 1981); data on federal support to nonprofits from Salamon and Abramson 1982.
   a. Includes a limited amount of income assistance aid not covered in the total spending column.

This pattern of government reliance on nonprofit organizations to deliver publicly funded services is even more clearly apparent in table 6.2, which is based on data assembled through The Urban Institute Nonprofit Sector Project from sixteen representative field sites of varying sizes throughout the country, and which covers state and local as well as federal spending in five human service fields.[2] These data show that, on average, over 40 percent of all government spending in the five fields goes to support the provision of services by private nonprofit groups. In some fields, such as social services, the nonprofit share is even higher. In addition, another 19 percent of total government spending in these fields goes to for-profit businesses. By comparison, government agencies deliver about 39 percent of the services they fund in these fields. In other words, nonprofits deliver a larger share of publicly funded services in these fields than do government agencies. Although the inclusion of a number of very large sites that make extensive use of nonprofits (such as New York) inflate these figures somewhat, the picture does not change much when median values are used instead of weighted means. Nonprofits still emerge as major providers of publicly financed services.[3] (For additional details on local sites see, for example, Musselwhite, Hawkins, & Salamon 1985; Grønbjerg, Musselwhite, & Salamon 1984; Harder, Musselwhite, & Salamon 1984.)

In addition to the direct government support to nonprofits identified above, nonprofits also receive indirect support in the form of the tax deductions provided to their contributors. These deductions represent revenue that would otherwise go to the U.S. Treasury but that the tax laws allow taxpayers to channel to nonprofit organizations instead as an incentive to private giving. According to U.S. Office of Management and Budget estimates, these "tax expenditures" provided an additional $8.4 billion in support to voluntary organizations in 1980, of which probably $5.5 billion went to nonreligious organizations (U.S. Office of Management and Budget 1981).[4]

Distribution of Government Support among Types of Nonprofits

The extensive support that government provides to nonprofit organizations is not distributed evenly among all areas of nonprofit activity. Rather, nonprofits in some fields receive far more than do those in others. This is so because both the overall extent of government spending and the share of that spending that goes to nonprofits vary from field to field.

Reflecting this, health providers receive the lion's share of all federal support to nonprofit organizations. In particular, as noted in table 6.3, over 60 percent of all federal support to the nonprofit sector in 1980 went to hospitals and other health providers, and about 15 percent each went to social service organizations and educational or research institutions. The remaining 10 percent was split among community development, international assistance, and arts organizations.[5]

During the early 1980s, federal support to the nonprofit sector shifted even more heavily toward health care pro-

2. The data reported here cover only the central city/county of each site, not the entire standard metropolitan statistical area. In the case of the Twin Cities area of Minnesota, data are reported separately on Hennepin and Ramsey counties.

3. Using the medians, nonprofits account for 36 percent of all spending, government for 41 percent, and for-profits for 20 percent.

4. The estimate of the share of the tax expenditures attributable to religious organizations is based on the assumption that 46 percent of all private giving flows to religious congregations, but that itemizers (who alone receive the tax deduction) give a smaller proportion of their total charitable contributions to religious congregations than do nonitemizers.

5. The distribution of funds shown in table 6.3 differs from that in table 6.1 because table 6.3 reports estimated receipts by *type of organization* and some programs distribute funds to several different types of organizations. This is particularly true of the employment and training program, which channeled funds to employment and training, social service, community development, and arts organizations.

TABLE 6.2   SHARE OF GOVERNMENT-FUNDED HUMAN SERVICES DELIVERED BY NONPROFIT, FOR-PROFIT, AND GOVERNMENT AGENCIES IN SIXTEEN COMMUNITIES, 1982 (WEIGHTED AVERAGE)[A]

| Field | Proportion of Services Delivered by | | | |
	Nonprofits	For-Profits	Government	Total
Social services	56%	4%	40%	100%
Employment/training	48	8	43	100
Housing/community development	5	7	88	100
Health	44	23	33	100
Arts/culture	51	*	49	100
Total	42%	19%	39%	100%

Source: The Urban Institute Nonprofit Sector Project.
*Less than 0.5 percent.
a. Figures are weighted by the scale of government spending in the sites. Percentages shown represent the share of all spending in all sites taken together that fall in the respective categories.

viders. This is a product of the continued rapid growth of federal health expenditures coupled with budget reductions in the nonhealth fields enacted during the early years of the Reagan administration. As a result, although the inflation-adjusted value of total federal support to nonprofit providers remained relatively constant between fiscal years 1980 and 1985, the share of that total absorbed by health care providers increased from under 60 percent to over 70 percent, and the share left for all other types of nonprofits shrank from 40 percent to under 30 percent.

Government Support as a Share of Total Nonprofit Income

Given the extent and distribution of government reliance on nonprofit organizations charted above, it should come as no surprise to learn that government support constitutes a major share of total nonprofit income. In fact, government has become the single largest source of support for the nonprofit sector, outdistancing the other major sources of support—fees and endowments as well as charitable contributions from corporations, foundations, and individuals.

TABLE 6.3   DISTRIBUTION OF FEDERAL SUPPORT AMONG TYPES OF NONPROFITS, FY 1980 ($ BILLIONS)

| Type of Organization | Revenues from Federal Sources | |
	Amount	As Percentage of Total
Social service	$6.5[a]	16%
Community development	2.3	6
Education/research	5.6	14
Health care	24.9	61
Foreign aid	0.8	2
Arts/culture	0.3	1
Total	$40.4[a]	100%

Source: Salamon and Abramson 1982, 43.
a. Includes a limited amount of income assistance aid.

This point is evident in table 6.4, which compares the extent of federal support for private nonprofit service organizations to the total revenues of these organizations, as estimated from U.S. Census and Internal Revenue Service data.[6]

6. Nonprofit organizations other than churches are required to file information Form 990 with the Internal Revenue Service each year, reporting on total receipts, sources of revenues, major categories of expenditure, and selected additional financial and program information. The IRS prepares a standard extract of the data available on these forms, which is available for public use. Unfortunately, the standard extract contains only a limited amount of information. And more serious, the activity code system the IRS uses to classify organizations makes it exceedingly difficult to ferret out which organizations belong in which subcategory, or even which organizations are service providers as opposed to fund-raisers or funding intermediaries (for example, United Way or Blue Cross organizations). This is particularly true in view of the fact that many organizations are miscoded even in terms of the IRS system. As a result, the IRS data have serious double-counting problems built into them. In addition, the data are incomplete and mostly unverified even for internal consistency.

To adjust for these problems, we analyzed two samples of organizations in the IRS data tapes—one composed of all large organizations and one a random sample of the remaining organizations—to identify the extent of miscoding in the data set. On this basis, we developed correction factors to apply to the remainder of the IRS data set. As an additional check, we aged the 1977 Census of Service Industries data to 1980 and used this as a second measure of the size of the components of the sector and of the sector as a whole. The estimates reported in table 6.4 are a composite of the estimates derived from these two sources. For a more detailed discussion of the methodology used to develop our estimate of sector size, see Salamon and Abramson (1982, 13–14 and n5).

Three other recent estimates of the size of the nonprofit sector are also available. One, by Rudney (1982), utilizes the 1977 Census of Service Industries data described above, aging them to 1980 by assuming that the sector as a whole, and its component parts, bear the same relationship to the gross domestic product in 1980 as the census reported they did in 1977. On this basis, Rudney estimates that the nonprofit sector in 1980 had expenditures of $129.2 billion including religion, and $107 billion excluding religion—slightly smaller than our $116.4 billion estimate (see also chapter 4 of this volume). A second estimate, developed by Smith and Rosenbaum (1981) utilizes the IRS 990 tabulations. It differs from our use of these data, however, in that it takes the IRS activity code system as given and does not make adjustments for the inappropriate coding of organizations and resulting double-counting in

TABLE 6.4   NONPROFIT REVENUES FROM FEDERAL SOURCES AS A SHARE OF TOTAL NONPROFIT REVENUES, 1980

Type of Organization	Total Revenue	Revenues from Federal Programs	Revenues from Federal Programs as Percentage of Total Revenue
Social service[a]	$13.2	$7.3	55%
Community development[b]	5.4	2.3	43
Education/research	25.2	5.6	22
Health care	70.0	24.9	36
Arts/culture	2.6	0.3	12
Total	$116.4	$40.4	35%

Sources: Total revenues based on estimates developed from IRS and census data. Government support is based on estimates developed in Salamon and Abramson 1982, 44.

   a. Includes international assistance.

   b. Includes civic associations and other.

As the table shows, we estimate that federal support accounted for 35 percent of the total expenditures of nonprofit service organizations (excluding religious congregations) in 1980.[7] For some types of organizations, however, the federal share is even higher than this—55 percent for social service organizations and over 40 percent for community development organizations. At the opposite end of the spectrum, arts organizations on average received only 12 percent of their revenues from federal program sources.

An even clearer picture of the role of government support in the funding of nonprofit organizations is evident in table 6.5, which draws on the results of a survey of some 3,400 nonprofit human service agencies—exclusive of hospitals and higher education institutions—conducted by The Urban Institute Nonprofit Sector Project in sixteen field sites across the country. (For further details, see Salamon 1984a, 1984b; Gutowski, Salamon, & Pittman 1984; Lukermann, Kimmich, & Salamon 1984; Grønbjerg, Kimmich, & Salamon 1984.) According to this survey, federal, state, and local governments together accounted for 41 percent of the income of these agencies as of 1981. Service fees and charges provided the second largest source of income, accounting for 28 percent of the total, well behind the government share. Private giving—individual, corporate, and foundation—ranked third, with 20 percent. The results of this survey thus confirm the picture that emerged from the top-down estimates discussed above: that government is the largest single source of income for nonprofit service organizations, outdistancing private giving by a factor of two to one.

As table 6.5 also shows, however, there is some variation in the extent of reliance on government funding among different types of nonprofit agencies. In fact, it is possible to discern three more or less distinct types or "models" of nonprofit agencies in terms of their funding structures. The first, and most common, is the government-dominant model, which applies to those types of agencies for which government is the dominant funding source. As table 6.5 shows, seven of the ten major types of nonprofit agenices we identified fit this model. For each of these types of agencies, government accounts for close to half or more of total income, and in three of the cases it accounts for more than 60 percent of the total. These types of agencies do vary in terms of where they get the remainder of their income, however. For legal services/advocacy and social services organizations, for example, the principal nongovernmental source of funds is private giving. For mental health and institutional/residential care organizations, in contrast, the principal nongovernmental source of funds is fee income. Nevertheless, for all these types of organizations the principal source of support, accounting for half or more of the total, is government.

The second nonprofit funding pattern is what might be called the fee-dominant model. The largest single source of income for agencies that follow this pattern are service fees and charges. As reflected in table 6.5, two types of agencies fit this model—health providers (exclusive of hospitals) and education and research institutions (exclusive of higher education institutions, which were not covered by our survey). In the case of health organizations, service fees constitute over half of total agency income. In the case of education/research organizations, fees exceed all other sources of income, but do not by themselves provide more than half of the total.

The final type of nonprofit funding pattern is the charity-dominant model, in which private giving—whether from individuals, corporations, or foundations—is the largest single source of income. This is the model that best fits the conventional image of the nonprofit sector, but as table 6.5 makes clear, only one set of agencies out of the ten exam-

the IRS system. On this basis, Smith and Rosenbaum estimate that nonprofit revenues in 1980 totaled $180 billion including religion, and $156 billion excluding religion—quite a bit higher than our estimate. A third estimate, developed by Hodgkinson and Weitzman (1984) using national income account data, places the current expenditures of nonprofit service organizations, exclusive of religious congregations and foundations, at $117.9 billion—almost identical with our estimate.

7. Using a different approach, Rudney (1982 and chapter 4 of this volume) estimates *total* government support for nonreligious nonprofits in 1980 at 35 percent.

TABLE 6.5   SOURCES OF SUPPORT OF NONPROFIT HUMAN SERVICE AGENCIES, 1981

Funding Pattern Type of Agency (n)[a]	Percentage of Total Income from				
	Government	Private Giving[b]	Fees	Other	Total[c]
Government Dominant					
Mental health (63)	67%	7%	23%	4%	100%
Housing/community development (91)	62	16	19	3	100
Legal services/advocacy (80)	62	23	10	5	100
Social services (538)	57	25	13	5	100
Employment/income assistance (103)	55	13	10	23	100
Institutional/residential (151)	51	11	32	5	100
Multiservice (314)	47	25	22	6	100
Fee Dominant					
Health (196)	31	13	51	5	100
Education/research (278)	28	25	31	16	100
Private Dominant					
Arts/culture/recreation (448)	15	30	27	27	100
All Agencies (2,304)	41%	20%	28%	10%	100%

Source: The Urban Institute Nonprofit Sector Project Survey.

a. Figures in parentheses represent the number of responding agencies in each category. Because some agencies failed to provide complete financial data and others neglected to provide information on their service focus, the number of respondents reflected in this table is smaller than the total respondents to the survey and the number that provided both financial and service-area data is slightly smaller than the number that provided just financial data.

b. Includes foundation, corporate, federated, and individual giving.

c. Some rows may not add to 100 percent because of rounding.

ined—arts, culture, and recreation—fits this model. And even here the fit is far from perfect since arts and cultural organizations as a group received almost as large a share of their income from fees and charges as from private giving, and they might well have received more were we to take account of the sales of products, which are included in the "other" category.

To be sure, the groupings of agencies noted here obscure a considerable degree of diversity among individual agencies within each type. Whereas social service agencies as a group received 57 percent of their income from government, for example, many social service agencies doubtless received little or no income from government and many others received 90 to 100 percent. Nevertheless, these data serve to confirm again how faulty the conventional image of the funding structure of the voluntary sector really is. Although the sector is typically identified exclusively with its private philanthropic base, in fact government is its principal source of support.

This conclusion finds still further support, moreover, in a body of data assembled by United Way of America from information supplied to it by its local affiliates. According to these data, which are partially summarized in table 6.6, government support is strong among United Way member agencies in most of the mainline nonprofit fields of service, such as child welfare, aging, community development, and legal aid. This is particularly significant in view of the fact that United Way agencies not only have access to United Way support but also tend to be older and more established organizations with good access to other private sources of support as well.

The Forms of Government Assistance to Nonprofits

Not only is government support to the nonprofit sector extensive and therefore an important part of the sector's total income, but this support also reaches the sector in a variety of forms and through numerous routes. In some programs, assistance takes the form of outright cash grants. In others, purchase-of-service contracts are used, and in still others government provides loans or loan guarantees. In the international assistance arena, government support to private voluntary organizations has taken even more varied forms, including ocean freight reimbursement, excess government proper-

TABLE 6.6   GOVERNMENT REVENUE AS A SHARE OF TOTAL REVENUES FOR SELECTED UNITED WAY AGENCIES, 1980

Type of Agency	Percent of Total Income from Government
Legal aid	84%
Community/neighborhood development	74
Aging	73
Child welfare	72
Planned parenthood	55
Catholic charities	46
Crippled children/adults	36
Cancer	29
YWCA	22
Salvation Army	17
Catholic youth organizations	13
Jewish community centers	7

Source: United Way of America 1981.

ty, surplus food, operational program grants, development program grants, institutional support grants, and several others as well (Bolling 1982).

Reflecting these different forms of assistance, federal aid reaches nonprofit organizations through a variety of routes. One such route involves direct financial dealings between nonprofit organizations and particular federal agencies, including such quasi-governmental or independent agencies as the National Science Foundation, the National Endowment for the Arts, and the National Endowment for the Humanities.

Federal assistance can also reach nonprofit organizations *indirectly*, through state and local governments that receive federal grants but retain substantial discretion in deciding whether to deliver the subsidized services themselves or to contract with nonprofit agencies or other public or private providers. The Social Services Block Grant (formerly the Title XX Social Services Block Grant program); the Administration on Aging grant programs; alcohol, drug abuse, and mental health programs; and the Community Development Block Grant program are all examples of federal assistance that reaches nonprofits through this route.

A third route for federal assistance to nonprofit organizations involves payments to individuals or to financial agents acting on their behalf. Perhaps the classic example here is Medicare, which reimburses individuals for certain hospital-related expenses but leaves to the individual the choice of whether to utilize a private nonprofit, a public, or a for-profit institution. A similar pattern prevails with the college student assistance programs, which provide important financial aid to nonprofit colleges and universities, but channel this aid to the students, who retain the choice about which type of institution—public, private nonprofit, or private for-profit—to attend.

These differences in the mechanisms of assistance have important implications for the nature of the relationship between government agencies and nonprofit providers. Generally speaking, federal influence is greatest in those programs where the form of assistance is a direct contract or grant between a federal agency and a particular nonprofit organization. It is weakest where the assistance is provided to private citizens who are then free to purchase services from providers of their choice in the market. At the same time, however, the direct route is more certain, whereas nonprofits have no guarantee of aid when the assistance is channeled through the client.

In view of this, it is significant, as reported in table 6.7, that the direct route, involving contractual relationships between the federal government and nonprofit organizations, is the least heavily used of these three forms of federal assistance. Only 20 percent of all federal aid to nonprofits took this route in 1980. In contrast, 53 percent of the federal aid to the sector was channeled through individuals, and another 27 percent reached nonprofits through state and local governments. Clearly, if the federal government is affecting the nonprofit sector, it is doing so indirectly. What is more, because the budget cuts of the early 1980s hit harder at the

TABLE 6.7 FEDERAL GOVERNMENT SUPPORT OF NONPROFIT ORGANIZATIONS BY AVENUE OF ASSISTANCE, FY 1980 ($ BILLIONS)

Avenue of Federal Assistance	Nonprofit Revenue from Federal Sources	
	Amount	As Percentage of Total
Direct to nonprofits	$7.9	20%
Through state/local governments	10.9	27
Through individuals	21.6	53
Total	$40.4	100%

Source: Salamon and Abramson 1982.

direct federal aid programs and those involving grants to state and local governments than those involving payments to individuals, the trend is toward even greater use of this voucher-type mechanism.

Regional Variations

One final characteristic of the existing pattern of governmental support of nonprofit organizations worth noting is its variation among different parts of the country and among communities of different sizes. This is shown in table 6.8, which reports the extent of government reliance on nonprofit organizations to deliver publicly funded services in the sixteen local sites examined as part of The Urban Institute Nonprofit Sector Project. As this table shows, the proportion of total government spending that goes to support service delivery by nonprofit organizations in five major service fields ranges from a high of 50 percent in Allegheny County (Pittsburgh) to a low of 12 percent in rural Tuscola County, Michigan. Although it is dangerous to draw conclusions on the basis of sixteen observations, the data in table 6.8 suggest two generalizations: first, government reliance on nonprofits to deliver publicly funded services tends to be less extensive in the South than in the Northeast and West; and second, such reliance also seems to be less extensive in small communities than in large ones. Thus of the eight sites reporting nonprofit shares of total government spending that are at or below the sixteen-site average, all either are in the South or are small sites, or both. In contrast, the sites at the high end of the scale are usually the large northern and western areas. What is more, with some notable exceptions (for example, Cook County, where the power of the city machine and its employees is unusually strong and contracting out is less extensive), this pattern holds even when health spending, which is quite large and somewhat unusual, is excluded.

Not only do regional variations exist in the extent of governmental reliance on nonprofits, but there are also regional variations in the share of nonprofit income that comes from government. This is apparent in table 6.9, which records the share of the income of nonprofit social service agencies that comes from government in the twelve metropolitan field sites covered by The Urban Institute survey. As

TABLE 6.8 EXTENT OF GOVERNMENT RELIANCE ON NONPROFIT ORGANIZATIONS IN SIXTEEN SITES, 1982

Site County (City)	Share of Total Public Spending Flowing to Nonprofits	
	All Fields[a]	All Except Health
Allegheny (Pittsburgh)	50%	39%
Cook (Chicago)	48	26
New York	43	46
Rhode Island	40	34
Ramsey (St. Paul)	40	26
San Francisco	40	39
Maricopa (Phoenix)	37	34
Hennepin (Minneapolis)	38	34
Warren (Vicksburg, Miss.)	34	47
Ada (Boise, Idaho)	33	18
Genessee (Flint)	28	15
Dallas	27	25
Fulton (Atlanta)	27	20
Hinds (Jackson)	23	23
Pinal, Ariz.	16	39
Tuscola, Mich.	12	25
All Sites (average)	34%	31%
All Sites (weighted average)	42.4%	30.4%

Source: The Urban Institute Nonprofit Sector Project.
a. Covers the fields of social services, health, employment and training, housing and community development, and arts and recreation.

this table shows, the government share ranges from a high of 82 percent in Jackson, Mississippi, to a low of 30 percent in Phoenix. Although the patterns are less pronounced here, there is some tendency to find higher levels of reliance on government support in the smaller communities and those in the South than in the larger communities and those in the North and West.

What accounts for these variations in government reliance on nonprofits to deliver services, and in nonprofit reliance on government for income? One factor appears to be the availability of private charitable support and the extent of private

TABLE 6.9 PERCENTAGE OF SOCIAL SERVICE AGENCY INCOME COMING FROM GOVERNMENT, BY SITE, 1981

Site	Government Share of Income
Jackson, Miss.	82%
San Francisco	74
Atlanta	70
Flint	65
Providence	65
Dallas/Fort Worth	59
Minneapolis/St. Paul	56
New York	54
Pittsburgh	53
Boise	42
Chicago	40
Phoenix	30
All Sites	57%

Source: The Urban Institute Nonprofit Sector Project Round I Survey.

TABLE 6.10 REGIONAL VARIATIONS IN THE SCOPE OF THE NONPROFIT SECTOR

Region	Nonprofit Organizations per 100,000 Population	Nonprofit Expenditures per Capita
Northeast	58.2	$522
North Central	50.2	$348
West	48.4	$262
South	36.8	$208
United States average	47.1	$323

Source: Computed from U.S. Census Bureau, 1981.

nonprofit activity to start with. As it turns out, substantial differences exist among different sections of the country and different sizes of communities in the extent of nonprofit activity. As reflected in table 6.10, the regions in which government relies most heavily on nonprofits to deliver publicly funded services (the Northeast and North Central regions) also turn out to have the highest number of nonprofit organizations and the largest nonprofit expenditures per capita. In contrast, the region in which government makes the least use of nonprofits (the South) also has the least well-developed nonprofit sector. What this suggests is that where nonprofit organizations are a major presence government has turned to them extensively for help in delivering publicly funded services. Conversely, where the sector is less fully developed, government agencies have carried more of the human service delivery burden themselves, but nonprofits have had fewer private charitable resources to draw on, too. These data thus raise doubts about the conventional image of government and the nonprofit sector as competitors. The conclusion that emerges from the data, rather, is that both government and nonprofits are responses to the same desire for collective goods, and that where this desire is strong both government activity and nonprofit activity are extensive.

Summary

The data currently available thus make clear that government support of private nonprofit organizations is extensive, that it is particularly important to social service and community development organizations, that most of it reaches nonprofit organizations indirectly—through individuals or state and local governments—and that it varies markedly among different sections of the country. Taken together, these data suggest that, whatever else its impact, government has certainly not supplanted or displaced nonprofit organizations. Rather, it has become a major force underwriting nonprofit operations, providing, in this capacity, a larger portion of the revenues of nonprofit service providers (exclusive of churches) than does private giving.

TOWARD A THEORY OF GOVERNMENT-NONPROFIT COOPERATION

Despite its immense scale and importance, the interaction between government and the nonprofit sector has attracted little serious attention, and what attention it has attracted has generally been hostile. In fact, after a flurry of interest in the late nineteenth and early twentieth centuries (Warner 1894; Fetter 1901–02; Fleisher, 1914; Dripps 1915), the subject of government-nonprofit relations largely disappeared from public debate and scholarly inquiry, as did the broader question of the role of voluntary organizations in the modern welfare state. More recently as well, a blind spot has persisted with respect to the relationships between the voluntary sector and government. A major three-year project on mediating structures conducted by the American Enterprise Institute in the mid-1970s, for example, advanced as its major conclusion the proposal that government should rely on voluntary organizations to deliver publicly funded services without ever acknowledging the extent to which current government operations already embody this approach (Berger & Neuhaus 1977). In his influential *Power and Community,* sociologist Robert Nisbet (1962) posits an inherent conflict between voluntary organizations and government, attributing to government much of the responsibility for the weakening of voluntary institutions and the resulting rise of alienation and anomie in the modern world. This theme finds expression as well in other treatments of the voluntary sector, which portray a mythical ''golden age'' of voluntary-sector purity that has been corrupted by receipt of government funds.[8] This is ironic not only because no such golden age existed but also because the early turn-of-the-century students of government-nonprofit cooperation objected to government support of nonprofits not because it would hurt nonprofits (the current concern) but because it might inhibit the development of the new welfare institutions of government, which were viewed as more comprehensive and fair. What has been lacking throughout, however, has been an analysis that takes account of the true history of government-nonprofit relationships and that comes to terms with the current shape of government-nonprofit ties.

That this is so is not simply a result of a lack of research. The reality of extensive governmental support of the voluntary sector has been too apparent for too long to accept this as an adequate explanation, especially since other aspects of voluntary-sector operations—such as board structures, staff-board relations, and professional-volunteer interaction—have come under closer scrutiny. That this reality was not perceived, or was perceived inappropriately, must therefore be attributed as much to a conceptual as to an empirical problem. Both students of the voluntary sector and students of the welfare state have failed to appreciate the reality of extensive government-nonprofit relationships because of faults in the conceptual lenses through which they have been examining this reality. To come to terms adequately with the facts, therefore, it is necessary to reconfigure the lenses, not simply add more information. To do so, we must first examine what the existing lenses look like, and determine how they have distorted our view. It may then be possible to fashion an alternative body of theory with greater power to let us see what has been going on.

The Shortcomings of Prevailing Theories

Two sets of theories are largely responsible for the widespread neglect of the role of government-nonprofit partnerships in the American welfare state: first, the theory of the welfare state, and second, the prevailing theories of the voluntary sector.

The Theory of the Welfare State

At the core of the misperception of government's relationship with the nonprofit sector in the American context has been the prevailing conception of the American welfare state. Focusing on the dramatic expansion of government social welfare expenditures that began in the Progressive Era, and accelerated during the New Deal and the Great Society, most observers have jumped easily to the natural conclusion that what has been underway in the United States has been a gigantic enlargement of the apparatus of government—particularly the national government—at the expense of other social institutions, among them private nonprofit groups. The central image has been that of a large bureaucratic state, hierarchic in structure and monolithic in form. It was this image that Nisbet (1962) apparently had in mind when he concluded:

> The conflict between the central power of the political state and the whole set of functions and authorities contained in church, family, guild, and local community has been, I believe, the main source of those dislocations of social structure and uprootings of status which lie behind the problem of community in our age. (p. 98)

> The real conflict in modern political history has not been, as is so often stated, between state and individual, but between state and social group. (p. 109)

Similarly, Berger and Neuhaus (1977, 35) bewail the tendency of government ''to establish a state monopoly over all organized activities that have to do with more than strictly private purposes.'' ''The logical conclusion of our present course,'' Kerrine and Neuhaus (1979, 18) pointed out in the mid-1970s, ''is that the state eventually becomes the sole provider of all social services.''

Whereas conservatives have had an incentive to exaggerate the growth and power of government in order to emphasize the threat that government poses to private action, liberals have had a corresponding incentive to downplay the role of voluntary agencies in order to buttress the case for a government role. This tendency has been encouraged as well by the focus of much of the national policy debate and most policy analysis on the *formulation* of policy, which has

---

8. Nielsen (1980) criticizes conventional scholarship on the voluntary sector because of this tendency, though Nielsen himself also takes a generally critical stance toward government support to nonprofits. For one of the few early alternative views, see Pifer (1966).

moved decisively into the public realm, rather than on its *implementation,* which is where nonprofits have retained a substantial role.[9] The overall result has been to emphasize the expansion of the state, to convey an impression of governmental dominance of societal problem solving and service provision, and to downplay in the process the role of private voluntary groups.

The Theories of the Voluntary Sector

While the prevailing conception of the modern welfare state has left little room for a vibrant private nonprofit sector or for a blossoming government-nonprofit partnership, the existing images of the voluntary sector similarly fail to create much expectation for effective cooperation between nonprofit organizations and the state. The current conception of the voluntary sector took shape, in fact, as part of a broader effort during the late nineteenth and early twentieth century to differentiate the public and private sectors in America in order to provide a conceptual basis for private business expansion unfettered by governmental control. The private voluntary sector thus came to be viewed for the first time as something apart from and better than government, and private agencies grew increasingly disdainful of public support.[10]

This tradition finds reflection, however, in the more formal theories of the voluntary sector that have surfaced in recent years. Broadly speaking, two such theories have been advanced to explain the existence of the voluntary sector, and neither provides much rationale for government-nonprofit cooperation.

The first of these theories views the existence of the voluntary sector as a product of "market failure," of inherent limitations of both the private market and government in producing collective goods (Weisbrod 1978). "Collective goods" are products or services like national defense or clean air that, once produced, are enjoyed by everyone whether or not they have paid for them. Providing these goods exclusively through the market will thus ensure that they are in short supply since few consumers will volunteer to pay for products they can enjoy free. In economic theory this is known as the free-rider problem. The need to produce such collective goods serves in traditional economic theory as the major rationale for government, since government can tax people to produce such goods. But there are circumstances in which one part of a political community feels a need for a range of collective goods but cannot convince a majority of the community to go along. It is to handle such circumstances, the argument goes, that a private voluntary sector is needed. Private nonprofit organizations thus exist to supply a range of collective goods desired by one segment of a com-

munity but not by a majority. From this it follows that the more diverse the community, the more extensive the nonprofit sector is likely to be. But because the nonprofit sector is viewed as a substitute for government, providing goods and services that the full political community has not endorsed, government support to nonprofit organizations has no theoretical rationale. To the contrary, under this theory, to the extent that nonprofits deliver services that government underwrites, they violate their theoretical raison d'être, which is to supply the goods government is not providing.

The second broad theory of the voluntary sector attributes the existence of voluntary organizations to a different kind of market failure, what one theorist terms contract failure (Hansmann 1981; see also chap. 2). The central notion here is that for some goods and services, such as care for the aged, the purchaser is not the same as the consumer. In these circumstances, the normal mechanisms of the market—which involve consumer choice on the basis of adequate information—do not obtain. Consequently, some proxy has to be created to offer the purchaser a degree of assurance that the goods or services being purchased meet adequate standards of quality and quantity. The nonprofit form, in this theory, provides that proxy. Unlike for-profit businesses, which are motivated by profit and therefore might be tempted to betray the trust of a purchaser who is not the recipient of what he buys, nonprofit firms are in business for more charitable purposes and may therefore be more worthy of trust.

Since most government programs involve a substantial amount of regulation, however, this theory also provides little rationale for government reliance on nonprofits or at least for government regulation of nonprofits (Rose-Ackerman 1985). In fact, since government agencies might be expected to have even less reason to betray trust than nonprofits, this theory might lead one to expect more reliance on government agencies than on nonprofit ones.

Toward a New Theory of Government-Nonprofit Relations

Given the prevailing perceptions of the American welfare state and the prevailing theories of the voluntary sector, it comes as no surprise that there is so little awareness of the continued vitality of the nonprofit sector or of the immense importance of government-nonprofit cooperation. In neither set of theories is there much hint that the nonprofit sector should play as substantial a role as it does. How, then, are we to account for this phenomenon? Is the continued vigor of the nonprofit sector and the extensive pattern of government-nonprofit cooperation accidental, or is there some theoretical rationale that can better help us come to terms with these developments?

I believe that the answer to these questions lies in certain shortcomings in the prevailing theories. Both the theory of the welfare state and the theory of the voluntary sector, moreover, are deficient, though for different reasons. To bring the prevailing reality into better focus, therefore, both sets of theories need to be reworked.

---

9. On the neglect of implementation research, see Hargrove (1975).

10. On the general movement to establish an intellectual basis for emphasizing the superiority of private over public action, see Hartz (1948). On the implications for the voluntary sector, see Nielsen (1980, 14–18), Stevens (1982, 550–56), and Whitehead (1973, 1–25).

Third-Party Government and the Theory of the Welfare State

The central problem with the theory of the welfare state as it has applied to the American context is its failure to differentiate between government's role as a provider of funds and direction and its role as a deliverer of services. In point of fact, it is largely in the former capacity that government—certainly the national government—has grown in the United States. In contrast, for actual delivery of services, the national government has turned extensively to other institutions—states, cities, counties, universities, hospitals, banks, industrial corporations, and others. The extensive pattern of government support of nonprofit organizations is thus but a part of a broader pattern of government action in this country that I have elsewhere called "third-party government" (Salamon 1981). The central characteristic of this pattern is the use of nongovernmental, or at least non–federal governmental, entities to carry out governmental purposes, and the exercise by these entities of a substantial degree of discretion over the spending of public funds and the exercise of public authority.

This pattern of government action is evident in a wide assortment of domestic program areas and involves a diverse array of actors. Under the more than nine hundred grant-in-aid programs, for example, the federal government makes financial assistance available to states and local governments for purposes ranging from aid to families with dependent children to the construction of interstate highways. Under the federal government's loan guarantee programs, close to $150 billion is lent by private banks to individuals and corporations, with federal backing, for everything from home mortgages to college educations.

In each of these programs the federal government performs a managerial function but leaves a substantial degree of discretion to its nongovernmental, or nonfederal, partner. In the Aid to Families with Dependent Children program, for example, the federal government reimburses states for a portion of their payments to mothers with dependent children, but leaves to the states the decision about whether to have such a program, what the income eligibility cut-offs will be, and even what the benefits will be.

This form of government action reflects America's federal constitutional structure, with its sharing of governmental functions between federal and state governments (Grodzins 1966; Elazar 1972). But third-party government extends well beyond the domain of relations among the different levels of government. It also applies to governmental relationships with a host of private institutions. As such, it reflects as well the conflict that has long existed in American political thinking between the desire for public services and hostility to the governmental apparatus that provides them. Third-party government has emerged as a way to reconcile these competing perspectives—to increase the role of government in promoting the general welfare without unduly enlarging the state's administrative apparatus. Where existing institutions are available to carry out a function—whether it be extending loans, providing health care, delivering social services—they therefore have a presumptive claim on a meaningful role in whatever public program might be established.

This pattern of government action is also encouraged by the country's pluralistic political structure. To secure needed support for a program of government action, it is frequently necessary to ensure at least the acquiescence, if not the wholehearted support, of key interests with a stake in the area. One way to do this is to give them a piece of the action by building them into the operation of the program. Thus private banks are involved in running the government's mortgage guarantee programs; private health insurers and hospitals, in the operation of the Medicare and Medicaid programs; and states and private social service agencies, in the provision of federally funded social services.

Finally, this pattern of government action is motivated in part by concerns about efficiency and economy. Where existing institutions are already performing a function, government can frequently carry out its purposes more simply and with less cost by enlisting them in the government program, thereby avoiding the need to create wholly new organizational structures or specialized staffs. This is particularly true where programs are experimental. This way of organizing government services also makes it easier to adapt program operations to local circumstances or individual needs and thus avoid some of the drawbacks of large-scale governmental bureaucracy. Finally, some argue that the use of outside contractors lowers costs by stimulating competition and promoting economies of scale, though the evidence here is far from conclusive (Fitch 1974; Savas 1984; Spann 1977).

In short, the extensive pattern of governmental support of nonprofit institutions is just one manifestation of a much broader pattern of third-party government that reflects deep-seated American traditions of governance as well as more recent concerns about service costs and quality. Instead of the hierarchic, bureaucratic apparatus pictured in conventional images of the American welfare state, third-party government involves an extensive sharing of responsibilities among public and private institutions and a pervasive blending of public and private roles. Because a number of different institutions must act together to achieve a given program goal, this pattern of government action seriously complicates the task of public management and involves real problems of accountability and control (Salamon 1981; Smith 1975; Staats 1975). But it also has much to recommend it. It makes it possible to set priorities for the expenditure of societal resources through a democratic political process while leaving the actual operation of the resulting public programs to smaller-scale organizations closer to the problems being addressed. It thus creates a public presence without creating a monstrous public bureaucracy. And it permits a degree of diversity and competition in the provision of publicly funded services that can improve efficiency and reduce costs.

So long as the image of the welfare state in America remained tied to its conventional European model stressing the expansion of the centralized bureaucratic state, the phenomenon of extensive governmental support for voluntary organizations had no apparent place and therefore tended to be overlooked. But once we adjust our conceptual lenses to take account of the reality of third-party government, it becomes clear why nonprofits play so important a role. In many fields, after all, private nonprofit organizations were involved before government arrived on the scene. In addition, nonprofits usually have objectives that are akin to, though hardly identical with, those of the public sector. Indeed, as noted above, until the late nineteenth century, private nonprofit organizations were considered part of the public sector since they were designed to serve public purposes. Given a welfare state that is characterized by an extensive pattern of third-party government, widespread government reliance on nonprofit organizations is thus not an anomaly but exactly what one would expect.

Voluntary Failure: A New Theory of the Voluntary Sector

If the failure to acknowledge the reality of third-party government in the conventional image of the American welfare state explains part of the neglect of government-nonprofit cooperation in recent decades, shortcomings in the existing theories of the voluntary sector explain the rest. Essentially, as we have seen, these theories explain the existence of the voluntary sector in terms of failures of the market system and of government. The voluntary sector is thus seen as derivative and secondary, filling in where other systems fall short.

It is possible, however, to turn this discussion on its head, to reject the view that the voluntary sector is merely a residual response to failures of government and the market and to see it instead as the *preferred mechanism* for providing collective goods. Government would then be viewed, under this theory, as the residual institution, needed only because of certain shortcomings or failings of the voluntary sector.

The central argument for this approach is that the creation of a sense of social obligation of the sort that is required to support collective action on community problems is best done on a voluntary basis and at the local or group level, where individuals can participate with their neighbors without sacrificing their freedom of choice (Schambra 1982). The more the fostering of a sense of social obligation moves away from this level, therefore, the more tenuous it becomes. Treating government, particularly the national government, as the first line of defense for the provision of needed collective goods, as is done in economic theory, thus creates a far less secure basis for the provision of these goods than voluntary action can provide. Government action thus becomes appropriate under this alternative theory only to correct for "voluntary failures," for inherent shortcomings of the voluntary sector. Viewed from this perspective, government support to voluntary organizations, and government-nonprofit partnerships, emerge as the least disruptive form that such governmental response to voluntary failure can take.

This alternative perspective is certainly more consistent with the history of government-nonprofit relationships in this country and makes far better sense of the fundamental reality of extensive government-nonprofit ties. What is more, it suggests a theoretical rationale for these ties that fits into a broader, and more positive, conception of the voluntary sector, thus rescuing this fundamental fact of voluntary-sector life from the limbo to which it has been consigned by existing theories.

But what are the voluntary failures that thus justify government involvement and governmental support for the voluntary sector? Broadly speaking, there are four: philanthropic insufficiency, philanthropic particularism, philanthropic paternalism, and philanthropic amateurism.

Philanthropic Insufficiency.   The central failing of the voluntary system as a provider of collective goods has been its inability to generate resources on a scale that is both adequate enough and reliable enough to cope with the human service problems of an advanced industrial society. In part, this is a reflection of the free-rider problem inherent in the production of collective goods. Since everybody benefits from a society in which those in need are cared for whether or not they have contributed to the cost of the care, there is an incentive for each person to let his neighbor bear most of the cost. Only when contributions are involuntary, as they are through taxation, are they therefore likely to be sufficient and consistent. As one early student of American charity put it: "The law is primarily an agency for bringing up the laggards in the march of progress, and when the community on the average wants benevolent work done, this is the method of pushing forward those who hang back. . . . The stingy man is not allowed to thrive at the expense of his benevolent neighbor" (Warner 1894, 306). Since the range of "benevolent work" that is thought necessary has expanded considerably over the years, moreover, this problem has grown increasingly important over time.

Beyond the free-rider problem, however, philanthropic insufficiency also results from the twists and turns of economic fortune. The fluctuations that have accompanied the growing complexity of economic life mean that benevolent individuals may find themselves least able to help others when those others are most in need of help, as happened with disastrous results during the Great Depression. Similarly, the voluntary system often leaves serious gaps in geographic coverage, since the locus of the resources frequently does not correspond well with the locus of the problems. In short, the voluntary system, despite its advantages in terms of creating a meaningful sense of social obligation and legitimacy, nevertheless has serious drawbacks as a generator of a reliable stream of resources to respond adequately to community needs.

Philanthropic Particularism.   If resource inadequacy is one source of voluntary-sector weakness, the particularism of the voluntary sector constitutes another. Particularism—the tendency of voluntary organizations and their benefactors to focus on particular subgroups of the population—is, of course, one of the purported strengths of the voluntary sector. Voluntary organizations provide the vehicle through which subgroups—ethnic, religious, neighborhood, interest, or other—can come together for common purposes.

Indeed, in some theories, as we have seen, it is precisely this particularism that provides the theoretical rationale for the existence of the nonprofit sector.

But particularism also has its drawbacks as the basis for organizing a community's response to human needs. For one thing, some subgroups of the community may not be adequately represented in the structure of voluntary organizations. Even voluntary organizations require resources, after all, and it is possible that those in command of the needed resources—financial as well as organizational—may not favor all segments of the community equally. As a result, serious gaps can occur in the availability of services. Up through the early 1960s, for example, the lion's share of child welfare services in New York City were provided through Catholic and Jewish agencies. Since most of the poor blacks who migrated to the city in the post–World War II era were Protestants, however, they did not immediately find a ''home'' in the established agency structure (Beck 1971, 271). Other subgroups—gays, the disabled, Hispanics, women—have found similar difficulties establishing a niche in the voluntary system and locating a source of support for their activities. More generally, the private nonprofit sector has long had a tendency to treat the more ''deserving'' of the poor, leaving the most difficult cases to public institutions. Indeed, our survey of 3,400 human service organizations revealed that the poor were the majority of the clients of only about 30 percent of the agencies, and that for half of the agencies, the poor constituted less than 10 percent of the clientele.

Not only can particularism, and the favoritism that inevitably accompanies it, leave serious gaps in coverage; it can also contribute to wasteful duplication of services. Voluntary organizations and charitable activity are motivated by considerations not only of social need but also of communal or individual pride. Each subgroup wants its ''own'' agencies, and appeals to donors are frequently made along religious, ethnic, or sectarian lines. The upshot is that the number of agencies can increase well beyond what economies of scale might suggest, reducing the overall efficiency of the system and increasing its costs. This was a great concern of early students of American social welfare policy, who viewed the duplication of facilities and the resulting waste of resources as one of the great drawbacks of the private voluntary system (Fetter 1901–02, 380; Fleisher 1914, 111). As Warner (1894, 359) put it in his classic treatise on American charity: ''The charities of a given locality, which should for useful result be systematically directed to the accomplishment of their common purposes, are usually a chaos, a patchwork of survivals, or products of contending political, religious, and medical factions, a curious compound, in which a strong ingredient is ignorance perpetuated by heedlessness.''

Left to their own devices, therefore, voluntary organizations may leave significant elements of the community without care and make wasteful use of what resources are available.

Philanthropic Paternalism. A third class of problems with the voluntary system of responding to community problems results from the fact that this approach inevitably vests most of the influence over the definition of community needs in the hands of those in command of the greatest resources. This is so despite the importance of volunteer effort in this sector. For one thing, voluntarism itself requires resources of time and knowledge. But, in addition, the growing need for professional approaches to social problems has made it necessary to go beyond voluntary effort. So long as private charity is the only support for the voluntary sector, those in control of the charitable resources can determine what the sector does and whom it serves. The nature of the sector thus comes to be shaped by the preferences not of the community as a whole but of its wealthy members. As a consequence, some services favored by the wealthy—such as the arts— may be promoted, while others desired by the poor are held back. Since these private contributions are tax deductible, moreover, they have the effect of allocating not only private expenditures but forgone public revenues as well, though without the benefit of any public decision process.

This situation is both undemocratic and potentially self-defeating since it can create a debilitating sense of dependency on the part of the poor. Aid is provided as a matter of charity, not of right. What is more, it was often accompanied in the past by moral preachments of the sort George Bernard Shaw immortalized in his play *Major Barbara*. A central premise of much early philanthropic activity, in fact, was that the poor were responsible for their own destitution and needed to be uplifted religiously and morally through the work of sectarian agencies. Even in more recent times, close students of social policy have criticized the funneling of funds ''into the hands of upper-class and middle-class people to spend on behalf of the less privileged people'' as ''the most pernicious effect'' of the private charitable system because of the dependency relationship it creates (Beck 1971, 218). In short, for all its strengths and value, private charitable support cannot easily escape its ''Lady Bountiful'' heritage and establish a claim to assistance as a right.

Philanthropic Amateurism. One final problem with the voluntary system has been its association with amateur approaches to coping with human problems. In part, this has reflected the sector's paternalism noted above: for a considerable period of time, the problems of poverty and want were attributed to the moral turpitude of the poor. Care of the poor, the insane, the unwed mother was therefore appropriately entrusted to well-meaning amateurs and those whose principal calling was moral suasion and religious instruction, not medical aid or job training.

As sociological and psychological theory advanced, however, these approaches lost favor; attention turned to more professional treatment modes involving trained social workers and counselors. Voluntary agencies, which stressed volunteer efforts and were limited by dependence on contributions from offering adequate wages, were in a poor position to attract professional personnel. It was partly for this reason that social welfare advocates of the late nineteenth and early twentieth centuries opposed public support for private charitable institutions, fearing this would siphon off resources needed to build an adequate system of professional *public* care. As one of these advocates put it in 1914: ''No appropriations should be made to charities under private management until the reasonable needs of the charities managed and supported by the state have been fully met and an adequate system of state institutions developed'' (Fleisher 1914, 112).

Summary: A Theory of Government-Nonprofit Partnership

In short, for all its strengths, the voluntary sector has a number of serious drawbacks as a mechanism for responding to the human service needs of an advanced industrial society. It is limited in its ability to generate an adequate level of resources, it is vulnerable to particularism and the favoritism of the wealthy, it is prone to self-defeating paternalism, and it has at times been associated with amateur, as opposed to professional, forms of care.

Significantly, however, the voluntary sector's weaknesses correspond well with government's strengths, and vice versa. Potentially, at least, government is in a position to generate a more reliable stream of resources, to set priorities on the basis of a democratic political process instead of the wishes of the wealthy, to offset part of the paternalism of the charitable system by making access to care a right instead of a privilege, and to improve the quality of care by instituting quality-control standards. By the same token, however, voluntary organizations can personalize the provision of services, operate on a smaller scale than government bureaucracies, reduce the scale of public institutions needed, adjust care to the needs of clients rather than to the structure of government agencies, and permit a degree of competition among service providers.

Under these circumstances, neither the replacement of the voluntary sector by government nor the replacement of government by the voluntary sector makes as much sense as collaboration between the two. In short, viewed from a theoretical perspective that acknowledges the widespread pattern of third-party government in the American version of the modern welfare state, and that posits the voluntary sector as the preferred mechanism for providing collective goods, but one that has certain inherent limitations or ''failures,'' extensive collaboration between government and the nonprofit sector emerges not as an unwarranted aberration but as a logical and theoretically sensible compromise. The voluntary failure theory of the voluntary sector and the third-party government theory of the American welfare state outlined here thus allow us to come to terms with the reality of government-nonprofit relationships far more effectively than the prevailing concepts now in use. Given the fundamental importance of these relationships, this is reason enough to lend credence to these alternative theories.

GOVERNMENT AND THE NONPROFIT SECTOR IN PRACTICE

To say that a strong theoretical rationale exists for government-nonprofit cooperation is not, of course, to say that this cooperation has worked out in practice the way the theory would suggest. To the contrary, any relationship as complex as this one is likely to encounter immense strains and difficulties, especially given the somewhat different perspectives of the two sides. Government officials, for example, must worry about the problems of exercising management supervision, ensuring a degree of accountability, and encouraging coordination when decision-making authority is widely dispersed and vested in institutions with their own independent sources of authority and support. Within the philanthropic community, the issues raised by the prevailing pattern of government support of nonprofit organizations are of a far different sort. Of central concern here are three other potential dangers: first, loss of autonomy or independence, particularly the dilution of the sector's advocacy role; second, ''vendorism,'' or the distortion of agency missions in pursuit of available government funding; and third, bureaucratization or overprofessionalization and a resulting loss of the flexibility and local control that are considered the sector's greatest strengths.

In the absence of a firm theoretical basis for government-nonprofit relations, neither government officials nor nonprofits have managed to develop a meaningful and coherent set of standards in terms of which to guide their interactions. Rather, both sides have tended to view the relationship from their own perspective and to apply standards that are rigid and absolute.

The concepts developed above, however, suggest a more meaningful and balanced set of criteria by which the relationships between government and the nonprofit sector can be judged. To the extent that cooperation between government and the nonprofit sector reflects a fit between the respective strengths and weaknesses of the two, as is argued above, the appropriate standard is one that acknowledges the need to correct the shortcomings of the two sectors without doing unnecessary damage to their respective strengths. In practice, this means that government's need for economy, efficiency, and accountability must be tempered by the nonprofit sector's need for a degree of self-determination and independence of governmental control; but that the sector's desire for independence must in turn be tempered by government's need to achieve equity and to make sure that public resources are used to advance the purposes intended.

Regrettably, the empirical data needed to evaluate how successfully this partnership has met this test are sparse. As one student of the subject pointed out in 1975: ''Although the potential hazards and benefits of government contracting for the purchase of service can be readily identified in the literature, little systematic research has been reported on failure or benefits that have actually come about. The concern is real, but the facts are not certain'' (Wedel 1976, 102).

Although the situation has not changed much since Wedel wrote, it is possible to reach some tentative judgments about how this partnership has been working. In particular, the message that emerges from the limited analysis to date is that many of the concerns about the partnership have not materialized to anywhere near the extent feared. Let us look first at what is known about the impact of this partnership on the nonprofit world, and then examine how it has operated from the perspective of the public sector.

The View from the Nonprofit Sector

Agency Independence

Perhaps the central concern on the part of those worried about nonprofit involvement in government programs has been the fear that such involvement would rob nonprofits of their "independence." A fundamental feature of the nonprofit sector, in this view, is its availability as a reservoir of novel or unpopular ideas and its role as an agent of social and political change. To the extent that the sector becomes an "agent" of the state, the argument goes, it will lose this capability and be vulnerable to political retaliation. What is more, it will come to tailor its activities to the priorities of far-away political representatives rather than to those of the communities it serves. A more subtle version of this argument takes the form of a concern that undue stress on the service delivery function of the sector can "straitjacket" nonprofit organizations and dilute their advocacy role.

Although instances of governmental infringement on agency autonomy doubtless exist (most recently in the battle over Office of Management and Budget Circular A-102 designed to prevent the use of federal funds to promote advocacy activities), the preponderance of empirical evidence casts doubt on this line of argument. A recent study of private agencies serving the handicapped by sociologist Ralph Kramer (1980, 292, 160), for example, concluded that "voluntary-agency autonomy is seldom compromised by the accountability requirements of governmental funding sources. More often, there is a low level of regulation and a closeness based on mutual dependency. . . . the impact of governmental funds in controlling voluntary social service organizations may be much less than is commonly believed."

The concern about the potential challenge to agency independence posed by government agencies must be evaluated, moreover, in the light of the challenge that can be posed by private funding sources as well. The notion that the nonprofit sector is independent, after all, can be misleading. Financially, the sector is almost inevitably dependent—on private sources of funds if not public ones. And historically, private funds have often come with strings every bit as onerous and threatening to agency independence as any government has devised.[11] At the very least, the valid concerns about the potential loss of independence as a result of receipt of public funds need to be balanced by a recognition of the challenge to

the independence of at least some kinds of organizations that can be posed by sole reliance on private funding as well.

Vendorism

An offshoot of the independence issue is the concern that government funding can distort agency missions by enticing agencies to concentrate their efforts in areas that may not coincide with what the nonprofit organization itself thinks is important or would like to do. Of particular concern here is the possibility that voluntary boards of directors can lose effective control of the agencies as a consequence, since the professional staff can develop funding sources outside of board influence or control.

Here, again, the empirical evidence is not supportive. A study of New York nonprofit agencies conducted by the New York United Way, for example, found little evidence that government funding had distorted agency missions (Hartogs & Weber 1978, 8–9). To the contrary, most agencies reported that government funding enabled them to carry out their existing missions better. Similarly, our survey of over 3,400 nonprofit agencies in sixteen local areas across the country turned up little evidence of agency concern that government had distorted agency missions. In only one significant respect did the agencies we surveyed report a change in their mission in response to receipt of government funds: they credited government with inducing them to focus more of their services on the poor. However, this fits well with the notion of philanthropic particularism cited above as one of the rationales for government involvement. Evidently, governmental support is having the effect that the theory developed here claimed for it—overcoming some of the favoritism of the nonprofit sector. Kramer's work on nonprofit agencies serving the handicapped reached a similar conclusion. As he phrased it: "Generally, agencies did what they always wanted to do, but for which they previously lacked the resources" (1980, 163).

Here as well, moreover, pressures to alter agency purposes can also emanate from private nongovernmental funding sources. These sources frequently have their own priorities and concerns that may or may not accord with the priorities of voluntary agencies. Foundations, for example, have frequently been accused of preferring new experimental programs, making it difficult to find support for mainline services. Similarly, many advocacy groups feel that corporations and foundations tend to shy away from potential controversy. Over half of the respondents in our survey of nonprofit organizations, in fact, felt that corporations do not support their types of programs. This was particularly true of social service and advocacy organizations serving minorities and the poor. In the absence of government support, these agencies might be forced to alter their programs to fit the funding priorities of private funders.

Agency Management and Bureaucratization

A third major issue surrounding government support of nonprofit organizations has been a concern that involvement with

---

11. Until recently, for example, little private support was available for inner-city minority organizations, particularly those with an advocacy mission. In recent years, many local United Way and corporate donors have insisted that agencies raise more of their funds from fees and charges and make other management changes, such as merging with other organizations. In addition, many foundations have standing policies against ongoing institutional support, which makes it necessary for nonprofit organizations to generate successive "novel" or "experimental" programs to attract foundation support.

government programs tends to produce an undesirable degree of bureaucratization and professionalization in the recipient agency. While relying on nonprofits to create a greater degree of heterogeneity and flexibility in service delivery than they can often provide themselves, government agencies must nevertheless guarantee that some features of program operations remain standard, even if carried out by nonprofits. These include effective financial management and accounting, maintenance of minimum quality standards, promotion of basic program objectives, and adherence to certain national policy goals such as equal opportunity, handicapped rights, and environmental protection. Government programs therefore often involve more red tape, cumbersome application requirements, and regulatory control than is common with other forms of financial support. In fact, over half (53 percent) of the respondents in our survey of nonprofit agencies agreed that "it is easier to deal with corporate and foundation funding sources than government funding sources," and less than a quarter disagreed. To cope with the financial accountability standards of government programs, the voluntary agency frequently has to develop internal management processes that reduce the agency's flexibility and often threaten its informal, voluntary character. In addition, government programs sometimes carry with them regulatory provisions that lead to greater reliance on professional staff and less on volunteers. Facilities sometimes must be certified and governmental guidelines on client/staff ratios, employment practices, provision for the handicapped, and so on adhered to (see Berger & Neuhaus 1977; Rosenbaum 1982).

Of all the concerns raised about the impact of government funding on nonprofit organizations, this one probably is the most credible. But there is a tendency to ascribe more of the apparent bureaucratization and professionalization of nonprofit organizations to government support than is probably justifiable. The pressures for improved agency management, tighter financial control, and use of professionals in service delivery do not, after all, come solely from government. Increased professionalization has been a major trend for decades within the fields in which nonprofit organizations are active: social services, health, education, even arts and community organization. In fact, the push for professionalization came in part from the voluntary sector, and government has been used to spread the professional standards developed in individual fields. In addition, many private funders increasingly expect sound financial management on the part of the agencies to which they provide resources. This is particularly true, for example, of United Way.

In contrast to the perception that agencies may be overbureaucratized and preoccupied with internal management, moreover, a study of the impact of government funding carried out by the Greater New York Fund in the mid-1970s concluded that voluntary agencies may pay *too little attention* to this dimension of their operations: they often do not charge government enough to carry out publicly funded services and must dip into their own resources to help. As the authors of this study concluded: "The enemy to survival is not from without, i.e., the government, but from within the agency's own management practices" (Hartogs & Weber 1978, 10).

The View from Government

That the partnership between government and the nonprofit sector may not have worked out as badly for the voluntary sector as many have feared is due in part to the fact that the instruments for accountability and control available to government have often been far weaker than is assumed. For one thing, as we have seen, much government aid to the nonprofit sector takes the form of payments to individuals or reimbursements for services rendered to them. Under such arrangements, government's ability to hold the nonprofit institution to account for the cost and quality of service is limited. In fact, in the massive Medicare program, and to a lesser extent in Medicaid, government has been obliged to underwrite virtually any costs that private hospitals claim are needed, with little opportunity for effective cost control. The elaborate licensing and regulatory procedures put in place for new facilities and for equipment purchase are merely efforts to come to terms with this fundamental fact of life, and they are imperfect efforts at that.[12]

Although more effective means of control are potentially available in the direct-grant and purchase-of-service arrangements, things have often not worked that way in practice because of the absence of some of the crucial prerequisites of cost-effective contracting—such as meaningful competition among providers, effective measures of performance, and government decision making geared to performance. Too often, decisions about whether to contract out services, and with whom, have been made under the pressures of unreasonable program deadlines, with too little information, and with little opportunity to search out potential contractors. As a consequence, governments have often had to accept the services the prevailing network of providers could supply rather than seek those the needs of the target population required. What is more, because performance criteria have been difficult to fashion and apply, government has often resorted to accounting controls and application and reporting procedures that increase the burdens on agencies without providing an effective means of oversight for government (DeHoog 1985).

Summary

Taken as a whole, then, the research to date on the impact of government funding on nonprofit organizations suggests that many of the fears that surround this relationship have not been borne out in practice. Clearly dangers to agency inde-

---

12. This changed somewhat in 1982 with the adoption of the diagnostic-related group (DRG) system of reimbursement, under which the federal government has fixed the amount it will pay under Medicare for treatment of certain ailments and thus created incentives for hospitals to reduce costs.

pendence, pursuit of agency purposes, and internal management style may result from involvement with public programs, but these dangers do not appear to be so severe as to argue for dismantling the partnership that has been created. More troubling, in fact, may be the concerns on the public side—that reliance on nonprofits to deliver publicly financed services can undermine public objectives and inflate costs. Perhaps the safest conclusion is that this relationship has involved excesses on both sides because of a failure to examine it closely or to develop a reasonable set of standards to guide it. By bringing this relationship into clearer empirical and theoretical focus, as this chapter has sought to do, it may be possible to move toward the more balanced assessment that is desperately needed.

CONCLUSION

For better or worse, cooperation between government and the voluntary sector is the approach this nation has chosen to deal with its human service problems. Though largely overlooked both in treatments of the voluntary sector and in analyses of the American welfare state, this pattern of cooperation has grown into a massive system of action that accounts for at least as large a share of government-funded human services as are delivered by government agencies themselves and that constitutes the largest single source of nonprofit-sector income. Despite its problems, this partnership has much to recommend it, combining as it does the superior revenue-raising and democratic decision-making processes of government with the potentially smaller-scale, more personalized service delivery capabilities of the voluntary sector. What is more, the partnership has deep roots in American history, testifying to its fit with basic national values.

In view of this, it is curious indeed how little serious attention the government-nonprofit partnership has attracted and how little account has been taken of it in conventional theories of the welfare state and of the voluntary sector. This chapter has argued that this neglect is a function of deficiencies in both sets of theories. The reconceptualization offered here, stressing the phenomenon of third-party government and the voluntary failure theory of the nonprofit world, provides a corrective to these deficiencies. Equipped with these concepts, it should be possible to rescue the government-nonprofit partnership from the intellectual no-man's land to which it has long been consigned and to come to terms with it as a basic and generally attractive feature of the American policy landscape.

REFERENCES

American Association of Fund-Raising Counsel, Inc. 1981. *Giving USA: 1981 Annual Report.*

Beck, Bertram M. 1971. "Governmental Contracts with Nonprofit Social Welfare Corporations." In Bruce L. R. Smith and D. C. Hague, *The Dilemma of Accountability in Modern Government.* New York: St. Martin's Press.

Berger, Peter, and John Neuhaus. 1977. *To Empower People: The Role of Mediating Structures in Public Policy.* Washington, D.C.: American Enterprise Institute.

Bolling, Landrum R. 1982. *Private Foreign Aid: U.S. Philanthropy for Relief and Development.* Boulder, Colo.: Westview Press.

Commission on Private Philanthropy and Public Needs. 1975. *Giving in America: Toward a Stronger Voluntary Sector.* Washington, D.C.: Commission on Private Philanthropy and Public Needs.

DeHoog, Ruth Hoogland. 1985. "Human Services Contracting: Environmental, Behavioral and Organizational Conditions." *Administration and Society* 16:427–54.

Dripps, Robert D. 1915. "The Policy of State Aid to Private Charities." In *Proceedings of the National Conference of Charities and Correction.* Chicago: Hildman Printing Co.

Elazar, Daniel. 1972. *American Federalism: The View from the States.* New York: Thomas Y. Crowell.

Fetter, Frank. 1901–02. "The Subsidizing of Private Charities." *American Journal of Sociology*, pp. 359–85.

Fitch, L. C. 1974. "Increasing the Role of the Private Sector in Providing Public Services." In *Improving the Quality of Urban Management,* edited by W. D. Hawley and D. Rogers, 264–306. Beverly Hills, Calif.: Sage.

Fleisher, A. 1914. "State Money and Privately Managed Charities." *Survey* 33:110–12.

Grodzins, Morton. 1966. *The American System.* Chicago: Rand-McNally.

Grønbjerg, Kirsten A., Madeleine Kimmich, and Lester M. Salamon. 1984. *The Chicago Nonprofit Sector in a Time of Government Retrenchment.* Washington, D.C.: The Urban Institute Press.

Grønbjerg, Kirsten A., James C. Musselwhite, Jr., and Lester M. Salamon. 1984. *Government Spending and the Nonprofit Sector in Cook County/Chicago.* Washington, D.C.: The Urban Institute Press.

Gutowski, Michael, Lester M. Salamon, and Karen Pittman. 1984. *The Pittsburgh Nonprofit Sector in a Time of Government Retrenchment.* Washington, D.C.: The Urban Institute Press.

Hansmann, Henry. 1981. "Why Are Nonprofit Organizations Exempted from Corporate Income Taxation?" In *Nonprofit*

Firms in a Three-Sector Economy, edited by Michelle J. White. COUPE Papers. Washington, D.C.: The Urban Institute Press.

Harder, Paul, James C. Musselwhite, Jr., and Lester M. Salamon. 1984. *Government Spending and the Nonprofit Sector in San Francisco*. Washington, D.C.: The Urban Institute Press.

Hargrove, Erwin. 1975. *The Missing Link*. Washington, D.C.: The Urban Institute Press.

Hartogs, Nelly, and Joseph Weber. 1978. *Impact of Government Funding on the Management of Voluntary Agencies*. New York: Greater New York Fund, pp. 8–9.

Hartz, Louis. 1948. *Economic Policy and Democratic Thought: Pennsylvania, 1776–1860*. Cambridge, Mass.: Harvard University Press.

Hodgkinson, Virginia, and Murray Weitzman. 1984. *Dimensions of the Independent Sector*. Washington, D.C.: Independent Sector.

Kerrine, Theodore M., and Richard John Neuhaus. 1979. "Mediating Structures: A Paradigm for Democratic Pluralism." *Annals of the American Academy of Political and Social Sciences* 446.

Kramer, Ralph. 1980. *Voluntary Agencies in the Welfare State*. Berkeley: University of California Press, p. 163.

Lukermann, Barbara, Madeleine Kimmich, and Lester M. Salamon. 1984. *The Twin Cities Nonprofit Sector in a Time of Government Retrenchment*. Washington, D.C.: The Urban Institute Press.

Musselwhite, James C., Jr., Winsome Hawkins, and Lester M. Salamon. 1985. *Government Spending and the Nonprofit Sector in Atlanta/Fulton County*. Washington, D.C.: The Urban Institute Press.

Nielsen, Waldemar. 1980. *The Endangered Sector*. New York: Columbia University Press, p. 47.

Nisbet, Robert. 1962. *Power and Community*. 2d ed. New York: Oxford University Press.

Pifer, Alan. 1966. "The Nongovernmental Organization at Bay." In *Carnegie Corporation Annual Report*.

Rose-Ackerman, Susan. 1985. "Nonprofit Firms: Are Government Grants Desirable?" Mimeographed.

Rosenbaum, Nelson. 1982. "Government Funding and the Voluntary Sector: Impacts and Options." In *Volunteerism in the Eighties: Fundamental Issues in Voluntary Action*. Washington, D.C.: University Press of America.

Rosner, David. 1980. "Gaining Control: Reform, Reimbursement and Politics in New York's Community Hospitals, 1890–1915." In *American Journal of Public Health* 790:533–42.

Rudney, Gabriel. 1975. "The Scope of the Private Voluntary Charitable Sector." In Commission on Private Philanthropy and Public Needs, *Research Papers*. Washington, D.C.: U.S. Department of the Treasury, 1:135–41.

———. 1982. "A Quantitative Profile of the Nonprofit Sector." Yale University, Program on Non-Profit Organizations Working Paper no. 40.

Salamon, Lester M. 1981. "Rethinking Public Management: Third-Party Government and the Changing Forms of Public Action." *Public Policy* 29:255–75.

———. 1984a. "Nonprofit Organizations: The Lost Opportunity." In *The Reagan Record*, edited by John Palmer and Isabel Sawhill. Cambridge, Mass.: Ballinger.

———. 1984b. "Nonprofits: The Results Are Coming In." *Foundation News*, July-August, pp. 16–23.

Salamon, Lester M., and Alan J. Abramson. 1982. *The Federal Budget and the Nonprofit Sector*. Washington, D.C.: The Urban Institute Press.

———. 1985. "Nonprofits and the Federal Budget: Deeper Cuts Ahead." *Foundation News* 26:45–54.

Savas, E. S. 1984. *Privatizing the Public Sector: How to Shrink Government*. Chatham, N.J.: Chatham House.

Schambra, William. 1982. "From Self-Interest to Social Obligation: Local Communities vs. the National Community." In *Meeting Human Needs: Toward a New Public Philosophy*, edited by Jack Meyer, 34–42. Washington, D.C.: American Enterprise Institute.

Smith, Bruce. 1975. "The Public Use of the Private Sector." In *The New Political Economy: The Public Use of the Private Sector*, edited by Bruce L. R. Smith, 1–45. London: Macmillan.

Smith, Bruce, and Nelson Rosenbaum. 1981. "A Quantitative Profile of the Voluntary Sector." Unpublished manuscript.

Spann, B. M. 1977. "Public vs. Private Provision of Government Services." In *Budgets and Bureaucrats*, edited by T. E. Borcharding. Durham, N.C.: Duke University Press.

Staats, Elmer. 1975. "New Problems of Accountability for Federal Programs." In *The Political Economy: The Public Use of the Private Sector*, edited by Bruce L. R. Smith, 46–67. London: Macmillan.

Stevens, Rosemary. 1982. "A Poor Sort of Memory: Voluntary Hospitals and Government before the Depression." *Milbank Fund Quarterly/Health and Society*. 60, no. 4.

U.S. Bureau of the Census. 1981. *1977 Census of Service Industries*. Washington, D.C.: U.S. Government Printing Office.

U.S. Office of Management and Budget. 1981. *Budget of the United States Government for FY 1982*. Washington, D.C.: U.S. Government Printing Office.

United Way of America. 1981. *United Way Allocations, 1981*. Alexandria, Va.: United Way of America.

Warner, Amos. 1894. *American Charities: A Study in Philanthropy and Economics*. New York: Thomas Y. Crowell Co.

Wedel, Kenneth R. 1976. "Government Contracting for Purchase of Service." *Social Work* 21.

Weisbrod, Burton. 1978. *The Voluntary Nonprofit Sector*. Lexington, Mass.: Lexington Books.

Whitehead, John S. 1973. *The Separation of College and State: Columbia, Dartmouth, Harvard, and Yale, 1776–1876*. New Haven: Yale University Press.

7

Nonprofit Organizations and the Market

RICHARD STEINBERG

M any people believe that nonprofit firms, un-
sullied by considerations of profitability,
provide needed social services in a trustworthy and efficient fashion. Others deride nonprofit firms, believing that without a profit
motive there is little incentive either to produce services in an
efficient manner or to accommodate the desires of consumers. Believers in the first school of thought are likely to
stress the advantages of publicly subsidizing nonprofit firms
through grants, tax exemption, deductibility of donations,
and exemption from onerous regulatory requirements. They
may even propose that for-profit firms should be legally
prohibited from providing certain services (such as day care
or nursing homes). Believers in the second school wish to
remove subsidies, arguing that they promote unfair competition that worsens the overall quality of service provision.

This chapter reviews the relevant literature and argues
that the behavior and performance of nonprofit firms cannot
properly be understood by looking at firms in isolation.
Nonprofit firms compete with one another in the markets for
donations, membership, clients, and sales. The nonprofit
sector as a whole competes with the for-profit and government sectors in the markets for skilled labor, sales, and
reduced (or zero) cost service provision. This competition is
often tempered by intrasectoral cooperation (in the form of
united fund-raising organizations and buying cooperatives)
and intersectoral transfer payments (corporate donations and
government grants). Overall, market structure seems to determine both behavior and performance.

Of course, one cannot analyze the impact of market structure without a clear understanding of the relevant facts.

I would like to thank Avner Ben-Ner, Paul DiMaggio, Henry Hansmann, Walter Powell, Susan Rose-Ackerman, Gladys Topkis, Cecile
Watters, and Charles Weinberg for a number of valuable comments on
drafts of this chapter.

Unfortunately, consistent and complete data sets for determining the market structures of various nonprofit industries
do not exist. Further, there are definitional issues to be
resolved. The next section of this chapter summarizes our
current understanding of these market structures.

On the surface, nonprofit and for-profit firms appear to
possess very different internal structures. Nonprofits receive
donations and conduct fund-raising campaigns, unlike for-
profits. Workers at nonprofit firms often donate their time—
indeed, the members of the nonprofit firm may be required to
pay dues if they wish to continue with the organization.
Nonprofit foundations and united fund-raising organizations
appear to have no structural analogues in the for-profit world.
And yet, as the third section of this chapter argues, these
differing internal structures perform similarly in the production, marketing, and distribution of services.

Although several theories of nonprofit firm behavior have
been proposed, certain types of behavior would not survive
inter- or intrasectoral competition. The fourth section examines some implications of market structure on the conduct of
nonprofit firms and summarizes some empirical tests of these
implications.

The market structure is thus found to be an important
determinant of performance by nonprofit and for-profit firms.
Although this structure may be regarded as fixed in the short
run, in the long run it is determined by the inherent advantages and disadvantages of the nonprofit, for-profit, and
governmental forms as well as by tax and regulatory advantages conferred upon the different sectors. Several studies
have examined the importance of these factors in determining the nonprofit share of output, and these studies are summarized in the fifth section. Using these empirical results, the
government could indirectly improve overall market performance, altering the nonprofit share by employing these tax
and regulatory levers.

Space considerations preclude discussion of other important regulatory issues. For example, when should nonprofit firms be exempt from antitrust legislation? How should non-profit incorporation laws be structured? Should cross-subsid-ization of services by nonprofit firms be regulated? Formal analysis of these issues is just beginning,[1] and considerations of the issues raised in this chapter can only help such anal-ysis.

MARKET STRUCTURE

In many industries, nonprofit firms compete not only with other nonprofits but with for-profits and governments in both input and output markets. A consistent set of data charac-terizing the three-sector structure of industries containing nonprofit organizations does not seem to exist, but evidence from a variety of sources has been compiled in table 7.1. The shares of employment, revenue, enrollment, and facilities owned by nonprofit organizations vary enormously across industries, though (perhaps because of definitional inconsis-tencies in extant data sets) there seem to be no empirical analyses of cross-industry differences in nonprofit share. Shares within each industry vary enormously from state to state and among metropolitan areas.[2]

Economists like to classify market structures by the ability of the firm to control price. Thus, a perfectly competitive firm is unable to affect the market price (or is ignorant of its power to do so) and selects only a production level. A monopoly, on the other hand, can select any price/quantity combination that consumers are willing to purchase. Oligopoly is an intermediate case, where firms may have control over price, depending on the reactions of competi-tors.

The price control framework is clearly inadequate for many markets containing nonprofit firms. For one thing, not all nonprofits charge a price for their charitable output. For another, nonprofit firms can sustain prices that are below market equilibrium levels if their patrons and donors are willing to subsidize losses to obtain some social goal (H. Schlesinger 1981; James 1983). Thus, even firms in competi-tive situations have some freedom to choose their prices (though they cannot charge higher than market rates).

How then are we to characterize market structures? A completely satisfactory approach has not been offered, but Feigenbaum (1980b) suggests that traditional indicators of

the distribution of firm sizes (such as the Herfindahl index[3] or the concentration ratio) can be used to characterize the eco-nomic power of nonprofit firms. Table 7.2 summarizes the market structure of several nonprofit industries, utilizing the four-firm concentration ratio—the share of total market reve-nues received by the four largest nonprofit firms in the rele-vant (local) market. By this measure, country clubs are reasonably competitive, whereas museums are somewhat monopolistic.

Certain ambiguities beset the concentration ratio index. Does the relevant market include competing government and for-profit firms? Presumably, the answer depends on whether the outputs of the different sectors are sufficiently similar, so that consumers regard them as one good (technically, the intersectoral cross-price elasticity of demand must be suffi-ciently high). No one seems to have estimated such cross-price elasticities of demand, though several researchers have examined differences in quality across sectors (Johnson 1971, Rushing 1974, Bays 1977, Kushman & Nuckton 1977 for hospitals; Titmus 1971 for blood; Kushman 1979 for day care).

Second, there is a problem defining the geographical extent of the market. Do hospitals compete for the same patients when they are located in the same metropolitan area or only when located in the same neighborhood?[4]

Third, there is a problem defining the appropriate measure of economic size. Do we wish to include donative revenues and membership fees or only sales revenues? How do we account for endowments in defining market structure? On the descriptive level, any arbitrary resolution of these difficulties will do when the details of index construction are spelled out. However, if theories of market structure and firm behavior are to be tested, or procompetitive policies are proposed, case-by-case resolution of these difficulties seems necessary.

Though all three sectors compete in the same markets, they do not all play by the same rules. The market structure is not complete without a description of the regulatory environ-ment. Government is defined by its monopoly of legitimate coercive power, and governments can obtain resources in any fashion supported by a majority of citizens and allowed by the relevant constitutions. Governments set the rules of competition, and they have set different rules and regulations for the nonprofit and for-profit sectors.

Nonprofit firms are granted exemption from the corporate income tax if they refrain from earning too much unrelated

1. See Hansmann (1981a) and Ellman (1982) on nonprofit corpora-tion laws; Rose-Ackerman (1980) and Bartlett (1982) on united fund-raising organizations and antitrust laws; ''Antitrust and Nonprofit En-tities'' (1981) on antitrust laws and other types of nonprofit firms; Rose-Ackerman (1982a) and Giancola (1984) on protecting for-profits from nonprofit competition; White (1979) on protecting nonprofits from for-profit competition; and Joseph (1975), Harris (1979), White (1979), Clark (1980), Caulfield (1981), James (1983), and Bays (1983) on regulating cross-subsidization by nonprofit firms.

2. For example, Hansmann (1982) cites evidence that the percent-age of nongovernmental hospital beds in nonprofit hospitals in 1975 varied from a high of 100 percent in Minnesota to a low of 32 percent in Nevada.

3. The Herfindahl index sums the squares of the market shares of each firm in an industry. It obtains a maximum value of 1 if the industry contains a single firm and declines with increases in the number of firms or with increased equality in shares among a given number of firms.

4. Marketing researchers worry very much about the appropriate definition of a market and have suggested various methods for dealing with these and other problems. See Day, Massy, and Shocker (1978) for definitions appropriate in an antitrust context, and Day, Shocker, and Srivastava (1979) or Urban and Hauser (1980) for definitions appropri-ate for marketing managers seeking to identify competitors and untapped market niches. These definitions need modification when applied to nonprofits.

business income (I.R.C., §501). They can receive tax deductible donations if they refrain from too much political lobbying (I.R.C. §170). They are often exempt from local property and sales taxes (Hansmann 1982) and face differing standards of antitrust regulation ("Antitrust . . ." 1981; Bartlett 1982). They receive special treatment with respect to Social Security (42 U.S.C. §410 (a)(8)(b) 1976), unemployment insurance (I.R.C. §§3306(b)(5)(A), (c)(8)), the minimum wage (19 U.S.C. §203(r) 1976; 29 C.F.R. §779.214 1979), securities regulation (15 U.S.C. §77c(a)(4) 1976), bankruptcy (11 U.S.C.A. §303(1) (West Supp. 1979)), copyright (17 U.S.C. §§110, 111(a)(4), 112(b), 118(d)(3) 1976), and postal rates (39 U.S.C.A. §3626 (West Supp. 1979)). Yet nonprofit firms also face many of the same regulations as for-profits, though their response to regulations may differ.

TABLE 7.1 SECTORAL COMPOSITION, BY INDUSTRY

Industry	Measurement Basis	NP Share[a]	FP Share[a]	G Share[a]
Health Services				
Short-term and general hospitals	Facilities[b]	53%	12%	35%
	Beds[b]	62	8	30
	Expenditures[b,c]	65	7	27
	Employment[b,d]	66	6	28
Psychiatric hospitals	Facilities[e]	18	26	56
Chronic-care hospitals	Facilities[e]	29	7	64
Homes for mentally handicapped	Facilities[f]	38	46	16
Nursing homes	Facilities[f]	34	61	5
	Facilities[g]	18	82	N.A.
	Beds[r]	20	69	11
	Employment[h,i]	24	76	N.A.
Education				
Elementary and secondary education	Enrollment[q]	10	1	89
Secondary	Revenues[k]	14	3	83
Postsecondary[l]	Revenues[k]	20	33	47
Higher education	Enrollment[j]	24	N.A.	76
Social Services				
Day-care centers	Facilities[n]	14	52	7
	Facilities[m]	43	57	N.A.
	Enrollment[n]	63	27	N.A.
	Employment[h,i]	56	44	N.A.
Individual and family services	Employment[h,i]	96	4	N.A.
Legal services	Employment[h,i]	2	98	N.A.
Culture and entertainment				
Theater, orchestra, and other performing arts	Employment[h,i]	26	74	N.A.
Radio and television broadcasting	Employment[h,i]	5	95	N.A.
Art museums	Revenue[o]	65	5	30
Research				
Research and development	Expenditures[p]	15	72	13
Basic research	Expenditures[p]	67	18	15

a. Where government share is not available, nonprofit and for-profit figures are shares of private-sector activity. When for-profit share is not available separately, private-sector share is reported in the nonprofit column.

b. Source: American Hospital Association 1981. Federal hospitals were not apportioned between long and short term, and all were included above.

c. Excludes new construction.

d. Full-time equivalent.

e. Source: National Master Facility Inventory, U.S. National Center for Health Statistics 1980.

f. Source: Survey of Institutionalized Persons, U.S. Department of Commerce 1976.

g. Source: National Master Facility Inventory, U.S. National Center for Health Statistics 1976.

h. Source: Rudney & Weitzman 1983.

i. Full- and part-time employment.

j. Source: U.S. Department of Commerce 1981, 1977 data.

k. Source: Bendick 1979.

l. Including vocational.

m. Source: U.S. Department of Commerce 1981, 1977 data.

n. Source: Coelen, Glantz, & Calore 1979; data are from 1976–77 and exclude small day-care centers serving less than thirteen children each.

o. Source: Clarkson 1979.

p. Source: U.S. National Science Foundation 1981. Data are 1982 estimates, by performance sector. Government includes only the federal government.

q. Source: U.S. Department of Health, Education, and Welfare 1978.

r. Source: Hirschoff, forthcoming. Public/private breakdown is by enrollment; for-profit/nonprofit breakdown is by number of schools.

TABLE 7.2 NONPROFIT FOUR-FIRM CONCENTRATION RATIOS, BY INDUSTRY

	Fiscal Year		
Industry	1974	1975	1976
Museums, zoos, etc.	86.2	89.6	86.7
Hospitals	41.8	41.0	40.3
Health clinics	83.9	81.9	83.2
Aid to handicapped	57.8	53.8	49.5
Medical research	65.8	65.2	62.9
Country clubs	36.0	35.6	34.9
Defense of rights	81.0	81.4	77.0
Aid to poor	91.2	88.8	83.5

Source: Feigenbaum 1980b. Largest four firms' combined share of total market revenues, simple average concentration ratio across seven SMSAS, nonprofit firms only.

FIRM STRUCTURES

For-profit firms raise initial capital through various debt instruments and obtain continuing resources through sales of goods and services. On the surface, this is a very different structure than the one employed by nonprofit firms. Initial resources are obtained through grants and bequests, and continuing resources are obtained through gifts, grants, contributions, dues, and fees as well as sales. Yet, as I shall show, the formal internal structures are not as different as they appear.

Table 7.3 summarizes the sources and uses of funds in

five broadly defined nonprofit industries. Some firms rely almost exclusively on sales (Hansmann's "commercial nonprofits" [1980]), whereas others rely heavily on donations (Hansmann's "donative nonprofits"). Weisbrod's "collectiveness index" (1980; and see table 7.4) measures the share of revenues derived from gifts, grants, and donations and indexes the extent to which nonprofits are devoted to public needs. The idea behind this index is that member needs are met through payment of dues and client needs are met through purchases. Thus, donations primarily meet public needs (but see below).

Sales and Advertising versus Donations and Solicitation

Although sales of goods and services and donations appear to be different structures for obtaining resources, they possess strong similarities. Buyers make explicit trades, obtaining goods or services in return for money. Donors often make implicit trades, obtaining direct benefits (a front-row seat at the opera, public recognition as a good citizen, job advancement), indirect benefits (the gratification of helping to eliminate poverty, a lower crime rate), and Kantian benefits (enjoyment of the act of giving). Clearly, if direct benefits motivate giving, a donation is not different from a purchase. Amos (1982) discusses ways in which indirect and Kantian motives may be empirically distinguished from direct motives (though his method is not free from problems [see Steinberg 1984]).

TABLE 7.3 INCOME AND WEALTH STATEMENTS FOR NONPROFIT ORGANIZATIONS[a]

	Welfare n = 199	Health n = 93	Education n = 167	Arts n = 30	Research n = 30
Source of Funds					
Sales	166	4545	3534	1418	9474
	(45%)	(91%)	(84%)	(92%)	(78%)
Dues and fees	30	13	7	5	37
	(8%)	(0%)	(0%)	(0%)	(0%)
Contributions and grants	174	431	664	116	2686
	(47%)	(9%)	(16%)	(8%)	(22%)
Uses of Funds					
Cost of goods sold	30	391	108	35	143
	(8%)	(8%)	(3%)	(3%)	(1%)
Fund-raising	56	147	157	16	110
	(15%)	(3%)	(4%)	(1%)	(1%)
Administration	88	3474	395	132	4186
	(24%)	(70%)	(9%)	(9%)	(34%)
Program	168	627	3218	126	6734
	(45%)	(13%)	(77%)	(8%)	(55%)
Retained earnings[b]	28	350	326	1229	1022
	(8%)	(7%)	(8%)	(80%)	(8%)
Wealth Measures					
Assets	620	5955	8351	1170	16141
Liabilities	170	2216	1117	150	4789
Net worth	450	3739	7234	1019	11352

a. Sample consists of tax Forms 990 filed in 1975 in four metropolitan areas—Philadelphia, Minneapolis/St. Paul, Houston/Galveston, and Los Angeles. Accounting procedures are not always uniform across sectors. For a complete description of the sample selection criteria and method of classification by sector, see Steinberg (1983a, 173–78). Figures are organizational means, in 000s of 1975 dollars. Shares are in parentheses.

b. Retained earnings are calculated as the difference between total sources of funds and all other listed uses of funds.

TABLE 7.4   INDEX OF COLLECTIVENESS, 1973–75

Type of Organization	Collectiveness Index (C)	Sample Size
Cultural	90	28
Religious	71	32
Public affairs	47	29
Social welfare	41	40
Agricultural	41	50
Educational	34	33
Legal, public administration and military	20	50
Veteran, hereditary, and patriotic	12	45
Athletic and sports	11	28
Honor societies	9	51
Scientific, engineering, and technical	6	51
Ethnic	3	37
Labor associations and federations	3	70
Trade, business, and commercial	2	58
Health	2	35
Hobby and avocational	1	20
Chambers of commerce	0	27
All Types	20	684

Source: Weisbrod 1980. Derived from IRS tax Form 990 data. Accounting procedures are not always uniform across types of organizations.

Even when nonprofit organizations do not provide obvious services in exchange for donative resources, the method of obtaining resources is similar to that of sales in for-profit firms. Fund-raising programs are expenditures by the nonprofit firm to produce donative payments in the same sense that expenditures on marketing result in sales in for-profit firms. Thus, criteria for maximizing the surplus generated by a fund-raising program are identical to criteria for maximizing the profits generated by production and marketing (Weinberg 1980; Steinberg 1983b). Except for minor technical qualifications, net returns are maximal when an additional dollar of fund-raising expenditure adds exactly one dollar to donations—that is, when the "marginal donative product of fund-raising" (MDPF) equals 1.[5] If MDPF exceeds 1, additional fund-raising will generate more in additional contributions than in additional costs, so firms whose MDPF exceeds 1 are doing too little fund-raising.[6] Eventually, additional fund-raising yields diminishing returns; when MDPF falls to 1, no further net gains are available from further expenditures.

Although donations can thus be modeled as a trade in which nonprofit firms provide literature soliciting funds in return for donations, the exact nature of the good received by

5. There are, however, additional complications when a nonprofit firm has revenue from sales as well as from donations (Weinberg 1980). For a precise statement of the technical qualifications on this optimizing rule and a discussion of the various ways MDPF has been statistically estimated, see Steinberg (1985a).

6. In this case, too little fund-raising is taking place from the perspective of the nonprofit firm, but fund-raising may still be excessive from a social standpoint. See Steinberg (1985a) for a further discussion of this point.

donors is subject to question. Tullock (1966) posited the rather extreme example of a nonprofit firm that provided no charitable service but sent donors handsome literature alleging (falsely) that donations were helping the starving millions. The donor would get a feeling of satisfaction and pride, the firm would get donations, and so both are "better off"; yet society gets no charitable output.

At the other extreme, when fund-raising literature is truthful, information is traded for donations, and social allocations are likely to be improved. Ehrlich and Fisher's model of advertising (1982) can be applied to fund-raising (Steinberg 1983a). In this model, donors are uncertain which nonprofit firms have the most desirable characteristics in terms of the type of service provided, the quality of service, or the efficiency with which donations are converted into service. Donors could obtain the relevant information on their own, but this is so costly that few would bother. As a result, total donations are low, as donors are not certain they can obtain desirable results from donating. Fund-raising literature is provided free by nonprofit firms. If it is regarded as reasonably truthful (say, because claims are monitored by legal authorities), the donor's cost of information is drastically reduced, and total donations will rise.

Fund-raising and Contract Failure

The fund-raising/donative trade appears to differ from most other trades for contract failure reasons (see chapter 2 in this volume). With most goods and services, buyers can be reasonably certain the quantity purchased is the quantity they contracted for, as they receive the merchandise. When donors "purchase" services for others, they do not usually observe the quantity received by nonprofit clients; thus they seek institutional guarantees that their donation will be fully applied. Hansmann (1980) argues that contributions are not made to for-profit firms because donors cannot be certain whether their donations will be used to increase stockholder dividends or to provide incremental charitable service. He argues further that the nondistribution constraint that defines the nonprofit sector provides assurance that donations will not be diverted to stockholders.

Hansmann does not analyze a different source of potential contract failure—the potential leak of donations to fund-raising. If half of each donation is used to increase fund-raising expenditure, then the donor's "price" of a dollar of charitable service expenditure appears to be two dollars. If donors find it difficult to obtain information on the diversion of contributions toward fund-raising, they will be uncertain about the price and reluctant to donate.

Steinberg (1986) argues that this source of potential contract failure is not likely to prove bothersome when the price is properly calculated. He considers a wide range of possible objectives underlying nonprofit firm behavior (including service maximization and budget maximization as special cases), and (with minor technical exceptions) demonstrates that the price of charitable service is exactly one dollar regardless of the share of fund-raising in the overall budget.

The basic reason is that the optimal level of fund-raising does not change when a (small) additional donation is made, so that 100 percent of additional contributions is available for charitable service provision. This implies that (small) donors do not need to monitor fund-raising levels to be certain of the quantity of charitable expenditure resulting from their donation. Thus contract failure that is due to fund-raising does not arise.

Dues and Fees

Another way in which nonprofit firms obtain resources is through dues and other membership and affiliation fees. There seems to be no clear analogue in the for-profit sector, but the recent spate of take-back contracts negotiated in the steel, airline, and automobile industries has some of the same flavor—member/employees are contributing for the survival of the organization. Affiliation fees are clearly analogous to franchising fees, and the local-national structure of many nonprofit firms (such as United Way of America and the National Cancer Society) serves many of the same functions as the franchise structure (such as that of McDonald's). The national parent organization obtains economies of scale in purchasing and enforces uniform quality standards on locals to protect the reputation of the organization as a whole. In this way, donors are further assured that their contributions will be well spent.

Very little has been written about the economic role of membership fees. The economic literature on clubs (Buchanan 1965; Sandler & Tschirhart 1980) and two-part pricing rules (Oi 1971) suggests some of the elements of an adequate theory of membership fees. Downing and Brady (1981) modeled the behavior of a citizens' interest group (CIG) that acts to maximize the present value of member net benefits. In their model, the behavior of the CIG determines which individuals will choose to become members. One determinant of the probability of membership is the cost to the individual of joining, largely consisting of dues but also including the value of the member's time outside the organization and other factors. Although their model is one of the very few to take dues into account, there is room for a great deal more analysis than they conducted, for in their model the only way to contribute is through membership. A model of the donor choice between nonmember donations and membership dues is clearly called for.

Access to Capital

Another difference between nonprofit and for-profit organizations is in their ability to obtain financial capital. Hansmann (1981c) notes that equity capital is not available to nonprofit organizations because of the nondistribution constraint. Although debt financing is available to some extent, Hansmann argues that the costs become prohibitive beyond some point well short of 100 percent debt financing. Donations are an uncertain and inadequate source of capital in many cases, leaving retained earnings as a necessary source of growth capital. Hansmann argues that nonprofit exemption from corporate income tax permits faster growth by allowing firms to retain more earnings. Thus, both external constraints on borrowing and internal subsidization through tax exemption bias the nonprofit capital structure toward retained earnings.

Though regular banks are reluctant to lend initial capital to nonprofit organizations, nonprofits obtain analogous services in the form of foundation grants. These grants often provide long-term capital rather than operating funds and are frequently designed to provide seed money for new organizations and new programs at existing nonprofit firms (Kramer 1981).

Foundations have the potential to assist service-providing nonprofit firms to reallocate resources over the business cycle. Steinberg and Perlman (1982) note that in times of recession nonprofit firms have greater needs for funds, and yet donations are likely to fall. A policy of retaining more earnings (building endowment) during economic booms and running down the endowment during recessions can improve the allocation of service provision over time; but there are limits to the ability of firms to compensate for the business cycle with internal financial policy. Foundations can function countercyclically, however, providing more grants in times of recession and rebuilding their assets in times of boom.

Labor Utilization

For-profit and nonprofit firms appear to differ substantially in the utilization of labor. For one thing, volunteers provide some of the labor for nonprofit organizations, a rare phenomenon in for-profit firms. For another, even when labor is paid for in both sectors, the rate of compensation appears to differ for comparable jobs. Finally, there is reason to believe that labor unions have different effects in for-profit and nonprofit firms.

On the first issue, it is not obvious that volunteer workers are uncompensated and cost the firm nothing. Mueller (1975) details four potential personal benefits to volunteers: pleasure from the act of giving, prestige, influence over the composition and allocation of charitable output, and development (or signaling) of skills that will help them in future (paid) employment. Mueller analyzes the last two sources of gain, and finds statistical support for their influence on volunteer time among professional women. Schiff (1984) considers an additional benefit—donors can gather information on the quality and efficiency of competing nonprofit firms by working as volunteers at the respective organizations before allocating their monetary donations. Havrilesky, Schweitzer, and Wright (1973) note one more benefit—volunteers may serve as role models who encourage other individuals to contribute time and money to services valued by the volunteer. They contend that this benefit explains why many community leaders are early volunteers in and early dropouts from public good causes.

Unpaid workers thus appear to be compensated, but not

by direct payments from the firm. Does this imply that volunteer labor is a free resource to the nonprofit firm? I know of no empirical analysis of this issue, but the answer is almost surely no. Volunteers may get in the way of full-time paid workers, reducing their productivity. Volunteers require the firm to obtain more supplies and perhaps purchase more insurance. But most important, they must be attracted to the firm, trained for their positions, and encouraged to stay, all of which cost money and staff time (Weinberg 1980; Lovelock & Weinberg 1984; Schiff 1984). Although nonprofit firms may not pay salaries to their volunteer labor force, they must be attentive to turnover costs.

Thus, there is some question from the perspectives of both firm and worker regarding the extent to which volunteer labor differs from compensated labor. Yet, if there is a real difference, it remains a puzzle why nonprofit firms attract volunteers and for-profit firms do not.[7] Is a volunteer worker at a for-profit hospital less likely to obtain Mueller's four benefits? How does the nondistribution constraint affect the potential benefits of volunteering? A way to get at this question empirically would be to obtain data on volunteer labor at hospitals that converted from nonprofit to for-profit status or vice versa. I know of no work being done along this line.

The only relevant literature I have found discusses the general question of why people donate to nonprofit firms—combining donations of time (volunteer labor) and money in one explanatory model. General models of donor motivation are reviewed elsewhere in this volume (see chapters 2 and 18). But such models do not explain volunteer labor, for Schiff (1984) shows that when the nondistribution constraint is the sole reason donors prefer nonprofits, donations would come (almost) exclusively in the form of money. With minor exceptions, donors could provide more charitable service if they spent their time earning money (and contributed incremental earnings) than if they volunteered.

Though it is not clear why volunteer labor is directed exclusively to the nonprofit sector, several researchers have modeled the donor's choice between gifts of time and money (Long 1977; Menchik & Weisbrod 1981; Schiff 1984). Morgan, Dye, and Hybels (1977) note the simple correlation between the two and speculate that "anything that reduced dollar giving by 10% might reduce time given by as much as 4%" (p. 175). More sophisticated statistical analyses by Dye (1980), Menchik and Weisbrod (1981), and Schiff (1984) obtained results that were generally consistent with Morgan, Dye, and Hybel's.

Even when all workers are paid, nonprofit firms seem to differ from for-profit firms and governments in their utilization of labor. Coelho (1976) analyzed the institution of tenure

in nonprofit organizations as a means of encouraging reliable information flows between workers and the board of directors (a similar point is made in Weisbrod and Schlesinger 1986). Freeman (1975) concluded that in general, nonprofit firms are likely to be more sensitive to wages and output in their hiring decisions than their for-profit counterparts. However, universities should be less sensitive to these fluctuations because of the institution of tenure and the goal of many universities to reward comparable faculty similarly regardless of nonacademic opportunities. Finally, he concluded that changes in external circumstances will affect the quality of faculty more than the quantity.

Borjas, Frech, and Ginsburg (1983) found that nonprofit nursing homes (especially those with religious affiliation) pay substantially lower wages to comparably skilled workers than for-profits, and government-operated homes pay substantially higher wages. A more sophisticated paper by Weisbrod (1983) disentangles the influences on the wage structures in for-profit law firms and nonprofit public interest law firms. He found that comparably skilled lawyers are paid substantially less in public interest law firms, that they know this, that the financial sacrifice is permanent, and that they are willing to sacrifice income because of their strong preference for public interest work. This confirms that the type of sorting/screening mechanism discussed by Young (chapter 10 in this volume) in the case of entrepreneurs also applies to workers at nonprofit firms.

A reanalysis of Weisbrod's data by Goddeeris (1984) confirmed that public interest lawyers are systematically different from other lawyers but does not confirm that they accept lower salaries in the nonprofit sector because of these differences in preferences. Rather, he found that apparently comparably skilled lawyers in the two sectors (on the basis of measured characteristics) do not have the same earnings potential in the for-profit world and that salary differences are due to the unmeasured factors that cause this earnings potential to differ. Thus, while nonprofits appear to obtain labor at a bargain price, it may be that these workers are of lower quality and do not impart competitive advantage on the sector.

A natural question arises as to whether unions have differing effects on labor utilization in the two sectors. Faine (1972) argues that in a nonprofit arts organization, such as a museum or an opera company, a strike is often welcomed by management as a means of reducing the deficit. For-profit firms, on the other hand, resist strikes, as they reduce profits. Where profits are available, unions have something to strive for, but this is not the case in nonprofits.

A deeper analysis of this question is probably warranted. It is true that nonprofit arts groups rarely cover costs through sales (Hansmann [1981b] argues that this represents a desire for voluntary price discrimination in order to cover the fixed costs of production), but they receive donative income which unions may strive to capture by striking. When donations serve only to increase union wages, however, donations may cease. The relationships among strikes, sales revenue, and donations need more careful analysis.

---

7. For-profit firms in particular industries attract volunteers, but to a much smaller extent than nonprofit firms. For example, figures presented in Coelen, Glantz, and Calore (1979) indicate that 17.2 percent of for-profit and 49.6 percent of nonprofit day-care firms utilized unpaid staff. These figures overstate the use of volunteers, for they include staff paid by outside agencies (such as CETA) as well as volunteers. The occasional use of volunteers by for-profits further complicates the puzzles cited in the text.

Foundations

So far I have concentrated on the structure of nonprofit service-providing agencies, including donative and commercial nonprofits, operated for the benefit of members or for clients. There are at least two other types of nonprofit organizations with different internal structures—foundations (private, public, community, and operating foundations) and united fund-raising organizations (such as the United Ways). (Ben-Ner in chapter 24 considers additional structures such as producer cooperatives.)

Very little has been written on the internal structure and functioning of foundations. Boulding (1972) advanced a few tentative hypotheses on the ''pure theory'' of foundations, but these are little more than a rehash of why people make donations of any sort. Steuerle (1977) and Steinberg and Perlman (1982) have analyzed the effect of the distribution requirements of the Tax Reform Act of 1969. Steinberg and Perlman note that the law as currently structured limits the ability of foundations to act as nonprofit banks—making large grants to service-providing organizations in times of recession and rebuilding assets at other times—since, in the case of private nonoperating foundations, grants must exceed a specified percentage of assets in each year. They propose an amendment that would positively encourage countercyclical grant making. But the lack of an adequate theory of foundation behavior hampers their analysis. The financial objectives of the foundation are unknown, as are the forces explaining the birth and death of foundations. Thus, analysis of policy impacts are incomplete and speculative.[8]

United Fund-Raising Organizations

The best analysis of the structure of united fund-raising organizations to date is by Rose-Ackerman (1980). She notes that membership in a united fund is determined by mutual advantages of current members and potential entrants. Current members enjoy greater contributions than they could obtain on their own for several reasons. First, since competitive fund-raising expenditure (fund-raising that seeks to divert donor dollars from one charity to another) is reduced, donors may believe their donations are more efficiently spent and thus may give more. Second, since united funds assess needs and audit performances of member agencies, donors may be convinced that their contributions will be better spent. In any case, donors need not devote as much time and effort to deciding which charities are meritorious and efficient, and this reduction in required donor effort encourages

---

8. There have been several studies of patterns of giving by foundations. Rhode (1975) examined the effect of asset levels, stock market prices, and bond prices on foundation support of health research and development. Wheatley (1978) analyzed patterns of giving in Chicago; Wolpert, Reiner, and Starrett (1980) analyzed giving in Philadelphia; and Steinberg and Perlman (1982) looked at grant making in four major metropolitan areas. But, without an understanding of the underlying determinants of foundation behavior, it is difficult to project how these patterns would change in response to governmental policies.

---

giving. Third, when donors disagree about which organizations are meritorious, tying donations into one package may help all donors. Though any one donor will find that some of his donations to the united fund are allocated to less preferred organizations, he is compensated by the fact that other donors provide funds for his favorite organization (Fisher 1977; Rose-Ackerman 1980). Finally, united funds often have local monopolies on access to payroll deduction plans.

A potential entrant, when deciding whether to seek membership, compares the advantages of membership (fund-raising costs are lower, while contributions received may be higher) with the disadvantages (loss of independence, united fund auditing requirements, restrictions on independent fund-raising that conflicts with the united fund campaign). Existing members compare the advantages of admitting a new entrant (one less fund-raising competitor, possible improvement in the fund's overall attractiveness to donors) with the disadvantages (a controversial or badly managed firm may reduce the fund's overall attractiveness to donors). Once membership is determined, the allocation process is constrained—if an organization is slighted in its allocation of the funds raised it may quit, often to the disadvantage of continuing members. In some cases, powerful members may negotiate special status within the united fund in return for their continued membership. Thus, for example, the American Cancer Society has negotiated special partnership agreements with United Ways in six states (''UW, Cancer Society . . .'' 1979).

Some writers (such as Wenocur et al. 1984) have criticized the united funds for supporting only older, middle-of-the-road philanthropies. Given the determinants of membership structure discussed above, this allocation pattern is not surprising—an organization that supported a controversial cause would endanger the total donations received, and existing members would find it in their interest to oppose its entry.

Controversial causes can obtain some of the advantages of United Way fund-raising without threatening total donations through the recently emerging donor-option plans. Under these plans, donors can leave their donations undesignated (in which case they are distributed to United Way member organizations) or designate that their contribution go to any tax-exempt human service organization (eligibility requirements vary across the plans). Nonmember organizations obtain access to payroll-deduction plans, but they do not receive the other advantages of a united fund. Thus, a number of alternative funds (with central monitoring and restrictions on independent fund-raising) have arisen—more than fifty by 1983 (Wenocur et al. 1984). They serve large clusters of donors with related preferences that are too controversial for United Ways.

These new institutions certainly complicate analysis of united fund-raising organizations. Some United Way organizations are concerned that their overall campaigns will suffer if they adopt donor-option plans, but no data are available that support this fear (Cook et al. 1981). Donor-option plans reduce the antipathy of some donors to United Way giving and thus may benefit member organizations. However, with donor-option plans in place, the incentive for nonprofit firms to become members of the United Way (and thus reduce competitive fund-raising) is reduced. Local United Way organizations are confused as to whether a donor-option program is in their interest, and sometimes they administer the program in a fashion that supports the suspicion that their real aim is to stifle competition for workplace contributions rather than provide open access (Wenocur et al. 1984). Nonetheless, the Board of Governors of the United Way of America has endorsed the donor-option concept and has urged local United Way organizations to implement the plans (United Way . . . 1982). Under a court order, the Combined Federal Campaign has also adopted a donor-option plan.

EFFECTS OF MARKET STRUCTURE ON PERFORMANCE

A common approach in the economics literature is to model the behaviors of for-profit, nonprofit, and government providers of service separately. Typically, analysts assume that for-profit firms wish to maximize profits and that their behavior can be derived and evaluated from this assumption. A different objective is postulated for nonprofit firms, such as enrollment maximization, medical-demand maximization, budget maximization, service maximization, quality/ quantity maximization, or expense-preference maximization (these models are reviewed in chapter 2 in this volume).[9] Predictions about nonprofit firms' behavior are derived under these alternative assumptions and contrasted with predictions about the behavior of for-profit firms.

I share the view in much of the existing literature that this approach is flawed for two reasons. First, nonprofit, for-profit, and government providers of service coexist in many markets. Except when there are explicit structures protecting nonprofit firms from competition, competition from these other sectors would eliminate many of the postulated nonprofit objective functions. A nonprofit firm that sought to maximize, say, managerial expense-preference objectives would be driven out of business by a for-profit firm acting to maximize its profits. Second, it is not clear that for-profit firms that compete in the same market as nonprofits would actually seek to maximize profits. ''For-profit'' is a legal designation, not a description of objectives, and economists have detailed a number of situations where for-profit firms would not seek maximal profits. Thus, predictions about differences in behavior between legally designated for-profit and nonprofit firms should not be predicated on the profit motive. The motives and behavior of both types of firms

should be derived and analyzed in a framework incorporating the market structure.

A Simple Market Competition Model

To emphasize the impact of market structure on nonprofit firm behavior, let us start with a simple and unrealistic competitive model, draw some conclusions, and then consider the impact of real-world complications. We shall assume that nonprofit and for-profit firms coexist in a market and that for-profit firms seek an output/quality mix and production technique that will maximize their profits. We shall assume nothing about the goal of nonprofit firms, for our argument does not depend on which theory of nonprofit behavior is relevant. Nonprofits have no special tax or regulatory advantages and receive no donations or dues. Costs of production and consumer demand for outputs are identical across sectors. Indeed, the only structural distinction allowed in this model between a nonprofit and a for-profit firm is the legal nondistribution constraint. Finally, potential entrepreneurs can enter the market as either nonprofit or for-profit firms without competitive disadvantage—there is no special cost advantage or name-brand recognition advantage possessed by preexisting firms. (Newhouse [1970], Pauly & Redisch [1973], and Rose-Ackerman [1982b] discuss alternative models of entry by nonprofit firms.)

In such a world, for-profit and nonprofit firm behavior must be identical (Manning 1973; White 1979). If any particular firm, profit-seeking or nonprofit, tried to charge a higher price (quality fixed) or sell a lower quality product (price fixed) than the prevailing market levels, that firm would lose all its business and would not survive. If a firm tried to charge a lower price (quality fixed) or sell goods of a higher quality (price fixed), its competitors would be forced to match this action or go out of business. There would still be diversity in quality levels, but an increase in product quality must be exactly (marginally) counterbalanced in the minds of consumers by an increase in product price. This is the theory of compensating differentials. The sorting out of firms by quality level is essentially arbitrary, and there is no reason to think that quality would systematically differ between the two types of firms.

All firms would have zero economic profits (economic profits are essentially equal to the difference between accounting profits and a ''normal rate of return''). If any price/quality combination represented in the marketplace allowed a firm to make economic profits, a new profit-seeking firm would enter with a lower price/higher quality package that would be profitable and drive the first firm out of business. A nonprofit firm might also enter the market (depending on the unspecified objective of nonprofit entrepreneurs), but this is not essential.

All the optimality properties of perfectly competitive idealized economies typically taught in introductory economics classes apply to this hybrid model. Consumer needs are well met by total production levels and quality spectra, and production responds appropriately to changes in consumer preferences.

---

9. Enrollment maximization was proposed by Krizay and Wilson (1974); medical-demand maximization by Pauly and Redisch (1973); budget maximization by Tullock (1966) and Niskanen (1971); service maximization by Weinberg (1980) and Steinberg (1983a); quality/quantity maximization by Newhouse (1970), Carlson, Robinson, and Ryan (1971), Lee (1971), and Hansmann (1981b); and expense/preference maximization by Clarkson (1972), Keating and Keating (1975), Feigenbaum (1980b), Borjas, Frech, and Ginsberg (1983), and James (1983).

Nonprofit Competitive Advantages and the Theory of Property Rights

Let us make the model more realistic by introducing grants and donations. As Hansmann has argued, donations are given only to nonprofit firms because of contract failure. Thus, donations relate specifically to the nondistribution constraint we have retained in this simplified model.

Donations allow nonprofit firms to behave differently and survive competition from for-profits. A nonprofit firm can now, if it chooses, produce an unprofitable price/quality package, with losses subsidized by donations (James 1983). Indeed, every nonprofit firm can behave differently, and all will survive the competition of the market when donors are willing to subsidize the losses caused by these disparities.

It is in this framework that the property-rights literature (Alchian & Demsetz 1972) becomes relevant. Proponents of this approach argue that nonprofits are likely to behave inefficiently (by wasting resources or producing the "wrong" output/quality mixture) because of the nondistribution constraint. If any firm produces efficient price/quality combinations (desired by the public), it is rewarded by profits. In for-profit firms, the owners get to keep these profits, either directly in the form of dividends or indirectly through capital gains when they divest their stock. Thus, owners have a financial incentive to ensure that production is efficient as this would maximize their claim on the firm's residual. When owners do a poor job of ensuring efficiency, the firm becomes ripe for a takeover bid, which would restore efficiency, or is driven out of business by other profit-maximizing firms.

At nonprofit firms, ownership is attenuated. Although there is a board of directors with the legal authority to control the firm's actions, board members are legally prohibited from obtaining the residual. Furthermore, this same non-distribution constraint drastically reduces the incentive for others to mount a takeover bid (Frech 1980). This attenuation of property rights reduces the board's incentive to ensure efficient production.

In our initial model, property rights have little relevance, for inefficient firms are driven out of business and survivors are efficient. Donations allow nonprofit firms to behave as property-rights theorists predict and still survive. Such theorists argue that the donative advantage will be spent on managerial emoluments (or slack)—those aspects of the job environment that managers want at a zero price but would not want at their actual cost in terms of the residual. These emoluments include pleasant coworkers (who may be overpaid to ensure they will remain pleasant), discriminatory hiring practices, long lunch hours, magnificent offices, and larger, more prestigious market shares. In a (profit-maximizing) for-profit firm, such emoluments are valued by owners at actual cost, and managers and coworkers are given perks only when necessary to retain a worker who is significantly more valuable than available replacements. In a nonprofit firm, no one owns the residual, so no one has a financial incentive to restrict emoluments. Property-rights theorists

are skeptical about the power of nonfinancial incentives (board preferences for efficiency per se) to constrain emoluments.

Legislators and citizens have expressed outrage over reported incidents of self-dealing, where board members of nonprofit firms covertly obtain shares of the firm's residuals for their personal use. According to property-rights theorists, this concern is misguided, for self-dealing restores the incentive for the firm to produce efficiently and market the price/quality combination most desired by consumers.[10]

Residual Claimants and Monitoring

The inefficiency conclusions are weakened when self-dealing (directly or indirectly) is practiced or when external agents have the ability to monitor and affect nonprofit performance through regulation or indirect incentives. Thus, many of the empirical studies to be cited below examine the extent to which medical societies dominate Blue Cross/Blue Shield. They argue that medical societies have an interest in minimizing administrative costs and managerial emoluments in order to maximize the demand for medical care and increase doctor income. This is a form of indirect self-dealing. One of the studies (Frech & Ginsburg 1981) argues that the quality of insurance will be higher than optimal in doctor-controlled Blues (in the sense that resources devoted to quality increments are better devoted to alternative uses), though most view medical-society control as efficiency improving. Medical societies retain imperfect control in most Blues, and a political compromise is struck between those desiring emoluments and those desiring administrative efficiency. Thus, the authors expect a negative correlation between measures of medical-society control of Blues and administrative costs and a positive correlation between control and doctor income.

Eisenstadt and Kennedy (1981) find that medical-society control of Blue Shield has no impact on administrative costs in states where Blues lack tax advantages (and are therefore constrained by competition with for-profit health care insurers) but has a significant negative impact on costs in other states. Empirical studies by Kass and Pautler (1979), Sloan (1981), Arnould and Eisenstadt (1981), and Arnould and Debrock (1982) found that physician control of Blue Shield caused higher physician prices, whereas Lynk (1981) found the opposite.

A number of other forces reduce inefficiency in certain cases. Political pressures have increasingly caused consumers to be selected for seats on the board of directors. Ben-Ner (1986) argues that only a few consumers or donors have to be involved in controlling the firm when it provides public goods. In many charities (especially medical research foundations), board members are intensely devoted to the chari-

10. See the discussions of residual claimants in Frech and Ginsberg (1978, 1981), Kass and Pautler (1979), Arnould and Eisenstadt (1981), Eisenstadt and Kennedy (1981), Sloan (1981), Lynk (1981), Arnould and Debrock (1982), and Hay and Leahy (1984).

ty's mission, often because family members would benefit from the resulting discoveries. A charity that desired the fund-raising advantages of membership in a United Way would have to submit to United Way oversight procedures and government attempts to monitor and regulate nonprofit performance more generally. Rose-Ackerman (1983) cites evidence that both United Way and government monitoring are minimal, however, and Boyle and Jacobs (1979) found that measures of state enforcement stringency had no effect on fund-raising costs as a share of funds raised. (Rose-Ackerman's paper [1982b] on the constraining influence of competitive entry on fund-raising behavior perhaps explains the irrelevance of regulation here.) The Better Business Bureau publishes ratings of various charities, but it is doubtful that these ratings are a major constraining influence. Donors can better monitor performance if they volunteer their labor rather than money (Mueller 1975). Grant-making agencies (governments and foundations) may require certain disclosures and/or management practices as a precondition for aid.

In many cases, the quality (price given) of a service product (education, day care, mental health care, and so on) can be evaluated by consumers only after some experience. Some clients are subsidized publicly or by some other nonprofit firm, and the subsidizer may have trouble discerning whether any particular firm is providing an efficient price/quality package. In such cases, the observed behavior of paying customers reveals firm efficiency, and subsidizers can structure their reimbursement policies to ensure efficiency by requiring that each firm serve at least one paying customer and reimburse the care of other clients at the same rate charged paying customers. Efficiency through "proxy shopping" was first proposed for the day-care industry by Nelson and Krashinsky (1973), and more generally and carefully by Rose-Ackerman (1983).

Critique of the Property-Rights Theory

At least five major criticisms can be made about received property-rights theory. First, for-profit firms are socially inefficient when contract failure applies. As Thompson noted (1980, 134), reduced efficiency owing to attenuated property rights "is often overshadowed by the increased efficiency in satisfying the customers that their contributions are being put to good use."

Second, the discretion afforded nonprofit managers allows nonprofits to act efficiently in an important class of situations wherein for-profit firms act inefficiently. The for-profit efficiency argument assumes that the (marginal) social benefit of an output mix can be captured by a firm in the form of (marginal) sales revenue. Weisbrod (1975) notes that many of the outputs sold by nonprofit firms provide external benefits (or are public goods, a special kind of externality). In such a case, it is well known that for-profit firms either leave the market or produce less than the efficient quantity (Atkinson & Stiglitz 1980, 505–07). If the nonprofit firm's decision maker values the provision of such goods, then it would

count as an emolument that helps society as well as the manager. Managerial discretion, allowed by contributions and the nondistribution constraint, can be an efficient mechanism for the provision of goods with external benefits. This argument hinges on the "correctness" of preferences of the nonprofit decision maker, and so the entrepreneurial sorting and screening mechanisms discussed by Young in chapter 10 become relevant.

When sorting and screening mechanisms fail to ensure that nonprofit managers have the "right" preferences, nonprofit firms may nonetheless improve market provision of goods possessing external benefits. Preston (1984) has argued that nonprofit managers seeking to maximize the residual (in order, say, to raise their salary) would be forced to consider external benefits. This is because donations, she argues, depend on the social content of the goods provided. She shows that the overall market product mix is improved when such nonprofit firms are allowed to compete with for-profits.

In cases where service demand fluctuates (such as medical care), capacity is a public good, for excess capacity reduces the risk that any individual will be denied use of facilities in times of excess need (epidemics, major accidents, and so on). Holtman (1983) argues that for-profit firms provide too little capacity, so that once again nonprofit firms may improve social welfare. However, this result may depend on his assumptions that nonprofit managers value only the output level of the organization and that they are constrained to have zero profits in each period, assumptions not derived from the nondistribution constraint.

Third, the property-rights theory is incomplete. Nonprofit firms need not use all the discretion afforded by contributions to increase emoluments. Some of the slack could be used to produce a lower price/higher quality product and eliminate all competition from for-profit firms (although other nonprofits might still compete). The circumstances in which nonprofits would act to eliminate for-profit competition have not, to my knowledge, been discussed in the literature, but the lack of for-profit competition in products sold by many donative nonprofits suggests that this phenomenon may be commonplace (though of course there are a number of alternative explanations of this phenomenon).

Fourth, when there are informational asymmetries (where sellers are aware of the quality of their products but buyers are not), for-profit managers are more likely to exploit consumers. Weisbrod and Schlesinger (1986) discuss the case of nursing homes, where it is difficult to ascertain quality in advance and costly to move if the consumer (or his or her relatives) discovers upon use that the actual quality is different from the anticipated quality. In this situation, the for-profit manager could maximize the firm's residual by misleading potential consumers about the subjective aspects of quality. Further, managers who valued honesty as well as their income would tend to segregate themselves into the nonprofit sector.[11] Thus, Weisbrod and Schlesinger (1986)

11. In some cases, sorting would work the other way. If it were

conclude, "The resulting failure to maximize profit could be socially efficient; the social inefficiency resulting from the profit distribution constraint on nonprofits could offset the inefficiency resulting from the proprietary firms' taking advantage of their informational superiority over their customers." Their statistical analysis of Wisconsin nursing homes supports this conclusion. Controlling for a variety of factors, they find that the number of client complaints to regulatory authorities is significantly lower in all categories of nonprofit than in for-profit nursing homes.

Finally, the advantages of the for-profit legal form are exaggerated, for there are several important situations wherein nominally for-profit firms do not act to maximize their profits. Indeed, managerial discretion–emoluments models were originally developed and applied to for-profits. The owners of the modern for-profit corporation (stockholders) do not directly manage the firm. It is costly for the owners to engage in the kind of detailed monitoring necessary to ensure that managers maximize profits, and a certain level of inefficiency is expected. Increasingly elaborate models of this phenomenon have appeared in the literature (Berle & Means 1932; Simon 1959; Williamson 1964; Leibenstein 1966; Marris & Mueller 1980; De Alessi 1983). Moreover, many industries in which nonprofits and for-profits coexist are regulated, and Alchian and Kessel (1962) argue that regulated for-profits are likely to suffer from the same managerial discretion inefficiencies predicted for nonprofits.

Since the nominally for-profit firms that compete with nonprofits may not seek to maximize their profits, models that assume profit maximization are flawed. It would seem to be preferable to derive the objectives of each type of firm explicitly from the legal constraints defining each sector and the market structure. Some tentative progress in this direction has been achieved by Clarkson (1980), but other technical problems must be resolved before firm and meaningful conclusions are derived from this approach.

Tests of Property-Rights Theories

Many nonprofit firms receive few or no donations. Property-rights theorists extend their models to commercial nonprofits that receive tax and/or regulatory advantages. The industry most frequently analyzed by such theorists is the health insurance market.

Three types of firms compete in health insurance: the Blues (Blue Cross/Blue Shield, organized as commercial nonprofits), mutual firms (consumer cooperatives that distribute the residual to policyholders in the form of dividend checks), and for-profit firms. Property rights are most attenuated in the Blues and least attenuated in for-profits. Blues had regional monopolies during all the periods studied, and for-profit and mutual health insurance markets were reasonably competitive, with easy entry (Frech & Ginsburg 1981).

The property-rights model implies that Blues would purchase more managerial emoluments, which can be approximately measured by reported expenditures on administration (per claim processed, per enrollee, per dollar of claims paid, or as a share of premiums paid, depending on the study). Differences in administrative costs survive competition because Blues are typically granted a 2 percent lower tax rate on premiums. Frech and Ginsburg (1981) calculate that when Blue Cross administrative costs are 30 percent higher than a competitor's, overall costs are typically only 2 percent higher, so the Blues' tax advantage allows up to 30 percent administrative inefficiency. However, the tax advantage enjoyed by Blues varies from state to state. Property-rights theorists predict that Blues will have higher average administration costs and that larger tax differentials will be positively correlated with higher Blue costs.

These predictions have been statistically tested by a number of authors[12] using multiple-regression analysis (which attempts to find out how much of the variation in administrative costs is due to tax differentials or property-rights differences and how much to other factors, such as level of coverage, local cost of living, and so on). Not surprisingly, results were mixed, and each study developed its own flaws. Most of the studies confirm property-rights hypotheses, but Blair, Jackson, and Vogel (1975) and Kass and Pautler (1981) suggested contrary conclusions. Overall, I find the evidence in support of administrative inefficiency to be more persuasive.

Property-rights hypotheses have also been tested with data on nursing homes and hospitals. Borjas, Frech, and Ginsburg (1983) tested M. Feldstein's (1971, 68) philanthropic wage conjecture—that the "rents of nonprofit organizations are partly 'spent' in overpaying workers as a philanthropic or charitable act"—using data from the nursing home industry. They obtained mixed results: church-related nursing homes pay significantly lower wages and other nonprofit nursing homes pay insignificantly higher wages than for-profit homes. Schlenker and Shaughnessy (1984) analyzed overall costs and nursing costs in Colorado nursing homes. They found that nonprofit nursing homes had significantly higher costs even after controlling for differences in case mix and quality of care.

Other studies have compared costs at for-profit and nonprofit hospitals,[13] attempting to uncover the portion of the cost difference that is due to nonprofit status per se, but many of these studies failed to control for case-mix differences that were due to cream-skimming by for-profit hospitals. Bays (1979) controlled for case-mix differences and concluded

---

impossible to inhibit self-dealing by nonprofit managers, dishonest managers might prefer to work in the nonprofit sector in order to obtain a share of the tax and other subsidies granted this sector (Clark 1980).

12. See Blair, Ginsburg, and Vogel (1975), Blair, Jackson, and Vogel (1975), Frech (1976, 1980), Vogel and Blair (1976), Vogel (1977), Frech and Ginsberg (1978, 1981), Berman (1978), Kass and Pautler (1979, 1981), and Eisenstadt and Kennedy (1981).

13. See Cohen (1963, 1970), Berry (1967), Carr and Feldstein (1967), Ingbar and Taylor (1968), Francisco (1970), Clarkson (1972), Ruchlin, Pointer, and Cannedy (1973), Rafferty and Schweitzer (1974), Lewin (1978), Vignola (1979), and the discussion in Clark (1980, 1460–62).

that for-profits are, in general, no less costly than nonprofits, but that chain for-profits are significantly less costly. This finding supports the contention that not all for-profits are efficient and is consistent with the Steinwald and Neuhauser (1970) argument that hospitals managed by physician-owners (a typical arrangement for nonchain for-profits) are less efficient than a typical for-profit because the physicians must divide their time between medical practice and management. Bays (1979) also speculates that the cost difference may be due to economies of scale in management that are attainable only by a chain of hospitals.

A different approach is taken in Wilson and Jadlow (1982). To minimize the impact of case-mix differences, they examined the provision of nuclear medicine services by hospitals. These services are generally offered by a self-contained unit within the hospital, and there appear to be no systematic differences among for-profit, nonprofit, and government nuclear medicine units in caseload or types of services offered. Using a variety of statistical techniques, they found that the legal status of the hospital explained 19 to 22 percent of the variation in hospital efficiency, and for-profits were significantly more efficient than nonprofits. It should be noted that their definition of efficiency is a narrow one: they examined whether outputs were maximal given the chosen input combinations but did not examine whether the input and output proportions were the correct ones (in economic jargon, they looked at technical efficiency, ignoring productive and allocative efficiency).

Competition among Nonprofit Firms

Very little attention has been devoted to analyzing the effect of competition among nonprofits in an industry containing only nonprofit firms. Rose-Ackerman's analysis (1982b) of competition among nonprofit firms that receive all their revenue from donations is illuminating. In her model, new nonprofit firms enter the market whenever the potential net revenues from a fund-raising campaign are positive, an assumption she admits is extreme for certain types of analysis. In the long run, entry eliminates all net returns from fund-raising; thus firms wasting resources on managerial emoluments are driven out of business (the article does not discuss slack, but this implication seems clear). A certain type of inefficiency is thereby eliminated, though a different sort replaces it: fund-raising continues in the long run (a firm that eliminated fund-raising would go out of business) even though the net return from fund-raising is zero.

The only empirical study of the effect of competition among nonprofits seems to be the analysis of the medical research charity market provided by Feigenbaum (1983). She argues that donors are unable to monitor the efficiency of their donations (in terms of the quantity and quality of output resulting from their donation), and governmental and umbrella group monitoring is imperfect, allowing managers to divert some resources toward emoluments. Competition among nonprofits does not reduce this inefficiency directly (owing to the monitoring problem) but indirectly reduces

emoluments through effects on fund-raising activities. In a highly competitive market, firms must devote a greater share of their slack resources to fund-raising and reduce spending on emoluments.

This prediction was confirmed by regression analysis, which revealed that charities in highly competitive markets spent on average over 20 percent less revenue on administration than charities in less competitive areas, and fund-raising costs were 10 percent higher in competitive markets. Research expenditures constitute a greater share of revenues for larger firms, which are presumably monitored more closely by donors and the IRS. However, one prediction of the model was not borne out. Competition should affect only the allocation of slack between fund-raising and administrative expenditures, not the shares of revenues devoted to slack and to research expenditures; yet Feigenbaum found that competition significantly increases research share. If this result can be explained and replicated, it would seem to imply that efforts at merging charities to avoid "needless" overlap and duplication are misguided (see also Rose-Ackerman 1983).

Competition with Government

Although Rose-Ackerman (1981) has analyzed the effects of government grants on nonprofit firm performance, I am unaware of any work that discusses the effects of direct government competition in service provision. Property-rights and public-choice theorists are fond of arguing that governments are inefficient providers of service. Indeed, Niskanen (1971) modeled the behavior of government bureaus in the same fashion that he modeled the behavior of nonprofit firms. Borjas, Frech, and Ginsburg (1983) found that government-owned nursing homes paid employees 6.6 percent more than for-profits (about 10 percent more than church-related nonprofits and 5 percent more than other nonprofits), and Wilson and Jadlow (1982) found that nuclear medicine units in government hospitals produced significantly lower outputs at each level of inputs than nonprofits. Thus, it seems unlikely that governmental competition provides the same spur to efficiency that for-profit competition does.

DETERMINANTS OF SECTORAL SHARES

Many factors have been adduced to explain the shares of output produced by for-profit, nonprofit, and governmental organizations. The few that have been tested empirically include the nature of the good or service provided and differences in the cost of provision, state regulation, and community characteristics. These factors can explain whether coexistence is expected as well as the shares provided by each sector.

Theories of the relationship between the nature of the good provided (public or private, quality observable prior to sale or only through use) and the sectoral shares are discussed by Hansmann in chapter 2 and will be dealt with only briefly here. Theories of the detailed determinants of personal and corporate donations and of foundation and government grants (which indirectly determine output shares) are reviewed in chapters 6, 18, and 19 in this volume. The effect of government provision on charitable donations, however, will be considered here, as this is a more direct intersectoral determinant. Space does not permit a general review of the determinants of government spending (Atkinson & Stiglitz [1980, chap. 10] provide an excellent introduction to the subject), though I will note the explicit considerations of voters when choosing between governmental provision and personal donations.

Government and Nonprofit Shares

Quite a few analysts have attempted to explain the coexistence of the third sector and government.[14] Most of this literature ignores for-profits (but see Holtman 1983), typically by restricting attention to industries in which for-profits could not compete profitably (such as welfare services, whose beneficiaries can hardly be expected to compensate a firm for services provided, or public goods industries more generally) or by assuming that for-profits are unaffected by the factors determining nonprofit and government shares. Some models examine the response of donations to changes in government expenditure on related services, but the resulting empirical analyses are subject to endogeneity bias. If, for example, a $1 million increase in government spending is correlated with a $500,000 increase in charitable donations, these models do not enable us to discern whether the government spending increase *caused* the donative increase or whether both were caused by, say, a change in tastes in favor of the service provided. At least three of the models (Seaman 1979; Roberts 1984; Steinberg 1985b) enable one, in principle, to sort out the causal from the spurious correlations by analyzing the simultaneous determination of donations and government spending.

Steinberg (1985b) suggests that the effects can be sorted out by adding local government spending to the model. When federal nonmatching aid to a community goes up, causality is much more likely to run from federal aid to local donations and local government spending than the reverse, as taste factors that might affect local community expenditures almost certainly do not cause federal aid to the community to change. In addition, this model is particularly suited for analyzing the predictions of Reagonomics that local government and charitable donations will pick up the slack when federal expenditures on social services are cut.

In Steinberg's model, both the act of giving and the total provision of the good provide utility to the donor, and these two sources of utility are imperfect substitutes for each other. That is, if you contribute a dollar to my favorite charity, I will be made happier, but my joy is not the same as when I contribute a dollar. In response to your increased contribution, my joy from my own contribution would be reduced somewhat, but not to zero.

Thus, each donor responds to the total donations of other donors and to total government spending. When government spending goes up, I would be tempted to lower my own contribution (the crowd-out phenomenon) but it would be difficult to figure out by how much since I would expect other donors to adjust as well.

Local voters would do well if they considered the effective price of local government spending relative to the effective price of donating. The effective price indicates out-of-pocket expenses necessary to provide a dollar's worth of additional service output. Both prices are reduced by federal income tax deductibility, but this does not alter the relative attractiveness of the two service-financing options. Differential efficiency affects the relative prices: if the leak of resources to managerial emoluments is greater in governments than in nonprofit firms, then nonprofits become better buys.

Two factors are somewhat more subtle. When government spending increases, private donations respond. If crowd-out is 100 percent, an increase in taxes and local government spending accomplishes nothing in the way of increased service output (the effective price is infinite). If crowd-out is negative (matching behavior), the price of output becomes quite low. Thus, all else being equal, we would expect communities with higher crowd-out parameters to rely more heavily on nonprofits.[15] This conclusion has not yet been subjected to empirical testing.

The final factor determining the effective price is the leverage effect of public provision. If I as donor devote a dollar to service provision, then total provision goes up by only a dollar. If I as politician or as decisive voter raise taxes and spending by a dollar per person, then total provision goes up by many dollars, and it costs me only a dollar. This leverage lowers the relative price of government.

When federal grants to a community go down, voters and donors face a very complicated decision process. The change in federal grants may affect the price of local government relative to nonprofit provision. There may be direct federal crowd-out (raising donations) and indirect crowd-out effects (as donors respond to induced changes in local government spending). Using the concept of Nash equilibrium to calculate long-run results, Steinberg demonstrates that any of four reactions of total spending (federal plus local plus donative) to federal spending cuts is theoretically possible—partial crowd-out (total spending falls by less than a dollar when federal spending falls by a dollar), total crowd-out (total spending is unaffected by federal spending), super crowd-out (total spending rises following federal cuts), or negative crowd-out (total spending falls by more than federal spending). The reaction is determined by the distribution of preferences in the community, and partial crowd-out seems most likely in most industries.

14. See Ireland and Johnson (1970), Hochman and Rodgers (1973), Wolpert (1977), Abrams and Schmitz (1978), YoungDay (1978), Seaman (1979), Kushman (1979), Rose-Ackerman (1981), Weiss (1981), Sugden (1982), Steinberg (1983a, 1985b), Jones (1983), Paqué (1983), Holtman (1983), Schiff (1984), and Roberts (1984).

15. Some technical qualifications to this conclusion are pointed out in Steinberg (1983a).

In Steinberg's model (1985b), nonprofit organizations are passive recipients of donations. Although this simplification allows for the derivation of certain results, Rose-Ackerman (1981) obtained results by simplifying the political model while complicating the nonprofit model. She found that, despite a general presumption that federal grants to a nonprofit firm would reduce donations, there are many circumstances where the reverse is true. Grants may be made on a matching basis, reducing the price of donation. Donors may regard grant reception as a sign that those with greater ability to monitor performance have approved the efficiency of the nonprofit firm and thus may increase their own donation. Finally, grants may encourage the organization to take a less extreme ideological position, increasing the popularity of the firm among donors.

Empirical Studies of Government's Effect on Nonprofit Share

Steinberg (1983a) estimated his model for two industries—hospitals and recreation. A number of statistical and data problems contaminated his results, but they remain suggestive. He found that a one-dollar increase in federal grants targeted to recreation caused local government spending to fall by about 65 cents and local donations by about 2 cents. Thus, total spending increased by only 33 cents. An increase in nontargeted federal aid led to small increases in both categories of recreation spending. Results were mixed for the hospital sector, with crowd-out appearing small or negative. A reanalysis of the same data (Steinberg 1985b), which incorporated governmental user fees, found super-crowd-out in the recreation sector.

Preliminary estimates provided by Hansmann (1982) suggest that governmental competition raises the share of private nursing home output provided by nonprofit firms. He obtained a similar result for vocational schools but found that governmental competition lowers the nonprofit share of the private hospital industry. Kushman (1979) found that differing types of federal aid have differing effects on the provision of day care by local governments, nonprofits, and for-profits. The Appalachian Regional Program of federal-state aid substantially increased nonprofit care in eligible counties, at the expense of for-profit centers. However, AFDC uniformly increased day-care provision by all three sectors.

Abrams and Schmitz (1978) explained the variations over time and income class in aggregate donations with three measures of government spending on related goods. They found partial crowd-out: a one-dollar increase in government transfers per person caused a 28 cent decrease in donations. A second study by Abrams and Schmitz (1984) also found partial crowd-out when they analyzed the variation in average itemized donations across states. Donations were found to be responsive both to the percentage of families in poverty and to governmental spending, with crowd-out estimated at 30 cents on the dollar. Reece (1979) analyzed the variation in individual donations across metropolitan areas and obtained a similar result. Although the level of statistical significance was low, his estimates suggest that a 1 percent increase in

government spending would cause donations to fall by 0.08 to 0.19 percent. Amos (1982) explained state variation in itemized donations with measures of state transfer payments and found that a 1 percent increase in state spending caused a 0.0005 to 0.6 percent decrease in donations. This translates to crowd-out of up to 46 cents on the dollar.

Wolch and Geiger (1983) found that both the number and the revenues of philanthropies in a community go up when intergovernmental grants constitute a larger portion of the local government budget. They also found significant interjurisdictional spillovers—resources of nonprofits are well explained by the income of neighboring communities. Seaman (1979) found that a local government decision to subsidize museums is well explained by the tax price of donation (as predicted in his model of simultaneous donor/voter choice), but the level of subsidy is not easily explained.

At least two studies have been conducted using foreign data. Paqué (1982), using aggregated tax data from the Federal Republic of Germany found that donations fell by 0.06 to 0.35 percent when state "social service expenditures" rose by 1 percent; state expenditures on "higher education and research" had no significant effect, but state expenditures on "health and recreation" and "cultural affairs" significantly increased donations. Thus, the literature contains statistical support for the negative crowd-out predicted for some industries by Steinberg (1985b) and Rose-Ackerman (1981). Jones (1983) explained temporal variation in charitable donations in the United Kingdom with governmental expenditure on social services and housing. He found that a 1 percent governmental increase caused donations to fall by 1.41 to 1.52 percent. Because aggregate donations are somewhat smaller in the United Kingdom, this large percentage change amounts to a small absolute change in donations—crowd-out is about one and one-half cents on the dollar. A reanalysis of the same data by Steinberg (1985c) found that crowd-out was a bit smaller (about half a cent on the dollar), but still statistically significant.

One study examined the effect of government spending on donations of time as well as money. Analyzing survey data from individual donors, Schiff (1984) found that the extent of crowd-out varied significantly with the type of government spending and the level of government doing the spending. For example, he found that a 1 percent increase in state government expenditures on noncash welfare increased donations of money to welfare organizations by 4.56 percent and decreased donations of volunteer labor by 4.96 percent. In contrast, a 1 percent increase in state cash assistance reduced donations of money by 2.88 percent and increased donations of time by 4.75 percent. An increase of 1 percent in local government welfare spending caused donations of money to rise by 0.47 percent and donations of time to fall by 0.27 percent.

Tax and Regulatory Advantages

Tax, regulatory, and donative advantages enjoyed by nonprofit firms are often cited to explain the share of output provided by each sector, but a careful theoretical exposition of this relation has not yet appeared. We do not know exactly how nonprofit firms decide whether to utilize these cost and revenue advantages to increase their market share (by undercutting or out-advertising for-profits), build market size, increase emoluments, or all three (though an introductory analysis of this problem is presented in Frech and Ginsburg [1981]). In some cases, these advantages merely compensate for other disadvantages, such as lack of access to financial capital (Hansmann 1981c). Nonetheless, preliminary estimates provided in Hansmann (1982) strongly suggest that at least part of the tax advantage is devoted to share increases. He estimates that if three types of state tax advantages were eliminated (property, sales, and corporate income tax exemptions), the share of private nursing home beds provided by nonprofit firms would fall from the current level of 24 percent to a level of between 3 and 10 percent. He finds a smaller effect in the hospital industry, where the nonprofit share would fall from 91 percent to about 90.5 percent, and intermediate-sized effects in the primary/secondary education and vocational education industries.

Two studies by Frech and Ginsburg examined the extent to which premium tax advantages are split between slack and share goals in Blues. Residual claimants (in the form of physician-controlled boards) would utilize the cost margin to undercut competitors and increase market share, whereas other board members and staff would seek increased managerial emoluments. Their 1978 study found that the Blue Cross market share is sensitive to the size of the tax advantage; their 1981 study found that both share and cost increase with tax advantages. However, their 1981 study also found that tax advantages raise costs but do not raise share for Blue Shield plans. They explain the disparity by noting that Blue Cross plans were more tightly controlled by physicians than were Blue Shield plans during their sample period.

Regulatory advantages are not randomly imparted by political systems, nor are they always designed to maximize social welfare. Proponents of the economic theory of regulation assert that "as a rule regulation is acquired by the industry and is designed and operated primarily for its benefit" (Stigler 1971). Industries with an identifiable self-interest in regulation compete in a political arena for desired changes. The group with the largest potential net gain is likely to prevail, as it will lobby the hardest and provide the most campaign contributions.

This theory was tested by Wendling and Werner (1980) for the hospital industry. They found that passage of certificate-of-need laws, which regulate entry of new hospitals and expansion of existing hospitals, was well explained by the potential net hospital industry gains from the regulation. Specifically, "in states where the hospital industry faces strong competitive pressures and industry organization costs are low, the likelihood of enactment of certificate-of-need regulation increases" (p. 7). Further support for these theories is provided by historical analysis (Bays 1983), empirical studies of health planning agency decisions (May 1967; Hyman 1977), and opinion surveys (Havighurst 1982, 363–65). Thus, regulatory advantages seem to be explained by market structure as well as the reverse.

Other Factors

Three facets of the good provided are important determinants of shares. First, nonprofit and governmental provision are more likely for public goods (consumption is nonrival), and for-profit provision is ruled out for nonexcludable public goods (where it is not feasible or economical to exclude nonpayers) (Weisbrod 1975). Welfare is one such good, for the benefits of poverty reduction accrue to everyone in the community. For-profit firms do not sell this good because potential buyers are hoping that someone else will pay for it so that they can benefit at no personal cost. Second, nonprofit provision is more likely in cases where the complex nature of the good and informational problems lead to contract failure (Hansmann 1980; Easley & O'Hara 1983; Weisbrod & Schlesinger 1986). Any time consumers wish to make donations, they prefer nonprofit firms because it is costly or impossible to determine whether a donation to a for-profit firm added to profits or to service. Nursing and day care are examples of another aspect of informational problems. Here, consumers may prefer nonprofit firms because they are more assured that the quality level contracted for is actually provided. Third, nonprofit provision is more likely if the demand for the good is variable and capacity must be precommitted (Holtman 1983). Emergency health care facilities are one such good—there is no time to build a new hospital when an epidemic or major accident hits a community. To my knowledge, none of these predictions has been carefully tested.[16]

Weisbrod's theory (1975) suggests that communities with more diverse preferences are likely to provide greater support to nonprofit firms, since greater diversity increases the extent to which higher than average demanders of a service will be dissatisfied with public provision. His theory has not been applied to industries in which all three sectors coexist. Feigenbaum (1980a) points out that donative provision will, in turn, reduce governmental provision, as voters take advantage of donors in order to cut back their tax burden. Thus, she predicts and tests the proposition that nonprofit provision is greater and governmental provision lower when a community is more heterogeneous (as measured by the coefficient of variation of a number of demographic variables). Analyzing income redistribution by government and by donors, her hypotheses are generally confirmed (though the level of statistical significance is low, a typical result when variables are badly measured, as they are here).

Another factor often thought to influence nonprofit share is the growth rate of overall demand for the service provided. For-profits are thought to be better able to respond to rapid increases in demand, for a variety of reasons. First, for-profits are likely to be efficiently managed because of the property-rights link. Second, for-profits often have less trouble (or face lower costs) securing capital to finance expan-

16. Preliminary evidence in support of the Holtman argument is found in Holtman and Ullman (1984), who concluded that nonpatient revenues of nursing homes (a proxy for donations) are highly related to the provision of extra capacity by these organizations.

sion. Third, the sense of community that overcomes donor free-riding incentives may not develop in rapidly growing communities (Steinwald & Neuhauser 1970). Preliminary estimates provided by Schlesinger (1980) and Hansmann (1982) confirmed this theory, but other studies of the hospital industry obtained mixed results (Kushman & Nuckton 1977; Bays, forthcoming). It is particularly difficult to test this factor, for nonprofit firms may respond one way to rapidly increasing demand when the increase is predicted long in advance and quite another way when the demand increase is a surprise. Further, if demand fluctuates (rather than growing steadily), Holtman (1983) has indicated that nonprofit firms will hold excess capacity, but for-profit firms will not. No study has properly accounted for these complications.

The final factor to be considered here is court-ordered desegregation. Desegregation seems to have led many students away from public elementary and secondary schools, but it is not immediately apparent whether private for-profit or nonprofit schools were the beneficiaries. If nonprofits respond slowly to sudden increases in demand, we would expect the for-profit share to rise. Hansmann's estimates (1982) seem to confirm this.

SUMMARY AND CONCLUSION

Nonprofit organizations do differ from their for-profit counterparts, but the differences are not as pronounced as they first appear. Advertising is in many ways analogous to fundraising, foundations play the role of the stock market in providing initial equity capital, and sales of goods and services are important sources of revenue for both types of organization.

Although the lack of a profit motive allows nonprofits to provide needed social services in a trustworthy fashion, it also fosters inefficiency. But there can be no monolithic theory of nonprofit behavior, for the forces of competition and regulation are paramount—the functioning of each nonprofit organization depends on the level of competition by government, for-profit firms, and other nonprofits. Competition is often tempered by special regulatory and tax advantages conferred on each sector by the government, and these advantages in turn are major determinants of the respective sectoral shares. Thus, the market structure paradigm seems invaluable for understanding the functioning and performance of nonprofit organizations.

REFERENCES

Abrams, Burton, and M. Schmitz. 1978. "The 'Crowding-Out' Effect of Governmental Transfers on Private Charitable Contributions." *Public Choice* 33:29–37.

———. 1984. "The 'Crowding-Out' Effect of Governmental Transfers on Private Charitable Contributions: Cross-Section Evidence." *National Tax Journal* 37:563–68.

Alchian, Armen, and Harold Demsetz. 1972. "Production, Information Costs, and Economic Organization." *American Economic Review* 62:777–95.

Alchian, Armen, and R. A. Kessel. 1962. "Competition, Monopoly and the Pursuit of Money." In *Aspects of Labor Economics*, 157–75. Princeton: Princeton University Press.

American Hospital Association. 1981. *Hospital Statistics—1980.* Chicago: American Hospital Association.

Amos, Orley M., Jr. 1982. "Empirical Analysis of Motives Underlying Individual Contribution to Charity." *Atlantic Economic Journal* 10:45–52.

"Antitrust and Nonprofit Entities." 1981. *Harvard Law Review* 94:802–20.

Arnould, R., and L. Debrock. 1982. "A Re-examination of Medical Society Control of Blue Shield Plans." Paper presented at the Eastern Economics Association Meeting, Washington, D.C.

Arnould, R., and D. M. Eisenstadt. 1981. "The Effects of Provider-Controlled Blue Shield Plans: Regulatory Op-

tions." In *A New Approach to the Economics of Health Care*, edited by M. Olson, 337–58. Washington, D.C.: American Enterprise Institute.

Atkinson, Anthony, and Joseph Stiglitz. 1980. *Lectures on Public Economics.* New York: McGraw-Hill.

Bartlett, Richard. 1982. "United Charities and the Sherman Act." *Yale Law Journal* 91:1593–1613.

Bays, Carson W. 1977. "Case-Mix Differences between Nonprofit and For-Profit Hospitals." *Inquiry* 14:17–21.

———. 1979. "Cost Comparisons of For-Profit and Nonprofit Hospitals." *Social Science and Medicine* 13(c):219–25.

———. 1983. "Why Most Private Hospitals are Nonprofit." *Journal of Policy Analysis and Management* 2:366–85.

———. Forthcoming. "Patterns of Hospital Growth: The Case of Profit Hospitals." *Medical Care.*

Bendick, M., Jr. 1979. "Essays on Education as a Three Sector Industry." In *The Voluntary Nonprofit Sector*, edited by Burton Weisbrod. Lexington, Mass.: D. C. Heath.

Ben-Ner, Avner. 1986. "Nonprofit Organizations: Why Do They Exist in Market Economies?" In *The Economics of Nonprofit Institutions: Studies in Structure and Policy*, ed. Susan Rose-Ackerman. New York: Oxford Univ. Press.

Berle, A., and G. Means. 1932. *The Modern Corporation and Private Property.* New York: Macmillan.

Berman, H. 1978. "Comment" (on Frech and Ginsberg chapter

in same book). In *Competition in the Health Care Sector: Past, Present and Future,* edited by W. Greenberg, 189–206. Germantown, Md.: Aspen Systems.

Berry, R. 1967. "Returns to Scale in the Production of Hospital Services." *Health Service Resources* 2:123.

Blair, Roger, Paul B. Ginsburg, and Ronald J. Vogel. 1975. "Blue Cross–Blue Shield Administration Costs: A Study of Non-Profit Health Insurers." *Economic Inquiry* 13:55–70.

Blair, Roger, J. R. Jackson, and Ronald Vogel. 1975. "Economies of Scale in the Administration of Health Insurance." *Review of Economics and Statistics* 57:185–89.

Borjas, George J., H. E. Frech III, and Paul B. Ginsburg. 1983. "Property Rights and Wages: The Case of Nursing Homes." *Journal of Human Resources* 17:231–46.

Boulding, Kenneth. 1972. *Towards a Pure Theory of Foundations.* New York: Nonprofit Report.

Boyle, Stanley E., and Philip Jacobs. 1979. "Fundraising Costs." *Philanthropy Monthly,* April, pp. 5–12.

Buchanan, James M. 1965. "An Economic Theory of Clubs." *Economica* 32:1–14.

Carlson, Robert, J. Robinson, and J. M. Ryan. 1971. "An Optimization Model of a Nonprofit Agency." *Western Economic Journal* 9:78–86.

Carr, W. J., and P. J. Feldstein. 1967. "The Relationship of Cost to Hospital Size." *Inquiry* 4:45.

Caulfield, Stephen. 1981. *Cross Subsidies in Hospital Reimbursement.* Washington, D.C.: Government Research Corporation.

Clark, Robert C. 1980 "Does the Nonprofit Form Fit the Hospital Industry?" *Harvard Law Review* 92:1416–89.

Clarkson, K. 1972. "Some Implications of Property Rights in Hospital Management." *Journal of Law and Economics* 15:363–85.

———. 1979. "Economics of Art Museums." Paper presented at the Conference on Institutional Choice, Madison, Wis., October 23–25.

———. 1980. "Managerial Behavior in Nonproprietary Organizations." In *The Economics of Nonproprietary Organizations,* edited by K. Clarkson and D. Martin. Greenwich, Conn.: JAI Press.

Coelen, C., F. Glantz, and D. Calore. 1979. *Day Care Centers in the U.S., Final Report of the National Day Care Study.* Vol. 3. Cambridge, Mass.: Abt Associates.

Coelho, P. 1976. "Rules, Authorities, and the Design of Not-for-Profit Firms." *Journal of Economic Issues* 10:416–28.

Cohen, H. A. 1963. "Variations in Cost among Hospitals of Different Sizes." *Southern Economics Journal* 33:355.

———. 1970. "Hospital Cost Curves with Emphasis on Measuring Patient Care Output." In *Empirical Studies in Health Economics,* edited by H. E. Klarman. Baltimore: Johns Hopkins University Press.

Cook, Richard V., Nancy L. Steketee, and Stanley Wenocur. 1981. *Study of United Way Donor Option Program.* Washington, D.C.: National Committee for Responsive Philanthropy.

Day, George S., William F. Massy, and Allan D. Shocker. 1978. "The Public Policy Context of the Relevant Market Question." In *Public Policy Issues in Marketing,* edited by John F. Cady. Cambridge, Mass.: Marketing Science Institute.

Day, George S., Allan D. Shocker, and Rajendra K. Srivastava. 1979. "Customer-Oriented Approaches to Identifying Product-Markets." *Journal of Marketing* 43:8–19.

De Alessi, L. 1983. "Property Rights, Transaction Costs and X-Efficiency." *American Economic Review* 73:64–81.

Downing, Paul B., and Gordon Brady. 1981. "The Role of Citizen Interest Groups in Environmental Policy Formation." In *Nonprofit Firms in a Three Section Economy,* edited by M. White. Washington, D.C.: Urban Institute.

Dye, Richard F. 1980. "Contributions of Volunteer Time: Some Evidence on Income Tax Effects." *National Tax Journal* 33:89–93.

Easley, David, and Maureen O'Hara. 1983. "The Economic Role of the Nonprofit Firm." *Bell Journal of Economics* 14:531–38.

Ehrlich, Isaac, and Lawrence Fisher. 1982. "The Derived Demand for Advertising: A Theoretical and Empirical Investigation." *American Economic Review* 72:366–88.

Eisenstadt, David, and Thomas Kennedy. 1981. "Control and Behavior of Nonprofit Firms: The Case of Blue Shield." *Southern Economic Journal* 47:26–36.

Ellman, Ira M. 1982. "Another Theory of Nonprofit Corporations." *Michigan Law Review* 80:999–1050.

Faine, H. R. 1972. "Unions and the Arts." *American Economic Review* 62:70–77.

Feigenbaum, Susan. 1980a. "The Case of Income Redistribution: A Theory of Government and Private Provision of Collective Goods." *Public Finance Quarterly* 8:3–22.

———. 1980b. "The Identification and Estimation of Inter-Industry Relationships within the Nonprofit Sector." Claremont Working Papers in Economics, Business and Public Policy, Claremont Colleges, Calif.

———. 1983. "Competition and Performance in the Nonprofit Sector: The Case of Medical Research Charities." Unpublished manuscript.

Feldstein, Martin. 1971. *The Rising Cost of Hospital Care.* Washington, D.C.: Information Resources Press.

Fisher, Franklin. 1977. "On Donor Sovereignty and United Charities." *American Economic Review* 67:632–38.

Francisco, E. W. 1970. "Analysis of Cost Variations among Short-Term General Hospitals." In *Empirical Studies in Health Economics,* edited by H. E. Klarman, 321–32. Baltimore: Johns Hopkins University Press.

Frech, H. E., III. 1976. "The Property Rights Theory of the Firm: Empirical Results from a Natural Experiment." *Journal of Political Economy* 84:143–52.

———. 1980. "Health Insurance: Private, Mutual, or Government." In *The Economics of Nonproprietary Organizations,* edited by K. Clarkson and D. Martin. Greenwich, Conn.: JAI Press.

Frech, H. E., and P. Ginsberg. 1978. "Competition among Insurers." In *Competition in the Health Care Sector: Past, Present and Future,* edited by W. Greenberg. Germantown, Md.: Aspen Systems.

———. 1981. "Property Rights and Competition in Health Insurance: Multiple Objectives for Nonprofit Firms." *Research in Law and Economics* 3:155–72.

Freeman, Richard B. 1975. "Demand for Labor in a Nonprofit Market: University Faculty." In *Labor in the Public and*

Nonprofit Sectors, edited by Daniel S. Hammermesh, 85–133. Princeton: Princeton University Press.

Giancola, Jeffrey S. 1984. *Unfair Competition by Nonprofit Organizations with Small Business: An Issue for the 1980s.* 3d ed. Washington, D.C.: Office of the Chief Counsel for Advocacy, U.S. Small Business Administration.

Goddeeris, John H. 1984. "Compensating Differentials and Self-Selection: An Application to Lawyers." Econometrics Workshop Paper no. 8405, Department of Economics, Michigan State University, East Lansing.

Hansmann, Henry. 1980. "The Role of Nonprofit Enterprise." *Yale Law Journal* 89:835–901.

———. 1981a. "Reforming Nonprofit Corporation Law." *University of Pennsylvania Law Review* 129:497–623.

———. 1981b. "Nonprofit Enterprise in the Performing Arts." *Bell Journal of Economics* 12:341–61.

———. 1981c. "The Rationale for Exempting Nonprofit Organizations from the Corporate Income Tax." *Yale Law Journal* 91:54–100.

———. 1982. "The Effect of Tax Exemption and Other Factors on Competition between Nonprofit and For-Profit Enterprise." Draft.

Harris, Jeffrey E. 1979. "Pricing Rules for Hospitals." *Bell Journal of Economics* 10:224–43.

Havighurst, Clark C. 1982. *Deregulating the Health Care Industry.* Cambridge, Mass.: Ballinger.

Havrilesky, Thomas, Robert Schweitzer, and Scheffel Wright. 1973. "The Supply of and Demand for Voluntary Labor in Behalf of Environmental Quality." *Proceedings of the Business and Economic Statistics Section of the American Statistical Association,* pp. 170–79.

Hay, Joel W., and Michael J. Leahy. 1984. "Competition among Health Plans: Some Preliminary Evidence." *Southern Economic Journal* 50:831–46.

Hirschoff, Mary-Michelle Upson. Forthcoming. "An Overview of Public Policy toward Private Schools: A Focus on Parental Choice." In *Private Education and Public Policy,* edited by Daniel Levy. New York: Oxford University Press.

Hochman, H., and J. Rodgers. 1973. "Utility Interdependence and Income Transfers through Charity." In *Transfers in an Urbanized Economy,* edited by K. Boulding, M. Pfaff, and A. Pfaff. Belmont, Calif.: Wadsworth.

Holtman, A. G. 1983. "A Theory of Non-Profit Firms." *Economica* 50:439–49.

Holtman, A. G., and Steven G. Ullman. 1984. "Non-Profit Firms and Donations: Some Empirical Evidence." Paper, University of Miami, Department of Economics.

Hyman, Herbert H. 1977. *Health Regulation: Certificate of Need and 1122.* Baltimore: Aspen Systems Corporation.

Ingbar, M. L., and L. D. Taylor. 1968. *Hospital Costs in Massachusetts.* Cambridge, Mass.: Harvard University Press.

Ireland, Thomas R., and David B. Johnson. 1970. *The Economics of Charity.* Blacksburg, Va.: Center for the Study of Public Choice.

James, Estelle. 1983. "How Nonprofits Grow: A Model." *Journal of Policy Analysis and Management* 2:350–66.

Johnson, Richard L. 1971. "Data Show For-Profit Hospitals Don't Provide Comparable Service." *Modern Hospital* 65:116–18.

Jones, P. R. 1983. "Aid to Charities." *International Journal of Social Economics* 10:3–11.

Joseph, Hyman, 1975. "On Interdepartmental Pricing of Not-for-Profit Hospitals." *Quarterly Review of Economics and Business* 12:33–44.

Kass, D., and P. Pautler. 1979. *Physician Control of Blue Shield Plans.* Staff Report to the FTC, Washington, D.C.

———. 1981. "The Administrative Costs of Non-Profit Health Insurers." *Economic Inquiry* 19:515–21.

Keating, Barry P., and Maryann O. Keating. 1975. "Nonprofit Firms, Decision Making and Regulation." *Review of Social Economy* 33:26–42.

Kramer, Donald W. 1981. "Foundations as a Source of Venture Capital." *Delaware Valley Agenda,* November 25, p. 9.

Krizay, John, and Andrew Wilson. 1974. *The Patient as Consumer: Health Care Financing in the United States.* Lexington, Mass.: D. C. Heath.

Kushman, J. E. 1979. "A Three-Sector Model of Day Care Services." *Journal of Human Resources* 14:543–62.

Kushman, J. E., and Carol F. Nuckton. 1977. "Further Evidence on the Relative Performance of Proprietary and Nonprofit Hospitals." *Medical Care* 15:55–67.

Lee, M. 1971. "A Conspicuous Production Theory of Hospital Behavior." *Southern Economics Journal* 38:48–58.

Leibenstein, Harvey. 1966. "Allocative Efficiency vs. 'X-Efficiency.'" *American Economic Review* 56:392–415.

Lewin, Larry. 1978. *Investor Owned Hospitals: An Examination of Performance.* Washington, D.C.: Lewin & Associates.

Long, Stephen H. 1977. "Income Tax Effects on Donor Choice of Money and Time Contributions." *National Tax Journal* 30:207–11.

Lovelock, Christopher H., and Charles B. Weinberg. 1984. *Marketing for Public and Nonprofit Managers.* New York: John Wiley.

Lynk, W. 1981. "Regulatory Control of the Membership for Corporate Boards of Directors: The Blue Shield Case." *Journal of Law and Economics* 24:159–74.

Manning, W. G. 1973. "Comparative Efficiency in Short-Term General Hospitals." Ph.D. diss., Stanford University.

Marris, Robin, and Dennis Mueller. 1980. "The Corporation, Competition, and the Invisible Hand." *Journal of Economic Literature* 18:32–63.

May, Joel J. 1967. "Health Planning—It's Past and Potential." Health Administration Perspectives no. A5. Chicago: Center for Health Administration Studies, University of Chicago.

Menchik, Paul, and Burton Weisbrod. 1981. "Volunteer Labor Supply in the Provision of Collective Goods." In *Nonprofit Firms in a Three-Sector Economy,* edited by Michelle White. Washington, D.C.: Urban Institute.

Morgan, J. N., R. F. Dye, and J. H. Hybels. 1977. "Results from Two National Surveys of Philanthropic Activity." In Commission on Private Philanthropy and Public Needs, *Research Papers,* vol. 1, 157–323. Washington, D.C.: U.S. Treasury Department.

Mueller, Marnie W. 1975. "Economic Determinants of Volunteer Work by Women." *SIGNS: Journal of Women and Culture in Society* 1:325–38.

Nelson, R., and M. Krashinsky. 1973. "Two Major Issues of Public Policy: Public Subsidy and the Organization of Supply.'' In *Public Policy for Day Care of Young Children,* edited by D. Young and R. Nelson. Lexington, Mass.: Lexington Books.

Newhouse, Joseph. 1970. ''Toward a Theory of Non-profit Institutions: An Economic Model of a Hospital.'' *American Economic Review* 60:64–73.

Niskanen, William A., Jr. 1971. *Bureaucracy and Representative Government.* Chicago: Aldine-Atherton.

Oi, Walter Y. 1971. ''A Disneyland Dilemma: Two-Part Tariffs for a Mickey Mouse Monopoly.'' *Quarterly Journal of Economics* 85:77–96.

Paqué, Karl-Heinz. 1982. ''Do Public Transfers 'Crowd Out' Private Charitable Giving? Some Econometric Evidence for the Federal Republic of Germany.'' Kiel Institute of World Economics Working Paper no. 152, Kiel, Federal Republic of Germany.

———. 1983. ''Public Subsidies to Private Charitable Giving: Some Arguments Revisited.'' Unpublished manuscript.

Pauly, Mark, and Michael Redisch. 1973. ''The Not-for-Profit Hospital as a Physicians' Cooperative.'' *American Economic Review* 63:87–99.

Preston, Ann E. 1984. ''The Non-Profit Firm: A Potential Solution to Inherent Market Failures.'' Wellesley College, Department of Economics, Working Paper no. 77.

Rafferty, J., and S. Schweitzer. 1974. ''Comparison of For-Profit and Nonprofit Hospitals: A Re-evaluation.'' *Inquiry* 11:304–09.

Reece, W. S. 1979. ''Charitable Contributions: New Evidence on Household Behavior.'' *American Economic Review* 69:142–51.

Rhode, William. 1975. *U.S. Private Foundation Support of Health Research and Development.* DHEW no. (NIH) 76–996.

Roberts, Russell D. 1984. ''A Positive Model of Private Charity and Public Transfers.'' *Journal of Political Economy* 92:136–48.

Rose-Ackerman, S. 1980. ''United Charities: An Economic Analysis.'' *Public Policy* 28:323–50.

———. 1981. ''Do Government Grants to Charity Reduce Private Donations.'' In *Nonprofit Firms in a Three Sector Economy,* edited by Michelle White. Washington, D.C.: Urban Institute.

———. 1982a. ''Unfair Competition and Corporate Income Taxation.'' *Stanford Law Review* 34:1017–39.

———. 1982b. ''Charitable Giving and Excessive Fundraising.'' *Quarterly Journal of Economics* 97:193–212.

———. 1983. ''Social Services and the Market: Paying Customers, Vouchers, and Quality Control.'' *Columbia Law Review* 83:1405–39.

Ruchlin, H., D. Pointer, and L. Cannedy. 1973. ''A Comparison of For-Profit Investor-Owned Chain and Nonprofit Hospitals.'' *Inquiry* 10:13–23.

Rudney, Gabriel, and Murray Weitzman. 1983. ''Significance of Employment and Earnings in the Philanthropic Sector, 1972–1982.'' Yale University, Program on Non-Profit Organizations Working Paper no. 77.

Rushing, William. 1974. ''Differences in Profit and Nonprofit Organizations: A Study of Effectiveness and Efficiency in General Short-Stay Hospitals.'' *Administrative Science Quarterly* 19:474–84.

Sandler, Todd, and John Tschirhart. 1980. ''The Economic Theory of Clubs: An Evaluative Survey.'' *Journal of Economic Literature* 18:1481–1521.

Schiff, Jerald. 1984. ''Charitable Contributions of Money and Time: The Role of Government Policies.'' Ph.D. diss., University of Wisconsin at Madison.

Schlenker, Robert E., and Peter W. Shaughnessy. 1984. ''Case Mix, Quality, and Cost Relationships in Colorado Nursing Homes.'' *Health Care Financing Review* 6:61–71.

Schlesinger, Harris. 1981. ''A Note on the Consistency of Non-Profit-Maximizing Behavior with Perfect Competition.'' *Southern Economic Journal* 48:513–16.

Schlesinger, Mark. 1980. ''Ownership and Dynamic Behavior.'' Paper submitted for Abt Associates Award.

Seaman, Bruce A. 1979. ''Local Subsidization of Culture: A Public Choice Model Based on Household Utility Maximization.'' *Journal of Behavioral Economics* 8:93–131.

Simon, Herbert. 1959. ''Theories of Decision Making in Economics and Behavioral Science.'' *American Economic Review* 49:253–83.

Sloan, F. 1981. ''Physicians and Blue Shield: A Study of the Effects of Physician Control on Blue Shield Reimbursements.'' In *Issues in Physician Reimbursement,* edited by N. Greenspan. Washington, D.C.: Department of Health and Human Services, HCFA/ORDS.

Steinberg, R. 1983a. ''Two Essays on the Nonprofit Sector.'' Ph.D. diss., University of Pennsylvania.

———. 1983b. ''Economic and Empiric Analysis of Fundraising Behavior by Nonprofit Firms.'' Yale University, Program on Non-Profit Organizations Working Paper no. 76.

———. 1984. ''A Comment on Motives Underlying Individual Contributions to Charity.'' *Atlantic Economic Journal* 12:61–64.

———. 1985a. ''Optimal Fundraising by Nonprofit Firms.'' Virginia Polytechnic Institute, Department of Economics Working Paper no. E85–01–01.

———. 1985b. ''Voluntary Donations and Public Expenditures.'' Virginia Polytechnic Institute, Department of Economics Working Paper no. E84–07–01 (revised June 1985).

———. 1985c. ''Empirical Relations between Government Spending and Charitable Donations.'' *Journal of Voluntary Action Research* 14:54–64.

———. 1986. ''Should Donors Care about Fundraising?'' In *The Economics of Nonprofit Institutions: Studies in Structure and Policy,* edited by Susan Rose-Ackerman. New York: Oxford University Press.

Steinberg, R., and Scott Perlman. 1982. ''A Study of Foundation Behavior and a Proposal for Regulatory Reform.'' University of Pennsylvania, Department of Regional Science, Metropolitan Philanthropy Project Working Paper.

Steinwald, B., and D. Neuhauser. 1970. ''The Role of the Proprietary Hospital.'' *Law and Contemporary Problems* 35:817.

Steuerle, Eugene. 1977. ''Distribution Requirements for Foundations.'' In *Papers and Proceedings of Annual Meeting.* Columbus, Ohio: National Tax Association–Tax Institute of America.

Stigler, George J. 1971. ''The Theory of Economic Regulation.'' *Bell Journal of Economics and Management Science* 2:3–21.

Sugden, Robert. 1982. "On the Economics of Philanthropy." *Economic Journal* 92:341–50.

Thompson, Earl A. 1980. "Charity and Nonprofit Organizations." In *The Economics of Non-Proprietary Organizations*, edited by K. Clarkson and D. Martin, 125–38. Greenwich, Conn.: JAI Press.

Titmus, Richard. 1971. *The Gift Relationship: From Human Blood to Social Policy*. New York: Pantheon.

Tullock, Gordon. 1966. "Information without Profit." *Papers on Non-Market Decision Making* 1:141–59.

U.S. Department of Commerce, Bureau of the Census. 1976. *Survey of Institutionalized Persons*, Current Population Reports, Special Studies Series, p. 23, no. 69, Washington, D.C.: U.S. Government Printing Office.

———. 1979. *Statistical Abstract of the United States*. Washington, D.C.: U.S. Government Printing Office.

———. 1981. *1977 Census of Service Industries*, SC77–A–53, p. I. Washington, D.C.: U.S. Government Printing Office.

U.S. Department of Health, Education, and Welfare. 1978. *Health, U.S., 1978*. DHEW Publication no. PHC78–1232. Washington, D.C.: U.S. Government Printing Office.

U.S. National Center for Health Statistics. 1976. *Health Resources Statistics*. Washington, D.C.: U.S. Government Printing Office.

———. 1980. *Health Resources Statistics*. Washington, D.C.: U.S. Government Printing Office.

U.S. National Science Foundation. 1981. *National Patterns of Science and Technology Resources*.

United Way of America. 1982. *Donor Option*. Alexandria, Va.: United Way of America.

Urban, Glenn, and John Hauser. 1980. *Designing and Marketing New Products*. Englewood Cliffs, N.J.: Prentice-Hall.

"UW, Cancer Society, Have Pacts in 6 States." 1979. *New Haven Register*, February 12.

Vignola, Margo L. 1979. "An Economic Analysis of For-Profit Hospitals." Paper presented at the Western Economic Association Meeting, Las Vegas, Nevada.

Vogel, Ronald J. 1977. "The Effects of Taxation on the Differential Efficiency of Nonprofit Health Insurance." *Economic Inquiry* 15:605–09.

Vogel, Ronald J., and Roger D. Blair. 1976. *Health Insurance Administrative Costs*. Lexington, Mass.: Lexington Books.

Weinberg, Charles P. 1980. "Marketing Mix Decision Rules for Nonprofit Organizations." *Research in Marketing* 3:191–234.

Weisbrod, Burton. 1975. "Toward a Theory of the Voluntary Non-Profit Sector in a Three Sector Economy." In *Altruism,*

Morality, and Economic Theory, edited by Edmund Phelps. New York: Russell Sage.

———. 1980. "Private Goods, Collective Goods: The Role of the Nonprofit Sector." In *The Economics of Nonproprietary Organizations*, edited by K. Clarkson and D. Martin, 139–70. Greenwich, Conn.: JAI Press.

———. 1983. "Wage Differentials between the Private For-Profit and Non-Profit Sectors: The Case of Lawyers." *Journal of Labor Economics* 1:246–63.

Weisbrod, Burton, and M. Schlesinger. 1986. "Public, Private, Nonprofit Ownership and the Response to Asymmetric Information: The Case of Nursing Homes." In *The Economics of Nonprofit Institutions: Studies in Structure and Policy*, ed. Susan Rose-Ackerman. N.Y.: Oxford Univ. Press.

Weiss, Jeffrey. 1981. "The Ambivalent Value of Voluntary Provision of Public Goods in a Political Economy." In *Nonprofit Firms in a Three-Sector Economy*, edited by Michelle White. Washington, D.C.: Urban Institute.

Wendling, Wayne and Jack Werner. 1980. "Nonprofit Firms and the Economic Theory of Regulation." *Quarterly Review of Economics and Business* 20:6–18.

Wenocur, Stanley, Richard V. Cook, and Nancy L. Steketee. 1984. "Fund-Raising at the Workplace." *Social Policy* 14:55–60.

Wheatley, Steven C. 1978. "Foundation Giving in Chicago—1976." Mimeographed.

White, William. 1979. "Regulating Competition in a Nonprofit Industry: The Problem of For-Profit Hospitals." *Inquiry* 16:50–61.

Williamson, Oliver E. 1964. *The Economics of Discretionary Behavior: Managerial Objectives in a Theory of the Firm*. Englewood Cliffs, N.J.: Prentice-Hall.

Wilson, George W., and Joseph M. Jadlow. 1982. "Competition, Profit Incentives, and Technical Efficiency in the Provision of Nuclear Medicine Services." *Bell Journal of Economics* 13:472–82.

Wolch, Jennifer, and Robert Geiger. 1983. "The Distribution of Urban Voluntary Resources: An Exploratory Analysis." *Environment and Planning* 15:1067–82.

Wolpert, Julian. 1977. "Social Income and the Voluntary Sector." *Papers, Regional Science Association* 39:217–29.

Wolpert, Julian, Thomas Reiner, and Lucinda Starrett. 1980. *The Metropolitan Philadelphia Philanthropy Study*. University of Pennsylvania, Department of Regional Science.

YoungDay, D. J. 1978. "Voluntary Provision of Public Goods: A Theory of Donations." Ph.D. diss., University of Wisconsin.

ORGANIZATION AND MANAGEMENT

8

Nonprofit Boards of Directors: Beyond the Governance Function

MELISSA MIDDLETON

Governing bodies for incorporated charitable institutions have been mandated by state statute since the end of the eighteenth century, the precedent having been set by Harvard College in 1636 (Hall 1984). Today, thousands of men and women sit on nonprofit boards and are, in fact, trustees for the over $125 billion that is used to provide services to millions of people (Rudney 1981).

Despite this important responsibility, many board members and managers alike contend that boards often function poorly. One recent article states, "Most of the problems that befall arts groups stem from the fact that boards have, over the years, translated [their] mandate with as much variety as husbands and wives interpret the vows to love, honor, and obey" (Saline 1982). Although here pertaining to arts organizations, this quotation could readily be applied to the boards of major health, educational, and social service institutions as well.

Only a meager amount of literature is available to help frustrated board members and managers. Material written by practitioners is typically prescriptive, focusing on the explicit internal functions of boards. The scholarly literature derives primarily from researchers interested in boards of directors as a mechanism that organizations can use to deal with uncertainties in their external world.

The perspective developed in this chapter is that boards are part of *both* the organization and its environment. *Environment* means all external elements that are salient to the organization as a whole, its subunits, or its members in their

performance of activities that are organization related but that fall outside its authority (Thomas 1984). These elements include other organizations, such as competitors and funding and regulatory agencies, as well as unorganized groups, such as donors and beneficiaries. Boards of directors are part of the organization because they are responsible in the broadest sense for its well-being and for ensuring that it fulfills its stated purpose. They are part of the external environment in the sense that their members are drawn from and often have primary affiliations to other groups in the community. Thus, boards, as boundary-spanning and control units, have an important role in regulating exchanges of information and resources across boundaries.

In its position as part of the organization and part of the environment, the board becomes a resource for each to use. To control any external dependencies, an organization can place on its board representatives of important external groups or constituencies and define as one of the board's functions the task of mediating its relationships with these key elements. On the other hand, board members and the groups they represent can also use nonprofit boards for their own purposes, such as enhancing their prestige in the community.

This view of boards as resources is particularly appropriate for nonprofit organizations because:

- Their goals are often vague, hard to quantify, and open to multiple interpretations (Powell & Friedkin 1982; Perrow 1963, 1978).

- Nonprofits often experience conflicting claims made on them by diverse constituencies such as donors and beneficiaries.

- Nonprofits rely heavily on interpersonal networking to

I wish to thank Paul DiMaggio, Woody Powell, John Simon, and Gladys Topkis for their many helpful comments and editorial advice on earlier versions of this chapter.

141

facilitate the flow of resources into and out of the organization (Boorman & Levitt 1981). Trustees provide connections to these important resource networks.

Trustees' networks of relationships and their influence on the organization is a theme of the first section of this chapter, which explores the board-environment relationship. The second section focuses on internal board issues and the board-organization interaction. Here, trustee relationships with one another and with staff and management are examined as well as a variety of other structural and organizational factors that influence board behavior. Throughout this chapter, some commonly held assumptions about the behavior and purposes of nonprofit boards of directors are challenged.

THE IMPLICIT AND EXPLICIT FUNCTIONS OF BOARDS

Great hope is often expressed for the crucial roles nonprofit boards of directors could play in this society: ''As I see it, there is no other way that as few people can raise the quality of the whole American society as far and as fast as can the trustees and directors of our voluntary institutions using the strength they have now in the positions they now have'' (Greenleaf 1973). Throughout this century, however, critics have castigated boards for their lack of expertise and the unhelpful roles they play in organizations: ''Indeed, except for a stubborn prejudice to the contrary, the fact should readily be seen that the boards are of no material use whatsoever; their sole effective function being to interfere with the [academic] management in matters that are not of the nature of business and that lie outside their competence and outside the range of their habitual interests'' (Veblen [1918] 1957).

Given this range of opinion, one might begin an inquiry into the behavior and functions of nonprofit boards by asking, ''What do they do?'' This section addresses that question from a variety of perspectives: what the practitioner-oriented literature tells board members about their importance and roles; the legal status of nonprofit boards; what board members say they do; and finally, what scholars say regarding the functions and importance of boards.

The Practitioner's Perspective

Material written by experienced board members stresses the governance and control functions of nonprofit boards. In the most general sense, these writings discuss board responsibilities for ''maintaining the continuity, stability, and integrity of the trust'' (Nason 1982) and for giving management support and guidance (C. Brown 1976). This literature explains the internal functions of boards, such as policy-making, budgetary and fiscal control, and supervision of management, but it rarely examines in depth the difficult issues surrounding the board-management relationship. The external function it describes most frequently is fund-raising;

it mentions less frequently helping the organization establish legitimacy and power in the community.

Although Nason (1977) asks, ''To whom are the trustees responsible, donors or beneficiaries?'' most of the practitioner literature has paid little attention to trustee accountability. The question of accountability and responsibility is important because it can help define the board's purpose, functions, and status within the organization. One might expect that the law regarding nonprofit organizations could clarify that question, but state statutes on nonprofit corporations do not provide a clear framework. Case law, however, is beginning to address this issue.

The Legal Status of Nonprofit Boards

Boards of charities have an unclear legal status, which falls between the law of trusts and the law of business corporations. The law of trusts prohibits self-dealing, holds trustees liable for simple errors of judgment, and disallows delegation of management responsibilities. Business corporation law, on the other hand, is less stringent. It allows self-dealing when there is proper disclosure, holds directors liable only for gross negligence, and allows for delegation of management duties with the board maintaining supervisory responsibilities (''The Fiduciary Duties . . . '' 1978). Boards of charities are left on their own to negotiate the gray area between these two ends of the legal continuum.

Some authors suggest that the lack of clarity regarding the nonprofit board's legal responsibilities has resulted in an attitude on the part of trustees that they are accountable to no one (Mace 1976; K. Brown 1977). In general, donors and beneficiaries lack standing to sue nonprofit trustees for breach of their fiduciary duties. This authority is given to state officials who infrequently exercise it (Hansmann 1981). In fact, any cases involving the liability of nonprofit directors have been infrequent. In the last decade, however, as private corporate law has increasingly stressed director responsibility, similar concerns have begun to arise in the nonprofit sector.

One important case was settled in 1974. In *Stern* v. *Lucy Webb Hayes National Training School*, commonly referred to as the *Sibley Hospital* case (381 F. Supp. 1003 [D. DC, 1974]), patients brought a class-action suit against the corporation charging mismanagement, nonmanagement, and self-dealing by several hospital trustees. The suit alleged that these trustees sought to enrich themselves by depositing money belonging to the hospital in banks of which the trustees were directors. It further charged that the trustees had failed in their fiduciary responsibilities by not attending board meetings and by failing to convene the finance committee.

Judge Gerhard A. Gesell found the trustees liable for nonmanagement because they had failed to hold meetings and to supervise the management of investments by hospital employees. To some extent, he applied the law of business corporations, stating that financial management can be delegated but must be supervised, and not totally prohibiting self-dealing. On the other hand, his standards for supervision of financial management and conflict of interest were higher than those usually applied under corporate law (Mace 1976).

The *Sibley Hospital* case was important in that it recognized the right of a group of beneficiaries (in this case, patients) to bring suit and emphasized trustee responsibilities for the active supervision of management. The legal status of nonprofit boards, however, remains ambiguous and contributes to the vagueness surrounding their explicit functions and status in organizations. With minimal guidance board members are left to answer these questions for themselves, assuming that they raise them at all.

What Do Board Members Say They Do?

One of the most comprehensive studies of trustees focused on four hundred business executives in ten cities who volunteered their time on nonprofit boards (Fenn 1971). They described their five most common functions as fund-raising, establishing operating procedures, enlisting the support of others, budgeting and fiscal control, and balancing the organization with a different point of view. It is interesting to note that neither supervising management nor broad policy-making is mentioned in this list despite the amount of attention both functions receive in the material written by practitioners. Instead the emphasis is on the more specific functions of financial oversight and operational procedures or on vague notions of expanding the organization's point of view and support network.

The study also asked executive volunteers what they would like to do as board members. Their answers included establishing operating procedures (which they said they do now) and deciding on public relations strategies for the organization. They did not want to initiate projects on behalf of the organization but enjoyed implementing tasks given to them by staff. In contrast, staff members wanted the trustees to play more of a leadership role in initiating projects.

Although it must be kept in mind that the sample for the Fenn study was composed of business executives and did not represent a broad range of board members, several important points emerge. First, these executive volunteers saw themselves as following the direction of staff, not as leading the organization. This contrasts with some assertions in the professional literature about broad-ranging leadership functions. Second, board and staff were not in agreement over the board's primary functions. The lack of clarity regarding board members' legal responsibilities and the unanswered question concerning trustee accountability may increase the likelihood that board members and staff will develop separate and inconsistent notions of what a board of directors should do. Not only may this produce an uneasy tension between board and management, but it may mean that board functions are determined on a short-term ad hoc basis. Third, the lack of clarity concerning the expectations of board members also raises the possibility that functions will be driven in part by their personal and social needs. In the Fenn study, board members said they preferred tasks that heightened organization credibility (establishing operating procedures) and visibility (designing public relations strategies). Both of these tasks, one may hypothesize, also heighten the credibility and visibility of board members themselves, which may represent important benefits they receive from their work.

Boards and the Organization's Environment

Most of the scholarly work on nonprofit boards has been written by researchers interested in the relationship between organizations and their environments. This framework stresses the ways in which organizations attempt to reduce external constraints and adapt more effectively to their environments. And one instrument available to help the organization do this is its board of directors. Pfeffer and Salancik (1978) state that "boards provide an opportunity to evolve a stable, collective structure of coordinated activity through which interdependence is managed."

In essence, boards are special boundary-spanning and control units that keep organizations connected to parts of their environment while also differentiating them from external elements. The major functions boards perform in this capacity include the following:

- They develop exchange relationships with external parties to ensure the flow of resources into and out of the organization.

- They process information gained from these exchanges to make the internal organizational adjustments necessary to meet environmental demands.

- They buffer the organization from the environment and thus protect it from external interference.

- They reduce environmental constraints by influencing external conditions to the organization's advantage.

The first function reduces organizational uncertainty by developing stable patterns of interaction with the environment. Through these interactions, the boundary unit acquires external information that is important to organizational functioning and may necessitate altering the input or output processes to keep the organization adaptive to changes. Boundary units also absorb external information without passing it along to the rest of the organization. For example, a trustee may be able to address informally a constituent's criticism without necessitating the involvement of the rest of the organization. In this capacity, they function as protectors of organizational activities. They also act as external representatives for the organization in its attempts to position itself more effectively in the external world and thus reduce the constraints under which it is operating.

To perform these functions boards provide interorganizational linkages through affiliations of board members to a variety of outside groups. For example, a social service nonprofit may place on its board an active member of the local chamber of commerce, who it is hoped will link the organization to the business community. The interorganizational linkage, then, creates a channel for information and resources to flow between enterprises.

To understand more fully the importance of these linkages, one must go beyond the fact that trustees connect organizations through overlapping memberships. The notion of ties between people in a linking relationship is useful in this regard. Granovetter (1973) states that "the strength of a tie is a (probably linear) combination of the amount of time spent, the emotional intensity, the intimacy (mutual confiding), and the reciprocal services which characterize the tie" (p. 1361). Reciprocal services can be examined using the notion of economic and social exchange relationships. Economic exchanges involve exchanges of equivalent resources such as money, information, or tangible products. Social exchanges entail extending oneself to another as part of the exchange—giving and receiving love or friendship, status and respect, and services (Foa 1971). They have an ongoing quality in that what is given is not necessarily immediately repaid with an equivalent resource.

The line between economic and social exchanges is not a clear one, for many ongoing economic relationships become overlaid with social content (Granovetter 1983). This blurring is particularly important in the nonprofit sector because board members are part-time volunteers who may serve as trustees for a variety of noneconomic reasons, such as the desires to become more fully integrated into the community, to develop new circles of friends, and to gain status and prestige. In fact, a board's ability to help manage the interdependence of the organization and external elements arises in part from the friendships that are developed among board members and with staff. These friendships over time increase members' identification with the organization and their feeling of responsibility for its survival and well-being. It is important, therefore, to stress that the notion of ties used here includes a historical dimension, a socioemotional component, and a description of the kinds of reciprocity or exchange involved.

In one of the first studies to examine directly the importance of board members' ties to external groups, Price (1963) analyzed the governing boards of two wildlife management agencies. The majority of the boards' work entailed external representation functions in that the boards interacted with the commercial fishermen and sportsmen who were the primary clientele of the two agencies. In this capacity, board members listened to criticisms of agency performance and regulations, defended agency policy to the clientele, and often mediated disputes between agency staff and the sportsmen. Price found that the boards were not involved in either establishing the budget (an internal economic function) or gaining staff compliance regarding internal policy (an administrative function). Rather, they performed a political function for the agencies. The board members, all gubernatorial appointments, had extensive political and social connections and were well positioned to provide the needed external representation role for the agencies.

Staff, on the other hand, criticized board members for their lack of wildlife management expertise and complained of the time it took to explain management technology to them. Members were undoubtedly appointed because of their political and social connections, not their management expertise. Staff, however, expected assistance with their detailed regulatory work, which board members neither could nor would provide. Therefore, the very characteristics that legitimated the boards' external representation functions created tensions between board and staff.

Pfeffer's study of government, religious, and private nonprofit hospital boards (1973) more explicitly addressed the issue of external linking functions. He posited that board functions would be related to sources of hospital funding and that board composition and size would be related to those functions. He also hypothesized that organizational effectiveness, measured by percentage increases in growth of services and financial resources, would be related to how the hospital board's functions, composition, and size matched the resource dependencies faced by the hospital. His hypotheses were upheld. Religious hospitals, not dependent on local resources, had boards that performed administrative functions. They were not composed of local influentials but were representative of the range of ethnic and socioeconomic groups in the community. He concluded that this broad-based board composition was related to the religious hospitals' needs for patient flow. Private nonprofit hospitals, dependent on community financial resources, maintained boards that concentrated on external functions such as resource acquisition, were composed of local influential business leaders, and were large, compared to the boards of other hospital types. Those private nonprofits that conformed most closely to this pattern were also found to be most effective, as defined by his measures.

The Price and Pfeffer studies both demonstrate that board functions are related to the external environment of the organization. Pfeffer emphasizes that the kind of resource dependence facing an organization influences its selection of board members, the size of the board, and its functions. In the Price study, the boards performed needed buffering and external representation functions and were ill equipped to meet internal administrative needs.

The composition of nonprofit boards is a particularly important aspect from which to examine interorganizational linkages. One must look at composition from two perspectives. The first relates to the diversity of external organizations represented on the board; the second emphasizes the range of social group memberships of the board (that is, race, gender, age, profession, and socioeconomic status). These two distinctions are necessary because a board can be diverse with respect to the range of organizations represented but homogeneous regarding social group memberships. The reverse can also be true: board members may come from similar organizations but represent diversity across group identities. Data on board composition suggest that across a variety of nonprofit types, the former pattern is more often the case. Nason (1977) estimates that there are 100,000 to 130,000 foundation trustees in this country. Drawing on several recent studies, he describes trustees as predominantly white, male, Protestant, in their fifties or sixties, wealthy, and in business or law. Women represent approximately 19 percent of the members of foundation boards, and minorities, a mere 0.3 percent. Kohn and Mortimer (1983) give the following breakdown for the approximately 38,000 college and university trustees: 85 percent male, 93 percent white, 65 percent over fifty years old, 90 percent with a bachelor's degree, and 75 percent in business or the professions. Kramer (1981) studied the composition of boards of organizations that work with the mentally and physically handicapped: two-thirds to three-quarters of these boards' members were male professionals. Few had by-laws stipulating participation on the board by consumers.

These data suggest that many nonprofits are linked through their boards to a relatively narrow range of the social strata. This is likely to be true because of the uncertainty many nonprofits face in their external environment. Consumers of service, women, and minorities often do not have access to needed economic, social, and political resources. Board member connections to upper echelons within communities, although potentially helpful for one aspect of organizational well-being, raise other issues for organizations. The next section explores this issue in more detail.

Mutual Cooptation: Community Elites and Nonprofit Boards

To understand the other concerns board composition raises for nonprofits, it is necessary to reemphasize the notion of ties and the exchange relationships that develop among board members, the environment, and the organization. Cooptation, as defined by Selznick (1949) in his classic study of the relationship between board behavior and external demands, is a process whereby crucial outside parties are absorbed into the leadership or policy-making structure in order to avoid threats to the organization's stability. Selznick and others have noted that cooptation is a two-way street. The organization takes the risk that external coopted members will influence the organization for their own purposes, which may differ from those of the organization. In some cases, these purposes represent a link between community power and involvement on local nonprofit boards of directors.

Studies of community power have developed alternative perspectives regarding the degree of power centralization found in a local area. The pluralist view maintains that power is distributed among a number of organized groups and that it shifts depending on the issue. Complementing this view is the belief that local business leaders are a fragmented group and have become less interested in civic involvement as their corporations have become part of national conglomerates (Schultze 1958). Other studies, suggesting an elitist view of community power, argue that the lack of involvement is illusory: "in civic matters, the corporation seeks not only to protect and foster its own interests but to promote a conservative, business-oriented ideology" (Pellegrin & Coates 1956). As Perrucci and Pilisuk (1970) point out, both views state that power resides in institutional systems, in inter-

organizational linkages that deal with the allocation of scarce resources. In order to examine community power structures, one must examine these networks and learn how they involve nonprofit organizations.

A rich set of network analyses has examined the extent of corporate director interlocks and involvement on nonprofit boards. Salzman and Domhoff (1983) distinguish between "full-tie networks," communication networks for information sharing and the creation of common viewpoints across corporations, and "strong-tie networks," networks that reinforce the hierarchical ordering of corporations relative to their status and power within a community. They found that nonprofits were central to the full-tie networks and concluded that nonprofit boards serve an important function by providing a place where business elites in a community meet to exchange information, create common viewpoints, and thus reinforce class cohesion. These data do not describe what actually occurs at board meetings. Rather, they indicate that through informal relationships, facilitated by common board memberships, and through board discussion of social, economic, and political issues affecting the organization, elites strengthen their ties with one another. Not only do community leaders serve the needs of the nonprofit organizations, then, but the nonprofits serve functions for the corporate community.

Ratcliff, Gallagher, and Ratcliff (1979) looked at whether positional power (the hierarchy of status and influence) among local banks and corporations was duplicated in the degree of involvement by bank and corporate members on the boards of civic organizations. They found that "upper-class prominence" (multiple corporate directorships and membership in elite social clubs) predicted civic involvement—92 percent of these prominent people were on the board of at least one United Way agency and over 50 percent were on several nonprofit boards.

The history of nonprofit organizations gives ample evidence of the role of nonprofit boards in facilitating the cohesion of local elites (Hall 1975; 1982). Hall's analysis of wealth in mid-nineteenth-century America (1982) suggests that "without cultural institutions to complement its for-profit corporate activities, the community's leaders could neither socialize their sons to the civic values necessary for sustaining economic autonomy, nor could it mediate the relations between new and old money and between ethnic groups."

The research on community elites as well as the previous discussion of boards as instruments for controlling organizations' environments indicate that boards fulfill related roles within organizations and the community at large. By providing a linking function for the organization to its environment, boards become a mechanism for integrating certain community groups. Through this process, they seem capable of generating power that extends beyond their role in organizational governance. The next set of issues to be addressed, then, includes "to whom does this power accrue?" and "what are the implications of this for resource allocations within communities?"

Power for Whom?

To answer this question, one must consider the selection pattern of trustees for certain nonprofit boards, the reasons for this pattern from the trustee's point of view, and what consequences ensue for organizations in terms of their resource-acquiring capacity.

In examining the relation of nonprofit boards to community elites, one cannot assume that this link exists for all nonprofits. The two studies mentioned earlier—Salzman and Domhoff and Ratcliff, Gallagher, and Ratcliff—used as their sample nationally and regionally prominent organizations. Neither study sampled from the smaller, less prestigious nonprofit organization; hence, one might question whether influential business and community leaders are members of the boards of these nonprofits. It appears that they are not.

Considerable evidence suggests that high-status members in a community tend to sit on the boards of nonprofit organizations that are seen as particularly significant in that community (Babchuk, Massey, & Gordon 1960; Zald 1967; DiMaggio & Useem 1982). Nonprofits judged to be central to the community include hospitals and colleges whose boards are dominated by men holding multiple corporate directorships. Large arts organizations frequently maintain boards composed of local elites. "Less vital" nonprofits include social service agencies whose boards more often consist of women and of men with few corporate ties. Although studies often do not define what is meant by a nonprofit's central or vital position in the community, it is reasonable to assume that key social, political, and economic groups within communities are critical to that determination.

In studying a particular kind of nonprofit trustee—business executives—Fenn (1971) found that they were more comfortable in "traditional" than in "contemporary" nonprofits. In traditional agencies members tend to be homogeneous with respect to socioeconomic status, ethnicity, and values. Their staff members decide what to provide to those in need. Contemporary agencies, on the other hand, are heterogeneous organizations whose members come from a mix of racial and socioeconomic strata. Consumers of service, not just staff, are involved in designing and implementing the programs that serve them. One may hypothesize that the business executives in Fenn's study felt more comfortable sitting on the boards of traditional agencies because of the social positions and values they shared with organization members.

The self-selection process of trustees onto certain nonprofit boards is also heightened by their personal and career motivations. Many executive volunteers express altruistic motivations for joining nonprofit boards. For example, some say, "The organization needed my skills," or "What am I really here for if not to make a contribution?" (Fenn 1971). Their reasons for volunteering may also include heightening their own visibility in the community, acquiring an opportunity to mobilize the resources of many organizations on behalf of policies and institutions they favor, and increasing their social and professional connections (Useem 1979; Auerbach 1961; McSweeney 1978).

Philanthropic work has become a career expectation for managers seeking to advance within corporations. Some companies have policies encouraging volunteer services that implicitly or explicitly tie pay and promotional benefits to that service (Fenn 1971). A demonstrated ability to participate effectively in civic matters may lead to more corporate responsibilities; therefore, a junior executive can build a reputation quickly through visible participation in philanthropic work (Pellegrin & Coates 1956). A career in philanthropy, however, is often dependent on a career in business, and thus there is a parallel between the position one holds in a corporation and one's official position on a board (Ross 1954). It is plausible to assume, then, that the executive or junior executive more readily gravitates toward the larger, more prestigious agencies that permit a wider scope of action, are perceived to have greater community value, and provide a larger stage for self-aggrandizement (Zald 1967).

An important relationship seems also to exist between an organization's ability to raise and maintain resources and its development of a high-prestige board (Zald 1967; Pfeffer 1973; Provan 1980). The Provan study found that organizations with high-status boards maintained higher funding levels from the United Way and other funding sources than those nonprofits whose trustees were less influential. Power boards did not, however, help organizations *increase* their basic level of financial assistance from these sources. Provan concludes that status boards are useful primarily in protecting already established resources.

This research contradicts Pfeffer's earlier finding (1973) that hospital boards composed of local influentials were related to measures of funding increases. The discrepancy between these findings, however, may be due to changes in funding climate. During the 1970s, political pressures on funding agencies like the United Way increased, forcing them to modify their allocation patterns to include less traditional organizations and those serving poor and minority populations. Powerful boards of established organizations could help maintain existing funding levels but could not quiet the demands being made to fund other constituencies.

The overlapping social and organizational networks of high-status trustees may have also decreased their ability to sense political changes taking place among poor and minority constituencies. The stronger the ties among network members, the less likely it is that members have access to different information and resources (Granovetter 1973). One could reasonably argue, therefore, that boards composed of interconnecting, high-status members did not have the capacity to gather and act on information about changes occurring outside of those networks. In this sense, they were ill equipped to meet the adaptation needs of their nonprofit organizations.

The question of for whom nonprofit boards generate power, then, is a complex one. The preponderance of data suggests that high-status members increase the power (resource-acquiring ability) of the traditional established agencies on whose boards they sit. In exchange, they use board memberships to solidify network relationships and to strengthen their positions in the community. Under situations of rapid change in the environment, this exchange may not always enhance the adaptive capacities of organizations. At a community level, however, the interlocking power relationships have implications for the allocation of resources.

Implications for Resource Allocation Schemes

In the case of federated fund-raising agencies (such as the United Way), many of the people sitting on the boards are themselves the representatives of the major donor sources—corporations in the community. In situations of limited resources, board members may treat these community resources as their own in the sense that the socioeconomic power of a grantee agency's board and its clientele, rather than the substantive content of its program, becomes the standard for allocation. Although these business elites may not always use their economic power to control welfare functions, their class interests may prevail in matters involving large expenditures or large populations of people (Wilensky & Lebeaux 1955).

Ratcliff, Gallagher, and Ratcliff (1979) expand the notion that board members act in ways that are consonant with their own group interests when they discuss the United Way, the Arts and Education Council, and the Regional Commerce and Growth Association in St. Louis:

> We have seen that the policies and programs these organizations have typically pursued have emphasized the maintenance of existing patterns of resource distribution and ideological tone within the metropolitan area. . . . A strong basis exists for enduring policy, program, and ideological control by an integrated core group of capitalists in the structural realities of power within the civic organizations involved.

Although the nonprofit sector is often conceptualized as the independent sector, able to experiment and innovate because it is less encumbered than the public and private sectors, it appears that the board structure of many of these organizations—the most enduring and stable ones in fact—leads them to emphasize the status quo.

The concept of "embeddedness" is important in understanding the ramifications of this apparent influence. Relations among groups within an organization are shaped by how those groups are embedded in the organization and how the organization is embedded in the social structure of the external environment. Power differences among groups create the effects of embeddedness (Alderfer & Smith 1982).

In the case of many boards of nonprofit organizations, we find patterns of embeddedness that are congruent with existing relations of power. The influence of high-status board members, the organizations and the groups they represent, and the prestigious nonprofits on whose boards they sit are mutually reinforcing situations of power that serve to maintain the status quo. When lower-status community members

serve on boards, as they do less frequently, they sit on boards of lower-status nonprofits. These organizations are more likely to be involved in efforts to reallocate resources to citizens who have little political capital, such as the poor and minority members of a community. Not surprisingly, both their lower status within the community and their reduced access to resources make it difficult for redistributive nonprofits to work effectively toward changing existing allocations of resources.

Board member networks facilitate the connection of nonprofits to certain external groups. A frequent and undiscussed consequence of these connections is the conservative role played by nonprofits. Some nonprofit boards may generate power that contributes to the maintenance of existing patterns of resource allocation and class and racial divisions.

Board member ties, while influencing the position of the nonprofit organization in the broader social structure, may also have consequences for internal board behavior and the board-organization relationship. The next section will explore these effects in more detail.

BOARD BEHAVIOR AND THE REST OF THE ORGANIZATION

As open systems, organizations import information about group relations, social and cultural values, and economic and political demands and constraints (Thomas 1984). The behavior of boards is influenced by the information that trustees bring with them, but internal board dynamics are not determined solely by external factors. Trustees' relationships with one another and with staff also influence the processes of decision making. This section will first examine important factors that influence the board's own internal work. The discussion then examines the board-management relationship as a political process that significantly affects organizational decision making.

Internal Board Behavior and Decision Making

> Every member of a board has a duty to speak to the overall public interest and not for a single interest. In reality, however, each member brings to the board perceptions of priority and morality grounded in his or her life experiences and conditions. Boards composed of only white, Anglo-Saxon, Protestant males with backgrounds in business affairs and drawn from more affluent socio-economic groups do not mean to speak only or substantially for WASPs. They may intend the public welfare; but they are handicapped in achieving it not being exposed to the aspirations and perceptions of the many constituencies they serve. The member of a racial minority group or other group will labor under a like disability in achieving the theoretical level of representing only the overall public interest. The rationale for a board drawn from diverse elements is grounded in the irrefutable fact that no one can get out of his skin. The-

ory and reality are not at war in this instance. It is indeed bad policy for a board member to regard himself as speaking for a constituency; but it is both inevitable and right for him or her to speak as a member of a group. (Eugene C. Sturckhoff, vice president for the Council on Foundations, as quoted in Nason 1977, 43–44)

The importance of this quotation lies in its clear acknowledgment of the personal frame of reference everyone brings to his or her work because of racial, gender, socioeconomic, and professional group memberships. The data presented earlier on board composition suggest the paucity of diversity on many nonprofit boards with respect to these memberships. Even though trustees represent a variety of professions and organizations, the similarity of their social group identities may produce a homogeneity of outlook. Strong ties among board members will increase this similarity even further (Granovetter 1973).

The selection process of many boards appears to facilitate homogeneity in board composition and outlook. It is reasonable to argue that boards use *both* explicit criteria and interpersonal networking in the recruitment and selection of board members. Criteria for board candidates may include such items as familiarity with the organizational activity, amount of time available for board work, and, an important point, the kinds of resources to which candidates have access. These strategic considerations that organizations use in selecting board members have been documented by researchers interested in the role nonprofit boards play in reducing organizational resource dependence (see the discussion above of the Pfeffer study). The organization is also concerned with less tangible attributes of board members, such as their values and attitudes concerning the organization's work, the extent to which they will be compatible with incumbent board members, and the prestige they will bring to the board. As with the job search and hiring process (Granovetter 1974), interpersonal networks act as screening devices for these less publicly acknowledged qualities. Candidates known to other board members are more likely to be recruited.

This process has been described as a self-perpetuating system whereby boards select only those who fit in (Nason 1977; Kramer 1965) and rid themselves of those who are seen as radical or deviant. One could hypothesize that a truly self-perpetuating board is one in which intangible qualities take on maximum importance and are perpetuated through the strong ties of existing board members. Through this process, similarity in board members' outlook and status is increased while the more strategic considerations of organizational needs are neglected. For example, it is often said that an unstated purpose of some arts organizations is to maintain certain class distinctions in society, so that the arts become a crucial part of elite screening and socialization. Their boards are composed of members of wealthy families who have contributed to the arts for years. Arts managers, who less frequently come from an elite stratum, see the need for the

organization to diversify funding sources and audiences and to bring more business expertise onto the board. Consequently they push for the recruitment of corporate executives. This move is often strongly resisted by elite board members because they see it as an attempt to dilute "high culture" and extend decision-making control beyond the elite stratum (DiMaggio & Useem 1982).

The structure of the board—that is, its officer positions and committees—also influences the degree to which diverse opinions are expressed. Some boards develop a hierarchy of committees with high-status members on the influential executive, fund-raising, and nominations committees and low-status members on the less prestigious program and personnel committees (Auerbach 1961). This kind of apportionment may reduce opportunities for lower-status members to express opinions and be heard.

The more powerful committees themselves can play important roles in determining the breadth of opinion actually utilized by the full board. The nominations committee is especially influential because it is the gatekeeper through which new members are recruited and oriented. The composition of the committee will strongly affect the types of members recruited. If narrowly composed, this committee can over time decrease the range of viewpoints represented on the full board. The executive committee is often a powerful committee even if its formal responsibilities are limited in the by-laws. It is typically composed of the officers and committee chairpersons, who frequently are also the most active board members. This group can easily become an inner core of the board because of the amount of time spent together on organizational activities. In addition, the large size of many nonprofit boards often makes decision making a cumbersome task. As a result, the board itself may place pressure on the executive committee to make more decisions in order to avoid protracted discussions at board meetings. This may increase the efficiency of the meetings, but overuse of the executive committee may reduce the opportunity for newer members or those not part of the inner core to participate fully in board deliberations.

Many boards may not have a well-developed formal structure or they may not use it in actual decision making. Instead an informal arrangement may exist whereby subgroups or individual members interact outside of meetings to discuss board business. Members who see one another often through social or business ties may be more likely to be involved in this informal decision making than those who are connected only through the formal process of board meetings. Again, the result is to narrow the range of information and resources brought to bear on board issues while increasing the strength of the ties among certain members.

The structure of the board, then, may both reflect existing patterns of board member relationships and provide opportunities to strengthen those relationships. There is a functional aspect of this process for the organization in that it may increase the time and degree of commitment some board members have for the organization. It becomes less functional when the ties among board members become exclusionary and reduce opportunities for others to become involved in board activities.

Under more exclusionary circumstances, decisions may look as if they are being made by consensus when in fact they have been made by an inner core. In this sense, consensus-style decision making is used as a protective device to maintain the power of the more influential members over the less influential (Spencer 1981). Peripheral members may allow this kind of decision making to continue if they are frequently rebuffed in their attempts to challenge the process and decide that it is not worth the time and energy to try to alter the patterns.

It is not surprising, then, that nonprofit boards are often described as conflict-averse—they seek to avoid anything controversial (Zald & Denton 1963; C. Brown 1976; Nason 1977). Conflict or controversy may call into question the legitimacy of existing power relationships and decision processes and may alter the pattern of relationships among members. Some kinds of controversial issues may also threaten relationships that are external to the board; members who belong to a number of other organizations may wish to avoid decisions that conflict with those interests (Kramer 1965).

Not all nonprofit boards are conflict-averse, however. The degree of conflict that surfaces seems to be related to the diversity of membership and specifically to the degree of constituent participation on the board. In a study of hospital boards, Whisler (1982) described them as ''noisy'' constituent bodies that corporate executives cannot dominate. These boards, with their subgroups of interests, frequently disagree over goals and organizational policies; the result is a bargaining style of decision making.

Cole (1980) studied twelve nonprofit organizations that had begun to include client members on their boards, including universities, museums, and mental health and health agencies. He defined client members as recipients of the organizations' services. Although he concluded that their participation did not hamper organizational innovation, he identified a confrontational stage experienced by the boards when client members were being integrated into them. One can surmise that, during the assimilation process, these boards experienced an increase in conflict and disagreement resulting from the added diversity in their membership.

One consequence of the noisy behavior of constituent boards is that they may intervene directly with the administrator and interact frequently with external parties related to the organization, something Whisler contends is not normal practice on corporate boards. With regard to administrative intervention, Cole found that the managers of the twelve nonprofits were skeptical of the value of client participation and fearful that these members would become too involved in daily administrative matters.

Although data on the behavior of conflict-averse and noisy boards are slim, they suggest that diversity in composition, particularly with regard to social group memberships, is

the salient dividing line between the two types of board behavior.

Conflict-averse boards may be composed of trustees who are relatively homogeneous, and this similarity reinforces strong ties among members. As these relationships strengthen, the desire increases to avoid controversial issues that might disrupt them. This may be especially true if board member ties extend beyond the organization. The exchange relationships among trustees and between trustees and the organization become more social than economic: they are characterized by the giving and receiving of friendship, status, and respect. The instrumental needs of the organization may take second place to the exchange of social resources. The ultimate threat is that as board member ties become increasingly strong, the board will become closed off to crucial elements in a changing environment.

Noisy boards, on the other hand, have relatively weak ties among members, resulting in part from the diversity of social group memberships. Trustee relationships revolve primarily around board business and may not extend past meetings. The exchange relationship, while in part social, is also economic in nature, and members share information and other resources. Extremely weak ties among trustees may result in a board that has no coherent sense of identity separate from staff. Unclear authority relationships between board and management may develop, and the board may encroach on staff's administrative functions. Lacking a sense of direction and purpose, the board may become too faction-ridden to make decisions crucial to organizational functioning and may contribute to an organization's lack of a sense of boundaries.

One should examine the interests management has in maintaining either a conflict-averse or a noisy board. A board that avoids conflict may also avoid challenging managerial competence and scrutinizing difficult program issues. The manager then remains relatively safe in his or her position and domain of influence. However, this kind of board may not be prepared to deal with important issues facing the organization, and management may feel a lack of board support at critical points. A noisy board may present management with more points of view from which to resolve issues. The process may become political, however, as various factions fight for control. In this case, it is doubtful that management stands to gain much from the diversity of opinions.

At this point it is important to delve more closely into the complexities of the board-management relationship and to discuss other organizational factors that affect the pattern of board behavior.

Board-Management Relations: ''Strange Loops and Tangled Hierarchies''

The professional literature does not devote much attention to the relationship between the board and top management of nonprofits, but it does recognize the delicate balance that must exist between their roles and responsibilities. The literature describes several factors that influence the balance:

- The board hires, fires, and supervises the executive; thus the executive is a subordinate of the board.

- The board is responsible for making final policy decisions and should not become "a captive of the palace guards."

However:

- The executive often has the important information and thus serves as an educator of the board.

- As implementors of policy, executives may in fact be the functional authority.

Much of the writing is prescriptive and suggests that the relationship is a partnership, one that depends on mutual trust; it should be harmonious, and it fails if communication about roles and responsibilities is ineffective.

Empirical studies of this relationship are scant. Those that have been made have emphasized not that it is harmonious but that it is often conflictual (Kramer 1965). Tension is an inherent aspect of the relationship because of the executive's informal power, role in shaping policy, and leadership position in the organization (Odendahl & Boris 1983). Odendahl and Boris quote one foundation president: "There has to be tension; there is always tension when you have an assertive staff. Boards *react* well; they don't create well."

In contrast to the descriptions in the literature, the board-management relationship is a dynamic interaction; to state that it is a partnership implies a resolution of the tension rather than a complex shifting of power.

The socioeconomic status differences between management and board members affect the likelihood of executive domination of the board. As described above, board members are frequently recruited from the business and professional elites, whereas "the executive is usually a middle-class member of an emerging middle-range status profession" (Kramer 1965). As a result, the executive may develop feelings of impotence. Under these conditions, overt executive domination of the board is unlikely (Kramer 1981). In the case of smaller nonprofits, however, they rarely attract trustees of means with ample time to spare. Thus, these volunteers rely on the executive for the flow of information and evaluation of organizational goals, making executive dominance more likely (Unterman & Davis 1982).

Closely linked to socioeconomic status is the degree to which the executive is recognized by the board as being a professional. In Zald and Denton's classic study of the YMCA (1963), they described the director as someone who came up through the ranks and lacked a professional ideology. With no external power base, he saw his own job success as intimately tied to the board and accepted its domination. A similar dynamic has been described recently among executives of various professional trade associations (Low 1978).

The more frequently noted pattern is one in which the executive has professional status and the board is composed of people who either are not professionals or are from professions different from that of the executive. The influence of professionals derives from their external power base (a professional identity group outside of the organization), their professional ideology, and their possession of information and knowledge about the technologies important to organizational activities. This command over information and knowledge may be particularly important in organizations dealing with complex technologies (Senor 1963). Kramer (1981) found that in those organizations in which the administration possessed a high degree of technocratic professionalization, particularly in combination with financial security, the power of the board was reduced to that of nominal policymaker.

Given these components of professional status, the executive may not trust the board members' ability to make decisions regarding organizational goals, policies, or programs. He or she may additionally distrust the prestige motivation of board members and, in a sense, wish to protect the organization and his or her professional status from misuse by board members. Finally, the executive has his or her own needs for status and recognition that may compete with the same needs of board members (Auerbach 1961).

Differences in socioeconomic status and professional affiliation, among other factors, may also represent ideological differences between board members and executives. As Kramer points out, ideological congruence is important because decisions are a result of the interaction of perceived facts (which are influenced by ideology) and predisposing values. He cites three studies where board members were largely more conservative than staff regarding the need for services, the institutionalization of patients, the role of government, and the economy in general.

The degree to which differences in socioeconomic status, professionalism, and ideology will cause serious tensions between board and management is influenced by several factors. First, executives will not always operate in accordance with the ideology of their professions, nor will board members always react on the basis of their socioeconomic positions. For example, informal social relations between board members and the executive, length of history with the organization, and type of issue presented may mitigate the effects of these differences.

Second, most board decision making is not of an ideological nature. As we have seen, boards tend to ratify policy rather than create it, and minutiae occupy many board meetings. The executive may steer the board away from policy and program matters, saying that they are really professional matters. He or she will instead stress reports that "educate" the board, which some label a non-decision-making process. Similarly, the executive may keep the board focused on external matters. For example, in a study of school superintendent–school board relations, Kerr (1964) found that the superintendent used his "inherent rights" as a professional in combination with his "emergent rights" as the executive to control the agenda for meetings and hence the flow of information to the board. In this way, he was able to use the board to legitimate the school to the community instead of having the board represent the community to the school.

This description of factors influencing the board-management relationship and board decision-making process has emphasized the importance of individual and group characteristics. Another way of viewing the salient factors is to look first at who is performing organizational tasks that are especially critical because of such factors as community needs and changes in technology (Perrow 1963).

According to Perrow, critical tasks include securing needed inputs, establishing legitimacy, providing specialized skills, and coordinating both organization members and relations with those outside the organization. Perrow demonstrates how the ideology, social background, and personal interests of those who perform the critical tasks will dominate the organization and determine operative goals. He begins, therefore, with an analysis not of individual or group characteristics but of the critical tasks that confront the organization. He then examines the importance of personal characteristics in determining organizational goals.

Critical tasks are variously important at different stages in an organization's life, and thus power shifts over time among key groups. In Perrow's study of the evolution of hospital goals, he describes four chronological stages: trustee domination, medical staff domination, administrator control, and finally multiple leadership. Decision making under multiple leadership can occur through the fortuitous convergence of short-term interests; through a decision made by one group that has ramifications for other groups but, once made, goes unreviewed; and through successive approvals of minor steps that culminate in an irreversible decision. This type of decision making sacrifices the assessment of long-term consequences in favor of short-term harmony and parochial gains. In short, the organization avoids open confrontation of differences in values and interests.

Other relationships within the organization as well as other organizational characteristics influence the board-management interaction. For example, the relationship will be affected by the extent to which the board is physically, socially, and psychologically removed from the organization and, conversely, by the degree to which the organization itself is isolated and rigidly bounded. In either case, the board may view its role as missionary work at a distance and thus may not want to become too involved with the program or its clients (Senor 1963). Although this may appear to lessen tension between board and staff, the board's isolation and distance may make it slow to notice and react to crucial changes within the organization.

The relationships among the board, the executive, and the rest of the program staff may also influence board-management dynamics. If agency staff members strongly support the executive, that may enhance his or her power relative to the board. They may collude with the executive to cover up his or her mistakes and covertly refuse to implement board decisions (Senor 1963). On the other hand, board-staff relationships may form through informal interactions or through various board committee activities involving staff. These relationships may result in undermining the executive's power both with the board and with staff.

The first instance of executive-staff collusion may be more likely to occur when the board is isolated from the rest of the organization. Neither management nor the board freely gives or receives information, thus providing ample opportunity for staff-executive collusion. The second instance of board-staff alliance may be more likely to occur when the board lacks a sense of its own identity, thus making authority relations within the organization even more unclear.

Finally, Zald (1969) describes certain strategic contingencies that can affect the extent of board power. For example, the life-cycle stage of an organization is an important factor when trustees are more dominant during the start-up stage since they supply needed resources and legitimacy (Perrow 1963; Nason 1982). Second, identity crises such as mergers or joint undertakings may force the board into a powerful position because it must fulfill its role as final decision maker in such matters. Third, when an executive director must be chosen and the responsibility falls to the board, its power may be enhanced relative to the rest of the organization.

These latter two situations carry the potential of raising basic questions of organizational mandate, character, and identity (Zald 1969). These questions in turn may initiate or heighten major conflicts among subgroups on the board and between the board and the rest of the organization. If this conflict has lain dormant or been held in check by the forces of competing interests, its eruption could disrupt the organization's functioning. In organizations already dealing with high degrees of conflict, these situations could exacerbate instability and vulnerability.

As we have seen in the description of factors influencing the board-management relationship, research in this area is not a simple matter. Compositional characteristics of the board affect how it relates to management and to the rest of the organization. Organizational factors such as degree of structural and technological complexity are additional influences. Informal relationships among any of the parties may relate to board behavior and influence. Finally, specific situations or crises may affect the board's functioning and power.

Any single research effort is not likely to untangle this laundry list of important variables. However, what emerges from the list is the importance of recognizing both structural and behavioral factors that significantly influence the board-management relationship. It is an interdependent relationship between people who see the organization from different perspectives. Understanding these differences and the inevitable tensions that result is an important first step for practitioners and researchers alike.

CONCLUSION

Given the discussion in this chapter, we can conclude that empirical studies of nonprofit boards, although scarce, are adequate to challenge much of the conventional wisdom. Below are three commonly held assumptions about nonprofit boards and a summary of the contradictory data regarding each assumption.

Assumption One:

Nonprofit boards are policy-making, goal-evaluating organizational units.

Most of the data indicate that boards do not formulate policy but rather ratify policy that is presented to them by staff. The executive committee in concert with top management may be the only place within the board structure where policy is designed. Certain situations (such as organizational transformations) may increase the likelihood that boards enact policy, but as a rule they do not. Instead, they are used more or less effectively for external linking functions.

Assumption Two:

Nonprofit boards are noisy constituent boards, characterized by bargaining behavior.

Some boards, especially those with strong ties among high-status members, appear to be conflict-averse and do not engage in discussions concerning controversial organizational issues, since they may disrupt the exchange relationships among members who stress the sharing of friendship, status and respect. Other boards whose members have weaker ties with one another fit the noisy-bargaining model. These boards may have a lower-status, constituent membership with more of a stake in organizational goals and mission.

Assumption Three:

The board-management relationship is a partnership built on mutual trust and effective communication.

The board-management relationship is essentially paradoxical. For many important decisions, the board is the final authority. Yet it must depend on the executive for most of its information and for policy articulation and implementation. The executive has these emergent powers but also is hired and can be fired by the board and needs the board for crucial external functions. As with all paradoxes, resolution is not possible. Instead the relationship is dynamic, and its movement depends on a number of individual, group, and organizational factors.

These commonly held assumptions regarding nonprofit boards of directors obscure the fact that their behavior and functioning is important in shaping both resource allocation systems in communities and the adaptability and survival capacity of organizations. Through understanding the nature of relationships trustees have with external groups, with other trustees, and with management, one can begin to determine the extent and kind of influence nonprofit boards exert on their external environments and on the organizations they govern.

"Sometimes boards don't use their power well; sometimes they misuse it. But the board is top dog" (Saline 1982).

REFERENCES

Alderfer, Clayton P., and Ken K. Smith. 1982. "Studying Intergroup Relations Embedded in Organizations." *Administrative Science Quarterly* 27:35–65.

Aldrich, Howard. 1979. *Organizations and Environments.* Englewood Cliffs, N.J.: Prentice-Hall.

Auerbach, Arnold J. 1961. "Aspirations of Power People and Agency Goals." *Social Work* 6:66–73.

Babchuk, Nicholas, Ruth Massey, and C. Wayne Gordon. 1960 "Men and Women in Community Agencies: A Note on Power and Prestige." *American Sociological Review* 25:399–403.

Boorman, Scott A., and Paul R. Levitt. 1981. "Cultural Conflicts and the Roots of Nonprofit Social Structure." In *Network Matching: Nonprofit Structure and Public Policy.* Yale University, Program on Non-Profit Organizations Working Paper no. 61.

Brown, Courtney C. 1976. *Putting the Corporate Board to Work.* New York: Macmillan.

Brown, Kristen M. 1977. "The Not-for-Profit Corporation Director: Legal Liability and Protection." *Federation of Insurance Counsel* 28:57–88.

Cole, Richard L. 1980. "Constituent Involvement in Non-Profit Organizations." Yale University, Program on Non-Profit Organizations Working Paper no. 18.

DiMaggio, Paul, and Michael Useem. 1982. "The Arts in Class Reproduction." In *Culture and Economic Reproduction in Education,* edited by M. W. Apple. London: Routledge & Kegan Paul.

Fenn, Dan H., Jr. 1971. "Executives and Community Volunteers." *Harvard Business Review* 49, no. 2:4ff.

"The Fiduciary Duties of Loyalty and Care Associated with the Directors and Trustees of Charitable Organizations." 1978. *Virginia Law Review* 64:449–65.

Foa, Uriel G. 1971. "Interpersonal and Economic Resources." *Science* 171:345–51.

Granovetter, Mark S. 1973. "The Strength of Weak Ties." *American Journal of Sociology* 78:1360–80.

———. 1974. *Getting a Job: A Study of Contacts and Careers.* Cambridge, Mass.: Harvard University Press.

———. 1983. "Labor Mobility, Internal Markets, and Job Matching: A Comparison of the Sociological and Economic Approaches." Unpublished manuscript.

Greenleaf, Robert K. 1973. "The Trustee: The Buck Starts Here." *Foundation News* 14:30–35.

Hall, Peter Dobkin. 1975. "The Model of Boston Charity: A Theory of Charitable Benevolence and Class Development." *Science and Society* 38, no. 4:464–77.

———. 1982. "Philanthropy as Investment." *History of Education Quarterly* 22, no. 2:185–203

———. 1984. *The Organization of American Culture, 1700–1900: Private Institutions, Elites and the Origins of American Nationality.* New York: New York University Press.

Hansmann, Henry. 1981. "Reforming Nonprofit Corporation Law." *University of Pennsylvania Law Review* 129, no. 3:500–623.

Kerr, Norman D. 1964. "The School Board as an Agency of Legitimation." *Sociology of Education* 38:35–59.

Kohn Patricia F., and Kenneth P. Mortimer. 1983. "Selecting Effective Trustees." *Change* 15, no. 5:30–37.

Kramer, Ralph. 1965. "Ideology, Status, and Power in Board-Executive Relationships." *Social Work* 10:107–14.

———. 1981. *Voluntary Agencies in the Welfare State.* Berkeley: University of California Press.

Low, James P. 1978. "Principles of Partnership." *Leadership*, pp. 9–12.

Mace, Myles L. 1976. "Standards of Care for Trustees." *Harvard Business Review* 54, no. 1:14ff.

McSweeney, Edward. 1978. *Managing the Managers.* New York: Harper & Row.

Nason, John. 1977. *Trustees and the Future of Foundations.* New York: Council on Foundations.

———. 1982. *The Nature of Trusteeship: The Role and Responsibilities of College and University Boards.* Washington, D.C.: Association of Governing Boards of Universities and Colleges.

Odendahl, Teresa, and Elizabeth Boris. 1983. "A Delicate Balance: Foundation Board-Staff Relations." *Foundation News* 24, no. 3:34–45.

Pellegrin, Roland J., and Charles H. Coates. 1956. "Absentee-Owned Corporations and Community Power Structures." *American Journal of Sociology* 61:413–19.

Perror, Charles. 1963. "Goals and Power Structures, a Historical Case Study." In *The Hospital in Modern Society,* edited by Eliot Friedson. New York: Macmillan.

———. 1978. "Demystifying Organizations." In *The Management of Human Services,* edited by R. C. Sarri and Y. Hasenfeld. New York: Columbia University Press.

Perrucci, Robert, and Marc Pilisuk. 1970. "Leaders and Ruling Elites: The Interorganizational Bases of Community Power." *American Sociological Review* 35, no. 6:1040–57.

Pfeffer, Jeffrey. 1973. "Size, Composition, and Functions of Hospital Boards of Directors: A Study of Organization-Environment Linkage." *Administrative Science Quarterly* 18:349–63.

Pfeffer, Jeffrey, and Gerald Salancik. 1978. *The External Control of Organizations.* New York: Harper & Row.

Powell, Walter W., and Rebecca Friedkin. 1982. "Political and Organizational Influences on Public Television Programming." Paper presented at the American Sociological Association Annual Meeting.

Price, James G. 1963. "The Impact of Governing Boards on Organizational Effectiveness and Morale." *Administrative Science Quarterly* 8:361–77.

Provan, Keith C. 1980. "Board Power and Organizational Effectiveness among Human Service Agencies." *Academy of Management Journal* 23:221–36.

Ratcliff, Richard E., Mary Elizabeth Gallagher, and Kathryn Strother Ratcliff. 1979. "The Civic Involvement of Bankers: An Analysis of the Influence of Economic Power and Social Prominence in the Command of Civic Policy Positions." *Social Problems* 26:298–303.

Ross, Aileen D. 1954. "Philanthropic Activity and the Business Career." *Social Forces* 32:274–80.

Rudney, Gabriel. 1981. "A Quantitative Profile of the Nonprofit Sector." Yale University, Program on Non-Profit Organizations Working Paper no. 40.

Saline, Carol. 1982. "The Board Game." *Philadelphia.*

Salzman, Harold, and G. William Domhoff. 1983. "Nonprofit Organizations and the Corporate Community." *Social Science History* 7:205–16.

Schultze, Robert O. 1958. "The Role of Economic Dominants in Community Power Structures." *American Sociological Review* 23:3–9.

Selznick, Phillip. 1949. *TVA and the Grass Roots.* Berkeley: University of California Press.

Senor, James M. 1963. "Another Look at the Board-Executive Relationship." *Social Work* 8:19–25.

Spencer, Anne. 1981. "What Non-Executives Don't Do." *Management Today,* May, pp. 50–53.

Thomas, David. 1984. "Reflections on the Relationship between Organizations and Their Environments: A Micro-level Perspective." Unpublished manuscript, Yale School of Organization and Management.

Unterman, Israel, and Richard Hart Davis. 1982. "The Strategy Gap in Not-for-Profits." *Harvard Business Review* 60, no. 3:30–40.

Useem, Michael. 1979. "The Social Organization of American Business Elite and Participation of Corporation Directors in the Governance of American Institutions." *American Sociological Review* 44:553–72.

Veblen, T. [1918] 1957. *The Higher Learning in America.* New York: Hill & Wang.

Whisler, Thomas L. 1982. "A General Model of Organizational Governance Applied to Hospital Boards." Unpublished manuscript, University of Chicago, Graduate School of Business.

Wilensky, Harold L., and Charles Lebeaux. 1955. *Industrialization and Social Welfare.* New York: Russell Sage Foundation.

Zald, Mayer N. 1967. "Urban Differentiation, Characteristics of Boards of Directors and Organizational Effectiveness." *American Journal of Sociology* 73:261–72.

———. 1969. "The Power and Functions of Boards and Directors: A Theoretical Synthesis." *American Journal of Sociology* 75:97–111.

Zald, Mayer N., and Patricia Denton. 1963. "From Evangelism to General Service: The Transformation of the YMCA." *Administrative Science Quarterly* 8:214–34.

9

Doing Well while Doing Good: Dilemmas of Performance Measurement in Nonprofit Organizations and the Need for a Multiple-Constituency Approach

ROSABETH MOSS KANTER
DAVID V. SUMMERS

We know, for instance, that we have to measure results. We also know that with the exception of business, we do not know how to measure results in most organizations.   Peter Drucker, *The Age of Discontinuity* (1968)

An important part of the strategic management process is assessing performance. Managers, employees, and others need to gauge whether an organization is doing well or poorly with respect to its standards for performance.

Although the measurement of performance is not a simple matter in any kind of organization (a task force at a major auto company recently identified over a hundred measures of organizational performance currently in use in the company), it is even more complicated for nonprofit organizations. Financial measures are central in for-profit organizations not only because profits can be measured easily but also because they are a good test of both market-need satisfaction and the capacity of the organization to run itself efficiently. But the

We would like to thank Woody Powell for his comments and editorial suggestions.

"test" in nonprofits is different: these organizations have defined themselves not around their financial returns but around their mission, or the services they offer. And services, of course, are notoriously intangible and difficult to measure. The clients receiving them and the professionals delivering them may make very different judgments about their quality, and donors may hold still another standard. And "doing good" is a matter of societal values about which there may be little or no consensus. It is this factor—the centrality of social values over financial values—that complicates measurement for nonprofit organizations.

Profit-making organizations are more flexible with respect to the deployment and redeployment of resources in any number of areas, as long as bottom-line criteria of financial performance are satisfied. But the centrality of mission for nonprofit organizations places limitations on their flexibility of action. Money can be obtained in a number of ways;

154

social values cannot. Therefore, an organization that establishes itself to make a profit *via* providing health care (financial goals first, mission second) has more flexibility to change fields, move across systems, or deflect resources from one set of activities to another than an organization in which financial goals are subordinated to mission.

The apparent freedom of major for-profit corporations to redefine their missions as making money rather than making widgets, thereby permitting themselves to move in and out of businesses at will, has been decried by business critics. But nonprofit organizations have no such apparent freedom. Without their mission, the organizations' reason for being collapses. Indeed, one critical test for whether an organization can attain nonprofit status is whether it claims to be "doing good" in one of the areas that society, or some segment of it, recognizes as valuable.

Admittedly, the lines dividing for-profit and not-for-profit organizations with respect to performance measurement are blurring. For-profit organizations are coming to stress social mission and values as a result of a new awareness of the role of values in highly successful corporations (Ouchi 1981; Peters & Waterman 1982; Kanter 1983). At the same time, nonprofits are increasingly setting more stringent financial goals, reporting "operating income" as though it were "profit," discussing strategic planning, "repositioning" themselves to take advantage of "market niches," and considering such market tests of performance as revenues from clients/customers as more important than the raising of nonmarket funds from donors. We have observed this dual evolution in major profit-making corporations, on the one hand, and in nonprofit health care systems in Virginia, Illinois, and North Dakota, on the other.

Still, if there is a distinction left, issues of performance measurement for nonprofit organizations are complicated by the absence of an overarching measure like financial performance and by the mission-directedness of the organization. The nonprofit organization, then, faces these dilemmas: (1) knowing when it is doing well, and (2) being able to make changes, or to redirect resources, when members of the organization suspect it is *not* doing well with respect to its "market," but can still attract resources by nonmarket means from nostalgic or believing donors.

We argue further that nonprofit organizations also have organizational rigidities—owing to the difficulty of effectiveness measurement and the varying standards of clients, donors, and others—that make it difficult for them to innovate or change. The question of values is always a politicized one, and the larger the number of groups claiming to define values for a nonprofit organization the more difficult measurement and making needed adjustments become.

In this chapter, we will indicate why performance measures are important and what functions they serve. We will see the many constituencies involved in defining organizational performance—constituencies that actively prefer different measures because of their own reasons for participating in the organization and their own uses for the data. Behind this argument is a view of organizations not as impersonal instruments guided by managers but as temporary alliances of separate groups, each interpreting the organization's purpose a little differently.

We will review the common ways in which organizational performance can be measured and then argue that, because of the existence of multiple constituencies or stakeholders, no one of these alone can guide an organization. Rather than present a way out of the dilemma of performance measurement for nonprofit organizations, we propose instead that acknowledgment of the realities of multiple constituencies and explicit attempts to develop multiple measures is the only sensible course. We will illustrate these ideas by drawing on a case study of a large nonprofit hospital and nursing home chain.

WHY AN ISSUE EXISTS: PROBLEMS WITH MEASURING GOAL ACCOMPLISHMENT

It would seem, on the surface, that measurement of organizational performance should be a simple matter: determine the organization's objectives, and then assess whether they have been attained. But the social science literature, particularly that related to nonprofit organizations, makes clear why this is difficult to do.

A long tradition in organization research defines effectiveness in terms of outputs and goal accomplishment (for example, Georgopolous & Tannenbaum 1957; Etzioni 1964; Price 1968; Campbell 1977; Hall 1978). But another long tradition criticizes this approach—most recently, and perhaps most important, on the grounds that because organizations are complex entities, the specification of their goals is itself problematic. Organizations may have many goals, and they can be inconsistent, contradictory, or incoherent; it is often unclear even at what level or with respect to what units the attainment of goals should be measured. As one author claims, goals may even be a mystification (Perrow 1981). This is one reason simple financial tests like "profits" are so appealing, and it is so often hard to get consensus on goals beyond this broad one.

The multiplicity of goals is fairly well recognized by analysts in the field, who define *effectiveness* as the "balanced attainment of many goals" (Kirchoff 1977), which they then seek to catalog and weigh. In the behavioral objectives model, for example, effectiveness is measured by getting "experts" in the organization to specify (1) a catalog of concrete observable organizational objectives; (2) the conditions under which the organization should be able to achieve them; and (3) the degree to which each objective should be satisfied (Campbell 1977). Pennings and Goodman (1977) define *effectiveness* similarly; but they do not explain how goals are to be identified, nor do they treat the complex issues that arise when there is more than a single ultimate criterion. Complexity is aggravated by the fact that some goals may be incoherent, unstated, or defined post hoc by the organization to justify its actions.

Organizations differ in their complexity, of course, as well as in the degree of coherence among subunits. Relatively autonomous subunits in their turn are likely to pursue multiple and sometimes inconsistent objectives. Such "loosely coupled systems" are especially prevalent in non-profit, governmental, and service organizations, such as a state university system, which has been described as an "organized anarchy" (March & Olsen 1976). Hospitals, too, are multiproduct organizations serving many purposes, only one of which is patient care, so that, as Scott and his colleagues have pointed out (1978), effectiveness with respect to one set of objectives (such as intensive care) might not generalize to others (say, teaching), and structural features of various segments of the organization may not correspond.

Thus goals exist at a variety of levels and may be differentially pursued by various parts of the organization. As Kirchoff (1977) notes, "Operational definitions have failed to clarify distinctions between organizational effectiveness, managerial effectiveness, and manager and subordinate behaviors and attitudes." Which units, then, are to be measured? Should one examine individual performance, behaviors, and satisfaction (Argyris 1962; Lawler, Hall, & Oldham 1974); contribution of and coordination among subunits (Pennings & Goodman 1977); or subunit goal attainment, treating each as an autonomous "profit center" (Manns & March 1978, for academic departments in universities)? Which cut through an organization is most appropriate for the measurement of effectiveness? Regarding human service organizations, Herzlinger (1979) notes the choice that must be made whether to generate cost data by *organizational unit* or by *program,* when the latter might cut across many functional, geographic, or client-defined divisions.

Finally, there is the related question of whether to measure outcomes in terms of holistic-categorical or aggregated-individual data. For some analysts, for example, the effectiveness of higher education is measured by its impact on individual consumers (Astin 1968, 1971, 1977; Feldman & Newcomb 1969; Bower 1977), just as that of hospitals can be measured by outcomes for individual patients. It can also be argued, however, that more global goals such as "education" or "health" are insufficiently measured by aggregated individual experiences.

When goals are vague or ill defined, effectiveness criteria may themselves become substitutes for goals, particularly when they are more precise and suggest concrete actions. This is one of the central issues generated by the necessity to operationalize goals in order to measure performance. For example, when the effectiveness of police departments is defined as "production rates"—the number of tickets written, or the percentage of arrests resulting in convictions—the measures may create informal quota systems (Marx 1976). Without regard to their larger mission, police workers may gear their activities to improving rates. Although organizations need criteria in order to achieve consensus about what constitutes effective individual and joint effort, they must beware of letting a measurement system define the organization's purpose (Epstein, Flamholz, & McDonough 1977; Farris 1975). Otherwise, specific goals can become the mini-

mally acceptable standards, with performance dropping to that level.

Drucker has offered incisive comments on this point:

It may sound plausible to measure the effectiveness of a mental hospital by how well its beds—a scarce and expensive commodity—are utilized. Yet a study of the mental hospitals of the Veterans' Administration brought out that this yardstick leads to mental patients being kept in the hospital—which, therapeutically, is about the worst thing that can be done to them. Clearly, however, lack of utilization, that is, empty beds, would also not be the right yardstick. How then does one measure whether a mental hospital is doing a good job within the wretched limits of our knowledge of mental disease?

And how does one measure whether a university is doing a good job? By the jobs and salaries its students get twenty years after graduation? By that elusive myth, the "reputation" of this or that faculty which, only too often, is nothing but self-praise and good academic propaganda? By the number of Ph.D.'s or scientific prizes the alumni have earned? Or by the donations they make to their alma mater? Each such yardstick bespeaks a value judgment regarding the purpose of the university—and a very narrow one at that. Even if these were the right objectives, such yardsticks measure performance just as dubiously as the count of bed utilization measures performance in mental hospitals. (1968, 196–97)

When immediate effectiveness measures set the standards for the organization, a tendency can arise to favor the short term over the long term—to maximize the score on indicators of today's performance. But very different criteria may be appropriate to the short, intermediate, and long runs—for example, short term: production, efficiency, satisfaction; intermediate term: adaptiveness, development; long term: survival (Gibson, Invanevich, & Donnelly 1973). When effectiveness is defined in terms of adaptability it is sometimes clear how short-term and long-term measures can conflict. If short-term efficiency and production-oriented measures tend to produce ritualistic behavior geared toward quantity rather than quality, then the "random, deviant" behavior that enhances an organization's ability to be "creative [and] flexible" (Weick 1977) may be lost.

Task-effectiveness or goal-attainment criteria may vary with an organization's life stage (Scott 1977) because every stage brings different key problems (Kanter & Stein 1979, sec. IV). Thus, when we measure effectiveness, we must include an assessment of how well an organization handles the critical issues of each period. Kimberly (1979) defines three stages of development of a new medical school: initiation, innovation, and institutionalization. Initially the school's problem is to carve out a niche; later, to survive and grow. Kimberly notes the paradoxical nature of success: "Success by later standards may undermine the very activities that have made the organization effective." Moreover, over time, goals are displaced (Thompson & McEwen 1958).

The problems of operationalization lead to a meaning/measurement dilemma for any organization whose output is not easily quantifiable (Warner 1967). On the one hand, efforts designed to meet standards of objectivity (for example, use of quantitative indicators such as number of grants, or mortality rates after surgery) are vulnerable to skepticism about their intrinsic meaning. On the other hand, efforts designed to convey high levels of meanings (such as grantors' assessments of the impact of projects, or physicians' judgments about community health) may be criticized for their subjectivity (Epstein, Flamholz, & McDonough 1977, 72).

Such a dilemma appears when we consider efficiency measures in higher education—costs per student, student/faculty ratios, costs per faculty member, or costs per square foot (Bowen & Douglas 1971; O'Neill 1971; Meeth 1974; Hartmark 1975). Such measures—which of course seem more important in times of financial stringency—can be challenged as not capturing anything meaningful about the quality of education or the experience of students. Campbell (1977) argues that effectiveness measures should always be subjective and based on the views of organizational members (which raises the question of ''which members'').

But measures of quality or experience are subjective and intangible. This is one of the reasons agreement among those who rank organizations or their units on effectiveness tends to be low (Seashore 1972). The criteria used to make meaningful subjective assessments of effectiveness tend to be uncorrelated or negatively correlated. Furthermore, supposedly ''hard'' objective measures sometimes turn out to be ''soft'' and subjective—for example, survey data, derived from judgments of organizational participants, translated into scalar terms. In short, it may be inadvisable to search for universal, objective, operational performance criteria centering around goal attainment because they tend to (1) replace larger goals and become the standard that motivates organizational behavior; (2) favor shorter term over longer term criteria; and (3) decrease the meaningfulness of the assessment process.

Another major problem with the goal-attainment tradition is one of substance, not measurement. Some writers argue that outcome measures of effectiveness are never pure indicators of performance quality because other factors enter in, the most notable being the characteristics of the materials or objects on which the organization performs, the available technology (Mahoney & Frost 1974), and a variety of environmental factors beyond the organization's control. For organization-design experts, effectiveness in accomplishing objectives can be affected by (1) theoretical bottlenecks—people don't know how to do it; (2) resource bottlenecks—people don't have the resources the job requires; and (3) organizational bottlenecks—people cannot put the resources together (Galbraith 1977). Whereas the latter two can perhaps be said to constitute indications of ineffectiveness, the first is often beyond the control of the organization.

Furthermore, desirable outcomes are often achieved not by aspects of the organization itself but by client characteristics (Lefton 1975). Outcome measurements for hospitals, for example, are affected both by medical knowledge and by patients' prior states. Hospitals that attract patients who possess features associated with greater health (such as high income or occupational status) may appear to be more effective in turning out healthier patients (may register lower mortality rates, for example, or shorter illnesses) (Scott et al. 1978). This factor may explain why elite universities turn out better students—they select the better students in the first place. Thus, it is often difficult to draw conclusions about comparative effectiveness unless a variety of other factors are controlled.

These contingency factors affecting goal attainment have led to two different perspectives on the measurement of effectiveness. According to one, effectiveness measures should be confined to accomplishments directly under the organization's control (Campbell 1977). According to the other, measures should factor in the favorability of technological knowledge, environmental support, and raw-material quality, thus taking these extraorganizational issues into account.

Frustrated by the problems of measuring effectiveness outlined above, some analysts (for example, the population ecologists such as Hannan & Freeman 1977; Aldrich 1979) have suggested that organizational survival be the ultimate criterion. At least, they implicitly argue, survival is as concrete an issue as profits, it can be measured easily, and it indicates ipso facto an organization's success on such critical effectiveness dimensions as resource attraction and internal organization.

Adaptation to the environment seems particularly critical to many researchers in the organization-environment tradition. First, characteristics of the environment strongly influence what kinds of organizations will be effective and which internal structures and processes are likely to fit their environment (Burns & Stalker 1960; Lawrence & Lorsch 1967; Thompson 1967; Osborn & Hunt 1974; Leifer & Delbecq 1978, Aldrich 1979). Second, for some organizations effectiveness may be a matter of convincing dominant actors in their environment that they *are* effective so that they can attract resources (for example, Yuchtman & Seashore 1967). In this view, measures of performance used to win such confidence may be decoupled from measures of the organization's achievement of more abstractly defined goals (Meyer & Rowan 1977). The organization's own actions, then, may have little to do with its apparent ''successes.'' It may simply be located in a favorable environment (Aldrich 1979). Thus, survival is a sign of adaptive capacity (though it might also signify the power to hold on even if no longer adaptive in an objective sense).

In the domain of nonprofit organizations, survival can indeed be an appropriate effectiveness standard. In alternative, or utopian communities (residential and economic arrangements owned cooperatively by and for the benefit of members), a survival measure—longevity—can be a success criterion (Kanter 1972). In this case longevity appears to cover other effectiveness dimensions because (1) the communities' overriding goal was to exist (goal attainment); (2) longevity was an indicator that the communities were satisfying their members since members continued to support them (morale, and perhaps appropriate structure/process); and (3) longevity suggested that they had weathered crises (flexibility, adaptation) and earned sufficient income (resource attraction). Of course, longevity does not tell us whether the communities did as well as they could have, only that they did well enough to continue operating.

There are some obvious limitations on the use of survival as a measure. First, it is highly skewed since there is a general "liability of newness" for virtually all organizations (Stinchcombe 1965; Freeman, Carroll, & Hannan 1983). Second, it provides no guide to short-term decision making by either managers or other constituencies. Third, survival is sometimes artificial: organizations may survive because a benefactor or owner is willing to support them despite their ineffectiveness. Finally, to the extent that organizations act as though survival were their ultimate goal (as many do), they may lose sight of other purposes, including their reasons for existing in the first place. Public service organizations are often accused of responding not to public needs but to the demands (real and imagined) of funding agencies and budget allocators (Herzlinger 1979).

Survival may also be unrelated or even negatively related to impact, another ultimate criterion. *Impact* can be defined more broadly than goal attainment (although they might be connected) as a long-term influence on the state of the environment surrounding the organization. Many of the utopian communities that were successful in surviving had little or no impact on their environments in terms of such measures as their ability to effect changes in adverse laws or to encourage others to form or join similar alternative communities (Kanter 1972).

Impact may even threaten survival. The impact of the March of Dimes—eradication of polio, the disease for which it raised funds—might have killed the organization; but members had sufficient stake in its continuation that they adopted a new mission to keep it alive (Sills 1957). Impact can also threaten the survival of organizations with avowedly political goals. The more they take a low profile and reduce their impact, the more they may be able to protect themselves; but they may elicit opposition to the extent that they start having impact (Marx 1974).

BEHIND GOALS: MEASURES FOR WHOM AND WHY?

The significant questions about performance measurement are thus not technical but conceptual: not *how* to measure effectiveness or productivity but *what* to measure and how definitions and techniques are chosen and are linked to other aspects of an organization's structure, functioning, and environmental relations. Problems plaguing this field are not mere annoyances to be brushed aside as soon as better mea-

surement techniques are invented; instead, they are fundamental aspects of modern organizations—profit making as well as nonprofit.

Recent models of organizations have moved away from rationalistic and voluntaristic assumptions about goal consensus, unity of purpose, and the possibility of discovering universal performance standards. The new models emphasize instead more political views, in which multiple stakeholders both inside and outside compete to use an organization for their purposes and to set performance standards that will advance their interests to make their jobs easier (Kanter 1980). Furthermore, political models make it clear that organizations may not control all the factors that influence how their effectiveness is defined and whether they meet effectiveness standards (Mintzberg 1983; Pfeffer 1981; Pfeffer & Salancik, 1977); the older, voluntaristic models were more likely to see the organization as controling all variables. Thus, the search for objective standards has declined. Multiple constituencies and multiple environments require multiple measures.

Constituency interests play a role in definitions of effectiveness via the uses to which various groups wish to put the data. Actors in and around an organization may require different kinds of effectiveness measures for different kinds of decisions and purposes. No single indicator will suffice.

Classic definitions of organizational effectiveness and models of measurement often favored, implicitly if not explicitly, some constituencies over others. Certainly profit (though supposedly an objective market measure of effectiveness, based on the efficiency with which input could be transformed into output) makes the interest of owners or shareholders paramount. Those analysts who define effectiveness as the ability of an organization to adapt to, manipulate, or fulfill expectations of the external environment (such as Bidwell & Kasarda 1975; Hirsch 1975; Katz & Kahn 1978) use the "supersystem" as the judge, thus making paramount the interests of supporters, sponsors, clients, regulators, and so on. Those who consider the satisfaction of customers (Gartner & Riessman 1974) or participants (Cummings & Molloy 1977) to be the central criterion similarly emphasize one set of interests over others.

A multiple-constituency or multiple-stakeholder approach to effectiveness is thus warranted (Bluedorn 1980; Connolly, Conlon, & Deutsch 1980). But simply to acknowledge the existence of many passive points of view is not enough. Different constituencies *actively* prefer different kinds of effectiveness measures. For example, managers might prefer structural measures of organizational characteristics because they have control over such factors; the rank and file might prefer process measures of activities because they control their own performance; and clients and customers prefer outcome measures because they want results, not promises or mere effort (Scott et al. 1978). Inside organizations, too, standards—and therefore measures—differ by field and function. Mahoney and Weitzel (1969) show that managers of research and development units in corporations apply models of effectiveness differently than do managers of more general business operations, perhaps because of differences in their perceptions of the production process and their more technological environments. Perrow (1977) states it simply: power affects the definition of effectiveness. In short, the interests involved are based not only on position but also on politics.

While acknowledging the existence of numerous interests and perspectives, some analysts still argue that a single standard of effectiveness can be developed based on the definition held by the organization's "dominant coalition" (Yuchtman & Seashore 1967; Gross 1968; Price 1968; Pennings and Goodman 1977). Buried in the notion of a dominant coalition is the idea that the various constituencies have already engaged in a bargaining process that has given them input into the organization's goal statement. Indeed, in the conflict-and-bargaining model of effectiveness, definitions of dominant coalition members prevail. Effective organizations are those that achieve the purposes established by the winning actors in the bargaining process (Elmore 1978). (The problem with this definition is its subjectivity. An individual's view of the organization's success or failure is determined by his or her position in the bargaining process.)

Organizational development models go even further in tying effectiveness to the achievement of consensus in the bargaining process (see Cunningham's reviews [1977, 1978]). Here the effective organization is one that "can build consensus between policymakers and implementors so as to create joint commitment to the goals of the organization"; thus better decisions occur with better relationships between constituencies (Elmore 1978). Research confirms that inside and outside constituencies (such as branch bank employees and customers) can agree on standards, especially when the inside group occupies a boundary-spanning role (Schneider, Parkington, & Buxton 1980).

Even those who reject the view that the dominant coalition's definition of organizational effectiveness should prevail still consider the coalition the most appropriate source of operational information about some dimensions of effectiveness. For example, Cameron (1978) argued that if one measures effectiveness by organizational characteristics, the dominant coalition (meaning the official, titled leaders) comprises the appropriate informants, since they have organizationwide information. But even though this is a statement about data sources rather than effectiveness definitions, if one follows this line of reasoning, it is likely that dominant coalition interests would be most strongly represented in the measurement process.

In contrast, another strong school of thought holds that the existence of multiple interests must be acknowledged in both the definitional and the data collection stages. Scott (1977) argued that criteria for evaluating organizational effectiveness and the data collected to assess it must be chosen from a variety of sources. This contemporary multiple-goal model (Scott 1978) sees organizations as composed of shifting coalitions of subgroups, both inside and outside, with differing views of what the organization should produce. Extending this view, Cummings (1977) defined effectiveness as the degree to which the organization is instrumental for both its inside and outside constituencies, since organizations are instruments of outcomes. This approach is limited by Cummings's identification of the individual rather than the organization as the appropriate unit of analysis.

This review leads us to several important conclusions. In general, organizational performance measures serve three kinds of functions, reflecting different aspects of an organization:

1. *Institutional functions:* measures to provide evidence that the organization is meeting standards or engaging in activities that confer legitimacy upon it; and to provide indicators of "progress" or "improvement" to instill pride in the organization's key constituencies, thus reaffirming their decision to support the organization and encouraging others to join them. The primary institutional functions of measuring performance thus revolve around *legitimacy renewal* and *resource attraction.* The constituencies served involve those linking the organization to its environment. In nonprofit organizations these might be boards, volunteers, and donors.

2. *Managerial functions:* measures to provide information to enable adjustment of activities to better meet standards; to provide knowledge of progress toward desired states; to spot trouble or potential trouble so that corrective action can be taken; and to allocate resources (budgets) and rewards among organizational participants and units. The primary managerial functions thus revolve around *structure and process corrections* and *internal allocation.* The constituencies served are the various levels and types of managers and professionals. In nonprofit organizations the managers may want different information for different reasons than the professionals, and the two may split into conflicting constituencies.

3. *Technical functions:* Measures to provide information on the efficiency or quality with which the organization delivers its basic products or services. The constituencies served are the customers or clients.

The contradictions between some of these measurement purposes and the gap between the constituencies create problems for all organizations. For nonprofits, these problems are exaggerated because of two kinds of loose coupling: between *sources of legitimacy* and *standards of management* and between those *providing resources* (donors of funds or time) and those *receiving services* (clients). In between are the managers and professionals, who have their own view of what the organization should be doing.

HEALTHCO AND ITS EFFECTIVENESS DILEMMAS

Healthco (a pseudonym) is a multiunit, nonprofit health care organization, which operates and leases over fifty hospitals and nursing home facilities. In its forty-six-year history, the organization has provided health care services in rural areas now covering thirteen states, mostly in the West and upper Midwest. Although the individual facilities are small (usually under a hundred beds), Healthco's operations are relatively diverse and complex, encompassing a full range of medical care and treatment programs (long term, acute, clinics, chemical dependency, and more).

We studied issues of organizational performance measurement and organizational change by assessing Healthco's level and capacity for innovation in early 1984. Nearly fifty Healthco managers were interviewed in depth along with top management informants. A review of internal systems also was carried out. Interview data were analyzed both qualitatively and quantitatively. (Note that the focus was on managerial issues at Healthco, so professional staff without administrative roles were not included, although obviously their perspectives are important, too.)

It is possible to "audit" and assess the level and type of innovation within an organization, profit or nonprofit, and to develop measures of the underlying structural factors that are either inhibiting or encouraging the process of innovation (Kanter 1983). We can thereby glean important information on the level of effectiveness and the views of key organizational constituencies on this matter. We can also slice the evaluation of organizational effectiveness two ways—assessing it on the individual level and on the organizational level. Auditing the level and types of innovation requires several steps in data collection: conducting a series of intensive interviews with both senior and middle managers and professionals (focusing on their individual accomplishments or innovations); administering a questionnaire on key themes in the organization that support or impede innovation; and reviewing the human resource system.

Healthco has been a relatively stable organization during the past four decades. Growth has been moderate, turnover low because many employees have made their career with the organization, and changes in top-level positions infrequent (there have been only three presidents). The founders of Healthco all came from a strong Protestant tradition and worked hard to inculcate religious values into the operating philosophy of its health care programs (to this day all but one member of the board of directors are members of the original denomination). However, a number of changes have occurred in the past few years, raising important issues about the future direction of the organization as well as concern about its overall effectiveness. As competition in the health industry increases and government regulations create more external control, Healthco is taking a serious look at its effectiveness.

Within Healthco some critical changes are taking place. This includes a significant amount of growth in staff (the total number of employees is over eight thousand), especially as new professional functions are added at the home office, as well as the acquisition, construction, and enlargement of facilities. Many new forms of technology, too, are being developed and used throughout the organization—not only medically related equipment but also new information systems, word processing, and the like. In the past few years a major reorganization has established a number of central

functions at headquarters in relatively new areas like marketing and management information systems.

The issue of effectiveness looms large for Healthco regardless of the conceptual approach we may use (system resource, goal attainment, determining the "right" areas in which a health care organization should operate) since there are multiple and competing constituencies, each with a stake in the determination and measurement of effectiveness. Thus it is important to know that the locus of control in Healthco is bifurcated. The executives at the headquarters office report to a board of directors (an active board that takes a keen interest in Healthco's operations). At the local level where each facility operates, an administrator is in charge who functions more independently (not unlike the CEO of any organization) but works with a board composed of community members. These two levels are linked through a series of regional managers who serve as liaison between the field and the headquarters office.

Constituencies in a Nonprofit Health Care Organization

Previous research on nonprofit hospitals suggests that there may be competing interests that influence the process of decision making and the determination of effectiveness (Rushing 1974). It is clear that within Healthco issues of power, politics, and the influence of stakeholder groups are important, although often disguised. Throughout the organization, overt displays of conflict and the exercise of power are discouraged. Nevertheless, a number of important constituencies exist within the company, each trying to have some input and influence over the organization's future.

To begin with, the board of directors takes an active and direct role in the operations and management of Healthco. It reviews quarterly virtually all major decisions made by the top officers. Numerous policy decisions are also elevated to the board's jurisdiction for final approval. Our interviews with middle managers made it clear that the board plays an important role in approving or disapproving the proposals, suggestions, and projects they generate. Since most managers have little formal contact with board members, they have few opportunities for establishing alliances with important members. As a whole, the body retains considerable veto power within the organization.

The consensus is that the board's role is to maintain the mission of Healthco: to provide health care in the spirit of "Christian compassion" through services to communities that might otherwise not have access to medical treatment facilities. In line with this goal, the board's interests may lie in maintaining the organization's present form, particularly in keeping the headquarters office in its current location with its regional orientation. Effectiveness for this constituency is gauged primarily by Healthco's ability to continue its basic services and keep alive the values and religious commitment of its founders.

Healthco's managers represent another significant constituency within the organization; however, they tend to fall along a dividing line of tenure and professionalism. Several managers have grown up with the organization and some, in fact, whose parents also made careers within Healthco, are "second generation." During the past five years, a large number of managers and professionals have joined Healthco, in most cases bringing in greater expertise and professional training. As one person we interviewed commented, "Everyone here is either sixty years old or twenty years old."

The recent generation of managers is clearly trying to move the organization in a direction compatible with the increased demands placed on health care organizations for more sophisticated technology, managerial techniques, and methods. In their view, the organization's future depends on its ability to offer high-quality medical services while controlling costs. This involves adopting new forms of office technology and automation, reaching out into the environment for new resources (through grants and cooperative ventures), and, most important, questioning the organization's current direction and shape. This last point is crucial, since managers within this constituency are considering moving Healthco toward a holding company, perhaps through merger with other multiunit systems.

The second managerial constituent group consists of middle managers who have been with the organization for more than five years. They are clearly less aggressive and politically oriented, more likely to conform to existing standards and the current mission than to explore new opportunities and a change in orientation. However, these managers are caught in a nexus of change and somewhat subtle tension as pressures mount to alter the existing structure and direction. As one representative manager commented, "I'm a company man, I guess, but I can see things changing. I'm loyal and I expect people to be the same." Persons in this constituency appear to be relatively powerless in their jobs. They express great concern and dissatisfaction over their inability to obtain resources, to get reliable information on various parts of the health care system, and to develop strong working relationships with their peers.

The final constituency that emerged in our interviews with Healthco members encompassed those managers serving as administrators of local hospitals and nursing home facilities. This field component of the organization is clearly distinct and functions relatively autonomously. The chief concerns of these managers are twofold: managing and controlling their own facilities, and developing and maintaining effective relations with their communities. Although the home office is likely to move the administrators around to various facilities on a semiregular basis, the administrator's position and ties to the immediate community are of great concern. The local area serves as an important resource base through both fund-raising efforts and the time contributed by participants in the facility's local board of directors. Hostile relations with the community must be avoided since bad press and negative community reactions toward the facility place undue pressure on the administrator. As might be expected,

the focus on effectiveness in the field was limited and concerned primarily the local environment rather than the overall health care system.

Although Healthco has an officially promulgated mission statement, each major constituency defines the mission and overall strategy in terms of its own interests. The official statement covers such areas as the organization's commitment to high-quality medical service, adherence to religious ideals, a declaration of nondiscrimination, and concern with cost-effectiveness and fiscal responsibility. This publicly stated mission is most congruent with the interests of the board of directors and indicates the important historical tradition the group seeks to continue.

In a nonprofit system such as Healthco, however, where the interests of the major constituencies are diverse both politically and geographically, it is difficult for the organization to find a focal mission and strategy upon which members can agree. Effectiveness becomes a key issue since it is also difficult to decide which areas in the organization are central to the mission and which require evaluation to determine strategic concerns, let alone which process of measurement is appropriate. Persons in the recently hired management constituency are concerned with making Healthco into a holding company and with the future of the nursing homes. For some it is questionable whether the organization should even continue to operate such facilities in the future. However, there is at present no central arena in which such issues might be decided. Most of the discussion takes place at the boundaries of constituencies, where individual members and constituency spokepersons exchange views with one another but do not make decisions or try to gather information on alternative perspectives.

The argument has been made that in for-profit organizations economic criteria dominate decision making, but such criteria are far from superordinate in the case of a nonprofit like Healthco. Here there are competing criteria (religious values and tradition, the primacy of local community needs and interests, and so on), and each one, it has been argued, has been vital to the organization's overall level of effectiveness in the past. As a result, both current strategy and future direction remain unclear and unresolved, although the members of each constituency are keen on seeing a focused strategy emerge.

Organization Effectiveness and the Process of Innovation

We argued that dilemmas of performance measurement increase rigidities for nonprofit organizations. We examined this issue by auditing the amount of innovation and focusing on Healthco's capacity to develop and implement new policies, new services, new organizational structures, and new methods of doing the work. Innovation is a crucial element of organizational effectiveness because it addresses the organization's potential to meet future demands, to take advantage of opportunities and resources within the environment, and to use resources (both human and material) to generate new products and services. We had two empirical referents for studying innovation within the organization: the individual employees who generate and carry out innovative ideas, and the system-level elements that may be at work to support or discourage employees in their innovations.

To measure the overall level of innovation we interviewed respondents about their accomplishments and categorized these into two groups: those considered innovative (because the new idea was implemented and put into practice) and those considered part of the basic and more routine job. Using this innovation index we found that the overall level of innovation was slightly over 50 percent or moderate (for a discussion of this methodology, see Kanter 1983). Innovation was also concentrated in two areas: the development of new methods for doing work (new technologies, approaches, techniques) and new opportunities (mostly new products or services).

At the system level at Healthco there were at least three rather striking structural elements that encouraged innovation. First, innovation was far more likely when there was a significant amount of senior-level management sponsorship, interest, and support for the accomplishments of middle-level managers and professionals. This often involved persons at the top directing their subordinates to produce certain results, leaving it to their discretion to invent and develop the actual methods. Second, innovation was more likely to occur when teamwork and collaborative mechanisms existed that brought together individuals from across internal organizational boundaries and functions. In most cases this occurred through such formal vehicles as established task forces, committees, and review boards. Finally, when external resources were widely available to managers and professionals, they were more likely to attempt innovation and succeed in completing it. This included their having access to external expertise and assistance through consultants, the academic community, and their counterparts in other hospital organizations, as well as community-level support. (In the case of field administrators this last included public commitment and interest as well as funding.)

In addition, some critical factors worked to systematically discourage innovation throughout the organization. The first involved various forms of resistance to managerial accomplishments, of both an active and a passive nature. Passive forms of opposition were seen in the home office and included a lack of commitment on the part of other staff (mostly peers and those higher in the organization) and foot-dragging on decisions. Managers in the field were likely to encounter active and passive forms of resistance to their work and so faced more direct forms of conflict and often hostile reactions from their local community.

A number of managers also commented on conditions discouraging attempts at innovation that we may summarize as a widespread form of powerlessness. This was due to the managers' possessing little control over important forms of resources (such as money and staff), their difficulties in obtaining adequate amounts of reliable information (of both a technical and political nature), and their weak ties to other managers who might have been helpful in the innovation process. This last factor was most evident in the general absence of working relations among peers within the organization—persons at the same level, whether within or outside of functional departments.

And finally, a characteristic of Healthco that appears to dissuade managers from pursuing innovations is a lack of rewards and recognition. The only formal recognition available to employees is a citation for completing a five-year increment of service. No rewards are provided to either individuals or teams for distinguished efforts or contributions, and managers who receive a salary increase feel it has little connection with their performance on the job.

At the individual level, we also evaluated managerial effectiveness in pursuing innovation. For instance, we found evidence that middle-level managers take little initiative in generating new ideas or projects, often relying on directions or suggestions from above or from outside consultants. Many were also weak in political skills, or the capacity for identifying and using available power sources and supporters, managing conflict, or making exchanges and promises to obtain necessary resources.

As a result of these issues, Healthco's effectiveness in stimulating and creating innovation was limited. Persons in almost every constituency were affected by some significant widespread conditions in Healthco's structure and culture. Not only did this keep the amount of innovation at a moderate level; it segmented the constituencies in a way that made it difficult for them to come together and address issues related to the organization's effectiveness.

Healthco as a Nonprofit Service Organization

Much of the distinctive character of Healthco may be attributed to its status as a nonprofit organization providing direct services. Therefore, we can identify some key factors that separate Healthco from profit-making organizations. First, the use of financial criteria in making decisions is not as evident as it would be in for-profit companies. One manager commented, "For years, we never used a budget." Another remarked that requests for major expenditures of money (made to a senior officer) never involved estimations of final costs, only the start-up costs and the perceived benefits.

Second, managers perceived the organization to be less concerned with financial objectives or bottom-line measures of performance than with human values and an observable commitment to Christian compassion and service. Finally, there appeared to be no formal financial incentives or rewards available to employees. The perception that individual financial benefits or incentives were unavailable is illustrated in the comment by one person that "we couldn't give bonuses here to people because we're nonprofit."

The other primary attribute of Healthco that renders it distinctive is its service-oriented technology. This is seen first in its lack of focus on product development, a characteristic that may be declining over time as certain product areas are identified and given greater attention (for example, a chemical dependency program and a facility for the education of severely disabled children). One result is that managers may tend to remain generalists, without developing specific forms of expertise in what could be construed as potential product or service areas (like long-term care, acute care, or special programs). Similarly, according to certain members, the organization is slowly developing professional expertise in what might be construed as product-related support areas such as marketing, project management and control, and financial systems.

DILEMMAS OF NONPROFIT PERFORMANCE MEASUREMENT

At Healthco we see in operation the characteristics constraining a nonprofit organization's ability to assess its performance and use the data it gets to make appropriate adjustments.

Generally, nonprofit organizations tend to provide services rather than manufacture goods, but service is often intangible and hard to measure (Thompson & McEwen 1958; Newman & Wallender 1978). Indeed, outcomes in some cases may be inherently unknowable (Drucker 1968). This issue is, of course, shared with for-profit service organizations as well (and there are those who argue that *all* organizations are at root providing services, even if they do it via selling goods).

But the intangibility of the measurement of services is compounded in not-for-profit organizations by the weaker influence clients—the recipients of services—have on their operations compared to the customers of profit-making organizations. Since the income of nonprofit organizations depends only partially (if at all) on fees for services, then marketlike measures of performance oriented around client- or customer-related measures tend to be rejected outright or to play a nondominant role. The needs of donors (of money or time) may play a much bigger role. Although it is often argued that the performance of service organizations should be a function of consumer involvement and satisfaction (Gartner & Riessman 1974), some nonprofits face little competition, and the market is virtually unlimited. With little competition, recipients of services do not tend to provide feedback (Selby 1978). A nonprofit like Healthco may receive feedback only during periods of growth, when efforts are made to build new facilities in communities not served by any hospital. At such times there may be two or three competing health care organizations, but the competition is framed in terms of *promises* for services, since nothing can be delivered until one organization is selected and begins its operations. Of course, as nonprofits and for-profits start to compete head-on, as is happening in health care in some communities, we can expect the two kinds of organizations to begin to converge in their performance measures.

Second, goal conflicts interfere with rational planning (Wheeler & Hunger 1984). Because of the existence of divergent goals and objectives, owing to the many constitu-encies involved and particularly to the dependence on donations unrelated to services, management may refrain from stating the organization's goals in anything but broad terms for fear of alienating major donors. There is no clear market check, and the influence of clients is reduced because clients may not be the organization's major source of funds. These two factors permit goal ambiguity and diversity of values to persist. But without clear specific statements of intended results, it is difficult to assess performance. In general, goal accomplishment is difficult when feedback from the environment is relatively fuzzy and signals indicating unacceptable goals are less effective and take longer to come (Thompson & McEwen 1958).

Third, the focus in nonprofit organizations is likely to shift away from output to input. Rather than focus on results (delivery of services, attainment of goals), these organizations are likely to concentrate on resource attraction. Since nonprofit organizations tend to provide services that are hard to measure, there is rarely a new bottom line. Thus, planning becomes more concerned with fund-raising or resource inputs than with service, in part because of the greater ease of measuring the former. Although the success of nonprofits rests in part on resource attraction, products or specific benefits do not tend to be available to donors (Shapiro 1973), and therefore performance criteria for resource allocation (service delivery) might be unrelated to criteria for resource attraction. In profit-making organizations, generating profits is an end in itself, with less interest in their allocation, but in nonprofits generating funds is only a step, and allocating them is key.

As a consequence, a fourth characteristic develops. The existence of ambiguous operating objectives creates opportunities for internal politics and goal displacement, for loose coupling between official or stated mission and operative goals. Because objectives are stated vaguely and planning concentrates on resource acquisition, managers inside the organization gain considerable leeway in their activities, opening up the possibility for political maneuvering or for ignoring the needs of clients while trying to please powerful donors—or for playing one constituency off against another.

In any nonprofit organization with a wide gap in the incentives, personnel, and procedures available for resource allocation (or service delivery), we can expect either a high degree of conflict (reflected in arguments about performance measures) or attempts to insulate donors or funders from allocators or deliverers (reflected in statements about professionalism and the need for independence), either of which tends to reduce the willingness to have performance measured at all.

Fifth, in nonprofit organizations like Healthco, where professionals play important roles, professional standards create rigidities and interfere with new responses to changing constituency needs. Where professionals hold power, as many sociologists have pointed out, they often operate to maintain a monopoly on delivery of particular services by restricting entry, requiring that preexisting standards be met that reinforce repetition of past behavior, and erecting legal barriers to clients seeking services elsewhere. Professional power of this kind flourishes in nonprofit organizations because of the absence of direct market tests of client satisfaction and because of the willingness of donors to encourage organizations to repeat behaviors and activities even when the clients appear to be less than satisfied. Witness the desire of university alumni donors to maintain the university as they remember it, whether or not it meets today's student needs; this desire reinforces the power of the faculty to declare that they know better than the students what the students need (although faculty standards may also conflict with alumni desires).

Furthermore, the worthiness of a nonprofit's activities may tend to be assumed, so that its mere existence is seen as indicative of "good works" or "social-moral contributions" and there is no need to show returns and results (Drucker 1968). Whereas financially weak for-profit organizations might find greater difficulty raising capital for continuing operations because of its financial problems, financially weak nonprofit organizations might use that circumstance as an occasion for rallying donors to contribute additional funds to shore up its operations—simply because of the belief in the worthiness of the organization. Indeed, to some donors the organization's very difficulties might provide confirmation of the need for its existence—and the more problems it encounters fulfilling its mission because of the new wrinkles in goal attainment, then the more vigorously its efforts should be pursued. Since nonprofits tend to believe in their own functioning, failure to achieve goals is taken not as a sign of weakness in the organization but as a sign that efforts should be intensified.

The existence of this impressive set of dilemmas may account for the virtual absence of control systems in human service organizations—even the separate elements of control, such as measuring effectiveness and efficiency or monitoring and evaluating performance (Herzlinger 1979). But the difficulty of assessing performance should not deter managers and boards of nonprofit organizations from trying to set objectives and assess results—to determine if they are indeed "doing well while doing good."

The ideal performance assessment system in a nonprofit organization would acknowledge the existence of multiple constituencies and build measures around all of them. It would acknowledge the gap between grand mission and operative goals and develop objectives for both the short term and the long term. It would guard against falling into any of the traps outlined in this chapter by developing an explicit but complex array of tests of performance that balance clients and donors, board and professionals, groups of managers, and any of the other constituencies with a stake in the organization.

A balanced approach would provide the data to help the organization know whether it is "doing well" on any of the dimensions of performance with which an active constituency might be concerned. Conflicts between measures can be better adjudicated when the data are clear. The ultimate test of performance for a nonprofit organization is, of course, whether those representatives of society that allowed it to join the category of "do-good" organizations (starting with the Internal Revenue Service) continue to feel it deserves this status. The test lies beyond the scope of management science and in the realm of social values.

REFERENCES

Aldrich, H. 1979. *Organizations and Environments.* Englewood Cliffs, N.J.: Prentice-Hall.

Argyris, Chris. 1962. *Interpersonal Competence and Organizational Effectiveness.* Homewood, Ill.: Irwin.

Astin, Alexander W. 1968. *The College Environment.* Washington, D.C.: American Council on Education.

———. 1971. *Predicting Academic Performance in College.* Riverside, N.J.: Free Press.

———. 1977. *Four Critical Years.* San Francisco: Jossey-Bass.

Bidwell, Charles E., and John D. Kasarda. 1975. "School District Organization and Student Achievement." *American Sociological Review* 40:55–70.

Bluedorn, A. C. 1980. "Cutting the Gordian Knot: A Critique of the Effectiveness Tradition in Organizational Research. *Sociol. Soc. Res.* (July):64.

Bowen, Howard R., and Gordon K. Douglas. 1971. *Efficiency in Liberal Education: A Study of Comparative Instructional Costs for Different Ways of Organizing Teaching-Learning in a Liberal Arts College.* New York: McGraw-Hill.

Bower, Joseph L. 1977. "Effective Public Management." *Harvard Business Review* (March-April). (Available in *HBR* reprint series, Management of Nonprofit Organizations, Part 2.)

Burns. T., and Stalker, G. M. 1960. *The Management of Innovation.* London: Tavistock.

Cameron, Kim. 1978. "Measuring Organizational Effectiveness in Institutions of Higher Education." *Administrative Science Quarterly* 23 (December):604–32.

Campbell, John P. 1977. "On the Nature of Organizational Effectiveness." In *New Perspectives on Organizational Effectiveness,* edited by Paul S. Goodman and Johannes M. Pennings, 13–55. San Francisco: Jossey-Bass.

Connolly, T., E. J. Conlon, and S. J. Deutsch. 1980. "Organizational Effectiveness: A Multiple-Constituency Approach." *Academy of Management Review* 5:211–17.

Cummings, Larry L. 1977. "Emergence of the Instrumental Organization." In *New Perspectives on Organizational Effectiveness,* edited by Paul S. Goodman and Johannes M. Pennings, 56–62. San Francisco: Jossey-Bass.

Cummings, Thomas G., and Edmond C. Molloy. 1977. *Improving Productivity and the Quality of Work Life.* New York: Praeger Publishers.

Cunningham, J. Barton. 1977. "Approaches to the Evaluation of Organizational Effectiveness." *Academy of Management Review* 2, no. 3 (July):463–74.

———. 1978. "A Systems-Resource Approach for Evaluating Organizational Effectiveness." *Human Relations* 31:631–56.

Drucker, Peter. 1968. *The Age of Discontinuity.* New York: Harper & Row.

Elmore, Richard F. 1978. "Organizational Models of Social Program Implementation." *Public Policy* 26, no. 2 (Spring): 185–229.

Epstein, Marc J., Eric G. Flamholtz, and John J. McDonough. 1977. *Corporate Social Performance: The Measurement of Product and Service Contributions.* New York: National Association of Accountants.

Etzioni, Amitai. 1964. *Modern Organizations.* Englewood Cliffs, N.J.: Prentice-Hall.

Farris, George F. 1975. "Chicken, Eggs, and Productivity in Organizations." *Organizational Dynamics* 3, no. 4 (Spring): 2–16.

Feldman, Kenneth A., and Theodore M. Newcomb. 1969. *The Impact of College on Students.* San Francisco: Jossey-Bass.

Freeman, John, Glenn R. Carroll, and Michael T. Hannan. 1983. "The Liability of Newness: Age Dependence in Organizational Death Rates." *American Sociological Review* 48:692–710.

Galbraith, Jay R. 1977. *Organization Design.* Reading, Mass.: Addison-Wesley.

Gartner, Alan, and Frank Riessman. 1974. *The Service Society and the Consumer Vanguard.* New York: Harper & Row.

Georgopolous, Basil S., and Arnold S. Tannenbaum. 1957. "The Study of Organizational Effectiveness." *American Sociological Review* 22:534–40.

Gibson, James L., John M. Ivanevich, and James H. Donnelly, Jr. 1973. *Organizations: Structure, Process, Behavior.* Dallas: BPI.

Gross, Edwards. 1968. "Universities as Organizations: A Research Approach." *American Sociological Review* 33:518–44.

Hall, Richard P. 1978. "Conceptual, Methodological, and Moral Issues in the Study of Organizational Effectiveness." Working Paper, Department of Sociology, SUNY-Albany.

Hannan, Michael T., and John Freeman. 1977. "Obstacles to Comparative Studies." In *New Perspectives on Organizational Effectiveness,* edited by Paul S. Goodman and Johannes M. Pennings, 106–31. San Francisco: Jossey-Bass.

Hartmark, Lief. 1975. *Accountability, Efficiency, and Effectiveness in the State University of New York.* SUNY-Albany: Comparative Development Studies Center.

Herzlinger, R. E. 1979. "Management Control Systems in Human Service Organizations." Paper delivered at Conference on Human Service Organization and Organization Theory, Center for Advanced Study in the Behavioral Sciences, Stanford, Calif., 2–3 March.

Hirsch, Paul M. 1975. "Organizational Effectiveness and the Institutional Environment." *Administrative Science Quarterly* 20:327–44.

Kanter, Rosabeth Moss. 1972. *Commitment and Community: Communes and Utopias in Sociological Perspective.* Cambridge, Mass.: Harvard University Press.

———. 1980. "Power and Change in Organizations: Setting Intellectual Directions for Organizational Analysis." Presented at the Plenary Session of the American Sociological Association Annual Meeting, New York.

———. 1983. *The Change Masters.* New York: Simon & Schuster.

Kanter, Rosabeth Moss, and Barry A. Stein, eds. 1979. "Growing Pains." In *Life in Organizations: Workplaces as People Experience Them.* New York: Basic Books.

Katz, Daniel, and Robert L. Kahn. 1978. *The Social Psychology of Organizations.* New York: Wiley.

Kimberly, J. 1979. "Issues in the Creation of Organizations: Initiation, Innovation and Institutionalization." *Academic Management Journal* 22:437–67.

Kirchoff, Bruce A. 1977. "Organizational Effectiveness Measurement and Policy Research." *Academy of Management Review* 2, no. 3 (July):347–55.

Lawler, Edward E., Douglas T. Hall, and Greg R. Oldham. 1974. "Organizational Climate: Relationship to Organizational Structure, Process, and Performance." *Organizational Behavior and Human Performance* 11, no. 1 (February):139–55.

Lawrence, P. R., and J. W. Lorsch. 1967. *Organization and Environment.* Boston: Harvard Business School Div. Res.

Lefton, M. 1975. "Client Characteristics and Organizational Functioning: An Interorganizational Focus." In *Interorganization Theory,* edited by A. R. Negandhi, 128–41. Kent, Ohio: Compar. Admin. Res. Inst.

Leifer, R., and A. Delbecq. 1978. "Organizational/ Environmental Interchange: A Model of Boundary-Spanning Activity." *Academic Management Review* 3, no. 1:40–51.

Mahoney, T. A., and P. J. Frost. 1974. "The Role of Technology in Models of Organizational Effectiveness." *Organizational Behavior and Human Performance* 11, no. 1:122–39.

Mahoney, Thomas A., and William Weitzel. 1969. "Managerial Models of Organizational Effectiveness." *Administrative Science Quarterly* 14:357–65.

Manns, Curtis L., and James G. March. 1978. "Financial Adversity, Internal Competition, and Curriculum Change in a University." *Administrative Science Quarterly* 23 (December): 541–552.

March, J. G., and G. P. Olsen. 1976. *Ambiguity and Choice in Organizations.* Bergen, Norway: Bergen Universitetsforlaget.

Marx, Gary T. 1976. "Alternative Measures of Police Performance." In *Criminal Justice Research,* edited by E. Viant, 179–93. Lexington, Mass.: Heath.

———. 1974. "Ironies of Social Control: Authorities as Possible Contributors to Deviance through Non-Enforcement, Covert Facilitation, and Escalation.'' Paper presented at meetings of the International Sociological Association, Toronto.

Meeth, R. L. 1974. *Quality Education for Less Money*. San Francisco: Jossey-Bass.

Meyer, John W., and Brian Rowan. 1977. ''Institutionalized Organizations: Formal Structure as Myth and Ceremony.'' *American Journal of Sociology* 83, no. 2:340–63.

Mintzberg, Henry. 1983. *Power In and Around Organizations*. Englewood Cliffs, N.J.: Prentice-Hall.

Newman, William H., and Harvey W. Wallender, III. 1978. ''Managing Not-for-Profit Enterprises.'' *Academy of Management Review* 3, no. 1 (January):24–32.

O'Neill, June. 1971. *Resource Use in Higher Education: Trends in Outputs and Inputs*. New York: McGraw Hill.

Osborn, R. N., and J. D. Hunt. 1974. ''Environment and Organizational Effectiveness.'' *Admin. Sci. Q.* 19:231–46.

Ouchi, William. 1981. *Theory Z*. Reading, Mass.: Addison-Wesley.

Pennings, Johannes M., and Paul S. Goodman. 1977. ''Toward a Workable Framework.'' In *New Perspectives on Organizational Effectiveness*, edited by Paul S. Goodman and Johannes M. Pennings, 146–84. San Francisco: Jossey-Bass.

Perrow, Charles. 1981. ''Disintegrating Social Sciences.'' *New York University Education Quarterly* 12, no. 2 (Winter):2–9.

———. 1977. ''Three Types of Effectiveness Studies.'' In *New Perspectives on Organizational Effectiveness*, edited by Paul S. Goodman and Johannes M. Pennings, 96–105. San Francisco: Jossey-Bass.

Peters, Thomas J., and Robert Waterman. 1982. *In Search of Excellence*. New York: Harper & Row.

Pfeffer, Jeffrey. 1981. *Power in Organizations*. Boston: Pitman.

Pfeffer, Jeffrey, and Gerald R. Salancik. 1977. ''Organization Design: The Case for a Coalitional Model of Organizations.'' *Organization Dynamics* (Autumn):15–29.

Price, James L. 1968. *Organizational Effectiveness: An Inventory of Propositions*. Homewood, Ill.: Irwin.

Rushing, W. 1974. ''Differences in Profit and Nonprofit Organizations: A Study in Effectiveness and Efficiency in General Shortstay Hospitals.'' *Admin. Sci. Q.* 19:474–84.

Schneider, B., J. J. Parkington, and V. M. Buxton. 1980.

''Employee and Customer Perceptions of Service in Banks.'' *Admin. Sci. Q.* 25:252–67.

Scott, W. Richard. 1977. ''Effectiveness of Organizational Effectiveness Studies.'' In *New Perspectives on Organizational Effectiveness*, edited by Paul S. Goodman and Johannes Pennings, 63–95. San Francisco: Jossey-Bass.

———. 1978. ''Measuring Output in Hospitals.'' Stanford University, Background paper for Panel to Review Productivity Measures, May.

Scott, W. Richard, Ann Barry Flood, Wayne Ewy, and William H. Forrest, Jr. 1978. ''Organizational Effectiveness: Studying the Quality of Surgical Care in Hospitals.'' In *Environments and Organization*, edited by M. Meyer and Associates. San Francisco: Jossey-Bass.

Seashore, Stanley E. 1977. ''The Measurement of Organizational Effectiveness.'' Paper presented at the University of Minnesota, Minneapolis (cited in Campbell 1977).

Selby, Cecily Cannan. 1978. ''Better Performance from 'Nonprofits.' '' *Harvard Business Review* 56 (September-October):92–98.

Shapiro, Benson P. 1973. ''Marketing for Nonprofit Organizations.'' *Harvard Business Review* (September-October). (Available in *HBR* reprint series, Management of Nonprofit Organizations.)

Sills, David. 1957. *The Volunteers*. Glencoe, Ill.: Free Press.

Stinchcombe, Arthur L. 1965. ''Social Structure and Organizations.'' In *Handbook of Organizations*, edited by James G. March, 142–93. Chicago: Rand-McNally.

Thompson, James D. 1967. *Organizations in Action*. New York: McGraw-Hill.

Thompson, James D., and William J. McEwen. 1958. ''Organizational Goals and Environment.'' *American Sociological Review* 23 (1958):23–31.

Warner, W. Keith. 1967. ''Problems in Measuring the Goal Attainment of Voluntary Organizations.'' *Adult Education* 19, no. 1 (Fall):3–15.

Weick, Karl E. 1977. ''Re-Punctuating the Problem.'' In *New Perspectives on Organizational Effectiveness*, edited by Paul S. Goodman and Johannes M. Pennings, 193–225. San Francisco: Jossey-Bass.

Yuchtman, Ephraim, and Stanley E. Seashore. 1967. ''A System Resource Approach to Organizational Effectiveness.'' *American Sociological Review* 32:891–903.

10

Executive Leadership in Nonprofit Organizations

DENNIS R. YOUNG

Scholars have devoted substantial study recently to the questions of how the management of organizations differs from one economic sector to another. To date, however, attention has been focused primarily on managing in government versus managing in business, largely ignoring the private nonprofit sector. For example, in *The Two Faces of Management,* Bower (1983) distinguishes technological from political styles of management—the latter being correlated (imperfectly) with high-level public-sector leadership, whereas the former is more characteristic of the functioning of business executives. Other contributions by Lynn (1981) and Perry and Kraemer (1983) focus on public management and how it differs from business management.

Comparisons of management across sectors are not simply of academic interest but bear on important policies, operational issues, and educational questions. For example, to what extent can business methods be used to improve the management of public and nonprofit organizations? How can leaders of the various sectors, each acclimated to different administrative environments, learn to appreciate one another's problems well enough to interact effectively as these sectors become more interdependent? These considerations lie at the heart of the current debate (Weinberg 1983) on whether management of government organizations should be taught in business schools or management schools, or whether it requires a separate institution with its own methods, values, and perspectives.

Though the literature focuses on business versus government, the question of how the executive function in nonprofits resembles or differs from that of government and business organizations is just as interesting conceptually, as important to the development of effective methods of administration, as significant to effective interaction among sectors, and as relevant to the training of future executives.[1] Thus, this chapter will explore on two levels how the problems of nonprofit chief executives compare with those of chief executives in other sectors. Most of the points made here will apply to other high-level managers as well.[2] On the

I would like to thank Woody Powell and John Simon for their comments on earlier drafts.

1. In the process of developing master's-level pilot programs in generic nonprofit management education, a small cadre of contemporary educators has had to consider the institutional context—business schools, public administration schools, or independent programs—in which such training can most effectively take place. Pilot programs utilizing various contexts have been developed, or are under development, at the University of Colorado at Denver, the University of San Francisco, the University of Missouri–Kansas City, Case Western Reserve University, the New School for Social Research, the State University of New York at Stony Brook, and elsewhere.

2. The discussion here draws on two principal research projects underwritten by the Yale University Program on Non-Profit Organizations (PONPO). The first is a study of entrepreneurship, published in a book of theory of nonprofit-sector behavior (Young 1983) and a book of case studies (Young 1985). Selected cases from the latter book are supplemented here by three additional unpublished cases of ventures in the proprietary human-service sector (Young 1981). The second research project, on which discussion of the inside role of executive leadership is based, is a survey of personnel practices in nonprofit organizations (Young 1984). The analysis of the internal problems of executive leadership is based on research in a cross section of fields including nonprofit hospitals, nursing homes, community health centers, theaters, opera companies, orchestras, dance companies, museums, social service and mental health agencies, fund-raising charities, and colleges and universities. The analysis of external leadership (entrepreneurship) draws on research more specifically focused on the fields of social and mental health services for children and youth. Throughout the discussion, an effort is made to compare consistently across proprietary, nonprofit, and government sectors by "holding the industry constant." Thus, comparisons of entrepreneurship, for example, are made within the general field of social and mental health services. This restriction reflects a basic principle of research design and also sensitivity to a common criticism of other discussions of differences in managing public- versus private-sector organizations—namely, that they tend to compare apples and oranges in the nature of services offered.

first level—their outside function—nonprofit executives will be considered in their role as entrepreneurs, as initiators and developers of new programs and resources. On the second level—their inside function—they will be viewed in their role as managers of people, with responsibility for maintaining incentives for employee performance.[3]

FUNCTIONS OF THE EXECUTIVE

A chief executive is responsible for managing the relationships between the organization and its social, economic, and political environment and for setting the tone and maintaining control of the organization's internal operations. Each of these broad, interrelated areas of responsibility consists, of course, of many component functions. Externally, relationships with trustees or stockholders, customers or clients, regulators, and funders or investors must be maintained on a day-to-day basis and cultivated in special circumstances. The executive must anticipate problems stemming from environmental change and identify and exploit new opportunities. Internally, he must allocate resources and make decisions concerning the work force, evaluate the performance of departments, make personnel decisions—recruitment, promotions and rewards, transfers, and discharges—attend to employees' morale, articulate plans and policies, and deal with internal crises.

Our focusing on entrepreneurship and personnel management permits a conceptual coalescing of many of the component functions, providing a compact comparison of nonprofit versus proprietary and governmental executive leadership. In particular, entrepreneurship establishes the circumstances under which an organization can draw sustenance from its environment in exchange for services rendered; personnel management maintains the incentives for workers to contribute their efforts for organizational purposes. Thus, entrepreneurship helps create the surpluses from which internal incentives for participation are generated. The guidance of this system of incentives generation and distribution is the heart of executive leadership as understood by Barnard (1938), Simon (1959), and other pioneers of organizational research.

Entrepreneurship

The term *entrepreneurship* has been defined in a variety of ways, though it is most commonly associated with the organization of new ventures in the business sector. (For reviews of different conceptions and definitions of entrepreneurship, see Peterson [1981] and Young [1983]. Key contributions to the literature include Schumpeter [1949], Collins & Moore [1970], Kirzner [1973], Cole [1959], Josephson [1962], Marshall [1964], and Coase [1937].) Generically, however, entrepreneurship is an activity characteristic of organizations in all sectors. Following Schumpeter (1949), we can define it

as the organizing and catalytic effort responsible for bringing about new economic activity (new goods or services) or the provisions of these products in some innovative way or, in Schumpeter's words, bringing about "new combinations." Entrepreneurship requires the melding of ideas and opportunities with resources and overcoming whatever constraints lie between the conception and the successful implementation of a project.[4] The activity may manifest itself as the formation or spin-off of new organizations or the cultivation of new projects or programs within existing organizations.[5]

Though its role is not fully appreciated outside the context of business, entrepreneurship is important to the vitality of organizations in all sectors because the environments of all organizations are constantly changing, often in a manner that either threatens their sources of sustenance or creates new opportunities for development—in either case, setting the stage for entrepreneurship. Some organizations are especially vulnerable to such changes, whereas others are better protected or insulated (Hirschman 1970). Vulnerability depends on such factors as market share, legal mandates, resource reserves, and supporting constituencies, but most organizations, whether vulnerable or not, ignore changes in their environments only at their peril.[6] Otherwise, they will eventually fail or need rejuvenation (often by new leadership) through fresh enterprising activity. Indeed, a prime source of inspiration for entrepreneurial behavior in organizations in all sectors is the need to solve a serious—often environmentally related—organizational problem (Young 1983, 1985; Peterson 1981).

Personnel Management

The performance of an organization obviously depends substantially on the quality of its work force and how well its members are motivated to contribute to the organization's purposes. Thus, a major challenge to executive leadership is to recruit desired employees in the labor market and adminis-

---

3. See Vroom (1983) for discussion of this dichotomy of responsibilities of organizational leaders. For additional perspectives on the functions of organizational leadership, see Stogdill (1981).

4. The broad definition of *entrepreneurship* specified here is not universally subscribed to. Within the nonprofit sector, the term has been more narrowly interpreted by some to connote commercial activity designed to provide extra revenues for nonprofit organizations. While the definition used here includes such commercial activity, the implications of the two definitions are different. As Crimmons and Keil (1983) suggest, the enterprise function, interpreted narrowly, can be compartmentalized; indeed, they suggest that nonprofits should employ separate enterprise directors—a simple extension of the commonly employed position of development director. In our broad definition, however, entrepreneurship is a more intrinsic function of executive leadership, not simply the facilitation of commercial activity.

5. The latter has been called "intrapreneurship" (see Kanter 1983). Peterson (1981) also points out that organizations can structure opportunities for entrepreneurship in a variety of ways—through franchising and contracting, establishing entrepreneurial divisions, or installing enterprise as a general operating milieu.

6. Even organizational giants such as the Bell System, H.E.W., New York City, and Chrysler Corporation, not to mention hundreds of other private and nonprofit organizations, have not been immune to environmental change in recent years.

ter evaluation and reward systems that will effectively retain good performers and maintain the morale and incentives for the work force as a whole.

Nonprofit organizations are highly concentrated in the service areas of the economy and hence tend to be labor intensive (see chapter 4 in this volume). For instance, philanthropic (tax-deductible, private) nonprofit organizations spend 60 percent of their annual budgets on salaries and benefits (Rudney 1981). Thus, the inside function of the nonprofit chief executive as ultimate manager of the organization's human resources is critical.

Nonprofits and other kinds of organizations differ in important ways in the problems of personnel management, although these differences have not been fully explored in the literature. (For discussions of the subject, see Nash [1983] and Slavin [1978].) As elaborated below, nonprofits have certain comparative handicaps as well as advantages in offering benefits to attract or retain specific types of employees. Moreover, the management of nonprofits is often disadvantaged in measuring employees' performance or in offering or manipulating rewards or penalties to motivate them.

THE EXECUTIVE AS ENTREPRENEUR

How does the entrepreneurial function in nonprofit organizations differ from that in counterpart governmental and proprietary organizations? Elsewhere, I have focused on differences in motivation for enterprise and on the processes of screening through which entrepreneurs with alternative values tend to sort themselves out among sectors and industries (Young 1983).[7] In this chapter, however, the factors inhibiting venture activity (the risks and constraints facing entrepreneurs) are the subject. Thus we ask, if an entrepreneuring executive wishes to engage in a project for whatever reason, what difficulties and restraining forces does he face, and how do these differ by sector?

Some of the literature on the rationale for nonprofit organizations is informative here. For instance, as residual providers of public goods (Weisbrod 1975; Douglas 1983), nonprofits face special free-rider problems in generating financial support for the services they propose to offer. And, required to observe the prohibition against distributing financial surpluses to owners, nonprofits are distinctively limited in their abilities to raise capital (Hansmann 1981a). Still, the nonprofit sector has proven to be the fastest growing sector of the economy in recent years (Rudney 1981). Hence, the constraints on nonprofit entrepreneurship, although they may be different from those in other sectors, are not obviously more binding.[8] In an effort to ferret out the more subtle

differences in entrepreneurial constraints among sectors, the following discussion will use as its points of reference, nine case studies—three social and mental health service ventures in each of the three sectors. These cases are as follows:[9]

P1: the founding of a new proprietary residential school for emotionally fragile children in New Jersey in 1969. In this case, the headmaster of such a school for children with emotional problems was discharged by an owner with whom he had professional and personal differences; the headmaster went on to establish his own proprietary school, serving the same clientele as before. The new school allowed the headmaster to continue his professional career as his own boss and to enhance his economic livelihood.[10]

P2: the corporate evolution of a proprietary mental health agency for youth in Massachusetts in 1976. Here a clinical psychologist, in cooperation with a few professional and financial partners, established a proprietary mental health agency of which he became executive director. This development followed seven years of unstable and failed partnership arrangements that led the entrepreneur to recapitalize and reorganize his mental health service under a more formal corporate structure.[11]

P3: the establishment of a new residential unit for violent children on the campus of a large proprietary child-care agency in Florida in 1972. The development of a secure on-campus residence for temporary care and restraint of violent children reflected the need for a facility to segregate violence-prone children from others on an episodic basis and the difficulty of securing such services from off-campus institutions. This initiative was part of an overall effort of the entrepreneur to respond to a growing interstate market for serving difficult-to-place handicapped, emotionally disturbed, and older children.[12]

G1: the establishment of a new town youth bureau on Long Island in 1977. In this venture, a former college professor of social work singlemindedly pursued the establishment of a youth bureau in Brookhaven Township over a period of several years, succeeding after a change in town

---

7. This work on screening expands on the suggestion of Hansmann (1980) that entrepreneurs or managers sort themselves out between nonprofit and proprietary sectors according to their pecuniary and nonpecuniary preferences; it is consistent with the works of Weisbrod (1983) and Mirvis and Hackett (1983), which find systematic differences, respectively, in the motivation of lawyers and workers generally, employed in the nonprofit versus other sectors.

8. For general and theoretic discussions of nonprofit versus other

sector constraints, see Clarkson (1981) and Clarkson and Martin (1980). For further insights, see Legoretta and Young (1986) for a review of case studies of organizations that moved from the government or business sectors of the economy into the nonprofit sector. The latter analysis indicates that the nonprofit form offers greater flexibility to entrepreneurs originally located in government, while it provides a means of reducing long-term financial liability and retaining administrative control for proprietors in the business sector who seek to ensure continuity in the missions of their organizations.

9. These cases, described in detail in Young (1981, 1985), concern organizations firmly rooted in their own sectors and involve few if any explicit choices of sector. For an analysis of cases focused on sector transitions, see Legoretta and Young (1986).

10. See "Chartwell Manor" in Young (1981).

11. See "Institute for Family and Life Learning" in Young (1981).

12. See "Paisano Maximum Care Unit: Montanari Clinical School" in Young (1981).

administrations. The bureau underwrites an array of services for youth throughout the town. The entrepreneur became the youth bureau's first director.[13]

G2: the establishment of a program for runaway youth in the Huntington Town Youth Bureau on Long Island in 1976. Originally, idealistic youth bureau social workers had developed ad hoc arrangements to house runaway teenagers on a temporary basis, but they faced practical and legal problems. The encouragement of the youth bureau's director and federal grant opportunities eventually made possible the formalization and expansion of this sanctuary program.[14]

G3: the development of a new outpatient program in a New York State children's mental hospital on Long Island in 1974. A psychiatrist appointed to head the Sagamore Children's Center (mental hospital) set out to redefine its emphasis from inpatient to outpatient service, consistent with state-of-the-art professional thinking on services for retarded and autistic children. A timely federal grant opportunity was the catalyst for the project. The outpatient program succeeded for a time but dissipated when the grant expired and the entrepreneur left for another position.[15]

NP1: the establishment of a nonprofit foster care agency for older boys on Long Island in 1972. A core group of entrepreneurs left secure professional positions in a state hospital on Long Island to establish an agency for teenage boys whose needs they felt could not be adequately addressed in the state facility. Despite great start-up difficulties associated with government regulations, the new agency achieved stability within a few years.[16]

NP2: the development of a new program for disturbed children on the campus of a large voluntary child-care agency in New York in 1973. The executive director of the agency, working closely with the director of one of the agency's campuses, established a residential facility for children who were more violence-prone, emotionally disturbed, and ethnically mixed than the agency was used to serving. The new facility served as a wedge to stimulate reform in the agency as a whole, enabling it to serve the city's changing clientele more effectively.[17]

NP3: the formation of a corporate umbrella structure to coordinate a large successful nonprofit residential child-care agency in Florida in 1977. The agency's chief executive established the corporation in order to consolidate the finances and administration of separately incorporated campuses for girls' and boys' programs. The effort was part of an overall strategy to break a charitable trust that prohibited

coed programming and to put in place a more efficient structure for soliciting donations and facilitating agency growth.[18]

Risks

In the proprietary sector cases, financial risks are common yet sometimes nominal. In both P1 and P2, for example, the entrepreneurs invested much of their own time and money. However, the ventures were relatively uncontroversial, and banks and investors assumed most of the financial liability. And in both cases, if the ventures had failed, the entrepreneurs could fall back on other professional employment.

The case of P3 is a bit different. The entrepreneur here had more of his own wealth and a lifetime of effort invested, the venture itself was riskier, and there were no obvious avenues of alternative employment. If the volatile mix of clientele introduced to the residential campus as a result of the project had exploded, the viability of the whole enterprise could have been jeopardized. Although bankruptcy would not have meant impoverishment, it did promise major financial and psychic loss and legal entanglement.

The three governmental cases entail the assumption of a variety of personal risks. In G1, the entrepreneur put aside his professional career and endured substantial unemployment, financial sacrifice, and career interruption, with no solid assurance of success. In G2, the social workers, in their idealism and under pressures of a situation involving temporarily homeless teenagers, put themselves in legal jeopardy by setting up a shelter program that was not officially sanctioned. Though these workers were not executives, they operated with authorization of the youth bureau administration, which thus put itself at risk. In G3, the entrepreneur jeopardized her standing in the psychiatric profession, as well as her career as a health care administrator, by radically altering the balance of inpatient and outpatient services in her facility to the point where it introduced potentially dangerous instability into the inpatient program.

In the nonprofit cases, the risk to entrepreneurs are also varied. In NP1, the entrepreneurs gave up secure jobs and good incomes in government service for the uncertain compensation and instability of a fledgling nonprofit agency, with no assurance that they could return if the venture failed. Another risk in NP1 was more subtle. The entrepreneurs were testing their abilities to survive economically on their own, and they might have found themselves inadequate to the task. In NP2, the risks involved potential damage to professional reputations. If the introduction of violence-prone children into an otherwise conservative agency had led to a serious incident, the wisdom, professional reputation, and tenure of the executives involved would have been called into question by staff, trustees, and social work peers. In NP3, the project represented a long-term gamble that the court would overturn a restrictive trust and allow the orderly growth and diversification of the agency. The strategy was to

---

13. See "Brookhaven Youth Bureau" in Young (1985).

14. See "Sanctuary Program: Huntington Youth Bureau" in Young (1985).

15. See "Outpatient Clinic: Sagamore Children's Center" in Young (1985).

16. See "Melville House" in Young (1985).

17. See "Pleasantville Diagnostic Center: Jewish Child Care Association" in Young (1985).

18. See "Florida Sheriff Youth Fund, Inc." in Young (1985).

set up a new (nonprofit) corporation for each new program and ultimately argue that these arrangements were too cumbersome to administer, thus requiring consolidation. If the entrepreneur had lost this case, he would have been stuck with an unwieldy organizational structure and concomitant difficulties of administration.

Comparing these cases across sectors yields few clear-cut distinctions, and perhaps that is the surprising conclusion in view of the conventional wisdom that businessmen/entrepreneurs are the quintessential risk takers in our economy. Although the proprietary ventures all involved financial risk taking, the risks were not unique to this sector, nor did they necessarily fall heavily on the entrepreneurs themselves. Indeed, one case each in the public and nonprofit sectors (G1 and NP1) involved as much personal financial jeopardy as any of the proprietary cases.

Risk to professional standing and reputation seems to characterize in common the public and nonprofit cases, though this element also enters the proprietary cases somewhat. Sacrificing personal reputation for an idea that might not work and indeed might backfire or invite ridicule (as in cases G3 and NP2) seems the most serious difficulty these entrepreneurs invited.

That risks pervade the undertaking of entrepreneurial activity regardless of sector and that they may not differ radically from sector to sector are hypotheses worthy of further investigation. The financial liabilities of proprietary entrepreneurs are commonly hedged by financial institutions, whereas those of nonprofit and public entrepreneurs may be just as real but less insured.[19] Moreover, the need to put one's personal reputation and credibility on the line seems to cross sector boundaries as well.

Constraints

Unlike personal risks, the economic and institutional barriers to implementing and fostering the various projects appear to differentiate themselves across sectors. In the proprietary cases, a key constraint was the ability to secure sufficient capitalization to ensure project viability, particularly in the early years. But constraints deriving from governmental and political considerations also played a part. In both P1 and P2, decisions were made to include or exclude particular clientele groups and programs on the basis of program restrictions associated with government funding. In P1, funding for handicapped children was rejected because it would have required the development of a separate program, segregated from the school's main agenda. In P2, a program for adults was dropped to comply with state child-care funding provisions that prohibited having adult programs in the same facility as those for children. In the case of P3, the entrepreneur had to pay attention to local sensitivities concerning the

potential exposure of community residents to violent children, and cultivate relationships with officials in charge of zoning.

In the governmental cases, political and bureaucratic considerations were much more imposing. In G1 and G2, attention had to be paid both to obtaining support of relevant political party interests and to balancing potential benefits geographically throughout the townships involved. In G3, the executive of the state facility had to be sensitive to the interests of the local community.

In all three public-sector cases, bureaucratic elements tended to stifle initiative. In G1, the youth bureau represented potential competition to the existing recreation department and was subtly resisted by that agency. In G2, potential sources of funds from state agencies were avoided because their requirements would have distorted the design and intent of the sanctuary program. In G3, the state civil service system presented monumental difficulties to an entrepreneur who was trying to appoint the right people to key staff positions in her program. In addition, inertial forces in the state bureaucracy opposed the major change of staff and purpose of the state hospital and, over the long run (after the entrepreneur left), succeeded in turning back the project and returning the hospital to its initial status as primarily an inpatient facility. This is not to argue that such bureaucratic repression is unique to governmental activity. Similar experiences occur within large profit-making corporations and large nonprofit universities or hospitals, for example. However, for self-contained agencies of modest size and scope, such as those reviewed here, those that operate in the public sector rather than in an independent private context seem necessarily to be more entangled in stifling relationships with other agencies in the same sector. A small government agency is less in control of its own destiny than an agency of similar size elsewhere in the economy.

The nonprofit cases present a more diverse set of constraints. For NP1, the primary barriers were state (architectural, programmatic, organizational) regulations that had to be satisfied before a facility could be opened and state childcare funding secured. The regulators were as much a problem as the regulations themselves, imposing delays, inconsistent decisions, and the like. The per-diem reimbursement system of funding also caused severe cash-flow problems because clients had to be served before any money was forthcoming, and banks were reluctant to take the promise of government funds as collateral. In cases NP2 and NP3, the constraining factors were more internally derived. The entrepreneurs in NP2 had to cope with the fears, conservatism, and dissenting professional judgments of staff reluctant to deal with a new client mix, as well as the worries and predispositions of trustees and contributors concerned with the programmatic and fiscal integrity of the agency and the maintenance of service to its traditional (ethnic) clientele.

In the case of NP3, the restrictions on funds and programs derived from donor preferences were the principal source of restraint. Having decided to avoid the entanglements of governmental funding entirely, this agency had to break through

19. Compare this view, however, to Legoretta and Young (1986) who find that once a proprietary organization is in financial jeopardy, proprietors who wish to preserve it while minimizing their personal financial liability may seek to convert it to nonprofit status.

the limitations imposed by the original restrictive trust governing the agency and to devise mechanisms, strategies, and programs that would appeal to new donors. The growth of NP3 into a multimillion-dollar child-care agency in the 1960s and 1970s, virtually without a penny of government money, is a monument to one entrepreneur's creativity in dealing with the preferences imposed by donor funding.

The constraints are nominally similar from sector to sector, but they differ in emphasis because entrepreneurs in different sectors have to play to different constituencies and sources of support, and they must abide by different rules. Though fund-raising is important for nonprofits and even government agencies, market potential and availability of venture capital dominate proprietary enterprise concerns. Partisan and geographic politics, bureaucratic interests, and system rigidities characterize the restraints on ventures in the public sector more than elsewhere. For nonprofits, an intermixture of three factors is apparent. First, a substantial dependence on government operating funds and/or certification can impose serious barriers to program implementation. Yet rejection of public support, if feasible, leads to the substitution of donor preferences as a source of influence and possible difficulty. Nor does diversification of support necessarily provide relief. In the case of NP2, for example, traditional sources of philanthropic support inhibited change, and pressure to change (to respond to societal needs for services) came largely from city and state government, which provided some 80 percent of the agency's revenues. Yet even government funding programs held back the project until a loophole in the funding laws could be found to pay for the special facility.

Lack of access to capital is another constraint commonly associated with nonprofit activity. Crimmins and Keil (1983), for example, note not only the absence of equity capital but also a reluctance of lending institutions to finance loans to nonprofit organizations (see also Hansmann 1981a). Case NP1 gives special credence to this difficulty, as start-up funds from personal sources were required to finance the venture until government reimbursement funds could be received, well after operations had begun.

An internal regime of shared power and influence over policy decisions in the nonprofit organization seems to impose special restraints on the nonprofit entrepreneur. This again is best seen in NP2, where staff members exerted their own professional judgments on decision making, and trustees pressed the views of members of the agency's traditional philanthropic support community. This internal participative regime, which loosens the administrative control of the executive and makes it more difficult for him to translate his intents into action, seems distinctly more prominent in nonprofits. Within executive agencies of government, where administrative authority follows a well-defined hierarchy or chain of command, or in the profit sector, where ownership signals who is in charge, the discretion of the executive is relatively less challenged within his own bailiwick (though in the case of government it may be severely challenged from outside or constrained by unions and civil service). In the

nonprofit cases, despite the presence of strong executive personalities, catering to divergent internal interests seems more intrinsic than elsewhere, because the executive's discretion is more circumscribed by independent judgments of staff professionals and by trustee interests.

THE EXECUTIVE AS PERSONNEL MANAGER

Like entrepreneurship, personnel management in nonprofit organizations involves constraints and other influencing factors that differentiate the character of the nonprofit executive's task from that of his counterparts in the other sectors. In particular, the nonprofit organization tends to present special problems but also certain advantages in competing for personnel in the labor market and in motivating personnel through the use of incentives.

This section summarizes findings of a survey of compensation and personnel practices across a range of industries in which nonprofits prominently participate. Through interviews and literature survey, this study broke new research ground and generated various hypotheses for further investigation.[20] However, as for any such initial effort, available sources of information were often subjective and incomplete. Thus, the results reported below should be considered preliminary and impressionistic.

The survey included health care, social services, performing arts, museums, charities, foundations, associations, and colleges and universities. Although the results varied by industry, some general patterns distinguished the nonprofit sector from the others.

Competing for Personnel

To recruit effectively in the labor market requires the ability to offer competitive salaries and benefits and/or offsetting nonpecuniary advantages. In the case of nonprofits, there appear to be four main factors that influence the types and levels of personnel compensation that can be offered to desired candidates for employment: (1) a preoccupation with quality; (2) a sensitivity to the organization's image as a charitable or public service institution; (3) special resource constraints; and (4) the ability to provide compensating nonpecuniary benefits in lieu of financial reward. These factors define boundaries within which the nonprofit executive must work in developing and maintaining the work force. Their relative intensity in various industries helps explain why nonprofits pay more than their public- and private-sector counterparts in some industries and personnel categories but less in others. Another source of explanation, however, is the

---

20. The methodology included a review of available industry compensation surveys, review of contributions to the general literature, and extensive interviews with several dozen leaders of industry associations and operating organizations. In the discussion that follows, sources of published information are cited where possible. Otherwise, statements are based on original interviews and analysis of documents, cited in Young (1984).

set of restraints operant in *other* sectors, particularly in government, where singularly high salaries for certain high-level positions may be politically if not statutorily infeasible.

That nonprofits are necessarily more concerned with, or less likely to neglect, quality than counterpart organizations in other sectors is a long-standing view supported by research (Newhouse 1970; Hansmann 1980; Douglas 1983; Nelson & Krashinsky 1973; Reder 1965). In brief, nonprofits are not so strongly subject to the financial incentives facing profit-seeking organizations (Hansmann 1980) or the pressure to serve all comers equally (Douglas 1983) faced by government agencies that must respond to a political majority. Rather, as suggested by Majone (1984), James (1983), Pauly and Redisch (1973), Young (1983, 1985), Vroom (1983), and others, nonprofits tend to be domains in which professions and professional thinking dominate, and agendas are shaped by a quest for professional excellence and prestige.

Nonprofit organizations have paid more for top hospital and nursing home administrators, and for top administrators and distinguished faculty in universities, than their public- or proprietary-sector counterparts. This is understandable in view of the quality orientation of such institutions and the kinds of key personnel required to maintain and enhance a reputation for quality (Vladeck 1976). Hospitals compete for patients on the basis of quality reputation as perceived by physicians who seek affiliation. Universities attract graduate students and research funds on the basis of the reputation of top faculty and the ability of key administrators to set the proper tone and garner resources from the community. Nonprofit nursing homes, viewing themselves as extensions of the professional health care system, also seek top administrators and medical personnel who will promote quality and hence attract the desired clientele and resource contributions. In these cases, nonprofits enjoy a certain advantage in competing with governmental organizations. As already noted, government tends to put a lid on top salaries, which allows private institutions to lure away the best executive and professional talent. Lower down in the personnel ranks, however, government is less restrained, as salaries are less visible or spectacular and hence less of a political liability and more prone to support by active public-sector unions. Thus differentials between public and nonprofit scales diminish or even reverse themselves at these levels.

The quality orientation of nonprofits works in two ways, however. In some cases, nonprofits are able to pay less because their stronger quality orientation provides other personal benefits or satisfaction to employees. Although systematic comparisons on this phenomenon are scarce (Young 1984), available information indicates that physicians in nonprofit hospitals, particularly teaching institutions, receive less compensation than they would in less prestigious proprietary or public hospitals (in addition to Young [1984], see B. Cole [1982] and B. Cole & Warren [1981] for hospitals; and *Academe*, July–August issues for the 1981–84 period, Miller, Miller, & Landauer [1982], and Freeman [1979] for universities). Similarly, social workers may work for less in nonprofit-sector agencies than in government

partly because the work environment and the perceived quality of care they can deliver are better there.

Aside from the magnet of quality, nonprofits frequently can offer certain compensating benefits that allow them to pay lower wages. Indeed, this is seen in the extreme in many organizations that successfully mobilize large numbers of volunteers. But even for paid employees, the environment of the nonprofit often is regarded as a special benefit. Nonprofits frequently provide a less intense or controlled or a more collegial or caring environment in which to work (Mirvis & Hackett 1983). They are often flexible enough to employ—in clerical positions, for example, and at lower wages than necessary to attract more technically qualified individuals—some people with less skill, experience, and formal credentials. Government civil service certification and test requirements and profit-sector preoccupation with short-term productivity may preclude such flexibility. But nonprofit social agencies and arts organizations, for example, may serve as training grounds for some individuals who may ultimately find better paying jobs elsewhere.

The use of volunteers and the flexibility to employ less experienced personnel reflect another characteristic that sometimes differentiates nonprofits from counterparts in other sectors—namely, resource constraints and heavy demands for programmatic use of existing resources. In the arts, for example, the economics are such that operating resources are typically very scarce, especially for nonprofit organizations committed to artistic values and reluctant to pursue commercially lucrative activities appealing to popular tastes. (For analyses of the economics of performing arts, see Baumol & Bowen [1966] and Hansmann [1981b].) In social agencies and charities, demands for programmatic expenditures constitute a bottomless pit of worthy causes and immediately pressing social needs. In many instances, trustees and volunteers exert considerable pressure to keep personnel costs down and devote as many dollars to direct service as possible, though this may not always be the most productive long-run practice.

The charitable nature of activities in certain industries brings with it other restraining forces on nonprofits' abilities to pay high wages. Trustees, for example, who have been asked to volunteer their own time to work for charities, social agencies, arts organizations, and the like may feel that regular employees should also incorporate an element of charity in their compensation packages. Moreover, charitable agencies are relatively open organizations, subject to scrutiny by government on behalf of the contributing public. In this fishbowl environment, it can be difficult to pay high managerial salaries, which might look out of line and embarrassing in the context of charity, despite whatever justification exists for the need to attract and retain superior administrative talent.

Differences in compensation practices among sectors are not equally strong for all categories of employees. For rank-and-file workers, such as secretaries, bookkeepers, technicians, custodial staff, and even regular staff nurses, caseworkers, and lower-level administrators, there tend to be relatively small differences among the various sectors in the nature of the work. Hence, relatively uniform compensation levels across sectors are determined by the general market for these categories of employees, except where trade unions dominate one sector more than another. This is not to argue that wage differentials accounting for such factors as the engagement by nonprofits, at lower pay, of individuals with less formal training or job qualifications, or differences in the quality and pace of the work environment, are not important, but only that differentials tend to be less prominent for rank-and-file workers than for other employee categories.

For professional staff and upper-level management, more prominent differences seem to occur across sectors. Professionals and some middle-level administrators may be paid less in nonprofit organizations because they are willing to accept compensation differentials in exchange for institutional prestige or better work environments. But nonprofit agencies commonly pay premiums for their very top administrators and distinguished professionals in order to promote or maintain their quality orientations.

Providing Incentives

Nonprofit organizations can present special constraints to executives wishing to utilize performance-based financial rewards to motivate personnel. Interviews with nonprofit executives and professionals reveal that several important factors affect the use of such rewards (Young 1984). These include (1) the element of volunteerism, (2) external expectations of altruism, (3) the emphasis on professionalism, (4) the lack of a bottom-line criterion, (5) the screening of employees by motivation, (6) absence of managerial traditions, and (7) the special statutory character of nonprofit organizations. These factors interact in various ways and affect managerial practices to different degrees by industry, but together they form a tapestry of both barriers and potentials facing nonprofit executives wishing to use performance-based rewards in their organizations.

Nonprofit organizations in such areas as charities, social services, nursing homes, and the arts depend strongly on volunteers. The intimate involvement of volunteers in the work of these nonprofits can affect their capacities to utilize performance reward systems in a number of ways. First, volunteer workers are obviously insensitive to direct monetary inducements. Moreover, volunteers can command a fair degree of discretion in how and what they do in exchange for the free labor they provide. But the presence of volunteers can also affect the nonprofit executive's ability to manage paid staff. In some organizations executives can be undermined by the ability of volunteers to circumvent management, not only in controlling their own terms of work, but also in influencing organizational policy.[21] In particular, volunteers can have policy agendas of their own as well as

political connections with (volunteer) trustees to whom they can appeal over the head of the executive. This can obviously create basic problems both in defining coherent goals for the organization from which performance criteria can be derived and in undermining the executive's ability to control the resources necessary to provide performance-based rewards.

Another aspect of this problem is the clubbiness of the work environment that may derive from the presence of large numbers of volunteer staff members. Indeed, the organization may be viewed by many as serving a social function per se rather than having a coherent set of service goals along which performance can be determined. This clubbiness can affect paid staff, not only in loss of coherence and service-oriented behavior, but also in terms of how paid staff are selected in the first place. If politically active volunteers populate an organization, paid staff positions can represent a source of patronage to be doled out on political grounds rather than on the basis of objective merit.

Finally, the fact that the trustees of nonprofit organizations are usually volunteers has implications of its own. Such trustees may expect altruistic motivation from paid staff and may thus be reluctant to approve an executive's proposal for reward systems that would pay employees for better performance. This psychology seems surprisingly common in view of the fact that nonprofit board members are often businessmen who might be expected to have a more coldly rational attitude. In some instances, though, businessmen-trustees may encourage merit-based rewards over the objections of other groups such as unions and professionals. Arts organizations and social service agencies appear more oriented toward the trustee psychology of altruism, whereas (generally larger) institutions of higher education or hospitals seem more inclined to a businesslike trustee psychology.[22]

Expectations of altruism and the concomitant reluctance to indulge in performance reward schemes extend beyond

---

21. Discussion of this point in Young (1984) is based largely on interviews held with an official of the National Mental Health Association. See also Cole (1980) and Selby (1978).

22. Various factors may explain this apparent diversity of trustee attitudes. Each trustee may struggle to juxtapose his or her own sacrifice of time on behalf of a charitable organization against the realization that the organization must pay reasonably well to attract competent employees. Just as individuals weigh these considerations differently, alternative boards of trustees may be expected to exhibit a variety of views. In addition, laymen trustees may exhibit different attitudes toward workers in fields where different stereotypes prevail. Artists may be viewed as eccentric, or social workers may be held in low esteem, neither therefore requiring or deserving, in some minds, much financial reward. In contrast, health or higher education professionals may be held in greater esteem, thus eliciting more sympathetic policies of remuneration. Another possibility is that trustees view some fields of activity as more businesslike than others. Universities or hospitals may be seen more as major service-producing enterprises compared to "charitable" social agencies or "cultural" arts organizations—the latter thus demanding less rigorous or formal personnel policies. Finally, the size and complexity of organizations may influence the selection as well as attitudes of trustees. Larger organizations, such as hospitals and universities, may simply be able to attract more enlightened, experienced, or sophisticated board members. For a review of other factors influencing board composition, competence, and problems in relations with staff, see Stein (1978).

trustees. It was noted earlier that some nonprofits operate in an environment of public scrutiny deriving from their charitable missions and the fact that they are chartered as vehicles of public purpose and receive tax exemptions and other economic benefits by law. In this context, any public perceptions that these organizations are being used as means of personal enrichment can be damaging. This is one reason that nonprofit organizational policies tend to be biased against the use of bonuses or other practices that might be interpreted as profiteering at the expense of the needy. Nonprofit workers must be seen to pursue service objectives of their own volition, uncorrupted by selfish financial objectives.

That many nonprofit organizations, which employ substantial numbers of professionals, tend to emphasize professional values more than proprietary and governmental organizations (Majone 1984; Young 1983; Mirvis & Hackett 1983) creates other problems for the use of performance-based reward systems. Professionals value their autonomy to make independent service judgments and depend on their peers more than on executives for guidance and evaluative feedback.

Moreover, professionals tend to resist the use of managerial systems of performance measurement to determine financial rewards (Newman & Wallender 1978; Young 1982). Professionals also prefer operating in a collegial environment, which entails strong elements of both egalitarianism and personal autonomy (Brinkerhoff & Kanter 1980; Majone 1984; Milofsky 1979, 1980). This in itself is at odds with the idea of providing differential rewards to individuals according to their performance. Indeed, the collegial environment often leads to the practice of ''protecting one's own,'' in which poor performers are shielded from punitive measures that otherwise might be imposed by management. The professional mode of decision making has both positive and negative properties in this connection. Usually, there are more careful screening mechanisms applied in the decision to hire someone or to grant tenure. However, for members of the inner group of professionals, there may be precious few other means by which an executive can tailor rewards or penalties according to merit-based criteria (Brinkerhoff 1979). Doctors in hospitals and faculty in universities provide the most obvious examples. (For relevant discussions, see Starr [1982], Reder [1965], and Friedson [1975] for the medical profession, and Tuckman [1979] and Cyert [1975] for universities.) But these practices pervade a much wider context, and they tend to be stronger in nonprofits than in other sectors that employ professionals.

The fact that nonprofit organizations have neither a clear political mandate nor the license to maximize and distribute profits also affects the ability of executives of these organizations to implement or use performance-based reward practices. Lack of a bottom-line criterion means that nonprofits have difficulty reconciling competing demands for services and use of organizational resources. If a coherent set of goals in lieu of profit or a political mandate cannot be articulated, organizational performance cannot be measured, making it difficult to specify performance criteria for organizational

subunits and ultimately for individual employees. Without such criteria, of course, the principle of performance-based reward becomes meaningless. Moreover, without an overriding organizational performance criterion, long-term resource development needs, such as investments in physical facilities or in personnel, may be neglected. A short-term organizational psychology of attempting to satisfy pressing service needs may restrain the nonprofit executive from setting aside funds for performance rewards.

The presence of professionals coupled with the absence of an overall performance criterion leads to potential conflict between staff workers and executive management. Without clear performance criteria, management may have considerable leeway in defining what is expected from staff members. And as professionals, staff members may have their own ideas of what they should do and how they should be judged. Moreover, staff members may fear that managers, having no adequate criteria by which they themselves can be held accountable, may be capricious in their judgments or may exhibit favoritism. Without a common measuring rod to reconcile the two perspectives, there is substantial potential for conflict and hence strong motivation for the executive to avoid this possibility entirely by having personnel benefits determined on other than performance measurement grounds.[23]

It was previously noted that certain differentials in the level of compensation by nonprofit versus other types of organizations may derive from nonpecuniary benefits of the nonprofit work environment. That is, some nonprofit workers may select these benefits in exchange for what might otherwise be a higher wage (Weisbrod 1983; Preston 1983). The same observation may apply to personnel practices, including policies governing benefits, promotions, and job security. Although Mirvis and Hackett (1983) found no differences among sectors in job security in general, interviews reveal that in some areas, such as charities or social service, nonprofit organizations do offer an intentionally secure and relaxed work environment, which itself appears to grow out of an implicit bargain struck between the organization and its employees. This bargain may even become explicit where nonprofit organizations incorporate service objectives into their personnel policies through employment preferences for members of their clientele groups, who may be handicapped in some way. Obviously, if such a policy prevails, it would be very difficult to implement performance-based personnel reward systems because they would be resented by employees, who would view their implicit contracts as being violated. Moreover, they would require that performance-based compensation be carried out by managers who them-

---

23. This view was articulated in the context of interviews concerning supervisors and caseworkers in social services but carries over to other categories such as deans versus faculties in universities or supervisors versus nurses in health care. See Young (1984) and also Staw (1983). Reluctance of managers to engage in performance appraisal arises in private-sector corporations employing professionals as well. See Meyer, Kay, and French (1969).

selves have been acculturated to a different stance in personnel matters.

The screening of non-performance-oriented managers into nonprofit organizations reflects a more general problem in many of these organizations—the lack of any strong internal management tradition. In particular, many nonprofits place people in management who have no formal management training. Nonprofits in the arts, social services, higher education, and other fields normally promote disciplinary professionals into administration, where they learn to manage only by trial and error.

This practice is explained by a combination of disciplinary biases, market factors, and weaknesses in the present system of management education. The professionals who often dominate nonprofit organizations tend to feel that a background in the profession per se—whether it be art, social work, health, or higher education—is the most important prerequisite for successful administration because it takes an "insider" to understand the problems and to gain the respect and confidence of professional staff in the field. There is an element of truth in this contention—which mirrors contemporary criticism of management in the business sector of the U.S. economy that MBA-trained managers lack sufficient appreciation of the technical processes of production and the nature of the product (see, for example, Peters & Waterman 1983; Kanter 1983). Few, however, would argue that disciplinary training in a profession plus on-the-job experience is a satisfactory substitute for formal management education.

Regrettably, schools of management, business, and even public administration rarely offer training sensitive to the special requirements of nonprofit organizations. Thus, opportunities for relevant managerial education in nonprofit-oriented fields are confined to concentrations in schools of education, social work, health, or arts that do not view management as their principal missions and tend not to have the most current managerial knowledge and technology or draw upon the most outstanding management faculties.

Finally, nonprofit organizations, even when they are inclined to do so, may have difficulty competing for formally trained managers because of the high salaries offered by the business sector. However, the works of Weisbrod (1983), Mirvis and Hackett (1983), and Preston (1983) suggest that some substantial number of prospective formally trained managers might be willing to sacrifice financial rewards for the special advantages of working in a nonprofit environment.

The absence of a formal management orientation in nonprofits can manifest itself in several ways at odds with performance-based reward systems. These include (1) the absence of managerial systems, particularly statistical data bases and measures that might be helpful in performance assessments; (2) a reluctance to make differential judgments about subordinates in favor of professional and peer judgments (a strong managerial tradition is required to overcome the natural tendencies to avoid the supervisory hassles and employee contentiousness associated with distributing rewards un-

equally and to take into account economic criteria in establishing compensation levels and benefit structures); and (3) a lack of discipline and methods of allocating funds for alternative purposes, including setting aside separate funds for merit purposes. In short, a performance-based personnel reward system requires both training and a managerial mind-set—both often in short supply in nonprofit organizations.

Finally, there are certain structural constraints on nonprofits that affect their capacities to use performance-based reward systems. The most obvious of these is the lack of access to benefits such as stock options and profit-sharing plans available to organizations in the profit sector. Another is the dependence of nonprofits on certain limited sources of revenues, such as charitable contributions and government and foundation grants. Although in times of fiscal stringency such reliance creates some pressure for greater efficiency and hence support for executive emphasis on performance, the need to meet pressing commitments assumed with the acceptance of the revenues can, as we have noted, crowd out opportunities for setting aside funds for merit-based rewards.

The nondistribution constraint for nonprofit organizations—the requirement that all revenues must be used for organizational purposes and that no "profit" may be distributed—may also create difficulties for the implementation of a performance reward system. One view of this constraint is that accumulation of surplus funds (which look like profits) should be avoided. If this concept is coupled with another common notion—that performance rewards must be generated from available surpluses—then obvious problems beset any initiative to develop such a system.

Clearly, a nonprofit CEO need not interpret the nondistribution constraint in this manner (see Nash [1983, chap. 7] for a discussion of IRS guidelines on the generation and use of surpluses by a nonprofit hospital for an employee retirement incentive plan). However, not to do so requires explicitly recognizing not only that it is legitimate to hold surpluses but also that a pool of merit funds is an important expenditure category in its own right, not just a leftover or luxury. Moreover, the allocation of merit funds requires some substitute for the bottom-line performance criteria available to organizations in other sectors. This is why a number of prominent nonprofit organizations, such as the Independent Sector, United Ways, and others, have experimented with management-by-objectives (MBO) systems. (See Wiehe [1978], Raider [1978], and McConkey [1975] for other examples of the use of MBO in nonprofit organizations.) In principle, MBO systems can identify the programmatic goals of merit fund expenditures and, in the process, specify the guidelines an executive can use to develop policies for allocating these funds among staff members.

CONCLUSION

It is clear that the rigors facing the nonprofit executive are considerable and substantially different in many ways from those facing executives in business or government. Thus, it is understandable if relatively few individuals are fully successful in meeting this challenge. But the improvement of management and leadership in the nonprofit sector would appear to depend not only on the engagement of the necessary individual talent but also on more explicit recognition of management as a critical area of activity in nonprofit organizations, and an activity that requires adaptation and development of an appropriate mix of skills and perspectives, some of which are more commonly associated with other sectors. This conclusion emerges from analyzing both the external entrepreneurial function of the executive and the internal personnel management function.

With respect to the entrepreneurial function, nonprofit chief executives must be prepared to take risks like their counterparts in other sectors. Risk taking is a well-established feature of business-sector leadership, but it seems not to be so well recognized in the nonprofit area. Yet the cases reviewed here and elsewhere (Young 1983, 1985) indicate that nonprofit executives almost inevitably put themselves in some kind of jeopardy—financial, professional, legal—if they are to get things done. And these risks can be at least as serious as those faced by businessmen in commercial ventures. If, as some have observed (Crimmins & Keil 1983), nonprofit organizations tend to be highly conservative, all the more determination is required for an executive to engage successfully in entrepreneurship.

The constraints associated with nonprofit ventures reflect a mix of business and politics at which the nonprofit executive/entrepreneur must be adept. Like the businessman, he must worry about raising capital, overcoming cash-flow problems (as in case NP1), and marketing his ventures—if not among potential customers or service recipients, then certainly among granting agencies or philanthropic donors. Indeed, (as suggested by case NP3), soliciting contributions from the latter may require the most imaginative of marketing strategies.

But unlike the commercial venturer, the nonprofit entrepreneur cannot rest on a successful marketing strategy. He must also be adept at coping with the regulatory agencies that control the funding and certification of services financed or overseen by government. In this role, the nonprofit executive resembles the government bureau chief dealing with higher levels of administration. Of course, proprietary-agency executives also become involved in the regulatory processes associated with government funding or supervision. But proprietary agencies, perhaps reflecting the strong value their leaders appear to attach to autonomy (Young 1983), tend to select market niches that allow them to avoid heavy governmental entanglement; nonprofits, on the other hand, usually define their mandates as more fully coincident with services and client groups entailing government support and supervision (Weisbrod 1980).

Indeed, where nonprofits avoid governmental entanglement, as in the case of NP3, they may do so by intensifying involvement with what might be termed "community and philanthropic politics." In this process, trustees and large donors must be cultivated and the public image of the agency as a socially responsible organization must be enhanced by association with civil groups and causes.

Finally, the nonprofit executive must be a politician within his own agency. Not only must he gain the support of his trustees in venture activity; he must also make special efforts to bring his staff along, particularly where the staff consists largely of professionals or influential volunteers.

The internal functions of the nonprofit executive also call for a mix of skills and a unique mind-set. Like the businessman, the nonprofit executive must be concerned with the performance of his agency (including its financial survival) and with selecting and motivating personnel in a manner that contributes to this objective. Yet the special problems of doing this in the nonprofit context also require a particular sensitivity to political factors.

In the competition for personnel, the nonprofit executive must know the marketplace as a businessman. He must be aware, for example, that he may have a wage advantage in recruiting certain personnel: he can offer less money because of amenities in his agency's work environment or because of a greater opportunity for training, compared to organizations in other sectors. But he must be politically sensitive to the constituencies for quality in his domain—the professional work force, trustees, volunteers, donors—which require a willingness to pay more for "stars" who can maintain or enhance the organization's reputation.

Similarly, the process of devising appropriate rewards for personnel already on board is both a businesslike and a political problem. On the business side, technologies must be developed that will adequately measure the achievement of organizational objectives and the contributions of individual staff members toward those objectives. Moreover, financial discipline must be applied to allocate funds for performance rewards in an orderly way that successfully balances immediate service needs against long-term personnel development.

Yet in trying to implement a compensation system that rewards merit and performance, the nonprofit executive must be attuned to restraints of a political nature. Paying bonuses or high salary increments can tarnish an agency's public charitable image. Differentiating among employees may threaten the professional collegial milieu. And establishing explicit objectives and performance criteria may invite conflict with influential volunteers.

Richard Neustadt (1960) once described alternate images of the chief executive of the United States: a "President in Boots" and a "President in Sneakers." From the overview presented in this chapter, the appropriate model for the nonprofit executive is not the political wheeler-dealer, the capitalist venturer and marketer, the disciplined technical manager, or the master of interpersonal relations—but a special mix of all these things.

REFERENCES

Barnard, Chester. 1938. *The Functions of the Executive.* Cambridge, Mass.: Harvard University Press.

Baumol, William J., and William G. Bowen. 1966. *Performing Arts: The Economic Dilemma.* New York: Twentieth Century Fund.

Bower, Joseph L. 1983. *The Two Faces of Management.* Boston: Houghton Mifflin Co.

Brinkerhoff, Derrick W. 1979. "Review of Approaches to Productivity Performance and Organizational Effectiveness in the Public Sector: Applicability to Non-Profit Organizations." Yale University, PONPO Working Paper no. 10.

Brinkerhoff, Derrick W., and Rosabeth M. Kanter. 1980. "Appraising the Performance of Performance Appraisal." *Sloan Management Review* 21 (Spring):3–16.

Clarkson, Kenneth W. 1981. "Institutional Constraints and Art Museum Management." In Michelle J. White, ed., *Non-Profit Firms in a Three-Sector Economy.* Washington, D.C.: Urban Institute, pp. 35–60.

Clarkson, Kenneth W., and Donald L. Martin. 1980. *The Economics of Nonproprietary Organizations.* Greenwich, Conn.: JAI Press.

Coase, R. H. 1937. "The Nature of the Firm." *Economica,* November, pp. 386–405.

Cole, Arthur H. 1959. *Business Enterprise in a Social Setting.* Cambridge, Mass.: Harvard University Press.

Cole, Ben S. 1982. "Compensation." *Modern Healthcare,* December, pp. 67–90.

Cole, Ben S., and Thomas T. Warren. 1981. "Compensation Survey." *Modern Healthcare,* December, pp. 71–82.

Cole, Richard L. 1980. "Constituent Involvement in Non-Profit Organizations." Yale University, PONPO Working Paper no. 18.

Collins, Orvis, and David G. Moore. 1970. *The Organization Makers.* New York: Appleton-Century-Crofts.

Crimmins, James C., and Mary Keil. 1983. *Enterprise in the Non-Profit Sector.* New York: Rockefeller Brothers Fund.

Cyert, Richard M. 1975. *The Management of Non-Profit Organizations.* Lexington, Mass.: D. C. Heath.

Douglas, James. 1983. *Why Charity?* Beverly Hills, Calif.: Sage Publications.

Freeman, Richard B. 1979. "The Job Market for College Faculty." Chapter 4 in Daniel R. Lewis and William E. Becker, eds., *Academic Rewards in Higher Education.* Cambridge, Mass.: Ballinger.

Friedson, Eliot. 1975. *Doctoring Together.* New York: Elsevier.

Hansmann, Henry B. 1980. "The Role of Non-Profit Enterprise. *Yale Law Journal,* April, pp. 837–43.

——. 1981a. "Why Are Non-Profit Organizations Exempted from Corporate Income Taxation?" In Michelle J. White, ed., *Non-Profit Firms in a Three-Sector Economy.* Washington, D.C.: Urban Institute, pp. 115–34.

——. 1981b. "Non-Profit Enterprise in the Performing Arts." Yale University, PONPO Working Paper no. 3.

Hirschman, Albert O. 1970. *Exit, Voice and Loyalty.* Cambridge, Mass.: Harvard University Press.

James, Estelle. 1983. "How Non-Profits Grow: A Model." *Journal of Policy Analysis and Management,* Spring, pp. 350–65.

Josephson, Matthew. 1962. *The Robber Barons.* New York: Harcourt, Brace, and World.

Kanter, Rosabeth M. 1983. *The Change Masters.* New York: Simon & Schuster.

Kirzner, Israel M. 1973. *Competition and Entrepreneurship.* Chicago: University of Chicago Press.

Legoretta, Judith M., and Dennis R. Young. 1986. "Why Organizations Turn Non-Profit." In Susan Rose-Ackerman, ed., *The Economics of Nonprofit Institutions: Studies in Structure and Policy.* Oxford: Oxford University Press.

Lynn, Laurence E. 1981. *Managing the Public's Business.* New York: Basic Books.

Majone, Giandomenico. 1984. "Professionalism and Non-Profit Organizations." *Journal of Health Politics, Policy and Law,* 8:639–59.

Marshall, Alfred. 1964. *Economics of Industry.* London: Macmillan.

McConkey, Dale D. 1975. *MBO for Non-Profit Organizations.* New York: AMACOM.

Meyer, Herbert H., Emanual Kay, and John R. P. French, Jr. 1969. "Split Roles in Performance Appraisal." In L. L. Cummings and W. E. Scott, Jr., eds., *Readings in Organizational Behavior and Performance.* Homewood, Ill.: Richard D. Irwin, pp. 714–21.

Miller, Jan P., Stephen S. Miller, and U. E. Landauer. 1982. "1981–82 Administrative Compensation Survey." Washington, D.C.: College and University Personnel Association.

Milofsky, Carl. 1979. "Not for Profit Organizations and Community: A Review of the Sociological Literature." Yale University, PONPO Working Paper no. 6.

——. 1980. "Structure and Process in Self-Help Organizations." Yale University, PONPO Working Paper no. 17.

Mirvis, Philip H., and Edward J. Hackett. 1983. "Work and Work Force Characteristics in the Non-Profit Sector." *Monthly Labor Review,* April, pp. 3–12.

Nash, Michael. 1983. *Managing Organizational Performance.* San Francisco: Jossey-Bass.

Nelson, Richard R., and Michael Krashinsky. 1973. "Two Major Issues of Public Policy: Public Subsidy and Organization of Supply." In Dennis R. Young and Richard R. Nelson, eds., *Public Policy for Day Care of Young Children.* Lexington, Mass.: D. C. Heath.

Neustadt, Richard E. 1960. *Presidential Power.* New York: John Wiley.

Newhouse, Joseph. 1970. "Toward a Theory of Non-Profit

Institutions: An Economic Model of a Hospital." *American Economic Review* 60:64–74.

Newman, William H., and Harvey W. Wallender. 1978. "Managing Not-for-Profit Enterprises." *Academy of Management Review,* January, pp. 24–31.

Pauly, Mark, and Michael Redisch. 1973. "The Not-for-Profit Hospital as a Physicians' Cooperative." *American Economic Review* 63:87–99.

Perry, James L., and Kenneth L. Kraemer, eds. 1983. *Public Management: Public and Private Perspectives.* Irvine, Calif.: Mayfield.

Peters, Thomas, and Robert H. Waterman. 1982. *In Search of Excellence.* New York: Harper & Row.

Peterson, Richard A. 1981. "Entrepreneurship and Organization." In Paul C. Nystrom and William H. Starbuck, eds., *Handbook of Organizational Design.* Vol. 1. Oxford: Oxford University Press, pp. 65–83.

Preston, Anne. 1983. "The Non-Profit Firm in a For-Profit World." Ph.D. diss., Harvard University.

Raider, Melvyn C. 1978. "Installing Management by Objectives in Social Agencies." In Simon Slavin, ed., *Social Administration.* New York: Haworth Press, pp. 283–92.

Reder, M. W. 1965. "Some Problems in the Economics of Hospitals." *American Economic Review,* May, pp. 472–80.

"Rocky Road through the 1980's: Annual Report on the Economic Status of the Profession, 1980–81." 1981. *Academe,* August.

Rudney, Gabriel. 1981. "A Quantitative Profile of the Non-Profit Sector." Yale University, PONPO Working Paper no. 40.

Schumpeter, Joseph A. 1949. *The Theory of Economic Development.* Cambridge, Mass.: Harvard University Press.

Selby, Cecily C. 1978. "Better Performance from 'Nonprofits.'" *Harvard Business Review,* September-October, pp. 92–98.

Simon, Herbert. 1959. *Administrative Behavior.* New York: Free Press.

Slavin, Simon, ed. 1978. *Social Administration.* New York: Haworth Press.

Starr, Paul. 1982. *The Social Transformation of American Medicine.* New York: Basic Books.

Staw, Barry M. 1983. "Motivation Research versus the Art of Faculty Management." *Review of Higher Education,* Summer, pp. 301–21.

Stein, Herman D. 1978. "Board, Executives and Staff." In Simon Slavin, ed., *Social Administration.* New York: Haworth Press, pp. 204–16.

Stogdill, Ralph M. 1981. "Leadership and Management in the Working Situation." In *Stogdill's Handbook of Leadership: A Survey of Theory and Research.* Revised and expanded by Bernard M. Bass. New York: Free Press, pp. 273–88.

"Surprises and Uncertainties: Annual Report on the Economic Status of the Profession: 1981–82." 1982. *Academe,* July-August.

Tuckman, Howard P. 1979. "The Academic Reward Structure in American Higher Education." Chapter 8 in Darrell R. Lewis and William E. Becker, Jr., eds., *Academic Rewards in Higher Education.* Cambridge, Mass.: Ballinger, pp. 165–90.

Vladeck, Bruce C. 1976. "Why Non-Profits Go Broke." *Public Interest,* Winter, pp. 86–101.

Vroom, Victor H. 1983. "Leaders and Leadership in Academe." *Review of Higher Education,* Summer, pp. 367–86.

Weinberg, Martha W. 1983, "Public Management and Private Management: A Diminishing Gap?" *Journal of Policy Analysis and Management,* Summer, pp. 107–15.

Weisbrod, Burton A. 1975. "Toward a Theory of the Voluntary Non-Profit Sector in a Three-Sector Economy." In E. S. Phelps, ed., *Altruism, Morality, and Economic Theory.* New York: Russell Sage.

———. 1980. "Private Goods, Collective Goods: The Role of the Non-Profit Sector." In Kenneth W. Clarkson and Donald L. Martin, eds., *The Economics of Nonproprietary Organizations.* Greenwich, Conn.: JAI Press, pp. 139–77.

———. 1983. "Non-Profit and Proprietary Sector Behavior: Wage Differentials among Lawyers." *Journal of Labor Economics* 1, no. 3:246–63.

Wiehe, Vernon R. 1978. "Management by Objectives in a Family Service Agency." In Simon Slavin, ed., *Administrative Behavior.* New York: Haworth Press, pp. 276–82.

Young, Dennis R. 1981. "Human Service Enterprise: Case Studies of Entrepreneurship in Child Welfare." Draft manuscript. Yale University, PONPO, Section II on Proprietary Organizations.

———. 1982. "Incentives and the Non-Profit Sector." Yale University, PONPO Working Paper no. 53.

———. 1983. *If Not for Profit, for What?* Lexington, Mass.: D. C. Heath.

———. 1984. "Performance and Reward in Non-Profit Organizations: Evaluation, Compensation and Personnel Incentives." Yale University, PONPO Working Paper no. 79 and ISPS Working Paper no. 2079.

———. 1985. *Casebook of Management for Non-Profit Organizations.* New York: Haworth Press.

11

Organizational Change in Nonprofit Organizations

WALTER W. POWELL
REBECCA FRIEDKIN

Our standard wisdom about organizations tells us that there are considerable differences between nonprofit and for-profit organizations. For-profit organizations are highly plastic. Their ultimate purpose—that of earning profits for their shareholders—allows considerable freedom in the means for accomplishing this goal. A firm can switch product lines, discontinue services, buy or sell other companies—all in the pursuit of greater financial return. But the nonprofit organization's mission—be it charitable, educational, or cultural—places much greater limitations on its flexibility of action. (Kanter and Summers make a similar point; see chapter 9 in this volume.)

This is a widely held view. Few would dispute a firm's mandate to change its activities in pursuit of financial gain, but many people would question a nonprofit's deviation from its professed mission. In fact, abandoning that mission can invite a host of legal and tax problems.

But is the issue really that simple? Is there such a stark contrast between organizational change processes in business firms and in nonprofits? We suggest not. Recent research, although not questioning the legitimacy of efforts by for-profit firms to alter their strategies, has raised questions about their capability to change successfully. Hannan and Freeman (1984) argue that organizations display a high degree of inertia. New practices and products rarely come from established organizations, they say, but are more likely to be created by new generations of start-up companies. Nelson and Winter (1982) suggest that the menu of choices available to most for-profit organizations is not broad, but narrow and idiosyncratic, and that this menu is built into the firm's operational routines. Most of the choices in organizations are made by automatically selecting one of the existing routines. This line of research argues that business firms may be less capable of managing change than is commonly assumed.

We suggest that nonprofits may be both more subject to pressures that induce them to change and more capable of responsive change than our standard accounts would have us believe. In part this is due to the absence of a single overarching measure, like financial return, on which to judge nonprofit performance. Because goals are highly politicized and do not lend themselves to easy objective measurement, a wide range of plausible interpretations for various and sundry activities can be offered. Moreover, precisely because nonprofit organizations depend on external sources for support, they may find it necessary to bend and shift with the prevailing political and economic winds. In addition, large nonprofit organizations frequently have multiple stakeholders—that is, a variety of constituencies making demands upon them. Responding to these demands often requires considerable flexibility.

AGENDA

Our aim in this chapter is to examine the issue of organizational change in the nonprofit sector. We hope to provide a better understanding of both the internal processes that lead to change and the external factors that contribute to organizational transformation. Although we will not be able to ascertain whether nonprofit organizations are more likely to change than for-profit organizations or whether they are better or worse at this process, the cases we have selected for review illustrate that nonprofits can be highly adaptive to changed circumstances and responsive to new demands. The important questions for our purposes concern the *sources* of

We would like to thank Paul DiMaggio for his comments on an earlier draft.

organizational change: what are the *motivations* for change? whose *interests* are best served by change? We also ask to what extent an organization's mission constrains or facilitates change and whether the process of change threatens or weakens the organization's stated purpose.

We suspect that the fundamental difference between nonprofit and for-profit organizations does not turn so much on intrinsic differences in organizational form or capability, or even on legal criteria that distinguish nonprofits from for-profits, as on differences in the availability of resources and the constraints associated with their acquisition.

In the next section we review current theories of organizational change, which highlight a variety of factors that help account for organizational change. We then introduce ten case studies drawn from research on the nonprofit sector. Each deals with the issue of organizational missions or goals and examines their adaptation or transformation. We then assess them by looking at the aggregate properties of all the cases. When viewed in this manner, our attention is drawn to elements that are common to many of them. These commonalities help inform our theories of organizational change and suggest several important implications about the process of change in contemporary nonprofit organizations.

THEORIES OF ORGANIZATIONAL CHANGE

We will briefly review three explanations for organizational change. Each is a generic one, that is, it has been offered as an explanation for change in all types of organizations—public, private, or nonprofit. We will highlight those aspects of the theories that seem most germane for nonprofit organizations, but the reader should keep in mind that similar processes take place in organizations in all sectors.

The first explanation focuses on internal organizational conditions and processes. Change may be developmental, a result of particular stages in an organization's history, or reactive, a response to such factors as performance, clientele, culture, or goals. The other two explanations focus on change as a result of organizational adaptations to the external environment. Both the organization's resource base and its institutional context are important. Resource-dependency theory suggests that organizations adjust in response to changes in the amount and type of resources available to them—for example, changes in funding, demand, or competition (Pfeffer & Salancik 1978). Institutional explanations are based on the view that an organization mirrors and incorporates the larger social structure of which it is a part (Meyer & Rowan 1977; DiMaggio & Powell 1983). Organizational change is seen as a response to shifts in the ideology, professional standards, and cultural norms of the field or sector in which an organization is situated. In a related vein, organizations are seen as mirrors of the larger society, as tools used by actors in the context of larger schemes (Selznick 1949). An extreme version of this approach would suggest that nonprofits are a type of ''organized anarchy,'' with competing interest groups pursuing different motives and agendas (March & Olsen 1976). As a result, change may be either a political outcome or a random event, a process characterized by drift as much as debate.

Internal Conditions

A distinguished research tradition associates organizational change primarily with reactions to internal conditions—in particular, growth, decline, and crisis. In this view, organizational change is an outcome of the dynamic qualities of organizations and their internal subsystems. Chandler's magisterial account (1977) of the rise of the multidivisional firm belongs in this category. He explains the change in organizational structure among major American firms from a functional to a multidivisional form as a consequence of the internal need to coordinate and manage large-scale growth and expansion.

Other internal features—in particular, goals and procedures—have also drawn the attention of researchers. Many scholars have argued that organizational change can sometimes be understood as being due to a natural tendency of operational goals to supplant purposive ones (Simon 1957; Blau 1963). In order to accomplish their goals, organizations establish a set of standard operating procedures. In the course of following them, however, the subordinates or members to whom authority and functions have been delegated often come to regard the procedures as ends in themselves rather than as means toward the achievement of goals. The actual activities of the organization then become centered around the proper functioning of procedures rather than upon the achievement of the initial goals. Selznick (1957) has called this ''the tragedy of organization'': the tendency of organizations to defeat the very purposes for which they were established.

Another source of change in organizational goals, one that is particularly relevant for nonprofit voluntary associations, is the desire of participants to retain their high-status positions in the organization. To accomplish this, they tend to focus their energies on self-serving rather than goal-directed activities. Michels (1962), in his famous study of political parties, discovered what he called ''the iron law of oligarchy,'' according to which ''it is organization which gives birth to domination of the elected over the electors, of the mandatories over the mandators, of the delegates over the delegators. Who says organization,'' Michels intoned, ''says oligarchy.''

The reasons for this tendency toward minority rule are many. The very structure of many nonprofit organizations may encourage this development. Large size, heterogeneous membership, and sporadic participation among the rank and file may move the leaders to feel they are the only ones who are really devoted to the organization. Or perhaps the leaders are the ones with the necessary skills and have control over the apparatus for communication; as a result, their control is perceived as appropriate, as a pursuit of their professional mandate and responsibility. Whether it is through a process of selection or by virtue of their professed competence, the tendency toward some form of minority rule in organizations is widespread.

But is this process inevitable? Michels asserted that minority rule invariably leads to a blunting of the purposes for which the organization was established. The case studies we examine, however, suggest that these goals are not always displaced when a small cadre assumes control. The centralization of leadership may in some cases be perceived as legitimate authority; in other situations, minority rule may lead to a more intense and radical pursuit of the espoused goals.

Resource Dependence

A second explanation of organization change is the resource-dependence model (Pfeffer & Salancik 1978), which emphasizes the tendency of organizations to alter their structures and goals in order to obtain the resources needed to survive. Researchers have used this model to explain the composition of hospital boards of trustees (Pfeffer 1973); the behavior of United Ways (Pfeffer & Leong 1977); and the allocation of university budgets (Pfeffer & Salancik 1974). Similarly, we have employed the resource-dependence perspective to account for changes in program decision making at a public television station (Powell & Friedkin 1986). We showed how the decline in both federal and foundation financing, and the subsequent increase in corporate and member support, have made it harder to present either politically controversial or artistically experimental works. Corporate underwriters naturally prefer ''safe,'' conventional, splendidly produced shows that reflect favorably upon the program's sponsor. Members are more attracted to popular music shows and natural history programs than to demanding, innovative work.

The core of resource-dependence theory is the view that organizations will (and should) respond to the demands of those groups in the environment that control critical resources (Pfeffer & Salancik 1978). Because organizations are not internally self-sufficient, they require resources from the environment; hence, they become dependent upon those elements that provide the most needed forms of support. The managerial task, according to this approach, is to respond to environmental demands and constraints and attempt to mitigate these influences. A good example of this process was shown in our analysis of the relationship between the multiple funding sources and the programming staff who were involved in producing the public television series, ''Dance in America'' (Powell & Friedkin 1986). As long as resources were abundant, the staff was able to manage the divergent demands of the different funders either by playing them off against one another or by attending to them sequentially. But when resources shrank and only a few funding sources provided the bulk of the money, the staff lost its room to maneuver and the funders gained much greater say in program content.

Institutional Models

DiMaggio and Powell (1983) have argued that many aspects of organizational change can be explained as a result of institutional isomorphism—processes that lead organizations in specific organizational fields to become more similar to one another over time, without necessarily becoming more efficient. Modern societies are marked by the increasing ''structuration'' of organizational fields. An ''organizational field'' refers to ''those organizations that, in the aggregate, constitute a recognizable area of institutional life: key suppliers, resource and product consumers, regulatory agencies, and other organizations that produce similar services or products'' (DiMaggio & Powell 1983, 148). Structuration is a four-part process characterized by increases in the amount of interaction among organizations in a field, which, in turn, accelerates the exchange of information, and may lead to the development of structures of prestige and domination within the field. These processes help create an ideological construction, or institutional self-definition, in which certain organizations and their practices are viewed (both by themselves and other members of the field) as being most central. These organizations serve as role models for other organizations; in so doing, they contribute to the development of an ''institutionalized mind-set''—widely shared assumptions about what the organization should look like and how its work should be performed (Galaskiewicz 1985).

Organizations perceived as not adhering to fieldwide norms may lose legitimacy and, as a result, face sanctioning by regulatory or central funding organizations. They may also lose clients and customers, particularly if transactions are based on complex contingent contracts requiring stability and accountability. Organizations that deviate from fieldwide norms may also encounter difficulty in recruiting staff, especially in those industries in which careers are built across organizations rather than within internal labor markets. More deviant organizations may find that access to financial markets is restricted. Peripheral organizations are also likely to have difficulty collecting information owing to their relative distance from the centers of fieldwide information networks.

Homogeneity within a field will tend to increase when organizations alter—either reluctantly or willingly—their structures and behaviors to conform to fieldwide norms. This process can occur in discrete steps (as when organizations acquire certified professionals, such as accountants, or start new departments) or gradually (as when organizations add to their administrative staff or offer more mainstream programs). An apt example is the case of a structural reorganization at a large metropolitan public television station. With the advice of a leading consulting firm, the station switched from a functional design to a multidivisional structure. The stations' executives were a little skeptical as to whether the new structure was more efficient; in fact, some services were now duplicated across divisions. But they were convinced that the new design would carry a powerful message to the for-profit firms with whom the station regularly dealt. These firms, whether in the role of corporate underwriters or as potential partners in joint ventures, would view the reorganization as a sign that ''the sleepy nonprofit station was becoming more business-minded'' (Powell 1986).

Researchers have suggested that organizational change

will be most influenced by external institutional forces when organizational technologies are poorly understood; when organizations are not closely evaluated or when they are located in a field in which market tests of efficiency do not operate strongly; when goals are ambiguous or highly politicized; and when organizations are enmeshed in elaborate relational networks and their environment is highly organized (Meyer & Rowan 1977; DiMaggio & Powell 1983). These arguments have obvious relevance to the nonprofit sector, where organizations frequently must cope with a high degree of uncertainty. In addition, the growing professionalization of the nonprofit field further contributes to institutional pressures, as organizations seek to show they can provide the same services as their competitors.

CASE STUDIES OF ORGANIZATIONAL CHANGE

The methodology of case studies is typically used in research when the issues under investigation are complex, multifaceted, nonrepetitive, and highly contextual, making more formal analysis impossible. Yet the authors of an individual case study usually present relatively simple explanatory arguments. Within the context of the story, these explanations have a ring of authenticity. The ideal case study offers plausible explanations and develops a detailed picture of the complexity of the issues that are involved in the case. The rich contextual material that is presented may also enable the reader to develop alternative explanations. When ethnography is done well, the richness of detail presented in an individual case can take our understanding well beyond the simple structures of the causal arguments developed by the author.

We have chosen ten case studies from the literature on organizational change. Nine of these cases deal explicitly with nonprofit organizations; one, by Burton Clark, deals with a community college, which is a public institution. The majority of the studies are regarded as classics; they have long been recognized as enduring contributions to research on organizations. The more recent studies have not yet attained this lofty status, but they share common elements with the classics: detailed attention to the natural history of an organization; a view that the present state of affairs is rooted in past events and decisions; and a concern with the informal features of an organization, its soft underbelly consisting of a tangled web of relationships, dependencies, conflicts, politics, and values. The common theme running through these studies is how organizational goals are changed—weakened or subverted—or successfully maintained in the face of altered external conditions and changing internal pressures.

Social Services

In his analysis of social service organizations for the blind, Scott (1967) found that, although stated agency goals are to enhance the welfare of the blind, factors other than client need more strongly influence service delivery. Organiza-

tional persistence and the interests of major benefactors were the major forces that Scott identified as responsible for goal displacement.

Although most blind people are female, elderly, and only partially blind, the majority of services are directed at children and employable adults. When services for the blind were first provided over a hundred years ago, children and otherwise healthy adults composed the needy population, and organizations for the blind addressed the problems of education and employability. That these emphases have continued is, in part, attributable to the institutionalization of early programs.

Fund-raising concerns, however, also explain the lack of attention paid to the majority of the blind population. Blind children evoke more sympathy from funders than do the elderly blind, and programs to employ blind adults appeal to widely shared values of personal independence. Whether accurate or not, agency administrators perceive that programs for the young, educable, and employable will enjoy better funding than those for the elderly.

This focus on service delivery to only a small portion of the blind population is obviously detrimental to the majority of the blind people whom these agencies are ostensibly intended to serve. Programs that are targeted to the young and employable force the agencies to compete for those few blind people who can take advantage of these services. These "marketable" blind persons assist the organization in its fund-raising efforts. The process of goal displacement is completed when, rather than fostering independence, the agencies guard their "desirable" blind and increase their clients' dependence by providing housing, employment, and recreation.

Our next example is Mobilization for Youth (MFY), a social welfare agency on Manhattan's Lower East Side concerned with the problem of juvenile delinquency. Helfgot (1974, 1981) analyzed MFY's history through 1972, including its four-year planning stage, its founding in 1962, and its subsequent ten years of operations. In general, MFY's history is a story of organizational change generated by a dependency on external sources for resources.

The relatively brief history of MFY was marked by several distinct changes in philosophy, strategy, and program. Born as the centerpiece of the federal government's "war on poverty," MFY's primary funders—the National Institutes of Mental Health (NIMH), the President's Committee on Juvenile Delinquency and Youth Crime (PCJD), and the Ford Foundation—were searching for innovative solutions to the problems of juvenile delinquency and poverty. The funders were attracted to new theories that argued that poverty and delinquency were the products of community-level factors rather than of individual inadequacy or maladaptation. The first proposal for MFY, however, was predicated on a more traditional service delivery model. Conceived by a local settlement house, MFY was intended to be a coordinating service as well as an organizational base to generate greater resources for area social work agencies. Although NIMH rejected the initial proposal, it suggested changes that would make the project more attractive to the government. Among its suggestions were close collaboration with academic social scientists to develop a theoretical basis for a program, a two-year planning phase, and a major research component to measure effectiveness. The other major funders, the Ford Foundation and the PCJD, had similar demands. Another influential factor in MFY's future development was the financial and decision-making participation by municipal government. New York City was initially reluctant to get involved with MFY; but, under pressure from the federal government, city agencies joined in sponsoring MFY as a pilot effort in the prevention and control of juvenile delinquency. The final proposal bore little resemblance to the original idea conceived by the Lower East Side settlement houses. Instead, it was heavily influenced by the interests and demands of organizations outside of the community that MFY would serve.

MFY's ideas were based on an eclectic mix of delinquency theories, the most distinctive of which was an explicitly structural theory about the nature of poverty. In the translation of theory into practice, however, this structural thrust was severely watered down. The staff of MFY found there was little they could do to influence the larger social structure; as a result, a culture of poverty theory soon pervaded MFY's programs. Helfgot argues that the emphasis on cultural inferiority, though inconsistent with MFY's initial rationale, was consistent with the objectives of MFY's elite sponsors. Far from being interested in fundamental reform, the funders desired greater social control, enforced by the community itself.

For most of the period of Helfgot's research, the powerful sponsors maintained control over MFY's programs and philosophy. Yet during a period of almost a year and a half MFY did become involved in militant community action, including rent and school strikes, civil rights demonstrations, voter registration drives, public attacks on federal and local agencies, and legislative lobbying. The initial structural approach was reemphasized: issues of power and discrimination, rather than cultural adjustment, became primary concerns, and staff members became "advocates" rather than "enablers." This period of militancy was short-lived; it provoked an intense public attack on MFY, including "charges of communist infiltration, misappropriation of funds, and precipitation of riots" (Helfgot 1981, 69). Although MFY was eventually cleared of all charges, this crisis forced a permanent withdrawal from militancy and its accompanying focus on structural change. The agency became one of professionals trying to help individuals adjust to existing institutions.

Two transitions, then, demand explanation: the shift to aggressive community-based action and the retreat from this vigorous program of protest. With respect to MFY's increasing militancy, Helfgot argues that the structural orientation of the initial proposal attracted militant professionals to the organization. When they found that cooperation with powerful institutions was no more successful than traditional social work in bringing about real change, these professionals turned to militant community action. The agency's contact with other movement organizations also contributed to its radicalization, as the staff was influenced by their more radical tactics. Moreover, MFY spawned several community action organizations, which became more militant than MFY itself and pushed the parent organization in the same direction: "MFY was thus seen as responsible for the movement organizations it created, becoming defined as more militant in the process" (Helfgot 1981, 87).

The shift toward conservatism was similarly driven by a mix of external and internal factors. Perhaps most important were the external funding sources and arrangements. The start-up grants were multiyear commitments, giving the new program some stability. When the initial grants expired, however, new funds were allocated on a yearly basis. The change to annual funding coincided with the transition from the Kennedy and early Johnson administrations, and their emphasis on innovative antipoverty programs, to the later Johnson and Nixon administrations, and their greater emphasis on individual adjustment. Just as MFY faced a financial crisis, a new funding source developed—the U.S. Department of Labor (DOL)—and MFY was designated a Manpower Research Center, entitling it to long-term support, but requiring both a shift in program emphasis and different measures of accountability. New programs concentrated on personal adjustment through vocational training, the success of which was assessed by DOL-mandated measures. The Department of Labor, along with the like-minded New York City Human Resources Administration (HRA), supplied 75 percent of MFY's budget. Another characteristic of the late Johnson-Nixon years was the channeling of grants through state and local governments, thus reducing MFY's direct control over its budget and programs.

An internal factor accounting for the shift in goals was the heavily professional component of MFY's organization. Over half of MFY's staff had completed college and a quarter held advanced degrees. Helfgot argues that this professionalism contributed to the emphasis on organizational maintenance, particularly as evidenced by the acceptance of DOL and HRA money, at the expense of original goals.

Social Movements

The previous examples describe conservative change. Indeed, Michels (1962) has argued that organizational change is inherently conservative because key staff members will always seek to protect their positions, even to the point of abandoning stated goals. But, in some cases, the capture of an organization by its staff can lead to greater militancy or more intense commitment to the espoused goals (see the discussion by Jenkins in chapter 17 of this trend in advocacy groups). An example of a radical transformation of organizational programs is provided by Jenkins's study (1977) of the National Council of Churches (NCC). He analyzed the history of the NCC, focusing on its increasing involvement in broad social change movements in the 1960s. A detailed analysis of the Migrant Ministry, an agency of the NCC, shows that it was so completely transformed that it essentially merged with the California farm workers' movement.

The NCC was founded as a federation of about thirty Protestant denominations, which contribute to the council proportionate to their congregational membership. The council provides services to its members, such as educational programs and literature, and sponsors agencies concerned with specific programs, such as giving aid to migrant farm workers (the initial goal of the Migrant Ministry).

The NCC's social involvement had traditionally been limited to charitable social work and teaching—a social gospel approach. In the late 1950s some agencies, including the Migrant Ministry, began to take a more activist approach to serving their clientele. By the early 1960s the goals of the NCC itself came to be identified as activist social change, particularly racial equality, in spite of the more conservative attitudes held by most congregation members—the nominal constituency of the NCC. Such activities as lobbying, community organizing, and political advocacy became important NCC undertakings.

As the activist programs became publicly visible, the NCC came under attack from its conservative laity. As a result, automatic contributions to NCC agencies were discontinued and denominations were allowed to select those activities to which they would contribute. Lay opposition did not result in the elimination of activist programs, however, although their growth was curbed and some existing programs were consolidated. Jenkins notes that the NCC continued to provide valuable services to the denominations and that denominational leaders, for prestige and career reasons, favored continued association with the NCC, thus helping to keep the council together. The general radicalization of the NCC, unlike that of Mobilization for Youth, continued despite criticism. In fact, the withdrawal of automatic contributions to the Migrant Ministry seemed to hasten its radicalization by lessening the ministry's dependence on "hostile" funding sources and thus increasing its autonomy. Although budgetary reductions were required, the Migrant Ministry invested all its effort in the Farm Workers' Union; as a result, the Migrant Ministry and the farm workers' movement soon became indistinguishable.

Several factors help explain the NCC's transformation. The growth of the Protestant church in the 1950s was important in several respects. Increasing membership meant more available funds for the NCC and its agencies. A surge in professional training for the clergy and the development of liberation theology contributed to the growth of a radical definition of the clergy's mission. A combination of self-selection and church personnel policies aimed at avoiding open conflict in the church channeled activist clergy into the NCC, which became a relatively insulated arena in which radicalism could flourish. In addition, the NCC's reward structure emphasized mission over money, encouraging staff members to develop programs in which they believed strongly.

Consistent with Michels's argument, the growth of the NCC required a larger administrative staff and increasing reliance on trained professionals, which gave the staff considerable control over decision making. Jenkins identifies several mechanisms by which this transfer of power occurred. For example, the volunteer status of members of the board of directors and the professional training of staff and executives encouraged an expert-client relationship between the NCC staff and its board. In addition, NCC executives held voting rights on the board, giving them ample opportunity to push their arguments at board meetings. Several reorganizations were intended to increase the accountability of the NCC to its board and the constituent denominations by centralizing budgetary control and increasing communications. In fact, executive control over the agencies and influence over volunteer board members increased, and NCC executives could push virtually any program through the board, as long as it did not decrease services available to the denominations. In addition, the dependence of NCC agencies on denominational funds decreased as monies became available from foundations, investments, individual donors, and nondenominational agencies. As a result, the NCC found itself relatively affluent. The combination of abundant resources and a secure domain were the principal factors that allowed the NCC to pursue radical goals that were widely divergent from its conservative lay constituency.

In contrast, Messinger's analysis (1955) of the transformation of the Townsend movement is a story of goal deflection, a case in which the organizational apparatus remained intact long after the social movement lost its original impetus. The Townsend movement was founded in the 1930s to advocate national pensions for the elderly as a mechanism for economic recovery. Even following the depression and later World War II, the organization remained committed to a specific program of pensions and economic reconstruction. The failure to respond to changing social conditions led to a steep decline in membership, even as pension issues gained political visibility in the 1950s. From a national membership of 2,250,000 in 1936, the movement shrunk to 56,656 in 1951. The decreasing political relevance of the Townsend plan halted recruitment of new members, and the advanced ages of existing members rapidly depleted the membership base. Moreover, other organizations, which did a more effective job of mobilizing political support for economic aid to the elderly, attracted many Townsend members to their ranks.

A key consequence of the sharp drop in Townsend membership was financial difficulty. In what Messinger refers to as a "tendency to salesmanship," the movement began lending its name to consumer products (candy bars and soaps) in order to raise money. The purchase of these items—unlike those in previous sales efforts, such as bumper stickers with political slogans—implied no commitment to the movement. These activities focused organizational efforts on the business of raising money rather than on the pursuit of political goals. Potential members ceased to be regarded as converts and came to be seen as customers. The leaders of the Townsend movement shifted their goals from a political agenda to a concern with organizational maintenance, even to the point that this entailed the death of the original mission. Membership activities changed, turning ''what were once the incidental rewards of participation into its only meaning.'' A politically active, value-oriented social movement was transformed into a recreation club, offering dances and card-playing for its remaining elderly members.

Voluntary Associations

Sills's analysis (1957) of the National Foundation for Infantile Paralysis contrasts sharply with Messinger's study of the Townsend movement. This is a case not of goal transformation but of the successful achievement of the foundation's major goal—namely, the eradication of polio. Rather than closing up shop, the foundation used its effective organizational structure and volunteer corps to broaden its mission to include research on all birth defects. In 1958, the name was changed to the National Foundation, dropping ''for Infantile Paralysis.'' Two decades later, in 1979, the name was changed again, to the March of Dimes Birth Defects Foundation. Sills argues that the organizational structure of the foundation was essential in keeping its activities centered on its stated goals and facilitated the subsequent decision to pursue related goals, once polio was conquered.

The foundation's structure was corporate in nature, with a national headquarters and local branches, rather than a federation of semiautonomous affiliates. Thus, ultimate control for foundation policy and the direction of its activities was retained by the national headquarters. This centralization was balanced, however, by a clear-cut division of responsibility. The foundation engaged in three distinct activities, each of which was the main purview of a separate part of the foundation: fund-raising, the disbursement of funds in local communities to aid victims of infantile paralysis, and research to eliminate the disease. The research function was administered by the national headquarters.

The foundation is perhaps best known for its annual fund-raising drive, the March of Dimes. This massive effort is the responsibility of local March of Dimes organizations, which are temporary in nature, rather than of the local foundation chapters, although the chapters participate in the drive. The march is directed by the national headquarters, which appoints campaign directors for each city. The position of director does not entail year-round effort, and new directors are often appointed each year. A huge number of volunteers is mobilized yearly and then dispersed upon completion of the drive. The local chapters of the foundation are primarily concerned with patient care. Half the money raised by the March of Dimes was returned to the chapters for disbursement in the community, primarily to give financial assistance to victims of polio.

Sills suggests that all voluntary associations face two potential sources of organizational failure. The first is member apathy, which stems from the upward delegation of authority from the rank and file to the leaders in large organizations where work is controlled by specialized staff professionals. The second is goal displacement, or the substitution of means for ends, stemming from the downward delegation of authority from the leadership to those responsible for day-to-day activities. In the case of the foundation, each of these problems was mitigated by its organizational characteristics.

Although the National Foundation is a large organization, the size of local chapters is kept small, and members are kept actively involved through a system of assigning them specific tasks. The temporary nature of the large March of Dimes organizations focuses volunteer involvement on the task at hand, namely, fund-raising. In addition, the high turnover among March of Dimes volunteers seems to help sustain enthusiasm. Responsibility for chapter affairs remains with volunteers largely because chapters are prohibited from electing a physician or public health professional as chairman. Professional guidance is available when needed from a Medical Advisory Committee, and from the state representative, a national headquarters employee.

A common reason for goal displacement is that members, especially paid staff, become more concerned with maintaining or improving their positions within the organization than with the pursuit of the organization's stated goals. This tendency was minimized at the foundation for three reasons. First, there is no state-level organization, eliminating an entire layer of paid staff positions and an important rung on the career ladder. Second, there is little opportunity for paid professionals to become widely known outside the organization itself. Finally, few paid staff members are ex-volunteers, so there is no visible upward career ladder for volunteers.

The tendency to focus on rules rather than on the intended objectives can also bring about goal displacement. The foundation's formal rules concerning its major activities were written in such a way that they help avoid this problem. The rules include prohibitions on chapter activities (for example, funds may not be used for the construction of hospitals), but they have little to say about day-to-day judgments that must be made to carry out foundation work. Thus, it is difficult for the technical requirements of the rules to become more important than the goals of the foundation.

Sills contends that the foundation was successful largely because of its organizational structure, which both allowed volunteers to become actively involved in the organization, but not in such a way as to displace the goals, and permitted headquarters to retain responsive control over the local chapters. The strong corporate structure was also important in the foundation's decision to broaden its purpose in the late 1950s. A record of success, local involvement combined with a lean and effective national leadership, and a clear delegation of functions made the search for a new organizational purpose much easier than would have been the case in other voluntary organizations, where continued existence might have been perceived as in the interest of the paid staff, not the larger public.

Gusfield's analysis (1955, 1963) of the Women's Christian Temperance Union (WCTU) portrays an organization in decline because its original goals and strategies were adhered to even in the face of significant social change. After the repeal of Prohibition the WCTU faced an increasingly hostile environment but continued to strongly oppose drinking.

Gusfield's explanation for this inability to adapt focuses on the WCTU leadership. During the WCTU's heyday it occupied a prestigious position in middle-class society. The social status of its leadership provided some legitimacy for its reformist posture, which was directed largely at the lower classes. With the end of Prohibition, however, these middle-class members left the organization and the social status of WCTU leadership declined. As the leadership came to be rooted in the lower and lower middle classes, the WCTU could no longer maintain a "superior," reformist posture. Instead, there was a growing resentment of the middle class who had abandoned the movement, and WCTU rhetoric became marked by moral indignation.

A second important factor in the decline of the WCTU was the rate of leadership turnover. Presidential tenure was rather long, and the slow pipeline to top positions groomed future leaders in terms of present policies. Although some members were well aware of their organization's waning popularity and tried to recruit and develop younger members and to support new leaders, the continuing presence of the old guard negated their efforts.

Zald's study (1970; Zald & Denton 1963) of the Young Men's Christian Association (YMCA) in the United States is an analysis of a successful organizational transformation. It is called successful because, although the organization's activities and efforts were altered in important ways, the changes enabled it to reach a larger audience without sacrificing its basic mission. Zald analyzed the history of the YMCA from its founding in the mid-1800s to the mid-1960s, and did a case study of the large Chicago YMCA from 1961 to 1967.

Founded as an interdenominational Protestant organization to provide Christian fellowship to young men, the YMCA quickly took on a strong evangelical character, as revivalism grew in the late 1850s. After the Civil War there were disagreements within the federation over the appropriateness and viability of evangelism in the YMCA. The New York association adopted a model of general service to young men, and by 1889 the International Committee (the national executive committee for the federation) officially opposed evangelism as a YMCA goal. The New York model gradually spread throughout the country, changing the YMCA from an organization dedicated to the moral salvation of young Protestant men to a secular, broad-based, fee-for-service organization pursuing general character development.

This shift in organizational goals, as well as the programmatic means of attaining them, was effective, and the YMCA grew both in resources and in membership. In contrast, the WCTU, which was also an organization with a strong moral component, did not adapt to external changes and lost its viability. What factors account for the YMCA's capacity for adaptive change? Zald addresses this question by examining the organization's political economy and its institutional development.

Four main factors explain the transformation of the YMCA's mission from evangelism to general service. First, the group's economic base as a religious organization was unstable. Resembling a Protestant denomination in its activities and the incentives offered to its members, the YMCA competed with the church for members and contributions and was vulnerable to the ups and downs of both revivalism and the business cycle. This financial insecurity made clear the need for alternative funding sources. Three programmatic innovations helped change the character of the YMCA. Various fee-for-service programs, such as lecture series and vocational education programs, were easy to implement and could be discontinued if demand declined. The widespread construction of dormitory residences, beginning in the 1870s, was a second innovation. These hostels provided income for the association and were widely perceived as a general public service. Finally, the development in 1885 of the YMCA gymnasium proved to be effective in recruiting members. These innovations were steps toward the organization acquiring a diversified economic base, supported by fees for various services. The residences and gymnasiums represented large capital investments and, in turn, programmatic commitments, making the YMCA a building-centered organization. Perhaps more important for future changes in programs and goals, the developing enrollment economy linked YMCA programs to the demands of its clientele.

Changes in the availability of resources, then, were clearly a driving force in the transformation of the YMCA, but an exclusive focus on resource dependency would miss elements of the organization's structure and political processes that also facilitated its ability to adapt. First among these is the broad nature of the association's stated goals. Providing for the welfare of the whole man—physical, intellectual, social, and spiritual—permits various interpretations and emphases and allows considerable latitude in developing and rejecting programs. Although the organization's goals were originally religious in purpose, several factors prevented religious dominance of the YMCA. An interdenominational emphasis, the use of lay rather than clerical leadership, and the focus on association and fellowship rather than church activities alone minimized theological influence in the YMCA's early days, thus maintaining options for future development.

In contrast to Sills's analysis, Zald maintains that the federated structure of the YMCA permitted flexibility and responsiveness to local needs. Zald (1970, 64) argues that "it was the ability of local Associations to command the support of their own communities that accounted for the YMCA's staying power," not the limited power of the national association. The autonomy of local associations is evidenced by the fact that they often ignored national directives with impunity. Their importance is indicated by the observation that some local policies, such as admitting women to membership, were originally opposed at the national level but later became the norm.

The final facilitating factor in the YMCA's successful development is its reliance on lay rather than professional control. The organization's history emphasized democratic lay control, and policy-making was traditionally deemed the responsibility of the board rather than the secretary (the top-level administrator). This ideology was reinforced by a committee structure developed to involve laypeople in specific program areas as well as in overall policy direction. The historic importance of laypeople, however, does not necessarily ensure their continued dominance. Zald argues that several factors tended to reduce conflict between secretaries and their boards and to support board control of policy development. The secretaries did not belong to a professional association or ascribe to a professional ideology that might compete with the YMCA for their allegiance; hence, they could not lay claim to a specialized skill or knowledge base from which to buttress their policy positions. Zald also notes that their personalities typically predisposed them to accept and respect authority. As a result, the YMCA has been dominated not by its national professional staff but by local members.

Community Organizations

Cooper (1980) analyzed the development and subsequent bureaucratic transformation of a community organization in the Pico-Union neighborhood of Los Angeles. The Pico-Union Neighborhood Council (PUNC) was founded in 1966. The product of organizing efforts of a small group of community residents, PUNC enjoyed some early, visible successes, such as getting improved street lighting and cleaning, but was unable to make progress in the area it had targeted for action: housing. When both a private developer and the Los Angeles Community Redevelopment Agency (CRA) expressed interest in Pico-Union as a redevelopment site, PUNC entered its second phase. The Neighborhood Council sought assistance in developing expertise in housing and redevelopment and greatly expanded its membership. During the height of community participation, PUNC had a small paid staff and about five hundred members. The group effectively mobilized community residents, involved them in decision making, and established itself as a legitimate representative of community interests. Subsequently, however, active community involvement ceased, replaced by passive and often tacit support for a professional and bureaucratic organization.

The Pico-Union Neighborhood Council is unusual among our case studies because financial pressures appear to have been an insignificant factor in its development. A local foundation was the sole funder of PUNC, but it "attached very few strings" to its money. Cooper argues that it was not financial dependence but the necessity of interacting with organizations whose perspectives were different from those of a grass-roots community organization, as well as the technical and legal nature of the projects that PUNC undertook, that were ultimately responsible for PUNC's transformation.

The two organizations with which PUNC established ongoing relationships were the CRA and the University of California at Los Angeles (UCLA). Although the nature of these relationships was initially different—the CRA and PUNC battled over control of the redevelopment process, whereas

UCLA assumed more of an advocacy role—both organizations contributed to the professionalization and bureaucratization of PUNC. Faculty members at UCLA were instrumental in helping PUNC obtain funding, develop a base of technical expertise, and solicit and articulate community preferences. Independent funding required PUNC's incorporation as a nonprofit organization and the hiring of staff, thus introducing bureaucratic and legal elements into PUNC's structure and facilitating its interaction with other organizations. Although these steps were necessary for PUNC to have any influence in the redevelopment process, they also contributed to its bureaucratization and professionalization. Similarly, the CRA's official control of the redevelopment process necessitated that, if PUNC was to remain substantively involved, the two organizations would interact in a framework largely defined by the CRA.

The nature of the tasks undertaken by PUNC was also responsible for the organization's transformation. The group became increasingly involved in projects requiring high levels of technical expertise and legal accountability. Its initial housing success was a detailed plan for community redevelopment. Although PUNC required considerable technical assistance, its distinctive area of expertise was the coherent presentation of informed community opinion. The development and construction of low-income housing, PUNC's next major project, required far more technical, legal, and bureaucratic knowledge, and active community participation declined precipitously.

Education

Clark (1956a, 1956b) studied the transformation of adult education in California from a narrowly defined program of remedial and vocational training for high school dropouts to a general service program for all adults. The impetus for broadening the educational mission included the growth of immigrant education, or Americanization classes, in the 1910s and the demand for adult vocational education during World War I. These changes expanded the population base from adolescents to adults, but the relatively narrow foci served to limit the diversity of the adult education curriculum. In the 1920s, state financial aid to adult education increased in response to concerns about immigration, providing a stimulus for the general expansion of adult education. By 1925 the mission of adult education had grown to include all adults as potential students. Clark's primary concern is with the way in which adult education has developed since that year. His analysis centers on three environmental conditions to which adult education had to respond in order to survive: organizational marginality, diffuse goals, and an enrollment economy.

In the status order of higher education, adult education occupies a low-prestige position. This marginality heightens the vulnerability of adult education. Rather than being firmly established in an orderly sequence of higher education, adult education is a nonmandatory program that does not offer a terminal degree. Thus, it resides on the periphery of the educational system and has little legitimacy in the eyes of the public, educators, legislators, and interest groups. The long-term security of adult education would appear to lie in an effort to achieve educational respectability. This goal, however, conflicts with the short-term needs for organizational survival. This focus on short-run results is principally dictated by the enrollment economy that drives adult education. But, as Clark shows, the concern with enrollment leads to a sense of diffuseness and a lack of vision concerning the goals of adult education.

The stated mission of California's adult education program "embraces the learning achieved by adults during their mature years" (Clark 1956b, 330). This broad purpose allows administrators wide discretion but fails to provide guidelines for strategic and day-to-day administrative action. Thus when considering curriculum changes, an administrator has no overarching educational purpose upon which to base a decision. New courses typically are added to a program in response to demonstrated demand, rather than as part of an educationally integrated curriculum, thus exacerbating the problem of marginality within the educational community.

Finally, the enrollment economy on which adult education is based shapes course offerings, the composition of the teaching staff, and administrative policies of adult education in fundamental ways. State financing depends almost entirely on attendance: the higher the attendance, the higher the state appropriations, regardless of overall costs. Many features of the educational process are tied to the contingencies of an enrollment economy. For example, although the adult education system is highly decentralized, the state board of education sets the minimum enrollment policy, according to which all classes must have at least fourteen students in attendance at all times. Many districts have a no-tuition policy in order to maintain enrollments (although this creates obvious problems of low commitment on the part of students). Most courses require no examinations. Course content is structured so that every lecture can stand alone as a comprehensible unit of information, and some courses permit rolling registration so that a student may begin at any point during the term and simply cycle back to that point to complete the course.

The colleges responded to the problems created by a demand-driven curriculum by cosponsoring courses with local organizations, such as the Medical Assistants' Association or the Department of Motor Vehicles. This arrangement has several advantages for the adult college. Adequate enrollment is generally ensured, the administrative burden is shared with the cosponsoring organization, the cosponsor provides an organized clientele which allows the adult program to use its resources more effectively, and these organizational linkages may be used by the college to gain support from local centers of political power. Clark argues that this is a form of weak cooptation that, although contributing to the adult education program's survival, further removes decision making from it.

The composition of the teaching staff is also influenced by

the need for large enrollments. Most teachers have other primary occupations, teaching in these programs on the side. Recruitment is decentralized and based heavily on personality (ability to sustain student interest and commitment) rather than on civil service exams or measures of teaching competence. Although there are provisions for tenure, retention is ultimately based on course enrollments.

The exigencies of the enrollment economy serve to maintain the system in the short run, but in the long run they contribute to its marginality. The mechanisms used to sustain and legitimate adult education also help keep the system on the educational periphery. Clark suggests that the major justifications for adult education are: (1) its low cost to local school districts; (2) its ability to involve adults (that is, taxpayers) in the educational process, thus serving as a valuable public relations tool for the entire district; and (3) its responsiveness to public demand. Thus, the marginality, diffuse goals, and enrollment economy that characterize adult education result in service-dependent organization rather than an educational system based on professional competence and educational integrity.

The California Institute of the Arts was founded as an avant-garde art scene, a utopian community for artists of all media to experiment and create, unhindered by market pressures and lay opinion (Adler 1979). From its inception, however, Cal Arts labored under twin pressures: ideological and financial. Within two years of its establishment, Cal Arts was largely transformed into a more conventional and conservative private art school. Within five years, public statements of philosophy espoused a new, more professional direction and utopian proclamations were increasingly out of favor. As numerous institute members said, "the dream had died."

Ideologically, two major conflicts contributed to the demise of the initial vision. From the start there was a divergence of opinion on the part of trustees and artists. The former were concerned that they fulfill the dreams of Walt Disney, the institute's benefactor, who died shortly before final plans were approved. The Disney legacy was typified by elaborate public spectacles. The artists' conception of the institute was also grand, but in the service of artists, with little concern for public consumption. In Cal Arts' early days its members reveled in the "joke" they had pulled on the conservative funders who had committed apparently unlimited monies for a radical and spectacularly equipped artists' playground. It soon became apparent, however, that the "joke" was on the artists, as the trustees began to exercise their considerable control. The extent of this control became clear when the board refused to hire the philosopher Herbert Marcuse for a position in the School of Critical Studies.

There was also a fundamental contradiction in the premise on which the institute was founded. Cal Arts was based on an avant-garde culture, which was inherently anarchistic and called for the destruction of its institutionalization. Artists were lured to a utopian community based on total freedom from constraint of any kind, a promise that was impossible to fulfill. For example, the initial philosophy stressed collegial relations between faculty and students and opposed a formal curriculum. Pressures soon mounted for a more traditional curriculum, however, as faculty members found it difficult to limit student access to their time, as students failed to meet the faculty's inflated expectations, and as the distinction between professional and amateur was increasingly blurred. Similarly, artists were attracted to Cal Arts in part by the opportunity to work closely with artists of other media in a community of art professionals. In practice, however, many faculty members expected to have easy access to other artists but not to have to provide support in return. Although Cal Arts survived as a school, the avant-garde scene soon disappeared.

Financial difficulties also plagued Cal Arts even before the campus was built; hence, from the outset, many activities were evaluated in terms of their impact on the school's economy. Owing to lavish plans and cost overruns, the entire fund allotted by Disney for Cal Arts was used up well before construction was completed. This increased the school's already strong dependence on the Disney family and created a perpetual atmosphere of insecurity and crisis. Board members were selected on the basis of personal and financial ties to the Disney family rather than for their ability to raise and maintain a sufficient endowment. High-level administrators exacerbated the financial problem by nominating board members who were sympathetic to their academic disciplines, paying little, if any, attention to their fund-raising ability.

As the extent of the financial crisis became evident, faculty members who had purchased expensive homes with steep mortgages or had given up secure tenured positions at other schools became less willing to experiment artistically or to rock the boat. Control of the purse strings soon translated into control over educational policy, as those arts most useful in fund-raising, such as classical music and dance and conventional theater, grew in favor with the trustees, and less marketable arts were severely cut back or eliminated. The lay staff also facilitated the work of artists of whom they approved (those whose work required discipline, scheduling, and coordination and whose product they appreciated) through their control of access to technical facilities and their selection of artists to appear in public events and display their work in public spaces. As financial pressures increased, the utopian character of the institute dissipated and values originally scorned became the keys to survival. Professionalism, originally dismissed in favor of vanguardism, was perceived by the artists to be their only source of power vis-à-vis the trustees. Similarly, market success, which was to have been discarded in favor of recognition by colleagues, became legitimate currency at Cal Arts.

ASSESSMENT

Although the causal arguments we have abstracted from the individual cases (some of these arguments were more implicit than explicit in the original presentation) provide relatively simple explanations of organizational change, the process of change appears to be much more complex when the studies are considered simultaneously. The collective portrait is one of multiple types of causality and richly intertwined relationships. Our attention is drawn to certain features of organizational change that are important because they appear in many of our cases, although they may not be the focal concern in any particular study.

We suggest the cases can be clustered into three categories. We label the first two categories unsuccessful because they both reflect change that either weakened the organization's mission or decreased its viability. The third category can be regarded as adaptive changes that were largely successful because the organization's mission was not threatened. Although we caution that our point about multiple causality is true in each of these cases, we think there are three principal variants on the process of organizational change in the nonprofit sector.

One variant is change driven primarily by the desires of leadership to maintain the organization. In such cases, the goals of the organization were not achieved, but the organization continued to exist, albeit in a feeble state. The Townsend movement and the WCTU are the best examples of this type of change.

Pressures for organizational change, however, more commonly come from the outside. External pressures are a critical feature of the majority of the cases we have reviewed. In some, such as Scott's study of the agency aiding the blind, the external demands are directly tied to the interests of key funding sources (as resource-dependency theory would predict). In other cases, such as that of PUNC, the external constraints are more institutional and are related to professional demands and standards of accountability. In the study by Helfgot of the MFY and the Adler study of the California Institute of the Arts we find that both resource constraints and normative pressures combined to influence the direction of the organizations. What unites all these cases is a process in which the original goals were not met. Instead, because of powerful external demands, the goals were supplanted by alternative ones in the interest of organizational survival. What distinguishes these cases from the first category is not just the presence of the external pressures but the willingness of the leadership to bend to these pressures in order to keep the organization alive. For example, Clark suggests that adult educators in California shifted their product from education to service by popular demand in order to retain their jobs.

All the cases we have grouped in this second category (Scott, Clark, Helfgot, Adler, and Cooper) illustrate the difficulty of disentangling resource-dependency and institutional-context arguments. Sometimes the external constraints are strictly financial; in other cases they are primarily normative pressures. But more often the two pressures exist in tandem. Perhaps the best-known study that emphasizes the importance of both an organization's resource environment and its institutional environment in explaining the process of organizational change is Selznick's analysis (1949) of the Tennessee Valley Association (TVA) from 1933 to 1943. The necessity of securing political support and organizational resources from the local community—initially hostile to this federally imposed project—was met by the TVA with a strategy of cooptation of local interest groups. Eventually, however, this process transformed the TVA's goals and character. The TVA delegated its agricultural program to conservative agribusiness interests, represented by the land-grant colleges, in exchange for their support. Under their influence, the TVA gradually altered its basic mission: instead of being primarily a conservation agency for the public good, it became an advocate of land development interests that were contrary to those of environmentalists and small farmers. In this case, and in the ones we have reviewed, external demands cannot be neatly labeled. Fiscal, political, and professional requirements overlap and the organizations appear weak and unable to ignore them, even to the point of sacrificing their initial purposes.

The third class of organizational change also represents change that is largely a response to external conditions, but the changes do not result in goal transformation. We considered these cases successful because the original goals were pursued more intensely (Jenkins's study of the NCC); or new, related goals were adopted once the stated goal was achieved (Sills's study of the March of Dimes); or the initial mission was broadened in a manner that led to organizational expansion and enhanced viability (Zald's study of the YMCA). The common elements in these three cases are important. All three organizations had a certain degree of financial stability. They were not resource poor, nor were they dependent upon a small number of funding sources. Each of the three organizations also had a measure of pluralism associated with its governance. The YMCA avoided control by any one denomination and opened its doors to people of all religions and races. More important from the governance perspective was the commitment to lay, rather than professional, management. Although the YMCA's federated structure differs from the March of Dimes' more centralized organizational form, the latter also avoided capture by any one constituency. The March of Dimes has remained a lean organization in terms of its staff, as well as retaining a large enthusiastic volunteer component. The formal management structures of the YMCA, the March of Dimes, and the NCC are all different, but they share the common trait of pluralism. No one professional group or single constituency dominates the decision-making process.

CONCLUSION

The successful cases of organizational change suggest several important lessons with considerable contemporary relevance. Participation in many nonprofit organizations is often segmental and part time. (This is why social scientists refer to voluntary associations as secondary associations, in contrast to primary groups such as the family or the work group.) Many of today's nonprofits are seeking to increase their volunteer base as a means of coping with fiscal uncertainty. But frequently an expanded membership is seen as a financial strategy, not as a means to create wider participation in the governance of the organization. The inherent danger in this practice is that participation, which could be a sustaining force, instead becomes more segmental and part time, thereby undercutting enthusiastic support and pluralistic governance.

Similarly, many nonprofits find themselves turning more and more to external sources of support as their own resources dry up and unmet social needs increase. The cases we have reviewed suggest that there are trade-offs inevitably associated with outside sources of support. This is not to suggest that funding sources direct control or even that they desire to covertly influence organizations to pursue certain activities at the expense of others. The difficulty with external sources of financing or a more general emphasis on commercial activities is that it can lead organizations to change in unanticipated ways. The case studies we have reviewed are all examples of unplanned change. No one expected the organizations to move in the directions they did. The forces of change often work quietly, and frequently it is not until too late that the organization recognizes that its legitimacy has been eroded and its purpose neglected. For example, patrons or funders may donate considerable sums of money with no programmatic strings attached. But decentralized, loosely organized structures may give patrons pause; they prefer centralized executive leadership, accountants, and financial managers because they help ensure fiscal accountability. The organization may add these staff members and change its leadership structure to accommodate these concerns. Such a change may seem benign, but it can disenfranchise broad-based participants and lead to elite dominance. No one dictated this outcome; indeed it might not even be preferred. But these are the problems that nonprofits frequently face, dangers that are exacerbated by the fiscal shortages that typify the current economic climate.

Our reanalysis of these studies of organizational change permits us to speculate about what types of goals are more or less likely to be displaced. When are unplanned changes most likely to occur to nonprofit organizations? We suggest that three factors—political clout, financing, and technical complexity—are crucial. Goals that are favored by weak constituencies are likely to yield to those favored by stronger ones. Services that are provided to the powerless and the poor are more likely to be supplanted by services for middle-income groups who have more political influence. When financial resources are in short supply or controlled by a small number of supporters, nonprofits will be more inclined to change confrontational tactics or controversial programs into more mainstream and acceptable approaches. And as the activities and programs of a nonprofit become more complex and require sophisticated technical, legal, or financial knowledge in order to execute them, broad-based participation and pluralist governance is likely to decline, and a core staff of experts will come to dominate the organization. These tendencies are not inevitable, but they do suggest a particular set of circumstances under which a nonprofit is most vulnerable or susceptible to change in both its mission and its method of operation.

REFERENCES

Adler, Judith E. 1979. *Artists in Offices: An Ethnography of an Academic Art Scene*. New Brunswick, N.J.: Transaction Books.

Blau, Peter. 1963. *The Dynamics of Bureaucracy*. Chicago: University of Chicago Press.

Chandler, Alfred. 1977. *The Visible Hand*. Cambridge, Mass.: Harvard University Press.

Clark, Burton A. 1956a. *Adult Education in Transition*. Berkeley: University of California Press.

———. 1956b. "Organizational Adaptation and Precarious Values: A Case Study." *American Sociological Review* 21:327–36.

Cooper, Terry L. 1980. "Bureaucracy and Community Organization: The Metamorphosis of a Relationship." *Administration and Society* 11, no. 4:411–44.

DiMaggio, Paul, and Walter W. Powell. 1983. "The Iron Cage Revisited: Institutional Isomorphism and Collective Rationality in Organizational Fields." *American Sociological Review* 48:147–60.

Galaskiewicz, Joseph. 1985. "Professional Networks and the Institutionalization of a Single Mind Set." *American Sociological Review* 50, no. 5 (October):639–58.

Gusfield, Joseph R. 1955. "Social Structure and Moral Reform: A Study of the Women's Christian Temperance Union." *American Journal of Sociology* 61:221–32.

———. 1963. *Symbolic Crusade: Status Politics and the American Temperance Movement*. Urbana: University of Illinois Press.

Hannan, Michael, and John Freeman. 1984. "Structural Inertia and Organizational Change." *American Sociological Review* 49, no. 2 (April):149–64.

Helfgot, Joseph H. 1974. "Professional Reform Organizations and the Symbolic Representation of the Poor." *American Sociological Review* 39:475–91.

———. 1981. *Professional Reforming: Mobilization for Youth and the Failure of Social Science*. Lexington, Mass.: Lexington Books.

Jenkins, J. Craig. 1977. "The Radical Transformation of Organizational Goals." *Administrative Science Quarterly* 22:248–67.

March, James G., and Johan Olsen. 1976. *Ambiguity and Choice in Organizations*. Bergen, Norway: Universitetsforlaget.

Messinger, Sheldon. 1955. "Organizational Transformation: A Case Study of a Declining Social Movement." *American Sociological Review* 20 (February):3–10.

Meyer, John W., and Brian Rowan. 1977. "Institutionalized Organizations: Formal Structure as Myth and Ceremony." *American Journal of Sociology* 83:340–63.

Michels, Robert. 1962. *Political Parties*. New York: Free Press. (Originally published in 1915)

Nelson, Richard, and Sidney Winter. 1982. *An Evolutionary Theory of Economic Change*. Cambridge, Mass.: Harvard University Press.

Pfeffer, Jeffrey. 1973. "Size, Composition and Function of Hospital Boards of Directors." *Administrative Science Quarterly* 18:349–64.

Pfeffer, Jeffrey, and Anthony Leong. 1977. "Resource Allocations in United Funds: Examination of Power and Dependence." *Social Forces* 55:775–90.

Pfeffer, Jeffrey, and Gerald Salancik. 1974. "Organizational Decision Making as a Political Process: The Case of a University Budget." *Administrative Science Quarterly* 19:135–51.

———. 1978. *The External Control of Organizations*. New York: Harper & Row.

Powell, Walter W. 1986. "Institutional Effects on Organizational Structure and Performance." In Lynne Zucker, ed., *Institutional Patterns and Organizations*. Cambridge, Mass.: Ballinger Books.

Powell, Walter W., and Rebecca Friedkin. 1986. "Politics and Programs: Organizational Factors in Public Television Decision-Making." In P. DiMaggio, ed., *Nonprofit Enterprise in the Arts*. New York: Oxford University Press.

Scott, Robert A. 1967. "The Selection of Clients by Social Welfare Agencies: The Case of the Blind." *Social Problems* 14, no. 3:248–57.

Selznick, Philip. 1949. *TVA and the Grass Roots*. Berkeley: University of California Press.

———. 1957. *Leadership in Administration*. New York: Harper & Row.

Sills, David L. 1957. *The Volunteers: Means and Ends in a National Organization*. Glencoe, Ill.: Free Press.

Simon, Herbert. 1957. *Administrative Behavior*. Glencoe, Ill.: Free Press.

Zald, Mayer. 1970. *Organizational Change: The Political Economy of the YMCA*. Chicago: University of Chicago Press.

Zald, Mayer, and Patricia Denton. 1963. "From Evangelism to General Service: The Transformation of the YMCA." *Administrative Science Quarterly* 8, no. 2:214–34.

IV

FUNCTIONS OF THE
NONPROFIT SECTOR

12

Nonprofit Organizations in the Production and Distribution of Culture

PAUL DIMAGGIO

The purpose of this chapter is to summarize what we know about the role of nonprofit enterprise in the production and distribution of culture. I address two questions: What explains the varying prevalence of nonprofit enterprise among different cultural industries? And what behavioral consequences follow if a cultural organization is nonprofit in form as opposed to for-profit or public? By "culture," a notoriously slippery concept, I refer to symbolic works produced in formally organized sectors of the economy—that is, materials produced for an audience, widely recognized as "cultural artifacts," and distributed through established channels. I am not concerned with the many forms of culture—language, most humor, some kinds of folk art and music, other privately consumed amateur events—that are produced and distributed without recourse to formal organizations or markets. Within the domain of institutionalized culture, I focus solely on the arts very broadly defined and ignore science, religion, law, and industrial design.

WHERE ARE NONPROFIT SECTORS PREVALENT?

To answer this question, we require a system for classifying cultural work. If we opt for the conventional view that

Research for this paper was supported by the Andrew W. Mellon Foundation (through grants to the Yale Program on Non-Profit Organizations and the Center for Advanced Study in the Behavioral Sciences), and the Carnegie Corporation and the Hewlett Foundation (through grants to the Program on Non-Profit Organizations). Institutional support from the Center for Advanced Study and the Program on Non-Profit Organizations is gratefully acknowledged, as are helpful editorial readings by Henry Hansmann, Walter Powell, and Charles Perrow.

distinguishes between industries that produce and distribute "high culture" and those that traffic in "entertainment," our job is made easier, for most cultural fields are divided up in this way when statistics are collected. The American Symphony Orchestra League (ASOL), for example, reports on the number of orchestras in the United States, but does not attempt to estimate the number of jazz bands; the Census of Service Industries collects data on the number of musical groups, but does not report separately the population of nonprofit orchestras. Because the ASOL and the census count bands in very different ways, there is little we can say about the relative prevalence of the nonprofit form in the large-ensemble music industry.

The problem with accepting the conventional classifications of cultural work into genres is that it gives us circular answers to questions about organizational form. All American museums are nonprofit, according to the American Association of Museums (AAM), because the definition of *museum* that the AAM has adopted excludes proprietary enterprises that mount exhibits for public view (National Endowment for the Arts 1982). Such circular answers are not incorrect, but they are less interesting than others might be.

Economists classify firms on the basis of industry. Firms whose products are close substitutes for one another are in the same industry; those that do not compete are not (Porter 1980). This method is more easily applicable to manufacturers of inputs to the production of other goods (for example, safflower oil and linseed oil, which can be substituted in some foodstuffs) than to producers of consumer items or, especially, services. It is probably least applicable to producers of leisure services, a group that includes most of the cultural industries, for such services are intrinsically substitutable unless there are barriers of taste. For example, all but the most avid music enthusiasts may regard Puccini and Verdi operas (or recordings by Cheap Trick and Twisted Sister) as substitutable for one another. Those with less finely developed schemas will view Beethoven and Puccini, or country music and rock and roll, as substitutes for one another. The more catholic in preference may even be willing to substitute popular and classical works if the price differential is sufficient. Indeed, the willingness of most people to substitute one cultural good for another may depend, in large part, on the extent to which markets for the two goods have been segmented by producers. If this is the case, it is circular to define industries on the basis of consumer preference.

I prefer a modified version of the economic approach, assuming for the sake of argument that presentations and performances in similar artistic media—for example, music, print, visual art, theater, dance—are potential substitutes for one another, and asking how, within these broad classes, industry segments are defined and allocated among nonprofit, proprietary, and public organizations. Assuming nothing about qualitative differences between ''high'' and ''popular'' culture is a heuristic device that permits us to avoid tautology and to develop, if not answer, some potentially productive questions.

Decoding the Data

How are cultural industries, by which I mean collections of sellers specializing in broadly defined artistic forms, divided among the nonprofit, for-profit, and public sectors? Most of the available statistics do not address this question directly. Consequently, the estimates that follow are, in most cases, rough ones. I raise this point both to caution the reader and, more important, to illuminate something about the cultural world by observing the manner in which statistics about it are collected.

Available Data and Institutionalized Form

In many industries, statistics are collected separately for nonprofit and for-profit organizations, rendering comparison difficult. This is especially the case in those industries in which public agencies make grants to nonprofit, but not to for-profit, producers. Such agencies have an interest in compiling lists of their potential constituents, lists from which for-profit firms are absent by design. Indeed, the better institutionalized an artistic field, the greater the likelihood that segments of the field are considered separate industries, that firms in each segment have a characteristic form, and that available statistics for nonprofit and proprietary producers are not comparable.

In general, then, established industries maintain institutionalized definitions of what an organization is that render invisible those producers that do not adopt this form. Most statistical series on cultural organizations are collected by trade associations or funding agencies. Organizations that do not join the trade associations or apply for government grants—including, in many fields, all proprietary organiza-

tions—are less likely to be counted than those that adopt the conventional legal form and participate actively in the field's activities. Industries that are poorly institutionalized— where members do not have a typical organizational form, where producers are unorganized, and where industry boundaries are poorly defined—generally yield far less information than others. For example, a recent report (Chicago Community Trust 1982) notes that Chicago's minority and neighborhood arts organizations tend to be ''collectives of dedicated artists'' operating on irregular budgets. Although few if any such groups distribute a profit, most ''have never attempted to acquire a 501(c)(3) status or become affiliated with any one agency with such status.'' Other neighborhood groups are affiliates of social service agencies or community centers. In either case, they are institutionally invisible and unlikely to be counted by national surveys.

If some industries are defined on the basis of organizational form, making conclusions about the intersectoral division of labor tautological, in many other industries organizational form is simply not salient to those who collect statistics. Trade associations that represent both public and nonprofit organizations often play down differences among their members, preferring not to treat firms with different forms as distinct, even for record-keeping purposes. Trade directories produced by third parties usually fail to distinguish between nonprofit and proprietary producers because the distinction is not important to their purchasers.

The Ambiguity of Formal Typologies

Another set of problems derives from the fact that the distinctions among nonprofit, for-profit, and public agencies are often ambiguous, and these categories do not exhaust the organizational universe. Jeffri, for example, has noted the difficulty of defining what, in fact, a dance company is (1980, 48–49). Some are ''several large rotating companies whose members fill in for each other for specific events.'' Others are solo performers. One company split into two groups with different names, different artistic management, and different styles, but remained, for legal purposes, a single company. To make matters more complex, sets of nonprofit companies are, in some cases, managed by a single for-profit management firm; in others, companies without nonprofit charters may be managed by nonprofit umbrella management organizations (Jeffri 1980).

Indeed, there are important classes of culture producers and distributors that do not fit neatly into the nonprofit/proprietary/public typology at all. I have already mentioned the problem of neighborhood arts organizations, which are very often unincorporated and, consequently, not legally nonprofit, although they neither seek nor earn a surplus. Such unincorporated groups are common in most of the performing arts and in the craft and visual arts, where associations of producers mount exhibits or operate galleries. At times, the line between public and private nonprofit is an ambiguous one. For example, a substantial minority of local arts agencies are private nonprofits formally designated by their community's governments to execute municipal functions. Many culture-producing or distributing groups are sponsored by and officially part of other nonprofit or public organizations. Some theaters belong to settlement houses or social service agencies, some youth orchestras are affiliated with YMCAs, and some art galleries are part of profit-making corporations. The most significant sponsors of this type are universities, which house thousands of television and radio stations, theaters, musical ensembles, little magazines, and museums. University sponsorship presents a statistical problem in that reports on such cultural organizations rarely distinguish between public and private universities, and a substantive problem, as well, because public and private university-sponsored organizations may have much more in common with one another than with free-standing nonprofits or public agencies in the same field.

In attempting to generalize about the nonprofit share of cultural industries, then, we are confronted by the inadequacy of available statistics and by the inadequacy of our analytic typologies. The two problems are intimately related. The more closely culture-producing organizations hew to institutionalized definitions of appropriate organizational forms, the more likely they are to show up in the statistical record.

The Nonprofit Role

I focus in this section on the percentage of producers and distributors that are nonprofit organizations in each of several broadly defined industries. The reason for emphasizing firms rather than shares of assets or sales is simply that the available information permits inference about the former but not about the latter.

Music

Some sectors of the music industry are almost entirely proprietary in form—for example, the 403 for-profit establishments that manufacture musical instruments (Bureau of the Census 1982a). The record industry is similarly dominated by for-profits. Although there are a few nonprofit and public-sector producers (for example, the Smithsonian Institution), of the 548 proprietary firms that produce records (Bureau of the Census 1982a) a mere 7 proprietary corporations released over 90 percent of the best-selling records and tapes in 1981 (Belinfante & Johnson 1983). Nonprofit recording companies are restricted to a few specialists in certain kinds of classical and folk music; and even specialists, as a group, are usually proprietary in form if not in spirit. Similarly, retail outlets for records, tapes, and musical instruments are predominantly for-profit, although college stores and museum shops also sell recorded music.

Even when we look at live performance, the music industry is dominated by the proprietary form. The Bureau of the Census (1982b) reports the existence of 6,712 producers, orchestras, and entertainers. Of these, 1,610, scarcely 1 in 4, are nonprofit (National Center for Charitable Statistics 1985,

5). (The public sector, of course, weighs in heavily with numerous military and high school bands.)

The one segment of the music industry in which nonprofit organizations are dominant is in the live presentation of classical and fine-arts music. The American Symphony Orchestra League (1979) estimated that there were approximately 1,500 orchestras in the United States. Sixty of these, all nonprofits, were major or regional orchestras, which provide substantial employment to players on a contractual basis. Most of the approximately 200 metropolitan and urban orchestras, as well as the approximately 550 small community orchestras, are nonprofit, although a few are public. There are also 500 college orchestras, divided among both public and private universities, and approximately 200 youth orchestras, usually free-standing nonprofits but in some instances affiliated with high schools, conservatories, or other nonprofit agencies. A best guess, then, is that there are approximately 1,550 symphony orchestras in the United States and that more than three-quarters of these are nonprofit, about one-fifth (mostly affiliated with public educational institutions) public, and perhaps 3 to 5 percent proprietary. But among the largest and most prestigious orchestras, the nonprofit form is virtually universal.

The situation is similar in opera. According to the Central Opera Service, in 1980 there were 177 nonprofit opera companies, 390 other nonacademic nonprofit presenters (including associations, festivals, and nonprofit theaters), and 419 university presenters (both public and private) (Martorella 1982). All the major opera companies are nonprofit.

The third fine-arts segment of the music industry includes chamber ensembles, small groups of players who perform both classical chamber music and modern compositions for small ensembles. These groups are numerous, they form and terminate rapidly, and there are no comprehensive data on their numbers or legal form. Although many of the more established and prominent chamber groups are incorporated nonprofits, subunits of nonprofit symphony orchestras, or university affiliates, these are probably outnumbered by unincorporated partnerships (King 1980).

Theatrical Performance

The movie and television drama industries are dominated by for-profit enterprise. The motion picture distribution market is dominated by a few producers and distributors: in 1980, 10 major firms and 13 independents accounted for all 245 major releases (Gertner 1982). Motion picture productions are mounted by corporate studios and commercial one-shot partnerships. A small set of for-profit production companies likewise dominates dramatic television production. To this commercial production must be added films made by government (including 12 federal agencies with their own film bureaus [Gertner 1982]) and by independent filmmakers, mostly sole proprietors, who produce films for public television, media arts centers, and a few art cinemas.

By contrast, live theatrical performance is finely segmented and more evenly divided among the nonprofit, for-profit, and public sectors. The most artistically dynamic sector of the theater industry is the resident stage, which consists of more or less stable companies that produce several plays per season. Of approximately 900 such theaters (Mathtech 1980), the largest and most prominent, with the exception of 2 or 3 public theaters, are nonprofit in form. Many smaller, lower-budget ensembles are unincorporated, affiliated with other nonprofit organizations, or in a few cases, proprietary or public. (One listing of 89 theaters in the San Francisco Bay area [Theatre Communications Center 1984] contains 77 nonprofits, 6 public theaters, and 6 that are apparently proprietary.)

By contrast, Broadway theater is almost exclusively proprietary. In 1980, all 30 Broadway houses were for-profit, as were most of the 30 off-Broadway houses and many of the 200 off-off-Broadway settings (Mathtech 1980). Of course, we cannot compare these enterprises to resident theaters directly, for they are essentially real-estate operations that rent space to production companies that exist, in many cases, only for the run of a play. Proprietary production companies dominate Broadway, whereas nonprofit theatrical groups account for the bulk of off-off-Broadway performance.

Broadway producers frequently launch additional productions of a play for distribution on the road. A 1980 report (Mathtech) counted 309 houses for Broadway productions outside of New York; of these, only 12 percent were proprietary, 28 percent were colleges (public and private), and 60 percent were civic centers (predominantly public). Oddly, then, what the proprietary sector does in New York, the public sector does in much of the rest of the country. Proprietary organizations also dominate dinner theaters and large musical theaters (although a substantial minority of the latter are public or nonprofit in form). Summer stock is more diverse. Of an estimated 310 companies, a fifth are nonprofit, a fifth proprietary, and almost one half are sponsored by public and private colleges and universities. Colleges also sponsor an estimated 2,500 amateur theater companies, and various community organizations (mostly nonprofit associations) account for an equal number of nonprofessional groups (Mathtech 1980).

Visual Arts and Exhibitions

Visual arts production is primarily corporate or individual in organization. Advertising agencies and advertising and design departments of proprietary firms both create art works in-house and contract out to solo practitioners. (The Bureau of the Census [1982b] reported 10,316 photography, art, and graphics firms, almost all commercial.) Most craft artists, painters, and sculptors are solo practitioners operating directly in the market rather than as employees of organizations. The distribution of fine-arts painting, sculpture, prints, and crafts is dominated by proprietorships and partnerships, primarily galleries and dealers. Of the handful of galleries that deviate from this form, a few are 501(c)(3) nonprofits, but most are for-profit or nonprofit cooperatives (many of the

latter under the administrative wing of churches or other nonprofit agencies) (Jeffri 1980).

The nonprofit role is more important in the exhibition of art. Most of the new exhibition spaces—of which 213 applied for National Endowment for the Arts grants in 1983 (Hodsoll 1984)—are nonprofit in form. More important, almost three-quarters of America's art museums are nonprofit (if one includes the 13.5 percent sponsored by private educational institutions) (Macro Systems 1979). The public sector also plays an important role in exhibition: approximately 12 percent of American art museums are public agencies, and another 14 percent are affiliated with public educational institutions. Nonprofit organizations account for three-fifths of our history museums and about two-fifths of all science museums, with public museums composing the rest. (According to the National Center for Educational Statistics, there were 4,580 museums of all kinds in 1979 [Macro Systems 1979]. The Census Bureau counted 2,387 nonprofit museums, probably an underestimate, in 1985 [National Center for Charitable Statistics 1985]).

These generalizations, of course, accept the official definition of a museum as a noncommercial organization (National Endowment for the Arts 1982). If we broaden the definition to include proprietary museums, the figures look different. According to one guide, over 300 corporations in the United States and Canada have art collections, most of which are accessible, under certain circumstances, to the public (International Art Alliance 1983). Many tourist museums in the western United States are either fully proprietary or serve as drawing cards for retail sales operations. The most thorough recent survey counted 156 such proprietary museums (Macro Systems 1979), but an earlier study (Rogers 1969) found 232. In addition, some companies maintain their own private museums, with access limited to employees. Coleman (1939) identified 19 such museums in the late 1930s; and Rogers (1969) found 88 in 1967. If we assume arbitrarily that only a handful of proprietary museums and internal company museums are museums of art, the 300 corporate collections still increase the proprietary share of art-exhibiting organizations to 33 percent and lower the nonprofit share to about 40 percent.

Broadcasting

The three major networks, the cable companies, and all but a handful of public cable franchises are for-profit organizations, as are virtually all the production companies that sell programs and program ideas to the major producers. Nonprofit enterprise thrives only within the public broadcasting system. In 1984, according to an industry directory (Taishoff 1984), 308 (23 percent) of the 1,341 television stations were public or nonprofit, as were 49 of the 4,811 AM stations (1 percent) and 1,047 of the 5,040 FM stations (21 percent). According to the Corporation for Public Broadcasting (1979), 39 percent of the public television stations were community (nonprofit) stations, a third were university sponsored, 11 percent were under the control of local school districts, and 17 percent were administered by state government agencies. But the major producing stations for the public television system were among the nonprofits (Powell & Friedkin 1984).

Print Media

It is difficult to estimate the number of book publishers, magazine publishers, and newspapers in the United States, in part because many are so small and evanescent. Of over 8,800 newspapers (Bureau of the Census 1982a), virtually all are for-profit corporations. By my own count of entries in *Magazine Industry Marketplace* (Bowker 1982)—a trade directory that includes most magazines printed and published in the United States over 15 pages in average length and with circulations of over 3,000—some 694 of the 2,186 magazines listed are published by organizations that are identifiably nonprofit. (Since many nonprofit publishers presumably could not be identified, this figure undoubtedly underestimates the nonprofit share.) Magazines published by nonprofits include a few large-circulation periodicals—*National Geographic, Ms., Harper's, Nation*—but in most cases they are organs of churches, professional or trade associations, trade unions, museums, or other nonprofits. The proprietary sector's share of gross circulation is much higher than two-thirds, for most mass-circulation periodicals are published by for-profit corporations. Many government agencies publish periodicals with surprisingly large subsidized circulations, but their aggregate share of the magazine population is low.

Literary Marketplace (Bowker 1984a), which includes all reporting organizations that publish three or more titles a year, lists 1,589 book publishers. *Books in Print* (Bowker 1983), which attempts to catalog all books currently available, includes over ten times that many. Another directory (Hubbard 1983) lists over 7,100 presses in the United States and Canada. Most large publishers (except for the mammoth U.S. Government Printing Office) are for-profit corporations, but many small publishers are nonprofit. My own count of *Literary Marketplace* listees noted 95 university presses (both public and private nonprofit) and 107 other identifiably nonprofit presses (belonging to operating nonprofits and to professional associations and nonprofit industry service organizations). This yields a base estimate of the nonprofit/public share of book publishers of more than 12 percent: small, but not insubstantial. University presses, of course, publish the bulk of scholarly and academic monographs and materials, giving them an especially important niche in the industry (Powell 1985).

Nonprofit organizations may become increasingly important in the publication of fiction and poetry in coming years as public grants to nonprofit presses grow in visibility. Most of the 2,719 small presses and little magazines listed in the most thorough directory (Fulton & Ferber 1983) appear to be proprietary or unincorporated single-person operations. But some sense of the distribution of forms among the major

small presses and little magazines can be gleaned from an inspection of National Endowment for the Arts grants in 1983 (National Endowment for the Arts 1984). Of grant recipients in the literary magazine field, 37 percent were freestanding nonprofits, 34 percent university affiliates, and 7 percent associated with other nonprofit organizations. Twenty-three percent of the grants were made to individuals, presumably because the magazines they produce do not have nonprofit status. By contrast, more than half of the grants for small presses were awarded to individuals, indicating the continued dominance of the proprietary form in this field, and approximately one-fifth each went to the presses themselves or to university sponsors or other nonprofit organizations.

If print-media producers are predominantly proprietary, distributors are mixed. Retail bookstores are overwhelmingly proprietary. But even here there is some nonprofit and public enterprises, represented by 2,843 college and university bookstores and 303 museum shops (approximately 14 percent of the retail book outlets) (Jacques Cattell Press, 1984). By contrast, well over half, and probably more than two-thirds, of our libraries are public, with most of the rest nonprofit in form (Bowker 1984b).

Presenting Organizations

Presenting organizations sponsor cultural events on an occasional basis. Many organizations fall under this ambiguous rubric. In fact, an informal canvass in 1980–81 by the Mayor's Commission on Cultural Affairs, using an especially broad definition, found more than 1,000 in New Haven alone.

There are four major types of arts sponsors: universities, churches, museums, and local arts agencies. We have no data on churches, so little can be said except that many of them host arts events of various kinds, many more serve as homes for choral and gospel musical activity, and all are nonprofit. Data on university art sponsorship is little better: the Association of College, University and Community Arts Administrators (1981) reported that 223 universities and colleges responding to their membership survey presented approximately 8,250 performances in 1980. But the response rate was low, not all university arts administrators received the survey, and many universities sponsor cultural events without employing arts administrators. A survey of groups that received grants to sponsor dance concerts during three years of the National Endowment for the Arts' Dance Touring Program revealed that fully half were universities (National Endowment for the Arts 1975). Little is known about museum sponsorship of nonexhibition cultural activities, but one study reported 732 museums sponsoring performing arts events in 1973 (Mandl & Kerr 1975).

Local arts agencies (until recently known as community arts councils) originated in the 1920s, but have become numerous only since 1965. Overseeing the cultural lives of their communities, many provide services and sometimes grants to arts organizations, and most (but not all) sponsor performing arts events or exhibitions. No one knows exactly how many local arts agencies there are, but the service organization for the field, the National Assembly of Local Arts Agencies (NALAA; 1979), estimated that there were 2,000 in 1979. An NALAA membership survey revealed that 78 percent of the agencies were private nonprofit organizations and 22 percent were municipal agencies. But a substantial number of the nonprofits (14 percent of all agencies) were publicly designated quasi agencies of their local governments. An earlier survey found that the private agencies included several subunits of chambers of commerce, private universities, or other nonprofit organizations; and the public agencies included subunits of public universities, local school districts, and one public library (American Council for the Arts 1978).

A Few Observations

What are we to make of this profusion of data? First, the relative importance of the nonprofit form varies less between artistic media (visual, musical, dramatic) or organizational functions (exhibition, presentation) than within them. Most arts industries (broadly defined) have islands of nonprofit activity: scholarly and poetry presses, classical music presenters, visual art exhibitors, resident theaters, and fine-arts dance companies. Nonprofit organizations present most of what has traditionally been regarded as ''high culture'' or ''serious'' art. These art forms are particularly labor-intensive, relatively unlikely to use media technologies for distribution, and thus unable to realize substantial economies of scale.

As a first-order generalization, then, nonprofit organizations produce high culture, which involves labor-intensive technologies, whereas commercial organizations produce mass culture, which requires capital-intensive technologies. But there is more to the story than this.

For one thing, not all serious art is produced by nonprofits or public organizations. Some segments of high-culture production and distribution are dominated by for-profit producers: for example, literature (novels and most poetry), classical music recording, and commercial art galleries. To some extent, these anomalies can be explained by economies of scale and technology. Nonetheless, many proprietary poetry presses are labor-intensive relative to the number of copies they can hope to sell; and serious fiction and classical recordings do not net the profits of popular mass-media successes.

Second, most creators of high art—composers, novelists, playwrights—are, in effect, sole proprietorships, dealing by sale or contract with proprietary and nonprofit firms that buy or, in the case of musical compositions and plays, ''rent'' the use of their creations. Some artists, composers, and poets are employees of universities, but they are paid to teach (even if they use their salaries to subsidize their artistic work and benefit from access to supplies and technology).

Third, predominantly nonprofit industry segments often have islands of for-profit activity within them. Very small artistic groups—chamber trios, neighborhood arts organizations, theaters—are not as a rule 501(c)(3) nonprofits, even when their intentions are consonant with nonprofit status. Other organizational forms are able to profit from the activities of the core nonprofits: thus commercial art galleries sell to art museums and, more important, rely on them to encourage interest in the visual arts and to valorize the work of their artists through purchase or temporary exhibition. In other cases (for example, proprietary art museums and Broadway and dinner theater), for-profit organizations are essentially similar to nonprofits in function, although they may differ in structure or in program emphasis.

Fourth, for-profit cultural sectors, especially those that use mass-production and distribution technologies, spawn oases of nonprofit activity. Public broadcasting was stimulated by the frustration of educators and intellectuals with the perceived vapidity of commercial television entertainment. Nonprofit poetry and fiction magazines and presses respond to the difficulty that fledgling authors have in reaching the public. Most university presses publish meritorious works of scholarship for specialists too few in number to support commercial publication. Nonprofit media arts centers provide outlets for films and videos ineligible by virtue of format, content, or style for distribution via commercial broadcast or theatrical release. Note that these nonprofit oases are, with the exception of public broadcasting, relatively more labor-intensive and less capable of achieving economies of scale than are their commercial counterparts.

Not all labor-intensive artistic work is nonprofit, however. In forms not traditionally considered high art, performance is organized differently. Take, for example, the case of performers of popular music, including most jazz, rock, and country music. Their work is labor-intensive: only a handful benefit from recording contracts and, consequently, technological economies of scale. Nor is the cost borne by nonprofit enterprise. Instead, artists enter into short-term performance contracts with proprietors of commercial houses—nightclubs, dance halls, and sometimes concert halls. The contract protects the proprietor from long-term risk, transferring it instead to the performers, who ordinarily work for a small flat fee and a percentage of the gate. A similar system is employed in Broadway and much off-Broadway theater, except that here the risk is borne by the investors rather than by the artists themselves. The case of jazz ensembles is particularly interesting, for one might expect them to resemble chamber groups in organization. But only with the rise of university sponsorship and modest public support has a convergence begun to occur; even now, nonprofit jazz combos are virtually unknown.

If the respective roles of proprietary and nonprofit/public enterprise are difficult to sort out, the gulf between nonprofit and public is even harder to fathom. As we have seen, nonprofit and public organizations coexist in nearly all industry sectors that are not predominantly proprietary. Thus most art museums are private, but many are public; for history museums, the proportions are reversed. Libraries are predominantly public agencies, but local arts agencies are largely private. Most public broadcasting stations are agencies of government, but the most influential are private nonprofits. And when we take into account cultural organizations sponsored by public and private universities, the difference becomes even more obscure.

Two generalizations are possible. First, public enterprise is more often dominant in those noncommercial cultural sectors perceived to provide services of wide public appeal or great educational utility, most notably libraries and history museums. Second, public sectors rarely exist within cultural industry segments that are predominantly for-profit. In such industry segments—fiction and poetry publishing, music recording, dramatic television production, most retail sales of cultural products—nonprofit organizations constitute the noncommercial minority.

Note, however, that these generalizations do not take us very far. The products of predominantly public cultural organizations may be perceived as important and useful because of the long-standing public commitments. Public investment may create demand and, in that sense, be self-legitimating over time. More important, the distinction between public and private dominance by industry does not explain the many cases in which substantial public and private subsectors coexist.

An Inductive Summary

Let me close this empirical review with three generalizations and a set of unanswered questions:

Proposition 1: Labor-intensive cultural activities tend to be organized in the nonprofit (or public) form, whereas those that are capital-intensive are more often organized on a proprietary basis.

Proposition 2: Cultural activities associated with high-art forms tend to be organized in the nonprofit (or public) form, whereas those that are associated with popular culture are more likely to be organized on a proprietary basis.

Proposition 3: Within the noncommercial sectors, cultural activities that serve large publics or are closely tied to the official aims of public education tend to be organized as public agencies, whereas activities with narrower audiences or less clearly educational purposes tend to be organized as nonprofit organizations.

Question 1: Why are some high-culture forms produced or distributed by proprietary organizations? Why are art galleries commercial? Why are poetry presses largely proprietary?

Question 2: Why is the creative process in the high-culture forms usually outside the scope of nonprofit sponsorship? Why are most painters, sculptors, composers of serious music, and playwrights sole proprietors (rather than employees of museums, galleries, orchestras, or theater companies)?

Question 3: If labor intensity is crucial, why is most performance organized on a proprietary contract basis? Why

are there so few nonprofit jazz groups? Why are there relatively more nonprofit chamber ensembles?

Question 4: Why is proprietary enterprise present even in industries that are largely noncommercial? Why are there so many for-profit museums? Why are most very small performing and exhibiting organizations in all industries *not* nonprofit?

Question 5: Why do nonprofit and public organizations coexist in so many industries, whereas public and proprietary organizations coexist in relatively few (and in none without nonprofit sectors, as well)? Why are some museums, local arts agencies, and noncommercial broadcasters public and others private?

Question 6: What is the role of university sponsorship? Does it matter whether universities are themselves public or nonprofit? Why are so many noncommercial cultural organizations sponsored by other organizations rather than free-standing nonprofit or public agencies.

Question 7: How may we explain the existence of industry segments—performing arts sponsorship, art galleries and exhibitors, entertainment broadcasting—in which proprietary, private nonprofit, and public firms perform similar functions?

Our inquiry thus far has been largely inductive. For a literature that has developed a more deductive approach to some of these problems, let us consider some recent work by cultural economists.

Economic Explanations of the Nonprofit Cultural Enterprise

The literature on cultural economics has grown in quantity and quality over the past decade (see, for example, Feld, O'Hare, & Schuster 1983; Throsby & Withers 1979; Hansmann 1981; and the papers in Blaug 1976; Hendon, Shanahan, & MacDonald 1980; and Hendon & Shanahan 1983). Relatively little of this work, however, addresses directly the question of why certain cultural organizations are nonprofit and others are not.

Let us divide the question of origins into two components: First, why are some cultural organizations not proprietary? Second, why are some noncommercial cultural organizations voluntary nonprofits while others are public agencies?

Why Nonproprietary Arts Organizations?

The conventional explanation for the prevalence of nonproprietary organizations in some cultural fields is that there are no profits to be made there. According to the classic exposition of this view (Baumol & Bowen 1966), the arts are a service industry and, as such, are highly labor-intensive. In contrast to the situation of manufacturing firms, which can boost productivity by implementing technical innovations, productivity increases in the arts are sorely limited by intractable technologies of production. To use the famous example, one cannot simply order a symphony orchestra to play twice as quickly.

Arts organizations operate in an economy that contains a large manufacturing sector. As productivity rises in manufacturing owing to improvements in production efficiency, manufacturing wages increase. Because arts and other service-providing organizations compete for labor with manufacturing firms (at least in the long run), nonmanufacturing wages are likewise pulled upward. Increasing wages cause the production costs of arts organizations to spiral beyond what the organization can hope for in earned income. Thus live performing arts organizations require philanthropic subsidy.

Baumol and Bowen's analysis explains the need for subvention, not the nonprofit form per se. The fact that an organization needs subsidy to survive does not, of course, mean that it will get it. Many cultural dodoes—touring light-opera companies and producers of slides for kinetoscopes, for example (Becker 1982)—have become economically unviable and expired. Given that nonprofit organizations in the performing arts need subsidy, why do they get it?

Hansmann (1981) addresses this question directly. Such organizations as orchestras and resident theaters do not produce primarily public or collective goods: the vast majority of benefits accrue to the purchasers of tickets. Nor can it be argued convincingly that donors wish to keep prices down to provide access to the needy, for high-culture arts audiences are almost universally well educated and well-to-do. Why, then, do ticket prices not reflect costs?

Hansmann explains the reliance of nonprofit performing arts organizations on donations as a form of voluntary price discrimination whereby some consumers agree to pay more than others for the same service. He attributes this arrangement to the price structure of performing arts production. Fixed costs of maintaining a house and mounting a production represent a high percentage of the total cost of any presentation. The marginal cost of providing an extra performance of a play or concert program, or of accommodating an additional consumer, is relatively low. Consumer prices must be high enough to cover the total costs of production but low enough to reflect realistically the marginal cost of an additional performance or audience member. Because demand for the arts is limited, however, quantity cannot be increased to the point where fixed costs are covered: in economic terms, the demand curve is underneath the cost curve at any given price.

To survive, then, the performing arts organization must set prices to extract from each consumer the value the performance holds for him or her. Selling different quality seats for different prices is one means of accomplishing this; but there is a limit to the degree that seat qualities can be differentiated, and this strategy works only to the extent that people who value a performance more highly also place an unusually high value on good seats. Consequently, orchestras and theater companies solicit voluntary donations as a means of discriminating with respect to price. In support of this argument, Hansmann demonstrates that most regular attenders do

make donations and that the combination of ticket revenues and contributions is maximized at a lower ticket price than would yield the maximization of ticket revenues alone. Organizations that rely on donations are naturally nonprofit, for contributors could not trust proprietary concerns to use their gifts to create more or better art rather than distribute them as profits.

Taken together, the Baumol and Bowen and Hansmann arguments provide a compelling account of why some performing arts organizations are not proprietary. (And, as Hansmann [1981, 346] suggests, the argument applies as well to museums, which also have large ratios of fixed to marginal costs and experience relatively low demand.) But some questions remain unanswered.

The Cost Disease. Do the arts, as Baumol and Bowen contend, suffer from a cost disease such that they require ever greater quantities of subsidy? This argument is consonant with historical evidence that the performing arts were once almost universally proprietary in organization and that the cost per performance appears to have risen steadily throughout the twentieth century, at least until 1970. But, despite the elegance of the formulation and its wide acceptance, there are some reasons for skepticism.

First, it is difficult to disentangle productivity-driven increases in operating costs from the costs of organizational growth, especially in the 1950s and 1960s, the period for which Baumol and Bowen's data are best. Empirical analyses necessary to distinguish cost increases that are due to productivity lags from those resulting from investment in and maintenance of new plant or the expansion of administrative components (like Pick's [1983] study of the nineteenth-century London stage) have not been undertaken.

Second, it is difficult to distinguish productivity-driven declines in the percentage of income that is earned from those reflecting increases in the volume of funding available from foundations, corporations, and the public sector. Netzer, for example, argues that increases in labor costs during the late 1960s and early 1970s were spurred in large part by the availability of institutional funding rather than by inexorable economic pressures. Describing his own case studies, he reports that financial difficulties "were not traceable to the Baumol-Bowen trends but to unsuccessful ventures, a failure to develop expected support at the box office or elsewhere, a withdrawal of previously available support, or efforts to expand without either market or donor support visible" (1978, 153). Also on the basis of case studies, Cwi (1983) reports that the budgeting process in nonprofit arts organizations involves horse-trading between managing directors and artistic directors, with programming decisions based in part on anticipated levels of both earned and unearned income (see also Jeffri 1980, 134; Peterson, forthcoming; Zeigler 1977).

Third, if one follows the logic of the cost-pressure argument, one would predict that performing arts organizations would have expired shortly after the Industrial Revolution—the point at which manufacturing productivity began to increase rapidly. Why the cost disease should have required wholesale public assistance in the 1960s (rather than in 1900 or 1930) is not explained.

Note, too, that Baumol and Bowen's study, like other economic accounts, takes as given the enduring nature of artistic conventions. Baumol and Bowen did not predict the remission of the cost disease that occurred in the 1970s, in part because they did not foresee that organizations would offer more concerts by small ensembles or that theaters would present plays with smaller casts (thus lowering cost per production) (Baumol & Baumol 1980, 1984; Schwartz 1981; Shoesmith & Millner 1983; Throsby & Withers 1979, 44–46). As students or consumers of the arts, economists may deplore these trends; but as economists they must recognize them as available strategies for increasing productivity.

Similarly, it is notable that nonprofit arts organizations have failed to implement productivity-enhancing devices that commercial producers have exploited. For example, in the early 1970s, popular record producers began substituting a single synthesizer for string sections of three or more players in order to reduce studio costs. Orchestras have failed to do this, no doubt reflecting the tastes of their patrons and audiences. These tastes, not technology, make it difficult for orchestras to increase economic productivity. The analytic problem is to understand the affinity between the nonprofit form and artistic conventions that are strongly defended and slow to change.

The Problem of Industrial Organization. Hansmann's explanation of the prevalence of nonprofit organizations in the high-culture performing arts is a persuasive one, especially if one takes as given the existence of deficits. But, for the most part, he, too, takes for granted a conventional definition of the performing arts firm, characteristic of the nonprofit performing arts but less common in the proprietary sector, as combining performance and sponsorship within a single organization.

Recall that in Broadway theater, nonrecorded popular music, and jazz, the making of art and the sponsorship of performances are undertaken by different organizations, each proprietary, with performance and sponsorship articulated by contract rather than hierarchy. Owners of real estate book artists into their houses on a contractual basis, providing the performance and associated services to paying customers. This separation of performance and sponsorship would seem a more realistic proprietary alternative to nonprofit enterprise than would for-profit orchestras or resident theaters of the familiar type.

Moreover, commercial sponsors frequently differentiate their offerings—for example, by hosting a rock concert one week, a classical performance the next, and circus acts the week after—to reduce risk and, perhaps, to cross-subsidize the less profitable but more prestigious genres. There is no prima facie reason for the failure of high-culture performing arts firms to employ either of these strategies—articulation of performance and sponsorship through contract rather than merger and cross-subsidization of artistic work with more popular fare. Indeed, commercial halls do host some high-culture performing arts events, museums run shops, and

opera companies sell champagne between acts. A convincing theoretical explanation for why these strategies are not more widespread in the high-culture arts may be sought in the further development of the transaction-cost approach (implicit in Hansmann 1980, this volume, chap. 2; Williamson 1975), as well as in the noneconomic factors described below.

Public or Voluntary?

We have no theories of the relative prevalence of public and nonprofit enterprise among noncommercial culture producers and distributors. But the more general framework of Weisbrod (1977b) and his colleagues can be extended to the arts. According to Weisbrod, noncommercial organizations exist to provide "collective consumption goods": goods with benefits that cannot be limited only to those who pay for them (like clean water or lighthouses).

Drawing on the public-choice tradition, whereby the political system is assumed to translate voter/consumer preferences into public policy in a relatively neutral and plebiscitarian fashion, Weisbrod (1977a) suggests that public enterprise comes into being when voters agree about the desirability of a collective good and the amount that should be provided. Under these circumstances, the ability of government to tax (and thus to circumvent the free-rider problem) makes it the most logical provider.

Frequently, however, demand for collective goods varies widely from person to person. When this occurs, government provides a level of the collective good equal to that demanded by the average voter. Citizens who prefer a higher level of provision band together to create private voluntary organizations to supplement the government's production.

For any given good, demand develops gradually, at different rates for different people. In the early stages of this process, the collective good is valued by only a minority of citizens, who create private voluntary organizations. When demand diffuses throughout the citizenry, government enters as the provider of choice. As incomes rise, voter/consumers seek private substitutes, over which they can exert greater control, for collective goods (for example, ship radar instead of lighthouses). Consequently, Weisbrod anticipates that nonprofit organizations will be the first providers of any given collective good, followed (and perhaps supplanted) by government, which will grow until consumers become wealthy enough to replace collective goods with privately consumable substitutes.

Applied to the arts in the United States, Weisbrod's arguments provide substantial explanatory leverage. Thus private nonprofit museums emerged in the late nineteenth century, public museums became dominant in the early twentieth, and the art market (a private substitute) has developed steadily over the past sixty years. The theory is also consistent with the growth of public subsidy to nonprofit arts organizations as public demand for the arts presumably has increased.

Nonetheless, there is much that the Weisbrod approach does not explain. For one thing, as Hansmann (1981) points out, the performing arts are, for the most part, consumed privately by the same people who donate to the organizations whose tickets they purchase. The Weisbrod model cannot explain why we have nonprofit orchestras, theaters, and dance companies. What is more, Weisbrod (1977a) predicts that the larger the private-goods component in a mixed private/collective good, the greater the tendency for for-profit providers (rather than voluntary nonprofits) to supplement governmental provision. But, as we have seen, in the arts, public and proprietary enterprise never coexist in industries without substantial nonprofit components. Instead, nonprofit and proprietary enterprise appear to share markets for goods with strong private-consumption traits.

Empirical research is required to assess the ability of collective-goods theory to explain apparent anomalies in the development of public and nonprofit enterprise in some industries. In the museum field, for example, the entries in Coleman's 1932 directory suggest that public art museums were more prevalent in the early twentieth century than they are today. If the collective-goods argument is correct, the higher recent birthrate of nonprofit art museums must mean that public demand for art museum services has declined relative to the heterogeneity of that demand: either because demand has declined absolutely (which is unlikely) or because heterogeneity has increased at a faster rate. The latter proposition would gain support to the extent that recently founded private nonprofit museums disproportionately specialize in relatively arcane collection areas. Nonetheless, collective-goods theory cannot easily predict the circumstances under which increased proprietary demand will yield public subsidy of existing nonprofit rather than the creation of fully public institutions.

Local arts agencies pose an especially challenging empirical test for the collective-goods approach. The private and public arts councils included in one survey (American Council for the Arts 1978) were founded at roughly equivalent rates. If we assume that places with large populations have more heterogeneous demand than small towns, we would expect the former to be more likely to have nonprofit arts agencies and that those in the latter would be predominantly public. A hand count of results from another survey (National Assembly of Local Arts Agencies 1982) does indicate that the percentage of agencies that are public declines with community size, but the percentage of private nonprofits that are publicly designated to perform municipal functions increases markedly with population, a finding the theory would not predict. In short, then, the Weisbrod model provides a promising basis for empirical research on cultural industries in which comparable public and private nonprofit enterprises coexist, but both testing and theoretical refinement will be required for its explanatory adequacy to be assessed fully.

Noneconomic Explanations of Nonprofit Cultural Enterprise

If their arguments are borne out empirically, the economic approaches we have reviewed will take us a long way toward understanding the relative prevalence of different organizational forms in the production and distribution of culture. The Hansmann and Baumol approaches explain the preponderance of nonprofit enterprise in the production and distribution of art forms that are labor-intensive and, to the extent that labor-intensiveness is especially characteristic of the high arts, help explain the importance of nonprofit firms in these fields. The Weisbrod theory explains the relative dominance of public enterprise in the provision of services (by libraries or history museums, for example) that have large collective-consumption components. Economists have not, however, provided answers to the questions posed at the end of our inductive review: why, for example, we have nonprofit publishing houses and for-profit jazz combos. Most important, they have not explained why performance and sponsorship are combined within single firms in some artistic fields but articulated by contract in others.

To answer some of these questions, we must address two sets of issues that economic approaches have thus far neglected: first, the role of organized consumers in the founding of cultural organizations, the establishment of conventional definitions of the firm, the segmenting of markets, and the diffusion of tastes; and, second, the influence of government administrative procedures and definitions on the distribution of organizational forms in particular industries.

The Institutional Origins of the Nonprofit Role

To understand the prevalence of the nonprofit form in the high-culture arts, we must understand the origins of America's orchestras and art museums. (For a detailed discussion upon which these remarks draw, see DiMaggio [1982a, 1982b].) High culture, as we now define it, did not exist in the United States until after the Civil War, nor did many nonprofit organizations offering exhibitions or performances to the general public. Serious art and popular works intermingled promiscuously in public performance. Sponsoring organizations might present a relatively austere program of classical music one week and a popular extravaganza (for example, "Mr. Mutie, his African monkey, and several Chinese Dogs" [Johnson, 1953]) the next. Paintings were first distributed by lottery and then hung alongside natural curiosities in museums like Peale's and Barnum's. Both exhibition and performance were organized commercially (save for relatively closed voluntary associations of amateurs); and performance and sponsorship were organizationally distinct, as they are in the live commercial arts today.

The definition and institutionalization of a high culture, the integration of performance and sponsorship within the cultural firm, and the development of nonprofit enterprise in the arts occurred together and were intimately related. All were driven by the efforts of emerging urban upper classes to define and legitimate a body of art that they could call their own and that would serve as a source of honor and prestige to themselves and their peers. In order to do this, the cultural entrepreneurs of the late nineteenth century needed to exert greater control over the artist than they could through the market. They employed the nonprofit form to bring performers under the direct employment of elite patrons, merging the function of performance and sponsorship. Once this was accomplished, professional artists and curators were recruited to define a high-art canon, to expel artistic works outside this canon from the museums and orchestras, and to frame standards for the behavior of arts consumers and a set of norms that defined authentic aesthetic experience in a way that limited it to the initiated cadre of elites and their middle-class followers.

The institutionalization of high culture, and the creation of models for its organization under nonprofit auspices, was affected, but not determined, by market forces. Indeed, the creation of high-culture forms, and organizations to distribute them, can best be understood as an antimarket social movement, aimed at defining a corpus of sacred art beyond the reach of profane commercial concerns.

A number of the questions posed earlier can best be understood from this historical perspective. Take, for example, the consolidation of performance and sponsorship within a single organizational setting. In the field of classical music, the market failed to provide the programs the founders of the symphony orchestras sought. Even the most chaste professional performing groups interspersed serious European compositions with light music, gimmickry, and song. With no natural segmentation of the music market between the upper-class public for fine-arts music and the more numerous but less demanding middle-class consumers, the former could exert consumer sovereignty only by creating a new organizational form. (For an economic model of nonprofit entrepreneurship that takes consumer control of governance into account, see Ben-Ner [1986].) Only the power to hire and fire performers, to demand their exclusive services, and to place them under the authority of a conductor hired by the nonprofit entrepreneur or trustees enabled the orchestras of the twentieth century to develop a musical canon and modern performance standards. In purely market terms, the nonprofit form was less efficient than the conventional combination of proprietary band and proprietary sponsor; but it attained ends that were unrealizable through market exchange alone.

Similarly, the origins of the nonprofit form help explain why creative artists—composers, playwrights, painters— are rarely employed by nonprofit enterprise. The first art museums were established by their founders to exhibit only the best that civilization (as they defined it) had to offer. Their relations with contemporary painters were stormy on two counts. First, they displayed little contemporary American work and purchased even less for their permanent collections. Second, when the work of local artists was exhibited, the museums' antimarket ethos led them to prohibit efforts at salesmanship or the display of prices. The sacralization of serious art—the establishment of fine art as a category separate from the trivial or mundane—involved both the rejection of the market and the creation of ritual distance between artist and consumer. Artists have fit best into traditional museums when they have been distant or deceased. Indeed, the inability of artists to use noncommercial organizations to make

their livings, both in Europe (White & White 1965) and in the United States, is responsible for the development of the commercial gallery system. Similarly, since noncommercial performing arts groups of the nineteenth century primarily presented the work of creators who were dead or European, and since the market provided more original American work than they were prepared to perform, there was little motive to incorporate the creative artist in the nonprofit performing arts firm.

A historical view also explains why jazz and folk performance and (until relatively recently) live theater were not organized on the model of the nonprofit performing arts firm; for Afro-American and folk performance styles were of no interest to the cultural entrepreneurs of the nineteenth century, in part because of the low status of their performers. Theater remained morally suspect, especially in Boston, and nineteenth-century cultural ideologies regarded aesthetic experience as most authentic when it was uncontaminated by words. Thus the substantive representational content of drama militated against its incorporation into the nonprofit model. (On the affinity between this ideology and the status interests of elite patrons, see DiMaggio [1982b].)

The Influence of the State

Economic models tend to treat government as a neutral mediator of citizen demand for collective goods (Weisbrod 1977b). Frequently, however, the manner in which the state organizes its activities takes on an independent significance. Indeed, there is some evidence that the vitality of the nonprofit form and particularly its diffusion to nontraditional areas of cultural production and distribution have been direct results of government policies.

Direct federal support of nonprofit arts organizations commenced with the creation of the National Endowment for the Arts in 1965 (although some states and municipalities supported the arts much earlier). With few exceptions, proprietary cultural organizations are ineligible for public subsidy. Public donors (like the individual contributors described by Hansmann [1980, this volume, chap. 2]) seek assurance that their funds will not be redistributed as income to an organization's governors, and the nonprofit form provides protection against extreme abuses of this type. Moreover, public agencies in the United States (unlike those in many other countries) find it difficult to legitimate direct intervention in the cultural marketplace: proprietary firms, it is assumed, should be left to the discipline of the market and not aided in their competition with other for-profits.

In fields in which proprietary and nonprofit enterprise coexist, the existence of grant programs to the latter shifts the competitive balance and provides incentives for all producers to adopt the nonprofit form. Just as major proprietary theaters like the Actors' Workshop and the Arena Stage converted to nonprofit status in order to qualify for foundation and, later, public assistance in the 1960s (Zeigler 1977), so the larger resident theaters automatically incorporated as nonprofit organizations in the 1970s and 1980s. A similar pattern has been visible in dance, where the National Endowment for the Arts' Dance Touring Program encouraged the incorporation of many companies on a 501(c)(3) basis. According to Jeffri (1980, 49), nonprofit status in the dance world "reveals an external structural definition that explains little except a legal formality." Similar trends are evident among chamber ensembles (King 1980).

Organizational types that have emerged in response to the availability of public funding—media arts centers, for example—have automatically taken the nonprofit form. In some cases, organizational forms respond rapidly to public inducements: when Massachusetts established an "arts lottery," several hundred local arts councils and lottery commissions were founded virtually overnight to distribute the earnings. Many of these were created as public agencies, in large part because of the rapid response time required to take advantage of the new revenue source. By contrast, in such states as Washington (Fuller 1979, 6–7), statutory restrictions on home rule may make the creation of public arts councils difficult, if not impossible, for certain classes of towns or cities.

Once an organizational form comes to be viewed as appropriate and legitimate within a cultural industry segment, it is difficult for the creators of new organizations to deviate from it. Zeigler (1977, 171) reports that resident theaters founded after 1960 "chose a structure which their local Establishments already understood because it was like the structure of the university, the hospital, the symphony orchestra and the community chest." Once forms are institutionalized, models for and information about the mandated form become widely available. The American Symphony Orchestra League's reference guide for symphony orchestras (1979), for example, contains a section on how to become a 501(c)(3) organization. Similarly, in industries that are largely proprietary (such as publishing or musical recording), even entrants with noncommercial aims are likely to incorporate as for-profit firms.

Organizations that deviate from the form dominating their industries tend to be very small and peripheral. Small theater companies or chamber music ensembles too new to qualify for state or federal grants, or too unstable to plan into the future, may have few incentives to invest in incorporation. By contrast, proprietary art museums fail to incorporate as nonprofits because they can often earn a profit: the Museum of Western Art at Wall Drug in Wall, South Dakota, is one of many attractions in a large tourist retail complex, while other western commercial museums benefit from the absence of competing forms of entertainment and edification and from the implicit subsidy of the federal interstate system.

When nonprofit organizations emerge in predominantly for-profit industries, it is often as a result of public policy. Thus noncommercial broadcasting exists as a consequence of Congress's decision to reserve a certain number of broadcast frequencies for noncommercial use (Frost 1937). If a majority of small presses and little magazines ever become nonprofit, it will be in order to exploit opportunities for state and federal grants. Even the decision of some magazine pub-

lishers to shift from the proprietary to the nonprofit form has been influenced by their desire to take advantage of indirect tax benefits (Feld et al 1983). The legal form of such organizations is comprehensible only with reference to the regulatory and grant-making role of the state.

WHAT DIFFERENCE DOES FORM MAKE?

I have documented and explained the relative prevalence of nonprofit organizations in different areas of cultural production and distribution. Here, I shall ask what difference, if any, legal form makes to the behavior of cultural organizations, focusing on nonprofits. Theory in this area has come almost entirely from economists, whereas descriptive studies of nonprofit cultural organizations have been undertaken almost exclusively by sociologists, historians, and laypersons. One purpose of this section is to bring these disparate literatures into confrontation.

Economic Approaches to Behavioral Differences

Economists have rather successfully modeled the behavior of proprietary firms by assuming that owners and their agents seek to maximize profits and have sufficient information and control over other participants that the firm behaves in a profit-maximizing manner. It has been natural, then, for economic models of nonprofit firms, including cultural organizations, to begin by making certain assumptions about the goals, or objective functions, of these organizations and to adapt conventional models of firms to predict their behavior (Hendon, Shanahan, & MacDonald 1980; Hendon & Shanahan 1983). Almost all economic models have posited that nonprofit cultural organizations try to maximize two principal goals: artistic quality and audience size (Baumol & Bowen 1976; Hansmann 1981; Montias 1983; Owen 1983; Throsby & Withers 1979). The models then attempt to predict the behavior of nonprofit firms, in comparison to profit-maximizing firms, by analyzing how a joint quality and audience maximizer would behave under the constraints to which cultural organizations are subject, or to consider the welfare consequences of pursuit of different objectives consistent with nonprofit status.

A central focus of such models has been the trade-off between quality and quantity. In general, economists agree that the quality-maximizing culture producer will have smaller audiences or fewer performances than either the audience-maximizing nonprofit or the proprietary profit maximizer, and that the audience-maximizing arts nonprofit will have lower ticket prices and more performances than either the quality maximizer or the for-profit cultural firm (Baumol & Bowen 1976; Hansmann 1981; Montias 1983; Owen 1983; Throsby & Withers 1979).

Most cultural economists have been modest about the virtues of this approach, emphasizing "the inadequacies of this form of modeling to capture various interesting and important aspects of nonprofit firms" (Hansmann 1981). Peacock and Godfrey (1976, 197–98) have suggested that so little is known about the production functions of nonprofit cultural firms that attempts to model their behavior are premature. Indeed, a number of economists (Hansmann 1981; Frey & Pommerehne 1980) have suggested a variety of additional objectives likely to influence the behavior of nonprofit cultural organizations.

Varieties of Objectives

Because of the centrality of objectives to economic models, it may be useful to consider the putative and apparent goals of nonprofit arts organizations one at a time, reviewing both economists' assumptions about these goals and evidence from case studies of nonprofit cultural organizations.

Quality. Economists have distinguished between two kinds of artistic quality. The first has to do with *innovation* or other aspects of the works produced or displayed: for reasons that are seldom made explicit, high-quality repertoires are taken to be those that appeal only "to the most refined tastes" (Hansmann 1981; Throsby & Withers 1979, 14). Quality in its second sense has to do with *production values* such as virtuoso performance or high-quality stage settings or costumes.

The trade-offs between these two kinds of quality would seem to be a ripe issue for economists' attention. As Becker (1982) has pointed out, it is easier for performers to present a polished rendition of a familiar work than of highly innovative or original material. In opera, for example, stars may prefer to perform work they know well already, and sets and costumes for frequently performed operas are easily accessible (Martorella 1982; Salem 1976). Innovative work requires greater expense for rehearsal time as well. Consequently, it will not do to treat quality as a single objective.

Cultural economists have assumed that nonprofit cultural organizations attempt to maximize quality in one or both of these senses. But such an assumption may betray a naïveté both about artists and about the control of nonprofit firms. Although many artists and curators, especially those in the major professional organizations, strive for perfection in production values, it seems reasonable to assume that others, like mortals in other occupations, seek simply to get by. Surely the extent to which artists are committed to virtuosity—and the distribution of such commitment across different kinds of arts organizations—is an empirical question. Similarly, whereas many organizationally employed artists, especially those in small performing arts companies, are committed to innovation, it seems likely that many others (perhaps most of those who work in the many arts organizations that do not present innovative materials) are perfectly content to perform conventional works.

If we were to assume, for a moment, that all artists were perfectionist enthusiasts of the most highbrow or innovative art, could we then further assume that quality was the principal objective of the nonprofit cultural firm? Only if we believed that artists were dominant in the decision making of such organizations. Economists who study arts organizations are uniformly vague when they speak of "management" or

"the director." But economists who study proprietary firms frequently assume that owners (as represented by boards of directors) are supreme and that managers act as their agents. In the nonprofit field, we might likewise expect boards of trustees to hold ultimate authority (as the law, in fact, requires) and arts managers to act as their agents (being subject to replacement if they do not). If this is the case, then the goals of artists, curators, artistic directors, or even managers are of less interest in establishing the firm's objective function than are those of trustees.

What do we know about the goals of trustees? Certainly most boards desire virtuoso performance. Nonetheless, because few arts boards actually include artists, board members may be poorly equipped to recognize it when they see it. With respect to the second kind of quality, innovativeness or the selection of difficult repertoire, the evidence is even more equivocal. A variety of case studies, in fact, suggest that many boards of trustees may actually place a negative value on difficult or avant-garde work. A study of the Philadelphia Orchestra in the 1960s, for example, noted that "without exception every Board member interviewed felt that the artistic obligation of the Philadelphia Orchestra was simply to maintain a high level of excellence in performance. Most board members dislike modern music" (Arian 1971, 66). A study of opera companies reported that their board members' "preferences are best-sellers, those with the highest box-office returns. Patrons, too, prefer the standard repertoire, and they want their contributions to go to the most popular works" (Martorella 1982, 142). A case study of another orchestra suggested that an artistic director's commitment to modern music actually increased subscription sales, but angered board members, who eventually dismissed him (Hart 1973). (Indeed, there is some evidence [American Symphony Orchestra League 1981] that audiences, as opposed to patrons and trustees, may be less averse to modern music than is commonly believed.) In short, if one must generalize about the objectives of performing arts firms, avoidance of innovation is as plausible a goal as the reverse.

In fact, arts organizations vary both in the objectives of their boards, managers, and artistic directors and in the power that each of these holds relative to the others. If we assume that the need to raise funds through ticket sales constrains the arts nonprofit and that donated support permits it to pursue its objectives more directly (DiMaggio 1983a, 1984), there is some evidence that resident theaters, at least, do prefer innovative repertoire. Studies in both the United States (DiMaggio & Stenberg 1985) and Great Britain (Austen-Smith 1980) find higher percentages of subsidy and lower levels of dependence upon earned income associated with more innovative or highbrow programming. In television broadcasting, an area in which direct comparison between proprietary and nonprofit firms is possible, public and nonprofit stations in the United States, Great Britain, and Australia present more arts and information programs and less light entertainment than their commercial counterparts (Katzman & Wirt 1977; Withers 1983). It is possible, of course, that these differences reflect less the preferences of nonprofit broadcasters than the market niche that public stations occupy.

Audience Size. Economists have assumed, with few exceptions, that nonprofit arts providers prefer large audiences not simply as means to fiscal ends but as ends in themselves, and that, consequently, they set ticket prices lower and provide more performances than would an optimizing proprietary firm. The desire for audiences tends to be taken as a matter of faith, again under the assumption that the objectives of artists are good proxies for the objectives of their employers. A number of economists assume, as well, that arts organizations seek a broad and socially heterogeneous audience. Reifying the arts organization, Baumol and Bowen (1976, 221) have argued that because the nonprofit arts firm "normally considers itself to be a supplier of virtue, it is natural that it should seek to distribute its bounty as widely and as equitably as possible. The group is usually determined to prevent income and wealth alone from deciding who is to have priority in the consumption of its services." Displaying a common confusion about the locus of power in arts organizations, Throsby and Withers (1979) posit similar organizational goals because "practitioners of the performing arts tend to have a crusading spirit. . . . the larger the audience that can be attracted, the happier they are."

In fact, little evidence supports this view, and considerable evidence suggests that most decision makers in nonprofit arts organizations have a more complex and often ambivalent attitude toward their audiences. This ambivalence is most marked among trustees, the policymakers for the nonprofit firm. An experienced museum director, noting the decline of the private patron, suggests that "it is possible that the greater democratization of our museums has something to do with the waning enthusiasm of a number of former donors. In the past, some wealthy people have, consciously or not, thought of the museum as a kind of aesthetic country club" (Shestack 1978; see also Frey & Pommerehne 1980; and on the orchestra, Arian 1971, 31). The disinterest in audience expansion for its own sake would seem to extend as well to managers who, as a group, display little enthusiasm for marketing or promotion except in response to financial crises (Hirsch & Davis 1980; Permut 1980).

Indeed, case studies suggest that many programs that appear to reflect an interest in audience expansion or service to new publics are in fact means to other ends. Although advocates cite the rise of subscription sales in the performing arts as an indication of democratization (Newman 1978), the subscription marketing technology, which emphasizes targeting prime prospects, is useful only for recruiting new patrons of the same socioeconomic standing as those already attending (Zeigler 1977, 179). Similarly, educational programs appear to occupy a low status in the concerns of decision makers in orchestras (Hart 1973) and art museums (Zolberg 1974, 1984). A study of a major opera company reports that "the most essential motive [for audience development] seems to be its necessity to the process of legitimating the organization for its sources of survival" (Salem

1976, 37). A comprehensive review of symphony orchestras' educational programs concludes, "It is a rather unfortunate commentary on the symphonic institution that it has been forced into these innovative programs, many of them of important community service, less by creative planning within the organization than by the pressure of their musicians for year-round employment" (Hart 1973, 287).

Decision makers in most nonprofit arts organizations, I suspect, attempt to cultivate a special kind of audience: their objectives have more to do with audience quality than with size or social composition (although it seems likely that they value the relatively high status of the latter). In his memoir of the Guthrie Theatre's first year, Sir Tyrone Guthrie (1964) stressed his desire for an audience both large and, above all, loyal and indulgent of the theater's artistic aspirations. The desire for intimacy lay behind his decisions to build a thrust rather than a proscenium stage (a decision that reduced the number of patrons the theater could accommodate by more than 20 percent) and to present the first production of *Hamlet* with the cast in modern dress. Such considerations are remote from the objectives of audience maximization and social diversification posited by many economists.

What support exists for the importance of audience size as an end in itself comes from aggregate studies of the relationship between subsidy and ticket pricing in nonprofit performing arts organizations (Globerman 1980; Netzer 1978; Touchstone 1980). Such studies have employed crude methodologies and obtained mixed results. More important, it is likely that, as Hansmann (1981) has argued, low ticket prices represent rational means to other ends than audience size and diversity. There are, of course, many participants in arts organizations who hold the values that economists posit and some nonprofit cultural firms where these values are the dominant ones. But their extent and distribution are empirical questions. Any behavioral models that posit such objectives a priori will be of the most limited applicability.

Survival and Legitimacy. Economists have assumed that the nonprofit arts firm attempts to survive; but with only a few exceptions (Frey & Pommerehne 1980; Hansmann 1981), they have paid little attention to the complex nonmarket determinants of survival in a grants economy, especially the supreme importance of organizational legitimacy.

By contrast, case studies of nonprofit arts organizations universally stress the efforts of their managers to establish the organizations as legitimate institutions within the local—and in some cases, national—cultural community. A study of the California Institute of the Arts, which was created as an avant-garde training institution, notes that "by the end of the Institute's second year, members of all schools believed programs were modified in directions calculated to secure trustee goodwill" (Adler 1979, 124). Classical music was strengthened at the expense of avant-garde composition, traditional painting at the expense of conceptual art, and public performance at the expense of theater "research." The Guthrie Theater produced a four-hour version of *Hamlet* for its premier performance as a signal to the audience that they were taken seriously, and cast nationally known stars as a signal that the theater was not just another tiny regional company (Guthrie 1964). The flagship station of the public fleet, WNET, implemented a multidivisional organizational structure in part to signal their managerial sophistication to potential corporate donors (Powell 1985).

In some instances, legitimacy plays an important role in financial survival. Thus the Seattle Opera viewed money-losing innovative programs as necessary to enable it to compete for national grants (Salem 1976). And Arian (1971, 69) writes that the Philadelphia Orchestra board regarded cost-efficiency as a legitimate value in its own right.

Budget Maximization and Growth. Hansmann (1981) is unique among economists in modeling budget maximization as an objective of the nonprofit arts firm. For some nonprofit arts organizations, growth appears to be an important goal (Cwi 1982, 77). Institutionalization and growth, or at least administrative structures that require minimal levels of growth, are favored by many foundations and government agencies that support the arts (DiMaggio 1983a; Poggi 1968; Zeigler 1977). And the tax system encourages nonprofit arts firms to set growth as an objective by tempting them to overinvest in capital (Feld et al. 1983, chap. 5).

Participant Rewards. For practitioners in a discipline that has achieved its greatest successes by assuming the primacy of interest in personal gain in the determination of human affairs, economists have been surprisingly polite in their attribution of goals to arts organizations. Of the books and papers I have reviewed, only two suggest that participants in nonprofit cultural firms may try to use the organizations to achieve their own ends, and neither attempts to model this behavior (Frey & Pommerehne 1980; Hansmann 1981). Yet, as Perrow (1979) has pointed out, participants in organizations commonly use them as vehicles for personal advancement. It would be surprising if nonprofit cultural organizations were somehow exempt from this tendency.

Certainly the professional and pecuniary goals of artists sometimes influence the behavior of the organizations in which they work. Musicians in small orchestras, for example, have forestalled efforts at artistic upgrading or expansion because they feared they would be dismissed if standards rose or they would have to relinquish regular employment if daily rehearsals were instituted (Hart 1973). Investigating changes in the performing arts with increases in public subsidy, Netzer (1978) suggested that theaters and orchestras use grants primarily to boost actors' and musicians' earnings. Artists' goals are most likely to prevail in artist-run organizations with weak boards and no administrative staff. A case study of one small theater collective reports that the organization's principal objectives were to provide the actors with opportunities to perform, fellowship and social support, and occasions for fun (Lyon 1974).

If artists impose their personal goals on some arts organizations, trustees and managers impose theirs on others. In the late nineteenth century, Henry Lee Higginson used the Boston Symphony Orchestra as a personal band, sending it to play at Boston society and college alumni gatherings. Simi-

lar, if less straightforward, patronal uses of nonprofit cultural organizations are not unknown today. Art museum trustees have been accused of letting their own collecting interests influence their preferences with respect to exhibition policy (Meyer 1979); and numerous commentators have suggested that patrons may regard arts organizations as private social clubs (Arian 1971; Pick 1983). Similarly, where the power of artistic personnel and trustees is weak, organizational goals may be synonymous with the personal objective functions of managers (Frey & Pommerehne 1980). If we assume that administrators prefer to spend money on assistants for themselves and that discretionary income can be employed in accordance with managers' preferences, then the percentage of the budget allocated to administration should rise with increases in grant support. Only two studies report results applicable to this hypothesis: the results of a study of U.S. art museums are consistent (DiMaggio & Powell 1984), but the findings of research on Australian performing arts organizations (Throsby & Withers 1979) are not.

The Stability of Objective Functions

As we have seen, there is much heterogeneity of objectives within the universe of nonprofit cultural organizations. No single behavioral model will apply to all or even most arts nonprofits; and the objectives of quality and quantity that have so far dominated economic models may not be the most important goals that arts organizations pursue.

Quite apart from the issue of heterogeneity, there is also some evidence that the objective functions of individual arts organizations are not stable over time. In the short run, arts managers, like managers of other organizations, switch their attention from goal to goal as various problems arise. Students of organizations call this process "problemistic search" (Cyert & March 1963) and arts administrators call it "putting out fires" and "management by crisis." I have suggested elsewhere (DiMaggio 1984) that public agencies that provide grants for objectives that are in mutual tension, if not inconsistent, exacerbate tendencies toward sequential attention to different goals.

Moreover, large arts organizations avoid explicit trade-offs between objectives by vesting responsibility for different goals in different subunits. In museums, for example, directors may seek to maximize the museum's adherence to standards promoted by the museum profession, curators the historical value of exhibits, membership staff the number of popular exhibitions, and educators the museum's commitment to outreach and public service (Frey & Pommerehne 1980; Zolberg 1984). To the extent that the relative influence of these actors fluctuates from time to time, the museum's objective function will change as well.

Objective functions may also change over the course of the nonprofit cultural organization's life cycle. According to Salem (1976), the goals of the Seattle Opera evolved as the organization matured, shifting from financial solvency and survival through community acceptance, to national recognition through expansion and innovation, to international recognition and artistic growth. Similarly, Poggi (1968) contends that nonprofit theaters inevitably must expand and that, if they succeed in doing so, increases in fixed costs will enforce artistic conservatism (see also Zeigler 1977). Although little systematic research has been undertaken on this topic, it seems likely that most nonprofit arts firms' goals do change with growth and age, a factor that must be taken into account in any behavioral model.

The Ambiguity of Objective Functions

The objectives of a nonprofit cultural organization are likely to be ambiguous as well as varied. I mean this in two senses. First, it is questionable to what extent major decisions by such organizations are best described as goal-directed. In Guthrie's memoir (1964), for example, he reports that two critical initial decisions—the choice of a city in which to locate and the choice of a design for the theater's permanent quarters—were driven more by intuition or deadlines than by an assessment of the relationship between means and ends. Why did the Guthrie Theatre locate in Minneapolis? "We have discussed it often and we simply do not know" (1964, 60). A key factor was a chance meeting between one of the theater's organizers and a prominent Twin Cities philanthropist. Such reports lead one to question whether the rhetoric of decisions and objectives is the most accurate way of representing the behavior of nonprofit cultural firms (see also Cohen & March [1974] on universities).

Goals in many arts organizations are ambiguous in a second sense: official goals are so abstract as to admit to any number of interpretations. Goals are good banners under which to rally but poor guides to behavior. All nonprofit cultural organizations profess a commitment to education and artistic accomplishment, but few are prepared to define either with any rigor. Indeed, the ambiguity of goals permits participants with widely differing interpretations to coexist peacefully in the same organizations.

Students of nonprofit cultural organizations have documented the protean nature of their goals: "The history of public broadcasting . . . reveals a basic lack of agreement on what it is or on what its mandate should be. This system has multiple uses, no clear standard of evaluation, and few clear operational processes. The stated mission of public television is to offer all things to all people" (Powell & Friedkin 1984).

Frey and Pommerehne (1980), in a perceptive essay on art museums, suggested that this ambiguity performs an important function by rendering the museum's managers unaccountable to market or bureaucratic standards of performance. They contended that the museum "directorate" (a vague characterization of professional staff with influence and authority) actively cultivates ambiguity so that "the production function connected with the museum's services is actively hidden by the supplier and cannot easily be detected and controlled from the outside" (1980, 252) Whether managers and staff try to maintain goal ambiguity or whether ambiguity simply results from efforts to keep individuals

with different values and standards working together in a climate of moderate civility, the effects are those that Frey and Pommerehne noted. As Peacock and Godfrey (1976, 197) have written, it is difficult "to specify the relation between the outputs and inputs by some kind of production function, principally because of the difficulty of defining output." Are the outputs of arts organizations exhibitions and performances, the number of attendances, or some combination thereof, perhaps weighted by the quality of the presentations or the aesthetic experience derived? So long as goals are unclear, behavioral modeling will be difficult indeed.

If there is a conclusion to this review it is that the difference between nonprofit cultural organizations and their proprietary counterparts lies not in the "typical" objectives of the former but in the tendency for nonprofit objective functions to be *more heterogeneous* and *more ambiguous* than those of the profit-maximizing, for-profit firm. In the sections that follow, I shall suggest certain research directions and organizational tensions that follow from these differences.

Goal Heterogeneity and Organizational Behavior

If one believes that there is a modal objective function for the nonprofit cultural organization, one need attempt only to model its behavior. But if one agrees that objectives are heterogeneous, the analytic problem becomes, first, to predict the goals that any given cultural organization will emphasize and, second, to explain the degree of heterogeneity observable in any population of nonprofit cultural organizations. Let us consider each of these problems in turn.

What Predicts the Objective Function of a Nonprofit Firm?

Case studies of nonprofit cultural organizations suggest four major factors that influence the objectives such organizations pursue: size and degree of orientation to the market; the extent, respectively, of class versus public sponsorship; the respective roles of artists, managers, and trustees; and the niche the nonprofit sector occupies in a given industry.

Size and Market Orientation. Nonprofit cultural organizations vary in size from the three-person dance company with no permanent residence or inventory of costumes to such multi-million-dollar businesses as the Metropolitan Museum of Art. They vary as well in their dependence upon earned income, from the volunteer organization that can get by on member contributions to the symphony orchestra earning three-quarters of a sizable budget from subscription and ticket sales.

Large organizations tend to be risk-averse: they have high fixed costs, both in salaries and, frequently, in maintenance of physical plant. Organizations that depend on high levels of earned income are similarly risk-averse, for a box-office failure may spell financial disaster (DiMaggio 1983a).

Like their proprietary brethren, managers of cultural organizations operating under market pressures devote much of their attention to ensuring stable flows of revenues and less time to artistic innovation. In his study of the Philadelphia Orchestra, which earns an exceptionally high proportion of its income, Arian (1971) notes that Eugene Ormandy was brought from relative obscurity to replace the free-spending Stokowski by trustees who sought a more cooperative artistic director, one willing to program to the box office and the orchestra's recording schedule. In later years, the orchestra's business manager noted that he would intervene in programming decisions only in the event of ''a fiscal problem, that is, if there was anything that was going to be terribly expensive'' (Schwalbe & Baker-Carr 1976b). In the field of opera, where organizations are large and earned income is a significant source of support, ''production costs often take precedence over artistic and musical considerations'' and management mediates between artistic standards and fiscal constraint (Martorella 1982, 84; 1983).

Similar factors influence innovativeness in resident theaters, where growth and dependence upon the market may alter the firm's internal balance of power. ''Getting subsidies is a difficult and time-consuming task. . . . Sometimes a founder stops directing and gives over most of his time to this job. Sometimes a person with special skills takes over the role—and with it, the power'' (Poggi 1968, 234–35; see also Zeigler 1977). The single empirical study of this topic reported that resident theaters that were above average in rate of growth or that increased their dependence on earned income during the 1970s came to present more standard repertoires, whereas those that remained small and independent of the market actually became more unconventional in their choice of productions (DiMaggio & Stenberg 1985).

Class versus Public Sponsorship. The salience of education and audience diversity as goals is likely to vary with the extent to which the governance of an arts organization is dominated by members of cohesive local upper classes and the extent to which the organization depends upon the public sector for sponsorship, legitimacy, or financial support.

Arian (1971) reported that the Philadelphia Orchestra, with an especially aristocratic board, in the 1960s resisted broadening the social base of its trustees and dissociated itself from a popular program of free summer concerts in a public park. By contrast, during this period the Utah Symphony Orchestra, with a board comprising outsiders to Salt Lake City's social elite, and the Buffalo Orchestra, under the board presidency of an Italian-American lawyer whose father was a musician, developed a range of service activities (the latter as it increased its dependence on public subsidy) (Hart 1973).

The former director of the Yale University Gallery has compared the museum director of the 1920s—''a connoisseur and gentleman [whose] few additional professional obligations [were] primarily those closely connected to his social life [such as] wooing collectors [and] establishing and maintaining rapport with the trustees''—to his counterpart of the post-1960s era. Programs of public arts support, he argues, have led museum staff to devote as much time to public service and participation programs as to collecting and re-

search (Shestack 1978). Similarly, the availability of public money through Titles I and III of the Elementary and Secondary Education Act encouraged many orchestras to develop programs for schoolchildren during the late 1960s and early 1970s (Hart 1973).

Little comparative evidence is available to assess the generality of these assertions. One study documents a positive net influence of federal grant monies and a negative effect of endowment income (a proxy measure of patron influence) on the number of outreach programs offered by U.S. art museums in the late 1970s, but finds no such associations for a comparable sample of history museums (DiMaggio & Romo 1984).

Roles and Relative Influence of Artistic Staff and Trustees. I have already mentioned the tendency for different goals to reside in specialized subunits of cultural organizations. When this is the case, the relative importance of different goals will depend on the relative influence of these subunits. Where education departments are influential, for example, art museums may pay closer attention to programs of outreach and public access; where curators wield power, art museums will appear more committed to goals of scholarship and conservation (Zolberg 1981).

Perhaps the most important distinction is between cultural organizations that are dominated by their artistic staff and those that are most influenced by trustees. Artistic directors and staff are most likely to emphasize quality objectives, whereas trustees tend to focus upon legitimacy and survival. Indeed, changes of goals over the life cycle of an organization occur most frequently in cultural nonprofits founded by an artist/entrepreneur. In the first years, the organization tends to project the founder's vision, and contrary to conventional doctrine, the trustees, often handpicked, serve as agents of the founder. Frequently, as the organization grows, the board expands to include community influentials who eventually dismiss the founder or force her or him to cede responsibility to a full-time manager, who serves as an agent of the board (see, for example, Zeigler [1977] on this phenomenon).

The Nonprofit Niche. In many instances, the objectives that nonprofit and proprietary cultural organizations pursue are functions of the niches they occupy in their industries. Powell (1982) documents how university presses have expanded their trade lists as commercial publishers focus increasingly on the mass market. Montias (1983) describes the emergence of a commercial theater sector in the Netherlands as nonprofit theaters became increasingly avant-garde. And Poggi (1968, 147) reports the influence of producers with noncommercial values in bringing the works of playwrights like Ibsen, Shaw, and O'Neill to the commercial stage before the rise of the nonprofit theater.

What Determines the Heterogeneity of a Nonprofit Cultural Industry?

To complicate matters, nonprofit cultural industries differ in the degree of goal heterogeneity they display. The resident stage, for example, includes theaters devoted to avant-garde experimentation, classical revivals, commercial entertainment, and radical social change, and embraces formal bureaucracies, medieval autocracies, and participatory democracies. By contrast, nonprofit orchestras are similar in structure and, for the most part, relatively predictable in repertoire. What explains the degree of diversity in objective functions observable in different nonprofit art worlds?

I would hypothesize that three determinants are most important. The first is the degree to which organizations in the industry are dependent upon the marketplace for survival. Although nonprofit firms can react to market pressures in several ways (DiMaggio 1984), in general, market constraints lead organizations to behave similarly to one another and to their proprietary counterparts.

The second factor is the heterogeneity within the industry with respect to the attributes I have identified as influencing the nonprofit cultural organization's objective function: size and market orientation, class versus public sponsorship, and the relative influence of artists, administrative staff, and trustees. The resident theater field, for example, is marked by great heterogeneity along all these dimensions, whereas the orchestra industry is relatively homogeneous.

The third factor is the degree to which the nonprofit cultural field is institutionalized, by which I mean the extent to which both public and professional expectations about the structures, goals, and programs of the organizations in it are well established and invariant, and the extent to which these expectations are diffused and reinforced by a set of professional and trade organizations, newsletters, conferences, and funding agencies (see also DiMaggio 1983b; DiMaggio & Powell 1983). A student of the opera field reports the tendency for companies to imitate competitors "that have been successful in getting grants in the hope that similar results can be attained" (Salem 1976); and a historian of the resident stage notes the standardizing effects of a national service organization's emphasis on "administrative rules and manners" during the late 1960s (Zeigler 1977, 185).

The Characteristic Tensions of Goal Ambiguity

Nonprofit cultural organizations are distinguished from proprietary cultural firms by the ambiguity, as well as the heterogeneity, of their goals. I have already suggested that ambiguity of objectives plays a valuable role in masking goal dissensus so that participants can get on with their work and in sufficiently obscuring the nonprofit cultural organization's operating processes to afford it at least some insulation from its complex and demanding environment.

Ambiguity of purpose does, however, cause characteristic tensions in any organization, and such tensions are rife within the nonprofit arts. In this section, we shall consider three chronic dilemmas: tension between management and artistic professionals; tension between artists and management together and boards of trustees; and difficulties in evaluating managers and holding them accountable for their performance.

Tension between Administrative and Professional Staff. Having taken economists to task for leaning a bit too heavily on cultural stereotypes about the artist's commitment to excellence and innovation, I shall not suggest that artists cannot function comfortably in bureaucratic organizations. Indeed, within the for-profit cultural sector, advertising artists spin out copy, situation-comedy scriptwriters develop story lines, and Nashville songwriters pen hits in austere cubicles, all buoyed in their work by strongly developed craft ideologies consistent with their employers' proprietary goals (Becker 1982; Gitlin 1984; Schudson 1984; Stewart & Cantor 1982).

Nonprofit arts organizations, however, are somewhat different. As Majone (1980) has observed, the characteristic legitimating ideologies of nonprofit organizations are similar to those of the professions, stressing disinterested service and professional expertise. What is more, in the nonprofit cultural fields, artists' training is likely to emphasize innovation or virtuosity and to deemphasize the market or bureaucratic settings in which the future artists must support themselves. Like the training institutions, the nonprofit cultural organizations in which artists labor make little room in their official rhetorics of motive for the exigencies of the marketplace. The artists they employ are socialized, in many cases, into a professional perspective that, like the official doctrine of the museum or the symphony orchestra, denies the legitimacy of compromise with commerce. Although artists recognize the mundane constraints under which they labor, the professional rhetoric of virtuosity or experimentation and the organizational rhetoric of service and excellence represent useful resources in their struggles for greater autonomy and control. Indeed, those artistic personnel—and I include in this group artistic directors and curators—whose training most carefully cultivates the denial of market factors tend to staff precisely those elite arts nonprofits whose size and budgetary needs make them most dependent upon the marketplace.

The tension between creative and administrative goals is nowhere better documented than in Adler's history of the California Institute of the Arts (1979), an organization dedicated, at its creation, to the avant-garde. Adler notes the cultural breach between the institution's lay administrators and the artists whose work it was their job to facilitate:

> Many laymen shared yet another experience: having . . . come to the Institute to pray, they found they had stayed only to be mocked. If art in western culture has inherited some of the "spiritual," redemptive significance of religion, the Institute's initiates . . . (particularly those considering themselves avant-garde) distinguished themselves from the laity by playing in the temple and ridiculing the earnestness of those who wished to worship. (112)

Lay staff, Adler continues, "favored those arts which demanded organized cooperation and formal scheduling and whose performance was highly visible": above all, dance and classical music. Visual artists, actors, and composers were held in relative disfavor, for what they did was less recognizable as "work" and could sometimes embarrass the institution in front of its trustees or community. Administrators came to regard such artists "with apprehension as unreliable actors in the show it was their job to stage" (117).

Such tensions are evident in less dramatic form in other nonprofit cultural settings. Powell and Friedkin (1984), in a study of two public television stations, document the conflict between programming staff, committed to "quality programs," innovation, and local features, and fund-raising staff, who prefer programs for which it is easier to raise money and that enable them to reinforce enduring relationships with corporate donors.

Such conflict is common as well in the performing arts, where artistic directors who fail to stay within budget or who mount avant-garde productions that drive away paying audiences may be sanctioned or even dismissed (Hart 1973; Martorella 1982; Poggi 1968; Salem 1976; Zeigler 1977). Hart (1973) criticizes Arthur Judson, the former manager of the Philadelphia Orchestra and the New York Philharmonic, for promulgating what has become the conventional wisdom that the manager never interferes in artistic policy but only facilitates the work of the artistic director. On the basis of case studies of a diverse range of U.S. symphony orchestras, Hart maintains that this view obscures the actual division of authority within the orchestra (1973, 71). Indeed, my own surveys of marketing and audience-development staff of symphony orchestras and resident theaters reveal that three-quarters of such staff in the theaters and almost three-fifths in the orchestras were occasionally or routinely consulted about artistic programming decisions (DiMaggio 1984, 75). (These figures, of course, do not include the undoubtedly higher percentage of top administrators involved actively in such decisions.)

Even art museums, which are usually directed as well as staffed by professional art historians, experience similar tensions. New categories of personnel favor programs that make it easier for them to do their jobs. One art museum development officer spoke enthusiastically to an interviewer of that institution's public outreach programs: "The fact that museums are now recognizing themselves as educational institutions gives them a whole new image and approach. It is one that I find increasingly easy to promote, much more so than a purely cultural approach" (Schwalbe & Baker-Carr 1976a, 10). As art museum directors come, increasingly, from backgrounds other than curatorship (DiMaggio 1983c), such conflicts intensify. According to Vera Zolberg (1984), the postwar era has witnessed the rise of a new class of "bureaucratic managers" who "try to run museums as rationally as they claim modern firms function." In a study of the Chicago Art Institute, she notes the difficulty that such directors encounter in their efforts at control, owing to "the tenacity of precontractual understandings" between curators and trustees, which lead to an "endemic circumventing of channels of communication" (Zolberg 1974, 282).

The Problem of Boards of Trustees.   Where goals are ambiguous, power inheres in the ability to define their opera-

tional implications. In nonprofit cultural organizations, ambiguities of purpose lead to tension among boards of trustees, administrators, and artistic personnel. In the performing arts, conflict between boards and artistic directors over deficits and controversial work are commonplace (Hart 1973; Poggi 1968; Salem 1976; Zeigler 1977). In art museums such conflicts occur when conservative trustees oppose efforts to expand programs for the general public (Shestack 1978) or when individual curators and trustees form alliances around their shared aesthetic goals (Schwalbe & Baker-Carr 1976a, 44; Zolberg 1974).

Conflict often remains latent until a financial crisis requires trade-offs between artistic and fiscal imperatives. Under these circumstances, boards that previously have been content to serve as agents of administrators or artists demand that the agency relationship be reversed. In order to forestall such an event, the founder of one major resident theater created a dual board structure, with one board of influentials overseeing his theater's physical plant and another of hand-picked supporters taking responsibility for the performing group he headed (Wilk 1982).

The Difficulty of Evaluation.   When objectives are ambiguous, it may be as difficult to tell how well an organization and its administrators are doing as it is for social scientists to model its behavior, and for much the same reason. By what standards, in terms of what output, is evaluation possible? The problem of evaluation raises concerns among boards (as well as institutional donors) about the accountability of the administrators they employ. Indeed, attendant on this uncertainty is a widespread belief, even among some nonprofit arts managers themselves, that arts administrators, as a group, lack competence.

What is the evidence in support of this assertion? In practice, there is very little beyond the anecdotal. Often such allegations hinge on implicit comparisons to an idealized notion of proprietary-sector leadership—a notion that the pace of executive turnover in such industries as television, film, and recorded music should at least call into question. Although some economists have suggested that wages in the nonprofit cultural sector are so low that competent managers may not be attracted (Throsby & Withers 1979), if one controls for firm size and considers the nonpecuniary advantages of such positions (Young, this volume, chap. 10), the proposition is less evident. The only study with which I am familiar that compares the efficiency of nonprofit and proprietary cultural organizations in the same field—a comparison of public and commercial television stations in Australia—yields findings that are as equivocal as they are unsurprising: the noncommercial stations reach fewer viewers but produce more hours of programming per dollar spent (Withers 1983). Our own surveys of managers in four noncommercial cultural fields indicate that, as a group, they possess relatively high levels of formal education in the liberal arts, relatively little training in management per se, and widely variable experience in the artistic disciplines they oversee. But, in the absence of either detailed data on the achievements of managers of comparable private-sector firms or of agreement on the skills relevant to managing nonprofit cultural institutions, a comparative assessment of preparation is impossible.

If the question of competence must be begged, it is possible, however, to suggest some structural reasons that we might expect observers to question the competence of nonprofit arts managers, quite aside from the merits of the case. First of all, ambiguity of objectives, under conditions of dependence on grant income, makes it difficult to predict the effects of this year's programs on next year's revenues (Powell & Friedkin 1983). Despite the efforts of some state arts agencies and locally oriented private foundations to provide predictable long-term funding, uncertainty about the future financial state of the organization is invariably high. For many nonprofit cultural organizations, ensuring stability by developing a predictable paying market for one's services is either impossible (as in the case of public television) or inconsistent with aesthetic goals (as in the case of small experimental or socially oriented performing groups or highly specialized museums) (see DiMaggio 1984). Given such a high degree of uncertainty, the often decried lack of systematic planning in nonprofit cultural organizations may be a realistic response. The multiplicity of goals that nonprofit cultural organizations pursue provides protective coloration for the administrator, who will find that nearly anything he or she does will appear to further at least some of them (Frey & Pommerehne 1980). At the same time, goal ambiguity ensures that any course of action will be inconsistent with some participants' favored objectives. Where goal dissensus is high, few managers will satisfy many of their trustees or external critics. Ambiguity of purpose offers managers flexibility and slack at the same time it ensures that their successes are likely to be ambivalent ones.

The Behavior of Public and Private Cultural Organizations

Up to now, I have considered those characteristics of nonprofit organizations that make them distinctive from their proprietary counterparts, implicitly including public organizations among the former. There is less to say in a review about behavioral differences between public and private nonprofit arts organizations because we have little data on this topic and even less theory. In this section I shall summarize briefly the little that exists.

The characteristics of public firms depend to a very great extent on the specific regulations that govern their operations and their relationship to other governmental bodies. Many public cultural organizations, especially public municipal museums, are pseudononprofits, buffered from city or county government by a volunteer board of trustees and, in some cases, considerable private patronage. By contrast, some local arts agencies are line departments of municipal government. Factors governing the behavior of public agencies are often localized and specific. In the state of Washington, for example, municipal agencies, including public local arts agencies, are forbidden by state law from making grants (although they often circumvent this prohibition by "contracting" with beneficiary groups) (Fuller 1979).

Theoretical approaches to public/private differences in other fields cannot readily be applied to the arts. For example, Scott and Meyer's analysis of public and private schools (1984) locates differences between the two types in the greater centralization, federalization, and fragmentation of authority in the environments of the former, a characterization less easily applicable to public agencies in the arts. The rationalization of the environment to which Peterson (forthcoming) accords responsibility for the rapid growth of the arts administration profession in the 1960s and 1970s was peculiar neither to public nor to private nonprofits.

It is possible, of course, that "publicness" and "privateness" inhere not in juridical definitions of form but in the relative dependence of different organizations on public and private funding sources (see Levy, this volume, chap. 15). But even here, the influence of both public and private money is likely to vary with the instrumentalities through which they are delivered: for example, public support may be general-purpose or program-specific, locally or federally provided, direct or indirect through the system of taxation; and private revenues may come in the form of corporate grants, individual patronage, or market exchange (Feld et al. 1983; DiMaggio 1983a; DiMaggio & Romo 1984). Although Frey and Pommerehne (1980) develop a set of hypotheses predicting differences between noncommercial and commercial museums (a distinction that appears to have more to do with market orientation than legal form), their predictions are based on features peculiar to the European, and especially the German, system of public support.

Drawing on Weisbrod's median-voter theory, Bendick, in a paper on schools, suggests that private nonprofits will provide higher quality goods than comparable public organizations (1977). But Weisbrod himself, in a discussion that includes libraries, states that no systematic differences between public and nonprofit firms are to be expected (Lee & Weisbrod 1977).

Although there are several sources of data on public and private nonprofit organizations in two industries in which they coexist—museums and local arts agencies—available comparisons fail to control for factors (for example, size and program emphasis) that may influence results. Nonetheless, some zero-order differences between the two groups are intriguing.

Consider first local arts agencies, which include three dominant legal forms: public agencies, private nonprofit organizations, and private nonprofits publicly designated to perform municipal functions. Gibans (1982) suggests that the publics have greater access to public funds and services, that voluntaries offer greater flexibility, and that private designated councils offer the best of both worlds. She further contends that municipal agencies focus upon allocating public funds, employing artists, purchasing arts services, and commissioning works, whereas the privates emphasize fundraising from the private sector and redistribution.

My own hand analysis of two listings—one of approximately seven hundred cases from the American Council for the Arts Handbook (American Council for the Arts 1978), another of the National Assembly of Local Arts Agencies' (NALAA) 1981–82 membership directory (NALAA 1982)—suggest that the latter generalizations may be ill founded. In the earlier listing, only 5 percent of the private nonprofits (but none of the publics) raised and disbursed private funds; the types were about equally likely to sponsor public presentations, arts education programs, artists' residencies, exhibitions, art festivals, and film festivals.

In short, then, although there is much variation in the behavior of local arts agencies, most of it falls within rather than between legal forms. Nonetheless, there are some notable differences. In the 1976 data, the publics were more likely (59 to 46 percent) to make grants, whereas the private councils were more likely to offer coordinated information services (74 to 60 percent) and mailing lists (40 to 23 percent). Of the agencies surveyed in 1981–82 (of which 27 percent were public, 41 percent fully private, and 32 percent publicly designated), public and publicly designated agencies were substantially more likely than fully private councils to make grants (with more than half of each of the former types offering financial assistance, compared to just a third of the latter). These differences themselves varied with organizational budget size, however. Among the smallest agencies, the privately designated were more likely than either the publics and privates to make grants, whereas among the largest, the publics (78 percent) provided grants more frequently than the designateds (68 percent), which, in turn, were far more likely to provide financial assistance than the fully private (32 percent). Among the smallest agencies, the types were about equally likely to have volunteer leadership; but of agencies with budgets of more than $50,000, only the free-standing nonprofits did not have paid administrators.

The broadest array of data exist for the comparison of public and nonprofit museums, although the absence of appropriate controls in published analyses renders interpretation difficult. Comparing all public to all private museums, a 1965 Office of Education study (Rogers 1969) indicated that public museums (of all kinds) reported far more attendance than private museums, a finding that was replicated in a 1973 study (National Endowment for the Arts 1974). Although size differences between public and private museums seem too slight to account for the magnitude of the difference, it is possible that controlling for museum type would moderate it in degree. (Science museums, which are more often public, as a group report higher attendance than art museums, which are more often private.) It is also possible that public museums are more strongly tempted to inflate their estimates than are private nonprofits. The 1965 study indicated that nonprofits were more likely than publics to charge admission fees, and the publics, according to the 1973 study, reported serving greater numbers of students. The 1965 study reported that nonprofits and public museums were about equally likely to sponsor special programs for selected publics: the greater variation was between municipal and county museums (of

which 33 and 27 percent, respectively, offered such programs) and state and federal museums (with only 14 and 10 percent, respectively, reporting special efforts of this kind). Similarly, a multivariate analysis of a 1979 national museum sample reported that the net effects of form on provision of educational services of various kinds vary more among different kinds of public museums than between nonprofit and public as a whole (DiMaggio & Romo 1984). In short, the preliminary verdict with respect to public service is that there is no apparent consistent difference.

The 1965 Office of Education study attempted to measure a number of quality indicators reflecting the breadth and depth of the museums' services. Again the findings were equivocal. Private nonprofit museums were actually more likely than their public counterparts to publish formal annual reports (27 as compared to 15 percent), perhaps a sign of accountability; and more likely to provide such services to scholars as library services and substantive publication programs (such as catalogs). On the other hand, they were less likely than the publics to offer professionally designed exhibits and to employ full-time professional staff. One could infer from this that private museums attend more to scholarly goals and public museums are more concerned with mounting exhibitions for the public, but without controls for museum type and size, such an interpretation, given the relatively small differences, is unwarranted.

One difference of note (Rogers 1969) was that 75 percent of the nonprofit museums but just 18 percent of the public museums maintained paid membership programs in 1965. Curiously, a study of data from 1932 reported almost the reverse: 83 percent of institutionally controlled museums (public, corporate, university, library, and foundation) were membership organizations compared to but 3 percent of the private nonprofit associations (Johnson 1972, 21). Although the categories do not correspond exactly, the results do indicate a notable increase in emphasis in the private nonprofit museum sector (and perhaps a decrease in the public) on membership programs between 1932 and 1965, as the former expanded its definition of the community to include new, albeit still predominantly upper-middle-class portions of the public. Not surprisingly, the 1965 study reported that nonprofits receive more in-kind private assistance, and in 1973, 72 percent of the nonprofits but only 41 percent of the public museums reported the presence of volunteer staff.

The structures of the two kinds of museum appear similar. Nonprofits, of course, were more likely to report having a board of trustees or equivalent body. In museums that did have boards, nonprofit directors were more likely (86 to 63 percent) to report attending trustee meetings regularly than were the directors of public museums (National Endowment for the Arts 1974). Nonetheless, public and private museums were very similar in their allocation of staff and budget across functional areas. One study of art museums affiliated with public and private universities likewise found few differences by form: the two sets of museums were similar even in the extent of their endowment income (Sloan & Swinburne 1981).

A Note on Industries

In my efforts to review conscientiously the literature on behavior, I have focused upon the nature of the nonprofit firm, especially in comparison to the presumably profit-optimizing and goal-directed for-profit enterprise. Although students of cultural institutions have conducted their inquiries almost entirely at the level of the firm, it may be that the more fundamental differences between nonprofit and for-profit cultural organizations lie in differences between industries that are *predominantly* proprietary and industries that are *predominantly* nonprofit. Within most industries, definitions of appropriate structures, products, and means of organizing are usually so institutionalized that only modest differences exist among firms of different legal form. At the industry level, such underlying differences as may follow logically from nonprofit sponsorship are freer to emerge, even though they may be shared, in large degree, by proprietary and public organizations. What is more, comparisons between for-profit and nonprofit/public firms are often artificial exercises, for most kinds of cultural organizations are overwhelmingly one or the other. It is at the industry level where the greatest degree of variation can be observed.

Within nonprofit industries, firms tend to employ artists or such aesthetic experts as curators directly, influencing their work through hierarchical authority relations. By contrast, proprietary cultural industries characteristically deal with artists by means of contract: artists can maintain either short-term contracts with cultural producers or distributors (as in the recording industry) or work with several producers or distributors simultaneously (as in film, book publishing, or nightclub entertainment). To put this another way, firms in nonprofit industries buy the artist's time, whereas those in for-profit industries purchase his or her products.

Second, firms in nonprofit cultural industries are characterized by ambiguous success criteria, whereas for-profit culture producers rely on market criteria for evaluation of success. It follows from this that artists are more influential in nonprofit cultural industries than in proprietary cultural sectors. (Under conditions of great market uncertainty, however, artists can attain unusual if temporary power even in the latter [see Peterson & Berger 1975].)

Third, in nonprofit cultural industries, the lack of market criteria of success, the importance of aesthetic ideologies, and the significant role of class and status in governance fuse to create a situation conducive to the maintenance of small markets for specialized genres. The desire of professionally socialized artists to work in academically legitimated cultural categories and the preference of high-status trustees and members to celebrate their taste in isolation from the masses coincide to ensure strong product differentiation, narrow market segmentation, and weak marketing efforts that together preserve the existence of a relatively wide range of finely classified cultural forms.

By contrast, the dependence of firms in predominantly proprietary industries on the bottom line leads to efforts to aggregate market segments to make it easier to achieve economies of scale; to attempts to expand demand through aggressive marketing, particularly to gatekeepers of the flow of new products to the public (Hirsch 1972); and to the availability of fewer and/or more weakly classified genres or cultural forms. Thus, under the proprietary duopoly of Community Concerts and Civic Music in concert promotion in the 1940s, classical musicians were restricted to the limited repertoire the concert companies dictated, "chosen to appeal to the broadest segment of the community" (Hart 1973, 82). And when theater was almost exclusively in the hands of the Erlangers and Shuberts, the differentiation of dramatic genres was likewise restricted: "the idea of writing for a limited or special audience did not even occur to most American playwrights" before the decline of the road show and the emergence of the noncommercial theater movement (Poggi 1968, 260).

SUMMARY

The implications of this review of research on behavioral differences between nonprofit and proprietary organizations for future research can be summarized as follows:

1. Attempts to develop a single best objective-function-based model of the behavior of all nonprofit performing arts organizations have not been fruitful, nor are they likely to be. At the very least, economists who pursue this general approach must provide empirical evidence in defense of their choice of objectives and specify narrowly the scope conditions of the models they develop.

2. Nonprofit cultural organizations may differ from proprietary cultural concerns less in their modal objective functions than in the greater heterogeneity of their goals. Research must explain variation among nonprofit cultural firms in the goals they pursue and illuminate the factors that increase or decrease goal heterogeneity.

3. Nonprofit cultural organizations may also differ from their proprietary counterparts in the greater ambiguity of their objectives. Research should explore the consequences of ambiguity for the internal political systems and decision-making processes of the nonprofit cultural firm.

4. Although the topic is potentially one of considerable interest to public policy makers, we have little in the way of theory or data analyses relevant to the question of differences between nonprofit and public cultural organizations. Research on this topic is needed, although it is possible that the specific context of public and private sponsorship may turn out to affect behavior more markedly than legal form per se.

5. The most important differences between nonprofit and proprietary enterprises (and possibly public enterprise) may be discernible not at the firm but at the industry level. We may best understand these differences by comparing cultural industries that are predominantly for-profit, predominantly nonprofit, or predominantly public.

REFERENCES

Adler, Judith. 1979. *Artists in Offices*. New Brunswick, N.J.: Transaction Press.

American Council for the Arts. 1978. *Community Arts Agencies: A Handbook and Guide*. New York: American Council for the Arts.

American Symphony Orchestra League. 1979. *Resource Guide: A Reference Manual for Symphony Orchestras*. Vienna, Va.: American Symphony Orchestra League.

———. 1981. *Twentieth-century Music and the Box Office at Symphony Concerts*. Report. Vienna, Va.: American Symphony Orchestra League,

Arian, Edward. 1971. *Bach, Beethoven and Bureaucracy: The Case of the Philadelphia Orchestra*. University: University of Alabama Press.

Association of College, University and Community Arts Administrators. 1981. *Profile Survey IX-A: 1980–81 Season*. Madison, Wis.: Association of College, University and Community Arts Administrators.

Austen-Smith, David. 1980. "On the Impact of Revenue Subsidies on Repertory Theatre Policy." *Journal of Cultural Economics* 4, no. 1 (June):9–17.

Baumol, Hilda, and William J. Baumol. 1980. "On Finances of the Performing Arts during Stagflation: Some Recent Data." *Journal of Cultural Economics* 4, no. 2 (December):1–14.

———. 1984. "On Inflation and the Arts: A Summing Up." In Baumol and Baumol, eds., *Inflation and the Performing Arts*, 173–95. New York: New York University Press.

Baumol, William J., and William G. Bowen. 1966. *Performing Arts: The Economic Dilemma*. Cambridge, Mass.: MIT Press,

———. 1976. "On the Performing Arts: The Anatomy of Their Economic Problems. In Mark Blaug, ed., *The Economics of the Arts*, 218–26. Boulder, Colo.: Westview Press.

Becker, Howard S. 1982. *Art Worlds*. Berkeley: University of California Press.

Belinfante, Alexander, and Richard L. Johnson. 1983. "An Economic Analysis of the U.S. Recorded Music Industry." In William S. Hendon and James L. Shanahan, eds., *Economics of Cultural Decisions*, 232–42. Cambridge, Mass.: Abt Books.

Bendick, Marc, Jr. 1977. "Education as a Three-Sector Industry." In Burton A. Weisbrod, ed., *The Voluntary Nonprofit Sector: An Economic Analysis*. Lexington, Mass.: Lexington Books.

Ben-Ner, Avner. 1986. "Why Are There Nonprofit Organizations in Market Economies?" In Susan Rose-Ackerman, ed., *The Economics of Nonprofit Institutions: Studies in Structure and Policy*. New York: Oxford Univ. Press.

Blaug, Mark, ed. 1976. *The Economics of the Arts*. London: Martin Robertson.

Bowker Publications. 1982. *Magazine Industry Marketplace*. New York: Bowker Publications.

———. 1983. *Books in Print*. New York: Bowker Publications.

———. 1984a. *Literary Marketplace*. New York: Bowker Publications.

———. 1984b. *The Bowker Annual of Library and Book Trade Information*. 29th ed. New York: Bowker Publications.

Bureau of the Census. 1982a. *Census of Manufactures*. Washington, D.C.: U.S. Department of Commerce.

———. 1982b. *Census of Service Industries*. Vol. 1, *Establishment and Firm Size*. Washington, D.C.: U.S. Department of Commerce.

Chicago Community Trust. 1982. *A Report to the Executive Committee of the Chicago Community Trust on the Arts in Chicago*. Chicago: Chicago Community Trust.

Cohen, Michael D., and James G. March. 1974. *Leadership and Ambiguity: The American College President*. New York: McGraw-Hill.

Coleman, Laurence Vail. 1939. *The Museum in America: A Critical Study*. Vol. 3. Washington, D.C.: American Association of Museums.

Corporation for Public Broadcasting. 1979. *A Study of Public Television's Educational Services, 1978–79*. Washington, D.C.: Office of Educational Activities, Corporation for Public Television.

Cwi, David. 1982. "Merit Good or Market Failure: Justifying and Analyzing Public Support for the Arts." In Kevin V. Mulcahy and C. Richard Swaim, eds., *Public Policy and the Arts*. Boulder, Colo.: Westview Press.

———. 1983. "Challenging Cultural Institutions to Make a Profit: Emerging Decisions for Nonprofit Providers." In William S. Hendon and James L. Shanahan, eds., *Economics of Cultural Decisions*, 49–56. Cambridge, Mass.: Abt Books.

Cyert, Richard M., and James G. March. 1963. *A Behavioral Theory of the Firm*. Englewood Cliffs, N.J.: Prentice-Hall.

DiMaggio, Paul. 1982a. "Cultural Entrepreneurship in Nineteenth-Century Boston, Part I: The Creation of an Organizational Base for High Culture in America." *Media, Culture and Society* 4:33–50.

———. 1982b. "Cultural Entrepreneurship in Nineteenth-century Boston, Part II: The Classification and Framing of American Art." *Media, Culture and Society* 4:303–22.

———. 1983a. "Can Culture Survive the Marketplace?" *Journal of Arts Management and Law* 13, no. 1 (Spring):61–87.

———. 1983b. "State Expansion and Organizational Fields." In Richard H. Hall and Robert E. Quinn, eds., *Organizational Theory and Public Policy*, 147–61. Beverly Hills, Calif.: Sage Publications.

———. 1983c. "The American Art Museum Director as Professional: Results of a Survey." *Art Galleries Association Bulletin* (United Kingdom) (July 24):5–9.

———. 1984. "The Nonprofit Instrument and the Influence of the Marketplace on Policies in the Arts." In W. McNeil

Lowry, ed., *Public Policies and the Arts in the United States*, 57–99. Englewood Cliffs, N.J.: Prentice-Hall.

DiMaggio, Paul, and Walter W. Powell. 1983. "The Iron Cage Revisited: Institutional Isomorphism and Collective Rationality in Organizational Fields." *American Sociological Review* 82:147–60.

———. 1984. "Institutional Isomorphism and Structural Conformity." Paper presented at the annual meeting of the American Sociological Association in San Antonio, Texas.

DiMaggio, Paul, and Frank P. Romo. 1984. *The Determinants of Humanities Education Programming in U.S. Art and History Museums*. New Haven, Report to the National Endowment for the Humanities, Office of Planning and Policy Assessment.

DiMaggio, Paul, and Kristen Stenberg. 1985. "Conformity and Diversity in the American Resident Stage." In Judith Balfe and Margaret Wyszomirski, eds., *Art, Ideology and Politics*. New York: Praeger.

Feld, Alan L., Michael O'Hare, and J. Mark Davidson Schuster. 1983. *Patrons Despite Themselves: Taxpayers and Arts Policy*. New York: New York University Press.

Frey, Bruno S., and Werner W. Pommerehne. 1980. "An Economic Analysis of the Museum." In William S. Hendon, James L. Shanahan and Alice J. MacDonald, eds., *Economic Policy for the Arts*. 248–59. Cambridge, Mass.: Abt Books.

Frost, S. E., Jr. 1937. *Education's Own Stations*. Chicago: University of Chicago Press.

Fuller, Lucille. 1979. *Arts Commissions in Washington State*. Seattle: University of Washington Institute of Government Research.

Fulton, Len, and Ellen Ferber, eds. 1983. *International Directory of Little Magazines and Small Presses*. Paradise, Calif.: Dustbooks.

Gertner, Richard, ed. 1982. *International Motion Picture Almanac*. New York: Quigly Publishing Co.

Gibans, Nina Freedlander. 1982. *The Community Arts Council Movement*. New York: Praeger.

Gitlin, Todd. 1984. *Inside Prime Time*. New York: Pantheon.

Globerman, Stephen. 1980. "An Exploratory Analysis of the Effects of Public Funding of the Performing Arts." Pp. 67–78 In William S. Hendon, James L. Shanahan, and Alice J. MacDonald, eds., *Economic Policy for the Arts*. Cambridge, Mass.: Abt Books.

Guthrie, Tyrone. 1964. *A New Theatre*. New York: McGraw-Hill.

Hansmann, Henry. 1980. "The Role of Nonprofit Enterprise." *Yale Law Journal* 89, no. 5 (April):835–901.

———. 1981. "Nonprofit Enterprise in the Performing Arts." *Bell Journal of Economics* 12, no. 2:341–61.

Hart, Philip. 1973. *Orpheus in the New World: The Symphony Orchestra as an American Cultural Institution*. New York: W. W. Norton.

Hendon, William S., and James L. Shanahan, eds. 1983. *Economics of Cultural Decisions*. Cambridge, Mass.: Abt Books.

Hendon, William S., James L. Shanahan, and Alice J. MacDonald, eds. 1980. *Economic Policy for the Arts*. Cambridge, Mass.: Abt Books.

Hirsch, Paul M. 1972. "Processing Fads and Fashions: An Organization-Set Analysis of Cultural Industry Systems." *American Journal of Sociology* 77 (January):639–59.

Hirsch, Paul M., and Harry L. Davis. 1980. "Are Arts Administrators Really Serious about Marketing?" In Michael P. Mokwa, William M. Dawson, and E. Arthur Prieve, eds., *Marketing the Arts*, 59–64. New York: Praeger.

Hodsoll, Frank. 1984. "A Compilation of Excerpts from Remarks." In *Arts Review* (supplement). Washington, D.C.: National Endowment for the Arts.

Hubbard, Linda S., ed. 1983. *Book Publishers Directory*. 4th ed. Detroit: Gale Research Co.

International Art Alliance. 1983. *Directory of Corporate Art Collections*. 2d ed. New York: American Council for the Arts.

Jacques Cattell Press. 1984. *American Book Trade Directory*. 30th ed. New York: Bowker Publications.

Jeffri, Joan. 1980. *The Emerging Arts: Management, Survival and Growth*. New York: Praeger.

Johnson, H. Earle. 1953. "The Germania Musical Society." *Musical Quarterly* 39, no. 1 (January):75–93.

Johnson, Keith Roberts. 1972. "American Museums, 1932–1965: A Test Case for the Comparative Analysis of Organizations." Ph.D. diss., Syracuse University.

Katzman, Natan, and Kenneth Wirt. 1977. *Arts and Cultural Programs on Radio and Television*. Washington, D.C.: National Endowment for the Arts, Research Division.

King, Millie Mei-Vung. 1980. "Through the Eyes of Boston: The State of Chamber Music Today." Unpublished manuscript, New Haven.

Lee, A. James, and Burton A. Weisbrod. 1977. "Collective Goods and the Voluntary Sector: The Case of the Hospital Industry." In Burton A. Weisbrod, ed., *The Voluntary Nonprofit Sector: An Economic Analysis*. Lexington, Mass.: Lexington Books.

Lyon, Eleanor. 1974. "Work and Play: Resource Constraints in a Small Theatre." *Urban Life and Culture* 3, no. 1 (April):71–97.

Macro Systems, Inc. 1979. *Contractor Report: Museum Program Survey 1979*. Washington, D.C.: National Center for Educational Statistics.

Majone, Giandomenico. 1980. "Professionalism and Nonprofit Organizations." Yale University, Program on Non-Profit Organizations. Working Paper no. 24.

Mandl, Cynthia K., and Robert M. Kerr. 1975. *Museum Sponsorship of Performing Arts*. Madison: University of Wisconsin Center for Arts Administration.

Martorella, Rosanne. 1982. *The Sociology of Opera*. New York: Praeger.

———. 1983. "Rationality in the Artistic Management of Performing Arts Organizations." In Jack B. Kamerman and Rosanne Martorella, eds., *Performers and Performances: The Social Organization of Artistic Work*, 95–107. New York: Praeger.

Mathtech, Inc. 1980. *Conditions and Needs of the Professional American Theatre*. Washington, D.C.: National Endowment for the Arts, Research Division.

Meyer, Karl E. 1979. *The Art Museum: Power, Money, Ethics*. New York: William Morrow.

Montias, J. Michael. 1983. "Public Support for the Performing Arts in Western Europe and the United States: History and Analysis." In G. Ranis and R. West, eds. *Comparative Development Perspectives*. Boulder, Colo.: Westview Press.

National Assembly of Local Arts Agencies. 1979. *Membership Survey*. Washington, D.C.: National Assembly of Community Arts Agencies.

————. 1982. *Membership Directory, 1981–82*. Washington, D.C.: National Assembly of Community Arts Agencies.

National Center for Charitable Statistics. 1985. *Non-Profit Service Organizations: 1982*. Washington, D.C.: National Center for Charitable Statistics.

National Endowment for the Arts. 1974. *Museums USA*. Washington, D.C.: U.S. Government Printing Office.

————. 1975. *Dance Touring Program: Summary of Survey and Evaluation*. Washington, D.C.: National Endowment for the Arts.

————. 1982. *Museums: Application Guidelines, Fiscal Year 1982*. Washington, D.C.: National Endowment for the Arts.

————. 1984. *Annual Report, 1983*. Washington, D.C.: National Endowment for the Arts.

Netzer, Dick. 1978. *The Subsidized Muse: Public Support for the Arts in the United States*. New York: Cambridge University Press.

Newman, Danny. 1978. "Subscribe Now—Musings Expressed by Danny Newman." In Lee G. Cooper, Hope Tschopik, E. James Hannon, and Carolyn L. Cochran, eds., *Selected Proceedings of the 1978 UCLA Conference of Professional Arts Managers*. Los Angeles: University of California at Los Angeles Study Center for Cultural Policy and Management in the Arts.

Owen, Virginia Lee. 1983. "Technological Change and Opera Quality." In William S. Hendon and James L. Shanahan, eds., *Economics of Cultural Decisions*, 57–64. Cambridge, Mass.: Abt Books.

Peacock, A. T., and C. Godfrey. 1976. "The Economics of Museums and Galleries." In Mark Blaug, ed., *The Economics of the Arts*, 189–204. Boulder, Colo.: Westview Press.

Permut, Steven E. 1980. "A Survey of Marketing Perspectives of Performing Arts Administrators." In Michael P. Mokwa, William M. Dawson, and E. Arthur Prieve, eds., *Marketing the Arts*, 47–58. New York: Praeger.

Perrow, Charles. 1979. *Complex Organizations: A Critical Essay*. 2d ed. Glenview, Ill.: Scott, Foresman.

Peterson, Richard A. 1986. "From Impresario to Arts Administrator: Formal Accountability in Cultural Organizations." In Paul DiMaggio, ed., *Nonprofit Enterprise in the Arts*. New York: Oxford University Press.

Peterson, Richard A., and David G. Berger. 1975. "Cycles in Symbol Production: The Case of Popular Music." *American Sociological Review* 40:158–73.

Pick, John. 1983. *The West End: Mismanagement and Snobbery*. East Sussex, England: John Offord Publications.

Poggi, Jack. 1968. *Theater in America: The Impact of Economic Forces, 1870–1967*. Ithaca, N.Y.: Cornell University Press.

Porter, Michael. 1980. *Competitive Strategy*. New York: Free Press.

Powell, Walter W. 1982. "Adapting to Tight Money and New Opportunities." *Scholarly Publishing* 14, no. 1 (October).

————. 1985. *Getting into Print: The Decision-Making Process in Scholarly Publishing*. Chicago: University of Chicago Press.

Powell, Walter W., and Rebecca Friedkin. 1983. "Political and Organizational Influences on Public Television Programming." In E. Wartella and D. C. Whitney, eds., *Mass Communication Review Yearbook*, 413–38. Beverly Hills, Calif.: Sage Publications.

Rogers, Lola Eriksen. 1969. *Museums and Related Institutions: A Basic Program Survey*. Washington, D.C.: U.S. Department of Health, Education and Welfare, Office of Education.

Salem, Mahmoud. 1984. *Organizational Survival in the Performing Arts: The Making of the Seattle Opera*. New York: Praeger.

Schudson, Michael. 1984. *Advertising: The Uneasy Persuasion*. New York: Basic Books.

Schwalbe, Douglas, and Janet Baker-Carr. 1976a. *Conflict in the Arts: The Relocation of Authority—the Museum*. Cambridge, Mass.: Harvard University Arts Administration Research Institute.

————. 1976b. *Conflict in the Arts: The Relocation of Authority—the Orchestra*. Cambridge, Mass.: Harvard University Arts Administration Research Institute.

Schwartz, Samuel. 1981. "The Facts First: A Reply to Baumol and Baumol." *Journal of Cultural Economics* 5, no. 2 (December):85–88.

Scott, W. Richard, and John W. Meyer. 1984. "Environmental Linkages and Organizational Complexity: Public and Private Schools." Paper presented at the Conference on Private and Public Schools, Center for Educational Research, Stanford University.

Shestack, Alan. 1978. "The Director: Scholar and Businessman, Educator and Lobbyist." *Museum News*, November-December.

Shoesmith, Eddie, and Geoffrey Millner. 1983. "Cost Inflation and the London Orchestras." In William S. Hendon and James L. Shanahan, eds., *Economics of Cultural Decisions*, 65–76. Cambridge, Mass.: Abt Books.

Sloan, Blanche Carlton, and Bruce R. Swinburne. 1981. *Campus Art Museums and Galleries: A Profile*. Carbondale: Southern Illinois University Press.

Stewart, Phyllis L., and Muriel L. Cantor. 1982. *Varieties of Work*. Beverly Hills, Calif.: Sage Publications.

Taishoff, Sol, ed. 1984. *Broadcasting/Cablecasting Yearbook*. Washington, D.C.: Broadcasting Publications.

Theatre Communications Center of the Bay Area. 1984. *Theatre Directory of the San Francisco Bay Area (1983–84)*. San Francisco: Theatre Communications Center of the Bay Area.

Throsby, C. D., and G. A. Withers. 1979. *The Economics of the Performing Arts*. New York: St. Martin's.

Touchstone, Susan Kathleen. 1980. "The Effects of Contributions on Price and Attendance in the Lively Arts." *Journal of Cultural Economics* 4, no. 1:33–46.

Weisbrod, Burton A. 1977a. "Toward a Theory of the Voluntary Nonprofit Sector in a Three-Sector Economy." In Burton A. Weisbrod, ed., *The Voluntary Nonprofit Sector: An Economic Analysis.* Lexington, Mass.: Lexington Books.

———. 1977b. *The Voluntary Nonprofit Sector: An Economic Analysis.* Lexington, Mass.: Lexington Books.

White, Harrison C., and Cynthia A. White. 1965. *Canvasses and Careers: Institutional Change in the French Painting World.* New York: John Wiley.

Wilk, John Robert. 1982. "The American Conservatory Theatre: The Creation of an Ensemble." Ph.D. diss., Wayne State University.

Williamson, Oliver E. 1975. *Markets and Hierarchies: Analysis and Anti-Trust Implications: A Study in the Economics of Internal Organization.* New York: Free Press.

Withers, Glenn A. 1983. "The Cultural Influence of Public Television." In William S. Hendon and James L. Shanahan, eds., *Economics of Cultural Decisions,* 77–92. Cambridge, Mass.: Abt Books.

Zeigler, Joseph Wesley. 1977. *Regional Theater: The Revolutionary Stage.* New York: DaCapo.

Zolberg, Vera L. 1974. "The Art Institute of Chicago: The Sociology of a Cultural Organization." Ph.D. diss., University of Chicago.

———. 1981. "Conflicting Visions in American Art Museums." *Theory and Society* 10:103–25.

———. 1984. "American Museums: Sanctuary or Free-for-All?" *Social Forces* 63, no. 2 (December):377–92.

13

Nonprofit Organizations and Health Care

THEODORE R. MARMOR
MARK SCHLESINGER
RICHARD W. SMITHEY

The topic of this chapter—nonprofits and medical care—is mired in controversy. Comparisons of the historical roles of nonprofit, governmental, and for-profit health institutions have been contentious. And the appraisal of contemporary arrangements is marked by fundamental differences of value, perspective, and fact.

The history of nonprofits in American medicine has been variously portrayed. The nonprofit form for hospitals is undoubtedly the dominant legal organization today. Some interpret this as triumph over the profit-making small hospital. For others, however, the story describes an endangered species reeling under the competition of large hospital chains. Or they discern a changing balance among the different forms of hospitals and see convergence, not divergence, as the dominant theme. As with hospitals, so with physicians. They are alternately regarded as profit-making entrepreneurs cloaked in the misleading rhetoric of service professionalism or as technically expert professionals resisting the commercial blandishments of corporate medicine (Relman 1980, 967–68; Yordy 1986, 32). These conflicting perspectives shape the character, tone, and policy conclusions of much recent scholarship about the history of American medicine (Gray 1985; Starr 1982; Evans 1984).

Historical controversy spills over onto disputes about what is currently taking place in American medicine (Fox

1986). Change is everywhere reported (Goldsmith 1984; Gray 1983, 1985), but its dimensions, consequences, and meaning are bewildering. The supply of physicians is growing—a glut for some, a boon to competition for others. A new payment arrangement for hospitals—diagnosis-related groups (DRGs)—introduces case reimbursement into Medicare for the whole nation and sets in motion thousands of specialists offering to assist hospitals—of all forms—in playing the new game. Within the for-profit hospital sector, the number of hospitals organized in chains doubled between 1973 and 1982, and large for-profit corporations now own and manage hospitals that used to be publicly run, controlled by nonprofit boards, or owned by physicians (Gray 1985, 10–12). Some nonprofit hospitals form themselves into large systems and imitate the new corporate manner (Gray 1985, 13).[1]

The merging of substantial health-related institutions is not restricted to hospitals. Symptomatic of the vertical integration taking place in the health field was the proposed 1985 merger of the for-profit Hospital Corporation of America (HCA) with American Hospital Supply, a multibillion-dollar fusion of health giants (largest in their respective sectors) that dominated the nation's newspaper front pages for a few days

We want to thank Rachel Wagner and Jonathan Sherman for their research assistance and helpful comments. Elizabeth Auld and Heleri Ziou attended to the problems of producing a finished manuscript with their usual skill and unusual dedication, for which the authors are grateful. We thank Woody Powell for many helpful editorial suggestions.

---

1. As of 1982, there were 34 investor-owned multihospital systems comprising 773 hospitals and 139 nonprofit systems comprising 967 hospitals (up from 121 nonprofit systems in 1978). Of the almost 7,000 acute-care hospitals in the United States, 11 percent are proprietary, and another 4 percent are managed by proprietary organizations. Nonprofit hospitals account for approximately 50 percent of the total. The remainder are operated by federal, state, and local governments. See Gray (1985) for a current review of the growth of nonprofit and proprietary hospital systems and recent activity in institutions other than hospitals.

in March 1985.[2] And, to complicate matters, nonprofit hospitals themselves have increasingly taken to the corporate marketplace, spawning for-profit subsidiaries, seeking debt financing that differs from stocks and bonds in legal name only, and searching for ways to imitate insurance companies, consulting firms, and industrial park entrepreneurs (Gray 1985, 17–19).[3] Health maintenance organizations (HMOs), home health agencies, dialysis and urgent-care centers, and other extrahospital forms are increasingly managed by large proprietary conglomerates. All this takes place in full view of the national media, which are delighted to repeat the passionate exchanges of defenders of various faiths: markets, governments, and voluntarism.[4] No wonder, then, that rational appraisal of where we are and where we are going is difficult.

That appraisal is as controversial as the history and contemporary portraiture. The nonprofit form is lauded or derided, seen as inherently inefficient or as a benevolent community institution, regarded as threatened or on the verge of recovery (Clark 1980; Clarkson 1972). The growth of for-profit chains prompts journalistic categorization, and the new monikers produce an acronymic frenzy: AMI, PPO, HCA, DRG, VHA.[5] Arnold Relman's "New Medical Industrial Complex" (NMIC), modeled on President Eisenhower's dread military-industrial complex of the 1950s (Relman 1980, 963), is but the most inflammatory example. In a $400 billion industry, there is more than enough money to finance companies of public relations specialists and lobbyists, all of whom can be relied on to produce dear and dread emblems of a benevolent or beastly past, a wondrous or dangerous present, and a fearful or hopeful future.[6]

2. In the event, Baxter Travenol won the battle for American Hospital Supply, outbidding HCA to produce a huge $4 billion conglomerate. Had HCA succeeded, the result would have been the largest U.S. health care firm, a vertically integrated conglomerate with an estimated $7.6 billion in annual revenues (Waldholz 1985, 3; Koten & Waldholz 1985, 2; Koten 1985, 2).

3. This is a major trend among big-city voluntary hospitals. Its extent is evident from the recent incorporation of Voluntary Hospitals of America, recently formed by sixty-two voluntary hospitals. Its subsidiary activities, all of which are for-profit, extend to management services, physician recruitment, outpatient services, supply services, financing, and insurance.

4. One example is the debate in the *New England Journal of Medicine* over the propriety of proprietary agencies treating end-stage renal disease (Lowrie & Hampers 1981; Relman & Rennie 1980; Lowrie 1981; Gardner 1981).

5. American Medicorp International, Preferred Provider Organization, Hospital Corporation of America, and Voluntary Hospitals of America.

6. The clash of views is really quite stark. Compare the following examples: "Nonprofit hospitals may be operationally inefficient compared to their for-profit counterparts. Moreover the nonprofit form may have played a key role in leading to both wasteful overcapacity of medical facilities in some areas and slow response to demand in others, while promoting the development of extremely costly and not truly justified 'high technology' health care" (Clark 1980, 1417–18). Referring to the growth of proprietary organizations in health, Relman (1980) states: "The private health care industry can be expected to ignore relatively inefficient and unprofitable services, regardless of medical or social need. The result is likely to exacerbate present problems with excessive fragmentation of care, overspecialization, and overemphasis

Do the nonprofits behave inefficiently, or do they provide useful services that the cream-skimming profit-making competitors shun? Are doctors compromised by working in hospitals controlled by corporations seeking profit? Or is this debate mostly a battle over how to rationalize an industry that grew fat, sloppy, and uncontrollable in an era of increased subsidies for medical care, medical research, and medical tinkering? No study—of a hospital closing or a new technology in action—and few summaries of these issues manage to emerge without being cast in the language of good and evil, delight and doom, prudence and waste.

Change is apparent in contemporary medicine, and public policy must, if this change is to be humanely managed, adapt. But the character of the debate about the nonprofit form—and its competitors—has been sufficiently confused and ill considered that much of the controversy should be reconsidered. The debate has been both ideological—commercialism and profit versus service and professionalism—and practical—which form is more efficient? The challenge of public policy is to adapt public rules to the central realities of American medicine, not the shibboleths of shrill discourse. In the case of medicine, other things besides the form of legal ownership are more important in fashioning appropriate responses. And so, in a paradoxical way, the central conclusion of a chapter on nonprofits in medicine is that the environment facing decision makers in medical institutions and the rules by which they operate are more significant than what institutions call themselves on their legal charters.

This chapter aims to provide a more accurate and better balanced assessment of the role of nonprofit organizations in health. It addresses first the history of the nonprofit form in American medicine and attempts to set that story in the broader history of American medical care. It then sketches the current state of nonprofit health institutions. The next part addresses the role of nonprofits in an industry with a mix of nonprofits, for-profits, and government institutions, in light of some of the expected differences among these forms. It examines in detail arguments about the merits and disadvantages of the nonprofit and for-profit forms, emphasizing the paradigmatic claims about cost, quality, and access among the opposing camps and important writers. And finally we present a concluding discussion.

THE NONPROFIT FORM IN AMERICAN MEDICINE

The ongoing debate over the proper ownership of health institutions has been complicated by an unfortunate tendency to equate profit-making with market-based allocations of services, to equate the proprietary form with profit making, and to cast ownership-related issues as crucial to the future

on expensive technology" (p. 969). Relman (1983) later claimed, "Judged not as businesses but as hospitals, which are supposed to serve the public interest, they [investor-owned chain hospitals] have been less cost-effective than their not-for-profit counterparts" (p. 372).

The American College of Hospital Administrators (now American College of Hospital *Executives*) forecast that 60 percent of all hospitals will be investor-owned by 1995 ("Health Care . . . " 1984, 2).

evolution of American medicine. This is partly attributable to our public policies, since a large portion of American health legislation has encouraged private nonprofit providers as an alternative to proprietary institutions. There may be strong reasons to favor more or less use of markets in allocating some health services. But these can be separated in principle and practice from analyses of the appropriate role of for-profit or nonprofit health care (Enthoven 1980; Dunham, Morone, & White 1982). Changes in the ownership mix of health care providers may well have some important implications for health policy, but completely eliminating either for-profit or nonprofit providers would in itself remedy few if any of the problems facing American medicine.

Casting the argument in terms of a choice between legal forms in medical care obscures the historical sources of the present situation. What we are witnessing is a heightening of an old and fundamental tension within medicine over whose interests should predominate. The steady pressure of rising costs, accompanied by the opportunities to earn high returns in medical care, has caused this tension to resurface. To understand the present, one must first comprehend the special features of medical care as an industry.

First, the relationship between provider and consumer of medical services differs, in several important ways, from that for other services. The asymmetry of information between the provider and the patient is more pronounced than for most services,[7] even in other areas in which nonprofit ownership is common (Steinberg, this volume, chap. 7). The importance of these asymmetries is heightened by the emotional associations of life-saving treatment and the traumas of injury and dread disease. For many, it is crucial that the relationship between provider and patient be one of "care giving," for in no "business" except prostitution is the pursuit of profit alone seen as so antithetical to the professional relationship clients seek (Titmuss 1971).

These considerations have in part shaped the policies that constrain the practices of health professionals. The medical professions have gained unusual authority in the belief that professional norms and sanctions would appropriately limit medical behavior (Arrow 1972; Fox 1986). There have been extensive attempts to encourage the ethic of care giving—through education, honorific example, and nonmonetary rewards.[8]

The judgment that professional norms are insufficient to regulate the medical industry has led to extensive medical legislation (Starr 1982, 402; Brown 1986, 22–23). Some

policies promote access to care by those disadvantaged in a private market. Others aim to control the cost and quality of the services that all patients receive (Ruchlin 1979; Drake 1980; Raffel, 601–02). Many of these policies have been explicitly designed to promote nonprofit organizations, either by enforcing less stringent regulations on them or by providing subsidies not available to their for-profit counterparts. "Numerous statutes, regulations, and judicial doctrines," we are currently reminded, "discriminate against for-profit hospitals," including preferential access to construction grants, subsidies for training programs, and planning and operational assistance for a range of health services (Clark 1980, 1473).

Second, understanding the role of nonprofit organizations in health is also made more difficult by the complexity of medicine and the diversity of institutions providing services. Nonprofit organizations treat acute illness (for example, hospitals, health maintenance organizations, neighborhood health centers), palliate chronic conditions (home health agencies, nursing homes, renal dialysis centers), as well as provide supportive services such as insurance (Blue Cross, Blue Shield), education and lobbying (American Medical Association, American Hospital Association), and research (March of Dimes, American Cancer Society). The institutional missions and the roles of professionals vary greatly across these services. It would, therefore, not be surprising to find that the implications of ownership vary as well.

Medical care accounted for 60 percent of total charitable nonprofit organization revenues or expenditures in 1980 (Salamon & Abramson 1982, 15). And private nonprofit agencies, by the measure of dollar expenditure, dominate the provision of medical care. Such aggregated pictures, however, mask considerable variation. The proportion of nonprofits differs greatly from one service to the next as table 13.1 illustrates. For some services, nonprofit institutions serve as much as three-quarters of all consumers, for others, less than 10 percent.

Nonprofit organizations may be classified by the way in which they are financed: donative (largely by philanthropy), or commercial (payments by clients and third-party insurers). Over the last century the trend in health has been for donative nonprofits to become commercial nonprofits (hospitals) and for support that had been donative to be increasingly assumed by government (medical research and education).[9] The histories and identities of these organiza-

---

7. The nonprofit has traditionally been the protector of consumers or purchasers of services from "contract failure." By virtue of its distribution prohibition, the nonprofit protects the buyer against the misdelivery of services he can't monitor or understand (Hansmann 1980, and this volume, chap. 2). Given that, in the case of medical care, this protective role was vested in the doctor as the patient's agent, the traditional role of the nonprofit was really less important.

8. The importance of nonmonetary incentives in medical care has led Evans to define the "not-only-for-profit sector." This refers to individuals and firms "in which a legal claimant to profits is well-defined, but profits represent only one among several competing objectives of the firm's ownership and management" (1984, 127).

9. The for-profit health care provider usually takes on the familiar corporate form. In particular, the company is owned by its stockholders and managed by a board of directors elected by the stockholders. Capital is raised through the sale of equity and the issuance of debt. Any net earnings are distributed in the form of dividends to the stockholders or retained and reinvested by the corporation, rendering the stock more valuable.

The nonprofit corporation, in comparison, does not issue equity. Capital is raised by collection of donations and issuance of debt. A nonprofit may accrue net earnings, but no dividends are paid. Any net earnings must be retained by the corporation. (A commercial nonprofit organization must make a profit to survive, especially in medical care. The distinction between nonprofit and for-profit enterprise rests largely

TABLE 13.1 RELATIVE PROPORTIONS OF FOR-PROFIT, PRIVATE NONPROFIT, AND PUBLIC HEALTH CARE PROVIDERS IN THE UNITED STATES

Institutions Offering Services	Measured in Terms of	Percentage of Services Provided by		
		For-Profit	Nonprofit	Public
Acute hospitals	Beds	8.5%	69.6%	21.9%
Psychiatric hospitals	Beds	6.0	4.7	89.3
Nursing homes	Beds	67.6	21.3	11.0
Homes for mentally handicapped	Residents	46.2	37.7	16.5
Blood banks	Facilities	63.3	5.8	30.9
Dialysis centers	Facilities	38.5	44.3	17.2
Health maintenance organizations	Enrollees	15.8	84.2	NA
Health insurance	Enrollees	45.2	42.7	12.0
Home health agencies	Patients	25.5	64.1	10.4

Source: Schlesinger 1984.

tions have been shaped by changes in their financing—who paid them, how much, and by what methods. Other factors, such as demographic patterns and historical changes, have, of course, also influenced the location and character of non-profits in the health industry.

The relative importance of nonprofit and for-profit health institutions has fluctuated over time. Services that are now dominated by nonprofit institutions, such as acute-care hos-

on what is termed the nondistribution constraint—that is, profits cannot be distributed to individuals [Hansmann, this volume, chap. 2].) The corporation is managed most often by a board of directors, either elected by the membership (which can include either donors or beneficiaries) or self-perpetuating. Thus, unlike the for-profit corporation, there is no formal connection between an individual's financial interest in the venture and the power to select and control management. Furthermore, given the prohibition against equity sales and the often slow process of raising funds through donation drives, the nonprofits in health are at a relative disadvantage in terms of their ability to generate capital funds.

Some, but not all, nonprofit corporations are charities under Section 501(c)3 of the federal tax law, I.R.C. 501(c)3 (1982). All nonprofit hospitals, for instance, are characterized as charities, whereas a non-profit insurance company or testing laboratory would not be a charity. The charity status is important because donations to charitable organiza-tions are tax deductible to the donor, thus conferring a significant federal subsidy upon nonprofit charities that receive contributions. State and federal tax laws also define a category of nonprofits, broader than the category of charities, that are exempt from corporate income, sales, and other taxes.

Hansmann has developed a useful scheme for describing differences among nonprofits, which identifies two characteristics: the source of income and the form of management or control. The "donative non-profit" relies primarily on donation income; the "commercial non-profit" derives its income primarily from the sales of goods or services to paying consumers; the "mutual nonprofit" is run by a board selected by the donor or consumer members; and the "entrepreneurial nonprofit" is managed by a self-selected board. The dominant form of nonprofit in the health care industry is the entrepreneurial/commercial nonprofit. Non-profit hospitals, although they qualify as charities, receive the great bulk of their income from sale of services. Donations to a nursing home are more rare (Hansmann 1980).

The third set of actors in health care are the public providers. Cities, counties, states and the federal government all operate hospital and health facilities of various kinds. The capital funds are tax dollars, and the management is under the formal control of the sponsoring govern-ment.

pitals, were at one time predominantly investor owned. Ser-vices that now have a substantial proprietary sector, such as HMOs and renal dialysis facilities, were only fifteen years ago almost exclusively provided by private nonprofit and public agencies (Schlesinger 1984, 80). These historical fluctua-tions suggest that diverse and interrelated factors determine the scale and role of nonprofit enterprise in medical care. Three distinct historical periods of change in mix and owner-ship form throughout the medical care industry emerge from our investigations.

1900–1950: The Institutionalization of Health Care and the Dominance of Nonprofit Organizations

Throughout most of the nineteenth century, medical care was largely a cottage industry. Hospitals were principally facili-ties for caring for the sickly poor; those with higher incomes were treated at home by physicians. Hospitals and physicians coexisted, the former supported by religious organizations and government subsidies, the latter by fees from patients (Raffel, 241–46; Starr 1982; 145–79; Stevens 1982, 552–55). Because of their religious affiliations, most of the hospi-tals established during this period were nonprofit. Toward the end of the nineteenth century, however, the practice of medicine became more complex. Medical education was increasingly specialized and a number of new medical schools were opened. Hospitals evolved into the primary setting for treating the very ill and began to require patient fees for support (Starr 1982, 157–61).

In this evolution, for-profit and nonprofit hospitals re-tained many of the distinctions that had previously existed between doctors and hospitals. The for-profit facilities con-tinued for the most part to be operated by a single doctor or small group of physicians and to cater to wealthier patients (Starr 1982, 165). The usually larger nonprofit hospitals continued to rely heavily on philanthropic support. The ab-sence or presence of philanthropy led to pronounced regional variations in ownership mix. The East and Midwest, popu-lated by service-oriented religious groups and philanthrop-ically minded capitalists, were dominated by nonprofit hospitals. The West, however, lacked a strong philanthropic tradition, having been settled after hospitals had begun to rely more heavily on patient fees for support and after the charitable mission of care for the poor was no longer the hospital's central function. Here, for-profit hospitals were far more common (Starr 1982, 170–71).

During the late nineteenth century a rapid proliferation of proprietary hospitals and medical schools took place as the country grew to the west (Stevens 1971, 24–25). The growth of nonprofit facilities was further inhibited because state and local governments withdrew subsidies that had previously been available (Stevens 1982, 560). By 1900, this growth of proprietary institutions had significantly changed the ownership picture in American medicine: over half of the medical schools and 60 percent of the hospitals in operation were privately owned, in most cases by one doctor (Bays 1983a). There was not yet a technological justification for large hospitals and usually the small proprietary hospital/clinic corresponded well to the then-dominant solo practice (Bays 1983a).

The subsequent fifty years brought increased formalization, standardization, and institutionalization to American medicine. During the first several decades of this century, this pattern was reflected primarily in the emergence of a standardized, more technically oriented set of medical schools, hospitals, and to a lesser extent, nursing homes. The increasing complexity of medical care raised the cost of both medical training and treatment, creating a greater need for subsidization (Starr 1982, 118). This in turn favored the growth of new nonprofit institutions that could tap religious affiliations (Starr 1982, 169ff.; Vladeck 1980), offer tax deductions in return for donations, and remain largely exempted from growing government regulation (Nielsen 1979, 184).

A large proportion of the medical profession strongly favored the nonprofit form. The increased emphasis on technical aspects of medicine and the institutions' dependence on fee-paying patients allowed doctors to increase their authority to the point where they became the dominant decision makers in hospitals (Starr 1982, 161). Rejecting for-profit enterprise reduced the threat of corporate control on this authority (Starr 1982, 218). Since antitrust laws were only loosely applied, nonprofit institutions also provided a way to control entry into medicine and to enhance the financial returns of a medical practice (Horty & Mulholland 1983; Weller 1984, 613–15).

The combined influence of economic incentives and professional interest thus led to a diminished role for proprietary institutions. By the mid-1920s, proprietary medical schools were starting to disappear, the proportion of investor-owned hospitals had declined to just over a third, and virtually all the medically oriented nursing homes were nonprofit (Bays 1983a, 367; Vladeck 1980).[10] The remaining for-profit in-

stitutions were disproportionately located in rapidly growing areas, where population increased faster than philanthropic voluntarism could supply new capital (Steinwald & Neuhauser 1970, 819–20) or where the philanthropic tradition was weak.

This trend was reinforced, in the short run, by the introduction of health insurance during the early 1930s (Raffel 1980, 393–94; Starr 1982, 295–98). Faced with financially strained hospitals and proposals for national health insurance, the American Medical Association abandoned its earlier rigid opposition to hospital insurance (Nielsen 1979, 112). With the cooperation of the American Hospital Association and enabling legislation passed by state governments (Rorem 1939; Law 1974, 8–11), Blue Cross and later Blue Shield were established to offer hospital and medical insurance, respectively.

Both of these provider-sponsored plans were organized as nonprofit enterprises for several reasons. Physician autonomy was, as noted before, less threatened by the nonprofit corporate form.[11] In addition, the insurance plans worked closely with providers. Proprietary ownership of these health insurance companies might well have raised questions about the appropriateness of the nonprofit status of hospitals.[12] Finally, state enabling legislation granted to the Blues what were effectively state-sanctioned monopolies in providing service-benefit plans (Law 1974, 8ff.). Legislators no doubt favored nonprofit ownership in part to avoid the appearance of having sanctioned organizations that could extract near monopoly "profits" from the health industry (Law 1974, 11).

The appropriate legal status of these health insurance plans was a matter of considerable dispute. Half the states refused to grant the plans tax-exempt status, and the Internal Revenue Service ruled that donations to the plans were not tax deductible.[13] To bolster their claim to nonprofit status,

---

and protect their freedom from social or governmental controls. Nielsen asserts that because the individual states worked closely with and patterned their licensing statutes on those suggested by the American Medical Association (AMA) and state medical societies, the AMA was largely responsible for a 30 percent decline in the number of proprietary medical schools and a 50 percent decrease in the number of medical graduates (Nielsen 1979, 106).

11. For a review of AMA resistance to various other forms of health insurance as well as the "corporate" practice of medicine, see Starr (1982, 295ff.) and Nielsen (1979, 105–16).

12. In the case of *Associated Hospital Service Inc.* v. *City of Milwaukee* (1961), for example, the court concluded that the legislature had the right to grant nonprofit status to the Blue Cross plan specifically because it was closely associated with nonprofit hospitals. (The American Hospital Association owned the name "Blue Cross of America" until 1972.)

13. About half the states refused to grant the plans tax-exempt status. As of 1978 the twenty states that granted exempt status were Arizona, Arkansas, California, Connecticut, Georgia, Idaho, Illinois, Kentucky, Louisiana, Maine, Massachusetts, Michigan, New Jersey, New York, North Carolina, Ohio, Oklahoma, Vermont, West Virginia, and Wisconsin (Law 1974, 9n37).

According to Law (1974): "Special corporate status and exemption

---

10. One view suggests that American medicine became more mercenary in 1920 with a change of control in American medicine to a new group of leaders. Their purpose was to improve their economic position

the Blues adopted the policy of community rating—charging all residents of a community the same premium. This effectively subsidized the old and the poor, who had higher than average medical expenses—at least those who could afford to purchase insurance.[14]

The growth of Blue Cross and Blue Shield reinforced the dominant position of nonprofit organizations in medicine. By the early 1940s, nonprofit plans controlled more than two-thirds of the health insurance market (Schlesinger 1984, 79). Blue Cross negotiated lower reimbursement rates for proprietary hospitals than for their nonprofit counterparts. This accelerated the decline of investor-owned facilities: by 1946 they represented less than 10 percent of all hospitals (Steinwald & Neuhauser 1970, 819). In addition, nonprofit hospitals, faced with the loss of more lucrative patients to proprietary hospitals, relaxed their previous strict staff admission policies and absorbed physicians from proprietary hospitals (Starr 1982, 165–71). Physicians remained uncontested in their authority to control both the delivery and the financing of medical care, authority mediated first by the nonprofit hospitals and later by Blue Cross and Blue Shield. Nevertheless, the growth of insurance under the auspices of the Blues was to sow the seeds of the eventual rebirth of proprietary institutions in medicine.

1950–1975: Public Subsidies and the Renaissance of Proprietary Health Care

Following World War II, some federal policymakers became increasingly concerned with encouraging access to medical care. To this end, legislation was passed subsidizing the medical industry (Lave & Lave 1974; Rosenblatt 1978, 264–70). At first, funds were paid directly to providers who agreed to care for the poor. Later subsidies were directed at increasing the effective demand of patients for medical care: unsuccessful attempts at national health insurance in the 1940s precipitated the drive in the 1950s for government health insurance covering the elderly—the Medicare program eventually enacted in 1965 (Marmor 1973, 13–16).

Initially, the direct public financing of facilities tended to

enhance the position of nonprofit institutions. In fact, many financing programs were specifically designed to do so, by making funds available either exclusively or preferentially to private nonprofit or public agencies. The postwar Hill-Burton program, for example, subsidized construction of a variety of nonprofit and public health care facilities, though funds were allocated primarily to the construction of short-term general hospitals. Hill-Burton subsidized one-third of all hospital construction projects between 1947 and 1972, supplying about 10 percent of the total capital costs (Lave & Lave 1974, 16).

Because nonprofit agencies were relatively slow to respond to subsidies, however, their share of services increased only marginally as a result of these funds (Vladeck 1980, 41–42; Lave & Lave 1974, 45). Moreover, by stimulating the expansion of public facilities, government subsidies indirectly altered and to some extent undermined the traditional role of private nonprofit medical care. Health institutions operated by state and local government grew rapidly during this period. Between 1945 and 1960, beds in short-term public hospitals increased by 15 percent, in psychiatric hospitals by 20 percent, and in nursing homes by over 200 percent.[15]

The growth of public medical facilities shifted much of the responsibility for caring for the poor to these institutions and away from their private nonprofit counterparts (Gage 1985, 77; Feder, Hadley, & Mullner 1984). This shift, coupled with the availability of public funds for capital projects, reduced the apparent need for donative financing, itself one of the chief justifications for nonprofit status.

In the 1960s and continuing through the mid-1970s, governmental program subsidies expanded from facilities to health insurance and direct payment for care. The passage of Medicare and Medicaid in 1965 (Marmor 1973; Stevens & Stevens 1974) and amendments to Social Security in 1972 and 1974 reflected this development and had a significant impact on the mix of ownership in American medicine (see table 13.2).

Rapidly growing health insurance—public and private—has almost invariably led to an increased proportion of services provided by proprietary institutions (Vladeck 1980, 105). The reasons for this are complex, but they probably reflect both organizational conflicts within nonprofit agencies and the ability of investor-owned organizations to acquire capital more rapidly (Steinwald & Neuhauser 1970, 828). Whatever the causes, the link between increasing health insurance coverage and an expanded role for proprietary organizations is striking.

This pattern was first evident in the health insurance industry itself. Wage freezes during World War II and the

---

from federal and state taxes seem to be based on a concept of social reform and utility rather than on any particular concrete characteristics of the Blue Cross plans. Neither the legislative history nor cases involving the validity of the tax-exempt status provide much insight into the justification for the favored status of hospital service plans over commercial hospital insurers. State tax exemption has been challenged by tax collectors in five states. In all but one, the courts held that the Blue Cross was not entitled to exemption from payment of state taxes, even though it has been characterized as charitable or benevolent by the legislature" (p. 9).

Blue Cross plans are exempt from federal income tax under I.R.C. 501(c)4. A 501(c)4 organization is exempt from federal income tax, but contributions to such an organization are not tax deductible by the contributor (Law 1974, 9–10).

14. Coverage was rarely offered on a sliding scale or discounted in any other fashion for low-income subscribers (Starr 1982, 309; Feldstein 1978, 183; Law 1974, 12).

15. Between 1946 and 1960, the number of beds in short-term public hospitals increased from approximately 133,000 to 156,000. Between 1949 and 1959 the number of beds in public psychiatric hospitals increased from 596,000 to 672,000, and from 1954 to 1973 the number of beds in public nursing homes increased from 27,000 to 106,000 (Schlesinger 1984, 76–77).

TABLE 13.2 PUBLIC SUBSIDIES AND THE GROWTH OF FOR-PROFIT HEALTH CARE

Type of Facility	Change in Coverage	Market Share of Proprietary Agencies	
		3–5 Years Before	3–5 Years After
Acute hospitals	Medicare enacted 1965	5%	7%
Nursing homes	Medicaid enacted 1965	60	70
Dialysis centers	Medicare covered 1972	4	21
Home health agencies	Medicare adds coverage 1981	7	25
Psychiatric hospitals	States mandate private insurance coverage 1975–80	1	6
Residences for mentally impaired	Title XX enacted 1974	10	38

Source: Schlesinger 1984.

Korean War prompted unions to push for increases in non-wage benefits. The most prominent growth took place in health insurance, with the number of enrollees growing sharply from less than 13 million in 1940 to over 100 million in 1955 (Schlesinger 1984, 79). With this growth in health insurance coverage, the market share of commercial insurers increased from 37 percent in 1940 to 55 percent in 1960.

The growth of proprietary providers was even more pronounced after the enactment in 1965 of Medicare and Medicaid (table 13.2). Initial implementation of these two programs boosted the amount of services (relative to nonprofits) provided by investor-owned hospitals and nursing homes, respectively (Starr 1982, 434). The subsequent expansion of Medicare benefits in the 1970s encouraged the growth of for-profit renal dialysis centers and home health agencies, and similar expansions of investor-owned psychiatric facilities resulted from other public financing.[16]

The expansion of investor-owned insurers increased competitive pressures on nonprofit insurance organizations. Commercial insurers offered policies based on the experience of particular groups rather than the overall health care use in the community. For groups with below-average risk of illness, including many employee groups, this experience rating offered much lower premiums than did community rating. During the 1950s a number of employee groups shifted from the Blues to commercial carriers, and others threatened to do so. In the face of this competitive pressure, the Blues virtually abandoned community rating by the 1960s, eliminating the implicit subsidy to high-risk individuals (Krizay & Wilson 1974, 40).

16. Although the short-term growth of proprietary providers occurred for all these services, for some, such as hospitalization, the growth of for-profit facilities has been much more pronounced over the long term (Sloan & Vraciu 1983).

This was but the first example of a number of changes in the services offered by nonprofit health providers when faced by competition from investor-owned institutions. The breadth and significance of these changes, however, became apparent only in combination with additional changes in American medicine that occurred in subsequent years.

The impact of Medicare and Medicaid was far more profound than simply stimulating the resurgence of for-profit enterprises in American medicine. Together with the growth of private health insurance, Medicare and Medicaid sharply increased the flow of funds into the health industry. Third-party financing, in short, transformed medicine into a virtual gold mine for commercial nonprofit as well as for-profit enterprises.

The relative position of Blue Cross also improved as a result of Medicare. The implicit designation of Blue Cross as the dominant fiscal intermediary for Medicare's hospital plan had eased the bill's passage in 1965; this concession signified an accommodating disposition toward hospitals and physicians in Medicare's first years of operation (Starr 1982, 375; Feder 1977, 37; Marmor 1973, 141). Moreover, Blue Cross's cost-based scheme of hospital reimbursement, transferred nearly intact to Medicare, meant that Blue Cross assumed a far more important position than when it was simply in the business of selling group hospitalization insurance (Law 1974, 93–102).

Third-party payment was a key transformative factor for American medicine. Blue Cross and Blue Shield, like hospitals, did little to threaten the autonomy of physicians. The benign nature of Medicare's early administration and the regularity of its payment reinforced the earlier patterns of third-party private insurers. The result was that, both before and after Medicare's passage, the authoritative power to determine medical costs still lay within the medical profession, whose interests continued to be furthered through Blue Cross, although in less direct ways.

Government health insurance prompted a period of extended growth for American medical institutions. Medicare permitted generous depreciation allowances for capital and, by reimbursing capital costs which were then plowed back into the cost base, inserted an inflationary factor into its own payments, which were then determined by the provider-dominated insurers (Feder 1977, 113–17). It was thus no surprise that the rate of medical inflation rose to twice the annual increases in the consumer price index for the period 1966–72 (Marmor, Wittman, & Heagy 1983).

High levels of medical inflation continued through the 1970s (see table 13.3) as efforts for reform concentrated on new forms of health regulation and new methods of delivering care. Regulatory initiatives, Professional Standards Review Organizations (PSROs) and Health Systems Agencies (HSAs) among them, were begun with national health insurance in mind. National health insurance, however, never materialized, and both the federal government and the health industry were left with a fragmented set of controls. The inflationary forces at work in medicine—principally broad health insurance coverage, pluralistic financing, and weak

TABLE 13.3 NATIONAL HEALTH EXPENDITURES

Calendar Year	Total Amount (in billions)	Percentage of GNP
1960	$26.9	5.3%
1970	74.7	7.5
1980	249.0	9.5
1981	286.6	9.8
1982	322.4	10.5
1983	355.4	10.8

Source: Freeland and Schendler, *HCFA Review*, Spring 1984.

countervailing regulatory authorities—worked their will through the 1970s (Brown 1985). The decade began with marked medical inflation, witnessed frustrated public reform, and ended with a strong mandate for cost control in Washington (Starr & Marmor 1984).[17]

Confident as the center of scientific progress, financially rewarded, and imbued with considerable cultural authority, American medicine had experienced a golden age in the quarter century after World War II. But events of the period since 1965 have changed the industry's outlook. Inflationary concerns grew to a crescendo in the late 1970s, and several initiatives designed to bring access, cost, and humane health care into a reasonable equilibrium were almost all disappointing. It was in the context of the mid-1970s that the debate over the role and character of the nonprofit institution in health sharply increased.

17. The federal government passed the National Health Planning and Resources Development Act of 1974, 42 U.S.C. par. 300e–4, 300k et seq. (1976), which authorized a system of local health planning organizations or health systems agencies (HSAs) to be dominated by consumers, to be designed to cut the costs of medical care, and to guarantee the quality of and improve the access to that care. The restraining effects of these HSAs, however, were modest (Morone & Marmor 1983; Starr 1982, 416). Certificate of Need (CON) programs, which required state (and HSA) approval of construction, and large capital programs planned by medical institutions are other cost control devices (Starr 1982, 398). Other regulatory attempts to control medical costs have included requirements for prior authorization, restrictions on capital expenditures, and reductions in the number of hospital beds (E. Brown 1983, 936–37). See also Marmor, Wittman, and Heagy (1983); Enthoven (1980); Marmor and Dunham (1985); and Brown (1986).

An effort to control the quality as well as the cost of medical care were the Professional Standards Review Organizations (PSROs), which functioned "by reviewing admissions to a health care facility, certifying the necessity for continuing treatment in an in-patient facility, reviewing other extended or costly treatment, conducting medical evaluation studies, regularly reviewing facility, practitioner, and health care profiles of care and reviewing facility and practitioner records as applicable to a particular review process" (Raffel 1980, 282).

Increasingly numerous as an alternative are HMOs. Patients must pay a flat annual sum, and they directly receive a wide array of medical services. The HMO must provide services within a fixed budget determined by the number of providers. More recently, in the 1980s, the federal government has attempted to control costs by using DRGs, which establish price limitations on a variety of hospital services (Morone & Dunham 1985; Comptroller General 1980, 34–62; Brown 1985).

1975–1985: The Era of Cost Containment and Increased Competition

Policymakers' and Americans' increasing concern about medical inflation led to direct changes in the health industry—the growth of the prospective-payment system, the increased consolidation of insurance and service delivery within prepaid health plans, and the imposition of a variety of regulatory measures. Inflation has also had some indirect effects. These have included threats to the financial stability of government-operated health facilities and subtle shifts in popular expectations about the responsibility of health facilities to their local communities. Most pervasive, and perhaps most important as an influence on the roles of nonprofit and for-profit health providers, has been the increased price competition among suppliers of medical services.

This competition has taken a number of forms. A variety of negotiated arrangements, including "preferred provider" and "exclusive provider" agreements, have been established to channel patients to a single or small group of providers, in return for price discounts (Gabel & Ermann 1985). More active negotiation by third-party payers over prices has eroded the ability of hospitals to cross-subsidize particular types of care and patients (Sloan & Becker 1984, 677–78; Clark 1980, 1480–81). Health maintenance organizations—which historically have had lower rates of hospitalization and costs—have grown substantially, with enrollment increasing from less than 6 million in 1975 to over 12 million in 1983.[18]

These sectorwide increases in competition have had significant implications for the role of private nonprofit providers. On one hand, diminished cross-subsidization of patients and services has reduced the ability of nonprofit institutions to offer unprofitable services, which had previously distinguished them from their for-profit counterparts (Schlesinger & Dorwart 1984). On the other hand, the loss of

18. This growth should be interpreted with caution. In simple terms, doubling market share in any industry from 5 to 10 percent is easier than increasing that share from 10 to 20 percent or from 20 to 40 percent. The base of HMO enrollment was quite low a decade ago, and the doubling of its clientele from that base need not foreshadow similar rates of growth on the now higher base. Second, what counts as an HMO has, over time, been defined more loosely: it also includes groups of physicians coordinated under the prepayment rubric of IPAs (individual practice associations). Third, as HMOs have grown, they have increasingly come to be owned by other firms in the health industry: Blue Cross, Blue Shield, commercial health insurance firms like Prudential, and more recently, some for-profit hospital chains. These changes in corporate governance make the character of the HMO population quite different from the model organization envisioned in the HMO act of 1973. Finally, it hardly needs pointing out that it is the financial incentives of prepaid group practice, not the legal category of HMOs, that explain most of the cost-restraining effects associated in the literature with HMOs. Luft (1981) rightly cautions that most of the cost-saving effects arise from more restrained use of hospitalization, some of which in turn is explained by the healthier populations who joined the earlier groups. Over time, the rate of increase in HMOs' costs have paralleled medical inflation, thus suggesting that the effects of HMO growth on inflation control have been exaggerated (L. Brown 1983).

cross-subsidization and increased dumping of the sickest patients from private facilities has threatened the financial stability of many public institutions (Feder & Hadley 1985, 70). Between 1977 and 1983, 128 short-term hospitals operated by state and local governments were closed, a decline of 7 percent (American Hospital Association 1983). Ironically, the need for a charitable role for private health institutions seems to be growing at exactly the time at which nonprofit organizations are least willing to meet that need.

At the same time, there has been a subtle shift in popular expectations about the responsibilities of health providers. Patients have in the past placed considerable trust in a physician's competence and expected fiduciary responsibility from physicians. This trust seems to be eroding as the service ethic in health care has become demythologized and a more commercially oriented ethic has developed among providers. These changes have been accompanied by a loss of professional authority and autonomy; some of the power once wielded by physicians has shifted to those who previously supported them—the financial and operating officers of hospitals, prepaid group practices, and both Blue Cross and Blue Shield.

Increased competition and lessened professional autonomy have reduced or eliminated some of the goals and practices that once distinguished nonprofit and for-profit providers of health care. Nonprofit institutions increasingly mirror the institutional structure of their investor-owned competitors; they have established holding companies, for-profit subsidiaries, multifacility chains, and more overtly hierarchical organizations that create a stronger role and added discretion for nonphysician managers. As with the Blues in the late 1950s, practices of nonprofit and for-profit health care facilities have converged in many ways. At the 1985 annual meetings of the American Psychiatric Association, for example, Dr. Eisenberg of Harvard Medical School observed:

> The worst of it is that voluntaries, unable to cross-subsidize expensive but essential clinical services because of cost-competition, are becoming less distinguishable from the proprietaries, as they "market," and worse, "demarket," diversify, "unbundle," "spin-off" for-profit subsidiaries, develop "convenience-oriented feeder systems," attempt to adjust case mix and triage admissions by their ability to pay.

Summary: Historical Perspectives on the Role of Nonprofit Health Care Providers

Our historical review suggests several important patterns in and influences on the role of nonprofits in the health world. For one thing, for each service, there appears to be a life cycle in the role of nonprofit providers. As new services develop, through technological or social innovation, the initial pioneers are almost always private nonprofit agencies. This is in part because new services are typically expensive and require subsidization from public or philanthropic dona-

tions or other sources. Most likely, it also reflects as well the importance of nonpecuniary goals for the most innovative providers.

As a health service gains broader acceptance, however, two important changes occur. First, its use in the proprietary sector increases.[19] If the increase is sufficiently rapid, existing nonprofit providers may be unable to expand expeditiously to provide additional services. The resulting entry of proprietary institutions creates competitive pressures that tend to bring about a convergence between the behaviors of nonprofit and for-profit providers. And, second, policymakers become concerned with ensuring adequate access for those unable to pay for the service. This concern leads them to provide subsidies to public agencies to finance the poor and uninsured, which in turn tends to reduce the importance of charitable provision of care by private nonprofit agencies.

To understand the role of nonprofit medical care providers, then, it is important to know where a particular service lies in this life cycle. For the health sector as a whole, there will be some services at early stages, some at intermediate, and some at later stages. For example, HMOs are just now moving from the first to the second stage, and hospitals are entering the later stages.

The implications of ownership for the performance of health institutions depend most significantly on professionals, particularly physicians. This is evident, most crudely, in the relationship between the extent of physician involvement in delivery of care and the extent to which for-profit organizations are active in a particular service. As shown in table 13.1, for example, the services in which doctors play the least important role—health insurance, nursing homes, blood banks, and residences for the mentally impaired—are those in which proprietary enterprises deliver the largest portion of services.

There may thus be an important link between professional incentives and authority and the role of nonprofit health care facilities. The normative implications of this relationship have been the subject of much debate. Some view physician's authority in nonprofit agencies as essentially elitist, reflecting goals that diverge from other important social values (Clark 1980, 1439). Others see this same interaction as a means of preserving important nonmonetary social ends, including access to care for the poor, avoidance of undesirably low-quality care, and the promotion of a stronger fiduciary relationship between health institutions and the communities in which they are located (Relman 1980, 967–68).

To better understand the extent and ways in which competition between nonprofits and for-profits has led to a convergence in their practices and to better grasp the interaction of professional incentives and ownership, it is useful to review the literature on the comparative performance of contemporary for-profit and nonprofit health care institutions.

19. Most health insurance plans, for instance, do not cover the costs of experimental procedures. It is only when such care is provided on a sufficiently widespread basis that it is covered and thus affordable for most individuals.

COMPARATIVE STUDIES OF NONPROFIT AND FOR-PROFIT HEALTH INSTITUTIONS: THE EVIDENCE

American health policy has concentrated on three primary aims: promoting access to care, limiting the cost of treatment, and ensuring the provision of services of adequate quality. Past studies of the effects of ownership on the behavior of providers have understandably focused on these three areas.

Ownership and Medical Costs

Two substantial sets of empirical studies have been conducted on the relationship between ownership and economic performance—the first focusing on nursing homes, the second on short-term general hospitals. Over a dozen studies have compared average costs of care in nonprofit and for-profit nursing homes.[20] Using varying data bases and measures of costs, these studies have reached a common conclusion: controlling for characteristics of patients, range of services provided, and other attributes of the facility, for-profit homes have average costs 5 to 15 percent lower than their nonprofit counterparts.

In contrast, investigations of the hospital industry have found only small, inconsistent differences in reported costs of proprietary and nonprofit facilities. Cost per day is usually higher in for-profit facilities. But shorter lengths of stay have led to their relative cost per admission being measured as lower in some studies, higher in others, and roughly equal in the rest (Sloan & Becker 1984; Ermann & Gabel 1984; Pattison & Katz 1983; Sloan & Vraciu 1983, 34; Lewin, Derzon, & Margulies 1981, 52; Bays 1979).

This research also seems to indicate ownership-related differences in costs in facilities where physicians' roles are relatively attenuated (Koetting 1980), but not where there is a stronger professional presence.[21] This suggests that professional standards and incentives mitigate some of the incentives for cost reduction (either through increased efficiency or reduced quality) that might otherwise be associated with for-profit ownership.

Ownership and the Quality of Medical Care

Assessments of ownership-related differences in quality for the most part mirror the findings on cost of care. For those facilities in which physicians control the delivery of care, there seem to be few if any measurable differences in quality

(Schlesinger & Dorwart 1984, 959; Schlesinger 1985, 11). For example, a recent review concluded that there is no evidence that the profit motive induces physicians to compromise quality: "Unless new definitions of quality are proposed which are more rigorous, comprehensible, measurable, and widely acceptable than those noted above, there appears to be no basis for examining this dimension beyond the results of existing studies" (Sherman & Chilingerian 1984, 5).

On the other hand, where physicians play a less active role, the evidence suggests that lower quality care is found in for-profit settings. Whether there are differences in the *average* quality is a matter of debate.[22] There is fairly consistent evidence, however, that for-profit facilities are disproportionately represented among institutions offering the very lowest quality care (Vladeck 1980, 123; Smith 1981, 86; Koetting 1980, 18).

Ownership and Access to Medical Care

Throughout their history, for-profit institutions have labored under the suspicion that they treat only the more profitable patients. In 1970 it was noted that "the most serious indictment of proprietary hospitals is contained in the argument that has been labeled 'cream-skimming'" (Steinwald & Neuhauser 1970, 832).[23] Fifteen years later, the scale of proprietary operations has enlarged greatly, but the concerns of observers have not changed. The quest for profits is regarded as "an additional motive to private provider groups and institutions to engage in patient skimming and to discontinue needed but cost-ineffective services" (Nutter 1984, 918).

Private nonprofit institutions, however, are also reported to select carefully the patients they treat. In the mid-1970s, the National Health and Environmental Law Project received a number of reports from local legal service programs indicating significant channeling of "indigent patients who present themselves for treatment at private nonprofit hospital emergency rooms to municipal and county hospitals" (Silver 1974, 184). Based on these and other reports, some analysts have concluded that cream skimming is a major factor within the voluntary sector as well: "The suburban community hospitals avoid the poor. . . . The voluntary teaching hospitals prefer if they can to take the 'interesting cases' and send everyone else to the city or county hospital" (Neuhauser 1974, 240).

---

20. About half of these are reviewed and summarized in Bishop (1980). Since that review was published, additional research has been completed by Koetting (1980), Frech and Ginsburg (1981), Caswell and Cleverly (1983), and Schlenker and Shaughnessy (1984).

21. Related research supports this pattern. For-profit providers appear to have lower costs in the provision of laboratory services (Danzon 1982) and health insurance (Frech 1976), but to have equal or higher costs for renal dialysis centers (Held & Pauly 1982) and health maintenance organizations (Schlesinger, Blumenthal, & Schlesinger 1986).

22. Studies comparing for-profit and nonprofit nursing homes have concluded variously that for-profit institutions have quality that is equal to nonprofit homes (Holmberg & Anderson 1968; Ullman 1983), less than nonprofit facilities (Koetting 1980), or equal in some dimensions but less in others (Riportella-Mueller & Slesinger 1982; Weisbrod & Schlesinger 1981).

23. Critics argue that proprietary hospitals engage in two forms of cream skimming: those involving services and those involving the selection of patients. According to this view, they skimp on expensive and underutilized services and exclude patients with complex illnesses who are uninsured or covered by Medicaid and cannot pay their full charges (Steinwald & Neuhauser 1970, 832).

It is clear then that private nonprofit and for-profit health providers each engage in some screening of patients who seek care. If ownership affects restrictions on access, it will thus be reflected not in the presence but in the nature or extent of patient selection. Facilities may select among patients to further a variety of organizational objectives, including increased surplus (profits) or enhanced status as teaching or research institutions. We focus here on selection of patients on the basis of profitability since this can be most readily measured.

Providers of medical care can avoid unprofitable patients in three ways. First, facilities can simply be located away from low-income areas. Second, they can choose not to provide services used disproportionately by the uninsured or underinsured. Third, they can actively screen for and discourage admission by those unable to pay for care. This screening could be accomplished by requiring a means test prior to admission or by not offering sliding fee scales for patients unable to cover fully the costs of care. Evidence from past studies suggests that for-profit providers are more likely to use each of these methods, and that this occurs both for facilities in which physicians play an important role and for those in which they do not.

Screening and the Location of the Facility

To the extent that facilities avoid patients with limited ability to pay, one would expect them to locate in affluent areas. If for-profit providers are more sensitive to these incentives, they should provide a higher proportion of services in these areas than in less profitable localities. Most studies of the relationship between ownership and choice of location examine the location patterns of short-term general hospitals. These studies have in fact found that the share of services provided under proprietary auspices is highest in states with high per capita income (Kushman & Nuckton 1977, 201), rapidly increasing levels of income (Steinwald & Neuhauser 1970, 828), and extensive insurance coverage (Bays 1983, 855). These patterns persist whether one focuses on all for-profit hospitals or just those associated with multifacility chains (Mullner & Hadley 1984, 149). Similar patterns are seen within states, with investor-owned facilities disproportionately located in counties that have relatively few Medicaid patients (Homer, Bradham, & Rushefsky 1984).

Less research has been done on others types of care. However, for-profit psychiatric inpatient care is three times higher in states where private coverage for this care is required, and for-profit home health care is almost three times more prevalent in states with generous Medicaid programs (Schlesinger & Blumenthal 1986). (See table 13.4.)

Screening and Selection of Services

To screen out patients with limited ability to pay, a facility can be expected to avoid offering two types of services: (1) those that are not reimbursed or are underreimbursed by insurance plans, and (2) those that are used disproportion-

TABLE 13.4 INSURANCE COVERAGE AND MARKET SHARES OF PROPRIETARY HEALTH CARE FACILITIES

Type of Facility	Proportion of Facilities that Are For-Profit	
	States that Mandate Psychiatric Inpatient Coverage in Private Insurance[a]	States with No Mandate
Psychiatric hospitals	42.9%	13.4%
	States with Generous Medicaid Programs[b]	States with Less Generous Medicaid Programs
Home health agencies	8.3%	3.3%
	States with Special ESRD Medicaid Coverage[c]	States with No Medicaid ESRD Program
Dialysis centers	30.7%	24.5%

Source: Schlesinger and Blumenthal 1986.
a. Twenty-two states.
b. Twenty-one states in which Medicaid fees for specialists equals at least 90 percent of Medicare reimbursement.
c. Thirty-six states.

ately by patients who are uninsured or covered by Medicaid (Sloan & Becker 1984).

Psychiatric hospitals provide several good examples of the first type of service. Emergency telephone and suicide prevention services are generally unreimbursed, since the client is often unidentified and therefore cannot be billed. Home care and day care programs tend, for historical reasons, to be underreimbursed by insurers (Schlesinger & Dorwart 1984, 963). Facilities that screen on ability to pay would therefore tend to avoid such services, and, indeed, surveys of psychiatric hospitals show that for-profit institutions are four to five times less likely to offer such services than are either their private nonprofit or public counterparts (Schlesinger & Dorwart 1984, 964). A recent study of outpatient services in general hospitals found that for-profit facilities, particularly those affiliated with a multihospital corporation, were less likely to offer unprofitable services (Shortell et al. 1986).

Facilities that select patients on ability to pay can also be expected to avoid those services that are used disproportionately by the indigent. Low-income patients are likely to be either uninsured or covered by Medicaid, which in most states pays hospitals at a rate far lower than reimbursement from other insurers (Sloan & Becker 1984, 682).[24] In short-term general hospitals—where data on service mix are most readily available—investor-owned hospitals are again sig-

24. Thus hospitals use revenues from full-paying patients to subsidize the Medicare and Medicaid patients. Even for-profit hospitals accept a substantial discount on the cost of care (Sloan & Vraciu 1983, 33).

TABLE 13.5 PERCENTAGES OF HOSPITALS WITH LOW-INCOME SERVICES AVAILABLE, IN URBAN AREAS WITH BOTH PRIVATE NONPROFIT AND FOR-PROFIT SHORT-TERM GENERAL HOSPITALS

| | Type of Service | | | | |
| | | | | Chemical Dependency Unit | |
Type of Hospital	Psychiatric Outpatient	Outpatient Department	Dental	Inpatient	Outpatient
100–199 beds					
For-Profit	6.3%	35.4%	31.3%	12.5%	10.4%
Private, nonprofit	8.9%	57.1%	44.4%	26.7%	26.7%
200–299 beds					
For-Profit	16.7%	41.7%	41.7%	4.2%	4.2%
Private, nonprofit	19.1%	60.0%	48.9%	14.9%	14.9%

Source: Schlesinger and Blumenthal 1986.

Note: Statistics based on hospitals in Anaheim, Atlanta, Augusta, Chattanooga, Chicago, Corpus Christi, Dallas, El Paso, Ft. Worth, Houston, Little Rock, Los Angeles, Louisville, Memphis, Miami, Mobile, Montgomery, Nashville, New Orleans, New York, Phoenix, Richmond, St. Petersburg, San Antonio, San Diego, San Francisco, Seattle, and Tucson.

nificantly less likely to offer such services (Schlesinger & Blumenthal 1986). Controlling for size and local characteristics, private nonprofit hospitals are significantly more likely to adopt services used by indigent patients (Cromwell & Kanak 1982; Schlesinger & Blumenthal 1986). (See table 13.5.) Where a hospital is the sole local institution, these differences in behavior are smaller (Schlesinger & Blumenthal 1986, 12).

Screening and Admissions Policies

Admissions policies can influence the average ability to pay in a facility in two ways. First, exclusionary policies (for example, requiring a means test) can be used to screen out particular classes of payers, such as the uninsured or those covered by Medicaid. Second, by providing services at a reduced charge, facilities can encourage the patronage of lower-income patients. Facilities that seek more profitable patients can be expected to adopt the former policies but avoid the latter.

TABLE 13.6 PROPORTION OF PHYSICIANS REPORTING EXCLUSIONS OF PATIENTS OF VARIOUS TYPES

Independent

Type of Patient	Public	Nonprofit	For-Profit
Uninsured	0.14	0.20	0.43
Medicaid	0.03	0.05	0.15
Medicare	0.02	0.01	0.04

System-Affiliated

Type of Patient	Public	Nonprofit	For-Profit
Uninsured	0.09	0.19	0.52
Medicaid	0.03	0.05	0.16
Medicare	0.01	0.01	0.05

Source: Schlesinger and Blumenthal 1986.

For-profit institutions appear significantly more likely to fit this pattern. Surveys of physicians reveal that investor-owned hospitals are two to three times as likely to adopt policies to discourage admissions of uninsured or Medicaid patients (Schlesinger & Blumenthal 1986, 14). (See table 13.6.) Conversely, a survey of long-term care facilities, including nursing homes, psychiatric hospitals, and institutions for the mentally handicapped, found that proprietary facilities were one-half to one-quarter as likely to offer services at reduced charge as were their nonprofit counterparts (Schlesinger & Blumenthal 1986).[25] (See table 13.7.)

Discussion of the Empirical Findings

These findings suggest that ownership does influence facility performance. Differences in cost and quality of care were confined largely to institutions in which physicians play a minor role. However, virtually all investor-owned institutions appear more likely to select patients on the basis of their ability to pay. For-profit facilities are also more likely to locate in areas with higher incomes and to avoid offering services used most by indigent patients. And proprietary providers appear more likely to screen patients on insurance status and less likely to encourage patronage by low-income patients by offering sliding fee scales.

The evidence concerning selection on the basis of cost of care is considerably weaker, in part because there are relatively few data on access under prospective reimbursement. The evidence that does exist is consistent with the conclusion

25. The differences between predicted and current costs of "transferred" patients are small, on the order of 2 to 4 percent. Each individual difference is statistically insignificant, and the cost difference between patients in public nursing homes and those in for-profit homes is opposite of that predicted. Nonetheless, eleven of the twelve signs are as one would predict if for-profit facilities did screen patients on the basis of costs. This pattern would occur by chance with a probability of less than 0.003.

TABEL 13.7 LEVEL OF CHARGES AS A REASON FOR SELECTION OF FACILITIES

| | Ownership of Facility | | |
Industry	Proprietary	Nonprofit	Public
A. Percentage of administrators responding that the availability of service at no charge was an important reason for the selection of their facility by consumers.			
Psychiatric hospitals	11.2	27.3	34.9
Institutions for mentally handicapped	15.5	22.2	48.2
Nursing homes	6.6	22.2	48.7
B. Percentage of clients responding that the availability of service at reduced or no charge was an important reason for their selection of a facility.			
Psychiatric hospitals	4.7	9.0	16.7
Institution for mentally handicapped	8.0	12.6	20.7
Nursing homes	4.9	8.9	23.8

Source: Schlesinger 1985.

that proprietary facilities are more sensitive to the financial incentives to screen out the most costly patients.

All of these findings should be interpreted with caution. First, most of the comparisons reported above do not control for many of the factors other than ownership that can affect institutional policies. Second, there is considerable variation in the behavior of health care organizations within any ownership category. Among investor-owned institutions, undoubtedly many discriminate less than the average nonprofit facility. Wise policymakers will take this variation into account. Third, before reacting to ownership-related differences, such as access restrictions imposed by for-profit providers, policymakers should, however, understand the origins of those screening practices. Like all health institutions, for-profit facilities respond to prevailing financial incentives. If they differ from nonproprietary providers in this respect, it is because they seem to respond more vigorously to those incentives. The existence of large numbers of inadequately insured or uninsured citizens in this country creates incentives for all health institutions to screen patients on the basis of ability to pay. For-profit institutions are more likely to do so, but as the data presented above reveal, private nonprofit facilities also restrict access far more than do public health care providers.

Prospective-payment systems, like Medicare's DRGs, are specifically designed to encourage facilities to specialize in the care they deliver and thus to choose carefully the patients they treat (Comptroller General . . . 1980, 34–62). Hospitals are free, under this prospective-payment system, to "specialize" in the care of low-cost, uncomplicated patients. Indeed, under DRGs and other prospective-payment systems, all facilities, whatever their form of ownership, will benefit economically by specializing to some degree in treating such relatively profitable patients, and screening on the basis of cost will almost certainly increase among nonprofit

facilities. Here too, however, investor-owned facilities seem likely to respond to these economic incentives more vigorously than will other providers.

The greater responsiveness of for-profit providers to financial incentives can be an asset as well as a liability. From the mid-1950s through the mid-1970s, many policy initiatives sought to encourage the expansion of the industry. The investor-owned sector responded most vigorously (Schlesinger 1985; Vladeck 1980, 250), as the history of Medicare's end-stage renal disease (ESRD) program illustrates. The 1972 ESRD amendments to the Social Security Act were intended to assure unrestricted access to care for all those with renal failure. The for-profit sector reacted more rapidly to the economic opportunity created by this new entitlement, opening facilities in many communities that were disproportionately poor or populated by minorities, areas in which nonprofit providers had been unable or unwilling to operate (Plough et al. 1984; Lowrie & Hampers 1982, 191–204).

Policymakers should recognize, therefore, that the screening practices of for-profit health facilities result in no small measure from overt public policy decisions or from the failure of American government to alleviate some major social problems. The growth of proprietary institutions highlights that we have no clear policy toward, nor consensus about, what constitutes adequate access to medical care for our citizens. Nor is there any agreement on the responsibility of medical providers either to individuals seeking care or to the community in which providers are located.

While we struggle to reach such a consensus, the spread of proprietary health care will exact a price. Prospective-payment systems and increased reliance on for-profit institutions may threaten the viability of government-owned facilities (E. Brown 1983; Lewin & Lewin 1984, 9). In the hospital sector, for example, private providers will find it profitable to avoid costly patients within any particular DRG category. These patients will be channeled to public institutions (Feder, Hadley, Mullner 1984). For any particular DRG, then, costs in public institutions will grow over time, creating the impression that they are less efficient compared to the private sector. This will undoubtedly lead to pressures to close more public hospitals, further exacerbating restrictions on access. Local, state, and federal governments must face the need to protect the financial stability of these facilities, which, in many areas, ensure only a minimum level of access to medical care.

Over the long term, the rise of proprietary institutions will magnify the effect of prevailing incentives to discriminate against patients who are unable to pay for their care or whose treatment is particularly costly. As disparities in access to care among different groups of citizens become more glaring, American society may be driven sooner than it might otherwise have been into providing all citizens with protection against the cost of illness. It would be ironic if the spread of for-profit medicine created conditions that prompted massive new governmental interventions into the organization and financing of American medicine. It would be a further irony if private nonprofit institutions, in responding to the competitive challenge of proprietary chains, helped create these very same conditions on a scale much larger than the proprietary sector alone could produce.

CONCLUSION AND DISCUSSION

Three points are central to any discussion in the 1980s about nonprofits and American medical care. The first is that factors other than the legal form of organization—whether nonprofit, profit, or governmental—have dominated the shape of American medicine and still do. To date, who pays for whose health care and how, the number and distribution of physicians and nurses, the organizational characteristics of payers and providers, and the larger political and economic environment—all these factors dwarf changes in corporate form in giving shape to how doctors, patients, and health insurance interact.

Second, legal forms often are held to stand for other institutional features associated with but not identical to the nonprofit, profit, or governmental structure of ownership. The most prominent dispute of the 1980s—inaccurately labeled as the rise of profit-making firms in health—in fact stands for several developments. It represents in part medical capitalism in the form of large-scale corporate investment in medicine (as with HCA and AHS) (Goldsmith 1984, 5). It stands as well for a spirit of entrepreneurialism—to use one of the vulgarities—that denotes a newer orientation toward profit, innovation, marketing sensitivity, and the like (New York Academy of Medicine 1985). And, finally, it stands for the scale and geographic reach of new hospital units—religious, profit-making, or nonprofit—that range over many sites (chains) and may, as has HCA, vertically integrate with drug suppliers, insurance firms, or hospital product firms.

Our third point arises from the evidence on comparative performance set out above. Although we have emphasized the confusion and overstatement about the importance of ownership forms in medicine, there do appear to be systematic, ownership-related differences in the practices of health institutions. It thus seems reasonable to consider such differences as the basis for some public policies in the health industry.

Putting the Profit-Nonprofit Distinction in Perspective

A simple thought experiment brings out the first point of this conclusion. But consider first the reasonable and widely held view that American medicine has, for the last twenty years, been in considerable difficulty.

Access to adequate care remains a serious problem for millions despite the growth until recently of private insurance and Medicare and Medicaid. Although figures vary considerably, at least 20 million people are without insurance coverage at all, private or public. Another 10 percent of the population—some 22 million in 1980—have inadequate protection against the most substantial medical expenditures—hospitalization and physician services (Munnell

1986). And another 20 percent lack insurance against catastrophic expenses beyond 15 percent of annual income (Heineman 1985; Davis 1985; Marmor & Dunham 1985).

The *costs of care*—however financed—have inflated enormously over the past decade and a half, rising from some $70 billion in 1970 to more than $400 billion in 1985 without commensurate improvements in quality or utilization.[26] And finally, there is widespread concern that insurance costs and greater pressure for cost reduction threaten further the quality of care available to Americans when they get it.

The simple thought experiment is this: if one imagines removing all the recent developments in organizational forms—the growth of chains and profit-making hospitals—would any serious analyst of American medicine doubt that the above critique would remain substantially correct? We think the simple answer is no, one would not.

The continuing problems with access and costs point to the presence of fundamental, long-standing features of American medicine that only partially manifest themselves in the overheated debate about the proper legal form of organization.

Clarifying the Real Changes in American Medical Care

The contemporary growth of investor-owned health care facilities, for example, has been viewed by proponents as the elixir for all that ails the American health care system. Opponents see it as indicative of the virtual abandonment of a set of cherished social institutions and values. Both sides view the recent growth of the for-profit sector as foreshadowing a systemwide transformation of the health industry—and perhaps its complete conversion to proprietary auspices.

In fact, it seems unlikely that such radical changes will occur. As we have seen, there have historically been a number of pronounced shifts in the relative importance of nonprofit and for-profit health care providers. These will continue to occur in the future in response to changes in private wants and in public subsidies, the changing authority of medical professionals, and the introduction of new technologies and services.

Whatever the history of the nonprofit in American medicine, the evidence of its performance, relatively speaking, does not clearly support either side of the nonprofit or for-profit debate. What is clear is that there has been a massive shift in the *character* of American medicine, not a shift in the dominant *form*. The growth of the for-profit chains, the challenge to business-as-usual, and the consequent shifts in the behavior of nonprofits are missed if one concentrates on nonprofit market share alone. If anything, the infusion of new capital in medicine has promoted competitive behavior in the industry, further exacerbating and, at the same time, obscuring the very conditions that should be the central subject of debate, namely, access and cost.

26. The figures represent 7.5 percent of GNP in 1970 and about 11 percent in 1985 (table 13.3).

The Policy Implications of Differences in Nonprofit and For-Profit Health Institutions

We discussed above those differences and similarities revealed by the social science literature. We did not ask the question of to whom these differences would be important. Judging from the past behavior of nonprofit and for-profit health agencies, it seems inappropriate to relate simplistically ownership form to the achievement of socially valued goals. Both for-profit and nonprofit health care providers have, in different ways, served important public goals. The entry of for-profit providers has made available services that otherwise would have been too limited to meet rapidly growing or shifting patterns of utilization. The nonprofit form has provided a medium for innovative delivery of services and has provided, and continues in many instances to provide, an important source of care for those without the means (or insurance) to finance care.

Eliminating one form of ownership would neither obviate nor render catastrophically large existing policy problems, such as ensuring the availability of health services at reasonable cost and quality.[27] Although shifts in ownership are clearly neither the source of nor the solution to current failings of American medical care, the observed differences between nonprofit and for-profit performance are relevant to health policy. When health care costs $400 billion annually, the possibility of cutting costs by even 10 percent through shifting services to the most efficient providers is attractive. In a system, however, in which a large portion of consumers remains abysmally uninformed about their options for treatment and the quality of the care they receive, the threat of cutting quality in the pursuit of providers' self-interest is a real and important concern.

Similarly, although there exist cost differences of up to 10 percent between for-profit and nonprofit providers—the former higher for some services, the latter for others—prohibiting one form of ownership from offering services would have only a small effect on the spiraling inflation of medical costs.

To summarize our conclusions, there do not seem to be appreciable differences for most American patients in the care provided by for-profit and nonprofit hospitals. We are not saying no differences exist—indeed we document them—but we want rather to emphasize that the near-term effects of the loss of market share by nonprofit hospitals are not associated with the dire predictions of the critics.

Ownership and Directions for Future Health Policies

If one shifts the question slightly, however, our interpretation changes substantially. There appear to be large differences between the forms of ownership and management for medical care entrepreneurs, who want to take profits out of medical care in the form of stock ownership (and are big winners), and for doctors, who have been profit makers all along but are losing control to new profit takers.

It is unclear, given that doctors and other medical personnel have been making the functional equivalent of profits—and high ones indeed under the old regime—whether the total amount of profit and the level of cost will go up under the new regime.[28] Who will benefit, however, and who will be accountable to whom, will change. To state it briefly, the small entrepreneurs—particularly physicians—seem to be losing power to the larger organized corporate institutions exemplified by Humana and Hospital Corporation of America and, in part, by the new nonprofit systems. Some of the changes now occurring, particularly the vertical and horizontal integration of medical care facilities, are historically unprecedented in health. Yet this is a familiar stage in the development of Western capitalism—the displacement of smaller units by larger ones in the name of rationalization.[29]

The argument, therefore, is not solely over profits or profitmaking. It is over the *control* of patients, profits, and professional privilege. The argument is not so much about organizational forms as about the incremental decline of a service ethos—more naked in one sector, more camouflaged in the other. The culture of American medicine, already entrepreneurial and commercial by international comparison, will probably grow more so (Marmor & Klein 1985).

All one needs to add here are the memorable words of the executive vice president of American Medical International, who in a recent interview laid out the full view that medicine is nothing but an ordinary market service. In explaining why hospitals are justified in getting tough with patients who cannot pay for care, Mr. Bruce Andrews noted that ''we don't expect Safeway and A&P to give away free food for people who can't afford it.'' This casual remark—and especially its casual dismissal of centuries of concern that the care of the sick imposes special obligations on both the givers of care and the community as a whole—is terribly revealing. Of equal concern is the behavior of the religiously affiliated

27. To use these differences to further social ends, however, requires a fairly sophisticated and complicated set of policies. Past ownership-based interventions have often been crude and, as a result, have met with mixed success. When, for example California adopted a prepaid system of care for its Medi-Cal enrollees, policymakers were concerned that prepayment would create incentives to cut quality of care. To mitigate these incentives, they required that all participating prepaid plans be organized under nonprofit auspices, on the theory that this would prevent providers from having a monetary incentive to reduce quality. This strategy was circumvented by entrepreneurs who established a set of nonprofit dummy corporations that effectively funneled profits to subsidiaries, creating essentially the same incentives as if the plans had been organized as proprietary corporations (Goldberg 1975).

28. Surely the potential for growth exists. As Evans notes about the for-profit testing lab: ''The strong stimulus to 'more' which is a consequence of for-profit motivation justifies serious concern. Unnecessary testing is pure waste of resources. But for-profit organization does not, cannot, recognize unnecessary testing as an intellectual concept. Sales are their own justification'' (1984, 321).

29. As Morone has observed, ''For-profit chains scramble the traditional discourse over American health policy by setting the principles of free enterprise and physician autonomy into tension'' (1985, 4). Actually, this tension has long been present in American health care, but it took large and powerful corporations to take up the profession's ideology with a vengeance.

institution that carefully nurtures its sponsorship in its public relations while sending certain cases down the road to the local county hospital.[30] The relative triumph of commercialism and the long decline of professional authority mark contemporary American medicine, not particular forms within it.

The central place of nonprofits in American medicine had been, for some fifty years, largely unchallenged. The community hospital—nonprofit in form, local in roots, often religious in character, with physicians permitted to use its capital as they brought in patients—was ubiquitous, an American institution that by the 1950s had the quality of the familiar, the taken-for-granted. As the problem of medical inflation became epidemic in the late 1960s and 1970s, that form, along with much else in American medicine, was increasingly criticized, challenged, and sometimes even ridiculed.

The typical challenge was to point out the gap between the mission of the nonprofit and the reality, the ever-increasing revenues bargained for with insurance companies, governments, and patients with the zeal often associated with capitalist enterprise. For much of the postwar period, this critique was associated with the alternative of government regulation and, for some, with the dream of national health insurance. But by the end of the 1970s, a wholly different alternative had emerged from this common diagnosis. It was that competition—from health maintenance organizations and then from the chains of profit-making hospitals—would right the wrongs of medicine. Increased competition, it was argued, would help us all, and the pressure of profit seeking and the vaunted efficiencies of that for-profit model of corporate organization were widely touted (Marmor, Boyer, & Greenberg 1983). It is this fight that has set the context for our discussion of the role of nonprofits in medicine.

The vices of the for-profits do not exonerate the non-

---

30. Generally, both public and private hospitals have a duty to accept all patients who require emergency care. That duty does not extend, however, to nonemergency situations (Marsh 1985, 162; *Stanford Law Review* 1962; Grady 1986).

profits, although one could hardly tell from the high-minded preachiness of some in the nonprofit health world (Relman 1980). Nor does the inflationary history of the nonprofit health institutions of the past two decades make the proprietary institutions an answer to the costliness of American medicine. There are limits to what can be said by distinguishing among organizational forms; the differences are simply not that great. But there should be few limits to the vigilance with which we examine all health institutions and apply the appropriate constraints to the vices of their organizational virtues. There may be some areas where the innovative, energetic pursuit of profit will, under the right rules, bring social gain. Drug production and laboratory medicine now operate under such rules, with ambiguous results (Evans 1984, 209–31). More competition between providers will almost certainly bring increased sensitivity to patients (particularly well-insured ones) and the costs of their care. Whether that sensitivity will mean caring or coddling is uncertain. And whether the concern about costs will produce true efficiency gains is uncertain, but possible (Evans 1984, 225–26).

There are parallel considerations for the nonprofits in health. Will the patient screening that is now more profitable produce a reaction, particularly among physicians and nurses? Will the nonprofit rationale—the commitment to caring for the sick, however financed—reenter our debates in such a way that responsible action is fiscally rewarded or, at the very least, not penalized? Will physicians discover anew the advantages of the nonprofit form without our policymakers losing the distinction between autonomy that helps patients and independence that simply increases physician incomes (Majone 1984)? Will we, in short, recognize that health care has been, for very good reasons, a not-only-for-profit industry and that no amount of marketing hype will make vulnerable patients the wary consumers of Adam Smith's theoretical markets?

The challenge for public policy will be to discover rules of the medical game that constrain the vices of both rampant commercialism and complacent professionalism. The real uncertainty is whether our polity is capable of such sophistication.

REFERENCES

American Hospital Association. 1983. *Hospital Statistics*. Chicago: American Hospital Association.

Arrow, Kenneth. 1963. "Uncertainty and the Welfare Economics of Medical Care." *American Economic Review* 53, no. 5:941–73.

Bays, Carson. 1983. "Patterns of Hospital Growth: The Case of Profit Hospitals." *Medical Care* 21:950–57.

———. 1983a. "Why Most Private Hospitals Are Nonprofit." *Journal of Policy Analysis and Management* 2:367.

———. 1979. "Cost Comparisons for For-Profit and Nonprofit Hospitals." *Social Science and Medicine* 13:219–27.

Bishop, C. 1980. "Nursing Home Cost Studies and Reimbursement Issues." *Health Care Financing Review* 2 (Spring):47–64.

Brown, E. 1983. "Public Hospitals on the Brink: Their Problems and Their Options." *Journal of Health Politics, Policy and Law* 7, no. 4 (Winter):927–44.

Brown, Lawrence D. 1986. "The Proper Boundaries of the Role of Government." *Bulletin of the New York Academy of Medicine* 62, no. 1 (January-February):15.

———. 1985. "Technocratic Corporatism and Administrative Reform in Medicare." *Journal of Health Policy, Politics, and Law,* 10, no. 3 (Fall):579–99.

———. 1983. *Politics and Health Care Organizations: HMOs as Federal Policy.* Washington, D.C.: Brookings.

Caswell, R., and Cleverly, W. 1983. "Cost Analysis of the Ohio Nursing Home Industry." *Health Services Research* 18 (Fall):359–82.

Clark, Robert C. 1980. "Does the Nonprofit Form Fit the Hospital Industry?" *Harvard Law Review* 93, no. 7 (May):1416.

Clarkson, Kenneth. 1972. "Some Implications of Property Rights in Hospital Management." *Journal of Law and Economics* 15:363.

Comptroller General of the United States. 1980. *Rising Hospital Costs Can be Restrained by Regulating Payments and Improving Management.* Publication no. HRD–80–72. Washington, D.C.: U.S. Government Printing Office.

Cromwell, J., and Kanak, J. R. 1982. "The Effects of Prospective Reimbursement Programs on Hospital Adoption and Service Sharing." *Health Care Financing Review* 4 no.2:67–88.

Danzon, P. 1982. "Hospital 'Profits': The Effects of Reimbursement Policies." *Journal of Health Economics* 1 (May):29–52.

Davis, Karen. 1985. "Access to Health Care: A Matter of Fairness." In Center for National Policy, *Health Care: How to Improve It and Pay for It.* Washington, D.C.: Center for National Policy.

Drake, D. 1980. "The Cost of Hospital Regulation." In A. Levin, ed., *Regulating Health Care: The Struggle for Control* (*Proceedings of the Academy of Political Science* 33, no. 4:45–59).

Dunham, Andrew; Morone, James; and White, William. 1982. "Restoring Medical Markets: Implications for the Poor." *Journal of Health Politics, Policy and Law* 7, no. 2 (Summer):488–501.

Eisenberg, Leon. 1985. "The Right to Health Care: For Patients or For-Profits." Paper presented at the annual meeting of the American Psychiatric Association, Dallas, Texas, May 21.

Enthoven, Alain. 1980. *Health Plan: The Only Practical Solution to the Soaring Cost of Health Care.* Reading, Mass.: Addison-Wesley.

Ermann, D., and Gabel, J. 1984. "Multihospital Systems: Issues and Empirical Findings." *Health Affairs* 3, no. 1:50–64.

Evans, Robert G. 1984. *Strained Mercy: The Economics of Canadian Health Care.* Toronto: Butterworth.

Feder, Judith M. 1977. *Medicare: The Politics of Federal Hospital Insurance.* Lexington, Mass.: Lexington Books.

Feder, Judith, and Hadley, Jack. 1985. "The Economically Unattractive Patient: Who Cares?" *Bulletin of the New York Academy of Medicine* 61, no. 1 (January-February):68–75.

Feder, J.; Hadley, J.; and Mullner, R. 1984. "Falling through the Cracks: Poverty, Insurance Coverage, and Hospital Care for the Poor, 1980 and 1982." *Milbank Memorial Fund Quarterly* 62 (Fall):544–66.

Feldstein, P. 1978. *Health Associations and the Demand for Legislation.* Cambridge, Mass.: Ballinger.

Fox, Daniel. 1986. "The Consequences of Consensus: American Health Policy in the Twentieth Century." *Milbank Quarterly* 64, no. 1:76–99.

Frech, H. E. 1976. "The Property Rights Theory of the Firm: Empirical Results from a Natural Experiment." *Journal of Political Economy* 84:143–52.

Frech, H., and Ginsberg, P. 1981. "The Cost of Nursing Home Care in the United States: Government Ownership, Financing, and Efficiency." In J. Van Der Gaag and M. Perlman, eds., *Health, Economics, and Health Economics.* New York: North-Holland.

Gabel, John, and Ermann, Dan. 1985. "Preferred Provider Organizations: Performance, Problems, and Promise." *Health Affairs* 4:24–40.

Gage, Larry S. 1985. "Impact on the Public Hospitals." *Bulletin of the New York Academy of Medicine* 61, no. 1 (January-February):75–81.

Gardner, K. 1981. "Profit and the End-Stage Renal Disease Program." *New England Journal of Medicine* 305:461–62.

Goldberg, V. 1975. "Some Emerging Problems of Prepaid Health Plans in the Medi-Cal System." *Policy Analysis* 1 (Winter):55–68.

Goldsmith, Jeffrey. 1984. "Death of a Paradigm: The Challenge of Competition." *Health Affairs* (Fall):7–19.

Grady, Denise. 1986. "The Cruel Price of Cutting Medical Expenses." *Discover* 7, no. 5 (May):25–43.

Gray, Bradford H. 1985. "Overview: Origins and Trends." *Bulletin of the New York Academy of Medicine* 61, no. 1 (January-February):7–23.

Gray, Bradford H., ed. 1983. *The New Health Care for Profit: Doctors and Hospitals in a Competitive Environment.* Washington, D.C.: National Academy Press.

Hansmann, Henry. 1980. "The Role of Non-profit Enterprise." *Yale Law Journal* 89, no. 5 (April):835–901.

"Health Care Costs to Hit 12% of Gross National Product: Study." 1984. *Hospital Week* 20, no. 33 (August 17):2.

Heineman, B. W., Jr. 1985. "Introduction: Health Policy and Health Politics." In *Health Care: How to Improve It and How to Pay for It.* Washington, D.C.: Center for National Policy.

Held, P. and Pauly, M., 1982. "An Economic Analysis of the Production and Cost of Renal Dialysis Treatments." Working Paper 3064–03. Washington, D.C.: Urban Institute.

Holmberg, R., and Anderson, N. 1968. "Implications of Ownership for Nursing Home Care." *Medical Care* 6 (July-August):300–307.

Homer, C. G.; Bradham, D. D.; and Rushefsky, M. "Investor-Owned and Not-for-profit Hospitals: Beyond the Cost and Revenue Debate." *Health Affairs* 3, no. 1:133–36.

Horty, John F., and Mulholland, Daniel M. 1983. "Legal Differences between Investor-Owned and Nonprofit Health Care Institutions." In Bradford Gray, ed., *The New Health Care for Profit: Doctors and Hospitals in a Competitive Environment.* Washington, D.C.: National Academy Press.

Koetting, M. 1980. *Nursing-Home Organization and Efficiency.* Lexington, Mass.: Lexington Books.

Koten, John. 1985. "Baxter to Buy American Hospital Supply." *Wall Street Journal,* July 16, p. 2.

Koten, John, and Waldholz, Michael. 1985. "Baxter Travenol

Bids $3.6 Billion for Supply Firm.'' *Wall Street Journal*, June 24, p. 2.

Krizay, J., and Wilson, A. 1974. *The Patient as Consumer*. Lexington, Mass.: Lexington Books.

Kushman, J. E., and Nuckton, C. F. 1977. ''Further Evidence on the Relative Performance of Proprietary and Nonprofit Hospitals.'' *Medical Care* 15, no.3:189–204.

Lave, J., and Lave, J., 1974. *The Hospital Construction Act*. Washington, D.C.: American Enterprise Institute.

Law, Sylvia. 1974. *Blue Cross: What Went Wrong?* New Haven: Yale University Press.

Lewin, Lawrence S.; Derzon, Robert A.; and Margulies, Rhea. 1981. ''Investor-Owneds and Nonprofits Differ in Economic Performance.'' *Hospitals,* July, pp. 52–58.

Lewin, M. E., and Lewin, L. S. 1984. ''Health Care for the Uninsured.'' *Business Health* 1, no. 9:9–14.

Lowrie, E. G. 1981. ''Treatment of End-Stage Renal Disease.'' *New England Journal of Medicine* 304:356.

Lowrie, E. G., and Hampers, C. L. 1982. ''Proprietary Dialysis and the End-Stage Renal Disease Program.'' *Dialysis and Transplant* 11:191–204.

Luft, Harold. 1981. *Health Maintenance Organizations: Dimensions of Performance*. New York: Wiley.

Majone, G. 1984. ''Professionalism and Nonprofit Organizations.'' *Journal of Health Policy, Politics and Law* 8, no. 4 (Winter):639–59.

Marmor, Theodore R. 1983. *Political Analysis and American Medical Care*. Cambridge: Cambridge University Press.

———. 1973. *The Politics of Medicare*. Chicago: Aldine.

Marmor, Theodore R.; Boyer, Richard; and Greenberg, Julie. 1983. ''Medical Care and Procompetitive Reform.'' In Theodore R. Marmor, *Political Analysis and American Medical Care*. Cambridge: Cambridge University Press.

Marmor, Theodore R., and Dunham, Andrew. 1985. ''The Politics of Health Policy Reform: Origins, Alternatives, and a Possible Prescription.'' In *Health Care: How to Improve It and Pay for It*. Washington, D.C.: Center for National Policy.

Marmor, T. R., and Klein, R. Forthcoming. ''Cost vs. Care,'' *Health Matrix*.

Marmor, Theodore R.; Wittman, Donald A.; and Heagy, Thomas C. 1983. ''The Politics of Medical Inflation.'' In Theodore R. Marmor, *Political Analysis and American Medical Care*. Cambridge: Cambridge University Press.

Marsh, Frank H. 1985. ''Health Care Cost Containment and the Duty to Treat.'' *Journal of Legal Medicine* 6 (June):157–90.

Morone, James. 1985. ''The Unruly Rise of Medical Capitalism.'' *Hasting Center Report*, August, pp. 28–31.

Morone, James, and Dunham, Andrew. 1985. ''Slouching towards National Health Insurance: The New Health Care Politics.'' *Yale Journal on Regulation* 2:263.

Morone, James, and Marmor, Theodore. 1983. ''Representing Consumer Interests: The Case of American Health Planning.'' In Theodore R. Marmor, *Political Analysis and American Medical Care*. Cambridge: Cambridge University Press.

Mullner, Ross, and Hadley, Jack. 1984. ''Interstate Variations in the Growth of Chain-Operated Proprietary Hospitals, 1973–82.'' *Inquiry* 21:144–57.

Munnell, Alicia. 1986. ''Ensuring Entitlement to Health Care Services.'' *Bulletin of the New York Academy of Medicine* 62, no. 1 (January-February):61–74.

Neuhauser, D. 1974. ''The Future of Proprietaries in American Health Services.'' In C. C. Havighurst, ed., *Regulating Health Facilities Construction*. Washington, D.C.: American Enterprise Institute.

New York Academy of Medicine. 1985. ''The New Entrepreneurialism in Health Care: 1984 Annual Conference, New York Academy of Medicine.'' In *Bulletin of the New York Academy of Medicine* 61, no. 1 (January-February).

Nielsen, W. 1979. *The Endangered Sector*. New York: Columbia University Press.

Nutter, D. O. 1984. ''Access to Care and the Evolution of Corporate, For-Profit Medicine.'' *New England Journal of Medicine* 311:917–19.

Pattison, R. V., and Katz, H. M. 1983. ''Investor-Owned and Not-for-Profit Hospitals: A Comparison Based on California Data.'' *New England Journal of Medicine* 309:347–53.

Plough, A. L.; Salem, S. R.; Schwartz, M.; Weller, J. M.; and Ferguson, C. W. 1984. ''Case Mix in End-Stage Renal Disease: Differences between Patients in Hospital-Based and Free-Standing Facilities.'' *New England Journal of Medicine* 310:1432–36.

Raffel, M. W. 1980. *The U.S. Health Care System: Origins and Functions*. New York: John Wiley.

Relman, Arnold S. 1983. ''Investor-Owned Hospitals and Health-Care Costs.'' *New England Journal of Medicine* 309:370.

———. 1980. ''The New Medical Industrial Complex.'' *New England Journal of Medicine*. 303:963–70.

Relman, A. S., and Rennie, D. 1980. ''Treatment of End-Stage Renal Disease: Free but Not Equal.'' *New England Journal of Medicine* 303:996.

Riportella-Mueller, R., and Slesinger, D. 1982. ''The Relationship of Ownership and Size to Quality of Care in Wisconsin Nursing Homes.'' *Gerontologist* 22 (Winter):429–34.

Rorem, R. 1939. ''Enabling Legislation for Non-Profit Hospital Service Plans.'' *Law and Contemporary Problems* 6:528.

Rosenblatt, Rand E. 1978. ''Health Care Reform and Administrative Law: A Structural Appraisal.'' *Yale Law Journal* 88, no. 2 (December):243–336.

Ruchlin, Hirsch S. 1979. ''An Analysis of Regulatory Issues and Options in Long-Term Care.'' In V. LaPorte and J. Rubin, eds., *Reform and Regulation in Long-Term Care*. New York: Praeger.

Russell, L. B. 1979. *Technology in Hospitals: Medical Advances and Their Diffusion*. Washington, D.C.: Brookings Institution.

Salamon, Lester M., and Abramson, Alan J. 1982. *The Federal Budget and the Nonprofit Sector*. Washington, D.C.: Urban Institute.

Schlenker, R. E., and Shaughnessy, P. W. 1984. ''Case Mix, Quality, and Cost Relationships in Colorado Nursing Homes.'' *Health Care Financing Review* 61:6.

Schlesinger, M. 1985. ''The Rise of Proprietary Health Care.'' *Business Health* 2, no. 1:7–12.

———. 1984. ''Public, For-Profit, and Private Nonprofit Enterprises.'' Ph.D. dissertation.

Schlesinger, M., and Blumenthal, D. 1986. ''Ownership and

Access to Health Care: New Evidence and Policy Implications.'' *New England Journal of Medicine* (forthcoming).

Schlesinger, M.; Blumenthal, D.; and Schlesinger, E. 1986. ''Profits under Pressure: The Economic Performance of Investor-Owned and Nonprofit Health Maintenance Organizations.'' *Medical Care* (forthcoming).

Schlesinger, M., and Dorwart, R. 1984. ''Ownership and Mental Health Services: A Reappraisal.'' *New England Journal of Medicine* 311:959–65.

Sherman, H. David, and Chilingerian, Jon A. 1984. ''For-Profits vs. Nonprofit Hospitals: The Effect of the Profit Motive on the Management of Operations.'' Unpublished manuscripts.

Shortell, S.; Morrison, E.; Hughes, S.; and Coverdill, J. 1986. ''The Impact of Multi-Institutional Systems on Service Provision.'' In L. Rossiter, R. Scheffler, G. Wilensky, and N. McCall, eds., *Advances in Health Economics and Health Services Research,* vol. 7. Greenwich, Conn.: JAI Press.

Silver, L. H. 1974. ''The Legal Accountability of Nonprofit Hospitals.'' In C. C. Havighurst, ed., *Regulating Health Facilities Construction.* Washington, D.C.: American Enterprise Institute.

Sloan, F. A., and Becker, E. R. 1984. ''Cross-Subsidies and Payment for Hospital Care.'' *Journal of Health Politics, Policy and Law* 8, no. 4 (Winter):660–85.

Sloan, F. A., and Vraciu, R. A. 1983. ''Investor-Owned and Not-for-Profit Hospitals: Addressing Some Issues.'' *Health Affairs* 2, no. 1:25–37.

Smith, D. 1981. *Long-Term Care in Transition: The Regulation of Nursing Homes.* Washington, D.C.: AUPHA Press.

Stanford Law Review. 1962. ''Recent Development: Private Hospital Must Admit Unmistakable Emergency Cases.'' *Stanford Law Review* 14, no. 4 (July):910–18.

Starr, Paul. 1982. *The Social Transformation of American Medicine.* New York: Basic Books.

Starr, Paul, and Marmor, Theodore. 1984. ''The U.S.: A Social Forecast.'' In Jean de Kervasdoué, John R. Kimberly, and Victor G. Rodwin, *The End of an Illusion.* Berkeley: University of California Press.

Steinwald, B., and Neuhauser, D. 1970. ''The Role of the Proprietary Hospital.'' *Journal of Law and Contemporary Problems* 35:817–38.

Stevens, R. 1982. '' 'A Poor Sort of Memory': Voluntary Hospitals and Government before the Depression.'' *Milbank Memorial Fund Quarterly* 60 (Fall):551–84.

———. 1971. *American Medicine and the Public Interest.* New Haven: Yale University Press.

Stevens, R., and Stevens, R. 1974. *Welfare Medicine in America.* New York: Free Press.

Titmuss, R. 1971. *The Gift Relationship.* New York: Vintage Books.

Ullman, S. 1983. ''Ownership and Performance in the Long-Term Health Care Industry.'' University of Miami, Department of Economics Working Paper.

Vladeck, B. C. 1980. *Unloving Care.* New York: Basic Books.

Waldholz, Michael. 1985. ''American Hospital Plans to Merge with Hospital Corp. in Stock Swap.'' *Wall Street Journal,* April 1, p. 3.

Weisbrod, B. C., and Schlesinger, M. 1981. ''Benefit-Cost Analysis in the Mental Health Area: Issues and Directions for Research.'' In *Economics and Mental Health.* National Institute of Mental Health Series EN no. 1, DHHS Publication no. (ADM)81–1114. Washington, D.C.: U.S. Government Printing Office, 8–28.

Weller, Charles D. 1984. ''Free Choice as a Restraint of Trade in American Health Care Delivery and Insurance.'' *Iowa Law Review* 69, no. 5 (July):1351–92.

Yordy, Karl D. 1986. ''Current and Future Developments in Health Care.'' *Bulletin of the New York Academy of Medicine* 62, no. 1:27–38.

14

Voluntary Agencies and the Personal Social Services

RALPH M. KRAMER

Since Henry VIII dissolved the monasteries people have been talking gloomily about the declining role of voluntary organizations in the provision of social welfare services.
W. B. Harbert

V oluntary social service agencies, with the possible exception of religious institutions, are among the oldest nonprofit organizations whose distinctive role and relationship to government has long been controversial. Indeed, the history of social welfare in the United States could be written from the perspective of the changing allocation of responsibilities between government and voluntary organizations for the *personal social services*.[1]

These services refer to the social care provided to deprived, neglected, or handicapped children and youth, the needy elderly, the mentally ill—in short, all disadvantaged persons with substantial psychosocial problems. It includes such services as day care and foster care, institutional facilities, information and referral, counseling, sheltered workshops, homemakers, and vocational training and rehabilitation (Kahn 1973, 28–32; Sainsbury 1977, 3–4, 23–24). Typical provider agencies are Family Service agencies, community or neighborhood centers, Planned Parenthood federations, associations for the retarded, centers for independent living, halfway houses, Visiting Nurse associations, Catholic Charities, and others usually included in the United Way.

1. The referent of this chapter is the *personal social services*, but for the sake of brevity, *personal* will be dropped and the term used will be *social services* with the understanding that its meaning is restricted to the type of services mentioned in the text and that it does *not* include income maintenance, employment, housing, medical care, or education—all of which are sometimes described as the social services, particularly in Great Britain.

Over forty-one thousand voluntary nonprofit social service organizations employed 933,000 persons in the United States in 1980; their total expenditures amounted to $13.7 billion (Hodgkinson & Weitzman 1984, 61–62). These organizations, bureaucratic in structure, are governed by elected volunteer boards of directors and utilize professional and/or volunteer staffs to provide a continuing social service to clientele in their communities. Others are organized as self-help or mutual aid associations which provide services to their members or to those who share a particular problem. At various times voluntary agencies have been known as private charities or private agencies; only recently has their tax-exempt status been used to describe them as nonprofit organizations.

Although the periodic concern about the future of voluntary agencies in the United States has invariably been cast in terms of their relationship to government, since the 1960s the social service economy has become increasingly mixed, and much of the conventional wisdom regarding the character and role of the public and the private sectors and the distinctions between them is no longer appropriate. The obsolescence of traditional dichotomies is reflected in the growing use of such rubrics as the new political economy, the contract state, welfare pluralism, and private or nonprofit federalism (Smith 1971; Kamerman 1983; Morris 1982).

Not only are most social services available under both governmental and nonprofit auspices; many services are increasingly provided by profit-making organizations which may be locally owned or subsidiaries of national corporations.[2] This is particularly true in the field of child welfare where profit-making organizations have rapidly become the dominant contractors with government for the provision of residential treatment, day care, and group homes, as well as for substance abuse programs (Born 1983). In addition, there has been a similar growth in the number of employee assistance programs in which social services, including information and referral, are made available to employees by upwards of eight thousand business and industrial corporations (Akubas & Kurzman 1982). In this enlarged field of occupational welfare, a new professional specialization has emerged—industrial social work—and it is not unusual for Family Service agencies and private counseling firms to compete for contracts with an employee assistance program. These structured systems of service provision are in addition to those provided informally by family members, still the major source of care and treatment (Moroney 1976).

The principal relationships between these coexisting institutional systems can be summarized as follows: together with government and profit-making organizations, voluntary agencies may relieve, replace, or reinforce the primary social systems of family, neighbors, and friends. In the public sector, voluntary agencies also may substitute for, influence, extend, and improve the work of government, or they may offer complementary services different in kind, or they can function as a public agent or vendor. Voluntary agencies may also compete with profit-making organizations in many fields of social service.

This statement still begs the question of the significance of organizational auspices for the social services. Actually, little is known empirically about what difference it makes if government, a voluntary agency, a self-help or neighborhood group, or a profit-making organization provides a social service. Many social service professionals believe that organizational sponsorship or "ownership of the means of production" is much less significant than the manner in which the service is delivered—how is more critical than who. For example, it is possible that organizational size, degree of bureaucratization and professionalization, complexity, and the type of technology may be more decisive than the legal form of ownership in influencing utilization, cost, quality, accountability, and effectiveness (Glisson & Martin 1980; Gordon 1975, 102–05).

Although there are probably as many differences among voluntary agencies as between them and governmental organizations, many national leaders still claim that the former are preferable because of their flexibility and innovative capacity. For example, Wilber J. Cohen, former secretary of

health, education, and welfare, refers to "the continuing task of innovating in areas where public agencies lack knowledge or are afraid to venture. . . . The private sector is adept at innovation, and at providing the models government needs" (Filer . . . 1975, 42). But beliefs about the superiority of the voluntary agency have usually rested less on evidence than on a set of invidious organizational stereotypes whereby government is perceived as intrinsically rigid, riddled with bureaupathology, and offering mass standardized services that are dehumanizing (Kramer 1981, 63).

How did this view come about? As Boorstin (1965, 121) has observed, communities existed to care for common needs before government existed. Voluntary organizations first provided basic social and other services and later government followed with some direct provision, but mainly with financial support for the proliferating charitable organizations (McCarthy 1982; Huggins 1981). During the last quarter of the nineteenth century and until the 1930s, subsidies from state and local governments were the prevailing mode of financing most voluntary institutions for children and the physically and mentally handicapped in the United States (Warner 1894, 334–56). At the same time, "private philanthropy flourished in America partly because of the benevolence of the pious and well-to-do and partly because public charity was afflicted with political abuse and corruption" (Leiby 1978, 274). The widespread distrust of government assured the continuance of public subsidies to voluntary agencies and helped perpetuate a set of popular beliefs about the inherent superiority of voluntary social service agencies; they were seen as more humane, sensitive, and individualizing than governmental agencies.

These opinions were reinforced by the influential role of Charity Organization Societies (COS) in the large urban centers, which were successful in eliminating public relief as a municipal function in twelve cities toward the end of the nineteenth century (Watson 1922). Although they were a major factor in restricting government to a residual social service function,[3] they were also the source of many significant developments in the voluntary sector such as the establishment of family and children's agencies, the professionalization of social work and its methods of casework, the Community Chest, and the Councils of Social Agencies (Pumphrey & Pumphrey 1961). The first schools of social work were started by the COS, and until the 1950s, professional education for social work was dominated by the special interests of the voluntary sector.

The Great Depression, however, made it clear that voluntary social service agencies had assumed a task they could not meet: "to serve as a substitute for, and through the exclusion of, a broad program in dealing with poverty, misery, dis-

2. In the late 1970s it was estimated that governmental funds channeled through voluntary agencies accounted for at least two-thirds of all day-care services, half of recreational services, over 40 percent of family planning services, a third of placement services and residential care and treatment, 11 percent of counseling services, and 27 percent of employment services (Grønbjerg 1982, 16). Close to 80 percent of nursing homes are operated for profit and at least two-thirds of their income is derived from Medicaid funds (Senate Special Committee on Aging 1974, 20–25).

3. In contrast to the COS ideology, the settlement house movement in the two decades before World War I secured legislation to improve working conditions and housing and for social insurance. Pumphrey and Pumphrey (1961, 126, 198–230) document the rivalry of the COS and the settlements for the support of the philanthropic public (see also Davis [1967]).

tress, and economic maladjustment'' (Lubove 1966, 610). A new era of governmental responsibility was inaugurated in the 1930s under the New Deal, culminating in the Social Security Act of 1935. At the same time, policies were adopted to restrict public funds to governmental agencies because of past abuses of the subsidy system.

As is often the case, two extreme views emerged: those who saw only an emerging role for governmental social services and refused to grant them permanent status, and those who, with the advent of public programs, no longer saw any place for the voluntary social services (Cohen 1958, 182–206). A division of responsibility, originally proposed in 1934 by Linton Swift, subsequently had great influence on governmental and voluntary agency relationships. Government was to provide mass programs for routinized services and to meet economic needs, while voluntary social agencies would experiment, supplement, innovate, and specialize. Although governmental services did not remain so restricted, this image of the voluntary agency as a vanguard setting the pace and standards for government was widely accepted in professional social welfare circles, including the National Conference on Social Welfare, even though the expansion of the welfare state drastically changed these relationships.

Underlying these changes in the role of the voluntary agency during the last century have been two conflicting conceptions of social welfare. The *residual* view, which prevailed before the 1930s, holds that social welfare institutions should come into play only when the normal structures of the family and the market break down. It stresses self-reliance, charity, philanthropy, and voluntarism. The *institutional* view of social welfare regards the social services as essential requirements to meet the needs of all persons in an industrial society—not just the poor, the unfortunate and the handicapped. It is the philosophical basis of the welfare state. In practice these conflicting philosophies coexist uneasily, with the residual view periodically revived in protest against increased taxation and spending (Wilensky & Lebeaux 1965, 38–40). The residual view has been the official philosophy of the Reagan administration since 1980, and it has served as the ideological justification for substantial reductions in the growth rate of many of the social services (Salamon & Abramson 1982).

But if governmental services are seen as being stretched to the limits of existing resources, on what basis can policy decisions be made regarding who shall be served and by whom? If government has the choice between administering the service directly or contracting with a nongovernmental agency, what is known about voluntary social service agencies and what can be expected from them?

Despite their importance and the concern for their future in the welfare state, there is a scarcity of empirical research or theory that could contribute to a knowledgeable assessment of their distinctive organizational competence, vulnerability and potential. Because sponsorship—governmental, nonprofit, or for-profit—has rarely been regarded as a variable worth studying, voluntary organizations either have been ignored by social researchers or their influence and virtues exaggerated by enthusiastic supporters.[4] They are usually regarded as quasi-sacred symbols of altruism, charity, and civic benevolence, taken for granted as social institutions, but not considered worthy of serious study. Consequently, with a few exceptions, the literature on voluntary agencies is ideological or hortatory, with stereotypes and impressions filling the data gap.[5]

Most descriptions of the character, goals, or functions of voluntary agencies imply the performance of four organizational roles: (1) as *vanguard,* their purpose is to innovate, pioneer, experiment, and demonstrate programs, some of which may eventually be taken over by government; (2) as *improvers* or *advocates,* voluntary agencies are expected to serve as critics, watchdogs, or gadflies, pressuring government to extend, improve, or establish needed services; (3) as *value guardians* of voluntaristic, particularistic, and sectarian values, voluntary agencies are expected to promote citizen participation, develop leadership, and protect the special interests of social, religious, cultural, or other minority groups; and (4) as *service providers,* voluntary agencies deliver those services they have selected, some of which may be a public responsibility that government is unable or unwilling to assume directly or fully (Kramer 1981, 9).

In recent years voluntary agencies have been included in a special class of formal organizations called human service organizations, which, although differing in their auspices, size, structure, function, and client populations, are believed to share a common set of attributes and vulnerabilities (Hasenfeld 1983, 7–11). They work directly with people whom they seek to change, process, or care for by making available critical resources for their maintenance, enhancement, protection, or restoration of well-being. In contrast to other formal organizations, their ''raw materials'' are people; their multiple goals are ambiguous and problematic; they rely on professionals and an indeterminate technology in which staff-client relationships are the core; and they lack valid measures of effectiveness.[6] As organizations, they are said to be resistant to change and innovation, and even supporters such as Stuart Langton (1981) join in this somewhat bleak assessment by pointing to such ''typical undesir-

4. In the few instances that local social service networks have been studied, voluntary organizations tend to be regarded as peripheral, mainly because of the low volume of their services compared to the clientele of public agencies. See, for example, Galaskiewicz (1979), Knoke and Wood (1981), and Knoke and Rogers (1979).

5. Among some notable exceptions are Sills (1957), Holleb and Abrams (1975), Zald (1970), Young and Finch (1977), Scott (1981), and Kramer (1981). In a class by itself is an extensive ecological study over an eleven-year period of a population of four hundred voluntary organizations in Toronto by Tucker (1983).

6. This use of the umbrella term *human service organization* is strongly criticized as confusing and misleading by Stein (1982). Austin (1981), however, has attempted to develop a theoretically grounded taxonomy of human service organizations on the basis that it is not the absence of profit that distinguishes these social benefit organizations; rather, the public goods character of their outputs explains differences in the pattern of organizational performance and their relationship to their environment.

TABLE 14.1 SOME FORMAL DIFFERENCES AMONG GOVERNMENTAL, VOLUNTARY, AND FOR-PROFIT SOCIAL AGENCIES

	Governmental Agency	Voluntary Agency	Profit-Making Agency
Philosophy	Justice	Charity	Profit
Represents	Majority	Minority	Owners and managers
Legal basis of service	Right	Gratuity	Fee for service
Source of funds	Taxes	Contributions, fees, payments, and grants	Payments from customers or third parties
Determination of function	Prescribed by law	Selected by governing group	Chosen by owners/managers
Source of policy-making authority	Legislative body	Charter and bylaws authorizing board of directors	Owners or corporate board of directors
Accountability	To the electorate via a legislative body	To constituency via board of directors	To owners
Scope	Comprehensive	Limited	Limited to those who can pay
Administrative structure	Large, bureaucratic	Small, bureaucratic	Bureaucratic; may be a franchise operation or part of a national company
Administrative pattern of service	Uniform	Variable	Variable
Organization and program size	Large	Small	Medium to small

able tendencies in voluntary organizations as excessive bureaucratization, insufficient financing, wasteful, excessively narrow issue advocacy, insufficient opportunities for participation in decision making, ineffective accountability, increasing centralization, inadequate long-range planning, rigid allocational patterns and marginal utility.'' At best, these sweeping criticisms should be considered hypotheses to be tested, along with other similar but more laudatory generalizations such as the belief that ''private agencies may be able to generate efficiently and intelligently within their spheres, may be more sensitive to small-scale problems than government'' (Filer . . . 1975, 44).

Some of the formal differences among governmental, voluntary, and profit-making agencies are summarized in table 14.1.

This chapter will review what is known about selective aspects of the organizational character of voluntary agencies, drawing on the rather sparse research findings on their size and structure, governance, fiscal resources, and service delivery systems. The service provision function is first analyzed in terms of the increasing dependency on public funds and their impact on voluntary agency autonomy and future growth. A classification of interorganizational relationships between government and its social service providers leads to a suggested reformulation of the traditional roles ascribed to voluntary agencies and to a brief examination of some of the complexities in identifying their distinctive competence at a time when sectoral differences are increasingly blurred. This raises some serious questions about the significance of organizational auspices for service delivery and, in particular, the arguments for privatization and for the empowerment of nongovernmental organizations. Not unexpectedly, the chapter concludes with some suggestions for future research on these issues.

SIZE AND STRUCTURE

Because of the differences in their mandate and resources, size may be one of the critical ways in which voluntary agencies differ from governmental organizations.

Most of the estimated forty-one thousand voluntary agencies in the United States are considered small with respect to the size of their budgets and number of staff or clients served. In a 1982 national study of thirty-four hundred nonprofit social service and other agencies, 75 percent had annual budgets under $500,000, including 40 percent whose expenditures were less than $100,000. Over three-fourths of the expenditures were made by 15 percent of the larger agencies with budgets of a $1 million or more each. These large agencies were also older and more established than the others, two-thirds of which were founded during the 1960s, relying heavily on the increased availability of federal funding (Urban Institute 1983, 3–4).

Size by itself does not tell the whole story because the scope and type of an organization's influence depends on its purposes and the extent to which it emphasizes direct services or advocacy, public information or research; on whether it relies mainly on paid professional staff or volunteers; and on the number and types of other organizations concerned with its clientele. Nor is the amount of funds raised a clear indication of the relative incidence or seriousness of a problem condition addressed by an agency. Indeed, because of the comparatively open charity market in which voluntary agencies operate, the relationship is often an inverse one, with an organization's fund-raising capacity the most important determinant of its service programs. Typically, an agency serving a community's blind citizens has a budgeted income twelve times that of a multiple sclerosis society that serves about three times as many clients.

Related to the size of voluntary organizations is their characteristic structure. Although usually loose and informal in their early formative stages, particularly those described as alternative or community-based organizations (Glasscote et al. 1975; Clark & Jaffe 1975), most voluntary agencies become more bureaucratic and professionalized over time in their struggle for identity and a domain (Grønbjerg 1982). As they move through a rather predictable series of phases, they develop a hierarchical pattern of authority, including a division of responsibility and work rules based on policies adopted by the board. Presumably they are subject too to characteristic bureaucratic pressures toward ritualism, conformity, and insularity (Perlmutter 1969; Rosengren 1970; Holleb & Abrams 1975).

The structure of a voluntary agency is also affected by its fiscal environment (Pfeffer & Salancik 1978). To obtain allocations from a United Way or other centralized funding body in government, agencies must comply with various requirements and report regularly on their services and finances; in the process, they inevitably become more formalized (Milofsky 1980). For small agencies, this is often difficult and expensive, necessitating a trade-off between informality in service delivery and administration and more stable funding. Perrow (1972, 6) has suggested that many organizations are much too small and insufficiently formalized and professionalized to provide minimum levels of service, and that this is as much an organizational sin as bureaupathology. Marginal size may explain some of the frequent complaints about the prevalence of inefficient management as well as fragmentation in the voluntary sector. Small size may also account for the flexibility usually attributed to voluntary agencies, but at the same time, this advantage may be offset by their greater fiscal dependency and difficulties in complying with accountability requirements. Large or small, however, most voluntary agencies are unusually dependent on the quality of their executive leadership and, therefore, more subject to idiosyncratic rather than structural factors. The importance of the individual personality and intangible incentives for participation and support is suggested in the observation that "a non-pecuniary organization must tolerate a great deal of foolishness if it is to survive" (Wilson 1966, 209–10).

Despite their relatively small size, most voluntary agencies have been described as miniconglomerates, because they sponsor many different programs such as counseling, day care, family life education, information and referral, advocacy, and so on. The larger and more complex they become, the less distinguishable they are from their governmental or profit-making counterparts. Actually, during the last twenty years, public fiscal policies in making funds available to nongovernmental organizations have contributed to the blurring of differences among social service agencies, and they have all become more entrepreneurial, political, bureaucratic, and professional (Reichert 1977, 1982; Grønbjerg 1982).

Although different types of professionals can be found in the technostructure of voluntary agencies, a special historical linkage exists with social work, the dominant profession in the social services (Lubove 1965). There has been considerable movement back and forth between employment in governmental and voluntary agencies by social workers, in addition to burgeoning private practices, but many prefer to work in voluntary agencies presumably because of the greater possibilities for professional autonomy and more collegial forms of administration (Kahle 1969; Finch 1978). Because of agencies' smaller size and less hierarchical structures, there is probably less conflict between professional and bu-

reaucratic norms in voluntary as compared to governmental agencies (Rothman 1974; Reisch & Wenocur 1982).

GOVERNANCE

While the organizational structure of the voluntary agency expresses its bureaucratic character, its pattern of governance indicates its roots as a voluntary association. The distinctive hybrid nature of the voluntary agency as a blend of lay control and professional direction has the customary advantages and disadvantages of other citizen-sponsored organizations governed by democratic norms (Sills 1968, 368–69; Zald 1969).

Authority ultimately resides in the board of directors, but there is a dual system of authority in service delivery that defines the relationship between higher and lower participants in the agency's professional and staff structure. Unique in voluntary agencies is a system of parallel governance establishing both lay volunteer and professional authority, each with its own functions, values, and interests, but still interdependent (Slavin 1978, 111). There are, therefore, built-in possibilities for role strain and conflict between laypersons and professionals, and particularly between the board and the executive, that have received relatively little attention (Kramer 1983).

Although traditionally referred to as a partnership, the ubiquitous relationship between the board and the executive is more complex and fluid, reflecting significant differences in their statuses, norms, roles, authority, responsibilities, and, ultimately, power. (See table 14.2 comparing board members and executives on these and other attributes.) Attempts to delineate a suitable division of responsibility between the board and the executive by distinguishing between policy and administration have not been successful because they two share various aspects of the policy-making process.[7] The executive can define issues as professional or clinical and thus remove them from the jurisdiction of the board, or when only the board can adopt policy, he can influence the decision-making process by his control over virtually all information provided to the board. Also, the executive and staff—since they are responsible for implementation—can substantially modify the policy goals adopted by the board (Stein 1961; Brager & Specht 1973).

Some empirical support for the belief in the dominant role of the executive was found in one of the few surveys of boards of directors of nonprofit organizations; it reported that "many trustees ignore the task of discussing policy and accept the de facto decisions of the executive director, though such neglect and acceptance seems to vary with the size of the organization" (Unterman & Davis 1982, 36). Other factors that may tilt the balance of power in favor of the

---

7. Kouzos and Mico (1979) distinguish among the policy, management, and service domains in a human service organization and ascribe many of its dysfunctional aspects to the differences in the respective structures, measures of success, principles and modes of work of the three domains.

TABLE 14.2 COMPARISON OF BOARD MEMBERS AND EXECUTIVES ON SIX ATTRIBUTES

	Board of Directors	Executive
Social status	Volunteer Trustee Employer Community notable	Professional/expert Full-time employee Director of social agency
Behavioral norms	Altruism, best interests of community Proscription of self-dealing and conflicts of interests Collaborative partnership with executive and stewardship Participation in and support of the agency	Ethical, professional performance Subordination of personal interests to those of the agency and the decisions of the board Helping relationship to board members, including leadership development
Roles	Policymaker/trustee Employer Interpreter, supporter, advocate	Multiple and diverse: enabler, guide, manager, educator, expert, etc.
Responsibility For:	Governance: policy-making/adoption Resource acquisition, allocation, control Appointment of executive, adoption of personnel policies Community relations	Implementation of policy via administration of program Appointment, supervision of staff Assisting the board, liaison between it and the staff
To:	Community (membership, contributors, constituencies), clientele	Board of directors, clientele, staff, community, professional interests
Types of authority	Legal (formal/official) right as trustees to govern, receive and allocate funds Hierarchical—over executive	Professional expertise Hierarchical—delegated by board to implement policy (administer program), employ, supervise, evaluate staff
Power (resources for influence)	Status, authority as a corporate trustee Prestige as community notable Legitimation of organization Access to resources Personal knowledge, skill, time, energy Duration of service, intensity of commitment	Status as professional with expertise Administrative authority and responsibilities Full-time commitment; duration, continuity of service Access to organizational information Informal relationships with key persons

executive relate to the type of organization, situation, and issue, as well as certain personal attributes of the board members. (See table 14.3 on the conditions conducive to greater power for the executive.)

The celebration of voluntary organizations as an important democratizing force has also been called into question by the composition and the decision-making processes of their governing bodies and the prevalence of minority rule (Sills 1968, 368). Although the typical board of directors consists of twenty-five to forty members, policy-making tends to be concentrated in a small number of self-perpetuating board members—disproportionately self-selected white males

from the corporate business and professional community (Provan 1980). Because of these characteristics, voluntary agencies have been described as ''private governments'' subject to the ''iron law of oligarchy,'' which is inconsistent with their espousal of democratic citizen participation. Some sociologists, such as Perrow (1970, 114–15), have claimed, however, that whether voluntary agencies are internally democratic is less significant than their advocacy role in representing the special interests of diverse groups in the community. In this view, voluntary agencies should be judged not by the norms of internal democracy but by their contribution to pluralism as expressed through advocacy for

TABLE 14.3 CONDITIONS CONDUCIVE TO GREATER POWER FOR THE EXECUTIVE THAN THE BOARD

Organization	Board Members	Situation	Issue
Large size Complexity Bureaucratization Decentralization Professionalization Technical knowledge base Many small donors Reliance on governmental funds	Large number High turnover Infrequent meetings Little service utilization/benefit Multiple community loyalties Shared welfare ideology Relatively low knowledge, experience, status, prestige, and access to resources Weak agency identification Low degree of financial support	Severe time constraints Routine, absence of crisis	Substantively clinical, technical, professional, or interorganizational Less tangible, nonfiscal, or community related Non-precedent setting, less policy Low salience Noncontroversial Programmatic

and service to their client constituencies. Although this argument may have some merit, the costs of minority rule may outweigh or even cancel the contribution to pluralism. For example, the lack of turnover within a leadership group can result in serious problems of succession, organizational unresponsiveness, an excessively narrow focus of interest, inflexibility, and resistance to change, thus vitiating most of the ostensible virtues of a voluntary agency.

Others, such as Douglas (1983), have even questioned the desirability and the feasibility of voluntary organizations striving to be ''representative'' by including many different interests and groups in the community. Representativeness, they assert, is a political value, and the voluntary agency can never hope to compete with government in its capacity to reflect the interests of the various publics within the electorate. The virtue of the voluntary agency lies instead in its *particularism*, in its concern with such specialized interests as the handicapped, and in its contribution to pluralism by being a minority rather than a majority agency.[8] In contrast to the political process or profit incentive, the decision-making power to determine the goals and service pattern in a voluntary agency is substantially influenced by the values and interests of the board and professional staff and, to a lesser extent, by its funding sources (James 1983).

The scope of a voluntary agency, then, must inevitably be limited; nevertheless it still must depend on various forms of support from a variety of interests in the community if it is to obtain legitimation, goodwill, and credibility, as well as clientele and other required resources. Consequently, organizational maintenance may be more compelling than ideology as an incentive for voluntary agencies to seek a broader base of participation in their governance—which would, for example, include more consumers.

PUBLIC FISCAL POLICIES

As Geoffrey Vickers has suggested, the source of resources determines the types of and standards for success and failure, the character of decision making, accountability, and the external relations of an organization. Typically, voluntary agencies have relied on a wide range of funding sources, with contributions, including endowments and bequests, their traditional primary sources of income. Beginning in the 1960s, however, a decline in real giving and an increase in operating costs, aggravated by an inflationary spiral, coincided with a greater availability of public funds for purchase of services. The takeoff period for voluntary agency vendorism began with the 1967 amendments to the Social Security Act, which

8. Although there is much variation among voluntary agencies, perhaps as much or more as between them and government, the latter is obligated to serve on a universalistic basis, whereas voluntary agencies are inherently more particularistic because they can choose whom they wish to serve (Newman & Wallender 1978; Rainey et al. 1976). Yet in a study of 675 social agencies in Wisconsin, both governmental and voluntary agencies were found in virtually all fields of service, except those concerned with financial support and social control functions where only governmental agencies prevailed (Sosin 1982).

provided matching grants whereby the value of contributed funds was tripled. This was in sharp contrast to the practice from 1930 to 1967 when public programs were almost invariably implemented by governmental agencies, although there was always a modest use of voluntary agencies (Wickenden 1976). Beginning in 1967, the United Way abandoned its long-standing ideological opposition to the use of governmental funds and encouraged its member agencies to seek such income, but to preserve their autonomy while collaborating in public-private ventures. Since then, United Way allocations as a percentage of member-agency budgeted income have declined from 42 percent in 1968 to a national average of 15 percent in 1980, and the average received from all governmental funds rose to over 40 percent. Income from government funds varies greatly according to the type of agency, as can be seen in table 14.4.

The rapid expansion of the social services since 1967, the progressive loss of confidence in governmental capacity for implementation, and the preferences for nongovernmental agencies have produced new kinds of providers and a much more complex social service network in most communities. Public policies favoring deinstitutionalization have also encouraged the emergence of new types of nonprofit organizations, which are distinguished by the degree to which they rely on public funds and involve consumers in their policymaking. Alternative agencies—such as crisis centers, free clinics, hot lines, other community-based quasi-nongovernmental organizations like community mental health centers, and peer self-help groups—have proliferated. Many voluntary agencies have become vendors—that is, private public-service providers or public agents (Rice 1975; Hill 1971; Wedel 1980).

TABLE 14.4   GOVERNMENT FUNDS AS A SHARE OF TOTAL INCOME FOR SELECTED UNITED WAY AGENCIES, 1980

Type of Agency	Percent of Total Income from Government
Legal aid	84%
Aging	73
Drug abuse	72
Child welfare	72
Retarded citizens	66
Mental health	65
Home health	62
Women's crises	60
Alcoholism	59
Planned Parenthood	55
Catholic Charities	46
Family Service	45
Cripped children/adults	36
Cancer	29
YWCA	22
Salvation Army	17
Travelers Aid	13
Catholic Youth organizations	13
Boys' Clubs	10
Jewish community centers	7
YMCA	7

Source: United Way Allocations 1981, 65–74.

The next stage of development occurred in 1974, almost coincidental with the downward trend in the economy, which until then had supported a continually expanding social welfare system. Title XX of the Social Security Act in 1974 broadened the boundaries of eligibility for the personal social services and made it possible for state and local governments to purchase more tangible services for a larger number of middle-class clients traditionally served by voluntary agencies (Derthick 1975). As a result, there was an enormous increase in purchase-of-service arrangements, so that they approximated over two-thirds of the total expenditures under Title XX. Revenue from governmental sources rose to constitute approximately 40 percent of the income of voluntary agencies, although this varies greatly by fields of service and by states. For example, over 70 percent of the income of agencies in the field of child welfare, aging, and drug abuse is derived from government (U.S. Dept. of HEW 1978). Reliance on nonprofit agencies has also led to governmental demands for greater efficiency, accountability, and services integration, but these have met with an indifferent response.

Thus, many voluntary agencies have been able to more than compensate for the decline in contributions and have continued to expand their programs through a process that has been called "private federalism" (C. Gilbert 1975) or "third-party government" (Salamon 1981). It is estimated that in 1980 $6.5 billion in federal funds were channeled to the nonprofit providers of social services, which represented about a third more than the total of all private contributions to these organizations (Urban Institute 1983). Nationally, *governmental support has become a more important source of revenue in the social services than all private giving combined*. It is ironic that a national coalition of voluntary nonprofit organizations chose as its name the Independent Sector at a time when its constituents had become more dependent than ever on governmental support.

Why are voluntary agencies used by government to carry out a public purpose? When asked, governmental officials are likely to cite such "good" reasons as lesser cost, greater flexibility in starting and terminating services, and the ability to bypass bureaucratic constraints and serve hard-to-reach groups. Yet these same qualities of voluntary agencies are perceived as the source of their major disadvantages as a public agent: their lack of accountability, their inadequate management, and their readiness to use political influence (Kramer & Terrell 1984).

Insofar as it can be determined, the reliance on voluntary agencies is due less to a rational assessment of advantages and disadvantages of their distinctive competence than to the fact that it is a pragmatic expedient. If a voluntary agency in the community is interested in providing services that the government requires for its clientele at a reasonable cost, then it is likely that purchase-of-service arrangements will be made (Gibelman & Demone 1983). Local precedent is reinforced by the historical American practice of using nongovernmental organizations to deliver public services, more recently referred to as "public/private partnerships" in which there is mutual benefit and an exchange of resources.

This policy is supported by a "reluctant welfare state"—social services are wanted, but it is preferred that nongovernmental organizations deliver them.

Despite the importance of governmental purchase of social services, few empirical studies of the practice have been conducted, and much of the literature is impressionistic. For example, it is widely held that among the dysfunctional consequences of agencies receiving public funds are dependency, cooptation and a dilution of advocacy and autonomy, goal deflection and loss of an agency's voluntaristic character through increased bureaucratization and professionalization (Beck 1970; Manser 1974). Evidence collected during the last decade in independent studies in the United States, Canada, Australia, United Kingdom, Israel, and the Netherlands suggests, however, that these dangers are considerably exaggerated and that the impact of governmental funds in controlling voluntary organizations is much less than is commonly believed (Kramer 1981, 160–64; Carter 1974; Salamon 1983). A study of the Greater New York United Way in 1978 also found little data to support the belief that governmental funding had reduced agency autonomy. On the contrary, most agencies reported that governmental funding enabled them to carry out their existing programs more effectively by replacing previously lost resources (Hartogs & Weber 1978, 8–9). During the period of the greatest expansion of governmental funding that began in the 1960s, the number of voluntary organizations increased enormously, and many new alternative agencies and self-help groups were enabled to provide social services to previously underserved groups (Grossman & Morgenbesser 1980).

Similarly, an Urban Institute national survey in 1982 of 3,411 nonprofit organizations, approximately two-thirds of which were social service agencies in twelve metropolitan and four rural areas, turned up little evidence of agency concern that government had distorted their mission. Findings from an extensive survey of voluntary organizations in Australia and a more limited one in England also failed to show that either the independence or the basic purposes of the voluntary organization had been significantly altered as a consequence of governmental funding, nor was advocacy constrained (Graycar 1982; Judge 1981; Wolfenden Committee 1978, 18).

What might explain this conclusion that seems so contrary to the conventional wisdom that he who pays the piper calls the tune? Among the external factors that appear to reduce the constraining effects of public funds on agency autonomy are the following: the payment-for-service form of most transactions, which involves less control than grants or subsidies; the diversity of voluntary agency income sources, which lessens dependency on any one; the countervailing power of a voluntary agency oligopsony (few sellers) of a service required by a governmental agency for its clients; political influence of the voluntary agency; and the lack of incentives and capacity for stricter accountability by government (Kramer 1981, 160–64). Other conditions limiting governmental control over its agents or vendors are the fragmented structure of the social services, which makes

close supervision exceedingly costly, and the inherent difficulties of evaluating the outcomes of the social services.

The conventional dualism between organizational autonomy and accountability may therefore be more artificial than
real; there may be less of a strain between them because a
strong, independent agency can be more accountable when
government can pinpoint responsibility. Furthermore, accountability requirements that emphasize performance
monitoring and evaluation can be beneficial to a voluntary
agency that seeks to improve its efficiency and the effectiveness of its service programs. Of course, services vary greatly
in the degree to which performance criteria and outcomes can
be specified. For example, it makes a difference whether the
voluntary agency service purchased by government involves
meals, medical or nursing care, day treatment, residential or
foster care, education or training, community organization or
counseling. Perhaps the issue can be rephrased: it may be a
matter not so much of how to preserve voluntary agency
freedom as how to make public-service providers more accountable without restricting the very qualities of flexibility
and individualization that make them desirable in the first
place.

These considerations should not minimize the serious
problems connected with the use of public funds, such as
excessive and conflicting reporting requirements or cash flow
delays, so that agencies have to use their own resources to
cover deficits or nonrecoverable or unexpected costs (Young
& Finch 1977; Wedel, Katz, & Weick 1979; Gibelman &
Demone 1983). In addition to these risks and uncertainties, a
voluntary agency faces other fiscal dilemmas when it functions as vendor. If it does not receive full reimbursement,
then it must make up the deficit, which in one large-scale
study in New York City averaged almost 18 percent of the
provider's budget (Hartogs & Weber 1978, 51). If an agency
does charge the full cost, then the rate of reimbursement may
be sufficient to attract competing profit-making organizations. Finally, unless there is some cost advantage, the governmental agency may not be interested in contracting out the
service. Because there are good prospects for the continuance if not an increase in purchase-of-service contracting,
government will have to increase its capacity for more effective contract management in order to improve its specification of what is desired and its accountability requirements.
Voluntary agencies, on the other hand, will have to strive for
greater efficiency in service delivery and improved managerial capabilities, and they will have to accept a greater
measure of paperwork, more citizen participation, and some
program restrictions when they become private public-service providers (Kramer & Terrell 1984). In short, they will
have to become more democratic, rational, and accountable
when they serve as public agents.

The fiscal environment of the voluntary agency has
changed rapidly; it will become one of greater austerity or at
least slowed growth because of planned reductions in public
spending for the social services during the 1980s. Earlier
studies in California and Massachusetts revealed that voluntary agencies were among the first to feel the impact of

cutbacks when local governmental revenues were reduced
after tax limitation measures had been adopted (Terrell 1981;
Demone & Gibelman 1984). National data on the effects of
cuts in the federal budget indicated that during 1980–82 almost two-thirds of the social service agencies surveyed sustained losses in their income from governmental sources,
although the size of these reductions was not specified (Urban Institute 1983). These losses occurred against a background of increased demands for services resulting from
economic conditions and governmental cutbacks in income
maintenance, food stamps, medical care, legal assistance,
employment training, and so on.

To cope, voluntary agencies reported reducing or curtailing services, using volunteers more often, increasing their
fees and/or staff workloads, reorganizing their management
systems, and securing alternative funds from governmental
grants, corporations, or foundations. Despite the erosion of
some of their resource base through the decline in public
funding, about half of the agencies expected to increase their
income and most are surprisingly optimistic about the future
(Urban Institute 1983). The extent to which optimism is
warranted is related to the differential capacity of voluntary
agencies to replace reduced governmental funding by greater
reliance on internally generated sources of revenue and/or to
manage their diminished resources more efficiently.[9] Then,
too, agencies differ greatly in the proportion of their budget
obtained from government, as well as in the priority they
attach to services that have been supported by public funds.

In any case, public fiscal policies have generated a more
uncertain and competitive environment for all social service
providers regarding their future funding and clientele. Under
these circumstances, it would be useful to have more information about the factors influencing the differential capacity
of voluntary agencies to adapt to retrenchment in governmental spending. More studies are needed, too, of fiscal,
administrative, and other technical aspects of service delivery when voluntary agencies are used by government to
provide a public good.

SERVICE DELIVERY ISSUES

As noted earlier, until the 1930s, the voluntary organizations
was the chief form of collective action for social service
delivery outside of government. But public provision has
advanced so rapidly that now voluntary organizations are
usually perceived as a way of extending, complementing, or
substituting for government. Obsolete metaphors—such as
the theories of "parallel bars" or "extension ladders" that
originated in the nineteenth century—have been succeeded
by equally inappropriate and simplistic notions of "partnership," a term that not only masks the actual power relationships between governments and voluntary organizations

9. There is a growing literature on the business activities of nonprofit organizations as a source of operating income and as capital for
future growth (Mier & Wiewel 1983; James 1983; Skloot 1983; Young
1983).

but also tends to obscure the existence of other social service providers in the market and in the informal sector (Kamerman 1983).

A more valid model of interorganizational functional relationships is one of coexisting systems occasionally collaborating and exchanging resources, infrequently competing or in conflict, and involving one of four types of service relationships depending on the level of public provision: (1) the voluntary agency is the only or *primary* provider because there are few if any governmental counterparts (for example, a hospice); (2) it *complements* governmental provision with services that are qualitatively different in kind (sheltered workshops); (3) it *supplements* or extends the governmental system with similar services some of which may offer an alternative choice; or (4) it serves as a *substitute* for governmental provision (homemakers, day care, counseling). Substitution occurs either when the voluntary agency is a public agent delivering a service that has been purchased by government for its clientele or when it is filling a service gap on its own, compensating for the failure of government to provide the service adequately or at all (see table 14.5).

The latter role has been criticized on the grounds that it can deter extending governmental services to all who are entitled to them, or that it can perpetuate second-rate governmental services, when, for example, a voluntary agency over a period of time develops a vested interest in a program and finds it difficult to give it up if this becomes an option. Furthermore, compensating for a deficiency in a governmental service is a rather weak rationale for a voluntary agency if it seeks to define a distinctive function for itself.

Role Reformulation

In the past this strategy was sometimes justified as part of the *vanguard,* or service pioneer role—the function of a voluntary agency was to develop new services, paving the way for their adoption by governmental bodies. Although this mystique still persists, there is little support for the belief that the voluntary agency is one of the primary sources of innovation for government (Schorr 1970). For example, in a study of twenty voluntary agencies in the San Francisco Bay area during the 1970s, only 5 percent of the new voluntary agency programs were adopted by a governmental agency over a ten-year period; the rest were continued by the original sponsor,

most often with public funds providing support. Similar outcomes have been found on the few occasions in other countries when this has been studied. Among the constraints on the transfer to or adoption by government of new programs started by voluntary agencies are their inappropriate size; unacceptable values (for example, they may be too controversial); low priority in the governmental domain; or lack of administrative, fiscal, or political feasibility (Kramer 1981, 183–86). These factors were operative long before the retrenchment in governmental spending for the social services; consequently, the future adoption by government of new programs developed in the voluntary sector would seem to be even less likely now.

Further analysis of what is often regarded as innovative by voluntary agencies reveals that many programs are essentially small-scale, noncontroversial, incremental improvements or extensions of conventional programs with relatively few original features. This is not to deny the development by some voluntary agencies, usually early in their histories, of numerous changes in dealing with such groups as rape victims, battered wives, the frail elderly, drug addicts, and other previously neglected clients. The identification of these neglected and underserved groups at the boundaries of governmental welfare programs has come usually from newer, more indigenous, less bureaucratized and professionalized organizations, which are frequently regarded as demonstrating the cutting edge of voluntarism (Glasscote et al. 1975). If it is true that voluntary agencies are more likely to be trailblazers in their early stages, then their high birthrate, more than their proverbial low mortality, helps ensure change in the social services. Paradoxically, the often criticized proliferation of voluntary agencies may express a resurgent vitality and constitute one of the prerequisites for the performance of the vanguard role.

But perhaps the types of innovation produced at the inception of a voluntary agency are different from those that are likely to occur when they are institutionalized. It might be hypothesized that the discovery of previously underserved persons, as well as those requiring more specialized care, would be expected to occur more often among small voluntary agencies at an early stage of development. In the older, more established agencies, other forces inherent in the rationality of bureaucratic structure, the professional interests of the staff in improving and extending their skill, and the

TABLE 14.5   THREE TYPES OF SERVICE PROVISION RELATIONSHIPS

	Voluntary Services as Supplementary	Voluntary Services as Complementary	Voluntary Services as Primary
Basic character of voluntary service	Extension of similar governmental service	Qualitatively different from governmental service	No governmental counterpart of voluntary service provision
Power relationship	Asymmetrical; unequal power because one element (government) is basic or dominant	Symmetrical power relationship between voluntary and governmental organizations	Asymmetrical; voluntary agency is dominant
Duration of service	Ostensibly time limited, until governmental provision	Long term because governmental provision is unlikely	Uncertain; continues as long as there is no governmental provision

maintenance needs of the organization are more conducive to the development of new programs that extend and improve existing services. This may help explain the fact that generally the large, more bureaucratized and professionalized voluntary agencies have been found to be the leading initiators of new programs, as well as the most active advocates, promoters of voluntarism, and users of public funds (Kramer 1981, 257). This finding is in accord with Wilson's observations that "organizations that rely primarily on intangible incentives (as do voluntary associations) will display in an exaggerated form the contrary tendencies that determine the innovative capacity of other organizations" (1966, 210).

This suggests that the emphasis on innovation as a distinctive feature of voluntary organizations may be somewhat displaced, and that the vanguard role and some of the other traditional functions could be reformulated more realistically. For example, apart from its lack of conceptual clarity, innovation can be more appropriately conceived as one of several possible outcomes of a program change and not as a basic property of a voluntary agency (see figure 14.1). Because innovation can be promoted by government either directly or through funding, *specialization* in a particular problem or age group rather than pioneering or experimentation is a more reasonable expectation for a voluntary agency. As Lord Beveridge put it, "The philanthropic motive is in practice a specialist motive; it drives men to combat a par-

ticular evil, to meet a particular need that arouses their interests" (1948, 26).

As interest groups, voluntary agencies are intrinsically particularistic and selective in contrast to the more universal and comprehensive scope of governmental agencies. Although, in general, voluntary agencies are centrifugal (separating out), and governmental organizations are centripetal (consolidating), there are important departures from these designations. For example, the principle of universalism is compromised by the enormous variation in type and quality of public services that reflects variations in local eligibility and staffing.

The specific problem areas or population groups selected by a voluntary agency serve as a basis for their service delivery and community support through their individualization of groups that are overlooked or that may have a low priority for government or the market—for example, pregnant adolescent girls, immigrants, runaways, and battered women. Like a brand name, specialization contributes to the preservation of organizational identity and enables a voluntary agency to claim jurisdiction over a domain such as the mentally retarded, Catholic youth, or Jewish aged. Although a voluntary agency has no necessary monopoly, its specialized knowledge and experience are major sources of its legitimacy and credibility and are expressed in the structure of both service provision and advocacy. The particularism of

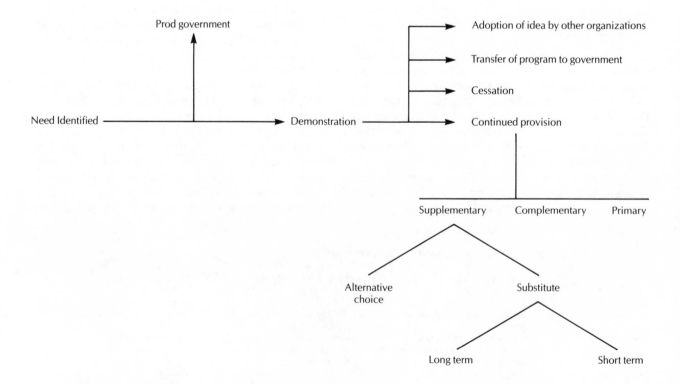

FIGURE 14.1. TYPOLOGY OF SERVICE PROVIDER ROLES

voluntary agencies is, at the same time, a source of the perennial criticism that they are overly specialized and excessively narrow in their focus in limiting services to victims of a particular disease or handicap or a specific problem or sectarian group.

Similarly, although voluntary organizations are the principal users of the time of unpaid *volunteers* in fund-raising, service giving, and policy-making, distinguishing them from profit-making and governmental organizations, this function, too, requires some qualification. Because relatively few nonprofit organizations involve volunteers in direct services and because various types of voluntarism can be promoted by government, *consumerism* more than voluntarism per se is a unique function that is not a substitute for or duplication of government. Consumerism refers to the involvement of clientele in policy-making in an organization designed for their welfare; it is expressed in its purest form in self-help or mutual aid associations. From this perspective, an organization is voluntaristic to the extent that it significantly involves the intended beneficiaries in decisions about goals and program policy, a practice not found among other governmental and profit-making social service providers. In addition to the promotion of citizen participation in their governance, voluntary agencies are also unique in the protection of other social, religious, cultural, and ethnic values through their service programs and advocacy.

The other major role, *advocacy,* has been called "the quintessential function of the voluntary sector" (O'Connell 1976). Historically, voluntary agencies have had the dual mission both of providing social services and engaging in social action—of "case and cause"—on behalf of their clientele. If neither governmental nor voluntary agencies have a monopoly on service innovation or the use of volunteers, then perhaps advocacy comes closest to being one of the few distinctive features of the voluntary agency (Filer . . . 1975, 45).

As organizational differences between governmental, voluntary, and profit-making social service organizations diminish because they are dependent on the same fiscal sources, policies, and regulatory environment, and as the social services in the welfare state become more universal, the historic mission of the voluntary agency to identify and articulate the interests of neglected and underserved groups in populations at risk takes on even greater importance. This does not imply an absence of concern for change among governmental or other interest groups, but rather, that advocacy is a more consistent and legitimate expectation of voluntary agencies.

Indeed, "change agentry" has even been proposed by Wolfensberger (1973) as the primary function for voluntary agencies servicing the mentally handicapped in welfare states with extensive programs of social services. This strategy is not feasible for ideological and practical reasons because most of the public support for voluntary agencies, and their influence, is derived from their legitimacy, credibility, and expertise as service providers and much less for their advocacy. Although exclusive concentration on advocacy,

for most agencies, may not be possible, there is justification for much greater stress on this function which is often more honored in principle than in practice.

Distinctive Competence

In one form of advocacy, however, the voluntary agency's claim to uniqueness, moral superiority, or altruism is somewhat questionable—that is, when advocacy is conducted on behalf not of the client directly but of agency interests. In these cases, the advocacy of voluntary agencies is not always distinguishable from the self-serving lobbying efforts of profit-making organizations who seek to influence legislation and regulations dealing with payment rates, definitions of eligibility, and other matters affecting them as contractors for the delivery of a public service. Under these conditions, the interests of the provider organization and those of the service beneficiaries for whom they purport to speak, such as preschool children, alcoholics, or refugees, are presumed to be the same. One major difference is that the board members of the voluntary agency, in contrast to the owners of a proprietary social service organization, do not derive any personal profit from their participation in its governance (Gelman 1983). This nondistributional constraint is regarded by Hansmann (1980) and others as a critical theoretical distinction between the two social service providers on the assumption that the absence of the profit motive inspires greater public "trustworthiness" in the character of the voluntary agency's services. It is believed that there will be less incentive to reduce quality or to sacrifice client interest for cost-cutting reasons. The nondistribution constraint[10] presumably affords an extra degree of protection of consumer interests under four conditions that often characterize the delivery of social services: (1) where there is a separation between consumer and purchaser of service as in third-party payments; (2) where the complexity or nonstandardized character of the service makes it difficult to compare and evaluate; and (3) where there is little choice either because the service involves the exercise of coercive power or (4) alternatives are not available (Gilbert 1983, 16).

Although the greater public accountability of nonprofit boards of directors and the superiority of the charitable ethos over the profit motive are widely assumed, some exceptions to these claims can be made. For example, voluntary organizations are equally concerned with breaking even and having secure financial conditions. Often what might be considered profit in a voluntary agency is also transformed not into program or improvements in services but into salaries and fringe benefits in such facilities as nursing homes, schools for

10. It is unclear how or why the nondistributional constraint operates in nonprofit organizations. What is it about their legal status that will result in greater concern for the protection of the client's interest? Is it the type of board members, executives, or staff who are self-selected and set higher standards for themselves and their services? Is it the linkage that voluntary agencies have had to government that gives them additional strength? Is it their philosophy, their norms, or their greater use of volunteers? See Douglas (1983) and Hansmann (1980).

the handicapped, sheltered workshops, and institutions for the blind and for juveniles (Gilbert 1983, 18). In many instances, the distinction between profit and nonprofit is more a matter of accounting definitions and practices to justify tax exemptions and contribution deductibility because, as one management consultant put it, ''nonprofits need surplus too in order to grow'' (Young 1983, 124). Also, it might be added, both types of social service providers have been accused of arbitrary selectivity—that is, of ''creaming'' whereby the most difficult and otherwise less desirable cases end up in governmental institutions and programs.

Although there have been attempts to identify social services as more appropriate for one or another auspice, few have succeeded in proposing criteria for a more coherent and consistent pattern. It may be that in many services the relative advantage of proprietary, governmental, or nonprofit sponsorship is marginal and only a few should be restricted to one or the other. Gilbert has suggested, for example, that the following conditions should make for a predisposition to nonprofit as against proprietary auspices: the extent to which the service is individualized or involves some degree of coercion, or is provided to clients who are vulnerable to exploitation owing to their diminished competence, such as children and mentally or emotionally handicapped persons (1983, 19–20).

Although such criteria seem cogent, Gilbert himself observes that many exceptions could be made in the personal social services including meals-on-wheels services, transportation services for the handicapped and elderly, telephone reassurance, and homemaker services, all of which could be standardized and made to conform to *either* proprietary or nonprofit auspices.

Further exceptions to these criteria are also found in a trend in the child welfare field, where in the course of the last decade there has been an almost fifteenfold increase in the share of purchase-of-service contracting by profit-making organizations: half or more of the contracts in residential treatment, institutional care, and group homes are now under proprietary auspices (Born 1983). It is ironic that these child welfare services conform so well to the conditions believed to be more conducive to nonprofits—they are nonstandardized, deal with a vulnerable population, and often involve some coercive authority.

Consequently, given the inherent diversity of nonprofit organizations as a class, one might be skeptical about discovering any overriding set of criteria or a theory that might explain or prescribe a more logical division of function. It may be, as is the case with hospitals and nursing homes, that legal status as a nonprofit organization is much less significant than other organizational variables, such as size, complexity, core technology, type of population and interorganizational relations, degree of professionalization and bureaucratization, and so on, as they affect cost, quality, effectiveness, and accountability. The task of studying these variables empirically, however, confronts many methodological obstacles in comparing profit and nonprofit organizations in the same field.[11] There are numerous technical difficulties both in defining operationally a set of indicators of the organizational variables and in controlling for the large number of relevant factors that affect performance. Agreeing on criteria for such qualities as trustworthiness, responsiveness, effectiveness, and innovation is exceptionally difficult when comparing organizations with characteristically ambiguous multiple goals and complex ill-understood technologies.

EMPOWERMENT AND VOLUNTARISM

Because the case for voluntarism has lacked empirical research, it is usually made on moral, ideological, and political grounds as is evident in virtually all the arguments for empowerment. Although greater use of profit-making organizations (privatization) is urged by conservatives (Drucker 1973; Savas 1982), a contrasting policy—empowerment, which also seeks to reduce the overload of government—is endorsed by both the Left and the Right (Janowitz 1976; Levitt 1973; Rich 1979). Empowerment places its faith in the nonprofit sector as a whole and encourages greater utilization by government of all mediating structures such as voluntary organizations, religious institutions, neighborhoods, and the more informal primary social systems. Two broad policy recommendations are made to ensure pluralism: public policy should protect and foster these mediating structures by not damaging them, and whenever possible, government should empower them with the resources for the realization of public purposes (Berger & Neuhaus 1977). Both in the United States and in Europe, advocates of empowerment are characteristically vague about funding sources, although it is usually implied that costs will be less (Hadley & Hatch 1981; Gladstone 1979).

Historically, we seem to have veered 180 degrees since the 1930s when government took over unemployment relief in the United States because voluntary organizations were no longer able to meet the demands; now there is a call for a greater use of the voluntary sector because government seems to have reached the limits of its capacity and legitimacy.

Supporters of empowerment, such as Kotler (1969), Glazer (1983), and Woodson (1981), tend, however, to lump together indiscriminately all forms of voluntarism and mediating structures and to regard them as equally desirable and effective in combating excessive governmental intervention. They overlook the considerable differences between the use of volunteers as unpaid staff and as peer self-help, among mutual aid, neighborhood, and community-based service organizations, among the diverse forms of citizen participation, and in the institutional structures of family and religion.

Sufficient attention has not been given to the great variation in the effectiveness of voluntary organizations as service

11. For an exception, see the pioneering study of Newton and Kagan (1983).

providers (Graycar 1983). Proponents of the voluntary sector, whether conservative, liberal, or radical, often fail to appreciate that its strengths are at the same time the source of its limitations: for example, where there is pluralism, fragmentation and duplication are the inevitable costs of particularism and individualization. Furthermore, whether based on locality, ethnicity, religion, or other sectarian interests, voluntary organizations as service providers are inherently narrow and exclusionary in their scope. Because the individual depends for social services on the initiative, resources, and capabilities of a particular group with which he is administratively identified, the substitution of voluntary for governmental agencies can result in even greater unevenness, inconsistency, and inequity in the distribution of social services.

Although evidence of their service delivery capability is rather sparse (Rich 1979), experience with various forms of decentralized neighborhood organizations and self-help associations suggests that they can become just as institutionalized, rigid, inaccessible, unresponsive, and undemocratic as professionalized service bureaucracies (Gilbert & Specht 1974, 174–77; O'Brien 1975; Furness 1974). For example, the use of small voluntary organizations, particularly alternative and more loosely organized ones in which advocacy, flexibility, responsiveness, and citizen involvement are sought, is often seriously compromised by the administrative demands of service delivery (Hartogs & Weber 1978). Although the use of contracts with a governmental body may be a highly desirable way of utilizing the resources of voluntary agencies to ensure accountability, formalization can vitiate the very qualities sought in alternative agencies or self-help groups in which responsibilities are more diffuse (Hartogs & Weber 1978). Often there is a choice between the haphazard performance and uncertain quality of a small-scale, voluntaristic, community-based program and that of a larger, more bureaucratic professional organization that may be able to provide better and more consistent services. This is part of the strain between pluralism-voluntarism and the desire for more comprehensive, cost-effective, and integrated social services. Still another consideration in the use of small, neighborhood-based, informal, consumer-oriented voluntary organizations is the possibility of their cooptation and subsequent decline as advocates because of the greater demands of service delivery.

Then there is also a romantic myth of a golden age of voluntarism in local communities in which neighbors helped one another. It is quite understandable in a shrinking economy that there would be a revival of interest in the use of volunteers as a substitute for paid staff. In California, supporters of reduced taxation fantasized about a wave of good neighborliness that would sweep the state in a collective volunteer effort to restore services lost as a result of tax and budget cuts. Not surprisingly, this did not occur, and experience showed that, when viewed as a cheap form of labor, paid or unpaid volunteers can exacerbate tensions among staff and between nongovernmental organizations and trade unions. They are no substitute for necessary services best delivered by professionals and other types of paid staff. Voluntarism is also no substitute for services that can best be delivered by government, particularly if coverage, equity, and entitlements are valued (Kamerman & Kahn 1976).

Beliefs about a golden age of voluntarism also underlay many proposals in the United States as well as those embodied in the 1982 Barclay Report in England, which advocated the provision of resources to informal networks of social relationships to deal with community care of the mentally ill, the infirm aged, physically and mentally handicapped persons, and so on. This recommendation was derided by Prof. Robert Pinker in his dissent from the Barclay Report as "a romantic illusion that we can miraculously revive the sleeping giants of populist altruism" (Barclay Report 1982, 244–45). Such substitutions of voluntary for governmental effort are subject to three sets of constraints: (1) the social networks may be nonexistent or unacceptable to the person in need of care, or the person may be unacceptable to the network (Segal 1979); (2) the available resources may not be adequate, or the informal relationships cannot be sustained with the required intensity, duration, and competence; and (3) such networks find it particularly difficult to be accountable for public funds and to perform a public function (White 1981, 30).

It is often forgotten that the present, more formalized modes of care and support developed because of the failure of local communities and the informal, more voluntaristic institutional systems to perform these functions.

CONCLUSIONS

All this suggests that thinking in terms of the traditional sectors may be less productive than asking some different questions. Apart from resting on a set of invidious organizational stereotypes and ignoring the blurring of sectoral boundaries, a focus on governmental versus voluntary versus profit-making auspices deflects attention from the major policy question of equity: *who* should get *what* services (Kamerman 1983)? This question takes on increasing urgency in view of the universalism manifested in the expansion of the welfare state into social services that are also available in the market, which in turn leads to a loosening of the boundaries between the social and economic markets.

Since we have little information about the differential impact of governmental, voluntary, or profit-making sponsorship on the quality, quantity, and effects on the clientele of a social service program, a less doctrinaire, more experimental and pluralistic approach would be more appropriate. One possibility is to design policies that might ensure a desired level of personal social services, using different funding devices and a variety of service providers, with the objective of optimizing such values as access, adequacy, accountability, cost efficiency, and effectiveness. In experimenting with different organizational mixes, we may learn more about the particular advantages and disadvantages of various types of providers of different types of personal social services.

Although the importance of organizational type may be less significant than is widely believed, nevertheless even distinctions that are blurred may still be meaningful. A concluding assessment of voluntary agencies should note their potential for particularism, the special advantage of their small size and scope as it contributes to their capacity for an individualized, flexible, and holistic approach, and their access to volunteers and contributors. They seem particularly suitable for clientele who have highly specialized needs or who are ineligible or unable to use governmental or proprietary services. At the same time, because of the inherent diversity and idiosyncratic character of voluntary agencies, public policies relying on them will be uneven in their impact.

In the light of these considerations, the following are some suggested items for a future research agenda:

1. Classifications and taxonomies of voluntary social service organizations and of their service programs.

2. Determination of the size and scope of the voluntary nonprofit social service sector in different fields of service.

3. The development of valid and reliable indicators for service delivery goals such as access, accountability, adequacy, continuity, choice, coherence, effectiveness, efficiency, and equity. If it proves feasible, comparative case studies in different fields of service could be made in which auspice would be one of the variables studied.

4. Case studies of different modes of funding between governmental and voluntary agencies, such as purchase of service agreements, grants, subsidies, and vouchers, and their impact on interorganizational relationships, on advocacy, and on clientele.

5. Studies of the costs and benefits of utilizing volunteers in direct services in agencies that employ professional social workers.

6. Studies of the governance patterns in different types of voluntary agencies with emphasis on the decision-making processes and the distribution of power among board, executive, and staff.

7. Studies of the influence of the type of problem condition, population at risk, and technology on the structure and function of voluntary agencies.

8. Longitudinal studies, using a life-cycle model, of the origin, growth and change—and possible decline—of voluntary agencies to learn how different types of agencies adapt to changing circumstances in their environment and to answer the question of why some organizations succeed better than others.

REFERENCES

Akubas, Sheila H., and Paul A. Kurzman, eds. 1982. *Work, Workers, and Work Organizations: A View from Social Work.* Englewood Cliffs, N.J.: Prentice-Hall.

Austin, D. M. 1981. "The Political Economy of Social Benefit Organizations: Redistributive Services and Merit Goods." In *Organization and the Human Services: Cross-Disciplinary Reflections,* edited by H. Stein, 37–88. Philadelphia: Temple University Press.

Barclay Report. 1982. "An Alternative View," by R. Pinker. In *Social Workers: Their Role and Tasks,* 236–62. London: Bedford Square Press.

Beck, Bertram M. 1970. "The Voluntary Social Welfare Agency: A Reassessment." *Social Service Review* 44:147–54.

Berger, Peter L., and Richard John Neuhaus. 1977. *To Empower People: The Role of Mediating Structures in Public Policy.* Washington, D.C.: American Enterprise Institute for Public Policy Research.

Beveridge, Lord William. 1948. *Voluntary Action: A Report on Methods of Social Advance.* London: George Allen & Unwin.

Boorstin, D. J. 1965. *The Americans: The National Experience.* New York: Vintage Books.

Born, Catherine E. 1983. "Proprietary Firms and Child Welfare Services: Patterns and Implications." *Child Welfare* 62, no. 2:109–18.

Brager, George, and Harry Specht. 1973. *Community Organizing.* New York: Columbia University Press.

Carter, N. 1974. *Trends in Voluntary Support for Non-Governmental Social Service Agencies.* Ottowa, Ontario: Canadian Council on Social Development.

Clark, T., and D. Jaffe. 1975. *Number Nine: Autobiography of an Alternative Counseling Service.* New York: Harper & Row.

Cohen, N. E. 1958. *Social Work in the American Tradition.* New York: Dryden Press.

Davis, A. F. 1967. *Spearheads for Reform: The Social Settlements and the Progressive Movement 1890–1914.* New York: Oxford University Press.

Demone, H. W., Jr., and M. Gibelman. 1984. "Reaganomics: The Impact on the Voluntary Not-for-Profit Sector." *Social Work* 29:5.

Derthick, M. 1975. *Uncontrollable Spending for Social Service Grants.* Washington, D.C.: Brookings Institute.

Douglas, J. 1983. *Why Charity?* Beverly Hills, Calif.: Sage Publications.

Drucker, Peter F. 1973. "On Managing the Public Service Institution." *Public Interest* 33:43–60.

Filer Commission on Private Philanthropy and Public Needs. 1975. *Giving in America: Toward a Stronger Voluntary Sector.* Washington, D.C.: Filer Commission.

Finch, W. 1978. "Administrative Priorities: The Impact of Employee Perception on Agency Functioning and Worker Satisfaction." *Administration in Social Work* 2, no. 4:391–400.

Furness, N. 1974. "The Practical Significance of Decentralization." *Journal of Politics* 36:958–82.

Galaskiewicz, J. 1979. *Exchange Networks and Community Politics.* Beverly Hills, Calif.: Sage Publications.

Gelman, S. R. 1983. "The Board of Directors and Agency Accountability." *Journal of Social Casework* 64, no. 2:83–91.

Gibelman, M., and H. W. Demone, Jr. 1983. "Purchase of Service: Forging Public-Private Partnership in the Human Services." *Urban and Social Change Review* 16, no. 1 (Winter):21–26.

Gilbert, C. 1975. "Welfare Policies." In *Policies and Policy Making: Handbook of Political Science* 6, edited by F. Greenstein and N. Polsby, 111–240. Reading, Mass.: Addison-Wesley.

Gilbert, Neil. 1983. *Capitalism and the Welfare State.* New Haven: Yale University Press.

Gilbert, Neil, and Harry Specht. 1974. *Dimensions of Social Welfare Policy.* Englewood Cliffs, N.J.: Prentice-Hall.

Gladstone, F. J. 1979. *Voluntary Action in a Changing World.* London: Bedford Square Press.

Glasscote, R., et al. 1975. *The Alternative Services: Their Role in Mental Health.* Washington, D.C.: Joint Information Service of the American Psychiatric Association and the National Association for Mental Health.

Glazer, Nathan. 1983. "Towards a Self-Service Society?" *Public Interest* 70:66–90.

Glisson, Charles, and Patricia Martin. 1980. "Productivity and Efficiency in Human Service Organizations as Related to Structure, Size and Age." *Academy of Management Journal* 23, no. 1:21–37.

Gordon, P. J. 1975. "Managing Diverse Organizational Strategies." In *The Management of Nonprofit Organizations,* edited by R. M. Cyert. Lexington, Mass.: Lexington Books.

Graycar, Adam. 1982. "Government Officers' Expectations of Non-Governmental Welfare Organizations." SWRE Reports and Proceedings no. 28. Kensington, New South Wales, Australia: Social Welfare Research Centre, University of New South Wales.

———. 1983. "The Interrelationship of Voluntary, Statutory and Informal Services." *British Journal of Social Work* 13, no. 4:379–93.

Grønbjerg, K. A. 1982. "Private Welfare in the Welfare State: Recent U.S. Patterns." *Social Service Review* 56, no. 1:1–26.

Grossman, Bart, and M. Morgenbesser. 1980. "Alternative Social Service Settings: Opportunities for Social Work Education." *Journal of Humanics* 8:59–76.

Hadley, R., and S. Hatch. 1981. *Social Welfare and the Failure of the State.* London: George Allen & Unwin.

Hansmann, H. B. 1980. "The Role of Non-Profit Enterprise." *Yale Law Journal* 89:835–901.

Hartogs, N. and J. Weber. 1978. *Impact of Government Funding on the Management of Voluntary Agencies.* New York: Greater New York Fund and United Way.

Hasenfeld, Y. 1983. *Human Service Organizations.* Englewood Cliffs, N.J.: Prentice-Hall.

Hill, William G. 1971. "Voluntary and Governmental Financial Transactions." *Social Casework* 52:356–61.

Hodgkinson, V., and M. Weitzman. 1984. *Dimensions of the Independent Sector: A Statistical Profile.* Washington, D.C.: Independent Sector.

Holleb, G. P., and W. R. Abrams. 1975. *Alternative Community Mental Health.* Boston: Beacon Press.

Huggins, N. 1981. *Protestants against Poverty: Boston's Charities 1870–1900.* Westport, Conn.: Greenwood.

James, E. 1983. "How Nonprofits Grow: A Model." *Journal of Policy Analysis and Management* 2, no. 3:350–66.

Janowitz, M. 1976. *Social Control of the Welfare State.* New York: Elsevier Scientific Publishing Co.

Judge, Ken. 1981. "Public Purchase of Social Care: British Confirmation of the American Experience." *Policy and Politics* 10, no. 4:397–416.

Kahle, J. H. 1969. "Structuring and Administering a Modern Voluntary Agency." *Social Work* 14, no. 4:21–28.

Kahn, Alfred J. 1973. *Social Policy and Social Services.* New York: Random House.

Kamerman, Sheila B. 1983. "The New Mixed Economy of Welfare: Public and Private." *Social Work* 28, no. 1:5–11.

Kamerman, Sheila B., and Alfred J. Kahn. 1976. *Social Services in the U.S.* Philadelphia: Temple University Press.

Knoke, David, and D. L. Rogers. 1979. "A Block Model Analysis of Interorganizational Relations." *Sociology and Social Research* 64, no. 1:28–50.

Knoke, David, and J. B. Wood. 1981. *Organized for Action: Commitment in Voluntary Associations.* New Brunswick, N.J.: Rutgers University Press.

Kotler, M. 1969. *Neighborhood Government: The Local Foundation of Political Life.* Indianapolis: Bobbs-Merrill.

Kouzos, J. M., and P. R. Mico. 1979. "Domain Theory: An Introduction to Organizational Behavior in Human Service Organizations." *Journal of Applied Behavioral Science* 15, no. 4:449–69.

Kramer, Ralph. 1981. *Voluntary Agencies in the Welfare State.* Berkeley: University of California Press.

———. 1983. "A Framework for the Analysis of Board-Executive Relationships in Voluntary Agencies." In *Voluntarism and Social Work Practice: A Growing Collaboration,* edited by F. S. Schwartz, 179–201. Lanham, Md.: University Press of America.

Kramer, Ralph, and Paul Terrell. 1984. *Social Services Contracting in the Bay Area.* Berkeley, Calif.: Institute of Governmental Studies.

Langton, Stuart. 1981. "The New Voluntarism." *Journal of Voluntary Action Research* 10, no. 1:7–20.

Leiby, James. 1978. *A History of Social Welfare and Social Work in the United States.* New York: Columbia University Press.

Levitt, T. 1973. *The Third Sector: New Tactics for a Responsive Society*. New York: Macon Press.

Lubove, Roy. 1965. *The Professional Altruist: The Emergence of Social Work as a Career: 1880–1930*. Cambridge, Mass.: Harvard University Press.

———. 1966. "The Welfare Industry: Social Work and the Life of the Poor." *Nation* 202:609–11.

McCarthy, K. D. 1982. *Noblesse Oblige: Charity and Cultural Philanthropy: Chicago, 1849–1929*. Chicago: University of Chicago Press.

Manser, Gordon. 1974. "Further Thoughts on Purchase of Service." *Social Casework* 55:421–34.

Mier, R. and W. Wiewel. 1983. "Business Activities of Not-for-Profit Organizations." *American Planning Association Journal* 49, no. 3:316–25.

Milofsky, C. 1980. "Structure and Process in Self-Help Organizations." Yale University, Program on Non-Profit Organizations Working Paper no. 17.

Moroney, Robert. 1976. *The Family and the State: Considerations for Social Policy*. London: Longmans.

Morris, R. 1982. "Government and Voluntary Agency Relationships." *Social Service Review* 56, no. 3:333–45.

Newman, W., and H. Wallender. 1978. "Managing Not-for-Profit Enterprises." *Academy of Management Review* 3:24–31.

Newton, J. W., and S. Kagan. 1983. *Survey on Profit and Quality in Child Care: A Report on the Pilot Study*. Yale University, Program on Non-Profit Organizations.

O'Brien, D. J. 1975. *Neighborhood Organization and Interest-Group Process*. Princeton: Princeton University Press.

O'Connell, B. 1976. "The Contribution of Voluntary Agencies in Developing Social Policies." New York: Council of Jewish Federations.

Perlmutter, Felice. 1969. "A Theoretical Model of Social Agency Development." *Social Casework* 50:467–73.

Perrow, Charles. 1970. *Organizational Analysis: A Sociological View*. Belmont, Calif.: Brooks/Cole.

———. 1972. *Complex Organizations: A Critical Essay*. Glenview, Ill.: Scott, Foresman & Co.

Pfeffer, J., and G. Salancik. 1978. *The External Control of Organizations: A Resource Dependence Perspective*. New York: Harper & Row.

Provan, K. G. 1980. "Board Power and Organization Effectiveness in Human Service Agencies." *Academy of Management Journal* 23, no. 2:221–36.

Pumphrey, R., and M. Pumphrey, eds. 1961. *The Heritage of American Social Work*. New York: Columbia University Press.

Rainey, H. G., et al. 1976. "Comparing Public and Private Organizations." *Public Administrative Review* 36:233–44.

Reichert, Kurt. 1977. "The Drift toward Entrepreneurialism in Health and Social Welfare: Implications for Social Work Education." *Administration in Social Work* 1:123–34.

Reisch, M., and S. Wenocur. 1982. "Professionalism and Voluntarism in Social Welfare: Changing Roles and Functions." *Journal of Voluntary Action Research* 11, no. 23:11–31.

Rice, Robert M. 1975. "Impact of Government Contracts on Voluntary Social Agencies." *Social Casework* 56:387–95.

Rich, Richard C. 1979. "Roles of Neighborhood Organization in Urban Service Delivery." *Urban Affairs Papers* 1:81–93.

Rosengren, William R. 1970. "The Careers of Clients and Organizations." In *Organizations and Clients: Essays in the Sociology of Service*, edited by William R. Rosengren and Mark Lefton, 117–36. Columbus, Ohio: Charles E. Merrill.

Rothman, J. 1974. *Planning and Organizing for Social Change: Action Principles from Social Science Research*. New York: Columbia University Press.

Sainsbury, E. 1977. *The Personal Social Services*. London: Pitman.

Salamon, Lester M. 1981. "Rethinking Public Management: Third-Party Government and the Changing Forms of Government Action." *Public Policy* 29, no. 3:255–75.

———. 1983. "Nonprofit Organizations and the Rise of Third-Party Government: The Scope, Character and Consequences of Governmental Support of Nonprofit Organizations." Paper presented at the Independent Sector Spring Research Forum, New York, May.

Salamon, Lester M., and A. Abramson. 1982. *The Federal Budget and the Nonprofit Sector*. Washington, D.C.: Urban Institute Press.

Savas, E. S. 1982. *Privatizing the Public Sector*. Chatham, N.J.: Chatham House.

Schorr, A. 1970. "The Tasks for Volunteerism in the Next Decade." *Child Welfare* 49:425–34.

Scott, R. A. 1981. *The Making of Blind Men*, New Brunswick, N.J.: Transaction.

Segal, Steven P. 1979. "Community Care and Deinstitutionalization: A Review." *Social Work* 24:521–27.

Senate Special Committee on Aging. 1974. *Nursing Home Care in the U.S.: Failures in Public Policy*. Washington, D.C.: U.S. Government Printing Office.

Sills, David L. 1957. *The Volunteers: Means and Ends in a National Organization*. Glencoe, Ill.: Free Press.

Sills, David L., ed. 1968. "Voluntary Associations: Sociological Aspects." In *International Encyclopedia of the Social Sciences*, 362–79. New York: Macmillan.

Skloot, E. 1983. "Should Not-for-Profits Go into Business?" *Harvard Business Review* 61, no. 1:20–25.

Slavin, Simon L., ed. 1978. "The Structure and Uses of Authority." In *Social Administration: The Management of the Social Services*, 111–16. New York: Haworth Press.

Smith, Bruce L. R. 1971. "Independence and the Contract State." In *The Dilemma of Accountability in Modern Government: Independence vs. Control*, edited by Bruce L. R. Smith and D. C. Hague, 3–69. New York: St. Martin's Press.

Sosin, Michael. 1982. "The Domain of Private Social Welfare: Comparisons with the Public Sector." Discussion paper 712–82. Madison: Institute for Research on Poverty, University of Wisconsin.

Stein, Herman D. 1961. "Some Observations on Board-Executive Relationships in Voluntary Agencies." *Journal of Jewish Communal Service* 38:390–96.

———. 1982. "The Concept of the Human Service Organization: A Critique." *Administration in Social Work* 4, no. 2:1–14.

Terrell, Paul. 1981. "Adapting to Austerity: Human Services after Proposition 13." *Social Work* 26, no. 4:275–82.

Tucker, D. 1983. "Environmental Change and Organizational Policy Making." In *Managing Voluntary Organizations,* edited by M. M. Moyer, 1–24. Downsview, Ontario: York University Faculty of Administrative Studies.

U.S. Department of Health, Education and Welfare. 1978. *Social Services U.S.A.* Washington, D.C.: Office of Human Development.

Unterman, I., and R. H. Davis. 1982. "The Strategy Gap in Not-for-Profits." *Harvard Business Review* 60, no. 3:30–32, 34, 36, 40.

Urban Institute. 1983. *Serving Community Needs: The Nonprofit Sector in an Era of Governmental Retrenchment.* Progress Report no. 3. Washington, D.C.: Urban Institute.

Warner, A. 1894. *American Charities: A Study in Philanthropy and Economics.* New York: Crowell.

Watson, F. 1922. *The Charity Organization Movement in the U.S.* New York: Macmillan.

Wedel, K. R. 1980. "Purchase of Service Contracting in Human Services." *Journal of Health & Human Resources Administration* 2, no. 3:327–41.

Wedel, Kenneth, Arthur Katz, and Ann Weick, eds. 1979. *Social Service by Government Contract: A Policy Analysis.* New York: Praeger.

White, T. 1981. "Recent Developments and the Response of Social Services Departments." In *A New Look at the Personal Social Services,* edited by E. M. Goldberg and S. Hatch. London: Policy Studies Institute.

Wickenden, E. 1976. "A Perspective on Social Services: An Essay Review." *Social Service Review* 50:586–600.

Wilensky, H. L., and C. N. Lebeaux. 1965. *Industrial Society and Social Welfare.* New York: Free Press.

Wilson, J. Q. 1966. "Innovation in Organization: Notes toward a Theory." In *Approaches to Organization Design,* edited by J. D. Thompson, 193–218. Pittsburgh: University of Pittsburgh Press.

Wolfenden Committee. 1978. *The Future of Voluntary Organisations.* London: Croom-Helm.

Wolfensberger, W. 1973. *The Third Stage in the Evolution of Voluntary Associations for the Mentally Retarded.* Toronto, Canada: National Institute for Mental Retardation.

Woodson, R. L. 1981. *A Summons to Life: Mediating Structures and the Prevention of Youth Crime.* Cambridge, Mass.: Ballinger.

Young, Dennis R., and Stephen J. Finch. 1977. *Foster Care and Nonprofit Agencies.* Lexington, Mass.: D. C. Heath.

Young, D. W. 1983. "Nonprofits Need Surplus Too." *Harvard Business Review* 60, no. 1:124–31.

Zald, Mayer N. 1969. "The Power and Functions of Boards of Directors: A Theoretical Synthesis." *American Journal of Sociology* 75:95–111.

———. 1970. *Organizational Change: The Political Economy of the YMCA.* Chicago: University of Chicago Press.

15

A Comparison of Private and Public Educational Organizations

DANIEL C. LEVY

BASES OF COMPARISON

I n education, as in many other fields where there is significant nonprofit activity, to compare private and public organizations is to grapple with complex material. Yet the challenges are compelling. Within and beyond the United States, disenchantment with the performance of public educational organizations has added a sense of urgency to the often substantial interest in examining alternatives. Thus private-public issues are crucial to many of the important educational debates of our time, as a growing policy literature illustrates (James & Levin 1983; Gaffney 1981; Everhart 1982; Breneman & Finn 1978; Levy 1986b). Instead of joining the policy debate, however, I step back in this chapter and try to identify and understand salient empirical differences between the two types of organizations.

The chapter concentrates on the potency of one basic concept—that of scope—and analyzes how well essential private-public differences can be appreciated by reference to it. To use terminology from organizational sociology, a limited scope (or "niche") characterizes "specialist" institutions; at the other end of a continuum, greater scope characterizes "generalist" institutions (Hannan & Freeman 1978, 152–53). Related to specialism are narrowness, selectivity, focus, and coherence; related to generalism are breadth, openness, looseness, and ambiguity.[1] The principal

I thank Paul DiMaggio and Walter W. Powell, as well as Roger L. Geiger and John W. Meyer, for comments on an earlier draft and the Andrew W. Mellon Foundation and Yale University's Program on Non-Profit Organizations for financial aid and institutional support.

1. Obviously, different terms can connote praise (for example, coherence, breadth) or criticism (narrowness, ambiguity), but I try to use them straightforwardly.

hypothesis here is that we can associate private more than public educational organizations with limited scope. Private *sectors* may often rival public sectors in breadth, but they tend to do so by adding narrow organization upon narrow organization.

The complexity of the private-public terrain in education ensures that no one hypothesis will prove accurate in nearly all cases. Observers have searched in vain for behavioral characteristics that consistently distinguish educational organizations labeled private from those labeled public: thus, many scholars, as well as partisans of one sector or the other, have belittled the private-public distinction (Levy 1986b, 170–92). I therefore define *private* and *public* only according to legal nomenclature, not scope or any other hypothesized criterion.[2] Notwithstanding the conceptual concern to dis-

2. The literature on for-profits is comparatively small and scattered in isolated institutional and policy reports rather than concentrated in scholarly works (Wine 1980; Trivett 1974, 48–54; Hartle 1976, 52–54; Levy 1986b, Introduction). Among other limitations not elaborated on in the text are the following: I deal only with formal teaching institutions, excluding the growing networks (often nonprofit) of nonformal, research, and interest group organizations in education. I do not compare the reasons for private and public growth nearly as much as the relevance of that comparison to scope could warrant; relatedly, I devote little attention to historically dominant private-public patterns. Additionally, I often group religious with other private institutions, not analyzing their special characteristics (Greeley 1969, 1982; Greeley, McCready, & McCourt 1976; McCluskey 1969, 1970; Bartell 1980), even though most or a very sizable minority of private enrollments are usually found in religiously affiliated institutions; U.S. schools and higher education provide respective examples. Finally, even though this chapter only selectively reviews the education literature with an eye toward private-public comparisons in scope, and even though it concentrates on only

cover private-public patterns, this then is an inductive approach, taking private and public organizations as labeled and proceeding to identify certain characteristics with them.

The private organizations analyzed here are private *nonprofit* ones. I restrict my comments about for-profits to capsule footnotes suggesting general contrasts to the other two sectors. I do so largely because for-profits have been far less important than the other two types. As a corollary, my private nonprofit versus public comparison naturally excludes single-sector educational systems. Although there are no fully private systems, many fully public ones exist, particularly in communist nations and in higher education (as in much of Western Europe and Africa).

Consequently, the thematic concern with private-public comparisons helps in the selection of this chapter's three principal geographical and educational contexts. These are (1) Latin American higher education, (2) U.S. schools, and (3) U.S. higher education, though I add footnoted comparisons to other settings, mostly Western European. The choice of U.S. contexts is obvious, given both readership interest and literature availability. I use Latin American higher education partly because it is my own area of expertise, and I can simplify the complex findings of my twenty-nation study without incurring an author's wrath.[3] More objective scholarly rationales for this choice relate to identified private-public characteristics in Latin American higher education.[4] In any case, conclusions from my own book become hypotheses for more general comparisons in most of the discussion below.

The analysis of private-public differences in our three principal contexts employs four categories: finance, governance, mission, and effectiveness.[5] The use of these categories could facilitate comparisons between education and

other major fields where private-public differences may be usefully considered in terms of specialism and generalism. Beyond this, the main reason for the four-part approach is to draw private-public educational comparisons over wider criteria than often considered. I believe that too much of the recent U.S. policy debate on private versus public in education has turned on an assessment of quality, as gauged by achievement test scores. Certainly the most discussed study comparing private and public educational organizations concerns these scores (Coleman, Hoffer, & Kilgore 1982b), dealing with matters like governance only as they may influence differential achievement. Yet even fuller measures of academic stature and pedagogical success would cover part of our effectiveness category only. Quality is merely one basis on which to compare private and public, either for our purposes of understanding differences between the two sectors or for making policy decisions based on those differences. And these other bases appear often to mark larger differences, offering greater alternatives for individuals and policymakers, alternatives relating to values such as equity, accountability, autonomy, pluralism, and contrasting notions of democracy.[6]

Finally, before proceeding to the heart of the chapter, a quick overview of the sectoral sizes in question is needed. Our three cases illustrate the rule that private educational sectors are typically smaller than public ones. The relationship holds in sixteen of the eighteen dual-sector systems studied in Latin America. The private enrollment share varies widely, from 6 percent or less in a few small nations, to nearly 60 percent in Colombia and roughly 70 percent in Brazil, with 10 to 15 percent fairly common. These figures represent startling private growth, largely a reaction to extraordinary growth and transformation in the public sector. Compared to only 3 percent in 1930 and 14 percent in 1955, the private share of the region's now roughly 5 million enrollments has reached 34 percent. In contrast, U.S. private school percentages dropped dramatically from the late nineteenth century through the first few decades of this century, mostly because of the growth of public high schools (Kraushaar 1972, 13–14). Recently, after a small decline between the mid-1960s and mid-1970s, the private share has been fairly stable, its more than 5 million students holding some-

certain geographical areas, it still ranges so widely (for example, including schools and higher education cross-nationally) that its major limitations are that it suggests more than it proves and that it underplays intrasectoral variation and intersectoral similarity.

3. All information on Latin American higher education is based on Levy (1986a), so I do not include the citation repetitively. The best book I know on Latin American private schools deals with Chile (Brahm, Cariola, & Silva 1971). I have analyzed Latin America's Jewish schools as a subset of private schools that illustrate many of the private-public contrasts found in this chapter (Levy, forthcoming).

4. As the text shortly shows, private universities throughout much of Latin America have grown greatly in importance in numerical and other terms. Yet the twenty nations are varied, providing many different political, economic, and social contexts for private-public comparisons; all these contexts are markedly different from U.S. ones, upon which most of the literature's private-public comparisons have been based. Additionally, important qualifications notwithstanding, "private" and "public" in Latin American higher education turn out to be extremely distinctive; the separate sectors are respectively characterized by striking privateness and publicness on most criteria employed to assess such qualities. More than any other major educational context I know of, this one provides fairly clear dual-sector categories from which to start.

5. These represent four of five concerns sometimes set forth as critical to Yale's Program on Non-Profit Organizations (Simon 1980, 5–11). Deleted is the power dilemma—how much nonprofits can or shall have power over decision making in the public and for-profit sectors.

6. While it is important to point out (Murnane 1986a) that Coleman's recent work contrasts with his influential earlier work that cast doubt on the impacts that schools make (Coleman 1966; also Jencks et al. 1973), contrasts in achievement scores would be far from the most crucial ways in which schools "make a difference." It is interesting that Coleman himself (as expressed in panel discussion comments at the Conference Comparing Public and Private Schools, Institute for Research on Educational Finance and Governance, Stanford University, October 25–26, 1984) regards the greatest contribution of his recent work as showing—contrary to some popular notions, often about private inferiority—that there is *not* a terribly decisive private versus public effect on achievement scores, thus allowing us to explore other explanations of differential achievement and, I take it, other bases of private-public comparisons. The 1984 conference just cited provides the basis for a volume (James and Levin, forthcoming) that will be a major addition to the literature comparing public and private schools.

thing over 10 percent of enrollments, slightly higher at the elementary level and slightly lower at the high school level (Erickson 1986; Williams et al. 1983, 4–8), though there is reason to suppose that the overall percentage could be a little higher (Cooper, McLaughlin, & Manno 1983, 95–97). By comparison, the private share is much higher, but has declined substantially, in U.S. higher education. Although it was still one-half in 1950, it dropped in the ensuing three decades to just over one-fifth (22 percent) of the now more than 11 million enrollments (Geiger 1986a).

Our three principal cases also illustrate the tendency for the private share of institutions to exceed the private enrollment share.[7] In the United States, the over 10 percent private enrollment share is spread over approximately 18 percent of the institutions (Erickson 1986), whereas the private sector's one-fifth share of higher education enrollments is spread over roughly one-half the institutions (Geiger 1986a). I have no reliable aggregate figure for Latin American institutions, but I have enough evidence to know that the private sector's institutional share exceeds its enrollment share in *each* of the eighteen dual-sector systems studied. In sum, private educational institutions are usually smaller than public ones.[8]

FINANCE: DEPTH VERSUS BREADTH

A crucial issue in comparing private and public educational organizations is who shoulders the financial burden. We can associate specialism with policies whereby individuals pay their own way directly to the institutions that serve them, and

7. It is difficult to generalize about private shares of Western European schooling, as there is variation by nation, primary-secondary within nation, and definition of private, though private can usually be read nonprofit (Mason 1983, 1, 19). Nevertheless, we can provide a loosely aggregated sketch here. Sweden and Norway have tiny private sectors, and Denmark, Great Britain, Greece, Italy, Luxembourg, and West Germany are less than 10 percent private, France and Spain go higher, and Belgium, the Netherlands, and Ireland go over one-half private (Neave 1983, 7; Rust 1982, 30; Mason 1983, 40). Private shares are generally smaller in Western Europe *higher* education. According to most assessments, the private sector is nonexistent or under 10 percent in almost all nations; the two striking exceptions are the Netherlands 23 percent and Belgium's 69 percent (Geiger 1986b; Levy 1982). Beyond Western Europe, percentages vary widely at all educational levels. Both Asia and Africa have many school systems with private sectors under 10 percent, over 30 percent, and in between (Cooper & Doyle, forthcoming). In Latin America, the private sector has a much longer tradition at the school than at the university level; but private percentages are now lower (roughly 16 percent; 13 percent primary, 28 percent secondary) at the school level. Even outside the communist world, *higher* education varies from insignificance in most nations to 80 percent in Japan and higher in the Philippines (Geiger 1986b; Levy 1982).

8. Private-public contrasts in average institutional size would be even greater if for-profits were included, certainly in U.S. schools and higher education (Katz 1978, 9) as well as English schools (Robinson 1971, 130). Private-public contrasts in sectoral size would sharpen expecially at the higher level, though much depends on how strictly we define both "higher" and "nonprofit." Higher can include multitudinous commercial schools, and nonprofit can include (as in Brazil) many small institutions that are behaviorally for-profit yet manage to retain nonprofit legal status. Clearly, in the United States and beyond,

broader scope with policies whereby institutions are funded through general tax revenues. In the former, there is a much tighter, well-identified relationship between paying for and receiving services than is the case in the latter.

Higher education finance in Latin America displays something approaching complete distinctiveness between the sectors. The public sector usually receives around 95 percent of its income from the national government. A basic rationale is that all education is a public good benefiting society at large, not just individual members. From Brazil to Venezuela to Mexico, students have blocked attempts to impose tuition, attempts based on notions of equity and the weakness of the public financial base.

In comparison, Latin American private higher education is funded overwhelmingly through private funds. Contributions widen the financial scope some, but are usually specific to particular universities; financial scope widens significantly in the private sector only when we add together the individually narrow but different bases of given institutions. Catholic universities receive funds and donated services from their religious communities, and elite secular universities draw support from domestic businesses as well as international businesses and foundations. Yet *tuition* remains the major source at all types of the region's private higher education organizations, and it is nearly the exclusive source at nonelite ones. Government subsidies are rare (although tax exemptions are available on the basis of the nonprofit status that virtually all the private institutions enjoy, nominally if not always in fact). The major exceptions regarding subsidies are found for some high-quality Catholic universities, as in Ecuador and Peru; they are based on the rationale that their missions tend to be the widest, or most publicly oriented, that the private sector undertakes. Nonelite institutions have cited their broadening socioeconomic status (SES) base in soliciting aid, but so far to little avail. The fundamental private-public difference remains that private institutions are privately funded, and public institutions are publicly funded.

How well can these private-public findings from Latin America be generalized? They can be rather strikingly extended to the United States, at least at the school level. Again there is great private-public distinctiveness, with the private sector relying mostly on tuition and adding other private funding, and the public sector relying even more exclusively on government funding. Although noteworthy, corporate donations to certain public schools, and the establishment of local private foundations to subsidize public school districts hit hard by government cutbacks, are still marginal in most states. Public financial responsibility for public elementary schools has long been seen as essential to the "public school tradition," and a similar responsibility was subsequently established for the high school level. The prime financial responsibility, however, has never been lodged with the

the for-profit sector is much more important at higher than at school levels. Whether U.S. corporations will be tempted to make a major effort at establishing for-profit schools (Levy 1986b, Introduction) remains to be seen.

national government, thus in some sense limiting the breadth of public-sector finance. Even the major shift away from local responsibility in recent decades has been toward the state level, not the national level, so that localities and the states now each contribute roughly 45 percent of public school income (Wirt & Kirst 1982, 237).

Private schools depend much less on support from any government level. Instead, they rely heavily on individual payments for individual benefits. As Erickson (1986) aptly puts it, fees are exacted "at the schoolhouse door," whereas public income depends on "sources far removed from the individual's pocketbook." Given that big endowments are a rarity, private secular schools usually receive more than 80 percent of their income through tuition, though the figure may drop below 50 percent in some Catholic schools, where expenditures are subsidized by parishes and donated services (Kraushaar 1972, 203–08). Recent figures, however, show that, overall, Catholic schools depend on tuition for roughly three-fourths of their income and on government for but 1 percent (Greeley 1981, 13). Turning back to non-Catholic private schools, there is substantial variation among the southern segregationist academies between tuition and donated services, often tied to fundamentalist congregations (Nevin & Bills 1976, 71–80, 118–19). Tuition more clearly dominates, running as high as $6,000 per year at the secular and some academically prestigious Protestant schools (Vitullo-Martin 1981, 39–40), thus narrowing the pools of potential applicants (Baird 1977, 36). In sum, notwithstanding the role of Catholic and certain other churches, most individual private schools are funded "narrowly and deeply" by their users and committed supporters. As with Latin American private higher education, only the addition of separately narrow bases makes the sector's financial base appear wide, though still not as wide as the tax-sustained public base.

Government aid has broadened the financial profile of U.S. private schools. Even the federal government has assumed an important role since 1965. The two major obstacles to government funding of private schools have been the broad commitment to public schooling and the idea that general funding for specialized private aims, especially religious ones, is inappropriate. Counterarguments emphasize the public benefits of private choice, the social or public character of private schooling, and the sometimes exclusive practices of *public* schooling.

Seeking compromises among such competing notions, government ties most of its private school aid to particular purposes deemed socially important. Federal aid goes largely to economically and physically disadvantaged students and is mostly handled by state and local authorities (Kutner, Sherman & Williams 1986). State aid goes largely for similar purposes, though also for public transportation, health services, textbooks, and other activities (Hirschoff 1986; Kraushaar 1972, 289–90). Especially important is the child-benefit theory whereby courts allow aid targeted directly for students but not for broad institutional support. Additionally, like other U.S. nonprofit organizations, more than 95 percent of private schools receive tax exemptions, notably on prop-

erty, and perhaps as much as one-fourth of total private school expenses are covered by government assistance (Encarnation 1983, 177, 187; Sullivan 1974, 92–95).

Even if we were to go beyond the U.S. school and Latin American higher education contexts and add Western Europe and much of the rest of the world, at both the school and university levels, U.S. *higher* education would stand nearly alone in having a public sector that draws significantly on private funds. Tuitions are higher than in any other public sector in the world, and no other nation has matched the U.S. corporate, foundation, and individual traditions of giving to public universities (Geiger 1986a). The public sector does depend on government over private sources by roughly a 4:1 ratio, but, as at the K–12 level, even most of the government funds do not come from as wide a base as found in the dominant worldwide tendency, where centralized national ministries are the key actors (Levy 1982). Indeed, only state governments provide annual institutional subsidies for U.S. public universities; even more local responsibility is the rule for public community colleges. Federal funding is mostly restricted to two concerns—one is student aid, the other, research (Carnegie . . . 1975b).

And these two federal concerns actually favor the private sector, where tuition is higher and a proportionally greater share of expensive research is conducted (Shils 1973; Geiger 1986a). Federal aid has also been sustained by the argument, upheld in *Tilton* v. *Richardson* (1971), that even church-related colleges are eligible, since higher education students are presumed to be "less impressionable" than grade school students. On the other hand, compared to federal aid, state aid for the private sector has been less important. Although most states provide such aid, it rarely equals 5 percent of either the state's higher education budget or the private sector's total income (Berdahl 1978, 349). Student aid is common, and support for the private institutions is most often targeted for service contracts or plants or is based on enrollment or degree formulas (Carnegie . . . 1976b, 80; Breneman & Finn 1978, 46). State aid tends to be greatest where private sectors are largest (Nelson 1978, 68; McCoy & Halstead 1979, 21); New York leads in this respect. This suggests a correlation between enrollment scope and financial scope. As at the school level, so at the higher education level, tax exemptions and deductions are important.

Thus, government finance further complicates a private-sector picture also characterized by a myriad of private financial contributors; but sectoral complexity can be simplified if we concentrate on subsectors (Geiger 1986a; Minter & Bowen 1978; Jellama 1973; E. James 1986a). The great majority of private colleges are not tied into a wide financial network, either governmental or private. Most rely greatly on tuition, perhaps adding the voluntary support of some local church or loyal alumni or other supporters (Bartell 1980; Jencks & Riesman 1968, 345). To be sure, the Harvards and Yales have wide national ties to private donors across the land; still, they represent the exceptions. Thus, intersectoral tuition gaps are frequently on the statewide order of 4:1 or 5:1, with major policy debates raging in state after state over the desirability of cutting that ratio, whether through more state aid to privates or higher tuition at publics; in fact, however, major policy changes have not occurred (Rusk & Leslie 1978; Carnegie . . . 1976b, 80; Breneman & Finn 1978, 12–13, 27). Justification for public tuitions rests partly on the belief that there is less government responsibility for higher education than for school education, in part because there is less need to foster widely shared beliefs at the higher level.

To sum up, U.S. finance proves to be much less intersectorally distinctive at the higher than at the school level.[9] The public sector draws considerably off private sources and the private sector has a much wider private (beyond tuition) and even government base in higher education. Nonetheless, even within U.S. higher education, private institutions tend to rely on much narrower bases than public ones. Most have a very narrow financial base tied to tuition. So even as we add U.S. higher education to the cases considered above, it is clear that public institutions typically rely overwhelmingly on the broad coverage of government, whereas private institutions rely much more on direct tuition payments, with other private contributions often tied by specific actors to specific institutions, and even government money, where available, often tied to specific rather than general institutional purposes.[10]

GOVERNANCE: CLOSE VERSUS OVERARCHING AND COMPLEX AUTHORITY

There are important parallels, some causal, in the financing and governing of educational organizations. Again private activity tends to concentrate rather closely in and around private institutions, whereas public institutions tend to be treated as parts of wider systems. Government is generally far more critical to the running of public institutions. And, notwithstanding the socially stratified basis on which it tends to function, government usually represents a wider array of groups and interests than individual private actors do. Consequently, differences in the scope of governance often relate to vital private-public contrasts in matters such as autonomy and accountability.

Latin American private and public universities are substantially distinct in governance, resembling the situation in finance except that the distinctiveness is not as great. Many public universities, though almost fully dependent on government funds, achieve considerable autonomy from government. Still, government is the overarching actor, playing an important role in virtually every public institution. On the other hand, governance within the public universities of many nations is characterized by a dispersion of power among administrators, faculty, students, and even office and physical plant workers (as in Mexico).

Most of Latin America's private universities, elite and nonelite alike, enjoy substantial autonomy from government, sometimes even under authoritarian regimes. This does not mean that they are more autonomous than public counterparts, however, for there is often a special, close, accountability to key financial and other authorities. These authorities, mostly businesses and churches, vary from institution to institution, making the private sector notably decentralized. But individual institutions have tightly packed, concentrated power structures, with the business or religious authorities appointing governing boards directly responsible to them. Nor is the power shared within institutions nearly as widely it is in the public sector. Most private universities are centralized and hierarchical institutions, allowing little room for dissent. Indeed, academic freedoms are not allowed to threaten the chosen, often specialized or restricted orientation of the organization. The private power structure is comparatively coherent, headed by authorities whose influence does not extend nearly as widely across institutions as the government's does, but instead penetrates more selectively and deeply.

Turning to U.S. schools, the private sector once had to struggle (though not as wrenchingly as in Latin American higher education) for the right to exist, until the *Pierce* case of 1925 provided legal security.[11] Since then there has been a near consensus that states should maintain some governance role but a far more limited one than in public schools (Erickson 1969; Campbell et al. 1980, 425). Within these bounds, and while the role has generally expanded over time, interstate variations has been enormous. This variation is found in all areas of state supervision—from safety codes to zoning, truth in advertising, admissions policy, and personnel credentials (Encarnation 1983, 187–93). Curriculum is another good example: control varies from slight in some

9. To bring for-profits into the financial analysis would be to make our private-public comparisons even starker. At both school and higher education levels, this sector is the most dependent on direct client payments; government aid is minimal, especially as for-profits do not get the exemptions and tax-deductible contributions that nonprofits do (Hirschoff 1986; Encarnation 1983, 177), though they can benefit from some money given to college students. On the other hand, our private-public comparisons would blur if either tuition tax credits or vouchers were implemented (James & Levin 1983; LaNoue 1972; Levy 1986b).

10. Compared to U.S. practice, school finance in Western Europe tends to show fewer private-public differences, as most nations now give substantial aid to private schools (especially where the private enrollment percentage is high), often through direct institutional subsidization, sometimes through vouchers (Neave 1983, 1–8; Rust 1982, 17–18, 25; E. James 1986b). Nonetheless, many private schools rely heavily on tuition and some receive no government support, whereas public schools are fully funded by the government (Mason 1983, 3; Halsey, Heath, & Ridge 1980, 39; Neave 1983, 1; Rust 1982, 23). In higher education, there is basically public funding of private institutions in the two nations where these institutions hold substantial enrollments, whereas private sectors with under 10 percent of enrollments typically rely on private funding; private-public distinctiveness is promoted, as almost all public sectors (even beyond Western Europe) are funded almost fully by government, usually through a widely standardized national role (Geiger 1986b; Levy 1982).

11. The Supreme Court struck down an Oregon law under which compulsory schooling (ages eight to sixteen) had meant public schooling only (Tyack 1968).

states to formidable equivalency requirements in others. Then too, regulations are often vague (Coons & Sugarman 1978, 168) and courts vary in what they uphold (although they rarely strike down regulations as unconstitutional). Moreover, just as in Latin America, some private institutions welcome government regulations (for example, in curriculum standardization) because they do not want to appear "too different" (Kraushaar 1972, 323) or illegitimate. For one thing, they may want to be distinctive in only one way, but to attract clients to that distinctive orientation, they have to assure them there will not be sacrifices along other lines. Such reasoning has been common among Catholic institutions, concerned to maintain decent and acceptable academic credentials, from the first private Catholic university in Latin America (Chile 1888) to some U.S. Catholic schools earlier in this century. In any case, the overriding rule in the United States is still that private schools are much freer than public schools from government commands tied to constitutional requirements and financial subsidies (Elson 1969, 104, 122–23; Hirschoff 1986; Kraushaar 1972, 316); this holds for the policies just cited, as well as for control over administrative boards, hiring, dismissal, programs for non-English speakers, and so forth. If approved, tuition tax credits could erode some of these private-public differences, as government money has already done (Glazer 1983, 196; Hirschoff 1986).

In accordance with the analysis of finance, however, we see again that there are both shorter and longer arms of government. A distinguishing characteristic of U.S. schooling has traditionally been local control (Ramírez & Robinson 1979; Meyer et al. 1977). By concentrating power closer to individual institutions than is the case in a nationally centralized system, local control limits public-private differences in governance scope.[12] But the trend in intergovernmental relations in the postwar period has been toward the higher levels, state and federal. This wider governance network has limited local authority to follow the distinctive desires of local constituencies. Even though at least the federal role often remains tied to specific concerns, and the impact of funding on governance varies (Meyer 1983, 187–88; Scott & Meyer 1983, 145–48; Kutner, Sherman, & Williams 1986), a broadened concept of publicness is reflected in court decisions, student rights, racial integration, mainstreaming of the handicapped, restrictions on prayer, and so forth (T. James 1983, 68; Hirschoff 1986; Coleman, Hoffer, & Kilgore 1982b, 163). This broadened publicness often promotes exits to private schools.

In contrast, the locus of private power remains much more tightly wrapped in and around individual schools. Boards of trustees, however they may be selected (Nevin & Bills 1976, 123), typically hold the fundamental authority to set policy

directions and delegate power to a principal who becomes "the captain of the ship," whereas the public school is more tied to the "uniformity, standardization and spelled-out procedures" of a comparatively distant central administration (Kraushaar 1972, 161, 144, 12, 173; Meyer 1983). Some Catholic schools collectively come under an overarching authority, but that varies, and real power often remains at the school level. Protestant, evangelical, and elite secular schools tend to be even more individually administered (Campbell et al. 1980, 430–32; McCready 1977, 74; Kraushaar 1972, 9, 144, 266–67). Therefore, the private sector's changing composition (Cooper, McLaughlin, & Manno 1983; Catterall 1984; Erickson 1986) makes the concentration of power around the school itself an increasingly salient private characteristic.

As in Latin American higher education, the issue is less the degree than the contours of instituitional autonomy versus external control. And these differing ties to the environment relate to the distribution of power *within* organizations. Again the privates tend to be more autocratic, though perhaps decreasingly so (Kraushaar 1972, 174, 267–68). Again shared assumptions, which are ensured by the school's authority to select its personnel and to dismiss them quickly if disputes arise, play a crucial role (Nevin & Bills 1976, 41–43; Kraushaar 1972, 163–64). Most participants, notably parents, exercise power through choice, and retain voice essentially through the implicit exit option (Hirschman 1970). Thus, while they may have little formal ongoing power within institutions, this power may be less cumbersome than that found in the public sector (Kraushaar 1972, 265, 102), a point sometimes cited in calling for public-sector reform (Coons & Sugarman 1978, 162–64, 177).

Several of these private-public contrasts in governance scope can be reinforced and elaborated by reference to some of the extensive work by Scott and Meyer (1984), including some empirical findings from a recent Bay Area sample. These authors argue that private decision making is much more likely than public decision making to occur within the school (where there is a higher administrator/student ratio) that is less constrained by external inspection and authorities over it (district, regional, or otherwise) (Scott & Meyer 1984, 25–38). Moreover, recent trends have enormously increased the complexity and reduced the clarity of public governance. Centralization has pushed decision making further from individual schools without, however, producing a clear top-down command structure. Instead, we see a mix of competing authorities at various levels, higher levels layered upon rather than replacing lower ones, thus producing a "fragmented centralization" with lots of "autonomous lateral relationships" (Meyer 1983, 181, 185) and a "much more elaborate organizational structure," with "a considerable cost in internal organizational consistency"; in sum, compared to private schools, public schools exist in a "complex and inconsistent controlling environment," as less "bounded and internally coherent organizations" (Scott & Meyer 1984, 32, 39).

Without probing the historical reasons, it is clear that U.S.

---

12. Of course, local control can mean different things in the two sectors. Much of the literature has explored how democratic the public sector is; Dahl's classic work (1961) found notable participation, but most subsequent research has emphasized how limited public participation is compared to the role of professionals and elites (Zeigler & Jennings 1974).

higher education has been characterized by less private-public distinction in terms of the breadth and complexity of governance than has been found in our other two educational contexts. Yet many similar patterns hold, even though in more blurred form.

The scope of government control is much wider in the public than the private sector. Granted, as at the U.S. school level, the federal role is limited even in the public sector (though not nearly so much as it was a few decades ago). But, outside the community college network, local control is hardly a factor; rather, state capitals tend to wield power across the breadth of their states' public institutions. Two more similarities to the school level further qualify the private-public contrasts in scope tied to the government role. One is that the government role varies greatly by state. Some state departments of education require teacher education programs to develop curricula leading to teacher certification, and others require the use of particular budget formulas and program-planning systems; certain state legislatures (as in Florida and New York) have even gone so far as to stipulate minimum numbers of classroom hours (Mortimer & McConnell 1978, 3–4, 207). A second qualification to the private-public tendencies I am emphasizing is that the government role has expanded even for the *private* sector. For example, some states have required or banned new course offerings, and there have been increased pressures with regard to such concerns as minority representation and rights. Nonetheless, the lengthening arm of government—the rule in state after state—shapes the public much more than the private sector.

Evidence on differing government roles according to sector accumulates from several related spheres of action. As at the school level, regulations (state and federal) have multiplied to hold especially the public institutions responsible for a host of wide social concerns (Bok 1980; Mortimer & McConnell 1978, 190). Newly active state legislatures (with vastly beefed-up staffs) turn their energies toward public more than private institutions. Similarly, most statewide coordinating boards have gone much further in trying to mold public than private institutions into their systemwide planning (Berdahl 1975; Odell & Thelin 1981). Along these lines, the role of the courts has increased over both sectors but differentially. In the most extensive study related to our interests, Kaplin (1978, 1–3, 19–21, 31, 97, 232) finds that the courts have recognized and reinforced the authority of private organizations to pursue distinctive ends. Private higher education, unlike its public counterpart, is not bound to the doctrine of religious neutrality (at least unless it seeks government funding). Additionally, private institutions are left much freer to bargain with their employees and to set and enforce disciplinary standards for students because the courts are inclined to view such matters as related to contractual relations between private institutions and the individuals associated with them by choice. Private institutions are also less bound than public ones by federal policy regarding discrimination. In many particulars, the degree of government imposition over private organizations depends largely on criteria concerning privateness; for example, universities receiving substantial government subsidization are less free than others from constitutional constraints and from the authority of coordinating boards (Mortimer & McConnell 1978, 220).

Largely because of the contrasting sweeps of government authority, the locus of the private policy-making process, much more than the public one, is centered around individual institutions themselves. This private-public contrast echoes what we found at the school level. An important difference in higher education, however, is that even many public institutions have considerable autonomy compared to public schools. They are much less tied to overarching authorities, thereby allowing much more interinstitutional differentiation, with the policy-making process more particularized by institution. Nevertheless, compared to private higher education institutions, public ones do not concentrate their power as tightly around individual institutions (Shils 1973).

Boards of trustees provide good illustrations of basic private-public differences. Even public universities have these bodies (normally more associated with private organizations), but with different tendencies. Public boards typically allow for a mjaor government role, through the appointment of most trustees, and are accountable to the states as broad representatives of the public interest. Private boards, on the other hand, tend to be appointed by, and remain more directly accountable to, particular constituencies, variable by institution but specific in most individual cases (Mortimer & McConnell 1978, 152–153; Millett 1973, 51; Epstein 1974, 37). Moreover, the close authority of individual boards over individual private organizations is not diluted by the formidable multiuniversity coverage found in the public sector, and, of course, it is less diluted by broad governmental authority. Consequently, the private organizations are generally less tied to standardized practices, whether in affirmative action plans, salary scales, tenure plans, or so many other concerns (Carnegie . . . 1975a, 61–65; Commission . . . 1973, 161, 180).

Finally, U.S. private higher education follows the patterns found for Latin American higher education and U.S. grade school education (though less sharply than either), not only by enjoying more autonomy from centralized government authority and less autonomy from closer private authorities, but also by tending to centralize *intra*institutional power more than public counterparts do.[13] Such intrainstitu-

13. As U.S. government regulation frequently accompanies its finance for nonprofits, so for-profits may operate with the relative absence of both. Coordinating boards, accrediting agencies, and courts have advanced the government role in for-profit higher education, but still minimally compared to what nonprofits face (Trivett 1974, 1–3, 38–42; Katz 1978, 7), though see Zumeta and Mock (1985). Another way in which for-profits add to the private-public contrasts in governance concerns their direct accountability to their owners, and their internal centralization, even authoritarian hierarchy, with little internal distribution of power (Katz 1978, 13); the principal of a for-profit school is less likely than his nonprofit counterpart to share power even with a governing board. In higher education, at least, these basic contrasts can be

tional centralization and lesser internal voice (for example, in student representation; Mortimer & McConnell 1978, 148) help sustain the private organization's clear and direct accountability to its board and specific external constituencies.[14]

MISSION: SELECTIVITY VERSUS COVERAGE

This section compares the missions of organizations that are financed and governed differently, exploring whether these missions differ, especially in scope.

In several important ways, the missions carved out by Latin America's private universities provide distinctiveness. There is distinctiveness across institutions, reflecting the heterogeneity in governance discussed earlier. And there is distinctiveness between sectors, despite some overlapping missions. A major concern related to the thematic private-public contrasts highlighted in this chapter is that the private missions tend to be narrower than the public ones.

One manifestation of the different breadth of private and public missions concerns student clienteles. Although Latin America's public sector rarely draws off more than a fifth of the age-relevant population, and although many unprestigious private institutions are no more elite than many public ones, the strong tendency is toward greater selectivity (in both academic and SES terms) within the private sector. This is especially true for the prestigious secular universities, but also for many Catholic ones. Among the latter, restrictive religious missions have become less common in recent decades yet still make for a marked distinction from public openness. Moreover, many Catholic and especially most other private universities can reasonably be described as narrower than public counterparts in their political orientations. The private universities are often identified with the political ideology and even the policies of the privileged, whereas the public ones are usually identified with calls for a much wider distribution of power and wealth. Beyond this

contrast, the private universities, more than the public ones, can be accurately identified with some particular ideology. Based largely on the disciplined private governance structure and selection process, there is less likelihood of ambiguity, incoherence, or widely heterogeneous ideologies.

These points apply well to another mission, an easily quantifiable one. Latin America's private sectors, in nation after nation, tend to be much more specialized in the academic areas of concentrations or fields of study (such as law) they offer to their students. The most striking private-public differences come when we compare organizations rather than sectors. In Venezuela, for example, where eight fields of study are offered, each of the four private universities holds a minimum of 64 percent of its enrollment in just one field of study, such as engineering, and none offers more than five different fields. By comparison, three of the four public-autonomous universities offer all eight fields, and none concentrates more than 36 percent of its students in any single field. Even when we aggregate data from the organizational to the sectoral level and across fifteen nations (those in which at least 90 percent of the enrollments could be categorized into fourteen identified fields), another powerful private-public difference related to scope is found: the private sector has proportionally more of its students in each of seven fields, with rough private-public parity in another, and every one of these seven fields is less expensive to offer than every one of the six fields where the public sector has the proportional lead. To illustrate, the private proportional edge is two to one in business fields, the public edge better than two to one in medicine.[15]

Important similarities to these private-public comparisons emerge for U.S. schools. Many have noted the extraordinary diversity among private schools compared to public schools. There are a multitude of different kinds of religious schools, segregationist academies, ghetto schools, progressive-experimental schools, boarding schools, and so forth (Cooper 1984; Erickson 1986; Esty 1974, 1–20). Even within most of these individual categories, there is great variation among institutions, as Baird (1977, 1–2) and Nevin and Bills (1976, 103) have shown for elite secular schools and segregationist academies, respectively.[16] The religious dimension is especially important; seven of eight private enrollments are in religiously affiliated institutions (Catterall 1984, 8). The Catholic subsector alone, despite strong proportional declines from the mid-1960s until the early 1980s, accounts for well over half the private enrollments (Cooper, McLaughlin, & Manno 1983, 94). Many Catholic institutions have lost

---

extended beyond the United States, where legally (for example, the Philippines; Geiger 1986b), and behaviorally (Brazil) for-profit institutions exist.

14. Private-public governance differences in Western Europe are limited by governments' extensive regulations over most of the private sectors it heavily subsidizes, usually the ones with the widest enrollment breadth (Neave 1983, 5–11; Rust 1982, 16, 19). However, this leaves considerable power with some private schools and their headmasters, and many nations free private schools from the public school stipulation of religious neutrality; moreover, on the Continent more than in Great Britain, the public sector is very widely controlled by standardized national government policy (Neave 1983, 3, 12–13; Mason 1983, 1–2). In higher education as well, we see some correlation between government finance and regulation of private sectors (though the relationship is by no means uniform), while also seeing (especially if we add some Asian cases) authority vested in boards or trustees orienting their institutions to specific constituencies (Geiger 1986b). Once again private-public contrasts are sustained in part because the public sector is typically so much more standardized to national government authority than in the United States (Clark 1983).

15. There are also striking private-public contrasts, beyond fields of study, concerning job markets. Private graduates are much more likely to seek employment in private enterprises, whereas public graduates have long depended heavily on government bureaucracies.

16. On Canadian counterparts to the kind of elite schools Baird (1977) discusses, see Gossage (1977); Gossage notes the limited enrollments, "independent" self-designation, nonprofit status, high tuition, absence of government subsidies, autonomous power through a private board, old-boy connections, and attractiveness as an alternative to decreasingly satisfying public schools.

some religious flavor over time (as the clientele they have served have become more integrated into the rest of society) but, as in Latin America, still preserve some distinctiveness from other institutions, both public and private. Other religious schools, such as the ''new Christian,'' or fundamentalist schools, tend to be at once more specialized and more intensive in their individual missions, insisting, for example, on particular prayers, theories of creation, and born-again fervor (Nevin & Bills 1976, 37–39; Skerry 1980, 21); examples of common curriculum notwithstanding, such schools tend to reinforce the interinstitutional distinctiveness characteristic of private sector missions.

While this interinstitutional diversity is often recognized, the intrainstitutional *lack* of diversity is perhaps equally noteworthy. Choice is ensured across private institutions much more than within them. As Nevin and Bills (1976, 2) observe for the segregationist academies that are so different from one another, ''Perhaps the single most important point about these schools is their sameness. . . . once you are inside you are in a fixed and unchanging world.'' The public dynamic is significantly different. As one would guess from its financial and governance profiles, the common school, at the elementary level, or the comprehensive high school is simultaneously intended to serve a considerable range of purposes and to be fairly similar one institution to the next. Clark (1984) laments that ''a substantial overload of conflicting expectations'' drives out the ''advantages of specialization,'' distinctiveness, and clarity as the ''huge hope of the system at large is thereby recapitulated in each of some sixteen thousand small worlds,'' the worlds of the ''unfocused'' comprehensive high school.

Beyond this, Erickson (1986) emphasizes how, by handling the bulk of the market, the public sector pushes the private sector to concentrate on a few special tasks. Similarly, Scott and Meyer's Bay Area sample (1984, 33, 38) shows public schools under many pressures to address a full range of needs, whereas private schools, receiving neither the pressure nor resources to do the same, instead seek discrete niches—thereby achieving greater goal coherence. Levin (1983, 28) and others have noted the ramifications for disenchantment with the public schools and for the growth of private alternatives.

The narrowness and depth of private missions clearly applies to self-consciously moral orientations, where there usually is a more rigidly defined sense of right and wrong than in public schools. Even in curriculum and the range of subjects offered, however, narrowness is often characteristic. Boarding and other elite schools are the most striking exceptions (Baird 1977, 4) and Catholic schools probably fit this generalization less than other private schools (Kraushaar 1972, 55). At the other extreme, some private schools portray their limited curriculum as relevant only for certain racial (Nevin & Bills 1976, 85, 13) or religious groups. For all the variation, a fair generalization might parallel my findings on Latin American universities (though in a diluted form) that private schools have a comparatively narrow focus. They offer a more restricted and specialized range of

courses (vocational, for example) and other activities, even if we control for size (Salganik & Karweit 1982, 155, 159; Coleman, Hoffer, & Kilgore 1982b, 72–84) or the percentage of minority students (Scott & Meyer 1984, 34–36). Beyond just the curriculum, private school offerings are often limited, though again one would have to distinguish the elite schools with their huge libraries, art galleries, and media and other special programs (Baird 1977, 4) from, say, the segregationist academies that ''offer bare bones education'' in terms of libraries, physical plants, health facilities, and so forth (Nevin & Bills 1976, p. 74). As James and Levin (1983, 8) point out, few private schools provide expensive services unless public finance and regulation alter the private profile, as with education for the handicapped (Weintraub 1981, 49–51; Kutner, Sherman, & Williams 1986). More generally, there is reason to doubt how well private choices can meet the broad challenges of a modern democratic society (Levin 1983; Hirschoff 1986).

Crucial to narrowly and coherently defined missions is the selection process. Here I consider students, as I did for Latin American higher education, though the selection of teachers and administrators is also important and follows a similar logic. Private schools tend to tap constituencies that fit in comfortably with the organization's complexion, that want a good deal of what in fact is offered in depth—and that are relatively unconcerned about (or even zealously do not want) what is not offered. Granted, there is controversy over how broadly representative the typical public school is (or ever was) and over whether its SES base has widened or narrowed.[17] Clearly we have some highly selective public schools, notably in New York City (Doyle & Cooper 1983), but these are still the exceptions.

One key generalization is that private schools tend to be aimed much more to privileged groups. Roughly 5 percent of families earning under $15,000 a year send their children to private schools versus roughly five times that percentage for families earning over $50,000 a year (Williams et al. 1983, 15). Second, beyond economic factors, private schools have been more oriented to preserving particular identities and beliefs than have public schools. Race has been a crucial example, though one must note that Catholic schools are attracting an increasing share of their students for nonreligious reasons, even attracting an increasing share of non-Catholics, including blacks. The black private enrollment proportion is still less than half that for whites, with Hispanics in between (Williams et al. 1983, 11; Catterall 1984, 18).

Turning to mission in U.S. higher education, one again finds, as in finance and governance, that private-public distinctiveness is less marked than at the U.S. school level, certainly less than in Latin American higher education. A

17. The view more cited in this essay is that the public sector has opened up (contributing to an exit by previously more satisfied groups). Another view, whose proponents have included Milton Friedman and James Coleman, holds that increased economic segregation by neighborhoods has increased the exclusiveness of individual public schools.

major factor is the interorganizational diversity characterizing even the public sector, where colleges and universities are not as bound as public schools to accommodate the range of interests found in given local geographical areas, nor as bound as Latin American public universities to nationwide standards set by ministries.

Nevertheless, even in U.S. higher education, organizational distinctiveness and specialized niches are especially associated with the private sector (Geiger 1986a). As Jencks and Riesman note (1968, 287–88), it is more difficult for public than private institutions to hold to unusual missions; this helps explain why there are "no public Amhersts, Oberlins, or Reeds." Herein lies one of the major reasons for the large U.S. support for the private sector, which performs "a function in our society that we cannot afford to lose" (Jellama 1973, x). An extensive array of Carnegie Commission and Council studies attests to this concern. The Carnegie classification finds private institutions extremely overrepresented among those types of institutions that tend to be most differentiated; 96 percent of all liberal arts and 67 percent of all specialized institution enrollments are in a private sector that includes one-half the institutions and fewer than one-fourth of overall enrollments (Carnegie . . . 1976a, xii, 36–40; El-Khawas 1976, 4).

Prominent examples of restrictive scope have involved race, gender, and (to a lesser extent) ethnicity, but also progressive experimentation and conservatism (Jencks & Riesman 1968, 346). Religion has been most important, though less than at the school level. Even if a sizable proportion of the private higher education institutions are religiously affiliated, that affiliation is often marginal and many Protestant institutions are very small. The contribution to diversity is nonetheless significant, as there is marked differentiation even among Catholic (Greeley 1967, 1–3) and especially among Protestant colleges (Pace 1974; Jencks & Riesman 1968, 312–14). Interinstitutional diversity has also been strong within other categories, such as women's colleges (Kendall 1975, 30).

Consequently, it is to the private sector that Burton Clark turns (1972, 178) to explore the "distinctive college" and the "organizational saga," that "collective understanding of a unique accomplishment in a formally established group," all beginning with a strong sense of mission. The ability to choose distinctive missions is often related to private governance and therefore freedom, leaving public institutions, tied to the state, at a relative disadvantage (Keeton 1971, 17–18; El-Khawas 1976, 43, 51). It is also often related to the much smaller average size of private than public institutions (Pace 1974; Kershaw 1976) mentioned above; and privates tend to be smaller within each category, such as doctorate-granting institutions (El-Khawas 1976, 13).

Some observers, however, have questioned whether the private sector is so characterized by interorganizational diversity. Perhaps conformity is the dominant tendency in U.S. higher education, public or private, with institutions prostituting themselves to extrauniversity financial interests (Goodman 1962, 169–71; Nisbet 1971). Perhaps private

universities have betrayed their distinct corporate identities in favor of a bland academic pluralism (Buckley 1977). Or perhaps almost all institutions really perform "public" missions (Silber 1975). For one additional example, it has been argued that, contrary to conventional wisdom, privates more often lapse into "institutional imitation," whereas public institutional missions can be anchored by law (Baldridge et al. 1978, 55–56). In any case, there is abundant evidence that many once highly distinctive private colleges have moved toward the mainstream, whether by mixing clienteles (by religion, race, gender, income), by pursuing academic quality, or by a controversial strategy of adapting to a changing environment through greater comprehensiveness (Pfnister & Finkelstein 1984).

Possibly the principal basis for downplaying private-public differences, however, is that other organizational categorizations can be more decisive. For example, a private doctorate-granting university is likely to have more in common with a public doctorate-granting university than with a private liberal arts college. Also, private research universities do not fit many of the indicators of narrow scope, and in forty-nine states the private sector attracts the higher out-of-state percentage (Carnegie . . . 1977, 50). Thus, even more than at the school level, prestigious private institutions reach out over a wide geographical scope.[18]

Nevertheless, ample grounds exist for associating privateness with an institution's ability to focus on a comparatively narrow clientele. We have already noted that some very strong correlations exist between private-public and other organizational categorizations. Additionally, private-public differences may hold in areas such as "public service" (McCoy & Halstead 1979, 39). Another example, applicable to the Latin American context as well, is regional distribution. Public institutions are more widely spread out across the nation and more responsible for meeting varied regional missions, whereas private institutions are freer to choose their own specialized missions (Carnegie . . . 1976a, 1–126; El-Khawas 1976, 11–13). In some sense, then, public institutions go to the clients, whereas the private institutions draw their clients. Finally, one of this century's most important transformations in the missions of U.S. private institutions has involved their increasing selectiveness (Grant & Riesman 1978, 291).

In considering clientele or any other factor related to mission, the distinction between sector and individual organization again proves crucial. For example, the private sector matches the public sector's black-to-total-student ratio as well as its female ratio largely by relying on distinctively black, and women's, colleges (El-Khawas 1976, 25). Similarly, individual private institutions are much more likely than public ones to cover only a narrow range of academic statures (whether high or low), curricula, religious or norma-

18. Furthermore, clientele differences are greater within than across sectors (El-Khawas 1976, 23; Monroe 1977, 1–13; Jonsen 1978, 9) and have been diminished by government regulation.

tive orientations, SES backgrounds, and so forth.[19] Even relatively homogeneous organizations, if different from one another, can build sectoral diversity, but we must appreciate how this diversity differs significantly from that based on institutions of broader scope.[20]

EFFECTIVENESS: CONVENTIONAL INDICATORS

In this section I will deviate from the analysis by region and educational level used to this point. Instead, drawing on evidence about those regions and levels, I discuss effectiveness in terms of two dimensions frequently invoked in making private-public comparisons, often invidious ones. The first is academic quality. Although usage varies in the literature as well as in popular discourse, I emphasize here the academic level, in terms of knowledge bases and skills, especially of students. A common measure is the achievement score. The second dimension of effectiveness considered below—client satisfaction—obviously addresses perceptions of effectiveness.

Accumulated, if scattered, evidence often suggests an average edge in the academic level of private over public educational institutions. Powerful qualifications are warranted, but first a bit of the evidence should be sketched. The private edge is possibly strongest where private-public distinctiveness has been most evident—in Latin American

higher education. As many as fourteen of eighteen Latin American countries with dual sectors show a private advantage, often a strong one; a public edge is evident in no more than two. For U.S. schools the Coleman, Hoffer, and Kilgore study (1982b; also Greeley 1982) offers the most publicized evidence; debate has turned mostly on whether private school policies produce higher achievement, not on the reality of a higher private standing. Even in U.S. higher education, where we have seen less private-public distinctiveness, most evidence again suggests an average private edge, based on surveys (since 1925), peer rankings, admissions to graduate schools, graduate training, research, and awards received (Cyert 1975, 48; Shils 1973, 8–9; Cartter 1966; Keeton 1971, 7–41; Jencks & Riesman 1968, 288; Carnegie . . . 1976b, 9, 79).

The qualifications should follow closely upon the sort of evidence just sketched, however. First, we often must fall back on prestige as a substitute concept for quality, as quantitative indicators of educational performance are frequently unavailable or questionable in terms of what they really measure; for example, seemingly impressive ratios of teachers, administrators, and expenditures per pupil may have as much to do with inefficiency as with quality, and achievement tests may be culturally or otherwise biased. A second qualification is that the private edge is usually an average edge, with considerable overlap between sectors and often greater gaps within each sector than between the average of each. This includes Latin American higher education, where the average private edge appears so large, for most observers base their private-public comparisons on the best-known institutions, and that is where the private edge tends to be clearest.[21] So it sometimes is in the United States, where people think more readily of the Harvards and Chicagos than of the lesser known colleges sometimes labeled "invisible" or "liberal arts II" (Astin & Lee 1972; Carnegie . . . 1976a; Roose & Anderson 1971), but many public institutions are superior to many private ones (Baldridge et al. 1978, 103). Similarly for U.S. schools, it makes a world of difference whether we focus on the elite boarding and prep schools (Baird 1977; Campbell et al. 1980, 435) or on the segregationist schools (Nevin and Bills 1976, 111). So great is the overlap that a few scholars reject the private claim to quality (Campbell et al. 1980, 448).

Even where private-public differences in quality remain notable in the face of institutional overlap, however, further qualifications are necessary. Crucially, are institutions academically superior because they provide more value added or simply because they start with an edge, as with better prepared or motivated students? This, most researchers agree, is a more important question than the popular one of which sector boasts higher average achievement scores or other

---

19. For-profit higher education weakens the private-public tendencies established here insofar as its students include a comparatively high percentage of minority and of less academically oriented students (Trivett 1974, 27–31). With its vocational orientations, for-profit institutions worldwide probably often attract a relatively low SES profile within the higher education context. On the other hand, the SES scope of individual institutions may still be narrow. More generally, most missions undertaken by for-profits are notable for their specificity and narrowness. They typically offer a limited curriculum, perhaps only one or a few disciplinary specializations, little general education, and "very limited services" (Katz 1978, 5, 8–9). Preparing students quickly for jobs is a major and measurable goal well suited to the profit motive (Trivett 1974, 16–17). The specific focus on job preparation to the exclusion of so many other missions pursued by nonprofits and especially public institutions, appears to characterize for-profit higher and school education outside the United States as well as in England (Robinson 1971, 129).

20. Although Western European public upper-secondary schools sometimes specialize more than comprehensive U.S. high schools (Clark 1984), most Western European private schools can choose more defined and narrow tasks than public schools. Religion has been critical, but political orientations, SES, and gender have also been factors (E. James 1986b; Mason 1983, 12; Halsey, Heath, & Ridge 1980). Also in higher education, alongside intersectoral similarities in missions where there is substantial government finance and regulation of private institutions that have relatively broad missions, peripheral private institutions generally choose niches with explicitly limited purposes (for example, preparation for business employment). As in finance and governance, a major factor producing private-public distinctiveness along lines related to scope concerns the role of national ministries in the public sector—the preoccupation, mostly alien to U.S. policy, for standardization (for example, in degrees granted and in civil service procedures) across public institutions.

21. In Colombia, for example, the private Los Andes and Javeriana universities could easily rank at the top, but Colombia also has many private universities of abysmal quality, offering its poorly prepared students few facilities or opportunities for learning; although many public universities share the low ground, others are above it.

measures of knowledge. There is by now important work relating client selection to achievement scores, much of it explaining variation in the latter largely in terms of the former, thereby casting doubt on whether private schools really bring about the superior scores often associated with them (Williams 1984; Murnane 1986a, 1986b; McPartland & McDill 1982). One key certainly lies in the admission of students, typically more selective, as we have seen, in the private sector. Where selection is more restrictive in the public sector, as in Brazilian, Japanese, and Philippine higher education, the average quality tends to be higher in the public sector (Geiger 1986b). Jencks and Riesman (1968, 270, 284), while emphasizing the growing similarity of private and public missions, identify differences in "raw material" as the determinant of still significantly different results; publics must constantly "play the numbers game," going "wide rather than deep," but privates "normally seek a small group" of "enthusiastic" followers. Thus, just as in Latin America, even the best public institutions usually have a comparatively heterogeneous clientele, more than the best private ones.[22]

In any event, quality is not the only component of effectiveness. In fact, not all educational organizations make quality their highest priority; most combine it with other goals, and some clearly subordinate it. Therefore, effectiveness can be thought of as fulfilling chosen missions, among which quality may be only one among several. As there are few longitudinal studies that measure the comparative success of educational organizations in producing the types of graduates they strive for, observers have often relied on client satisfaction.[23] Clients may cite effectiveness or success on any of many factors important to them, ranging from enforcing discipline to transmitting religious faith to instilling an interest in learning.

Concentrating here only on U.S. schools, there is substantial evidence of a private advantage. True, negative feelings about the public schools are easily and often exaggerated. Catterall (1984, 9–11) points out that there has in fact been no major shift from the public to the private sector and the School Finance Project (Williams et al. 1983, 56) finds that only 14 percent of parents are dissatisfied with their child's public school. Nonetheless, other observers see reasons to underscore a shift to the private sector, anticipating its acceleration (Cooper, McLaughlin, & Manno 1983), and the School Finance Project finds that only 3 percent of parents are dissatisfied with their child's private school. Kraushaar

(1972, 127, 130, 133, 107) finds the level of satisfaction for private students to be "extraordinarily high," despite complaints about competitiveness, limited "voice," and the "relative uniformity or lack of wide variation" within institutions. And parental satisfaction may run even higher. Baird (1977, 112–19) finds that students, teachers, and administrators believe that their elite schools fulfill proclaimed goals, and he attributes this to both the academic stature and the intensity of the environment. Intensity alone appears sufficient at the segregationist academies, where many students and parents readily express love for their schools, feel comfortable with the internal homogeneity, and even see many of the educational limitations in a positive light (Nevin & Bills 1976, 3, 39, 81, 143).

EFFECTIVENESS: COMPARING APPLES AND ORANGES?

If the private sector often surpasses the public sector on commonly utilized indicators, however, these indicators may be biased toward the former. We have already seen that higher achievement scores, for example, do not show that private schools necessarily educate more effectively. A broader point about the difficulty of comparing effectiveness between two sectors typically so different in scope can be forwarded by considering (1) the different meaning of client satisfaction between sectors and then (2) the more specialized nature of private-than public-sector endeavors.

The Different Meaning of Client Satisfaction

Without reference to our thematic contrast between private depth and public breadth, the data on client satisfaction cited above may be misleading. Most surveys gauge the support of the users of each sector; if the private schools please only a small group a good deal while the public schools please a larger group but only moderately, the former score higher. A different yet not necessarily more biased approach would gauge the satisfaction of the *general* public with each sector.[24] Relatedly, the widespread stability, high survival rate, and even historically striking expansion of public educational institutions (certainly including both the school and the university levels most closely considered in this chapter) probably reflect considerable popular support and an extraordinary effectiveness in garnering resources.[25]

22. I have no idea about the effectiveness of for-profit educational organizations, except in regard to academic stature for higher education. As one would expect from their SES compositions, they tend to achieve little academic prestige. Indeed, both in the United States (Trivett 1974, 4) and beyond, the question more often concerns academic legitimacy. Clearly, however, this does not mean that they are failing in their chosen missions.

23. Contrary to a widespread feeling that Catholic educational organizations have not been contributing to Catholic values, research has produced mixed to encouraging results (Greeley 1969; Greeley, McCready, & McCourt 1976).

24. I thank John Meyer (personal correspondence, November 1984) for highlighting this difference between private and public support. In fact, Meyer goes further when he argues that we should see school success at least partly as it is truly gauged and rewarded in the political process—by work or output less than by social and ritualistic functions; from this perspective, U.S. schools have generally been quite successful (Meyer & Rowan 1983a, 73, 92; Meyer 1983, 182). I would guess that this insight is applicable more to the public than the private sector, with the latter more likely to set and be measured by explicit work and performance standards.

25. On the other hand, to regard greater public than private survival rates as showing greater effectiveness is to use an indicator biased against the private sector, as specialist organizations assume the risks that often go with "putting all eggs in one basket."

Clearly, the demonstrable patron satisfaction with private schools is based heavily on the choice—reciprocal choice—characteristic of that sector. Individuals choose, and pay for, organizations that suit them (Esty 1974), and organizations try to choose individuals who will fit comfortably. There is a tight linkage here that is uncharacteristic of the public sector, where organizations tend to be more heterogeneous and less able or disposed to choose narrowly, and individuals link up with organizations more for reasons of physical than normative proximity and cannot count on encountering like-minded individuals; notably greater knowledge, care, and purpose appear to surround the choice of private than public schools in the United States and Canada (Kutner, Sherman, & Williams 1986; Erickson 1986).

The ways in which mutual matching between clientele and private institutions lead to either effectiveness or at least the perception of effectiveness have been explored by several authors (Kraushaar 1972, 106; Salganik & Karweit 1982, 152–54; Murnane 1986a, 1986b; Clark 1972, 182). Some evidence suggests that private teachers may give up $2,000 to $9,000 a year to teach in the private rather than the public sector (Chambers 1984, 39). Sizer (1984) argues that private curricula—though narrower and offering less choice than public curricula—are more effectively tailored to students. Coons and Sugarman (1978, 116–19) refer to a "stable integration," with some empirical evidence to support the notion that this is more likely to lead to effectiveness than is imposed heterogeneity, which often produces tensions. The correlation between focused choice and satisfaction, which both *tend* to be greater in the private than public sector, is also underscored by El-Khawas's findings (1976, 41) that the most specialized institutions in U.S. higher education, whether private or public, enjoy the highest satisfaction rates. Not surprisingly, then, some analysts are exploring ways in which more heterogeneous public institutions, for example, at the U.S. school level, could match people, structures, and programs more closely (Coleman 1984; Clark 1984).

More Specialized Endeavors

Connected with reciprocal choice are other considerations that help simultaneously to explain and qualify the perception and even the reality of private effectiveness as gauged by common indicators. One is that private organizations frequently select less difficult missions. We have already seen how private missions tend to be more specialized; the point here is that it is easier to be successful when one undertakes simpler tasks. It is more difficult to attend to a heterogeneous constituency. It is especially challenging to try to produce high test grades or secure enviable future educational and job placements for students who are from lower SES backgrounds and are often less educationally prepared. The same could be said of trying to achieve success in a wide range of curricula options, including expensive ones, as opposed to focusing on a few inexpensive ones. If society demands that an educational task be attempted, the private sector may have an option, the public sector a responsibility. The public sector more often tackles the difficult tasks, even the dirty work. In short, private-sector effectiveness often depends on public-sector coverage.

Choice must be seen in this context. Although private sectors are continually hailed for providing choice, it is unclear which sector generally provides more.[26] There is a pronounced tendency to take for granted the public sector and the choices it offers; the private sector is then regarded as the welcome addition. In truth, it is less the amount than the *contours of choice* that differ in characteristic ways between the sectors. Individual public organizations usually offer *more* choice than individual private ones, whereas inter-organizational distinctiveness among the latter produces choice within the sector. Therefore, although certain efforts to explain the creation of nonprofit private organizations postulate that these organizations offer something over the average that the public as a whole supports or receives, and there is evidence for that proposition in education (for example, in providing elite quality), there is also a strong sense in which private organizations provide *less* than the mean. This, of course, relates to the often heard normative reservations (for example, on elitism or racism) about the chosen exclusiveness of private organizational pursuits. Moreover, expanded choice for some in the private sector can lessen choice for others in the public sector. Where, for example, private institutions are socially or academically elite, they may in effect limit the options of public students regarding social interaction, further educational opportunities, and job selection.[27]

THE FINANCE-GOVERNANCE-MISSION-EFFECTIVENESS NEXUS

In wrapping up this exploration into the roots of private-public contrasts in *effectiveness,* we can logically bring to-

26. Before we control for its greater size, the public sector would usually have a substantial edge. An argument that has been made for both Latin American and U.S. higher education (Shils 1973, 29) is that the private sector's effective pursuit of certain specific goals helps preserve the public sector's ability to pursue broader functions.

27. Probing the quality/effectiveness issue, Halsey, Heath, and Ridge (1980, 210–13) find that British students in private schools do better, even controlling for material aspects of the home environment, but they believe that "*unmeasured*" (their italics) attitudes at home shape propensities (at least of primary school students) in an intersectorally significant way, as seen by sibling comparisons between the two sectors. In a follow-up article, the authors (forthcoming) conclude that "private education conferred some, albeit small, educational advantage" for a privileged cohort group, but they could not tell how much selectivity and home effects, as opposed to school effects, were responsible. Also see E. James (1986b) and Mason (1983, 3) on the roots of perceived private effectiveness in the Dutch and other Western European cases, respectively. In higher education, Geiger's eight-nation study, with four Western European cases, (1986a) concludes that neither the private nor the public sector has a consistent edge in quality, but that private institutions do tend to innovate and respond to environmental stimuli more readily and that public action is more contingent on government action.

gether prior points about our other major categories—finance, governance, and mission.[28] Strong bases of private effectiveness lie in the specialism we have found repeatedly in restrictively but deeply based finance, in narrowly concentrated governance, and in selectively limited mission. And a powerfully reinforcing basis lies in the comparatively coherent, tight connection among the three in the mutually reinforcing interactions among income sources, power holders, and chosen missions. In all this, we usually find the most persuasive explanations, both unflattering (elitism) and flattering (choice and commitment) for private effectiveness.

Private organizations are more likely than public ones to have identifiably chosen missions, backed by a centralized power structure, itself integrally tied to (if not largely overlapping) the key financial actors.[29] There is less propensity for conflict or countervailing tendencies as one comes closer (than in public organizations) to choosing the characteristics he desires, whether as student, parent, teacher, administrator, or donor. Fundamentally contradictory demands are therefore relatively rare—and can be dealt with convincingly—as organizational legitimacy rests less on voice and debate than on faithfulness to known and chosen orientations. In this connection, even the very narrow conceptions of morality that dominate in many private organizations—whether Mexico's socially very conservative Autonomous University of Guadalajara or a segregationist academy in the United States—are preserved, indeed, nurtured, more than coercively imposed (Skerry 1980, 24; Nevin & Bills 1976, 18). Furthermore, paying customers, and donors, expect a level of dedication to chosen missions and usually retain the governance reigns to secure the type of personnel who fit and promote these (Kraushaar 1972, 155–56, 182, 267; El-Khawas 1976, 38; Nevin & Bills 1976, 129; Erickson 1986), to ensure what Salganik and Karweit (1982, 155) call a "coherent set of attributes." Even in U.S. higher education, where the private-public differences tend to be less than in our other educational settings, Geiger (1986a) emphasizes the tight links between the financial services private institutions must seek and the distinctive purposes and intimate environment they must champion, in contrast to public coun-

terparts, which are more loosely connected to majoritarian pursuits. Shils (1973, 15) points out that the private research universities (in many ways the broadest institutions in the private sector and the ones most tied to government) "tend to have their centres of initiative and decision within themselves to a greater extent than is the case among the state universities, even the most eminent."

Although there are also linkages among finance, governance, and mission in public organizations, they are characteristically looser than in their private counterparts. The "state" and the "public" tend to be nebulous concepts, as ill-defined as they are wide ranging. Commitment is comparatively broad and thin. And so, frequently, is accountability. Private accountability is usually more defined, focused, direct; based on some understanding of mutual choice, it diminishes the importance of autonomy and the legitimacy of conflicting voices among various actors within the sector.[30] Consequently, generalizations concerning the relative ambiguity of educational (especially university) organizations, as opposed to other organizations (Weick 1976; Clark 1983, 18–26), apply better to public than private ones. Similarly, I read Meyer's work (1983, 182–83, 190–92) on the "loose coupling" within educational organizations, involving structures and activities, means and ends, policies and outcomes, as much more characteristic of the public than the private institutions I have considered, a contrast consistent with Meyer's belief that decoupling is often an adaptive strategy to cope with the complex layerings of governance associated earlier with the public sector.

CONCLUSION

Thematic attention to salient private-public comparisons leaves us with the question of how much characteristics normally associated with one sector can thrive in the other. For example, as Levin (1983, 31–34) points out, there already are a greater number of options available within the public school sector than most people think. One illustration cited above concerned New York City's special public high schools—with noteworthy specializations (like music or science) in mission and with selection procedures that diverge from the public school norm, creating a comparatively narrow environment with deep commitment and often achieving great effectiveness (Doyle & Cooper 1983). Other alternative public schools are also relevant (Campbell et al. 1980, 423–48), including magnet schools, which attract students from different neighborhoods to something distinctive. Yet

---

28. The varied and complex interrelationships in the nexus suggest to me that caution is warranted in tracing the roots of specialism or generalism to any one aspect. For example, we could say that certain institutions start with narrow missions and that this has implications for their financial base and governance structure. But others may see the process starting more on the governance side, as the state preempts most of the space for its public institutions, leaving private institutions as the leftovers that face the problems/opportunities of specialists with narrow niches. A particular danger in this second approach, however, is that it *may* assume a sequence and causality that does not operate, as when private institutions arise simultaneously or even before public ones. More generally, the partial validity of each of several such approaches argues for restraint in identifying just one as central.

29. Corollaries to such tendencies help explain the substantial association of privateness and small size. Thus, while small size relates to limited scope, that is a private-public factor. Additionally, much of our evidence links privateness with comparatively limited scope even when we control for size.

30. Where one dimension widens in scope it is likely that others will as well. Thus, among Latin American private universities, Catholic ones most often receive government money—and most often have the widest participatory governance base and offer the widest variety of fields of study. And of the three educational contexts considered here, U.S. higher education offers the most evidence of how a broadening in one category is likely to be accompanied by a broadening in others and by some loosening in the finance-governance-mission nexus; yet even the U.S. higher education context would be a weak example alongside Western European schooling.

nearly all tendencies found within a complex real world yield important exceptions, and one is struck by the absence of more such public schools around the nation. Additionally, evidence from Latin American higher education suggests, amid such great disenchantment with public institutions, that the implantation into public institutions of many characteristics (like tuition) associated with private ones has usually produced disappointing results, though sometimes mixed ones. It appears that public policy cannot easily alter the private-public distinctions examined here by experimenting in the public sector with certain characteristics more associated with the private sector.[31]

In practice, private-public differences have diminished, or blurred, less as a result of the public sector emulating the private one than the private one "becoming more public." And public policy, especially through increased funding and regulation, has provided much of the thrust. The relevant evidence in this chapter comes mostly from U.S. education at all levels, though Western European education, especially primary and secondary (Neave 1983; Rust 1982; Mason 1983) would provide even more potent corroboration, sustained by higher education transformations in nations such as Belgium and the Netherlands (Geiger 1986b). Latin American higher education has provided much less evidence, at least partly because most private universities are still comparatively new.

Future transformations and relevant policy issues notwithstanding, this chapter has emphasized empirically contrasting private-public patterns, trying to identify and understand them. Most important, it has found private-public differences to be substantial, despite intrasectoral variation, intersectoral similarities, and intersectoral blurring over time. These differences hold for all three educational contexts explored, especially for Latin American higher education and U.S. schools. The parallels found across disparate educational, social, economic, and political contexts suggest that the identified patterns are not random ones but are logically (though by no means inevitably) associated with privateness and publicness, a conclusion that apparently would be strongly promoted by the inclusion of additional geographic regions.[32] Private-public distinctions do make— or at least mark—crucial differences at both the institutional and the sectoral levels.[33]

Naturally, it is easier to identify than to conceptualize the private-public tendencies discussed here. Nonetheless, scope (as well as related concepts) seems to advance our understanding. Where private and public educational sectors differ, which is not always but often, those differences can be conceived of largely in terms of the scope found in finance, governance, mission, and effectiveness. The core in each of these categories tends to be more specialized and concentrated in the individual private than public organization, with private breadth and diversity attainable at the sectoral level through the aggregation of differentiated organizations. All this points to contrasting bases on which private and public should be understood in education.

31. Such general observations cast doubt on how much the private sector truly innovates in ways that serve as models for the public sector, but they also leave substantially open the vital questions of the *degree* to which valued private characteristics could be extended through public policy decisions, or how the public sector is affected by the private sector's presence. See, for example, how Coleman, Hoffer, and Kilgore (1981, 538–45; 1982b, 162–64) respond to those who dismiss the implications they derive regarding policies that affect achievement. At an extreme, Kraushaar (1972, 317) concludes: "In short, if there were no private schools, people would have to create them." Paradoxically, this could be true if publics really do learn from privates *or* if they do not and only privates can achieve certain goals.

32. For example, five or six (depending on how one assesses Belgium) of Geiger's seven non-U.S. higher education cases show considerable private-public differentiation (1986b).

33. Moreover, private-public differences would have been even more substantial had the for-profit sector been integrally included with the nonprofit sector in this analysis.

REFERENCES

Astin, Alexander W., and Calvin B. T. Lee. 1972. *The Invisible Colleges: A Profile of Small Liberal Arts Colleges with Limited Resources*. New York: Carnegie Foundation for the Advancement of Teaching.

Baird, Leonard L. 1977. *The Elite Schools: A Profile of Prestigious Independent Schools*. Lexington, Mass.: D. C. Heath.

Baldridge, Victor J., David V. Curtis, George Ecker, and Gary Riley. 1978. *Policy Making and Effective Leadership: A National Study of Academic Management*. San Francisco: Jossey-Bass.

Bartell, Rev. Ernest, C.S.C. 1980. *Enrollment, Finances, and Student Aid at Catholic Colleges and Universities*. Washington, D.C.: Association of Catholic Colleges and Universities.

Berdahl, Robert O. 1975. *Evaluating Statewide Boards: New Directions for Educational Research*. San Francisco: Jossey-Bass.

———. 1978. "The Politics of State Aid." In D. W. Breneman and C. E. Finn, Jr., eds. *Public Policy and Private Higher Education*, 321–52. Washington, D.C.: Brookings Institution.

Bok, Derek. 1980. "The Federal Government and the University." *Public Interest* 58:80–101.

Brahm, Luis A., Patricia Cariola, and Juan José Silva, eds. 1971. *Educación Particular en Chile*. Santiago: Centro de Investigación y Desarrollo de la Educación.

Breneman, David W., and Chester E. Finn, Jr., eds. 1978. *Public Policy and Private Higher Education*. Washington, D.C.: Brookings Institution.

Buckley, William F. 1977. Introduction to *God and Man at Yale*. South Bend, Ind.: Gateway Editions, 1951.

Campbell, Ronald F., Luvern L. Cunningham, Raphael O. Nystrand, and Michael D. Usdan. 1980. "Alternative Schools." In *The Organization and Control of American Schools*, 423–48. Columbus: Charles E. Merrill Co.

Carnegie Council on Policy Studies in Higher Education. 1975a. *Making Affirmative Action Work in Higher Education*. San Francisco: Jossey-Bass.

———. 1975b. *The Federal Role in Postsecondary Education*. San Francisco: Jossey-Bass.

———. 1976a. *A Classification of Institutions of Higher Education*. Berkeley, Calif.: Carnegie Foundation for the Advancement of Teaching.

———. 1976b. *The States and Higher Education*. San Francisco: Jossey-Bass.

———. 1977. *The States and Private Higher Education*. San Francisco: Jossey-Bass.

Cartter, Alan. 1966. *An Assessment of Quality in Graduate Education*. Washington, D.C.: American Council on Education.

Catterall, James S. 1984. "Private School Participation and Public Policy." Paper presented at the Conference on Public and Private Schools and Educational Policy, Stanford University, October 25–26.

Chambers, Jay G. 1984. "Patterns of Compensation of Public and Private School Teachers." Stanford University, Project Report no. 84–A18 of the Institute for Research on Educational Finance and Governance.

Clark, Burton R. 1972. "The Organizational Saga in Higher Education." *Administrative Science Quarterly* 17:178–83.

———. 1983. *The Higher Education System: Academic Organization in Cross-National Perspective*. Berkeley: University of California Press.

———. 1984. "The School and the University: What Went Wrong in America." Paper presented at the Rockefeller Institute of Government Policy Forum, Albany, N.Y.

Coleman, James S. 1966. *Report on Equality of Educational Opportunity*. Washington, D.C.: U.S. Government Printing Office.

———. 1984. "Public and Private Schools beyond Achievement." Paper presented at the 140th anniversary of the SUNY at Albany School of Education, September 21, Albany, N.Y.

Coleman, James S., Thomas Hoffer, and Sally Kilgore. 1981. "Questions and Answers: Our Response." *Harvard Educational Review* 51:526–45.

———. 1982a. "Achievement and Segregation in Secondary Schools: A Further Look at Public and Private School Differences." *Sociology of Education* 55: 162–82.

———. 1982b. *High School Achievement: Public, Catholic and Private Schools Compared*. New York: Basic Books.

Commission on Academic Tenure in Higher Education. 1973. *Faculty Tenure*. San Francisco: Jossey-Bass.

Coons, John E., and Stephen D. Sugarman. 1978. *Education by Choice: The Case For Family Control*. Berkeley: University of California Press.

Cooper, Bruce S. 1984. "The Changing Demography of Private Schools: Trends and Implications." *Education and Urban Society* 16:429–42.

Cooper, Bruce S., and Denis P. Doyle. Forthcoming. "Private Schools, Worldwide." In *International Encyclopedia of Education*. London: Pergamon Press.

Cooper, Bruce S., Donald H. McLaughlin, and Bruno V. Manno. 1983. "The Latest Word on Private-School Growth." *Teacher College Record* 85:88–98.

Cyert, Richard M., ed. 1975. "Public and Private Higher Education." In *The Management of Nonprofit Organizations*, 45–52. Lexington, Mass.: D. C. Heath.

Dahl, Robert A. 1961. *Who Governs?* New Haven: Yale University Press.

Doyle, Denis, and Bruce S. Cooper. 1983. "Is Excellence Possible in Urban Public Schools?" *American Education* 19, no. 9:16–26.

El-Khawas, Elaine H. 1976. *Public and Private Higher Education: Differences in Role, Character, and Clientele*. Washington, D.C.: American Council on Education.

Elson, John. 1969. "State Regulation of Nonpublic Schools: The Legal Framework." Pp. 103–34 In D. A. Erickson, ed.,

Public Controls for Nonpublic Schools, 103–34. Chicago: University of Chicago Press.

Encarnation, Dennis J. 1983. "Public Financing and Regulation of Nonpublic Education: Retrospect and Prospect." In T. James and H. M. Levin, eds., *Public Dollars for Private Schools*, 175–95. Philadelphia: Temple University Press.

Epstein, Leon D. 1974. *Governing the University*. San Francisco: Jossey-Bass.

Erickson, Donald A. 1986. "Choice and Private Schools: Dynamics of Supply and Demand." In D. C. Levy, ed., *Private Education: Studies in Choice and Public Policy*. New York: Oxford University Press.

Erickson, Donald A., ed. 1969. *Public Controls for Nonpublic Schools*. Chicago: University of Chicago Press.

Esty, John C. 1974. *Choosing a Private School*. New York: Dodd, Mead.

Everhart, Robert B., ed. *The Public School Monopoly: A Critical Analysis of Education and the State in American Society*. Cambridge, Mass.: Ballinger.

Gaffney, Edward McGlynn, Jr., ed. 1981. *Private Schools and the Public Good*. Notre Dame: University of Notre Dame Press.

Geiger, Roger L. 1986a. "Finance and Function: Voluntary Support and Diversity in American Private Higher Education." In Daniel C. Levy, ed., *Private Education: Studies in Choice and Public Policy*. New York: Oxford University Press.

———. 1986b. *Private Sectors in Higher Education: Structure, Function, and Change in Eight Countries*. Ann Arbor: University of Michigan Press.

Glazer, Nathan. 1983. "The Future under Tuition Tax Credits." In T. James and H. M. Levin, eds., *Public Dollars for Private Schools*, 87–100. Philadelphia: Temple University Press.

Goodman, Paul. 1962. *Compulsory Mis-education and the Community of Scholars*. New York: Vintage Books.

Gossage, Carolyn. 1977. *A Question of Privilege: Canada's Independent Schools*. Toronto: Peter Martin Associates.

Grant, Gerald, and David Riesman. 1978. *The Perpetual Dream: Reform and Experiment in American Education*. Chicago: University of Chicago Press.

Greeley, Andrew M. 1967. *The Changing Catholic College*. Chicago: Aldine Publishing Co.

———. 1969. *From Backwater to Mainstream: A Profile of Catholic Education*. New York: McGraw Hill.

———. 1981. "Catholic High Schools and Minority Students." In E. M. Gaffney, Jr., ed., *Private Schools and the Public Good*, 3–16. Notre Dame: University of Notre Dame Press.

———. 1982. *Catholic High Schools and Minority Students*. New Brunswick, N.J.: Transaction Books.

Greeley, Andrew M., William C. McCready, and Kathleen McCourt. 1976. *Catholic Schools in a Declining Church*. Kansas City: Sheed & Ward.

Halsey, A. H., A. F. Heath, and J. M. Ridge. 1980. *Origins and Destinations: Family, Class, and Education in Modern Britain*. Oxford: Oxford University Press.

———. Forthcoming. "The Political Arithmetic of Public Schools." In G. Walford, ed., *The British Public Schools*. London: Falmer Press.

Hannan, Michael T., and John H. Freeman. 1978. "The Population Ecology of Organizations." In Marshall W. Meyer and associates, *Environment and Organizations*, 131–71. San Francisco: Jossey-Bass.

Hartle, Terry. 1976. *Recent Research on Private Higher Education*. Washington, D.C.: American Council on Education.

Hirschman, Albert O. 1970. *Exit, Voice, and Loyalty: Responses to Decline in Firms, Organizations, and States*. Cambridge, Mass.: Harvard University Press.

Hirschoff, Mary-Michelle Upson. 1986. "Public Policy toward Private Schools: A Focus on Parental Choice." In D. C. Levy, ed., *Private Education: Studies in Choice and Public Policy*. New York: Oxford University Press.

James, Estelle. 1986a. "Cross-Subsidization in Higher Education: Does it Pervert Private Choice and Public Policy?" In D. C. Levy, ed., *Private Education: Studies in Choice and Public Policy*. New York: Oxford University Press.

———. 1986b. "Public Subsidies for Private and Public Education: The Dutch Case." In Levy, ed., *Private Education*.

James, Thomas. 1983. "Questions about Educational Choice: An Argument from History." In T. James and H. M. Levin, eds., *Public Dollars for Private Schools*, 55–70. Philadelphia: Temple University Press.

James, Thomas, and Henry M. Levin, eds. 1983. *Public Dollars for Private Schools*. Philadelphia: Temple University Press.

———. Forthcoming. *Comparing Public and Private Schools*. London: Falmer Press.

Jellama, William. 1973. *From Red to Black? The Financial Status of Private Colleges and Universities*. San Francisco: Jossey-Bass.

Jencks, Christopher, et al. 1973. *Inequality: A Reassessment of the Effect of Family and Schooling in America*. London: Allen Lane.

Jencks, Christopher, and David Riesman. 1968. *The Academic Revolution*. Garden City, N.Y.: Doubleday.

Jonsen, Richard W. 1978. *Small Liberal Arts Colleges: Diversity at the Crossroads?* AAHE–ERIC/Higher Education Research Report no. 4. Washington, D.C.: American Association of Higher Education.

Kaplin, William A. 1978. *The Law of Higher Education*. San Francisco: Jossey-Bass.

Katz, Neil. 1978. "A Review of the Literature on Non-Profit Organizations in Higher Education." Unpublished manuscript, SUNY at Stony Brook.

Keeton, Morris T. 1971. *Models and Mavericks*. New York: McGraw Hill.

Kendall, Elaine. 1975. *Peculiar Institutions*. New York: G. P. Putnam's Sons.

Kershaw, Joseph. 1976. *The Very Small College*. New York: Ford Foundation.

Kraushaar, Otto F. 1972. *American Non-Public Schools: Patterns of Diversity*. Baltimore: Johns Hopkins University Press.

Kutner, Mark, Joel D. Sherman, and Mary Williams. 1986. "Federal Policies for Private Schools." In D. C. Levy, ed., *Private Education: Studies in Choice and Public Policy*. New York: Oxford University Press.

LaNoue, George R., ed. 1972. *Educational Vouchers: Concepts and Controversies*. New York: Teachers College Press.

Levin, Henry M. 1983. "Educational Choice and the Pains of Democracy." In T. James and H. M. Levin, eds., *Public Dollars for Private Schools,* 17–38. Philadelphia: Temple University Press.

Levy, Daniel C. 1982. "Private versus Public Financing of Higher Education: U.S. Policy in Comparative Perspective." *Higher Education* 11:607–28.

———. Forthcoming. "Jewish Education in Latin America: Challenges to Autonomy and Group Identity." In J. Elkin and G. Merkx, eds., *The Jewish Presence in Latin America.* Winchester, Mass.: Allen & Unwin.

———. 1986a. *Higher Education and the State in Latin America: Private Challenges to Public Dominance.* Chicago: University of Chicago Press.

Levy, Daniel C., ed. 1986b. *Private Education: Studies in Choice and Public Policy.* New York: Oxford University Press.

McCluskey, Neil. 1969. *Catholic Education Faces Its Future.* Garden City, N.Y.: Doubleday.

McCluskey, Neil G., ed. 1970. *The Catholic University: A Modern Appraisal.* Notre Dame: University of Notre Dame Press.

McCoy, Marilyn, and D. Kent Halstead. 1979. *Higher Education Financing in the Fifty States: Interstate Comparisons Fiscal Year 1976.* Washington, D.C.: National Institute of Education.

McCready, William C. 1977. "Parochial Schools: The 'Free Choice' Alternative." In James S. Coleman et al., *Parents, Teachers, and Children: Prospects for Choice in American Education,* 67–75. San Francisco: Institute for Contemporary Studies.

McPartland, James M., and Edward L. McDill. 1982. "Control and Differentiation in the Structure of American Education." *Sociology of Education* 55:77–88.

Mason, Peter. 1983. *Private Education in the EEC.* London: National Independent and Schools Information Service.

Meyer, John W. 1983. "Centralization of Funding and Control in Educational Governance." In J. W. Meyer and W. R. Scott, eds., *Organizational Environments: Ritual and Rationality,* 179–98. Berkeley, Calif.: Sage.

Meyer, John W., Francisco Ramírez, Richard Robinson, and John Boli-Bennett. 1977. "The World Educational Revolution, 1950–1970." *Sociology of Education* 50:242–58.

Meyer, John W., and W. Richard Scott, eds. 1983. *Organizational Environments: Ritual and Rationality.* Berkeley, Calif.: Sage.

Meyer, John W., and Brian Rowan. 1983a. "Institutionalized Organizations: Formal Structure as Myth and Ceremony." In Meyer and Scott, eds., *Organizational Environments,* 21–44.

———. 1983b. "The Structure of Educational Organizations." In Meyer and Scott, eds., *Organizational Environments,* 71–98.

Millett, John D. 1973. "Similarities and Differences among Universities of the United States." In James A. Perkins, ed., *The University as an Organization,* 39–56. New York: McGraw Hill.

Minter, W. John, and Howard R. Bowen. 1978. *Independent Higher Education.* Washington, D.C.: American Association of American Colleges.

Monroe, Charles. 1977. *Profile of the Community College.* San Francisco: Jossey-Bass.

Mortimer, Kenneth P., and T. R. McConnell. 1978. *Sharing Authority Effectively.* San Francisco: Jossey-Bass.

Murnane, Richard J. 1986a. "Comparisons of Private and Public Schools: The Critical Role of Regulations." In D. C. Levy, ed., *Private Education: Studies in Choice and Public Policy.* New York: Oxford University Press.

———. 1986b. "Comparisons of Private and Public Schools: What Can We Learn?" In Levy, ed., *Private Education.*

Neave, Guy. 1983. "The Non-State Sector in the Education Provision of Member States of the European Community." Internal memo to the Educational Services of the Commission of the European Communities, Brussels.

Nelson, Susan C. 1978. "Financial Trends and Issues." In D. W. Breneman and C. E. Finn, Jr., eds., *Public Policy and Private Higher Education,* 63–142. Washington, D.C.: Brookings Institution.

Nevin, David, and Robert E. Bills. 1976. *The Schools that Fear Built: Segregationist Academies in the South.* Washington, D.C.: Acropolis Books.

Nisbet, Robert A. 1971. *The Degradation of the Academic Dogma.* New York: Basic Books.

Odell, Morgan, and John Thelin. 1981. "Bringing the Independent Sector into Statewide Higher Education Planning." *Policy Studies Journal* 10:59–70.

Pace, Robert C. 1974. *The Demise of Diversity? A Comparison of Eight Types of Institutions.* New York: McGraw Hill.

Pfnister, Allan O., and Martin J. Finkelstein. 1984. "Introduction." *Journal of Higher Education* 55:117–21.

Ramírez, Francisco O., and Richard Robinson. 1979. "Creating Members: The Political Incorporation and Expansion of Public Education." In John W. Meyer and Michael Hannan, eds., *National Development and the World System.* Chicago: University of Chicago Press.

Robinson, Gordon. 1971. *Private Schools and Public Policy.* Loughborough, England: Loughborough University of Technology.

Roose, Kenneth D., and Charles J. Anderson. 1971. *A Rating of Graduate Programs.* Washington, D.C.: American Council on Education.

Rusk, James, and Larry Leslie. 1978. "The Setting of Tuition in Public Higher Education." *Journal of Higher Education* 49:531–47.

Rust, Val D. 1982. "Public Funding of Private Schooling: European Perspectives." *Private School Quarterly,* Winter, pp. 11–34.

Salganik, Laura Hersh, and Nancy Karweit. 1982. "Voluntarism and Governance in Education." *Sociology of Education* 55:152–61.

Scott, Richard W., and John W. Meyer. 1983. "The Organization of Societal Sectors." In Meyer and Scott, eds., *Organizational Environments: Ritual and Rationality,* 129–54. Berkeley, Calif.: Sage.

———. 1984. "Environmental Linkages and Organizational Complexity: Public and Private Schools." Stanford University, Project Report 84–A16 of the Institute for Research on Educational Finance and Governance.

Shils, Edward. 1973. "The American Private University." *Minerva* 11:6–29.

Silber, John. 1975. ''Paying the Bill for College: The Private Sector and the Public Interest.'' *Atlantic Monthly* 235:33–40.

Simon, John G. 1980. *Research on Philanthropy*. An Independent Sector Research Report. Washington, D.C.: Independent Sector.

Sizer, Theodore R. 1984. *Horace's Compromise: The Dilemma of the American High School*. Boston: Houghton Mifflin.

Skerry, Peter. 1980. ''Christian Schools versus the I.R.S.'' *Public Interest* 61:18–41.

Sullivan, Daniel J. 1974. *Public Aid to Nonpublic Schools*. Lexington, Mass.: D. C. Heath.

Trivett, David A. 1974. *Proprietary Schools and Postsecondary Education*. Washington, D.C.: ERIC Clearing House on Higher Education Research Report.

Tyack, David B. 1968. ''The Perils of Pluralism: The Background of the Pierce Case.'' *American Historical Review* 74:74–98.

Vitullo-Martin, Thomas. 1981. ''How Federal Policies Discourage the Racial and Economic Integration of Private Schools.'' In E. M. Gaffney, ed., *Private Schools and the Public Good*, 25–43. Notre Dame: University of Notre Dame Press.

Weick, Karl E. 1976. ''Educational Organizations as Loosely Coupled Systems.'' *Administrative Science Quarterly* 21:1–19.

Weintraub, Frederick J. 1981. ''Nonpublic Schools and the Education of the Handicapped.'' In E. M. Gaffney, ed., *Private Schools and the Public Good*, 49–55. Notre Dame: University of Notre Dame Press.

Williams, Mary Frase, Linda Addison, Kimberly Small Hancher, Amy Hutner, Mark A. Kutner, Joel D. Sherman, and Esther O. Tron. 1983. ''Private Elementary and Secondary Education.'' Vol. 2 of a final report to Congress of the Congressionally Mandated Study of School Finance, July.

Williams, J. Douglas. 1984. ''Public and Private School Outcomes: Results from the High School and Beyond Follow-up Study.'' Stanford University, Program no. 84–B4 of the Institute for Research on Educational Finance and Governance.

Wine, Mary B. 1980. *Bibliography on Proprietary Postsecondary Education*. Washington, D.C.: Association of Independent Colleges and Schools.

Wirt, Frederick M., and Michael W. Kirst. 1982. *Schools in Conflict*. Berkeley, Calif.: McCutchan.

Zeigler, Harmon, and M. Kent Jennings. 1974. *Governing American Schools: Political Interaction in Local Districts*. North Scituate, Mass.: Duxbury.

Zumeta, William, and Carol Mock. 1985. ''State Policy and Private Higher Education: A Preliminary Research Report.'' Paper presented at the Association for the Study of Higher Education meetings, March 16, Chicago.

16

Neighborhood-Based Organizations: A Market Analogy

CARL MILOFSKY

M ost of the literature about managing neighborhood-based organizations (NBOS) is
rooted in the bureaucratic model of organizational structure. That model grows from
three axioms that define the unit of analysis,
the *organization:*

1. Organizations can be treated as whole social systems
with boundaries that are clearly defined, relatively imperme-
able, and stable over a period of years.

2. Organizations have a definite set of norms that legitimate a decision-making process and concentrate authority in
the hands of a few people.

3. Organizations perform specific characteristic functions. Members of the organization direct their attention and
their energies to carrying out these functions. People who
provide resources to the organization and those who obtain
services and resources from it expect it to perform these
functions (Selznick 1957; Thompson 1967; Milofsky 1980;
Freeman 1980).

The field of social work has generated a substantial academic literature that explores problems encountered in managing small nonprofit social service agencies with local community constituencies (Abels 1977; Skidmore 1983; Smith &
Freedman 1972; 196–211; Tucker 1981; D. W. Young
1979). Since social work agencies have adopted a rhetoric of
community involvement in their affairs, writers in this tradition have easily assumed that what is true for a group of social
case workers or community development specialists must
also be true for voluntaristic organizations created by people
living in a locale that provides social services—often vital
services. Thus, when people (especially funders and professional social workers) have worried about how to make
economic development organizations or community self-

help groups work better, they often have emphasized better
planning, management, and accounting procedures (see
Finch 1982; Hairston 1981). These alterations make it easier
for NBOS to interact with funding agents from outside the
community and, by making access to outside funding more
secure, may increase the chances that particular organizations will survive over time.

These discussions of administration techniques in small
nonprofits have not excited people outside of social work in
the way organizational theory since the late 1950s has informed the thinking of both social theorists and practitioners
in an array of institutions. It seems that few community
activists who launch and nurture community movements rely
on any written literature to guide their activities. This is
partly because there are no strong traditions of intellectual-
ism in community organizing and partly because there is very
little written that seems relevant to those working in the
trenches of community organizing (exceptions might be Baldock 1974, 60–82; and Zald 1967).

Social theorists interested in community and social movements would agree that the social work administration literature misses the point when it comes to understanding what is
most important about voluntary associations and NBOS.
Marx, Tocqueville, Durkheim, Toennies, and Simmel in
different ways described voluntary associations, embedded
in local community life and composed of shifting casts of
volunteers, that arise sporadically to attack particular local
problems while providing members with the pleasures of
community social interaction. They have argued that this
''web of affiliation'' knits the community together and helps
turn an aggregation of people living in the same area into a
cohesive, moral unit which provides a sense of purpose and
identity for individuals. In addition, these voluntary associations—vehicles of political mobilization and political educa-

tion—are the bedrock of democracy. At the same time, because Americans (in Tocqueville's eyes anyway) join many groups that address different political, economic, and social interests, voluntary associations also become an instrument of political stability. Crosscutting interest groups tend to undermine the appeal of single-issue mass movements. Thus mass-society theorists like Ortega y Gasset and Kornhauser saw voluntary associations as the main defense a democratic society had to offer against movements like Nazism and Stalinism.

Thinking about local voluntary associations as though they were little bureaucracies would seem foolish to social theorists in part because those interested in the fate of Western civilization usually are not interested in how one could make any particular association work more successfully. But more important the limited attention theorists of community and social movements have given to management issues comes from a set of underlying assumptions about what these organizations are. These assumptions are fundamentally different from those that underlie the bureaucratic model. This chapter offers an alternative perspective to the bureaucratic one for understanding management issues among NBOs and suggests some specific ways to use this new perspective in managing them.

The central contrast between the two perspectives is that organizations, rather than being seen as autonomous social systems, are treated as subordinate parts of a larger social system, the community. This means that where the bureaucratic model takes survival and growth as the central issues for each unit, my perspective recognizes that organizational death may be a viable solution to certain problems as long as it contributes to the overall well-being of the community. Another strength of the new perspective is that it demands that we see organizations in context—as parts of interorganizational systems or ecologies (Hannan & Freeman 1977, 1984; McPherson 1983) whose members make strong demands on one another. In particular, since NBOs usually control few resources internally, understanding their behavior requires that we place their dependency relationships at the center of the discussion.

Since the bureaucratic model offers as its underlying metaphor an autonomous social system whose actors strive to control uncertainty injected from outside by the environment, that model distorts our understanding of social units that do not stand alone but rather, by their nature, are components of a larger system. Searching for a more appropriate metaphor, this chapter depicts the relationship of NBOs to the community to be like the relationship of firms to an economic market. In classical economic theory, markets are composed of many small firms that together form industries. An industry as a whole produces products and distributes goods, and interaction among its members—competition—forces them to be disciplined and accountable to abstract laws of good economic practice.

For a comparison of communities and economic markets to make sense, however, we have to alter some ingrained ideas economists have given us about what a market is and what it does. Competition is the central feature of a market to economists, but it is not very important here. Within communities, in fact, there is strong pressure for organizations *not* to compete (Weiss 1978).

The market analogy helps our thinking because communities, like markets, are aggregate social structures that encompass many semiautonomous units (firms for markets, neighborhood organizations or voluntary associations for communities). As is the case with the study of markets, community analysts are most concerned with how the aggregate functions. Competition is important in market analysis because it is a mechanism by which inefficient firms are disciplined and eventually weeded out. The community is similar in that neighborhood organizations die when they no longer address a critical issue or serve a local need,[1] but their death need not represent a loss for the community. The death of particular neighborhood associations matters only if new organizations are not spawned and if former activists no longer participate in community affairs. In both the market and the community, the untimely survival of particular ineffective units (firms or NBOs) is deleterious. The system is healthiest when unproductive units fail, allowing their resources to be recycled into other, healthier units. The market and the community are similar in terms of the central importance of the birth/death cycle of constituent units.

A major goal of this chapter is to provide a framework to help local activists better understand the environment they confront and the operating issues that bear on their particular enterprises. I will devote relatively little space to specific propositions about the behavior of neighborhood-based organizations, because our knowledge is limited. Lacking a strong theoretical base, research has been misdirected or idiographic and fractionalized, so that we do not know much about how small participatory organizations function. The suggestions I offer here are primarily impressions gained from exploratory survey research and from informal case studies on a few organizations. One lesson this chapter *does* offer is that local activists must be prepared to let an organizing venture die and trust that new opportunities for action will arise.

This chapter has three sections. The first reviews the

---

1. Community studies have often suggested that voluntary associations are unstable and that they tend to fail from lack of community support. Rothschild-Whitt and Whitt (forthcoming) suggest there are few empirical data on the issue of whether in fact small participatory organizations fail more often than large, more formally structured ones. Organizational theorists like Hannan and Freeman (1977, 1984) might argue that if NBOs fail often it is more because they tend to be young than because they are democratic. New organizations—small businesses, for example—can have a mortality rate in excess of 50 percent. Given this general finding in organizational research, there is reason to believe that NBOs are substantially more likely to survive than their for-profit counterparts. Over two-thirds of two hundred organizations surveyed by the Program on Non-Profit Organizations at Yale University survived from 1978 to 1984 despite a harsh funding climate. This does not invalidate the conceptual point, however, that being structurally subordinate, voluntary associations may die out without damaging the health of the community.

traditional literature on communities, focusing on the integrating role voluntary associations play and on recent efforts at community organization represented in the War on Poverty as well as in private community mobilization efforts like the National Welfare Rights Organization (Piven & Cloward 1979). The task of this section is to define what we mean by "neighborhood-based organization" and to suggest some issues related to organizational structure that need clarification. In the second section, I propose a theory that emphasizes the similarity in structure between communities and economic markets. This causes us to look closely at the relationship between funding sources and structure in NBOS. The final section relates this market perspective on NBOS to several specific organizational issues that commonly arise in them.

NEIGHBORHOOD-BASED ORGANIZATIONS

For the purposes of this chapter, neighborhood-based organizations have the following characteristics:

1. They serve or are identified with a particular geographic region, usually a neighborhood or residential community.

2. They are organized to provide social services, to serve as a setting in which social or cultural activities may take place, and to act as an agent of advocacy or governance for a particular neighborhood or constituency.

3. They either are legally incorporated as nonprofits or are too small to be incorporated, or they may be incorporated as cooperatives but have an explicit goal of not making large profits for members (Rothschild-Whitt 1979).

4. They usually have an explicit commitment to represent the interests of their community rather than the private or professional interests of their founders. Often they are committed to democratic governance in organizational policy-making and have procedures for including community members in policy-making and program administration.

5. They usually are small with few layers of hierarchy and little internal specialization into formal departments.

This definition needs to be loose rather than precise because NBOS so often are small, fluid, and loosely structured. The structural variety among NBOS makes it hard to say exactly which attributes are necessary to include an entity in the category. Further, these organizations may have close relationships with or may evolve into organizations with a more formal structure. The definition is weak so that organizations like the YMCA (Zald 1970) or ACORN (a national federation of community organizations) are not excluded even though they have attributes of large-scale bureaucratic organizations. I also do not want to exclude organizations that have become more formal and bureaucratic by virtue of having successfully raised large amounts of money to provide services to neighborhood residents (Hannan and Freeman [1977] come to a different conclusion on this issue). Were we to define NBOS narrowly, saying perhaps that they are geographically focused participatory organizations

rooted in local community institutions, we would omit organizations that have evolved from informal to more formal ones but may one day evolve back in a more participatory direction as the funding climate changes. One community theater in the Midwest chose this direction after receiving funding for several years from the National Endowment for the Arts. Leaders of the theater objected to demands from NEA that it rationalize its administrative procedures. As federal funding became more difficult to get, they chose not to apply for funding renewal. Instead they sought to renew local participation which, members felt, had suffered during the period of federal funding.

Though large organizations are not excluded by the definition, this chapter primarily deals with problems that confront small participatory ones. To the extent that the former enter this discussion, it is because their basis of legitimacy lies with a community and with community involvement in their affairs. In particular, when broad-scale policy changes affecting funding occur, as has recently happened in the federal government, more formalized neighborhood-based organizations may have to jettison some of their formal structure to survive. Social theory (Michels' [1949] iron law of oligarchy, for example) tells us that this will not often happen. But the community theater example just mentioned suggests NBOS can be both flexible and tenacious. This conclusion is supported by a follow-up survey I recently conducted of two hundred NBOS, many of which had substantial federal funding when first surveyed in 1978. Over two-thirds of those organizations were still alive in 1984, despite federal funding cuts. Although the 1984 data are not detailed, phone conversations with activists in these organizations suggests that many sacrificed the one or two large programs the federal government had funded and replaced them with a diverse menu of small programs, many with strong participatory orientations.

Traditional Examples of Neighborhood-Based Organizations

If theory does not help us define neighborhood-based organizations, perhaps examples will. The term itself calls forth the image of organizations that have their roots in the social lives of residential neighborhoods. The traditional examples are organizations that arose in ethnic communities and that were a focus both of local social life and of a variety of mutual aid and community-betterment services. In some places a church—especially Catholic parishes (Fichter 1954) or Protestant churches in the black community—is the main generator of these organizations. Emphasizing spiritual awareness and concern for one's fellow beings, and enhancing community integration through ritual and expressive events, social organizations allied with churches are among the most important community-building agents (Warner 1959; Wood 1981).

In other communities there may be several primary institutions that, like the church, spin off collections of informal associations that become foci of the local social and political life. Thus, Kornblum (1974), in his study of the steelworker community of South Chicago, describes densely organized neighborhoods where social life revolves around four primary institutions: the union, the church, ethnic associations, and the political ward system. Wheeldon (1969), describing a colored (people of mixed black and white parentage) community in Rhodesia (now Zimbabwe), presents a similar complex interplay of primary institutions. The literature is rich in descriptions of this combination of social and institutional forces by which communities are knitted together with crosscutting and mutually supporting memberships in small voluntary associations (Simmel 1964; Warner & Lunt 1942; Warner & Low 1947; Warner & Srole 1945; Warner et al. 1963; Stein 1972)—what I term NBOs.

Neighborhood-based organizations are the vehicle by which a spirit of community grows within a residential area. Suttles (1968, 1972) and Hunter (1974), following Janowitz's seminal book (1967), argue that community is an ideology or abstraction that does not automatically develop in an area. It is a sense of identification with and commitment to a place, and this must be constructed through the efforts of individual actors and organizations. These community builders have specific self-interests in fostering loyalty to or identification with the people who live in an area or who share religious beliefs, ethnic background, a place of work, or political concerns.

The primary institutions of a community represent a partial list of agents who have an interest in fostering solidarity among the residents. Each of the institutions pulls its members in a different direction. The leaders tend to become zealots or professionals: priests, union organizers, politicians, social workers, teachers, professional community organizers, and recreational leaders. Residents, having an interest in one or more of these institutional spheres or perhaps just drawn along by the social tide, find themselves enmeshed in the push and pull of different specialized concerns. No one of these concerns is likely to dominate their lives. As involvements increase within one's daily life, however, the particularism of each interest group erodes. Community emerges as a common factor, shared by all the particular interests that spawn specific voluntary associations.

As an abstraction held in the public mind, community has no concrete social existence. It exists only as the sum of neighborhood social contacts and as a result of the ebb and flow of voluntary interest group affiliations. Shifting our focus to the neighborhood organizations that are the building blocks of community, we see that no one of them is intrinsically important. Just as a building can stand if a brick is removed from one of the walls, so communities are not endangered by the demise of particular neighborhood-based organizations. Not only are other organizations likely to arise but the people who belonged to an NBO during one period of activity usually stay in the community. If one of their involvements evaporates, they are likely to join another group (Merton 1976; Rothschild-Whitt & Whitt, forthcoming; Wheeldon 1969). In disappearing, voluntary associations may cause more problems for the analyst who would like to argue that particular neighborhood organizations have intrinsic importance than for the community members who abandon them.

Voluntary Associations as Agents of Community Self-Help

The traditional examples of NBOs emphasize their importance in building solidarity among residents (Warner et al. 1963), helping integrate immigrants from rural areas into urban society (Little 1965), and providing means by which citizens can be integrated into the broader democratic political culture (Eisenstadt 1956; Dahl 1961). In each case, NBOs are not the focus of discussion. Rather, they are an independent variable that helps explain some larger and presumably more important phenomenon—community solidarity, integration of immigrants, or democratic politics. Recognizing that all these good things come from voluntary associations, activists from Jane Addams (1961) forward have tried to build and use NBOs as a way of attacking social problems among the poor. If people in need can generate a strong community infrastructure, the logic goes, they can provide a variety of social services without relying on outsiders or being so heavily dependent for resources on them. Further, the mere presence of a strong community should build moral cohesion among the poor, combating the deviance that is born of social fragmentation and disorganization.

Since the 1890s, a variety of social action and intervention programs that follow this logic have been created to attack specific social problems—especially those related to poverty. Some of these efforts have been formal attempts by local leaders to mobilize resources and extend them to needy community members. Religious organizations have been especially important in this regard. Thus we have charitable groups like the Jewish Vocational Service (Seeley, Junker, & James 1957), which today are established social welfare organizations, and religious institutions like Catholic parochial schools (Sarason & Doris 1979), which also have roots in self-help efforts by people living in urban ethnic communities. Over time, many of these organizations have outgrown their community roots and become important providers of services to all urban residents.

Other community-building movements were initiated in the late nineteenth century by outsiders eager to improve, uplift, or mobilize the poor. The settlement house movement, begun primarily by middle-class women who laid the foundation for the modern profession of social work (Addams 1961; Lubove 1969), provided recreational and counseling services to residents of urban slums. Public education began in New York and other East Coast cities as a charitable service provided to children living in poor houses (Tyack 1974; Katz 1971). These and similar efforts laid the foundation for most contemporary social welfare services (for delinquency programs, see Platt [1969] and Schlossman [1977]; for workmen's compensation programs, see Nonet [1969]; for health care, see Freidson [1970] and Starr [1982]; for public welfare, see Piven and Cloward [1971]; for the YMCA, see Zald [1970]).

The growth of the labor movement and of succeeding social action movements championing the rights of the aged, blacks, welfare mothers, and other needy groups (Piven & Cloward 1979) added a new dimension to these community-based social action organizations. Where earlier groups had been concerned primarily with providing services, these later ones sought to represent the political and economic interests of residents. At first these movements championed particular issues. But in the 1930s and 1940s, Saul Alinsky articulated a political action philosophy that was not issue specific (Alinsky, 1969, 1972). Issues were important to Alinsky as devices that could mobilize residents through conflict and lead them to see the many parallel concerns they shared with those who lived near them. To Alinsky, people become politically effective when they become part of an active community, not when they act on only one issue. Political mobilization in the Alinsky tradition typically focuses on the failure of political and economic agents outside the community to provide services or to respect the physical and social integrity of a neighborhood. But political mobilization is more than a means for wresting concessions from the power structure. It also involves local residents in neighborhood social life and builds their sense of concern and responsibility for their neighbors. Thus, political mobilization is a device of community building that fosters local self-help efforts independent of outside sponsorship or support (Bailey 1974; Lancourt 1979).

The Alinsky organizing movement has spawned an impressive variety of community organizations across the country. And perhaps more important, it provided a model for the federal War on Poverty (Moynihan 1969; Rose 1972; Warren, Rose, & Bergunder 1974). The Office of Economic Opportunity (OEO) funded a variety of social services for the poor, which had built into their structure two elements of the Alinsky philosophy. First, there was a deliberate effort to include local residents in decision-making boards of the new social service organizations. Second, the new services were conceived as political tools. They were often outspokenly critical of established bureaucratic social service organizations like the public schools, urban renewal programs, and public welfare departments.

As Moynihan (1969) points out, the political activism and social criticism built into OEO led to its eventual demise. Local political leaders convinced federal legislators that it was politically dangerous to fund dissent in low-income communities. Its death did not eliminate OEO's policy innovations, however. To the contrary, OEO's programs were a template for succeeding generations of federal programs aimed at aiding the poor. Community representation on the policy boards of federally funded programs became a staple feature of local social service organizations. In addition, federal funding of social services shifted dramatically through the 1960s and 1970s from programs that provided large grants to local governments to numerous programs providing small grants (or categorical grants) for particular programs to nonprofit organizations located in communities. In his 1982 State of the Union address, President Reagan reported that a total of nearly $100 billion was spent on social programs in 1980 through about five hundred federal categorical grant programs ("Text . . ." 1982). His budgetary reforms have been directed, in part, at eliminating from the federal repertoire this device for funding and controlling local community programs.

Although the federal government may withdraw from directly supporting local organizations, twenty years of existence have made local social service organizations sponsored with outside funds a fixture on the community scene. Over these two decades, organizations that might have begun as local voluntary associations have grown and prospered by obtaining federal grants, building their budgets and staffs, and becoming more professional. In most communities there now exists a kaleidoscope of fractionalized service organizations, only loosely interconnected with one another but all committed to a rhetoric of serving local needs and representing local residents in their decision-making structures.

These local social service nonprofits should be included within the scope of our discussion of NBOs. Some of them do not conform to the characteristics outlined earlier since they have multimillion-dollar budgets, large professionalized staffs, complex administrative structures, and centralized decision-making structures. They may support the rhetoric of community involvement, but it is hard to argue that they are not large private social service bureaucracies similar to hospitals, mental health agencies, and private schools. These organizations are most appropriately studied using the conceptual tools of traditional organizational theory.

As noted above, many of these organizations grew out of neighborhood self-help efforts that successfully attracted large government and foundation grants, fueling organizational expansion and administrative formalization. Now federal funds are being sharply cut back or routed through state and local governments via block grants. Survival may require that these organizations become smaller and less formal, that they rediscover their community origins, mobilize volunteer workers, and attract diverse local resources. If they succeed in this, perhaps they will again become like voluntary associations.

THE MARKET AS METAPHOR

Neighborhood-based organizations, unlike formal bureaucracies, tend to have rapid membership turnover, fuzzy boundaries, democratic policy-making procedures, and a high death rate. A better analogue is the economic market. The economic theory of the firm emphasizes that each productive unit is part of and is shaped by the demands of a larger interactive system. That system is composed of competing firms, consumers, and sets of organizations that, on the one hand, provide the resources necessary for production and, on the other, absorb what a firm produces. The structure of any firm is a product of demands made by resource providers in the marketplace (that includes *both* providers of raw materials and consumers who provide revenues [Thompson 1967]), operational difficulties of manufacturing a product, and decisions made by the entrepreneur who runs the firm (Stinchcombe 1974, 1983). A theory of NBOs based on a market rather than a bureaucratic analogy emphasizes that (1) each organization in a community is subordinate to a larger whole and is not an autonomous social system; (2) demands of resource suppliers shape organizational structure; and (3) entrepreneurs, ready to launch new ventures after old ones fail, are keys to the existence of a vibrant set of NBOs in a community.

The Market and the NBO

The main unit of analysis in market theory is the industry—a collection of firms that produce similar products, serve an overlapping public, and compete with one another (Bain 1968; Cohen & Cyert 1965). The dynamics of a market differ in some respects from those of communities that spawn many neighborhood-based organizations. The key similarity is that the internal structure of individual firms is relatively unimportant when we talk about how the market functions and whether it is operating efficiently. Individual firms are born and die without upsetting the market. Only the rate of birth and death and the concentration of firms matter. So it is for communities and their NBOs.

Neighborhood-based organizations are not, of course, commercial, nor are there ways of measuring efficiency that directly compares with the concept of profitability. Business managers often are guided by signals the market provides in deciding what to produce, where to set prices, whether or not their workers are efficient, and whether or not the organization is doing well. In contrast, NBOs often rely on volunteers, define their domains by negotiating with other organizations to avoid duplication (which in business would be called competition), and sometimes consciously choose strategies that lose money to achieve some abstract purpose. Supply and demand may operate among NBOs, but these market-related concepts do not explain interorganizational dynamics as they do for firms competing within an industry.

The force of the analogy between the market and the community is that both use similar mechanisms for solving problems, mobilizing resources, and distributing them. Where organizational theory suggests there should be leaders who plan, attempt rationally to solve problems, and thus try to control and direct their closed social system, the market solves problems interactively. That is, the people who identify or are responsible for solving problems—whether intellectuals, policymakers, or entrepreneurs—recognize that they cannot anticipate how most problems will be solved, nor can they direct their solutions (Lindblom & Cohen 1979, 54–71). In an ideal competitive market, a collection of individuals, each acting in his or her own best interests, will solve problems automatically as a by-product of their interactions. These processes distribute commodities to the public, generate production with relatively little waste, and prevent excessive concentration of resources in the hands of a few actors.

We know, of course, that markets have flaws and that perfect competition never exists (Lindblom 1977, 76–89). But that does not detract from the appeal of the metaphor. It frees us from the responsibility of tracking every event, being concerned about the welfare of every firm, and figuring out how to achieve particular changes. If we understand rules that govern the interactive process (market competition) and know how the market departs from the ideal, we can do a good job of anticipating outcomes. This will become clearer when we talk about how NBOs relate to funding agents and how diverse NBOs may attract funds to a community from a variety of sources.

The market metaphor helps us understand NBOs because it turns our attention away from worrying about whether specific organizations are prospering and instead asks what makes a community "efficient" as an engine for mobilizing resources and making them accessible to a wide range of citizens. If there is a rich supply of NBOs in an area, then substantial in-kind resources will be mobilized. Individual citizens will find the associations and their attendant services that are accessible to them. They will be able to make their needs known and will have available the means to locate and acquire desired civic resources. In this way services should be better fitted to local needs than if some distant planner determines what services are provided and how they should be allocated.

The main hypotheses of this section are as follows:

H_1: If there is a rich supply of neighborhood-based organizations in an area, then the death of particular organizations will lead to the birth of new ones.

One of the main effects of participation is that citizens learn how to organize themselves. As they participate in more associations, they become better able to launch and shepherd new ventures. For NBOs to be continually created, there must be a pool of local activists available, just as for markets to grow and remain viable, there must be a pool of entrepreneurs ready to create new businesses when market conditions permit. Thus:

H_2: For a neighborhood to generate new associations as existing ones die out, there must be a supply of experienced residents who have some experience in voluntary associations, who see these organizations as a useful vehicle for achieving their personal goals, and who have the interest and energy to start or join a new project.

Observers of communities and voluntary associations have often discussed ways communities generate entrepreneurial activists. Rothschild-Whitt and Whitt (forthcoming) argue that an environmental attribute important to the health, survival, and regeneration of alternative organizations is a "movement orientation" among activists in a locale. Such activists do not see particular involvements as separate from the context of some broader political commitment. Wheeldon (1969) explores the importance of residents' personal careers within the social and political structure of a community as a process that encourages involvement. Young (1978, 1983, 1984) talks about varieties of entrepreneurship among leaders of small social service organizations. He compares them to the entrepreneurs who start small businesses and explores the reasons workers in a nonprofit organization might value setting up their employment in an entrepreneurial way. Lipset (1950) argues that becoming an officer in civic organizations tends to heighten political consciousness. Having been active, he asserts, one is more likely to become involved when one's personal interests are threatened. Janowitz (1967) discusses local industries (churches, real estate brokers, the YMCA) that have an economic interest in enhancing resident identification with a greographic neighborhood. He claims that these local businessmen generate civic associations to further their personal interests. Network theorists (Laumann 1973; Laumann & Pappi 1976; Mitchell 1969; McPherson 1981, 1982) suggest that the greater the density of social networks in a community, the more likely that bystanders will be recruited to participate when new issues arise.

The supply of activists and organizations within a community is important in the same way that the presence of many small firms is important in a market. If there are few organizations and few activists, there will be little organizing activity. This suggests another hypothesis:

> H_3: *Where there is little organizing activity in a neighborhood whose residents cannot afford to purchase social services, either citizens receive no services or services tend to be provided by a few large nonprofit firms (social service agencies) organized by people (often professionals) who live outside the community.*

Large professionalized organizations tend to fit the bureaucratic organizational model, which limits community involvement in decision making and program planning. Consequently:

> H_4: *If one or a few large nonprofits come to dominate local service provision, they tend to kill off small voluntary associations—unless the large supplier(s) are in fact federations or consortia of small, independent organizations.*[2]

2. Warren, Rose, and Bergunder (1974) argue that the dominant pattern is for nonprofit organizations that provide social services to communities to be monopoly suppliers of particular services. They call these organizations ''community decision organizations.'' There is substantial pressure within the social service system for agencies to ''cooperate,'' which, as Weiss (1978) points out, is in part language to legitimate agreements about dividing up the social service turf. In such an oligopolistic system, legitimate social service providers dominate access to major funding sources, so that alternative service providers are screened out. The United Way, for example, is explicitly structured so that new agencies that duplicate services of a present member agency cannot receive funding easily (Polivy & Milofsky 1981).

Although the dominant pattern is this cooperative division of service functions, agencies exist in some communities that represent federations of voluntaristic NBOs which, over the years, have joined together. Such an arrangement may allow sharing of administrative resources and technical skills. More important, as Hunter (1982) argues, federating is necessary so that community-based organizations can effectively address political institutions that encompass jurisdictions larger than the neighborhood. Thus, he argues, NBOs have tended to band together into stratified federations representing larger and larger jurisdictions. They

Conventional wisdom tells us that as NBOs seek and become dependent upon large grants from the federal government, large foundations, or the United Way their priorities are increasingly determined by concerns for accountability, fund-raising needs, and the norms of professionals. Community members cannot participate as fully as in smaller, less formal organizations. Activism tends to atrophy as opportunities for effective participation decline and as large organizations dominate access both to resources and to problems that need solving.

The market analogy helps explain the central problem for those interested in fostering NBOs: how to encourage resource mobilization at the community level without destroying voluntary associations by the very process of making resources available. If we make large grants available to local organizations, either those grants are won by large social service agencies or their size and accountability requirements transform voluntary associations into social service bureaucracies, destroying their participatory elements.

Focusing excessively on how to maintain the health and survival of *particular* organizations (examining NBOs using traditional organizational theory) threatens to institutionalize ineffective organizations just as protecting inefficient firms, perhaps by imposing tariffs on imported goods, threatens to burden the economy with inefficient firms. To have well-run NBOs (firms) it is important that the processes of birth and death continue. Services may be lost when an NBO fails, but the infrastructure of a community does not depend on this free clinic or that food cooperative persisting from decade to decade. What counts is that a community have activists and that those activists remain interested in launching new ventures. The death of organizations may make it hard for communities to provide a complete array of social services (just as the death of firms may cause serious local labor dislocations). But if we try to preserve *particular* firms, we tend to work against the health of a ''market'' of NBOs. This occurs if, to increase their chances of survival, we encourage organizations to become larger, more rational, and more bureaucratic. By focusing on the trees we ignore the forest. By focusing on particular organizations, we pay insufficient attention to ways of improving the health of the *collection* of NBOs in an area.

Perhaps this market rationale sounds suspiciously like

begin with federations of block clubs, extend to city- and statewide federations, and find their ultimate expression in national citizen lobbies. Presumably these federations are open to new members, so that, in contrast to oligopolistic social service agencies, federations do not necessarily monopolize access to funding sources. Although we may conceptually distinguish formalized social service agencies from federations of voluntary associations, the likelihood is that *empirically* it will be difficult to draw the line between the two types of organization. Extreme examples will be easy to distinguish, but there are numerous examples of voluntaristic community organizations whose success over time led them to swallow other organizations, to become more formal, and thereby to become functionally equivalent to more formal organizations, even though they retain the manifest structure of voluntary associations.

Nixon's philosophy of benign neglect, but it is not a justification for cutting funding support for community-based programming. Rather, understanding the relationship between the part and the whole, whether it be the firm and the market or the NBO and the community, is necessary if we are to develop an adequate understanding of voluntary associations.

In the next section we take the first step by introducing the concept of *funding arenas*. They are as important to community-based organizations as the concept of industry is to understanding market behavior. Funding arenas help us recognize how depending on outside funding agencies shapes NBOS. They show why entrepreneurial activists are essential to the growth and survival of community organizations. Funding arenas are most important, however, in throwing a spotlight on the central managerial issue in voluntary associations—the difficulties inherent in mobilizing resources and managing cash flow. The final task of this chapter will be to explore some relationships between cash-flow management and the structure of NBOS.

FUNDING INSTITUTIONS AND RESOURCE DEPENDENCY

In economic terms, industries are groups of firms that compete in selling particular products (Bain 1968). Usually an industry is defined by the products or services its firms produce and is limited to a narrow spectrum of products that are similar or are produced using a similar technology. Sometimes, as Stinchcombe (1983, 106–29) points out, things other than product similarity define the boundaries of an industry. Administrative procedures, labor relations, or the ecological structure of a technology can divide apparently similar products like steel and chemicals into separate industries. However one defines industries, they revolve around the production and distribution of products and services and they define markets.

Neighborhood-based organizations can be (and routinely are) divided into industries on a similar basis. The most important way this happens is in relationship to organizations that fund NBOS. Funding agents who normally provide money grants to NBOS often distinguish among local organizations on technical grounds. In particular, those that support services within a particular geographic area (such as the United Way, certain corporate foundations, and combined health charities) evaluate applicants for funds in terms of the local institutional division of labor. They ask, "What is the array of services that ought to be provided?" and they examine existing organizations to see whether there is duplication of effort or of granting-agency support (Polivy & Milofsky 1981; Weiss 1978). They make their funding decisions by defining a mix of necessary social service industries, allocating a percentage of their total budget to each one, and then dividing up these funds among a few agencies that have established themselves within that specialized industry—for example, child care, services to the elderly, or sheltered workshops for the handicapped.

Funding agents that serve larger regions, particularly national organizations like federal categorical grant agencies or national foundations, usually encourage specialization. Each administrative unit within these national funding organizations provides support for one or a few services at the local level. Thus HUD has separate programs to support housing rehabilitation, construction of new apartment complexes, local economic development, and local neighborhood organizations. This pattern is repeated from department to department in the federal government and within the foundation world as well. Large organizations like the Ford Foundation have different programs to provide aid to inner-city high schools and to stimulate housing or economic development in inner cities through revolving loan funds. Small foundations cannot be so internally differentiated. Consequently, many specialize in particular technical areas. Thus, the New World and Mott foundations fund community-organizing projects around the country, the Interreligious Foundation for Community Organization funds political organizations in minority communities, the Robert Wood Johnson Foundation funds health care projects, and the W. T. Grant Foundation funds programs that address children's health needs.

While distinctions among technical functions play a central role in structuring relationships among NBOS, they do not have the same meaning as in the market economy because the coordinative focus among community service organizations makes each industry like a monopoly. Technical specialties do not correspond to markets. Rather, certain organizations like the public schools, area agencies on the aging, or housing authorities are designated "community decision organizations" (CDOS [Warren 1967a]). These are empowered to seek funding and plan services on behalf of a local jurisdiction. Although CDOS may do their work well or poorly, they usually maintain their mandate because it is difficult for new organizations to challenge their legitimacy (Warren, Rose, & Bergunder 1974).

Competition within markets is not a source of innovation or discipline among NBOS as it is among for-profit firms. There is a parallel phenomenon, however, involving the grant application process. Although granting agencies often accept the legitimacy of CDOS as the main operating agency within a given technical area, this mandate may not extend to programs in allied technical areas. If funding is available for services not currently represented in a given community, new organizations can emerge and old ones can expand their domains by applying for grants to provide these services. Seeking such funding is relatively easy for NBOS experienced in dealing with a particular granting agency since, within any funding agency, application procedures tend to be similar across technical areas. In some cases individual grant givers work in several technical areas so that local leaders may get advice from old acquaintances—the old-boy network— about how to make a successful application.

Although there is little competition within any technical area, NBOS from one locale may compete vigorously across areas. If local people know how to write one kind of grant application, they can put their understanding and skills to work writing proposals to funders in several technical areas within a particular institutional sphere. Funding in a locality will grow if people are available who are capable of assembling proposals and applications. This suggests the following hypothesis:

H_5: *The number of people available to work on proposal and application development is a function of (1) the number of local organizations that have existed in the past that have sought funding in a particular institutional sphere, and (2) the extent to which professionals involved in those organizations have involved laypeople in fund-raising.*

Giving citizens fund-raising experience, then, is one way that local policymakers could (and in some communities do) stimulate long-term growth in the NBO sector.

While expertise in raising funds from federal categorical granting agencies or national foundations may be transferable across a group of similar funding organizations, it may not transfer easily across institutional boundaries. Thus, someone who can successfully write applications to federal agencies may not be so successful at writing applications to foundations. Leaders who have been able to raise funds through grass-roots appeals may be less able to write successful proposals for federal agencies.

Funding Arenas

The institutional spheres that provide resources to NBOs have boundaries and impose requirements that are likely to produce structural variation among NBOs. Thus it is useful to divide up this institutional array of ''places one can go to fund NBOs'' into a set of funding arenas. *A funding arena is an organization or a collection of organizations that provides resources and has a distinctive set of norms to govern the process of applying for grants or resources, a distinctive* *process for making funding decisions, and a specialized network of people who exchange information and influence.*[3] The following hypothesis defines the impact of funding arenas:

H_6: *Funding arenas are important determinants of behavior among NBOs to the extent that the norms of fundraising within an arena are so elaborate and costly to obey that leaders of NBO find it difficult to conform to the norms of more than one or two arenas simultaneously.*

Thus, one of the defining characteristics of funding arenas is that through their influence NBOs should become specialized, drawing most of their resources from one or two arenas. They should be pushed into functional specialization to the extent that funders demand it. The internal structure of NBOs should also become specialized to meet requirements imposed by decision-making agents within particular funding arenas.

Few data are available about funding arenas to tell us how sharply defined they are and what their contours might be. Table 16.1 shows, however, that funding arenas are important in this sample of 200 NBOs. Seventy percent of the sample received at least 70 percent of their funding from one source, and 82 percent of them received more than 50 percent from one source. The federal government was the leading funding source. Funding from a combination of federal,

---

3. When I speak of exchanging influence I am borrowing the language of pluralist political scientists like Dahl (1961) and Banfield (1961). They argue that political leaders govern by building consensus among leaders of many constituencies within a community. To forge a consensus, leaders exchange favors with those who represent local or special interest constituencies. By doing favors for these representatives, political leaders are later able to call in ''favor debts'' when they need support on a particular public issue. The capacity to acquire obligations for help is *influence*. Since favors are traded, influence may be exchanged.

TABLE 16.1   THE FUNDING OF NEIGHBORHOOD-BASED ORGANIZATIONS

| Percent of Funding | Federal Government | Local Government | Federal + State + Local Funding | Private Sources | | | | Total |
				Large Business	Foundations	Mass Funds + Church	Internal	
>70%	37 26% 100%	17 12% 100%	32 23% 67%	2 1% 50%	11 8% 69%	8 6% 67%	33 24% 87%	140 70%
60–69%			7 41% 15%	0 0% 0%	4 24% 33%	3 18% 25%	3 18% 8%	17 9%
50–59%			9 60% 19%	2 13% 50%	1 7% 6%	1 7% 8%	2 13% 5%	15 7%
<50%								28 14%
Total	37 18%	17 9%	48 24%	4 2%	16 8%	12 6%	38 19%	200 100%

Source: New World Foundation Survey of Community Self-Help Organizations, 1978 (see New World Foundation 1980).

state, and local government sources provided most of the resources to 102 organizations (51 percent). The next largest source was autonomous fund-raising by organizations (38, or 19 percent of the sample).

Strong as these data are, they do not indicate that funding sources necessarily are coercive. We may find that NBOS move freely between arenas, meaning that these institutional spheres are not so confining as the theory suggests. Given the dependence on government funding demonstrated in table 16.1, it is likely that NBOS have tried to change funding sources since these data were collected in 1978. On further examination we may also find that technical specialty is a much stronger determinate of organizational structure than funding source. Thus, in predicting structural patterns, it may be more important that an NBO provides housing or day care or cultural programming than that it receives funds from the federal government or local churches. We may find that such features as size, degree of democratic decision making, or organizational age are dominant factors. Most probably, there will be sharp differences between specific arenas—like the federal government and grass-roots funding sources—and more ambiguous boundaries between others. In this case, the concept of funding arenas is more useful as a metaphor that guides our thinking about the shaping of NBOS than as a device for measuring causal influences.

To explore these alternative possibilities and make the abstract definition of funding arenas clearer, let us consider the major funding arenas for NBOS: (1) the federal government, (2) local and state governments, (3) corporations and investment institutions (usually locally based), (4) national foundations, (5) local federated fund-raising organizations like the United Way and church-related charities, and (6) sources such as memberships, service fees, investment income, and business ventures that do not draw upon interorganizational contacts (Milofsky & Romo 1981).

Each of these arenas represents a separate entity of some kind.[4] Norton Long (1966) called a similar grouping of

institutions "games." David Ramage (New World Foundation 1980) spoke of them as different "cultures." These terms appropriately convey a sense that each arena is a rule-governed collection of actors whose relationships are bounded more by common understandings about how to act than by legal rules and boundaries. The arenas are institutions, not organizations (Meyer & Rowan 1977; Meyer, Scott, & Deal 1981). Organizations working in different technical areas will be differently constrained by arenas and may even make up different lists of arenas. People in some parts of the country (like New York State, for example) would have to include state governments as a separate funding arena—indeed, with the growth of block grants state governments everywhere are emerging as new arenas.[5] What defines the arenas are the perceptions and practices of the participants.

This much said, thumbnail sketches of each will help clarify what distinguishes the various funding arenas that are relevant to NBOS.

ing because sharply different kinds of organizations on occasion draw from the same arena—the federal government, for example. The organizations that make up one or another arena will shift as the target organizations that seek funding shift. What is more, particular funding organizations are likely to make different kinds of structural demands on different target organizations. Thus, the federal government relates differently to requests for funds from GM and from the South End Businessmen's Association.

5. That state and local governments are different legal entities does not mean that they should automatically be assigned to different funding arenas. Funding arenas are defined by constraints NBOS face that require structural adaptations to the demands of a funding entity. Local governments are a funding arena not just because they have traditionally been an important resource pool for NBOS. They also embody a unique decision-making structure. That structure is, on the one hand, open to public scrutiny and involvement but, on the other hand, often controlled by crystallized political ties built up over years of interaction between community influentials (see Dahl 1961; Banfield 1961; Laumann & Pappi 1976). A state like Connecticut, which is relatively small and has no dominant city like a Chicago or a Detroit, has a decision-making structure much like that described for large cities. Consequently, in small states, we should not necessarily separate state funding for NBOS from municipal funding. Large states like New York, on the other hand, may have decision-making structures more like that of the federal government. At both levels of government—large states and federal—decision makers are not likely to know much about NBOS that seek funds. Political intermediaries and demonstrations of expertise (both impersonal means by which an NBO may exert influence) are likely to determine the outcome of a funding application. Perhaps, therefore, large states should be treated as a separate funding arena or combined with the federal government in a single arena defined by the *decision mechanism*.

In addition to considerations of size, recent changes in federal policy have given states new funding authority. Since the absolute size of the federal contribution to social services has been cut at the same time allocation responsibilities have changed, the strategic changes required for NBOS to gain funding is perhaps not yet great. If public demand for government spending on social programs increases, however, states are likely to become increasingly active as funders of NBOS. Having acquired new responsibilities for distributing federal tax money, states should assume roles sharply distinct from those of federal and local decision makers, emerging as a progressively more important and distinct funding arena for NBOS.

4. Readers may disagree with the way I have assigned particular funding sources to arenas. For example, our research suggests that lumping together all funding sources that do not require interorganizational contacts is incorrect. Fees for services are characteristic of organizations that provide social services. This makes these organizations more like those that receive funding from the United Way than like those that raise money through bake sales. Similarly, organizations that receive funds from returns on investments are more like organizations that receive funds from corporations and financial institutions than like grassroots fund-raisers. Precise assignment of organizations to arenas must wait for empirical research of a kind yet unknown. The main point is that arenas exist that are distinct from one another in empirically meaningful ways. The likelihood is that when we try to define those arenas in some empirically precise way we will encounter enormous problems of quantification. This is partly because the arenas are symbolic as well as based on legal arrangements. It also is because relevant arenas shift from one type of organization to another. There should be an array of funding arenas for every kind of organization, not just for NBOS. Imagine how different the funding arenas for General Motors and the South End Businessmen's Association would be. The matter is made more confus-

The Federal Government

Because of its size and complexity there is no single way to characterize the federal funding arena that does not overlook some of the methods NBOs use to obtain funding. However, over the past twenty-five years categorical grant programs have played a critical role in the growth of NBOs performing a variety of technical functions. Categorical grants are funds allocated by Congress to address narrow problems. These funds are distributed and their use overseen by a large number of technically specialized offices in Washington to which NBOs must submit proposals if they wish funding. Categorical grant programs have been radically cut back since the later years of the Carter administration in favor of allocating funds to states in block grants. Nonetheless, there remain some categorical grant programs available to NBOs, and techniques for raising funds in Washington remain important to NBO leaders.

Federal fund-raising places a premium on grant-writing skills and on learning about the priorities of particular agencies. People working in those agencies receive many proposals from organizations they know little about. To choose among them, they look to see whether proposals are technically sophisticated, sensitive to current policy issues, and appropriately concerned with fiscal and administrative controls so that accountability is ensured. The difficulty of gaining attention of federal officials and of convincing them that one's NBO deserves funding is an important factor encouraging NBOs to become larger, more complex, and less fluid.

Raising funds from the federal government requires a heavy investment in learning about different programs so that NBOs can target agencies likely to be interested in the problems they confront. Also, NBOs must have personnel on staff with the technical and administrative planning skills necessary for writing acceptable proposals. To compete successfully for funding, large administrative staffs are needed. But federal grants tend to be large and tend to require that organizations be able to perform complex tasks. Thus, once organizations expand to carry out federal grants, they are progressively more likely to have staff who can write proposals that are well informed and technically competent.

Local Government

I argued above that the federal government is a unique funding arena more because of problems bureaucrats face gaining information and making decisions about small organizations like NBOs than because of the number and variety of programs the federal government sponsors. Studies of local government suggest that decision making within "small" political jurisdictions—a city the size of Chicago (Banfield 1961) is a small jurisdiction in this discussion—is sharply different. When categorical grant programs require that bureaucrats allocate funds to people and organizations unknown to them, localities often distribute funds through community leaders who are familiar players in the local political game or represent constituencies important to political officials. Members of Congress may on occasion intervene on behalf of NBOs applying for federal funds, but categorical grant programs still heavily emphasize universalistic criteria. Local decisions are based more on exchanges of influence and agreements among representatives of different neighborhoods about how indivisible governmental resources should be allocated (Dahl 1961). Urban political networks tend to be based on long-standing acquaintanceships and crystallized social networks (Laumann & Pappi 1976; Galaskiewicz 1979).

Compared to federal fund-raising, it is less important for NBOs to invest heavily in grant writing to acquire resources from local government than it is for their leaders to have close contacts with politicians. They must make a credible case that programs are needed, but the success of fund-raising efforts is likely to depend more on whether organizational leaders can work out exchanges of favors (perhaps by convincing a local politician that an organization's constituency can be important in his or her reelection) than simply on the technical competence of their applications. To be successful, leaders must invest in building strong ties within the local political culture—the logic is opposite to Granovetter's argument (1973) about the "strength of weak ties."

Corporations and Investment Institutions

Corporations tend to be idiosyncratic in their funding practices (see Useem, this volume, chap. 19). Some give grants to promote ideological or philosophic interests of corporate leaders (for example, welfare capitalists in Hall [1982]). Others give grants to improve their image in the community or with employees. Some industries invest in community organizations in the hope that they will make the cities in which their corporate headquarters are located more attractive and will improve employee relations. In other cities there is a tradition of corporate philanthropy that makes local corporate leaders feel obliged to support local causes (Galaskiewicz & Rauschenbach 1979).

To obtain corporate funding NBOs must be located in a community having either local corporations or an interested economic elite that might be tapped for support. The attack on Kodak by Alinsky's organization FIGHT (Freedom, Integration, God, Honor Today) in Rochester, N.Y., showed that corporations may need encouragement to enter the philanthropic realm (Lancourt 1979). To bridge the gap between the working-class communities they often serve and business leaders, NBOs need representatives who are socially compatible with the latter. This may mean recruiting sympathetic members of the business classes (middle-level managers or their wives, for example) to the NBO board (see Middleton, this volume, chap. 8). This strategy sometimes opens NBOs to the charge that they have sold out for money. An alternative is the creation of middleman organizations, like Greater Hartford Process in Connecticut (New World Foundation 1980), which mediate between the grass roots and the business community to help bridge the culture gap between the working and upper classes.

Foundations

National foundations share with the federal government the problem that they receive many applications from strangers whose organizations are hard to evaluate from a distance. Foundations are not constrained, however, by the need to provide equal opportunity to all applicants, and they are not vulnerable to the sort of political pressure that can be brought to bear on federal agencies by concerned members of Congress. Like federal agencies, foundations often define narrow sets of issues to which they will respond and intervention approaches they will support.

Foundations, however, tend to be less universalistic than the government in evaluating proposals (see Ylvisaker, this volume, chap. 20). Personal contacts with foundation officers can have an important impact on grant decisions. There also is a relatively small, crystallized network of people in the foundation circle—primarily officers of large and small foundations around the country and civic leaders who have received grants or provided advice to foundation officers in the past. Boorman and Levitt (1981) suggest that this is an old-boy network, which practices what they term "network matching," the trading of information and opportunities among network members. To raise funds from foundations it is important that members of the foundation circle know about and approve of an NBO's activities. This allows NBO leaders to use network contacts to gain access to and acceptance from foundations that might provide funding. It also allows foundation decision makers to make discrete inquiries about an NBO and to learn whether foundation dollars will be well spent. David Ramage (New World Foundation 1980) points out that these contacts are especially important where there is a cultural gap between members of an NBO's low-income community and those members of the economic elite who sit on foundation boards. Network intermediaries can give advice about the reliability of NBOs whose management styles do not exhibit the symbols of competence foundation officers expect to see. They may also advise applicants about how to write and present proposals so that they are acceptable to decision makers.

Federated Fund-Raising Organizations

The United Way is the most important federated fund-raising organization, but in some communities there also exist black United Funds, combined health charities, Catholic charities, or the United Jewish Appeal, each of which raises and distributes funds for local social services. They tend to allocate funds by assigning a base budget (Wildavsky 1964) to a collection of organizations that each fund has supported for a number of years. Thus, most of their resources are committed at the beginning of each budgetary period, and only a small portion of the annual grant budget is available for discretionary allocation to new organizations (Polivy 1982; Polivy & Milofsky 1981). Federated funds tend to favor established organizations because most were created by coalitions of social service organizations seeking to reduce competition in fund-raising. They legitimate their distributional practices by arguing that there should be no duplication of services in a locality. Consequently, new organizations that compete with old ones usually are not funded. This is an important reason that, as I suggested earlier, social services in most communities are monopolistic rather than competitive.

Organizations with no history of grants from a federated funding agent thus face an arduous task in seeking funding. Funding decisions are made by influential citizens working with professionals from the social service agencies that have been receiving funds. New organizations are most likely to garner funding if (1) they are performing a function that is locally recognized as important, (2) their functions are not performed and are not likely to be performed by any organizations currently supported by the fund, (3) they are not receiving support from the federal government or any other entity, (4) they find or place an advocate among the local influentials who make allocation decisions for the federated fund; and (5) they are prepared to reapply several years in succession to promote their case for funding. Where the United Way is concerned, Polivy (1982) argues that applicants are most likely to receive funding if prior support has come from local corporations.

Independent Fund-Raising

Neighborhood-based organizations can raise funds from membership dues, fees for services, donations from individuals, investments, fund-raising events, and business ventures, thus avoiding having to rely on outside forces or to shape themselves to fit outsiders' expectations. There has lately been special interest in what Boyd and Spiegel (1983) call the "business option"—entrepreneurial ventures launched by NBOs to raise money by acting like businesses. Churches have pursued this direction with great success over the years by organizing car washes, bingo games, publishing houses (Beckford 1975), toy companies (Zablocki 1980), economic development projects, camps, and the like. Most NBOs are limited in their ability to launch such projects because venture capital is required. Partnerships with businesspeople who invest capital in a project carries the risk that community-serving goals will be changed to meet the demands of business partners (McDonough 1983).

Autonomous fund-raising often leaves an NBO free to define its own goals and evolve its own distinctive style of organization. If a voluntary organization can generate a rich income stream and not rely on other groups, then members are freer to experiment with radical styles of organization. Traditional funding entities usually do not tolerate such experiments, as Taylor (1979) demonstrates in her analysis of a free clinic that changed from relying on panhandling for funds to receiving grants from the county health department.

Constraints of Funding Arenas

Two things are critical about each of these funding arenas: (1) for NBOS to successfully develop and promote proposals within each takes resources, often in substantial amounts, and (2) the decision makers in each arena have definite ideas about what makes a candidate NBO an appropriate recipient of funding. Demands placed upon an NBO by decision makers in one arena may, if accepted, make it difficult for the NBO to seek resources in another arena. Receiving federal money makes it difficult for an organization to be accepted into the family of United Way organizations. The informality of a grass-roots NBO that elicits support from leaders of local community organizations may convince decision makers in more institutionalized arenas that the NBO is not sophisticated enough to administer grant money successfully. Thus, NBOS may have difficulty raising funds from several arenas simultaneously because of conflicting values within the funding arenas. In most cases, organizations are limited to one or two arenas because they lack the resources to pursue fund-raising efforts in many directions at once. Thus:

> H_7: Funding arenas exercise the greatest constraint on small and informally structured organizations.

Large organizations are able to buffer internal departments from one another. They also are more able to free up resources for a funding search. Consequently they can simultaneously make overtures in several arenas (Stinchcombe, personal communication). Thus, the YMCA can successfully organize neighborhood support groups, obtain money from the United Way, and seek federal funds (Zald 1970).

Some organizations that work in technical areas specifically requiring that funding be sought by progressing from one arena to another seem to represent exceptions to H_7. Low-income housing organizations are the clearest example. They often begin as grass-roots movements and secure seed money from local funding sources like a church or a foundation. They may then receive an initial large grant from a nonlocal foundation, allowing them to launch a full-scale housing program. With an administrative structure in place, organizations then have the staying power to submit a proposal to the Department of Housing and Urban Development and survive until they are reimbursed for completed work. Polivy (1982) suggests that successful new grantees of United Ways also pass through a funding chain.

However, organizations that string together funding support from several arenas in ways *characteristic* of their technical area or of particular arenas that support them are not exceptions to the general funding-arena hypothesis. The goals of these organizations are shaped by the demands of funding entities as surely as are organizations wholly limited to one arena.

ORGANIZATIONAL ISSUES

The market metaphor shifts our attention from organizations as self-contained social systems to organizations as part of larger social systems. The main consequences of this shift of focus are twofold.

First, rather than the primary concern being how to ensure the survival and success of particular groups, organizational decline and death are viewed as common and sometimes desirable occurrences. Thus, where managers of a bureaucratic organization may devote great energy to finding ways of preserving their organization even though its primary goals have been accomplished (Sills 1957), leaders of an NBO might decide that both they as individuals and the community as a whole might be better off if the organization were allowed to die. Because the organization exists as part of a larger social system, an NBO's participants may turn their attention to other projects that better advance the goals of and social relationships within their community.

Second, the issue that most centrally shapes operating problems for the leaders of many NBOS concerns the mobilization of resources. As nonprofit organizations, NBOS are limited in their ability to raise capital. As small organizations, many have little slack and cannot easily tolerate shortfalls. Some of their most distinctive qualities come from leaders' preoccupation with resource mobilization problems.

Thus, for an organizational theory of NBOS to be adequate, we must understand the influence of funding arenas and recognize the strategies local entrepreneurs develop to generate necessary resources. None of this structural wisdom teaches us much, however, unless we also recognize the wear and tear on individuals that is inherent in community activism. I have suggested that bureaucratization is a danger to NBOS. This is true mainly because although it interferes with organizational democracy it also offers personal solutions to exhaustion and burnout for those who run NBOS. This chapter concludes, therefore, with some observations on the problems of regeneration in community activism.

Funding Arenas and Organizational Structure

If funding arenas are as coercive as I have suggested, then they should be responsible for sharp differences in the structure of NBOS. Organizations drawing resources from a given source should have a distinct organizational style or personality molded to the functional demands of that arena. These patterns are partly a matter of empirical description. Organizations funded by the federal government, for example, will have different attributes than those funded by local churches. The important effects of funding arenas, however, are also felt in aspects of NBOS that are not so easily observed or measured. They shape the strategies chosen by leaders and the actions NBO participants decide are possible to undertake. Thus, the discussion of funding arenas must be a structural/functional one. Strategic efforts by both NBO leaders and decision makers in funding organizations shape the structure of NBOS. By the same token, the concrete attributes NBOS take as they evolve shape the strategies that both leaders and funders consider reasonable and likely to succeed. To make sense of NBOS, we have to see that function shapes structure and structure shapes function.

The funding-arena theory is also structural/functional in the sense that each organization has to be seen in the context of larger social systems. Earlier I mentioned that NBOs are embedded in a broader community life. They are also embedded in a system of funding organizations that usually extends outside of the community. This goes beyond their relationships with specific funding organizations. It includes as well the universe of funding possibilities and the organizational transformations that would follow choosing one or another strategy of acquiring resources. Participatory organizations that consider seeking grant funds from the government or from a large foundation might consider in advance changes that would follow receiving such funds. Similarly, leaders of administratively complex NBOs whose organizations confront loss of grant funds might consider whether their organizations can or should change structurally to attract self-help resources from the community. Although the two kinds of organizations—participatory and administratively complex—seem different in kind, they are in fact joined by the opportunities and constraints presented by the system of funding arenas. We can imagine the universe of alternative strategies for action and survival that is open to NBOs only if we have a clear idea about the array of funding arenas NBOs confront and the choices entailed in participating in each one.

The discussion of particular arenas given earlier provides an outline of how particular arenas affect organizations. This outline needs fleshing out, but little research exists to do this. Some work has been done on how federal fund-raising shapes NBOs (Mayer & Blake 1981; Marshall & Mayer 1983), and Polivy (1982; Polivy & Milofsky 1981) has discussed the structural demands United Ways make on applicant organizations. Little is known, however, about what leads corporations or banks to make grants to NBOs, how NBOs can attract investments from private business (McDonough 1983), how local civic organizations come to support particular neighborhood development efforts (Janowitz 1967), or how states allocate resources to NBOs given their new responsibilities under block grants. The lack of research also reflects weak institutionalization in some arenas. Where funders are a fragmented group—individual donors or churches or corporations—they will lack the coherent funding policy we find in foundations or United Ways. Such coherence as exists lies in discoveries by NBO leaders that certain things work and certain things do not when raising funds from this or that source.

If more data on the characteristics of funding arenas were available, they would provide us with models of organizational behavior sharply different from those the bureaucratic approach gives us. First, rather than being based on broad generalizations, this theory is institutionally specific. Although there are certain system characteristics that shape the behavior of the federal government or local governments or United Ways relative to NBOs, the constraints imposed by different arenas remain heavily shaped by historical forces and the idiosyncrasies of particular organizations within each arena. The funding-arena theory also makes interinstitutional relations central (Meyer & Rowan 1977; Meyer, Scott, &

Deal 1981). Our data will describe the behavior of actors in particular organizations, but we imagine NBOs as part of a large complex system—the community—while we imagine funders as part of a different large complex system—the funding arena. *Relationships* are central in defining the behavior of actors at both ends. But throughout this chapter I have argued that the actors can change their affiliations without substantially changing the structures we care about. Thus, NBOs can shop around among federal offices looking for a granting program that will provide resources without changing the way the federal arena would constrain the NBO's behavior. Similarly, a particular NBO can go out of business without substantially changing the capacity of a community to attract resources—assuming that leaders of old NBOs remain in the locality. To understand how funding arenas shape NBOs, we must go beyond studying how funding from one or another source correlates with some structural feature of NBOs; we must also understand strategic considerations that are built into relationships between communities and various resource providers.

Entrepreneurs and Funding "Jigs"

Jigs are tools woodworkers build to carry out a particular job. One of the striking things about entrepreneurship in the world of NBOs is the enormous amount of institutionally specific information leaders build up: about how to survive, how to manage the idiosyncratic problems they encounter working with their clients, and how to cope with the agencies that provide resources to them. This information often leads them into behavior that seems mysterious and counterproductive to outsiders. Yet on close examination, that behavior often turns out to be a clever means for mobilizing or borrowing resources:

- A coop supermarket survived for years by capitalizing on the fact that supermarket suppliers do not require cash payment for wholesale deliveries and do not charge interest on money owed.

- A housing rehabilitation organization raised capital it needed to pay its grant-writing staff by borrowing funds it received from other grants intended to pay for management of property. These internal loans could be repaid when (and if) new grants were received.

- A Jewish agency serving orphans survived for years, despite efforts by the state and by established Jewish organizations to close it down (Young 1978, 1983, 1984), because of the ability of its director to maintain support from a neglected Orthodox subgroup in the Jewish community.

In each of these examples, NBO leaders discovered a "trick" for mobilizing and stretching resources that required that they have intimate familiarity with their kind of organization, with the funding sources available to them, and with their communities. These tricks are funding jigs—tools these entrepreneurs developed to solve administrative problems specific to their situations.

There are always tricks and bits of situated knowledge managers develop to make their organizations run better. For example, both Stinchcombe (1974) and Kornblum (1974) have described the importance of such tricks in steel plants. Line personnel (assembly-line workers) use the tricks to demand and to legitimize power in their relations to staff (professionals and managers). But NBOS differ from larger organizations in which institutionally specific tricks of the trade are shaped and constrained by formal structure. In large organizations universalistic expertise—about bookkeeping, methods of production, supervision of personnel, or the raising of capital—plays an important role and leads to governance by experts who possess general knowledge. This is one of the forces that leads to organizational isomorphism (Stinchcombe & Smith 1975; DiMaggio & Powell 1983).

Lacking much formal structure, NBOS tend to be strongly shaped by the idiosyncratic knowledge of their entrepreneurial leaders. The funding jigs entrepreneurs invent are standardized to the extent that within a particular funding arena and within a particular technology there may be certain rules one must follow to obtain resources. However, there also are limits on standardization. The tricks entrepreneurs think up are shaped by the tasks they are trying to carry out and by the particularities of their communities. There also is virtually no codification of funding jigs, so that entrepreneurs in one community do not learn what has worked for people in similar situations elsewhere.

This idiosyncrasy is the reason that if communities are to have a successful collection of NBOS they must generate a deep and diverse pool of neighborhood entrepreneurs. Because there is little isomorphism among NBOS, the knowledge needed to launch a successful project in one technical area is different from that required in another, just as the knowledge required to pry funding out of one funding arena is different from that required to obtain it from another. Among NBOS, general knowledge is scarce and particularism runs rampant. If there is to be organizational theory for NBOS, a critical part of that theory must be an attempt to describe and categorize funding jigs—means of generating and maintaining cash flow.

Bureaucracy and Burnout

Roland Warren (1967, 1–2) once argued that when thinking about social change people orient themselves toward one of two general values, which he characterized as "truth" and "love." The truth orientation, he explained, refers to "the impassioned conviction of the zealot, the person who is convinced he has come upon some fundamental moral value and wishes to see it embedded in the warp and woof of events." The love orientation, in contrast, is used "roughly in the sense of the Latin *caritas* and the Greek *agape*, and 1 Corinthians. I am using it not in the affective sense, but in the appreciative sense as a relationship of infinite appreciation and respect, perhaps best expressed by Stoic and Jew and Christian alike in the concept that men are all brothers, being children of the same loving Father." Warren claimed that, in

their purest form, these values tend to conflict with each other.

The substance of this value conflict does not concern us here. However, Warren's discussion does underline an essential element of leadership in social movements—that participation is heavily motivated by altruism rather than self-interest. Of course, we could argue endlessly about whether altruism ever is truly disinterested, a debate that would place Titmuss (1971) on one side arguing with Mancur Olson (1965) and Hardin (1982). But that would distract us from a real difference one sees between organizations that are fundamentally social movements—including many of the more democratic NBOS—and organizations that gain allegiance by distributing concrete benefits—usually money—to participants. This concern for personal advantage, an orientation toward pragmatism, is perhaps a third value motivating people to seek social change.

Leadership in participatory NBOS is extremely demanding, in part because there is little general knowledge leaders can bring to bear on the difficulties of mobilizing resources, gaining the support of a constituency, or legitimating their organizations. Because each situation and each organization tends to be different and tends to pose serious obstacles to successful organization, organizers must be unusually creative and energetic to make their ventures successful. This creativity is well illustrated in the case studies of entrepreneurship in social service nonprofits presented by Dennis Young in chapter 10 of this volume and elsewhere (1984).

Young's research, however, focused on organizations that usually were run by professionals and that sought to become solidly institutionalized. In this chapter I have argued that communities might best be served if some of these organizations avoided institutionalization (or bureaucratization, as I have called it), choosing instead to cease their activities. This is because pragmatism, as opposed to truth and love, tends to produce certain distinctive organizational structures that close off broad-based participation and crystallize a division of labor in a way that reifies expertise. Some (for example, Michels 1949) have suggested that these "distinctive structures" inevitably develop in participatory social movements. They argue that evolutionary processes are at work that necessarily undermine democracy in participatory organizations. This evolutionary conviction tends to discourage belief in the possibility for democratic social action.

By focusing on the organizational dynamics of NBOS I have tried to draw attention to certain practical problems that confront those who lead grass-roots social movements and wish to keep them informal and communal. Examining how some people manage to keep neighborhood movements alive, one quickly sees how hard this is to do. One understands why after a time people are inclined to give up trying to turn the intangibles of neighborhood life into a program that generates or attracts resources to a needy area.[6] Yet local activists should not feel reluctant or regretful about letting

6. This idea was suggested upon reading this manuscript by Charles Haun, a community organizer.

their efforts lapse. As long as activists retain their belief in truth or love and as long as they live in a community in which others share and support those beliefs, new movements can emerge.

It is hard for those immersed in a particular movement to see larger patterns of historical change and community development. Without this vision, however, activists can become martyrs, overextending and exhausting themselves. Rather than pulling out of a particular movement and saving their energy for another undertaking, such organizers may abandon community work or pursue initiatives that would make their organization more stable and institutionalized. Either way, the community may be a loser. If organizers become exhausted and leave the community, the human resources needed to generate new movements are lost. If organizers seek large grants or in some other way make their organizations more permanent and, presumably, more bureaucratic, the community is likely to lose control.

Emphasizing the practical difficulties of leadership in NBOs, one comes to see that should social movements shift to become more bureaucratic, the causes of change are not some opaque law of social entropy. One might assume that such dark forces are at play when reading Michels's phrase, "the iron law of oligarchy." Introducing changes that formalize their organizations, leaders of social movements usually are taking pragmatic steps to make their work easier and less stressful. It is hard to survive year after year not knowing whether one will have a job, so it is comforting to make one's organization permanent. It is uncomfortable to be underpaid, so it makes sense that starving activists might eventually seek to receive a reasonable wage. It is frustrating to see the lessons of long experience continually swept aside by inexperienced volunteers who only recently have become involved in a movement. It also is frustrating to be continually uncertain about which participants in an organization are responsible for which activities (Milofsky & Elworth, 1985). What I have called bureaucratization in NBOs largely refers to a set of adjustments that make it easier to keep track of what is going on, to take advantage of accumulated "organizational intelligence" (Wilensky 1967), and to guarantee continuity over time. All these are reasonable desires on the part of leaders once one recognizes the hardships of organizational maintenance.

Perhaps an organizational theory of NBOs should be directed to finding solutions that avoid these dilemmas of bureaucratization and burnout. But casting the problem in this way does violence to the nature of NBOs. The simple fact is that these neighborhood movements exist in their moment. They are generated when members of a community share a sense of problem and their actions are fueled by enthusiasm and social commitment. Their shape is strongly determined by the cast of characters who create the organization and by the structure of opportunities and constraints those characters perceive. When the charter members no longer feel an urgency to participate, there tends to be an organizational crisis that leads to a shift in administrative form, a rollover in central characters, or the death of the movement. An organizational theory of NBOs must recognize the vitality and energy inherent in transience and focus on the problems involved in building interest and in riding on a flood of collective enthusiasm. This chapter has argued that those problems mainly concern how resources can be mobilized and how constraints of resource dependency can best be managed.

REFERENCES

Abels, Paul. 1977. *The New Practice of Supervision and Staff Development: A Synergistic Approach*. New York: Association Press.

Addams, Jane. 1961. *Twenty Years at Hull House*. New York: New American Library.

Alinsky, Saul D. 1969. *Reveille for Radicals*. New York: Random House.

———. 1972. *Rules for Radicals: A Pragmatic Primer for Realistic Radicals*. New York: Vintage.

Bailey, Robert, Jr. 1974. *Radicals in Urban Politics: The Alinsky Approach*. Chicago: University of Chicago Press.

Bain, Joe. 1968. *Industrial Organization*. 2d ed. New York: John Wiley.

Baldock, Peter. 1974. *Community Work and Social Work*. London: Routledge & Kegan Paul.

Banfield, Edward C. 1961. *Political Influence*. Glencoe, Ill.: Free Press.

Beckford, James A. 1975. *The Trumpet of Prophecy: A Sociological Study of Jehovah's Witnesses*. New York: Halsted Press.

Boorman, Scott A., and Paul R. Levitt. 1981. "Network Matching: Nonprofit Structure and Public Policy. Chapter One: Cultural Conflicts and the Roots of Nonprofit Social Structure." Yale University, Department of Sociology, unpublished manuscript.

Boyd, Bruce, and Hans Spiegel. 1983. "Financing Community

Organizations: The Business Option.'' *Journal of Community Action* 1, no. 5:9–13.

Cohen, Kalman J., and Richard M. Cyert. 1965. *Theory of the Firm: Resource Allocation in a Market Economy*. Englewood Cliffs, N.J.: Prentice Hall.

Dahl, Robert A. 1961. *Who Governs? Democracy and Power in an American City*. New Haven: Yale University Press.

DiMaggio, Paul W., and Walter W. Powell. 1983. ''The Iron Cage Revisited: Institutional Isomorphism and Collective Rationality in Organizational Fields.'' *American Sociological Review* 48:147–60.

Eisenstadt, Schmuel N. 1956. ''The Social Conditions of the Development of Voluntary Associations—A Case Study of Israel.'' *Scripta Hierosolymitana* 3:104–24.

Fichter, Joseph. 1954. *Social Relations in the Urban Parish*. Chicago: University of Chicago Press.

Finch, William A., Jr. 1982. ''Declining Public Social Service Resources: A Managerial Problem.'' *Administration in Social Work* 6, no. 1:19–28.

Freeman, John H. 1980. ''The Unit of Analysis in Organizational Research.'' In Marshall W. Meyer et al., *Environments and Organizations*. San Francisco: Jossey-Bass.

Freidson, Elliot. 1970. *The Profession of Medicine: A Study of the Sociology of Applied Knowledge*. New York: Dodd, Mead.

Galaskiewicz, Joseph. 1979. *Exchange Networks and Community Politics*. Beverly Hills, Calif.: Sage Publications.

Galaskiewicz, Joseph, and Barbara Rauschenbach. 1979. ''Patterns of Inter-institutional Exchange: An Examination of Linkages between Cultural and Business Organizations in a Metropolitan Community.'' Paper presented at meetings of the American Sociological Association, Boston.

Granovetter, Mark. 1973. ''The Strength of Weak Ties.'' *American Journal of Sociology* 78:1360–80.

Hairston, C. F. 1981. ''Improving Cash Flow Management in Nonprofit Organizations.'' *Administration in Social Work* 5, no. 2:29–36.

Hall, Peter D. 1982. ''Philanthropy as Investment: An Essay Review of Burton K. Folsom, Jr., *Urban Capitalists Entrepreneurs and City Growth in Pennsylvania's Lackawanna and Lehigh Regions, 1800–1920*.'' Yale University, Program on Non-Profit Organizations.

Hannan, Michael T., and John H. Freeman. 1977. ''The population ecology of organizations.'' *American Journal of Sociology* 82:929–64.

———. 1984. ''Structural Inertia and Organizational Change.'' *American Sociological Review* 49:149–64.

Hardin, Russell. 1982. *Collective Action*. Baltimore: Johns Hopkins University Press for Resources for the Future.

Hunter, Albert. 1974. *Symbolic Communities: The Persistence and Change of Chicago's Local Communities*. Chicago: University of Chicago Press.

———. 1982. ''The Neighborhood Movement as Communal Class Politics: The State Construction of Community.'' Paper presented at the Program on Non-Profit Organizations, Yale University, May.

Janowitz, Morris. 1967. *The Community Press in an Urban Setting*. Chicago: University of Chicago Press.

Katz, Michael. 1971. *Class, Bureaucracy and Schools: The Illusion of Educational Change in America*. New York: Praeger.

Kornblum, William. 1974. *Blue-Collar Community*. Chicago: University of Chicago Press.

Lancourt, Joan E. 1979. *Confront or Concede: The Alinsky Citizen Action Organizations*. Lexington, Mass.: Lexington Books.

Laumann, Edward O. 1973. *Bonds of Pluralism: The Form and Substance of Social Networks*. New York: Wiley.

Laumann, Edward O., and Franz U. Pappi. 1976. *Networks of Collective Action: A Perspective on Community Influence*. New York: Academic Press.

Lindblom, Charles E. 1977. *Politics and Markets: The World's Political-Economic Systems*. New York: Basic Books.

Lindblom, Charles E., and David K. Cohen. 1979. *Usable Knowledge: Social Science and Social Problem Solving*. New Haven: Yale University Press.

Lipset, Seymour M. 1950. *Agrarian Socialism: The Cooperative Commonwealth Federation in Saskatchewan: A Study in Political Sociology*. Berkeley and Los Angeles: University of California Press.

Little, Kenneth L. 1965. *West African Urbanization: A Study of Voluntary Associations in Social Change*. New York and Cambridge: Cambridge University Press.

Long, N. E. 1966. ''The Local Community as an Ecology of Games.'' In R. L. Warren, ed., *Perspectives in the American Community*, 54–68. Chicago: Rand McNally.

Lubove, Roy. 1969. *The Professional Altruist: The Emergence of Social Work as a Career 1880–1930*. New Jersey: Atheneum.

McDonough, William. 1983. ''Neighborhood Fiscal Empowerment Analytic Paper.'' Prepared for Division of Community Planning and Neighborhood Studies, Office of Policy Development and Research, HUD. Hartford, Conn.: McDonough, Bond & Assoc.

McPherson, J. Miller. 1981. ''A Dynamic Model of Voluntary Affiliation.'' *Social Forces* 59:705–28.

———. 1982. ''Hypernetwork Sampling: Duality and Differentiation among Voluntary Organizations.'' *Social Networks* 3:225–49.

———. 1983. ''An Ecology of Affiliation.'' *American Sociological Review* 48:519–32.

Marshall, Sue A., and Neil S. Mayer. 1983. ''Neighborhood Organizations and Community Development.'' Washington, D.C.: Urban Institute.

Mayer, Neil S., and Jennifer L. Blake. 1981. *Keys to the Growth of Neighborhood Development Organizations*. Washington, D.C.: Urban Institute.

Merton, Robert K. 1976. ''Dilemmas in Voluntary Associations.'' In *Sociological Ambivalence*, 90–105. New York: Free Press.

Meyer, John W., and Brian Rowan. 1977. ''Institutionalized Organizations: Formal Structure as Myth and Ceremony.'' *American Journal of Sociology* 83:340–63.

Meyer, John W., W. Richard Scott, and Terrance E. Deal. 1981. ''Institutional and Technical Sources of Organizational Structure: Explaining the Structure of Educational Organizations.'' In Herman D. Stein, ed., *Organization and Human Services*. Philadelphia: Temple University Press.

Michels, Robert. 1949. *Political Parties*. Glencoe, Ill.: Free Press.

Milofsky, Carl. 1980. "Structure and Process in Community Self-help Organizations." Yale University, Program on Non-Profit Organizations Working Paper no. 17.

Milofsky, Carl, and Julie Elworth. 1985. "Charitable Associations." In Nicholas Hobbs and James Perrin, eds., *Issues in the Care of Children with Chronic Illness*. San Francisco: Jossey-Bass.

Milofsky, C., and F. Romo. 1981. "The Structure of Funding Arenas for Community Self-help Organizations." Yale University, Program on Non-Profit Organizations Working Paper no. 42.

Mitchell, J. Clyde. 1969. *Social Networks in Urban Situations*. Manchester: University of Manchester Press.

Moynihan, Daniel P. 1969. *Maximum Feasible Misunderstanding*. New York: Free Press.

New World Foundation. 1980. *Initiatives for Community Self-Help: Efforts to Increase Recognition and Support*. New York: New World Foundation.

Nonet, Phillipe. 1969. *Administrative Justice: Advocacy and Change in Governmental Agencies*. New York: Russell Sage.

Olson, Mancur, Jr. 1965. *The Logic of Collective Action: Public Goods and the Theory of Groups*. New York: Schocken.

Peters, Victor. 1965. *All Things Common: The Hutterian Way of Life*. Minneapolis: University of Minnesota Press.

Piven, Frances Fox, and Richard A. Cloward. 1971. *Regulating the Poor: The Functions of Public Welfare*. New York: Vintage.

———. 1979. *Poor People's Movements: Why They Succeed, How They Fail*. New York: Vintage.

Platt, Anthony M. 1969. *The Child Savers: The Invention of Delinquency*. Chicago: University of Chicago Press.

Polivy, Deborah K. 1982. "A Studies of the Admissions Policies and Practices of Eight Local United Way Organizations." Yale University, Program on Non-Profit Organizations.

Polivy, Deborah K., and Carl Milofsky. 1981. "Finding Funding in the 1980s: Some Useful Information on Funding Arenas and How to Approach Them." Paper presented at meetings of the National Association of Social Workers, Philadelphia, November 19.

Rose, Stephen M. 1972. *Betrayal of the Poor: The Transformation of Community Action*. Cambridge, Mass.: Schenkman.

Rothschild-Whitt, Joyce. 1979. "The Collectivist Organization," *American Sociological Review* 44:509–28.

Rothschild-Whitt, Joyce, and J. Allen Whitt. Forthcoming. *Work without Bosses*. Rose Monograph Series.

Sale, Kirkpatrick. 1973. *SDS*. New York: Random House.

Sarason, Seymour B. 1971. *The Culture of the School and the Problem of Change*. Boston: Allyn & Bacon.

Sarason, Seymour, and John Doris. 1979. *Educational Handicap, Public Policy and Social History*. New York: Free Press.

Schlossman, Stephen L. 1977. *Love and the American Delinquent: The Theory and Practice of "Progressive" Juvenile Justice. 1825–1920*. Chicago: University of Chicago Press.

Seeley, John R., B. R. Junker, and R. W. James. 1957. *Community Chest*. Toronto: University of Toronto Press.

Selznick, Philip. 1952. *The Organizational Weapon: A Study of Bolshevist Strategy and Tactics*. New York: McGraw Hill.

———. 1957. *Leadership in Administration*. New York: Harper & Row.

Sills, David. 1957. *The Volunteers: Means and Ends in a National Organization*. Glencoe, Ill.: Free Press.

Simmel, Georg. 1964. *Conflict and the Web of Group Affiliations*. New York: Free Press.

Skidmore, Rex A. 1983. *Social Work Administration, Dynamic Management and Human Relationships*. Englewood Cliffs, N.J.: Prentice-Hall.

Smith, Constance, and Anne Freedman. 1972. *Voluntary Associations: Perspectives on the Literature*. Cambridge, Mass.: Harvard University Press.

Starr, Paul. 1982. *The Social Transformation of American Medicine*. New York: Basic Books.

Stein, Maurice. 1972. *The Eclipse of Community: An Interpretation of American Studies*. Princeton, N.J.: Princeton University Press.

Stinchcombe, A. L. 1974. *Creating Efficient Industrial Administrations*. New York: Academic Press.

———. 1983. *Economic Sociology*. New York: Academic Press.

Stinchcombe, Arthur L., and Tom W. Smith. 1975. "The Homogenization of the Administrative Structures of American Industries, 1940–1970." Unpublished manuscript. University of Chicago, National Opinion Research Center.

Suttles, Gerald D. 1968. *The Social Order of the Slum: Ethnicity and Territory in the Inner City*. Chicago: University of Chicago Press.

———. 1972. *The Social Construction of Community*. Chicago: University of Chicago Press.

Taub, R., G. P. Surgeon, S. L. Holm, P. B. Otti, and A. Bridges. 1977. "Urban Voluntary Associations, Locality Based and Externally Induced." *American Journal of Sociology* 83:425–42.

Taylor, Rosemary C. R. 1979. "Free Medicine." In John Case and Rosemary C. R. Taylor, *Coops, Communes and Collectives: Experiments in Social Change in the 1960s and 1970s*, 17–48. New York: Pantheon.

"Text of President's Message to Nation on the State of the Union." 1982. *New York Times*, January 27, p. A16.

Thompson, James D. 1967. *Organizations in Action*. New York: McGraw-Hill.

Titmuss, Richard M. 1971. *The Gift Relationship: From Human Blood to Social Policy*. New York: Vintage Books.

Tucker, David J. 1981. "Voluntary Auspices and the Behavior of Social Service Organizations." *Social Service Review* 55:603–27.

Tyack, David. 1974. *The One Best System*. Cambridge, Mass.: Harvard University Press.

Warner, William Lloyd. 1959. *The Living and the Dead: A Study of the Symbolic Life of Americans*. New Haven: Yale University Press.

Warner, William Lloyd, and J. O. Low. 1947. *The Social System of the Modern Factory: The Strike: A Social Analysis*. New Haven: Yale University Press.

Warner, William Lloyd, J. O. Low, Paul S. Tunk, and L. Srole. 1963. *Yankee City*. New Haven: Yale University Press.

Warner, William Lloyd, and Paul G. Lunt 1942. *The Status System of a Modern Community*. New Haven: Yale University Press.

Warner, William Lloyd, and Leo Srole. 1945. *The Social Systems of American Ethnic Groups*. New Haven: Yale University Press.

Warren, Roland L. 1967a. "The Interorganizational Field as a Focus for Investigation." *Administrative Science Quarterly* 12:396–419.

———. 1967b. "Truth, Love and Social Change." Paper presented at the Seminar on Channeling Social Change, Institute on Man and Science, Rensselaerville, N.Y., October.

Warren, Roland L., S. M. Rose, and A. F. Bergunder. 1974. *The Structure of Urban Reform: Community Design, Organization and Stability and Change*. Lexington, Mass.: Lexington Books.

Weiss, Janet. 1978. "Coordination of Human Services: Substance vs. Symbol of Reform." Yale University, Institution for Social and Policy Studies Working Paper no. 805.

Wheeldon, Patricia D. 1969. "The Operation of Voluntary Associations and Personal Networks in the Political Processes of an Inter-ethnic Community." In J. Clyde Mitchell, ed., *Social Networks in Urban Situations: Analyses of Personal Relationships in Central African Towns*. Manchester, England: Manchester University Press.

Wildavsky, Aaron. 1964. *The Politics of the Budgetary Process*. Boston: Little, Brown.

Wilensky, Harold L. 1967. *Organizational Intelligence: Knowledge and Policy in Government and Industry*. New York: Basic Books.

Wood, James R. 1981. *Leadership in Voluntary Organizations: The Controversy of Social Action in Protestant Churches*. New Brunswick, N.J.: Rutgers University Press.

Young, David W. 1979. *The Managerial Process in Human Service Agencies*. New York: Praeger.

Young, Dennis. 1978. "Motives, Models and Men: An Exploration of Entrepreneurship in the Non-profit Sector." Yale University, Program on Non-Profit Organizations Working Paper no. 4.

———. 1983. *If Not for Profit for What? A Behavioral Theory of the Nonprofit Sector Based on Entrepreneurship*. Lexington, Mass.: Lexington Books.

———. 1984. *Casebook of Management for Nonprofit Organizations: Entrepreneurship and Organizational Change in the Human Services*. New York: Haworth Press.

Zablocki, Beniamin. 1980. *The Joyful Community*. Chicago: University of Chicago Press.

Zald, Mayer H. 1967. "Sociology and Community Organization Practice." In Mayer Zald, ed., *Organizing for Community Welfare*, 27–61. Chicago: Quadrangle.

———. 1970. *Organizational Change: The Political Economy of the YMCA*. Chicago: University of Chicago Press.

17

Nonprofit Organizations and Policy Advocacy

J. CRAIG JENKINS

I n what *Time* called "an era of strenuous clique and the vociferous claque" and *Newsweek* labeled the age of "me-first factionalism," political commentators have increasingly noted—and typically lamented—the recent upsurge of political advocacy. In his farewell address President Carter charged that the "special interests" had sabotaged his administration by mounting a massive lobbying campaign in the Congress. From across the Hill, Sen. Edward Kennedy echoed the complaint, claiming that Congress was "awash in a sea of special interest campaign contributions and special interest lobbying." Academic analysts, such as Bell (1976), Huntington (1976, 1981), and Ladd (1980), have offered an even more ominous diagnosis, claiming that the recent upsurge in "single-issue" and "special interest" political advocacy has produced a "crisis of democracy." The multiplication of demands and the uncompromising manner in which they have been advanced have, in their view, "overloaded" the polity, producing political paralysis, weakened authority, and political alienation. What brought about this general upsurge in political advocacy? What has been the significance of the recent increase in policy advocacy by nonprofit organizations? Have the nonprofit advocates been a corrective or a contributor to this apparent "excess of factionalism"?

NONPROFIT ADVOCACY AND THE PUBLIC INTEREST

The rationale offered by most nonprofit advocates is that they represent the noncommercial collective interests of the general public as opposed to the special economic interests of particular segments of society. In other words, the nonprofit advocacy is distinctively committed to the "public interest" defined in terms of noneconomic, collective or indivisible interests that have the general public as their intended bene-

ficiary. Berry (1977, 7), for example, in discussing the array of nonprofit organizations currently active in public interest lobbying in Washington, D.C., defines them in terms of their advocacy of "collective good[s], the achievement of which will not selectively and materially benefit the membership or activists of the organization." Similarly, Schuck (1977, 133), in discussing nonprofit public interest law firms, has argued that they pursue "collective interests shared by broad publics" as opposed to the narrow private economic interests advocated by the typical private law firm. More recently Tesh (1984, 29–31), contrasting what she calls "issue groups" with "interest groups," points out that the former have an open or nonexclusive membership and base their appeals for support in terms of "moral convictions about the rightness of policies" as opposed to narrow economic interests. The tax code also supports this interpretation, reserving the nonprofit form for charitable, social welfare, and educational activities that can be seen as benefiting the general public. By this logic, nonprofit advocacy would appear to be a corrective to the "excesses of factionalism," advancing collective interests of the general public against claimants representing the private economic interests of narrow groups.

This public interest conception of nonprofit advocacy has been challenged on several grounds, the most important being the question of objectivity. Who gets to say what the general or public interests are? Gone is the optimism of a Lippman (1955, 42) who could claim that "the public interest may be presumed to be what men would choose if they saw clearly, thought rationally, acted disinterestedly and benevolently." Interests are diverse and inherently subjective. One person's "public good" may be another's "public bad." Those who claim to speak in the name of the public can claim no privileged insight. In response, several nonprofit advocates have advanced an essentially procedural rationale in which the public interest is defined in terms of ensuring access to all "significant views that otherwise would go unrepresented" (Jaffe 1976, 31). Similarly, Rabin (1975, 207), speaking of law reform activities, identifies public interest advocacy with a "broadened range of value advocacy" created by "providing representation to groups that have been unable to organize effectively to compete in the marketplace for the services of skilled advocates." In other words, the public interest lies not in any specific policy or viewpoint but in expanding the diversity of interest representation so as to guarantee that all interested parties have a voice. By this logic, the impact of nonprofit advocacy on the problem of factionalism is more complex. Although nonprofit advocacy might counter the overrepresentation of more resourceful groups, it might also aggravate the overall problem by increasing the number and intensity of contending voices.

Significantly, however, neither of these two rationales can stand on its own. The first or substantive definition of the public interest correctly emphasizes the collective or indivisible character of the interests advanced by nonprofit advocates but suggests that all segments of society benefit equally and in the same manner. This contention, of course, gives rise to the dispute over objectivity. In general, the benefits of nonprofit advocacy flow disproportionately toward the unorganized and excluded interests in society, including those of the general public. In large part, this is a question of intent. Because nonprofits are officially committed to furthering charitable, social welfare, educational, and kindred values, the formal intent of their programs is typically to serve less advantaged groups. The collective interests at stake, however, are not necessarily those of the society as a whole. In fact, public interest advocates frequently find themselves speaking against the narrow interests of better organized and more powerful groups. The key requirement is that the benefits be nondivisible collective goods and that otherwise unrepresented groups, including possibly the general public, are the formally intended beneficiaries.

Nonprofit organizations are uniquely committed to aesthetic and cultural values; yet this does not exclude nonprofit advocates from concern with economic or commercial issues. In fact, nonprofit advocates frequently cast their claims in terms of the collective economic interests of the general public. The best formulation here is probably Tesh's (1984), emphasizing the moral and nonexclusive or generalized nature of their appeals for support. Since nonprofits are not formally committed to private economic interests, they must rely heavily on moral appeals to mobilize resources. Since their goal is to represent otherwise unrepresented interests, the nonprofits have to pitch their appeals for support to the general public. One need only be a citizen to be solicited by most nonprofits.

The second or procedural definition of the public interest also has its special virtues. It correctly argues that the nonprofit sector is biased toward the interests of those on the margins of society but, as typically formulated, ignores the nature of these interests and the bases of appeals. Nonprofit organizations go beyond merely adding new voices to the decision-making process by articulating specific kinds of interests—collective interests—and by relying on specific kinds of appeals—moral appeals, typically directed at the general public. In this sense, the older substantive definition of the public interest still has a special significance.

What is entailed by policy advocacy? A narrow conception is that of any attempt to speak for or on behalf of a specific position so as to influence formal governmental decisions. The conception used here is slightly broader. I will treat as policy advocacy any attempt to influence the decisions of any institutional elite on behalf of a collective interest. This conception opens up a broader range of methods and social arenas than conventionally recognized. The most prevalent nonprofit advocates are the public interest law firms and lobbies that are heavily engaged in litigation and lobbying, serving as representatives in formal court and administrative proceedings, and attempting to influence Congress and other governmental officials. They also, however, support law suits against private corporations and have been known to create their own forums for articulating positions. Campaign GM, for example, purchased stocks and attempted to use stockholder elections to alter the policies of a private corporation (Vogel 1978). The nonprofit organizations created by Ralph Nader have specialized in research and educational efforts, publishing books and articles, holding news conferences, and offering interviews to the press to generate publicity for their positions. Because it generates pressures as well as resources, many nonprofits also engage in direct organizing. Community organizations, for example, frequently mount grass-roots campaigns to mobilize a membership to pressure institutional elites and support the organization. Some nonprofit advocacy organizations blend advocacy with the direct delivery of services. It is critical to note, however, that advocacy and service delivery are analytically different. Advocacy focuses on changing policies and securing collective goods, whereas service delivery creates divisible or individual benefits and may be provided without actual changes in policies. The distinction is probably clearest in the area of nonprofit law. Some nonprofit law firms, such as the Legal Services Corporation, are primarily involved in legal services—for example, handling divorce cases for the indigent—whereas others, such as the NAACP–Legal Defense Fund, eschew legal services in favor of test-case litigation designed to create precedents benefiting broad classes or groups of individuals. The particular claimant serves merely as the agency for a collective bid and may, in fact, find individual interests sacrificed for the sake of the collective claim.

Nonprofit advocates usually rely on routine political channels, but not always. Direct actions like marches, demonstrations, and even riots have been used. It is also important to keep in mind that advocacy does not necessarily result in actual influence. Policy advocacy is a question of articulating positions or sets of demands, not necessarily securing them. Policy advocacy, then, is analytically distinct from actual policy enactment (the decision) and implementation (putting the decision into practice). One of our key concerns will be the factors that convert advocacy into decisions and implemented policies.

Nonprofit policy advocacy, then, can be defined in terms of attempts by nonprofit organizations to influence institutional elites. The demands will be posed in terms of collective benefits that are claimed to flow toward otherwise unrepresented groups, including the general public, and that are couched in terms of moral appeals directed the public. In the majority of cases, the political positions advocated will be similar to those of other liberal or reform-oriented political action groups, but this is by no means a necessity. As Walker (1983) found in his survey of advocacy organizations in Washington, D.C., nonprofit advocates generally advance positions entailing increased governmental services and regulations and find themselves at odds with the more privatistic positions taken by the special interest representatives of trade associations, corporations, professional societies, and unions, who often oppose these measures. Yet a growing and significant conservative nonprofit advocacy sector defines the public interest in terms of protecting private liberty and the competitive marketplace. For both wings of the nonprofit scene, litigation and lobbying are the favored methods, with occasional use of research, organizing, services, and even disruptive protests.

Because of their affiliation with unrepresented interests, nonprofit advocates are frequently on the margins of the institutionalized political system. Some are actually social movement organizations in the sense that they are routinely outside or excluded from centers of political decision making (see Gamson 1975, 16–8; Tilly 1978, 125–33). A significant factor, then, is the political status of the nonprofit organization. Is it politically ''vested'' (Roy 1981) in the sense that its views and interests are routinely taken into account by political elites? If it is, then advocacy efforts should meet with greater receptiveness. If, however, it advocates interests that are routinely ignored or, worse still, deliberately excluded in centers of political decision making, then the reception will be problematic and the organization may find it necessary to use more unconventional tactics. We therefore need to distinguish politically recognized advocacy organizations, or ''interest group organizations,'' from those that lie outside the institutionalized system of decision making, or ''social movement organizations.'' In addition, we need to distinguish organizations with a formal membership that contributes most of the resources from professional advocacy organizations that lack a genuine membership. The National Association for the Advancement of Colored People (NAACP) and NAACP–Legal Defense Fund, for example, differ significantly in terms of resource mobilization and programs, the former being a membership organization and the latter a professional advocacy organization. By combining these criteria, we can also distinguish between ''professional movement organizations'' (McCarthy & Zald 1973, 1977), possessing a paid staff but no members and standing outside the polity, from ''professional reform organizations'' (Helfgot 1981), which have political access. Among the membership organizations, we can also distinguish ''classical social movement organizations'' (McCarthy & Zald 1973, 1977), which have a base of contributing members but weak political standing, from ''interest group organizations,'' which enjoy membership support as well as routine political access.

THE FORMATION OF NONPROFIT ADVOCACY ORGANIZATIONS

There have been three general approaches to the formation of political advocacy organizations: traditional ''disturbance'' and ''entrepreneurial'' theories (Berry 1977, chap. 2; 1978), and the more recent ''political opportunity'' formulations (McAdam 1982; Walker 1983; Jenkins 1985a). Disturbance theories are centered around social changes that create strains or discontinuities in social relations or institutions. Truman's classic analysis (1951) of the formation of interest group organizations constitutes a prime example of disturbance theory. Wars, depressions, and social dislocations created by mass migrations and the like are seen as stimulating the formation of advocacy organizations designed to solve pressing social problems. In the study of social movements, such theories are known as discontent theories because of their emphasis on the grievances experienced by the supporters of advocacy organizations (Jenkins 1983b). Entrepreneurial theories, in contrast, focus on the issue definition and organizing efforts of leaders who play the key role in building a new advocacy organization. Salisbury (1969) has called this an exchange approach because of the central role of interpersonal exchanges between entrepreneurs and their supporters. The distinction also shows up in the social movement field where entrepreneurial theories are called resource mobilization theories because of the central role of entrepreneurial resources in creating new organizations (see McCarthy & Zald 1973, 1977). In this approach, entrepreneurs offer material, solidary, and purposive gains to galvanize support for the new organization. Recently several analysts have offered a political opportunity approach that emphasizes the emergence of favorable political settings for making demands. McAdam (1982), for example, has argued that the formation of new civil rights organizations in the late 1950s and early 1960s was due to a more opportune environment for advancing black political interests. Traditional social controls were weakened and black voters had greater leverage. Early victories, such as the Supreme Court ruling in *Brown* v. *Board of Education* and the Montgomery bus boycott, spurred the creation of new organizations, chiefly the Southern Christian Leadership Conference (SCLC) and the Student Nonviolent Coordinating Committee (SNCC). In this argument, the promise of success is the major spur to the formation of new advocacy organizations.

These analysts have often acted as if these are mutually exclusive approaches but, as Berry (1977, 22–23) has argued, each has useful insights that should be incorporated into a broader synthetic model. Berry's own research (1977, 23–44) on public interest lobbies provides support for both entrepreneurial and disturbance formulations, about two-thirds of the organizations originating from entrepreneurial efforts and a third from disturbances. Likewise, Useem's study (1980) of the supporters of an antibusing organization in Boston found that both grievances and exposure to organizing efforts were important in building the membership. The most thorough explication of the political opportunities theory is McAdam's analysis of the civil rights movement (1982, chap. 3). Here, too, disturbance and entrepreneurial elements enter into the explanation. Political opportunities created a "cognitive liberation" that led to collective redefinitions of conditions as unjust and mutable, which in turn led to a heightened sense of grievance. This occurred within an increasingly cohesive black community with indigenous leaders—chiefly black ministers—who served as political entrepreneurs. Most of these attempts at synthesis, however, have taken one approach as more general, attempting to subsume others as specific applications. Berry (1977, 22), for example, has suggested that entrepreneurial activities could be conceived as a form of disturbance. Reversing the order of synthesis, McCarthy and Zald (1977) have suggested that discontents are frequently manufactured by entrepreneurs. Likewise, McAdam (1982, chap. 3) has argued that political opportunities can set off collective redefinitions of conditions as "disturbing" and organizing campaigns. Yet the factors identified in these approaches are conceptually distinct, and the evidence points toward the independent importance of each factor.

How, then, might these approaches be fruitfully synthesized? In another context, Gamson, Fireman, and Rytina (1982) have suggested a useful approach from which we might borrow. In their study of collective rebellions, they found that a combination of five distinct factors had to be present. Singly, each factor was necessary but not sufficient; only the combination was sufficient. Each factor had to meet a basic threshold level, but increments beyond that were insignificant. Occasionally, surpluses in one factor compensated for defects in others. Extending this logic to our concern, disturbances, entrepreneurial efforts and new opportunities have to be present for the formation of new advocacy organizations. Each must be present at a minimal threshold and surpluses in one might compensate for others, but there is no fixed order or priority among these factors. In any particular setting, one or more of the three theories will be most relevant depending on the factors present.

In general, entrepreneurship and new opportunities, especially in the form of outside patronage, are the most important factors in the formation of nonprofit advocacy organizations. Crises and various disturbances may stimulate advocacy efforts among relatively cohesive and politically influential groups, but the groups represented by nonprofit advocacy tend to be disorganized and politically marginal. Grievances and disturbing conditions are ignored because the group is too disorganized and lacks leadership or political access. Entrepreneurship and the patronage of wealthy individuals and established organizations are frequently decisive in initiating a new organization. Consumers, for example, are a highly disaggregated group. The stake of any individual consumer is usually outweighed by the costs of mounting a

bid for change. Ralph Nader's entrepreneurship was decisive in launching the consumer movement during the 1960s (Pertschuk 1982), but the support of wealthy individuals and private foundations was essential in forwarding these new consumer advocacy organizations (McCarry 1972; Gorey 1975). Similarly, the major environmental organizations have drawn on entrepreneurial initiative and extensive patronage. The Environmental Defense Fund was organized by a group of natural scientists concerned about DDT's effects on bird nesting and was initially funded by the Rachel Carson Fund of the Audubon Society. The largest environmental law firm, the Natural Resources Defense Council, was launched after a group of prominent citizens fighting the Storm King power plant was brought together by the Ford Foundation with a group of Yale law students seeking a sponsor for an environmental law firm (Adams 1974).

Impoverished groups confront similar problems, lacking the cohesion and resources to mount their own advocacy efforts. Entrepreneurship, frequently in the form of outside leaders, and sponsorship by wealthy patrons or established institutions are often necessary. In many cases, the entrepreneurs are professional organizers from prior advocacy efforts. The National Welfare Rights Organization was launched in the late 1960s by former activists in the civil rights movement. Organizing funds came from private foundations and the National Council of Churches (Bailis 1974; Jackson & Johnson 1973; West 1981). The United Farm Workers union was originally organized as a nonprofit community organization sponsored by liberal church agencies, private foundations, and unions. Cesar Chavez had been on the staff of the Community Service Organization, a nonprofit civil rights advocate for urban Mexican-Americans in California (Jenkins & Perrow 1977; Jenkins 1985a). Entrepreneurs and sponsorship can also strengthen organizing efforts among relatively resourceful groups. The National Organization for Women (NOW), for example, was initially organized by political activists attending the White House–sponsored National Conference on the Status of Women in 1966. Although the Johnson administration had not intended to create an independent advocacy group for women, its sponsorship inadvertently organized an entrepreneurial cadre with heightened awareness of women's issues. Direct patronage by the United Auto Workers union and the Institute for Policy Studies kept the organization alive during the early years (Freeman 1975, 52–56). In a strikingly similar way, White House sponsorship of the Consumer Advisory Council in the Kennedy and Johnson years fostered the creation of the consumer movement by bringing activists together and creating sufficient cohesion that they could begin organization building (Creighton 1976).

It should therefore not be surprising that patronage was critical in launching the overwhelming majority of the nonprofit advocacy organizations currently active in Washington, D.C. (Walker 1983). Although professional advocacy organizations are more dependent on patronage, even membership organizations have found it necessary to solicit outside support before embarking on new advocacy projects.

The NAACP's historic move to create test-case legal advocacy was made possible by a grant from the Garland Fund in the 1930s (Kluger 1976; Rabin 1975). Without this support, the legal program would never have moved beyond a reactive service approach. As Walker (1983, 404) has concluded, the amount and issue focus of political advocacy in general and nonprofit advocacy in particular is at any point "largely . . . determined by the composition and accessibility of the system's major patrons of political action."

The explanation of the rise of nonprofit advocacy, then, turns out to hinge on the sources of entrepreneurship and institutional patronage. What gives rise to new entrepreneurship and patronage? Political entrepreneurs are almost invariably middle to upper-class in social origins, and college educated. The growth of the "new class" of symbol specialists and cultural producers occupationally committed to the creation, criticism, and transmission of culture has, no doubt, created an increased structural supply of potential political entrepreneurs: "intellectuals enamored with righteousness and possibility; college students for whom perfectionism is an occupational hazard; portions of the upper class freed from concern with economic self-interest; clergymen contemptuous of materialism; romantics derisive of Babbitt and Main Street" (Kirkpatrick 1976, 245). Yet equally important are the conditions that lead these natural allies of moralistic politics to turn to active proselytizing. As James Q. Wilson (1973, 201) has argued, "periods of rapid and intense organizational formation are periods in which the salience of purposive incentives has sharply increased. Organizations become more numerous when ideas become more important." In other words, this pool of potential cadres not only must expand but also must become more receptive to the moral calling of social reform. Unfortunately we know more about what facilitates entrepreneurs than what stimulates their receptiveness to ideals. Affluence and increasing autonomy, not increased grievances, apparently help, reducing the economic hardships associated with entrepreneurial activities and creating a broader audience for moral appeals. Similarly, new mobilization technologies—such as the daily newspaper for the Progressive Era muckrakers and televised interviews followed up with direct mail solicitation for contemporary public interest advocates—have facilitated entrepreneurial efforts. As numerous observers have noted, the economic affluence and enhanced prestige of professional occupations coupled with new mobilization techniques encouraged a general growth in middle-class political activism in the 1960s. The nonprofit sector was clearly a major beneficiary of this surge of activism. We witnessed the rise of direct-mail-supported public interest lobbies, increased volunteering for political campaigns, "guerrillas in the bureaucracy" who defined professional service in terms of advocacy, and "radical professionals" who put themselves at the service of the powerless (Milbrath & Goel 1977; Needleman & Needleman 1974; Perucci 1973).

Explanations of patronage have fallen into three main interpretations. My own research on the National Council of Churches (Jenkins 1977) has supported what might be called a "conscience" theory. Surplus resources and growing independence by staff professionals allowed moral visions of social reform to come to the fore, leading to active sponsorship of advocacy efforts ranging from the civil rights movement and the peace movement to welfare reform. Similarly, the gradual shift from amateur to professional leadership in the established conservation organizations led to support for a new wave of environmental political advocacy in the mid 1960s (Fox 1981). The same processes have also appeared among private foundations. The larger foundations that are staffed by professionals and institutionalized to the degree that the original family donors no longer control the board of trustees have been more likely to support political advocacy projects (Nielsen 1972; Jenkins 1984). In fact, Moynihan (1969) offered a generalized version of this thesis, arguing that economic affluence and institutional autonomy have led to a "professionalization of reform" in which the impetus for social change has shifted from mass movements to professional advocates. Building on this insight, McCarthy and Zald (1973, 1977) argued that affluence, professionalization, the prominence of the mass media, and groups with discretionary time schedules have created a new array of professional social movements relying on the support of "conscience constituencies." By this argument, patronage is rooted in affluence, professionalization, and autonomy and motivated by altruism and public-spiritedness.

McAdam (1982) has offered an alternative social control interpretation of patronage, arguing that the outside support for the major civil rights organizations was reactive, stimulated by the political threat of mass insurgency. Insurgency forced institutional elites to perceive racism and black poverty as significant social problems and to respond in an attempt to divert disorders into more peaceful channels. Support for the movement organizations, especially the moderate civil rights advocates, actually constituted efforts to control the movement. Key events, such as the Kennedy administration's active promotion of foundation support for the Voter Education Project and pressure on the American Bar Association to create the Lawyers' Committee for Civil Rights under Law, fit this interpretation (Navasky 1977). Both were reactive and designed to direct dissidence into routine channels. The patron had a clear interest in dampening insurgency and encouraging "responsible militancy" in its place. As McAdam has demonstrated, the general pattern of external funding for the civil rights organizations was reactive and focused on building up the moderate organizations.

My own work on farm worker organizations (Jenkins 1985a) offers still a third interpretation that, while incorporating the conscience and social control arguments, emphasizes the political advantages that patrons might hope to gain from sponsoring new advocacy efforts. The motives underlying sponsorship for farm worker advocacy were diverse. Organized labor was interested in expanding its organizational base and political position. The liberal churches and foundations acted out of conscience and their perception that Cesar Chavez represented a "responsible" approach to the resolution of significant social problems. Slack resources and an increasing role for staff professionals facilitated their involvement. Political disorders pricked their conscience as well as aroused concerns about social stability. Sponsorship was channeled toward "responsible" advocacy that abided by the rules of the political game. As McAdam found, advocates that challenged these conventions found their sponsorship withdrawn. Yet conscience and social control were not the sole considerations. Shifting national political alignments also made sponsorship feasible and advantageous for certain patrons. Sponsorship was weak and highly uneven during the 1950s when conservative Republicans and Democrats controlled national politics. As urban liberals gained influence in the 1960s, especially in Congress, potential patrons saw new opportunities for successful reforms. By the late 1960s they could hope to gain from their support of reform efforts, garnering sympathetic votes and bringing new allies into the political system. In short, patrons also make an assessment of the political setting and how new advocacy efforts might rebound to their own political advantage.

This "political advantages" interpretation also makes sense of other cases of elite patronage for nonprofit advocacy. White House sponsorship of the consumer advocates in the 1960s derived from the perception that consumer reform was a consensual "motherhood" issue that would entail few costs and create improved relations with Congress (Nadel 1971). An increase in the number of urban liberals in Congress made these calculations possible. This also makes sense of the fact that institutional support for new advocates often comes after, not before, the passage of major reform legislation. Pratt (1977), for example, found that the major advocacy organizations in the "gray lobby" of the 1960s were launched after the passage of the major reform bills. Likewise, the large outpouring of institutional patronage for the environmental advocates came after the passage of the Environmental Protection Act in 1970 (Andrews 1976). Reform legislation legitimizes the advocates' claims and assures potential patrons that their support will bring results.

Sometimes sponsorship is inadvertent, occurring through a working out of institutional processes already underway. Chief (then Appellate) Justice Warren Burger's 1966 ruling expanding the definition of legal "standing," for example, grew out of a general liberalization of legal procedures but was profoundly important in opening the way for public interest law. By allowing suits to be brought in the absence of clear economic damages and in the name of professional advocates rather than direct claimants, the ruling made it possible for public interest lawyers to claim a role and petition for foundation sponsorship (Orren 1976). Similarly, the series of congressional reforms that began in the early 1960s gradually decentralized authority, creating broader opportunities for nonprofit advocacy. Open hearings, reduced emphasis on seniority, restrictions on special interest lobbying, and the multiplication of subcommittees and staff created a more favorable environment for advocacy (Walker 1977; Heclo 1978; Schlozman & Tierney 1983). More access

points and possibilities for securing congressional sponsorship encouraged patrons to invest in new advocacy efforts.

The tax code and its administration have been an important regulator of elite sponsorship. The major issue has been the tax deductibility of contributions to nonprofit organizations involved in political advocacy. Tax deductibility is limited to "religious, educational, charitable, scientific, and literary" organizations (501–c3), which in turn are barred from "substantial political activity." In contrast, contributions to organizations involved in substantial lobbying and political advocacy (typically 501–c4) are prohibited for private foundations and nondeductible for individuals. Yet the meaning of "substantial political activity" for 501–c3 organizations has been ambiguous and only gradually clarified by legislation and IRS rulings. In 1955, conservative southern congressmen, piqued at the *Brown* v. *Board of Education* decision pressured the Justice Department to revoke the tax exemption of the NAACP–Legal Defense Fund, which had been incorporated as a nonprofit charitable (501–c3) organization in the 1930s. The claim was that legal advocacy constituted "political action." The Justice Department ultimately forced the Legal Defense Fund to break ties with the NAACP, a 501–c4 organization, but affirmed the tax deductibility of legal advocacy. In 1966, the IRS revoked the tax deductibility of the Sierra Club because of its challenge to the proposed construction of a dam that would have flooded part of the Grand Canyon. In this interpretation, "politics" included public education efforts, chiefly letter-writing campaigns and newspaper ads targeted primarily at an administrative agency.

The major clarifications came in the Tax Reform Act of 1969. Following revelations that a candidate had used a private foundation to fund his own electoral campaign and that the Ford Foundation had supported a voter registration campaign in Cleveland, Ohio, that helped elect the nation's first black big-city mayor, Congress voted to define "politics" narrowly as direct involvement in campaign activity or attempts to directly influence Congress and the executive branch. Appearances before Congress or administrative bodies were construed as legal so long as they were "educational"—that is, factual and solicited by the governmental body in question—or were an insubstantial portion of the organization's efforts, which most observers assumed to mean 10 to 20 percent. Public education efforts of the sort that had lead to the Sierra Club revocation were legal as long as they were not focused on congressional legislation. Voter registration was a suitable target of foundation support so long as the campaign was nonpartisan (separate from efforts of campaign organizations) and general (covering a five-state area). As Goetz and Brady (1975) have argued, the regulations were actually quite liberal. In fact, the voter registration rules spurred some foundations to expand their funding to cover larger projects. Yet the negative publicity, past punitive actions, and continued vagueness as to what constituted "substantial" and "political" discouraged foundation support for advocacy. In 1976 the restrictions were further liberalized, "substantial" being defined in terms of a sliding scale that allowed up to 20 percent of the first $500,000 budget and declining afterward. The act also legalized grass-roots lobbying by allowing unrestricted efforts to influence legislation via education of the public.

There has also been a continuing controversy over the granting of tax-deductible status. Generally the IRS has followed a lenient policy, merely requiring a coherent statement of purpose within the bounds of "religious, educational, charitable, scientific, or literary" activities. However, there have been several controversial cases. In 1969, the IRS refused to grant 501-c3 status to the Natural Resources Defense Council and the Project on Corporate Responsibility on the grounds that their activities were not "charitable." In the former, the argument was that public interest law, in contrast to civil rights and poverty law, did not have a clear constituency and hence did not entail sufficient prohibitions on barratry. Most observers concluded that the Nixon administration, then under attack by many of the nonprofit advocates, was using this as a device to prevent the formation of more critics. When the commissioner of the IRS resigned on the final issuance of the exemptions, this contention received support. In any case, the withholding destroyed the Corporate Responsibility Project and subjected the practice of public interest law to distinctive regulations. Public interest firms were barred from accepting fees from their clients and had to file annual reports specifying why their cases were in the public interest (Halperin & Cunningham 1971; Harrison & Jaffe 1971; Adams, 1974). More recently, IRS audits under the Reagan administration have challenged the tax-exempt status of the Foundation for National Progress, publisher of *Mother Jones* magazine, and several other politically oriented publications on the grounds that their articles have advocated specific legislation or their business operations were identical to those of the commercial press (MacKenzie 1981). Perhaps even more central, however, has been the vagueness of tax regulations and the high level of discretion enjoyed by IRS officials. Tax audits and the granting of exemptions are largely up to IRS officials and the appointed commissioner, leading to repeated charges of favoritism and political motivation in decisions to audit and grant exemptions.

Another constraint on patronage are the peer networks influencing potential patrons. Foundations occasionally follow fads, supporting projects that have recently been adopted by other prominent foundations. In part, this is because they rely on informal advisers, typically other foundation staff member, and, in the case of national grants to local community advocates, the advice of local business elites (Milofsky & Romo 1981). Joint or coordinated grants are also common in supports for policy advocacy groups, in part because this diffuses responsibility and potential negative publicity. Because larger foundations have more staff to evaluate potential grantees, smaller foundations often follow their lead, assuming that a competent evaluation has been completed. Foundations and other patrons have also supported specialized go-between organizations, such as the Youth Project and the Center for Community Change, whose function is to provide technical support and screen potential

applicants to ensure they are "responsible militants." Well-regarded advocates sometimes even enjoy the status of advisers, steering patronage toward their own political allies and away from rivals, much in the way that Cesar Chavez was able to block foundation grants from going to rival farm worker organizers.

In general, then, the formation of nonprofit advocacy organizations depends heavily on the availability of entrepreneurs, elite patronage, and a favorable political environment. The broad increase in nonprofit advocacy over the past three decades should be explicable in terms of an increase in all three elements. The scale of the upsurge itself was, by all accounts, unprecedented. There was a dramatic growth in nonprofit organization generally (Rosenbaum & Smith 1983; Salamon 1983) and in the visibility of nonprofit advocacy in particular (Ornstein & Elder 1978, 36–51; Greenwald 1977; Hayes 1978; Walker 1983). A wide array of new community organizations sprang up, asserting claims on behalf of previously unrepresented groups to control over municipal services, land development policies, and access to mortgage credit as well as federal legislation affecting the cities (Perlman 1976, 1978; Boyte 1980; Katznelson 1981; Hunter 1983; Castells 1983). Advocacy on behalf of weakly represented groups also expanded. The number and visibility of women's and consumer advocates grew exponentially (Carden, 1974, 1977; Berger 1980; Nadel 1971; Pertschuk 1982), and the budgets for minority advocates rose steadily. Probably the most innovative development was the creation of public interest law, giving rise to over a hundred nonprofit advocates involved in litigation, research, and publicity on behalf of previously unrepresented groups and interests (Harrison & Jaffe 1971; Jaffe 1976; McKay 1977; Council for Public Interest Law 1976, 1980).

The explosion of grass-roots social movements, especially the civil rights and antiwar movements, played a critical role in creating resources for these new advocacy organizations. The mass movements raised new issues, attracted new entrepreneurs, and created new organizational forms for mobilizing resources. The turbulence also brought issues like poverty and civil rights to elite attention and made professional advocates appear as "responsible militants." Behind these developments were, of course, broad economic and political changes. Sustained economic growth strengthened the position of professional symbol specialists and created slack resources for investment in discretionary issues like the environment and population control. Accompanying this was a general increase in political activism by the middle and upper-middle classes, who exhibited greater awareness of political issues and weakened loyalties to traditional partisan ties. A gradual liberalization of the national political elite created opportunities for the mass movements as well as encouraging elite patronage and entrepreneurial efforts to launch new advocacy efforts. Presidents sponsored consumer and women's rights efforts, foundations and wealthy donors contributed to new nonprofit advocacy organizations, and senators took the initiative in pressing through reform legislation. In response to rising insurgency, institutional elites also moved quickly to support nonprofit advocacy as a responsible alternative to disruption. With revelations about Vietnam and Watergate proliferating, public interest advocates capitalized on increasing skepticism about institutional authority. By pressing for procedural reforms to guarantee governmental openness and accountability, organizations like Common Cause and Public Citizen quickly became the "loyal opposition" (Berry & Fisher 1981), virtually taking over the role traditionally occupied by the political parties. It was clearly a political age and a favorable time for the formation of new nonprofit advocacy organizations.

THE "CARE AND FEEDING" OF ADVOCACY ORGANIZATIONS

James Q. Wilson (1973, 30) once defined the problem of organizational maintenance in terms of "not only survival, but also . . . producing and sustaining cooperative effort." The major discussions of the problem of organizational maintenance have stemmed from Olson's seminal *The Logic of Collective Action* (1965). Olson argues that organizations advocating "collective goods"—indivisible benefits that jointly advantage an entire group—will find it impossible to secure sufficient support by relying solely on appeals to these collective benefits. Potential supporters will recognize that they will benefit regardless of their contributions and will attempt to "ride free." Leaders, then, will have to use "selective" (divisible or individual) incentives, such as cheap insurance, special services, and coercive threats, to secure contributions. There are two other possible solutions. Privileged members who possess sufficient resources to outweigh the personal costs of securing the collective good might contribute. Or groups so small that the collective benefits outweigh individual costs might contribute. But large, less endowed groups will not. Consumers will not support consumer-advocacy organizations without the incentive of private benefits, such as the buyers' guides furnished by the Consumers Union. Or only the affluent will contribute since their personal costs will be nominal. Similarly, although everyone benefits from clean air, because the benefits are joint no one will pay the costs of securing this collective good without coercion or special incentives.

By this reasoning, the survival, much less maintenance, of nonprofit advocacy organizations is highly problematic. In fact, Salisbury (1969) and Frohlich, Oppenheimer, and Young (1971) have argued that the formation of advocacy organizations is also problematic because it requires entrepreneurs who perceive opportunities to advance their own careers and perhaps the patronage of privileged actors. Although the difficulties that most nonprofits confront in mobilizing resources and the importance of patronage could be taken as prima facie evidence in support of Olson's theory, the number and political significance of nonprofit advocates suggest that other factors must be at work. Most nonprofits do not rely heavily on selective incentives, and although the notion of privileged actors has some merit, most supporters (including patrons) appear to be more receptive to the advo-

cates' moral claims to public service. In the early years, Ralph Nader's Public Citizen organization included in its solicitation requests the promise that none of the contributions would be "wasted" on special reports or contributor services. Tillock and Morrison's study (1979) of Zero Population Growth and Forsythe and Welch's study (1981) of contributors to human rights advocacy groups found that supporters were indifferent to selective incentives. Furthering a moral vision was their sole overriding concern. Similarly, Faich and Gale (1971) found that the majority of Sierra Club members, especially newer members, did not even make use of club services but were politically motivated by concerns about the environment. It would seem that Olson's theory needs to be extended to incorporate moral and solidary incentives that may overcome free riding.

Mitchell (1979) has attempted to salvage Olson's theory by arguing that support for the environmental advocates has been due to their attack on "collective bads" from which there is no individual escape. In other words, if the collective good being sought is the avoidance of an otherwise inescapable disaster, then the logic of riding free will not hold. This, however, is like arguing that once supporters recognize the logic of riding free, they will act so as to override this logic. The major insight of these studies is that moral incentives are central and can override the free-rider problem, an insight that appears far more persuasive than the notion of unavoidable disasters.

The notion that moral and solidary incentives are central to organizational maintenance has received extensive attention (J. Q. Wilson 1973; Fireman & Gamson 1979; Marwell & Ames 1979, 1980; Moe 1980, 1981; Jenkins 1983a). Drawing on Clark and Wilson's classic theory of organizational incentives (1961), these analysts have argued that solidary and moral incentives are more important than Olson's selective material incentives. Solidary incentives may be selective (such as special honors) or collective (the self-respect of the group as a whole). Even more important are inherently collective purposive incentives. Commitment to a moral vision blurs the distinction between individual and collective gain. The individual internalizes the interests of the collectivity, acting out of a sense of conscience rather than personal gain. For example, my study of farm worker organizations found that the United Farm Workers mobilized a solid base of support where others had failed because of the central emphasis on ethnic solidarity, community ties, and the moral claims of *La Causa* (Jenkins 1983a). This argument about *collective* incentives is, as Fireman and Gamson (1979) have argued, different from a "soft selective incentives" argument that merely extends Olson's argument by switching the coin of rewards. Collective incentives are not selective—divisible and enjoyed by individuals—but inherently collective.

It is also important to recognize imperfect communications (Moe 1980). Walsh and Warland (1983) found in a study of supporters and opponents of the re-start-up of the Three Mile Island nuclear plant that large percentages on both sides of the issue were free riding because they were uninformed about the existence of advocacy organizations. Greater access to information is probably a key reason for higher levels of involvement in community advocacy organizations by those already active in other organizations (Von Eschen, Kirk, & Pinard 1971; Curtis & Zurcher 1973). Participation exposes people to new information, converting the network of already active participants into the prime recruiting ground for new activists.

Some groups are also more receptive to particular appeals. In general, the affluent are more receptive to moral appeals, whereas lower-class groups are more receptive to material and solidary appeals (J. Q. Wilson 1973, 62–67). The supporters of the consumer, environmental, and governmental reform movements have been drawn from college-educated, upper-middle-class professionals in the social service sector of the economy (Weisbrod, Handler, & Komesar 1978, 102–45; McFarland 1976; Lichter & Rothman 1983). Their public service ideology fits the goals of these movements, and they have the discretionary resources to contribute. Less affluent groups, in contrast, are more responsive to appeals that address their immediate needs. The classic Alinsky (1969, 1972) model of community organizing was built around immediate tangible benefits. The Massachusetts Welfare Rights Organization, for example, used special payments secured by organizers on behalf of welfare recipients and the selective solidary incentive of group recognition (Bailis 1974). Similarly, Brill (1971) has argued that organizers of lower-class rent strikes must attend to the direct material needs of tenants for hot water, heat, and building safety, not abstract goals like the transformation of society. In a comparative study of lower-class organizing, Withorn (1978) has argued that the strategic use of material selective incentives can be used to secure initial support, followed up by more durable solidary and purposive appeals.

The implication, however, is not that the Olson theory can be safely ignored. There are many examples of the problem of free riding. The Massachusetts Welfare Rights Organization collapsed because welfare officials recognized the organization's reliance on the special benefits and because core activists blunted the organization's impact in order to preserve access to their solidary rewards (Bailis 1974). Similarly, the Mobilization for Youth, a community development project in New York's lower East Side that served as a model for the War on Poverty's Community Action projects, failed in part because it did not use services as selective incentives (O'Brien 1975, 89–91). Likewise, farm worker organizations have failed to weather grower attacks because they cast their appeals primarily in terms of collective material gains (Jenkins 1983a). Free riding is a serious problem, as any organizer will attest. Walsh and Warland (1983) found extensive free riding even among informed ardent opponents of the Three Mile Island nuclear plant. Olson was correct that advocacy organizations cannot rely primarily on collective material incentives. He simply failed to recognize the role of moral and solidary appeals, especially collective ones.

Is institutional patronage more important in the maintenance of advocacy organizations than in their formation? In general, patronage is probably more critical in an organization's early years while indigenous bases of support are being built. There are notable exceptions, however, and it is well to keep in mind that organizational survival is not the same as maintenance. Over the past three decades the NAACP has become increasingly dependent on foundation and corporate grants and governmental contracts, strengthening the overall financial health of the organization (Aveni 1978). Meanwhile, membership and related fund-raising have stagnated, and the organization has been wracked by internal disputes over its mission and structure. Growing patronage has helped the organization launch research and legal advocacy projects but has not helped generate a growing base of indigenous support.

There are also cases in which patronage works against organizational maintenance. Among nascent community organizations, patronage often promotes rivalries among volunteers for paid staff positions and fosters a view of the organization as a dispenser of services rather than an advocacy project requiring volunteer contributions (Wellstone 1978). The Community Action Projects (CAPs) in the 1960s found that federal support was restricted to particular services and imposed strict fiscal controls that frequently collided with advocacy and indigenous mobilization efforts. In fact, several CAPs were closed down because of their advocacy efforts (Peterson & Greenstone 1977; Helfgot 1974, 1981). Indigenous support is critical to the effectiveness of patronized organizations. The National Committee against Discrimination in Housing was more successful in cities that had a significant base of volunteer support as well as patronage. High levels of patronage without indigenous support encouraged a professionalized service approach that weakened the advocacy effort (Saltman 1971).

THE STRUCTURE OF ADVOCACY ORGANIZATIONS

Zald (1970) has argued that the typical nonprofit organization has a federal structure. Each program and its relevant constituency has a significant degree of autonomy, yet there is a central staff to coordinate and mobilize resources. The organization can maximize community ties and pursue diverse goals while centralizing technical services. No doubt this blend between centralized bureaucratic organization and decentralized participatory organization has an important grain of realism. Most organizations actually fall someplace between the extremes of a perfect bureaucracy and a direct participation organization. But this has done little to still the often heated debate between proponents of these different forms. The primary reason is the importance of organizational structure to the realization of the humanitarian and democratic values typically identified with nonprofit organizations. If nonprofit organizations and nonprofit advocacy are central to the vitality of liberal democracy, then the degree of internal democracy and public accountability of these organizations is of critical importance.

Probably the most coherent formulation of the participatory decentralization position may be found in Gerlach and Hine's analysis of social movements (1970). They argue that the typical social movement has a "segmentary, poly-cephalous and recticulate" structure and that this cell-like structure of multiple groups loosely linked by common ideology, informal networks, and traveling evangelists is more effective. The decentralized structure maximizes solidary and purposive incentives, promotes active proselytizing by competition and multiple access points, facilitates tactical innovation and reliability because of internal diversity and duplication, and, like a many-headed monster, increases the chances of survival in a hostile environment. Other proponents have approached the question from a value stance, arguing the virtues of direct participation in decision making as a means of realizing democratic values (Pateman 1970; Rothschild-Whitt 1979; Breines 1982). There are drawbacks, however. In addition to classical objections about size, inefficiency, and the problems of reconciling strong minority sentiments with majority rule (Mansbridge 1982), decentralized structures also impose limits on goals and resource mobilization. Freeman (1973) has argued that the extreme decentralization of the early women's advocacy groups led to a "tyranny of structurelessness" in which the groups could not mobilize large numbers of activists or take on larger targets on behalf of institutional change.

The proponents of a centralized structure have seized on this latter issue, arguing that a clear hierarchy maximizes mobilization by converting diffuse expectations into clearly defined roles and enhances tactical readiness by increasing organizational learning and reducing coordination costs and internal frictions (Gamson 1975; Tilly 1978, 148–59). Probably the strongest evidence comes from Gamson's study (1975) of social movement organizations in which centralized groups were more successful. Schisms were far less likely and centralization facilitated focused attacks on particular targets.

There are several problems with the way in which this debate has traditionally been cast. Proponents have often acted as if their models were literal descriptions rather than ideal types. No organization actually operates purely according to one model; they only approximate the patterns. Moreover, analysts have often confused the question of the typical form with that of the effectiveness of different structures. It is possible that the typical form of nonprofit advocacy is not the most effective. Finally, analysts have often mixed normative and empirical arguments. Adhering to the empirical proposition that participatory democracy is unwieldy does not necessarily undermine the normative thesis that participation is desirable.

The first step is to clarify the meaning of democracy and its relevance to organizational structure. McFarland (1978) has identified three meanings of organizational democracy: (1) a polyarchal model according to which members control leaders by giving or withdrawing resources such as votes or dues amidst leader competition, (2) a participatory model in which members participate equally and freely in making significant collective decisions, and (3) a descriptive repre-

sentational model according to which leaders proportionately correspond to certain demographic characteristics of the membership. The first is clearly more compatible with a centralized structure. Members can influence leaders through elections or withholding dues and other contributions, and demand adherence to formally stated principles. The second model, of course, converges with the decentralized informal structure. Member control lies in their direct involvement in decisions. There are no formal structures to impede their influence. The third model stands separately, having only oblique relevance to the question of organizational structure.

Which model of democratic organizations is more empirically relevent? McFarland argued that the polyarchal model is more relevant to an organization like Common Cause, involved in national lobbying and relying on direct mail for contact with a nationwide membership. Lobbying requires a centralized structure with a paid professional staff able to maneuver without consulting members. Ironically, however, the chief mechanism of accountability is the leaders' commitment to a participatory ethic. Because Common Cause's chief goal is furthering governmental openness and accountability, leaders have applied stringent criteria to themselves. For example, members are periodically polled concerning the stance to be taken on various issues. Volunteering is encouraged, bringing staff into contact with at least a segment of the membership. Elections to the governing board are organized to ensure that handpicked nominees do not consistently win, and in line with the descriptive representational model, an attempt is made to include a cross section of the membership. Finally, members can easily withdraw their support, a factor that has altered staff priorities in several cases. The participatory model is approximated only insofar as volunteering and mailings increase interaction between staff and members.

Hertz (1981) has argued that the participatory democracy model was more relevant to the structure of the welfare rights movement. Drawing on Gerlach and Hine's notion of a decentralized movement structure, she argued that the voluntary nature of contributions and the high priority placed on personal commitment required a decentralized structure. As in the brown-lung movement (Judkins 1979), the geographic dispersion of a mass membership meant that locals were only loosely knit together by organizers and common ideology. The emphasis on changing people's values and personalities also made a decentralized face-to-face structure almost inevitable. In general, nonprofit organizations emphasizing personal transformation over institutional change and attempting to mobilize a mass membership rather than influence a handful of legislators will develop a decentralized structure that allows extensive participation in decisions (Curtis & Zurcher 1974).

This notion that different kinds of nonprofit organizations entail different structures has been developed by several analysts. Freeman (1979), for example, has argued that the "two wings" of the women's movement have drawn on different organizational traditions. The "older" wing—NOW, WEAL (Women's Equity Action League), NWPC (National Women's Political Caucus)—has mobilized the generation of women whose political experience was rooted in the labor and early civil rights movements. Their primary goal has been incremental institutional reform through lobbying and litigation; they favor a centralized national organization with a professional staff and polyarchal structures. The "younger" wing (consciousness-raising groups, radical feminists) has been centered among the generation whose primary political experience was the student New Left of the 1960s (Evans 1979). Their primary goal has been personal transformation so as to prepare the cultural grounds for a radical transformation of society. Structureless affinity groups with rotating or no formal leadership and participatory decision making have been the favored form. Similarly, Starr (1979) has analyzed the diverse organizational structures of the social movements of the 1960s and 1970s, contrasting the decentralized "exemplary" model adhered to by radical communes, law collectives, and the Student Nonviolent Coordinating Committee, with the heirarchical "adversary" model of the national advocacy organizations— NOW, CORE (Congress on Racial Equality), SANE, the Alinsky-styled community organizations, the public interest lobbies, and the alternative media projects. The former have typically adopted restrictive membership rules and requested intense commitments, whereas the latter have pursued less intense commitments from the general public.

Once in place, these organizational structures set severe limits on the tasks that can be pursued. The centralized wing of the women's movement has been able to pursue national legislation and court cases but has been less successful at educational and service tasks. Similarly, the decentralized wing has handled tasks that can be tackled by small groups with minimal division of labor (such as women's centers, bookstores) but has been unable to take on larger institutional targets (Freeman 1979). These structures also make nonprofit organizations more or less vulnerable to environmental pressures. The centralized adversary organizations of the antiwar movement rapidly collapsed once public interest in the issue declined; the more inward-oriented exemplary communes and coops were more insulated. Of course, this also meant that they tended over time to become encapsulated, cutting themselves off from the larger society and sources of new recruits. Another possibility is an organizational contradiction based on combining these forms. For example, SNCC held to exemplary goals while pursuing adversary activities, which introduced severe tensions that ultimately led to organizational collapse when high commitments could not be compromised with pragmatic politics (Stoper 1983).

It is also important to keep in mind that these structures are ideal types. As Lawson (1983) has argued, advocacy organizations are actually blends of these polar types. The tenant movement, for example, is characterized by different organizational units operating at different levels—centralized units involved in legal advocacy on a national, state, or citywide level, and a vast number of relatively informal building organizations of the residents of particular tenements involved in organizing and direct conflicts with landlords. The

movement as a whole, then, might be better characterized as a federal structure with a centralized staff. Similarly, the National Organization for Women is organized around a centralized national staff lobbying in Washington, D.C., supported by an array of highly autonomous state and local organizations and a set of special task committees pursuing their own projects (Carden 1978). This double structure, however, has not been without its strains. The local organizations have frequently rebelled at national directives, withholding dues and refusing to cooperate with national campaigns because of objections to an "autocratic" national staff and the acceptance of "the system" implied by a national lobbying program (Costain 1980, 1981; Costain & Costain 1983a).

The bugaboo underlying much of this discussion has been the problem of organizational transformation, especially leadership domination and institutional accommodation along the lines outlined by Michels (1962). In Michels's classic formulation, organizations inevitably become oligarchic and conservative, losing their oppositional and innovative qualities. Large size and tactical efficacy necessitate bureaucratization, which in turn gives professional staff de facto control over organizational policy. Because an adversarial stance threatens the survival of the organization and staff members have a major stake in organizational survival, staff dominance leads to institutional accommodation. The classic case is that of the Townsend clubs in the 1930s, which were converted from advocacy organizations to a network of social clubs for selling geriatric products (Messinger 1955). This "iron law of oligarchy," however, is not ironclad. Advocacy organizations that remain small, rotate leadership and job assignments, are strongly committed to participatory values, and make decisions at regular meetings have been able to sustain their participatory qualities for extensive periods of time (Rothschild-Whitt 1979). The cost, however, appears to be small size and social marginality. The goal transformation part of the thesis is also vulnerable to criticism. Zald and Ash (1966), for example, have argued that oligarchy does not necessarily result in the loss of an adversarial stance. Noting that leaders are often more committed to social change than members, they contend that oligarchy might in fact lead to greater adversarial efforts. The rising dominance of professional staff in the Sierra Club in the 1960s, for example, led to aggressive advocacy efforts that eventually culminated in David Brower's ouster and his launching of the Friends of the Earth to carry on a strict advocacy approach (Fox 1981). In a slightly different manner, the professional staff of CORE gradually forced a radical black-power stance on an integrationist organization, precipitating an organizational collapse (Meier & Rudwick 1973). Significantly, the more decentralized structure of CORE relative to the NAACP made it easier for the staff to carry the day (Rudwick & Meier 1970). In fact, the civil rights experience suggests that the trajectory of nonprofit advocacy might instead be toward increasing radicalism. Success breeds heightened expectations, frequently leading to broader demands and more militant tactics.

Pressures for organizational transformation also come from outside. The classic Michels argument focuses on internal sources of change. But given the precarious resources of many nonprofits, external pressures will often be more critical. Institutional patrons often require specific organizational structures as a condition of support. Private foundations, for example, need centralized executive leadership in order to ensure their fiscal accountability. Decentralized structures are also unfamiliar to foundation boards drawn from the corporate and university worlds, forcing nonprofits to adopt bureaucratic forms simply to survive (see DiMaggio & Powell 1983). Centralization coupled with pressures to abandon controversial tactics or demands produces Michels's accommodationism. The Woodlawn Organization in Chicago, for example, emerged in the early 1960s as a scrappy decentralized community organization attacking city hall and the University of Chicago, but after expanding into cooperative enterprises and building restoration, it turned to foundation and governmental grants. Such grants were available, however, only on agreement that the organization centralize decision making and drop its traditional adversarial stance (Fish 1973). Helfgot's study (1974, 1981) of Mobilization for Youth and Gittel's survey (1980) of citizen organizations have confirmed the notion that patronage, especially in the form of grants for service delivery, generally comes at the expense of internal democracy and militant advocacy for social change.

THE EFFECTIVENESS OF NONPROFIT ADVOCACY

The nonprofit advocates proclaim their task to be that of countering the dominance of the special interests by serving as a voice for the collective interests of the unrepresented and the general public. By their own measure, they have been more successful in raising issues and educating the public than in shaping the details of public policy or the operations of governmental agencies. Less accessible targets, like private corporations, have been even less affected, shaking off their public interest critics with a few token appointments to the board or the creation of a face-saving "social responsibility" committee. Yet the impact of the new nonprofit advocates has been more substantial than this portrait suggests, in terms of both specific policies and the general operation of the American political system.

Our major focus will be on public policy because it has been the major target for nonprofit advocacy. The first step in policy advocacy is creating an issue and interjecting it onto the political agenda. Of the numerous interests in society, probably only a fraction are ever actually organized into the policy process. Disorganization, privatistic values, and institutional procedures "bias the system," creating "nondecisions" (Bachrach & Baratz 1970) that keep interests and the potential issues tied to them off the political agenda. Entrepreneurship, consciousness raising, and dramatic crises are frequently necessary to bring an issue to bear, first on the "public agenda"—the set of issues that "have achieved a high level of public interest and visibility"—and then on the "formal agenda"—the "list of items which decision makers have formally accepted for serious consideration" (Cobb, Ross, & Ross 1977, 126). Because of their central role in molding public opinion, the mass media are primary arbiters in regulating access to the public agenda. Once an issue has been created, the focus shifts to getting it on the formal agenda and influencing the actual policies or formal decisions of public officials. Congress, the White House, and the courts are the primary arenas. Lobbying, legal cases, mass demonstrations, and even violence are critical tools in pressuring favorable decisions. Success here, though, does not necessarily mean that policies will actually be implemented. Governmental officials have considerable discretion over spending money and enforcing regulations. Courts are better at prohibiting actions than specifying new practices. Even the most farsighted policies can create unanticipated consequences. Potential beneficiaries like the poor may even have to be mobilized to make use of gains like new welfare programs. The ultimate test is whether the new policies are actually implemented in ways that actually advantage the intended beneficiaries.

Probably the most elusive factor is entrepreneurial skills. Ralph Nader's talent at converting a technical report on agency abuses into a public issue is legendary. David Brower was able in a short time to convert his following within the Sierra Club into the Friends of the Earth, a highly visible environmental lobbying organization, and John Gardner built Common Cause into a 200,000-member organization overnight largely through his personal reputation as a thoughtful reformer. The general field of nonprofit advocacy resembles that of religious advocacy, dominated by "institutionalized personalities" (Soreuf 1976) whose reputations outrun their organizations. Such personalities, however, are more effective in setting the public agenda, securing media coverage, and attracting public attention. Moving toward favorable policies usually takes organizational clout and favorable political allies.

If the "bias of the system" is the basic obstacle to getting on the formal agenda, then "socializing the conflict" by redefining the nature and scope of the issue is the favored tactic (Schattschneider 1960). By redefining an issue in abstract terms, drawing on favorable symbols like "equality" and "justice," advocates attempt to bring into a conflict groups that otherwise would stand quietly on the sidelines. Such issues are frequently viewed as general and enduring and, if posed in nontechnical terms, can arouse a broader public. Likewise, if clear precedents can be identified, the prospects for public support and elite receptiveness are improved (Cobb & Elder 1972, 96–122). Yet socializing the conflict can also work against the advocacy group. In general, proponents of change are disadvantaged—the burden of proof rests on them. Opponents need only raise serious doubts to discredit a proposal for change. Opponents can also convert the conflict into an ideological dispute by reinterpreting the issue as a threat to fundamental values. The opponents of the equal rights amendment have been quite successful at the latter, using the most dramatic and even irrational claims (its passage would lead to unisex bathrooms) to undercut the organizational advantages of the proponents (Boles 1979). In fact, their successes have led Gelb and Palley (1982) to contend that advocates of change are best off if they contain the scope of conflict by defining issues in narrow incremental terms. Demands for feminist reform cast in terms of "role equity" (equal treatment) as opposed to "role change" (altering women's role in society) have been more successful. Clear precedents can be identified. Legal and scientific specialists will be more supportive. Informational lobbying will be more persuasive. Opponents will find it difficult to convert the conflict into a rancorous ideological battle in which institutionalized values are seen as threatened. Along this line, Gamson (1975) has argued that social movements making narrow demands (single issues; reforms that do not displace antagonists) are more successful.

The mass media play a powerful gatekeeping role in defining the issues that reach the public agenda. Although advocates have often used the media to powerful effects (see Garrow [1978] on Martin Luther King's Birmingham and Selma campaigns), the frames and organizational features of the media operate as major constraints. Newsworthiness prizes exotic and bizarre events without context. Advocates therefore find it necessary to locate dramatic cases or "crises" that can capture media attention. This thirst for drama can also push advocates over the edge of credibility, encouraging them to use ever more exotic claims and bizarre actions to garner publicity. Nor are the media effective at covering underlying causes. Events stand out in sharp detail while their causes recede into the background. Complex reports and scientific studies lack the drama to receive attention, but bizarre behavior that may undermine public support for the cause will be publicized (Gitlin 1980). Nor are all media organizations created equal. In general, large city newspapers with middle- to upper-class readerships and national news organizations are more likely to cover advocacy claims (Goldenberg 1975). Because of the time pressures of meeting press deadlines, reporters depend heavily on official sources for continued cooperation, discouraging them from covering adversarial claims. At the minimum, official sources receive the last say.

Once on the agenda, the actual details of policy changes are more shaped by the organizational characteristics of the advocates. Presthus (1974) found that lobby organizations with a bureaucratic structure, a skilled permanent staff, an elaborate communications system, and a large membership were most effective. Interestingly, he also found that the age and political reputation of the lobby was of little importance. Virtually all observers have concluded that professional advocacy organizations are weaker than member-based organizations. Although they are more centralized and often enjoy excellent technical resources, they are vulnerable to patron controls and, without a membership base, to charges of elitism. As Tober (1984) has noted, Congress tends to view the claims of environmental advocates with skepticism, con-

sidering them staff-driven organizations without genuine membership support. Handler (1978) also concluded that membership helps litigation efforts, giving the organization more staying power. Professionalized nonprofit advocates have used several tactics to overcome these problems. The environmentalists have used public opinion polls showing strong public support for environmental protections. Another tactic is the formation of coalitional or umbrella organizations to represent a broad segment or general interest. The Consumer Federation is an organization of organizations, claiming to represent all consumers, much as the Leadership Conference on Civil Rights includes almost two hundred organizations supporting civil rights reforms. The question is whether these coalitions are worth their costs in internal battles. The Leadership Conference has been held up as an example of an acrimonious alliance that has as often weakened civil rights support by sharpening conflicts as strengthened it by creating consensus. The women's advocates have hit on an alternative formulation, relying on ad hoc coalitions that allow each organization to pursue its own priorities and ignore conflicting priorities yet line up behind consensual positions (Costain 1980). Similarly, legal advocates frequently file amicus curiae suits in support of their political allies.

What about the perennial question of working within the system or acting outside routine channels? The primary consideration is the political status of the group. Those outside the political system are unlikely to receive a hearing, much less a favorable decision. Disruptive events, like protests and rallies, are often necessary merely to get an issue onto the formal agenda. Piven and Cloward (1977), for example, have argued that poor people's movements succeed only when they generate institutional disruptions. Likewise, Gamson's study (1975) found that social movement advocates who used unruly tactics, including collective violence, were more successful. The impact of disruptions, however, may be limited to getting an issue onto the formal agenda. Demonstrations organized by the antiwar movement of the 1960s, for example, had a favorable impact on Senate roll-call voting, largely because they roused public attention and sensitized elites to the issue. Once on the agenda, however, demonstrations appeared to have a negative effect (Burstein & Freudenberg 1978). Advocates inside the system, in contrast, can use less demanding methods, hiring lobbyists, filing law suits, and supporting sympathetic candidates. Advocacy groups, however, rarely follow an exclusive program. The presence of a disruptive radical wing is often an advantage, as it was for civil rights moderates during the early 1960s. The Kennedy and Johnson administrations cultivated the NAACP and the Urban League in order to keep ahead of the increasingly strident militants in CORE and SNCC (Miroff 1981). Yet militant actions and radical demands can also unleash powerful counterforces, spurring countermovements and alienating potential allies. The urban riots of the late 1960s simultaneously generated short-term welfare gains (Button 1978; Hicks & Swank 1981) while undercutting the lobbying efforts of the moderate civil rights organizations by creating a white backlash and alienating moderate allies (Burstein 1979, 1981).

Most observers view informational lobbying as the most effective method for influencing the details of policy decisions (Presthus 1974; Forsythe 1980; Tober 1984). Testimony at public hearings is often pro forma with key representatives frequently absent. The "dirty dozen" campaigns of the Friends of the Earth have failed to remove targeted congressional representatives, and electoral campaigns are extremely expensive. Environmental litigation has been effective in halting construction projects and altering agency procedures but not in forcing changes in substantive policy (Davies & Davies 1975, 124–37; Andrews 1976, 7–19). In large part, this reflects the limits of the courts as a policy arena. The courts are best at prohibiting actions, not asserting new policies. They are generally unwilling to overrule Congress on substantive issues and even more reluctant to become involved in monitoring agencies. Unless targets can be shown to be violating legal procedures, as in the celebrated environmental impact cases, they are usually invulnerable to court actions. Proponents of change, then, find it difficult to secure more than temporary victories. The likelihood of success through legal reform is greatest when a single case or decision is involved, a technically simple solution is available, and administrative discretion, especially at the field level, is minimal (Handler 1978). The problem of administrative discretion is probably the most serious problem. Advocates concerned with racial and sex discrimination, for example, have pushed for quota-like regulations primarily to ease the burden of monitoring. Yet, significantly, nonprofit advocates are less likely to make use of such insider tactics as informational lobbying, public testimony, and private meetings with representatives, reflecting their relative political exclusion (Schlozman & Tierney 1983; Gais, Peterson, & Walker 1983). Outsider tactics, like demonstrations and grass-roots lobbying, are an essential part of their repertoire.

One tactic that has received almost universal condemnation is organizations participating in formal advisory committees and similar participatory devices. Although Levine (1970, 158–78) claimed that the participation of the poor in Community Action Projects forced city governments to be more responsive to minority and lower-class problems, most students have concurred with Alford and Friedland's contention (1975, 455–64) that the CAPs represented "participation without power." The agencies depended on federal funding and those that became involved in significant advocacy found their funding revoked. Similarly, Warren, Rose, and Bergunder (1974) found in a survey of community organizations participating in advisory committees that of 606 cases of "innovation" traceable to advocates, only 6 entailed significant policy changes. Similarly, Rothman (1974) found that participants in Environmental Protection Agency committees had no genuine impact. Administrators are usually able to select the representatives to be appointed, bringing in those already supportive of agency policies. Few are willing

to challenge the agency, deferring to its claims to expertise (Rosenbaum 1978). Although for a while nonprofit advocates saw the use of "intervenor funding" (financial support for participation in agency hearings) as a significant source of funding, congressional restrictions and the Reagan administration have brought its use to a halt. Nor is there clear evidence that it created significant influence. In a slightly different vein, the various nonprofit advocates who assumed top staff positions in the Carter administration in agencies involved with consumer rights, poverty, and the environment frequently found themselves hemmed in by past practices and thus affecting policy only at the margins (see Tober 1984). In general, participatory mechanisms appear to be a prime case of Edelman's "symbolic politics" (1964, 1971), generating the public image that interests are being taken into account without actually altering the substance of policy.

Nonprofit advocates, assuming that Congress and representative bodies are more receptive than agencies and courts, have made these their key targets. Yet representative institutions vary in their accessibility. For example, reform city governments with a city manager and an at-large elected council have been less responsive to lower-class and minority demands than those with a mayor and ward representation (Eisinger 1973). Receptiveness also varies across issues. From a study of congressional responsiveness to women's demands over a hundred-year period, Costain and Costain (1983b) concluded that Congress has played a gatekeeper role by responding more readily to demands for health and educational services and shunting economic and political rights issues to the side. Congress is more receptive to demands that can be treated as distributive benefits than those requiring regulations or redistributive controls. Benefit programs allow logrolling compromises, whereas regulations and redistributive measures typically entail clear costs imposed on particular groups (Lowi 1972).

The receptiveness of representative institutions also varies over time. The wave of congressional reform that began in the early 1960s (reapportionment, elected committee chairs, more subcommittees and staff, weakened leadership and seniority, restrictions on campaign spending and contributions) decentralized congressional decision making, creating a more diffuse and permeable policy system. Reforms weakened the hold of the traditional "iron triangles" of special interest lobbies, specialized congressional committees, and agency heads, creating a more diffuse "issue network" (Heclo 1978) system in which expertise and informal contacts among political entrepreneurs became more prominent. Decentralization created more targets for lobbying and encouraged representatives, especially in the Senate, to take an entrepreneurial role in defining the policy agenda and pressing reform legislation (Walker 1977; Gais, Peterson, & Walker 1983).

The structure of political opportunities is also shaped by shifting political alignments. A divided and weakened opposition creates a more favorable context for successful advocacy. The passage of the major consumer legislation during the 1960s, for example, stemmed from disarray within the business community in which larger corporations actively supported consumer reforms in the hope that this would temper their critics and reassure consumers (Nadel 1971). In contrast, by the late 1970s business associations like the Chamber of Commerce and the Business Roundtable mobilized to form a common front against consumer reforms, most notably blocking the Nader proposal for a Consumer Protection Agency to institutionalize his efforts (Pertschuck 1982). Environmental advocates active in the area of energy policy have similarly benefited from rivalries among alternative energy suppliers. In several cases their suits and lobbying against proposals for coal slurry pipelines in the West have been supported by eastern coal firms and the railways. Similarly, broad electoral realignments can bring reform-minded governments to power, weakening the hold of entrenched interests and giving advocates greater opportunities. The general liberalization of American politics during the 1960s and early 1970s facilitated the rise and policy successes of the public interest movement. Even more dramatic opportunities are created by generalized political crises in which alliances among established political actors become unpredictable. Entrenched groups fear losing their claims or perceive new opportunities for strengthening their position by supporting the bids of outsiders against their former allies (Tilly 1978, 126–28, 213–14). A mild form of political reshuffling appears to have occurred in the early 1960s when northern Democrats became open supporters of civil rights reforms, acting against their southern New Deal allies. Although the link between socioeconomic changes and political realignments is poorly understood, it seems plausible that fundamental socioeconomic crises lead to political crises and intense power struggles among established powers, creating unprecedented opportunities for advocacy. Such crises in effect set off reform periods that alter the political landscape by bringing new voices into the political system and institutionalizing new public philosophies (Tarrow 1983).

NONPROFIT ADVOCACY AND THE HEALTH OF THE AMERICAN POLITICAL SYSTEM

The proponents of nonprofit advocacy have seen it as a major force for the renewal of the American political system. The majority of the nonprofit advocates have adopted a kind of neoliberal political stance, affirming the liberal reform ideas behind Progressivism and the New Deal while rejecting many of the traditional liberal reform measures. In agreement with traditional liberalism, they have argued for increased use of scientific knowledge and governmental efforts to solve social problems. Yet, unlike their liberal forebears, these neoliberals have been skeptical of centralized public authority, advocating direct citizen access and decentralized authority. This flows from their conclusion that past liberal reforms have often been diverted or corrupted by the special interests. In general, they have accepted Lowi's critique (1979) of interest group liberalism, seeing governmental

agencies as captured by the well-organized special interest groups. Many of these captive agencies were originally created by liberal reformers to protect the public but, because of the persistent pressures of organized special interests, came under the control of these same interests. The neoliberal solutions, then, have emphasized accountability measures such as direct citizen participation, open access rules, freedom of information, clarity of legal standards, and judicial review. In several cases, such as the advocacy of a consumer protection agency, they have argued for a governmental agency captive to their own efforts to counterbalance the agencies already captured by private groups (Vogel 1978, 1981). In this vein, nonprofit public interest advocacy has been seen as a major device for countering the "iron law of decadence" (Lowi 1971), reinvigorating the political system by challenging the political stranglehold of special interests in the name of the public.

Not all nonprofit advocates, however, have adopted this neoliberal vision. In the past decade, there has also been a significant growth in nonprofit advocacy by neoconservative and New Right groups such as the American Enterprise Institute, National Affairs, Inc. (publisher of the *Public Interest*), and the Heritage Foundation. These organizations have been more closely associated with corporate leadership and espoused a more conservative view of government and the public interest. Although at several points they converge with their neoliberal brethren, especially in their shared skepticism of public authority, the neoconservatives have frequently been direct opponents of the neoliberals. Dan Burt (1982), for example, heads the neoconservative Capitol Legal Defense Fund, which, in addition to its right-to-work suits against unions and its advocacy in the General Westmoreland libel case against CBS, has charged that the network of organizations associated with Ralph Nader has withheld financial information from the public and promoted excessive governmental regulations. The clash is essentially philosophical. The neoconservatives have argued from a laissez-faire stance, emphasizing reduced social spending, strict moral standards, and greater reliance on self-help and market solutions. They have modeled their tactics on the neoliberals, using research, litigation, and public educational efforts. Yet, compared to their neoliberal brethren, they have enjoyed greater political access and resources because of their closer ties to corporate elites.

What assurance exists that the public interest is served by granting tax privileges to these obviously partisan organizations? Several critics have argued that their policy positions stem from the economic and political interests of their major contributors and leading entrepreneurs. The tax deduction, then, would seem to be merely a subsidy for the policy advocacy of particular sectional views and interests. Lichter and Rothman (1983), for example, have offered evidence on the salaries and political views of the staff of the nonprofit public interest lobbies, attempting to document economic privilege and liberal bias. Kristol (1977) and Tucker (1982) have argued that the public interest advocates are biased toward the interests of the upper-middle class and against those of the general populace. Public interest liberals are seen as advancing the career interests of public-sector professionals by promoting governmental spending, pressing for aesthetic goals like preserving wilderness areas for affluent backpackers at the expense of jobs for the less affluent, and instituting consumer protections for the well-to-do at the cost of economic inefficiency.

The central dispute has been over the purported bias of the public interest liberals. Significantly, the critics have ignored the advocates of a neoconservative, or New Right persuasion, implicitly treating them as legitimate nonprofit representatives. Yet the critics do have a point. The nonprofit advocates are generally liberal in orientation and dependent on the upper and upper-middle classes for contributions and policy entrepreneurs. The support for their other criticisms, however, is much weaker. As we have seen, many of the nonprofits have a precarious base of support and hence an ambiguous claim to a constituency. Their vulnerability to the charge of bias stems in part from this weak constituency base. Yet, given their advocacy of collective goods, it is difficult to imagine a different base of support. As Olson (1965) would predict, most citizens ride free, and as J. Q. Wilson (1973) would argue, the more educated and affluent are more receptive to moral incentives. This does not mean, however, that nonprofit advocates are unresponsive to their claimed constituencies or that they represent only the interests of their donors. If Common Cause were taken as the touchstone, the nonprofit advocates are far more open and accountable, both to the general public and to their contributors, than the private advocacy organizations that dominate national politics (Ornstein & Elder 1978; McFarland 1978). Liberal advocates like the Children's Defense Fund and the NAACP might draw their resources from elite groups, but the poor and minorities are the direct beneficiaries of most of their efforts and elites draw only derivative benefits like a good conscience and political stability. Nor are Lichter and Rothman's figures (1983) on the salaries of nonprofit advocates particularly condemning. The relevant comparison is the private special interest Washington lobbyists, beside whose organizational coffers and personal financial fortunes those of the nonprofit public interest liberals pale (Gelb & Palley 1982, 45–60; Walker 1983).

Actually, a far stronger case can be made that the nonprofit advocates are biased toward the views and interests of nonelite groups. In this sense, the tax privilege appears to be a subsidy on advocacy for these segments, not the general public or elites. If the public interest is defined in terms of the representation of otherwise unrepresented interests, then the nonprofit advocates would appear to have a strong claim to tax advantages. Although they cannot claim a privileged insight into the interests of the whole society, they can claim to expand the range of policy advocacy to otherwise unrepresented interests. In view of the overwhelming dominance of private special interest representation on behalf of elite groups like large corporations and the more affluent professions (see Greenwald 1977; Ornstein & Elder 1978; Salisbury 1983; Schlozman & Tierney 1983; Walker 1983), this

public interest counterforce would appear to be a healthy corrective. In short, the tax advantages may flow disproportionately toward more affluent groups, and nonelite groups may receive greater attention in public interest advocacy. But, given the overwhelming bias of the interest representation system toward elite groups, the nonprofit advocates appear to be a benign counterforce.

Another line of criticism has focused on the stridency and uncompromising terms in which single-issue nonprofit groups have pressed their claims, purportedly paralyzing government, overloading the system with demands, and ultimately leaving behind a legacy of citizen skepticism and withdrawal (Bell 1976; Huntington 1981). Here again, the argument has an element of truth but has been overdrawn. As Walker (1983) has shown, nonprofit advocacy has grown at about double the rate of private advocacy over the past two decades. Nonprofit advocacy groups are also less likely to compromise their positions. As Tesh (1984) has argued, general citizen organizations attract contributors precisely because of their emphasis on moral concerns, and moralists frequently find it difficult to strike compromises over indivisible symbolic issues. In this sense, the nonprofit advocates have frequently advocated positions that have been difficult to compromise.

The broader criticisms of nonprofit advocacy, however, have not been supported. The rising tide of skepticism about institutional authority made it possible for the nonprofit advocates to raise issues and mobilize support, but their efforts did not create the confidence gap. Declining confidence flowed primarily from major elite decisions like involvement in Vietnam and the Watergate scandal, political disasters like the Kennedy assassinations and the oil embargoes, and the economic stagnation of the 1970s (Lipset & Schneider 1983). In other words, nonprofit advocacy was strengthened by the decline in public confidence but it did not create it. Yet it is also true that the adversarial attacks of some of the nonprofits may have helped sustain the confidence gap in the late 1970s by hastening the decline of political parties, identifying more political scandals, and heightening public awareness of gaps between promise and performance (Berry 1980).

The political overload thesis has received even less support. Although we have witnessed a major increase in nonprofit policy advocacy over the past two decades, the private for-profit advocates continue to dominate the national pressure system. The number of nonprofit advocacy organizations has grown at about double the rate of the private advocates, but the overwhelming majority of Washington representatives are still private, and in terms of resources and political contacts, they have the nonprofits outgunned on the order of two to one (Walker 1983; Schlozman & Tierney 1983; Salisbury 1983). Nonprofit advocacy may be healthy and prospering. It does not appear to be an "endangered sector" (Nielsen, 1982) slated for oblivion. Yet, by the same token, its hold on the reins of power is far weaker than that of the advocates for the large corporations and the more affluent professions. In short, if there is an overload, it would seem to be rooted in the dominance of the special interests rather than in an excess of nonprofit advocacy. Ultimately the major problem with the thesis of an overload is that it is premised on a highly debatable value judgment. The proponents assume that an efficient political system—that is, one that reduces the gap between promise and performance—is preferable to one that is equitable and accessible—one that maximizes political access. The balance between efficiency and accessibility is ultimately a value judgment, not simply an empirical one.

The criticisms raised by sympathetic analysts have been more telling. The nonprofit advocates have been far more effective in raising issues and shaping the political agenda than in developing solutions and forcing compromises. As McFarland (1976) has noted, the public interest nonprofits are dependent on entrepreneurial skills and weak constituencies, making them less effective at interest aggregation and conflict resolution. They cannot take the place of coherent political parties and sustained mass social movements. Moreover, the professionalized advocacy organizations are vulnerable to the charge that their professionalized structure and focus on procedural reforms have reinforced tendencies in American society toward a new form of alienated politics:

Atomized Common Cause members receive communications from unseen persons in Washington requesting them to initiate some form of political activity, usually one conducted in solitary fashion such as writing letters. Such activity is generally oriented to the procedural mechanics of government and not to the substantive issues. The individual [receives] messages from the media that Common Cause is an effective political power. . . . His motivation is his desire to avoid the conflicts, disappointments, boredom, and failures incurred in direct action in politics. The member thus prefers to pay someone else to do his political work for him. (McFarland 1978, 328)

Another way of putting this is that professional nonprofit advocates cannot substitute for broad citizen participation.

A related criticism has been the charge of emerging corporatism, largely stimulated by the increasing dependence of the nonprofit advocates on governmental and elite patronage (Handler 1978; Wilson 1983). Although small contributors and grass-roots support have been critical to many of these organizations, institutional support has become increasingly important. Public interest law, for example, has become more dependent on governmental grants, which rose from 22 percent of their total revenues in 1975 to 33 percent in 1979 (Council for Public Interest Law 1980, 16). Meanwhile, private foundation support dropped from 37 to 31 percent, and, more significantly, public contributions, including membership dues, fell from 37 to 26 percent. In effect, rising governmental support meant that institutional patronage rose from 59 to 64 percent of total revenues. In part, this was because of the declining effectiveness of direct-mail fundraising. By the late 1970s, most observers saw the field of public interest advocacy as saturated with competing fund-

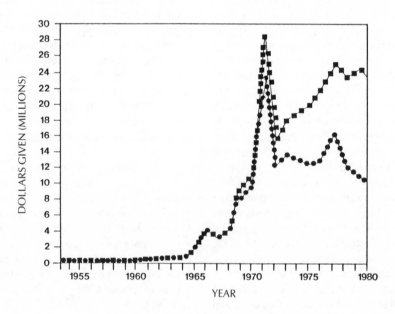

■ Private foundation grants to social movement organizations ($ millions current)

● Private foundation grants to social movement organizations ($ millions constant; 1967 = 100)

FIGURE 17.1. FOUNDATION GRANTS TO SOCIAL MOVEMENTS

raisers. Some issues, like prisoners' rights and auto safety, were unable to generate either a large public following or a set of small contributors. Others, like gun control and strip-mining controls, have received support only after highly publicized events like an assassination or a mining disaster. In a study of supports for social movement advocates (Jenkins 1985b), I found that foundation support grew rapidly from the early 1960s through 1971, dropped and then peaked again in 1977, and then declined through 1980 (see figure 17.1). For the social movements, this was a significant base of support, amounting in 1971 to $28.7 million. Yet, in terms of total foundation giving, this was minuscule, constituting only .705 percent of all foundation grants (figure 17.2). Paralleling the public interest law experience, foundation giving shrank in the late 1970s, dropping in constant dollar terms (1967 = 100) by 55 percent between 1971 and 1980 (see figure 17.1). The reasons for this rise and drop are complex, but probably the central factor was the pressure generated by the mass movements of the 1960s and early 1970s. The funding peak followed closely on the upsurge of the mass movements, and then, after the movements declined, funding gradually tapered off. Funding also went primarily to professional advocates who could be seen as "responsible militants" and whose major effort was to implement policy changes initiated by the movements.

The question of corporatism ultimately hinges on how these institutional supports shape the process of policy ad-

vocacy. If institutional elites can control or channel the advocacy process by funding particular organizations, then it would appear that this funding is ultimately a basis of elite control. Schmitter has defined corporatism as a system of state-sponsored interest representation in which

> the constituent units are organized into a limited number of singular, compulsory, noncompetitive, hierarchically ordered, and functionally differentiated categories, recognized and licensed (if not created) by the state and granted a deliberate representational monopoly within their respective categories in exchange for observing certain controls on their selection of leaders and articulation of demands and supports. (1976, 65)

Clearly, the interest representation system as a whole does not fit the corporatist model. In the United States, interest groups and movement organizations are voluntary, diverse, competitive, and relatively independent from state controls (Salisbury 1979). Yet, as John Wilson (1983) has argued, the corporatist model is an ideal type toward which the American polity could be seen as moving, which is particularly relevant in interpreting nonprofit advocacy. Several studies have emphasized the importance of institutional patronage in creating and sustaining nonprofit advocacy. The nonprofit organizations have been staff dominated (that is, hierarchically ordered), especially the professional advocacy organizations.

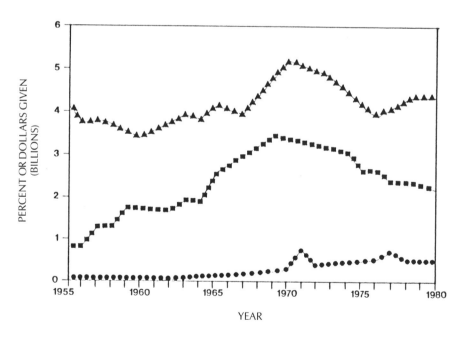

● Percent foundation grants going to social movements (constant $; 1967 = 100)

■ Total private foundation grants (constant $; 1967 = 100)

▲ Total social welfare philanthropy, all sources.

FIGURE 17.2. PHILANTHROPY AND SOCIAL MOVEMENT GIVING

Patronage has tended to convert the advocacy organizations into centralized service purveyors, demobilizing masses by emphasizing services and projecting images of elite responsiveness. Elite patrons clearly have a decisive say over the advocates, even if it is not the state that provides the major funding. The nonprofits have had their greatest impact in raising issues, not controlling policy decisions or their implementation. In short, elite patronage is a form of political control.

Several analysts have therefore argued that institutional support for nonprofit advocacy represents the leading edge of an emergent system of corporatist representation (Handler 1978, 222–33; John Wilson 1983). Institutional support for nonprofit advocacy gives elites greater control over policy advocacy, and the impetus for policy change comes increasingly from centralized professional organizations without grass-roots bases. Yet one feature that does not fit this corporatist interpretation is that of legitimacy. In Schmitter's analysis (1979), the major benefit of corporatism is increased legitimacy. Although it may be that support for nonprofit advocacy has kept legitimacy problems from becoming more serious, the persistence of the confidence gap suggests it has not solved the problem.

Ultimately the major issue is the effectiveness of nonprofit advocacy in shaping policy changes. Several nonprofit advocates have argued that increasing their organizational resources and reforming governmental procedures could counteract the power of the special interests. Although their net effect may have been to serve as a counterforce, this line of argument underestimates the political power of business in a capitalist society. As Vogel (1981) has argued, the special interests, especially the large corporations, do not derive their political influence simply from organizing, capturing governmental agencies, and lobbying. In a capitalist society, politicians must eventually defer to the preferences of business because they ultimately depend on the rate and location of corporate investment for political stability (Lindblom 1977). This means that the nonprofits' claim that they counter the special interests by simply organizing larger numbers and securing procedural reforms is naive. At best they can set up roadblocks that ensure consideration of a broader range of interests.

By this reasoning, strengthening professional nonprofit advocacy at the expense of mass social movements would appear to be a losing bargain. The political power of the nonprofits depends largely on their political context, especially the existence of mass movements and supportive elites. Although professional advocacy represents increased formal access, if this comes at the cost of greater organizational dependence on elites and diminished mass support, then the gain is probably negative. The best hope for strengthened nonprofit advocacy would appear to be a broad popular upsurge in political participation similar to that which emerged in the 1960s. In the context of such a general reform period, nonprofit advocacy would again enjoy not only an infusion of new resources but also expanded political opportunities for transforming the political agenda and carrying through major social reforms.

REFERENCES

Adams, John H. 1974. "Responsible Militancy—the Anatomy of a Public Interest Law Firm." *Record of the Association of the City of New York* 29:631–45.

Alford, Robert, and Roger Friedland. 1975. "Political Participation and Public Policy." *Annual Review of Sociology* 1:429–79.

Alinsky, Saul. 1969. *Reveille for Radicals*. New York: Random House.

———. 1972. *Rules for Radicals*. New York: Random House.

Andrews, Richard. 1976. *Environmental Policy and Administrative Change*. Lexington, Mass.: Lexington Books.

Aveni, Andrian. 1978. "Organizational Linkages and Resource Mobilization." *Sociological Quarterly* 19:185–202.

Bachrach, Peter, and Morton Baratz. 1970. *Power and Poverty*. New York: Oxford University Press.

Bailis, Lawrence. 1974. *Bread or Justice*. Lexington, Mass.: Lexington Books.

Bell, Daniel. 1976. *The Cultural Contradictions of Capitalism*. New York: Basic.

Berger, Margaret. 1980. *Litigation on Behalf of Women*. New York: Ford Foundation.

Berry, Jeffrey M. 1977. *Lobbying for the People*. Princeton, N.J.: Princeton University Press.

———. 1978. "On the Origins of Public Interest Groups." *Polity* 3:379–97.

———. 1980. "Public Interest vs. Party System." *Society* 7:42–48.

Berry, Jeffrey, and Bill Fisher. 1981. "Public Interest Groups as Loyal Opposition." *Citizen Participation* 2:14–15.

Boles, Janet. 1979. *The Politics of the Equal Rights Amendment*. New York: Longman.

Boyte, Harry. 1980. *The Backyard Revolution*. Philadelphia: Temple University Press.

Breines, Wini. 1982. *Community and Organization*. South Hadley, Mass.: Bergin.

Brill, Harry. 1971. *Why Organizers Fail*. Berkeley: University of California Press.

Burstein, Paul. 1979. "Public Opinion, Demonstrations and the

Passage of Antidiscrimination Legislation." *Public Opinion Quarterly* 43:157–72.

———. 1981. "Social Protest, Public Opinion and Public Policy." Paper presented at the 76th Annual Meeting of the American Sociological Association, Toronto, Canada.

Burstein, Paul, and William Freudenberg. 1978. "Changing Public Policy." *American Journal of Sociology* 84:99–122.

Burt, Dan. 1982. *Abuse of Trust*. Chicago: Gateway.

Button, J. W. 1978. *Black Violence*. Princeton, N.J.: Princeton University Press.

Carden, Maureen L. 1974. *The New Feminist Movement*. New York: Russell Sage.

———. 1977. *Feminism in the Mid-1970s*. New York: Ford Foundation.

———. 1978. "The Proliferation of a Social Movement." *Research in Social Movements, Conflict and Change* 1:179–96.

Castells, Manuel. 1983. *The City and the Grassroots*. Berkeley: University of California Press.

Clark, Peter B., and James Q. Wilson. 1961. "Incentive Systems." *Administrative Science Quarterly* 6:29–66.

Cobb, Robert, Jennie-Keith Ross, and Marc Howard Ross. 1977. "Agenda Building as a Comparative Political Process." *American Political Science Review* 70:126–38.

Cobb, Roger, and Charles Elder. 1972. *Participation in America*. Boston: Allyn & Bacon.

Costain, Anne N. 1980. "The Struggle for a National Women's Lobby." *Western Political Quarterly* 33:476–91.

———. 1981. "Representing Women: The Transition from Social Movement to Interest Group." *Western Political Quarterly* 34:100–13.

Costain, Anne, and Douglas Costain. 1983a. "The Women's Lobby." In A. Cigler and B. Loomis, eds., *Interest Group Politics,* 191–216. Washington, D.C.: Congressional Quarterly Press.

———. 1983b. "Movements and Gatekeepers." Paper presented at the Conference on the Women's Movement in Comparative Perspective, Western Studies Program, Cornell University.

Council for Public Interest Law. 1976. *Balancing the Scales of Justice*. Washington, D.C.: Council for Public Interest Law.

———. 1980. *Survey of Public Interest Law Centers*. Washington, D.C.: Council for Public Interest Law.

Creighton, Lucy Black. 1976. *Pretenders to the Throne*. Lexington, Mass.: Lexington Books.

Curtis, Russell, and Louis Zurcher. 1973. "Stable Resources of Protest Movements: The Multi-organizational Field." *Social Forces* 52:53–61.

———. 1974. "Social Movements." *Social Problems* 21:356–70.

Davies, James Clarence, and Barbara Davies. 1975. *The Politics of Pollution*. Indianapolis, Ind.: Bobbs-Merrill.

DiMaggio, Paul, and Walter Powell. 1983. "The Iron Cage Revisited: Institutional Isomorphism and Collective Rationality in Organizational Fields." *American Sociological Review* 48:147–60.

Edelman, Murray. 1964. *The Symbolic Uses of Politics*. Urbana: University of Illinois Press.

———. 1971. *Politics as Symbolic Action*. Chicago: Markham.

Eisinger, Peter. 1973. "The Conditions of Protest Behavior in American Cities." *American Political Science Review* 67:11–28.

Evans, Sara Jane. 1979. *Personal Politics*. New York: Knopf.

Faich, Ronald, and Richard P. Gale. 1971. "The Environmental Movement: From Recreation to Politics." *Pacific Sociological Review* 11:270–87.

Fireman, Bruce, and William Gamson. 1979. "Utilitarian Logic in the Resource Mobilization Perspective." In M. Zald and J. McCarthy, eds., *The Dynamics of Social Movements,* 8–45. Cambridge, Mass.: Winthrop.

Fish, F. H. 1973. *Black Power/White Control*. Princeton, N.J.: Princeton University Press.

Forsythe, David. 1980. "Humanizing Foreign Policy." Yale University, Program on Non-Profit Organizations Working Paper no. 22.

Forsythe, David P., and Susan Welch. 1981. "Citizen Support for Non-Profit Public Interest Groups." Yale University, Program on Non-Profit Organizations Working Paper no. 35.

Fox, Stephen. 1981. *John Muir and His Legacy*. Boston: Little, Brown.

Freeman, Jo. 1973. "The Tyranny of Structurelessness." *Ms.* 3:20–25.

———. 1975. *The Politics of Women's Liberation*. New York: McKay.

———. 1979. "Resource Mobilization and Strategy." In M. Zald and J. McCarthy, eds., *The Dynamics of Social Movements,* 167–89. Cambridge, Mass.: Winthrop.

Frohlich, N., J. A. Oppenheimer, and O. R. Young. 1971. *Political Leadership and Collective Goods*. Princeton, N.J.: Princeton University Press.

Gais, Thomas, Mark Peterson, and Jack Walker. 1983. "Interest Groups, Iron Triangles and Representative Institutions in American National Government." *British Journal of Political Science* 41:161–85.

Gamson, William A. 1975. *The Strategy of Social Protest*. Homewood, Ill.: Dorsey.

Gamson, William, Bruce Fireman, and Steve Rytina. 1982. *Encounters with Unjust Authority*. Homewood, Ill.: Dorsey.

Garrow, David J. 1978. *Protest at Selma*. New Haven, Conn.: Yale University Press.

Gelb, Joyce, and Marian Lelf Palley. 1982. *Women and Public Policy*. Princeton, N.J.: Princeton University Press.

Gerlach, Luther, and Virginia Hine. 1970. *People, Power and Change*. Indianapolis, Ind.: Bobbs-Merrill.

Gitlin, Todd. 1980. *The Whole World Is Watching*. Berkeley: University of California Press.

Gittel, Marilyn. 1980. *Limits to Citizen Participation*. Beverly Hills, Calif.: Sage.

Goetz, Charles, and Gordon Brady. 1975. "Environmental Policy Formation and the Tax Treatment of Citizens Interest Groups." *Law and Contemporary Problems* 39:213–16.

Goldenberg, Edie. 1975. *Making the News*. Lexington, Mass.: Lexington Books.

Gorey, Hays. 1975. *Nader and the Power of Everyman*. New York: Grosset & Dunlop.

Greenwald, Carol. 1977. *Groups, Power, Lobbying and Public Policy*. New York: Praeger.

Halperin, Charles, and Cunningham, John. 1971. "Reflections on the New Public Interest Law." *Georgetown Law Journal* 59:1095–1126.

Handler, Jack F. 1978. *Social Movements and the Legal System.* New York: Academic.

Harrison, Gordon, and Sanford Jaffe. 1971. "Public Interest Law Firms: New Voices for New Constituencies." *American Bar Association Journal* 58:459–67.

Hayes, Michael. 1978. "The Semi-sovereign Pressure Groups." *Journal of Politics* 40:45–78.

Heclo, Hugh. 1978. "Issue Networks and the Executive Establishment." In A. King, ed., *The New American Political System,* 87–124. Washington, D.C: American Enterprise Institute.

Helfgot, Joseph H. 1974. "Professional Reform Organizations and the Symbolic Representation of the Poor." *American Sociological Review* 39:475–91.

———. 1981. *Professional Reforming.* Lexington, Mass.: D. C. Heath.

Hertz, Susan H. 1981. *The Welfare Mothers Movement.* Washington, D.C.: University Press of America.

Hicks, Alexander, and Dwayne Swank. 1981. "Paying Off the Poor." Paper presented at the Annual Meeting of the American Sociological Association, Toronto, Canada.

Hunter, Albert. 1983. "The Neighborhood Movement as Communal Class Politics." Unpublished manuscript, Yale University, Program on Non-Profit Organizations.

Huntington, Samuel. 1976. "The United States." In M. Crozier, S. Huntington, and S. Watanuki, eds., *The Crisis of Democracy,* 59–118. New York: New York University Press.

———. 1981. *American Politics.* Cambridge, Mass.: Harvard University Press.

Jackson, Larry, and W. A. Johnson. 1973. *Protest by the Poor.* Lexington, Mass.: D. C. Heath.

Jaffe, Sanford. 1976. *Public Interest Law.* New York: Ford Foundation.

Jenkins, J. Craig. 1977. "The Radical Transformation of Organizational Goals." *Administrative Science Quarterly* 22:248–67.

———. 1983a. "The Transformation of a Constituency into a Social Movement." In J. Freeman, ed., *The Social Movements of the Sixties and Seventies,* 52–70. New York: Longman.

———. 1983b. "Resource Mobilization Theory and the Study of Social Movements." *Annual Review of Sociology* 9:527–53.

———. 1984. "Foundation Support for Social Movements." Paper presented at the Annual Meeting of the Council on Foundations, Denver, Colorado.

———. 1985a. *The Politics of Insurgency.* New York: Columbia University Press.

———. 1985b. "Funding of Progressive Social Movements." In Jill Shellow, ed., *The Grantseekers' Guide,* 2d ed., 7–17. Mt. Kisco, N.Y.: Moyer Bell.

Jenkins, J. Craig, and Charles C. Perrow. 1977. "Insurgency of the Powerless." *American Sociological Review* 42:249–68.

Judkins, Bennett. 1979. "The Black Lung Movement." *Research in Social Movements, Conflicts, and Change* 11:78–96.

Katznelson, Ira. 1981. *City Trenches.* Chicago: University of Chicago Press.

Kirkpatrick, Jeane. 1976. *The New Presidential Elite.* New York: Russell Sage Foundation and the Twentieth Century Fund.

Kluger, Richard. 1976. *Simple Justice.* New York: Random House.

Kristol, Irving. 1977. *Two Cheers for Capitalism.* New York: Norton.

Ladd, Everett Carll. 1980. "How to Tame the Special-Interest Groups." *Fortune* 36:66–80.

Lawson, Ronald. 1983. "The Decentralized but Moving Pyramid." In J. Freeman, ed., *The Social Movements of the Sixties and Seventies,* 119–32. New York: Longman.

Levine, Robert. 1970. *The Poor Ye Need Not Have with You.* Cambridge, Mass.: Harvard University Press.

Lichter, Robert, and Stanley Rothman. 1983. "What Interests the Public and What Interests the Public Interests?" *Public Opinion* 14:44–48.

Lindblom, Charles. 1977. *Politics and Markets.* New York: Basic.

Lippmann, Walter. 1955. *Essays in the Public Philosophy.* Boston: Little, Brown.

Lipset, S. M., and William Schneider. 1983. *The Confidence Gap.* New York: Free Press.

Lowi, Theodore. 1971. *The Politics of Disorder.* New York: Norton.

———. 1972. "Four Systems of Policy, Politics and Choice." *Public Administration Review* 32:298–310.

———. 1979. *The End of Liberalism.* New York: Norton.

McAdam, Doug. 1982. *Political Process and the Development of Black Insurgency.* Chicago: University of Chicago Press.

McCarry, Charles. 1972. *Citizen Nader.* New York: Saturday Review.

McCarthy, John, and Mayer Zald. 1973. *The Trend of Social Movements.* Morristown, N.J.: General Learning.

———. 1977. "Resource Mobilization and Social Movements." *American Journal of Sociology* 82:1212–41.

McFarland, Andrew S. 1976. *Public Interest Lobbies.* Washington, D.C.: American Enterprise Institute.

———. 1978. "Third Forces in American Politics: The Case of Common Cause." In J. Fishell, ed., *Parties and Elections in an Anti-Party Age,* 318–32. Bloomington: University of Indiana Press.

McKay, Robert B. 1977. *Nine for Equality under Law.* New York: Ford Foundation.

MacKenzie, Angus. 1981. "When Auditors Turn Editors." *Columbia Journalism Review* 9:29–34.

Mansbridge, Jane. 1982. *Beyond Adversary Democracy.* New York: Basic.

Marwell, Gerald, and R. Ames. 1979. "Experiments on the Provision of Public Goods, I." *American Journal of Sociology* 84:1335–56.

———. 1980. "Experiments on the Provision of Public Goods, II." *American Journal of Sociology* 85:926–37.

Meier, August, and Elliott Rudwick. 1973. *CORE.* New York: Oxford University Press.

Messinger, Sheldon L. 1955. "Organizational Transformation." *American Sociological Review* 20:3–10.

Michels, Robert. 1962. *Political Parties.* New York: Free Press.

Milbrath, Lester, and M. L. Goel. 1977. *Political Participation*. 2d ed. Chicago: Rand McNally.

Milofsky, Carl, and Frank Romo. 1981. "The Structure of Funding Arenas for Community Self-help Organizations." Yale University, Program on Non-Profit Organizations Working Paper no. 42.

Miroff, Bruce. 1981. "Presidential Leverage over Social Movements." *Journal of Politics* 43:2–23.

Mitchell, Robert C. 1979. "National Environmental Lobbies and the Apparent Illogic of Collective Action." In C. S. Russell, ed., *Collective Decision Making*, 87–135. Baltimore: Resources for the Future.

Moe, Terry M. 1980. *The Organization of Interests*. Chicago: University of Chicago Press.

———. 1981. "A Broader View of Interest Groups." *Journal of Politics* 43:531–43.

Moynihan, Daniel P. 1969. *Maximum Feasible Misunderstanding*. New York: Free Press.

Nadel, Mark. 1971. *The Politics of Consumer Protection*. Indianapolis, Ind.: Bobbs-Merrill.

Navasky, Victor. 1977. *Kennedy Justice*. New York: Atheneum.

Needleman, Martin L., and Carol E. Needleman. 1974. *Guerillas in the Bureaucracy*. New York: Wiley.

Nielsen, Waldemar. 1972. *The Big Foundations*. New York: Columbia University Press.

———. 1982. *The Endangered Sector*. New York: Columbia University Press.

O'Brien, David J. 1975. *Neighborhood Organization and Interest Group Processes*. Princeton, N.J.: Princeton University Press.

Olson, Mancur. 1965. *The Logic of Collective Action*. New York: Harvard University Press.

Ornstein, J. J., and S. Elder. 1978. *Interest Groups: Lobbying and Policymaking*. Washington, D.C.: Congressional Quarterly Press.

Orren, Karen. 1976. "Standing to Sue." *American Political Science Review*. 70:723–41.

Pateman, Carol. 1970. *Participation and Democratic Theory*. Cambridge: Cambridge University Press.

Perlman, Janice. 1976. "Grassrooting the System." *Social Policy* 7:4–20.

———. 1978. "Grassroots Participation from Neighborhood to Nation." In S. Langton, ed., *Citizen Participation in America*, 65–80. Lexington, Mass.: Lexington Books.

Pertschuk, Michael. 1982. *Revolt against Regulation*. Berkeley: University of California Press.

Perucci, Robert. 1973. "In the Service of Man." In P. Harmos, ed., *Professionalization and Social Change*, 179–94. Keele, England: University of Keele.

Peterson, P., and David Greenstone. 1977. "Racial Change and Citizen Participation." In R. Haverman, ed., *A Decade of Federal Antipoverty Programs*, 241–78. New York: Academic Press.

Piven, Frances, and Richard Cloward. 1977. *Poor People's Movements*. New York: Pantheon.

Pratt, Henry. 1977. *The Gray Lobby*. Chicago: University of Chicago Press.

Presthus, Robert. 1974. *Elites in the Policy Process*. New York: Cambridge University Press.

Rabin, Robert. 1975. "Lawyers for Social Change." *Stanford Law Review* 28:207–61.

Rosenbaum, Nelson, and Bruce L. R. Smith. 1983. "Composition of Revenues and Expenditures in the Voluntary Sector." In *Since the Filer Commission*. Washington, D.C.: Independent Sector.

Rosenbaum, Walter R. 1978. "Public Involvement as Reform and Ritual." In S. Langton, ed., *Citizen Participation in America*, 81–96. Lexington, Mass.: Lexington Books.

Rothman, Jack. 1974. *Planning and Organizing for Social Change*. New York: Columbia University Press.

Rothschild-Whitt, Joyce. 1979. "Conditions for Democracy." In J. Case and R. C. R. Taylor, eds., *Communes, Coops and Collectives*, 215–44. New York: Pantheon.

Roy, William. 1981. "The Vesting of Interests and the Determinants of Political Power." *American Journal of Sociology* 86:1287–1310.

Rudwick, Elliott, and August Meier. 1970. "Organizational Structure and Goal Succession." *Social Science Quarterly* 51:9–24.

Salamon, Lester. 1983. *The Nonprofit Sector and the Rise of Third-party Government*. Washington, D.C.: Urban Institute.

Salisbury, Robert H. 1969. "An Exchange Theory of Interest Groups." *Midwest Journal of Political Science* 13:1–35.

———. 1979. "Why No Corporatism in America." In P. C. Schmitter and G. Lehmbruch, eds., *Trends towards Corporatist Intermediation*, 275–302. Beverly Hills, Calif.: Sage.

———. 1983. "Interest Representation: The Dominance of Institutions," *American Political Science Review* 78:64–76.

Saltman, Juliet. 1971. *Open Housing as a Social Movement*. Lexington, Mass.: Lexington Books.

Schattschneider, E. E. 1960. *The Semi-Sovereign People*. New York: Holt, Rinehart, & Winston.

Schlozman, Kay Lehman, and John T. Tierney. 1983. "More of the Same: Washington Pressure Group Activity in a Decade of Change." *Journal of Politics* 45:351–77.

Schmitter, Phillipe. 1979. "Modes of Interest Intermediation and Models of Societal Change in Western Europe." In P. Schmitter and C. Lehmbruch, eds., *Trends towards Corporatist Intermediation*, 117–46. Beverly Hills, Calif.: Sage.

Schuck, Peter. 1977. "Public Interest Groups and the Policy Process." *Public Administration Review* 37:137–40.

Soreuf, Frank. 1976. *The Wall of Separation*. Princeton, N.J.: Princeton University Press.

Starr, Paul. 1979. "The Phantom Community." In J. Case and R. C. R. Taylor, eds., *Communes, Coops and Collectives*, 245–73. New York: Pantheon.

Stoper, Emily. 1983. "The Student Nonviolent Coordinating Committee." In J. Freeman, ed., *The Social Movements of the Sixties and Seventies*, 320–34. New York: Longman.

Tarrow, Sidney. 1983. *Struggling to Reform*. Ithaca, N.Y.: Cornell University Western Studies Program.

Tesh, Sylvia. 1984. "In Support of 'Single-Issue' Politics." *Political Science Quarterly* 99:27–44.

Tillock, H., and D. E. Morrison. 1979. "Group Size and Contribution to Collective Action." *Research in Social Movements, Conflicts, and Change* 2:131–58.

Tilly, Charles. 1978. *From Mobilization to Revolution*. Reading, Mass.: Addison-Wesley.

Tober, James. 1984. "Wildlife and the Public Interest." Yale University, Program on Non-Profit Organizations Working Paper no. 80.

Truman, David. 1951. *The Governmental Process*. New York: Knopf.

Tucker, William. 1982. *Progress and Privilege*. Garden City, N.Y.: Doubleday.

Useem, Bert. 1980. "Solidarity Model, Breakdown Model, and the Boston Anti-busing Movement." *American Sociological Review* 45:357–69.

Vogel, David. 1978. *Lobbying the Corporation*. New York: Basic.

———. 1981. "The Public Interest Movement and the American Reform Tradition." *Political Science Quarterly* 95:607–27.

Von Eschen, D. J., J. Kirk, and Maurice Pinard. 1971. "The Organizational Substructure of Disorderly Politics." *Social Forces* 49:529–44.

Walker, Jack L. 1977. "Setting the Agenda in the U.S. Senate." *British Journal of Political Science* 7:423–45.

———. 1983. "The Origins and Maintenance of Interest Groups in America." *American Political Science Review* 77:390–406.

Walsh, Edward, and Rex H. Warland. 1983. "Social Movement Involvement in the Wake of a Nuclear Accident." *American Sociological Review* 48:764–80.

Warren, Roland, Stephen Rose, and Ann Bergunder. 1974. *The Structure of Urban Reform*. Lexington, Mass.: Lexington Books.

Weisbrod, Vernon, Jack Handler, and Neil Komesar, eds. 1978. *Public Interest Law*. Berkeley: University of California Press.

Wellstone, Paul. 1978. *How the Rural Poor Got Power*. Amherst: University of Massachusetts Press.

West, Guida. 1981. *The National Welfare Rights Movement*. New York: Praeger.

Wilson, James Q. 1973. *Political Organizations*. New York: Basic.

Wilson, John. 1983. "Corporatism and the Professionalization of Reform." *Journal of Political and Military Sociology* 11:53–68.

Withorn, Ann. 1978. "To Serve the People." Ph.D. diss. Brandeis University.

Zald, Mayer. 1970. *Organizational Change*. Chicago: University of Chicago Press.

Zald, Mayer, and Roberta Ash. 1966. "Social Movement Organizations." *Social Forces* 44:327–41.

V

SOURCES OF SUPPORT FOR NONPROFIT ORGANIZATIONS

18

Who Gives to What?

CHRISTOPHER JENCKS

Not all nonprofit organizations depend on voluntary giving. But political groups get almost all their income from gifts, churches get more than 90 percent of their income this way (Interfaith Research Committee 1977), and universities, hospitals, health funds, social welfare organizations, arts groups, and many other nonprofits rely on gifts for a significant fraction of their income. This chapter summarizes what we know about the people who give money to nonprofit organizations in America. It focuses on gifts from living individuals to tax-deductible organizations, as defined by the Internal Revenue Service (IRS), ignoring corporate giving, bequests, gifts to individuals, and gifts to political parties, candidates, and pressure groups.

The chapter discusses five questions:

1. How do Americans distribute their philanthropic gifts among different types of organizations?
2. How does personal income affect philanthropic effort (that is, the percentage of income an individual or couple gives away)?
3. How do other personal characteristics affect philanthropic effort?
4. How much does tax deductibility affect the amount individuals give to philanthropic causes?
5. How has donors' propensity to give changed over time?

I will take these questions up in order and then conclude with a brief discussion of how important gifts are to the recipients.

I am indebted to the Center for Urban Affairs and Policy Research at Northwestern University for support while working on this chapter, and to Jill Graham, now at the University of British Columbia, who led me through the historical statistics on charitable giving while she was a Fellow at the center. In addition, Charles Clotfelter generously gave me a prepublication copy of his comprehensive book on charitable giving (Clotfelter 1985), without which this chapter would have been even less complete than it now is, and made helpful comments on an earlier draft. Paul DiMaggio, Walter Powell, and Richard Steinberg also provided useful suggestions.

WHO BENEFITS FROM PHILANTHROPY?

Table 18.1 shows how Americans distributed their gifts in 1962 and 1978–81. The 1962 data come from the IRS, which asked itemizers how they had distributed their gifts in that one year. My estimates assume that nonitemizers distributed their gifts in the same way as low-income itemizers. The 1978–81 data come from two Gallup surveys that asked random samples of Americans how much they gave to various causes in 1978 and 1981. The Gallup surveys almost certainly undersampled the rich, and they may also be biased by selective recall of different kinds of giving.

Roughly two-thirds of all gifts went to churches throughout this period.[1] Gifts to hospitals and educational institutions climbed from 4 to 15 percent of total giving.[2] Gifts to other health and social welfare groups, such as the March of Dimes, the Heart Fund, the Red Cross, the Salvation Army, and the YMCA/YWCA, held fairly steady at 12 to 14 percent of the total.[3] Gifts to all other organizations—youth groups,

1. Since the 1978–81 estimates underrepresent large donors, and since large donors gave a smaller fraction of their money to churches in 1962 than small donors did, the 1978–81 data may slightly exaggerate the percentage of personal income given to churches. Given the small sample size and other vagaries of the Gallup data, no significance should be attached to the decline in the fraction of all giving that went to churches between 1978 and 1981. Kahn (1960, 82) cites data from consumer expenditure surveys suggesting that churches got 77 percent of total giving in 1935–36, 71 percent in 1941, and 67 percent in 1950, but the sample coverage changes from year to year.

2. The actual increase may be even greater, since the 1978–81 data underrepresent the very rich. In 1962, those with incomes over $50,000 constituted only 0.1 percent of all American families, but they accounted for almost half of all the money given to both hospitals and educational institutions (Feldstein 1975b). The top 0.1 percent of all families would be represented by three individuals in the 1978–81 Gallup samples, and all three of these individuals might well have refused to participate. Whether for this or other reasons, the Gallup surveys do not appear to have covered anyone who made a very large gift to either a hospital or an educational institution.

3. Given the uncertainties surrounding the boundaries of this category, probably no significance should be attached to the small apparent decline between 1962 and 1978–81.

TABLE 18.1   DISTRIBUTION OF PHILANTHROPIC GIVING BY TYPE OF RECIPIENT, 1962–81

Type of Recipient	Percent of Philanthropic Giving		
	1962	1978	1981
Churches and other religious organizations	62%	68%	63%
Educational institutions	3	10	9
Hospitals	1	5	7
Other health and social welfare organizations	14	11	13
All other organizations	19	7	8
Total	100%	100%	100%

Sources: For the distribution of giving in 1978–81, see Independent Sector (1982) and Gallup Organization (1979). For the distribution among itemizers in 1962, see Feldstein (1975b). For nonitemizers I assumed total 1962 gifts of $1 billion, which is the difference between itemized 1962 giving ($9.5 billion) and the American Association of Fund-Raising Counsel's (1983) estimate of total 1962 giving ($10.5 billion). I then assumed that nonitemizers distributed this $1 billion in the same way as itemizers with 1962 incomes below $5,000. The results are hardly altered by using the distribution for itemizers with incomes below $10,000 instead of $5,000.

environmental groups, veterans' associations, organizations sponsored by police and fire departments, ethnic organizations, consumer groups, and so forth—appear to have fallen from 19 to 8 percent of the total.[4]

The diversity of the activities to which Americans contribute poses a terminological problem. Research on giving has recently been dominated by economists, almost all of whom label philanthropic gifts as "charity." Although this term has a pleasing simplicity, it is misleading. To most people—including economists—"charity" conjures up images of the rich helping the poor: medieval lords endowing almshouses, John D. Rockefeller giving away dimes, or the average citizen tossing money in the Salvation Army kettle at Christmas. Very few of the contributions covered by table 18.1 are "charitable" in this sense. They are almost all meant to "do good," but the prospective beneficiaries are seldom indigent and are often quite affluent.

Most of the money that congregations contribute to local churches, for example, pays for services to the members of the congregation. According to the Interfaith Research Committee (1977), local churches typically allocate only 4 percent of their income to "social welfare" activities and organizations. Likewise, gifts to hospitals usually provide new facilities—or occasionally new services—for all patients. They are seldom earmarked for people who could not otherwise afford to use the hospital. Most gifts to colleges and universities are also intended to upgrade the institution as a whole by providing new facilities, new professorships, or more money for general operating expenses. Only a small fraction of all gifts to colleges and universities goes for

scholarships to help poor students. Gifts to symphonies, art museums, and other arts groups are equally unlikely to be aimed at making art available to those who could not otherwise afford it.

I do not mean to suggest that philanthropic giving is *never* "charitable" in the traditional sense of the term. Gifts to Catholic Charities, the 100 Neediest Cases, Boys Clubs of America, and CARE, for example, are primarily meant to help those less fortunate than the donor. Roberts (1984) estimates that less than a tenth of philanthropic giving is charitable in this sense. I suspect the figure is slightly higher, but not much. Whatever the actual fraction, it seems best to use the term "philanthropy" to describe gifts in general, and to reserve the word "charity" for those gifts that are specifically aimed at the poor or the needy.

DO THE RICH GIVE MORE GENEROUSLY?

Many of us think of philanthropy as a luxury on which people spend money only after they have paid for necessities like food, housing, medical care, and transportation. This view is obviously encouraged by using the term "charity" to describe all forms of philanthropy. If it were correct, the poor would give virtually nothing to others. Both the absolute level of giving and the percentage of total income given to philanthropy would then rise as income rose. In the language of economics, which I will adopt here since there is no vernacular alternative, the income elasticity of philanthropic giving would be greater than 1.00. This simply means that a 1 percent increase in income would increase philanthropic giving by more than 1 percent. If the income elasticity of philanthropic giving were greater than 1.00, the fraction of income given to philanthropy—what I will call "philanthropic effort"—would also rise as income rose.[5]

For many years the IRS has published data on the amount that taxpayers who itemized their deductions said they gave to philanthropic organizations. At least in recent years, these taxpayers' reports appear to be very accurate. The IRS's Taxpayer Compliance Measurement Program has found that itemizers can document 97 percent of the charitable contributions they list on their tax returns. This finding holds at all income levels (Clotfelter 1985).

Table 18.2 shows the mean amount given to charity by itemizers in various income brackets in 1981. In that year, almost all taxpayers with incomes over $50,000 itemized, so the table provides an almost complete picture for these taxpayers. Within this group philanthropic effort rose rapidly as income rose. Those with incomes of $50,000 to $100,000 typically gave away 2.9 percent of their income, while those with incomes over $500,000 typically gave away 8.9 per-

4. This apparent decline may just reflect the fact that taxpayers make more effort than Gallup respondents to identify every gift.

5. In using the term "philanthropic effort" to describe the fraction of income allocated to philanthropic causes, I do not mean to imply that when the rich and the poor both allocate the same percentage of their income to philanthropy, they are making equal "sacrifices." This is clearly not the case. I use the term "effort" simply as shorthand for "the fraction of income allocated to philanthropy," a phrase that grows tedious with repetition.

TABLE 18.2   CHARITABLE DEDUCTIONS CLAIMED BY TAXPAYERS WHO ITEMIZED IN 1981

Adjusted Gross Income (AGI)	Mean Charitable Deduction	Deductions as a Percent of AGI	Total Contributions (in billions)	Percentage of Taxpayers Who Itemized
Under $5,000	$ 181	6.1	$ 0.1	3.1%
$ 5,000–9,999	490	6.3	0.7	8.4
$ 10,000–14,999	574	4.5	1.4	17.7
$ 15,000–19,999	595	3.4	2.1	32.2
$ 20,000–24,999	613	2.7	2.6	47.3
$ 25,000–29,999	643	2.3	2.9	63.5
$ 30,000–49,999	885	2.3	9.5	80.3
$ 50,000–99,999	1,709	2.7	5.5	93.6
$100,000–499,999	6,560	4.1	4.0	96.9
$500,000 or more	90,880	8.9	1.8	98.9
All itemizers	$ 976	2.9	$30.8	33.1%

Source: Internal Revenue Service (1983).

cent. Since many taxpayers with incomes below $50,000 do not itemize, and since we know from sample surveys that nonitemizers give less than itemizers in the same income bracket, table 18.2 exaggerates the generosity of lower-income taxpayers. Still, it is striking that as income rises from $5,000 to $30,000, itemizers give a *declining* fraction of their income to philanthropic causes. The relationship between income and philanthropic effort thus appears to be U-shaped, with the rich and the poor making more effort than those in the middle. Median family income was $22,000 in 1981, and detailed examination of the data suggests that the tipping point at which philanthropic effort began to rise was about twice the median.

The U-shaped relationship between income and philanthropic effort is not a by-product of the fact that rich itemizers save more on taxes when they give to philanthropy. The same U-shaped pattern recurs when we look at itemizers who had different incomes but ended up in the same tax bracket.

Furthermore, the tipping point was still about twice the median family's income in 1970.[6]

To see whether this U-shaped relationship between income and philanthropic effort persists when we take account of those who do not itemize their deductions, we can look at how much Gallup respondents said they gave to charity in 1981. Table 18.3 summarizes these reports.[7] Philanthropic

6. See table 18.5. If we eliminate those who for various reasons fell in a much lower tax bracket than one would ordinarily expect based on their adjusted gross income (shown in parentheses in table 18.5) philanthropic effort fell until income reached about $20,000 in 1970. Among taxpayers in the same tax bracket with income above $20,000, the proportion of after-tax income allocated to philanthropy rose steadily as income rose. Median income was $9,900 in 1970.

7. One problem with the Gallup data is that Gallup asks respondents how much they and their spouse (if any) gave to charity last year, but does not classify respondents according to how much income they and their spouse received ("taxpayer income"). Instead, Gallup classifies

TABLE 18.3   CHARITABLE GIVING IN 1981 AS REPORTED TO GALLUP

Household Income	Mean Contribution[a]	Percentage of Income[b]	Religious Gifts as a Percentage of Income	Other Gifts as a Percentage of Income	Sample Size[c]
Under $5,000	$ 238	9.5%	4.8%	4.7%	90
$ 5,000–9,999	289	3.9	2.5	1.4	170
$ 10,000–14,999	305	2.4	1.5	0.9	200
$ 15,000–19,999	440	2.5	1.9	0.6	180
$ 20,000–49,999	620	2.0	1.3	0.7	465
$ 50,000–99,999	1,019	1.6	1.2	0.4	65
$100,000 or more	NA	NA	NA	NA	15
All	$ 497	2.1%	1.3%	0.8%	1,185

Source: Independent Sector (1982).

a. These means are for the respondent and spouse, not for all household members. In the original report, the means for specific types of recipients add to more than the grand mean. Mary Malecha of Independent Sector writes that this is because, in computing the grand mean, "the Gallup Organization knocked out some large numbers." Since large contributions are in fact common, I chose to estimate the grand mean from the means for specific types of recipients, which had not been purged of "large numbers."

b. For income intervals below $20,000, I used the midpoint to estimate the mean. For intervals above $20,000, I used IRS data on mean AGI for the relevant interval. I estimated the mean for the total sample from the interval means and the sample Ns.

c. Ns rounded in the original report.

effort clearly falls as income rises from $5,000 to $50,000. Indeed, it appears to keep falling above $50,000, but the Gallup figures for households over $50,000 are probably not reliable.[8] The Gallup survey tells almost exactly the same story about giving in 1978 (Gallup 1979). The Gallup data thus reinforce the notion that philanthropic effort fell until income reached about $50,000 in 1981. Taken together, the Gallup and IRS data imply a U-shaped relationship between income and philanthropic effort.

This relationship is not new, and it is not a by-product of combining data from two different sources. In 1963–64 the Federal Reserve Board conducted a sample survey of both itemizers and nonitemizers. Unlike Gallup, this survey over-sampled the rich and got good data from them. Table 18.4 shows the mean amount that respondents at various income levels said they gave to philanthropy in 1963. Philanthropic effort fell until income reached about $12,500. Since median family income was $6,249 in 1963, the tipping point appears to have been about twice the median in 1963 as well as in 1970 and 1981. A broadly similar pattern recurs in consumer expenditure surveys going back to 1941 (Kahn 1960, 82).

The one survey that does not show a similar U-shaped relationship between income and philanthropic effort is the National Survey of Philanthropy (NSP), conducted in 1973 by the University of Michigan's Institute for Social Research and the U.S. Bureau of the Census. The NSP was the largest and most detailed survey of giving ever conducted in America, so we cannot dismiss its findings as a fluke. If we set aside the handful of NSP respondents with incomes below $4,000, it seems to show that philanthropic effort rises steadily as income rises (Morgan, Dye, & Hybels 1977).

Unfortunately, neither this result nor any other based on the NSP is trustworthy. Despite the care with which the NSP was conducted, its results are consistently at odds with every other source of data on philanthropic giving in America. After weighting to correct for the fact that it deliberately oversampled affluent respondents, for example, the NSP indicates that Americans gave $26 billion to $32 billion to charitable organizations in 1973 (Morgan, Dye, & Hybels 1977). The actual figure was on the order of $18 billion to $21 billion (Nelson 1977; Nelson 1986). The NSP indicates that itemizers accounted for 86 percent of total giving in 1973, or $22 billion to $28 billion. The IRS (1975) reports that itemizers deducted only $14 billion in 1973. Like all sample surveys,

TABLE 18.4 PERCENTAGE OF INCOME DONATED TO PHILANTHROPY: 1964 FEDERAL RESERVE BOARD SURVEY

Income Class (in thousands)	Amount Given[a]	Percentage of Income[b]	Percentage of Families in Income Class[c]
0–5	$ 59	2.4%	36.4%
5–10	150	2.0	43.7
10–15	193	1.5	14.5
15–20	315	1.8	3.3
20–50	670	2.2	2.0
50–100	2062	3.4	0.1
100 or more	22,528	NA	0.1
Total	$ 157	NA	100.0%

a. Feldstein and Clotfelter (1976)
b. Column 1 divided by interval mean, estimated from IRS data.
c. U.S. Bureau of the Census (1984), Table 14, data for families in 1963.

the NSP overestimates the percentage of taxpayers who itemized (57 percent according to the NSP, compared to the IRS's figure of 35 percent). But unlike most sample surveys, the NSP also overestimates the average amount that itemizers gave to charity ($775 in the NSP, compared to $525 reported to the IRS). This upward bias increases with itemizers' reported income.[9] As a result, the NSP exaggerates charitable giving among rich itemizers while underestimating it among low-income itemizers. I do not know what went wrong with the NSP, but because of these problems all results based on it are suspect.[10]

So far as I can discover, no one has tried to explain the U-shaped relationship of income to philanthropic effort.[11] My own very tentative explanation is that philanthropy takes two distinct forms which I will call "paying your dues" and "giving away your surplus." The U-shaped distribution shown in tables 18.2 through 18.4 is a by-product of pooling these two kinds of philanthropy.

"Paying your dues" is best illustrated by giving to local churches. In deciding how much to give, all members feel a desire to do their fair share, but in deciding what is fair, members must balance two conflicting feelings. On the one hand, they feel that everyone should contribute according to his or her ability to pay. Taken literally, this implies that the rich should contribute at least as large a fraction of their income as the poor—by tithing, for example. Indeed, one might argue that the rich should give a *larger* percentage of

---

respondents according to their total *household* income. Some respondents with low taxpayer incomes have quite high household incomes. This is the case, for example, when Gallup interviews a twenty-year-old undergraduate living with affluent parents, an elderly mother living with affluent children, or a secretary living with three roommates. As a result, table 18.3 underestimates both the relationship of household income to household contributions and the relationship of taxpayer income to taxpayer contributions.

8. The problems discussed in footnote 7 are especially serious in the top income group. Also, compare the Gallup mean for those with incomes of $50,000 to $99,999 to the IRS mean for itemizers in this income range in 1981. Many households with incomes above $50,000 include individual taxpayers with incomes far below $50,000.

9. Compare Morgan, Dye, and Hybels (1977, 193) to Internal Revenue Service (1975, 53).

10. Because of these problems, I will report most NSP findings in footnotes. See, for example, note 32.

11. Clotfelter and Steuerle (1981) note the relationship and present data indicating that it persists with the price of giving (tax benefits) controlled. Feldstein and Taylor (1976) and Feldstein (1975a) also present income elasticities with price controlled that imply a U-shaped relationship between income and philanthropic effort. But Clotfelter and Steuerle are the only writers who comment on the U-shaped relationship, and even they offer no hypothesis to explain it.

their income than the poor, since giving up 1 percent of your income represents less "sacrifice" if you are rich than if you are poor. On the other hand, many members also feel that their church should be a community of equals. This encourages the development of uniform norms about what all members should give to remain in good standing. Poorer members often feel that even if their income is less than the average for the congregation it would be demeaning to contribute significantly less than the average. This is especially likely to be the case if their income is only temporarily low. The richer members often feel that although they should contribute somewhat more than the average member, they should not be expected to contribute a lot more. The whole point of being rich, after all, is to make your economic obligations less burdensome, and many people see no reason this should not apply to their religious obligations as well. Church members seem to compromise these conflicting conceptions of their obligations by giving more as their income rises, but not giving proportionately more.[12] As a result, the proportion of income allocated to churches declines sharply as income rises.[13]

Workplace gifts to organizations like United Way are also a form of "paying your dues," and they too probably claim a declining fraction of income as income rises.[14] I suspect that the same is true of gifts to organizations like the Heart Fund and the Cancer Society that solicit door to door.[15] Once asked, many people feel obliged to give "something" but look for the minimum respectable gift (their "dues"). As a result, door-to-door solicitations probably get a declining fraction of income as income rises. Table 18.3 suggests that most gifts made by families with incomes below $50,000 follow this pattern.

Giving away "surplus" income is a different phenomenon. Some people have essentially unlimited material wants and feel no inhibitions about gratifying them. These people never have surplus income, no matter how much they make. But beyond a certain biologically necessary minimum, most

people's material aspirations depend largely on how their friends live. Money is only one of many criteria people use to select friends. The rich, therefore, tend to have friends with somewhat less money than themselves. If they consume at the socially expected level for their circle of acquaintances, they are likely to have money left over at the end of the year. Some rich people respond to this situation by acquiring richer friends and spending more money. Some respond by saving. But some give away part of the surplus.

If contributions to the local church are the prototypical form of "paying your dues," contributions to hospitals and major universities appear to be the prototypical way of disposing of surplus income. Feldstein (1975b) found that in 1962 people gave a rising fraction of their income to hospitals and educational institutions as their income rose, and this remained true even with tax bracket controlled. There is no reason to suppose this situation has changed since 1962.[16] Gifts to some other organizations almost certainly follow the same pattern as gifts to hospitals and universities.[17] It seems likely, for example, that gifts to the arts follow this pattern.

The high income elasticity of giving to education may at first seem to contradict my general argument. Alumni account for roughly half of all gifts to higher education (American Association of Fund-Raising Counsel 1983), and alumni giving has many of the social and moral features of "paying your dues." Thus, if we surveyed the alumni of specific colleges, the income elasticity of giving might well be less than 1.00. But when we look at the population as a whole, we find a very different pattern, for two reasons. First, alumni giving is largely confined to graduates of good private colleges and universities, most of whom have relatively high incomes. Second, almost half the money given to colleges and universities comes from nonalumni. I know of no hard data on these donors, but impressionistic evidence suggests that they are usually very rich and that they usually give to major universities. Rich inventors who build a new laboratory for a local university and rich Ukrainians who endow a chair in Ukrainian studies to keep their old culture alive are examples. Giving is more a way of disposing of surplus income (or capital) for such donors than of meeting a well-defined social obligation.

I do not want to claim too much for the distinction between "giving away your surplus" and "paying your dues." The percentage of income given to some organizations (such as churches) clearly falls as income rises, whereas the percentage given to other organizations (such as hospitals)

---

12. Scholarly organizations seem to resolve the same problem in the same way, setting up sliding scales that demand higher dues from more affluent members, but setting ceilings and floors that ensure income elasticities well below 1.00.

13. Feldstein's (1975b) table 3 implies that constraining the coefficient of price to be zero would yield an income elasticity of 0.79 for itemizers' gifts to churches in 1962. The income elasticity of giving to churches in the Gallup data is about 0.6 (see my table 18.3). In theory, these elasticities could be low simply because fewer upper-income respondents are church members, but in practice the Gallup data indicate that upper-income respondents are slightly *more* likely than lower-income respondents to report having given something to a church. It follows that if we calculate the income elasticity for those who gave at least $1, it is lower than for the population as a whole, at least in the Gallup data. For earlier data on this point, see Kahn (1960, 82).

14. Reece (1979) reports an income elasticity of 0.355 for gifts deducted from the donor's paycheck, but this estimate has such a large standard error that it is hardly conclusive.

15. Long (1976) provides data on the relationship of income to gifts in response to door-to-door solicitations, but his functional form does not yield an elasticity.

16. The Gallup surveys contain too few affluent respondents and too little overall giving to educational institutions and hospitals to determine whether this pattern still held in 1978–81.

17. The percentages of income given to both "other health and social welfare" organizations and "all other" organizations exhibit a U-shaped relationship to income (Feldstein 1975b). This presumably reflects the fact that these categories are very heterogeneous, including both groups like symphonies and art museums and groups like United Way. My argument implies that if we could disaggregate these categories the percentage of income given to specific organizations would seldom show a U-shaped relationship to income.

clearly rises as income rises. The U-shaped relationship between income and total philanthropic effort is a by-product of aggregating gifts to these two kinds of organizations. But my description of the motives behind these two distinct patterns of giving is pure conjecture.

NONECONOMIC DETERMINANTS OF PHILANTHROPIC GIVING

If scholars had divided up the study of philanthropy in the conventional way, economists would have concentrated on the effects of income and taxation, sociologists would have studied the effects of race, sex, occupation, and other social influences, and social psychologists would have studied the effects of personal experiences and attitudes. In fact, sociologists have hardly studied philanthropic giving at all, and psychologists, although interested in many other forms of altruism, have not studied people who give away their money in real-life situations (Staub 1978; Gonzalez & Tetlock, n.d.). As a result, we do not know much about the noneconomic determinants of philanthropic giving. What we do know is largely a by-product of economists' work on economic determinants of giving.

Age

Other things being equal, old people give away more money than young people. After adjusting for income, tax bracket, wealth, education, and other demographic factors, Feldstein and Clotfelter (1976) found that in 1963 a one-year increase in a household head's age was associated with a 1 percent increase in average giving. When Clotfelter (1980) and Clotfelter and Steuerle (1981) looked at the behavior of itemizers during the early 1970s, they found even larger age differences, again with income, tax bracket, and family structure controlled.[18] Such differences could arise in either of two ways. One possibility is that people become more generous as they get older. The other possibility is that those born in the late nineteenth and early twentieth centuries have been more generous throughout their lives than those born in later decades. Such differences between birth cohorts would lead to age differences at any particular moment in time.

In order to choose between these two alternatives we need longitudinal studies of the way in which specific individuals change their level of giving as they get older. Only one such study exists. When Clotfelter (1980) followed itemizers from 1970 to 1972, he found that those under thirty-five typically gave 13 percent more in 1972 than in 1970, even after controlling for changes in their income and tax bracket. Those between thirty-five and sixty-four did not change their

level of giving. Those over sixty-five reduced their giving by an average of 7 percent after controlling for changes in income and tax bracket.

If aging had the same effect throughout the twentieth century that it had between 1970 and 1972—a very large "if"—the cross-sectional age differences found in all studies of giving during the 1960s and 1970s must have had two distinct sources. Among those under about thirty-five, age differences in giving must have reflected the fact that people's propensity to give increased up to the age of about thirty-five. Anyone who has lived with a child—or a teenager—is likely to find this plausible.[19] Among those over thirty-five, in contrast, age differences in giving must have reflected lifelong differences between individuals born in different years. Individuals born in the late nineteenth and early twentieth centuries must have given more at every stage of their lives than individuals in similar circumstances born in more recent decades. If this explanation were correct, of course, the historical record should also show a decline in the overall level of giving during much of the twentieth century, at least after we take account of changes in income and tax rates. As we shall see, there is some evidence for such a decline.

Family Structure

Studies of taxpayers who itemize their deductions have almost always controlled marital status, on the grounds that a couple with an adjusted gross income of, say, $30,000 cannot afford to give as much as a single individual with the same income. In fact, however, married couples typically give 20 to 40 percent more to philanthropic causes than single individuals with the same income and the same marginal tax rate.[20]

If philanthropy were due solely to having more money than you need, having dependents should also reduce charitable giving. In fact, couples with dependents give more than those with the same income and no dependents, and this remains true even after controlling their tax bracket. Each dependent increases a family's expected level of giving by about 6 percent (Clotfelter 1980). Among couples between thirty-five and fifty-five the effect is even larger. Those with dependents give almost 50 percent more than those in the

18. Morgan, Dye, and Hybels (1977, 64) also report that giving increased about 2 percent a year with age after controlling income and education in the 1973 NSP. The Gallup surveys show weaker zero-order age effects in 1978 and 1981 than the 1963 Federal Reserve Board survey or the 1973 NSP, perhaps for reasons discussed in footnote 7. No one has conducted a mutivariate analysis of the Gallup data.

19. My own unpublished work with the General Social Survey shows that the proportion of individuals who say that other people are usually helpful, fair, and trustworthy also rises with age. This holds not only in cross sections but when one follows cohorts over time. Since most people spend most of their time with others of their own age, young people's judgments about others are likely to be primarily judgments about the young, and older people's judgments are likely to be primarily judgments about the middle-aged and elderly. Although such judgments need not be accurate, my guess is that they are. Data on the age at which people commit crimes against others also suggest that consideration for others increases with age, at least up to thirty or so.

20. This estimate is based on the work of Feldstein and Taylor (1976) using 1962 and 1970 tax returns and on the work of Clotfelter and Steuerle (1981) using 1975 returns. For reasons that are not clear to me, Clotfelter (1980) found far smaller effects in some of his models.

same income and tax bracket with no dependents (Clotfelter & Steuerle 1981).

These findings suggest that concern for others is not usually a zero sum sentiment, in which family members "use up" their concern for others on one another and have nothing "left over" for outsiders. Instead, our supply of concern for others appears to expand when we live with other people. As a result, couples with children at home seem to have more left over for others than childless couples of the same age, and childless couples have more left over than those of the same age who live alone. Perhaps living with others makes us care more about others in general, including those with whom we do not live. In addition, those who care about others may be more likely to marry, more likely to stay married, or more likely to decide to have children.

The fact that couples with children at home give more than other couples may also reflect the fact that organizations serving children are more likely to seek voluntary contributions than organizations serving adults. Many adults believe that children's access to services should not depend on their parents' willingness or ability to pay. Most organizations that serve the young therefore try to minimize their fees. This leaves them constantly short of funds and forces them to solicit extra contributions from parents. A Little League team that needs new equipment, for example, will often ask for contributions. A gymnasium for adults that needs new equipment will just raise its fees. The net result, at least in my experience, is that organizations which serve children depend more on gifts than organizations which serve adults. So parents probably get more requests for gifts than other people do.

Gender

Much current thinking suggests that women are more concerned with other people's welfare than men are (but see the review in Staub 1978). One might therefore expect women to give away a larger fraction of their income than men. But women are also socialized to be efficient consumers and hence to take pride in spending their money prudently. Waiters and waitresses often report that women tip less generously than men, and taxi drivers habitually report the same thing, though I know of no quantitative data on tipping.

The evidence on whether women give more or less to philanthropy than men with comparable resources and obligations is inconclusive. Studies of married couples almost invariably pool spouses' incomes and gifts. So far as I know, no one has investigated how couples decide about their joint gifts, so we do not know whether husbands or wives are more inclined to give. To assess the relative generosity of men and women we must look at differences among single individuals. The 1963 Federal Reserve Board survey found that women gave 9 percent more than men, once income, wealth, tax bracket, and various demographic characteristics were controlled, but this difference was not statistically significant. Morgan, Dye, Hybels (1977) also reported that unmarried women gave more than unmarried men in the NSP, but

they did not report the size or statistical significance of the difference. Thus, although the available evidence suggests that women are more generous than men, the evidence is hardly conclusive.

Ethnicity and Religion

The Federal Reserve Board survey found that with income and tax status controlled whites gave 28 percent more than nonwhites in 1963, but because the survey covered relatively few nonwhites, this difference was not statistically significant. No subsequent study appears to have looked at the effects of race on giving. Nor has anyone looked at ethnic differences among whites. Folklore suggests that Jews give more than Gentiles, but Jews also have higher incomes than Gentiles (Greeley 1977; Jencks 1983), and folklore is a notoriously unreliable guide to multivariate relationships.

Gallup found that Protestants gave 87 percent more than Catholics in 1978 and 52 percent more in 1981. Since Protestants and Catholics have almost exactly the same average income (Greeley 1977), it seems to follow that Protestants give more than Catholics with the same income. The NSP found much smaller differences (Morgan, Dye, & Hybels 1977).

Education

The Gallup surveys found that an extra year of schooling was associated with an 11 percent increase in the typical respondent's giving in both 1978 and 1981.[21] Something like half this relationship is probably traceable to the fact that schooling increases an individual's income.[22] This suggests that among those with the same income, an extra year of school or college increases an individual's philanthropic effort about 5 percent.[23]

21. This estimate is based on grouped data presented in Gallup Organization (1979) and Independent Sector (1982). The estimate is virtually identical for both surveys and is roughly linear for the broad educational categories that Gallup uses.

22. This estimate is based on the fact that an extra year of schooling is typically associated with an 11 percent increase in family income (U.S. Bureau of the Census 1984), and that the income elasticity of giving is on the order of 0.5 in the Gallup sample.

23. Feldstein and Clotfelter (1976) report that college graduates in the Federal Reserve Board sample gave 34 percent more than nongraduates, once income, tax bracket, community size, and other demographic factors were controlled, but this estimate has a sampling error of 22 percentage points. College graduates had about seven years more schooling than the typical nongraduate in 1963, so if the effects of schooling were linear, each year of school would have raised philanthropic effort by about 5 percent, with a sampling error of 3 percentage points. Morgan, Dye, and Hybels (1977, 163) indicate that with income and age controlled a year of school typically raised giving by about 4.4 percent in the NSP, though they found weaker effects after controlling marital status, family size, and the length of time people had lived in their current neighborhood. Since these variables barely affect giving in the NSP, it is hard to see how controlling them could appreciably reduce the estimated effect of schooling.

Community Ties

Most of us would expect people with strong community ties to give more than those with weak ties. Strong community ties imply both vulnerability to social pressure and a high likelihood of feeling that your community's interests are your own. Home ownership is one obvious proxy for community ties, since home owners usually have a stronger commitment than renters to staying in their present community, and they are also more likely to live in neighborhoods where people know one another. Home owners do give more than renters, but this difference disappears when we control income and wealth (Feldstein & Clotfelter 1976; Morgan, Dye, & Hybels 1977). The length of time people have lived in their present community should also affect their willingness to give, but at least in the NSP it didn't (Morgan, Dye, & Hybels 1977).

Community Characteristics

The Federal Reserve Board survey found that with income controlled respondents in communities with 250,000 to 1 million inhabitants gave twice as much as those in communities of more than 1 million and two-thirds more than those in communities of less than 250,000. These differences were statistically significant at the 0.001 level (Feldstein & Clotfelter 1976).[24] Hochman and Rodgers (1973) found that donors gave more in metropolitan areas with a high level of income inequality, and Clotfelter (1985) reported unpublished work by Abrams and Schmitz showing that with other factors controlled contributions were higher in states with a lot of poor people. Such findings provide some support for the notion that recipients' "need" encourages giving, although the evidence is far from conclusive.

Family Background

The NSP is the only philanthropic survey that has collected data on respondents' family background. According to Morgan, Dye, and Hybels (1977), those who grew up in cities were average donors. Those who grew up on farms gave more than the average, while those who grew up in small towns gave less. Those who said their parents were "pretty well off" gave 15 percent less than those who described their parents as "average" and 20 percent less than those who described their parents as "poor." Those who said their parents gave regularly to "religious or charitable" organizations gave 19 percent more than those who said their parents did not give regularly.[25] All these differences could have been due to sampling error.

THE EFFECTS OF TAXES ON CHARITABLE GIVING

Both the federal government and most states allow taxpayers to deduct philanthropic gifts from their taxable income. This means that if you give, say, $100 to a philanthropic cause and itemize your deductions, your after-tax (disposable) income falls by less than $100. If, for example, you face a marginal tax rate of 40 percent and you itemize, a $100 gift reduces your disposable income by only $60. Taxpayers need not itemize their deductions, however. Instead, they can take the standard deduction. Since very few people make philanthropic gifts that exceed the standard deduction, very few itemize unless they also have substantial deductions for state and local taxes, interest, medical expenses, or casualty losses. The rich almost always itemize, whereas the poor almost never do. For the middle classes the decision varies according to whether they own their home, live in a state with high taxes, or have high uninsured medical bills.

The effects of the deduction on the level of giving have been hotly debated in recent years. Congress gradually raised the standard deduction from $1,000 to $3,200 between 1970 and 1977, reducing the proportion of taxpayers who itemized from 48 to 26 percent. A number of philanthropic organizations opposed raising the standard deduction on the ground that those who no longer itemized would give less. Giving allegedly fell from 1.96 to 1.90 percent of personal income during this period (American Association of Fund-Raising Counsel 1984), exacerbating recipients' fears. Partly in response, Congress decided in 1981 that by 1986 all taxpayers should be allowed to deduct their philanthropic contributions even if they did not itemize their other deductions. This proposal is now being reexamined, however.

Economists' views about the effects of the philanthropic deduction also changed during the 1970s. In the 1960s most economists viewed the deduction as a loophole whose main effect was to reduce the effective tax rate on the rich. The pioneering empirical work of Taussig (1967) appeared to support this view, since it suggested that those who faced high marginal tax rates gave no more than those with similar incomes who for various reasons faced lower marginal tax rates. Had this finding held up, it would have implied that deductibility merely lowered tax revenue without raising the level of giving. Taussig's work was technically flawed, how-

---

24. Hochman and Rodgers (1973) found negative but insignificant effects of population on mean giving in thirty-two metropolitan areas, but they did not test for nonlinear effects of the kind Feldstein and Clotfelter report. Hochman and Rodgers also tested for regional effects, which were generally insignificant. Morgan, Dye, and Hybels (1977, 220) report that community size did not affect giving in the NSP, but they do not report the categories they used or the coefficients they obtained, so one cannot tell whether their findings differ significantly from Feldstein and Clotfelter's. Clotfelter (1985) reports a study by Dye showing that among NSP respondents with the same income, those living in communities with a lot of poor people gave more away, but Reece (1979) did not find this using the Consumer Expenditure Survey. The NSP is too unrepresentative and Reece's sample is too small for these findings to carry much weight. Wilson (1983) found that mean income was the only community characteristic with a consistent effect on giving in the 1950, 1960, and 1972 Consumer Expenditure Surveys, but he used only aggregate data.

25. Since children seldom know much about their parents' finances, the fact that adults who give generously report that their parents did likewise could also be due to selective perception.

ever (Feldstein 1975a), and empirical work during the 1970s and early 1980s—mainly by Martin Feldstein, Charles Clotfelter, and their collaborators—suggested that the charitable deduction exerted a major effect on philanthropic giving.[26]

In analyzing the effect of taxes on contributions, economists begin by calculating the "price" of giving. If you itemize your deductions and you are in the 40 percent tax bracket, for example, you can buy $1.00 worth of philanthropy by forgoing only $0.60 worth of personal consumption or saving. Your price of giving is thus 0.60. If you do not itemize or do not pay income tax, your price of giving increases to 1.00—an increase of 67 percent. To predict the effect of tax deductions on contributions, economists estimate the price elasticity of giving. If, for example, a 1 percent price increase leads to a 1 percent decline in giving, the price elasticity is -1.00.[27]

As I will try to show below, the best available evidence suggests that the price elasticity of giving in contemporary America is on the order of -1.25. This means that a 1 percent increase in the price of giving (from 0.600 to 0.606, for example) lowers an individual's expected contributions by 1.25 percent (from $100.00 to $98.75, for example). To see what this implies, imagine a husband and wife in the 25 percent bracket who gave $400 to deductible causes in 1980 but did not itemize their deductions. If they began to itemize for some reason, giving $400 would reduce their disposable income by only $300. This would constitute a 25 percent reduction in their price of giving. A price elasticity of -1.25 implies that they would respond to this price change by giving 43.3 percent more, bringing their total contributions to $573.[28] Giving $573 would cost them $(0.75)(573) = 430 after taxes. Their aftertax cost would thus rise by $30. An elasticity of -1.25—or *any* elasticity greater than 1.00— thus implies not just that taxpayers increase their gifts when they are deductible but that taxpayers increase their gifts *by more than they save on the deduction.* As a result, charitable organizations gain somewhat more than the government loses. In this case, deductibility increases contributions by $173 while lowering tax receipts by only $143. The $30 difference is made up by the donors, who either save or consume $30 less.

At first glance, the idea that donors will give more *after taxes* because they can deduct their gifts may seem counterintuitive. But if we think of deductibility as a special kind of federal matching grant, the notion that it encourages people to give more is less startling. In the example given, the

couple who were spending $400 to buy $400 worth of charitable activity would spend another $30 in order to buy another $173 in charitable activity. The idea that people are willing to spend more on something when the price falls, even if this means buying less of everything else, should be familiar to every bargain hunter: "He made me an offer I couldn't refuse."

Economists have estimated the price elasticity of giving using three kinds of data: (1) cross-sectional data on itemizers; (2) cross-sectional data that include nonitemizers; and (3) longitudinal data on itemizers. Although no one body of data is likely to persuade a skeptic, the fact that all three approaches consistently suggest price elasticities between -1.0 and -1.5 is quite persuasive.

Cross-sectional Studies of Itemizers

Because of certain esoteric provisions of the tax code, not all taxpayers with the same taxable income have always faced the same marginal tax rate, even when they itemized. Some have been able to average their income for several years, some have been able to reduce their taxes by taking advantage of the fact that the maximum tax on earned income differed from that on unearned income, some have been subject to a minimum tax despite the fact that they had many deductions, and so forth. If the price of giving influences the amount given, itemizers who face high tax rates should give more than itemizers with similar incomes who face low tax rates.

If we set aside Taussig's flawed work, there have been two major cross-sectional studies of itemizers' philanthropic giving. With income, marital status, and age controlled, Feldstein and Taylor (1976) obtained price elasticities of -1.09 in 1962 and -1.29 in 1970. Clotfelter and Steuerle (1981) obtained an elasticity of -1.27 for 1975.[29]

These cross-sectional studies could easily yield upwardly biased price elasticities. The Internal Revenue Code is not an experiment in which taxpayers with the same income are randomly assigned different tax rates. Congress assigns taxpayers with the same income to different tax brackets partly because it believes that income is an imperfect proxy for ability to pay. That is why taxpayers with low incomes in the recent past have been allowed to average their incomes over several years, and it is at least one reason taxpayers who get $100,000 a year in dividends have paid more than taxpayers who get $100,000 a year from earnings. If tax rates reflect taxpayers' ability to pay taxes, they presumably reflect taxpayers' ability to give to philanthropy as well. Taxpayers with low marginal rates may thus contribute less because

26. The reader who wants a full review of the evidence should begin with Clotfelter and Steuerle (1981) and then turn to Clotfelter (1985).

27. More formally, let P be an individual's price of giving, e be the individual's price elasticity of giving, G be the amount the individual gives, and G^* be the amount the individual would give if P were 1.00. Then $G = (G^*) (P)^e$, and $\log G = \log G^* + (e)(\log P)$. If $e = -1$, $G = G^*/P$.

28. The formula is $G_2 = (G_1) (P_1/P_2)^{1.25}$, where G_1 and G_2 are the amounts given at times 1 and 2, and P_1 and P_2 are the prices at times 1 and 2. In this case, $P_1 = 1.00$, $P_2 = 0.75$, and $G_1 = 400, so $G_2 = (400)(1.43) = 573.

29. Dennis, Rudney, and Wyscarver (1983) obtained substantially lower price elasticities using the 1979 Treasury tax file, but they use a different income measure and a different specification. Although some of their criticisms of the traditional approach strike me as persuasive, others do not, at least in the absence of strong supporting evidence, which they do not provide. They present no estimates of the sensitivity of their results to specific assumptions.

they have less to give, not because they get less of a tax break.[30]

Cross-sectional Surveys that Include Nonitemizers

Nonitemizers pay a higher price for giving than itemizers. But if the tax code works the way it is supposed to work, nonitemizers should have *fewer* unavoidable expenses and should be able to give more to charity than itemizers with the same taxable income.[31] Thus, if cross-sectional studies of itemizers exaggerate the price elasticity of giving by confounding the effects of price with the effects of ability to pay, including nonitemizers should introduce an opposite bias and lower the estimated price elasticity of giving. In fact, including nonitemizers hardly alters the estimated price elasticity. Using the 1963 Federal Reserve Board survey, Feldstein and Clotfelter (1976) found a price elasticity of −1.15. Using the 1972–73 Consumer Expenditure Survey, Reece (1979) found a price elasticity of −1.19. The close agreement between the "upwardly biased" results for itemizers and pooled results that include "downwardly biased" estimates for nonitemizers suggests that both biases are minor.[32]

Longitudinal Studies

Schwartz (1970) was the first to study changes over time in philanthropic giving. Because of the way he disaggregated his data, his estimated price elasticities had very large standard errors, but they are still surprisingly low, averaging only −0.4. This seems to reflect the fact that he used very broad income classes, defined in terms of current rather than constant dollars. Using more detailed data, Feldstein (1975a) obtained a price elasticity of −1.24 for the period from 1948 to 1968. Abrams and Schmitz (1978) obtained values between −1.00 and −1.13 for 1948 to 1972.

Feldstein and Taylor (1976) estimated the impact of the 1964 tax cut by comparing the charitable giving of taxpayers with the same real income in 1962 and 1970. They found that giving had declined in every income bracket. After allowing

for the secular decline in giving at all income levels during the 1960s, the estimated price elasticity was −1.58. Clotfelter and Steuerle (1981) applied this same method to rate changes between 1970 and 1975, most of which were due to bracket creep, and obtained a price elasticity of −1.09.[33]

There is one major exception to the general finding that the price elasticity of charitable giving is between −1.0 and −1.5. Clotfelter (1980) followed individual itemizers with incomes below $50,000 from 1968 to 1970, from 1970 to 1972, and from 1972 to 1973. He found that over these short intervals a 1 percent change in the price of giving lowered contributions by only 0.33 to 0.45 percent. He argues that these elasticities are low because taxpayers take several years to respond to tax changes. This is plausible. Many people become aware that their marginal tax rate has changed only when they file their return. This means that it takes at least a year for a change in these people's tax rate to affect their level of giving. If, as seems likely, tax rates often affect giving by affecting the donor's unconscious mind-set rather than by affecting explicit calculations of costs and benefits, the lag is likely to be even longer. Consistent with this assumption, Clotfelter and Steuerle (1981) found a higher price elasticity (−0.88) when they looked at the effect of changes in itemizers' tax rates for the five-year interval from 1968 to 1973. Clotfelter's elasticities may also be low because they exclude taxpayers in the top 0.5 percent of the family income distribution, and these are the people who seem to be most sensitive to price changes.

Taken together, the three kinds of studies described above are surprisingly consistent. The overall price elasticity of charitable giving is between −1.0 and −1.5 in almost every study. Such close agreement between cross-sectional and longitudinal studies is extremely rare in the social sciences. It is also very reassuring.

Income Differences in Tax Sensitivity

Although a $1 tax deduction almost certainly increases the "typical" donor's contribution by more than $1, some individuals are inevitably more tax sensitive than others. The rich, for example, respond more strongly to tax incentives than do those with lower incomes. Table 18.5 shows the percentage of income that itemizers gave to deductible organizations in 1970, broken down by both income and tax bracket. At first glance, no uniform pattern is obvious, but this is because many cells in table 18.5 include only individual's who, for various unusual reasons, paid significantly less tax than the norm for their income group. Table 18.5 shows these low-tax cells in parentheses. Low-tax itemizers with incomes below $50,000 give a much larger fraction of their income to philanthropic causes than normal itemizers in the same income bracket. This is exactly the opposite of what economic theory (or any other theory) would lead us to

30. Feenberg (1982) tries to get around this problem by looking at the impact of *state* income tax rates on charitable giving. He finds that residents of states with high income tax rates give more than residents of states with low rates or no income tax at all. The estimated price elasticity is −1.23. Skeptics may wonder, however, whether residents of high-tax states give more solely because giving costs them less after taxes. These states could have a high level of giving for the same reason they have high taxes, namely that their residents have an unusually strong tradition of concern for the common good.

31. Since home ownership is the prime determinant of whether it pays to itemize, the validity of this argument depends on the assumption that home owners have more out-of-pocket expenses than renters. This seems plausible in the short run, unless one assumes that renters save as much as home owners add each year to their equity, which seems unlikely.

32. Boskin and Feldstein (1977), Dye (1977), and Long and Settle (1979) report much larger elasticities, ranging from −2.1 to −2.5, when nonitemizers are included, but their estimates are based on the NSP, which is suspect for reasons discussed earlier.

33. The estimates in the text weight income classes by the number of taxpayers in each class. Unweighted estimates are much less stable than weighted estimates. The 1970–75 rate changes are too small to justify any strong conclusions.

TABLE 18.5   PERCENTAGE OF INCOME GIVEN TO PHILANTHROPY BY MARRIED ITEMIZERS UNDER AGE 65 IN 1970, BY TAX BRACKET

Net Income (in thousands)	Marginal Tax Rate[b]						
	0–14	14–22	22–28	28–39	39–54	54–63	63–69
Under 2	(32.6)[c]	d	—	—	—	—	—
2–10	(7.8)	4.4	4.4	d	—	—	—
10–20	(7.4)	3.5	2.9	3.1	—	—	—
20–50	(7.8)	(7.4)	4.0	3.3	3.9	4.9	—
50–100	(3.6)	(6.3)	(6.4)	(6.1)	5.3	5.5	7.9
100–500	(2.8)	(2.0)	(3.4)	(3.8)	5.7	9.2	15.0
Over 500	(1.8)	(1.5)	(2.2)	(1.5)	(2.4)	(5.8)	36.2
	Sample Sizes[e]						
Under 2	111	d	—	—	—	—	—
2–10	598	5,429	251	d	—	—	—
10–20	55	2,670	11,428	2,480	—	—	—
20–50	58	179	1,090	5,334	6,045	1,410	—
50–100	37	40	63	308	2,099	5,845	2,768
100–500	113	108	91	313	1,599	2,333	5,097
Over 500	24	11	9	16	53	54	168

Source: Feldstein and Taylor (1976).
a. Adjusted gross income minus tax liability in the absence of any gifts.
b. In the absence of any gifts.
c. Parentheses indicate taxpayers who paid unusually low taxes relative to their income.
d. Less than five cases.
e. High-income taxpayers were deliberately oversampled.

expect. The most likely explanation is that table 18.5 underestimates these low-tax itemizers' true income, much of which is subject to special tax treatment. It is hardly likely, for example, that the 111 itemizers with nominal incomes below $2,000 in this sample really lived on less than $2,000, or that they really gave away $1 for every $2 they spent on themselves, as the table implies. No useful conclusions can be drawn from data on such individuals until we know more about their real income and about why their taxes were so low. Studies that include such individuals—which is to say almost all the studies cited up to this point—could easily be misleading. But if we ignore these individuals, table 18.5 is very instructive.[34]

Among "normal" taxpayers, tax rates show no consistent relationship to philanthropic effort until the marginal tax rate exceeds 38 percent. Tax increases beyond 38 percent are associated with substantial increases in philanthropic effort. This suggests that people become tax conscious only when their marginal tax rate is relatively high. An inevitable corollary of this finding is that tax rates had no consistent effect on giving among itemizers with incomes below $20,000 in 1970, since such taxpayers never faced tax rates above 38 percent. Table 18.5 suggests that tax sensitivity depends more on taxpayers' current tax bracket than on their income, but one would need a multivariate statistical analysis to be sure about this.[35]

34. Table 18.5 aggregates Feldstein and Taylor's (1976) original categories in order to minimize random sampling error and dramatize the underlying pattern of the data. The conclusions in the text are not a byproduct of this aggregation process.

35. While both Feldstein and Taylor (1976) and Clotfelter and

Longitudinal studies tell pretty much the same story. Feldstein and Taylor (1976), for example, looked at changes in giving between 1962 and 1970 among itemizers in the same (real) income bracket. They found that the price of giving rose significantly among itemizers with incomes above $20,000 (in 1962 dollars), largely because of the 1964 tax cut. Each 1 percent price increase lowered giving by 1.5 percent among those with incomes of $20,000 to $50,000, by 1.8 percent among those with incomes of $50,000 to $100,000, and by 2.1 percent among those with incomes over $100,000.[36] When Feldstein (1975a) looked at the effects of rate changes from 1948 to 1968, the price elasticity of giving was significantly higher among high-income itemizers.[37]

Feldstein (1975b) also found that gifts to churches had a price elasticity of only about −0.5, whereas gifts to educa-

Steuerle (1981) present regression results that speak to this question in one way or another, both include low-tax donors in their samples. Since including low-tax donors may distort the relative impact of income and tax bracket on giving, their findings on this point could be misleading.

36. These are unweighted means of the arc-elasticities in column 9 of Feldstein and Taylor's table II. Clotfelter and Steuerle (1981) also estimated the effects of rate changes between 1970 and 1975 that were due to inflation-induced bracket creep, but rates hardly changed from 1970 to 1975 for those with incomes above $40,000. Since these are the only taxpayers who appear to have been sensitive to tax rates in Feldstein and Taylor's 1970 baseline data, it is not surprising that rate changes between 1970 and 1975 have no consistent effect on the level of giving.

37. See Feldstein (1975a, n31). I am not sure how to reconcile his note 31 with his equations 7 through 9, but it is broadly consistent with his equation 4, which shows nonlinear effects of ln$P$ on ln$G$ with income controlled.

tional institutions and hospitals had a price elasticity of more than −2.0.[38] This is precisely what we would expect from table 18.5, since gifts to churches come mainly from lower-income taxpayers, who do not appear to be very tax sensitive, whereas gifts to educational institutions and hospitals come mainly from higher-income taxpayers, who are quite tax sensitive.

Policy Implications

Brannon (1981) has estimated that the charitable deduction increased charitable giving by $5.5 billion in 1975, costing the Treasury $5.2 billion. Since personal income was $1,255 billion in 1975, Brannon's figures imply that the charitable deduction diverted about 0.4 percent of personal income from the government to private charitable organizations. Since individual giving totaled about $24 billion in 1975, Brannon's figures also imply that deductibility raised the level of giving by about a quarter.

Advocates of tax simplification have frequently urged Congress to eliminate the deduction, or at least restrict it to large donors. This might significantly reduce the revenue of private universities and hospitals, which are supported primarily by the tax-sensitive rich. It would probably not have much impact on churches, which get relatively little money from the tax-sensitive rich. Reducing the marginal tax rate for the rich would also reduce giving to universities, hospitals, and similar groups. Unfortunately, most econometric estimates of the effect of tax changes are based on extremely simple assumptions, especially with regard to the "true" incomes of those who appear to pay unusually low taxes relative to their nominal income. As a result, econometric estimates of the likely effects of a given change in the tax code must be treated with extreme caution.

TRENDS IN GIVING

The IRS has reported the total amount that taxpayers deducted for philanthropic contributions since 1917, when Congress first established the deduction. Unfortunately, these data do not cover most potential donors. Until World War II the personal exemption was so high that most families did not have to file a tax return. Congress lowered the personal exemption repeatedly during the early 1940s, so that almost all families had to file returns, but it also introduced the standard deduction in 1944, so that only a minority of those who filed returns had to itemize their contributions. Nonetheless, a number of individuals and organizations have tried to estimate the overall level and trend in individual giving from IRS data. The American Association of Fund-Raising Counsel (AAFRC) publishes the best-known estimates, which appear every year in *Giving USA* and are reproduced every year

in the Census Bureau's *Statistical Abstract of the United States*. They go back to 1955. Less well known, but perhaps more accurate, is Ralph Nelson's series (1977), most of which appears in *Historical Statistics of the United States* (U.S. Bureau of the Census 1976). This series ends in 1972. Andrews (1950) and Kahn (1960) provides estimates for the years from 1924 to 1954.

To illustrate the dangers of taking such estimates at face value, table 18.6 uses the Kahn and AAFRC series to estimate the percentage of personal income given to philanthropy from 1929 to 1982. Kahn's estimates suggest that philanthropic effort increased sharply between 1930 and 1932, increased again between 1938 and 1940, and then increased steadily from 1944 to 1954. The AAFRC estimates show very little change from 1956 to 1982—though there is a slight upward drift from 1956 to 1970 and a slight downward drift from 1970 to 1980. Anyone familiar with the history of the federal income tax will immediately note that these apparent trends in philanthropic effort mostly mirror changes in the tax code. The Hoover administration lowered filing requirements in 1932, increasing middle-income families' incentive to give, and estimated giving rose, too. The Roosevelt administration lowered filing requirements repeatedly from 1940 to 1942, again increasing the incentive to give, and estimated giving rose again. It is true that the Roosevelt administration also introduced the standard deduction in 1944, which eliminated most taxpayers' incentive to give, and that estimated giving did not fall as a result. But the percentage of itemizers rose steadily from 1948 to 1970, and estimated giving did the same, until 1962. Congress repeatedly increased the standard deduction from 1970 to 1977, lowering middle-income families' incentive to give, and estimated giving fell. If we discount 1940–44 on the grounds that the tax code changed so rapidly that giving did not have time to adjust fully to the new incentives, table 18.6 seems to show that tax changes largely explain trends in giving.

In fact, table 18.6 shows no such thing. The relationship between the tax code and the estimated level of giving is an assumption, not a genuine finding. It is built into the procedures that Kahn, AAFRC, and everyone else uses to estimate total giving. Since everyone assumes that nonitemizers give less than itemizers, any change in the percentage of itemizers automatically produces the "expected" change in total giving. Such changes probably do occur, but without direct measurement of nonitemized contributions we cannot prove it.

In the absence of genuine data on nonitemizers' gifts, the only way to learn much about trends in giving is to focus on itemizers. Column 3 in table 18.6 shows the percentage of adjusted gross income that itemizers claimed to have given to philanthropy from 1924 to 1982.[39] There is no clear trend in itemizers' philanthropic effort from 1924 to 1940, although

---

38. Reece (1979) reports exactly the opposite pattern, but all his estimates have such large sampling errors that they cannot be given much weight.

39. The IRS did not calculate adjusted gross income (AGI) until the 1940s, but Kahn (1960) estimated AGI from published data for earlier years.

TABLE 18.6   PHILANTHROPIC CONTRIBUTIONS, TAX RATES, AND PROPENSITY TO GIVE, 1924–82

	(1) Total Contributions as Percentage of Personal Income	(2) Itemizers' Share of AGI	(3) Itemizers' Contributions as Percentage of Their AGI	(4) Itemizers' Mean Marginal Tax Rate	(5) Itemizers' Propensity to Give	(6) Index of Propensity to Give (1954 = 100)	(7) Ratio of Itemizers' Mean AGI to All Taxpayers' Mean AGI	(8) Propensity to Give for Itemizers with Mean AGI for All Taxpayers
1924			2.05	.12	1.74	94		
1926			2.04	.11	1.76	95		
1928			1.97	.13	1.66	90		
1929	1.28	.37	1.94	.12	1.66	90		
1930	1.27	.34	2.32	.11	2.01	109		
1932a	1.50	.37	2.57	.15	2.10	113		
1934	1.47	.33	2.15	.16	1.72	93		
1936	1.44	.37	1.98	.20	1.49	80		
1938	1.47	.38	2.20	.15	1.79	97		
1940a	1.61	.57	2.20	.15	1.80	97		
1942a	1.59	.56	2.44	.27	1.64	89		
			Standard deduction adopted: see text.					
1944	1.56	.24	3.80	.36	2.18	85		
1946	1.74	.25	4.08	.34	2.42	94		
1948	1.87	.24	4.09	.28	2.73	106		
1950	1.92	.27	4.01	.28	2.65	103		
1952	2.03	.31	4.14	.35	2.43	95		
1954	2.15	.37	4.11	.31	2.57	100		
			Estimation procedures changed: see text.					
1956b	1.82	.45	4.08	.22	2.84	99	1.15	2.99
1958	1.88	.50	4.05	.22	2.96	103	1.12	3.09
1960	1.90	.57	3.73	.22	2.73	95	1.14	2.87
1962	1.92	.61	3.53	.26	2.42	84	1.04	2.46
1964	1.91	.62	3.41	.24	2.42	84	1.18	2.58
1966b	1.93	.62	3.13	.25	2.18	76	1.53	2.56
1968	1.93	.67	3.02	.22	2.21	77	1.23	2.39
1970	1.96	.71	2.87	.25	2.00	70	1.16	2.12
1972b	1.91	.58	3.03	.28	2.01	70	1.32	2.51
1974	1.91							
1976b	1.91	.55	2.89	.32	1.78	62	1.36	2.02
1978b	1.89	.54	2.78	.36	1.59	55	1.42	1.82
1980	1.84	.57	2.78	.37	1.56	54	1.39	1.80
1982	1.88	.62	2.89	.33	1.75	61	1.28	1.92

Sources by Column

1. Gifts for 1929–54 from Kahn (1960), p. 66, col. 2. Gifts for 1956–82 from Nelson (1986), p. 49. Nelson's estimates will appear in future AAFRC reports and replace those in earlier reports, which contain serious errors for years prior to 1970. Personal income for 1929–82 from Economic Report of the President (1985).

2. Data for 1929–54 from Kahn (1960), p. 63. Data for 1956–82 from Internal Revenue Service, *Statistics of Income*, various years. AGI = Adjusted Gross Income.

3. Data for 1924–54 from Kahn (1960), p. 49. Data for 1956–82 from Internal Revenue Service, *Statistics of Income*, various years.

4. The 1924–54 means weight each dollar of income equally and come from Kahn (1960), p. 57. The 1956–82 means are the marginal rates for married couples with incomes at the mean for all itemizers. The 1924–54 procedure yields an estimate of 0.32 for 1956, whereas the 1956–82 procedure yields the estimate of 0.22 shown in the table. The difference is primarily due to the fact that the 1956–82 procedure weights small incomes as heavily as large ones.

5. (Column 3)(1 − Column 4)$^{1.25}$

6. Column 5/K_p, where K is a constant that varies by period. For 1924–42, K = (.0257)(1.57/2.18), since Column 5 = 2.57 in 1954, 1.57 in 1943, and 2.18 in 1944. (The 1943 estimate uses Kahn's estimates of Columns 3 and 4 for that year.) For 1944–54, K = .0257. For 1956–82, K = (.0257)(2.84/2.54), since the 1956 value for Column 4 is 2.54 using Kahn's procedure for estimating marginal tax rates and 2.84 using my less satisfactory method.

7. Internal Revenue Service, *Statistics of Income*, various years.

8. (Column 5)(Column 7)/(Column 7)$^{.62}$ The exponent of 0.62 is the income elasticity of giving from Clotfelter's (1985) time series regression for 1948–80.

a. Filing requirements had changed significantly since the previous year shown. Comparisons with prior years may be affected.

b. The standard deduction had changed since the previous year shown. Comparisons with prior years may be affected.

there is some suggestion that giving declined less than income in the depths of the depression. Itemizers' philanthropic effort almost doubled from 1940 to 1946, for reasons I will discuss shortly. There is no clear trend in philanthropic effort from 1946 to 1958, a sharp decline from 1958 to 1970, and no clear trend after 1970.[40]

To assess the impact of changes in tax rates on itemizers' philanthropic effort, I estimated the percentage of income that itemizers would have given in the absence of tax benefits. I will call this estimate the donor's underlying "propensity to give." Column 5 of table 18.6 shows these estimated propensities.[41] The estimates in column 5 assume that tax changes exert their full effect on contributions in the year they come into effect. As noted earlier, changes in tax rates actually take some years to exert their full effect on contributions. As a result, column 5 usually shows a decline in the apparent propensity to give just after a tax increase (for example, 1936, 1942, or 1952). Readers should ignore these short-term fluctuations, which are probably spurious, and focus on long-term trends instead.

Before discussing trends in itemizers' propensity to give, two further problems must also be dealt with. First, the introduction of the standard deduction in 1944 led disproportionate numbers of low contributors to stop itemizing. As a result, the remaining itemizers' propensity to give was much higher. Second, my simple method of estimating trends in itemizers' marginal tax rates from 1956 to 1982 implies a lower average rate than the procedure Kahn used for 1924–54. My procedure therefore inflates itemizers' estimated propensity to give. Column 6 tries to eliminate these two discontinuities in the 1924–82 series. It presents an index of

the propensity to give that is standardized to a value of 100 for those who itemized in 1954.[42]

The index of itemizers' propensity to give shows no long-term trend worthy of the name from 1924 until around 1960. It then declines fairly steadily from 1960 to 1980, at an average rate of 2.8 percent a year. There is a small increase between 1980 and 1982, but readers should not put much weight on this reversal unless it continues after 1982. Unfortunately, IRS data beyond 1982 were not available when I wrote this chapter.

One possible explanation for the decline in itemizers' propensity to give after 1960 is a gradual change in the kinds of people who itemized, analogous but opposite to the change that occurred in 1944. We know, for example, that middle-income families give a smaller share of their income to philanthropy than the rich, even when the price of giving is the same. If such families constituted a growing fraction of all itemizers after 1960, this could have pushed down itemizers' average propensity to give. But column 7 of table 18.6 shows that although the percentage of income going to itemizers rose in the 1960s, itemizers' incomes were only marginally higher than the average taxpayer's income in 1960 and the same was true in 1970. Column 8 estimates the propensity to give among itemizers with the same income as the average taxpayer in a given year, and it still shows an average annual decline of 2.3 percent a year from 1960 to 1980. Other kinds of selection bias could be at work, but if we assume that wider use of the standard deduction *always* brings in less generous contributors, we must explain why itemizers' propensity to give did not fall from 1948 to 1958, when their share of total income doubled. We must also explain why itemizers' propensity to give did not rise after 1970, when their share of total income fell.

The proposition that the propensity to give fell from 1960 to 1980 is consistent with, but not identical to, other investigators' findings. Feldstein's (1975a) data indicate that the underlying propensity to give fell by about 1.8 percent a year from 1948 to 1968 for itemizers with incomes between $4,000 and $100,000, but he does not distinguish trends before and after 1960.[43] Clotfelter's estimates for 1948 to 1980 imply an average annual decline of 1.5 percent a year for itemizers with incomes over $4,000, but again he does not distinguish trends before and after 1960.[44]

---

40. Kahn (1960) presents data on total giving from 1935 to 1950 derived from consumer expenditure surveys, and the U.S. Bureau of Labor Statistics (1964) presents similar data for 1960. Within the broad limits imposed by changes in definitions and samples, these data tell roughly the same story as the IRS data in table 18.6. Total giving was 1.3 percent of pretax money and nonmoney income in 1933–36 for a sample of families of two or more. Adding single individuals hardly alters estimated philanthropic effort in 1960, and it probably would not have done so in 1935–36. Excluding nonmoney income would, however, have appreciably raised estimated philanthropic effort, since a large fraction of the population still lived on subsistence farms in 1935–36. Total giving was 1.7 percent of pretax money income for families and individuals in 1941. This probably represents a small increase over 1935–36, though it is hard to be sure because nonmoney income is excluded from the denominator in 1941. Table 18.6 shows a similar increase. The 1950 and 1960–61 consumer expenditure surveys covered only urban families and individuals. Gifts amounted to 1.8 percent of money income in the 1950 survey and 2.2 percent in the 1960–61 survey. Including rural families and individuals would probably lower these figures by 0.1 or 0.2 percent. The implied trend from 1941 to 1950 is consistent with table 18.6. The implied trend from 1950 to 1960 is not.

41. Column 5 estimates the percentage of income that itemizers would have given in the absence of tax benefits if the price elasticity of giving was −1.25. When I repeated the exercise using price elasticities of −1.00 and −1.50, the trend was almost identical. Note that those propensities to give do *not* control the effect, if any, of changes over time in either nominal or real income, so they differ from the secular trends reported by Feldstein (1975a) and Clotfelter (1985).

42. Like most indexes of this kind, column 6 assumes that the percentage change in the estimated propensity to give at the time of transition from one series to another applies to all other years as well. This assumption is surely false, but the likely direction of the bias is not clear, at least to me.

43. Feldstein does not estimate the trend in giving with only price controlled. Using pooled cross sections, he obtained $\ln G = .806 \ln Y - 1.1271 \ln P - .014 \text{Year} - 1.649$, where G is the amount given, P is price, and Y is the donor's income in constant dollars. Since itemizers' real income rose by an average of 2.26 percent a year from 1948 to 1968, net giving with only price controlled must have risen about $(1.0226^{.806}/1.014) - 1 = 0.41$ percent a year. Philanthropic effort must therefore have fallen by $1 - 1.0041/1.0226 = 1.8$ percent a year.

44. Clotfelter's equation for 1948 to 1980 is $\ln G = .621 \ln Y - 1.656 \ln P - .00813 \text{Year} - .070$. Itemizers' real income rose by an average of

Why should prospective donors' underlying propensity to give have fallen from 1960 to 1980? One possible answer is simply that their income changed. For philanthropic effort, as I have defined it, to remain constant, a 1 percent income change must lead to a 1 percent change in giving. We noted earlier that the income elasticity of giving only exceeded 1.00 among families with incomes more than twice the median. In cross-sectional studies of the population as a whole, the income elasticity of giving averages about 0.80 (Feldstein & Taylor 1976; Feldstein & Clotfelter 1976; Clotfelter & Steuerle 1981). If the same pattern held when mean income changed over time, giving would rise (or fall) by a smaller percentage than income. This means that the *percentage* of income allocated to philanthropy would tend to fall as mean income rose. The logic here is no different from the logic that leads us to expect that increases in real income will lead to declines in the percentage of income allocated to food, clothing, or any other good for which the income elasticity of expenditure is less than 1.00.

But there is no compelling reason to believe that changes in the mean income of the population as a whole have the same effect on giving as differences in relative income at a single point in time. Increases in per capita income have historically been associated with increases in the cost of the ''standard package'' of goods and services Americans thought they needed (Rainwater 1974). This has meant that when per capita income rose, families at any given real income level felt worse off. This being so, I would not expect a 1 percent increase in mean income to raise giving as much as a 1 percent increase in an individual's income relative to the mean. Such evidence as we have supports this hypothesis. When Feldstein (1975a) calculated the effects of both mean income and individual income relative to the mean, he found that a 1 percent increase in mean income raised giving by 0.2 percent between 1948 and 1968, and a 1 percent increase in an individual's income relative to the mean raised giving by 0.8 percent. If a 1 percent increase in per capita income yields only an 0.2 percent increase in giving, then each 1 percent increase in per capita income will lower the typical donor's propensity to give by 0.8 percent, at least if we define this propensity in percentage terms.

Table 18.6 suggests, however, that the elasticity of mean giving with respect to mean income has varied over time. Real disposable income rose almost as fast from 1940 to 1960 as from 1960 to 1980. Giving kept pace with income from 1940 to 1960 but not from 1960 to 1980. So the question of why things changed remains a puzzle.

A family's underlying propensity to give presumably depends on three factors: its perception of its own consumption and saving needs relative to its income, its perception of prospective recipients' needs, and its moral judgment about how it ought to make trade-offs between its own and other people's needs. All three factors can change over time.

Families' perceptions of their own needs seem to be largely determined by their income. But if income remains constant while material aspirations rise, families will presumably feel short of cash and less inclined to give it away. Many observers thought this happened in the 1970s. Conversely, if the general economic mood is optimistic, families may feel less obliged to provide for the future and may give more to others. Many observers thought this was happening in the 1960s. Nonetheless, the propensity to give appears to have fallen in the 1960s, just as it did in the 1970s. All things considered, this kind of explanation does not seem promising.

Prospective donors' perceptions of other people's needs presumably depend partly on the extent and visibility of economic hardship. Since the rich seem to give more in communities with a lot of poor people (see above), we would also expect them to give more during hard times, such as the 1930s. But this logic applies only to redistributive giving, and as we have seen, only a small fraction of total giving has redistributive goals.

Even when gifts do not have redistributive goals, donors' judgments about the potential recipient's need are still likely to affect how much they give. If a hospital solicits money for a major addition to its physical plant, for example, and if prospective donors know that the hospital can also get the money from the federal government or (indirectly) from Blue Cross, they may not give as much as they would if they thought the addition could not be built without their money. Likewise, if a university solicits funds for an addition to its physical plant, and if prospective donors believe that the university could get the money by raising tuition, they may give less than they would if they thought the university's students could not afford higher tuition. Economists, showing their usual flair for value-free terminology, label the effect of government spending on philanthropy as ''crowding out'' (Abrams & Schmitz 1978). They do not discuss the effect of user charges.

Government transfers to the needy rose dramatically during the 1930s, and Roberts (1984) makes a persuasive case that private charity was reduced as a result. Government transfers rose again in the late 1960s and early 1970s. So did government subsidies to private hospitals, universities, the arts, and social welfare groups. User charges also rose dramatically in many of these institutions. Taken together, these trends might explain why people's propensity to give to such institutions fell in the 1960s and 1970s. Clotfelter (1985) found, however, that governmental social welfare spending rose so steadily from 1948 to 1982 that he could not distinguish the effect of government spending from the effect of any other linear trend. Furthermore, even if crowding out explains the decline in giving to specific institutions, it is not clear why overall giving should have declined rather than just being directed to new recipients.

All sorts of other factors could, of course, contribute to the decline in donors' propensity to give. Theories that pur-

---

1.92 percent a year from 1948 to 1980, so the net change in giving with price controlled is about $(1.0192)^{.621}/1.0081 - 1 = 0.37$ percent a year. It follows that the propensity to give fell by $1 - 1.0037/1.0192 = 1.5$ percent a year.

port to explain the decline must, however, also explain why the propensity to give did *not* decline from 1924 to 1960. This means we cannot invoke such old chestnuts as urbanization, the rise of individualism, or any of the other developments allegedly associated with "modernity." All these phenomena have been at work for the better part of two hundred years and were certainly at work from 1924 to 1960. The phenomenon that interests us is only twenty-odd years old, so the explanation must be of equally recent origin.

Theories that purport to explain donors' declining propensity to give must also avoid excessive generality. This is important because such evidence as we have suggests that although donors' propensity to give *money* has fallen, their willingness to give *time* has risen. Table 18.7 presents data on volunteering in 1965, 1974, and 1981. The data for different years are not as comparable as we might wish, but they seem to show an increase in volunteer activity, not a decline. This is contrary to conventional wisdom, which focuses on the decline of full-time female volunteers. But full-time volunteers account for a trivial fraction of all volunteer activity. If table 18.7 is right, we must reject theories that explain Americans' declining propensity to give money to philanthropy in terms of broad changes in values, attitudes, or character traits, since such broad changes would almost inevitably imply a parallel decline in volunteering.

We must also consider the possibility that several different factors were at work. If, for example, we were to construct a multivariate model that took account of changes in age, marital status, and numbers of children, we might find that these factors pushed up giving in the 1950s and pushed it down in the 1960s and 1970s. If we then added the percentage of income going to itemizers to our model, we might be able to explain both the net stability of the 1950s and the decline of the 1960s and 1970s. This is, however, a task for the future.

CONCLUSIONS

Although donors' underlying propensity to give probably declined during the 1960s and 1970s, it is not obvious that anyone suffered as a result. We know very little about the way in which individual giving affects the recipients.[45] In the

45. It is even harder to survey recipients than donors. No one respondent can usually provide complete information on a large organization, and surveys that require multiple respondents usually have low response rates for obvious reasons. Furthermore, even when a respondent has the information we want, he or she may not provide it, since organizations are generally far more secretive than individuals. In addition, most organizations have a unique internal structure that is known to participants and shapes the way participants talk about the organization to each other. Survey researchers who do not formulate their questions in these terms have trouble finding out much. Individuals are also unique, of course, but since they seldom spend a lot of time talking to themselves unless they are poets or schizophrenics, they are more likely to think about themselves in terms that are shared by all members of their society, including survey researchers.

absence of evidence, a few general observations about the impact of individual giving on nonprofit organizations must suffice.

The importance of individual contributions to an organization depends on its alternative sources of income. The two main alternatives are usually government subsidies and user charges. User charges have clearly come to play a larger role in financing some kinds of nonprofits over the past generation. Private colleges and hospitals, in particular, have developed new mechanisms that make it much easier for users to pay for their services. Hospital patients have never had much money when they were sick because they were by definition unable to work, and many were unable to return to work even if they left the hospital alive. The development of private hospital insurance, Medicare, and Medicaid has largely solved this problem, allowing hospitals to charge most users the full cost of their services. Private colleges and universities faced a similar problem for many years. Their clients were young and could seldom earn enough to both support themselves and pay the full cost of their schooling. The growth of loan programs has not completely solved the problem of financing private higher education, but it has created a framework within which this problem can in principle be solved. Many students are still *unwilling* to pay the full cost of private higher education, since they can get it cheaper in publicly subsidized institutions, but that is an altogether different problem.

Despite these developments, user charges have obvious limitations. Sometimes it is hard to identify those who benefit from an activity or to charge them for it. Basic research is a classic example. We usually assume that the benefits of such activities are diffused throughout society and that the federal government should therefore pay for them, but there is no market mechanism for determining how much basic research is worth or how much the federal government ought to spend on it. Nor does there seem to be much political consensus on this point.

In other cases, users simply cannot afford to pay for the services they want and others want them to get. Those who do not have insurance, for example, can seldom pay for hospital care if they become ill. If we want to care for the uninsured, either the government or private philanthropy must pay. Nor can we expect user charges to solve the problems of the homeless, the mentally ill, the alcoholic, and so on. By the same token, experience shows that pregnant teenagers will not pay for prenatal care or advice about how to prevent future pregnancies. If we want them to get such services, we must provide them free. Indeed, it seems that we must often bribe teenagers to use them.

In cases of this kind, as in cases where the user is hard to identify, government subsidies are the only alternative to private giving. Government subsidies certainly grew far faster than private giving declined during the 1960s and 1970s, so the nonprofit sector as a whole flourished. But as nonprofits learned to their sorrow after 1980, government largesse is subject to sudden, unpredictable fluctuations. The

TABLE 18.7 TRENDS IN HOURS OF VOLUNTEER WORK, 1965–82

	November 1965[a]	April 1974[b]	March 1981[c]
Mean Hours Volunteered per Week by Persons Over 14			
For health, educational, service, recreational, and civic community action organizations.[d]	.20	.43	.51
Other nonreligious, nonpolitical organizations[e]	.08	.15	.26
Religious organizations[f]	NA	.30	.24
Political organizations	NA	.03	.06
Total for all organizations	NA	.92	1.07
Percent Doing Any Volunteer Work			
Within past year for any organization[g]	18.1	23.5	47
Within past year for a nonreligious organization[h]	NA	19.4	NA
Within past week for any organization[i]	7.0	9.9	NA
Within past week for a nonreligious, nonpolitical organization[j]	5.0	NA	NA

a. Calculated from U.S. Department of Labor (1969).

b. Calculated from ACTION (1975).

c. Calculated from Gallup Organization (1981), p. 22. The Gallup question covers the three months prior to the interview, so I divided by 13 to get a weekly average. Use of a longer time period could encourage exaggeration. On the other hand, comparison of the total hours shown on page 22 of the report with the frequency distribution on page 18 suggests that Gallup probably coded respondents who said they volunteered more than 92 hours over the previous three months (9 percent of all respondents) as volunteering 99 hours. This is surely too low. The net effect of these two offsetting biases is unknown.

d. Since more detailed questions may lead to more complete recall, it is important to recognize that questions have, in fact, become more detailed. The 1965 survey categories were as follows: Hospital or clinic; Other health or medical; Educational; Social or welfare service (such as home for aged or orphans, legal aid, travelers' aid); Civic or community action; and Other (specify).

The 1974 categories were: Health (hospitals, mental health clinics, March of Dimes, other health drives); Education (teachers' aides, tutors, etc.); Justice (court volunteers, legal aides, etc.); Citizenship (Scout leader, VFW officer, etc.); Recreation (activity leaders, Little League coaches, etc.); Social and welfare (home for the aged, orphanages, etc.); Civic and community action (consumer groups, environmental protection, etc.); Religious (usher, choir, Sunday school teacher, etc.); Political (fund-raiser, poll watcher, campaign worker, etc.); and Other (specify).

These changes had no apparent effect on the distribution of responses. "Other" organizations accounted for 23 percent of all the nonreligious organizations for which respondents said they had volunteered in 1965, whereas the new categories of Justice, Citizenship, and Political, along with Other, accounted for only 22 percent in 1974. The kinds of organizations explicitly listed in 1965 accounted for 74 percent of volunteer hours in 1974. The 1965 report did not give hours for each type of organization, so I assumed that the organizations explicitly listed accounted for (74)(100 − 23)/(100 − 22) = 73 percent of all hours in 1965.

The 1981 survey added more categories and more examples. Rescue squads were added to Health; school boards and college fund-raisers to Education; civil liberties to Justice; Jaycees and Junior League to Citizenship; the Salvation Army, NAACP, family

planning, drug rehabilitation, and hot lines to Social and welfare; neighborhood groups to Community action; and party officials and unpaid office holders to Political. New categories were added for Arts and culture, Work related (labor union, professional association, safety patrol, etc.), and general fund-raisers for United Way, Catholic Charities, Jewish Federations, and the like. Perhaps as a result, Education, Health, Recreation, Social/Welfare, and Community action accounted for only 67 percent of all the activities mentioned, compared to 78 percent in 1974.

e. The increase in hours spent on "other" activities between 1974 and 1981 may be partly a methodological artifact, attributable to underreporting of such activities—especially those that are "work related"—in earlier surveys.

f. Because the 1965 survey did not indicate that volunteer work for a church "counted," such work was seriously underreported (.09 hours per week). Because the 1974 survey took place during Holy Week, the level of religious volunteering was atypically high. Thus, no inferences should be drawn from these data about trends in religious volunteering.

g. Because religious volunteering was not explicitly listed in 1965, the 1965 figure undoubtedly understates the percentage of individuals who had volunteered during the previous year.

h. The 1965 survey did not ask respondents whether the volunteer work they had done over the past year was for religious or nonreligious organizations. Nonetheless, the 1974 report, apparently drawing on the first table in the text of the 1965 report, indicates that 16 percent did nonreligious volunteer work in 1965. Internal evidence indicates that this table was constructed by assuming that the number of individuals who did exclusively religious volunteer work during the week prior to the survey was the same as the number who did exclusively religious volunteer working during the year prior to the survey, which is unlikely. The actual percentage who did nonreligious work during the previous year could be as high as 18.1 (if all those who did religious work in the prior week did some nonreligious work in the course of the year), or as low as 5.0 (if all those who volunteered during the course of the year but not during the week prior to the survey did exclusively religious work when they did any at all).

i. The 1965 figure is undoubtedly biased downward because the survey instrument did not explicitly ask about church work. The 1974 figure is inflated by the fact that the week before the survey was Holy Week, so more people did church work than in an ordinary week. The 1981 survey did not ask about the previous week.

j. The 1974 survey could have been analyzed to estimate participation in nonreligious activities during the previous week, but for reasons known only to ACTION, it wasn't.

same is true of individual gifts, of course, but the overall ups and downs of private giving are usually more gradual than the ups and downs of government subsidies. Private donors may replace some of the money that is lost when government subsidies fall, but they almost never make up the entire loss.

A more fundamental problem with government subsidies is that they lead to drastically different kinds of public accountability. A nonprofit that depends heavily on individual gifts must constantly attend to its public image, but it does not necessarily need to avoid controversy. It can afford to make enemies, so long as it wins friends in the process. This is far less true of nonprofits that depend primarily on government money. For them, the absence of enemies is usually worth more than the presence of friends. Government subsidies also bring an emphasis on procedural regularity at the expense of results.

Nonetheless, it seems to me that we should not view

donors' declining propensity to give with undue alarm. Given the immense growth in government support for the nonprofit sector over the past generation, and the nonprofits' increasing capacity to impose user charges, the need for private gifts has surely declined. The real question is whether gifts to the organizations that can neither charge users for their services nor get the government to pay for their activities have declined. I know no data on this point, but the growth of giving to political groups of various kinds leads me to suspect that when alternative sources of money are not available individual giving is at least as generous as in the past.

REFERENCES

Abrams, Burton A., and Mark D. Schmitz. 1978. "The 'Crowding-out' Effect of Governmental Transfers on Private Charitable Contributions." *Public Choice* 33:29–39.

ACTION. 1975. *Americans Volunteer–1974*. Pamphlet no. 4000–17. Washington, D.C.: U.S. Government Printing Office.

American Association of Fund-Raising Counsel. 1983 (and earlier years). *Giving USA*. New York: American Association of Fund-Raising Counsel.

Andrews, Emerson. 1950. *Philanthropic Giving*. New York: Russell Sage.

Boskin, Michael, and Martin Feldstein. 1977. "Effects of the Charitable Deduction on Contributions by Low Income and Middle Income Households: Evidence from the National Survey of Philanthropy." *Review of Economics and Statistics* 59:351–54.

Brannon, Gerard. 1981. "Comment on Clotfelter and Steuerle." In Henry Aaron and Joseph Pechman, eds., *How Taxes Affect Economic Behavior*, 437–41. Washington, D.C.: Brookings Institution.

Clotfelter, Charles T. 1980. "Tax Incentives and Charitable Giving: Evidence from a Panel of Taxpayers." *Journal of Public Economics* 13:319–40.

———. 1985. *Federal Tax Policy and Charitable Giving*. Chicago: University of Chicago Press.

Clotfelter, Charles, and Eugene Steuerle. 1981. "Charitable Contributions." In Henry Aaron and Joseph Pechman, eds., *How Taxes Affect Economic Behavior*, 403–37. Washington, D.C.: Brookings Institution.

Dennis, Barry, Gabriel Rudney, and Roy Wyscarver. 1983. "Charitable Contributions: The Discretionary Income Hypothesis." Yale University, Program on Non-Profit Organizations, Offset.

Dye, Richard. 1977. "Personal Charitable Contributions: Tax Effects and Other Motives." *Proceedings of the National Tax Association*, November 9.

Economic Report of the President. 1985. Washington, D.C.: U.S. Government Printing Office.

Feenberg, Daniel. 1982. "Identification in Tax-Price Regression Models: The Case of Charitable Giving." Cambridge, Mass.: National Bureau of Economic Research, Offset.

Feldstein, Martin. 1975a. "The Income Tax and Charitable Contributions: Part I—Aggregate and Distributional Effects." *National Tax Journal* 28:81–100.

———. 1975b. "The Income Tax and Charitable Contributions: Part II—The Impact on Religious, Educational and Other Organizations." *National Tax Journal* 28:209–26.

Feldstein, Martin, and Charles Clotfelter. 1976. "Tax Incentives and Charitable Contributions in the United States." *Journal of Public Economics* 5:1–26.

Feldstein, Martin, and Amy Taylor. 1976. "The Income Tax and Charitable Contributions." *Econometrica* 44:1201–22.

Gallup Organization. 1979. *Survey of the Public's Recollection of 1978 Charitable Donations*. Princeton, N.J.: Gallup Organization.

———. 1981. *Americans Volunteer: 1981*. Princeton, Gallup Organization.

Gonzalez, A. Miren, and Philip Tetlock. N.d. "A Literature Review of Altruism and Helping Behavior." Yale University, Program on Non-Profit Organizations Working Paper no. 16.

Greeley, Andrew. 1977. *The American Catholic: A Social Portrait*. New York: Basic Books.

Hochman, Harold, and James Rodgers. 1973. "Utility Interdependence and Income Transfers through Charity." In Kenneth E. Boulding, Martin Pfaff, and Anita Pfaff, eds., *Transfers in an Urbanized Economy*. Belmont, Calif.: Wadsworth Publishing Co.

Independent Sector. 1982. *Patterns of Charitable Giving by Individuals*. Washington, D.C.: Independent Sector.

Interfaith Research Committee. 1977. "A Study of Religious Receipts and Expenditures in the United States." In *Research Papers Sponsored by the Commission on Private Philanthropy and Public Needs*, vol. 1, 365–450. Washington, D.C.: Department of the Treasury.

Internal Revenue Service. 1975. *1973 Statistics of Income—Individual Income Tax Returns*. Washington, D.C.: U.S. Government Printing Office.

———. 1983. *1981 Statistics of Income—Individual Income Tax Returns*. Washington, D.C.: U.S. Government Printing Office.

Jencks, Christopher. 1983. ''Discrimination and Thomas Sowell.'' *New York Review of Books,* March 3, pp. 33–38.

Kahn, Harry. 1960. *Personal Deductions in the Federal Income Tax.* Princeton, N.J.: Princeton University Press.

Long, Stephen H. 1976. ''Social Pressure and Contributions to Health Charities.'' *Public Choice* 16:55–66.

Long, Stephen H., and Russell F. Settle. 1979. ''Charitable Contributions: The Importance of Relative Income.'' Paper presented at the Econometric Society Meetings.

Morgan, James N., Richard F. Dye, and Judith H. Hybels. 1977. ''Results from Two National Surveys of Philanthropic Activity.'' In *Research Papers Sponsored by the Commission on Private Philanthropy and Public Needs,* vol. 1, 157–323. Washington, D.C.: Department of the Treasury.

Nelson, Ralph L. 1977. ''Giving in the American Economy, 1960–1972.'' In *Research Papers Sponsored by the Commission on Private Philanthropy and Public Needs,* vol. 1, 115–34. Washington, D.C.: Department of the Treasury.

———. 1986. ''The Amount of Personal Giving in the United States, 1948–1982.'' United Way Institute, United Way of America.

Rainwater, Lee. 1974. *What Money Buys.* New York: Basic Books.

Reece, William S. 1979. ''Charitable Contributions: New Evidence on Household Behavior.'' *American Economic Review* 69:142–51.

Roberts, Russell D. 1984. ''A Positive Model of Private Charity and Public Transfers.'' *Journal of Political Economy* 92:136–48.

Schwartz, Robert A. 1970. ''Personal Philanthropic Contribution.'' *Journal of Political Economy* 78:1264–91.

Staub, Ervin. 1978. *Positive Social Behavior and Morality: Social and Personal Influences.* New York: Academic Press.

Taussig, Michael K. 1967. ''Economic Aspects of the Personal Income Tax Treatment of Charitable Contributions.'' *National Tax Journal* 20:1–19.

U.S. Bureau of the Census. 1976. *Historical Statistics of the United States.* Washington, D.C.: U.S. Government Printing Office.

———. 1984. *Current Population Reports.* Series P–60, no. 142, ''Money Income of Households, Families, and Persons in the United States, 1982.'' Washington, D.C.: U.S. Government Printing Office.

U.S. Bureau of Labor Statistics. 1964. *Consumer Expenditures and Income: Detail of Expenditures and Income.* BLS Report 237–38, Supplement 3–Part A. Washington, D.C.: U.S. Government Printing Office.

U.S. Department of Labor. 1969. *Americans Volunteer.* Manpower Automation Research Monograph no. 10. Washington, D.C.: U.S. Government Printing Office.

Wilson, Mark. 1983. ''Family, Urban, and Regional Influences on Giving Behavior.'' *Papers of the Regional Science Association* 53:189–97.

19

Corporate Philanthropy

MICHAEL USEEM

orporate gifts to nonprofit organizations do not
constitute a major fraction of either's income.
Large firms typically give less than 1 percent
of their pretax income to charitable purposes;
major nonprofits seldom receive more than 10
percent of their income from corporate gifts. Yet the stakes
are significant for both sides of this gift relationship. Corporations frequently feature their giving programs as center-
pieces of company efforts to serve the community, and many
nonprofits depend on corporate gifts for the margin between
submersion and survival. Corporate contributions are thus an
important element in strategic planning by the business and
nonprofit sectors alike.

This chapter reviews what is known about the determinants, organization, and impact of corporate philanthropy for
the nonprofit sector. It draws on studies describing the major
trends in corporate support for nonprofit organizations, such
as those conducted by the Conference Board, and it builds on
a range of more analytic studies of the reasons for company
giving. I will characterize the levels and patterns in corporate
gifts to nonprofit organizations, identify the main explanations for why some companies are more forthcoming than
others, and assay the impact of corporate philanthropy on
both donors and recipients.

THE ORGANIZATION OF
CORPORATE PHILANTHROPY

The level of corporate giving is keyed to company income.
Though the correlation is not lockstep, as business income
rises, so too does the amount of company donations. Thus, as
the American economy has expanded, contributions to the
nonprofit sector have expanded as well. The income of business firms before taxes totaled $10 billion in 1940, and
business contributions that year stood at $38 million. By
1960, company income had risen to $49.8 billion, and gifts
had correspondingly grown to $482 million. Corporate in-
come soared to $242 billion in 1980, and contributions are

estimated to have reached $2.6 billion. By 1982, they
reached nearly $3 billion (Troy 1984; table 19.1).

The concept of corporate giving dates to the turn of the
century and the rise of the modern corporation. In its early
decades, corporate philanthropy was uneven in practice,
limited in scope, and subject to legal and populist dispute.
Since World War II, however, the debate has shifted from
whether or not to give to how much to give, and most major
corporations now engage in regularized giving programs.
Even the level has become increasingly uniform. During the
past three decades, contributions by major firms have usually
averaged just under 1 percent of corporate income, although
the precise percentage has varied from year to year. The
business norm of nearly 1 percent is the best single predictor
of future levels of corporate philanthropy. When a company's profits increase by $1 million over the previous year's
income, its annual contributions according to one cross-
sectional study can be expected to rise by $6,500 to $9,500,
or just under 1 percent of the income rise. When a good year
follows a bad one, a large company's income can increase by
$100 million or more, implying additional gifts to the non-
profit sector of up to $1 million or over. When bad follows
good, the reverse prevails. A study of all companies in 1977,
based on U.S. Treasury records, found that of firms reporting
a profit that year, 35 percent made a contribution; of companies in the red, however, only 2 percent made an offering
(Karl & Katz 1981; Karl, n.d.; McElroy & Siegfried 1985;
Smith 1983; United Way 1981; Chemical Bank 1984).

As a counterpoint for comparison, individual charitable
contributions for the past decade have averaged double the
corporate rate, about 1.9 percent of personal income. It
should be noted, too, that virtually all corporate giving is by
the nation's major firms. Less than a quarter of the 2.2
million companies make any contribution, and only 7.5
percent provide more than $500 per year. Of the nation's
1,127 corporations whose assets exceeded $0.5 billion in
1977, more than 80 percent made contributions; and though
these firms composed less than 0.1 percent of all companies

TABLE 19.1 CORPORATE INCOME AND CONTRIBUTIONS, 1940–82

Year	Net Income before Taxes ($ billions)	Contributions ($ billions)	Contributions as Percentage of Pretax Income
1940	10.0	0.038	0.38%
1950	42.9	0.252	0.59
1960	49.8	0.482	0.97
1970	75.4	0.797	1.05
1975	132.1	1.202	0.90
1980	234.6	2.359	1.01
1981	227.0	2.600a	1.14
1982	174.2	2.950a	1.69

Source: Troy 1984.
a. Estimated by the Council for Financial Aid to Education.

with income, the total dollar value of their contributions constituted 50 percent of all corporate gifts. As in most areas of corporate social and political activity, discussion of corporate philanthropy is thus primarily a consideration of the practices of *large* corporations (United Way 1981; Smith 1983; American Association . . . 1984, 11; Troy 1984).[1]

Four major aspects of the organization of corporate giving are (1) the composition of company philanthropy, (2) the major types of recipients, (3) company decision-making procedures and organization, and (4) the criteria companies use to allocate funds and select recipients.

The Composition of Corporate Giving

Corporate giving is predominantly in the form of cash, but property gifts are common as well. Companies can claim federal charitable tax deductions for cash contributions up to 10 percent of pretax net income (the maximum was raised from 5 percent in 1981). For equipment contributed to education institutions for research purposes, the cost may be deducted plus 50 percent of the difference between the cost and selling price of the product, but most other product donations must be deducted at cost only. There is no provision for deducting contributed management time (Feld et al. 1983).

Manufacturers of computer equipment have taken particular advantage of the educational product deduction, and IBM, Digital Equipment Corporation, Hewlett-Packard Company, and Apple Computer, among other firms, contributed large amounts of computer equipment to schools and universities in the early 1980s. In 1982, for instance, IBM's charitable cash contributions of $43 million were supplemented by nearly $10 million in loaned and contributed equipment; Apple Computer gave $20 million worth of computer equipment to schools in California, the state in which it is headquartered (Teltsch 1983; Turner 1984).

Still, of the estimated $3 billion given by corporations in 1982, a figure that included both cash and deductible noncash

contributions, the great majority was cash. A Conference Board survey of the practices of more than 500 large firms in 1982 found that only 11 percent of the total deductible contributions were in the form of company products and property. Moreover, only 1 in 5 of the corporations made any noncash deductible gift. Another national survey of 229 large companies in 1980–81 found that in-kind contributions of all kinds equaled only 13 percent of the cash contributions. Thus, close to 90 percent of the total value of corporate charitable gifts to the nonprofit sector has been in the form of cash (Troy 1984; Siegfried & McElroy 1981, 6).

Companies also contribute a range of gifts they do not treat as deductible charitable gifts, including the use of corporate facilities and services, company products, and even some cash. Among the services, for instance, is technical assistance in accounting, management, marketing, and corporate fund-raising, and at times managers are even loaned to nonprofit organizations on a full-time basis. Some firms also extend loans to nonprofit organizations at rates below current market charges. More than half of the nation's largest companies reported some gifts in 1982 that were not deducted from their federal income tax. The value of the nondeductible contributions by large firms in 1982 are estimated to have been the equivalent of approximately 20 percent of the value of the deducted cash and property contributions (Koch 1979; Weber & Lund 1981; Troy 1984; Wall 1984; Teltsch 1983).

Senior managers also contribute substantial amounts of uncompensated time to the governance of nonprofit organizations. Virtually all such managers of large corporations are approached to serve on boards, and most major companies have policies, often written, explicitly encouraging community work of this kind. Consequently, volunteering their services is a nearly universal practice among top corporate officers. A 1978 survey of the presidents and chairmen of more than 500 large American corporations found that one-third serve on the board of a cultural organization, one-third are trustees of a health or human service institution, and two-thirds sit on the governing board of a university. Eighty percent serve on the board of at least one nonprofit organization. Another study of the presidents and chairmen of 380 large American corporations in 1975 found that better than half were affiliated with five or more such organizations. The weekly demand was, on average, three hours of company time and three hours of personal time, a total approaching 10 percent or more of the entire workweek (the median workweek of chief executives of large U.S. corporations is fifty-six hours).[2]

Not surprisingly, in many instances, "civic duties become a beastly burden for chief executives," as the *Wall Street Journal* lamented (June 11, 1981, 1). Even then, the relative contribution of staff and management time pales before the cash offerings of most firms. One survey estimates

---

1. Corporate contribution practices in other advanced industrial democracies are described in Mauksch (1982).

2. Fenn (1971); Bonfield (1980); Harris and Klepper (1976); Burck (1976). Other studies and discussion of business trustees on nonprofit boards can be found in Ratcliff et al. (1979); Useem (1979); Salzman and Domhoff (1983); Unterman and Davis (1982); and Middleton (1983).

that donated employee time is equivalent to less than 3 percent of the direct financial contributions of the firms; another puts the total at less than 2 percent (Siegfried & McElroy 1981; Troy 1984).

Major Types of Recipients of Corporate Philanthropy

Education is the leading beneficiary of corporate dollars, receiving more than two-fifths, or 40.7 percent (see figure 19.1). Sectoral variations are large: banks contributed only 23 percent of their gifts to education, whereas chemical companies allocated 43 percent. Support for health and human services—gifts to hospitals, federated campaigns, and separate projects for youth, employees, the family, and the aged—consumes nearly a third of the typical contributions budget (31 percent). Sectoral preferences are often reversed here: banks gave 46 percent of their monies to health and human services, but chemical firms allocated only 31 percent. Approximately half of the corporate contributions in the area of health and human services is channeled through the United Way and other federated campaigns (Troy 1983, 1984).

Cultural organizations and the arts receive between 11 and 12 cents of the corporate contributions dollar. Civic and community affairs, including grants to local and state government and local projects on transportation, housing, and environment, benefited from about the same level of support. Culture and the arts was the area of greatest relative expansion during the 1970s, expanding from 5.3 percent of total contributions in 1970 to 11.4 percent in 1982. The allocation of company monies displays greater variation in these smaller areas than for education and health and human ser-

vices. Among the quarter of companies giving the least fraction of their contribution budget to culture and the arts, for instance, the median percentage was 5.3, whereas among the quarter of most generous companies, the percentage was nearly triple this level.

In even more specific areas of giving, corporate support is often still more uneven. In a study of support of humanities programs (such as preservationist activities, historical studies, humanities fellowships) by forty-seven large companies during the 1977–79 period, for instance, four of the firms, all petroleum companies (Exxon, Mobil, Atlantic Richfield, and Sun), were found to account for nearly half of all the humanities giving; another study of corporate gifts to public television found a comparable concentration of oil company support. A breakdown of the allocation of corporate gifts within the five major areas is provided in table 19.2 (Fremont-Smith 1972, 49; Troy 1981, 1984; Office of Program and Policy Studies . . . 1983; Ermann 1979).

By tradition, corporations do not usually contribute to religious organizations (the biggest single recipient of individual contributions), and by law they cannot contribute to explicitly political organizations. But within the broad classes of nonprofit organizations to which donations are made, potential recipients are treated far from equally. Companies prefer recipients that are prestigious, large, and located near headquarters or plants with large staffs. In a study of the thirty to forty premier educational and cultural organizations and major corporations in Minneapolis and St. Paul, Galaskiewicz and Rauschenbach (forthcoming) found that strong predictors of the number of firms giving to each and the amount contributed are the size and prestige of the nonprofit organizations. Moreover, size and stature are independently influential: more prestigious organizations receive

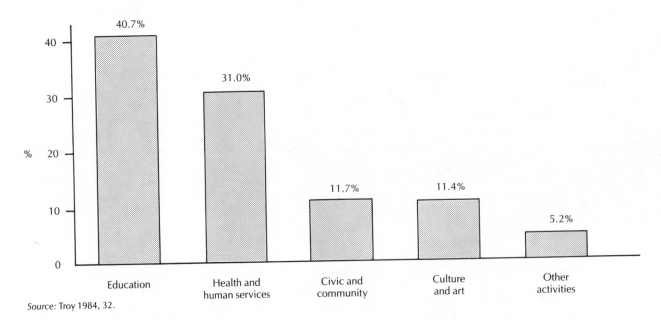

Source: Troy 1984, 32.

FIGURE 19.1. DISTRIBUTION OF COMPANY GIFTS AMONG MAJOR BENEFICIARIES, 1982

TABLE 19.2   DISTRIBUTION OF THE CONTRIBUTIONS OF 534 LARGE CORPORATIONS, 1982

Area	Contributions Amount ($1,000s)	Percent of Total
Health and Human Services:		
Federated drives: United Ways and the like	$182,384	14.2%
National health agencies	9,831	0.8
National welfare agencies	15,226	1.2
Hospitals		
Capital grants	26,985	2.1
Operating grants	10,694	0.8
Employee matching gifts for hospitals	2,157	0.2
Youth agencies	30,517	2.4
Agencies for senior citizens/elderly	3,964	0.3
Other local health and welfare (human services) agencies	44,603	3.5
Subcategory not identified	70,946	5.5
Total health and human services	397,305	31.0
Education:		
Higher education institutions:		
Unrestricted operating grants	57,352	4.5
Student financial aid	23,154	1.8
Departmental and research grants	114,562	8.9
Capital grants (including endowment)	46,845	3.7
Employee matching gift programs	71,167	5.5
Grants to state and national fund-raising groups	17,381	1.3
Precollege educational institutions:		
Employee matching gifts	5,197	0.4
All other support	14,028	1.1
Scholarships and fellowships	34,568	2.7
Education-related organizations:		
Economic education	23,896	1.9
All other support	28,158	2.2
Other	40,908	3.2
Subcategory not identified	44,997	3.5
Total education	522,213	40.7
Culture and Art:		
Music	19,492	1.5
Museums	31,714	2.5
Public TV/Radio	18,346	1.4
Arts funds or councils	9,341	0.7
Theaters	10,062	0.8
Cultural centers	10,533	0.8
Dance	4,238	0.3
Libraries (other than academic)	2,974	0.2
Employee matching gifts for culture and art	4,312	0.4
Other	14,272	1.1
Subcategory not identified	20,554	1.6
Total culture and art	145,838	11.4
Civic and Community Activities:		
Community improvement	48,214	3.8
Environment and ecology	13,783	1.1
Justice and law	7,001	0.5
Housing and urban renewal	12,751	1.0
Research organizations other than academic	15,220	1.2
Other	27,683	2.2
Subcategory not identified	24,600	1.9
Total civic and community activities	149,252	11.7
Other:		
Religious activities	1,396	0.1
Women's causes	3,434	0.3
Groups in U.S. whose principal objective is aid to other countries	18,555	1.4
Activities other than above	36,532	2.8
Subcategory not identified	7,081	0.6
Total other	66,998	5.2
Grand total	1,281,606	100.0

Source: Reprinted from Kathryn Troy, *Annual Survey of Corporate Contributions, 1984 Edition.* © The Conference Board, 1984.

greater corporate support, regardless of size; and larger organizations receive more company backing, whatever their stature.

Companies also prefer recipients near their operating locations, with most firms allocating the majority of their funds within this regional preference. Among geographically dispersed corporations there is a strong skew toward the headquarters location. According to one large-firm study, companies give approximately $40 per employee at plant locations but five times this amount—more than $200 per employee—in the headquarters area. More than 75 percent of the firms' funds go to the region of the main office, and less than 10 percent is given to national causes. A study of corporate giving in one city, Philadelphia, revealed a similar disparity, with locally headquartered firms giving far more to nonprofit organizations in the Philadelphia area than companies with local plants but head offices located elsewhere; other city studies have reported comparable levels of local concentration (Fremont-Smith 1972, 41; Siegfried & McElroy 1981; McElroy & Siegfried 1985; Wolpert & Reiner 1980; Reiner & Wolpert 1981; Donors Forum of Chicago 1980).

Personalized connections also channel corporate donations to certain nonprofit organizations over others. A conventional fund-raising strategy used by many nonprofits is to invite a senior manager onto the governing board as a first step toward soliciting large-scale support from his or her firm. Moreover, well-known and well-connected managers are often able to deliver support not only from their own company but from other enterprises as well. This principle is well understood by most participants, who have no illusions about a nonprofit's purpose in inviting them to join a governing board. David M. Roderick (1982), when chief executive of U.S. Steel and trustee of several educational, arts, and community organizations, described his fellow business trustees: "'Every person who comes to a [nonprofit] board has connections of one kind or another, and this may be the chief criterion for selecting most board members. . . . The network of sources that provides funds, services, and goods, not to mention the channels to other people with parallel and interlocking networks of their own, are what really oil the board activity of every group.'"

Consistent with this personalized channeling of corporate contributions, Galaskiewicz and Rauschenbach (forthcoming) report that Minneapolis and St. Paul organizations attracting large numbers of corporate trustees also attract large numbers of company grants. Another study of the corporate contributions raised by 340 universities revealed that institutions whose governing boards are populated by well-connected company managers are four to five times more successful in raising business support than universities whose boards lack such executives (Useem 1984).

Company Decision-Making Procedures and Organization

Among smaller companies, corporate contributions are often allocated on a relatively ad hoc basis, with few fixed rules and procedures for setting priorities and selecting recipients. For large companies, however, the rules of professional management now generally prevail. The professionalization of corporate giving accompanied the more general elevation of the public affairs function during the 1970s. Only a handful of large firms maintained a formal public affairs office in 1970, but more than 80 percent of the top five hundred manufacturing firms did so by 1980. A range of functions became centralized in the public affairs office, including government relations, media contact, community programs, and philanthropic programs. Moreover, three-quarters of such offices are now headed by managers with the rank of vice president, indicating the ascent of public affairs—and its contributions function—into the higher reaches of the organizational chart (Preston 1981a; Keim 1981; Murray 1982; Post et al. 1983; Wall 1984).

Direct study of the contributions process by Siegfried and McElroy (1981) revealed widespread formalization of the giving procedure and, of particular note, its integration into general company planning at the highest level. Eighty percent of 240 major firms surveyed in 1980–81 had developed formal policies on gifts, and 60 percent had issued written policies. Though company contributions represent only a tiny fraction of the cash flow that senior managers oversee, the top levels of management are almost always responsible for the broader outlines of the contributions program, including the levels of giving, allocations among broad classes of recipients, and rules for selecting beneficiaries. In four out of five companies, contributions policies are primarily set by a committee of executives, the chief executive, board of directors, or chairman of the board (table 19.3). Similarly, a survey of 440 major firms in 1975 revealed that general gift policies are usually developed at the highest levels of management. Two-thirds of the firms reported that the chairman and president play a major role in setting goals, priorities, and budget levels for their contributions programs. A study of 62 Massachusetts companies in 1984 found a similar pattern (Siegfried et al. 1983; Harris & Klepper 1976; Useem & Kutner 1986).

The actual allocation process is typically managed by a corporate officer, often working with an advisory committee or an allocations committee which largely approves the of-

TABLE 19.3 PRIMARY POLICY SETTER AND PRIMARY MANAGER OF COMPANY CONTRIBUTIONS, 229 MAJOR COMPANIES, 1980–81

Manager or Mangerial Group	Primary Policy Setter	Primary Manager
Committee of executives	27.5%	25.3%
President or chief executive	22.7	9.2
Board of directors	17.9	2.6
Chairman of board	10.9	2.2
Trustees of foundation	9.2	7.0
Designated officer	7.9	49.8
Committee of foundation executives	3.5	3.1
Plant committee	0.4	0.9

Source: Siegfried et al. 1983.

ficer's recommendations. This structure is adopted by half of major companies (table 19.3). In other cases primary responsibility for allocations is held by a committee of executives, the president, or other managers or groups, but such arrangements are exceptions. The contributions officer is assisted by staffs comprising as many as fifteen full-time employees in firms contributing tens of millions of dollars. The typical staff allocation, however, is relatively modest, consisting of an executive devoting a quarter of his time, a half-time secretary, and a committee that meets occasionally. Even this staffing is more than most small companies can manage. Among companies whose annual sales range between $25 million to $50 million, most decisions on both the level and the targets of giving are taken by the chief executive alone (Siegfried et al. 1983; White & Bartolomeo 1982, 49–50; Galaskiewicz 1986).

The professionalization of corporate giving during the 1970s was accompanied by the creation of numerous company foundations. Approximately half of the nearly eight hundred large firms surveyed by the Conference Board in 1981 maintained a company foundation, and foundation donations accounted for two-fifths (42 percent) of all corporate giving. Foundations typically operate alongside a company's regular giving procedures, accounting for some but rarely all of a given corporation's contributions. Foundations permit a company to shield a portion of its gifts from internal management pressures and, more important, from the vagaries of fluctuating income. Regular contributions are closely tied to annual company income, but foundation contributions derive in part from separate reserves. Though the reserves also derive from income, foundations draw from them in lean company years and contribute to them in better years. Company profits were near a postwar low in 1981, for example, and 64 percent of the company foundations gave out more than they received from their firms; two years before, prior to the worst of that recession, more than half—53 percent—reported a positive income flow (Lahn 1980; Troy 1983).

The Exxon Corporation's direct and foundation contributions practices are typical of many of the nation's largest firms (see figure 19.2). In 1982 the company made direct contributions of $40.5 million in more than 2,000 grants to such recipients as the American Enterprise Institute ($200,000), Stanford University ($21,000), National Urban League ($125,000), the New York Philharmonic ($225,000), and the Educational Broadcasting Corporation ($5.2 million). The Exxon Educational Foundation also contributed another $26.0 million to more than 1,500 recipients, including Cornell University ($184,500), Colorado School of Mines ($102,000), Colby College ($50,750), Colonial Williamsburg Foundation ($25,000), and the American Arbitration Association ($30,000).

Criteria Used in Allocating Corporate Contributions

Critical decisions on company gifts occur at two levels, with distinct criteria applied at each. The first is the company's

decision on the overall level of contributions; the second is its allocation of funds among deserving recipients.

Virtually all major companies consider contributions sufficiently significant to merit a place in the annual budget, and most use a relatively simple procedure for determining the overall amount. A survey by Siegfried and McElroy found that nearly 60 percent of the major companies they surveyed calculate the amount as a percentage of the firm's pretax net income, and nearly 30 percent base it on the company's contributions the year before. Other factors enter into the decision, but the primary driving force is the level of company earnings. The importance of corporate income can be seen in the relative rating corporate contributions officers attach to twelve factors in setting their giving levels. The leading factors were, following the discretion of the chief executive, the size of the company's previous year's contribution budget and its current earnings (table 19.4). Still, other considerations, including a sense of general obligation to give—and to give to the local community—entered into the decision (Siegfried, McElroy, & Biernot-Fawkes 1983).

Contribution officers and committees review requests for gifts with criteria in mind that are generically akin to those used by private foundations and government agencies. Among the leading considerations are the nonprofit organization's general reputation, the quality of the proposed program, and the likelihood of effective and successful completion.

The survey by Siegfried and McElroy asked responsible managers to rate the importance of various qualities of a potential donee in reviewing a gift request. The leading element, specified by 53 percent, was the effectiveness of the organization in delivering its services. In assessing effectiveness, about a third of the companies examined the ratio of the organization's administrative expenses to the services delivered. The quality of the administration of the requesting organization was the next most important factor (48 percent), followed by organization's reputation (29 percent) and the philosophy guiding the organization's services (18 percent) (Siegfried, McElroy, & Biernot-Fawkes 1983).

Professional administration of charitable programs among large companies is the norm, but nonbureaucratic and personal factors still play a large role. Chance events at times determine how monies are allocated among the major classes of beneficiaries. One New York company, for instance, abruptly entered the leading ranks of corporate benefactors of the visual arts. The origin of the decision to invest in an area in which the firm had no previous record can be traced to the sudden interest of the company's chief executive. An acquaintance, a chief executive of another major firm, bemusedly described the conversion: "You couldn't get [the chief executive] to look at a picture, period. Then somebody persuaded him to sponsor something at the Whitney Museum, and suddenly everybody in his company was interested. They went to a formal cocktail party at this [exhibit] they had sponsored. He got very excited about the whole scene, being invited to the Whitney and having the company sponsor it. And now, the next thing I know, Christ, he's

EXXON CORPORATION

Sponsoring Company: Exxon Corp.
Sales: $97.17 billion
Profits: $4.19 billion
Fortune Rank: 1 (1982)
Employees: 173,000
Headquarters: New York, NY
Major Products/Industry: petroleum exploration, production, refining, and marketing; chemicals; electro-mechanical equipment

WHO TO CONTACT

Richard F. Neblet
Manager, Contributions
Exxon Corp.
1251 Avenue of the Americas
New York, New York 10020
(212) 398-3690

HOW MUCH THEY GIVE: $40,502,242 (1982); $35,992,033 (1981); $30,057,541 (1980)

GRANT TYPES: award, capital, department, general support, matching, project, research/study, scholarship

OTHER SUPPORT: loaned executives workplace solicitation (United Way only)

THEIR PRIORITIES

International: Around 35% of total contributions. Between 40% and 45% of these funds to education; between 35% and 40% to health, welfare, and community services; between 10% and 15% to arts & humanities; remainder to public information and policy research. Around 45% of these funds awarded in Canada; between 20% and 25% in the Far East; around 15% in Latin America; between 10% and 15% in Europe, with remainder in Africa and the Middle East.
Public Broadcasting & the Arts: Around 25%. Over half of these funds awarded to underwrite PBS *Great Performances* and *The MacNeil/Lehrer Report* programs. Remainder to variety of disciplines, with emphasis on music, museums and galleries, and theater groups. Company also administers matching gifts program for the arts.
Civic & Community Services: Around 10%. Funds variety of causes with emphasis on community funds, public service loans, neighborhood revitalization programs, jobs programs, and traditional youth groups. Company also administers volunteer involvement fund which supports agencies in which company employees are involved.
Public Information & Policy Research: About 10%. Supports broad range of organizations with primary emphasis on public policy, international affairs, and energy conservation. Other interests include legal, economic, and women's issues.
United Funds & Health: Just under 10%. Over two thirds to united funds. Remainder primarily to hospitals and medical centers, medical research, and health organizations.
Education: Around 5%. Over two thirds to higher education emphasizing education and research in areas related to petroleum exploration and production, Middle Eastern studies, and minority engineering scholarship programs. Remainder to precollege education with emphasis on energy, minority engineering, and economic programs.
Other: Also supports variety of environmental causes and minority social service organizations.

TYPICAL RECIPIENTS

Arts & Humanities: arts centers, arts institutes, arts organizations, dance, drama, historic preservation, museums/galleries, music, opera, performing arts (general), public broadcasting
Civic & Public Affairs: business/free enterprise, civil rights, economics, environmental affairs, international affairs, law and justice, philanthropic organizations, professional & trade associations, public policy/government, urban and community affairs,
Education: business education, colleges and universities, economic education, educational research, minority education, science/technology education, social sciences education, student aid
Health: health organizations (national), hospitals, medical rehabilitation, medical research, mental health, outpatient health care delivery, pediatric health
International: foreign educational institutions, international arts, international health care, international relief
Science: engineering/technology, physical sciences, scientific organizations
Welfare: child welfare, community service organizations, delinquency and crime, drugs and alcohol, employment, handicapped, legal aid, united funds,

WHERE THEY GIVE: internationally, nationally, and near corporate operating locations

WHERE THEY OPERATE: CA (Benecia), CT (Darien), FL (Coral Gables), GA (Athens, Gainesville, Newman, Stone Mountain), IL (Franklin Park), IN (Columbus, Madison, Mishawaka), KY (Lawrenceburg), LA (Baton Rouge), MN (Mankato), MT (Billings), NJ (Florham Park, Linden), NM (Pinos Altos), NY (New York), NC (Greensboro), OH (Cleveland), PA (Dubois, Washington), SC (Greenville, Saint Stephen, Spartanburg), TN (Rogersville), TX (Baytown, Felder, Houston, Mont Belvieu), WV (Wayne County), WY (Gillette), Canada (Toronto)

FIGURE 19.2. GIVING PROGRAM OF EXXON CORPORATION, 1982

Continued on next page

FIGURE 19.2., *Continued*

GIVING OUTLOOK

—Analysts expect earnings to drop for the third straight year at Exxon as company profits are held hostage to Saudi oil prices (which are at least $2 a barrel over world market prices). Despite the slump in earnings, however, company contributions have climbed steadily over the past few years. Given that the percentage decrease in company earnings won't be as sharp as in 1982, past company performance indicates that giving may well continue to increase this year.

WHO RUNS THE COMPANY

Clifton C. Garvin, Jr.: chmn, ceo, dir: Exxon Corp *B* Portsmouth VA 1921 *ED* VA Polytechnical Inst 1943 1947 *CORP AFFIL* dir: PepsiCo, Citicorp, Sperry Corp *NONPR AFFIL* mem: Am Chemical Soc, Am Inst Chemical Engrs; dir: Am Petroleum Inst; vchmn, trust: Sloan-Kettering Inst; chmn: Business Roundtable; vchmn: Un Way Am; trust: Teachers Insurance & Annuity Assn Am
Howard C. Kauffmann: pres, dir: Exxon Corp *B* 1923 *ED* OK Univ BSME *CORP AFFIL* dir: Chase Manhattan Corp. Chase Manhattan Bank NA, Pfizer Inc *NONPR AFFIL* dir: Am Petroleum Inst

WHO RUNS THE CONTRIBUTIONS PROGRAM

Richard F. Neblet: mgr contbs: Exxon Corp

THEIR PHILOSOPHY

"At Exxon, our efforts in support of these charitable activities reflect our belief that the corporate role cannot—and should not—be limited to the purely economic. We strive to safeguard the health of our employees, conform to equitable employment practices, and conduct our operations in a manner that is compatible with sound environmental standards. But like other citizens, we also share in the responsibility for preserving the well-being of society as a whole. We honor this obligation by providing financial support for hospitals, colleges and universities, civic groups, museums and performing arts groups, research institutions, and other nonprofit organizations on whom all of us depend for essential services and whose activities help enrich our lives."

HOW TO APPROACH THEM

Initial Contact: proposal outline not exceeding five pages to Richard F. Neblet, manager of contributions for Exxon Corp.
Include Information On: contact person, key individuals, project goals and need addressed, amount requested, project description, how project differs from and expands upon related work in field, project evaluation criteria, detailed budget (including other funding sources), project duration
When to Submit: any time

OTHER THINGS YOU SHOULD KNOW

—Exxon is America's most profitable company and one of its most generous corporate philanthropies. In addition to its massive direct giving program, Exxon also supports Exxon Education Foundation (see following profile). Contributions from these two sources totalled $66.5 million in 1982.
—Exxon's substantial international giving reflects the international nature of its business. Over 50% of Exxon's operating earnings are collected abroad; only about one third of its proven reserves are located in the United States.
—Company has expanded number of grants to provide management assistance to nonprofit organizations.

RECENT GIVING

Total Grants: 40,502,242
Number of Grants: 2,133*
Average Grant: $18,988
Highest Grant: 750,000
Lowest Grant: under $5,000

Typical Range: $5,000 to $25,000
Period: calendar year 1982
NOTE: Includes several lump-sum figures representing unspecified contributions under $5,000

RECENT GRANTS

Arts & Humanities

$5,150,000	Educational Broadcasting Corporation, Great Performances (PBS) — 2 grants
500,000	Metropolitan Opera Association
350,000	Meet the Composer — composers-in-residence program
225,000	New York Philharmonic — general support ($525,000, 1981-83)
168,850	Business Arts Fund, Houston, TX
100,000	Lincoln Center for the Performing Arts — corporate fund

Civic & Public Affairs

$200,000	American Enterprise Institute for Public Policy Research — general support
125,000	National Urban League
85,000	World Wildlife Fund
60,000	NAACP Special Contribution Fund — general support

Education

$158,000	Council for Chemical Research ($474,000, 1982-84)
50,000	Consortium on Energy Impacts
21,000	Stanford University, Exploration Project
15,000	New York University, Center for Near Eastern Studies, Tulips, Arabesques & Turbans Exhibit
1,000	Princeton University, Program in Near East Studies

Health

$150,000	Memorial Sloan-Kettering Cancer Center — general support
100,000	University of Pennsylvania — liquid membrane-artificial blood research
45,700	Foundation for Chemical Dependency Centers
40,000	Fairleigh Dickinson University — liquid membrane-periodontal research
25,000	National Homecaring Council

International

$312,000	Lago Scholarship Foundation
200,000	Intercol Foundation
100,000	European Institute of Advanced Studies in Management
87,488	Melbourne University — fission tracking study
70,000	American University of Beirut
70,000	American University of Cairo
51,876	European Community Youth Orchestra
43,400	Thailand Office of University Affairs — scholarships
35,000	La Guajira Museum of Science
30,519	Sydney University, Faculty of Engineering
26,234	University of Birmingham, Institute of Occupational Health
25,000	Universidad del Norte
20,833	International College

Welfare

$964,000	United Way, Houston and Harris County, TX
750,000	New York Community Trust (Community Funds) — Exxon community fund
30,000	YMCA, Houston Downtown
25,000	Citizens Crime Commission of New York City
15,000	Boys' Clubs of America

Source: Reprinted from *The Taft Corporate Giving Directory, 1985* with permission of Taft Group, Inc., Washington, D.C.

TABLE 19.4   FACTORS IDENTIFIED BY COMPANY MANAGERS AS INFLUENCING THE LEVEL OF CORPORATE CONTRIBUTIONS, 229 MAJOR COMPANIES, 1980–81

Factor	Percentage of Managers Reporting Factor to Be "Very Important"[a]
Discretion of chief executive officer	67.7
Size of previous year's contribution	64.6
Earnings in current year	48.0
Size of firm relative to community	36.7
"Fair Share" obligation	33.8
Earnings in previous year	30.1
State of the economy	27.1
Number of employees	8.7
Volume of requests	8.3
Number of customers	5.7
Marginal tax rates	1.7
Stockholder relations	1.3

Source: Siegfried et al. 1983.

a. Manager rated factors as very important, slightly important, or irrelevant.

calling up people including myself: 'Say, would you host a little party of artists that are coming together?' '' Despite the professionalization of management, then, individual preferences and contacts among a company's senior officers are as important here as anywhere in corporate decision making (Useem 1984, 122–23).

THE DETERMINANTS OF CORPORATE PHILANTHROPY

Some firms give generously, whereas others contribute little to nonprofit organizations. Some corporations allocate large shares of their philanthropic budget to cultural organizations, whereas other companies prefer universities. Company policies are by no means uniform, and in this diversity are answers to the fundamental question of why companies give money to the nonprofit sector.

The four main determinants of corporate philanthropy are (1) a set of factors related to the immediate corporate goals of securing reputation and profitability, (2) management attitudes toward corporate social responsibility, (3) metropolitan and national business cultural attitudes concerning the proper public role of the modern corporation and the appropriate level of giving, and (4) government policy toward charitable giving.

Company Self-Interest

Charitable contributions are part of a broader set of social and political activities in which most large corporations are involved—activities designed to change or influence conditions not normally considered part of a firm's immediate economic concerns. These conditions interest such constituencies of the firm as employees', civil rights, and women's organizations, which are concerned with issues of equity in hiring and promotion, environmental and consumer groups,

government agencies, other organizations lobbying the corporation, and the public itself.[3]

Company activities directed at these constituencies include efforts to enhance the quality of employee work life, affirmative programs in hiring and promotion, voluntary environmental clean-up efforts, the contribution of time to advising government agencies, routinized contact with the media, and the channeling of money to candidates for federal office through political action committees. The activities are often grouped under the rubric of corporate social responsibility or performance. Since the level and direction of a company's giving are largely determined by its overall concept of socially responsible behavior, its philanthropy cannot be understood apart from it.

The forces underlying corporate responsiveness can be most readily identified through systematic comparison of the major corporate leaders and laggards. To make such a comparison, Parket and Eilbirt (1975) formulated these questions: ''What variables would help account for the difference in social responsibility activities among firms? Why do some appear to be more active than others? What determines or governs or limits such activities?''

A leading variable accounting for many of the differences is the firm's perception of its self-interest. If a firm's managers feel that making gifts will benefit employee morale, promote product sales, enhance the company's reputation, or reduce government interference, they are likely to do so; but if they see no payback for the company, they are far less likely to make contributions.

The importance of the corporate calculus can be seen in a study of the philanthropic programs of America's fifty-five largest investor-owned electric utilities. Levy and Shatto (1980) found that the percentage of a utility's gross income contributed to nonprofit organizations is strongly correlated with the company's advertising and customer service expenditures. Since advertising and customer service are surely not alternative forms of charity, it is fair to conclude that charity is, in part, an extension of advertising and customer relations. Similarly, when comparing interindustry variations in expenditures for advertising and philanthropy, Levy and Shatto (1978) and Burt (1983) found high correlations between the two, again implying that philanthropy is partially driven by company marketing strategies. Fry, Keim, and Meiners (1982) reported that industries with high levels of contact with the public, such as insurance, retail, and lodging, maintain significantly larger advertising and contributions programs than do mining, construction, primary metals, and other industries whose contact with the public is far more limited.

Corporate self-interest is also evident in the varying emphases among areas of giving of companies in different sectors. In 1982, the manufacturers of electrical machinery and equipment contributed less than 0.8 percent of their pretax net income, whereas banks gave at nearly twice that

3. Discussion of these issues can be found in Sethi (1978); Vogel (1978); and Preston (1978, 1980, 1981b, 1982).

rate. Moreover, of the monies allocated, banks gave a far greater share to civic and community affairs than did the electrical manufacturers (15 versus 6 percent). Commercial banks are not permitted to engage in interstate banking, and their prosperity depends strongly on the condition of the local economy. Community gifts are viewed as contributing to the quality of life in the region and thus, indirectly, to local prosperity and the future earnings of the bank. Thus, for example, Citibank, New York City's premier commercial bank and the second largest in the nation, allocated 80 percent of its nearly $5 million in contributions in 1980 to recipients in the New York metropolitan area. Selling in a national market, electrical equipment manufacturers are, by contrast, far less dependent on, and therefore less likely to be concerned with, regional prosperity. General Electric Company thus distributed its $12 million in 1980 among recipients, primarily colleges and universities, located throughout the country. These contrasting sectoral attitudes are encoded in the tactical thinking of local fund-raisers. In seeking support for a major community project, such as a public-private partnership to revitalize the city's schools, civic fund-raisers share a common premise that the first call should be made to the area's major banks. University fund-raisers, by contrast, are more likely to approach the major electrical manufacturers (Troy 1984; Public Management Institute 1983; Fremont-Smith 1972, 44).

High-technology companies, which are far more dependent on the graduates and research products of universities than are retail firms, give much more to higher education than do retail companies. Similarly, petroleum companies give exceptionally high fractions of their contributions budgets to the arts and culture, perhaps indicating the value of such gifts to refurbish an especially tarnished corporate image. Exxon Corporation finds evidence from its own surveys that generous support of cultural programs has improved its image among the country's opinion leaders. Corporate patronage of the arts is believed to be particularly effective in reaching those who count (Ermann 1979; Brooks 1976; Council for Financial Aid to Education 1978, 1979).

The utility of corporate largesse for bringing the right image to the right people could be seen in company sponsorship of the 1983–84 traveling exhibition of nineteenth-century American paintings. Shown at the Museum of Fine Arts in Boston, the Corcoran Gallery of Art in Washington, D.C., and the Grand Palais in Paris, "A New World: Masterpieces of American Paintings 1760–1910" was the largest single exhibition of its kind—and was made possible by a grant from the United Technologies Corporation. "I am proud and pleased that United Technologies is a partner in this breathtaking exhibition," wrote Harry J. Gray, chief executive of one of the nation's largest industrial firms. The advertising staff was probably pleased as well, for the company's name appeared on the exhibition poster seen by thousands of exhibit visitors, subliminal reminder of United Technologies' public-spiritedness (Stebbins et al. 1983).

Studies of individual companies provide corroborating evidence. One large manufacturer invested extensively in the visual arts, for instance, contributing especially large amounts to major New York museums. That cultural contributions cultivate more than aesthetic ideals is the working axiom of the company's chief executive, whom I interviewed. "There's an indirect editorial kind of credibility to arts giving," he said. "You can take ads and say, 'Look how good we are,' but if you *do* things, you get editorial attribution, which I think is more believable. The payoff is not readily discernible, but I do think it is incremental, and I do believe that over time you get a larger and larger audience that has a better opinion of you" (Useem 1984).

Transnational companies carry the corporate calculus to wherever their operations may be located. In 1980, IBM United Kingdom underwrote new productions of the Royal Ballet, Royal Opera, and Royal Academy. An IBM spokesperson explained the motive in seeking regal affiliation: "IBM as a major multinational obviously has an interest in making sure that its corporate image is associated with something both creative and culturally laudable" (Otten 1981). The study of corporate giving in Minneapolis and St. Paul by Galaskiewicz and Rauschenbach (forthcoming) confirmed the importance of the underlying principle: company giving in culture and the arts is strongly skewed toward the most prestigious organizations in the region. Corporate patronage of the arts is undertaken with discretion, but it is a discretion exceedingly well placed.

Finally, the concentration of company resources within an industry has a bearing on many areas of corporate behavior, and it influences the levels of giving as well. In sectors in which there are a few large dominant firms, giving rates are higher than in sectors populated by many firms, each with modest market shares, even taking varying profit levels into account. Large firms in concentrated markets, less constrained by the competitive fray of the less concentrated sectors, are more able to invest in trade associations, the acquisitions of other firms, candidates for political office, and nonprofit organizations (Pittman 1976; Burt 1983; Scherer 1980; Staber 1982; McElroy & Siegfried 1985).

Management Culture

The corporate calculus in company philanthropy consists of those factors predisposing a firm to make large contributions in the furtherance of company goals—above all, profits. Yet these factors are not more than *predisposing* conditions, encouraging but never ensuring a firm's responsiveness. The attitudes and actions of senior management are usually what make the final difference.

The importance of management culture can be seen in the case studies conducted by Merenda (1981) of five exemplary programs of corporate social responsibility. He interviewed top managers, reviewed the minutes of key meetings, and digested whatever evidence remained in the wake of the establishment of five innovative programs: General Electric's effort to increase minority representation among its managerial ranks, Raytheon's establishment of an inner-city job training center, Cabot Corporation's expansion of its corporate contributions, Eastern Gas and Fuel's evolution of a system of social audit and reporting, and Hancock's program to assist the Boston school system through a troubled period of court-ordered desegregation. In all five cases, he concluded, "the chief executive is the pivotal figure when it comes to the initiation of voluntary social programs." The factors distinguishing executives who act from those who do not are sometimes a matter of personal biography, other times a product of chance events, but ultimately not reducible to strictly corporate calculus.

If the top leadership is critical for starting and enlarging contributions programs, a more general culture of management commitment is a main ingredient for sustaining them. Organizational elements are not absent: in Merenda's five case studies, routine always follows innovation, with programs soon becoming ordered and bureaucratized. Yet undergirding successful routinization of the programs is the formation of a conducive managerial culture, a culture supporting the new programs and insulating them from the vagaries of sudden company misfortunes. From their 1981 study of four hundred large-company public affairs offices, of which three-quarters managed their firms' contributions, Post and his colleagues (1983) concluded that widespread management commitment to public affairs is required if programs are to take root. "To achieve this institutionalization," they said, "it is important to obtain administrative participation and commitment from managers at all levels of the firm—and from general managers in particular."

Metropolitan and National Business Cultures

Corporate communities evolve distinct climates of giving among their members. Local metropolitan business communities vary in their attitudes toward company giving, and so too do separate national communities. Whatever a firm's level of managerial commitment to and private stakes in a contributions program, if its metropolitan or national business community considers generous giving an obligation, it will tend to be more responsive.

Firms' mutual influence on one another's philanthropic policies is evident in the frequent contact maintained by contributions officers of different companies. Groups of contributions managers meet informally in many metropolitan areas to compare policies and share information on potential recipients, and, more generally, public affairs managers share a range of concerns through meetings sponsored by the Public Affairs Council.

Nearly a third of the corporate executives responsible for giving programs of 440 major firms reported in response to a 1975 survey by the Conference Board that "peer company comparisons" are a major factor in setting the contribution dollar level. Similarly, the 1980–81 survey of major companies by Siegfried and McElroy found that most firms are relatively well informed about the policies of other companies: one-third directly solicited information from other companies, and four out of five were aware of other firms' giving policies. Two-thirds of the companies reported that

pressure from other firms was a very important influence on their giving decision, ranking equally with the nature of the appeal. Corroborating the importance of peer pressure within the local corporate community, systematic intercity analysis revealed that a company's contributions increase when other firms in the same region increase their gifts (Harris & Klepper 1976, 21; Siegfried & McElroy 1981; McElroy & Siegfried 1985; Siegfried et al. 1983).

Large firms in Minneapolis and St. Paul also frequently consult one another about a nonprofit organization they are considering funding. Galaskiewicz (1986) found that two-fifths of major companies (but only one in twenty of smaller firms) frequently share information, a process attributed to company efforts to reduce risk in a decision-making environment inherently fraught with high levels of uncertainty. An important by-product, Galaskiewicz's study revealed, is the evolution of similar knowledge and attitudes about potential nonprofit recipients among corporate managers who are in frequent communication.

Corporate giving levels consequently vary considerably from city to city. Minneapolis and St. Paul's corporate community, led by such firms as Pillsbury Company and Minnesota Mining and Manufacturing Company, has long been among the most generous in the country. In 1981, sixty-two major firms gave at the then maximum deductible rate of 5 percent, among the largest number for any metropolitan area in the country. Extensive interviews of Twin Cities contributions officers conducted by Galaskiewicz (1980) offered direct evidence that companies there do indeed attempt to keep up with one another. Their "corporations become the 'patron' of a prestigious cultural organization," he wrote, "to enhance their image in the eyes of their fellow executives." Business culture in other cities, however, is far less forceful on company giving. The percentage of pretax income allocated by major companies varies among metropolitan regions by a factor of more than two: San Francisco firms on average gave 0.87 percent of their pretax income in 1982 and New York firms gave 0.79 percent, whereas the rate among Minneapolis and St. Paul firms was 1.72 percent (Council for Financial Aid to Education 1984).

Indirect evidence would also suggest that an important medium for transmitting such interfirm influence is contact among the companies' general managements. Ratcliff and his associates (1980) examined the personal political contributions of the directors of all seventy-eight commercial banks in St. Louis during the 1976 and 1978 elections. Regardless of the bank's size and a range of other characteristics, its board members contributed considerably more if the bank shared many directors with other large corporations. Moreover, Ratcliff also found that board members with such banks, regardless of their personal characteristics, also gave more of their personal time to local civic organizations. The stronger a bank's ties with the corporate community, the more generous were its directors.

More direct evidence on the importance of peer influence comes from a study of sixty-nine publicly held companies in Minneapolis and St. Paul by Galaskiewicz (1986). The most generous companies were found to be those whose senior managers are in close contact with local philanthropic luminaries and the social elite. These companies are more generous in the percentage of pretax income they give; moreover, their donations are distinctively large even after taking into account variations in the levels of company income. If peer pressures encourage companies to give at rates other than what their own logic would otherwise dictate, there is nonetheless some individual payback to the companies that do respond. The most generous companies, this study found, also acquired a reputation within the local business community as the most successful companies. When top managers were asked to rank the business success of the cities' major firms, companies with the largest giving programs emerged at the top, and this ranking remained even when the firms' actual earnings and other measures of performance were controlled.

Metropolitan business cultures can thus encourage or discourage local rates of company giving, though this is only one of several factors accounting for intercity differences. Among the other factors are the size and development of the nonprofit sector itself—a better organized third sector successfully extracts more corporate money—and the relative presence and self-conscious identity of old families of wealth—a strong tradition of upper-class noblesse oblige reduces the amount of locally contributed corporate money. The latter is the case in Boston, for example, where one of the nation's strongest and most public-minded patrician traditions has long generated ample private giving and thus inhibited corporate giving. By one estimate, business contributions provided more than 14 percent of the operating budget of cultural organizations in Minneapolis and St. Paul, 7 percent in Houston, and under 2 percent in Boston (Baltzell 1979; Story 1980; DiMaggio 1982; Garvin 1982).

Business giving is influenced by the national corporate culture as well. Large corporations extensively share one another's directors, and they often own major fractions of one another's stock, lending an element of both organizational and economic interdependence. A social and political interdependence exist as well, a product of the formation of common action groups, such as the Business Roundtable, and a sense of shared adversity in the face of government regulation and a distrustful public. A by-product in recent years has been the emergence of a national business culture stressing social responsiveness.

Business self-interest, however, is just beneath the surface. Half of the presidents and chairmen in a survey of large corporations in the mid-1970s agreed that "corporations should be a leader in public service activities," because "this is required for [businesses'] long-term success and survival" (Harris & Klepper 1976). The tone is different, however, from the usual expression of the corporate calculus. Reference to divisible benefits accruing directly to the contributing firm is not missing, but there is accompanying allusion to the joint benefits that may be shared by all large firms.

The chief executives of many large firms, because of their direct personal involvement in the affairs of other companies as outside directors and the affairs of government through the Business Roundtable and other associations, have acquired a concern for the business environment that extends far beyond the particular interests of their own company. As a consequence, they are willing to spend some of their own time and the resources of their own company to help create a better climate for the entire business community. Contributions to the nonprofit sector are among the leading vehicles for doing so.

Not all top managers, nor all large firms, share the view that companies should be more socially responsive, whatever the immediate return to their corporation. But evidence from my own research reveals that managers and firms that are more involved in the networks of the national business community are also more generous with their personal and corporate contributions. Managers who are serving as directors of several large companies, for example, are also several times more likely than other top managers to be serving on the governing board of a university and to be raising large amounts of money for it. Similarly, companies whose officers are involved in this intercorporate network are also far more active in supporting educational and cultural programs. As at the metropolitan level, the culture of the broader corporate community thus encourages firms to support the nonprofit sectors at levels substantially above those dictated by corporate logic alone (Useem 1982, 1984).

Government Policy

Government policies can have a direct bearing on both the overall level of corporate contributions and the giving levels of individual companies. Tax policies are an important factor, though other government initiatives may have an impact as well, including matching-grant programs, local government grants to nonprofit organizations, federal support for the nonprofit sector, and formation of public-private partnerships.

Tax Policies

Corporations have been allowed federal income tax deductions for charitable contributions since 1935. The ceiling for cash and product deductions was raised under the Economic Recovery Tax Act of 1981 from 5 to 10 percent of the firm's taxable income. Federal income taxes in 1981 could range as high as 46 percent of a corporation's income, though the effective rate averaged considerably below that and varied substantially from sector to sector. The overall effective corporate tax rate in 1981 averaged 35 percent: pharmaceutical firms paid at a rate that equaled 36 percent of their income, petroleum companies were taxed at an effective rate of 19 percent, and commercial banks were taxed at only 2 percent (Fremont-Smith 1972; Feld et al. 1983).

The deductibility of corporate contributions from federal taxes is an incentive toward overall higher giving. Tax policies may also increase contributions among firms in higher effective tax brackets: pharmaceutical companies give relatively more compared to banks (1.76 versus 1.32 percent of their pretax net income), and this may be partly a product of the highly disparate effective tax rates in the two sectors. Changes in the deductibility elements of federal law, however, may or may not alter giving patterns. The raising of the maximum allowable charitable deduction from 5 to 10 percent in 1981 had modest impact, for instance, since only one in ten firms were at or above the 5 percent giving level when the law was changed. Outright elimination of the charitable deduction, on the other hand, would considerably reduce the level of corporate giving. The 1981 tax law provision permitting a special deduction for a product donated to education—a provision in which the cost of the product plus half of the difference between the cost and selling price may be deducted—is generally credited for an increase in manufacturers' gifts of equipment, especially computers, to higher education. A similar special deductible provision has been available since 1976 for product gifts intended to benefit infants, the needy, and the ill, and it may partly account for the exceptionally high rate of product donations by pharmaceutical firms (Feld et al. 1983, 48–50, 195–96; Smith 1983; Turner 1984; Council for Financial Aid to Education 1984; Troy 1984).

Matching Grants

Matching-grant programs, in which federal agencies provide a nonprofit organization with support contingent on its raising two or three times the amount in private gifts, is another government incentive that may increase corporate giving. The National Endowment for the Humanities, for example, has offered grants to universities if they are able to attract three additional private dollars for every federal dollar received. Matching-grant programs are known to generally increase private giving, including that of corporations. Government policy-making in this area has a much more targeted bearing than tax policies on the specific allocations of corporate monies. In selecting recipients for matching grants, federal agencies in effect draw corporate money to recipients of the government's choosing and away from others (Rose-Ackerman 1980).

Local Government Support of Nonprofit Organizations

Even without matching-grant provisions, changes in government support of nonprofit organizations can influence company giving, either favorably or unfavorably. A significant reduction in government support could help establish new standards of public behavior, possibly triggering reduced corporate giving as well. Yet a reduction in government support might also inspire many corporations to make up the difference, especially if the change in government policy were accompanied by a plea for more private giving.

Limited evidence at the metropolitan level suggests that the overall impact of the possibly countervailing effects of a sharp reduction in government spending may be more nega-tive than positive, however. In a comparison of government and corporate giving in fourteen metropolitan areas, one study found that regions with lower local government expenditures on health and human services are also those with lower levels of local corporate giving (Siegfried & McElroy 1981). It is thus possible that a significant drop in local government spending could trigger a downward spiral in company philanthropy as well.

Federal Government Support of Nonprofit Organizations

The national administration's decision to reduce government spending on nonmilitary programs in 1981–85 constituted a kind of natural experiment on the impact of sharp changes in government spending at the national level. Salamon and Abramson (1982) estimated that the fiscal 1982 federal budget and budgets projected for 1983–85 would reduce the national outlays for nonprofit organizations by $115 billion below the level prevailing in fiscal 1980 (in constant dollars). This cut in federal support would reduce government support for the nonprofit sector during a four-year period by almost 20 percent.

With total corporate contributions in 1982 totaling just under $3 billion, an overnight doubling of company gifts could at best make up for only a tiny fraction of the $115 billion federal reduction. But even a quick doubling of company giving is extremely unlikely in any event. Corporate philanthropy is tightly disciplined by the flow of corporate income, and, short of a very large growth of company income during this same period, only a small fraction of the federal reduction is likely to be compensated by increased corporate giving.

Realistically foreseeing no doubling of corporate income, the national administration launched a campaign in 1981 to instill in the business culture a more favorable attitude toward private giving, hoping that many firms would be willing to go far beyond the 1 percent rule. Some firms did indeed announce new contributions in response to President Reagan's appeal for a "new federalism," an era that would see less government and more private support for education, culture, health, and human services. The predominant response, however, was corporate inertia: only 6 percent of more than four hundred major firms surveyed in 1981 indicated that they would increase their giving in response to the federal cuts. "There is a feeling in this country—wrongly so—that corporations are to step up to fill the void," commented David Roderick, chief executive of U.S. Steel, speaking for most company managers in 1981. "It should be obvious that we can't do it all." Some firms suggested that the impact of the government's withdrawal could even be counterproductive: a vice president of AT&T, for example, testified before Congress that the federal retreat could precipitate a similar withdrawal by the private sector (McGuire & Weber 1982; Frederick 1983; Wyszomirski 1983).

If rhetorical appeals had little impact, major reductions in federal support for the nonprofit sector could still indirectly stimulate corporate giving. Cutbacks in government spending were based in part on the national administration's premise that lowered domestic spending would generate new business prosperity. If this happened, then the resulting corporate income should in turn be followed by enlarged contributions budgets. While plausible, there is no evidence to demonstrate that government reductions in support of the nonprofit sector indeed produced this kind of indirect business stimulus. The results of this natural experiment of the early 1980s suggest that large-scale federal policy changes toward the nonprofit sector are not likely to act as a stimulant of corporate largesse. But, on the other hand, there is no *systematic* evidence that such changes depress corporate giving.

Public-Private Partnerships

Public-private partnerships are defined as collaborative efforts undertaken by government, business, and nonprofit organizations. The purposes range from employment training to scientific research. The vehicle is often a new program or organization jointly sponsored and managed by business and a nonprofit or government organization. One product is a more direct involvement of business in the fruits of its philanthropy.

The federal Job Training Partnership Act of 1983, for instance, mandated the delivery of employment services through local "private industry councils." At least half of the council's membership, 51 percent, must be drawn from business. Local companies thus contribute executive time to council meetings, and the national government funds the programs approved by the business-dominated councils. Similarly, Stanford University and a number of high-technology companies, including Honeywell, Xerox Corporation, Intel Corporation, and General Electric Company, jointly run Stanford's Center for Integrated Systems. With funding and guidance from industry, this university center is devoted to graduate education and research in one of the frontiers in computer and semiconductor development—very large-scale integrated systems—of direct practical interest to its industrial cosponsors.[4]

Public-private partnerships acquired considerable attention from both sectors during the early 1980s. For government and nonprofit organizations, partnerships promised more corporate support; for business firms, they offered more corporate control. When systematic evidence becomes available on the impact of the rise of partnership activity, it will probably reveal that firms invest more time and money as a result. Other consequences are anticipated as well: com-

pared to traditional company giving practices, the "new corporate philanthropy" is probably more closely aligned to immediate corporate self-interest, more professionalized in execution, and more transforming of the recipient organizations.

CONSEQUENCES OF CORPORATE PHILANTHROPY FOR DONORS

Corporate philanthropy is perceived to be consequential by most major donors. The case is compelling enough for internal proponents in most large companies successfully to advocate growth in nearly every year's budget.

The public affairs managers surveyed by Murray (1982) reported that they track the effect of their programs on public opinion, legislation, and the company's competitiveness and income. The last criterion is among the most significant in the long run, for if corporate contributions do not yield some payback to the firm's profitability, investment is likely to remain modest in scale, marginal to company planning, and fragile at best.

We know that more profitable corporations make large contributions, but there is less certainty whether large contributions make corporations more profitable. One study focusing on twenty-eight firms in four industries, for instance, found that companies better rated for social responsibility also reported better growth in earnings. Yet other inquiries have more typically found no association between socially responsive behavior and profits. One investigation, for instance, rated forty-seven companies for their overall level of social responsibility and found no correlation between the rating and the market performance of the company's stock. A study of thirty commercial banks in Texas found little systematic correlation between five separate measures of performance—including contribution levels—and income. Analysts reviewing the studies on corporate philanthropic and social programs generally side with Preston's conclusion from his own review "that there is practically no evidence of any strong association among socially relevant behaviors, whether desirable or undesirable, and any of the usual indicators of economic success." Highly profitable enterprises are as diverse in social performance as product. "For every Xerox there seems to be a J. P. Stevens," Preston observed, "and low-profit firms can be cited at both ends of the spectrum as well" (Aldag & Bartol 1978; Kedia & Kuntz 1981; Sturdivant & Ginter 1977; Alexander & Buchholz 1978; Preston 1981a).

If analysts are able to find little compelling evidence that company contributions enhance income, contributions officers will have even less evidence. Yet gifts to the nonprofit sector continue to grow in absolute if not relative terms. This would suggest that there are consequences, but that they are to be found elsewhere than in the enhancement of a firm's short-term income. A range of evidence points to two important outcomes, one still a matter of corporate calculus, but the other transcending it.

---

4. Descriptions of partnerships between business and higher education can be found in National Science Board (1983); descriptions of local public-private partnerships in one state where they have been particularly active, Massachusetts, are available in Governor's Task Force on Private Sector Initiatives (1983); discussion of partnerships for urban revitalization is contained in Committee for Economic Development (1982).

Several kinds of studies suggest that corporate contributions have a favorable impact on company image, if not immediate profits. In selecting recipients for donations, for instance, firms display a strong bias toward highly visible and prestigious institutions (Galaskiewicz & Rauschenbach, forthcoming). The skew is consistent with the strategy of enhancing company reputation through proper association.

Similarly, other studies reveal that companies usually do not have good information on how their recipients are using donations. Most firms require no accounting from, or evaluation of, the beneficiaries. This suggests that the simple act of associating with the recipient is often more important to a company than how the recipient applies the gift (Duca Associates 1978; Galaskiewicz 1980; Cmiel & Levy 1980).

Direct studies of the impact of company giving also show that, as intended, contributions usually improve a firm's public standing. One national survey, for instance, revealed that the public is aware that firms vary in social responsiveness—and that the public's perceptions correlate with the actual level of company contributions (White 1980). An improved public image may have no immediate payback for a firm, but it does expand a company's latitude in dealing with matters of interest to the public, whether it be union negotiations, plant closing, or tax legislation. With such evidence in hand, a vice president for corporate public affairs can have ample reason to defend if not expand image-building contributions by the company.

The second consequence, one transcending the goal-directed logic of the individual firm, is alteration of the general social and political environment of business. The political mobilization during the 1970s of a range of corporate "stakeholder" groups—civil rights, consumers', women's, and environmental—moved the business climate to the forefront of the corporate agenda. Reginald Jones, chairman of General Electric Company during this period, expressed an assessment that had become widespread in the highest circles of corporate management by the end of the decade: "It is no exaggeration to say that for most managers, their main problems—the main obstacles to achieving their business objectives—are external to the company. . . . the main problems these days are . . . determined in the arena of public policy." And public opinion fueling the public policy process had turned notably against the large corporation (Vogel 1978; Freeman & Reed 1983; Lipset & Schneider 1981; Jones quoted in Windsor & Greanias 1982, 84).

Evidence scattered through a number of studies supports the assessment of Preston (1981a, 13) in reviewing many of the works that "the bulk of corporate philanthropic activity has no connection whatsoever with profit-seeking behavior or any other conventional business management goal. It does, however, have a great deal to do with the preservation of the social system within which the corporation operates." If so, this would help explain why so little evidence links individual company profits to good social performance. The link is at a different level: contributions improve the climate in which all major firms can prosper, with little private capture of benefits by the giving corporation.

CONSEQUENCES OF CORPORATE PHILANTHROPY FOR RECIPIENTS

Corporate philanthropy grew rapidly during the latter part of the 1970s. The total more than doubled between 1975 and 1979, rising from $1.2 billion to over $2.4 billion, and the growth rate outstripped that of all other forms of private giving. Even then, however, corporate gifts still came to constitute only 5 percent of all giving. If donations to religious organizations, largely by individuals, are excluded from the total giving figure, company philanthropy stands at 10 percent of all gifts. But with only one contribution dollar in ten coming to the nonprofit sector from business, the impact of corporate giving relative to other sources of private donations is necessarily limited.

Moreover, the great bulk of the income of the nonprofit sector derives in any case from sources other than gifts. Of the $116 billion in revenues received in fiscal 1980 by non-religious, nonprofit service organizations, only 22 percent came from private giving. Corporate giving thus constitutes little more than 2 percent of the total income of the nonprofit service sector. A detailed analysis of the revenue of nearly 13,000 charitable organizations reporting to the state of California in 1981–82, for instance, reveals that government grants constituted 21.6 percent of total charitable income, but corporate grants furnished only 2 percent. Similarly, a national survey of 3,400 nonprofit organizations in sixteen regions conducted in 1982–83 found that while government funds comprised 39.1 percent and United Way and other federated campaigns provided 6.8 percent of their fiscal 1982 revenues, direct company gifts supplied only 2.9 percent. In the case of colleges and universities, major beneficiaries of corporate largesse, company support contributed a mere 1.3 percent to their total expenditures in 1982–83 (Salamon & Abramson 1982; American Association . . . 1983, 91–93; Nonprofit Sector Project 1983; Council for Financial Aid to Education 1984).

If they were spread evenly, corporate contributions would thus be expected to have no significant influence on recipients. But most nonprofit organizations receive no business underwriting, and a few receive much. Managers of the favored institutions assert that business largesse erodes neither programming autonomy nor administrative independence. The director of one of the nation's most successful solicitors of corporate contributions, Anthony Bliss of the Metropolitan Opera of New York, flatly denies any external influence by the opera's benefactors. When donors offer to finance a new production, he states that he accepts the backing only if such a production would have been a product of his artistic judgment as well (Feld et al. 1983, 164).

Yet the condition permitting the Metropolitan Opera to retain such fierce independence—numerous generous contributors—is not enjoyed by most nonprofit organizations. Studies of the more usual conditions under which one organization is more subject to the influence of another reveal that organizational autonomy is greater if (1) an organization's reliance on external resources is low, (2) outside contributors are large in number and diverse in purpose, (3) no outside contributor accounts for a disproportionate share of the gifts, and (4) there is an ample supply of alternative potential contributors (Aldrich 1979; Pfeffer & Salancik 1978).

Thus, nonprofit organizations highly dependent on the gifts of a small set of large corporate contributors are least able to resist the benefactors' preferences. The specific preferences vary by type of firm and recipient. In the visual arts, for instance, company sponsors prefer to back large high-visibility exhibits with widespread appeal. Art museums seeking external backing are thus understandably fond of large and aesthetically accessible exhibitions. "Corporations are primarily interested in representational art," observed the director of development for New York's Whitney Museum, since "the masses of people relate to it more surely. The masses do *not* relate to abstract art. Corporations are interested in improving their image, and if they spent money on an exhibition which the bulk of the people do not relate to, they would in their view be doing more harm than good" (Rosenbaum 1977). Thus, blockbuster exhibitions drawing mass publics and publicity are especially attractive to corporate sponsors, a preference not lost on resource-starved museum directors (DiMaggio 1983a).

Similarly, university administrators seeking corporate sponsorship may also be drawn to improve their science and engineering curriculum and applied research capabilities, rather than their humanities programs, to entice business interest, especially by manufacturing firms. Managers of social service organizations may quietly discourage programs, such as community organizing or abortion counseling, that could embarrass or anger company contributors. Public television programmers seeking company backing may be encouraged to develop programs that are meant for national rather than local broadcast, that appeal to influential audiences (younger and male), and that are uncontroversial (Powell & Friedkin 1983).

Corporate sponsorship has an impact not only on the programs of nonprofit organizations but on administrative structures as well. "Organizational isomorphism"—the tendency for organizations to acquire the attributes of other organizations upon which they depend—applies here as well as anywhere. DiMaggio and Powell (1983) have observed that organizations come in time to resemble—sometimes unconsciously, sometimes out of necessity—their sponsors. If corporations favor sound fiscal management, strong marketing and public relations, and a professionalized administration, then nonprofits seeking corporate money will favor them, too. Funding by public agencies of cultural organizations is achieving precisely this kind of organizational change, according to a study by DiMaggio (1981, 1983b). Policies of the National Endowment for the Arts and of other agencies, for instance, have encouraged recipients to move toward better accounting, more vigorous lobbying, and professionalization of management practices.

Corporate sponsorship of nonprofit organizations, finally, in some instances may leverage additional support. Nonprofit organizations prominently announce their leading corporate sponsors when seeking private funding from other firms, foundations, and private individuals. The presence of such highly respected companies as IBM, Bank of America, or General Motors on a contributors' list is used by fundraisers to open a door if not always to pin down a gift. The imprimatur of the nation's leading firms implies that the recipient has passed their review and thus is a safe investment for other companies with little time to perform a detailed review.

TABLE 19.5 NATIONAL ORGANIZATIONS CONCERNED WITH CORPORATE PHILANTHROPY

American Association of Fund-Raising Counsel
25 West 43rd Street
New York, NY 10036
212-354-5799

Business Committee for the Arts
1501 Broadway
New York, NY 10036
212-664-0600

The Conference Board
845 Third Avenue
New York, NY 10022
212-759-0900

Council for Financial Aid to Education
680 Fifth Avenue
New York, NY 10019
212-541-4050

Council on Foundations
1828 L Street, N.W.
Washington, DC, 20036
202-466-6512

The Foundation Center
888 Seventh Avenue
New York, NY 10106
212-975-1120

The Independent Sector
1828 L Street, N.W.
Washington, DC 20036
202-223-8100

National Committee for Responsive Philanthropy
810 18th Street, N.W.
Washington, DC 20036
202-347-5340

Yale University Program on Non-Profit Organizations
16A Yale Station
New Haven, CT 06520
203-436-0155

Public Affairs Council
1220 16th Street, N.W.
Washington, DC 20036
202-872-1790

Public Management Institute
358 Brannan Street
San Francisco, CA 94107
415-896-1900

United Way of America
801 North Fairfax Street
Alexandria, VA 22314
703-836-7100

EXPANDING AND IMPROVING
CORPORATE PHILANTHROPY

The importance of corporate philanthropy to donors and recipients alike has spawned a small industry devoted to improving the giving process. Guidance on targeting requests and optimizing prospects is available to recipients from a variety of sources. Assistance in selecting recipients and maximizing impact is available to donors as well.

For recipients in search of support, the contributions programs of large corporations are profiled in several sources. The Foundation Center (1983) publishes a guide to the programs of more than six hundred company foundations; the Taft Corporation (1984) publishes profiles of the giving programs of most major corporations; and the Public Management Institute (1984) issues a guide to the programs of more than five hundred of the most active major corporations. All include the firms' funding priorities, sample grants, and the names of responsible officials or members of contributions committees. A profile, from one of these guides, of the nation's largest industrial firm, Exxon Corporation, appeared above in figure 19.2. A related source book contains information on the public affairs offices of fifteen hundred major companies, including skeletal data on their foundations (Columbia Books 1984). Regional profiles are available for some metropolitan areas as well, typically including a number of smaller companies that the national directories are unable to cover. More than two hundred Chicago-area companies, for example, are described in a directory published by the Donors Forum of Chicago (1983).

In the field of higher education, the Council for Financial Aid to Education (1978) publishes detailed descriptions of leading business programs of support for colleges and universities. For culture and the arts, the Business Committee for the Arts (1980) and American Council for the Arts (1983) offer graphic descriptions of the contributions of many major firms. Annual reports are also usually published by companies with major giving programs, such as Exxon, Chase Manhattan Bank, and Polaroid Corporation.

Nonprofit organizations in search of grants can also avail themselves of services provided by these and other organizations, including seminars on corporate fund-raising, guidelines on how best to approach corporate contributions officers, forums for contributions officers and fund seekers, and even some brokerage between firms and nonprofit organizations seeking a suitable contribution program or partnership. The Associated Grantmakers of Massachusetts (1982), for example, is an organization of twenty-two major corporations and fifteen foundations created to assist those who seek the more than $40 million annually given by its members' organizations. For the nonprofit fund-raiser, the association maintains a clearinghouse of information on corporate giving programs, runs a training program on the practical tasks of fund-raising, and sponsors a "meet the donors" luncheon series. Direct assistance in fashioning a new appeal for corporate donations can be obtained as well.

Corporations in search of assistance can turn to the Council for Financial Aid to Education, Business Committee for the Arts, Council on Foundations, the Independent Sector, Conference Board, and other national organizations concerned with corporate philanthropy listed in table 19.5. The Independent Sector, for instance, publishes an informational newsletter called *Corporate Philanthropy*. Guidance in developing an organizational structure and justifying philosophy for a contributions program can be found there (related Council for Financial Aid to Education publications include its 1981 and 1982 documents; related Conference Board publications include McGrath 1976, 1977; and Troy 1980; also see Council on Foundations 1982; Council of Better Business Bureaus 1984). To identify which nonprofit organizations might be most suitable for a partnership effort or outright grant, companies often consult with state and local government agencies and private organizations for names and brokerage efforts. State and local government agencies often maintain an office devoted to facilitating public-private partnerships and enhancing local corporate giving as well.

REFERENCES

Aldag, Ramon J., and Kathryn M. Bartol. 1978. "Empirical Studies of Corporate Social Performance and Policy: A Survey of Problems and Results." In *Research in Corporate Social Performance and Policy*, vol. 1, edited by Lee E. Preston, 165–99. Greenwich, Conn.: JAI Press.

Aldrich, Howard. 1979. *Organizations and Environments*. Englewood Cliffs, N.J.: Prentice-Hall.

Alexander, Gordon J., and Rogene A. Buchholz. 1978. "Corporate Social Responsibility and Stock Market Performance." *Academy of Management Journal* 21 (September):479–86.

American Association of Fund-Raising Counsel. 1983. *Giving USA: 1983 Annual Report*. New York: American Association of Fund-Raising Counsel.

———. 1984. *Giving USA: 1984 Annual Report*. New York: American Association of Fund-Raising Counsel.

American Council for the Arts. 1983. *Guide to Corporate Giving 3*. New York: American Council for the Arts.

Associated Grantmakers of Massachusetts. 1982. *Annual Report, 1981*. Boston: Associated Grantmakers of Massachusetts.

Baltzell, E. Digby. 1979. *Puritan Boston and Quaker Philadelphia*. New York: Free Press.

Bonfield, Patricia. 1980. *U.S. Business Leaders: A Study of Opinions and Characteristics*. New York: Conference Board.

Brooks, John. 1976. "Fueling the Arts, or, Exxon as Medici." *New York Times,* January 24, pp. D1ff.

Burck, Charles G. 1976. "A Group Profile of the Fortune 500 Chief Executive." *Fortune,* May, pp. 173ff.

Burt, Ronald S. 1983. *Corporate Profits and Cooptation*. New York: Academic Press.

Business Committee for the Arts. 1980. *Triennial Survey of Business Support of the Arts*. New York: Business Committee for the Arts.

Chemical Bank. 1984. "Giving and Getting: A Chemical Bank Study of Charitable Contributions, 1983 through 1988." New York: The Not For Profit Group, Chemical Bank.

Cmiel, Kenneth, and Susan Levy. 1980. *Corporate Giving in Chicago, 1980: A Study of the Giving Patterns of 51 Major Chicago Corporations*. Chicago: Chicago Library Research Report Series.

Columbia Books. 1984. *National Directory of Corporate Public Affairs*. 2d ed. Washington, D.C.: Columbia Books.

Committee for Economic Development. 1982. *Public-Private Partnership: An Opportunity for Urban Communities*. New York: Committee for Economic Development.

Council for Financial Aid to Education. 1984. *Corporate Support of Education, 1982*. New York: Council for Financial Aid to Education.

———. 1982. *Guidelines: How to Develop an Effective Program of Corporate Support for Higher Education*. New York: Council for Financial Aid to Education.

———. 1981. *Corporate Social Responsibility: Policies, Programs, Publications*. New York: Council for Financial Aid to Education.

———. 1979. *Corporate Support of Higher Education, 1978*. New York: Council for Financial Aid to Education.

———. 1978. *The Casebook: Aid-to-Education of Leading Business Concerns*. New York: Council for Financial Aid to Education.

Council of Better Business Bureaus. 1984. *A Window on the World of Philanthropy*. Arlington, Va.: Council of Better Business Bureaus.

Council on Foundations. 1982. *Corporate Philanthropy: Philosophy, Management, Trends, Future, Background*. New York: Council on Foundations.

DiMaggio, Paul. 1983a. "Can Culture Survive the Marketplace?" *Journal of Arts Management and Law* 13:61–87.

———. 1983b. "State Expansion and Organizational Goals." In *Organizational Theory and Public Policy*, edited by Richard H. Hall and Robert E. Quinn, 147–61. Beverly Hills, Calif.: Sage.

———. 1982. "Cultural Entrepreneurship in Nineteenth-Century Boston: The Creation of an Organizational Base for High Culture in America." *Media, Culture and Society* 4:33–50.

———. 1981. "The Impact of Public Policy on Organizations in the Arts." Yale University, Program on Non-Profit Organizations.

DiMaggio, Paul, and Walter W. Powell. 1983. "The Iron Cage Revisited: Institutional Isomorphism and Collective Rationality in Organizational Fields." *American Sociological Review* 82:147–60.

Donors Forum of Chicago. 1983. *Chicago Corporate Connection*. 2d ed. Chicago: Donors Forum of Chicago.

———. 1980. *Corporate Giving in Chicago, 1980*. Chicago: Donors Forum of Chicago.

Duca Associates. 1978. *Colorado Corporate Contributions Survey, 1978*. Denver: Duca Associates.

Ermann, David. 1979. "Corporate Contributions to Public Television." *Social Problems* 25:505–14.

Feld, Alan L., Michael O'Hare, and J. Mark Davidson Schuster. 1983. *Patrons Despite Themselves: Taxpayers and Arts Policies*. New York: New York University, 1983.

Fenn, Dan H., Jr. 1971. "Executives as Community Volunteers." *Harvard Business Review* 49 (April-May).

Foundation Center. 1983. *Corporate Foundation Profiles*. 3d ed. New York: Foundation Center.

Frederick, William C. 1983. "Corporate Social Responsibility in the Reagan Era and Beyond." *California Management Review* 20:145–57.

Freeman, R. Edward, and David L. Reed. 1983. "Stockholders and Stakeholders: A New Perspective on Corporate Governance." *California Management Review* 25 (Spring): 88–106.

Fremont-Smith, Marion R. 1972. *Philanthropy and the Business Corporation*. New York: Russell Sage Foundation.

Fry, Louis W., Gerald D. Keim, and Roger E. Meiners. 1982. "Corporate Contributions: Altruistic or For-Profit?" *Academy of Management Journal* 25:94–107.

Galaskiewicz, Joseph. 1986. *Gifts, Givers, and Getters: Business Philanthropy in an Urban Setting*. New York: Academic Press.

———. 1980. "Prestige, Power and the Provision of Collective Goods." Unpublished paper, Department of Sociology, University of Minnesota.

Galaskiewicz, Joseph, and Barbara Rauschenbach. Forthcoming. "The Corporate-Culture Connection: A Test of Interorganizational Theories." In *Resource Dependency and Community Organizations,* edited by Carl Milofsky.

Garvin, Michele. 1982. "Analysis of Survey of Corporate Support for the Arts in Massachusetts." Boston: Massachusetts Council on the Arts and Humanities.

Governor's Task Force on Private Sector Initiatives. 1983. *Report*. Boston: Commonwealth of Massachusetts.

Harris, James F., and Anne Klepper. 1976. *Corporate Philanthropic Public Service Activities*. New York: Conference Board.

Johnson, Orace. 1966. "Corporate Philanthropy: An Analysis of Corporate Contributions." *Journal of Business* 39:489–504.

Karl, Barry D. N.d. "Corporate Philanthropy: Historical Background.'' Unpublished paper, Department of History, University of Chicago.

Karl, Barry D., and Stanley N. Katz. 1981. ''The American Private Philanthropic Foundation and the Public Sphere, 1890–1930.'' *Minerva* 19 (Summer):236–70.

Kedia, Banwari L., and Edwin C. Kuntz. 1981. ''The Context of Social Performance: An Empirical Study of Texas Banks.'' In *Research in Corporate Social Performance and Policy,* edited by Lee E. Preston, 133–54. Greenwich, Conn.: JAI Press.

Keim, Gerald D. 1981. ''Foundations of a Political Strategy for Business.'' *California Management Review* 23 (Spring):41–48.

Koch, Frank. 1979. *The New Corporate Philanthropy: How Society and Business Can Profit.* New York: Plenum Publishing.

Lahn, Seth M. 1980. ''Corporate Philanthropy: Issues in the Current Literature.'' Yale University, Program on Non-Profit Organizations.

Levy, Ferdinand K., and Gloria M. Shatto. 1980. ''Social Responsibility in Large Electric Utility Firms: The Case for Philanthropy.'' In *Research in Corporate Social Performance and Policy,* vol. 2, edited by Lee E. Preston, 237–49. Greenwich, Conn.: JAI Press.

———. 1978. ''The Evaluation of Corporate Contributions.'' *Public Choice* 33:19–28.

Lipset, Seymour Martin, and William P. Schneider. 1981. *The Confidence Gap: How Americans View Their Institutions.* New York: Macmillan.

Maddox, Katherine E. 1981. ''Corporate Philanthropy.'' Ph.D. diss., Vanderbilt University.

Mauksch, Mary. 1982. *Corporate Voluntary Contributions in Europe.* New York: Conference Board.

McElroy, Katherine Maddox, and John J. Siegfried. 1985. ''The Effect of Firm Size on Corporate Philanthropy.'' *Quarterly Review of Economics and Business* 25 (Summer):18–26.

McGrath, Phyllis S. 1977. *Action Plans for Public Affairs.* New York: Conference Board.

———. 1976. *Managing Corporate External Relations: Changing Perspectives and Responses.* New York: Conference Board.

McGuire, E. Patrick, and Nathan Weber. 1982. *Business Voluntarism: Prospects for 1982.* New York: Conference Board.

Merenda, Michael J. 1981. ''The Process of Corporate Social Involvement: Five Case Studies.'' In *Research in Corporate Social Performance and Policy,* vol. 3, edited by Lee E. Preston, 17–41. Greenwich, Conn.: JAI Press.

Middleton, Melissa. 1983. ''The Place and Power of Non-Profit Boards of Directors.'' Yale University, Program on Non-Profit Organizations.

Murray, Edwin A., Jr. 1982. ''The Public Affairs Function: Report on a Large-Scale Research Project.'' In *Research in Corporate Social Performance and Policy,* vol. 4, edited by Lee E. Preston, 129–55. Greenwich, Conn.: JAI Press.

National Science Board. 1983. *University-Industry Research Relationships.* Washington, D.C.: National Science Foundation.

Nonprofit Sector Project. 1983. *Progress Report No. 3.* Washington, D.C.: Urban Institute.

Office of Program and Policy Studies, National Endowment for the Humanities. 1983. ''Corporate Giving for the Humanities, 1979–1981: A Pilot Study of Method and Approach Using 50 Corporate Giving Programs.'' Washington, D.C.: National Endowment for the Humanities.

Otten, Alan L. 1981. ''English Corporations: Art's New Tudors?'' *Wall Street Journal,* April 3.

Parket, I. Robert, and Henry Eilbirt. 1975. ''Social Responsibility: The Underlying Factors.'' *Business Horizons* 18 (August):5–10.

Pfeffer, Jeffrey, and Gerald R. Salancik. 1978. *The External Control of Organizations: A Resource Dependence Perspective.* New York: Harper & Row.

Pittman, Russell. 1976. ''The Effects of Industry Concentration and Regulation on Contributions in Three 1972 U.S. Senate Campaigns.'' *Public Choice* 27 (Fall):71–80.

Post, James S., Edwin A. Murray, Jr., Robert B. Dickie, and John F. Mahon. 1983. ''Managing Public Affairs: The Public Affairs Function.'' *California Management Review* 26 (Fall):135–50.

Powell, Walter W., and Rebecca Friedkin. 1983. ''Political and Organizational Influences on Public Television Programming.'' In *Mass Communication Review Yearbook,* vol. 4, edited by E. Wartella and D. C. Whitney, 413–38. Beverly Hills, Calif.: Sage.

Preston, Lee E., ed. 1982. *Research in Corporate Social Performance and Policy,* vol. 4. Greenwich, Conn.: JAI Press.

———. 1981a. ''Corporate Power and Social Performance: Approaches to Positive Analysis.'' In *Research in Corporate Social Performance and Policy,* vol. 3, edited by Lee E. Preston, 1–16. Greenwich, Conn.: JAI Press.

———, ed. 1981b. *Research in Corporate Social Performance and Policy,* vol. 3. Greenwich, Conn.: JAI Press.

———, ed. 1980. *Research in Corporate Social Performance and Policy,* vol. 2. Greenwich, Conn.: JAI Press.

———, ed. 1978. *Research in Corporate Social Performance and Policy,* vol. 1. Greenwich, Conn.: JAI Press.

Public Management Institute. 1984. *Corporate 500: The Directory of Corporate Philanthropy.* 3d ed. San Francisco: Public Management Institute.

———. 1983. *Corporate 500: The Directory of Corporate Philanthropy.* 2d ed. San Francisco: Public Management Institute.

Ratcliff, Richard E., Mary Beth Gallagher, and David Jaffee. 1980. ''Political Money and Ideological Clusters in the Capitalist Class.'' Unpublished paper, Department of Sociology, Washington University.

Ratcliff, Richard E., Mary Elizabeth Gallagher, and Kathryn Strother Ratcliff. 1979. ''The Civic Involvement of Bankers: An Analysis of the Influence of Economic Power and Social Prominence in the Command of Civic Policy Positions.'' *Social Problems* 26:298–313.

Reiner, Thomas S., and Julian Wolpert. 1981. ''The Non-Profit Sector in the Metropolitan Economy.'' *Economic Geography* 57:23–33.

Roderick, David M. 1982. ''A Few Practical Concerns.'' *American Arts,* March.

Rose-Ackerman, Susan. 1980. ''Do Government Grants to

Charity Reduce Private Donations?'' Yale University, Program on Non-Profit Organizations.

Rosenbaum, Lee. 1977. ''The Scramble for Museum Sponsors: Is Curatorial Independence for Sale?'' *Art in America* 65 (January-February):10–14.

Salamon, Lester M., and Alan J. Abramson. 1982. *The Federal Budget and the Nonprofit Sector.* Washington, D.C.: Urban Institute Press.

Salzman, Harold, and G. William Domhoff. 1983. ''Non-Profit Organizations and the Corporate Community.'' *Social Science History* 7:205–16.

Scherer, F. M. 1980. *Industrial Market Structure and Economic Performance.* 2d ed. Chicago: Rand McNally.

Sethi, S. Prakash. 1978. ''Dimensions of Corporate Social Responsibility: An Analytical Framework.'' *California Management Review* 17:58–64.

Siegfried, John J., and Katherine Maddox McElroy. 1981. ''Corporate Philanthropy in America: 1980.'' Unpublished paper, Department of Economics and Business Administration, Vanderbilt University.

Siegfried, John J., Katherine Maddox McElroy, and Diane Biernot-Fawkes. 1983. ''The Management of Corporate Contributions.'' In *Research in Corporate Social Performance and Policy,* vol. 5, edited by Lee Preston. Greenwich, Conn.: JAI Press.

Smith, Hayden W. 1983. *A Profile of Corporate Contributions.* New York: Council for Financial Aid to Education.

Smith, Lee. 1981. ''The Unsentimental Corporate Giver.'' *Fortune,* September 21, pp. 121–34.

Staber, Udo Hermann. 1982. ''The Organizational Properties of Trade Associations.'' Ph.D. diss., Cornell University.

Stebbins, Theodore E., Jr., Carl Troyen, and Trevor J. Fairbrother. 1983. *A New World: Masterpieces of American Painting 1760–1910.* Boston: Museum of Fine Arts.

Story, Ronald D. 1980. *The Forging of an Aristocracy: Harvard and the Boston Upper Class, 1800–1870.* Middletown, Conn.: Wesleyan University Press.

Sturdivant, Frederick D., and James L. Ginter. 1977. ''Corporate Social Responsiveness: Management Attitudes and Economic Performance.'' *California Management Review* 19, no. 3:30–39.

Taft Corporation. 1984. *Taft Corporate Directory, 1984 Edition.* Washington, D.C.: Taft Corporation, 1984.

Teltsch, Kathleen. 1983. ''Survey Says Companies Gave Record Amount to Charities.'' *New York Times,* November 21, p. B16.

Troy, Kathryn. 1984. *Annual Survey of Corporate Contributions, 1984 Edition.* New York: Conference Board.

———. 1983. *Annual Survey of Corporate Contributions, 1983 Edition.* New York: Conference Board.

———. 1981. *Annual Survey of Corporate Contributions, 1981 Edition.* New York: Conference Board.

———. 1980. *Managing Corporate Contributions.* New York: Conference Board.

Turner, Judith Axler. 1984. ''IBM Increased Its Support of Education More Than 50 Pct. in 1983.'' *Chronicle of Higher Education,* January 25, p. 9.

United Way of America. 1981. *Scope and Trends: Some Aspects of Philanthropy in the United States.* Alexandria, Va.: United Way of America.

Unterman, Israel, and Richard Hart Davis. 1982. ''The Strategy Gap in Not-for-Profits.'' *Harvard Business Review,* May-June, pp. 30–40.

Useem, Michael. 1984. *The Inner Circle: Large Corporations and the Rise of Business Political Activity in the U.S. and U.K.* New York: Oxford University Press.

———. 1982. ''Classwide Rationality in the Politics of Managers and Directors of Large Corporations in the United States and Great Britain.'' *Administrative Science Quarterly* 27:199–226.

———. 1979. ''The Social Organization of the American Business Elite and Participation of Corporation Directors in the Governance of American Institutions.'' *American Sociological Review* 44:553–72.

Useem, Michael, and Stephen I. Kutner. 1986. ''Corporate Contributions to Culture and the Arts: The Organization of Giving, and the Influence of the Chief Executive Officer and Other Firms on Company Contributions in Massachusetts.'' In *Nonprofit Organizations in the Production and Distribution of Culture,* edited by Paul DiMaggio. New York: Oxford University Press.

Vogel, David. 1978. *Lobbying the Corporation: Citizen Challenges to Business Authority.* New York: Basic Books.

Wall, Wendy L. 1984. ''Companies Change the Ways They Make Charitable Donations.'' *Wall Street Journal,* June 21, p. 1.

Weber, Nathan, and Leonard Lund. 1981. *Corporations in the Community.* New York: Conference Board.

White, Arthur H. 1980. ''Corporate Philanthropy: Impact on Public Attitudes.'' In *Corporate Philanthropy in the Eighties,* 17–19. Washington, D.C.: National Chamber Foundation.

White, Arthur H., and John Bartolomeo. 1982. *Corporate Giving: The Views of Chief Executive Officers of Major American Corporations.* Washington, D.C.: Council on Foundations.

Windsor, Duane, and George Greanias. 1982. ''Strategic Planning Systems for a Politicized Environment.'' In *Research in Corporate Social Performance and Policy,* vol. 4, edited by Lee E. Preston, 77–104. Greenwich, Conn.: JAI Press.

Wolpert, Julian, and Thomas A. Reiner. 1980. *The Metropolitan Philadelphia Philanthropy Study.* Philadelphia: School of Public and Urban Policy, University of Pennsylvania.

Wyszomirski, Margaret Jane. 1983. ''The Reagan Administration and the Third Sector: The Case of the Arts.'' Unpublished paper, Department of Political Science, Rutgers University.

20

Foundations and Nonprofit Organizations

PAUL N. YLVISAKER

Foundations may loom large in the minds and lives of many, but by any numerical indicator they are a mere speck on the canvas of American society. The 23,600 active foundations identified by the Foundation Center from Internal Revenue Service (IRS) files and profiled in the introduction to its *Foundation Directory* (1985) represented only 3 percent of the 785,000 independent-sector organizations enumerated in *Dimensions of the Independent Sector*. Their combined assets ($64.5 billion) were only roughly half the total assets ($125 billion, estimated by *Forbes* in 1984) of the country's four hundred wealthiest individuals; their annual grants ($4.8 billion) were 3.7 percent of the independent sector's estimated total operating expenditures ($131 billion in 1980) and roughly 0.5 percent of the federal government's budget ($1 trillion); their employees (about 6,000) accounted for only 0.1 percent of the independent sector's 6.2 million employees and 0.006 percent of the nation's employed workforce.[1]

Though they contribute less than four cents out of every dollar spent by independent-sector organizations and are outmatched by total federal spending at a ratio of approximately 200:1, foundations are still generally credited with—and often resented for—playing a disproportionately influential role in the private and public sectors of American society. This chapter will describe their role and the ways in which they do their work. I hope it will also provide a perspective useful both in understanding foundations and in dealing with them.

CHARACTER, SCALE, AND INTERESTS OF AMERICAN FOUNDATIONS

The Dominant Foundations

Given the extreme bimodal distribution in size, the mass of private philanthropy is highly concentrated in America. A relatively few foundations dominate the scene. The 4,402 foundations that in 1985 met the requirements for listing in the *Directory*—grant-making organizations with assets over $1 million or annual giving over $100,000—comprised only 18.7 percent of all foundations but accounted for 97 percent of total foundation assets, 85 percent of total grants, and practically all paid staff.

Within that select group, there is even more concentration. Ninety-six foundations, each with assets of over $100 million or more, owned over half of all foundation assets, made 35.8 percent of all *Directory* grants, and employed an overwhelming proportion of the paid foundation personnel. Fifteen foundations with assets of $500 million or more alone accounted for approximately 28.2 percent of total assets, 13.6 percent of total grants, and the majority of paid staff.[2]

Foundations are also geographically concentrated. No

I am indebted to Patty Unkle and Carla Shepard for their help in the preparation of this chapter, and to Woody Powell and John Simon for their careful readings of earlier drafts.

1. Foundation statistics in this chapter are taken from Foundation Center (1985, pp. v–xxiii) unless otherwise noted. Data are based primarily on 1983 foundation returns filed with the Internal Revenue Service. Figures on the independent sector in the first paragraph are from Hodgkinson and Weitzman (1984, pp. 1–4, 37). It should be pointed out that the survey makes a distinction between nonprofit organizations and independent-sector organizations. The data are based on 1980 information for independent-sector organizations (such as not-for-profit, tax-exempt organizations that are voluntary organizations, churches, private schools, foundations, and social welfare and civic organizations).

2. The fifteen foundations listed in Foundation Center (1985, p. xiii) with assets of $500 million or more are the Ford Foundation, J. Paul Getty Trust, John T. and Catherine T. MacArthur Foundation, W. K. Kellogg Foundation, Robert Wood Johnson Foundation, Pew Memorial Trust, Rockefeller Foundation, Andrew W. Mellon Foundation, Lilly Endowment, Kresge Foundation, Charles Stewart Mott Foundation, Duke Endowment, McKnight Foundation, Carnegie Corporation of New York, and W. M. Keck Foundation.

state or sizable community is without one; but 56.5 percent of the assets of the 4,402 foundations listed in the 1985 *Directory* were owned by foundations in the Middle Atlantic and East North Central regions, approximately 20 percent in New York City alone. Happily, this disparity is significantly offset by two factors: the faster growth rates in recent years of foundations in other regions, documented in the *Directory*, and the large number of the more concentrated foundations that invite requests from outside their immediate locale.

The Striking Diversity among Foundations

Diversity in Kind

There are, by law and label, five significantly different types of foundations.[3] Four of these are regularly tabulated by statisticians in the field: company-sponsored foundations, independent foundations, operating foundations, and community foundations. The fifth—so-called public foundations—have recently attracted attention as possible prototypes of future philanthropy.[4]

The first three types all bear the same statutory designation as "private foundations." Given their differences, however, that may be stretching a single term past its breaking point.

Company-sponsored foundations (723 of them large enough to be included in the 1985 *Directory*, with annual grants totaling $803.6 million, or 19.7 percent of all foundation grants listed) are legally indistinguishable from independent foundations; they file the same reports, meet the same requirements, and similarly commit their funds to a public purpose. But they live within the corporate frame, ultimately having to satisfy the shareholders that what they do is definably in the interests of the corporation. As many a corporate foundation has proved, that definition has become flexible enough to encompass the proposition that what is in the general public's interest is also in the corporation's. Still, the tension is always there, pulling at corporate giving to move closer to a narrower calculus.

Independent foundations, on the other hand (and they are by far the most numerous, accounting for 80 percent of foundations listed in the 1985 *Directory*, 71 percent of total grants, and 83.6 percent of total assets), enjoy the greater latitude their classification suggests. They are duty bound to honor the trust and charter under which they were created, but they are not subject to the constraints of corporate inter-

ests and voting shareholders. Because they are freer, these foundations have periodically aroused the suspicion and ire of the public, particularly when they are perceived to be indulging self-interest under the cloak of altruism. In the searing episode of 1969, Congress was provoked enough to pass a punitive Tax Reform Act explicitly designed to make private foundations pay a price for their independence, roughly proportionate to their distance from public participation and other restraining influences.[5]

Some *operating foundations*, the third form of private foundations, are very large (the Wilder Foundation, for example, ranks among the 50 largest), and some are household names (Kettering, Russell Sage, the Twentieth Century Fund). They are, however, few—only 79 out of the 4,402 listed in the 1985 *Directory*, and 2,126 in the current IRS records—and by law, their grant making to other nonprofit agencies is limited to 15 percent of total income. Their work is performed mostly in-house (usually in the form of direct service and/or research) and only occasionally by subsidizing the activities of others.[6]

Community foundations have proliferated throughout the country. In her survey for the Council on Foundations, Scanlan (1985) identified 305 community foundations, 86

---

3. There are also "foundations that are not foundations." One variety bears the name but in actuality raises money rather than giving it. Another growing category includes personal giving by individuals who are assisted by professional staff but have not created a separate legal entity—for example, the Windom Fund.

4. Williams (1984) looks at one of the prototypes of future philanthropy—alternative funds. Unlike private foundations, these so-called public foundations (like their community foundation counterparts) are actually public charities under the tax code. Their broad base of donors enables them to escape the restrictive rules placed on private/independent foundations by the 1969 Tax Reform Act.

5. In the early 1960s, Texas congressman Wright Patman began a crusade against foundations, charging them with engaging in a variety of questionable practices. At his urging, the Treasury Department launched an investigation of foundation financial dealings, discovering a number of abuses. As a result of Treasury's 1965 report and Patman's continued insistence, the House Ways and Means Committee (under the chairmanship of Congressman Wilbur Mills) began a new investigation of foundations in 1969. Combined with Treasury's 1965 report and a general perception of foundations as symbols of wealth and power, shrouded in secrecy and controlled by only a few, the climate for foundations was not propitious. After hearing a number of witnesses, the committee's response was to tighten the reins of private/independent foundations by creating a number of measures they felt would correct the abuses of the past. These measures included an excise tax on investment income (to cover expenses associated with Internal Revenue Service regulation of foundations—originally 4 percent of assets, later reduced to 2 percent and 1 percent in certain circumstances); a minimum payout requirement based on either 5 percent of foundation assets or all income, whichever was greater (this was later changed to a payout based on 5 percent of assets only); a limit on individual deductions for gifts to foundations; provisions against self-dealing (transactions between a foundation and a disqualified person—donor, trustee, relative, and so on); a limit on the amount of stock a foundation and its disqualified persons could own in a business (excess business holdings); a tax on investments that jeopardize the foundation's ability to carry out its purpose; and a tax aimed at prohibiting or regulating foundation activities dealing with grants to individuals, other foundations, nonexempt organizations, legislative matters, or political campaigns. The hearings also resulted in tougher reporting requirements for foundations. The Form 990 was expanded to include reporting on the provisions approved in 1969, and foundations were told to make public a notice announcing its availability. Foundations were also required to begin filing copies with states where they were incorporated and maintain their principal office. Further reading on the subject can be found in U.S. Treasury (1965); Nielsen (1972; pp. 5–20, 365–98); Cuninggim (1972; pp. 190–216).

6. A more detailed description of operating foundations and their activities can be found in Foote (1985a, 1985c).

more than reported in the last council survey (1975); 134 qualified for listing in the 1985 *Directory*, with assets totaling $2.8 billion.

A few, such as the San Francisco and Cleveland foundations, are very large, with assets running into the hundreds of millions of dollars. Most, however, are quite small. What sets them apart is their relatively close and structured ties to the communities they serve. The committees controlling their grant making are appointed by varying combinations of trustee banks and local dignitaries, ensuring at least a modicum of local accountability. These foundations are also required by federal law to meet a "public support" test—having to raise each year a specified fraction of their total revenues from the broader public as against gifts from a few large donors. They qualify thereby as public charities under the Internal Revenue Code; and in recognition of their more evident accountability, they have been given favored treatment in federal tax legislation.

Public foundations also qualify as public charities, annually raising the money they then give away for specified causes and constituencies. Although they engage in grant making, they have not been separately tabulated in the various counts of American foundations, nor has the Internal Revenue Code given them special attention or designation. They include a broad range of both conventional and innovative organizations, ranging from the Philadelphia Bar Foundation to the Haymarket People's Fund and the Wonder Woman Foundation. They all enjoy the advantages of not being chartered as private foundations with the encumbrances imposed by the Tax Reform Act of 1969. What is of interest is the emergence, in some of the more intrepid members of this growing classification, of what may be a prototype of future American philanthropy: organizations that face the democratizing challenge of the market and are willing to experiment with governing mechanisms less elitist than those of traditional private foundations. The Council on Foundations voted in 1984 to admit qualifying applicants from this group into full membership, symbolically recognizing their growing significance.

Diversity in Growth Rates

The different types of foundations have varying rates of growth. The total number of *Directory*-size foundations grew by 2,384 from 1977 to 1984 (700 were dropped because they failed to meet the criteria for inclusion). Some of the growth can be attributed to the 685 foundations established during the 1970s and early 1980s and to those established earlier that received substantial gifts or additions to their endowments during that period. A second factor leading to the increase in *Directory*-size foundations is the market conditions over the past decade. Foundation assets in current dollars are sharply depreciated when converted to constant dollars, because of inflation. Moreover, the declining value of the dollar (from $.551 in 1977 to $.335 in 1981 based on 1967 dollars) has made it possible for a number of foundations to meet the requirements for inclusion in the *Directory*.

On a positive note, the 1985 *Directory* reports that real assets have risen for the first time since 1972. This follows a period of sharp decline in asset value between 1972 and 1975 (from $25.2 billion to $17.8 billion in constant dollars for *Directory*-sized foundations) and a steady plateau between 1975 and 1981.

Independent foundations fared the worst. The decline in the foundation birthrate that began gently in the 1960s plunged rapidly in the 1970s—according to the General Accounting Office, dropping off by 59 percent.[7] Much of that has been attributed to the discouraging provisions of the 1969 Tax Reform Act. But there may well be other reasons woven more subtly into the changing culture and climate of contemporary America. (Some of these factors will be discussed later.) The facts of the years 1975–81 speak for themselves. Assets grew nominally by $16 billion ($25.5 billion to $41.5 billion), but in constant dollars declined by $609 million. Although this decline reversed in the period from 1981 to 1983 when assets increased by $11.2 billion in current dollars and by $2.4 billion in constant dollars, it was the first increase that independent foundation assets had had in constant dollars since 1975. Overall independent foundation giving increased by over $315 million (12.2 percent) in current dollars and almost $23 million in constant dollars between 1981 and 1983. In 1983, these foundations received $1.3 billion in gifts or additions to endowments. Over half of that went to 23 foundations, including 6 that appeared in the 1985 *Directory* for the first time.[8]

Company-sponsored foundations fared much better. Between 1975 and 1983, the number of *Directory*-size foundations in this category jumped by 56.5 percent (462 to 723). Their combined assets more than doubled in current dollars ($1.2 billion to $3 billion) and rose by 28.6 percent in constant dollars. Their grants increased by 229.2 percent in current dollars ($244 million to $804 million), or 77.9 percent in constant dollars.

Community foundations did even better. Between 1975 and 1983, the number of *Directory*-size community foundations grew by 86 percent, assets in current dollars by 140 percent (constant dollars, 30 percent), and grants by a striking 250 percent (constant dollars, 84 percent). And it was not only the larger and more established community foundations that flourished. Given the blessing of the Tax Reform Act of 1969, community foundations began cropping up throughout the United States. Currently, the Council on Foundations reports receiving an average of fifty inquiries a year from

---

7. The General Accounting Office (1984) states that "4,143 grantmaking foundations were formed in the 1970s compared with 10,077 in the 1960s—a 59% drop." Additional research on trends in foundation formulation, growth, and termination is currently being conducted by the Council on Foundations and the Yale Program on Non-Profit Organizations. Preliminary findings can be found in Odendahl (1985, pp. 513–23).

8. The six foundations are G. Harold and Leila Mathers Charitable Foundation, Horace W. Goldsmith Foundation, Lucille P. Markey Charitable Trust, J. Roderick MacArthur Foundation, Wilbur D. May Foundation, and Lloyd Fry Foundation.

groups interested in establishing community foundations for their areas, some of them regional or statewide in scope. The 1985 *Directory* includes 134 community foundations, up 86 percent (62 new foundations) since 1975.

No breakouts are available for private operating foundations or for public foundations—the latter already mentioned as having lately taken on new life.

Diversity in Activities and Processes

Foundations are also becoming more diverse as they expand their activity beyond grant making. Foundations do a lot more than give money. It has long been recognized that their wealth puts them in an influential position. What is strikingly different about philanthropy over the past decade is the explicit and expansive way in which the more enterprising foundations are developing such roles as lender, investor, insurer, adviser, venturer, partner, convener, monitor, gadfly, evaluator, catalyst, ethicist ("the Good Housekeeping Seal of Approval"), and banker of social talent, knowledge, and memory. With a dozen and more roles to select from and then combine and emphasize in individual fashion, the differentiation of foundations is inevitable and can go on almost infinitely.

Although certain basic processes are generic to philanthropy, there are wide variations in the way foundations carry them out. These processes can be grouped under seven headings.

Governance. The ultimate authority and responsibility within foundations rest with trustees—with the clear exception of community foundations, where grant making is given over to distribution committees, and the somewhat blurred exception of company-sponsored foundations, where trustees, even when not identical with management, operate within reach of corporate policy. Aside from that, generalization is difficult. There does seem to be a correlation between foundation size and the character of trustee involvement; the smaller, the more intimate; the larger, the more confined to policy determination, external relations, and general monitoring of staff performance. But there are many explicit exceptions. For example, trustees of the MacArthur Foundation—one of the nation's largest—are directly responsible for designated foundation programs and are paid accordingly. And every major foundation, whatever its classification, has had its moment when trustees—for sometimes good and sometimes questionable reasons—have involved themselves deeply in the operation and management of the enterprise. Donors, their families, and friendly lawyers and bankers they may have "trusteed" can be said generally to display a more aggressive interest, but again the rule is tested by the many examples of restraint on the part of well-positioned trustees who might be expected to act otherwise.

Congress has shown an interest in foundation governance, being apprehensive about both elitism and self-dealing. In the 1969 tax act it acted explicitly on the latter, but only indirectly on the former (for example, giving less favored tax treatment to private foundations with self-per-

petuating boards of trustees). And as noted earlier, public foundations are experimenting with new forms of governance. One such is the Haymarket People's Fund of Boston; its expanding network of socially diverse individuals share in the fund's decision making.[9]

All told, there are presumably over 140,000 foundation trustees in the United States (a conservatively estimated average of 6 for each of 23,600 foundations). On that scale, they outnumber paid staff by 23 to 1. Obviously, there are far more foundations without staff than with staff. In those cases, governance means trustee involvement in every aspect of the foundation's activity.

Not all trustees are active, however. When John Nason researched his definitive study of foundation trustees in America, *Trustees and the Future of Foundations* (1977), the sputtering performance of so many dismayed him. Without the analog of the "due diligence" rule that disciplines corporate directors, the required public reporting of attendance below 75 percent, and continuous monitoring by regulatory agencies, improved overall trustee performance may be slow in coming. But the pace may be quickened by the awakening interest within philanthropy, dwindling nonprofit budgets, increasing litigiousness, and sobering thoughts about possible liability.

Staffing. It would be difficult to find greater diversity than along the continuum extending from the giant foundations with their highly professional and extensive staffs to the tiniest of grant makers with only one or two trustees, a post office box, and sometimes not even a telephone listing. Staffing is correlated with size, but by no means predictably. Within blocks of each other in New York City is one foundation granting almost $1 million annually whose only employee is a part-time bookkeeper and another foundation granting half as much which employs full time one of the most professional and experienced philanthropists in the nation—plus an office manager.

One can, however, discern a trend toward more staffing and more professionalism, certainly among *Directory*-size foundations. But there are complications. The Federal Tax Act of 1984 put a cap on administrative expenses that can be counted to meet payout requirements;[10] that constraint, along with tightening budgets, will hardly encourage a significant expansion in foundation employment. And the very question of whether philanthropy can or should be a career or a profession is arguable. The job market is minuscule; appointments are idiosyncratic; lateral and upward mobility is limited; skill comes mostly from experience, and experience is not widely accepted as transferable; and even the professionals wonder if long service in philanthropy is good for

9. The prototype for organizations with broader forms of governance was the Vanguard Public Foundation. An explanation of the structure can be found in Vanguard Public Foundation (1977).

10. The 1984 tax act enabled most foundations to reduce their federal excise tax from 2 to 1 percent and to reduce the difference in tax treatment for gifts to public charities and foundations. The one disappointing provision of the act for foundations set a limit on the administrative costs that can count toward meeting the payout requirement.

them or for society.[11] Nor are foundations model employers; biennial surveys by the Council on Foundations show significant lapses and disparities in employment practices, with only modest improvements over time. The 1984 *Foundation Management Report* found that top management of foundations is still largely male (73 percent overall, 94 percent for foundations with over $100 million in assets); women, although they are now the majority of paid staff (68 percent), are far from achieving parity in pay or promotional opportunity; and minorities, although gaining (now 13 percent of reported employment), are still at the margin.

For all that, most of those who work in foundations find it a fascinating and challenging occupation, a vantage point from which they can survey, sort out, and perhaps influence seemingly all of life. And even if they make mistakes or do only a mediocre job, they retain their influence: the money they dispense is still good and the world still comes flatteringly to their door. One of the most important dimensions of diversity in philanthropy is the way in which staff differentially respond to the sense of power that goes with the position. It is telling that arrogance is universally recognized as the chief occupational hazard in the field—the central concern of addresses by J. Irwin Miller and Alan Pifer at the 1984 annual conference of the Council on Foundations.

A close second as an occupational hazard—surely, both parties would agree—is the almost inescapable tension between board and staff.[12] These tensions stem from differences among trustees in which staff can easily get caught; differences in personalities and perspectives; conflicting interpretations of board and staff prerogatives; the constant need for staff to deal reliably and authoritatively with applicants, and the imperative for trustees to reserve judgment; the inherent subjectivity in analyzing and deciding social issues; the impatience, particularly among younger staff, to "accomplish something" and the understandable conservatism of board members, many of whom "have seen it all before"; and intermittently the reverse: a board growing weary of former novelty that has become routine and pressuring staff to come up with something exciting.

This is a hazard, but not a constant condition. The intervals of harmony are nearly as frequent. But anyone dealing with foundations should know that these dynamics are constantly in play.

Investing.   Until recently, investment of foundation assets has been handled conventionally by designated trustees, financial officers, and portfolio managers. But recent events have stirred a much broader concern, and foundations are further differentiating themselves in how directly and rapidly they are responding to the changes. Understandably, given the growing disparity between social needs and philanthropic

resources, all foundations are reviewing their portfolio performance.

The new concerns are ethical, on the one hand, and pragmatic, on the other. Simply put, the first addresses the question: is the foundation through its investments reinforcing or offsetting the social benefit it is trying to achieve through its grant making and other activities? The question does not submit to easy answers, as anyone who has struggled with the issues of South Africa, nuclear energy, and the like can attest. But it is increasingly recognized that trustees cannot sidestep responsibility for deciding explicitly the policies and procedures for addressing the ethical issues raised by shareholder resolutions and possible incongruities between the foundation's mission and its financial holdings.

The second development is pragmatic and innovative— the use of some portion of the foundation's endowment for "program-related investments," making monies available for housing, community development, minority enterprises, and other ventures of higher risk and lower return than those available on the open market. Once thought to be incompatible with the test of the prudent investor, this use of a foundation's corpus is now widely accepted and encouraged as a way of stretching scarce resources and nourishing managerial discipline in those organizations committing themselves to repayment.[13]

Defining Mission and Programs.   Sooner or later the question arises whether and how a foundation can define and communicate more precisely what it hopes to accomplish. This is true even of community foundations, whose very purpose is to be of general use to the broad range of constituencies they serve—if in no other way, by focusing the allocation of their discretionary funds.

There are many reasons for sharpening focus: the need to make most efficient use of scarce resources, to avoid wasting client and foundation time on countless proposals that go nowhere, to concentrate on areas where trustee interest is high and staff expertise is greatest, to create a distinctive public image and a set of consistent criteria for judging requests.

Sharpening focus can be a difficult task; many foundations deal with it simply by ducking it. But peer group and applicant pressures are coming down heavily on the side of focused grant making, so much so that the imperative of clearly defined policies, priorities, and guidelines has been incorporated into the Council on Foundations "Recommended Principles and Practices" to which all members subscribe.[14] State-of-the-art practice usually involves a sys-

---

11. Odendahl, Boris, and Daniels (1985) explore the personal and professional concerns of women and men in the grant-making field. Foote (1985b) provides an overall look at what foundations and the Council on Foundations are doing to provide professional development opportunities for staff and trustees.

12. Odendahl and Boris (1983) examines the delicate balance between board and staff.

13. Knowles (1985) deals with the link between a foundation's investment policy and its program goals. Foundation involvement in emergency loan funds is chronicled in Youkstetter (1981). Additional information on alternative investments can be found in Council on Foundations (1985), the selected and edited proceedings of a conference on the subject.

14. The Council on Foundations "Principles and Practices" are included in Viscusi (1985). She also profiles the history leading up to the adoption of the statement and offers examples of foundations whose actions echo these views.

tematic canvassing of social needs and trustee interests falling within the range of the foundation's chartered purpose. Suggestions are winnowed and options narrowed, preferably in special meetings of staff and trustees, until a consensus is reached on a manageable set of focused objectives. Some room is left for flexibility in dealing with the unanticipated and taking advantage of what in the trade are rather fondly described as "targets of opportunity."

The process is continuous as board and staff watch the ebb and flow of unmet needs and the shifting marginal utility of a particular pattern of grant making. Adjustments can be made in annual or biennial policy meetings, with major program changes placed on the agenda at longer intervals. (Where foundations have in fact placed their bets over the past thirty years will be detailed and discussed below.)

Judging and Deciding. Foundations range from being extremely active—assertively promoting their objectives and soliciting proposals—to being extremely passive, accepting whatever requests come their way. Most operate somewhere in the middle, leading when they are confident of trustee support and know what they want to accomplish, but following when they are in a noncommittal and exploratory mode or are not prepared to take on the public responsibility and controversy that may follow from exercising an initiative.

Whatever their mode, foundations eventually have to get down to the arduous business of analyzing and judging the proposals on their desks. Obviously this is easiest to do when mission and criteria are clear (although, admittedly, strong staff and trustee prejudice can also, and too often do, make the task a simplistic one: the die is cast if trustee X or executive Y or someone in their club "wouldn't go for that in a million years!"). But even clarity of mission and criteria does not readily resolve all the subjectivities and imponderables that go into deciding whether a particular proposal is worth the investment. At this point, competent staff can be of inestimable value: to make site visits where applicants can be seen and judged on their own turf (far superior, when such visits can be managed, to stilted conversations in the foundation's office); to check out the results of proposals that have been tried before; to solicit the judgments of knowledgeable people; to work through the details of budgets, tables, backgrounds of project personnel—all the steps that, if not attended to, can turn a promising grant into a disaster.

Trustees may or may not participate in this early stage of the judgmental process. If there is no staff, of course, they must, and some have become not only expert but ingenious in handling these exploratory details. One family foundation will not consider a proposal until it has been fully scouted by one of the family trustees, who then as its advocate must defend the project and his or her judgment of it at a board meeting.

Even where there are staff, some foundations encourage trustees (and obviously, there are some trustees who need no encouragement) to join in site visits and in other ways to assist directly in preselection activities. Often in family foundations, their trustees tend to want a more intimate involve-

ment. One such foundation, with assets in the tens of millions of dollars and a highly professional staff, regards close involvement as a distinguishing mark of trustee responsibility. It holds two meetings rather than one during a given round of grant making. At the first, screening session, staff members present a large assortment of proposals, which are then put to a vote of descending preference; those that survive are presented for final decision at a second meeting a month later.

Not all foundations—certainly not the very large ones—can impose that kind of a work load on trustees or sustain the dedication and give-and-take such a process requires. The far more common practice is for the staff to do the preliminary screening and then present a docket of proposals to the full board. What happens then also varies. Some foundations expect that management's judgment will prevail; trustee rejection of any substantial number of proposals over time is taken as a signal for a significant change in direction or a CEO resignation. In other very large foundations trustees insist on choice and indulge—sometimes collegially, sometimes not—in spirited debate. Simply to show the range, one large foundation schedules meetings on a single docket that go on regularly from early morning till midnight.

Most sizable foundations expedite the grant review and decision-making process by allowing the CEO to make discretionary grants of a specified smaller order, the usual limits being between $5,000 and $25,000. These grants, as well as proposals screened by staff, are usually scanned by trustees at a subsequent board meeting—a form of protective monitoring of policy and staff adherence.

Grant Processing and Evaluation. All sorts of minutiae are involved in grant processing, and none is insignificant enough to be dismissed. Given the conditions that foundations exact of grantees and that governments in turn exact of foundations, a lengthy paper trail of communications, audits, and reports keeps adding file cabinets, computers, and specialized personnel to philanthropic budgets.

Without discounting the importance of the managerial and record-keeping task, a more fundamental question for foundations concerns the evaluation of their own and their grantees' performance. How do they determine whether they are making a difference, doing as much good as they are intended to do, accomplishing the objectives they have set for themselves?

The first step is to evaluate individual grants. Until the 1969 Tax Reform Act persuaded them otherwise, foundations were only glancingly engaged with this issue. Their judgments were made more or less informally (more explicitly, in cases of grant renewal), and they tended to keep their distance from grants, once they were made. But since 1969, evaluation has become a preoccupation, and more and more foundations are requiring applicants to state in advance how they intend to assess their own performance. Foundations themselves too may conduct or commission evaluations selectively and often by highly sophisticated methods. The thorny question in all these assessments is whether any device, no matter how quantitative or methodical, can capture all the subtle indicators of failure or success, and over what period of time. But though the process has many elements of the search for the Holy Grail, there is no question that engaging in the search introduces a healthy discipline into both the donor and the applicant communities and, what is more, that it has been made imperative by the growing need to make the most of scarce philanthropic resources.

The broader quest—determining the overall effectiveness of a foundation's activity over time—is equally necessary, problematic, and healthy. It is most productive when staff and especially trustees spend considerable time listening to outside observers who are capable of taking the long view and judging particulars in context. Rarely do categorical answers emerge from technical analyses, although these are essential in arriving at defensible conclusions. But in the swirling environment that foundations live and struggle with, judgment and convictions are in the end inescapable. (See chapter 9 for a further discussion of assessment among nonprofits.)

Relating with Applicants, Grantees, and the Public. The most trenchant and persistent criticism of foundations has been directed at their alleged aloofness, inaccessibility, and closed circuits of communication. Examples are not hard to come by as one scans the behavior of many individual foundations, the writings even of friends of philanthropy, the successive reports of independent commissions, and not least the spotty record of public reporting by foundations, even when legally required.[15]

Although it is hard to assess the progress of foundations in responding to this criticism, it is clear that the environment in which they now operate is far more insistent on open and forthcoming behavior. The 1969 Tax Reform Act lit a fire under foundations with its more stringent requirements for filing and making publicly available annual accounts of grants, finances, and other data. The Filer Commission added its strong exhortation and, by giving the Donee Group a chance to be heard, touched off a movement that led to the establishment of the National Committee for Responsive Philanthropy, with its continuing scrutiny of foundation behavior.[16] The Council on Foundations has exerted its influence, making openness, accessibility, and full reporting key elements of its "Principles and Practices" as well as of its conference agendas and its professional development program.[17] Undergirding all this is the growing public insistence

that institutions claiming a role in public life deal openly and equitably with every segment of the community.

Matters are still far from ideal, but there are solid indications that foundations are becoming more responsive. Thanks to more widespread reporting and to the Foundation Center, regional grant-making associations, and an expanding number of scholars and activists doing research on philanthropy, both grant seekers and the public have available much more information on foundations and how to approach them. "Technical assistance" is becoming a standard item in the foundation repertoire, whereby they share know-how as well as money with nonprofit agencies, including help in formulating programs and preparing grant proposals. A few foundations, such as the Boston, Bush, and Mary Reynolds Babcock foundations, have experimented successfully with public meetings, analogous to those required of American corporations. Not least, foundations have become more agile, congenial, and collaborative in their relations with governmental bodies, including Congress. The benefits were evident in the cordiality of the 1983 hearings of the House Ways and Means Committee—in vivid contrast to the chill of 1969.[18]

Diversity in Foundation Culture

Diversity is also inherent in the culture of American philanthropy. Foundations were not legislated into existence as a class; each was created in its own mold, has its own history, prides itself on its own individuality, has developed its own sense of mission, and almost instinctively sets itself apart. The goal of a foundation is to do what is unique and will be seen to be unique. In recent years, this surge toward diversity has been at once tempered and intensified. Two contrary forces have been at work.

On the one hand, congressional criticism in the late 1960s showed foundations how unprepared they were to defend themselves in a single voice. They were part of a profession that had failed to monitor its own performance or to cure its own ills. A drive toward a common defense, a shared identity, collaboration, and professionalism ensued—witness the work of the Filer Commission, the creation of regional associations of grant makers, and the stepped-up efforts of the Council on Foundations to raise standards.[19] Cutbacks in

15. Reports by the Commission on Private Philanthropy and Public Needs (1975, 1977) and the Commission on Foundations and Private Philanthropy (1970) and books by Cuninggim (1972) and Heimann (1973) offer criticism of certain foundation practices. A more critical perspective can be found in Nielsen (1972, 1985), the National Committee for Responsive Philanthropy (1980) and the Donee Group (1977).

16. In the course of its deliberations the Filer Commission invited testimony from a group of concerned nonprofit organizations, largely representing minorities and advocacy institutions. This group organized more formally and wrote its own report, which was included in the Filer Commission's *Research Papers*. Later the group established the National Committee for Responsive Philanthropy with offices in Washington, D. C.

17. Two examples are Unkle and Ylvisaker (1984), a self-assessment tool for foundation boards, and the five-day Institute for New Staff,

a biennial workshop offering both practical as well as philosophical sessions for newcomers to the field.

18. In June 1985, the Subcommittee on Oversight of the House Ways and Means Committee met to determine whether current rules enacted in 1969 ensured that only private foundations operating for the public benefit were enjoying favorable tax treatment. Although critics raised several issues of concern, a number of grantee organizations testified to express their support for foundations, and the overall atmosphere was thought to be both positive and fair. See U.S. House of Representatives (1983) for the committee's report and recommendations.

19. Regional associations are local, statewide, or regional networks of grant makers (and in some cases, grantees) that were created for the most part after the 1969 Tax Reform Act. Reacting to the hostility evident at these hearings, foundations joined together, vowing never to be caught in the same situation. The associations' purposes include

governmental programs and the pressure on philanthropy to fill the resultant gap in social expenditures also promoted more extensive collaboration among foundations as a logical way of maximizing scarce resources.[20]

But a splintering movement is also at work, reflecting the ascendancy of political conservatism in American society and the assertiveness of conservative philanthropy.[21] New foundations have sprung up, and some older ones newly encouraged, to counter the alleged dominance of liberal thought, especially among the staffs of the more prominent foundations. Although there is a certain irony in the fact that those now called liberal have more often than not been castigated in the past for being too conservative, it is clear that the political and philosophical diversity of American foundations is being intensified—or at the very least, more bluntly articulated.

Diversity in Grant Making

Diversity is reflected—but even more submerged—in the patterns of aggregated grant making over time. The nation's 23,600 foundations make hundreds of thousands of individual grants each year; taken one by one, their variety is overwhelming. Every cause, every constituency, every discipline, every point on the philosophical continuum somehow finds a niche no matter how tiny in the dispensation of foundation monies. Much of this variety is a function simply of the idiosyncratic interests of donors, which range from bird feeding to world hunger, from neighborhood parks to

---

increasing communication and sharing of information among members, educating the public about the role of foundations, and representing grant makers' interests and concerns with public officials. Foote (1982) offers a historical perspective and highlights the activities of individual regional associations. The Council on Foundations' communications assistance service is designed to assist grant makers in handling questions from the press. It is also designed to encourage and provide technical assistance for foundations that are publishing an annual report for the first time or that need advice on a communications question.

20. Northern California Grantmakers (1985) offers an excellent description of the efforts and lessons learned by grant makers in the northern California area.

21. Nielsen (1985, pp. 37–58) explores the rise of conservatism in the last thirty years and analyzes the role played by foundations and corporate givers. He looks at the movement's origins, leaders, and financial supporters and their emphasis on public policy research as a means for affecting change in society. The *Washington Post* (January 4, 1981) charted what it called the "conservative network"—a mapping of over one hundred donors, research institutes, journals, and special-purpose organizations. Listed donors included the John M. Olin Foundation, Fred C. Koch Foundation, Bechtel Foundation, Adolph Coors Foundation, Smith Richardson Foundation, Sarah Mellon Scaife Foundation, J. Howard Pew Freedom Trust, Lilly Endowment, Samuel Noble Foundation, and a score of corporations. The same newspaper (December 25, 1984) more recently canvassed the activities of some of the "alternative foundations" that "support social change and . . . spurn usual philanthropies"—that is, the liberal end of the donor continuum, such as the Haymarket People's Fund, Vanguard Foundation, and Funding Exchange. What is intriguing about these alternative funds is that their leading figures are from families of great wealth and corporate antecedents.

global pollution, from juvenile delinquency to schistosomiasis. As the public becomes more aware of these waiting resources, and as data and technical assistance become more accessible to the nation's increasingly needy and aggressive applicants, it is likely that the range of philanthropic interests will expand.

Much of this diversity lies obscured within the published aggregates of foundation grants as traditionally classified. A high proportion of foundation support monies may go to "higher education" or "welfare"; but these simple labels do not reveal the variegated and often contradictory nature of the grants they include. One foundation may fund dissident elements challenging the academic and welfare establishments, whereas another may simultaneously finance a self-congratulatory study by the professional elite; both grants will be classified and reported under the same label. Trends are similarly obscured: at the very peak of philanthropic concentration on certain fields of interest or modes of activity, venturesome foundations will almost certainly be incubating new ideas, testing moves in contrary directions.

Attempts to categorize foundation interests—and by categorizing to detect general characteristics and trends—are also plagued by the paucity and incomparability of data. Recent efforts by a variety of researchers and analysts—notably the Foundation Center, the Council on Foundations, the Independent Sector, and the Yale Program on Non-Profit Organizations—have made substantial dents in the problem. But the failure of many foundations to report, the differing schemes of grant classification, the incomparability of data over time, and the almost insuperable difficulty of capturing the dynamics of foundation grant making (philosophy, motivation, changes of mind and mission, and one-time megagrants) all conspire against precision in communicating the past, present, and emerging interests of American foundations.

Nevertheless, something can be learned in the attempt. Presented below are two sets of data that—though far from being either comparable or complete in their coverage—provide a rough profile of philanthropic interests over the past thirty years.

PATTERNS OF GRANT MAKING: A THIRTY-YEAR PERSPECTIVE

The first set of data (tables 20.1–20.4) draws on a hitherto unpublished study by Karla J. Shepard with support from the Twentieth Century Fund. Several years ago, noting the inadequacy of available information on foundation giving, Shepard and her associates made a path-breaking effort to create a systematic, uniform, longitudinal data base covering the programs of the nation's largest (noncorporate) private foundations. The resulting information is especially valuable because (1) *all* grants, rather than just those over $5,000, as in other published series, were included; (2) a consistent and highly sophisticated classification was used, which had been developed with the aid of an expert advisory group; (3) grants were given multiple classifications reflecting the several cat-

TABLE 20.1 FIELDS OF INTEREST, 1955–79

Fields of Interest	1955	1960	1965	1970	1975	1979
Arts, culture, humanities, religion						
# %[a]	21.2	24.7	24.2	22.8	27.5	27.8
$ %[a]	9.5	13.9	15.2	17.4	18.5	20.5
Health, medical						
# %	20.8	17.3	19.6	17.4	15.7	16.8
$ %	17.4	16.4	13.4	24.2	30.2	27.4
Social, community services						
# %	19.7	14.1	17.3	16.8	17.3	21.8
$ %	5.8	4.1	3.9	7.0	9.4	13.9
Types of education						
# %	18.3	27.6	26.8	29.6	27.3	22.0
$ %	45.0	47.9	53.9	33.6	28.6	29.4
Educational issues						
# %	1.3	4.1	3.8	3.4	4.2	3.8
$ %	3.9	4.4	5.4	4.8	4.8	3.1
Social sciences						
# %	8.5	8.0	5.5	6.1	6.0	4.3
$ %	13.4	9.5	6.6	6.5	5.5	4.6
Physical, natural sciences						
# %	12.2	11.8	8.9	6.7	5.3	4.6
$ %	5.3	12.9	10.0	7.8	5.8	5.9
Public issues of community and society						
# %	16.0	19.7	18.7	24.4	25.2	25.9
$ %	30.0	28.9	30.3	34.0	26.3	25.5

Source: Shepard/Twentieth Century Fund, *47 Independent Foundations with over $100 Million in Assets.*
a. # % = percent of total number of grants; $ % = percent of total dollars granted.

TABLE 20.2 INTENDED BENEFICIARY, 1955–79

Intended Beneficiary	1955	1960	1965	1970	1975	1979
Age Group						
0–18						
# %[a]	14.5	16.2	19.1	20.8	19.1	19.1
$ %[a]	6.5	7.8	9.8	7.9	11.4	10.5
Young adults						
# %	16.3	24.3	22.8	22.8	19.4	15.6
$ %	42.8	39.2	49.2	27.7	24.6	27.1
Elderly						
# %	1.0	.8	1.1	.4	1.4	2.2
$ %	.5	.6	1.2	.3	1.0	1.9
Ethnic Groups						
Blacks						
# %	1.7	1.7	2.8	5.4	2.0	1.7
$ %	.7	.6	3.4	5.0	3.0	1.8
Hispanics						
# %	.1	.2	.1	.6	.8	1.4
$ %	—	.1	—	.5	1.5	1.8
Native Americans						
# %	.3	.2	.2	.7	.8	.7
$ %	—	—	—	.3	.1	.5
Other Targeted Groups						
The poor						
# %	2.0	1.6	2.6	3.4	3.1	1.7
$ %	.4	.7	2.7	2.4	1.6	1.6
Refugees, immigrants						
# %	.7	.2	.2	.2	.1	.3
$ %	.2	—	—	—	—	.2

Source: Shepard/Twentieth Century Fund, *47 Independent Foundations*
a. # % = percent of total number of grants; $ % = percent of total dollars granted.

TABLE 20.3 RECIPIENT INSTITUTIONS, 1955–79

Auspices	1955	1960	1965	1970	1975	1979
Public						
# %[a]	14.4	18.8	14.8	15.3	14.5	13.7
$ %[a]	16.9	23.6	20.5	15.0	13.8	15.2
Private-Profit						
# %	.2	.1	.2	.4	.1	.3
$ %	.1	—	.1	.6	—	.1
Private-Nonprofit						
# %	57.0	55.9	60.8	64.8	61.8	66.7
$ %	75.2	66.1	69.6	76.3	72.8	71.1
Sectarian						
# %	13.1	13.4	13.8	11.4	17.5	14.6
$ %	4.1	6.3	7.3	5.6	10.1	10.8
Individual						
# %	14.9	11.4	10.2	8.0	5.9	4.6
$ %	3.6	3.9	2.5	2.5	2.6	2.8
Type of Institution (Example: Education)						
Preschool through 12						
# %	2.1	1.8	2.7	3.5	2.4	2.6
$ %	.9	.7	.9	1.3	.7	1.3
Community colleges						
# %	.1	.2	.4	.6	.4	.4
$ %	—	—	.4	.5	.3	.3
Colleges, universities						
# %	26.6	36.3	30.8	31.4	29.1	25.5
$ %	40.0	55.3	57.7	39.3	35.8	38.6
Citizen, public interest						
# %	6.4	5.2	7.4	8.6	10.4	10.9
$ %	4.3	2.9	6.1	7.1	6.8	7.5

Source: Shepard/Twentieth Century Fund, *47 Independent Foundations*
a. # % = percent of total number of grants; $ % = percent of total dollars granted.

egories they often simultaneously touched upon, yielding a much more faithful and versatile portrait of foundation interests (thus a grant for a neighborhood multiservice center might simultaneously be tallied under health, welfare, and community development); and (4) a longer time period was covered than by other series of comparable sophistication. The data base unfortunately reports grants only through 1979.

Tables 20.1–20.4 have been aggregated from those data. They represent the total giving of 47 independent foundations at five-year intervals from 1955 to 1979, each of which in at least one of those selected years reported assets of over $100 million. These foundations had total holdings of $15 billion in 1979, about 35 percent of all foundation assets and 45 percent of the assets of independent foundations listed in the *Directory.* The number of their grants was only a tiny proportion of all foundation grants, but accounted for 25 percent of total dollars given by all foundations and nearly 40 percent of total dollars granted by independent foundations.[22]

Juxtaposed to the Shepard/Twentieth Century Fund time series is a second set of tables (20.5–20.8) drawn from data gathered by the Foundation Center and published in both the

Grants Index and the *Directory.*[23] The two sets are *not* comparable: the *Grants Index* covers only those grants of $5,000 or more awarded by the 100 largest foundations, together with another 350 foundations (including corporate and community foundations) that voluntarily report their grants directly to the Foundation Center; grants, although coded in multiple categories (by field of interest, geography, and so on), are not given multiple classification within fields of interest as in the Shepard/Twentieth Century Fund breakdown; categories are by no means identical; and different people, with differing criteria and subjective judgments, have done the coding and classifying. This data set is also skewed in its sampling, being very sensitive to large grants and changes in program direction on the part of the giant foundations.

Although not amenable, then, to precise analysis and conclusions, the juxtaposed data sets, when approached with caution, can provide a historical sweep of large-foundation activity that provokes some general observations. A few will be ventured here.[24]

23. The 465 foundations included in the Foundation Center's (1984) sample, accounted for 45 percent of all foundation giving. Seventy-four percent of total grants given by these 465 foundations came from the 101 largest.

24. By far, not all the breakdowns available in the Shepard/Twentieth Century Fund and Foundation Center data series are covered by the tables and analysis in this section. Readers interested in further explora-

22. The Ford Foundation alone accounted for 16 percent of all grants and 36 percent of total dollars among the foundations in these tabulations.

TABLE 20.4   GEOGRAPHIC LOCATION, 1955–79

Recipients	1955	1960	1965	1970	1975	1979
Domestic						
# %[a]	88.0	87.1	90.2	93.1	89.5	91.4
$ %[a]	85.2	84.5	87.3	92.4	93.6	94.3
Northeast						
# %	31.9	28.4	30.2	29.3	21.3	21.2
$ %	34.6	32.4	36.6	40.6	23.2	24.3
Mid-Atlantic						
# %	10.9	12.6	14.7	16.0	18.8	16.3
$ %	9.7	11.0	9.7	13.2	22.7	18.7
Southeast						
# %	7.0	7.0	6.6	8.1	7.5	7.8
$ %	6.7	7.5	9.5	9.7	11.4	12.1
Midwest						
# %	15.4	17.7	15.5	16.5	18.7	17.7
$ %	27.8	12.4	13.9	12.7	21.6	15.9
Northwest						
# %	.6	1.0	.8	.8	1.4	2.8
$ %	.5	.4	.6	.7	1.4	1.8
Central						
# %	4.5	4.8	3.1	3.5	2.9	3.2
$ %	2.5	2.3	6.3	4.7	2.3	3.2
West and Southwest						
# %	17.5	15.4	19.0	18.7	19.0	22.4
$ %	3.4	18.4	10.6	10.5	10.8	17.9
Noncontinental						
# %	.3	.2	.3	.2	.5	.4
$ %	—	.2	.2	.1	.2	.5
Foreign						
# %	11.7	12.3	9.4	6.8	10.5	8.6
$ %	14.8	15.3	12.7	7.6	6.3	5.6
Western Europe						
# %	3.6	3.3	1.9	1.7	1.8	1.7
$ %	2.5	2.4	2.2	1.6	.9	.9
All Others						
# %	8.0	9.0	7.5	5.0	8.7	6.9
$ %	12.3	12.9	10.4	6.0	5.4	1.7

Source: Shepard/Twentieth Century Fund, *47 Independent Foundations*
a. # % = percent of total number of grants; $ % = percent of total dollars granted.

1. By far the bulk of foundation grants have gone to domestic institutions engaged in education, health, and, to a lesser extent, cultural activities; the largest single share has gone to educational organizations and activities.

2. Over time, education's share has steadily diminished; welfare's share has increased (markedly, in recent response to governmental cutbacks, increasing social hardship, and the rising percentage of philanthropic activity directed to localized social services); health's share seems to have peaked in the 1970s and then gently declined; and culture's share oscillated, rising in the 1970s and holding more nearly constant in very recent years.

3. Shares going to the physical and social sciences fell steadily until the late 1970s but seem again to be on the rise, particularly in the grants of the larger foundations.

4. Concern with public issues has greatly increased, as expressed in the growing number of grants since the late 1960s.

5. Special groups in the American population—minorities, refugees, immigrants, children, women, and the elderly—have consistently been the beneficiaries of very small shares of foundation giving, these modest shares seeming to rise and fall with demographic changes, cycles of public awareness, and perceived constituency strength.

6. Colleges and universities have long been the major instruments and beneficiaries of foundation giving, though their share of total funding has abruptly declined in recent years. Table 20.9 documents the still heavy reliance on colleges and universities as foundation instrumentalities and recipients.

7. Schools have received a surprisingly small fraction of foundation monies, the pattern indicating scant attention during the very years in which the nation's educational "crisis" was developing and breaking.

tion will find a great number of revealing characteristics of foundation giving. To cite a few from the Shepard series: general purpose/unrestricted grants decreased from 40 percent in 1955 to 15 percent in 1979; recipient institutions that are local in scope have been increasing, accounting in 1979 for half of all grantees; and renewal grants decreased dramatically between 1955 and 1979, with most grants going to new recipients.

TABLE 20.5 FIELDS OF INTEREST, 1980–83[a]

Fields of Interest	1980 All Reporting Foundations	1981 All Reporting Foundations	1982 101 Largest Foundations	1982 343 Other Foundations	1983 101 Largest Foundations	1983 364 Other Foundations	1984 100 Largest Foundations	1984 360 Other Foundations
Cultural								
# %[b]	15.2	17.4	14.8	18.1	15.2	16.9	15.1	17.6
$ %[b]	13.5	15.3	13.8	14.6	15.0	16.9	13.0	16.3
Religion								
# %	3.3	1.8	2.5	1.8	2.0	2.1	2.2	2.6
$ %	2.4	2.0	2.1	1.2	1.8	2.9	2.2	2.5
Health								
# %	16.2	16.7	16.3	17.7	15.3	18.1	16.0	18.9
$ %	25.1	22.5	21.6	19.1	21.1	23.5	23.8	23.6
Welfare								
# %	31.6	32.4	31.5	35.2	32.9	35.4	30.9	35.0
$ %	24.5	26.2	25.6	27.0	28.0	29.7	26.5	30.3
Education								
# %	21.9	20.2	20.5	17.2	18.8	17.0	19.8	15.8
$ %	22.4	21.1	22.2	28.0	15.8	16.3	18.3	14.9
Social sciences								
# %	5.5	5.8	7.5	4.9	7.8	6.0	7.6	6.2
$ %	5.7	6.0	7.7	5.0	7.9	6.0	7.7	7.6
Sciences								
# %	6.3	5.7	6.9	5.1	8.0	4.5	8.4	3.9
$ %	6.4	6.9	7.0	5.1	10.4	4.7	8.5	8.4

Source: Foundation Center Grants Index: 400+ Foundations[c]
a. "Years" indicate when compiled by Foundation Center. Grants actually made in preceding year.
b. # % = percent of total number of grants; $ % = percent of total dollars granted.
c. For all years, these include the 101 largest foundations. The remainder are sampled foundations which provided complete listings of grants over $5,000. The numbers indicated in 1982 and 1983 (444 and 465) represent an increase of about 207 over 1980 and 1981.

8. Grants abroad have declined over the thirty-year period as a share of foundation giving; they have been cut roughly in half. Well over 95 percent of foundation funds currently go to domestic recipients.

9. Regional disparities within the United States have marginally lessened, the most noticeable change being a

TABLE 20.6 INTENDED BENEFICIARY

Beneficiary	1980	1981	1982	1983	1984
Children and youth					
$ %[a]	7.3	9.8	8.9	10.1	10.8
Aged					
$ %	2.0	1.4	2.1	2.2	3.3
Women and girls					
$ %	1.7	2.9	2.5	2.8	3.6
Men and boys					
$ %		1.0	0.9	1.3	1.0
Minorities					
Blacks					
$ %	1.9	2.8	2.2	2.6	3.0
Hispanics					
$ %	.6	.8	1.0	1.0	1.0
Native Americans					
$ %	.4	.4	.3	.3	.4
Asian-Americans					
$ %		.1	.1	.1	.2
General minorities					
$ %	1.9	1.9	2.3	1.6	1.7

Source: Foundation Center Grants Index: 400+ Foundations
a. $ % = percent of total dollars granted.

trend toward equalization between the Northeast and West-Southwest.

10. The share going to individuals has steadily declined, markedly so after the 1969 Tax Reform Act with its more burdensome requirements on grants made to individuals.

11. Viewed in the aggregate, foundations do not emerge as a force out in front of—certainly not at odds with—American society and its other institutions. Foundation interests lag as much as they lead. The pattern of governmental expenditures (witness the attention to minorities and the poor in the 1960s and the rapid adjustment to the new conservatism thereafter) appears to be at least as sensitive to social change as that of philanthropy—again, viewed in the aggregate.

The special quality and contribution of philanthropy cannot be deduced from quantitative measures of its collective behavior. Rather, it lies in the statistical certainty that in the midst of aggregate stability (conservatism?), individual foundations (not always the same) will be restlessly prowling every social and scientific frontier, nudging society along with as yet untested ideas.

FOUNDATION INFLUENCE: THE ART OF SELECTING AND LEVERAGING

Tiny though they are against the larger canvas of American society, foundations have managed to exert a significant

TABLE 20.7   RECIPIENT INSTITUTIONS

Institutions	1980	1981	1982	1983 101 Largest	1983 364 Other	1984 100 Largest	1984 360 Other
Government agencies							
# %[a]	1.8	2.3	2.5	2.7	2.4	2.8	2.8
$ %[a]	2.7	2.9	3.2	2.5	2.7	3.3	2.9
Churches and temples							
# %	1.3	1.3	1.2	1.8	1.6	2.0	2.4
$ %	.8	.8	1.7	1.1	2.0	1.2	1.9
Educational institutions							
All types							
# %	31.2	31.2	30.6	32.2	26.3	32.3	25.4
$ %	38.4	41.0	42.5	35.0	30.9	36.8	30.8
Schools							
# %	4.5	5.2	5.4	3.1	5.9	2.7	5.8
$ %	2.4	4.2	4.9	2.1	5.4	2.2	4.4
Two-year colleges							
# %	.3	.3	.3	.3	.4	.7	.4
$ %	.2	.3	.3	.5	.5	.5	.3
Public universities and colleges							
# %	(not separately	6.5	6.4	8.4	4.9	9.4	5.0
$ %	tabulated)	7.0	8.5	6.2	5.4	9.6	5.6
Private universities and colleges							
# %	23.0	15.2	14.4	15.7	12.0	14.6	9.8
$ %	29.6	22.2	23.1	19.2	14.4	18.3	13.5
Graduate schools							
# %	3.4	4.0	4.1	4.6	3.0	4.9	4.4
$ %	6.2	7.3	5.7	7.2	5.2	6.2	7.0

Source: Foundation Center Grants Index: 400+ Foundations
a. # % = percent of total number of grants; $ % = percent of total dollars granted.

influence (not always benign) on the nation's private and public affairs. Partly, but only partly, this is due to the simple fact of their having what everyone in society would like a piece of: money and the power that goes with it. That power is magnified when it comes trailing the explicit or silent

TABLE 20.8   GEOGRAPHIC LOCATION, 1983 BREAKDOWN OF 32,165 INDIVIDUAL GRANTS

	# %	$ %
Foreign Recipients[a]	2.6	2.9
International-Domestic Recipients	3.1	4.1
Domestic Recipients	94.3	93.0
Northeast[b]	24.0	25.0
Mid-Atlantic	17.0	11.0
Southeast	9.0	10.0
Midwest	17.0	18.0
Northwest	3.0	2.0
Central	4.0	3.0
West and Southwest	20.0	21.0
Noncontinental	1.0	3.0

Source: Foundation Center Grants Index: 471 Foundations
a. # % = percent of total number of grants; $ % = percent of total dollars granted.
b. Regional aggregates comparable to Twentieth Century Fund breakdown (cf. table 20.4).

influence of the corporate and cultural elite in whose name the money has been given. One has only to browse through the histories of the Rockefeller and other great-fortune philanthropies to appreciate the web of influence they have spun.

But there are other reasons, and substantial ones, why foundations have become influential. These reasons go directly to the generic role and art of philanthropy: its ability to choose, concentrate, and leverage.

Where philanthropic resources have concentrated, however, is not entirely a matter of choice: strictures of the tax code, not solely the altruistic instincts of philanthropy, have limited the activity of foundations overwhelmingly to the world of the nonprofits (though with a significant rise in recent grant making to government agencies). Within that more concentrated universe, foundations have further focused predominantly on nonprofit service providers. In that smaller terrain of some 125,000 agencies with total annual budgets running at about $130 billion, foundations are still vastly outnumbered and outspent.

Clearly, the quantitative contribution of foundations even to this limited segment of the nonprofit sector is minimal. Further evidence: a sample survey by the Urban Institute indicates 1981 revenue sources of this segment as follows: private giving by corporations/foundations, 6 percent, and by individuals, 14 percent; investment income, 5 percent; service charges, 28 percent; government, 41 percent; and other, 6 percent (Salamon 1984). Still another indicator:

religious giving for the charitable provision of social services has recently been estimated by the Council on Foundations at $7.5 billion to $8.5 billion annually;[25] foundation grants flowing to sectarian service institutions (Shepard/Twentieth Century Fund tabulations cited above) historically have amounted to no more than 5 to 10 percent of foundation total giving and only 2 percent of all religious contributions.

These are minimal shares. Nevertheless, foundations can and do have a significant and sometimes determining influence on nonprofits—and ultimately on the larger society these institutions are so vitally engaged with. Among the ways they can and cannot exert such influence are the following:

1. *Foundations can expand and influence the choice not only of goals but also of the means of implementing them.*

Nonprofit agencies are constantly constrained by limited budgets and by such forces as constituency pressures, obdurate circumstances, and the stubbornness of past orthodoxies. Foundations can and sometimes do offer an alternative and liberating source of money, ideas, and legitimacy, which allow nonprofits, and through them, the public, to entertain options not otherwise available.

In doing so, they help create and maintain a system that opens four main avenues for social action rather than the single choice of government alone. The first option is simply that: to work exclusively through government, initially securing the passage of laws and appropriations and then turning to the executive/administrative branch for implementation. A second is to win the approval of a private funding source and then to get the job done through a nongovernmental agency. The other two are hybrids of these: public funding and private instrumentation, and private funding and public administration.

Foundations play a significant role in making all four of these choices available. Though barred from lobbying, they can stimulate governmental action through the research, education, experimentation, conferencing, and publications they finance. Second, they can independently initiate and fund programs that are then governmentally administered. Third, they become partners of legislatures, jointly authorizing and paying for services provided by nongovernmental organizations. Fourth, they can—and mostly do—turn directly to nonprofit agencies to implement what they have chosen to finance.

2. *Foundations cannot do much in the way of general support.*

Total foundation giving is around $4.8 billion annually, as against the $130 billion budgeted by nonprofit charitable service agencies alone. The inability of foundations to bankroll those budgets was made painfully obvious with the Reagan cutbacks, which trimmed the federal contributions to those same nonprofit agencies by more than 20 percent (1984 versus 1980, not including Medicaid and Medicare pay-

25. See Reckard and McDonald (1985). A summary of the project was done by McDonald (1984).

ments). It would have taken all foundation income and a good deal more simply to make up that deficit. In no way could foundations have come more than selectively to the rescue.

3. *Foundations can—and necessarily do—maximize their influence by being selective.* That imperative is observed in many ways:

a. By selecting fields of concentration where particular foundations perceive the greatest social need and/or promise of payoff. Thus the Robert Wood Johnson Foundation has chosen health; the Spencer Foundation, educational research; the Kresge Foundation, the provision and rehabilitation of physical facilities; and so on.

b. By selecting ideas and approaches that by their currency, inherent force, and challenging or innovative nature have the power to move people and institutions.

c. By selecting points of leverage that convert small inputs into the greater energy needed to redirect larger forces.

d. By selecting people and institutions of unusual capacity and/or social influence, to set the pace and standards for others.

e. By selecting for survival (through triage) those critical people, ideas, programs, and institutions threatened by generally diminishing resources and/or public support.

4. *Foundations can serve as a countervailing force to governmental and other private influences:*

a. By counterbalancing patterns of resource allocation. If government is concentrating on or neglecting one set of social concerns and corporate and individual givers another, foundations can shift in contrary directions and attend to other constituencies.

b. By providing complementary support that helps nonprofit agencies fend off or cure distortions of their priorities, terms of reference, or operating modes caused by overdependence on other funding sources.

c. By offsetting or neutralizing the political and special interests that often accompany governmental, corporate, and personal giving.

d. By taking a longer and broader view than other funding sources can or will adopt.

5. *Foundations can enhance their influence through collaboration* with other funding sources. Notable examples are the joint creation by national and community foundations of arts stabilization and community development funds—at scales no one foundation could or would likely venture.

6. *Foundations in the nature of things cannot act as a monolithic force.* Given their penchant for differentiation and autonomy and their philosophical and chartered diversity, the probability that all foundations will simultaneously exert influence in a single direction is zero.

7. *Foundations can, however, set trends, and sometimes fads, and otherwise dominate patterns in social spending and action simply by the power of their initiative* and their ability to command public attention.

8. *Foundations can magnify their influence by seizing the*

TABLE 20.9   THE TOP 25 RECIPIENTS OF GRANTS FROM FOUNDATIONS WITH ASSETS OF $100 MILLION OR MORE

Recipient	Grants Amount[a] (millions)	Number of Grants[b]
University of California	$12	71
Harvard University	10	60
Columbia University	7	47
Boy Scouts of America	2	42
Yale University	6	39
Council on Foundations	2	39
University of Pennsylvania	11	36
Stanford University	5	35
University of Chicago	3	31
Case Western Reserve University	3	31
Johns Hopkins University	4	30
Massachusetts Institute of Technology	3	29
University of Texas	2	29
University of Michigan	5	28
Cornell University	2	25
New York University	3	23
National Academy of Sciences	5	22
Northwestern University	3	22
University of Washington	2	20
Cleveland State University	.9	20
Princeton University	3	19
University of Pittsburgh	.9	19
Urban Institute	3	18
American Red Cross	1	18
Vanderbilt University	1	17
University of Minnesota	1	17

a. Only two nonacademic institutions received more than the University of California, and both were beneficiaries of large one-time contributions. When ranked by "most money received," 13 of the top 25 recipients were institutions of higher education, eight of them represented in table 20.9 (California, Harvard, Columbia, Yale, Pennsylvania, Stanford, Johns Hopkins, and Michigan).

b. *Foundation Grants Index,* 13th ed. (Reporting Year 1983), includes only grants of $5,000 or more. From a special computer run done by the Foundation Center for the author.

initiative: by giving challenge and matching grants; by being the first to spot a trend or emerging social problem; by acting when all others are inert or stymied.

9. *Foundations can extend their influence* through commissioned studies and (increasingly) through the device of leadership statements in annual reports, professional conferences, and grant announcements.

10. *Foundations can bring to social action a distinctive spirit and motivation* supportive of the charitable instinct historically associated with nonprofit institutions and the tradition of voluntarism. Unfortunately, they can also violate this instinct through actions motivated by purposes other than altruism.

These are the potentials of foundations as they seek, against the numerical odds, to be a leavening influence within the nonprofit community and in society at large. And what of the record?

The simple fact that philanthropic practice has generated such an abundant repertoire of leveraging strategies is evidence enough of the important role foundations have played in the life, vitality, and effectiveness of America's voluntary sector. Behind every strategy there is a storehouse of accumulating experience and vivid examples too bulging to inventory here. Similarly persuasive is the net judgment of the nation's elected representatives that foundations have earned their place as a respected institution and creative social force.

Admittedly, there are disparities between potential and performance. *In the aggregate,* foundation giving has favored the *more established* agencies, *conventional* fields of interest and modes of operation, and *more advantaged* constituencies (see table 20.9). Foundations collectively have not responded with great agility or countervailing force to shifting public needs and patterns of financial support. Nor has the *net* activity of foundations over time served significantly to reduce disparities between rich and poor, majorities and minorities—as one might expect of philanthropy, given its original conception. But given also the massiveness of modern society and the resistant forces at work, all that may be too much to expect of foundations whose resources are so comparatively tiny.

THE ROLE OF FOUNDATIONS IN AMERICAN SOCIETY

Foundations were first given legal definition in the English Statute of Charitable Uses in 1601. As charitable trusts and instruments of localized giving, they were a familiar part of the American scene even in colonial times. But it was not until the turn of the twentieth century that they became of substantial size and prominence, and not until after World War II that their numbers and scale of activity caused them to be seriously considered as an important social institution. It is worth remembering that roughly three out of four of America's larger foundations (*Directory*-size) did not exist prior to 1950.[26]

It has taken Americans—and, for that matter, grant makers themselves—some time to get a sense of what modern philanthropy is all about. It both is and is not the personal kind of charity that lingers on in the stereotype of the fortunate giving to the unfortunate. Many foundations, and much of what they give, are still in that tradition. But other concepts have flowed into the philanthropic mix and have given foundations some different and sometimes clashing colorations.

Much in the newer tradition stems from the rhetoric of Andrew Carnegie: amassing wealth carries with it the responsibility of helping improve the condition of society.

26. Following are the dates of establishment of *Directory*-size foundations (assets of $1 million or more or grants of $100,000 or more) according to the Foundation Center (1985, p. viii): Before 1900: 38; 1900–1909: 20; 1910–1919: 68; 1920–1929: 141; 1930–1939: 183; 1940–1949: 678; 1950–1959: 1,510; 1960–1969: 973; 1970–1979: 563; 1980–1984: 169; Data not available: 106; Total: 4,402.

Along with the rhetoric came some new realities: the scale of such wealth, which moved the potential of philanthropy onto an entirely new plane, and the corporate form of organization, which transformed personal into more professionalized and impersonal giving. Another molding factor emerged from the early Rockefeller philanthropies: the belief that a partnership between philanthropy and science could probe beneath the incidence of social ills to find and deal with their root causes.

By 1950, the opening of two decades of explosive foundation growth, these newer concepts of philanthropy were firmly in place; to speak of foundations was to speak first of all about Carnegie and Rockefeller. Planning for the Ford Foundation in that year started with those concepts and went a step beyond—explicitly designating "public affairs" as a major involvement of that soon to be dominant foundation.[27]

Other concepts of philanthropy had also been germinating. Cleveland a generation before had pioneered with the notion of a community foundation, an institution that would by its currency avoid "the dead hand of the past" and be more immediately responsive to public needs.[28] The model was quickly adopted in other metropolitan communities. More slowly, but just as surely, first the courts and then shareholders accepted the notion of corporate giving for social purposes.[29]

The foundation movement was ready for takeoff by 1950; lift was provided by a federal and state tax structure that made foundations an attractive shelter for the great personal and corporate affluence of the postwar period. That affluence also awakened two other philanthropic motivations: renewed guilt over the continued existence of misery amid plenty, and a burgeoning confidence that America's rapidly accumulating wealth, allocated privately as well as publicly, could solve the nation's social and other problems.

Foundations had periodically rubbed up against critical segments of the public; but when they proliferated and became a conspicuous factor in public affairs after 1950, they came under almost continuous attack. Most of the salvos were launched by particular persons and groups with particular vexations (Taft Republicans angered by the support given Eisenhower by liberal Republicans closely associated with the Ford and other foundations; Congressman Patman un-

forgiving of Huntington Hartford's A&P for driving his father out of the grocery business and ever-suspicious of the eastern financial establishment). The fact was that foundations had grown beyond public understanding, and they became easy targets not only for these focused attacks but for some wilder charges of being subversive—all the more confusing when knowledgeable critics simultaneously were charging American foundations with being too conservative.

The year 1969 marked the beginning of greater public sophistication about foundations, even though this chapter of their history was written in essentially negative terms. The sins of philanthropy were indeed exposed, but the important finding was that they did not include subversion. Even in the rather punitive legislation that followed, Congress accepted foundations as legitimate and useful instruments of a democratic society. So did American conservatives, who for a time had spend their energies trying to limit the influence of foundations but have since decided to use philanthropy aggressively for their own purposes.

Now in the mid-1980s, the place of foundations in American society seems generally accepted. The Filer Commission in the 1970s had helped in two ways: it provided a wealth of information and in the process greater public understanding of the work of foundations, and it forged a security link between foundations and the better-known world of churches and social service agencies, all henceforth to be banded together as America's third, or independent sector. Also, as discussed earlier, foundations after 1969—thanks in large part to the Tax Reform Act—behaved better and more openly, and the attitude of America's legislators turned from negative to positive.

This is not to argue that all confusion has been clarified, all apprehensions quieted, or the systemic role of foundations in contemporary society fully rationalized. The familiar rhetoric about foundations and their raison d'être ("change agents," "contributors to diversity," "incubators of new ideas," "social testing grounds," "society's passing gear," and so on) is liturgically comforting, but it supplies only fragments of an explanation of how foundations—in all their divergent forms and idiosyncrasies—fit into the structure and workings of society. That philanthropy has now become the focus of scholarly and political efforts to understand its niche is evidence enough of its arrival and acceptance.

The evolving political effort—understandably but ironically (given the heralded origins of philanthropy in altruism)—has been carried on predominantly within the confining arena of tax legislation. If one wants to read the "constitutional charter" of American foundations, most provisions will be found in the Internal Revenue Code and accompanying regulations.[30] The effect is both limiting and preoccupying, tax considerations shaping the perception, practices, and too often the motives and philosophy of foundations. The occasional great moments when the nation contemplates the

27. A more detailed discussion of the Ford Foundation and its development can be found in Magat (1979).

28. An excellent source for learning about the historical background as well as the practical issues of operating a community foundation is Struckhoff (1977).

29. In 1953 the U.S. Supreme Court upheld a decision of the N.J. Supreme Court establishing the legitimacy of corporate giving. The case involved a contribution to Princeton University by the A. P. Smith Manufacturing Company. The report of the Chancery Division of the Supreme Court of New Jersey, *A. P. Smith Company* v. *Barlow*, 1953 stated: "The contribution here in question is towards a cause which is intimately tied into the preservation of American business and the American way of life. Such giving may be called incidental power, but when it is considered in its essential character, it may well be regarded as a major, though unwritten, corporate power. It is even more than that. In the Court's view of the case, it amounts to a solemn duty."

30. An easy reference source for the Internal Revenue Code and regulations dealing with private foundations can be found in Freeman (1981, Appendix 20).

role and assesses the performance of foundations come when the Ways and Means Committee of Congress holds its hearings; and there the justification of philanthropy begins and ends with the rationalization of tax advantage.

Recent scholarly attention is a welcome though still struggling effort to provide a much broader understanding. A growing cadre of insightful historians (for example, Barry Karl, Stanley Katz, Peter Hall, and Kathleen McCarthy) are tracing the origins and evolution of American foundations, correlating their behavior with changing social forces and recording their metamorphosis from isolated charities to a distinctive social process. Economists and political scientists (for example, Lester Salamon, Burton Weisbrod, Henry Hansmann, Aaron Wildavsky, and Gabriel Rudney) are taking up the generic question of the place foundations and other nonprofit agencies occupy in a market economy; similarly, other disciplines are trying to develop a workable theory of the collective role and behavior of American philanthropy that encompasses all varieties.

It could be that the quest is an impossible one, that foundations can be understood only by learning to know them each and every one, that there is no way of comprehending within one theory the range of motivations from pure altruism to blatant self-interest, of philosophies from the far Right to the far Left, of practices from assertiveness to passivity, of vision from farsightedness to myopia, or of size from the minuscule to the mighty.

But if there is a valid and simplifying perception of foundations and their role, it derives from two maxims about a massive democratic society. The first is Gregory Bateson's observation that as an organism grows larger it must correspondingly miniaturize. The second is the democratic imperative of maximizing choice.

These twin principles are expressed in philanthropy's progression from charity to social process. The larger the society has become, the more predictably and compulsively Americans have created a plethora of devices enabling them to gain some leverage on the system without having to go through the wearying process of winning total control or consensus. Similarly, this society (and increasingly other democratic societies) has searched for ways of allowing the coexistence of alternatives, even when contradictory, thereby expanding options among philosophies to live by, goals to be achieved, and the means by which to attain them.

This miniaturization and spreading out of decision making are essential aspects of the logic of an ever-enlarging democracy—a logic manifested in the growth of foundations and the proliferation of nonprofit agencies in general. As that logic would predict, by far the greatest numbers of these institutions have been established within the past generation.[31] Notable, too, is the fact that both government and business, in the course of their own growth, have found it expedient to foster the parallel development of these more freewheeling and adaptable structures. They are more wieldy; they are more credible among their several constituencies; they allow more flexibility in accommodating to local circumstance, even when those accommodations create inconsistencies; they can be dealt with contractually rather than as permanent obligations; they can extend the range of challenge and experimentation beyond what is available through either corporate or governmental decentralization alone; and they can be turned to as either allies or fall guys depending on the calculated advantage of the moment.

It is no accident either that both business and government adopted the philanthropic device of grant making as an expanding facet of their own operations. The rapid spread of foundations within government (such as National Endowment for the Arts, National Endowment for the Humanities, National Institute of Health, National Science Foundation) and the corporate sector is itself evidence of how congenial grant making is to the functioning of large organizations.

But philanthropy is far more than grant making; it is a constitutional statement by society that there should be a private counterpart to the legislative process, a freestanding alternative that allows for independent considerations of the public interest and private allocations of resources for public needs. As Nason (1977) put it, foundations are "public bodies privately organized." And as the Internal Revenue Code states, foundations must distribute their monies explicitly for a public purpose.

This larger social role of foundations is still obscured by the traditional clothes they wear. One layer is charity; another is privatism ("This is my money and it's nobody's business how I give it"). But inexorably, those who practice modern philanthropy and those who are affected by it have come to realize that this process of private considering and giving for the public interest is itself a matter of the public interest. And so the body of professional standards and governmental requirements accumulates, marking the boundaries within which these "private legislatures" can operate (for example, no lobbying), defining the terms on which they will be publicly accountable (reporting and disclosure), and ensuring the integrity of their operations (no self-dealing).

Judged from this broader viewpoint—do foundations individually and together serve effectively as private alternatives to governmental definition of public needs and priorities?—the performance of foundations has been mixed. On the positive side, foundations have scored some brilliant successes in both complementing and challenging the patterns of publicly legislated decisions, in the short run and over time. They have at critical junctures provided access to scarce resources and public attention to causes and constituencies that could not hope to win the support of voting majorities. They have incubated new ideas and programs that could not survive the heat of too-early debate. They have brought perspective and dispassion to issues otherwise left to burn in partisan controversy. They have taken a longer view of public needs than public legislators can politically afford. They are experimenting with promising new modes of governance and public accountability and finding imaginative ways of listening to and serving the interests of a broader

---

31. See Salamon (1984) for a discussion of these patterns of growth.

representation of the American citizenry. And even in their collective conservatism and individual contrariness, they have provided a gyroscopic stability to the nation's determination of need and appropriate response.

But there is also a formidable list of entries to be made on the debit side. Of the 140,000 foundation trustees, relatively few see themselves as fulfilling anything more than a discrete and essentially private purpose; broader discussions of public needs and philanthropic responsibilities are perfunctory if engaged in at all; outlook and giving are narrowed to unquestioned assumptions and favored recipients. Assets, governance, and management are still heavily tilted toward wealth, toward social homogeneity, and, in the corporate world, toward institutional self-interest. Access has been limited, reporting sluggish, and some hard philosophical questions (for example, should governance of foundations be inheritable?) slow to be raised. And there are now warning signs that the philanthropic process may become more politicized, mirroring rather than enlightening the quality of public dialogue.

What is most encouraging is the rapidity (speaking in historical terms) with which the philanthropic role in modern society is being consciously accepted by the public and self-consciously dealt with by philanthropists themselves. Sensitive monitoring and continuous self-improvement are now the prevalent mode, and that augurs well.

REFERENCES

Andrews, F. Emerson. 1956. *Philanthropic Foundations.* New York: Russell Sage Foundation.

Boris, Elizabeth T., and Carol A. Hooper. 1984. *1984 Foundation Management Report.* Washington, D.C.: Council on Foundations.

Commission on Foundations and Private Philanthropy (Petersen Commission). 1970. *Foundations, Private Giving and Public Policy.* Chicago: University of Chicago Press.

Commission on Private Philanthropy and Public Needs (Filer Commission). 1975. *Giving in America.* Washington, D.C.: Department of the Treasury.

———. 1977. *Research Papers.* Washington, D.C.: Department of the Treasury. Vol. 1, *History, Trends and Current Magnitudes;* Vol. 2, *Philanthropic Fields of Interest;* Vol. 3, *Special Behavioral Studies, Foundations and Corporations;* Vol. 4, *Taxes;* Vol. 5, *Regulation.*

Council on Foundations. 1985. *Alternative Investment Strategies.* Washington, D.C.: Council on Foundations. (Selected and edited proceedings of a conference on Alternative Investment Strategies for Institutions, March 6–7, 1985, New York City.)

Cuninggim, Merrimon. 1972. *Private Money and Public Service: The Role of Foundations in American Society.* New York: McGraw-Hill.

Donee Group. 1977. "Private Philanthropy: Vital and Innovative or Passive and Irrelevant." In *Research Papers,* vol.1:49–88.

Foote, Joseph. 1982. "RAGTIME." *Foundation News* 23, no. 5 (September-October):5–13.

———. 1985a. "Service Unlimited." *Foundation News* 26, no. 4 (July-August):11–19.

———. 1985b. "Stretching the Career Ladder." *Foundation News* 26, no. 1 (January-February):24–28.

———. 1985c. "You Name It, They Do It." *Foundation News* 26, no. 5 (September-October):14–25.

Forbes. 1984. 134, no. 8 (Special issue; October 1):156.

Ford Foundation and Kathleen Hallahan. 1983. "Philanthropy Goes to Congress." *Foundation News* 24, no. 3 (May-June):12–21.

Foundation Center. 1985. *The Foundation Directory.* 10th ed. New York: Foundation Center.

———. 1984. *The Foundation Grants Index.* 13th ed. New York: Foundation Center.

Freeman, David F. 1981. *The Handbook on Private Foundations.* Washington, D.C.: Council on Foundations.

General Accounting Office. 1984. "Statistical Analysis of the Operations and Activities of Private Foundations." (GAO/GGD–84–38).

Goulden, Joseph. 1971. *The Money Givers.* New York: Random House.

Hall, Peter Dobkin. 1980. "The Community Foundation and the Foundations of Community: H. C. Trexler Estate of Allentown, Pennsylvania—A Preliminary Report." Yale University, Program on Non-Profit Organizations Working Paper no. 34.

Heimann, Fritz F., ed. 1973. *The Future of Foundations.* Englewood Cliffs, N.J.: Prentice-Hall, for the American Assembly.

Hodgkinson, Virginia Ann, and Murry S. Weitzman. 1984. *Dimensions of the Independent Sector: A Statistical Profile.* Washington, D.C.: Independent Sector.

Karl, Barry D., and Stanley Katz. 1983. "The American Private Philanthropic Foundation and Public Sphere 1890–1930." *Minerva* 19, no. 2 (Summer 1981; published in March 1983).

Knowles, Louis. 1985. "Alternative Investments: Helping

Communities the Old-Fashioned Way." *Foundation News* 26, no. 3 (May-June):18–23.

Longstreth, Bevis, and H. David Rosenbloom. 1973. *Corporate Social Responsibility and the Institutional Investor*. A report to the Ford Foundation. New York: Praeger Publishers.

Magat, Richard. 1979. *The Ford Foundation at Work: Philanthropic Choices, Methods and Styles*. New York: Plenum Press.

McCarthy, Kathleen D. 1983. "Private Philanthropy and Public Needs: The Historical Perspective since the Filer Commission." Paper prepared for History, Theory and Functions Panel, May 3.

———. 1984. "25 Years of Change." *Foundation News* 25, no. 6 (November-December):14–21.

McDonald, Jean A. 1984. "Survey Finds Religious Groups Strongly Favor More Collaboration." *Foundation News* 25, no. 5 (September-October):20–24.

Miller, J. Irwin. 1984. "Time to Listen." *Foundation News* 25, no. 3 (May-June):16–23.

Nason, John W. 1977. *Trustees and the Future of Foundations*. New York: Council on Foundations.

National Committee for Responsive Philanthropy. 1980. *Foundations and Public Information: Sunshine or Shadow?* Washington, D.C.: National Committee for Responsive Philanthropy.

Nielsen, Waldemar A. 1972. *The Big Foundations*. New York: Columbia University Press.

———. 1985. *The Golden Donors*. New York: Truman Talley Books/E. P. Dutton.

Northern California Grantmakers. 1985. *Perspectives on Collaborative: Funding: A Resource for Grantmakers*. San Francisco: Northern California Grantmakers.

Odendahl, Teresa J. 1985. "Private Foundation Formation, Growth and Termination: A Report on Work in Progress." In *1985 Spring Research Forum: Working Papers*, 513–23. Washington, D.C.: Independent Sector and United Way Institute.

Odendahl, Teresa J., and Elizabeth T. Boris. 1983. "A Delicate Balance: Foundation Board-Staff Relations." *Foundation News* 24, no. 3 (May-June):34–45.

Odendahl, Teresa J., Elizabeth T. Boris, and Arlene Kaplan Daniels. 1985. *Working in Foundations: Career Patterns of Women and Men*. New York: Foundation Center.

Petska, Thomas B., and Daniel Skelly. 1982. "Private Foundations, Federal Tax Law, and Philanthropic Activity." In *1981 Proceedings of the American Statistical Association*. Section on Survey Research.

Pifer, Alan. 1984. *Speaking Out: Reflections on 30 Years of Foundation Work*. Washington, D.C.: Council on Foundations.

Reckard, Edgar C., and Jean A. McDonald. 1985. *The Philanthropy of Organized Religion*. Washington, D.C.: Council on Foundations.

Reilly, Raymond, and Donald Skadden. 1981. *Private Foundations: The Payout Requirement and Its Effect on Investment and Spending Policies*. University of Michigan, Graduate School of Business Administration (For the Council of Michigan Foundations).

Richman, Saul. 1973. *Public Information Handbook for Foundations*. New York: Council on Foundations.

Rudney, Gabriel. 1981. "A Quantitative Profile of the Nonprofit Sector" Yale University, Program on Non-Profit Organizations Working Paper no. 40.

Russell, John M. 1977. *Giving and Taking: Across the Foundation Desk*. New York: Teachers College Press.

Salamon, Lester M. 1984. "The Results Are Coming In." *Foundation News* 25, no. 4 (July-August):16–23.

———. 1985. *Government and the Voluntary Sector in an Era of Retrenchment: The American Experience*. Washington, D.C.: Urban Institute. (Prepared for delivery at the International Conference on Philanthropy meeting, Venice, Italy. September 27, 1985.)

Salamon, Lester M., and Alan J. Abramson. 1982. *The Federal Budget and the Nonprofit Sector*. Washington, D.C.: Urban Institute.

———. 1985. "Nonprofits and the Federal Budget: Deeper Cuts Ahead." *Foundation News* 26, no. 2 (March-April):48–54.

Scanlan, Joanne B. 1985. *1985 Community Foundations Survey*. Washington, D.C.: Council on Foundations.

Shepard, Karla J. 1981. "The Nation's Largest Foundations, 1959–1979." Unpublished manuscript, Twentieth Century Fund.

Struckhoff, Eugene C. 1977. *The Handbook for Community Foundations: Their Formation, Development and Operation*. 2 vols. New York: Council on Foundations. (Contains 1975 Community Foundation Survey prepared by the council.)

U.S. House of Representatives. 1983. *Report and Recommendations Concerning Federal Tax Rules Governing Private Foundations*. Subcommittee on Oversight, Committee on Ways and Means (September 28).

U.S. Senate. 1973. *The Role of Foundations Today and the Effect of the Tax Reform Act of 1969 upon Foundations*. Report of Proceedings, Subcommittee on Foundations, Committee on Finance (October 1–2).

———. 1974. *Impact of Current Economic Crisis on Funds and Recipients of Foundation Money*. Report of Proceedings, Subcommittee on Foundations, Committee on Finance (November 25).

U.S. Treasury. 1965. *Treasury Department Report*. (Submitted to the Committee on Finance and the House Ways and Means Committee, February 2.)

Unkle, Patricia A., and Paul N. Ylvisaker. 1984. "Self-Study Guide for Foundation Boards." Draft; Council on Foundations.

Vanguard Public Foundation. 1977. *Robin Hood Was Right: A Guide to Giving Your Money for Social Change*. San Francisco: Vanguard Public Foundation.

Viscusi, Margo. 1985. "Coming of Age." *Foundation News* 26, no. 3 (May-June)26–35.

Weaver, Warren. 1967. *U.S. Philanthropic Foundations: Their History, Structure, Management, and Record*. New York: Harper & Row.

Whitaker, Ben. 1974. *The Philanthropoids: Foundations and Society*. New York: William Morrow.

Williams, Roger M. 1984. "All in the Family." *Foundation News* 25, no. 4 (June-August):42–49.

Youkstetter, Dennis. 1981. "Meeting Special Needs Quickly." *Foundation News* 22, no. 1 (January-February):25–29.

Young, Donald R., and Wilbert E. Moore. 1969. *Trusteeship and the Management of Foundations*. New York: Russell Sage Foundation.

Zurcher, Arnold J. 1972. *The Management of American Foundations: Administration, Policies, and Social Role*. New York: New York University Press.

Zurcher, Arnold J., and Jane Dustan. 1972. *The Foundation Administrator*. New York: Russell Sage Foundation.

Publications dealing with philanthropy:

Foundation News. Washington, D.C.: Council on Foundations (published bimonthly).

The Grantsmanship Center News. Los Angeles: Grantsmanship Center (published bimonthly).

Newsletter. Washington, D.C.: Council on Foundations (published biweekly).

The Philanthropy Monthly. New Milford, Conn.: Non-Profit Report (published eleven times a year).

21

Enterprise and Commerce in Nonprofit Organizations

EDWARD SKLOOT

INTRODUCTION: RESOURCE SCARCITY AND THE RISE OF COMMERCIAL ACTIVITY

In the conventional wisdom of nonprofit organizations, a distinction has long existed between doing charitable works and earning money. Although numerous examples of decades-old nonprofit enterprise can be found in all service delivery areas, they are commonly perceived as isolated instances running counter to the norm. In fact, however, these examples are part of a long-standing and increasingly apparent movement by nonprofit organizations to diversify their sources of revenue. In the last five years, the trend has become particularly notable.

Before about 1980, little attention was paid to enterprise and commerce in the voluntary sector. The Filer Commission (Commission . . . 1975), for example, focused on philanthropic sources of revenue, on the danger of escalating costs of operation, and on the complex interrelationships of the voluntary sector with government. The existence and appropriateness of income-earning activities, even fees for service, received scant notice.

Nor was attention paid in academia, either. For example, little interaction occurred between the faculty and students of business schools and those of, say, social work, arts, or public health. Almost no research on nonprofit enterprise was undertaken. (See Appendix 2 for a brief review of the recent literature.) In the philanthropic community, the story was the same. Earned income strategies for foundations or their nonprofit grantees (other than investment policy) were seldom agenda items at meetings of the Council on Foundations. Moreover, foundation programs designed to support revenue-enhancing activities were rare.

Nevertheless, pockets of commercial activity have long existed. Dating from the early part of the century, business ventures were established to serve groups of members, alumni, or friends of nonprofit organizations. For example,

the Metropolitan Museum of Art has sold copies of photographs of its collections for more than eighty years, and it established its first official sales shop in 1908. Several university presses were established before World War I to enhance scholarship and make it available to a limited national audience. Later, colleges set up bookstores to provide course material for faculty and students as well as to serve as places to exchange books.

The scope and magnitude of enterprise activities in the nonprofit sector has expanded greatly since 1980 for four major reasons. First, the double-digit inflation of the late 1970s resulted in sharply rising expenses. New sources of revenue were needed, and it was apparent to some nonprofits that traditional fund-raising approaches would not be sufficient.

Second, the Reagan administration enacted major reductions in federal domestic spending in areas where nonprofits were traditionally active. This was a major policy shift. In the 1960s and 1970s the federal government had often used nonprofit organizations to deliver mandated services. Nonprofits acted as agents of the government, and this role served both sectors well (Salamon 1981; 1983, 5, 24). With funding for services now threatened, nonprofits looked for new sources of money to keep their programs going.[1]

Third, the new administration persistently called for increased "self-reliance" by nonprofit organizations. Its own preference for turning over established public-sector tasks to the private sector—from selling gold coins to providing census data—suggested to some nonprofits that using com-

1. One authoritative research group projected a decline of 21 percent in federal spending for fiscal years 1982–86 in fields where nonprofit organizations were active. The shortfall is measured in constant 1980 dollars (Nonprofit Sector Project 1983, 5).

mercial strategies of the private sector to provide their services was a viable approach.

Finally, while corporate and foundation giving was holding fairly constant, the competition for these dollars was growing increasingly stiff. This, too, encouraged the search for new streams of income.

As nonprofits cast about for new revenue opportunities, income-generating projects—once dismissed as illegal, irrelevant, or inconsequential—took on a particularly attractive cast. Nonprofit executives began to investigate their organizations' possibilities. A few foundations began to fund earned income projects. Journalists even began to write about successful nonprofit enterprises. Thus, in the past few years, some nonprofits have established, and many more have contemplated, a wide variety of earned income ventures.

Establishing income-generating ventures is only one of several possible responses to current or projected financial need. The strategy is not the only recourse, and it certainly is not feasible for all. Indeed, for some organizations, income-generating ventures can be dangerous. They can compromise the organization's charitable mission, disrupt operations, raise thorny legal issues, and cause substantial financial harm. (See Appendix 1 for a discussion of legal issues in enterprise for nonprofits.) On the other hand, at their best, earned income activities can diversify the nonprofit's revenue base, measurably strengthen its finances and management, and nurture new program initiatives.

As increasing numbers of nonprofits engage in income-generating activities, they and the social and economic environment in which they provide their services will change. Some changes have already occurred. The purpose of this chapter is to describe the kinds of entrepreneurial activities increasingly in favor among nonprofits and to chart the impact of these activities on three levels:

- The way individual nonprofit organizations operate

- The way they interact with both the private and the public sectors

- The role they play in society

THE VARIETIES OF ENTREPRENEURIAL BEHAVIOR

Enterprise has a fuzzy and sometimes negative connotation among the staff and board members of nonprofit organizations. Many actively shy away from words like *profit* and *earnings*. For some, this is due to the erroneous belief that nonprofits cannot earn money. For others, it is due to a lack of experience or training in commerce, which makes business terminology and commercial strategies unfamiliar and sometimes unwelcome.

For our purposes, enterprise has a clear definition: *it is sustained activity, related but not customary to the organization, designed to earn money.* Examples of entrepreneurial activity are plentiful and diverse. They can be categorized according to the product or service being sold in the commercial arena.

1. *Program-related products:* Nonprofits develop products for sale to organization members, participants, and the public at large. These products are closely identified with the organization on a local or national level. They promote its mission as well as earn money.

Perhaps the best-known example of program-related products are the cookies of the Girl Scouts of America. Young people learn responsibility while they promulgate the Scouts' mission. In 1982, the Girl Scouts sold 125 million boxes of cookies for gross revenues in excess of $200 million.

Publishing is an activity to which environmental and cultural organizations have long been attracted. Sierra Club calendars and books, for example, detail the natural beauty of the environment and sell well commercially. Other conservation organizations, like the National Geographic Society and the Museum of Natural History, publish widely read magazines. In 1982, *National Geographic* took in $22 million in (taxable) advertising revenue in addition to its $152 million (untaxable) subscription and membership revenues.

Health-related nonprofits sell products, too. The Planned Parenthood® Federation of America recently introduced its own house-brand condom for sale to its affiliates and clinics (see below). The American Red Cross and many local blood centers sell fractionated blood products commercially and for research.

Across the nation a wide range of program-related products is sold by a diverse group of organizations. Products range from wearable goods associated with "A Prairie Home Companion" radio program, sold through mail-order catalogs by Minnesota Public Radio, to a book on how to choose a nursing home by FRIA, a small consumer-activist organization based in New York City.

2. *Program-related services:* Nonprofits provide ancillary commercial services to members, friends, and alumni, which enhance the tax-exempt mission of the organization. The services may be available to the public as well. Some services are run by the organization, whereas others are leased to concessionaires, usually for a percentage of gross revenues.

A typical program-related service is the gift shop commonly found in cultural institutions and hospitals. Perhaps the best known is run by the Metropolitan Museum of Art, whose overall merchandise revenues exceeded $25 million in 1982. Some of these shops are run largely or entirely by volunteers. The New York City Ballet Gift Bar is one such enterprise. It is open one-half hour before dance programs and during program intermissions. Gross revenue of the Gift Bar exceeds $125,000 annually; the net to the City Ballet is more than half that amount.

Parking lots are another source of revenue. Clients, patrons, and the public need places to park near the facility they are visiting, and they are willing to pay for the service.

Another area is food sales—even self-service vending machines. Cultural institutions, hospitals, and educational institutions run restaurants or cafeterias for the convenience of relatives visiting a patient, for patrons at an exhibition, or for ticket holders during the intermission of a concert or play. For example, the Smithsonian Institution in Washington, D.C., grosses more than $10 million in food and beverage sales annually.

There are many other related services. For example, organizing tours and travel packages for the members, students, faculty, and graduates of educational and cultural organizations are now commonplace activities. The Museum of Natural History and the American Jewish Congress are especially well known for their tour programs.

3. *Staff and client resources:* Nonprofit organizations use the expertise of their staff members and clients in commercial ventures. These ventures may offer similar services to new groups of consumers or new, related services to current ones.

For example, in the arts, the Guthrie Theatre in Minneapolis offers its computerized box-office system and assistance to set it up to other nonprofit theaters. The New York PBS station, WNET, provides its production and postproduction services to corporate and nonprofit clients. The Spence School in New York provides computer support to a dozen other private schools in Manhattan. Museum staffs do appraisals of art work for members and nonmembers and advise on the purchase or preservation of works of art for a fee. Librarians consult on book preservation and bookbinding.

Numerous social service organizations have consulted for the private sector in designing alcoholism and drug treatment programs, and some are now designing comprehensive employee assistance programs as well. The Miami Valley Hospital in Dayton, Ohio, offers financial and management consulting services to other hospitals in the local area.

Possibly the most lucrative area to develop in recent years is the long-term research contract between private corporations (the contractor) and universities. It is also one of the most problem ridden. These contracts, which often involve large amounts of money, can raise such issues as the dedication of staff time, the use of tax-exempt university facilities for profit-making clients, academic freedom, the integrity of research, and the ownership and control of patents.[2] Harvard, Stanford, and Washington University in St. Louis have contemplated or signed long-term contracts with sponsoring corporations, and agreements involving several other universities and corporations are in the offing.

Some social service nonprofits also employ their own clients in commercial activities. These ventures are most commonly conducted in sheltered workshops operating through federal or state contracts under strict regulation.

2. See, for example, Daniel Steiner, ''Technology Transfer at Harvard University,'' Discussion Memorandum, Office of the General Counsel, Harvard University, October 9, 1980; Ann Crittenden, ''Industry's Role in Academia,'' *New York Times*, July 22, 1981, p. D1; and David E. Sanger, ''Corporate Links Worry Scholars,'' *New York Times*, October 17, 1982, sec. 2, p. 4.

Owing to their large social service and training components, few ventures earn much profit, although the sheltered workshop operations of Goodwill Industries and of the Volunteers of America are among the financially strongest.

4. *Hard property:* The sale, lease, and rental of land and buildings is an increasingly common source of earned income. Much of the income derives from making use of facility downtime—fixed resources that lie idle during some part of the day.

For example, many schools and colleges rent excess dormitory and cafeteria space during slack summer months to special conventions or traveling adult education programs. Some private schools and universities lease their stadia to professional sports teams for training and practice; others use their tennis courts for tennis camps and their ice rinks for community or private leagues. Renting auditoriums, kitchen facilities, and even equipment is increasingly common. National Public Radio even leases transponders on its satellite during its broadcast downtime.

The Rensselaer Polytechnic Institute in Troy, N.Y., has taken the concept further. It has set aside campus facilities to ''incubate'' high-technology industry and encourage successful ventures to stay in the local area. It charges a low rent for the facilities.

In another hard-property area, the National Audubon Society has for decades leased sections of its Rainey Bird Sanctuary in Louisiana for mineral exploration, under tightly controlled agreements. Universities in the western part of the United States lease land to ranchers and farmers for grazing and irrigation.

The sale of air rights is a notable, if infrequent, occurrence. In the 1970s, the Museum of Modern Art sold the air rights over its building for $17 million plus substantial annual payments to a tax-exempt trust created by state legislation. More recently, sale-leaseback transactions involving land and buildings of the Oakland Museum and Bennington College have been arranged, but sale-leaseback transactions by nonprofit organizations have now been sharply curtailed by Congress in its Tax Reform Act of 1984.

Finally, some organizations expand into new space more than sufficient for their needs and lease out the excess. For example, the Municipal Arts Society of New York City purchased the north wing of the landmark Villard Houses in Manhattan. It receives commercial rents from the lease of two floors of the building and uses the money to subsidize its own operating costs on the remaining floors.

5. *Soft property:* Soft property encompasses a cluster of income-earning assets that includes copyrights, patents, trademarks, art and artifacts, and even mailing and membership lists.

Two especially active organizations in licensing products for royalty payments are Children's Television Workshop and the National Wildlife Federation. The workshop licenses its ''Sesame Street'' characters for adaptation in books, toys, records, and soft products to for-profit commercial firms. In 1982, the organization grossed $9 million in royalties from its agreements. Similarly, the federation licenses its well-known Ranger Rick character. On a different front, the Bank Street College of Education recently developed the Bank Street Writer, a piece of word processing software now licensed for sale to the commercial and educational market (see below).

Some organizations permit their names to be used by, and often contribute to, commercial publications of high quality, which are related to their own activities. One such case is the National Audubon Society, which licenses its name for the Audubon and Peterson Field Guides, as well as for the Audubon Elephant Folio, published in limited reproductions.

Commercially attractive products are also reproduced from collections of art, artifacts, and furniture. For example, Winterthur and the Museum of the City of New York license reproductions of period furniture. The Metropolitan Museum of Art has derived a substantial income from licensing artistic designs from its collections to textile design and production companies.

CASE STUDIES

Business ventures, regardless of who owns them, must progress through at least eight stages of development in order to be successful. These stages are:

- Defining the business clearly and following a coherent business plan

- Establishing a viable organizational structure appropriate to the business

- Raising sufficient start-up or expansion capital

- Finding, developing, and maintaining a market niche for the product or service

- Employing a management team able to develop the business

- Promoting the business via various marketing strategies

- Expanding the business at a pace consistent with managerial talent and financial resources

- Revising operations when results indicate the need for a change

The case studies below describe how four nonprofit organizations progressed through these eight stages in defining, establishing, promoting, and expanding or terminating their earned income ventures. They also illustrate a number of principles of enterprise applicable to all nonprofit organizations.

Planned Parenthood® Federation of America

Early in 1981, the Planned Parenthood® Federation of America, Inc. (PPFA), began to discuss the development of a house-brand contraceptive product. Having become aware that other nonprofits were creating earned income ventures to help fund program services, PPFA decided to survey its resources to identify its own prospects.

At first, the senior staff of PPFA thought of developing an oral contraceptive. The organization deferred the idea after arranging for a favorable purchase agreement with a private-sector company. The staff then turned to the idea of developing and/or selling condoms through its network of 190 affiliates and over 700 clinics.

Condoms were a good choice for several reasons. First, the price of condoms purchased by its affiliates and clinics was increasing every year and PPFA wanted to contain the costs. Second, PPFA affiliates, clinics, and clients formed a natural distribution network. Staff members were in continuous regular contact with the 1.5 million individuals served by PPFA affiliates annually, of whom 23 percent were known to be condom users. Third, condom use appeared to be increasing as a result of widespread concern about sexually transmitted diseases. Fourth, condoms were inexpensive products, easy to transport, store, and distribute. Finally, and possibly most important, increasing the use of condoms was a desirable social goal, wholly consonant with PPFA's exempt purposes. Linking condom sales to family planning was natural.

The national headquarters staff decided to investigate the purchase, distribution, and sale of condoms to affiliates and clinics, who would then sell (or give) condoms to their clients. In mid-1982, the national board of PPFA and several leadership groups representing affiliate directors approved the concept. Headquarters then conducted two polls. It sampled twenty-two, or 11.6 percent, of its affiliates nationwide to test interest in marketing condoms to clients and to estimate the number of condoms that might be distributed annually. Interest was high, as were the estimates of national distribution.

A private consulting firm was hired to survey a national sample of five hundred women to determine interest in using PPFA products and to estimate the number of potential non-client purchasers. The results pointed to intense interest in the product. The organization also appointed a senior-level staff member to run the project on a full-time basis, reporting directly to its executive vice president. After investigating legal, tax, and product liability issues of condom sales, its legal staff and outside counsel advised that the product was well within the scope of its exempt purposes; sales would not adversely affect PPFA's tax status. The preservation of tax-exempt status was a crucial consideration. Additional product liability coverage was purchased.

The staff then sought bids from three major condom manufacturers to supply the product, possibly under license to PPFA. Only one, the Fuji Latex Company, a large international supplier of latex surgical gloves and condoms, responded.

As interest in the project grew among PPFA affiliates, the national board chose to act. Early in 1983, it authorized a contract with Fuji Latex for the purchase of 1.5 million condoms.

A second consulting firm was then enlisted to research the national condom market, to prepare financial projections, and to design a product introduction strategy for its affiliates.

The report, completed late in the spring of 1983, projected a break-even on investment fourteen months from start-up, with progressively increasing profits thereafter.

In March 1983, the condoms were shipped to the United States, attractively packaged with the federation's logo. In May and June, PPFA test marketed the condom and a centralized distribution system, and a formal business plan was prepared. Also designed was a sales strategy based on pre-payment from affiliates and chapters who would then receive their orders from a central warehouse facility in Maryland.

In July 1983, PPFA condoms went on sale at a price competitive with other manufacturers' products. At the end of the first six months, sales were slightly below projections, although the percentage of affiliates and chapters participating in the project was approaching the goal set by national headquarters.

At the end of nine months, PPFA asked its consulting firm to review the project and suggest course-correcting strategies, for PPFA had decided to move the project to profitability quickly and saw that its own local chapter and affiliate market was too small to generate substantial income. In the summer of 1984, as a result of the review, PPFA entered discussions with several national corporations to consummate a licensing arrangement for the condom and other products. At this writing, negotiations are underway.

In the two years it took to develop and market its house-brand condom, PPFA had executed a variety of orthodox planning and implementation steps. Although planning did not follow a fixed course and timetables were perhaps too short, most of the key steps in creating a venture had been followed. The responsibility for the project was clear, board support was constant, research was strongly positive, start-up funding was available, marketing themes were well defined, and the business plan was prepared and executed.

The PPFA example illustrates four principles of nonprofit enterprise. First, entrepreneurial activities succeed on the basis of formal, thorough written plans. The halfhearted or partial implementation of a business plan will doom a venture and may hurt the nonprofit itself. Second, at select times, hiring consulting assistance can be a good investment. Most nonprofits do not have the range of planning skills in-house necessary to mount a venture. A consultant can be helpful, as long as responsibility for the entire project rests with the client. Third, earned income activities are most likely to succeed when they build on the natural resources of the organization—that is, on what the organization is already doing. Staff members will readily understand the connection and clients may welcome it. Fourth, the name, reputation, and clientele of an organization may provide a competitive marketing advantage. The nonprofit organization should be willing to use them all as one element of a comprehensive marketing strategy.

Bank Street College of Education

The Bank Street College of Education has long been associated with high-quality teacher training and educational re-search. It has also been known for its Bank Street Reader Series, which has been used for three generations to teach countless schoolchildren to read. During the 1970s the Bank Street Reader Series generated in excess of $1 million in royalties. Until five years ago, however, no systematic effort to develop and market educational products had been undertaken.

In 1979, the new president of the college, Richard R. Ruopp, moved to change the situation. Ruopp believed the college's mission could not be fulfilled without developing high-quality educational products for use in and out of the classroom. Also, he was persuaded that generating substantial amounts of unrestricted related earned income could nurture new innovative programs that might need an infusion of cash.

One of Bank Street's first commercial efforts was begun in 1980. It was *Three-to-Get-Ready,* a family-oriented Sunday newspaper supplement. Two venture capitalists contracted with Bank Street to create the magazine for bimonthly distribution. At its height the supplement reached 9.5 million subscribers of eighty-two newspapers. Advertising revenue was not sufficient, however, and the venture folded early in 1981.

Despite this failure, the Bank Street board of trustees remained supportive of entrepreneurial activity. Ruopp had raised the subject with the trustees from the first, specifically discussing new product development and expanding Bank Street's early childhood services, like day care.

In August 1979, Ruopp had created the Center for Children and Technology to research and evaluate new educational products for young people. One interest of the center was the process by which children learn to write well. In the fall of 1981, the center received a $70,000 foundation grant to investigate the impact of microcomputer-based word processing on children's writing and editing skills. One of the center's first findings was that none of the available word processing software was designed for young people. The center concluded that the best way to test word processing software for children was to design the product from scratch.

Ruopp was put in touch with a private-sector curriculum developer, Intentional Education, Inc. (IEI), which had the design and programming capability. Bank Street had designers, teachers to teach writing, children in a "researchable" laboratory environment, and the capability to field test any software. In April 1982, the two organizations agreed to develop word processing software for children, and a joint development budget of $160,000 was set. Bank Street put up $45,000 in cash and invested $35,000 in staff time, essentially funded by grants and contracts.

From this point the project moved quickly. Design of the word processing software was completed in the late fall of 1982. The two partners then entered negotiations to license the software with commercial distributors. They demanded and obtained a high-quality/low-cost pricing strategy that would ensure that the package of teaching materials would be affordable by consumers and the discs would be highly competitive in the marketplace.

Licensing agreements for the new Bank Street Writer were signed with Scholastic Incorporated for sale to the school market for an advance against royalties, and with Broderbund for sale to the popular consumer market for a guarantee plus royalties.

The Bank Street Writer reached the marketplace in January 1983, only nine months after conception of the idea. By summer, the Bank Street Writer, with a dozen rave reviews behind it, had become the second largest selling word processing software in the United States, with expectations of becoming the leader in sales in 1984 when it would be issued in IBM-PC- and PCjr.-compatible format.

The Bank Street Writer has been both a financial and educational boon to the college. It produced royalty income net of expenses in excess of $60,000 in 1983, which would more than quadruple in 1984. Bank Street's earned income from various projects in 1983 equaled $300,000, comprising 2.5 percent of its $12 million budget, but 7.5 percent of all unrestricted funds. Seen another way, the $300,000 in earned income was the functional equivalent of a $3 million increase in Bank Street's endowment.

No less important than the financial rewards, Bank Street became the codeveloper of a high-quality educational product, available nationally at an affordable price. It did so with a relatively small but critically important investment of its own capital, which enabled it to retain a 45 percent equity position.

Besides the transforming effect on writing skills across the country (the Writer is popular with both adults and children), Bank Street's own teachers have now been trained to use microcomputers, using the Writer as a prime teaching tool. This involvement has helped break down resistance to the idea that educationally sound material can also be commercially successful. Finally, the Bank Street Writer has also enhanced the college's national reputation and enabled it to share some of its experience with other institutions through training and consultancies.

The Bank Street example illustrates three principles of nonprofit enterprise. First, board commitment must be sustained. Business ventures take time to prove out, and some will fail despite the best planning efforts. Boards must be ready for the inevitable highs and lows of enterprise. Second, development costs must be clearly identified and budgeted, budgets must be treated seriously, and timetables must be closely followed. That Bank Street and IEI produced the software in nine months gave them a major jump on the competition in a progressively more crowded computer software field. Third, joint-venturing a business undertaking with a private-sector firm is a viable, often preferable, strategy for nonprofit organizations to pursue. Joint ventures can diminish risk, infuse additional professional expertise, and reduce costs to a nonprofit.

The Film Forum

The Film Forum is a small nonprofit organization in New York City. It screens the work of independent filmmakers who traditionally have difficulty in obtaining adequate distribution of their finished work. The screenings give them much-needed exposure to an informed New York City audience and to critics—whose reviews often open up new or expanded distribution opportunities.

In its first two years, the Film Forum presented experimental films made by American artists, producers, and directors. In 1972, when Karen Cooper, the current director, took over, she expanded the range of films shown (to include non-American filmmakers) and the kinds of films shown (to include documentaries, and so on). By the mid-1970s, the Film Forum was a thriving small enterprise. It operated on a mix of grants and ticket-sales income and had a budget of approximately $75,000.

In 1975, with the organization's lease about to expire, Cooper located larger quarters in an old theater in Greenwich Village. She arranged to lease for five years the two-hundred-seat house—four times larger than their previous space. The Ford Foundation made a three-year $35,000 grant to help cover basic expenses in the new location.

But the theater had structural limitations: it was too cramped for comfortable seating; the rake of the seats was such that subtitles were hard to read; the projection area was too small to show 35mm films, the most common medium used in Europe; and office and concessions areas were nonexistent. In addition, other film houses began to compete for the Film Forum's audience. Although attendance was strong, the fidelity of audiences could not be taken for granted.

For the Film Forum, these structural limitations were inhibiting program development and affecting its ability to compete. The organization's future was in jeopardy, and Cooper sought a way to move to better quarters. After investigating two alternate sites with the help of a Ford Foundation–provided consultant, Cooper found a building that had once been used as an automobile garage. She sought a rehabilitation loan from the Office of Program-Related Investments of the Ford Foundation. The problem was that ticket-sales revenues were insufficient to cover loan repayments. To get a loan, she had to create a new stream of income, preferably one closely related to her organization's ticket-sales revenue.

The solution was an imaginative one. If two theaters could be constructed in the garage, the second one could be leased to a private entrepreneur, whose rent payments would produce the income stream needed to cover the loan repayment. This aspect was critical, since it would markedly diminish the risk to the foundation and thus increase its willingness to make a loan. But the "right" subtenant had to be found. Cooper sought out a leading exhibitor of independent films of high artistic quality. Since his audiences shared the same interests as Cooper's, the synergistic effect of adjacent film houses could be expected to boost traffic in both. He agreed to a ten-year rental agreement with a renewal option and personally guaranteed the first year's rental payments. Cooper retained the right to operate the food concessions in both houses.

The Ford Foundation then made a $400,000 loan to reconstruct the garage and create a two-theater complex. The new facility was opened in September 1981, and since then, the Film Forum, better able to market its services, has scored major program and financial successes. It has expanded to a full-day, seven-day-a-week, year-round schedule, and screenings have increased tenfold. The organization has also met all financial expectations, too. It is current in its loan payments to the Ford Foundation, and its operating budget for both theaters now exceeds $700,000. The Film Forum is now self-sustaining in its new home.

The Film Forum example illustrates two principles of nonprofit enterprise. First, there are several possible sources of financing for nonprofit ventures, not just commercial banks and other lending institutions. Foundations are one untraditional source of nongrant funds, and others may be board members, staff members, even clients. Second, the private sector can be a willing ally in the development of a venture, even if it is not an equity holder. The possibilities for cooperation are numerous if the imagination exists to create a mutually beneficial, viable proposition.

Children's Television Workshop

Children's Television Workshop (CTW) was founded in 1969 to use broadcast television to educate children and young adults. The primary vehicle for this purpose was the television program "Sesame Street." Soon after CTW's establishment, its chairman, Lloyd N. Morrisett, and president, Joan Ganz Cooney, saw that the organization would have to develop financial support from other than the government and foundations in order to implement its educational mission.

In the early 1970s, CTW began to license books and records based on "Sesame Street" and its other television production, "The Electric Company." It soon expanded into games, toys, and other functional products, international TV sales, and later, commercial TV production and theme parks. Also in the early 1970s, CTW sought to enter the booming business of wiring urban communities for cable TV. The initiative was rooted in a decision by CTW's board to pursue a venture with both financial and social goals.

Staff members and consultants knew that the companies bidding on franchises to wire urban areas had to offer both local programming services and the capacity to produce locally packaged materials. They believed the Workshop's expertise in video production could enhance the bids of cable companies and make a major educational contribution to local communities. Accordingly, CTW established a Program Advisory Service (PAS) that would give technical assistance to local communities in need of programming expertise.

The Workshop had two objectives in setting up PAS. Its social objective was to empower schools, community groups, and neighborhood institutions to create programs that would meet their local needs. Its financial objective was to obtain an equity position, at low investment cost, in the new cable systems. To this end, CTW would commit PAS, its technical assistance arm, in exchange for a share of the equity in a cable franchise.

The responsibility for running the PAS and CTW's participation in urban cable was given to two consultants, who later became part of the Workshop's senior staff. This small team came to see that the bidding-and-building process of an urban cable system might take at least five years—a lead time unacceptable for CTW's social and financial objectives.

Thus, CTW changed its approach. It identified the partially built urban cable system in Honolulu, whose owners had not fully met the terms of their franchise. In 1972, CTW, a Canadian corporation, and a group of local investors bought the franchise in a forced sale. The board of CTW, through CTW Communications, Inc., its for-profit subsidiary, allocated $650,000 for the purchase, for which it received 24 percent of the company. The funds came from a large exit grant made to CTW by the Ford Foundation, which CTW's board decided to use as risk capital. A healthy 20 percent return on the investment was projected. The total investment by all parties was able to leverage $11 million of debt to put toward the completion of construction of the Honolulu system.

The Workshop had assumed that its strong suit was community outreach and its expertise in TV production. But as CTW became more deeply involved in the Honolulu cable business, the staff discovered that its production experience was not relevant to the perceived need. For example, to perform training activities in Honolulu, the PAS had to hire non-CTW personnel who had little connection to, or experience in, the Workshop's educational mission. The PAS gradually learned that local community and political leaders were not prepared to make the long-term commitment needed to become sophisticated television producers.

Another issue was that the CTW staff pressing for the development of a technical assistance service and investment in cable systems was not the core staff of CTW. The activity was generally held at arm's length by other CTW personnel.

By the mid-1970s, CTW realized the Honolulu cable franchise would take longer to mature than anticipated. In the interim, in order to fund PAS's $250,000 annual cost, CTW marketed the service to other cities and cable systems. Although it became involved in two other franchise awards, CTW's interest in wiring urban cable systems was fast declining. Its participation increasingly looked like a risky financial investment with fewer and fewer socially relevant aspects. However, it held on to the franchise (it even invested another $100,000 in the system) for several more years. By 1980, the financial projections made in the early 1970s finally began to materialize, and CTW put its share of the business on the market, selling it in 1981 to a major cable company for $5 million.

The estimated costs of PAS and other in-house expenses totaled $1.7 million over the life of the project. Thus, although the sale of equity ensured that the Workshop exceeded its financial goals, CTW never reached its social ones. It discovered that the comparative advantage of its production staff was illusory and that, far more important, the linking of social and financial goals had to be extremely well calibrated in order to be successful.

The Workshop had made its decisions on the basis of reasoned analysis. Its board was willing to take risks and to stay with the investment for a considerable period of time. But the success of the cable project depended on a large number of uncontrollable variables working out favorably. When they did not, CTW reevaluated its commitment to participating in the construction of urban cable systems and decided to withdraw from the business.

The CTW example illustrates three principles of nonprofit enterprise. First, all business ventures demand constant course correction. Initial assumptions seldom bear out exactly as projected. Management must be willing to rethink and alter its approach or else face loss of the entire enterprise. Second, nonprofits can create and use for-profit subsidiaries to take on financial risk and protect the organization from financial liability. The Workshop had its own for-profit arm and used it for the cable venture and other investment activity. Various legal and structural options exist and they should always be investigated before starting a venture. Third, the marketplace is an excellent communicator and the ultimate judge of a product or service. If it does not want your product or service, it will let you know.

The Distinguishing Features of Nonprofit Enterprise

The four case studies, and the numerous examples of enterprise cited earlier, suggest seven characteristics that distinguish nonprofit enterprises from traditional business ventures.

First, a charitable purpose is linked closely with, and often animates, commercial ventures. In nonprofit enterprises, earning income is rarely the only, and usually not the primary, consideration in starting a business. Ventures are simultaneously a way to promulgate the mission of the organization and to diversify its revenue base. At the same time, of course, the businesses must succeed on their own terms in the marketplace.

Second, although net income is crucial in determining the viability of ventures, it is seldom the only measure of success. For example, organizations may choose to earn less than commercial entrepreneurs if their core activities might be compromised by the business. The choices that are made are spelled out in the business plan.

Third, commercial ventures are usually a secondary activity of the organization. Earned income as a percentage of total income is usually a small number, commonly less than 25 percent. This percentage applies to nonprofits of all sizes and functional areas.

A fourth distinguishing feature is how the income is used. Since nonprofit organizations are forbidden by law to distribute profits to their members, employees, or board members, all net income must be returned to the organization. This does not mean that the income is plowed back exclusively into the commercial venture. In general, it is returned to the operating fund for distribution to ongoing or new programs.

Fifth, the early stages of commercial ventures by nonprofits are commonly capitalized from internal funds, directly or indirectly through philanthropic or governmental sources. Most organizations do not have lines of credit or venture capital connections. Joint ventures with the private sector are increasingly common. They may provide start-up capital and special expertise to the nonprofit partner.

Sixth, commercial ventures in nonprofit organizations sometimes mix paid professionals and voluntary labor. Volunteers may be board members who shepherd a project through, or friends who donate skills for little or no compensation. This is not to suggest that the ventures are not professionally run or managed, only that not all "employees" are paid.

Finally, many nonprofit commercial ventures pay no federal income tax and often only some local taxes. Although in recent years the Internal Revenue Service has viewed commercial activities more stringently, the legal precedent for the untaxability of "substantially related" income is strongly rooted in law and amplifying rulings.

KEY ISSUES IN NONPROFIT ENTERPRISE

Earned income activities can have a number of positive results for the nonprofit organization. These include, directly or indirectly, improved financial stability, strengthened program activity, increased organizational visibility, enhanced fund-raising capacity, and improved managerial ability.

Still, as we have seen, entrepreneurial ventures by nonprofit organizations can be risky. They may not always be successful, or they may take several years until success is manifest. Many problems arise at the start, when nonprofit organizations seek to execute both charitable programs and earned income ventures.

The first part of this section describes several of the most common operational problems. The last two parts briefly describe other more wide-ranging issues that arise as more nonprofit organizations seek to earn income. The impact of these issues can be seen across the voluntary sector as well as at the points where the activities of the public, private, and nonprofit sectors intersect.

Enterprise at the Level of the Individual Organization

The issues here primarily involve the financial and managerial capacity of organizations simultaneously to enter ventures and accomplish their charitable purpose. There are times when commercial and charitable activities conflict, resulting in a stressful, possibly unproductive working environment—and an unsuccessful enterprise.

Commercial activities are not easily absorbed within nonprofit organizations, at least not at first. They often bring with them new legal structures, management styles, and reporting procedures that run counter to less formal, possibly less rigorous approaches.

For example, attention to the bottom line may encourage organizations to review their pricing policies, and the review can lead to new charges and fees that approximate real costs of service delivery. Revising fee structures thus can lead to increased income, but the effort can also bring to the surface philosophical differences based on theories of equity and the public service role of nonprofit organizations.

Enterprise can also exacerbate the traditional conflicts over resource allocation. Under ordinary circumstances, nonprofits are often short of capital, personnel, and space. Starting or nurturing income-earning ventures can add another claimant for these resources. Organizations may have to reallocate funds, or even borrow money, which, arguably, might better go for program services. If borrowed money is involved, the expenditure of resources can be even harder to justify.

The tension between earned income activities and charitable purposes may cause conflicts at the operating level. Priorities can conflict. Staff loyalties can become divided between old and new projects. Communications can temporarily suffer until ventures are comfortably absorbed. Furthermore, time demands on key staff members may increase and they may not be able to meet them without endangering the exempt purposes of the organization. New business ventures may absorb as much as 30 to 50 percent of the chief executive officer's time over many months. His or her unavailability for other matters might exacerbate staff tension even more.

Compensation is a particularly troublesome issue. In order to attract and keep skilled professionals with business experience, nonprofit organizations may have to pay higher salaries or arrange other benefits, thus creating two levels of compensation. Moreover, if the ventures do succeed, the staff members associated with them may be attracted to the private sector by promises of better compensation. On the other hand, without adequate compensation, earned income projects may not attract the talented staff they need to succeed. (Commercial ventures can also provide career opportunities for qualified employees who wish to move on.)

At the board level, board members may be concerned about personal financial liability. Some may be uncomfortable with enterprises about which they have no substantive knowledge. Others may reject the idea of commercial ventures as inappropriate to the charitable purposes of the organization. Since board members are legally responsible for the organization, their clear support, or at least the support of key members, is crucial to the success of a venture. Indeed, financial or other professional assistance from board members can measurably improve the chances of success of earned income ventures.

Finally, there is the danger of "too much" success. High levels of earned income can raise serious legal and tax issues and threaten to tip an organization away from its mission. The issue here is not that "the commercial tail will wag the program dog" but that sustained profitability may make staff members complacent or distant from the primary purpose of their organization.

Enterprise at the Level of the Nonprofit Sector

The issues at this level pertain to how nonprofits relate to one another and the publics they serve, their sources of unearned income, and their federal tax-exempt status.

The public associates nonprofit activity with charity. Some staff and board members believe that the more they engage in commerce the less individual or philanthropic support will be forthcoming. Informal discussions with dozens of nonprofit executives have shown this to be a needless concern. In fact, several have stated that successful ventures enhance their fund-raising appeal by making them look like "winners." Moreover, commercial activities may open up sources of money not previously available to nonprofits. These include program-related investments and revolving loan funds that have become popular in recent years.

There is reason to believe, however, that the organizations in greatest need of funds to replace federal grants and contracts—social service, criminal justice, and environmental organizations and advocacy groups—are those least able to create commercially viable ventures. Their natural resources—that is, the things they do—may be less commercially viable while the populations they serve may well be the neediest. In such instances, as "the rich get richer," commercial ventures might separate some groups even further from others, enhancing their visibility and possibly their fund-raising ability at the expense of others.

Another near-term possibility is that competition for the same clients or customers will increase. For example, in some cities, hospitals have added vocational rehabilitation and clinical services, often on an outpatient basis, expanding into areas traditionally served by other social service providers.[3] Cultural institutions, YMCAs, colleges, and universities now compete head-to-head in providing adult education programs. Where competition increasingly occurs, strains can develop in jointly sponsored projects, in community outreach, and in professional relationships. Of course, competition can also energize organizations and encourage them to improve the services they offer.

Although there is no indication that nonprofits turn off public support by starting commercial enterprises, the same cannot be said for their effect on the Internal Revenue Service (IRS). Even though earned income is a distinctly minor part of the budgets of most nonprofits, the IRS has become increasingly aggressive in its search for unrelated business income.

Some nonprofits are concerned that well-publicized individual cases of commercial activity in such areas as retail sales, research contracting, and publishing will result in an across-the-board increase in involvement by the IRS, state and local agencies, and politicians. They also point to certain

3. See, for example, two articles by Michael Waldholz in the *Wall Street Journal*, "Some Hospitals Are Entering Diverse Businesses, Often Unrelated to Medicine, to Offset Losses," August 12, 1981, p. 46, and "To Keep Doors Open, Nonprofit Hospitals Act Like Businesses," December 29, 1982, p. 1.

activities seen most recently in the health and hospitals field, where organizations are seeking ways to shelter certain earned income ventures, the proceeds of which might be claimed by governments under reimbursement guidelines. An unknown but apparently growing number of hospitals and nursing homes are busily establishing limited partnerships, for-profit subsidiaries, controlled companies, and even complex holding companies. As they transform their legal and organizational structures along lines more prevalent in the private sector, they may attract just that IRS attention they seek to avoid.

Expanding earned income activities may also affect how Congress and the executive branch view their support of the entire voluntary sector. For example, the case to retain nonprofit mailing status at reduced rates, essentially a fiscal subsidy voted by Congress, may be harder to make, as the nonprofit sector appears to act more and more like its for-profit counterpart.

Enterprise at the Level of the Three Sectors

The issues here include the impact of increased competition for earned income, including competition for government contracts, the erosion of traditional service distinctions between the for-profit and voluntary sectors, and the heightened need for a rationale to continue service delivery by nonprofit organizations if such service can be provided by the private sector with the same quality and at a lower price. Strictly speaking, these issues do not flow directly out of the development by nonprofits of ancillary commercial activity. They arise because such activity is part of an overall trend toward the restructuring of service delivery patterns across all three sectors.

As nonprofits extend their commercial endeavors, they will increasingly compete with private-sector firms providing comparable services and products. In recent years, lawsuits have challenged the tax exemption of nonprofits who run educational tours, act as travel agents, engage in retail trade, use nontaxpaying facilities for commercial activities, and rent excess space.[4] Court decisions have invariably upheld the right of nonprofits to engage in earned income activities, so long as they are substantially related to their exempt purposes.

Nevertheless, as nonprofits extend their range of commercial operations, private-sector groups and individuals will mount their opposition. They will claim unfair competition by tax-exempt organizations that are endowed with cheap mailing rates, untaxed property, and protected charitable status. Some agencies of the government have begun to respond to the cries for relief, even though the arguments for

action are often flimsy and occasionally erroneous. A recent U.S. Small Business Administration (SBA) report (1983) focused these concerns and called for stringent measures against nonprofits—despite the fact that its proposals were not based on empirical findings.

On its side, the private sector will increasingly expand into areas traditionally reserved for nonprofits. Since the mid-1970s, for example, large corporate providers like Humana, Upjohn, and Baxter-Travenol have bought or expanded into all phases of facility-and-home-provided medical care that were once the near-exclusive domain of nonprofit organizations.[5] Nonprofit and for-profit institutions increasingly compete for the same client base.

The expansion is less apparent but perhaps even more extensive in child welfare and day-care programs, where for-profits are widely used as contractors for residential treatment, institutional care, and group-home settings. In 1977, for example, private firms provided a majority of these services under contract to local agencies, and their presence is expanding (Born 1983). In day care, publicly traded companies like Kindercare are now moving aggressively into the field.[6]

Private-sector firms will not only compete with nonprofits; they will also seek to use or absorb them. In the educational field, fears of commercial interference in university research through huge multiyear research contracts have prompted serious debate over the benefits and dangers of ties to large international corporations (Bouton 1983; Bok 1981). In the health field, the recent attempt by the Hospital Corporation of America to purchase McLean Psychiatric Hospital, part of Harvard Medical School, prompted vociferous faculty opposition and the withdrawal of the offer (Culliton 1984).

The federal government affects this two-way expansionary policy by direct appropriation and by subsidy, sometimes in conflicting ways. As noted earlier, by cutting back on the funds available to the voluntary sector, it pressures nonprofit organizations to look toward earned income activities to make up their budgetary deficits. By reducing corporate taxes and easing depreciation schedules, it erodes tax-based distinctions and makes it easier for corporations to compete in low-margin services traditionally provided by nonprofits. By pressing for a reduction of entrepreneurial activity on the grounds of unfair competition with the private sector, as the SBA and the IRS are increasingly doing, government forecloses an option to promote the continuing fiscal health of nonprofits. Given the crosscutting and inherently complex nature of the issues, a coherent and uniform federal approach toward nonprofit enterprise probably will not evolve for some time. What is certain, however, is that efforts by the nonprofit sector to compete will not be greeted kindly by the private and public sectors.

4. See, for example, "When Should the Profits of Nonprofits Be Taxed?" *Business Week*, December 5, 1983, p. 191, and Karen J. Winkler, "America's Colleges vs. Pharmacies, Bookstores, Restaurants, Hotels, and Travel Agents," *Chronicle of Higher Education*, July 27, 1983, pp. 5–6.

5. "The Big Business of Medicine," *Newsweek*, October 31, 1983, pp. 62–73.

6. Myron Magnet, "What Mass-Produced Child Care is Producing," *Fortune*, November 28, 1983, pp. 157–74.

Moreover, state and local government policies, particularly with regard to privatization of public services, will increasingly affect nonprofit organizations. Many governments in their search for higher productivity and lower cost have begun to contract out social, health, and even protective services to private-sector firms and to nonprofit groups.[7] As the trend toward privatization gains momentum, contracts will increasingly be awarded on the basis of performance and cost-effectiveness, and less often on the basis of tradition or past association. Government policies at this level will thus spur competition between private-sector firms and nonprofit organizations.

The boundaries between the private and voluntary sectors are thus increasingly permeable. In the next few years, boundary disputes across the sectors will inevitably increase. A possible near-term scenario is that the private sector will gradually impoverish parts of the voluntary sector by skimming off clientele able to pay or by seeking and winning government service contracts that traditionally have gone to nonprofit organizations.

In the long run, if the private sector can deliver certain services common to nonprofits in a consistently cheaper and equally effective manner, nonprofit organizations may have to review nothing less than their philosophical premises for existing—as well as the way they operate.

---

7. See, for example, "Want to Buy a Fire Department?" *Newsweek,* April 25, 1983, pp. 55–56, and John Herbers, "Cities Turn to Private Groups to Administer Local Services" *New York Times,* May 23, 1983, p. 1, as well as Born (1983).

APPENDIX 1

LEGAL ISSUES

The income-producing activities of nonprofit organizations are subject to federal income tax law considerations in two basic ways.[8] First, the activities may be unrelated to the organization's exempt purpose *and* so large in terms of its overall operations that the organization's tax-exempt status is thrown into jeopardy. Second, the activities may not jeopardize the organization's tax exemption but may still necessitate the payment of an unrelated business income tax (UBIT).

Real-world examples of the first case are rare, although one of the most notorious was the ownership of the C. F. Mueller Company, a pasta manufacturer, by New York University Law School.[9] The second case—paying a tax on income-producing activities—is more common and relevant to this discussion. A federal tax is imposed on income-earning activities that are not related to the organization's purposes. A related business activity, according to tax law, is one that "contributes importantly" to the accomplishment of the nonprofit's exempt purposes. Income from a related activity neither raises questions about the tax-exempt status of the nonprofit nor is taxed.

There are two questions that must be asked before an organization focuses on the matter of relatedness. First, is the activity a "trade or business"? The Treasury Department defines the term as including "any activity carried on for the production of income from the sale of goods or the performance of services." All entrepreneurial activities discussed in this chapter fit this definition.

The second question is whether the activity is "regularly carried on." The standard for this test is whether the activity is performed with a frequency and in a manner comparable to non-tax-exempt organizations: is the activity conducted commercially? Under this definition, an occasional bake sale, flea market, or benefit dance do not qualify as "regularly carried on."

The organization must then ask if the income-earning activity is "substantially related"—that is, if it "contributes importantly" to the accomplishment of its exempt purposes. This is known as the "relatedness test."

Among the factors that are examined in determining whether an activity is related to the nonprofit's exempt purposes are (1) whether the organization's charter, articles of incorporation, bylaws, and other relevant documents contain clear references to the related income-earning activity in which it is engaged, and (2) whether the organization is operating its business in a way that is substantially related to its exempt purposes.

It is *not* relevant to the relatedness test that an organization

---

8. Numerous pamphlets, articles, and tax services discuss legal matters. Among the most useful are works by Bromberg (1981), Galloway (1982), Hopkins (1982), Lehrfeld (1980), Troyer and Boisture (1983), and Turkel (1983).

9. See John Brooks, "The Marts of Trade: The Law School and the Noodle Factory," *New Yorker,* December 26, 1977, pp. 48–54.

uses its earned income for exempt purposes. In determining relatedness—and taxability—the nonprofit must look to where the income comes from, not the use to which it is put. The organization should consider the nature of the activity and its scope, and be sure that a clear, substantial causal relationship exists between the income-producing activity and the nonprofit's purposes. On the other hand, if a nonprofit's venture is deemed (by itself or by the IRS) unrelated, the activity is neither illegal nor necessarily threatening to its exempt status. The organization may pay tax on the net income of the activity, like any for-profit commercial endeavor.

In recent years, the IRS has increasingly fragmented organizations' activities to define related and unrelated business in order to identify the portion of income it deems taxable. For example, retail items in museum stores are increasingly separated out according to their relatedness to the educational purpose of the museum. In magazine publishing, income from subscriptions is considered related, whereas advertising income is usually considered unrelated.

There is no fixed ratio of unrelated activity to gross revenue wherein an organization's tax exemption may be cast in doubt. Legal opinion and a sense of the marketplace suggest a danger zone: when gross income from unrelated activities exceeds 20 to 30 percent of gross revenue, the organization should seriously review its activities. As an organization considers entering a commercial venture, it is wise to contact a skilled and informed tax attorney to help determine relatedness and to discuss the best organizational form for the enterprise. Depending on the nonprofit's purposes, a wide range of income-producing activities can pass the relatedness test.

Finally, it is important to note that certain income from commercial ventures is specifically excluded from payment of UBIT. These exclusions fall into two categories. The first is passive investment income. It includes rents from real property that is not debt financed, royalties, interest payments, and dividends. Recently, nonprofits have been especially active in licensing products or characters they have developed to for-profit firms in return for royalty payments.

The second category of exclusions involves more active involvement in commerce by the organization. It includes, for example, activities substantially performed by volunteers, activities primarily conducted for the convenience of an organization's members, students, employees, and so on, and activities involving the sale of donated merchandise.

APPENDIX 2

LITERATURE REVIEW

Although enterprise in nonprofit organizations has existed for many years, the literature on the subject is of very recent origin. It ranges from the analytical to the practical, and several key works are discussed below. One important area, the rationale for the existence of nonprofit activities, as principally discussed by Hansmann (1980) and Weisbrod (1977), is of broad theoretical interest, but not directly relevant to our discussion. (See chapter 2 by Hansmann in this text.)

One area of research deals with the relationship between government financing and nonprofit organizations. It is particularly useful to understand the growth of, and interdependency between, the public and voluntary sectors. The steady contractions in federal funding, the impact on the operations of nonprofits, and the search for alternative sources of revenue are discussed comprehensively by Salamon and Abramson (1982). Their book can be read as a warning to those who do not realize the depth of sectoral interdependence and the destabilizing effect large federal cutbacks will have on service delivery. Salamon and his colleagues have continued their valuable research through the Urban Institute's Nonprofit Sector Project. Also active in this area is the Center for Responsive Governance, especially in the work of Smith and Rosenbaum (1981).

Several recent books and articles have begun to define the range of nonprofit enterprises and to spell out the dangers of precipitous entry into the marketplace. An extensive overview is found in Crimmins and Keil (1983), whose survey of 130 nonprofits found only 22 percent of the groups sampled earned more than 10 percent of their income through enterprise. They present case studies of 11 innovative nonprofits, emphasizing that entrepreneurship (in their definition) may encompass a variety of activities from bartering to product marketing on a wholesale level. They suggest that without tight bottom-line-oriented management nonprofits cannot hope to succeed in enterprise.

Crimmins and Keil offer a number of provocative suggestions to nonprofits seriously committed to earned income strategies. One is the hiring of a director to run all commercial enterprises. A second is that a new kind of nonprofit entity be created, the 501(c)(3)x organization, which would be permitted to earn up to 80 percent of its revenues from enterprise tax free. The authors also suggest the creation of a nonprofit enterprise development corporation that would funnel venture capital into nonprofit ventures.

The availability of business skills is discussed in a report by Brown and Associates (1983), consultants to the Twin Cities Regenerative Funding Project of Minneapolis/St. Paul. The report concludes that although most agencies appear to have some potential for increasing their earned income, few consulting services or teaching tools are available to help them. It highlights certain common denominators of nonprofits—a shortage of capital to invest, a need to protect their tax-exempt status, and a reliance on consensus in decision making. Brown and Associates created a series of assessment workshops designed to help the staff and board members of nonprofit organizations determine whether they should pursue earned income opportunities.

Several articles written from the perspective of direct business experience have recently appeared. Skloot (1983) suggests five necessary ingredients for success in nonprofit enterprise: a product or service directly linked to the organization's purposes, the availability of management talent,

trustee support, entrepreneurial spirit within the organization, and money or the ability to get it. He also describes a nine-step process nonprofits must work through before they undertake commercial activities. The process begins with a full review of the goals and objectives of the organization and ends in the implementation of a comprehensive business plan.

Cagnon (1982), Duncan (1982), and Williams (1982) also discuss the opportunities and pitfalls that nonprofit organizations face when they try to enter commercial ventures. Cagnon and Duncan are especially observant in pointing out the scale of effort and the talent needed to turn a profit in the *private* sector. They chasten nonprofits to think hard and often before they turn toward commerce. (Both authors speak from the perspective of long experience.) Williams and Cagnon both provide several examples of commercial successes by nonprofit organizations. Nevertheless, Williams also cautions the reader about the odds against success.

Finally, a very valuable handbook spelling out the kinds of legal and organizational forms nonprofit commercial ventures can take, and presenting the advantages and disadvantages of each, is Wiewel et al. (1982).

REFERENCES

Bok, Derek. 1981. "The President's Report: Business and the Academy." *Harvard* 83:23–25.

Born, Catherine E. 1983. "Proprietary Firms and Child Welfare Services: Patterns and Implications." *Child Welfare* 62:109–18.

Bouton, Katherine. 1983. "Academic Research and Big Business: A Delicate Balance." *New York Times Magazine,* September 11, pp. 62ff.

Bromberg, Robert S. 1981. *Tax Consequences of Expanding Income-Producing Activities of Charities and Business Leagues.* Prentice-Hall Tax-Exempt Organizations Service. Englewood Cliffs, N.J.: Prentice-Hall.

Brown, Peter C., and Associates. 1983. *In Search of Cash Cows: Exploring Money-Making Options for Nonprofit Agencies.* Minneapolis: Self-published.

Cagnon, Charles. 1982. *Business Ventures of Citizen Groups.* Helena, Mont.: Northern Rockies Action Group.

Commission on Private Philanthropy and Public Needs (Filer Commission). 1975. *Final Report.* Washington, D.C.: Department of the Treasury.

Crimmins, James C., and Mary Keil. 1983. *Enterprise in the Nonprofit Sector.* Washington, D.C.: Partners for Liveable Places.

Culliton, Barbara J. 1984. "University Hospitals for Sale." *Science* 223:909–11.

Duncan, William A. 1982. *Looking at Income-Generating Businesses for Small Nonprofit Organizations.* Washington, D.C.: Center for Community Change.

Galloway, Joseph M. 1982. *The Unrelated Business Income Tax.* New York: Wiley.

Hansmann, Henry. 1980. "The Role of Nonprofit Enterprise." *Yale Law Journal* 89:835–901.

Hopkins, Bruce R. 1982. "The Tax Implications of Profit-Making Ventures." *Grantsmanship Center News* 10:38–41.

Kotler, Philip. 1982. *Marketing for Nonprofit Organizations.* 2d ed. Englewood Cliffs, N.J.: Prentice-Hall.

Kramer, Ralph M. 1982. *From Voluntarism to Vendorism: An Organizational Perspective on Contracting.* Yale University, Program on Non-Profit Organizations Working Paper no. 54.

Lehrfeld, William J. 1980. *Federal Tax Treatment of Unrelated Business Income.* 2d ed. Washington, D.C.: Chamber of Commerce of the United States.

Lovelock, Christopher H., and Charles B. Weinberg. 1978. "Public and Nonprofit Marketing Comes of Age." In *Review of Marketing,* ed. Gerald Zaltman and Thomas V. Bonoma,

413–52. Pittsburgh: American Marketing Association and Graduate School of Business, University of Pittsburgh.

The Nonprofit Sector Project. 1983. *Progress Report No. 3.* Washington, D.C.: Urban Institute.

Rein, Richard. 1973. "PRI: Will Its Time Ever Come?" *Foundation News* 13 (November-December):13–24.

———. 1978. "A Better Mousetrap But No Mice." *Foundation News* 18 (January-February):28–30.

Rose-Ackerman, Susan. 1982. *The Market for Loving Kindness: Day Care Centers and Demand for Child Care.* Yale University, Program on Non-Profit Organizations Working Paper no. 55.

———. N.d. *Unfair Competition and Corporate Income Taxation.* Yale University, Program on Non-Profit Organizations Working Paper no. 37.

Rosenbaum, Nelson. 1983. "New Approaches to Revenue Generation in the Voluntary Sector: An Entrepreneurial Perspective." Working Papers for Spring Research Forum: Since the Filer Commission. Washington, D.C.: Independent Sector.

Salamon, Lester M. 1981. "Rethinking Public Management: Third-Party Government and the Changing Forms of Government Action." *Public Policy* 29:255–75.

———. 1983. "Nonprofit Organizations and the Rise of Third-Party Government: The Scope, Character, and Consequences of Government Support of Nonprofit Organizations." Paper for Independent Sector Research Forum.

Salamon, Lester M., and Alan J. Abramson. 1982. *The Federal Budget and the Nonprofit Sector.* Washington, D.C.: Urban Institute Press.

Skloot, Edward. 1983. "Should Not-for-Profits Go into Business?" *Harvard Business Review* 61:20–27.

Smith, Bruce L. R., and Nelson Rosenbaum. 1981. *The Fiscal Capacity of the Voluntary Sector.* Washington, D.C.: Center for Responsive Governance.

Troyer, Thomas A., and Robert A. Boisture. 1983. "Charities and the Fiscal Crisis: Creative Approaches to Income Production." Proceedings of the New York University Thirteenth Conference on Charitable Organizations. Albany, N.Y.: Matthew Bender.

Turkel, Mark D. 1983. "Business Activities (Related and Unrelated) of Tax-Exempt Organizations and Their Tax Consequences." Proceedings of the New York University Thirteenth Conference on Charitable Organizations. Albany, N.Y.: Matthew Bender.

U.S. Small Business Administration. 1983. *Unfair Competition by Nonprofit Organizations with Small Business: An Issue for the 1980s.* Washington, D.C.: Office of the Chief Counsel for Advocacy.

Weisbrod, Burton. 1977. *The Voluntary Nonprofit Sector.* Lexington, Mass.: D. C. Heath.

Wiewel, Wim, James H. Ridker, Robert Mier, and Robert Giloth. 1982. *Business Spin-Offs: Planning the Organizational Structure of Business Activities.* A Manual for Not-for-Profit Organizations. Chicago: Center for Urban Economic Development, University of Illinois at Chicago Circle.

Williams, Roger. 1982. "Why Don't We Start a Profit-Making Subsidiary?" *Grantsmanship Center News.* 10:14–23.

VI

COMPARATIVE PERSPECTIVES

22

The Nonprofit Sector in Comparative Perspective

ESTELLE JAMES

The purpose of this chapter is to summarize our knowledge of the nonprofit sector abroad and to examine what light this throws on the theory of nonprofit institutions. As we shall see, the nonprofit sector varies greatly in absolute and relative size from one country to another. However, most significant, we find that the organizations that do exist behave in strikingly similar ways. This chapter uses these empirical observations as the basis for a theory of why and where nonprofits develop and grow.

The theory presented here contrasts with previous theoretical paradigms of nonprofit organizations (NPOs), such as those of Hansmann (1980, 1981), Easley and O'Hara (1983), and Ben-Ner (1986), developed with the American context in mind. In attempting to explain why NPOs are found in some areas but not in others, these theories concentrate on the comparative advantage of NPOs versus profit-maximizing organizations (PMOs), rather than NPOs versus government. They stress that NPOs arise in response to asymmetric information between producer and consumer; the incentive that profit-maximizing managers have to downgrade quality is allegedly removed by the nonprofit constraint. For similar reasons, nonprofits are considered more likely to use donations for the intended purpose, so people are more willing to make philanthropic contributions to NPOs, and this is seen as another raison d'être for their existence. Thus, nonprofits develop, and constitute an efficient contractual form, where

I wish to thank the numerous people in the United States and abroad who helped me with various parts of the studies that have been summarized in this paper. I especially appreciate the capable data analysis carried out by my research assistants, R. R. Huang, Janice Mullaney, Steve Broughman, H. K. Lee, and Li Chi Wann. I also acknowledge the financial support received for the various parts of this study from the Exxon Education Foundation, the National Endowment for the Humanities, the Social Science Research Council, the Agency for International Development, and the Program on Non-Profit Organizations at Yale University.

trustworthiness is important because many small customers or donors do not have adequate information about output characteristics.

Although these theories, which I shall label the "conventional wisdom" about NPOs, seem to fit the American situation, they fit other countries less well. First, they do not explain why the size of the nonprofit sector varies so widely from one country to another; does informational asymmetry also vary? Since we have no independent objective measure of informational asymmetry, the predictive ability of these models cannot be tested, with respect to either differences across industries or differences across countries.

Second, these theories ignore the fact that NPOs usually produce quasi-public goods—that is, goods that yield both public and private benefits—and do so in competition with government, not PMOs. Therefore, we need to explain the division of responsibility between government and NPOs, even more than between NPOs and PMOs.

Third, we observe that, whereas government is a substitute for NPOs in production, it is a complement in financing. Indeed, from a worldwide point of view private philanthropy is insignificant, whereas governmental subsidies are a major source of funds, particularly in countries where the nonprofit sector is large. Therefore, we need to explain why governments, rather than many small donors, contribute resources to NPOs.

Fourth, these paradigms ignore a simple but crucial empirical observation that is surely relevant to a theory of nonprofit origins—universally, the major founders of NPOs are organized religious (or other ideological) groups.

This chapter develops an alternative approach that emphasizes private supply-side variables and government policy toward production and financing, in explaining why founders choose and governments support the nonprofit form, when consumers choose nonprofit services, and in what circumstances (industries, countries) we will find a large nonprofit sector. Our theory seems to fit the American experience as well as that of other countries. One value of the comparative approach is that it forces you to look at the United States with fresh eyes; another value is that it enables you to develop more generally applicable theories. My hope is that the hypotheses generated here inductively, by empirical observations from several countries, will be confirmed as they are tested further in a larger number of settings.

In Part 1 I argue that the relative size of the private nonprofit sector is determined by both excess demand and differentiated demand for quasi-public goods and by the supply of religious entrepreneurship in the society and industry under examination. These demand-side variables were set forth in previous works by Weisbrod (1975, 1977) in explaining private-sector production of certain collective goods; this chapter develops that idea further and emphasizes supply-side variables in explaining why the private sector took the form of nonprofits rather than for-profits in areas such as education, health, and social service. Part 2 analyzes the sources of venture capital and operating funds for NPOs and how this varies depending on whether their raison d'être is excess demand or differentiated demand. The most important finding is their heavy reliance on government subsidies; private management does not necessarily mean private funding. Part 3 compares public and private service provision with respect to costs, one of their more measurable aspects, and attempts to draw inferences regarding relative efficiency and quality; this, however, is the most problematic and inconclusive section. The impact of subsidies on costs and autonomy, including the convergence of large private and public sectors, is explored. The conclusion pulls together the empirical findings of our comparative approach as well as the light thrown on the theory of nonprofit organizations and public policy related thereto.

Examples in this chapter are drawn heavily from the field of education, the major service provided by NPOs throughout the world, and from a group of industrialized and developing countries whose nonprofit sectors have been intensively studied by me (James 1982a, 1982b, 1984, 1986a; James and Benjamin 1987). More tentative evidence suggests that the same generalizations apply to nonprofits in other industries and countries as well. However, this chapter is, to a large extent, a progress report about what needs to be done in the future rather than a final report on what has been done in the past.

PART 1. DEMAND AND SUPPLY OF PRIVATE NONPROFIT SERVICE PROVISION

Definition of Terms and Literature Survey

First, a brief note on the definition of "nonprofit organization." One of the first problems encountered in comparative research is the need to redefine terms and categories in a way that is meaningful in other countries as well as the United States. Suppose we start by defining NPOs in their basic legal-structural sense as "organizations that are legally prohibited

from earning and distributing a monetary residual." Such organizations are found throughout the world and, in different variations, have been amply studied by social scientists. Included in this category, for example, are political parties, interest groups, labor unions, organized religion, voluntary associations, and trade associations. In fact, these are the kinds of organizations that most people abroad assume you are interested in, when given this broad structural-legal definition.

This category, obviously, is far too broad to cover in a single essay or even in a single volume. Much of the discussion of the nonprofit sector and nonprofit theory in the recent American literature focuses on a subset of organizations that are tax-exempt and eligible to receive tax-deductible gifts because they are serving a public purpose—that is, the 501(c)(3) organizations. These organizations combine three important attributes: (1) they are legally and structurally nonprofit, as described above; (2) they provide "socially useful" services; and (3) they are philanthropies, deriving a large part of their revenues from (tax-deductible) contributions. Our tax laws, then, define for us a subset or organizations that have all three characteristics and are deemed to be a useful category to study.

Other countries, however, do not have the same tax laws, so, from an international perspective, this definition fails. Tax deductions may not exist, and typically, private philanthropy is not as important as it is here. Thus, we must find some other way to describe our topic.

The focus of this chapter is on organizations that (1) are primarily service-providing rather than social or income redistributive, and (2) qualify as NPOs from the legal-structural point of view. Excluded are organizations such as the family or social clubs that do not enter GNP and labor unions, political parties, or trade associations which, I would argue, are coalitions designed to alter the distribution of economic wealth and political power rather than to expand the productive frontier.

What do we know about the role of nonprofit organizations abroad? Separate studies of the educational, social service, and health systems in various countries, especially England, sometimes (but not always) include the role of and data about the private nonprofit sector (Hatch 1980; Rooff 1957; Goodman Committee 1976; Wolfenden Committee 1978; Morris 1969; Glennerster & Wilson 1970; West 1970). The same may be said of World Bank, UNESCO, and other multicountry statistical compilations. One occasionally finds references to private services in larger works on the welfare state, particularly for countries such as the Netherlands which relies heavily on voluntary organizations for the provision of quasi-public services (Pryor 1968; Flora & Heidenheimer 1981; Lijphart 1968; Wilensky 1975). In the development literature, one reads about voluntary rural development groups, community self-help groups, clan and caste associations, and international voluntary organizations in building human capital (Smith & Freedman 1972; Smith 1982, 1983; Tendler 1982; Little 1965). However, little has been written analytically about the role of the indigenous nonprofit sector from a comparative perspective, cutting across industries and/or countries and attempting to relate these facts to the theoretical paradigms of nonprofit growth and behavior (among the few previous cross-country studies are Kramer 1982; Geiger 1984; Levy 1984). This chapter attempts to fill this gap.

The Varying Size of the Nonprofit Sector

To what degree do different countries rely on the private (nonprofit) sector in their provision of goods and how can we explain the diverse choices made by different societies? Are there uniformities across countries in the services that NPOS provide and, if so, how can we explain these uniformities?

These turn out to be difficult questions to answer, even at the most basic level of quantification, since most countries do not keep separate data on the set of organizations we are considering. In national income statistics, expenditures of NPOS are often grouped together with "household expenditures" and cannot be readily distinguished. A subset of expenditures, those financed by public subsidies, are often included with "government expenditures": this applies, for example, to teacher salaries which may be paid directly by the government. Typically, there is no central data source on government grants to NPOS. Nor do we have accurate records on voluntary contributions; tax returns, which are an important data source in the United States, are not very useful in numerous countries where donations are not tax deductible and/or income taxes are not paid. The organizations themselves usually guard their financial data, claiming this to be private, not public information.

Thus, data on the size of the nonprofit sector are not yet available for a large number of countries. However, I have compiled such information for Holland and Sweden, two polar cases which I shall use for illustrative purposes throughout this chapter (see table 22.1). For comparison, data on government spending are also included.

Gross spending by Dutch NPOS was approximately 15 percent of GNP, 35 percent of combined spending by government plus NPOS. In contrast, in Sweden outlays by NPOS was barely 1.6 percent of GNP, only 3 percent of the combined government plus NPO total. Consistent with the aggregated figures, the private sector's share of total educational expenditures varies from 6 percent in Sweden to 61 percent in Holland. However, in both countries education is the key activity of NPOS, constituting about 35 percent of total nonprofit production.

Spotty supporting data are available from other countries. Although the definitions and categories vary from study to study, certain common features emerge. Thus, a 1981 survey of all nonprofit associations and foundations in Japan showed that the largest number (33 percent of the total) are in the field of "education and culture" and fall under the jurisdiction of the minister of education (Tanaka & Amemiya 1983, 26, 30) and a similar percentage is related to health, welfare and environmental issues (see table 22.2). For Sri Lanka we have data on "charitable organizations," among which educa-

TABLE 22.2 MAJOR ACTIVITIES OF NPOS IN JAPAN, 1981 (PERCENTAGE BREAKDOWN BY NUMBERS OF ORGANIZATIONS)

Education and culture	33%
Health, welfare, environment	33
Aid to private industry (trade associations)	26
Quasi government	8
Total	100%

Source: Tanaka and Amemiya 1983, 26, 30.

TABLE 22.1 TOTAL EXPENDITURES BY GOVERNMENT AND NPOS

	Sources of Expenditure (%)		Sources of NPO Revenues (%)		
Activity	Direct Government Expenditure	NPO Expenditure	Government and Compulsory Insurance	Private Revenue	Share of NPO Expenditure
A. Holland					
Education	39%	61%	93%	7%	37%
Culture and recreation	49	51	85	15	7
Health	18	82	84	16	32
Social service and old-age homes	24	76	98	2	15
Religion	—	100	3	97	2
Other (nonprofit and government areas)	96	4	81	19	71
Total	65%	35%	88%	12%	100%
B. Sweden					
Education	94%	6%	75%	25%	35%
Culture and recreation	70	30	67	33	37
Health	100	—	—	—	—
Social service and old-age homes	100	—	—	—	—
Religion	77	23	4	96	14
Other (nonprofit and government areas)	99	1	100	0	14
Total	97%	3%	65%	35%	100%

Source: Compiled from James 1982b, 53–54, 61–63. Details of data derivation are given in that source.

TABLE 22.3 MAJOR ACTIVITIES OF APPROVED CHARITIES IN SRI LANKA, 1979 (PERCENTAGE BREAKDOWN BY NUMBERS OF ORGANIZATIONS)

Education	35%
Health and family planning	14
Homes for orphans and elderly	14
Sports, recreation, and environment	10
Aid to needy and emergency relief	34
Religion	34
Other	6
Total	147%[a]

Source: James 1982a.

a. Total is more than 100% because two activities were counted for many organizations.

tional activities again predominate—especially significant since private schools are not counted as "approved charities" and hence would be additional to these numbers (see table 22.3).

More work has been done in assembling data for the United States, but this, too, has proven a difficult task, with different analysts coming up with somewhat different numbers. It is clear, however, that the size of the American nonprofit sector falls somewhere between the polar extremes of Holland and Sweden. Estimates of nonprofit expenditures for 1980 range between 6 and 9 percent of U.S. national income (Hodgkinson & Weitzman 1984, 9, 16, 51; Smith & Rosenbaum 1981, 12–13).[1] Within the nonprofit sector, education and health constitute almost two-thirds of total expenditures, nonprofit outlays exceeding federal government spending in these areas (Hodgkinson & Weitzman 1984, 48, 51; Salamon & Musselwhite 1983, 8–9). (See tables 22.4 and 22.5.)

Thus, the data suggest that different countries make very different choices about the size of their nonprofit sectors, but

1. It should be emphasized that these are gross figures which exceed value added since they include expenditures on raw materials. In 1960, approximately 3.5 percent of our national income originated in the nonprofit sector, a figure that increases to 6 percent if imputed value of volunteer labor is included (Hodgkinson & Weitzman 1984, 9). Unfortunately, we do not have the net figure or data on volunteers for Sweden and Holland.

those organizations that do exist are engaged in similar types of activities throughout the world. Many of these activities are "quasi-public goods"—that is, goods that yield a combination of private benefits to the individuals concerned and external benefits to society at large. Among these, education appears most consistently. The main competitor to NPOs for the production of these goods is usually the government, not the profit-maximizing sector. Nonprofit activities also tend to be labor-intensive and human capital–enhancing. These are the stylized facts we shall try to explain below.

Demand-Side Explanations: Excess Demand

How do we explain the diverse choices made by different societies? Although we have theoretical models predicting the types of industries in which nonprofits will be located, we do not have a theory predicting their location by country. In this section I suggest two sets of demand-side variables—excess demand and differentiated demand—that provide part of the answer. These demand-side explanations view the private sector as a market response to a situation wherein large groups of people are dissatisfied with the amount or type of government production. Private production of quasi-public goods will be larger in countries where these conditions exist. Thus, to explain private-sector behavior we must first model government behavior—a difficult task because no generally accepted model exists. In the next section I add a supply-side variable that explains why the private production

TABLE 22.5 SOURCES OF NONPROFIT REVENUES IN THE UNITED STATES

	Government	Private Contributions	Private Fees	Other
Education	16%	16%	53%	15%
Health	34	9	49	8
Religion	—	86	—	14
Social service	34	30	25	11
Arts and culture	24	62	10	4
Other	22	23	15	40
Total	25%	28%	39%	8%

Source: Hodgkinson and Weitzman 1984, 44.

TABLE 22.4 NONPROFIT VERSUS GOVERNMENT EXPENDITURES IN THE UNITED STATES

	Federal Government Spending (in b $)	NPO Resources (in b $)	NPO Current Expenditures	Share of Total NPO Expenditures
Education	$22.5	$36.7	$31.2	21%
Health	53.7	74.3	65.1	44
Religion	—	18.0	12.9	9
Social service	53.5	15.9	13.7	9
Arts and culture	.6	5.0	2.5	2
Labor unions, political parties trade associations		21.0	17.2	12
Other nonprofit areas	$18.4	10.0	5.8	4
Total nonprofit		$180.9	$148.4	100%

Source: Hodgkinson and Weitzman 1984, 44, 48, 51, 52; Salamon and Musselwhite 1980, 9.

is nonprofit and provides an alternative theory about why nonprofits concentrate in education and other human resource industries.

Theory of Excess Demand

First, private production has been a response to an excess demand for education and other quasi-public goods in the face of a limited government supply. Weisbrod (1977, 51–77) has shown that, with a given tax structure, if the government satisfies the median voter (in order to maximize its votes in a two-party democracy), some people will have a ''leftover'' demand which they will attempt to satisfy privately. Although this is difficult in the case of pure collective goods (for example, national defense), it is feasible for quasi-public goods which can be parceled out and from which people can be excluded if they do not pay the price. Moreover, if private benefits do not overstate social benefits, the development of a private sector adds to efficiency in this case.

The question then arises: why does government limit production? Our basic idea is that people will vote to expand public production so long as their probable (external plus private) benefits from expansion exceed their tax shares; but at the quantity chosen by the majority some people may still have high marginal benefits which they will satisfy in the private sector. Assume first that public and private service provision per unit of output are equally costly. If tax shares (costs) are the same for everyone (for example, under a head tax system), the groups limiting government production will be those with lower marginal benefits—that is, with lower willingness to pay owing to less income or less taste for the public goods. The high-benefit (high-income) groups buy additional services in the private market; this limitation on public supply is the price they are paying for a non-benefit-based (regressive) tax system. On the other hand, if tax shares differ while marginal benefits are relatively constant across people, the groups limiting government production will be those with higher tax shares; this limitation on service is potentially the price paid by the lower classes in a very progressive tax system. In both cases the limitation on the public sector and growth of the private sector stems from the redistributive function of government provision, that is, from the disparity between benefits and taxes for different groups. These cases are developed in greater detail in James (1986a).

The number of people voting to restrict government output increases if public provision is more costly than private provision. In later sections I discuss some of the reasons—bureaucratic rules, above-market civil service wages, and so on—that may lead to higher costs in the public sector. A particularly important reason is the deadweight loss from taxation, including the cost (and sometimes the impossibility) of implementing an effective tax collection system. The higher the costs of government production relative to private, the smaller the level of public provision chosen by the median voter, leaving a greater excess demand for the private sector to fill.

The median voter theory may not work so neatly if different people have different degrees of political power—for example, if certain groups don't vote, are underrepresented in the legislature, have less economic resources to invest in influencing decisions, or if police and military power rather than free elections are the basis of the government. Then, the outcome will depend on the preferences of the ruling coalition, which may not include the median voter or represent the majority will. Nevertheless, the point remains that a private sector will develop when the perceived benefits and costs of government production of quasi-public goods vary, and the groups with lower benefits or higher taxes succeed in choosing their preferred point.[2] Unfortunately, no generally accepted model of political economy exists to predict which coalition will dominate or how much the government will produce. However, in the examples given below I shall try to indicate the relative costs of public and private production as well as the groups that gain and lose from the policies that different governments have adopted.

Empirical Examples of Excess-Demand-Driven Nonprofit Sectors

The excess-demand model clearly applies to education in developing countries, where small-scale production and subsistence agriculture, industries with a low return to education, still predominate, but contrast sharply with the growing urban areas where the private return is high. The difficulties in raising tax revenues from rural areas and the reluctance of the urban upper class to subsidize a large public sector from which others will benefit imply a coalition of low demanders and high taxpayers that effectively restricts the supply of government schools.

One might expect this coalition to be strongest at the secondary level. At the primary level, where private benefits are substantial in rural as well as urban areas and where externalities are most often perceived, the group of low demanders may be relatively small. At the university level, high taxpayers may be willing to pay a disproportionate amount of the public bill if they also get disproportionate access. At the secondary level, however, rural benefits may be lower than for primary and access not as income-biased as for university; hence the low demanders and the high taxpayers form a coalition to restrict government production. At

2. This approach merely leads us one step further back to ask: what determines the tax system? Once the tax system is viewed as an endogenous variable, the same coalitions that determine the distribution of taxes may simultaneously determine the quantities of government services, complicating the analysis. For example, the tax burden may be heavily concentrated by a ruling majority on a minority too small to limit taxes or government production. The majority, which benefits, may then opt for generous provision of public services paid for by the minority, until this process is halted by the disincentive effect of taxation or the possibility of ''exit'' (emigration). Along similar lines, if a high-tax, low-benefit coalition is powerful enough to limit government production, why don't they also reduce taxes for the former? Perhaps the high-tax shares they are paying reduces the effective opposition of outside groups and thereby helps keep them in power.

the same time, as primary school graduates increase, and as the incentive to acquire higher education (often heavily subsidized) rises, many urban middle- and working-class families become anxious to send their children to secondary school, even if they must pay themselves. By the above reasoning we would predict that the private sector will be relatively small at the primary level and much larger at the secondary level, and the two would not be highly correlated, in developing countries where exess demand is the moving force. We would expect to find a somewhat smaller (though still substantial) private sector in higher education as well. Indeed, this prediction is roughly consistent with the empirical evidence: the relative role of private education is much larger at the secondary than the primary level and the correlation between the two is low for developing countries (James 1986b). The reasons much of this private growth takes place in the nonprofit rather than the for-profit sector will be discussed in the section on supply-side influences.

Among industrialized countries, Japan best fits this excess-demand model: over one-quarter of all high school students and three quarters of those in higher education attend private nonprofit institutions. Japan today can hardly be characterized as a developing country, but it has made the transition to modern industrial state more rapidly and recently than most Western countries and its large private education sector may be a legacy of earlier periods. In addition, Japan has, since the end of World War II, been controlled by the conservative Liberal Democratic party (LDP), which has maintained the lowest rate of government expenditure and taxation among modern developed countries. This policy of limited government production, as applied to education, meant that only the minimum quantity deemed necessary for national purposes was provided publicly, while everything else was considered a consumer good, left to private enterprise. It is hardly surprising that the supporters of the LDP (top managers, small shopkeepers, farmers—groups with a low taste for education or high tax shares) constituted a majority coalition benefiting from this policy of limited public spending on education. Demand far exceeded the limited government supply, however, as evidenced by high application rates, low acceptance rates, and the large number of *ronin*—students who, having failed the entrance exam to universities the first time round, spend a year or two cramming and try again. (This phenomenon is found in other developing countries, too, such as India.) Thus, private funding and management of secondary and higher education flourished, particularly in the years after World War II (see James & Benjamin 1987).

It is instructive to contrast the Japanese with the Swedish case, since the party in power in Sweden during this period, the Social Democratic party (SDP), is the mirror image of Japan's LDP. The SDP's working-class constituency wanted—and got—a redistributive tax structure combined with a high quantity of government service, a vast expansion of education and other social services provided by the government at the expense of middle- and upper-class taxpayers. In Sweden, 90 percent of each cohort now stays in school until age eighteen and one-third go on to higher education—proportions that are very similar to those in Japan—but almost all are accommodated in government institutions (Marklund 1979; James 1982b, 48). Clearly, there was no leftover demand here for the private sector.

Does the ability to tax as well as the median voter's willingness to spend on education and other quasi-public goods increase with economic development, leaving less leftover demand for the private sector? We would expect the group of low demanders to decline with development, given the high income elasticity of demand for these goods. Thus, the quantity of government-funded services chosen by the median voter should rise. In the case of Japan, as agriculture declined and the urban working class increased, the LDP did indeed find it necessary to form new coalitions in order to maintain itself in power. Policies were modified in the late 1960s and 1970s to include more government spending on education and social service programs. However, this increase took the form of subsidies to the well-established private sector rather than increased government production; sectoral shares were deliberately stabilized (James & Benjamin 1987). The implications of government subsidies to NPOs will be discussed later. Here, we simply note that a shift from private to public financing does not necessarily imply a shift from private to public production. The latter occurred earlier in England and Sweden but has not occurred in Japan and does not appear to be an inevitable consequence of development.

Differentiated Tastes: Another Demand-Side Explanation

A second demand-side model views private nonprofit production of quasi-public goods as a response to differentiated tastes about the *kind* of service to be consumed (rather than differentiated tastes about *quantity*) in situations where that differentiation is not accommodated by government production. The private sector would then grow larger if (1) peoples' preferences with respect to product variety are more heterogeneous and more intense, owing to deep-seated cultural (religious, linguistic, ethnic) differences, (2) this diversity is geographically dispersed so it cannot be accommodated by local government production, (3) government is constrained to choose a relatively uniform product, and (4) the dominant cultural group is not determined to impose its preferences on others; hence private production is a permissible way out. The differentiated-demand model appears to explain the development of private educational sectors in modern industrial societies.

Differential preferences about quality, one group demanding a ''better'' product than the median voter choice, may also lead to the development of a private alternative. Since quality of education and other services probably has a high income elasticity of demand, this situation is likely to occur where the income distribution is more dispersed. This phenomenon has been observed in some American cities, in selected Japanese cities such as Tokyo, and in developing countries with a disparate income distribution, such as India, and Latin America. The elite private schools play an important role in the economic and social structures of their countries. They are, however, small in number, so quality considerations do not explain the existence of large private sectors. Indeed, their very eliteness comes, in part, from their scarcity value. It is unlikely that large groups of people hold preferences about quality intense enough to induce them to pay for a private school when a free or low-cost public school is available. Moreover, the public system can and has been structured in many countries to accommodate differentiated preferences about quality (for example, selective schools, internal tracking, residential segregation). In fact, although some private schools may accommodate tastes for higher quality, average quality in the private sector cannot generally be considered higher than in the public sector. More will be said about this later, when we discuss cost and quality differences between the two sectors and policy alternatives that might increase the attractiveness of public schools. For all these reasons, when I discuss different preferences about product type in this section, I will be referring primarily to cultural, not quality, variables.

Economic models usually assume that local governments provide quasi-public goods, that people will move to a geographic community offering the kinds of services they prefer, and that those with like tastes will therefore congregate together to get the product variety of their choice. The hypothesis proposed here is that barriers to mobility often stop this process at a point where considerable heterogeneity still exists within a local political unit. Yet, economies of scale and standardization or other political constraints prevent the local government from satisfying this diversity. Then NPOs may be considered a "community of interest" constituting an alternative to geographically based communities—an institutional mechanism for responding to diverse tastes that cut across geographic communities without requiring movement costs or overcoming other movement barriers. The characteristics of variety and choice are, potentially, the great advantage of a system of private service provision—although, as we shall see, that advantage is not always realized.

In countries of great religious and linguistic uniformity (as in Sweden), a centralized public educational system may suffice. In societies where cultural groups are concentrated in different geographic areas (as in Switzerland), local government production achieves the desired diversity. In nations where a dominant group seeks to impose its language or values on others, private schools may be prohibited or restricted; this was the position of Holland and France during earlier anticlerical periods. The melting-pot theory and the general belief in assimilation of minorities to majority values led to the common-school movement in the nineteenth- and twentieth-century United States; the growth of Catholic private schools was a response by a group that did not want to be fully assimilated. However, the cultural heterogeneity model best explains the development of large private sectors in countries such as Holland and Belgium today.

Dutch society has long been characterized by deeply felt cultural (religious) cleavages. In particular, control over their own education was especially important to the Catholics and Calvinists (orthodox Protestants) who constitute approximately 50 percent of the population. These two groups formed a political coalition at the turn of the century which, after much battling, succeeded in bringing about state subsidy of private schools, a principle embodied in the 1917 Dutch Constitution (James 1984; Geiger 1984). In the years to come not only education but most other quasi-public goods, such as health care and social service, were to be produced by private organizations, though financed mainly by the state (Kramer 1982)—hence the large numbers we presented earlier for the Dutch nonprofit sector. Similar cleavages along linguistic and religious lines may be found in Belgium.

In India, too, private schools and colleges are often differentiated by language (associated with region of origin), religion (Muslim, Parsee, Sikh), or caste group. The same is true of Malaysia (Chinese and Indian minorities). In Israel, most private schools are run by and for very Orthodox Jewish groups, who are dissatisfied with the secular public schools.

Since densely populated urban areas will be characterized by greater diversity, with a market large enough to support several schools, the cultural heterogeneity argument leads us to expect private provision of education to be positively associated with urbanization and density indices. This is one of the hypotheses that will be tested below.

More generally, I would expect differentiated demand rather than excess demand to be the moving force behind large private sectors in modern industrial societies equally at the primary and secondary levels. Desire for cultural homogeneity is likely to be greatest at the primary level, for this is the age at which linguistic ability and religious identification develop, values are formed, and so on. It is also true, however, that residential segregation in public systems may accomplish this purpose better at the primary than the secondary level, since the catchment area is often larger for the latter. Quality considerations as a motivation for choosing private schools are likely to be larger at the secondary level. The partially counteracting effect of these three forces (desire for homogeneity, size of catchment area, quality considerations) could easily lead to a relatively large private primary sector, but a relatively small disparity in private-sector size at primary and secondary levels in societies where differentiated demand is the raison d'être for private education. These predictions are roughly consistent with the empirical evidence: the private sectors at primary and secondary levels are close in relative size and highly correlated for most modern industrial countries, except Japan (James 1986b).

Who Starts Private Schools and Why? Supply-Side Explanations and the Theory of Nonprofit Organizations

Who starts private schools and why? Ordinarily, we do not ask this question in the theory of the firm. We assume that enterprise founders are an anonymous group of people seeking profits and willing to start a new business wherever a profitable opportunity presents itself. Since we "know" their objective, profit maximization, any further information about their identity, tastes, and motives is irrelevant.

In situations where education is characterized by huge excess demand, we do indeed find many ordinary profit-maximizing private schools, the Philippines and parts of South America being prime examples. However, more commonly, private schools are established as nonprofit organizations. Why do the founders choose the nonprofit form? In the absence of a profit motive and reward, who provides the entrepreneurship and venture capital for private schools and for the nonprofit sector more generally, and what do they hope to gain? Will the supply of nonprofit entrepreneurship automatically respond to demand? I suggest that differences in the availability of nonprofit entrepreneurship exert a potentially powerful supply-side influence on size of the nonprofit sector and, indeed, evidence from different countries (and different states within a given country) supports this hypothesis. Examining the sources of entrepreneurship also helps us understand why the nonprofit sector is concentrated in education and other human resource industries, and why it often plays a more important role there than the for-profit sector.

Disguised Profit Distribution

One major motive for founding is the possibility of disguised profit distribution, and there is a popular belief in many countries (for example, Japan, Colombia) that this takes place, particularly in areas where nonprofit status may be a legal requirement for schools and universities. Although called nonprofit, these organizations are, allegedly, really profit-making entities. The illegal ways of distributing profits are only rarely brought to light, as when student places or professional appointments are "sold" to families giving large gifts to the school's administrator or kickbacks are given to influential people after successful equipment sales. The legal ways are more interesting but very difficult to detect or prove. For example, the founder may become the headmaster or director and be paid a salary beyond the market wage—that is, beyond what he could earn elsewhere; he is, in effect, receiving monetary profits, albeit in disguised form. Even more valuable disguised profit distribution is said to take place in nonmonetary, hence nontaxable form— expense accounts, free houses, and cars (James & Benjamin 1987).

Although opportunities may exist for earning profits in areas characterized by excess demand for education, they seem less prevalent in countries where differentiated demand is the moving force: many people may be willing to pay a profit-generating price where there is no government alternative but not where some alternative, albeit inferior, exists. Thus, we must look for other motives, particularly in the latter case.

Status, Prestige, and Political Power

Benefits to founders may also take intangible form: perpetuation of a family name on a school or status and prestige from being connected with an important institution. In effect, by creating these status distinctions (and thereby exacerbating prestige inequalities), a society is increasing the coinage at its disposal and using some of it to pay for nonprofit entrepreneurship. Those motivations are common, too, in the United States. In Sweden, on the other hand, private philanthropy is actually frowned upon as a source of undesired status differentials.

Another intangible benefit to school founders in many countries (for example, Japan, India, Kenya) is the political support they gain in a local community. The community may be beholden to an individual who starts a school or hospital there; he gains a potential cadre of worker and consumer supporters. Thus, political ambition is often pointed to as a motivation for founding NPOs.

Religious Motivation

However, another motivation seems much more potent when we observe that most founders of private schools (and other NPOs) are not randomly drawn individuals seeking personal gain but rather are "ideological" organizations—political groups (as in colonial countries such as India and Kenya before independence), socialist labor unions (as in Sweden), and, first and foremost, organized religion. Universally, religious groups are the major founders of nonprofit service institutions. We see this in the origin of many private schools and voluntary hospitals in the United States and England, Catholic schools in France and Latin America, missionary activity in developing countries, services provided by Muslim *wacfs* (religious trusts), and so on. Usually these are proselytizing religions, but other religious/ideological groups often must start their own schools as a defensive reaction (for example, the "independence schools" in Kenya and the caste-dominated schools in India were started partly to provide an alternative to the Western mission schools). Typically, their costs of production are lower than those of government schools. This supply-side variable suggests that the private-school sector will be more important in countries with strong, independent, proselytizing religious organizations competing for clients.

These conditions were obviously satisfied in Holland in the early twentieth century, when 95 percent of all private schools were started by religious groups, and in Latin America in the same period, when Catholic universities were started in reaction to the secular ideology of the public universities. They are present in countries with a history of missionary activity, as in Japan, India, and Kenya. On the other hand, they are absent in Sweden, the country which, as observed earlier, has a very small private educational sector. The Church of Sweden, to which 95 percent of the people nominally belong, is an established church with little opposition, closely tied to and financially dependent on the government. Historically, the church has relied on government funding, and in return, the government has the right to make decisions about church procedures and personnel. In effect, the Church of Sweden could be viewed as part of the Swedish government, with neither the need for nor the ability to supply a competing service. Thus, both demand- and supply-side variables would predict a small private sector in Sweden, and that is exactly what we find.

Why Nonprofit?

This simple observation—that religious groups are the major founders of private schools and other NPOs—has important implications for nonprofit theory. It explains why nonprofits are concentrated in areas such as education and health and it suggests a particular reason the nonprofit form was chosen by the founders: their object was not to maximize profits but to maximize religious faith or religious adherents and schools are one of the most important institutions of taste formation and socialization. Similarly, hospitals are a service for which people will have an urgent periodic need; hence they constitute an effective way for religious groups to gain entrée and goodwill in a society. The nonprofit form was chosen because the main objective was often not compatible with profit-maximizing behavior. For example, religious schools set up to keep members within the fold and/or attract new believers may have to charge a price below the profit-maximizing level in order to compete with government schools and entice the largest numbers in.

Once these religious schools and hospitals are founded they have a comparative advantage over their profit-maximizing alternatives. First, they have a semicaptive audience; as discussed in the previous section, parents may prefer to send their children to a school with a particular religious orientation. The service suppliers, the religious group itself, may "advertise" that this is a good thing to do. Second, some people may trust such schools and hospitals precisely because they are run by religious groups, not because of their nonprofit legal status. Third, religious groups have, in the past, had access to low-cost volunteer labor (such as priests and nuns) and donated capital, which allow them to undercut their secular rivals and compete with government schools. Fourth, once a school or hospital has been founded by a religious group, it develops a reputaton that may allow it to continue attracting a clientele even if it later loses its cost advantage. Often, institutional prestige is correlated with age (James & Benjamin 1987). Finally, the religious group may be politically powerful enough to secure government subsidies and to require that only nonprofits be eligible for them. Thus, the religious motive for founding provides a powerful supply-side explanation for where nonprofits are found, why the nonprofit form is used, which services are provided by nonprofits, and how these institutions may compete effectively with a public or secular profit-maximizing alternative.

Statistical Testing of Demand and Supply Effects

Statistical testing of the demand- and supply-side hypotheses presented above is not an easy task. Ideally, if we were attempting to explain the differential size of the private nonprofit sector across a large number of countries, we would need information, for each country, on the amount of government and private production; the quality, religious, and linguistic orientation and differentiation of public services; various indicators of quantity demanded; the degree of cultural heterogeneity within the population, including some index of the strength of religious and linguistic identification; the availability of (non-profit) entrepreneurs; and the amount of government subsidy to existing and prospective NPOs. In practice, these data are exceedingly difficult to obtain. Data gaps and definitional differences from one country to another make cross-national statistical analyses problematic in general. In this case, uniform data are often not available on degree of (religious and linguistic) differentiation within the public system or government subsidies to the private system. In addition, objective measures do not exist for some other subjective variables we would want to include, such as "intensity of preferences" for religiously differentiated schools. For example, the Catholics and Calvinists strongly wanted their own privately controlled schools and made this their major political objective in Holland, a country that is almost 100 percent Christian; similarly the very Orthodox Jews wanted their own schools in Israel, a Jewish state. These two countries would not show up as very heterogeneous by international standards; yet the subjectively felt heterogeneity and desire to achieve more homogeneous groupings were obviously great. Moreover, the definition of public versus private is by no means an unambiguous concept; we really have a continuum of public versus private funding and control.

To reduce these problems in statistical testing (multiple regression analysis), I have focused on differences in private-sector size across states or provinces *within* several of the countries studied, particularly Holland, India, Japan, the United States, and, to a lesser extent, Sweden. The advantage of this approach is that definitions are more uniform within countries, and some of the variables that are most difficult to measure, such as degree of differentiation in and religious control of the public schools and subsidies to the private schools, may be relatively constant across states or provinces in a given country. Therefore, we are left with a smaller set of more easily quantifiable variables. The public/private division of responsibility for education (%PVT) was taken as my dependent variable; this differs greatly both within and across countries. In the case of the United States, Holland, and India this was measured as "percentage of schools that are private"; in the case of Japan, "percentage of total enrollments in private schools" was used. Somewhat different models were used for each country, because of data availability or because the relevant models (underlying raison d'être for the private sector) seemed to vary. Whenever possible a common set of independent variables—per capita income, density, urbanization, per student spending in public schools, and religious factors—were tested. Per capita income (PCI) was taken in some cases as an indicator of excess demand (for example, see the discussion of Japan in James & Benjamin 1987), in other cases as evidence of ability to pay for differentiated private education (for example, in the United States a high PCI enables people to buy an education that differs from that provided by the state, just as it enables people to buy anything else, in the private market). Density and urbanization were included as indicators of heterogeneous demand within a geographically limited area. Per student spending was used as a proxy for public school quality and the quality motive for attending private school. Religious variables, as discussed above, capture both demand- and supply-side effects.

Summary of Results

In all cases the religion variable turns out to be highly significant. While this combines both a demand and supply effect in Holland, Sweden, and the United States, in India and Japan, where many people who attend Christian schools are not Christians, we are probably observing primarily a supply-side phenomenon. Per capita income is also generally significant as an indicator of excess demand and/or the financial ability of parents to purchase a preferred type of education for their children. Density and urbanization appear to be correlated with "percent private," but this effect often disappears when PCI is included, suggesting that these three variables are exerting a common influence. Per student spending in public schools plays a very limited role except in U.S. secondary schools. Also of interest is the importance of a historical factor—that is, the early founding of private schools. This shows up, for example, in the importance of the "literacy" variable in India and "presence of pre–World War II Christian schools" in Japan. It suggests that once private schools are founded they disappear only with a long lag, even if the initial conditions disappear.

These results are all roughly consistent with the hypotheses given above concerning the impact of demand and supply variables, and, perhaps most important, the role of religious entrepreneurship in determining relative size of the private nonprofit sector. Although the five countries considered here differ greatly in terms of stage of development, political system, cultural values, and size of the private educational sector, they are remarkably similar in terms of the variables determining the geographic distribution of private schools within each country, and these variables are consistent with my hypotheses regarding the formation of NPOs. For a paper presenting my analysis in detail, see James (1986a).

(Yet another statistical analysis I have done across thirty-eight developing countries and twelve modern industrial countries further confirms these conclusions, especially the importance of cultural heterogeneity in the latter and religious entrepreneurship in both [James 1986b].)

PART 2. PUBLIC FINANCE IN THE PRIVATE NONPROFIT SECTOR

Where do NPOs get their venture capital and their operating funds? Venture capital is a problem because ordinarily, in profit-maximizing firms, this is provided on an equity basis by private entrepreneurs seeking a return (in the form of dividends or capital gains) in exchange for their waiting and risk; this return, of course, is unavailable in the nonprofit sector. Operating funds are a problem because nonprofits often provide services that compete with free government-produced alternatives (such as schools) or are specifically designed as a redistributive device to a clientele that does not have the ability to pay (such as social services).

Venture Capital

We should note, first of all, that NPOs tend to be concentrated in small-scale enterprises and labor-intensive industries, such as education, health, and social service, where the capital requirements are relatively low. Thus, we have another supply-side explanation for the industrial concentration of nonprofits, this time focusing on the nature of the inputs required rather than the nature of the output or the general availability of entrepreneurs. Even within these narrow areas, private nonprofit organizations tend to be concentrated in the most labor-intensive niches. For example, private universities in Japan, Colombia, and Brazil do teaching rather than research, they are specialized rather than general purpose, and they teach management or liberal arts subjects, rather than expensive laboratory sciences. It is not clear that a vast expansion of pure science or basic research could take place on a privately financed nonprofit basis.

Nevertheless, even in these labor-intensive areas, some initial capital is needed. Religious organizations clearly have an advantage here, since they have access to seed money from the parent organization. Indeed, this access to venture capital is one reason for their predominance in the nonprofit sector; other potential entrepreneurs would have a hard time finding sources of risk capital without a risk return. Foundations that provide seed money for operating NPOs in the United States are, in a sense, their secular equivalent.

In countries characterized by excess demand, hence high potential profits, much of the venture capital for new NPOs comes from retained earnings of older operating NPOs that are legally required, after all, to reinvest their net revenues. Thus, we find vertically integrated chains and horizontally integrated branches of schools in countries such as India and Japan. In Japan, where debt financing plays a major role in private enterprise generally, nonprofit high schools and universities are also debt financed; in this sense, NPOs operate very much like PMOs. During the rapid expansionary period of the mid-sixties, over two-thirds of all private secondary and higher educational capital outlays were loan financed, and debt service constituted 15 to 20 percent of total expenditures (James & Benjamin 1987).

In Kerala, India, where the government sets generous salary floors for private school teachers, far in excess of their opportunity cost, large donations (equivalent to several years' wages) are often unofficially required for a job. In effect, this provides the capital for the classroom in which they will teach. (The male teachers, in turn, may finance their job acquisition by the higher dowry price they can demand, as a consequence of their improved job prospects.)

In developing countries the venture capital problem for NPOs is merely a small part of the general shortage of capital for all purposes. One common solution is the contribution of labor by groups of underemployed workers to build much-needed social overhead capital under the auspices of a (formal or informal) NPO. Examples are the *shramadama* (work camp) construction activities in Sri Lanka, in which (young) people are assembled to build roads or hospitals, and the *harambee* secondary schools in Kenya, built with community contributions, sometimes volunteer labor.

The international Western NPO (for example, Ford Foundation, YMCA, Dutch religious organizations) is also a major source of venture capital for indigenous Third World NPOs. Indeed, the latter were often set up specifically to receive funds from the former—an example of the international transmission of capital and institutional forms. But Western NPOs, in turn, get much of their funds from their governments (James 1982a). This brings us to our final and most important source of venture capital—the government.

Government support was needed for the bank loans to Japanese private schools extended during a period of credit rationing, and the provision of funds through international NPOs similarly depends on financing by Western governments. But the clearest case of governmental provision of venture capital occurs in modern welfare states. The few private schools in Sweden typically occupy buildings made available to them at below-market rentals by their municipalities. The Danish government extends low interest loans to cover construction costs of private schools. In Holland, where NPOs are strongest, the government goes further still, constructing buildings for and turning ownership over to each private school. Both in Sweden and Holland, sports facilities are constructed and maintained by local governments, but used by nonprofit sports organizations.

Thus, many solutions exist to the venture capital problem, with donations from wealthy individuals, so common in the United States, only a small part of the total picture, and government the largest part, from the international point of view.

Operating Funds

The contrast between American experience and that of other countries is even more striking with respect to operating funds—for example, funds to cover wages and other current expenses. In the United States, NPOs have historically obtained a large part of these revenues from voluntary sources—fees for services and donations. Indeed, the study of philanthropy and the study of NPOs have been viewed as synonymous and much NPO theory tries to explain this connection.

One quickly finds, however, that in other countries it is essential to distinguish between private service provision and private funding. In particular, philanthropy is very limited abroad. Nevertheless, nonprofit production is substantial in some of these countries, sometimes even larger (in relative terms) than in the United States. Where excess demand is strong, much of this funding comes from fees. In modern industrial societies, however, recurrent funding for these large nonprofit sectors, even more so than venture capital, comes primarily from the government.

This is well illustrated in table 22.1, which shows that 88 percent of NPO spending in the Netherlands and 65 percent in Sweden is government financed. Most of the rest comes from fees and rents of various sorts, except for religious organizations, which receive donations. Teachers and other workers in Dutch private schools are paid by the government and are considered civil servants. Likewise, the state is responsible for teacher salaries in many private schools in Belgium and France. Most private schools in India and England are "aided" schools, receiving over 50 percent of their funds from government subsidies. In Japan, which long resisted increased government spending on education, subsidies now cover 30 percent of private educational expenditures. Similar subsidies were recently instituted for Australian (largely Catholic) private schools. In Kenya, the nongovernmental harambee schools were initially self-supporting but have pressured the government for aid, usually for government-paid teachers. Even in the United States, where philanthropy is more common, government subsidies cover a large and increasing proportion of total nonprofit costs, the estimates ranging from 25 to 35 percent, depending on whether religious organizations are excluded and implicit tax subsidies are included. In the latter case, public finance far exceeds private donations.[3]

Thus, from the international perspective, reliance on nonprofit service provision and substantial government support go together. A ranking of the eleven member states of the European Community by the relative share of their private sectors in education shows that the top seven receive direct government subsidies, while three of the bottom four do not. Heading the list are Holland, Belgium, and Ireland, where virtually all the bills are paid by the state (Neave 1983, 5A). This positive correlation occurs as both cause and effect: such support, in many cases, seems necessary for the private sector to grow large (for example, Holland); in other cases a large private sector is politically powerful enough, having a potent combination of students, teachers, and entrepreneurs, to obtain government subsidies (for example, France and Japan). In both cases, it appears that large private nonprofit sectors cannot be long sustained without substantial government support.

Public Finance, Private Production

Why, then, does the government choose to delegate production rather than producing itself, and when does it delegate to nonprofit rather than for-profit enterprises? The answer to

---

3. See table 22.5. Figures given by Rudney (1981, 4–5) and Salamon and Musselwhite (1983, 10–12) show even larger amounts of government support.

these questions, I believe, throws new light on the theory of nonprofit organizations.

My work suggests three important reasons why subsidized private production is sometimes chosen by the government over pure public production of quasi-public goods. First, we have already seen that certain groups (often religious) want to control the schools and may engage in logrolling to obtain this control together with full or partial government subsidies. By delegating production, the party in power gains their political support. In many European countries, the religious group itself has a strong political party, able to implement the subsidies directly. These pressures may be particularly relevant in situations where cultural heterogeneity has motivated the growth of the private sector, on the demand side. The subsidies in such cases may cover most of the costs, as in Holland and Belgium.

Second, the share of total costs borne by the government is often less when production is delegated to private organizations. Private schools and hospitals face less political pressure against imposing fees; they are willing and able to meet some of their own costs in return for some decision-making autonomy. Thus, tuition and fees have covered well over half of private educational expenditures in the United States and Japan; small fees are even levied in Dutch private schools, despite generous government grants (Smith & Rosenbaum 1981, 20; James 1984; James & Benjamin 1987). Kramer (1982) documents that subsidized nonprofit social service organizations are expected to cover some of their expenses from private sources. The subsidies encourage private production and thereby bring about expansion of service at lower taxpayer costs.

Third, private schools and hospitals also benefit from cost-cutting devices, which usually involve lower labor costs than government institutions would face. Volunteer labor, for example, has been characteristic of nonprofit institutions. Although estimates vary, the most recent calculation indicated that its value exceeded total cash contributions in the United States (Hodgkinson & Weitzman 1984, 11, 44). In Sri Lanka, where labor is relatively more plentiful, volunteer time was estimated as 400 percent of domestic monetary contributions (James 1982a, 117). Religious schools and hospitals, in particular, have benefited from volunteer services of priests and nuns—although this has been declining in recent years (see Muller [1983] for data on the United States). Even when volunteer labor is not used, the private nonprofit-sector wage bill is often much less than in the public sector. For example, salaries of teachers in American private schools have historically been lower than those of public school teachers. Similarly, in Kenya and India (unsubsidized) private school teachers are typically paid much less than their public counterparts, the latter receiving wages far in excess of opportunity cost. In labor-surplus developing countries low-paid labor employed by NPOs may be a socially acceptable way of circumventing a minimum wage constraint that is above the market-clearing level.

In a later section I discuss at greater length the sources and

implications of the lower cost incurred by NPOs, its relationship to quality, and the impact of government subsidies on these variables. Suffice it here to point out that cost saving is, initially, a powerful rationale for the government to delegate production of quasi-public goods to private organizations. This may be particularly relevant in situations where excess demand in the face of limited government spending has motivated the growth of the private sector. In such cases, government may institute subsidies to encourage private production, but we would expect subsidies to cover only a modest portion of total costs, as in Japan and many developing countries.

Now, in cases where government subsidies are involved, nonprofit status of private schools and hospitals is often required. This suggests yet another reason for the choice of nonprofit status by the founders and for the predominance of NPOs over PMOs in these human services: NPOs are eligible to receive government grants and tax privileges. We must ask, then, why government prefers to donate to NPOs rather than PMOs. Earlier, I suggested that religious groups may lobby for subsidies and to restrict competition, may urge that only NPOs be eligible. In addition, in industries such as education that are characterized by many small enterprises, providing services rather than countable objects, monitoring each one by the government would be very costly. The one-way term *subsidy* or *grant* rather than the reciprocal term *purchase* suggests the difficulty in measuring quid pro quo. Nonprofit status assures the government that its subsidy will indeed be used to increase inputs providing (some of) the services in question, not simply distributed as profits. Politicians may have a high preference for avoiding scandal, and subsidies to NPOs may be considered "safer" than payments to PMOs, in situations where output cannot be readily observed.

NPO theory stresses the connection between nonprofit status and private philanthropy, the idea being that NPOs are considered more trustworthy than PMOs by potential donors who cannot directly monitor the use of their donations; hence NPOs survive in philanthropic areas. I have questioned this theory on grounds that, from a worldwide point of view, private philanthropy is unimportant, NPOs compete in production with government rather than with profit maximizers, and international differences in size of nonprofit sector are left unexplained. I now suggest that, for the reasons given above, governments may sometimes choose to delegate production of quasi-public goods, may buttress this delegation with subsidies, and, partially for monitoring reasons, may prefer to subsidize NPOs. Thus, asymmetric information and transactions costs do indeed enter into the preference for the nonprofit institutional form. They enter, however, not because of the attitude of many small donors but, rather, because of one large donor with the power to set certain basic contractual terms—the government.[4]

4. It is interesting to note that in concentrated industries (for example, defense, space) the government deals with PMOs, since it can more easily monitor and/or regulate a small number of large firms. However, even these contracts are often written on a cost-plus basis, in effect

Government Regulation

What is the relationship between government funding and government regulation? Does more of the former imply more of the latter? If so, the government controls could obviate some of the advantages (and disadvantages) of the private sector, which stem from its independence, differentiated product, and ability to respond rapidly and economize on costs. My research suggests that nonprofits can be regulated with or without subsidies, but usually do pay a price in terms of loss of autonomy as subsidies increase. The regulations may be imposed simultaneously with the subsidies, but, more commonly, they are added after the private organizations have become dependent on government funds. The normative rationale is that, once public funds garnered by compulsory taxation are given, society also has a right (duty) to exert some control over how these funds are spent. A positive rationale is that, once having given funds, politicians have the power to demand a quid pro quo, and they use this power to establish rules and standards that gain them goodwill from diverse constituencies.

This finding seems to conflict with that of Kramer (1982) who finds subsidized social service organizations to be largely uncontrolled. This apparent conflict, however, probably stems from the fact that he is concentrating on output restrictions; I have observed that many government regulations apply to inputs rather than outputs. For example, in Dutch private schools teacher numbers and salaries, as well as required teacher credentials, are centrally determined, as are hours and other conditions of work; we also find rigid restrictions on the school's ability to fire teachers. In Kenya, government-paid teachers are supplied directly by the public Teachers Service Commission. Salaries and qualifications of teachers in aided private schools in Sweden, France, and India are regulated. One rationale is that inputs are easier to measure and control than outputs; these regulations may be used in situations where inputs are readily observable but outputs (including quality) are not. In addition, this observation is consistent with the hypothesis, discussed below, that government financing is a response to producer as well as consumer interests, and the regulations are designed in large part to protect the producers.[5]

Direct controls over outputs also exist in these countries (for example, over curriculum, length of time spent on each subject, examination and degree requirements). These, however, seem less tied to subsidies, often applying to unaided as well as aided schools. Controls over quantity are more commonly tied to subsidies: government permission may be needed to start new schools or expand old ones. In Japan an informal agreement to stabilize sectoral shares seemed to accompany the institution of government subsidies (James & Benjamin 1987).

Controls extend, too, over the distribution of service and the criteria for selecting students in subsidized schools. For example, the price for government support to the mission schools in postindependence Kenya is that they agree to forgo religion as a basis for selection. Schools that receive aid must use centrally determined student selection criteria. Government in Holland and Sweden places a ceiling on the fees that subsidized private schools can charge (James 1982b). In India tuition floors are set in some states, ceilings in others, for aided schools, reflecting different philosophies about whether the regulations are designed to enhance quality (floors) or equality (ceilings). Dutch schools are proscribed from excluding students who do not pay; at the university level, students are allocated among private institutions by a central governing body (James 1984). In Sweden the government has claimed the right to assign students to the private vocational schools it supports (James 1982b). In France private schools are eligible for subsidy only if they agree to become part of the regional educational plan, accepting students from a catchment area designated by the government (Neave 1983, 18).

One of the most interesting regulations found both in Sweden and in Holland concerns the decision-making process in NPOs. For example, Swedish nonprofit organizations for youth and immigrants, encouraged by the government, are required to be "democratic," "representative," and "participatory" in order to qualify for subsidy. Similarly, Dutch workers and, to a lesser extent, consumers have a mandated role in the decision-making process of private schools and social service organizations (James 1982b). Aided French schools must accept representatives of state and local governments on their boards of directors (Neave 1983, 19). In NPOs, where profits are not the predetermined goal, choices about output and technology depend on the preferences of the decision makers. Consequently, changing the composition of decision-making bodies can change the way the organization behaves, one way of maintaining social control yet permitting decentralization at the same time.

Finally, subsidized private schools are usually required to submit detailed financial statements to the government in order to enable detection of disguised profit distribution. This was one of the few regulations accompanying the subsidies in Japan. If successfully implemented, this would mean that some private-school founder/managers have become worse rather than better off as a consequence of the subsidy scheme (and some Japanese schools have voluntarily turned down the subsidy as a result).

Thus, private nonprofit schools and other organizations clearly face a trade-off between more autonomy and more funds. These rules are designed partially to maintain quality control and/or increase equality, but they come at the expense of the variety and choice a privatized system is supposed to provide. It also follows that, while "private non-

---

turning part of the PMO into a constrained-profit enterprise for purposes of dealing with the government.

5. For a discussion of input-based (financial) controls rather than output-based (programmatic) controls in the case of public television, see Powell and Friedkin (1986). The output controls are long run and implicit: if programming is consistently counter to government intentions, funding may be cut off at some point in the future.

profit'' may remain an unambiguous legal category, the public-private breakdown of decision-making power is much more mixed and continuous; pure private management, like pure private funding of NPOs, is rare.[6]

PART 3. COST AND QUALITY IN THE NONPROFIT SECTOR

Lower Cost: Does This Mean Lower Quality or Higher Efficiency?

As noted earlier, one rationale for the government to delegate production responsibilities to nonprofit organizations is the lower cost thereby incurred. Should the lower cost incurred by NPOs, before subsidization, be interpreted as evidence of lower quality or higher efficiency as compared with public institutions? This is what we would like to know and it is most difficult to ascertain. The former interpretation assumes that efficiency is the same in the two sectors, so lower valued inputs must mean less value added. The latter assumes that value added by the two sectors is the same, so lower costs imply greater efficiency in processing inputs, usually ascribed to more skillful management and better incentives in the private system. I shall analyze this issue with particular attention to the case of education. I also present some observations on the impact of subsidies on costs.

A definitive examination of this question would require an accurate measure of value added, a task that is greatly complicated by differences among schools in their student inputs as well as ambiguities concerning the appropriate measure of output. The output of education has been variously interpreted as amount earned by graduates (that is, incremental lifetime earnings), amount learned (for example, incremental scores on achievement tests), or willingness to pay (that is, the consumer's subjective evaluation of all the investment and consumption benefits of education); these three measures may give different gross outputs. To ascribe differential output effects to a school type requires us, furthermore, to control for student input, so that we are measuring ''net value added'' by the school itself, independent of the value of the incoming student or peer group effect. Unfortunately, these data are generally not available. The most careful study of this issue, based on a longitudinal survey of U.S. high school sophomores and seniors, concluded that private schools were more effective (see Coleman, Hoffer, & Kilgore 1981, 1982), but this finding has been vigorously attacked by many critics (Murnane 1983a; Murnane, Newstead & Olsen 1983; Goldberger & Kane 1982). Thus, even when excellent data are available and supposedly objective econometric techniques are used, it turns out that the results are highly sensi-

tive to choice of statistical methodologies with different underlying assumptions; hence the definitive answer continues to elude.

In other countries we simply do not have the data necessary for sophisticated econometric analyses. I have, however, approached this issue in another way, conducting a careful examination of how private schools coexist with public schools and trying to evaluate whether, when costs are lower, the sources of cost saving and the consumer response imply lower quality or greater efficiency.

Consider, first, the converse case of Holland. Dutch public and private schools receive the same subsidy per student, and the private schools charge a small fee as well, so their cost per student is actually (slightly) higher than in public schools. Does this mean that their value added is also greater? The problem in analyzing this is that the student inputs are, by definition, differentiated along religious lines. For example, relatively few Catholics have historically gone on to the university; is this due to a Catholic school effect or an effect stemming from the student's cultural background?

We can, however, use a more direct market-based test to examine public-private differences in school quality and efficiency in the Netherlands. Since people have a choice, which is not biased by unequal subsidies, we can simply observe their actions to make inferences about perceived benefits and costs—the approach we usually use in economic analysis. The fact that 70 percent of all parents choose to send their children to private schools, which charge a small fee (despite the presence of free public schools nearby), suggests they believe they are getting more for their money there. Part of this preference, of course, comes from religious identification and from the desire for religious segmentation. However, since the proportion attending private schools has not declined with the increasing secularization of Dutch society, other forces must also be at work. Many people with whom I discussed this issue believe that the private schools are more personal and responsive to consumer wishes, more careful about how they spend their funds than the publics. Private schools are considered more flexible, less bureaucratic, and effectively overseen by a board of directors specifically concerned about the welfare of the school, rather than by a generalized municipal administration. We also know that, on the average, private and public schools spend their discretionary funds somewhat differently, the latter paying more for ''maintenance and cleaning,'' the former having more left over for various ''educational facilities'' (James 1984). Although objective proof is not available, the majority of parents have revealed their preference for (belief in the greater efficiency of) the private schools.

As a second case we consider Japan, which in many ways is a polar opposite to Holland (see James & Benjamin 1987). In Japan, public high schools and universities are generally preferred by parents, both because their tuition is much lower owing to generous government subsidies and because their prestige is higher. Students at public institutions, on average, achieve higher test scores and lifetime earnings, suggesting that their gross output is indeed greater. However, the stu-

---

6. As one example of a hybrid organization, consider the case of the Kenyan hamambee school, which is built with volunteer contributions of money and labor from local communities on an informal basis, often has a teacher whose salary is paid by the central government, therefore faces regulations over criteria for admitting students, and is managed (at the request of the community) by a mission group, one of the few groups with educational managerial experience. Is this private or public, secular or religious?

dent input is also superior at these schools, which are highly selective, and employers may use them for their screening rather than human capital-building function, making it unclear whether social value added is also greater there.

On average, the private sector in Japan operates at much lower cost per student than the public sector; in 1973, before substantial government subsidies were instituted, the private-public cost ratio was .72 for high schools and .38 for higher education (James & Benjamin 1987). Indeed, this is characteristic of most countries (Brazil, Philippines, India) where the private sector has developed in response to excess demand (see Levy [1983] on Latin American higher education). To what can we attribute this cost differential?

I found that in Japan part of it stemmed from product mix differentials (for example, more teaching and liberal arts, less science and research in the private sector); these are independent of both quality and efficiency implications. Part of the cost differential stemmed from lower input-output ratios (for example, more students per faculty member, larger class size) in private schools. American consumers tend to assess large classes as low quality, but the Japanese do not make the same subjective evaluation and they may be right—the objective research evidence is inconclusive despite numerous studies on this topic. (For a summary of this literature, see Hanushek [1981].)

However, much of the cost differential is due to lower wages paid to workers, especially teachers. The use of low-paid teachers in Japan is facilitated by the presence of enclaves of underemployed workers who do not have full access to the labor market, namely young women and retired men. The disproportionate presence of these groups in the private sector keeps wages low there, despite the fact that formal credentials of teachers are comparable to those in the public sector. Part-timers are also heavily employed in private universities; they are not paid fringe benefits, which they receive from their regular jobs, and the moonlighting wage rate tends to be lower as well. Lower wages are, in fact, a characteristic of unsubsidized private schools (except for a few elite ones) in most countries I have studied—for example, Sweden, India, Kenya, and even the United States, where "volunteer" labor by priests and nuns kept Catholic schools financially solvent for many years.

Is this evidence of greater efficiency or lower quality? Do the lower wages available to these groups stem from their lower productivity or simply from an artificial segmentation of the labor market, which arbitrarily makes different opportunities available to different kinds of people? By the former interpretation, the private sector is offering lower quality teaching. By the latter interpretation, the private sector is able to take advantage of these labor market imperfections and hire equivalent services at lower cost, whereas the public sector is proscribed by custom or law from paying market-clearing wages and, instead, rations jobs by a variety of nonprice criteria, such as age, sex, nepotism, or bribery, which are often not related to quality. Even if these criteria are quality related on average, there may be much variance in individual cases, which can only be assessed subjectively.

Relaxation of these formal credentials may be ruled out in public schools but permitted in private schools, which can therefore, with good subjective judgment, hire equally effective workers with a different bundle of observable attributes at lower cost. In the absence of objective measures of value added and productivity, I leave it to the reader to draw his or her own conclusions about relative quality and efficiency. Relevant to this judgment are calculations of the social rate of return to university education in Japan using market measures of cost, which showed lifetime earnings to be lower but the social rate of return higher to graduates of the private sector. Perhaps a combination of lower quality and greater efficiency (that is, poorer student inputs, possibly lower value added per pupil, but higher value added per unit of expenditure) is provided by many private educational organizations.

The Perverse Impact of Government Subsidies

However, as we have seen, the very growth of the private sector ultimately sets up political pressure for subsidies and a major effect of the subsidies, in Japan and elsewhere, is to reduce the cost advantage. In particular, wages rise dramatically when subsidies are instituted; indeed, this is commonly required as a condition of the subsidy. In Japan, higher quality (costs) in private schools was a stated object of the subsidies that began in the early 1970s and cover 30 percent of private schools' costs today. The public/private cost differential did indeed decline, but almost all of this decline was due to an increase in private school teacher salaries. While private school teachers were paid much less than those in public schools before the subsidies were introduced, by 1983 they were actually paid more (James & Benjamin 1987).

Paid teachers replaced volunteer labor and salaries rose rapidly when subsidies were granted to Dutch private schools at the turn of the century, when the Swedish government took over the private girls' schools in the 1920s and instituted subsidies to adult education over the last two decades (James 1982b; 1986a), and when the communist government in Kerala, India, instituted subsidies to private schools in the 1950s. In each case, teachers were major gainers. Similar observations have been made concerning the impact of government subsidies in the arts and social services (Netzer 1978; Kramer 1982).

How can we explain this common phenomenon? In some cases the government may have required higher wages in exchange for the subsidy; indeed, this may have been their major intent. In other cases higher wages are not required by law but are exacted by unions as the financial security of the private schools and the value of their workers grows because of government support.

The higher salaries may enable more and better staff to be hired and rapid expansion without downgrading quality; at least, this was often their ostensible intent. However, the inframarginal workers gain a "profit"—the subsidy constitutes, in part, a redistribution of income to them. Thus, both consumer and producer interests are involved in government subsidies to NPOs. Once private schools and other NPOs have been started, new interest groups coalesce—of teachers and other workers—and they may exert pressure on politicians. Whereas economic efficiency arguments are usually couched in terms of consumer interests, the data given above suggests that the latter are at least equally important in the political process that creates and maintains these subsidies. Ironically, NPOs may be subsidized because of an initial cost advantage, but owing to this dynamic process, this cost advantage disappears after substantial subsidies are introduced.

CONCLUSION

In summary, I have offered an alternative to the conventional theory of NPO formation, based on a few simple observations from the international scene. The fact that most NPO founders were religious organizations, with the objective of maintaining and increasing their adherents rather than maximizing profits, explains why the nonprofit form was chosen by them and why it is found in such socializing or crucial life-and-death institutions as schools and hospitals. The difficulty in raising capital for NPOs explains further their concentration in labor-intensive industries such as education, health, and social service. Their access to donations and low-cost labor, such as priests and nuns, as well as their religious "brand name," gave them an advantage over secular PMOs. Religious NPOs, in effect, have a lower supply price than PMOs, and NPOs will dominate in industries chosen by the religious group. Thus, a theory based on entrepreneurship and input characteristics is offered in place of theories that stress lack of consumer information about output characteristics, in explaining which services are provided by nonprofit rather than for-profit organizations.

These services also tend to be quasi-public goods—that is, goods that yield both public and private benefits—and are therefore often government financed. Indeed, we have seen that, in most countries, government subsidies to NPOs are large and private philanthropy small. Given the political power of organized religious groups and the difficulties in monitoring many small enterprises, government often requires subsidy recipients to have nonprofit status; nonprofits are also eligible for varying tax privileges in different countries. This special treatment by government further builds the comparative advantage of NPOs over PMOs in the provision of quasi-public goods. Indeed, there is no empirical evidence that market forces alone could lead to NPO dominance.

While NPOs have a cost advantage over PMOs under these circumstances, government services usually have a price advantage over NPOs. Therefore, coexistence of the latter two must also be explained. I suggest that NPOs flourish where excess demand exists, in the face of limited government production, or where intensely felt preferences over product variety (religious, linguistic, quality) make people willing to pay a higher price for a differentiated product. These demand-side variables explain why a private market exists for the production of quasi-public goods and the supply-side variables explain why nonprofits develop to different extents in different countries, and are often able to prevail over for-profits in this private market.

This view of the nonprofit sector as depending on tastes and domestic policies within a country needs to be modified slightly when dealing with Third World countries, where much of the nonprofit sector is financed from abroad. There, preferences of and cultural diversity among foreign donors and policies of foreign governments may be more important than purely domestic factors (James 1982a). Although today private schools and hospitals are mainly financed by domestic sources, many were originally established by missionary entrepreneurs. Other indigenous nonprofit organizations are largely financed by grants from foreign governments or international nonprofit organizations (especially church groups). (See chapter 23 by Anheier.) In fact, the indigenous organizations are sometimes set up primarily to receive this revenue—an example of the export of an institutional form from West to East, going together with the export of funds.

A major potential advantage of private service provision is that this often permits some reliance on voluntary payments, thereby revealing and implementing people's preferences and reducing the necessary amount of taxation and tax-induced disincentive effects. The political decision about how much education and other services to provide publicly may lead to an excess demand which people are willing to purchase on the private market; if the private rate of return does not exceed the social, these purchases are efficient. The corresponding disadvantage is that this may discourage further expansion in the public sector, thereby limiting the access of low-income groups. In fact, in many countries the high private benefit of education and the large government subsidy to private schools seem to mitigate this problem; whether this would also be true of other quasi-public goods is less clear.

A second source of comparative advantage for the private sector in quasi-public-good production arises in cases where product variety is possible, tastes are differentiated, and economies of scale are relatively small. Diverse organizations may be better able than government to offer a heterogeneous product mix and enable people to make separate choices about different services, rather than tying together a bundle of public goods, as is done through local governmental provision. The corresponding disadvantage is the possible segmentation of society into many small religious, linguistic, and racial groups. Although this can be prevented by specific integrationist policies, it certainly has happened in some courtries (such as Holland and Belgium) with large private educational sectors.

A third advantage of privatization is the lower costs often implied initially; private organizations may be able to avoid constraints on factor utilization, wage floors, and bureaucratic red tape which keep government costs high. This may facilitate large increases in quantity consumed. The corresponding disadvantage is the possibility that lower costs may mean lower quality.

For example, had all the enrollment expansion in Japan been confined to the public sector, it probably would have involved more uniform and higher expenditures per student and possibly better quality, hence a greater opportunity cost of education. The total social cost would have been greater yet because of the deadweight loss of tax financing versus fee financing. The trade-off between cost of quality on the one hand and quantity on the other would have meant that fewer students, including low-income students, could have been accommodated. The private sector, then, enabled more rapid enrollment growth, but it may have led to a lower enrollment share for and less redistribution to low-income groups than a more heavily subsidized system would have.

Most of the examples in this chapter have been drawn from the field of education. To what extent are these observations generalizable to other services provided by nonprofits as well? I would argue that many, but not all, of the ideas presented above apply also to quasi-public goods, such as health care and social services, that are produced both by government and private nonprofit organizations. In all cases, religious entrepreneurship plays a key role in the private sector. In all cases, the private sector develops to provide a service that is not being provided (in type or amount) by the government. In all cases, public funding (through direct subsidies, tax benefits, or social insurance) is important. However, there are major differences in the nature of demand for these other services, in the relative supply of the nonprofit form, and in the welfare evaluation of public versus private provision.

In the case of health care, private hospitals have developed where people are dissatisfied with either the amount or the quality of government hospitals and have an effective demand (ability and willingness to pay) for the private service. Since much health care is covered by third-party payers—voluntary or compulsory medical insurance—neither public nor private provision can be said to reveal peoples' true preferences about the value of these services. Cultural heterogeneity as a source of demand, hence private-sector advantages stemming from responsiveness to differentiated tastes, are less important for health care than for education.

Many private hospitals, both here and abroad, were founded by religious organizations (missionaries, for example), and these are nonprofit.[7] But private for-profit enterprise also flourishes in the health industry, particularly in developing countries. These often take the form of doctors' practices and clinics (small hospitals) attached thereto. Preliminary investigations suggest that government hospitals are the largest and most capital intensive and for-profit practices and clinics the most numerous in many other countries. Thus, the health care industry has components in all three sectors, with the nonprofit sector possibly the least important, abroad. Since medical care is often cited as a service whose quality consumers are unable to evaluate and hence should prefer "trustworthy" nonprofit hospitals, this obser-

vation about their relative importance in other countries casts further doubt on informational asymmetry theories of nonprofit development.

The provision of many other social services, such as services for the poor, the handicapped, and so on, are different from health and education in that they are designed for particular groups whose present and expected future income is relatively low; hence the "need" of the direct recipients cannot be translated into effective demand in the private market. Effective demand, then, comes from recipients of external benefits or people who wish to redistribute real income in the form of particular services, and the redistribution may take place through a public or private transfer system—that is, through government grants or private philanthropy. Neither of these mechanisms reveals true preferences—government fails because it uses compulsory taxation and the private sector fails because of the free-rider problem inherent in a system of voluntary donations.

Once again, religious entrepreneurship plays a major role in the private sector and uses the nonprofit form. In contrast to health care, private for-profit provision of (charitable) social services, dependent on philanthropy, is rare. Are people then willing to donate (labor and money) because they trust the nonprofit legal form or because they belong to and trust the religious group that runs it? Is the organization set up as a nonprofit to encourage donations or because the religious entrepreneurs had some other nonpecuniary objective in mind? In line with my earlier discussion, I would argue for the importance of religious motivations, both for founding and donating.

In education, health, and social service, government support (in grants, tax privileges, or insurance) plays a major role in large private sectors, displacing fees (education) and donations (social service) as the key source of funding. Indeed, as we have seen, private-sector growth and government subsidies usually go hand in hand; large private sectors are rarely sustained for long periods without government support. The dependence of NPOs on public funding means that, whereas the two sectors may be substitutes in production, they are complements in expenditures. Once a division of production responsibilities has been determined, expenditures by NPO sector and size of government budget will be positively correlated.

The subsidies facilitate private-sector growth, but they also enable the government to extract concessions in return, in the form of regulations over inputs, outputs, and other characteristics that satisfy diverse constituencies. The subsidies, and the regulations and market forces that accompany them, have the effect of raising costs. This development is not inevitable, but it certainly is common. Thus, the very factors that originally created the demand for a private sector also set in motion forces making the private sector more like the public; as the private sector grows, with government funding and regulating, it becomes quasi governmental. This possible convergence between public and large private sectors, in a variety of industries, is one of the many topics needing further study as we examine the nonprofit sector from a comparative international perspective.

7. Other sources of nonprofit entrepreneurship also exist in the American health care industry. Hospitals may be organized by medical schools as teaching facilities; hence they have education, as well as health and earnings, as goals. Or they may be organized by doctors as cooperatives designed to maximize physicians' incomes; hence they constitute an avenue for disguised profit distribution. These secular nonprofits seem to be less prevalent abroad, and secular for-profits are more common.

REFERENCES

Ben-Ner, Avner. 1986. "Nonprofit Organizations: Why Do They Exist in Market Economies?" In *The Economics of Nonprofit Institutions: Studies in Structure and Policy,* edited by Susan Rose-Ackerman. Oxford: Oxford University Press.

Coleman, James, Thomas Hoffer, and Sally Kilgore. 1981. "Questions and Answers: Our Response." *Harvard Educational Review* 51 (November):526–45.

———. 1982. *High School Achievement: Public, Catholic and Private Schools Compared.* New York: Basic Books.

Easley, David, and M. O'Hara. 1983. "The Economic Role of the Nonprofit Firm." *Bell Journal of Economics* 14.

Flora, Peter, and Arnold J. Heidenheimer. 1981. *The Development of Welfare States in Europe and America.* New Brunswick, N.J.: Transaction Books.

Geiger, Roger. 1984. *Private Sectors in Higher Education: Structure, Function and Change in Eight Countries.* Mimeographed.

Glennerster, Howard, and Gail Wilson. 1970. *Paying for Public Schools.* London: Allen Lane/Penguin Press.

Goldberger, A. S. 1964. *Econometric Theory.* New York: Wiley.

Goldberger, Arthur, and Glenn Kane. 1982. "The Causal Analysis of Cognitive Outcomes in the Coleman, Hoffer, and Kilgore Report." *Sociology of Education* 55:103–52.

Goodman Committee. 1976. *Charity, Law and Voluntary Organizations.* London: Bedford Square Press of the National Council of Social Service.

Hansmann, Henry. 1980. "The Role of Nonprofit Enterprise." *Yale Law Journal* 89:835–98.

———. 1981. "Nonprofit Enterprise in the Performing Arts." *Bell Journal of Economics* 12:341–61.

Hanushek, Eric. 1981. "Throwing Money at Schools," *Journal of Policy Analysis and Management,* Fall.

Hatch, Stephen. 1980. *Outside the State: Voluntary Organizations in Three English Towns.* London: Croom-Helm.

Hodgkinson, Virginia, and Murray Weitzman. 1984. *Dimensions of the Independent Sector: A Statistical Profile.* Washington, D.C.: Independent Sector.

James, Estelle. 1982a. "The Nonprofit Sector in International Perspective: The Case of Sri Lanka." *Journal of Comparative Economics* 6:99–129.

———. 1982b. "The Private Provision of Public Services: A Comparison of Holland and Sweden." Yale University, Program on Non-Profit Organizations Working Paper no. 60.

———. 1983. "How Nonprofits Grow: A Model." *Journal of Policy Analysis and Management* 2:350–65.

———. 1984. "Benefits and Costs of Privatized Public Services: Lessons from the Dutch Educational System." *Comparative Education Review* 28:605–25.

———. 1986a. "The Public/Private Division of Responsibility for Education: An International Comparison." *Economics of Education Review.*

———. 1986b. "Differences in the Private Educational System in Modern and Developing Countries." Mimeographed.

James, Estelle, and Gail Benjamin. 1987. *Public versus Private Education: The Japanese Experiment.* London: Macmillan.

Kramer, Ralph. 1982. *Voluntary Agencies in the Welfare State.* Berkeley: University of California Press.

Levy, Daniel. 1983. "An Evaluative Overview of Latin American Private Higher Education." Mimeographed.

———. 1984. *The State and Higher Education in Latin America.* Mimeographed.

Lijphart, Arend. 1968. *The Politics of Accommodation: Pluralist and Democracy in the Netherlands.* Berkeley: University of California Press.

Little, Kenneth. 1965. *West African Urbanization: A Study of Voluntary Associations in Social Change.* Cambridge: Cambridge University Press.

Marklund, Sixten. 1959. *Educational Administration and Educational Development.* Stockholm: Institute of International Education.

Marklund, Sixten, and Gunnar Bergendal. 1979. *Trends in Swedish Educational Policy.* Stockholm: Swedish Institute.

Mecham, J. Lloyd. 1966. *Church and State in Latin America.* Chapel Hill: University of North Carolina Press.

Morris, Mary. 1969. *Voluntary Work in the Welfare State.* London: Routledge & Kegan Paul.

Muller, Carol Blue. 1983. "The Social and Political Consequences of Increased Public Support for Private Schools." In *Public Dollars for Private Schools,* edited by Thomas James and Henry Levin, 39–55. Philadelphia: Temple University Press.

Murnane, Richard J. 1983. "Comparisons of Public and Private Schools: Lessons from the Uproar." Yale University, Program on Non-Profit Organizations Working Paper no. 73.

Murnane, Richard, Stuart Newstead, and Randol J. Olsen. 1983. "Comparing Public and Private Schools: The Puzzling Role of Selectivity Bias." Yale University, Program on Non-Profit Organizations Working Paper no. 68.

Neave, Guy. 1983. "The Nonstate Sector in the Education Provision of Member States of the European Community." Brussels: Report to the Education Services of the Commission of the European Community.

Netzer, Richard. 1978. *The Subsidized Muse.* Cambridge: Cambridge University Press.

Owen, David. 1964. *English Philanthropy, 1660–1960.* Cambridge, Mass.: Belknap Press of Harvard University.

Powell, Walter W., and Rebecca Friedkin. 1986. "Politics and Programs: Organizational Factors in Public Television Decision Making." In *Nonprofit Enterprise in the Arts,* edited by Paul DiMaggio. New York: Oxford University Press.

Pryor, Frederick. 1968. *Public Expenditures in Communist and Capitalist Nations.* New Haven, Yale University Press.

Rooff, Madeline. 1957. *Voluntary Societies and Social Policy.* London: Routledge & Kegan Paul.

Rudney, Gabriel. 1981. "A Quantitative Profile of the Nonprofit Sector." Yale University, Program on Non-Profit Organizations Working Paper no. 40.

Salamon, Lester, and James C. Musselwhite, Jr. 1983. "Voluntary Organizations and the Crises of the Welfare State." Washington, D.C.: Urban Institute.

Smith, Brian. 1982. "Churches as Development Institutions: The Case of Chile, 1973–80." Yale University, Program on Non-Profit Organizations Working Paper no. 50.

———. 1983. "U.S. and Canadian Nonprofit Organizations (PVO's) as Transnational Development Institutions." Yale University, Program on Non-Profit Organizations Working Paper no. 70.

Smith, Bruce, and Nelson Rosenbaum. 1981. "The Fiscal Capacity of the Voluntary Sector." Washington, D.C.: Brookings Institution.

Smith, Constance, and Anne Freedman. 1972. *Voluntary Associations: Perspectives on the Literature.* Cambridge, Mass.: Harvard University Press.

Tanaka, Minoru, and Amemiya, Takako. 1983. *Philanthropy in Japan '83: Private Nonprofit Activities in Japan 1983.* Tokyo: Japan Association of Charitable Corporations.

Tendler, Judith. 1982. "Turning Private Voluntary Organizations into Developmental Organizations. Questions for Evaluation." Washington, D.C.: A.I.D. Discussion Paper no. 12.

Weisbrod, Burton. 1975. "Toward a Theory of the Voluntary Nonprofit Sector in a Three-Sector Economy." In *Altruism, Morality and Economic Theory,* edited by Edmund Phelps, 171–95. New York: Russell Sage Foundation.

———. 1977. *The Voluntary Nonprofit Sector.* Lexington, Mass.: Lexington Books.

West, E. G. 1970. *Education and the State.* London: Institute of Economic Affairs.

Wilensky, Harold. 1975. *The Welfare State and Equality.* Berkeley: University of California Press.

Wolfenden Committee. 1978. *The Future of Voluntary Organizations.* London: Croom-Helm.

Zellner, Arnold, and T. H. Lee. 1965. "Joint Estimation of Relationships Involving Discrete Random Variables." *Econometrica* 33:382–94.

23

Indigenous Voluntary Associations, Nonprofits, and Development in Africa

HELMUT K. ANHEIER

This synthesizing review of the relevant literature on indigenous third-sector organizations in Africa south of the Sahara[1] covers a great variety of organizational forms: voluntary associations, rotating credit associations, self-help groups, improvement societies, village associations, cooperatives, public corporations, and nongovernmental organizations, among others. All are alike in that they are neither governmental agencies nor true for-profit enterprises. They range, however, from modern to traditional groups, from genuinely African to imported forms, from more or less governmentally controlled to grass-roots organizations, from organizations created in the course of development projects with excellent ties to international funding agencies to organizations existing in the backwaters of African societies. As in the West, there is no prototype of the African third-sector organization.

Although the importance of voluntary associations in the African context was identified by anthropologists as early as the 1920s (Lowie 1925; Westermann 1935), it was not until the 1960s that they received detailed attention by social scientists. By this time the problems of rapid urbanization had worsened: rural surplus extraction persisted and often increased; countries were beset by political instability and mismanagement of programs; and Western "rationalizers"

(markets and bureaucracies) seemed to create more problems for African societies than they solved. In response to the failure of many large-scale programs and development plans, a new approach to the problems was emerging (Schumacher 1973). Advocated by some international development agencies and donor organizations, this approach entailed the use of private voluntary associations (PVO) in the course of development. Rather than simply replacing local social structures with large-scale forms of production and administration, the new method focused on maintaining and reinforcing indigenous organizations in order to achieve a gradual improvement of living conditions.

Earlier modernization theories were criticized for failing to take account of two crucial factors now coming to be regarded as essential to effective development: local participation and initiative, and self-help and self-management by the people affected. Development programs were no longer to be "implemented" but rather to be "facilitated." What once had been planned on a macrolevel—the development of whole African societies or entire regions—was now to be conducted at the community level. Catchphrases—like "bottom-up" versus "top-down" administration, "development from above" versus "development from below," and "blueprint" versus "greenhouse" approaches—were heard that illustrated well the divergent paths to development.[2]

The post–World War II confidence in large-scale planning, massive technology transfer between societies, and

I gratefully acknowledge the financial support received from the Ford Foundation and the Program on Non-Profit Organizations, Yale University. I wish to thank Juan J. Linz, Paul DiMaggio, Woody Powell, and Gladys Topkis for supplying helpful critiques of an earlier draft.

1. Because the Republic of South Africa represents a special case, literature dealing with that country's third sector is not included in this discussion.

2. For a very influential work concerning the development ideology of many religious private voluntary organizations (PVOS), see Freire (1972). In reference to changing policies in developing countries, see, for example, the U.S. Foreign Assistance Act of 1962 as amended, 1973.

capital-intensive projects gave way to a more "humble approach, implying that development is primarily a matter of trial and error with as many unanticipated consequences as anticipated. The Promethean spirit marked by such characteristics as controlled experimentation, manipulation and functional rationality is no longer the dominant force on the intellectual scene" (Hyden 1983a, IV–7). The encouragement of private and voluntary efforts, a reliance on local initiatives rather than planned interventions, and the creation of incentives to use local know-how rather than Western technology and its models of rational organization characterize what came to be called the "greenhouse" approach. In this context African third-sector organizations fit well and are now in great favor among planners and social scientists. The new approach to development, however, is based on several crucial assumptions that are often left unspecified but that will become clear in the following pages. At this point, I will simply note three important factors.

First, the ideological shift from a macrolevel, large-scale approach to local, small-scale initiatives had its origin in Africa and Latin America, but its support came chiefly from outside the developing world.

Second, the ideological shift has not been without a substantial dose of irony. Earlier modernization theory was based on the notions of a free market economy and a free, or at least increasingly free, society. Yet in practice, development efforts in the context of the theory required far-reaching state interventions, which resulted in planned economies. It was a theory originating in the for-profit world, but in practice it turned out to be a governmental program of national development plans assisted by bilateral and multilateral agencies. Entrepreneurs, central to modernization theory, were replaced by planners and bureaucrats. Although the greenhouse approach contains several elements also present in modernization theory, in practice they diverge—for example, in the matter of decentralized local action. Thus, the development-from-below approach in the end resembles more closely the unplanned, individually oriented society and is conceptually closer to a market economy. Self-help organizations and private voluntary efforts require spontaneous, participatory, and creative personalities—not unlike the classic profit-seeking entrepreneur. But in contrast to him, participants in self-help groups are expected to aim for the common good rather than maximum private returns (see, for example, Hyden 1983b, 120).

Third, ultimately, both approaches must be judged by their patterns of success and failure, but making judgments is difficult. For one thing, the available evidence on the benefits of working through indigenous third-sector organizations is far from clear; the data are insufficient and unreliable. Moreover, the two approaches imply two different notions of what constitutes development. And however "development" is defined, the very process of definition involves making decisions that are implicitly or explicitly ideologically grounded.

What strategy is called for in a given situation and evaluating its success depends on whether the end product of development is seen as an increase in per capita GNP, a more equitable income distribution, a higher level of awareness among the rural poor, or some combination of these. Because the two approaches employ such strikingly different criteria, it is almost impossible to compare them. We are faced with a missing yardstick, so to speak. I have, however, devised several questions that are central to any evaluation of the role and behavior of African third-sector organizations in development.

1. What types of organizations constitute the indigenous African third sector? And, related to this, how closely does the African situation resemble its equivalent in developed Western societies?

2. How reliable are the social science descriptions of these organizations?

3. What is the developmental potential of indigenous third-sector organizations?

However they do it, African societies must develop soon to avoid a social and economic disaster within the next decade (Todaro 1977; Acharya 1981). The overall performance of all but a few African countries in social, political, and economic terms has been disappointing during recent years; most parts of the continent are relatively more underdeveloped today than they were ten years ago. Twenty-two of the thirty-six poorest countries in the world are in Africa, and by any criterion for measuring level of development, the continent is the least developed in the world (Kiros 1981; World Bank 1983). Thus, all organizations in Africa have ultimately to be judged from a developmental point of view: to what extent do they contribute to a solution for this deep social and economic malaise?

THE PROBLEM OF HETEROGENEITY: SEARCHING FOR A UNIFYING THEME

Most previous attempts to define and classify third-sector organizations in Africa have not contributed to conceptual clarification for several reasons.

First, as mentioned earlier, there is no prototype of a third-sector organization (Ben-Ner 1982), which helps account for the diversity of definitions, terms, and acronyms. In the search for a unifying terminology, Muenckner (1979) and Seibel (1981) suggested applying the term "self-help group" to such diverse phenomena as traditional indigenous forms of cooperation and modern cooperatives and related organizations. Hamer (1981), Parvey (1972), and Kerri (1974) opted for "private voluntary associations" (PVO) and defined them as shared interest groups established independently of kinship or territorially based groups. Their acronym PVO is most frequently used by American development agencies (Tendler 1982). Development organizations related to the UN tend to use "nongovernmental organization" (NGO) to indicate the broad category (Van Heemst 1981; Barclay 1979; Fayossewo 1974–75; Dahlen 1978; Epps 1976). None of these definitions, however, contributes to an analytical understanding of third-sector organizations in Africa. Most of these conceptualizations, while lamenting the heterogeneity of the organizations, fail to recognize that understanding the reasons for the diversity might bring one closer to understanding the organizations than does any attempt at devising a global terminology.

Second, conceptual confusion also arises from the gap between official description and organizational reality. Tendler (1982) demonstrates that the portrait voluntary associations draw of themselves is not always an accurate one. This discrepancy prevails throughout African third-sector organizations. Many cooperatives, for example, are de facto governmental agencies, merely labeled "cooperative" without in fact adhering to cooperative principles. Some are clearly for-profit organizations, whereas others are nonprofit. Some cooperatives and community development projects are recorded on paper, whereas others, like tribal associations or many informal self-help groups, are never mentioned in official reports. These biases in the accounts contribute considerably to the unreliability of official statistics.

Third, development plans and programs are a further source of conceptual confusion. Planning activities frequently lead to the creation of apparently new organizational forms, which, when combined with shifts in ideology, create a need for new terms. The acronyms PVO and NGO are good examples.

A final reason for conceptual confusion is the ahistorical manner in which the organizations are approached. Many scholars simply state there is a connection among cooperatives, self-help organizations, and the traditional African mode of production (in fact, cooperatives are now described as traditional self-help modes made effective by formal organization). Unexplored is Africa's history as if the continent were never subject to changing social and economic experiments, development ideologies and strategies, and all kinds of imported and homemade solutions for its problems—a history that makes it difficult to differentiate what is indigenous from what is not.

Cooperative Theory

Cooperative theory developed primarily in agricultural economics (Helmberger 1964). Mather defined cooperatives according to three basic principles that distinguised them from for-profit businesses: service at cost, democratic control, and limited return on capital (1969, 14–19). Given that profits constitute the reward for entrepreneurial efforts and that cooperatives are nonprofits, cooperatives do not rely on the presence of entrepreneurs. This reasoning, of course, has made cooperatives particularly attractive for developing countries, where the lack of indigenous entrepreneurship has been seen as an obstacle to further development.[3]

Cooperative theory postulated that cooperatives in developing countries are primarily an instrument of market

reform—that is, an organizational remedy for market imperfections and failures with the ultimate goal being the establishment or reestablishment of more perfect market conditions. (The four major sources of market imperfections are production inefficiencies—nonoptimal factor combinations—inefficiencies in scale, inefficiencies in pricing, and suboptimal vertical integration [Buse & Helmberger 1969, 201–09]). Cooperatives as instruments of structural reform, then, are considered almost a transitory organizational form. As "conditions in the market improve, the cooperative is in a position to step into the market and take advantage of whatever comparative advantages its members may have" (Buse & Helmberger 1969, 209).

The limitations of cooperative theory are obvious. Cooperatives are examined solely within a market framework (though an imperfect market) with almost no consideration of state activities, which are the most important factor of cooperative promotion in developing countries. Furthermore, cooperative theory does not recognize the colonial legacy of early cooperative efforts in Africa (to be discussed later) and simply ignores all nonmarket systems, despite their immense importance. More fundamental is E. C. Smith's (1969, 358) point that cooperative theory is based on the same assumptions as neoclassical economic theory and thus presumes the existence of developed markets and institutions, identifiable goods of known characteristics, equal access to capital and information, and developed demands for inputs and supply for outputs. All these assumptions, however, are highly questionable in the case of African economies.

Theories of Nonprofit Organizations

Economists' concern with NPOs in developing countries is of more recent origin than cooperative theory. Sommer (1979, 8), has suggested the following definition: NPOs are established to fulfill a public charitable purpose. The universe of NPOs is divided into two large subsets: private voluntary agencies, such as CARE or Catholic Relief Service (PVOs), and endowed foundations, like the Ford or Rockefeller foundations (cf. Friedman 1981, 1; Bolling 1983).

In regard to Africa, we can distinguish between international and indigenous NPOs. The indigenous NPO sector can be further divided into two parts, following James's classification: "The first part consists of organizations providing some shared facility or service where the people who pay (through membership or usage fee) are also the direct and principal beneficiaries and exclusion is possible (e.g., community pools and consumer cooperatives)" (1980, 5). James assumes that under certain conditions of increasing costs or congestion, for-profits could carry out these functions optimally—an implicit reference to cooperative theory. In other words, in organizational settings where patterns of contribution and benefits can be attributed to the same group, NPOs can also be seen as an instrument for market reform. Once market imperfections give way to more perfect market conditions, indirect contact via impersonal supply and demand is preferable. But more often the role of this NPO type is

---

3. See Youngjohns (1982) on profit versus nonprofit issues of NGOs; Duelfer (1974) on the objectives of cooperatives in general; Migot-Adholla (1970, 1972) on entrepreneurship and cooperatives.

defined in relation to the state and international development agencies. In this respect, NPOs act as providers of public and semipublic goods (often in the sense of a spillover effect) to supplement for state inactivities and misallocation, and they operate as information management and feedback systems for development agencies (to be discussed later).

The second category of indigenous NPOs consists of organizations in which the groups of beneficiaries and of contributors do not *directly* coincide. This second category, then, James calls the true nonprofit sector.

Indigenous NPOs in the form of large-scale foundations and true nonprofits in James's sense are still rare in Africa. There are several reasons for this. First, international NPOs preempt some of the potential areas for indigenous NPO activity. African countries act as hosts for American and European NPOs, and it is the interaction between international and indigenous NPOs that seems to set agendas for the growth and direction of the latter. The involvement of international NPOs goes far beyond the redistribution of capital or food from developed countries. International NPOs provide know-how and technological and managerial assistance (Sommer 1979). In many cases, this extensive involvement has had a serious side effect in that indigenous NPOs have become more and more reliant on outside help. In other cases, the involvement of international NPOs furthered the penetration of a money economy in excluded rural areas after they became the target of developmental or relief programs. In yet other instances, such as Northern Togo,[4] food distributed in rural areas in the course of child nutrition programs was sold by international NPOs at below market value. This created a new local market for imported food, but it also led to a partitioning of the small local communities involved in the program into those qualified for the child nutrition program, who subsequently could sell their acquired products on local markets, and those who, for one reason or another, failed to qualify as food recipients.[5] This example brings two questions to mind. To what extent is the involvement of international NPOs counterproductive in terms of the development and emergence of indigenous NPOs and enterprises?

In answer to the first question, we can say (disregarding badly conceived and implemented projects) that the involvement of international development and relief organizations tends to be counterproductive in the second- or third-order consequences of given projects. Because local African social and economic structures are extremely complex and highly interrelated, and because most projects are implemented on the basis of insufficient data, projects can easily have unintended results. These results, or repercussions in indigenous

social and economic structures, are not necessarily negative in nature; what is important is that they are often unforeseen.

In regard to the second question, it is certainly true that although monetary, technological, and managerial dependency inhibits the emergence of indigenous NPOs, the presence of international agencies nevertheless fosters their creation. This is so because international NPOs search for indigenous counterparts and assist in their development—albeit in accordance with their own objectives via grant-making policies.

A second reason indigenous NPOs are rare in Africa is that the state takes over many functions they could provide, as do international NPOs, UN organizations, and the state in combined projects.

The public enterprise or corporation—a legal entity halfway between government and private enterprise, with its own accounts and property but ultimately state owned—is an important form of state involvement in developing countries. The form is by and large based on a legal importation from Great Britain (Pozen 1972). Under colonialism, public enterprises were used mainly in the field of agricultural marketing to maintain production levels and to provide African cash-crop farmers with price stability. After they attained independence, many African countries extended the role of the public corporation, for several reasons.

First, they permitted state ownership of the means of production, which meant they could be more easily controlled and adjusted to changing developmental policies and programs than could stock corporations and enterprises. Second, it was assumed that this control could be exercised without large-scale bureaucratic structures like those of socialist countries in Eastern Europe. Finally, it was hoped that if public corporations could successfully pioneer or experiment in new markets, these new entrepreneurial areas would then be taken over by private enterprises—a reasoning similar to the structural-reform argument in cooperative theory.

Although few data are available on the performance of public corporations in Africa, a study of such enterprises in twenty-four developing countries around the world found an average operating surplus before depreciation of about 1.3 percent of gross domestic product (GDP) in 1977 (Short 1983; see also Grantt & Dutto 1968; Shirley 1983, 10). When interest payments, subsidies, depreciation, and taxes were taken into account, the African public corporations included in the study ended in the red. This, in turn, forestalled their use of self-financing techniques. As a result, public corporations are responsible for 30 percent or more of all domestic credit outstanding in Benin, Gambia, Senegal, Mali, and the Ivory Coast and up to 87 percent in Guinea (Shirley 1983, 13). A fundamental reason for this situation is that public corporations ''are expected to pursue both commercial and social goals and to answer many different constituencies'' (Shirley 1983, 17). As in many state-controlled cooperatives, conflicting objectives and a lack of clear goal assessments has led to constant conflicts between managers and politicians.

This built-in conflict between substantive and formal ra-

4. This example is based on information gathered in the course of my field research in Togo.

5. With the exception of emergency situations, relief organizations hardly ever distribute food free of charge, in order to discourage welfare attitudes among recipients. Because of their nonprofit status and their contractual relations with the government, they are obliged to sell at cost—an externally induced price much below local market prices.

tionality (Weber 1947) has had perverse effects in some cases. For some public enterprises created to serve the rural poor, the World Bank observed: "The costs of subsidies are shifted from the consumer to the taxpayer, or, if the deficit is financed through inflationary monetary expansion, to the public at large. Given the regressive nature of taxes in many developing countries and the impact of inflation on the poor, the effect may be to increase income inequalities" (1983, 76–78). Such negative side effects are difficult to assess beforehand, and they may block any intended positive achievement.

A third factor working against indigenous NPOs is the low level of economic and social differentiation in most African countries. This reduces the demand for a variety of services typically provided by NPOs in Western countries. Under the extended family system, for example, there is no need for day-care centers or homes for the elderly.[6] Or because art is a matter of ritual symbolism in everyday life and is not subject to large-scale, specialized organization, nonprofit museums and theaters are unnecessary.

A final factor is a common problem of African economies: they lack investment capital for further development. By their nature, NPOs do not create surplus capital, so that true NPOs are of secondary importance as development organizations. This is especially true of charity organizations and endowed foundations. Capital must be generated and accumulated in a private economy before it can be redistributed. Foundations with headquarters in Africa are either heavily reliant on American and European inputs (for example, Enda, Environment, and Development in the Third World in Senegal) or religiously oriented (COCIN, Church of Christ in Nigeria, or the Foundation Cheick Mbacke in Senegal, a Muslim PVO, linked to the religious hierarchy.) Otherwise, NPOs like the Aga Khan Foundation, part of whose endowment fund originated in Africa, tend to be administered from Europe or America. Reasons for this may be found in the international monetary system (many African currencies are not convertible on world markets) and in the communication and transportation problems within and among African countries.

Cooperatives, as compared to NPOs, are conceptually closer to market organizations. Under certain conditions the economic functions fulfilled by cooperatives can be provided by market-oriented, for-profit organizations. This substitution hypothesis, however, does not apply to the true nonprofit sector. Hansmann's trustworthiness and contract-failure theory (1980), Weisbrod's median-voter theory (1977), and Ben-Ner's conceptualizations of NPOs as special cases of backward vertical integration of consumers attempting to increase their welfare in excludable public goods (1982) all demonstrate that goods provided by NPOs can only suboptimally be supplied by for-profit enterprises and the state.

Thus, there is little social and economic space for indigenous true NPOs to which these theories could readily be applied.

Sociological and Anthropological Conceptualizations

As compared to economics, the conceptual situation in sociology and anthropology is less clear and systematic. Anthropologist Michael Banton (1968, 357) has defined voluntary associations as groups "organized for the pursuit of one interest or several interests in common. Associations are usually contrasted with involuntary groupings serving a greater variety of ends, such as kin groups, castes, social classes and communities." Voluntary associations are seen as an indicator of social evolution in the development from undifferentiated to differentiated societies. This line of thought is akin to classical sociological evolutionary dichotomies like Maine's status versus contract, Toennies's *Gemeinschaft* versus *Gesellschaft,* and Durkheim's mechanical versus organic solidarity.

Within the field of anthropology, two main areas of investigation have emerged. The first deals with the origins of voluntary associations in undifferentiated primitive societies; the second focuses on the emergence of voluntary associations under conditions of social change. Pioneering work on the origins of voluntary associations was done by Schurtz (1902), who traced the origin of voluntary groupings to the antogonism between generations leading to a classification based on age, and Webster (1932), who maintained that secret societies arise out of a natural grouping together in life (Hamer 1981, 113).[7]

Tardits (1956) and Gosselin (1976) have attributed the emergence of voluntary associations among the Fon of Dahomey to socioeconomic tensions arising from particular forms of division of labor between the sexes. Writes Gosselin, "Women have a monopoly of all the local trade. Now, nothing is free in the villages; everything is bought, even between husband and wife. Men are obligated to assume irregular but heavy expenditures. They are responsible for the basic support of their wives and children" (1976, 56). For most men, one solution for their financial dilemma lies in participating in tontines, a widespread rotating credit association.

Another example involves a centralized, more statelike society: the Yoruba Kingdoms (Forde 1951). Here the Ogboni association played an important role in politics and the judicial system. To some extent, the Ogboni association ran parallel to a hierarchical political structure based on inheritance and status ascription. This association provided one of the few opportunities for upward mobility within a rigid and closed status system. Among the Mende of Sierra Leone, the Poro society served as an organ for social control covering several realms of activity: Njayei treated insanity, Humui

---

6. In recent years day-care centers have sprung up in higher-income residential areas of large African cities. Most day-care centers are part of Western-type women's associations like the YWCA.

7. See also Vierkandt (1931), Hoebel (1949), and Lowie (1925) on cooperative organizations in primitive societies.

supervised sexual behavior, and Kpa was responsible for minor physical disorders. Paralleling Poro, which was restricted to men, was Sande, a women's association (Little, 1949; Banton 1968).

Hamer (1981, 113) suggests that "it is possible to see certain attributes in these historic forms of solidarity that may provide a key to understanding certain pre-conditions for forming modern cooperatives and self-help associations." Although this is certainly the case for some precolonial voluntary associations, it is argued that in more complex societies, such as the Yoruba, the Edo, the Kingdom of the Congo, and the Tanzanian highlands, voluntary associations may well have been embryonic social classes (Balandier 1968; Meillassoux 1975; Gutkind, Cohen, & Copans 1978).

To generalize, in traditional African societies voluntary associations served any of the following functions:

- They were social-control mechanisms to cope with the problem of deviance in the broadest sense.

- They operated as integrative organizations crosscutting family structures and thereby avoiding potential cleavages within communities.

- They were born out of economic necessity because of contradictory divisions of labor and inequitable income distributions.

- They acted as alternative mobility strata in societies with rigid, often hereditary, status systems.

- They were embryonic social classes in which membership brought economic advantages after an initial investment in the form of a (usually comparatively high) membership fee.

This brings us to the evolutionary aspects of voluntary associations. Although anthropologists identified the importance of voluntary associations under changing social and economic conditions as early as the 1920s (see, for example, Martin 1923, 244–48, on the Cape Coast; Green 1964, 43, on Eastern Nigeria; Westerman 1935, 45, on Togo; Little 1949, 1950, on West Africa), it was not until the 1960s that African voluntary associations received renewed attention (Wallerstein 1964, 319; Kerri 1974, 1976, 27–29; Koll 1969; Little 1962a, 1962b, 1964, 1965, 1967, 1972; Meillassoux 1968; Lloyd 1953; Plotnicov 1967, 72–74; Seibel & Koll 1968; among others).

The majority of these studies focused on the diverse functions served by the associations, particularly their power to enhance adaptation (seen as a gradual acculturation to the modern urban environment and the minimization of uncertainties and disruptions connected with rapid social change); to fulfill the mobilization function (either politically or socially); and, to a lesser degree, to generate income and provide employment opportunities (Geertz 1962; Eisenstadt 1956; Hamer 1976a, 1976b; Barnes 1973; Parkin 1966; Ruel 1964; Imaogene 1967; Anderson 1970).

These multiple functions made PVOs especially attractive in view of an increasingly discouraging social and economic situation. Implicitly, it was assumed that a compatibility between social and economic functions could be retained during and after the transformation of PVOs into more contractual relationships and legal forms. Too often, the literature disregarded Gide's Paradox (1930), which states that the more successful a cooperative society socially, the more likely it is to fail in economic terms, and vice versa (see Nash, Dandler, & Hopkins 1976). But it is the degree of compatibility and the tensions between alternative functions that determine the developmental potential of PVOs on a microlevel.

In a widely accepted sociological definition, Sills (1968, 362–63) views voluntary associations as spare-time participatory organizations, as opposed to businesses, cooperatives, and trade associations. This definition addresses a subset of "true" nonprofit organizations: private NPOs in Sommer's terminology (1979). Within the African context, such a conceptualization of voluntary associations poses serious problems: for the unemployed and the underemployed in urban and rural areas and for subsistence farmers, the terms *leisure* and *spare-time* are misleading. The sociological conceptualization applies to only a very small sector of Africa's population: the economic and political elite in particular and, to some extent, the skilled industrial work force—the modern sector of society.[8]

THE COOPERATIVE MOVEMENT IN AFRICA: A HISTORICAL OUTLINE

Since the turn of the century, when cooperatives were first introduced in Africa, they have enjoyed an impressive and almost uninterrupted growth. Today in no other region in the world are cooperatives as numerous as in Africa (Cooperative Chronology 1973, 45), and nowhere else has the cooperative movement been subject to such radically different political ideologies.

Colonial Period

In English-speaking colonies, cooperatives were first regulated following the Indian Act as a legal model—a modification of Raiffeisen-type cooperatives, first introduced in India. Indigenous forms of cooperation were neglected by the colonial powers. Strickland, an English cooperative expert sent to Nigeria to investigate the adaptability of indigenous cooperatives to modern forms, called them "fraudulent and improvident" (1934). His report became highly influential in the codification of cooperative matters. Cooperative ordinances first came into effect in Nigeria, Tanzania, Uganda, and Kenya (see, for example, Cooperative Societies Ordinance No. 9 of 1935 for Nigeria). With the enactment of

---

8. These professional and leisure-time associations should not be confused with the countless social clubs prevalent all over Africa. Most social clubs are tribal and/or village associations.

ordinances, the initiative to sponsor cooperatives was shifted from the central government to local colonial authorities in accordance with the spirit of British indirect rule (Brink-schulte 1976, 287). The main economic objective of these early cooperatives was the collective marketing of cash crops for world markets in order to level fluctuating prices and ease the debt problem for many African farmers who, through the introduction of taxation and a money economy, faced financial distress.

The reaction to the ordinances and bylaws was mixed. The cooperative registrar in Lagos observed that many would-be members "have come . . . only to recoil disappointed that cooperation, so far from being a bed of roses, is strewn with thorny regulations difficult to comprehend and more difficult to observe. Others turned a blind eye to these discouraging documents and wrote again, only to find that they had no stomach for the formidable set of bylaws" (Nigeria, Cooperative Registrar, par. 48). Problems arising from the legal preoccupation of the colonial powers were usually attributed to the indigenous population (see Engelmann's review of early annual reports of Ugandian cooperatives [1968]). This failure to comprehend indigenous social structures led to a colonial ideology asserting that the correct policy was the implementation of Western types of cooperatives.

In the French colonies, cooperative development took a different path, following the French colonial pattern of direct centralized rule (Ghaussy 1964, 75; Raulin 1976). Some forty years before the French government enacted the first cooperative law for their colonies in 1947, the Sociétés de Prévoyance were established (Engelmann 1968, 9). The main objectives were to provide a rudimentary infrastructure in rural areas and to serve as a social security institution for farmers via the collection of membership fees. Membership was compulsory, however, and contributions to the sociétés were "imposed and collected like taxes" (Engelmann 1968, 10). In addition, the indigenous population was excluded from any administrative decision-making power. Despite their apparently bureaucratic setup, the sociétés created mistrust of governmental aid and institutions. They prevented the exercise of private initiative at the grass roots and led to widespread corruption by société officials.

In contrast, the cooperative law of 1947 (Loi No. 47–1775 du 10 septembre 1947) was a "liberal" creation. According to the French Code de Commerce, cooperatives are a modification of a joint stock company—that is, a for-profit enterprise (Duelfer 1974)—unlike cooperatives in English-speaking colonies, where their nonprofit status was legally recognized (Adeyeye 1978, 47). This complex legal structure was difficult for cooperative members to comprehend. When combined with a liberal handling of foundation procedures, such as the transformation of precooperatives into cooperative societies, it resulted in the creation of many nonviable cooperatives (Comboulives 1967, 22). As a consequence the cooperative law of 1955 (Décret No. 55–184 du février 1955) increased the legal requirements for the transition of precooperatives and reestablished further state involvement in cooperative affairs.

The Cooperative Movement after Independence

After independence, African countries continued to foster the development of cooperatives largely within the legal frameworks left by the colonial powers. In most new nations, the cooperative movement came more and more under state influence and control. Ghana, for example, opted to centralize the cooperative movement (Ghaussy 1964, 66), with the result that cooperatives came to depend on state financial assistance but also became quasi-governmental organizations. The former French colonies maintained governmental control and influence over cooperative affairs, and only the Ivory Coast chose a decentralizing policy (Brinkschulte 1976, 288). Our focus here will be on cooperative developments in Nigeria and Tanzania, two countries in which the movement took strikingly different forms.

From 1951 to 1976, the cooperative movement in Nigeria grew at an impressive rate. Adeyeye (1978, 73) lists 821 registered societies for 1951 and 10,591 societies for 1976, having a total of 589,775 members (an average of 56 members per cooperative). The federal government provided such basic infrastructure as educational centers for cooperative managers and created large-scale banks to meet cooperative demands. Within the framework of an open economy, where the state assumes a nurturing role for industry and agriculture (Hopkins 1973; Kilby 1969, 2), cooperatives competed with for-profit enterprises in the same markets.

On a federal level, active incentives to foster cooperatives were included in the Third National Development Plan (1975–80). The plan reflected two changes in governmental policies toward cooperatives: the federal government would take an active role in cooperative development, and cooperatives were now seen as a form of voluntary self-help. Although all Nigerian states incorporated the federal guidelines into their programs, the *Second Progress Report* for the third plan indicates a very limited plan implementation rate of 15 percent.[9]

Under the guidelines for the Fourth National Development Plan (1981–85), the federal government addressed the difficulties encountered by its cooperative program in the previous plan period: "perhaps the most serious is the lack of effective leadership and qualified personnel to manage cooperatives along modern lines" (Nigeria: Federal Ministry . . . 1981–85, 42). The government expressed concern that an apparent lack of enthusiasm for the cooperative movement

9. In fact, achievement estimates provided by state governments are highly unreliable. Seven out of nineteen states and the federal government itself were unable to provide any information on actual plan fulfillment. Estimated achievement rates range from zero (Anambra State) to an exceptional 88 percent in the case of Kano State. Bendel State indicated a 4 percent achievement, and Lagos State reported a 7 percent achievement rate; Oyo State provided no information.

reflected an "ignorance on the part of the general public about the existence of the movement and about its potentials for the welfare of the individual" and criticized the tendency of "some state governments to exercise excessive control over cooperatives" as well as the fraudulent practices of some state officials in implementation of programs. While acknowledging these difficulties, the Fourth National Development Plan follows much the same strategies and guidelines as those in the previous plan. This implies a continued attempt to exercise government control over cooperatives in order to "develop" such associations "along modern lines," a phrase left unspecified in the guidelines for the fourth plan.

Tanzanian cooperatives, during the first of two periods, developed in a fashion similar to that in Nigeria under British rule. Cooperatives began in rural areas as multipurpose marketing organizations. As Westergaard (1970, 124–25) notes, the first Tanzanian cooperative, the Kilimanjaro Native Planters' Association (KNPA), was soon able to develop a marketing monopoly for coffee, the major agricultural export product. Paulus (1964) describes how the ICNCU (which developed out of the KNPA) was considered by peasants to be a governmental and colonial institution.

The years until independence showed slower growth in the number of cooperatives than in Nigeria. In 1940, there were 40 registered cooperatives, and only 172 in 1952 (Westergaard 1970, 127). After independence the growth was dramatic: from 1961 to 1970 the number of registered societies rose to 1,937. Kaplan (1978, 45) notes that the Indian population, which migrated to Tanzania under British rule, exerted a very important economic influence on the peasantry and acted as middlemen between producers and merchants from overseas. With the rise of nationalism beginning in the early 1950s, cooperatives were seen as an instrument to bypass the Indian mercantile class. In Tanzania as well as in Uganda (Kasfir 1970; Vincent 1976) and Kenya (Karanja 1974) "cooperatives became a symbol of unity against all forms of colonial exploitation" (Migot-Adholla 1970, 29–31. Giant cooperatives such as the Victoria Federation of Cooperative Unions were intended to combat entrenched marketing systems and middlemen.

Much earlier than in Nigeria, cooperatives were thought of as a remedy for Tanzania's social, political, and economic problems (see Saul 1971). This development paved the way for Tanzania's second cooperative movement, which impressed its ideological stamp on many of the continent's countries—African socialism. The movement began in 1967 with the adoption of J. K. Nyerere's *Arusha Declaration*, in which he laid the ideological and political groundwork for Tanzania's future social and economic transition: *Ujamaa Vinjini*, socialism and development.

Nyerere sees the ujamaa, the traditional mode of production, as the starting point for further development (Cliffe 1970, 39). In his words: "We must take our traditional system, correct its shortcomings, and adapt to its service the things we can learn from the technologically developed so-

cieties" (Nyerere 1967, 4). The three basic principles of traditional ujamaa living are "mutual respect and obligation . . . ; a common obligation for everyone to work; and the common ownership of the basic goods" (Cliffe 1970, 39–40).

Nyerere's first step in implementing his policy was to transform existing and newly founded villages into large producer-cooperatives according to ujamaa principles. But even strong governmental efforts to promote ujamaa villages could not overcome peasant reluctance to move to ujamaa settlements, and in 1969 only 400 new ujamaa villages were registered (Hyden 1980, 102). With continued governmental promotion, however, and even coercive action, 90 percent of the population lived in ujamaa villages by 1977. But confidential reports quoted in Weaver and Kronemer (1981, 843) indicate that only 25 out of 8,229 registered ujamaa villages actually adhere to ujamaa principles. Nyerere's attempt to combine tradition and modernity in the form of "appropriate technology," a large-scale social experiment, had devastating consequences for Tanzania's economy. Today Tanzania faces severe shortages and relies on imported agricultural products to avert starvation (see also Roth 1976; Meister 1969; Omari 1976).

Cooperativism in Crisis, and the Self-help Movement

After the early 1970s, ideological shifts and changing social and economic conditions led to a revival of cooperatives as voluntary self-help organizations. No longer were cooperatives regarded as an alien form implemented from above; rather, they became a synonym for Africa's new answer to her developmental dilemmas: self-help and self-reliance.

There are three related causes for this development. First, beginning with independence, Africa's new elites underwent an ideological shift. As they became more disenchanted with the West, many African leaders rediscovered their own cultural traditions, stressing "traditional" values like "African solidarity" and "African cooperation." This new attitude toward cooperatives is reflected in Ijere's introduction to *New Trends in African Cooperatives* (1975). He believes that the ethical and economic characteristics of cooperatives "come close to the African social structure and custom [and] that in discussing them one finds a lot that is in common between the modern and the indigenous" (Ijere 1975, 5). Ijere does not specify what it is that indigenous social structures and cooperatives share. But he goes on to state that because of their close affinity, "Africans have accepted cooperation with greater enthusiasm and understanding than they have capitalism and socialism." Viewed as an alternative to capitalism or socialism, cooperatives appear in a radically different light. Despite their introduction as an alien organization and their declared objective to penetrate and control local economies, cooperatives are seen by Ijere as African organizations. His categorical statement indicates the "indigenization" and "Africanization" of the cooperative movement by the elite. Of course, not everyone characterizes African cooperatives as does Ijere (see Essien 1975, 113–14, for a more realistic interpretation; also Gagnon 1976), but the elitist orientation he expressed (1975) marked a new period in cooperative history.

A second reason for the revival of cooperatives as self-help organizations is changing social and economic conditions, namely, declining food production (Todaro 1977, 207), rural poverty (ILO 1979, 44), rapid urbanization with the emergence of the informal sector in urban areas (Hake 1977; ILO 1973; Sethuraman 1981; Fapohunda 1981), and unemployment and underemployment (Gugler 1982).

The reaction of social scientists and development planners to a discouraging social and economic situation is yet a third reason for the increased attention to cooperatives (United Nations Research . . . 1969, 1970, United Nations Commission . . . 1975; Miracle 1969; ILO 1973; Lassen 1979; Emerij 1974; Madujibeya 1976). This perspective focused on maintaining and reinforcing the resources of indigenous organizations and the informal African "social security system" (Gerdes 1975). In contrast to earlier planning efforts wherein indigenous forms of cooperation, judged as backward, were to be replaced by large-scale modern organizations, the new approach assumed that modern cooperatives would constitute simply a new version of traditional indigenous cooperation.

It is apparent that this assumption, like the modernization theories that the new approach heavily criticized, was based on a simple traditionality-modernity dichotomy. Nevertheless, it enjoyed widespread popularity among social scientists and planners (Ijere 1975; Lombard 1959; Trappe 1966; Seibel 1968, 1970). It was not until the mid-1970s that more critical voices were heard (COPAC 1978; Hyden 1973, 223; Illy 1978, 1980, 91; Texier 1975, 2; Ollawa 1977, 412; Apthorpe 1977, 5). The central question in this debate was whether self-help efforts and self-reliant developmental attempts are best served within the framework of modern cooperative organizations or of indigenous traditional forms.

Governmental attempts to control, nurture, and even implement indigenous self-help organizations and cooperatives at the grass roots have been subject to much criticism. The most vehement critic by far has been Apthorpe, who writes: "Government and United Nations agencies in the Third World have been convinced by their [the cooperatives'] golden promise of popular participation in social and economic development and like the colonial powers before them have blithely promoted cooperative associations. But experience has fallen far short of expectations" (1977, 4). He goes on to say, "The actual record of cooperatives in developing countries has, after the very high expectations, been a matter of much disappointment—to many members of society, to non-governmental and governmental promoters and aid donors" (5). Brinkschulte (1976, 292), Eicher (1969, 337), and Hyden (1970, 12–13) claim that many cooperative successes exist only on paper and that many governments, under pressure to implement development projects successfully, are reluctant to confess expensive and wasteful failures.

Essien concludes, "In general the cooperative movement in Nigeria is destined to grow in a society where neither sufficient motivation nor adequate understanding for it is present but where few who find it worthwhile, backed by the governments, organize and promote it" (1975, 114). Similarly with regard to East Africa, Migot-Adholla (1970, 33) showed that the most ardent promoters of cooperatives were usually not farmers and cultivators; rather, they were often found in a situation of status incongruency between the traditional and the modern stratification systems, and in this respect, cooperatives provided welcome opportunities for upward social mobility.

The literature overall gives the impression that most attempts to transform indigenous forms of cooperation into modern institutions were failures. Texier (1975, 3) even denied that traditional forms of cooperation could be considered a vehicle for the introduction of modern cooperatives. In his view, the two types of institutions rest upon distinctly different principles, and every attempt to combine them will lead to socially and economically unstable organizations. Gosselin (1976) warned that it can be dangerous to resurrect ghosts, in this case the ideological ghost that views traditional African social structures and economies as fertile grounds for "participatory and integrated" development. It was as if Strickland, the colonial cooperative expert, had called it right when—almost fifty years ago—he wrote, "I am not hopeful for a reform of *Esusu,*" an indigenous voluntary association among the Yoruba (1934, 14).

By the end of the 1970s, the promising hypothesis of a relationship between modern cooperatives and traditional forms of cooperation was largely rejected. At the same time, a search for indigenous voluntary associations backed by a larger part of the population itself began (Nash, Dandler, & Hopkins 1976; COPAC 1978). Kerr criticized Apthorpe by stating that "this condemnation of cooperative associations contrasts markedly with my own specific experiences with certain Nigerian voluntary associations which seemed to be contributing significantly to rural development. These voluntary associations were initiated from within their communities and have been there for decades; they are not the 'cooperatives' promoted by agencies from outside the communities, which Apthorpe is talking about" (1978, 88).

Recently, the distinction between development from above versus development from below has also been criticized. Tendler argues that advocates of a bottom-up development approach neglect the importance of local elites. She introduces the factor of *local elite control* as an intervening variable determining the outcome of developmental self-help efforts. This implies a critique of all theoretical positions that assume on an a priori basis that all self-help groups and community projects are participatory in the sense of genuinely representative decision making: "It misspecifies local-elite control as participatory . . . . And it mistakenly assumes that local-level control is synonymous with favorable benefit distributions" (1982, v). Tendler's criticism points to a new perspective that is also taken up by Gow and Morss (1981), who argue that none of the divergence in views between opponents of working through indigenous social structures (such as Gosselin 1976, 64) or proponents (such as Seibel & Massing 1974) can be proved universally right. Muenckner (1980, 1981), Gow and Morss (1981), Kerri (1976), and COPAC (1978) demonstrate a greater readiness to analyze and evaluate each local situation on its merits, thus adding a more inductive flavor to an ongoing controversy.

TRADITIONAL VOLUNTARY ASSOCIATIONS AND INDIGENOUS THIRD-SECTOR ORGANIZATIONS TODAY

It is only in the most biased circles that traditional African societies are equated with a version of the Garden of Eden (Nnoli 1981), a far from accurate picture. On a slightly different level are statements that the way to a "truly" African cooperative has not yet been found (Lipeb 1980, 68). These points of view are reflected among proponents of self-help groups and voluntary associations who assume that such organizations provide a virtually conflict-free environment for development; that African peasants and the urban poor are naturally participatory; that voluntary associations are (or have been) voluntary in a Western sense; that these groups are generally egalitarian and highly democratic institutions; and, finally, that their members exhibit a strong altruistic bent toward the betterment of the community at large.

As mentioned before, Tendler's work (1982) provides evidence that the first two assumptions are fallacious. Drawing on my earlier discussion of voluntary associations in traditional societies, I argue that three components have been carried into the indigenous voluntary associations and self-help groups of today: economic necessity, alternative mobility paths and private economic advantages, and social and economic control. A fourth factor is that of religion: voluntary associations are often church-related organizations.

Economic Necessity

Two examples will demonstrate that participation in self-help groups and voluntary associations is not necessarily altruism but is in fact an economic necessity for the people involved.

Harambee in Kenya

Harambee as a concept embodies the ideas of joint efforts, mutual aid, and community self-reliance. Although it is conceptually similar to ujamaa in Tanzania and humanism in Zambia, harambee, unlike ujamaa, has not become ideologized by a political elite in Kenya. Harambee became a national slogan under Kenyatta's presidency, but it has never been regarded as the key to Kenya's development. Similar forms of mutual aid are found all over Africa—for example, *Nnoboa* and *nkabon* in Ghana, *kuu* among the Kpelle of Liberia, and *ematonyok* among the Masai.

Orora and Spiegel (1981) estimate that harambee contrib-

uted about 11.4 percent of all national development expenditures between 1967 and 1973. Mbithi and Rasmusson say that harambee arose "from the disenchantment or cleavage of a strongly traditional periphery . . . with a planning economic and political centre" (1977, 32); this peripheral disenchantment crystallized in the design of local efforts, attracting the center's resources.

Obviously, some harambee projects have been successful; others have not. According to Mbithi and Rasmusson (1977), successful harambee projects were associated with democratic leadership selection and continuity and a diversified contributional network with special emphasis on the use of local resources, but with their limitations in mind. The projects, then, avoided financial dependency, as well as the danger of becoming a showcase for conspicuous donors. Unsuccessful projects were characterized by conflicts between individual and communal goals, local dependency on outside resources, government interventions, the existence of too many harambee projects competing for local resources, and, finally, undemocratic leadership selection and leadership discontinuity.

Harambee projects are local in character and pertain to specific areas, communities, and populations.[10] Thus, when combined with traditional forms of social control, they are able to avoid the free-rider problem.[11] This has been an important factor in the failure of projects in highly urbanized communities. Mbithi and Rasmusson (1977) found no successful harambee projects in Nairobi itself, where competition for scarce resources and increased individualization rendered traditional control mechanisms steadily more ineffective. Hake (1977) reported that self-help groups in the informal sector, once they became moderately successful, were unable to withstand the pressures economic success forced upon social relationships. One self-help group, for example, that started as an informal land-developing cooperative changed to a real estate agency operating on a for-profit basis in a relatively short period of time. This example demonstrates that voluntary associations, although a form of collective action, can act as an organizational mechanism to make profit-seeking activities possible.

---

10. "Local" does not necessarily imply that all contributors to local self-help groups actually reside in a given area. For example, the Association des Jeunes de Thilogne, a Senegalese self-help group in the Sahel, has about 350 members. Monthly contributions are 100 CFA (or 25 cents) minimum, varying according to economic and social status. Because most inhabitants of Thilogne have migrated to the Ivory Coast, France, or Dakar, an elaborate contribution network is employed to ensure regular donations to an annual budget of 420,000 CFA.

11. The free-rider problem was first stated by Wicksell (1896, 81): "If the individual is to spend his money for private and public uses so that his satisfaction is maximized, he will obviously pay nothing whatsoever for public purposes (at least if we disregard fees and similar charges). Whether he pays much or little will affect the scope of public services so slightly, that for all practical purposes, he himself will not notice it at all. Of course if everyone were to do the same, the State would soon cease to function" (cited in Green & Laffont 1979, 6). The free-rider problem in PVOs can be formulated in a manner parallel to Wicksell's argument (see also Olson 1965).

In this respect, we should distinguish between two types of PVOs. One provides semipublic goods and is similar to dike organizations among Dutch farmers facing the collective problem of tidal floods. In such cases, the existence of an identifiable commonly shared problem with high risks and opportunity cost attached leads to collective action in the form of voluntary associations. The second type represents a more transitory organization. What may start as a mutual aid group—a potential nonprofit organization—changes to a business when necessary. In these cases, PVOs, particularly self-help groups, are the nuclei of joint for-profit ventures and represent a reservoir for entrepreneurial development.

Credit and Savings Associations

Although credit and savings associations have been described in ethnological and anthropological literature (such as Meyer 1940, Cameroun; Westermann 1935, Togo; Green 1964, the Gold Coast; Bascom 1952 and Nadel 1942, Nigeria; Balandier 1955, the Congo; Little 1959, Ghana; Pankhurst & Eshete 1958, Ethiopia), they were first systematically studied and put into cross-cultural focus by Ardener (1964) and Geertz (1962). Since then their work has been expanded by Bouman (1977, 1979) and Miracle, Miracle, and Cohen (1980).

Geertz regards these indigenous associations as middle-rung economic institutions, able to bridge the gap between large-scale modern agricultural institutions of banking and commerce and the traditional economy. Participation in these associations trains peasants and small-scale traders to participate in modern institutions, thus ultimately facilitating modernization (1962, 261). More recently, Geertz's middle-rung assumption has been criticized by Kurtz (1973). Given the reinforcing cycle of poverty, extremely scarce resources, inflation, the lack of modern social security institutions, and an overburdened family system, and hampered by restrictive and inefficient practices that exclude the majority of the population from access to formal banks, credit and savings institutions may be the only available adaptation to social and economic conditions outside the modern economy. The advantages of these associations lie in their easy accessibility, their effectiveness in regulating membership eligibility at almost no cost, and their ability to mobilize resources in informal capital markets (Bouman 1977).

A disadvantage of credit and savings associations is that a liquidity rate of 1 offers no credit multiplication because the organizational setup demands a member coverage of 100 percent.[12] And, Haggblade (1978) showed that a total contribution of $20,000 is the upper limit for rotating credit associations; beyond this threshold, default rates increase disproportionately.

12. This disadvantage could be easily overcome if banks would provide their services to informal credit and savings associations—accepting securities, providing credit, and so on. This, however, implies a considerable change in present banking policies.

Alternative Mobility Paths and Economic Advantages

We have already seen that the cooperative movement was initiated and promoted not so much by the peasantry or target groups as by the government and parts of a rural and urban elite who found themselves in a situation of status incongruency. It should not be too difficult to find analogies in the current self-help movement in the form of local grant "entrepreneurs" who maintain an excellent donor network, thus gaining a higher social status within local communities.

As another example, most villages have more than one village association in large *urban* centers. These associations comprising people from the same village now living in a city are stratified according to the prestige and often private benefits that can be derived from participation. Because they are stratified, they are able to provide public and semipublic goods for the village (such as building roads and market facilities or providing the means for electrification), but at the same time achieving private benefits (being awarded contracts or eliciting the increased loyalty of fellow villagers). Because of stratification, therefore, it is possible to avoid the free-rider problem—at least to the extent that private benefits are derived from participation and contributions. In a community large enough to incur a potential free-rider problem, thereby rendering participation economically unattractive, credit and savings associations provide credit facilities—without interest for members, but often at considerable interest for nonmembers.

These examples demonstrate how fine the line is between private and public benefits in the associations, a central reason for their intrinsic social and economic instability.

Social and Economic Control

In general this type of association caters less to the provision of public and semipublic goods than to the provision of benefits for a specific group of people in the same trade, craft, or industry—not unlike unions or guilds in European countries. Good examples are informal associations among craftsmen in urban areas (Koll 1969) and more formal guilds like the Sudanese Chamber of Crafts. Although craft and small-scale and industry-related associations contribute substantially to the development of the urban informal and semiformal economic sector, some associations among traders (such as those of market women in West African cities) help create inequitable terms of trade by limiting the number of competitors or creating artificial scarcities of often essential goods. Equally distorting are landlord associations in urban slum areas; they not only keep rents artificially high but also boycott many attempts to upgrade the slums.

Religious Motivation

As mentioned before, it has become increasingly difficult to differentiate the traditional from the modern, and the indigenous from the imported in Africa. The most prominent example of this is represented by religious (Christian or Islamic) PVOs. Whereas Islam has not provided fertile ground for PVO development (Clarke 1982; Anheier 1986), the Christian churches have been actively involved in the fields of health services and education since the precolonial period (see chapter 22). The history of missionary societies all over Africa, however, demonstrates that Christian PVOs by no means provide a conflict-free environment for development (Kalu 1978; Clarke 1982; Ajayi 1965). The use of missionary societies by the secular colonial powers to further their political influence led to persistent secular-religious conflicts in most African countries. Similarly, the societies' attempts to bring the gospel to as many unbelievers as possible introduced a competitive element in interdenominational affairs, once the number of missionary societies operating in Africa had increased. There also existed a built-in conflict between church-related PVOs and laity organizations, for ultimately, worldly objectives like education and, increasingly, development efforts were subordinated to the religious objective of salvation.[13]

Besides the secular-religious conflict inherent in development-oriented Christian PVOs, churches in Africa continue to be influenced by the indigenization debate, involving two opposed positions. The first claims that a viable church in Africa has to be founded on the social and religious values and customs of the indigenous population, whereas the second position argues that the unity of the church requires the suppression of indigenous cultures and their replacement by the Western expression of Christianity (see, for example, Catholic Church . . . 1982, 2).

In any case, the alleged secular character of *the* African PVO, implicit in much of the literature (although in fact they often tend to be religiously oriented), represents one of the myths surrounding the popularity of PVOs in development. The religious character of many PVOs has consequences, too, for their assumed participatory nature. Whether participation takes place in a secular setting or in a religious context makes a strong difference. The "one man, one vote" principle of cooperatives does not apply to organizations linked to and sponsored by the Catholic hierarchy. To some extent, that proponents of PVOs in development publicize their participatory and grass-roots democratic character is a direct ideological reaction to the bureaucratic top-down approach that accompanied modernization practices.

13. One additional goal conflict for African churches is introduced by the theology of liberation. The inner-worldly component contained in the equation of missionary and developmental activity results in the collectivization of salvation. It is here that we can find a basic dilemma for the Christian church in Africa; it contrasts sharply with the Protestant ethic. This displacement of God into society implicit in the holistic approach to development (where religious, moral, and social development become synonymous) reversed the individualization of salvation. In their theological aspects, churches in Africa are moving backward to a pre-Calvinist era as far as objectives are concerned, while becoming more secular in their activities.

VOLUNTARY ASSOCIATIONS AND DEVELOPMENT

It is tempting to describe PVOs as organizations that fill the gap left by the state and for-profit businesses in the delivery of goods, services, and social security. The description, however, fails to capture the underlying dilemmas of the African situation.

As we have seen, since the beginning of colonialism, African governments have steadily tried to reshape their economies and societies, albeit under strikingly different and changing ideologies. Overall, governments rate poorly in these areas of activity. Many citizens, the poor in particular, are bypassed in the delivery of public and semipublic goods. For one thing, large proportions of the population are simply hard to reach with conventional service-delivery systems. Moreover, African social and economic systems are extremely complex, riddled with externalities, red tape, severe communication problems, and overregulation. In other words, the current social and economic situation in Africa makes it impossible for governments to control both the free-rider problem and the problem of negative externalities.

Like the state, PVOs try to combine substantive and formal rationality, economic and noneconomic objectives. Unlike the state, which must report to many different constituencies, PVOs are usually well defined in membership by ethnic, religious, economic, class, or political characteristics and interests. Thus, PVOs are in a better position to avoid and control free riders. Being local in character and usually modestly scaled, PVOs can employ a wide range of mechanisms in allocating and redistributing resources. They are in a more advantageous situation to control the effects and impacts of their projects than is the state—that is, they can control the problem of negative externalities. These two advantages constitute the great potential of PVOs for reorienting and distributing public and semipublic goods, both in the sense of information management and in the sense of a feedback mechanism.

Contributors, Beneficiaries, and Development

Saying that PVOs flourish in environments in which the state can operate with only limited effectiveness does not imply that all types of PVOs contribute equally to the development of African societies.

I have demonstrated that the indigenous African third sector is heterogeneous and that it has become so during recent decades. Cooperative history in Africa and Tendler's work (1982) showed that organizatonal articles of faith and organizational reality do not necessarily coincide. In the African third sector, perhaps more than elsewhere, the saying *nomen est omen* certainly does not apply. Most local PVOs and self-help groups are informal part-time associations characterized by multiple membership; they employ a complex network of resource allocation and redistribution, not necessarily in monetary terms but in kind or loyalty. In many instances, the associations cross the boundaries of a strict nonprofit world, and they are well connected to many echelons of government activity. In other words, PVOs are embedded in their environment to such an extent that the exact nature of their resource allocation and distribution is not easily discerned. It is almost impossible, too, to judge from the outside whether, for example, the Youth Progressive Union of Ijebu-Ode or the Amicale de Jeunesse de Sokode contributes to development, or whether they are elite organizations controlling local communities or organizations extracting local surplus to urban areas.

For these reasons, the classification of indigenous PVOs should be taken as a guideline for empirical research only (see figure 23.1). Following James's suggestion (1980), we divide the true indigenous third sector into two large classes: organizations in which the contributors coincide with the beneficiaries and those in which they are two distinct groups.

In those cases where contributors and beneficiaries coincide, we can distinguish three further cases.

1. The group of contributors is smaller than the group of beneficiaries. This is typical of community development groups that provide public and semipublic goods and bring benefits to the whole community, such as environmental cleanup or road construction.

2. The group of beneficiaries is identical to the group of contributors. This case comprises two types of organizations: nonprofit cooperatives on the one hand, and elite organizations, professional associations, and crafts associations on the other.

3. The group of contributors is larger than the group of beneficiaries. Examples are religiously based development organizations largely funded through congregational donations. In this case, the religious community contributes to a development project from which only a small proportion will benefit. A second group comprises social service organizations financed largely through donations and levies, such as local YMCA/YWCA chapters.

Voluntary Associations and Outside Assistance

The new attention to PVOs has increased the number of joint projects involving PVOs and both governmental agencies and international development organizations.

As mentioned earlier, their ability to combine economic rationality with some substantive objective makes PVOs attractive as a development tool. At the same time, this combination is the main source of their social and economic instability. That indigenous PVOs are deeply embedded in local social and economic structures implies their very limited formal accountability. They are successful on a local level because they are only to some degree ''monetarized'' in economic terms and yet entertain an elaborate system of institutional memory in social terms. Their embeddedness

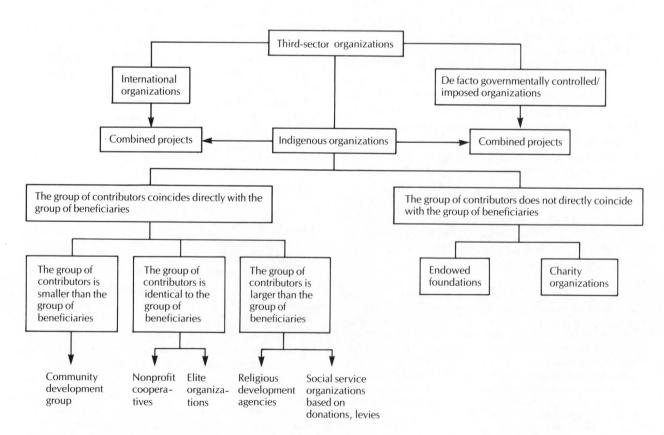

FIGURE 23.1. THIRD-SECTOR ORGANIZATIONS IN AFRICA

also implies that outsiders, such as development organizations or the government, have to operate somewhat blindly concerning actual local conditions and structures.

If they are engaged in joint projects with development organizations or are funded by them, PVOs must obtain official status and governmental recognition, and they must introduce formal accountability and bookkeeping. This "institutionalized suspicion" (Dore 1971) can change the character of many informal associations—often to their members' disadvantage. Transforming informal relations among members, and between the association and its environment, to formal ones can easily result in the loss of many channels of resource allocation. More important, the delicate balance between formal and substantive rationality is disturbed by new opportunities and monetary inputs from outside. Again, Gide's Paradox comes to mind concerning the internal dynamics of voluntary associations—dynamics that seem to culminate when PVOs become targets of development programs. As a result, PVOs tend to lose much of their comparative advantage over formal bureaucracies in general and state agencies in particular. And it is here that Hyden's statement (1983a) that development is a process of trial and error with as many unanticipated consequences as anticipated finds its true context.

REFERENCES

Acharya, S. N. 1981. "Perspectives and Problems of Development in Sub-Saharan Africa." *World Development* 9, no. 2:109–49.

Adeyeye, S. O. 1978. *The Cooperative Movement in Nigeria Yesterday, Today, and Tomorrow*. Gottingen: Vandenhoek & Ruprecht.

Ajayi, J. F. 1965. *Christian Missions in Nigeria, 1841–1891*. London: Longman.

Anderson, R. T. 1970. "Voluntary Association and Social Change: A Search for Regularities." *International Journal of Comparative Sociology* 2:245–50.

Anheier, H. K. 1986. "Private Voluntary Organizations, Networks, and Development in Africa: A Comparative Analysis of Organizational Fields in Nigeria, Senegal and Togo." Ph.D. diss., Yale University.

Apthorpe, R. 1977. "The Cooperatives' Poor Harvest." *New Internationalist* 48:4–6.

Ardener, S. 1964. "The Comparative Study of Rotating Credit Associatons." *Journal of the Royal Anthropological Institute* 94, no. 2:201–29.

Balandier, G. 1955. *Sociologie des Brazzavilles noires*. Paris: Colin.

———. 1968. *Daily Life in the Kingdom of the Kongo*. London: Allen & Unwin.

Banton, M. 1968. "Voluntary Associations: Anthropological Aspects." In *International Encyclopedia of the Social Sciences*, vol. 16, pp. 357–62. New York: Macmillan and Free Press.

Barclay, A. H., Jr. 1979. "The Development Impact of Private Voluntary Organizations." *Development Digest* 17, no. 3:105–24. Development Alternatives.

Barnes, S. T. 1973. "Voluntary Associations in a Metropolis: The Case of Lagos." Paper presented at 16th Annual Meeting of Africa Studies Association in Syracuse, New York, October-November.

Bascom, W. 1952. "The Esusu: A Credit Institution of the Yoruba." *Journal of the Royal Anthropological Institute* 82, no. 1

Ben-Ner, Avner 1982. "A Theory of Non-Profit Organizations." Yale University, Program on Non-Profit Organizations Working Paper no. 51.

Bolling, L. R. 1983. *Private Foreign Aid. U.S. Philanthropy for Relief and Development*. Boulder, Colo.: Westview Press.

Bouman, F. J. A. 1977. "Indigenous Savings and Credit Associations in the Third World: A Message." *Savings and Development, Quarterly Review* 4, no. 1, or *Development Digest* 16, no. 3.

———. 1979. "The ROSCA: Financial Technology of an Informal Savings and Credit Institution in Developing Economies." *Savings and Development* 4.

Brinkschulte, B. 1976. *Formen und Funktionen wirtschaftlicher Kooperation in traditionellen Gesellschaften West Afrikas*. Meisenheim: A. Hain.

Buse, R. C., and P. G. Helmberger. 1969. "Potential and Feasibility of Cooperatives as Instruments of Market Reform." In *Agricultural Cooperatives and Markets in Developing Countries*, edited by K. R. Anschel, R. H. Brannon, and E. D. Smith, 197–211. New York: Praeger.

Catholic Church of Nigeria. 1982. *The History of the Catholic Church in Nigeria*. Lagos: Academy Press/Macmillan Nigeria.

Clarke, Peter B. 1982. *West Africa and Islam: A Study of Religious Development from the 8th to the 20th Century*. London: Arnold.

Cliffe, L. 1970. "Traditional Ujamaa and Modern Producer Cooperatives in Tanzania." In *Cooperatives and Rural Development in East Africa*, edited by C. Widstrand. New York: Africana Publishing Corp.

Comboulives, M. 1967. *L'organisation coopérative au Sénégal*. Paris.

Cooperative Chronology. 1973. Supp. No. 2. Geneva: ILO.

COPAC. 1978. *Cooperatives against Rural Poverty.* Var Gard: Saltjoebaden.

Dahlen, O. 1978. "NGO Organizations for Action." *Transnational Associations* 30:1–14.

Dore, R. 1971. "Modern Cooperatives in Traditional Communities." In *Two Blades of Grass: Rural Cooperatives in Agricultural Modernization,* edited by P. Worsley, 43–60. Manchester: Manchester University Press.

Duelfer, E. 1974. *Operational Efficiency of Agricultural Cooperatives in Developing Countries.* F.A.O.

Eicher, C. K. 1969. "Reflections on Capital-Intensive Moshav Farm Settlements in Nigeria." In *Agricultural Cooperatives and Markets in Developing Countries,* edited by K. R. Anschel, R. H. Brannon, and E. D. Smith, 327–46. New York: Praeger.

Eisenstadt, S. N. 1956. "Sociological Aspects of the Economic Adaption of Oriental Migrants in Israel: A Case Study in the Problem of Modernization." *Economic Development and Cultural Change* 4:269–78.

Emerij, L. 1974. "A New Look at Some Strategies for Increasing Productive Employment in Africa." *International Labour Review* 4:269–73.

Engelmann, K. E. 1968. *Building Cooperative Movements in Developing Countries.* New York: Praeger.

Epps, D. 1976. "The Role of NGO Cooperation in Establishing a New World Order." *International Associations* 28:257–59, 271.

Essien, A. E. 1975. "Introducing Management Principles into Nigerian Cooperatives." In *New Trends in African Cooperatives: The Nigerian Experience,* edited by M. O. Ijere, 112–250. Enugu: Fourth Dimension Publishers.

Fapohunda, O. J. 1981. "Human Resources in the Lagos Informal Sector." In *The Urban Informal Sector in Developing Countries,* edited by S. V. Sethuraman, 70–83. Geneva: ILO.

Fayossewo, A. A. 1974–75. *NGO Partner and Programme Identification.* Mission to the Sahel, F.A.O., Rome.

Forde, D. 1951. *The Yoruba-Speaking Peoples of South-Western Nigeria. Ethnographic Survey of Africa. Western Africa, Part IV.* London: International African Institute.

Freire, P. 1972. *Pedagogy of the Oppressed.* New York: Herder & Herder.

Friedman, R. 1981. "The Role of Non-Profit Organizations in Foreign Aid: A Literature Survey." Yale University, Program of Non-Profit Organizations Working Paper no. 32.

Gagnon, G. 1976. "Cooperatives, Participation, and Development: Three Failures." In *Popular Participation in Social Change,* edited by J. Nash, J. Dandler, and N. Hopkins, 365–80. The Hague: Mouton Publishers.

Geertz, C. 1962. "Rotating Credit Associations: A 'Middle Rung' in Development." *Economic Development and Cultural Change* 10, no. 3:241–63.

Gerdes, V. 1975. "Precursors of Modern Social Security in Indigenous African Institutions." *Journal of Modern African Studies* 13, no. 2:209–28.

Ghaussy, G. A. 1964. *Das Genossenschaftswesen in den Entwicklungslaendern.* Freiburg: Rombach.

Gide, C. 1930. *Communist and Cooperative Colonies.* London: G. G. Harrupt.

Gosselin, G. 1976. "Traditional Collectivism and Modern Associations: The Example of Southern Dahomey." In *Popular Participation in Social Change,* edited by J. Nash, J. Dandler, and N. Hopkins, 55–70. The Hague: Mouton Publishers.

Gow, D. D., and E. R. Morss. 1981. "Local Organization, Participation and Rural Development: Results from a Seven-Country Study." *Rural Development Participation Review* 2, no. 2:12–17.

Grantt, I., and G. D. Dutto. 1968. *Financial Performance of Government-Owned Corporations in Less-Developed Countries.* IMF Staff Papers no. 25. Washington, D.C.: IMF.

Green, J. R., and Laffont. 1979. *Incentives in Public Decision-Making.* Amsterdam: North-Holland Publishing Co.

Green, M. M. 1964 (1947). *Ibo Village Affairs.* New York: Praeger.

Gugler, J. 1982. "Over-Urbanization Reconsidered." *Economic Development and Cultural Change* 4 (December).

Gutkind, P. C. W., R. Cohen, and J. Copans, eds. 1978. *African Labor History.* Beverly Hills and London: Sage Publications.

Haggblade, S. 1978. "Africanization from Below: The Evolution of Cameroonian Saving Societies into Western Style Banks." *Rural Africana* 2.

Hake, H. 1977. *African Metropolis, Nairobi's Self-Help City.* London: Sussex University Press.

Hamer, J. H. 1976a. "Prerequisites and Limitations in the Development of Voluntary Self-Help Associations: A Case Study and Comparison." *Anthropological Quarterly* 49, no. 2:107–34.

———. 1976b. "Voluntary Associations as Structures of Change among the Sidamo of Southwestern Ethiopia." *Anthropological Quarterly* 49, no. 2:73–91.

———. 1981. "Preconditions and Limits in the Formation of Associations: The Self-Help and Cooperative Movement in Sub-Saharan Africa." *African Studies Review* 24.

Hansmann, H. 1980. "The Role of Non-Profit Enterprise." *Yale Law Journal* 89, no. 5:835–901.

Helmberger, P. 1964. "Cooperative Enterprise as a Structural Dimension of Farm Markets." *Journal of Farm Economics* 46, no. 3:603–17.

Hoebel, E. A. 1949. *Man in the Primitive World.* New York: McGraw-Hill, 302–12.

Hopkins, A. G. 1973. *An Economic History of West Africa.* London: Longman.

Hyden, G. 1970. "Can Co-ops Make It in Africa?" *Africa Report* 15:12–16.

———. 1973. *Efficiency versus Distribution in East African Cooperatives.* Nairobi: East African Literature Bureau.

———. 1980. *Beyond Ujamaa in Tanzania: Underdevelopment and an Uncaptured Peasantry.* Berkeley: University of California Press.

———. 1983a. *Rural Community Development: Role of Community-Based and Intermediary Organizations.* Concepts and Issues Paper. New York: Ford Foundation.

———. 1983b. *No Shortcuts in Progress: African Development*

Management in Perspective. Berkeley: University of California Press.

Ijere, M. O., ed. 1975. *New Trends in African Cooperatives: The Nigerian Experience*. Enugu: Fourth Dimension Publishers.

Illy, H. F. 1978. "How to Build in the Germs of Failure." *Rural Africana* 2.

———. 1980. "Afrikanische Solidaritaet und europaeisches Genossenschaftswesen: Kreditgenossenschaften im frankophonen Kamerun." In *Wege zu einer afrikanischen Genossenschaft*, edited by H. H. Muenckner, 91–106. Marburg: Institut fuer Kooperation in Entwicklungslaendern.

ILO. 1973. *Employment, Incomes and Equality: A Strategy for Increasing Production Employment in Kenya*. Geneva: ILO.

———. *Profiles of Rural Poverty*. Geneva: ILO.

Imaogene, S. O. 1967. "Mechanisms of Immigrant Adjustment in a West African Community (Sapele Town)." *Nigerian Journal of Economic and Social Studies* 9, no. 1.

James, E. 1980. "The Non-Profit Sector in International Perspective: The Case of Sri Lanka." Yale University, Program on Non-Profit Organizations Working Paper no. 32.

Kalu, O. U. 1978. *The Divided People of God: Church Union Movement in Nigeria: 1875–1966*. New York: NOK Publishers.

Kaplan, I. Ed. 1978. *Tanzania: A Country Study*. Washington, D.C.: American University.

Karanja, E. 1974. "The Development of a Cooperative Movement in Kenya." Ph.D. diss., University of Pittsburgh.

Kasfir, N. 1970. "Organizational Analysis and Ugandian Cooperative Union." In *Cooperatives and Rural Development in East Africa*, edited by C. G. Widstrand, 178–208. Uppsala: Almquist & Wiksell.

Kerr, G. B. 1978. "Voluntary Associations in West Africa: Hidden Agents of Social Change." *African Studies Review* 21, no. 3:87–100.

Kerri, T. N. 1974. *Anthropology, Voluntary Associations and Voluntary Action: The Romance of the Intimate and the Reticent—A Review*. Washington, D.C.: Association of Voluntary Action Scholars.

———. 1976. "Studying Voluntary Associations as Adaptive Mechanism: Review of Anthropological Perspectives." *Current Anthropology* 17:23–47.

Kilby, P. 1969. *Industrialization in an Open Economy: Nigeria 1845–1966*. Cambridge: Cambridge University Press.

Kiros, F. G. 1981. *The Least Developed Countries of Africa and the Prospects for a New International Economic Order*. Addis Ababa, Ethiopia: United Nations.

Koll, M. 1969. *Crafts and Cooperation in Western Nigeria*. Duesseldorf: Bertelsmann.

Kurtz, D. V. 1973. "The Rotating Credit Associations: An Adaption to Poverty." *Human Organizations* 32:49–58.

Lassen, C. 1979. "Reaching the Assetless Rural Poor." *Development Digest* 17, no. 1:3–28.

Lipeb, M. 1980. "Verbaende und trennende Elemente bei autochthonen Selbsthilfeorganisationen und Genossenschaften-Möglichkeiten und Probleme einer Synthese." In *Wege zu einer afrikanischen Genossenschaft*, edited by H. H.

Muenckner, 53–68. Marburg: Institut fuer Kooperation in Entwicklungslaendern.

Little, K. 1949. "The Role of the Secret Society in Cultural Specialization." *American Anthropologist* 51, no. 2.

———. 1959. "The Organization of Voluntary Associations in West Africa." *Civilizations* 9, no. 3.

———. 1962a. "The Urban Role of Tribal Associations in West Africa." *African Studies* 21, no. 1.

———. 1962b. "Some Traditionally Based Forms of Mutual Aid in West African Urbanization." *Ethnology* 1, no. 2.

———. 1964. "The Role of Voluntary Associations in West African Urbanization." In *Africa: Social Problems of Change and Conflict*, edited by Van den Berghe. San Francisco: Chandler Publishing Co. Also in *American Anthropologist* 59.

———. 1965. *West African Urbanization: A Study of Voluntary Associations in Social Change*. Cambridge: Cambridge University Press.

———. 1967. "Voluntary Associations in Urban Life: A Case Study of Differential Adaption." In *Social Organization: Essays Presented to Raymond Firth*, edited by M. Freedman. London: Cass.

———. 1972. "Voluntary Associations and Social Mobility among West African Women." *Canadian Journal of African Studies* 6, no. 2:275–88.

Lloyd, P. C. 1953. "Craft Organizations in Yoruba Towns." *Africa* 23.

Lombard, J. 1959. "Le collectivisme Africain, Valeur socioculturelle traditionelle: Instrument de progrès économique." *Présence Africaine* 26:22–51.

Lowie, R. H. 1925. *Primitive Society*. New York: Boni & Liveright, chap. 10, 11.

Madujibeya, S. A. 1976. "Oil and Nigeria's Economic Development." *African Affairs* 75(300):284–316.

Martin, E. C. 1923. "Early Educational Experiments on the Gold Coast." *Journal of the African Society* 23.

Mather, L. L. 1969. "The Principles, Functions, and Benefits of Cooperation: The Traditional Model." In *Agricultural Cooperatives and Markets in Developing Countries*, edited by K. R. Anschel, R. H. Brannon, and E. D. Smith, 13–27. New York: Praeger.

Mbithi, P. M., and R. Rasmusson. 1977. *Self-Reliance in Kenya: The Case of Harambee*. Uppsala: Bohnslaningens AB.

Meillassoux, C. 1968. *Urbanization of an African Community: Voluntary Associations in Bamako*. Seattle and London: University of Washington Press.

———. 1975. *L'esclavage en Afrique précolonial*. Paris: Maspero.

Meister, A. 1969. "Ambitions and Risks of Cooperative Socialism in East Africa: Kenya, Uganda, Tanzania." *Journal of Asian and African Studies* 4, no. 4:241–74.

Meyer, E. 1940. "Kreditringe in Kamerun." *Koloniale Rundschau* 31.

Migot-Adholla, S. E. 1970. "Traditional Society and Cooperatives." In *Cooperatives and Rural Development in East Africa*, edited by C. G. Widstrand, 17–37. Uppsala: Almquist & Wiksell.

————. 1972. "The Politics of Mechanization in Sukumaland." In *African Cooperatives and Efficiency,* edited by C. G. Widstrand, 81–104. Uppsala: Almquist & Wiksell.

Miracle, M. 1969. "An Evaluation of Attempts to Introduce Cooperatives and Quasi-Cooperatives in Tropical Africa." In *Agricultural Cooperatives and Markets in Developing Countries,* edited by K. R. Anschel, R. H. Brannon, and E. D. Smith, 301–15. New York: Praeger.

Miracle, M., O. S. Miracle, and L. Cohen. 1980. "Informal Savings Mobilization in Africa." *Economic Development and Cultural Change* 28, no. 4:701–25.

Muenckner, H. H. 1979. *The Legal Status of Pre-Cooperatives.* Bonn: Friedrich-Ebert-Stiftung.

————. 1980. *Wege zu einer afrikanischen Genossenschaft.* Marburg: Institut fuer Kooperation in Entwicklungslaendern.

————. 1981. *Possibilities and Problems of Transformation of Local Village Groups into Pre-Cooperatives.* Amsterdam: IUAES Intercongress.

Nadel, F. 1942. *A Black Byzantium: The Kingdom of Nupe in Nigeria.* London: Oxford University Press.

Nash, J., J. Dandler, and N. S. Hopkins, eds. 1976. *Popular Participation in Social Change: Cooperatives, Collectives and Nationalized Industry.* The Hague and Paris: Mouton.

Nigeria, Cooperative Registrar. *Annual Reports 1935–37.* Lagos.

Nigeria: Federal Ministry of Economic Development. *Third National Development Plan, 1975–1980.* Lagos.

Nigeria: Federal Ministry of Economic Development. *Third National Development Plan, 1975–1980. Second Progress Report.* Lagos.

Nigeria: Federal Ministry of National Planning. *Guidelines for the Fourth National Development Plan 1981–1985.* Lagos.

Nnoli, O., ed. 1981. *Path to Nigerian Development.* Dakar: Codesria.

Nyerere, J. K. 1967. *Socialism and Rural Development.* Dar es Salaam: Government Printer.

Ollawa, P. E. 1977. "On a Dynamic Model for Rural Development in Africa." *Journal of Modern African Studies* 15:401–23.

Olson, M. 1965. *The Logic of Collective Action: Public Goods and the Theory of Groups.* Cambridge, Mass.: Harvard University Press.

Omari, C. K. 1976. *Strategy for Rural Development: Tanzania's Experience.* Dar es Salaam: East African Literature Bureau.

Orora, J. H., and H. B. C. Spiegel. 1981. "Harambee: Self-Help Development in Kenya." *International Journal of Comparative Sociology* 21, nos. 3–4:243–53.

Pankhurst, R, and E. Eshete. 1958. "Self-Help in Ethiopia." *Ethiopia Observer* 2:11.

Parkin, D. 1966. "Urban Voluntary Associations as Institutions of Adaption." *Man* 1, no. 1.

Parvey, C. F. 1972. "The Role of Voluntary Associations in Third World Development: Some Questions for Exploration." *Journal of Voluntary Action Research* 1:2–7.

Paulus, M. 1964. "Das Genossenschaftswesen in Tanganyika und Uganda." *Afrika Studien* 15.

Plotnicov, L. 1967. *Strangers to the City.* Pittsburgh: University of Pittsburgh Press.

Pozen, R. C. 1972. "Public Corporations in Ghana: A Case Study in Legal Importation." Yale Law School, Program in Law and Modernization Working Paper no. 8.

Raulin, H. 1976. "Organized Cooperation and Spontaneous Cooperation in Africa (Niger Republic)." In *Popular Participation in Social Change,* edited by J. Nash, J. Dandler, and N. Hopkins, 35–43. The Hague: Mouton Publishers.

Roth, W. 1976. "Traditional Social Structure and the Development of a Marketing Cooperative in Tanzania." In *Popular Participation in Social Change,* edited by J. Nash, J. Dandler, and N. Hopkins, 45–53. The Hague: Mouton Publishers.

Ruel, M. J. 1964. "The Modern Adaption of Associations among the Banyang of West Cameroon." *Southwestern Journal of Anthropology.* Spring:1–14.

Saul, J. 1971. "Marketing Cooperatives in a Developing Country: The Tanzanian Case." In *Two Blades of Grass,* edited by P. Worsley, 347–70. Manchester: University of Manchester Press.

Schumacher, E. F. 1973. *Small is Beautiful. Economics as if People Mattered.* New York: Harper & Row.

Schurtz, H. 1902. *Altersklassen und Maennerbuende: Eine Darstellung der Grundformen der Gesellschaft.* Berlin: Reimer.

Seibel, H. D. 1968. "Landwirtschaftliche Entwicklung in Africa." *Zeitschrift fuer auslaendische Landwirtschaft* 7:219–32.

————. 1970. "Indigenous Economic Cooperation and Its Developmental Function in Liberia." *Cooperative Information* 46:7–53.

————. 1981. "Indigenous Self-Help Organizations and Rural Development: Some Liberian and Ghanian Cases." *Rural Development Participation Review* 3, no. 1:11–16.

Seibel, H. D. and M. Koll, 1968. *Einheimische Genossenschaften in Afrika. Formen wirtschaftlicher Zusammanarbeit bei west-afrikanischen Staemmen.* Duesseldorf: Bertelsmann.

Seibel, H. D. and A. Massing. 1974. *Traditional Organizations and Economic Development. Studies of Indigenous Cooperatives in Liberia.* New York: Praeger.

Sethuraman, S. V. 1981. *The Urban Informal Sector in Developing Countries.* Geneva: ILO.

Shirley, M. M. 1983. "Managing State-Owned Enterprises." World Bank Staff Working Paper no. 577. Management and Development Series no. 4.

Short, P. 1983. *Appraising the Role of Public Enterprise: An International Comparison.* IMF Occasional Paper Series. Washington, D.C.: IMF.

Sills, D. L. 1968. "Voluntary Associations II. Sociological Aspects." In *International Encyclopedia of the Social Sciences,* vol. 16. New York: Macmillan and Free Press.

Smith, E. C. 1969. "Adopting Cooperatives and Quasi-Cooperatives to Market Structures and Conditions of Less-Developed Countries: A Summary Economic View." In *Agricultural Cooperatives and Markets in Developing Countries,* edited by K. R. Anschel, R. H. Brannon, and E. D. Smith, 349–73. New York: Praeger.

Sommer, J. G. 1979. *Beyond Charity: U.S. Voluntary Aid for a*

Changing Third World. Washington, D.C.: Overseas Development Council.

Strickland, C. F. 1934. *Report on the Introduction of Cooperative Societies into Nigeria.* Lagos: Government Printer.

Tardits, C., et al. 1956. *Société paysanne et problèmes fonciers de la palmeraie dahoméenne.* Paris: L'Homme d'outre Mer.

Tendler, J. 1982. "Turning Private Voluntary Organizations into Developmental Agencies: Questions for Evaluation." A.I.D. Program Evaluation Discussion Paper no. 12.

Texier, J. M. 1975. "Promotion of Cooperatives in Traditional Areas." *Cooperative Information* 51:1–9.

Todaro, M. P. 1977. *Economic Development in the Third World: An Introduction to Problems and Policies in a Global Perspective.* New York: Longman.

Trappe, P. 1966. *Die Entwicklungsfunktion des Genossenschaftswesens am Beispiel ost-afrikanischer Staemme.* Neuwied: Luchterhand.

United Nations Commission for Africa. 1975. *Revised Framework of Principles for the Implementation of the New International Order in Africa. 1976–1981–1986.*

United Nations Research Institute for Social Development. 1969. *A Review of Rural Cooperatives in Developing Areas.* Geneva: United Nations.

———. 1970. *Rural Cooperatives and Planned Change in Africa: Case Materials,* edited by R. Apthorpe. Geneva.

Van Heemst, J. J. P. 1981. *The Role of NGOs in Development: Some Perspectives for Further Research.* The Hague: Institute of Social Studies.

Vierkandt, A. 1931. "Die genossenschaftliche Gesellschaftsform der Naturvoelker." In *Handwoerterbuch der Soziologie,* edited by A. Vierkandt. Stuttgart: Enke.

Vincent, J. 1976. "Rural Competition and the Cooperative Monopoly: Ugandian Case Study." In *Popular Participation in Social Change,* edited by J. Nash, J. Dandler, and N. Hopkins, 71–97. The Hague: Mouton Publishers.

Wallerstein, I. 1964. "Voluntary Associations." In *Political Parties and National Integration in Tropical Africa,* edited by T. S. Coleman and C. C. Rosberg. Berkeley: University of California Press.

Weaver, J. H., and A. Kronemer. 1981. "Tanzanian and African Socialism." *World Development* 9, no. 10.

Weber, Max. 1947. *Theory of Social and Economic Organizations.* Translated by A. R. Henderson and T. Parsons, and edited by T. Parsons. Glencoe, Ill.: Free Press.

Webster, H. 1932. *Primitive Secret Societies.* New York: Macmillan.

Weisbrod, B. A., ed. 1977. *The Voluntary Non-Profit Sector.* Lexington, Mass.: D. C. Heath.

Westergaard, P. W. 1970. "Cooperatives in Tanzania as Economic and Democratic Institutions." In *Cooperatives and Rural Development in East Africa,* edited by C. Widstrand. New York: Africana Publishing Corp.

Westermann, D. 1935. *Die Geidyi-Ewe in Togo.* Berlin: W. deGruyter.

Wicksell, K. 1896. *Finanztheoretische Untersuchungen und das Steuerwesen Schwedens.* Jena: G. Fischer.

World Bank. 1983. *World Bank Development Report 1983.* Oxford: Oxford University Press.

Youngjohns, B. J. 1982. "Cooperatives and Credit: A Reexamination." *Development Digest* 20, no. 1:3–9.

24

Producer Cooperatives: Why Do They Exist in Capitalist Economies?

AVNER BEN-NER

I n capitalist economies, where the major resource allocation mechanism is the market, the main ownership mode
is private, and the prevalent motivating force is self-
interest—the dominant type of organization is the capitalist firm. But apart from capitalist firms and state-
operated organizations, there also exists a substantial fringe
composed of nonprofit organizations and cooperatives.
These organizations, sometimes referred to collectively as
the third sector, differ from capitalist firms in various ways.
In particular, whereas in capitalist firms capital alone has the
right to control the firm, hire labor, and appropriate monetary
profits, in the third sector the economic role of capital is
largely superseded by that of labor or consumers. Third-
sector organizations may be viewed as special cases of vertical integration: parties engaged in repeated transactions
merge instead of interacting on the market or signing contracts as separate entities. One party assumes control over the
activities of the other, and the resulting integration eliminates
the harmful consequences engendered by the conflicting objectives of the separate parties (Williamson 1975; Grossman
& Hart, 1986). In nonprofit organizations and consumer
cooperatives, consumers gain welfare by controlling the
goals and actions of what otherwise would be independent
sellers (Ben-Ner 1986a). In producer cooperatives, I suggest

in this chapter, workers own and control capital in order to
increase their welfare by internalizing the conflicts of interests between labor and owners of firms. Within the third
sector, then, organizations differ from one another. One
important way is that nonprofit organizations, unlike cooperatives, are constrained from distributing any monetary profits
to their workers, manager, or owners of their capital.

Economic theory and the other social sciences highlight
the congruity between capitalist firms and the capitalist economic system. It is therefore interesting to understand the
reasons for the emergence of third-sector organizations in
capitalist economies. Hansmann (this volume, chap. 2)
focuses on nonprofit organizations and reviews the economic
theories that attempt to explain their existence; this chapter
concentrates on another major component of the third sector,
producer cooperatives. The discussion parallels the study of
nonprofit organizations in capitalist economies I have presented elsewhere (Ben-Ner 1986a), attempting a thorough
theoretical analysis of the reasons for and the circumstances
of formation of producer cooperatives, complemented by
empirical surveys and illustrations. This study draws from
many contributions that have provided useful theoretical
insights and empirical evidence regarding the formation of
producer cooperatives, the most notable of which are by
Jones (1980, 1984), Shirom (1972), Aldrich and Stern
(1983), Bradley and Gelb (1983), Pryor (1983), Putterman
(1982, 1984), Cornforth (1983), and Ireland and Law
(1982).

A *producer cooperative* (PC) is an organization controlled by member-workers who share profits among themselves. They own the PC's capital (collectively or through
individual shares) or rent it from others (Gui 1984). Although
there may be shareholders who do not work in the PC, such

The helpful comments by Saul Estrin, Benedetto Gui, Bertrand
Horwitz, Derek Jones, John Michael Montias, Walter Powell, Frederic
Pryor, Louis Putterman, and Teri Van Hoomissen, as well as financial
support from the Program on Non-Profit Organizations at Yale University, are gratefully acknowledged. The Southampton Economic Research Unit at the University of Southampton and the Centre for Labour
Economics at the London School of Economics, where much of the
paper was written during visits in the summers of 1984 and 1985,
provided stimulating environments and research facilities.

owners may not enjoy majority control over the firm. Similarly, a minority of nonmembers may be hired to work for wages in the PC without enjoying controlling rights. (See Pryor [1983] and Putterman [1984] for more detailed definitions.)

The lines of demarcation among types of organizations are not always clear. Pauly and Redisch (1973) have suggested that some organizations that are called nonprofit organizations are in fact producer cooperatives. I have argued (Ben-Ner 1986a) that most nonprofit organizations are initially very similar to consumer cooperatives, and have claimed that many PCs grow to resemble capitalist firms (Ben-Ner 1984, 1986b). In addition, some firms that fit the above definition are not legally incorporated as PCs. This chapter concentrates on those organizations that comply with the PC definition at the time of their *formation,* excluding agricultural PCs and communes.[1]

Numerous past and present organizations correspond to the definition of PCs suggested above and therefore fall within the scope of investigation here. A few examples may indicate the empirical range of this study. The plywood cooperatives in northwestern United States, with work forces ranging in the few hundreds, are owned by their workers, though not by all of them since they employ hired wage laborers as well. Individual shares can be sold by departing member-workers to incoming members. Members participate in management directly on a one-man-one-vote basis or via elected representatives. Another type is represented by small-scale PCs in various countries, often concentrated in service industries. Many offer no individual shares, but are owned collectively by their workers; hence departing members receive no compensation nor do new members pay entry fees. The governance of many such PCs is based on direct democracy. Large manufacturing and service firms that were bought by their employees from former owners serve as yet another example of organizations the birth of which I hope to explain in this chapter. Such firms, frequently neither incorporated as PCs (even when the legal form is available) nor commonly called by that name, have various ownership and governance structures. For instance, many have a formal separation of ownership and labor; thus shares can be sold and bought by workers as well as by nonworkers such as community organizations or individuals. Such PCs are seldom managed by the workers; their governance structure resembles that of capitalist firms in that shareholders meet infrequently and do not get involved in day-to-day managerial issues.

The chapter is organized as follows: the next section deals with the theory of PC formation. I suggest that in a capitalist economy there exist inherent biases against the formation of PCs, expecially in that entrepreneurs will in general prefer to establish capitalist firms where they can appropriate profits to themselves, rather than establish PCs where they must share profits with others and bear high costs of entrepreneurship. Nevertheless, circumstances may arise that favor the establishment of PCs either as new firms or by conversion of capitalist firms. The emergence of such circumstances may validate advantageous features enjoyed by PCs and generate sufficient additional profits and welfare to make PCs viable where capitalist firms are not and to overcome the entrepreneurship problem, consequently rendering PCs superior to capitalist firms. The special advantageous features stem mainly from the elimination of conflicts between owners and workers; the favorable circumstances include support by PC promoters, exercise of labor market power by capitalist firms, threat of shutdown of capitalist firms in declining industries or during generalized recessions, dissatisfaction of workers with workplace characteristics in capitalist firms, and, in general, superior performance by PCs relative to capitalist firms.

The following section commences with a survey of the PC sector in a few capitalist economies and continues with empirical illustrations of PCs formation, employing the theoretical analysis presented in the first part. The final section summarises the key arguments and ventures some generalizations regarding the birth of PCs.

FORMATION OF PCs: THEORY

The Problem of Entrepreneurship

The formation of a new economic organization hinges on the successful completion of several actions: identifying an economic niche for the new organization; raising the financial capital; assembling physical capital, labor, and other inputs; organizing and coordinating production, marketing, investment, and other economic functions; and allocating risk bearing (see Casson 1982). Although these various actions can be carried out by different groups or individuals, they must be integral parts of a general blueprint designed to achieve the formation and sustenance of the economic organization. The design of the blueprint and the assignment of actions to different groups define the entrepreneurial role. Successful completion of this role requires the possession of certain skills: acquaintance with market conditions in the intended area of operation, knowledge of possible sources of financial capital, expertise in relevant technical matters, administrative skills, and ability or willingness to assume some of the risk involved in setting up the new organization. Some of these skills may, in part, be delegated to others. Whoever performs these tasks—whether one person or a group—will be referred to here as the entrepreneur.

A self-interested entrepreneur will establish a new organization if he or she can make a profit from this act. Under broad circumstances, such an entrepreneur will have no incentives to share the profits generated by the new organization with others. Therefore, if both types of organizations are equally efficient, a self-interested entrepreneur will establish a capitalist firm rather than a PC.

---

1. For agricultural and consumer cooperatives, see Heflebower (1980); for communes and agricultural cooperatives, see various articles in Dorner (1977). Pryor (1983) is a useful introduction to all these organizations.

This bias against the formation of PCs in capitalist economies stems from the scarcity of individuals possessing entrepreneurial skills. But even if these skills were more widely distributed than they actually are, the bias would still persist. Entrepreneurial skills as developed in capitalist economies are best suited for the establishment of capitalist firms, so that the exercise of PC-formation entrepreneurship entails additional costs of learning and adaptation on the part of individuals.[2] Thus the bias against PCs—the entrepreneurial problem—is a bias in favor of the organizational status quo.[3]

This analysis has provided a powerful negative result regarding the possibility of establishing PCs in capitalist economies. The rest of this section is devoted to the derivation of positive results—that is, to the analysis of circumstances that *favor* the formation of PCs. All input providers would receive at least their alternative incomes, and at least some of them would receive more in a PC as compared to a capitalist firm. In particular, the entrepreneur's net gain (in monetary terms or, more generally, in utility terms) from forming a PC must exceed his or her gain in an alternative course of action, including the formation of a capitalist firm. The gain of entrepreneurs and of other providers of inputs may be generated by transfers from promoters of PCs or by the domination of the PC form of organization, both of which will be discussed below.

Support by PC Promoters

Support for the creation of a PC may come from groups or individuals other than prospective member-workers, such as political movements, trade unions, cooperative umbrella organizations, philanthropists, or the state. This support may be granted for a number of reasons. One is the view that cooperation at the workplace—involving the elimination of conflict between employers and employees, worker participation in management, and worker ownership—is desirable both in itself and as a means toward other welfare-related goals and economic efficiency, and should therefore be encouraged (see, for example, Horvat 1982; Pateman

2. The actions concerning the establishment of PCs and capitalist firms are somewhat different. The difference regards, for example, recruitment of workers and of equity capital (as in a PC a majority of workers must also participate in control and in ownership of the firm), establishment of decision-making procedures (more democratic in PCs), adoption of accounting methods (regarding the definition of the cost of labor, distribution of profits, and so on), or the assumption of legal status (incorporation as a cooperative or other available forms). See also Abell (1983), Aldrich and Stern (1983), and Putterman (1982). For a somewhat different view of the entrepreneurial problem emphasizing the limited information at the disposal of prospective PC members, see Estrin (1979).

3. There exist additional impediments to the routine formation of PCs in capitalist economies. Workers, who have less wealth than capitalists, are more risk averse and can also raise less capital using their personal wealth as collateral. Furthermore, the PC form of organization is less known to potential lenders, who therefore will view it as a riskier venture worth of fewer loans and at higher interest rates. (See Ben-Ner [1986b] for a more detailed analysis.)

1970; Vanek 1970, 1975; Oakeshott 1978). Another reason may stem from a recognition that workers' welfare, especially employment, can be improved at a lower cost by promoting PCs rather than through capitalist firms or the provision of welfare payments. (See Bradley and Gelb [1980, 1983] for a related view.)

Several authors have argued that PCs may be desirable for workers but may be unattainable. Miller (1981) and Putterman (1982, 1984) claim that the interaction between PCs' attributes of internal organization and their capitalist environment puts PCs at a disadvantage (by too little investment or inability to attract capable managers, for example), and they cannot compete successfully with capitalist firms. Therefore, in order to ensure the viability of PCs and permit workers to express their preferences for the PC form, state aid is needed. The entrepreneurial problem may create similar opportunities for state support for PCs.

Vanek (1970), Horvat (1975b), and others have emphasized the problems PCs have with their environment: limited access to capital, discrimination in input and product markets, and so on. They conclude that in order to overcome these disadvantages support organizations must promote the formation and continued existence of PCs.

The support of promoters can bear on the formation of PCs in three ways, all of which reduce the problem of entrepreneurship. First, promoters capable of fulfilling the entrepreneurial role may be willing to share the prospective organization's profits with member-workers. Second, promoters may award grants to PCs, making them a relatively more profitable and hence a dominant type of organization; a sufficiently large grant may provide an entrepreneur a profit share that is larger than the total profit obtainable from a capitalist firm. In the absence of other facilitating circumstances such grants may have to be very large and increase with the size of the prospective PC. Third, PC promoters may help improve the entrepreneurial abilities of prospective members through educational programs. To ensure that the gain in abilities will be not be used for the formation of capitalist firms, promoters may inculcate workers with cooperative ideology, or may provide each of them with limited entrepreneurial skills so that only their combination of skills will be useful for the formation of a new firm, a PC.

Circumstances when PCs Dominate Capitalist Firms

PCs' Internal Organization and Economic Performance

PCs can be formed only if they enjoy a special advantage relative to capitalist firms that permits them to overcome the entrepreneurial problem. This advantage can be generated by external support or by the existence of special features that render PCs superior to capitalist firms. There are two such special features inherent in PCs' internal organization. The first stems directly from the construction of PCs as organizations controlled by workers. This control internalizes the conflict of interests between them and owners of capital, something that cannot be achieved in firms controlled by owners of capital.[4] The crucial difference lies in capital's being an inanimate object; once ownership or rental of it is acquired by workers, it can be subordinated to their will. The second special feature of PCs' internal organization results from workers' management and ownership of capital, which improves their motivation and induces them to work better (Vanek 1970, 1975; Horvat 1982; Blumberg 1968; Oakeshott 1978).

The first feature, elimination of conflicts between firm owners and workers, eliminates asymmetries of information, distrust, opportunism, exercise of intrafirm monopolistic or monopsonistic power, and contractual inflexibilities that prevail between the two parties in capitalist firms.[5] This in turn frequently alters (reduces) the effective prices of capital and labor faced by the PC and enables it to behave more efficiently than the capitalist firm (Ben-Ner 1985). In particular, as discussed below, PCs can be established when capitalist firms are deterred by barriers to entry raised by labor-market oligopsonists or when capitalist firms cannot operate profitably because of unfavorable market conditions. PCs can also be formed when workers desert capitalist firms because of dissatisfaction with workplace conditions. In activities in which centralized monitoring is difficult to carry out, mutual monitoring and better incentives for worker-members help overcome shirking and make for superior performance of PCs (Russell 1985; Stiglitz 1974). The second feature, improved motivation to work, enables PCs to produce from the same amount of inputs more output than capitalist firms can produce.

The first special feature of PCs' internal organization confers advantages upon them only under circumstances that make conflict in capitalist firms detrimental to production. In contrast, the second feature's benefits can be reaped regardless of economic circumstances, as they entail a permanent shift in the productive capacity of PCs relative to capitalist firms.

The benefits derived from workers' management and ownership are challenged by some authors. They argue that workers are inefficient decision makers, that they have insufficient incentives for monitoring and supervising one another because of diffusion of profits, and that they invest too little (Webb & Webb 1914, 1921; Alchian & Demsetz 1972;

Furubotn 1976; Jensen & Meckling 1979; Williamson 1980). It is not possible to determine here the relative merits of these arguments (but see Putterman's detailed and incisive criticisms of them [1982, 1984]). Suffice it to say that the claimed disadvantage of PCs is, like the second special feature's advantage, independent of economic circumstances.

The rest of this section concentrates on circumstances that cause PCs to dominate capitalist firms by permitting workers to capitalize on PCs' first feature. The existence of favorable circumstances, however, does not ensure that PCs' special advantage will outweigh entirely the entrepreneurial problem. When that happens, social welfare can be improved by granting support to PCs by the state or other PC promoters.

Labor Market Power of Capitalist Firms

Consider capitalist firms operating in perfectly competitive markets for their products. In small and relatively isolated localities, a few such firms may still be able to maintain market power, and thus restrict employment and keep wages below their competitive level (Addison & Siebert 1979). Although the (oligopsonistic) profits enjoyed by extant firms would tend to attract new capitalist firms, such a situation can persist if information about labor market conditions is not available to potential entrants, or if there are some barriers to entry. Barriers may be erected through administrative means as a result of successful weilding of local political power by extant firms. Entry may also be deterred if the firms are able to coordinate their activities to maintain strategic excess capacity. Extant firms can threaten to use the excess capacity in response to attempts to enter (or even use it occasionally to send signals to potential entrants), thereby increasing their demand for labor. Their demand alone may raise wages to the competitive level, and if some entry materializes, wages will exceed the competitive level, not only eliminating profits but possibly causing losses; thus such a strategy may deter potential entrants. (See Williamson [1968] and Salop & Scheffman [1983] for related analyses.)

If entry of new capitalist firms is successfully prevented, workers can adopt one of a few strategies to improve their wages: (1) leave the locality for the higher competitive wage elsewhere, (2) organize to bargain with the firms for a higher wage, (3) buy out capitalist firms and convert them into PCs, or (4) establish new firms as PCs.

The first possibility is limited by the cost of acquiring information about jobs available elsewhere and that entailed by moving; this in fact defines the ability of capitalist firms to exercise power in the labor market. The second possibility depends on workers' ability to organize in the locality. Nevertheless, bargaining will improve their wage but not enable them to attain the competitive wage, and some oligopsonistic profits will remain with the capitalist firms (De Menil 1971).[6]

---

4. Workers' participation in management and profit sharing in capitalist firms attenuate somewhat the conflict between owners and workers (Cable 1984), whereas the possible existence of nonworker shareholders (or inegalitarian shareholding by member-workers) in PCs prevents the complete elimination of that conflict. Nonetheless, the more extreme cases treated in the text serve well in making the point of this section, as the conflict cannot be larger in any PC than in any participatory capitalist firm. A similar comment applies to the second special feature.

5. All conflict and its consequences can be entirely eliminated only if agency problems do not exist and workers are homogeneous. Although neither condition is likely to be fulfilled in reality, the comment made in the previous footnote still holds true.

6. Greenwald (1979) demonstrates that "very" strong unions can achieve the maximum feasible wage, which in the present context is the competitive wage. The union strength presumed by such a result ex-

The third solution attempts to eliminate the conflict of interests between workers and owners by bringing the firm under worker control. In this case, a capitalist firm converted into a PC will be able to provide each worker an income equal to the competitive wage, which is the maximum wage a perfectly competitive firm can pay. Nevertheless, unless workers manage to buy out most local firms, their gain from conversion is likely to be very small. If workers in one firm decide to buy it, they must pay its owners at least the price of its capital plus the present value of the stream of future profits that would be earned if the firm continued to be operated as a capitalist firm. If no other firms are converted, the one in question can continue to operate as an oligopsony and earn supernormal profits by keeping wages low; hence its owners will sell it only if they are paid at least the oligopsony price. Conversion of only one firm means, in fact, that workers have to pay their own wage differentials—hence they have no gain at all. Only if workers in many firms attempt to buy them out will conversion offer a valuable strategy.

The solution of extensive buy-outs presents several problems, however. First, it requires that there be workers to fulfill the entrepreneurial role in most local firms. Further, either these persons must be offered significant gains or they must be ideologically inclined towards PCs. Second, conversions must occur simultaneously if they are to constitute an effective pressure on the labor market and push down expected oligopsonistic profits to zero. Third, workers' organized attempt to buy out the local firms may be countered by owners' formation of a sellers' coalition in order to extract higher prices for their firms. As these requirements for the buy-out solution are onerous, the likelihood of its occurrence is very low.[7]

The fourth solution is the creation of new PCs. As in the previous case, members of PCs attain the competitive wage, but this time they do not have to compensate owners of capitalist firms for their forgone profits. Formation of new PCs is the only sure way to increase participating workers' wages to the competitive level, and it is therefore their most preferred solution. Moreover, the creation of new PCs, unlike the bargaining and buy-out solutions, benefits participating workers even if they constitute only a small minority of local workers.[8]

It is important to emphasize that the excess capacity strategy of extant firms cannot prevent entry of PCs. Workers

in the locality who are capable of forming a firm face three alternatives. First, they may remain employed with extant firms, where their expected wage is below the competitive wage. Second, they may establish capitalist firms where they can earn the competitive wage plus zero economic profits, or even make losses; that is, their expected earnings are below the competitive wage. Third, they may form PCs where they agree with their fellow workers to pay themselves (that is, all workers, which in this case must be members) the highest feasible wage; in the PC their expected wage is the competitive wage. Such an agreement can be sustained because it is in the best interest of all members to isolate themselves from local wage fluctuations generated by the entry-deterrence strategy of extant firms. A similar agreement cannot be sustained in a capitalist firm where workers do not share in profits. Only if these firms raised and then kept wages credibly at the competitive level could they prevent capable workers from forming PCs. If they did so, the need for PCs would disappear (given the present assumptions). However, capitalist firms do not have to go to such extremes if only a relatively few workers are involved in forming PCs. In this case capitalist firms would need to raise wages only enough to accommodate the increase in demand for local labor (thus benefiting the unorganized workers), but they will not have to raise wages to a competitive level.

PCs, then, will be formed only if the difference between the local wage and the competitive wage (the PC-attainable income per worker) is large enough to induce the entrepreneurial effort. This critical difference may be achieved, for example, because local wages fall owing, say, to an increase in the local labor supply as a result of natural population growth, or because of the demise of local firms, which depresses the demand for labor, or because of tighter organization of the oligopsony. Such situations increase the gain from forming PCs. This gain may be greater if a general improvement in economic conditions raises also the PC-attainable income per member (more than the local wage), if grants are accorded to PCs, or if the entrepreneurial role is assumed by outsiders.

Declining Industries

Consider now a capitalist firm operating in a declining industry. At some point firm owners may decide that at current and expected demand and cost conditions, current and expected profits call for the shutdown of the firm. The firm's workers lose their incomes, and because of a drop in their demand for services, the incomes of other workers and firms in the locality may fall as well. In addition, the wealth of dismissed workers and others will drop with the reduction in real estate values resulting from lower incomes. These costs of firm shutdown, borne by workers and the rest of the local community, are temporary and very small if the locality in which the shutdown occurs is large and firms that operate in nondeclining industries can absorb the unemployed workers. However, if the locality is small and its labor market relatively isolated, and if the closing firm is a major employer,

---

empts the union even from the need to bargain and is well beyond what can be imagined in the present context. Even in trade union–run firms it is likely that workers will earn less than the maximum economically feasible (Ben-Ner & Estrin 1985).

7. Conversely, the likelihood of buy-outs under these circumstances is greater the fewer the local firms since both the incentives to form PCs are greater (because of better exploitation of oligopsonistic power) and the organizational demands placed on workers are lower.

8. The possibility of creation of new PCs may exert a downward pressure on the price of existing capitalist firms that are candidates for worker buy-out. Together with the lower demands placed on entrepreneurship in the case of a buy-out, this may reduce the advantage of new PCs relative to buy-outs, but it is unlikely to eliminate it entirely.

the costs borne by workers and community may be very large. But even in large localities with numerous firms the costs borne by redundant workers may be very high if their skills are job-specific (Bluestone & Harrison 1982; Bradley & Gelb 1983).

If entry of new firms (lured by low wages following the unemployment) is sluggish, unemployed workers without overly restrictive job skills may decide to migrate out of the locality to get jobs elsewhere. In so doing they bear the costs of moving, of severance of social ties, and of the loss of real estate value (which increases with the size of the migration). Related costs may also be borne by the rest of the community.

As the costs of shutdown borne by workers and community mount, both groups have increasing incentives to prevent it happening. They may offer wage and tax concessions to the capitalist firm, or they may attempt to buy it out and convert it into a PC, possibly with community participation. The maximum value of concessions workers and the community would make or the price they would pay for the capitalist firm depends on their alternative incomes and wealth in the three alternative outcomes: shutdown, continued operation as a capitalist firm, and continued operation as a PC. The minimum value of concessions or the price firm owners would require depends on the value of its assets in case of shutdown. If the maximum is strictly greater than the minimum, firm owners will negotiate with workers and community regarding the choice of concessions versus buy-out, and the extent of concessions or the price to be paid for the firm. The choice between shutdown, concessions, or buy-out and conversion into a PC will usually be determined by such factors as relative risk aversion, asymmetry of information, and distrust, whereas the actual size of concessions or the price of the firm depend on these factors, on the minimum and maximum values discussed above, and on the bargaining skills of the parties. The discussion below concentrates on the case when the maximum amount that workers and the community are willing to pay for the continued operation of the firm (either as concessions or as a purchase price) exceeds the minimum acceptable to the firm's owners. Hence the analysis focuses on the institutional choice between a capitalist firm and a PC.[9]

Consider the case when workers and the community, because of their lesser wealth or their social attitudes, are more risk averse than the capitalist firm's owners. In this case they are willing to buy insurance that will relieve them from assumption of some of the employment and wage risk entailed by the firm's operation on the market. If they operated the firm as a PC, workers and the community would not be able to purchase such insurance because they cannot sell the PC's risk-bearing equity to outsiders (if they could, the firm

would have been a capitalist firm).[10] However, workers and the community can pay an "insurance premium" in the form of greater wage and tax concessions to the less risk-averse capitalist firm's owners in exchange for stabler employment and wages. Thus, workers and the community are willing to pay more in the form of concessions than in the form of price for the firm, by the magnitude of the insurance premium. Therefore, concessions will be negotiated.

The decline of an industry reduces individual firms' expected profits, and it also may reduce the variance of profits. Lower variance is equivalent to lower risk, in which case the insurance element in employment in a capitalist firm becomes less important for workers, and buy-out will be preferred to concessions.

The success of the concessions solution may hinge on the parties' fulfillment of actions contingent on future events, such as adjustment of wages to changing demand conditions. If there is distrust between workers and the community on one hand and the firm on the other in the sense that each party fears that the other may renege on its obligations, they will be unable to sign contracts or will sign suboptimal ones. To safeguard themselves against the other side's future violation of contracts, the firm may invest too little and workers may acquire too few firm-specific skills (Grout 1984; Ben-Ner 1985). Consequently, profits and wages will be lower than if there were trust between the two. In a PC the antagonistic relations between employer and workers and the resulting distrust are dissolved by the abolition of one party. Obviously, a similar solution cannot be achieved within the framework of a capitalist firm (see also Ben-Ner 1984; Miyazaki 1984). Therefore, the deeper the mutual distrust, the likelier it is that the buy-out solution will dominate the concessions solution. Mutual distrust is typically heightened during the stress and strife induced by the necessity of dividing a diminishing pie.

Not having access to a firm's accounts and sources of information regarding its profitability, workers and the community may believe that the firm is falsely portraying a bleak profits picture in order to obtain greater concessions. Again, the parties will be unable to sign contracts, or the contracts they negotiate will be suboptimal (Hart 1983). In a PC the reasons for maintaining asymmetric information are absent. As a result, if asymmetry of information is believed to exist, workers and the community may be willing to pay a price for the firm higher than the amount of concessions they are willing to make, and since the firm is indifferent to the two options (everything else being equal), a buy-out will more likely take place.

On the other hand, if workers or the community expect that they will be unable to sell their PC ownership shares in the future (perhaps because of a limited market for them), they will prefer to make concessions rather than buy out the capitalist firm. If, in addition, the firm's equipment is expected to last longer than workers' or the community's de-

9. For a more detailed and technical analysis, see Ben-Ner (1985). See also Bradley and Gelb (1980) for an analysis of buy-out conditions with state support, and Stern and Hammer (1978) for a study of various aspects of buy-outs, including issues of workers and community organization.

10. Markets for insurance against profit fluctuations do not exist in general because of problems of "moral hazard."

sired affiliation with the firm, implying a loss of a portion of initial investment, the advantage of concessions is further increased. Concessions can be spread over the life of the equipment and therefore are preferable in this case. Similarly, if workers believe that a PC's economic performance would be inferior to that of the capitalist firm's, they will prefer a concessions solution. In addition, if capital markets are imperfect in that workers and community have less access to borrowed funds than other entrepreneurs do, and if the workers' and community's own resources are insufficient for a buy-out, concessions may be necessary.

The availability of entrepreneurial skills will, of course, influence the choice between concessions and buy-out. Both solutions require organization of workers, but the buy-out possibility is more demanding in terms of entrepreneurship. The buy-out solution, however, entails the advantages of a PC discussed above, which if sufficiently large, may induce prospective members of the PC to make an entrepreneurial effort.

Yet another alternative open to workers and the community is to form a new PC. This option, however, is likely to be dominated by the buy-out option if the expected decline of the industry is not very large, for several reasons. First, the entrepreneurial skill necessary for a buy-out is relatively simple and limited in scope as compared to that of forming a new PC. Second, workers may be limited in their choices of occupations by their job-specific skills and therefore prefer to remain in the industry in which they presently work. In addition, a retiring plant is immediately available for operation, and its purchase price is likely to be lower because of its lack of alternative uses (and therefore easier to finance). However, if the decline of the industry is very large or if (for reasons of a generalized recession, see below) workers are already unemployed, a new firm may be feasible as a PC but not as a capitalist firm. (The foregoing analysis, which focused on the relationship between workers and the capitalist firm's owners within an existing firm, applies also, with appropriate differences, to the expected relationship between workers and owners within a potential capitalist firm.)

The conditions analyzed here determine what will happen to a capitalist firm and its workers when the firm operates in a declining industry: whether the firm will shut down and its workers will become unemployed or migrate to a different locality, whether workers and the community will make concessions to the capitalist firm, whether they will buy it out and convert it into a PC, or whether they will establish a new PC altogether. As noted earlier, an exogenous change is needed to make possible the creation of a PC. In the present case, the decline of an industry provides the impetus for starting the process that may culminate with the establishment of a PC.

Recessions

The case of an individual capitalist firm facing shutdown because of a generalized recession is similar to that of a capitalist firm operating in a declining industry. The main difference is that the alternative wages attainable by workers in other firms are also falling; hence obtaining employment elsewhere is less attractive or infeasible. Consequently, buy-outs of capitalist firms and their conversion into PCs as well as concessions are both likely to be more frequent.[11] Moreover, if economic activity is equally affected in different industries, the relative attractiveness of purchasing a firm in a different industry is eliminated. The weight of the factors listed at the end of the discussion on declining industries will dominate, and in comparison to the declining-industries case, workers in firms threatened with closure will form PCs more often by buying out these firms than by establishing new ones.

During generalized recessions the number of unemployed workers might be substantial, and the conditions for establishing a viable PC may be ripe. Nonetheless, as unemployed workers are not currently associated with one another or with physical capital (and therefore the PCs they form will be new firms), they will face a greater entrepreneurial problem than would workers in firms threatened with closure. In any event, contrary to capitalist firms, the formation of PCs of the type discussed presently is countercyclical.

Provision of Workplace Characteristics

In the discussion so far it has been implicitly assumed that the wage is the only work-related variable that workers care about. In general, however, firms provide workers with bundles of desirable and undesirable workplace characteristics: wages, physical and mental demands, job security, participation in decision making, job safety, regimentation of work, division of labor, cleanliness of the workplace, and more. Workers may have preferences about the levels at which the various characteristics are provided, just as consumers have preferences about the amounts of goods they consume.

The profit-maximizing bundle of characteristics provided by a capitalist firm coincides with the workers' welfare-maximizing bundle (subject to the economic viability of the firm) only if there are many firms among which workers can choose (Dréze 1976; Dréze & Hägen 1978). In such a case, workers can choose their firm according to the combination of workplace characteristics offered, and competing firms may end up providing the most desirable bundle to workers. Two problems arise if only a few firms operate in an industry or locality. First, these firms may use their market power to provide too little of the desirable and too much of the undesirable characteristics (when relevant cost conditions prevail). Second, because management cannot distinguish among workers with different preferences for workplace characteristics, it treats all of them as if they were like the average worker. However, if workers had somehow disclosed their preferences to the management, it could use this information to further increase its market power vis-à-vis the workers and

11. It is difficult, however, to predict how a recession might affect the choice between buy-outs and concessions.

increase profits at the expense of a further reduction in workers' welfare.

The foregoing analysis also assumed that capitalist firms are interested in profits only and have no preferences about the bundle of workplace characteristics. Nevertheless, Braverman (1974), Marglin (1974), Reich and Devine (1981), Pagano (1985), and others have argued that capitalist firms are interested not in total profit generated by the firm but in the share of the profit that accrues to firm owners. This share is inversely related to the power wielded by workers, which is positively related to their control over the firm. To reduce worker control, firms choose excessive degrees of division of labor, too low skill requirements, and exaggerated hierarchy in decision making. In this way, these authors claim, the profit accruable to capitalist firms' owners is higher, despite the possibility that costs might be higher.

Whatever the source of the inefficiency, capitalist firms may provide bundles of workplace characteristics that do not coincide with the workers' most preferred and economically feasible bundles. The smaller the competition among firms in terms of workplace characteristics, the greater will be the departure from the workers' preferred solution. Workers can improve their situation by organizing and negotiating with firm owners over bundles of workplace characteristics. If the power of their organization is small, and an industry-level (rather than firm-level) trade union is incapable of sufficiently improving their lot or is negotiating similar contracts for dissimilar firms or workers, then workers have two options left: they may buy out the capitalist firm in which they are employed or form a new PC. Either option would give them the possibility of running the firm according to their preferences by internalizing the antagonistic relations prevailing between the owners and themselves (that is, they would become both worker and manager, thus relieving the conflict). Moreover, the worker-run PC may be a vehicle to provide workplace characteristics according to the expressed preference of workers rather than the preferences of the average worker.

Of the two options, the buy-out is likely to materialize only if most workers in the relevant industry or field organize to buy out the capitalist firms in which they are employed (for the same reasons discussed earlier). Hence, all things being equal, incorrect provision of workplace characteristics will stimulate the creation of new PCs rather than conversion of capitalist firms. The problem of entrepreneurship in this case is similar to that we saw earlier. In order for a PC to be formed, some change must occur so as to create a gain large enough to cover the costs of entrepreneurship involved in the creation of PCs. Such a change may come from a change in the bundle of workplace characteristics being offered. For example, an organizational innovation may be introduced increasing the extent of hierarchical decision making without a compensating change in other characteristics, inducing some workers to want to form a PC. Or a general economic improvement that raises wages may increase the demand of some workers for democratically run PCs. Thus as before, a change in outsiders' policies regarding support for PCs may

induce their creation. When preferences of workers in a given workplace are very different, those with average preferences have the least incentives to engage in forming a PC, whereas workers with extreme preferences have the strongest incentive to do so. In such cases only some workers will depart from an existing capitalist firm in order to form a PC of their own.

FORMATION OF PCs: EMPIRICAL SURVEY AND ILLUSTRATIONS

PCs appeared first in the United Kingdom in the late eighteenth century shortly after the advent of the factory system. Thousands of PCs have been established since then in various countries, mainly in industrialized economies, with a recent upsurge occurring in the 1970s and 1980s. This section provides first a selective survey of PCs during those years in various capitalist economies.[12] Then some confrontation of theory with empirical findings is attempted through the analysis of information regarding the formation of PCs in various countries and times according to the theoretical categories discussed earlier. Although not intended as a comprehensive survey of the formation of PCs in capitalist economies, the discussion will pinpoint essential trends in and reasons for the formation of a large number of them.[13]

A Survey

The largest PC sector is in a noncapitalist country, Yugoslavia, where essentially all industrial production and a good many other nonagricultural activities are carried out in PCs. This situation was initiated in the early 1950s and matured in the mid-1960s under the auspices of the state, which permits only PCs in industry (see, for example, Horvat 1982; Pryor 1983). As table 24.1 suggests, the size of the PC sector elsewhere is much smaller, although it has grown appreciably during the 1970s and continues to grow in the 1980s. Italian PCs are second in number and economic importance only to Yugoslav PCs (2.4 percent of the Italian nonagricultural work force is employed in PCs). Slightly more than 40 percent of Italy's PCs are in construction,[14] another

12. For a survey of cooperatives in various countries not covered here, see Pryor (1973).

13. There appears to be no published systematic statistical or econometric work on the reasons for the formation of PCs. Attempts to identify relationships between various economic and social variables have been made by the authors cited at the end of the second paragraph of this chapter as well as by Estrin (forthcoming). This section relies considerably on these contributions. For detailed studies of contemporary cases (mainly of buy-outs) at the firm level, see Davy (1983), Woodworth (1982 and 1985), and various studies in Jackal and Levin (1984) and Lindenfeld and Rothschild-Whitt (1982). Organizations that are PCs by this chapter's definition but are incorporated as partnerships are not included in this survey.

14. The Italian statistics overstate, because of their special definitions, the number of PCs in construction at the expense of industrial branches such as metalworking (Estrin, Jones, & Svejnar, forthcoming).

TABLE 24.1 PRODUCER COOPERATIVE STATISTICS IN SELECTED COUNTRIES

	Italy			France			United Kingdom			Netherlands		
	1970	1976	1981	1970	1976	1981	1970	1976	1981	1970	1976	1981
Number of PCs[a]	4,370	5,893	11,203	522	559	933	17	47	468	10	13	40
Number of workers	ND	229,800	427,900	29,200	29,000	32,500	1,600	3,000	7,000	1,350	1,430	1,870
Number of worker-members	ND	212,460	390,200	8,400	11,000	18,100	420	900	6,000	350	330	800
Revenue in $U.S.[b]	ND	ND	8,235	270	ND	965	18	ND	212	16	52	110
New PCs	ND	1,076	2,102	52	50	228	1	16	138	2	5	21
Number of workers in new PCs	ND	41,970	80,380	800	800	3,200	ND	ND	ND	ND	800	120
Failed PCs[c]	ND	560	1,040	48	35	92	0	3	8	ND	ND	ND
Number of workers in failed PCs	ND	21,840	39,860	ND	ND	2,260	0	150	140	ND	ND	10
National Nonagricultural employment in 1980	17,978,000			17,511,000			23,760,000			4,309,000		

Sources: For PCs: CECOP 1982, Annex III, pp. 16–17. For nonagricultural employment: UN Statistical Yearbook, 1982.

a. Data regard only PCs affiliated with the main cooperative umbrella organization in each country: Italy = FEDERLAVORO-LEGA, France = GC SCOP, UK = ICOM, Netherlands = ABC. The data do not include most partnerships in such professions as law, accounting, or medical practice.

b. It is not clear in which year's prices the CECOP revenue data are included.

c. Failed PCs refer to PCs that were erased from the PCs' registry for any of several possible reasons (bankruptcy, sale to a capitalist firm, transformation into a capitalist firm, and so on).

40 percent in services, and a little under 20 percent in industry. Within industry, PCs are found in most branches, though more than a quarter of the 11,203 industrial PCs in 1981 were in textiles, clothing, and leather branches. Other concentrations of PCs are in construction materials (379), wood products (156), and printing and publishing.

In 1981, there were 933 PCs in France (employing 0.2 percent of the nonagricultural workforce): 364 in construction, 293 in industry, and 276 in various services. Industrial PCs were concentrated in the metal and mechanical branch (96 cooperatives) and in printing and publishing (92). At the same time, United Kingdom PCs (with 0.03 percent of the nonagricultural employment) were more heavily concentrated in industry (particularly in printing and publishing, metal and mechanical, and textile, clothing, and leather branches) and relatively less concentrated in construction (56); there were 175 PCs in services. In Holland in 1981 there were 6 PCs in construction, 14 in industry, and 20 in services. (Data on these four countries may be found in CECOP 1982, Annexe 2).

PCs exist in other capitalist countries as well, though in many their weight, albeit growing, is very small. Although there are relatively few PCs in Spain, in and around the Basque town of Mondragon a remarkable cooperative system consisting of more than 70 industrial PCs with 16,000 workers (all members) supported by financial, technical, educational, and consumer cooperatives has developed since the 1950s. The PCs operate in a great variety of industrial branches and are mostly capital intensive employing modern technologies. This cooperative system has grown steadily and serves as an example for would-be PCs elsewhere (Thomas & Logan 1982).

Denmark's 800 PCs in 1980 were distributed as follows: 200 in construction, 250 in industry, and 350 in services (CECOP 1982, 90). In West Germany and Belgium the num-

ber of PCs is insignificant. In the United States, there were only about 100 PCs in the late 1970s with a work force of about 10,000 (Jackall & Crain 1984); since then a few large capitalist firms have been converted into PCs, but the cooperative sector remains proportionally very small. The cooperative sector in Israel is proportionally very large if trade union- and kibbutz-owned firms are included (more than a quarter of industrial employment). However, exclusive of these, the PC sector alone is much smaller (employing 1.5 percent of the nonagricultural workforce) and has been shrinking during the past two decades as well as losing its cooperative character by employing more hired workers than members. In 1981 there were 53 PCs in industry with 2,723 workers (of whom only 709 were members), 3 public transport PCs with 13,553 workers (7,986 members), and 33 PCs in services and transportation with an employment of 2,940 (766 members) (Israeli Cooperation Centre 1983).

This survey suggests that, although PCs can be found in most realms of economic activity, they tend to concentrate in a few industries such as textiles, leather, clothing, wood and metal works, printing, construction, and services.[15] These industries bear some characteristics that make them more suitable for PCs. First, concentration can be expected on account of a smaller entrepreneurial problem in activities that employ relatively simple techniques but a fairly skilled and homogeneous labor force, and that produce a few products. Second, these techniques are comparatively labor intensive as PCs and their members have only limited access to equity and debt capital. Third, PCs created in response to decline of

15. It is not only that most PCs are concentrated in these industries, as presented in the text, but that PCs are better represented in these industries relative to other industries. See Ben-Ner (1986b, tables 4 and 4a) for comparative statistics with capitalist firms' industrial concentration in several countries.

industries are concentrated in the old industries, as the survey indicates. Fourth, PCs established as new firms may be attracted to lower risk industries because of members' relative risk aversion (Ben-Ner 1986b).[16]

Promoters' Support

Political movements, social philosophers, trade unions, cooperative umbrella organizations, philanthropists, and the state have historically provided some support for PCs. It is difficult to deduce from their pronouncements the reason for their support. It is also difficult to evaluate their actual contribution to the formation of PCs since their support was typically a supplementary rather than the main or initiating factor. Thus, this discussion can convey only a coarse picture of the role of PC promoters.

Most left-of-center as well as some right-of-center political parties have lent limited support to PCs, mainly by promoting state legislation favorable to them (see below) and in a very few cases by actively promoting cooperative ideology (for example, the Cooperative party in the United Kingdom). Few trade unions have lent active support for the creation of PCs, most viewing their role as improving the lot of employees vis-à-vis employers. Nonetheless, there are a few exceptions. For example, the Knights of Labor provided ideology, encouragement, and loans to help form some two hundred PCs during the 1880s in the United States (Jones 1980; Aldrich & Stern 1983). Italian unions have lent some support to PCs (see Thornley 1983), and Belgian, Welsh, and other trade unions, especially since the late 1970s, have helped form PCs primarily by promoting the idea among workers and providing funds for feasibility studies.

PC umbrella organizations have existed in many countries (but not in the United States—for example, where the Cooperative League has not embraced them). Apart from extending ongoing support to existing PCs by providing various central services or securing contracts for them, these organizations have helped create new PCs by providing educational programs for future cooperators, aiding with establishment grants (mostly in the form of loan insurance or cheap loans), supplying technical services, and occasionally even fulfilling the entire entrepreneurial role. Active organizations exist in Italy, the United Kingdom, France, Spain, the Netherlands, Israel, and other countries (see CECOP [1982] for details on the activities of umbrella organizations in different countries.) The Spanish-Basque cooperative organization in Mondragon is special in that it often fulfills the entire entrepreneurial role necessary for the establishment of PCs and provides afterward a myriad of support services (Thomas & Logan 1982).

Social philosophers provide justification for support for

PCs and help create a preference for participation in them. Among the better known thinkers were Owen, Proudhon, Blanc, Kropotkin, and G. D. H. Cole, although their actual influence was probably very low. (See Hovart [1975a], Cole [1944], and Lambert [1963] for accounts of the theories of various thinkers and their presumed influence.)

Owners of firms have rarely handed them over to workers. The United Kingdom seems to have been the main location for such events. Robert Owen's creation of PCs by granting plants to workers in the first half of the nineteenth century seems not to have been followed up until the 1960s and 1970s when about a dozen such grants took place. (The better known cases are the large firms of the Scott Bader Commonwealth and the John Lewis Partnership; see Cornforth [1983] and Derrick [1981].)

In many countries the PC is a legal form of incorporation. Like other legal forms it is designed to lend state support for those who choose to govern their internal affairs in certain ways; in this sense it confers no advantage to PCs over other forms of organization. Nevertheless, companies that satisfy certain criteria required for PC incorporation (minimum membership, minimum levels of equity capital, and so on) are granted in some countries limited financial advantages.

In the United States, for example, legislation dating from the late 1970s makes it slightly cheaper to convert a capitalist firm into a PC rather than sell it to another capitalist firm (Bradley & Gelb 1983; Latta 1979); nevertheless, public assistance has been granted only in a minority of conversions (Bradley & Gelb 1983). The PC status does not confer any other advantages on members in the United States, although it does in some Western European countries. The advantage stems from the fact that profits distributed to members are partly exempt from company taxes (this is so in Ireland, France, and the United Kingdom, whereas in Italy distributed profits are treated as preferred small savings; see CECOP 1982, Annexe 1). Since the 1970s, limited state assistance is granted in some Western European countries for the conversion of capitalist firms into PCs, although similar assistance has been granted to capitalist firms in economic difficulties (Bradley & Gelb 1983). In general, state aid to PCs seems to be forthcoming mostly during recessions as a means of providing jobs and income at a lower cost to the state than alternative income maintenance schemes. In addition to the aid of the 1970s, the most remarkable case of state aid was the creation of some 250 self-help PCs with federal aid during the Great Depression in the United States (Jones 1980).

However, the state also imposes some restrictions on the use of profits by PCs, requiring a certain share (about 20 percent) to be kept in reserve, sometimes imposing distribution of profits to nonmembers, and so on. (CECOP 1982, Annexe 1). Moreover, legislation regarding PC incorporation has been only lately enacted and is viewed as unsatisfactory in several countries, putting PCs at a disadvantage relative to capitalist firms (Carnoy & Shearer 1980; CECOP 1982). As mentioned earlier, grants enjoyed by PCs are in fact accorded to all firms of similar size or firms engaged in

16. PCs are also concentrated in service industries, such as taxicabs, medical services, refuse collection, accountancy, and law, where centralized monitoring is particularly difficult (Russell 1985). Many of these organizations are incorporated as partnerships which, as mentioned earlier, are not covered in this survey.

similar lines of business or operating in certain regions. Overall it seems that, to the extent that a net gain is conferred on members of PCs by the state, it is of very modest magnitude (see CECOP 1982 Annexe 1, espec. pp. 171–73, and 106–31 passim).

The support for the creation of PCs has sometimes been offset, at least in part, by the hostility of the environment toward the form. PCs in various places, especially during the nineteenth century but also occasionally in recent times, have been discriminated against by financial institutions and business associates, experiencing difficulties in obtaining loans or in finding suppliers of materials or buyers for their products (see, for example, Shirom 1972; Carnoy & Shearer 1980).[17]

Although it is impossible to gauge the exact influence of external support on the formation of PCs, the empirical literature seems to suggest that external support *alone* has been the reason for the formation of an insignificant proportion of PCs and has more often been a *complementary* factor when PCs otherwise became a superior form of organization. When PCs are able to generate higher profits or welfare than capitalist firms, yet not enough to provide a sufficient share to entrepreneurs, external support plays an important role in their formation and in improving social welfare.

Circumstances of PC Superiority

Economic Performance Issues

Several studies have concentrated on issues related to the performance of PCs. Conte (1982) reported work that indicates that the majority of U.S. plywood PCs are probably more efficient than their capitalist counterparts. Jones (1979) considered a few general indicators of comparative efficiency in U.S. PCs and capitalist firms that operate in similar industries and found that the record is mixed. Mondragon PCs are, according to Thomas and Logan (1982), more efficient than comparable Spanish capitalist firms. Articles in books edited by Jones and Svejnar (1982) and Stephen (1982) claim that many, though by no means all, PCs in various countries are more efficient than capitalist firms. Bradley and Gelb (1983) and Davy (1983) suggest that among PCs created through conversion of failing capitalist firms there has been a decisive improvement in economic performance. In a study of PCs in several countries, Estrin, Jones, and Svejnar (forthcoming) found that for given amounts of inputs an increase in such variables as participation by members in decision making and equity capital vested in members usually raises output; as these variables differentiate PCs from capitalist firms, the study can be interpreted as lending support for the claim of superior performance in PCs.

None of these empirical studies made an attempt at a direct empirical substantiation of the theoretical claims out-

17. The reasons for discrimination vary from ideological opposition to PCs, aversion for dealing with an unfamiliar form of organization, a belief that workers as owners cannot be reliable business associates, or lack of acquaintance with PCs and fear that they may be more volatile than capitalist firms (Ben-Ner 1986b).

lined earlier in the chapter. In particular, no detailed study of the economic performance of PCs and capitalist firms within similar environments (same industrial branch, geographical location, and time period) was carried out. Nevertheless, the existing studies can be interpreted as suggesting that many, perhaps most, PCs are more efficient than capitalist firms, whereas others are equally efficient or less so. Thus the PC sector is heterogeneous in its efficiency attributes relative to the capitalist sector. PCs seem not to have been established in order to capitalize on a general efficiency advantage owing to the second special feature of their internal organization, but as a reaction to external economic circumstances that validate the advantages stemming from their first special feature (internalization of conflicts).

Labor Market Power

Labor market power enjoyed by capitalist firms in small and isolated localities brings about lower employment and wage levels and fluctuations in both. According to Aldrich and Stern (1983), in American towns where employment was provided by just a few large companies (for example, in the timber industry), workers had no job security and suffered from low wages. Because of intense rivalry between trade unions (IWW and AFL), efficient collective bargaining was unfeasible. Some workers, imbued with a socialist or cooperativist political philosophy, decided to form new PCs as the best feasible solution to their problems (for example, pre–World War II plywood PCs and some shingle and weaving PCs established in the 1910s). Similar circumstances seem to have led to the formation of a few new PCs elsewhere, too. (See Thornley [1983] for Italian PCs and Rigge [1981] for Irish PCs.) There seems to be no record of instances of buyouts by workers in reaction to capitalist firms' labor-market power.

Declining Industries and Recessions

Decline of individual industries and generalized recessions have precipitated the formation of probably the largest number of PCs through conversion of failing capitalist firms and by creation of new firms by unemployed workers. Shirom (1972) provides considerable empirical support to the hypothesis relating recessions and PC formation during the late nineteenth and early twentieth century in the United States. Similarly, Jones (1980) suggests that the 1911–12 decline of the American shingle and weaving industries brought about the conversion of several capitalist firms into PCs, apparently at the initiative of their owners. In other industries, also at the beginning of this century, heightened conflict between owners and workers during recessions brought about the creation of PCs in such industries as cigar making, fish canning, and shoe manufacturing (Jones 1980). As mentioned earlier, the Great Depression prompted the U.S. government to provide large grants for the creation of PCs, and it is therefore impossible to estimate how many would have been created without this help. Other PCs were created during the same period without government aid by unemployed workers who bought out closed plants in mining and in sign painting (Jones 1980). Several of the well-known plywood PCs were also created through the conversion of failing capitalist firms during difficult times in the industry (Berman 1967).

A significant wave of PC formation took place in the United States during the 1970s and early 1980s. The number of PCs established and their economic importance exceeded that of any previous wave in American history and was precipitated by the recessions of that period and the decline of certain industries. In some cases worker buy-outs occurred without the involvement of local communities (for example, a supermarket chain in Pennsylvania, an insurance company in Washington, D.C., an airline in California, and an automobile bearing plant in New Jersey). In other cases some measure of local community involvement existed, varying from participation in funding feasibility studies and provision of leadership in the buy-out attempt to actual purchase of shares in the nascent PC. The common characteristic of these cases was the small size and distant location from industrial centers of the localities in which the shutdown took place (for example, a meat-packing plant in Iowa, a steel plant in Maryland, and an asbestos firm in Vermont). This provided both the necessary condition of material interest on the part of the communities, as well as the social connectedness that made possible the creation of a workers' community coalition and the generation of leadership. These conversions were aided somewhat by favorable legislation as well as by the efforts of a few individuals promoting PCs who brought the alternative to the attention of workers and helped fulfill part of the entrepreneurial role (Stern & Hammer 1978; Bradley & Gelb 1983; Hammer, Stern, & Gurdon 1982; Lindenfeld 1982; Rosen, Klein, & Young 1986).

In the United Kingdom many of the PCs formed during the last third of the nineteenth century were initiated during recessions or in declining industries; according to Thornley (1981), about two hundred PCs were formed between 1865 and 1880. The initiative for their creation often came from directly affected workers, or from trade unions, concerned individuals, and consumer cooperatives (Jones 1982; Cornforth 1983). An upsurge of PC formation took place in the United Kingdom in the 1970s and early 1980s. Many of them were initiated by workers who bought failing capitalist firms with little or no external support. The support actually granted by governmental development agencies or private organizations consisted mainly of initial promotion of the PC idea, fulfillment of some entrepreneurial functions, and supply of small loans at slightly preferred interest rates. Substantial government aid to two conversion attempts constituted the exception to this pattern (Derrick 1981; Bradley & Gelb 1983; Cornforth 1983). In addition, several new and conversion PCs were established in remote and declining areas with the aid of local communities and with financial support from regional development agencies that was granted to all similarly scaled firms. The communities provided equity capital and obtained the right to share in profits as well as to influence the operation of the PCs (Derrick 1981).

Since the second half of the nineteenth century, an un-

known share of the numerous Italian PCs was created either by conversion or as new firms during recessions and in declining industries, including a few hundred PCs formed in the 1970s (Thornley 1983; Zevi 1982; Patane 1979). During the 1970s and early 1980s, many hundreds of PCs were created in other European countries in reaction to similar phenomena. (See CECOP [1982] and Bradley and Gelb [1983] for various countries, Defourny, Estrin & Jones [1985] for France, and Defourny [1982] for Belgium.)[18]

Workplace Characteristics

Beginning in about the middle of the nineteenth century, many capitalist firms adopted both mechanization and hierarchical methods of management. Craftsmen lost control over the labor process, their status was lowered, and their independence was curtailed by increased supervision by owners and their agents (Montgomery 1979). Some craftsmen sought to regain their lost position by attempting to establish PCs; from their point of view, PCs were superior to capitalist firms because they allowed them to choose a more desirable bundle of workplace characteristics. Examples of this were cooperage and glassblowing PCs in the United States and cabinetmaking, shoemaking, and bakery PCs in France (Shirom 1972; Jones 1980; Aldrich & Stern 1983).

The quest for control over the workplace and the production process, often combined with the desire of individuals possessing entrepreneurial skills to work in cooperative environments, has been the impetus for the formation of many PCs during the last two decades in many developed countries. Such PCs, often referred to as "alternative cooperatives" or "collectives," were established mainly by middle-class workers who enjoyed higher incomes and a consequent rise in their demand for workplace democracy, a pleasant and informal working atmosphere, less regimentation, a more limited division of labor, and greater interest in the final product. Most of these PCs operate in nontraditional health services, bookshops, printing, retail health food, and so on (Rothschild-Whitt 1979; Cornforth 1983).

An important workplace characteristic that has been insufficiently provided relative to worker preferences and that has led to the formation of many PCs is job security. This is the case, for example, of many PCs in the construction industry, which is characterized by demand fluctuations (see Jones 1980, Zevi 1982; Derrick 1981; see Jones 1980 also for evidence on plywood and foundry PCs).

CONCLUSIONS

This chapter has asserted that producer cooperatives are not likely to be routinely formed in capitalist economies. Although conditions for their establishment may arise under various economic and social circumstances, PCs are most often created during economic slumps when capitalist firms

18. For statistical information regarding the mode of formation of PCs (new firms versus buy-outs) in France, the United Kingdom, Sweden, and the United States, see Ben-Ner (1986b, table 2).

cannot be created or cannot survive. When capitalist firms are not so threatened, producer cooperatives are less likely to be created. The explanation of this paradox lies in the interaction between basic features of the capitalist economic system and the special features of PCs' internal organization. Self-interest combined with (1) scarcity of entrepreneurial individuals and (2) relatively higher costs of PC formation (owing to their being a nonprevalent type of organization) implies that, if profits can be made, (1) scarce entrepreneurs will not want to share them with PC members, and (2) PCs will be relatively expensive to form. Therefore, capitalist firms will be established instead of PCs. Thus ordinary profit opportunities that invite entry by capitalist firms do not induce entry by PCs. This was called the entrepreneurial problem and was viewed as a fundamental bias against the formation of PCs in capitalist economies. PCs are created when they enjoy a sufficiently large advantage relative to capitalist firms that outweighs the entrepreneurial problem. This advantage may be generated by external support or by PCs' superior performance, and may or may not be affected by external economic circumstances. The advantage that stems from member-workers' better motivation (or, for that matter, the disadvantage that is claimed by some authors) is intrinsically unrelated to external economic circumstances, whereas the support granted to PCs by outsiders is likely to be in part correlated with economic circumstances. The advantage that stems from internalization of the conflict of interests between owners of firms and their workers is validated by a set of economic circumstances that includes persistence of labor market power of capitalist firms, decline of industries, recessions, and dissatisfaction by workers with the provision of workplace characteristics in capitalist firms. In order to detect historical patterns of PC formation, then, it is necessary to examine the factors that determine the economic circumstances that underlie such formation. In general terms, these factors can be characterized as follows.[19]

Labor market power can be enjoyed by capitalist firms in isolated areas. Economic development, which reduces geographical isolation, is therefore likely to reduce the potential for PC formation owing to labor market power. Decline of industries is accelerated by rapid technological change and by deep transformations in demand for final products because of changes in income. During such periods an increase in PC formation is likely to be witnessed. Other cyclical patterns that affect certain industries may also affect the entire economy and generate business cycles, including recessions, and induce periodic upsurges in creation of PCs.

Dissatisfaction of workers with workplace characteristics may be generated by many factors. Major technological changes are likely to be accompanied by restructuring of the workplace and by organizational innovations that may be rejected by some workers. Increases in income may raise the demand by workers for change in various workplace characteristics: management style, decision-making processes, division of labor, and so on. Without an increase in the number of firms and in the competition among them regarding workplace characteristics some workers' demands may remain unsatisfied, and the possibility of PCs' creation is enhanced. On the other hand, the development of trade unions and other forms of workers' organizations providing them with a collective voice may achieve some of the goals of PCs either directly at the workplace or through state involvement via legislation and regulation. Such developments may reduce the attractiveness of PCs.

Generally, the more prevalent PCs are in a certain region the easier it is to establish new ones. First, workers in such regions are more likely to be aware of the alternative and will consider it when confronted by circumstances that favor PC formation. Second, the special costs of PC formation that stem from this organizational form's scarcity obviously will be lower. Third, where numerous PCs exist, umbrella organizations may form that further reduce the costs of establishment.

PCs are created in response to some of the negative consequences of the conflict of interests between owners of firms and their workers, just as nonprofit organizations are formed in reaction to the undesirable outcomes stemming from the conflict of interests between profit-maximizing firms and their customers.

The incidence of these conflicts is pervasive, resulting from the pursuit of self-interest by individuals in capitalist economies. Furthermore, and contrary to Adam Smith's belief,[20] the consequences of these conflicts are probably as frequently negative as they are positive. The remedy to some of these problems is found in vertical integration and assumption of control by workers in PCs and consumers in nonprofit organizations. However, the incidence of PCs and nonprofit organizations is relatively rare because, as I argue in this chapter and in Ben-Ner (1986a), these types of organizations encounter fundamental obstacles to their formation in capitalist economies. Such obstacles can be overcome sometimes, but the creation of third-sector organizations is more difficult and depends on different circumstances than those necessary for the creation of capitalist firms.

PCs, like nonprofit organizations, increase the feasible set of capitalist economies by making possible certain actions that capitalist firms are incapable of performing.[21] As such, the existence of third-sector organizations is functional to the operation of the capitalist economy. In answering the question posed in the title of this chapter, I have focused on the stage of formation, dealing only tangentially with organizational evolution and demise. A more complete understanding of the role and function of PCs (and nonprofit organizations) in capitalist economies must be based on an analysis of their entire life cycle.[22]

19. I analyze the historical pattern of PCs' formation in more detail in Ben-Ner (1986b).

20. See the famous passage in Smith (1937), book 4, p. 423.

21. The clearest example of that is when PCs are formed instead of failing capitalist firms, acting as "organizational scavengers" of the economy.

22. I have made some attempts in this direction in Ben-Ner (1984, 1986b, 1986c).

REFERENCES

Abell, Peter. 1983. "The Viability of Industrial Producer Cooperatives." In *Organizational Democracy and Political Proceses,* edited by Colin Crouch, 73–103. New York: John Wiley.

Addison, T., and W. J. Siebert. 1979. *The Market for Labor: An Analytical Treatment.* Santa Monica, Calif.: Goodyear.

Alchian, Armen A., and Harold Demsetz. 1972. "Production, Information Costs, and Economic Organization." *American Economic Review.* 62:777–95.

Aldrich, Howard, and Robert N. Stern. 1983. "Resource Mobilization and the Creation of U.S. Producers' Cooperatives 1935–1935." *Economic and Industrial Democracy* 4:371–406.

Ben-Ner, Avner. 1984. "On the Stability of the Cooperative Form of Organization." *Journal of Comparative Economics* 8:247–60.

———. 1985. "Plant Shutdowns, Wage Concessions, and Worker Buy-Outs of Firms: A Game-Theoretic Approach." Paper presented at the Fifth World Congress of the Econometric Society, Cambridge, Mass., August.

———. 1986a. "Nonprofit Organizations: Why Do They Exist in Market Economies?" In *The Economies of Nonprofit Institutions: Studies in Structure and Policy,* edited by Susan Rose-Ackerman. Oxford: Oxford University Press.

———. 1986b. "The Life Cycle of Worker-Owned Firms in Market Economies: Empirical Survey and Theoretical Analysis." SUNY—Stony Brook, Harriman College. Mimeographed.

———. 1986c. "The Life Cycle of Nonprofit Organizations: Birth, Evolution, and Demise." In preparation.

Ben-Ner, Avner, and Saul Estrin. 1985. "What Happens When Trade Unions Run Firms?" London School of Economics, Centre for Labour Economics, Discussion Paper no. 217, April.

Berman, Katrina V. 1967. *Worker-Owned Plywood Companies: An Economic Analysis.* Pullman: Washington University Press.

Bluestone, Barry and Bennett Harrison. 1982. *The Deindustrialization of America; Plant Closings, Community Abandonment, and the Dismantling of Basic Industry.* New York: Basic Books.

Blumberg, Paul. 1968. *Industrial Democracy: The Sociology of Participation.* New York: Schocken Books.

Bradley, Keith, and Alan Gelb. 1980. "Worker Cooperatives and Industrial Policy." *Review of Economic Studies* 39:665–78.

———. 1983. *Worker Capitalism: The New Industrial Relations.* London: Heinemann.

Braverman, Harry. 1974. *Labor and Monopoly Capital: The Degradation of Work in the Twentieth Century.* New York: Monthly Review Press.

Cable, John. 1984. "Employee Participation and Firm Performance: A Prisoners' Dilemma Framework." European University Institute Working Paper no. 84/126, Florence.

Carnoy, Martin, and Derek Shearer. 1980. *Economic Democracy: The Challenge of the 1980s.* New York: M. E. Sharpe.

Casson, Mark. 1982. *The Entrepreneurs: An Economic Theory.* Oxford: Martin Robertson.

CECOP (European Committee on Workers' Co-operatives). 1982. *Role des cooperatives de production dans le maintien et la creation d'emplois.* Programme of Research and Action on the Development of the Labour Market, Study no. 82/8. Brussels: Commission of the European Communities.

Cole, G. D. H. 1944. *A Century of Co-operation.* London: George Allen & Unwin.

Conte, Michael. 1982. "Participation and Performance in U.S. Labour-Managed Firms." In *Participatory and Self-Managed Firms: Evaluating Economic Performance,* edited by Derek Jones and Jan Svejnar, 213–38. Lexington, Mass.: Lexington Books.

Cornforth, Chris. 1983. "Some Factors Affecting the Success of Failure of Worker Co-operatives: A Review of Empirical Research in the United Kingdom." *Economic and Industrial Democracy* 4:163–90.

Davy, Samuel I. 1983. "Employee Ownership: One Road to Productivity Improvement." *Journal of Business Strategy* 4:12–21.

Defourny, Jacques. 1982. "The Emergence of Workers' Cooperatives in Belgium." University of Liege, Belgium, CIRIEC Working Paper.

Defourny, Jacques, Saul Estrin, and Derek Jones. 1985. "The Effects of Worker Participation upon Productivity in French Producer Cooperatives." *International Journal of Industrial Organization* 3:197–217.

De Menil, George. 1971. *Bargaining: Monopoly Power versus Union Power.* Cambridge, Mass.: MIT Press.

Derrick, Paul. 1981. "European Workers' Co-operatives: Perspectives from the United Kingdom." In Programme of Research and Action on the Labour Market, *Prospects for Workers' Cooperation in Europe.* Brussels: Commission of the European Communities.

Dorner, Peter, ed. 1977. *Cooperative and Commune.* Madison: University of Wisconsin Press.

Dréze, Jacques. 1976. "Some Theory of Labor Management and Participation." *Econometrica* 44: 1125–40.

Dréze, Jacques, and K. Hägen. 1978. "Choice of Product Quality: Equilibrium and Efficiency." *Econometrica* 46:493–513.

Estrin, Saul. 1979. *Self-Management: Economic Theory and Yugoslav Practice.* Ph.D. diss., Sussex University, United Kingdom.

———. Forthcoming. "The Role of Producer Cooperatives in Employment Creation." *Economic Analysis and Workers' Management.*

Estrin, Saul, Derek Jones, and Jan Svejnar. Forthcoming. "The Varying Nature, Importance and Productivity Effects of Worker Participation: Evidence for Contemporary Producer

Cooperatives in Industrialized Western Economies." *Journal of Comparative Economics.*

Furubotn, Eirik G. 1976. "The Long-Run Analysis of the Labour-Managed Firm: An Alternative Interpretation." *American Economic Review* 66:104–24.

Greenwald, Bruce. 1979. "Existence and Stability Problems of Economies of Labour-Managed Firms and Their Relationship to Those of Economies with Strong Unions." *Economic Analysis and Workers' Management* 13:73–92.

Grossman, Sanford, and Oliver Hart. 1986. "The Costs and Benefits of Ownership: A Theory of Vertical Integration." *Journal of Political Economy.*

Grout, Paul A. 1984. "Investment and Wages in the Absence of Binding Contracts: A Nash Bargaining Approach." *Econometrica* 52:449–60.

Gui, Benedetto. 1984. "Basque versus Illyrian Labor-Managed Firms: The Problem of Property Rights." *Journal of Comparative Economics* 8:168–81.

Hammer, Tove Helland, Robert N. Stern, and Michael A. Gurdon. 1982. "Workers' Ownership and Attitudes towards Participation." In *Workplace Democracy and Social Change,* edited by Frank Lindenfeld and Joyce Rothschild-Whitt. 87–108. Boston: Porter Sargent Publishers.

Hart, Oliver. 1983. "Optimal Labour Contracts under Asymmetric Information: An Introduction." *Review of Economic Studies* 40:3–35.

Heflebower, Richard B. 1980. *Cooperatives and Mutuals in the Market System.* Madison: University of Wisconsin Press.

Horvat, Branko. 1975a. Introduction to *Self-Governing Socialism: A Reader,* Vol, 1, edited by Branko Horvat, Mihailo Markovic, and Rudi Supek, 3–66. White Plains, N.Y.: International Arts and Sciences Press.

———. 1975b. "Why Are Inefficiencies of Private Enterprises Tolerated?" *Economic Analysis and Workers' Management* 9:339–45.

———. 1982. *The Political Economy of Socialism.* White Plains, N.Y.: M. E. Sharpe.

Ireland, Norman J., and Peter J. Law. 1982. *The Economics of Labor-Managed Enterprises.* London: Croom Helm.

Israeli Cooperation Centre. 1983. *Producer Cooperative Statistics.* Mimeographed, Tel-Aviv.

Jackall, R., and J. Crain. 1984. "The Shape of the Small Workers Cooperative Movement." In *Worker Cooperatives in America,* edited by R. Jackall and H. Levin, chap. 5. Berkeley: University of California Press.

Jackall, Robert, and Henry Levin, eds. 1984. *Worker Cooperatives in America.* Berkeley: University of California Press.

Jensen, Michael C., and William H. Meckling. 1979. "Rights and Production Functions: An Application to Labor-Managed Firms and Codetermination." *Journal of Business* 4:469–506.

Jones, Derek C. 1979. "U.S. Producer Cooperatives: The Record to Date." *Industrial Relations* 8:342–56.

———. 1980. "U.S. Producer Cooperatives: An Interpretive Essay." Department of Economics, Hamilton College. Mineographed.

———. 1982. "British Producer Cooperatives, 1948–1968: Productivity and Organizational Structure." In *Participatory and Self-Managed Firms: Evaluating Economic Perfor-*

mance, edited by Derek C. Jones and Jan Svejnar, 175–98. Lexington, Mass.: Lexington Books.

———. 1984. "American Producer Cooperatives and Employee-Owned Firms: A Historical Perspective." In *Worker Cooperatives in America,* edited by R. Jackall and H. Levin. Berkeley: University of California Press.

Jones, Derek C., and Jan Svejnar, eds. 1982. *Participatory and Self-Managed Firms: Evaluating Economic Performance.* Lexington, Mass.: Lexington Books.

Lambert, Paul. 1963. *Studies in the Social Philosophy of Cooperation.* Trans. Joseph Letargez. Chicago: Cooperative League of the USA; Brussels: Société Genérale Cooperative.

Latta, Geoffrey. 1979. *Profit Sharing, Employee Stock Ownership, Savings, and Asset Formation Plans in the Western World.* Philadelphia: University of Pennsylvania, Wharton School, Industrial Research Unit.

Lindenfeld, Frank. 1982. "Workers' Cooperatives: Remedy for Plant Closings?" In *Workplace Democracy and Social Change,* edited by Frank Lindenfeld and Joyce Rothschild-Whitt, 337–52. Boston: Porter Sargent Publishers.

Lindenfeld, Frank, and Joyce Rothschild-Whitt, eds. 1982. *Workplace Democracy and Social Change:* Boston, Porter Sargent Publishers.

Marglin, Stephen. 1974. "What Do Bosses Do? The Origins and Function of Hierarchy in Capitalist Production." *Review of Radical Political Economics* 6:60–112.

Miller, David. 1981. "Market Neutrality and the Failure of Cooperatives." *British Journal of Political Science* 11:309–29.

Miyazaki, Hajime. 1984. "On Success and Dissolution of the Labor-Managed Firm in the Capitalist Economy." *Journal of Political Economy* 92:909–31.

Montgomery, David. 1979. *Workers' Control in America.* New Haven: Yale University Press.

Oakeshott, Robert. 1978. *The Case for Workers' Co-ops.* London: Routledge & Kegan Paul.

Pagano, Ugo. 1985. *Work and Welfare in Economic Theory.* Oxford: Basil Blackwell.

Patane, Olga. 1979. "Dans l'Italie en crise des cooperatives de chomeurs." *Autrement,* no. 20:234–39.

Pateman, Carol. 1970. *Participation and Democratic Theory.* Cambridge: Cambridge University Press.

Pauly, Michael, and Michael Redisch. 1973. "The Not-for-Profit Hospital as a Physicians' Cooperative." *American Economic Review* 63:87–99.

Pryor, Frederic L. 1973. *Property and Industrial Organization in Communist and Capitalist Nations.* Bloomington: Indiana University Press.

———. 1983. "The Economics of Production Cooperatives: A Reader's Guide." *Annals of Public and Cooperative Economy* 54:133–72.

Putterman, Louis. 1982. "Some Behavioral Perspectives on the Dominance of Hierarchical over Democratic Forms of Enterprise." *Journal of Economic Behavior and Organization* 3:139–60.

———. 1984. "On Some Recent Explanations of Why Capital Hires Labor." *Economic Inquiry* 22:171–207.

Reich, Michael, and J. Devine. 1981. "The Microeconomics of

Conflict and Hierarchy in Capitalist Production.'' *Review of Radical Political Economics* 12:27–45.

Rigge, Marianne. 1981. ''European Workers' Co-operatives: Perspectives from Ireland.'' In Programme of Research and Action on the Labour Market, *Prospects for Workers' Cooperation in Europe*. Brussels: Commission of the European Communities.

Rosen, Corey, Katherine J. Klein, and Karen M. Young. 1986. *Employee Ownership in America: The Equity Solution*. Lexington, Mass., and Toronto: Lexington Books.

Rothschild-Whitt, Joyce. 1979. ''The Collectivist Organization: An Alternative to Rational-Bureaucratic Models.'' *American Sociological Review* 44:509–27.

Russell, Raymond. 1985. ''Employee Ownership and Internal Governance: An 'Organizational Failures' Analysis of Three Populations of Employee-Owned Firms.'' *Journal of Economic Behavior and Organization*.

Salop, Steven, and David T. Scheffman. 1983. ''Raising Rivals' Costs.'' *American Economic Review Papers and Proceedings* 73:267–71.

Shirom, Arieh. 1972. ''The Industrial Relations System of Industrial Cooperatives in the United States, 1889–1935.'' *Labor History* 25:533–51.

Smith, Adam. 1937. *The Wealth of Nations*. Edited by Edwin Cannon. New York: Random House.

Stephen, Frank H., ed. 1982. *The Performance of Labour-Managed Firms*. London: Macmillan.

Stern, Robert N., and Tove Helland Hammer. 1978. ''Buying Your Job: Factors Affecting the Success or Failure of Employee Acquisition Attempts.'' *Human Relations* 31:1101–17.

Stiglitz, Joseph E. 1974. ''Incentives and Risk Sharing in Sharecropping.'' *Review of Economic Studies* 33:361–71.

Thomas, Henk, and Chris Logan. 1982. *Mondragon: An Economic Analysis*. London: George Allen & Unwin.

Thornley, Jenny. 1981. *Workers' Co-operatives: Jobs and Dreams*. London: Heinemann Educational Books.

———. 1983. ''Workers Co-operatives and Trade Unions: The Italian Experience.'' *Economic and Industrial Democracy* 4:321–44.

Vanek, Jaroslav. 1970. *The General Theory of Labor-Managed Market Economies*. Ithaca, N.Y.: Cornell University Press.

———. 1975. Introduction to *Self-Management: Economic Liberation of Man*, edited by Jaroslav Vanek, 11–36. Baltimore: Penguin.

Webb, Sidney, and Beatrice Webb. 1914. ''Cooperative Production and Profit Sharing.'' *New Statesman*, Special Supplement.

———. 1921. *A Constitution for the Socialist Commonwealth of Great Britain*. London: Longman.

Williamson, Oliver. 1968. ''Wage Rates as a Barrier to Entry: The Pennington Case.'' *Quarterly Journal of Economics* 85:85–116.

———. 1975. *Markets and Hierarchies: Analysis and Antitrust Implications: A Study in the Economics of Internal Organization*. New York: Free Press.

———. 1980. ''The Organization of Work: A Comparative Institutional Assessment.'' *Journal of Economic Behavior and Organization* 1:5–38.

Woodworth, Warner. 1982. ''Worker Takeover of a General Motors Plant: Toward a Robin Hood Theory of Change.'' Brigham Young University, mimeographed; paper presented at the Third International Conference on the Economics of Self-Management, Mexico City, August.

———. 1985. ''Difficulties in Attempting to Launch Self-Managed Firms in the U.S.'' Brigham Young University, mimeographed; paper presented at the Fourth International Conference on the Economics of Self-Management, Liege, July.

Zevi, Alberto. 1982. ''The Performance of Italian Producer Cooperatives.'' In *Participatory and Self-Managed Firms: Evaluating Economic Performance*, edited by Derek Jones and Jan Svejnar, 239–52. Lexington, Mass.: Lexington Books.

Index

451

About the Contributors

Helmut K. Anheier is an assistant professor in the Department of Sociology, Rutgers University, and a research scientist at the University of Cologne, West Germany. He is currently completing a comparative study of private voluntary organizations in West Africa. His research interests include comparative organizational sociology, social network analysis, and developmental studies.

Avner Ben-Ner, an assistant professor at the W. Averell Harriman College for Policy Analysis and Public Management and in the Department of Economics at SUNY–Stony Brook, studies various economic aspects of the life cycle of organizations. He has done theoretical and empirical research on cooperatives, nonprofit organizations, and communes, in addition to work on trade unions and various issues in comparative economic systems.

Paul DiMaggio is associate professor, Institution for Social and Policy Studies, Sociology Department, and School of Organization and Management at Yale University, and executive director of the Yale Program on Non-Profit Organizations. He has written widely on cultural policy and organizational aspects of the arts.

James Douglas graduated from Oxford University in 1941 and then spent nearly ten years as an administrative officer in the British civil service. In 1951, he joined the staff of the Conservative Party research department with which he remained until 1977 first as an economist and then in 1970–74 as director. He has held a variety of visiting appointments in a number of universities and worked with the Yale Program on Non-Profit Organizations for two years. He is the author of *Why Charity?*

Rebecca Friedkin is a doctoral candidate in sociology at Yale University. Her interests in organizational change have included analysis of the effects of changing technology on clerical work and study of the changes in the financing of public television (with W. W. Powell).

Peter Dobkin Hall is associate research scientist in the Program on Non-Profit Organizations at Yale University. He is author of *The Organization of American Culture, 1700–1900: Institutions, Elites, and the Origins of American Nationality.*

Henry Hansmann is professor of law at Yale, where he also undertook his graduate training, receiving both a law degree and a doctorate in economics. He taught law, economics, and public policy at the University of Pennsylvania from 1975 until 1983, when he returned to Yale to join its law faculty. The author of a number of articles on the law and economics of nonprofit and cooperative organizations, he is interested generally in the economic analysis of legal rules and institutions.

Estelle James is professor and chair of economics, State University of New York, Stony Brook. She received her Ph.D. from MIT, has taught at Stanford University and University of California, Berkeley, and has held visiting appointments at Tel Aviv University, the Australian National University, and the Program on Non-Profit Organizations at Yale University. She has published numerous articles on applied welfare economies and the economics of education and is currently working on a comparative economic analysis of the role of the nonprofit sector, with particular reference to public versus private education.

Christopher Jencks is professor of sociology and a faculty associate of the Center for Urban Affairs and Policy Research at Northwestern University. He is the coauthor of *Who Gets Ahead?, Inequality,* and *The Academic Revolution.* A former editor of the *New Republic* (1961–63) and Fellow of the Institute for Policy Studies (1963–67), he has also taught at Harvard (1967–79) and the University of California, Santa Barbara (1977–78).

J. Craig Jenkins is author of *The Politics of Insurgency: The Farm Worker Movement of the 1960s* as well as nu-

461

merous articles on social movements and American politics. He is currently associate professor of sociology at Ohio State University, Columbus. He has taught at the University of Missouri, Columbia, and has been a research associate at the Center for Policy Research and a Visiting Fellow at the Program on Non-Profit Organizations, Yale University. His current research is on the politics of private philanthropy and the dynamics of political reform eras.

Rosabeth Moss Kanter is the Class of 1960 Professor of Business Administration at Harvard University. She was formerly professor of sociology and professor of organization and management at Yale University. She also serves as chairman of the board of Goodmeasure, Inc., a Boston management consulting firm, and is on the board of several national nonprofit organizations. She is author of eight books and over a hundred articles, including *The Change Masters* and *Men and Women of the Corporation*. The recipient of many academic honors and four honorary doctoral degrees, she was named a Woman of the Year for 1984 by *Ms.* magazine for her contributions to ''demonstrating that equity and fairness can be good business.''

Ralph M. Kramer is a professor in the School of Social Welfare at the University of California, Berkeley. Prior to joining the Berkeley faculty in 1964, where he also received his B.A. and M.S.W. degrees, Professor Kramer was employed for seventeen years as a psychiatric social worker, family service agency executive, and executive director of a social planning council. He is the author of numerous articles on citizen participation, social planning, and the voluntary sector. His books include *Voluntary Agencies in the Welfare State, Participation of the Poor,* and *Community Development in Israel and the Netherlands*. His recent research on government–voluntary agency relations focuses on the consequences of purchase-of-service contracting.

Daniel C. Levy, associate professor of educational administration and policy studies and of Latin American studies at State University of New York, Albany, was previously research associate with the Higher Education Research Group and the Program on Non-Profit Organizations at Yale University. His articles on the politics of higher education and on Latin American affairs have appeared in leading journals and have been published in many nations. His books include *University and Government in Mexico* and *Higher Education and the State in Latin America: Private Challenges to Public Dominance;* he is coauthor of *Mexico: Paradoxes of Stability and Change* and editor of *Private Education: Studies in Choice and Public Policy.*

Theodore R. Marmor received his B.A. and Ph.D. degrees from Harvard and taught at the universities of Wisconsin, Minnesota, and Chicago before coming to Yale in 1979 as chairman of the Center for Health Studies. He is professor of public management and political science in the Yale University School of Organization and Management and Department of Political Science. Professor Marmor is the author of *The Politics of Medicare* and numerous articles on the poli-

tics and policies of the welfare state, particularly emphasizing social security, national health insurance, and health planning. A number of these articles have recently appeared in a volume of essays, *Political Analysis and American Medical Care*. Editor of and contributor to *National Health Insurance: Conflicting Goals and Policy Choices,* he was also editor of the *Journal of Health Policy, Politics and Law* from 1980 to 1984.

Melissa Middleton is currently a Ph.D. candidate in the Department of Organizational Behavior at the Yale School of Organization and Management. She holds a B.A. degree in political science from the University of Pennsylvania and a master's degree in public and private management from Yale. Her research, as well as her consulting work, has focused on nonprofit boards of directors. Prior to graduate school, Middleton worked for ten years in the nonprofit sector as the founder/executive director of two human service organizations and as a member of several nonprofit boards and statewide commissions.

Carl Milofsky received his Ph.D. in sociology from the University of California, Berkeley, and currently is associate professor of sociology at Bucknell University. He is editor of a forthcoming volume on community organizations which is part of a research series sponsored by Yale's Program on Non-Profit Organizations. He also has written extensively on the sociology of special education.

Walter W. Powell is associate professor of organization and management and sociology at Yale University, and has long been affiliated with Yale's Program on Non-Profit Organizations. His books include *Getting into Print: The Decision-Making Process in Scholarly Publishing;* he is coeditor of *Conflict and Consensus: Essays in Honor of Lewis A. Coser* and coauthor of *Books: The Culture and Commerce of Publishing*. His primary interests are in the areas of organization theory, social networks, and the sociology of culture.

Gabriel Rudney is senior research associate, Program on Non-Profit Organizations, at Yale's Institution for Social and Policy Studies. He is consultant to the Treasury on tax-exempt organization matters and is also a member of the Internal Revenue Commissioner's Advisory Committee on Tax-Exempt Organizations. He has recently served as a consultant to the American Red Cross and the YMCAs of America, and has advised the Council on Foundations, the Independent Sector, and the American Association of Fund-Raising Counsel. He currently serves on the boards of the Trust for Philanthropy and the National Center for Charitable Statistics. He was research director of the Commission on Private Philanthropy and Public Needs (known popularly as the Filer Commission). His research at Yale concerns the measurement of the dimensions of the nonprofit sector and the theory and measurement of giving behavior.

Lester M. Salamon is director of the Center for Governance and Management Research and of the Nonprofit Sector Project at the Urban Institute. Between 1977 and 1980, he served as deputy associate director of the U.S. Office of Management and Budget. Prior to that he was associate professor of policy sciences at Duke University. Dr. Salamon's work at the institute has focused on alternative instruments of government action, the processes of policy formulation and implementation, and the character and role of private nonprofit organizations. His most recent publications include *The Reagan Presidency and the Governing of America*, *The Federal Budget and the Nonprofit Sector*, and "Voluntary Organizations and the Crisis of the Welfare State" in the *New England Journal of Social Sciences*.

Mark Schlesinger is research coordinator at the Center for Health Policy and Management at the Kennedy School of Government. His research interests include the influence of ownership on the behavior of health care institutions, the influence of prepaid and other innovative financial arrangements on the delivery of health care, and contemporary changes in access to care. He has served as coordinator on a collaborative Harvard/VA study of reform of the Veterans' Administration health care system and is co–principal investigator for a proposed three-year project to study the growth of for-profit psychiatric hospitals.

John G. Simon is Augustus Lines Professor of Law and deputy dean, Yale Law School, and chairman of the Program on Non-Profit Organizations at Yale. He has been engaged in teaching and research on philanthropy and the nonprofit sector since the early 1960s and has also served as officer or trustee of a number of nonprofit groups, including the Taconic Foundation (president), Cooperative Assistance Fund (founding chairman), Potomac Institute (secretary), the Foundation Center (trustee), Council on Foundations (trustee), and Rockefeller Archives Center (governing council member). He is coauthor (with Charles W. Powers and Jon P. Gunnemann) of *The Ethical Investor* and coeditor (with Deborah Stipek) of *Exit Age: Reconsidering Compulsory Education for Adolescents*. He has written many articles and book chapters on various topics in law, philanthropy, and education.

Edward Skloot is founder and president of New Ventures, a consulting firm that helps nonprofit organizations manage themselves better and increase their earned income. Before starting New Ventures in 1980, he served in a variety of public- and private-sector positions, including deputy administrator of parks, recreation, and cultural affairs of New York City, deputy commissioner of mental hygiene of New York State, and vice president of Griffenhagen-Kroeger, a management consulting firm. He has published widely in such journals as the *Harvard Business Review*, the *Entrepreneurial Economy*, and *Orbis*, and speaks frequently on entrepreneurship, nonprofit management, and intersectoral competition. He is a member of the Independent Sector's committee on competition between small business and the voluntary sector.

Richard W. Smithey is currently a doctoral candidate in political science at Yale University. He has written case

studies on medical care policy and the management of medical care institutions at the Yale University School of Management. His research interests include decision making, political beliefs, and medical care policy in the United States.

Richard Steinberg is an assistant professor, Department of Economics, Virginia Polytechnic Institute and State University; associate editor of *Evaluation Review;* an affiliate at the Center for Volunteer Development; and a research consultant for Yale's Program on Non-Profit Organizations. His area of specialization is economics of the nonprofit sector.

David V. Summers is manager of research services at Goodmeasure, Inc., a management consulting firm, and a doctoral candidate in sociology at Yale University, where he is completing a dissertation on coalition formation in organizations. He is also completing research on the use of alternative work arrangements in American industry and the conditions that give rise to power and elite groups within different organizational settings.

Michael Useem is director of Boston University's Center for Applied Social Science and associate dean of the College of Liberal Arts. His current research focuses on the social and political activity of corporations and their managers. His articles have appeared in *Administrative Science Quarterly, California Management Review, Sloan Management Review, American Sociological Review*, and the *New York Times*, and he is the author of *The Inner Circle: Large Corporations and the Rise of Business Political Activity in the U.S. and U.K.*

Paul N. Ylvisaker is Charles William Eliot Professor of Education at Harvard University. He is concerned with issues of public policy, especially as they relate to education and urban development, private philanthropy, and corporate social responsibility. He formerly was the director of the Public Affairs Program at the Ford Foundation and the first commissioner of community affairs in New Jersey. He has taught at Harvard, Swarthmore, Pennsylvania, Yale, and Princeton. He is a director-consultant of the Dayton-Hudson Corporation and a member of the board of the Van Leer Group of Companies and the Bernard van Leer Foundation, as well as India International, Inc., the Boston Foundation, the Mary Reynolds Babcock Foundation, the Edward W. Hazen Foundation, the Alaskan Natives Foundation, Outward Bound, and the Hispanic Policy Development Project. He served as chairman of the National Academy of Sciences' Commission on National Urban Policy and as cochairman of the National Commission on the Secondary Schooling of Hispanics. He is a regent of the Commonwealth of Massachusetts and senior consultant to the Council on Foundations.

Dennis R. Young is a professor in the W. Averell Harriman College for Policy Analysis and Public Management of the State University of New York, Stony Brook. He is also a visiting faculty member of the Program on Non-Profit Organizations at Yale University. Dr. Young received the B.E. degree from the City College of New York and the M.S. and

Ph.D. degrees from Stanford University in engineering–economic systems. His principal research interests are the economic organization of public services and the theory and management of nonprofit organizations. His books include *How Shall We Collect the Garbage? A Study in Economic Organization; Foster Care and Nonprofit Agencies* (with Stephen Finch); *If Not for Profit, For What? A Behavioral Theory of the Nonprofit Sector Based on Entrepreneurship; Casebook of Management for Nonprofit Organizations;* and *Subsidizing Inefficiency* (with Richard Silkman).